# The Complete Writings

## of

# Menno Simons

# THE
# COMPLETE WRITINGS
## OF
# MENNO SIMONS

## c.1496-1561

TRANSLATED FROM THE DUTCH
BY LEONARD VERDUIN AND
EDITED BY J. C. WENGER,
WITH A BIOGRAPHY BY HAROLD S. BENDER

*For other foundation can no man
lay than that is laid, which is Jesus Christ.*

I CORINTHIANS 3:11

HERALD PRESS
Scottdale, Pennsylvania
Waterloo, Ontario

# CONTENTS

# ILLUSTRATIONS

LOCATION OF MENNO'S WRITINGS IN VARIOUS EDITIONS

| Title | 1646 Opera | 1681 Opera Omnia | 1871 Works | 1876-1881 Werke | 1956 Writings |
|---|---|---|---|---|---|
| Foundation of Christian Doctrine | 1-142 | 1-70 | I 11-102 | I 17-148 | 105-226 |
| The True Christian Faith | 145-246 | 71-120 | I 103-164 | I 149-235 | 324-405 |
| The New Birth | 247-268 | 121-132 | I 165-178 | I 236-253 | 87-102 |
| The Cross of the Saints | 269-320 | 133-159 | I 179-212 | I 254-297 | 581-622 |
| Meditation on Psalm 25 | 321-348 | 160-176 | I 213-228 | I 298-320 | 65-86 |
| The Spiritual Resurrection* | (Unpaginated) | 177-184 | I 229-237 | I 321-331 | 53-62 |
| Instruction on Excommunication | 349-398 | 185-214 | I 239-268 | I 332-369 | 961-998 |
| The Nurture of Children | 399-410 | 215-222 | I 269-276 | I 370-377 | 947-952 |
| Reply to Gellius Faber | 411-611 | 223-324 | II 1-105 | II 1-156 | 625-781 |
| Supplication to All Magistrates | 613-621 | 325-330 | II 107-113 | II 157-165 | 525-531 |
| Defense to All Theologians | 623-630 | 331-335 | II 115-120 | II 167-174 | 535-540 |
| Clear Account of Excommunication | 631-656 | 337-350 | II 120-137 | II 177-199 | 457-485 |
| Some Questions | 894-904 | 473-478 | II 276-281 | II 400-408 | 477-485 |
| The Incarnation of Our Lord | 657-724 | 351-382 | II 139-177 | II 201-257 | 785-834 |
| Confession of the Triune God | 725-739 | 383-391 | II 179-188 | II 259-272 | 489-498 |
| Christian Baptism | 741-821 | 393-433 | II 189-231 | II 275-336 | 229-287 |
| Not Cease Teaching and Writing | 823-864 | 435-455 | II 233-255 | II 339-371 | 292-320 |
| Confession of the Distressed Christians | 865-893 | 457-473 | II 257-276 | II 375-400 | 501-522 |
| Reply to Sylis and Lemke | 905-925 | 479-490 | II 283-295 | II 409-426 | 1001-1015 |
| Reply to False Accusations | 927-974 | 491-516 | II 297-323 | II 427-466 | 543-577 |
| Brief and Clear Confession | 975-1020 | 517-542 | II 325-350 | II 467-502 | 422-454 |
| Reply to Martin Micron | 1021-1124 | 543-598 | II 351-401 | II 503-576 | 838-913 |
| Epistle to Martin Micron | 1125-1162 | 599-618 | II 403-424 | II 577-607 | 917-943 |
| The Blasphemy of John of Leiden | 1163-1185 | 619-631 | II 425-440 | II 609-629 | 33-50 |
| A Kind Admonition on Church Discipline | (Missing) | 631-637 | II 441-449 | II 631-641 | 409-418 |
| Meditations and Prayers for Mealtime | (Missing) | (Missing) | (Missing) | (Missing) | 955-958 |

* No. 2, The Spiritual Resurrection, is bound between fol. 348 and fol. 349 in some copies of the 1646 edition, and in other copies, at the end of the book.

# Introduction

•●••●••●••●••●••●••●••●••●••●••●••●••●••●••●••●••●••●••●••●••●••●••●••●••●••●••●••●••●••●••●••●••●••●••●••●••●••●••●••●••●••●••●••●••●••●••●••●••●••●••●••●••●••●••

The present generation has witnessed an unprecedented interest in the history and witness of the Anabaptists, including the Swiss Brethren, the Hutterian Brethren of Moravia, and the Dutch Mennonites. This is true both within and without the Mennonite brotherhood, and in Europe as well as in America. Of all the persons in early Anabaptist history none was so influential as Menno Simons, the Dutch priest who was converted in 1535, who united with the quiet Dutch Anabaptists called Obbenites in 1536, and who was ordained as one of their elders about a year later. Furthermore only three early Anabaptist leaders left writings of any considerable extent: Pilgram Marpeck of South Germany, and Menno Simons and Dirk Philips in the North. Marpeck's writings seem to have enjoyed but little circulation in the Mennonite brotherhood down through the centuries, while Menno's writings, especially his *Foundation* book of eight works, circulated widely in Mennonite circles, being translated from Dutch into German and English, and passing through many editions. Menno's writings have also been read much more than those of Dirk Philips.

One of the first collections of Menno's works in Dutch was the *Sommarie* of 1600-1, printed at Hoorn, Holland. A larger collection of Menno's writings was published in 1646, *Opera . . . ofte Groot Sommarie.* This was reprinted in 1681 in large folio form, and with the addition of his *Kind Admonition on Church Discipline* of 1541, together with ten of his letters to individuals and churches. The folio edition of 1681 was prepared by H. J. Herrison and was published at Amsterdam under the title, *Opera Omnia Theologica, of Alle de Godtgeleerde Wercken van Menno Symons . . . .* The first comprehensive collection of Menno's works in English was published by John F. Funk and Brother of Elkhart, Indiana, in 1871, *The Complete Works of Menno Simon (sic!).* Part I was a revision of the English edition of some of Menno's writings translated from the German by I. Daniel Rupp and was published at Lancaster, Pennsylvania, in 1863. Part II was translated from the Dutch by an Indiana schoolteacher named Piebe Swart. The entire manuscript was reviewed by Joseph F. Summers: but neither Swart nor Summers was a trained historical scholar. The 1871 English edition contained every item in the 1681 *Opera Omnia,* although the publisher considered it advisable to omit a total of about 760 lines (over 17 pages) from Menno's discussion of the incarnation. Funk also issued Menno's writings in German, *Die vollständigen Werke Menno Simons*, Elkhart, Indiana, 1876; *Zweiter Theil*, 1881. None of the previous Dutch or English editions of Menno's works contained the *Meditations and Prayers for Mealtime* of c. 1557; nor his two hymns; nor his letters to David Joris, to the Davidians, and to a church in Prussia; nor his Final Instructions on Marital Avoidance; nor the Wismar Articles.

The present edition of Menno's writings was translated by a competent scholar, Leonard Verduin of Ann Arbor, Michigan. He used the folio edition of 1681, *Opera Omnia Theologica*, but with constant reference to the earlier *Opera* of 1646. In cases of uncertain text the translator found that he could almost always correct the 1681 readings by a comparison with the 1646 edition. Throughout the work the translator sought to give in modern English a faithful rendering of what Menno had written in his long and involved Dutch sentences. Unless there was a special point in a Dutch rendering, the translator generally rendered Bible verses in the language of the King James Version. The translator sought to catch even the mood of Menno: at times he was eloquent, at other times sharp in the heat of theological debate, sometimes he used language which could only be rendered by that which approached modern slang. Menno wrote for common people and did not hesitate to use direct peasantlike speech. He did not attempt a polished rhetorical or artificial style. Usually Menno wrote either in Dutch or in the Oostersch dialect of the region in North Germany where he lived for many years after he left Holland. He wrote a few items in Latin, such as the epilogue to his book on Psalm 25. (This epilogue is missing in the 1681 edition and in all other translations heretofore.) Deepest gratitude is due the translator for the carefulness and accuracy of his work.

After the translator had completed his work, the translation was carefully edited by Beulah Stauffer Hostetler, Assistant Book Editor at the Mennonite Publishing House, in order to make this edition as readable as possible. Sometimes it seemed advisable to cut Menno's long sentences into two or more briefer ones in English but never at the expense of a faithful presentation of his thought.

The manuscript was then submitted to John Christian Wenger, Editor of this edition, who after much research located writings of Menno not included in any previous collection of his works and arranged them in chronological order (as nearly as could be determined). He read and checked the entire manuscript editorially, added clarifying footnotes, wrote an explanatory introduction to each section, and prepared the index.

Harold S. Bender revised his biography, *The Life and Writings of Menno Simons* (1936), for inclusion in this volume.

It should be noted that where parentheses occur in Menno's writings the material as enclosed is from Menno's own pen. This is also true of parenthetical remarks which are enclosed in brackets within the text of a Scripture verse.

Elsewhere material in brackets has been inserted into the text by the editor to clarify Menno's language.

It will be immediately evident to every reader that Menno was a sound evangelical, a true saint of God united to Christ by faith, born again and sanctified by the Holy Spirit, a teacher who sought to align his life and doctrine with the infallible Word of the Lord, the Holy Scriptures. Menno himself was of course not infallible. He sometimes quoted from Apocryphal books as if they were inspired. He also held to a theory of the incarnation that is unacceptable to Mennonites today. And he stood for a practice of *shunning* (breaking social fellowship with) excommunicated persons which seems harsh and unscriptural to many in the brotherhood now. Yet it is plain that Menno had a sound view of the Scriptures, the Trinity, the new birth, holiness of life, divine grace, God's keeping power, the need of perseverance in faith and obedience, the doctrine of love and nonresistance, Christian separation and nonconformity to the world, the baptism of believers only, the rejection of all oaths, and the necessity of obeying literally every New Testament command. It is right that the church he served should be called *Mennonite!*

This edition is issued with the hope that God may be pleased to use it to strengthen the Mennonite brotherhood in Christ Jesus, to promote a dynamic Christian life, and earnest obedience to His holy Word. May the book contribute to the recapture of apostolic Christianity in this era of secularism and spiritual lukewarmness. May it give to our people a new sense of their spiritual heritage, and may it introduce to Christendom at large a new vision of Christianity as redeemed discipleship. May it create a new loyalty to the Word of God as the only authoritative Guide, and thus bring to our congregations and members a deeper sense of Christian mission. To these ends it is sent forth with the prayer that God may be pleased, through this effort, to glorify His Son, and to edify His earthly body, the church.

*April 5, 1955*                                          JOHN C. WENGER

## Preface to the Fourth Printing, 1978

Research and publication on Menno continue unabated. Particular attention is called to Irvin B. Horst's splendid monograph, *A Bibliography of Menno Simons,* and his revised dating for some of Menno's publications.

Note also the description of Menno's person in Cornelius Krahn's unique contribution, *Dutch Anabaptism* (p. 184). At about fifty Menno was described as "a thick, fat and heavy man, with a wry facial expression and a brown beard, who had difficulty walking."

For this printing I have corrected typographical errors, and added a few footnotes as well as several items in the Index.

J. C. Wenger

# Preface to the Fifth Printing, 1986

It is a matter of great rejoicing that the continued demand for Menno's *Complete Writings* calls for another reprint. Various changes have been made in this new printing, the most important being the dropping of the Wismar Articles of 1554. This change was approved by both the Publisher and the Editor. For one thing, the text of the articles is not pure; further, they were not written by Menno as far as we know, therefore they do not belong in his *Writings*. We hope that the reader will approve of this decision.

Apart from his Autobiography (pages 668—674), the latter part of this volume is largely devoted to polemical material—against Gellius Faber, John a Lasco, Martin Micron, and Sylis & Lemke—and is somewhat tiring. But the essays from "The Spiritual Resurrection" to "Brief Defense to All Theologians" are crisp and attractive. Menno was our best sixteenth-century writer.

When the first edition of Menno's writings appeared, Professor Otto Piper of Princeton Seminary took it to class and spoke highly of Menno and the faith community which bears his name. Let us remember to follow Christ whom Menno sought to uphold in all his writing—ponder the Christology of page 884, for example, or the briefer summary on page 832.

*Soli Deo Gloria!*

J. C. Wenger
Goshen, Indiana

# A Brief Biography

## of

## Menno Simons

# A Brief Biography of Menno Simons

## By Harold Stauffer Bender

*•◦••◦••◦••◦••◦••◦••◦••◦••◦••◦••◦••◦••◦••◦••◦••◦••◦••◦••◦••◦••◦••◦••◦••◦••◦••◦••◦••◦••◦••◦••◦••◦••◦••◦••◦••◦••◦••◦••◦••◦••◦••◦••◦••◦•*

## *From the Preface to the 1936 Edition*

The year of the four hundredth anniversary of Menno Simon's renunciation of Catholicism finds us with no available biography of Menno in English. J. Newton Brown's very brief and inadequate sketch, *The Life and Times of Menno, the Celebrated Dutch Reformer,* published at Philadelphia in 1853, has long since been forgotten, and the modern biography by John Horsch, *Menno Simons, His Life, Labors, and Teachings,* published at Scottdale, Pennsylvania, in 1916, which has served us well for twenty years, has just gone out of print. In this anniversary year when the commemoration of Menno Simon's conversion revives our appreciation of the service which he rendered to the cause of evangelical Christianity and the cause of the Mennonite Church in particular, it is desirable that a comprehensive, popular account of his life and work be made widely available. This is particularly true at a time in world affairs when, in the midst of economic distress and fearful rumors of war, the voice of Menno Simons can profitably be heard with its calm but convinced insistence upon a thoroughgoing practical Christianity making the whole of life subject to the lordship of Christ, and with its demand that men resolutely abandon all carnal strife and live together in peace and love.

In preparing a popular biography of Menno Simons which might be read with pleasure and profit by both old and young, it seemed good to avoid both the style and the forms and thereby possibly the impediments of learning, without sacrificing scrupulous accuracy in detail. What is here presented is in essence based upon the work by John Horsch named above and the most recent biography of Menno Simons submitted as a doctoral dissertation at the University of Heidelberg, Germany, in February, 1936, by Dr. Cornelius Krahn. I am greatly indebted to these two good friends, to Dr. Krahn for the privilege of reading his manuscript before its publication, and to John Horsch for his careful reading of the manuscript and his many valuable suggestions.

*   *   *

The publication of the second edition of this biography in connection with the new edition of Menno's *Writings* has afforded me the opportunity of making a few necessary corrections in the text.

*Goshen, Indiana*
*February 26, 1955*

HAROLD S. BENDER.

# A Brief Biography of Menno Simons

By Harold S. Bender

## I. THE CATHOLIC PRIEST

About 1496, some years after the discovery of America, a child was born to a Dutch peasant family living in the village of Witmarsum in the province of Friesland in the far northwest corner of continental Europe. The father, whose name was Simon, called his son Menno, and according to the custom of the time the boy was called Menno Simons (Simon's Son). The village of Witmarsum lies in a fertile plain, about halfway between the cities of Franeker and Bolsward, less than ten miles from the North Sea.

Quite early the parents of Menno Simons decided to consecrate their son to the service of the church, the Catholic Church, and in preparation for that service committed him to the care of a monastery near his home, possibly the Franciscan Monastery at Bolsward. There for long years he devoted himself to the spiritual exercises required of a monk, and to the traditional course of theological study required of candidates for the high office of the priesthood. During his years of study he learned to read and write Latin quite well, learned also to read the Greek, and became well acquainted with many ancient writings in Latin, particularly the writings of the church fathers such as Tertullian, Cyprian, and Eusebius. But the greatest book of all, the Bible, he failed utterly to read. It was not until two years after he was ordained to the priesthood that he ventured with great trepidation to open the covers of this forbidden volume.

Menno Simons' ordination to the Catholic priesthood took place in the month of March, 1524, in the twenty-eighth year of his life, probably in the city of Utrecht, seat of the ancient bishopric of Utrecht which included practically all of modern Holland in its jurisdiction. His first assignment was as parish priest in the village of Pingjum which lay next to his home village of Witmarsum. Here he served for a period of seven years, 1524-31, as the second in rank of three parish priests. In 1531 Menno was transferred to his home village of Witmarsum where he served for five years as parish pastor until January, 1536, when he laid down his office in the Catholic Church and joined the small group of devoted evangelical brethren under the leadership of Obbe Philips, known as Anabaptists or Obbenites.

The twelve years of Menno Simons' service as a Catholic priest were outwardly spent, as far as man could see, in the performance of the usual round of duties of a Catholic priest in a small country village. He took his place in the regular worship of the church, performing the high ceremony of the mass as well as other rites and ceremonies. He offered prayers for the living and the dead, baptized the children of the parish, consecrated marriages, received confessions, administered discipline, and occasionally preached brief sermons in connection with the Sunday worship of the congregation. Like the typical village priest of the time he did not take his office nor his life very seriously. He gave little time or effort to study, but rather, as he himself confesses, joined his fellow priests in "playing cards, drinking, and frivolities of all sorts, as was the custom of such unfruitful men."

But outward appearances did not tell the full story of Menno's life during his twelve years in the priesthood. Very early doubts about certain dogmas of the church arose to plague his conscience, and his life was made increasingly miserable by an inner soul-struggle which did not cease until he broke the bonds which bound him to the Catholic Church and stepped forth in the faith and liberty of the Gospel. Let us trace this eleven-year struggle.

In the very first year of Menno's priestly service, in 1525, the same year that Conrad Grebel and his brethren were founding the Mennonite Church in Zurich, Switzerland, a grave doubt arose to disturb his carefree, frivolous life with its formal religion. As he was celebrating the mass, suddenly the thought arose that possibly the bread and wine were not actually changed into the flesh and blood of the Lord as he had been taught, and as he was teaching the people. At first he shrank back from the thought as a whispering of the devil; but he could not get rid of the doubt, even by the use of the confessional. How Menno came to doubt the dogma of transubstantiation as held by the Catholic Church is not clear. He must have come in contact in some way with the teaching of Martin Luther or the other reformers on this point, either in books, or through the circulation of such ideas by word of mouth. As early as 1521 a Hollander by the name of Hoen had begun to teach the view that the elements used in the Lord's Supper were not actually transformed, but were merely symbols of the suffering and death of Christ. Whether Menno had read Hoen's writings or not, the rise of doubt on this point in his mind is evidence that the influence of the Reformation had already begun to reach into far-off Friesland, for the attitude toward the mass was a touchstone in the matter of the new evangelical heresy.

For about two years Menno was tormented by doubts regarding the mass before he found a way to help himself. He finally decided to seek relief by a diligent search of the New Testament. This decision was one of the greatest steps in Menno's life. In fact, it was the decisive step which was certain to lead to his final conversion, for the fundamental principle of the Reformation was the sole authority of the Word of God as the source of truth for faith and life.

Now the decision of Menno Simons to search the Scripture for help in solving his doubts about the mass was not a decision to give up the authority of the church, for he probably hoped to find in Scripture a confirmation of the teaching of the church. The real problem came when Menno, having dared to open the lids of the Bible, discovered that it contained nothing of the traditional teaching of the church on the mass. By that discovery his inner conflict was brought to a climax, for he now was compelled to decide which of two authorities was to be supreme in his life, the church or the Holy Scriptures.

He had been taught by the church that disbelief in its doctrine meant eternal death. What should he do? Fortunately, as Menno himself repeats, he found help in the writings of Martin Luther, for Martin Luther taught him that violation of the commandments of men could never lead to eternal death. It is not known in which of Luther's writings Menno found his help, possibly in the 1518 pamphlet, *Instruction on Several Articles,* or possibly in the important booklet written in 1520 entitled, *On the Freedom of a Christian Man.*

When Menno Simons accepted Luther's view and dared to deny the dogma of transubstantiation as held by the Catholic Church because the Scriptures did not teach it, he found a way out of his doubts and struggles, a way to free his conscience and deliver his soul from eternal death. But in so doing he entered upon a road that would inevitably lead him out of the Catholic Church, for to follow the Scriptures in all matters of conscience was to forsake the fundamental principles of Catholicism. In making his decision on the mass, however, Menno did not follow Luther's teaching on this point; rather he developed his own interpretation of the Lord's Supper; he did not become a Lutheran in any way. What he was always grateful to Luther for, was the fundamental principle of the authority of Scripture as over against any human authority.

Menno's decision to follow the Scriptures was probably arrived at about the year 1528. It did not lead to his immediate abandonment of the Catholic Church, because at first he disagreed with the church only on the question of the mass, and no doubt thought that he could remain a loyal Catholic and teach his new view within the church. So like all the other reformers he made no haste to change his church membership. Such a change would have meant giving up a good position with its generous income, and Menno still "loved the world, and the world him" too much, as he later said, to take such a radical step. The fact is that he was still far from a real comprehension of the Gospel, far from a spiritual conversion. The next years, from 1528-31, were rather years of gradual enlightenment. He says of his own experience during this time, that "by the enlightenment and mercy of the Lord I increased in the knowledge of the Scriptures and soon was considered by a few, although undeservedly, as an evangelical preacher," that is, as one who preached sermons based upon the Scriptures. Men began to seek him because "it was said that I preached the Word of God and was a good man."

Menno's progress in the Gospel was slow. One pillar of his Catholic faith had broken down, namely, the mass, but he continued nevertheless, out of fear of men, to celebrate the mass as before. Outwardly he was still a loyal priest. He might never have left the Catholic Church had it not been that a second pillar of his Catholic faith also broke down, the pillar of baptism. The breaking down of this pillar was gradual. It is quite probable that it was begun by the reading of a small book by a certain Billican, a preacher in the South German city of Nördlingen, which advocated the principle of allowing liberty in the age of baptism. At least Menno refers to a book on baptism by certain preachers of Nördlingen. The book used arguments first given by Cyprian, one of the early Latin church fathers of North Africa. At first Menno paid little attention to the question, but he was forced to think seriously about baptism in the year 1531 while he was still at Pingjum by a very strange occurrence in the neighboring city of Leeuwarden. On March 20, 1531, a certain tailor by the name of Sicke Freerks Snijder was executed in that city for the strange reason that he had been baptized a second time. "It sounded strange in my ears," says Menno, "that a second baptism was spoken of." It seemed still more strange when Menno learned that Freerks was a pious, God-fearing man, who did not believe that the Scriptures taught that infants should be baptized but that they rather taught that baptism should be administered only to adults upon confession of a personal faith.

Freerks was an itinerant tailor who had been baptized in the city of Emden in East Friesland in the latter part of the year 1530 by a preacher named Jan Volkerts Trypmaker who had in turn been baptized and appointed lay preacher in the same city earlier in 1530 by a certain former Lutheran lay preacher named Melchior Hofmann. It has been claimed that Hofmann himself was baptized by certain radical Anabaptists in Strasbourg late in the year 1530. At any rate he began in 1530 to preach the new baptism and other similar doctrines of the Anabaptists, with Emden as his starting point. It should be said here that the main body of Anabaptists in Strasbourg, as well as in Switzerland and South Germany, had never had anything to do with Hofmann. Indeed, in 1538, in a public disputation with leaders of the Reformed Church in Bern, Switzerland, certain Swiss Anabaptist leaders publicly repudiated all connection with Hofmann. Hofmann preached certain radical and fanatical doctrines relating to the second coming of Christ and the establishment of an earthly kingdom of God at Strasbourg, and also gave many strange interpretations to prophecy including the designation of himself as a second Enoch. The doctrines which he taught were clearly perversions which he originated in his own fertile imagination, fanatical doctrines which he had learned neither from Luther, nor Zwingli, nor the Anabaptists, nor any evangelical teachers. So Hofmann cannot be called an Anabaptist in the same sense as the Swiss Brethren or the Mennonites, even though he taught baptism on confession of faith rather than infant baptism.

But Menno Simons knew nothing of all this when he heard about the execution of Sicke Freerks. What did mightily stir his mind was the thought that one should be willing to die for the sake of a "second baptism." Was it possible that the Catholic Church was wrong in the matter of infant baptism just as it was wrong in the matter of the mass? Once again the priest Menno found himself in a conflict of conscience due to the new doubt that had arisen. But this time he knew how to find the solution to his problem; as an "evangelical" preacher he turned at once to the Bible for light. Here, though he searched long, he "could find no report about infant baptism." He next turned for help to his superior at Pingjum, the pastor. The pastor finally admitted, after repeated discussions with Menno, that infant baptism had no basis in Scripture, but insisted that reason showed that it was necessary and justifiable. But Menno Simons, who had learned to trust the Word, was not willing "to trust his reason" alone. So he sought further for aid, this time searching diligently what the church fathers might have to say. They taught him that children needed baptism to be cleansed from original sin. But when Menno compared this teaching with the Scriptures he found a clear conflict, for did not the Scriptures teach that the blood of Christ the Redeemed, and not the water of baptism, was the only means for cleansing from sin? The church fathers were wrong.

As a last resort, Menno turned to his evangelical contemporaries, the reformers. All of them taught that children should be baptized, though for different reasons. Luther insisted that children could have faith, at least by proxy, and should be baptized on the basis of that faith; Butzer of Strasbourg urged that children be baptized as a guarantee that they would be reared in the ways of the Lord; whereas Bullinger of Zurich argued that children should be incorporated into the covenant people by baptism as the Jewish children had been incorporated into the covenant people by circumcision. But in spite of their various and diverse arguments, Menno noted that all alike failed to give Scriptural proof for infant baptism; each followed his own reason. Having arrived at the end of his diligent search with no proof that infant baptism was based on the Word of God, Menno concluded that "all were deceived about infant baptism"—the Catholic Church, priests at Pingjum, the church fathers, the reformers—and that baptism on confession of faith alone was Scriptural.

This momentous decision was the most significant one in Menno's entire career, for it sealed the breach with the Catholic Church and ultimately led him into the circle of the Anabaptists. Salvation by the sacrament of baptism was the cornerstone upon which the whole Catholic system of religion was built. One might conceivably remain a Catholic while denying transubstantiation, but how could one keep faith with a church whose essential mode of salvation was denied? On the other hand, the Anabaptists alone among the religious groups of the day denied the need for infant baptism and based membership in the church upon a personal experience of salvation of which water baptism was merely the outward symbol.

Yet this momentous decision, apparently arrived at in the year 1531, did not lead Menno at once to an outward breach with the church which he served as priest, and from which he drew his income. Five more years were to pass until this break came. Even though, as Menno asserts emphatically, his new beliefs in the matter of baptism (as well as the earlier change in the interpretation of the Lord's Supper) were received through the study of the Scripture under the guidance of the Holy Spirit by the grace of God, his new-won convictions did not lead to action. There were, apparently, small groups of Anabaptists in the vicinity, but Menno did not associate himself with them.

On the contrary, when he was offered the promotion of an appointment to be pastor at Witmarsum, he did not hesitate to accept it. The larger income stirred his "lust for gain," says Menno, and so out of weakness, he continued to live the double life of a hypocrite, continued to officiate at the mass, continued to baptize infants. Menno himself gives the explanation of his weakness, for he says that although he had indeed a knowledge of the Scriptures it had been made fruitless by his fleshly life. What had changed his mind had not yet affected his heart, the Word of God was not yet living within him. He describes his hypocritical life at this time in harsh words: "Relying upon grace I did evil. I was as a carefully whitened sepulcher. Outwardly before men I was moral, chaste, generous; there was none that reproved my conduct; but inwardly I was full of dead men's bones . . . . I sought mine own ease and my praise more zealously than Thy righteousness, honor, truth, and Thy Word."

The inconsistency between conviction and practice in the matter of baptism and the Lord's Supper did not let the new pastor at Witmarsum rest any more than it had the former priest at Pingjum. Menno's conscience constantly condemned him, for he suffered under a continuous inner conflict.

The matter of baptism was stirred up afresh about a year after Menno's arrival in Witmarsum by the entrance of several Anabaptists into the community. Menno says that he neither saw the persons who "broke into the church in the matter of baptism," nor knew who they were, nor whence they came. Still Menno remained quiescent.

But finally a far more serious "break" into his parish occurred when certain ones of the "sect of Münster" reached Witmarsum, and "deceived many pious hearts in our village." This occurred sometime in the year 1534, for the revolutionary kingdom of Münster was not set up until February of that year.

The grievous error of the "perverted sect of Münster," as Menno repeatedly called them, was a very serious matter to Menno. Since the grievous damage wrought by the Münsterites was the final cause of Menno's withdrawal from Catholicism and his adherence to the Anabaptists, and since the fight against this fanatical movement with every weapon at his command was Menno's chief concern in the years 1534 and 1535, it is well to consider briefly the character and effects of Münsterism.

Jan Matthys, an unlearned but egotistical baker of Haarlem, Holland, was one of the small group of followers of Melchior Hofmann who had joined the "Melchiorites" about the year 1531. When Hofmann was cast into prison in Strasbourg in May, 1533, and consequently lost his leadership over his followers, certain unsavory elements in the movement began to win influence and gradually assumed the leadership. Among these Matthys was the chief. He was a powerful personality, filled with hate for the upper classes, and equipped with an imagination capable of devising the most fantastic schemes. He succeeded in wresting the leadership to himself and swinging most of the Melchiorites with him in a radical revolutionary program, although some, like the brothers Obbe and Dirk Philips of Leeuwarden and others, totally rejected the strange new teachings of Matthys from the outset and refused to have anything to do with him even though they were threatened with persecution by his agents. In fact, Obbe Philips took the leadership of a group of Melchiorites who definitely rejected all the radical teachings of Hofmann as well as the perversions of Matthys and sought to build their faith alone on a sound interpretation of Scripture.

Meanwhile Jan Matthys heard that the evangelical laboring classes of the city of Münster in Westphalia in northwest Germany had overthrown the dominant upper classes including the Catholic bishop. Thrilled with the thought that this might furnish him an opportunity to secure a base to begin his campaign against the "godless" upper classes, he at once sent agents to Münster who succeeded in winning over the evangelical preachers Rothmann and Roll to his program in January, 1534. Soon Matthys himself came to the city, took over control with the willing acquiescence of the somewhat hysterical populace, and promised to establish the kingdom of God on earth, the new Jerusalem. When he was killed in a sortie in April, Jan of Leiden took his place and installed himself as king. The amazing doctrine was now announced that since the kingdom of God had come, judgment was to be executed upon the unbelieving world by believers and members in the new kingdom. "Apostles" were sent out repeatedly from Münster inviting "believers" everywhere to come to the new Jerusalem and participate in its blessings. Thousands believed the announcement, accepted the invitation, and set out, and although many of them were arrested on the way, hundreds reached the city. However the reign of the Münster kingdom was not to be long; the siege of the city, which was instituted by the army of the Bishop of Münster in March, 1534, led to the final capture and the overthrow of the "Kingdom" in June, 1535, after terrible suffering and indescribable scenes of brutality within the city.

Unfortunately the doctrine of vengeance and destruction of the ungodly by the godly had taken deep root in the circles of the former Melchiorites in Holland, so that lesser plottings and revolts were organized in other places of Münster, with consequent disaster. The terrible poison of the revolutionary fanaticism of Jan Matthys and Jan of Leiden wrought its deadly work among the harassed and persecuted Melchiorites of Holland.

Menno Simons came into contact with the "Münsterite perversion" sometime during the year 1534. Some of the more zealous and pious souls among his flock, doubtless some of those who had been influenced by his preaching and with whom he felt himself spiritually united, were swept away into the fanaticism of the Münsterite error. Even his own brother was among the number. Although Menno had been inclined to adopt the principle of adult baptism, he could not for a moment think of casting his lot with the Münsterites. He admitted that they had a commendable zeal, but declared that they erred grievously in their teaching. He was deeply distressed as he saw their abominable doctrines making inroads among the pious of his parish, and determined to throw himself heart and soul into the struggle against them

The fight against the Münsterite influence occupied Menno's chief attention for almost a year. He was so vigorous in his public denunciation of them in his sermons that he soon won the reputation of being able "to stop the mouths of the enemy very well." In his pastoral visits he sought not only to hold those who were in danger, but to win back those who had already been deceived and had slipped. He even succeeded in having one secret and one public meeting with "two fathers of the perverted sect." Finally Menno decided to carry the battle against them still further by writing. The result of his endeavors was a little pamphlet, written probably early in 1535, although printed for the first time in 1627, bearing the title: "A Clear and Indubitable Proof from Holy Scripture Against the Abominable and Great Blasphemy of Jan van Leiden." In this writing Menno vigorously attacked the claim of "King" Jan to divine authority, and proved that the taking of arms by the Münsterites was a gross sin and contrary to the will of God for the church, as well as contrary to the example and spirit of Christ. He appealed to all true Christians everywhere to separate themselves from such abominations and to follow after the example of Christ.

## II. CONVERSION AND RENUNCIATION OF CATHOLICISM, 1535-1536

But even while Menno was fighting vigorously the good fight of truth against the error of the Münsterites, he was becoming constantly more deeply involved in a serious inner conflict. He sought to keep the pious souls who were dissatisfied with the Catholic Church from following the heresy of the Münsterites, but unless he provided them with something better, did he not seem to be merely a defender and supporter of the Catholic Church? And when his Catholic friends used his name and arguments to strike down the Münsterites, was he not letting himself appear to be their ally in maintaining the rule of darkness in that church? The more successfully he fought the Münsterites the more intolerable the situation became to his conscience.

The climax of the conflict in his soul came with the tragedy at the Old Cloister near Bolsward when almost three hundred misguided souls lost their lives, among them his own brother in the flesh. The group was one of those referred to earlier, which had been imbued with the poison of the Münsterite revolution, and had decided to set up its own city of refuge and begin its own campaign for the kingdom of God in Friesland. In March, 1535, a large company of three hundred had seized an old monastery (Oude Kloster) outside of the city of Bolsward and entrenched itself therein. They were unable to hold out long against the siege of the forces of the government and after one hundred and thirty had been slain, the rest were captured and executed on April 7. The sight of these "poor misguided sheep," as Menno called them, giving their blood and their lives for their faith, even though it was a false faith, made an extraordinary impression upon Menno. He could not cast it off. They had given their lives for error, while he was not willing to give anything for the truth, but merely for fear of losing his reputation and his income continued to be a part of a system which his conscience had rejected. If he had had the courage to come out into the open, renounce Catholic doctrine and practices, and be a shepherd to these erring sheep, perhaps he could have saved them and averted the tragedy. Their blood, he felt, was upon his soul, and there it burned deeply to his shame. "The blood of these people," he said, "became such a burden to me that I could not endure it nor find rest in my soul." It was true that he had spoken against some of the abominations of the papal system, but out of fear of the "cross of his Lord" he had not made a clean breach with the whole system.

The tragedy of the Old-Cloisterites brought Menno to the parting of the ways; he now saw clearly his duty. As a servant of God he could not evade the responsibility to help the erring sheep, and as one who professed obedience and trust in God he dared no longer refuse to take up the cross of persecution and suffering whatever the cost might be. He could no longer go against his conscience and conviction.

In this extremity of his soul, Menno turned to God with sighing and tears, pleading for grace and forgiveness, pleading for a pure heart and courage to preach His holy name and His Word in all truth. In his own account of his conversion Menno describes his change of heart in the following words: "My heart trembled in my body. I prayed God with sighs and tears that He would give me, a troubled sinner, the gift of His grace and create a clean heart in me, that through the merits of the crimson blood of Christ He would graciously forgive my unclean walk and ease-seeking life, and bestow upon me wisdom, candor, and courage, that I might preach His exalted and adorable name and Holy Word unadultered and make manifest His truth to His praise." The Lord was gracious unto him, the decision was made, and Menno went forth with a sense of divine mission to a new life. Some may criticize Menno for having tarried so long with his decision, but such condemnation is hardly just. The full light dawned upon him but gradually and his was a slow-moving Frisian nature, not easily stirred and changed. What is important to note is that once Menno was stirred he was moved to the depths of his nature, and from the decision once made he never turned back. The change was so deep, so thorough, so complete, and gave him such a sense of divine mission, that he was enabled by the grace of God to be an inspired leader, a mighty tower of strength to his bitterly persecuted people, for more than twenty-five years. In reality, a comparison with Luther and Zwingli casts no discredit upon Menno Simons in respect to the speed of his break with Rome, particularly when we remember that Martin Luther had the powerful protection of the Elector of Saxony and endangered neither his reputation nor his income by his change, while Zwingli never moved until he had the support of the city council of Zurich, whose well-paid pastor he remained until his death on the battlefield of Cappell.

Menno Simons' decision to break completely with the Catholic Church probably occurred in April, 1535, soon after the tragedy at Bolsward. He began at once to preach openly from his pulpit in Witmarsum the truths which he had possibly taught in part in private earlier, the word of repentance, of true faith, of believer's baptism, of the right Lord's Supper. He dared now to attack openly all the evils of the church, for he was done with all calculations to save himself. He apparently determined to use the Witmarsum church as the platform for his new message as long as possible, as Luther had done at Wittenberg, and Zwingli at Zurich. The marvel is that for nine months he was permitted to do this, according to his own statement. During these nine months he carried on a double campaign: on the one hand he was striving mightily to save his people from the Münsterite abominations, and on the other hand he was seeking to lead them out of their old beliefs into the true faith of the Gospel. Note his own description of his attitude and activity during these nine months.

"In consequence, I began in the name of the Lord to preach publicly from the pulpit the word of true repentance, to direct the people unto the narrow path and with the power of the Scriptures to reprove all sin and ungodliness, all idolatry and false worship, and to testify to the true worship, also baptism and the Lord's Supper according to the teaching of Christ, to the extent that I at that time had received grace from God. I also faithfully warned every one of the Münsterite abominations, viz., king, polygamy, earthly kingdom, the sword, etc., until after about nine months when the gracious Lord granted me His fatherly Spirit, aid, power and help, that I voluntarily forsook my good name, honor and reputation which I had among men and renounced all the abominations of Antichrist, mass, infant baptism and my unprofitable life, and willingly submitted to homelessness and poverty under the cross of my Lord Jesus Christ; in my weakness I feared God, sought out the pious and, although they were few in number, I found some who had a commendable zeal and maintained the truth.

"Behold thus, my reader, the God of mercy, through His abounding grace which He bestowed upon me, a miserable sinner, has first touched my heart, given me a new mind, humbled me in His fear, taught me in part to know myself, turned me from the way of death and graciously called me into the narrow path of life, into the communion of His saints. To Him be praise forevermore. Amen."

But Menno's position as an evangelical preacher in a Catholic pulpit and parish could not long be maintained. His complete secession from the church was only a matter of time. Just when he was baptized is not clear, possibly soon after his conversion in April, but more probably not until his public secession from the church nine months later. During these nine months he may have introduced changes in the ceremonies and sacraments of the church as well as in the content of his preaching. It is possible that the mass was changed into a simple communion service in commemoration of the Saviour's suffering and death, and certainly all infant baptisms must have ceased. Finally it became apparent to Menno that he could no longer have any connection with the old church, with "Babel," even in a purely external way. Consequently he voluntarily, without compulsion, "forsook Babel and entered the true church, the house of his Lord." This he did by relinquishing his pulpit and his charge as a priest and by leaving the village of Witmarsum for other residence. The exact time of the renunciation of the papal church was probably Sunday, January 30, 1536. It may be assumed that he went to Obbe Philips in Leeuwarden to tell him of his decision, for Menno says that he first looked about him for God-fearing people.

But for the next few months after his secession what Menno wanted more than anything else was quiet to think over the implication of his decision, to read the Word of God and to meditate upon it, and to solve some of the theological questions which still troubled him. One of these questions concerned the exact mode of the incarnation. He had apparently learned of some peculiar views of the incarnation from some of the brethren, who may have gotten them originally from Melchior Hofmann, and wanted to decide for himself what he should believe. The problem which disturbed him was this: How could the sinless divine nature of Christ be incarnated in the flesh of sinful descendants of fallen Adam? Because of his earnest desire for the truth and his great fear of unbelief and error, Menno came into a serious conflict on this question. He fasted and prayed to God "that He might reveal to him the mystery of the conception of His blessed Son" in so far as this was necessary for the glory of God and the lightening of the burden of his conscience. Attempts to secure help from the brethren were unsatisfactory. After several months Menno felt that he had come to a satisfying conclusion on his question by adopting a theory of the incarnation which made the incarnation a new creation of the human flesh of Christ in Mary so that Christ took being in Mary but was not born of Mary's flesh. It was similar to Hofmann's view. Menno developed this theory chiefly to satisfy himself and seldom said much about it except when he was forced to do so in public debates by his enemies who found his peculiar view of the incarnation a weak spot. He complained repeatedly that he was compelled against his inclination to debate on this point. It is of interest to note that Menno's vagary on the mode of the incarnation was not acceptable to the Swiss Mennonites, and that although it continued to have influence on the thinking of some of the Dutch-North German Mennonites this theory of the incarnation never found its way into any authoritative creed or confession of the Mennonite Church.

The year following Menno's public renunciation of the Catholic Church in January, 1536, was spent in retirement, as has been stated above. Apparently Menno did not remain at any one place. Traces of his movements during this time have been preserved in the records of martyrs who were punished several years later for sheltering him. He traveled from Witmarsum to Leeuwarden, back to Witmarsum and to Groningen. Toward the end of the year he seems to have settled down in a retreat in or near the city of Groningen in northeast

Holland; it was in the province of Groningen that he was ordained as an elder or bishop.

Menno fails to mention the place of his ordination or the names of those who ordained him, but tells in detail the experience which led up to the final commission. It must be clear of course that after his secession Menno had continued to preach and to teach as he had occasion and opportunity; but he had assumed no definite responsibility or leadership among the Brethren since leaving Witmarsum. While he was giving himself to study and writing in his retreat near Groningen, six or eight of the brethren came to him and entreated him to accept the office of elder or chief shepherd and bishop of the brotherhood. The time of the call was "about a year after he left the papacy," that is, sometime during the winter of 1536-37. It was not easy for Menno to accept the call, for although he considered it his duty to aid in shepherding the "God-fearing ones," yet he knew what might await him out in the world if he should publicly appear as their leader. So he asked for time for prayer and consideration. When the brethren soon after repeated the call a second time, Menno yielded, though not without a struggle. He describes his decision thus:

"When I heard this [the call] my heart was greatly troubled. Apprehension and fear were on every side. For on the one hand I saw my limited talents, my great lack of knowledge, the weakness of my nature, the timidity of my flesh, the very great wickedness, wantonness, perversity and tyranny of the world, the mighty great sects [the persecuting state churches], the subtlety of many men and the indescribably heavy cross which, if I began to preach, would be the more felt; and on the other hand I recognized the pitifully great hunger, want and need of the God-fearing, pious souls, for I saw plainly that they erred as innocent sheep which have no shepherd.

"When the persons before mentioned did not desist from their entreaties, and my own conscience made me uneasy in view of the great hunger and need already spoken of, I consecrated myself, soul and body, to the Lord, and committed myself to His gracious leading, and I began in due time [i.e., after having been ordained to the ministry of the Word] according to His holy Word to teach and to baptize, to labor with my limited talents in the harvest field of the Lord, to assist in building up His holy city and temple and to repair the dilapidated walls."

The ordination must have taken place early in 1537, and was performed by Obbe Philips "in Groningen," as Obbe himself reports.

The significance of Menno's acceptance of the leadership of the brotherhood in northern Holland, known at that time as Obbenites, can scarcely be overestimated. As Menno himself says, the few who had remained faithful to Scriptural, evangelical doctrines under the leadership of Obbe and Dirk Philips, and had resisted the temptation to follow after the fanatical doctrines of Jan Matthys, were discouraged and scattered, eagerly looking for a strong leader. Obbe Philips himself finally lost heart, laid down his office as bishop, and left the brotherhood entirely a few years later, probably in 1541. Many of those who had been swept away in the Münsterite stream, disillusioned by the tragic failure of the "Kingdom," were helplessly confused as sheep without a shepherd. They perhaps could be won back to a true faith.

On the other hand other fanatical leaders were still trying to promote radical movements in spite of the collapse of Münster, and they were endangering the faith of many. Chief among them was Jan of Batenburg, the outstanding leader, whose program of violent vengeance degenerated more and more into simple banditry. A gathering of these revolutionary Anabaptists was held at Bocholt in Westphalia in August, 1536. Even David Joris, whom Obbe Philips had ordained as a bishop about the same time as he ordained Menno, turned out to be an ecstatic and visionary fanatic, whose foolish interpretations of Scripture were matched by his unclean and hypocritical character. It is not too much to say that the preservation of the Dutch and North German Anabaptists from complete annihilation or at least from absorption into the fanaticism of the Batenburgers and Davidians, and their rallying around a Biblical standard of faith and life, was due in large measure to the fruitful labors of Menno Simons, who yielded to the earnest appeal of his God-fearing brethren and in so doing yielded himself heart and body and soul to his God, and took upon himself "the heavy cross" of his Lord in a faithful, unremitting devoted ministry until his death at Wüstenfelde in Holstein in 1561.

## III. LABORS IN HOLLAND, 1536-1543

The field of labor assigned to Menno Simons at the time of his ordination was apparently not limited in any way. He was expected to visit the scattered brethren, to preach, to baptize, to build up the church of God as he had opportunity. Naturally he sought to fulfill his task first in the territory which lay near at hand. Very little direct evidence of his work during the first years of his ministry has been preserved. What is available shows that although he was married to a certain Gertrude in 1536 or 1537, he maintained no permanent residence, but traveled about a great deal. His first field of labor extended from East Friesland, where he baptized a certain Peter Jans at Oldersum in 1536, westward across the two northern provinces of Groningen and West Friesland. In the latter two provinces he spent most of his time until 1541.

Menno himself tells of one man whom he had baptized in West Friesland and who was executed January 8, 1539, because he had sheltered Menno.

"About the year 1539," writes Menno, "a very pious and God-fearing man named Tjard Reynders was apprehended in the place where I sojourned, for the reason that he had received me, a homeless man, out of compassion and love, into his house, although in secret. A short time after this he was, after a free confession of his faith, executed and broken on the wheel as a valiant soldier of Christ, according to the example of his Lord, although he had the testimony, even of his enemies, that he was an unblamable and pious man." It is noteworthy that in this statement Menno calls himself a homeless man.

He came to West Friesland several times a year until 1541, and was so effective in his work that he soon became known as the outstanding leader of the Anabaptists in the province. The provincial authorities had tried unsuccessfully for several years to extirpate "the accursed sect" and finally concluded that they would have no success until Menno himself was gotten out of the way. A plan was proposed to Mary, regent of the Netherlands, by which certain captured Anabaptists might be prevailed upon to betray Menno in return for pardon, but it failed to work. The letter, dated May 19, 1541, in which the plan was outlined, illustrates vividly the dangers which faced Menno in his labors.

"Most serene, right honorable, most mighty Queen, most gracious Lady. We offer ourselves as humbly as we can for Your Majesty's service. Most gracious Lady, although the error of the cursed sect of the Anabaptists which in the last five or six years has very strongly prevailed in this land of Friesland, but now—the Lord be praised—through the publication of divers placards and through executions which have been carried into effect against transgressors of that sort, this sect would doubtless be and remain extirpated, were it not that a former priest Menno Symonsz who is one of the principal leaders of the aforesaid sect and about three or four years ago became fugitive, has roved about since that time once or twice a year in these parts and has misled many simple and innocent people. To seize and apprehend this man we have offered a large sum of money, but until now with no success. Therefore we have entertained the thought of offering and promising pardon and mercy to a few who have been misled [by the Anabaptists] and who desire grace [having recanted their faith] if they would bring about the imprisonment of the said Menno Symons. However we would not be so bold as to do this ourselves but desire first to advise Your Majesty of it, praying to be informed of Your Majesty's good pleasure and command which we, to the extent of our power, are willing and ready to carry out, as knows God Almighty. May He long spare Your Majesty in good health and happy reign. Written at Leeuwarden on the nineteenth day of May, 1541. Your Majesty's very humble and obedient servants, the counsellors ordained of the Imperial Majesty in Friesland."

The offers of reward for Menno's arrest which had been announced by placards spread throughout the province of West Friesland brought no results, nor did they deter Menno from his labors in that region. At last the emperor himself, Charles V, was prevailed upon to publish a severe edict against Menno on December 7, 1542, which placed a price of 100 gold guilders on his head, and which further forbade giving aid or shelter to him in any way or reading his books. All his followers were likewise ordered to be arrested. Whoever should succeed in delivering Menno to the authorities was promised pardon for any crime which he might have committed. (See Horsch biography, 55-7.)

The severity of this edict indicates the intensity of the persecution which Menno and his followers experienced in Friesland at this time. Menno was fully aware of the danger which faced him but he continued to labor with unabated zeal and courage.  His spirit is well characterized by the following lines from a tract which he wrote about this time:

"And above all pray for your poor and willing minister who is sought with great diligence to be delivered up to death, that God, the gracious Father, may strengthen him with His Holy Spirit and save him from the hands of those who so unjustly seek his life, if it be His Fatherly will; and if it be not His will, that He may then grant him in all tribulation, torture, suffering, persecution and death such heart, mind, wisdom and strength," etc.

In the year 1541 Menno shifted his field of labor further south to the city of Amsterdam and the territory immediately surrounding it known as the province of North Holland.  Here he spent most of his time for the two years from 1541 to 1543, without breaking off his contacts with Friesland and Groningen.  While he doubtless baptized many in Amsterdam and vicinity during this time, the names of but two have been preserved, Lukas Lamberts and the bookseller Jan Claeszoon.  Both were executed as martyrs on January 19, 1544, shortly after Menno left this region.  Claeszoon or Claassen circulated Menno's writings and possibly even published some of them.  He was also an ordained minister.

During the seven years of labor in the Netherlands Menno was quite active in writing, and in circulating the booklets which he wrote.  A total of seven titles appeared, five of which were rather small pamphlets, varying in size from twenty to sixty pages of average book size.  The two most important books were *Foundation of Christian Doctrine,* a book of two hundred and fifty pages written in 1539, and *The True Christian Faith,* a book of one hundred and sixty pages also written in 1541.  *Christian Baptism,* a book of sixty pages published in 1539, is also of importance.  All of the writings of this period of Menno's life are substantial doctrinal expositions dealing with fundamental doctrines such as repentance, faith, the new birth, holiness, and similar themes. They are not learned treatises but rather simply written books well adapted to the common man, and deal with the great issues of the hour.  For this reason they were widely read and did splendid service in strengthening the faith of many who were disturbed and unsettled by the many conflicting currents of the day.  It is no wonder that the authorities were so anxious to suppress Menno's writings, and that they placed severe penalties upon those who read them or distributed them.

## IV. LABORS IN NORTHWEST GERMANY, 1543-1546

Feeling that a wider field of service was open to him in northwest Germany where the severe edicts of the emperor and the regent were not in force, Menno left Holland permanently in the fall of 1543 after seven years of arduous and fruitful labors there.  The remaining eighteen years of his life till his death in 1561 he devoted to building up the church in northwest Germany, the territory just immediately east of Holland.  The comparative length of his labors in the two countries shows that Menno was less of a Hollander than a German during his twenty-five years of service as a Mennonite bishop, a fact which has seldom been recognized as it should. Persecution was not so severe in the territories of northwest Germany as in Holland, first because the emperor, who was a stanch Catholic, had very little power or influence here, and second because many of the rulers and lesser nobility were inclined to be tolerant. Menno's life in Germany falls into three unequal periods which will be treated successively: (1) a few months in East Friesland, 1543-44, (2) two years in the bishopric of Cologne, 1544-46, (3) fifteen years in Holstein and the Baltic seacoast region, 1546-61.

In the early winter of 1543-44, Menno with his family appeared in East Friesland where the Countess Anna was reigning. The capital of this region was the seacoast town of Emden. At this time the territory was in transition from Catholicism to Protestantism; so the Anabaptists were temporarily tolerated. Anna had just appointed (1543) John a Lasco, a Zwinglian reformer and native of Poland who had been active in the province since 1540, to organize the proposed new Protestant state church. Just where Menno settled when he came to East Friesland is unknown, except that it was not in Emden, although there was apparently a fair-sized congregation of brethren here which had been established under the leadership of Obbe and Dirk Philips.

Because of the tolerance of the ruler, Countess Anna, several sects had found refuge in East Friesland in addition to the "Mennonites." Among them were the Batenburgers, who as followers of Jan van Batenburg still held to the bloody doctrines of Münster, and the Davidians, followers of that strange visionary fanatic, David Joris, a former co-worker of the Philips brothers who had separated from them in 1536. When John a Lasco entered upon his work as the reformer of East Friesland in 1543 he soon became aware of the difference between the fanatical, revolutionary sects and the peaceful, relatively orthodox Mennonites. Being seriously concerned with the development of a sound and just policy toward all, he was very glad to learn through some of the brethren of the arrival of Menno Simons himself as the leader in the province, and invited him to come to the capital for a discussion of theological questions. This discussion, called by some a debate or disputation although it really was more of a semipublic interview, was held with the consent of the ruler January 28-31, 1544, in the chapel of the former Franciscan monastery in Emden. Several Reformed ministers and others were present. Three days were necessary to cover the field of discussion, which included the following topics: the incarnation of Christ, baptism, original sin, and the calling of ministers. On two subjects, original sin and sanctification, Menno and a Lasco agreed; on the remaining three no agreement was possible. Menno himself testifies that he was treated with kindness, and that the only demand made was that he submit a written statement of his faith which might be presented to the authorities so that they might have definite and reliable information concerning the principles which Menno and his followers upheld.

The promised statement of faith was delivered by Menno three months later with the title, *Brief and Clear Confession*. It dealt at length (about seventy pages) with two of the disputed doctrines, the incarnation and the calling of ministers, and promised a further statement later on baptism, the third point. The latter statement was never given, and a Lasco proceeded to publish Menno's statement of principles without his consent. He intended to use it as a weapon against the Mennonites, whereas Menno had hoped by it to win recognition or at least tolerance. A Lasco published a reply in the form of a book written in Latin, which appeared at Bonn the following year, 1545. Years later, in 1554, Menno replied in turn in a book of about one hundred pages entitled, *The Incarnation of Our Lord*.

A Lasco's attitude toward the Mennonites was somewhat mixed. He undoubtedly advised the authorities not to permit the leaders such as Menno to remain in the territory, yet he seemed to be willing to grant a measure of toleration to the lay members, and took care to distinguish them from such radical groups as the Batenburgers. When Countess Anna in 1544 under pressure from Holland issued an edict banishing all "Anabaptists," a Lasco persuaded her to modify it so as to expel the radicals and permit the "Menists" milder treatment subject to examination by a Lasco, although banishment was retained as an ultimate penalty. This modified decree of 1545 is of historic interest as the first document in which the name "Menist" or Mennonite was used to refer to the followers of Menno Simons.

Before the middle of the year 1544, probably in May, Menno fled from East Friesland to find refuge and peace in the territory of the bishopric of Cologne. Two reasons probably drew Menno to the Rhineland. One was the existence in this territory of a number of flourishing congregations of the Brethren. The other was the very tolerant policy of Archbishop Herman von Wied, who was favorable to the Reformation and who was at that time engaged in transforming the bishopric into a Lutheran principality.

The two years (1544-46) which Menno was permitted to spend in the bishopric of Cologne until Herman von Wied was driven out by his Catholic enemies in 1546, were among the most peaceful and fruitful of his life. The few traces of his labors and movements which have been preserved reveal that he traveled a great deal, that his books were widely distributed and read, and that his name and fame were growing rapidly. In his own writings Menno later refers to some of his experiences here, mentioning the fact that he had been invited to discuss theological matters with the preachers at Bonn on the Rhine and also with the preachers at Wesel in the territory of Cleve. At Bonn the authorities, influenced by reports from John a Lasco and his friend, Hardenberg, finally rejected the plan, while the Wesel preachers in their reply to Menno's offer to come, offered to let the hangman instruct Menno, although they had previously told one of Menno's friends that they would be ready to meet him in a discussion.

Traces of Menno's labors in the Rhineland have been preserved in the

*Left*: Hans de Ries, 1553-1638, Dutch Mennonite bishop, historian, and religious writer. *Right*: The 1948 Portrait of Menno Simons by Arend Hendriks.

*Left*: Interior of the former Witmarsum Mennonite Church built in the early eighteenth century. Now the site of the Menno Simons Monument. *Right*: Dirk Philips, c. 1504-68 Menno's colleague, friend, and fellow-bishop.

Title page of the 1580 edition of the Dutch Mennonite martyrology, *Het Offer des Heeren* (The Lord's Offering).

Title page of the first edition of Menno Simons' *Foundation of Christian Doctrine*, 1539.

Scene from the 1685 edition of T. J. van Braght's *Martyrs Mirror*, drawn by Jan Luiken.

The only extant letter in the handwriting of Menno Simons, *Comforting Letter to a Widow*, c. 1549. (Note his initials, MS, following the Amen.) This letter is given in English translation on pages 1028, 1029.

confessions and testimones of some of the martyrs. Among the places mentioned where he preached are Fischerswert and Illekhoven. At the latter place
Menno lodged in 1545 with a deacon named Lemke. One martyr was executed
because he had transported Menno Simons and two other men in a boat from
his home at Fischerswert down the Meuse River to Roermond. When the
mild reign of Archbishop Herman came to an end by his deposition because of
the defeat of the Protestant princes in the Smalcald War in 1546, and Catholicism was restored throughout the province, Menno's time in Cologne was up
and he was forced to flee.

## V. LABORS IN HOLSTEIN, 1546-1561

Forced to leave the Rhineland, Menno fled with his sick wife and small
children to the territory of Holstein which lay east and north of Hamburg
along the Baltic seacoast. Already small groups of Mennonites fleeing from
persecution in Holland had found their way into this region which was under
the sovereignty of the king of Denmark and thus not under the anti-Anabaptist
laws of the empire. Where Menno first settled is unknown, although he did
live for a time in the city of Wismar; his later residence was in or near the
small village of Wüstenfelde not far from Oldesloe, about halfway between the
Hanseatic cities of Hamburg and Lübeck. The first evidence of Menno's
presence in Holstein was his participation in a theological discussion at Lübeck
in 1546 with Nicholas Blesdijk, a son-in-law and follower of the notorious
David Joris, and a leader of the sect of Davidians.

David Joris, a Fleming born at Bruges, was one of the most remarkable
and notorious characters which the Reformation produced. He early became
a zealous Lutheran, but in 1531 came under the influence of Melchior Hofmann's teachings and joined the group of Melchiorites. Later he associated
with the Obbenites and was apparently ordained a minister by Obbe Philips
before Menno Simons joined the group. However, when Joris became infected with Münsterite ideas and developed fanatical tendencies, which was apparently in the year 1536, the Obbenites disowned him. From that time on Joris
led a movement of his own which became known as the Davidians, although his
following never became large. Finally in 1544 under the stress of persecution
and tribulation he forsook his followers, assumed the name of John of Bruges,
and settled as a Reformed refugee in Basel where he died in 1556.

The teachings of Joris were a strange mixture of theological fanaticism
and antinomianism. He claimed to have a divine call to be a prophet and to
establish the kingdom of God on earth over which he was to reign as the third
David. He went so far as to teach that the work and revelation of Christ were
not adequate and that the Holy Scriptures were to be superseded by his own
literally inspired writings which contained the final revelation of God. His
conception of fleshly sin was such that he taught that the inner man was not
affected by what the flesh might do, and that hence the gross works of the

flesh were not to be counted as sin. As a consequence of such teaching, much sin and immorality appeared among the Davidians.

Menno had openly attacked David Joris and his teachings in his very first writings, 1536-39. Aroused by Menno's attack in the *Foundation,* Joris wrote a letter to Menno challenging him to prepare for a great battle. Menno replied vigorously to the challenge in a strong letter to Joris written in 1542, in which he pointed out that further contact between the two men was impossible because they stood on radically different platforms, since Menno followed Christ and His Word, whereas Joris followed his own foolish and egotistical dreams and hallucinations. He therefore requested Joris to cease writing to him, for he would not read any more of his writings until he had learned to respect and honor the Word of Christ.

When Joris disappeared from the world of affairs under the alias of John of Bruges, an end was put to the personal conflict, but not to contact between Menno and the Davidians. In a country place near Lübeck Menno engaged in an extended discussion with the above-mentioned Nicholas Blesdijk, in which baptism and other questions were debated. Menno was supported in the debate by Dirk Philips, Leonard Bouwens, Gillis of Aachen, and Adam Pastor. The record of the discussion was printed but seems to have been lost. However Blesdijk describes the meeting in several of his books, especially in one published in 1546 under the title, *A Christian Vindication and Refutation . . . of a Letter Written by Menno Simons.* Among the many points of difference between the Mennonites and the Davidians, one stands out sharply. Menno and his brethren held that the doctrine of the church and its correct organization and discipline was one of the most important doctrines of Christianity, whereas the Davidians would have nothing of the sort. For them the individual and a so-called "spiritual" interpretation of the Scriptures was the center and source of Christian doctrine.

The presence of the four brethren in the debate at Lübeck with Blesdijk, suggests organized co-operation among the leaders of the Mennonites at this time. There is good evidence to believe that about this time the bishops began to have occasional meetings or conferences, and that they worked out a plan of co-operation whereby a definite territory was assigned to each bishop within which he was permanently responsible for pastoral oversight, for discipline, and for baptizing new converts. Bouwens was given the West (Holland), Gillis of Aachen received the Rhineland, Dirk Philips was assigned the region of Danzig and its vicinity along the eastern Baltic, while Menno retained the central district from East Friesland to Holstein and was recognized as the chief among the bishops. Dirk Philips was apparently a bishop before Menno was ordained in 1537. Gillis of Aachen was ordained a bishop about 1542, while Bouwens was not made a bishop until 1551. Unfortunately, the first leader of the brethren, Obbe Philips, had lost heart about 1541 and turned back upon the movement which he had served so well. Menno considered him an apostate.

The bishops mentioned above, together with others, met occasionally at various places. At such meetings reports were given of conditions in the various fields, problems were discussed, serious cases of discipline decided, and regulations drawn up for the church. The meeting of Lübeck in 1546 on the occasion of the debate with Blesdijk is the first recorded meeting of the sort. At least two meetings were held in the next year, 1547, one in Emden and one in Goch. The chief matter considered at these meetings was the doctrinal error which had become apparent in the teaching of Adam Pastor (Roelof Martens), one of the leaders who had been ordained about 1542 by Menno Simons and Dirk Philips. Pastor erred in the doctrine of the divinity of Christ, for he held that Christ did not exist as the Son of God previous to His coming into the world, and was divine after His incarnation only in the sense that God dwelled in Him. He accepted the authority of the Bible as the Word of God but sought to find support for his heresy by certain peculiar interpretations. At the first meeting in 1547 in Emden the bishops still entertained hope that Pastor might be restored to his former doctrinal position. However, the hoped-for change for the better did not appear so that, at a second meeting held in the same year at Goch, Pastor was excommunicated. Pastor himself held Menno jointly responsible for the excommunication, although Dirk Philips was apparently the one who spoke the words of the ban in the name of the group.

At first Pastor succeeded in securing a following and making some trouble in the church. To counteract the influence of his teaching, Menno in 1550 wrote a tract on the deity of Christ called, *Confession of the Triune God.* In no uncertain tones he set forth the Scriptural teaching on this subject, and warned the church strongly against the new teaching as a violation of a fundamental doctrine of the Gospel. The tract, a pamphlet of about twenty pages, was first circulated among some of the churches in handwritten form. Later a copy made for the brethren in Groningen was printed.

The last contact between Menno Simons and Adam Pastor was at a debate at Lübeck in 1552. The purpose of the original excommunication in 1547 had been twofold, first to protect the church, and second to make the man consider the error of his ways with the hope that he might be won back. With the hope that Pastor might be persuaded to return, Menno agreed to the discussion in 1552. According to Pastor's own report of the meeting the discussion was fruitless. Little further is heard of the followers of Pastor. After a period of activity in the Rhineland and Westphalia, Pastor died in Münster. His following, which never was large, gradually disintegrated.

As was stated earlier, Menno's assignment as a bishop involved the pastoral oversight of the entire territory in northern Germany east of Groningen to Prussia, including East Friesland, Oldenburg, Holstein, Mecklenburg, and possibly Pomerania. His travels at times took him outside of these territories. In 1547 he attended the meeting of the elders in Goch; in April, 1549, he was in West Friesland near Leeuwarden; and in the summer of 1549 he visited the brethren in Prussia. The visit to Prussia is reported by Menno himself in a letter to the brethren in Prussia dated October 7, 1549. The letter consists primarily of an appeal to maintain the peace and unity which had been restored among the brethren after a serious controversy had been settled by Menno during his visit in the previous summer.

Scarcely had Menno returned from settling the controversy in Prussia until he found it necessary to make a trip to the western congregations in a similar mission. The influence of Pastor's heretical teaching concerning the deity of Christ was still making trouble, and other disputes had arisen over the application of the ban in matters of excommunication. On both subjects Menno wrote pamphlets in the year 1550. The one against Pastor has already been mentioned; the second pamphlet was entitled *Clear Account of Excommunication.* This latter writing, a pamphlet of about forty-five pages, was circulated among the churches in handwritten form. It was not printed until 1597. The pamphlet was a discussion of the function, practice, and extent of the ban, and was directed against those who wished it applied to spiritual matters only. In the course of the western trip a conference was held at Emden in 1549 at which among other things, one of the ministers, Francis Kuyper, was excommunicated by Menno because of having defended unscriptural views on justification by faith and other points.

Aside from these two briefer pamphlets of 1550 (which were not printed at once) and a few short letters and four brief petitions written in 1551 and 1552, Menno did not publish anything of importance between 1541 and 1554, except the *Reply to Gellius Faber* in 1552, a book of about two hundred and fifty pages. One reason was perhaps that he was too busy in his travels and in performing his duties as a bishop to have much time for writing. Another reason may have been the difficulty in finding a printer who would print his books for him. The four petitions mentioned above were addressed in a general way to the civil authorities and to the learned men and teachers of the Lutheran and Reformed state churches of Germany. The purpose of all the "petitions" was to refute the charges of heresy and fanaticism which were constantly being brought against the Mennonites by their enemies. In them Menno asserted in the strongest possible terms that he and his brethren had no connection whatsoever with Münster, and that their only purpose was to be truly Biblical Christian believers. He also appealed for public discussions in which he would have an opportunity to refute the false accusations of his enemies.

The *Reply to Gellius Faber* mentioned above was a lengthy discussion of six fundamental questions: the calling of ministers, baptism, Lord's Supper, ban, church, and incarnation. Faber, a Reformed minister in Emden, associate of a Lasco, had attacked the doctrines of the Mennonites, although not specifically directing his attack against Menno. This book is Menno's largest, though of little importance because it merely repeats the thought of his earlier writings. The most important thing in it is his account of his own conversion and call to the ministry, which has often been reprinted as a separate tract.

During the winter of 1553-54 Menno spent some time in the Hanseatic city of Wismar on the Baltic seacoast between Lübeck and Rostock. Here he fellow-shiped with a Mennonite congregation, although he endeavored to keep his place of residence hidden. In spite of the attempt to maintain secrecy he became involved in a very interesting fashion in a theological discussion with two Reformed ministers. It came about in this way. A boatload of Reformed refugees from London who had been driven out of England by persecution, arrived off the harbor of Wismar on December 21, 1553. The Mennonites of the city were the only ones willing to help the needy refugees whose ship had frozen fast in the ice some distance from shore. In the course of the contact the two groups became so involved in doctrinal discussions that the leader of the refugees, Herman Backereel, requested a discussion with Menno Simons. This discussion was held on December 26, 1553. Feeling the need of support, the Reformed group summoned to their aid Martin Micron of Norden in East Friesland, one of their leading ministers. Micron and Menno held two lengthy discussions in the presence of many interested friends, both of them being held in the house where Menno lived. The dates of the two meetings were February 6 and 15, 1554. All three discussions, the two with Micron and the one with Backreel, were held in strict secrecy with a pledge by the Reformed group not to reveal Menno's hiding place to the magistrates. The meeting of February 6 dealt with the topics of baptism, the incarnation, oath, divorce, calling of ministers, functions of the civil authorities. It concluded peacefully. The second meeting, by request of Micron who knew Menno's weakness, was confined exclusively to the question of the incarnation and ended with bitterness on both sides. No account of these meetings was published until 1556 when Micron published a book under the title, *A True Account*, which contained a partial and somewhat inaccurate account of the proceedings including charges of a personal nature against Menno. Menno replied promptly in 1556 with *Reply to Martin Micron*, containing about two hundred pages, one of his longest writings. Two years later, in 1558, Micron returned to the fray with a book entitled, *A Reckoning*.

Soon after the discussion with Micron in 1554, Menno took part in another important meeting in Wismar of a quite different character, a conference of bishops and leaders of the Mennonite Church. Various matters of discipline had been creating difficulties, so that a meeting of the bishops had become necessary to secure and maintain unity and harmony in the church. The outcome of the conference was a set of nine resolutions dealing with such topics as marriage with nonmembers of the church, application of the ban, use of the courts of justice, the bearing and use of arms, and the necessity of a commission from the church and the bishop in order to preach. Unfortunately the text in which the resolutions have been preserved is so corrupt that it is impossible to be sure of the original meaning. Seven bishops took part in the meeting, Menno Simons being the leader. Among the others were Dirk Philips, Leonard Bouwens, and Gillis of Aachen. In respect to the exercise of the ban the resolutions took a rather strict position, so strict at least, that a conference of Swiss and South German brethren at Strasbourg in 1557 felt it necessary to pass a resolution disagreeing with the Wismar resolutions, and sent two delegates to Menno Simons to ask him to moderate the position on the ban taken by the North German bishops.

The increasing pressure of the civil and ecclesiastical authorities in Wismar against the Mennonites finally made it desirable for Menno Simons to leave the city. He therefore changed his residence during the spring or summer of 1554 to a location some distance westward near the town of Oldesloe between Lübeck and Hamburg. A certain nobleman by the name of Bartholo-mew von Ahlefeldt who lived in this vicinity had permitted Mennonite refugees fleeing from persecution elsewhere to settle upon his estate called "Fresenburg" as early as 1543. A Mennonite printer of Lübeck, who had operated a secret press on which he printed a large number of Mennonite books as well as many Bibles and concordances which were distributed as far west as Amsterdam, was compelled to seek a safer place for his operations. He moved first to Oldes-loe, where ten casks full of books were confiscated, and finally to Fresenburg. He must have reached the latter place sometime during the latter part of 1554. Although it has not been definitely proved, it is altogether possible that the printer was Menno's printer, or even Menno himself, and that Menno ac-cordingly had gone from Wismar to Lübeck, thence to Oldesloe, and finally to Fresenburg. It is more likely however that the printer was a well-to-do member of the church and a friend of Menno, since it is well known that Menno remained a poor man to the end of his life. At this time then Menno settled permanently at Wüstenfelde, a village on the estate of Fresenburg.

As persecution increased in the neighboring regions, more and more Mennonites found a haven of refuge under the protection of Baron von Ahle-feldt at Fresenburg and Wüstenfelde. The King of Denmark tried to persuade von Ahlefeldt to change his policy of toleration and drive them away, but he refused to do so, for he had been deeply and favorably impressed in his younger days by the steadfastness of the Mennonites under persecution, suffering, and death. Here in Fresenburg and Wüstenfelde Menno had time and peace to revise many of his earlier writings and to translate them from the original Dutch into the dialect spoken in this region which is called the *Oostersch* or eastern dialect. All his new writings written after 1554 were written in this dialect. A total of at least ten books and pamphlets were printed at Lübeck and Fresenburg during the years 1554-61.

The last years of Menno's life were saddened by serious and at times bitter controversy among the churches of the West over matters of discipline, chiefly over the question of strictness in the matter of application of the ban and shunning of excommunicated members. As early as 1550, in his booklet *A Clear Account of Excommunication,* Menno had expressed the desire to be spared further trouble over this matter. The more serious divisions occurred after Menno's death.

The first news of the sharpened controversy over the ban reached Menno in 1555 in the form of a letter from five brethren "of good repute" living in Franeker in West Friesland, who reported that some desired that the ban be not imposed without preliminary warning three times except in cases of gross sin. Menno defended this more moderate procedure over against those who demanded an immediate and sharp application of the ban without warning

An allied question which made a great deal of trouble was the question of shunning or avoidance of excommunicated members, particularly when members of the same family were involved. As the controversy grew warmer, letter after letter was sent to Menno from Holland begging him to take sides in the matter. Leonard Bouwens supported the radicals in their extreme demands, and when he finally threatened to expel a married woman in Emden because she refused to shun her husband, Menno was forced to take a stand. In a letter dated November 12, 1556, he protested vigorously against extreme views and practices. He made a trip from Holstein to West Friesland in the hope of promoting unity and harmony, but met with only partial success, for a division still seemed to threaten. He returned home to Wüstenfelde, heartsore and grieving over the sad state of affairs in the church which he loved with all his heart. His feelings are well expressed in a letter addressed to his brother-in-law Reyn Edes in 1558: "O my brother Reyn! If I could only be with you even a half day and tell you something of my sorrow, my grief and heartache, and of the heavy burden which I carry for the future of the church. . . . If the mighty God had not strengthened me in the past year, as He is now doing also, I would have lost my reason. There is nothing on earth that I love so much as the church; yet just in respect to her must I suffer this great sorrow."

Menno's strict position on the ban was to make additional trouble for him with other groups of Mennonites in the Rhineland and in South Germany. In April, 1556, before he had gone to West Friesland, two brethren from the Rhineland, by name Sylis and Lemke, together with others, had visited him in Wüstenfelde to discuss the question of the ban and shunning. They were inclined to be less strict. They left Menno only partially convinced, but agreed to consider the matter further and lay it before certain South German brethren for counsel. Menno gave Sylis a written statement of his position to take along to show the South Germans.

When they finally reported Menno's views on the question of shunning to the very important conference in Strasbourg in 1557 at which over fifty bishops from many countries took part, they received a strongly negative reaction. The conference adopted a resolution rejecting the shunning of married partners and formulated a letter addressed to Menno and his fellow bishops in North Germany and Holland containing an earnest appeal for moderation in the matter of shunning. In the letter they expressed the strong desire to be one in peace and unity with the brethren in the North. They also indicated disagreement with Menno's peculiar theory of the incarnation.

The appeal of the Strasbourg conference was to be in vain. The unity was not reached, for the brethren in the North were implacable in the matter of shunning. In the year 1558 both Menno and Dirk Philips published strong tracts on the question. In Menno's tract, entitled *Instruction on Excommunication*, the strict position on shunning which demanded that all human ties, including those of marriage and the family, must give way under the ban of the church, was clearly taught. This pamphlet stirred up further controversy. Sylis and Lemke took the lead in opposing Menno, so that he felt it necessary to publish a tract against them in January, 1560, entitled *Reply to Sylis and Lemke*. In this pamphlet, which was his last writing, Menno defended himself, and finally announced that he could no longer regard the two men as brethren.

Menno's time after this episode was but short. His health had never been strong, and his life of hardships and privations, as well as the burden of the churches, undermined what health he had, particularly since he had been crippled in Wismar so that he had to use a crutch at times. His death came upon him on his sickbed January 31, 1561, just twenty-five years after his renunciation of Catholicism at Witmarsum. His wife had preceded him in death between 1553 and 1558, as well as two children, a daughter and a son. One daughter survived him. He was buried in his own garden in Wüstenfelde. Unfortunately the place can no longer be determined with accuracy because of the destruction of Wüstenfelde in the devastation of Fresenburg in the Thirty Years' War. The plot of ground was located as nearly as possible in 1906 when a modest memorial was erected by the Hamburg-Altona Mennonite Church in memory of Menno's labors in the service of God and the church he loved.

## VI. THE SIGNIFICANCE OF MENNO SIMONS

Menno Simons was not the founder of the Mennonite Church. The Mennonite Church was founded in Zurich, Switzerland, in January, 1525, by Conrad Grebel, Felix Manz, George Blaurock, and others, eleven years before Menno Simons renounced Catholicism. Nor did Menno found the church in Holland. If any one deserves that title it was Obbe Philips who began to gather the brethren in Friesland about 1533. Yet there is good historical reason for the Mennonite Church to bear the name of Menno Simons, for in the time of greatest need Menno Simons was the heaven-sent leader who rallied the scattered brethren and gave them the leadership in faith and spirit and doctrine which they needed. He it was who led them safely through the time of great tribulation "in spite of dungeon, fire, and sword."

Menno's greatness lay not so much in his eloquence, although he was a good preacher, nor in his literary craftsmanship, although he could write well for the common man. He was no great theologian, although he knew how to present the plain teachings of the Bible with force and clarity. He was not even a great organizer, although he rendered a real service in the guidance which he gave to the bishops and ministers of the growing church. Yet, Menno Simons was one of the great religious leaders of his day and land, perhaps the most outstanding religious leader of the Netherlands in his time. His work and influence have had permanent significance on the history of the people and church which bear his name, and through them his influence has reached the larger circles of the free churches of England and America.

The greatness of Menno Simons lies in three factors of influence, his character, his writings, and his message. His character was a steadying, heartening, building influence in the long, hard years of persecution and struggle from 1535 to 1560, based on deep conviction, unshakable devotion, fearless courage, and calm trust. His writings, though they seem at times, as gathered together in his complete works, to be repetitious and insignificant, included some admirable tracts for the times, pointed, plain, well adapted to their purpose. They reached the common people at the right time, and were powerful agents in the building and strengthening of the church and in winning new adherents. But most of all it was the message of Menno Simons which made him a great leader in a great cause. He built no great system of theology, nor did he discover any great new or long-lost principle; he merely caught a clear vision of two fundamental Biblical ideals, the ideal of practical holiness, and the ideal of the high place of the church in the life of the believer and in the cause of Christ.

On the basis of the first ideal he called for a genuine change of life and the faithful practice of the Christian way of life as Christ taught and lived it, the life of righteousness, holiness, purity, love, and peace. For him Christianity was more than faith only; it was faith and works. And this practical Christianity meant for Menno the resolute abandonment by the Christian of all carnal strife and war, indeed of the use of force in any manner, as well as a thoroughgoing separation from the sin of the worldly social order. The ideal of the church which Menno held was the organizing principle of Christian doctrine and life in his entire thinking. For him the church was the representative and agent of Christ on earth, and as such was to keep itself holy and pure in life and doctrine, and was to give a faithful witness for Christ until He came. These ideals of Menno have been the major formative ideals throughout the four hundred years of Mennonite history, for they were shared by the Swiss-South German Mennonites as well. They constitute the genius of the Mennonite Church. Out of them was born the ideal of complete separation of church and state, of toleration and freedom of conscience, of high moral and social ideals, of the preaching and practice of peace, of the supreme sovereignty of Christ over His own in this worldly world of ours—all ideals far in advance of their day, but which today have become the common and cherished possession of a large section of English and American Protestantism.

It is, therefore, not for the greatness of Menno Simons, the man, and his human achievements, that we bring this tribute—the tribute we bring is to the greatness of the ideals and convictions which possessed his soul and commanded his life, and which have blessed countless thousands since his day.

Throughout this volume the text followed in
the translation was generally that of the 1681 Dutch
folio edition, but occasionally corrected
by the 1646 Dutch edition of Menno's *Opera*.

# The Blasphemy of John of Leiden

*Tegens Jan van Leyden*

## 1535

*For other foundation can no man
lay than that is laid, which is Jesus Christ.*

I Corinthians 3:11

# Introduction

Menno was not converted until 1535. He tells the story of his change of heart in the latter part of the second section of his *Reply to Gellius Faber* (pp. 668-674 of this volume, a section early lifted out and made a separate booklet, and published as such many times in Dutch, German, and English: *Menno Simons' Renunciation of the Church of Rome*).

It was at about the time of his brother's death, which occurred April 5, 1535, that Menno wrote his sharp polemic, *The Blasphemy of John of Leiden*, evidently after his own utter surrender to Christ but before his formal renunciation of Roman Catholicism which occurred on or about January 30, 1536. In this booklet Menno seeks to overcome the awful errors of the Münsterites, a radical sect who sought to establish a theocracy by force of arms. The booklet was evidently circulated in manuscript form, for the first known print is of the year 1627. The full title reads: *A Plain and Clear Proof from Scripture, Proving that Jesus Christ is the Real, Spiritual David of the Promise, the King of Kings, the Lord of Lords, and the Real, Spiritual King of Spiritual Israel, that is, of His Church, which He has bought with His own Blood. Formerly written to all the true Brethren of the Covenant scattered abroad, against the great and fearful Blasphemy of John of Leiden, who Poses as the joyous King of all, the Joy of the Disconsolate, so Usurping the Place of God.* The title page, as in all Menno's works, included also I Corinthians 3:11. The "Brethren of the Covenant" were the peaceful Melchiorites (cf. p. 9).

The remarkable fact about the booklet is the theological maturity which it evinces. Menno has already laid the basic doctrinal convictions which he will stand upon the remainder of his life. There is, asserts Menno, but one true king and lord, namely, Christ Jesus. It is He who possesses all authority in heaven and on earth. It is He who is at the right hand of God, the place of all power. It is the church which is His spiritual kingdom. This kingdom is one of love and peace, one in which only spiritual weapons are wielded. Christians cannot bear arms or fight. They leave the punishment of evildoers to God and the nations of earth; they themselves as followers of Christ cannot undertake to punish or harm sinners. There is but one ultimate Judge, Christ Himself, who will mete out punishment to evildoers on the day of judgment when He comes again. And that day has not yet come. We are still in the age when wheat and tares grow together in the world. Let no one seek to root out the tares now.

The book abounds with Scripture citations and allusions. Menno is already a Biblicist. He has laid the foundation for a lifetime of Bible teaching.

The booklet is printed in Menno's *Opera Omnia Theologica*, Amsterdam, 1681, fol. 619-31, and in the *Complete Works* of 1871, II, 425-40.

J. C. W.

# The Blasphemy of John of Leiden

# 1535

●—●—●—●—●—●—●—●—●—●—●—●—●—●—●—●—●—●—●—●—●—●—●—●—●—●—●—●—●—●—●—●—●—●—●—●—●

## *Salutation*

Grace, peace, and mercy from God the Father, through Jesus Christ, be with all true brethren of the covenant scattered abroad [Melchiorites].

The eternal, merciful God who has called us from darkness into His marvelous light, yes, has led us into the kingdom of His beloved Son, Jesus Christ, must keep us upon the right way, that Satan by his wiles may not deceive us and no root of bitterness spring up among us to make confusion and many be defiled, as alas happens to some these days. It must be that sects arise among us that those who are approved may be made manifest.

Let none stumble at this but let all give heed to the Word of God and abide by it, that they may be delivered from the strange woman, as Solomon says (by which woman we should understand all false teachers), even from the stranger which flattereth with her words; which forsaketh the guide of her youth, and forgetteth the covenant of her God.

This is the true nature of all false teachers. They desert the pure doctrine of Christ and begin to traffic in strange doctrine. They get others under their spell so that they cannot believe the truth and they use smooth talk as Paul says: By good works and fair speeches, they deceive the hearts of the simple. They leave their master Christ, whom alone they should hear as the Father testifies saying: This is my beloved Son, in whom I am well pleased; hear ye him. But this voice from the Father all false teachers forget, and they leave their only master, Christ Jesus, for since they are not of His sheep, they do not hear His voice. The false teachers forget the covenant of their God, and that to which we should give most heed they ignore, as Christ reprovingly said unto the Pharisees: Ye pay tithe of mint and anise and cummin, and have omitted the weightier matters of the law, judgment, mercy, and faith: these ought ye to have done, and not to have left the others undone. Ye blind guides, which strain at a gnat and swallow a camel. Paul said, The end of the commandment is charity out of a pure heart and of a good conscience and of faith unfeigned, from which some having swerved have turned aside unto vain jangling; desiring to be teachers of the law; understanding neither that which they say nor whereof they affirm. So all false teachers forget the cove-

33

nant of God whereby they are bound to Him, as, O God, many do at present who have forgotten all that upon which they were baptized, namely, the cross, and would recommend and make use of the sword. May the Almighty God save all brethren of the covenant from this; may He give them wisdom and prudence to keep the covenant of God, and to be mindful of what kind of spirit Christ wants His disciples to be. Luke 9:55.

God grant that they may be aware of this strange woman, for her house is inclined to death and her ways to corruption. All those who enter in unto her will not come out again, nor do they get on the way of life. And since this strange woman is now very influential and deceives many as did and does the prophetess Jezebel, even as the serpent deceived Eve, therefore we will by the grace of God discover some things that those who are still blind may see and that even as they acknowledge Antichrist to be an abomination standing in the holy place, they may know seduction for what it is. And that even as they will not drink of the cup of the Babylonian harlot, they similarly avoid the venom of the serpent; and that if they be bitten by the serpent, they may become aware of it and get rid of the venom by looking at the true serpent and being cured. All of which God must give us.

We might have been excused from writing but necessity impels us, partly because we cannot tolerate the shameful deceit and blasphemy against God that a man be placed in Christ's stead, partly because we are not allowed to speak, and such deceit and abominable heresy concerning the promised David and other articles are defended with passages from the Bible. But it is the nature of all seductive and erring spirits to flee from the Word of God as Christ says, For every one that doeth evil, hateth the light, neither cometh to the light, lest his deeds should be reproved. But he that doeth truth cometh to the light, that his deeds may be made manifest that they are wrought in God. Therefore he that flees from the light, that is, from the Word of God, manifests that his deeds are not wrought in God.

But there are some who cannot see this. They need the eyesalve which is mentioned in the Revelation of John. O God, what perilous times these are! How the prophet Baal conspires now with the Moabite king against the Israel of God! The Egyptian sorcerers, how they stand now against the true Moses! The lying Pashur, how he is now heeded, because he prophesies prosperity which does not come! How the false Hananiah now deceives the pious children of Israel, and makes them trust in falsehood!

The Almighty God shall raise a Jeremiah to reprove the deceiver of the people, who shall speak nothing but that which God commands him to speak, and the Lord must place His Word in the mouth of this Jeremiah as a fire, and all false teachers as stubble. The Lord will do it so that truth may prevail. No matter how many prophets of Baal arise, yet the Lord will leave a Micah who shall proclaim the true Word of the Lord.

But enough of this. We will undertake the matter to the honor of God and to the edification of the church. In the first place it is certain that Almighty God has made His Son Christ Jesus our Lord King both of the earth and of His faithful church. That Christ is the King of all the earth is abundantly testified to by the Scriptures; particularly the prophet David, who says, The Lord most high is terrible; he is a great King over all the earth, and God is gone up with a shout, the Lord with the sound of a trumpet. Sing praises to God, sing praises; sing praises unto our King, sing praises. For God is the King of all the earth: sing ye praises with understanding. God reigneth over the heathen: God sitteth upon the throne of his holiness.

As certainly as Christ is God, so certainly is He King of all the earth. Paul testifies this in the letter to the Ephesians saying that God the Father raised him from the dead, and set him at his own right hand in the heavenly places, far above all principality, and power, and might, and dominion, and every name that is named, not only in this world, but also in that which is to come: and he hath put all things under his feet, and gave him to be head over all things to the church. Eph. 1:20-22.

Christ testifies of Himself that He is a mighty King, saying: All power is given unto me in heaven and in earth. Paul says that Christ is the express image of God, upholding all things by the word of His power. Christ is the King of all the earth even if the wicked may rebel against it. Therefore the prophet says: The Lord reigneth, therefore the people rage; he sitteth between the cherubim, the earth is moved.[1] Psalm 99:1. For they can do nothing more than the Lord allows them (John 19:11); and none can withstand Him. The mountains melt as wax before the Lord, the ruler of all the earth.

And that Christ is King of His believing church is clearly asserted in the Scriptures. For Isaiah says, Unto us a child is born, unto us a son is given; and the government shall be upon his shoulder: and his name shall be called Wonderful, Counsellor, The mighty God, The everlasting Father, The Prince of Peace. Of the increase of his government and peace there shall be no end. Isa. 9:6.

The house of Jacob is the believing church as everybody knows. Of it, Christ is King, as the angel testified, and as Jeremiah says concerning Christ, that He would be a King who should reign and prosper. Also Isaiah says, Behold, a king shall reign in righteousness, and princes shall rule in judgment.

Seeing then that Christ is King both of all the earth and of His believing church, as we have shown by the plain Scriptures, according to the grace received of God, how can John of Leiden call himself a joyous king of all, the joy of the disconsolate?

If he would be our king, our lord, then Paul and Isaiah must back down, for Paul says: For though there be that are called gods, whether in heaven or in earth, (as there be gods many, and lords many,) but to us there is but one God, the Father, of whom are all things, and we in him; and one Lord Jesus Christ, by whom are all things, and we by him. Isaiah says: The Lord is our judge, the Lord is our lawgiver, the Lord is our king.

[1] Dutch translation. *Tr.*

Behold, as certainly as Christ is our Lawgiver and as surely as He is our Judge, so surely is He our King. What then becomes of John of Leiden? Oh, abominable blasphemy against God, that a man should call himself the joyous king of all when it is written: O Lord God, creator of all things, who art fearful, and strong, and righteous, and merciful, and the only and gracious King, who alone art good, who alone art a mighty king, who alone art righteous, omnipotent and eternal, who deliverest Israel of all evil. Paul says: I give thee charge in the sight of God, who quickeneth all things, and before Christ Jesus, who before Pontius Pilate witnessed a good confession; that thou keep this commandment without spot, unrebukeable, until the appearing of our Lord Jesus Christ: which in his times he shall show, who is the blessed and only Potentate, the King of kings, and Lord of lords.

Again, it is the greatest blasphemy a man can speak that John of Leiden asserts that he is become the joy of the disconsolate. For Christ became our joy at His birth, according to the testimony of the angel to the shepherds: Behold, I bring you good tidings of great joy. For unto you is born this day, in the city of David, a Saviour, which is Christ the Lord. With this the words of David agree: Light is sown for the righteous, and gladness for the upright in heart. Rejoice in the Lord, ye righteous; and give thanks at the remembrance of his holiness. Make a joyful noise unto the Lord, all ye lands. Serve the Lord with gladness: come before his presence with singing. Know ye that the Lord he is God: it is he that hath made us, and not we ourselves; we are his people and the sheep of his pasture. Paul says, Rejoice in the Lord alway: and again I say, Rejoice. In this way all the Scriptures admonish us to rejoice in Christ our Lord; for it is He of whom the patriarch Jacob prophesied that He would be the expectation of the people, that is, the one for whom the people of God should look with great desire, even as Christ testifies: Your father Abraham rejoiced to see my day; and he saw it, and was glad.

Christ is the true Melchisedec, king of Salem, that is, the king of peace, who has made peace between God the Father and the human race. He is the pious Isaac who by His sacrifice has reconciled us with His heavenly Father, and His sacrifice remains in honor forever. Christ is the true David, who has slain the great Goliath, and has taken away the blasphemer of Israel. Yes, He has caused great rejoicing, as it is written: The Spirit of the Lord God is upon me; because the Lord hath anointed me to preach good tidings unto the meek; he hath sent me to bind up the broken-hearted, to proclaim liberty to the captives, and the opening of the prison to them that are bound; to proclaim the acceptable year of the Lord, and the day of vengeance of our God; to comfort all that mourn; to appoint unto them that mourn in Zion, to give them beauty for ashes, the oil of joy for mourning, the garment of praise for the spirit of heaviness.

How clearly it is shown here that Christ is become the joy of the disconsolate in whom all pious Christians rejoice, saying, rejoicing we will rejoice in the Lord, our souls shall rejoice in the Lord; for He has clothed us in raiments of righteousness and surrounded us with the mantle of righteousness, as a bride adorned with bracelets. To this the prophet Zechariah calls us saying: Rejoice greatly, O daughter of Zion; shout, O daughter of Jerusalem: behold, thy King cometh unto thee; he is just, and having salvation; lowly, and riding upon an ass, and upon a colt, the foal of an ass. Zech. 9:9. And the royal prophet David says: Sing unto the Lord a new song, and his praise in the congregation of saints. Let Israel rejoice in him that made him: let the children of Zion be joyful in their King. Let them praise his name in the dance; let them sing praises unto him with the timbrel and harp.

This all the saints of God did. David says: Our soul waiteth for the Lord: he is our help and our shield. For our heart shall rejoice in him because we have trusted in his holy name. And Isaiah: Lo, this is our God; we have waited for him, and he will save us; this is the Lord; we have waited for him, we will be glad and rejoice in his salvation. We see how all the saints have rejoiced in God.

But what joy man can give us, is written: Put not your trust in princes, nor in the son of man, in whom there is no help. His breath goeth forth, he returneth to his earth; in that very day his thoughts perish. Happy is he that hath the God of Jacob for his help, whose hope is in the Lord his God; who helps the needy and raises up those that are bowed down. He is their mighty protection and strong stay, a defense from the heat, and a cover from the sun at noon, a preservation from stumbling and an help from falling. He raiseth up the soul, and lighteneth the eyes; he giveth health, life, and blessing.

Christ is become our joy. Therefore everyone may judge for himself what an abomination it is in the sight of God that a man aspires to be that which our Saviour Christ is. Is this not an abomination standing in the holy place? And what is even worse, this John of Leiden is not satisfied with posing as the joyous king of all who is become the joy of the disconsolate, but he also claims to be the promised David of whom all the prophets testify and does not admit that Christ is the promised one.

Of such a mind are all false prophets and antichrists that they have on their heads names of blasphemy, and crowns like unto gold (by which pride is meant), as may be seen in the Babylonian harlot who was arrayed in scarlet, having a golden cup in her hand, full of abomination and the filthiness of her fornication. And she says in her heart, I sit a queen, and shall see no sorrow. But the Lord can not tolerate it and says, Babylon, the glory of kingdoms, the beauty of the Chaldees' excellency, shall be as when God overthrew Sodom and Gomorrah. Therefore shall her plagues come in one day. And not Babylon only, but also all antichrists, together with their deceit and false writings, shall be destroyed, as Christ says: Every plant which my heavenly Father hath not planted shall be rooted up. Matt. 15:13.

Greater antichrist there cannot arise than he who poses as the David of promise. This David is Christ as the Scriptures testify abundantly. He that hath ears to hear, let him hear.

The prophet Hosea says: For the children of Israel shall abide many days without a king and without a prince, and without sacrifice, and without an image, and without an ephod, and without teraphim; afterward shall the children of Israel return and seek the Lord their God, and David their king, and shall fear the Lord, and his goodness in the latter days.

It is incontrovertible that this King David can be none other than Christ Jesus, whom all must seek who want to be saved, as it is written: Seek the Lord and ye shall live. Isaiah says, Seek ye the Lord while he may be found, call ye upon him while he is near. For this reason David says, I sought the Lord and he heard me, and delivered me from all my fears. And Christ, the wisdom of God, says: He that findeth me findeth life, and shall have the pleasure of the Lord. What king shall the children of Israel have if not Christ Jesus, the true Melchisedec, king of Salem, which is, King of peace; of whom the whole number of the disciples have testified: Blessed be the King that cometh in the name of the Lord; peace in heaven, and glory in the highest.

The Jews despised this King Christ and therefore they were blinded. Yet they shall return and come to Christ, their King David, as Paul testifies, saying: Blindness in part is happened to Israel, until the fullness of the Gentiles be come in. And so all Israel shall be saved, as it is written: There shall come out of Zion the deliverer, and shall turn away the ungodliness from Jacob. For this is my covenant with them, when I shall take away their sins. Isa. 59:20. Since Israel is yet to be converted unto Christ, it follows incontrovertibly that the King David, whom Israel shall seek, can be none other than Christ.

Every righteous person will understand in what terrible error those are caught who do not allow that this David is Christ but look to another man. Of such Christ says, I am come in my Father's name, and ye receive me not; if another shall come in his own name, him will ye receive. John 5:43. But those who with Jerusalem will not receive Christ will also with Jerusalem be destroyed. Those who with the Pharisees oppose Christ and nevertheless think they are enlightened shall be blinded with the Pharisees. Let all pray to God for wisdom, and they shall understand that Christ is the true David.

Jeremiah says: It shall come to pass in that day, saith the Lord of hosts, that I will break his yoke from off thy neck, and I will burst thy bonds, and strangers shall no more serve themselves of him: but they shall serve the Lord their God, and David their king, whom I will raise up unto them.

Now the commandment of the Lord is: Thou shalt worship the Lord thy God, and him only shalt thou serve. Therefore this King David is no one but Christ, whom the Father has raised up unto us, saying, Yet have I set my king upon my holy hill of Zion. And the Christian Church acknowledges no other king, no other Lord than Christ. Therefore all the saints say, The Lord is our defense; and the Holy One of Israel is our King. Now who is the Holy One but He of whom Isaiah testifies, saying: For thus saith the high and lofty One that inhabiteth eternity, whose name is Holy. And in the Apocalypse: These things saith he that is holy . . . he that hath the key of David. Jeremiah says concerning Babylon, Recompense her according to her work; according to all that she hath done, do unto her; for she hath been proud against the Lord, against the Holy One of Israel.

We see that the Holy One of Israel is none other than the true God and Lord, Christ Jesus; therefore none but Christ can be the King of His believing church, even as the Spirit of God testifies to the prophet Micah, saying: The Lord shall reign over them in mount Zion, from henceforth, even forever. Who is this shepherd if not Christ, of whom it was prophesied: Behold, the Lord God will come with strong hand, and his arm shall rule for him; behold, his reward is with him, and his work before him. He shall feed his flock like a shepherd; he shall gather the lambs with his arm, and carry them in his bosom, and shall gently lead those that are with young.

Christ testifies of Himself that He is the shepherd, for He says: I am the good shepherd; the good shepherd giveth his life for the sheep. Christ truly pastures His sheep. He is the door of the sheepfold; all who enter into the fold through Him shall be saved and shall go in and out and find good pasture. Therefore David says: The Lord is my shepherd; I shall not want. He maketh me to lie down in green pastures: he leadeth me beside the still waters. And the apostle Peter says: For ye were as sheep going astray, but are now returned unto the Shepherd and Bishop of your souls. Moreover the Lord God says, My servant David shall be a Prince among them. Let no one stumble over the fact that God the Father calls His Son Christ a servant, saying: Behold my servant whom I uphold, mine elect, in whom my soul delighteth. And at another place, Behold my servant, whom I have chosen; my beloved in whom my soul is well pleased. At still another place the Father speaks concerning Christ: By his knowledge shall my righteous servant justify many.

This servant David is Christ, and He is the Christian prince. And who but He is a prince of the church of Christ, as Paul testifies that He alone is the Prince, and as the prophet says: Thou Bethlehem Ephratah, though thou be the least among the thousands of Judah, yet out of thee shall he come forth unto me that is to be ruler in Israel; whose goings forth have been from of old, from everlasting.

The Lord speaks through the same prophet: They shall be my people and I will be their God, and David my servant shall be King over them and they shall have one Shepherd. We have proved clearly enough by the Scriptures that God the Father has placed no other king over Zion than His Son Jesus Christ, nor will He place any other, and that He gave Him an eternal kingdom. Therefore it is needless to go over this again. And that God the Lord says: David my servant shall be King over them, and they shall all have one shepherd, is understood to be said of Christ, for no man can be our only Shepherd. For although God gives some apostles; and some prophets; and some evangelists; and some, pastors and teachers, yet the only Shepherd is Christ, and no one else, as may be plainly understood from the words of Christ: other sheep I have which are not of this fold; them also I must bring, and they shall hear my voice; and they shall be one fold and one shepherd.

All believers are the sheep of Christ and there is but one fold, of which Christ is the Shepherd. From this it must follow that Christ is the only Shepherd, and that no one else can be that. For this reason Peter calls Christ the chief Shepherd, and Paul says: Now the God of peace, that brought again from the dead our Lord Jesus, that great shepherd of the sheep, through the blood of the everlasting covenant, make you perfect in every good work to do his will.

Christ is the only Shepherd; for all believers must hear His voice and the voice of none other. From this it follows at once that He is also the promised David, according to the words of the Lord; David my servant shall be King over them; and they shall all have one Shepherd. Besides this God says, My servant David shall be their Prince forever. I trust that no one is so foolish (unless a root of bitterness be in him and he be given up of God to a perverse mind) as to understand these words of some man—that a man shall be our eternal prince—for it is written that God alone is eternal, He only has immortality and dwells in a light to which none can come. No man can be our eternal Prince. But Christ is our eternal Prince, and His kingdom is an everlasting kingdom as it is written, Thy throne, O God, is forever. Paul and Peter say that Christ's kingdom is eternal; and the angel said to Mary: The Lord God shall give him the throne of his father David, and he shall reign over the house of Jacob forever, and of his kingdom there shall be no end. Again the prophet says, His seed shall endure forever, and his throne as the sun before me. It shall be established forever as the moon, and as a faithful witness in heaven. From this everybody realizes that our eternal prince is none other than Christ; therefore our Promised David is none other than Christ.

In one of the Psalms we read: Then thou spakest in vision to the Holy One and saidst, I have laid help upon one that is mighty; I have exalted one chosen out of the people. I have found David my servant; with my holy oil have I anointed him. Who is this mighty one on whom God laid help, if not Christ Jesus who has all power in heaven and on earth, to whom God has submitted all things and to whom are committed all things pertaining to the church?

In this Christ the Almighty God has lodged help; for we are helped and saved by Him, as Christ says: If the Son therefore shall make you free, ye shall be free indeed. And Paul says: For what the law could not do in that it was weak through the flesh, God sending his own Son in the likeness of sinful flesh, and for sin, condemned sin in the flesh.

Christ is the strong Samson who broke the jaws of the lion; He is the pious David who slew the giant Philistine with whom none of the Israelites dared fight; He is the chosen one, whom the Father has chosen as His own

Son, saying, Behold, my servant whom I have chosen. This chosen one the Father has exalted among the people seeing that He has placed Him as King of His holy Mount Zion, as the Prince who shall rule His people. For this reason the church acknowledges Him to be their head and to be the most exalted of men on earth saying: As the apple tree among the trees of the wood, so is my beloved among the sons. I sat down under his shadow with great delight, and his fruit was sweet to my taste. Further the Lord says, I have found my servant David; with my holy oil have I anointed him.

This anointed David is Christ; for He is the truly anointed of the Lord to whom God the Father speaks, Thy throne, O God, is forever; a sceptre of righteousness is the sceptre of thy kingdom; thou hast loved righteousness, and hated iniquity; therefore God, even thy God, hath anointed thee with the oil of gladness above thy fellows. Christ says, The Spirit of the Lord is upon me, because he hath anointed me. Peter says, God anointed Jesus of Nazareth with the Holy Ghost and with power.

If anyone should still be in doubt (impossible to a man of understanding, so clear is the Scripture), then let him consider the following words: He shall cry unto me, Thou art my Father, my God, and the Rock of my salvation. Also, I will make him my first-born, higher than the kings of the earth. Christ is the first-begotten Son of God, as Paul says: God the Father has predestinated us to be conformed to the image of his Son, that he might be the first-born among many brethren. And to the Hebrews, When he bringeth in the first-begotten into the world, he saith, And let all the angels of God worship him.

Therefore as surely as Christ is the first-begotten Son of God, so surely is He the servant David whom the Father anointed with the holy oil, that is, with the Holy Ghost.

Moreover, the Lord says concerning His servant David: My mercy will I keep for him forevermore, and my covenant shall stand fast with him. His seed also will I make to endure forever, and his throne as the days of heaven. This seed is the children, for it reads further: if his children forsake my law. Now it is plain that this should not be understood of physical children of the figurative David, for they turned to idolatry and forsook the law of God. For this they were often punished and at last cut from the olive tree as unfruitful branches.

Nor did the external kingdom of David remain unbroken. It was destroyed as the holy patriarch Jacob and other prophets predicted. And to understand it as having reference to the physical children of David is contrary to the epistle of Paul to the Romans, for there Paul says: For they are not all Israel which are of Israel. Neither because they are the seed of Abraham, are they all children, but in Isaac shall thy seed be called. That is, they which are the children of the flesh, these are not the children of God; but the children of the promise are counted for the seed. Therefore we should not take this seed as referring to the physical children, but to the spiritual seed of which it is written: When my servant shall have given his life as a sacrifice, then he shall have seed and live long. This seed are all the true children of God, which are born again, not of corruptible seed, but of incorruptible, by the Word of God.

Christ says, Behold, I and the children which God hath given me. And these children of God abide in eternity; eternal joy and peace shall be upon them: they shall reign forever with Christ; Christ their King has an eternal kingdom, and His throne shall be as the days of heaven. This psalm quite agrees with the words of the prophet Nathan, which he spake unto David promising him Solomon. Even as we must not understand the words of the prophet Nathan as referring to Solomon merely, but rather to Christ, although the words in a literal sense are spoken concerning Solomon, so we should not understand the words of the psalm as referring to the literal David merely, but rather to the true David, Christ Jesus. And this the following text strongly implies which speaks of the passion of Christ.

This is our confession of the promised David. We might by the grace of God write a great deal more to show that Christ is our promised David; but we presume that enough has been written for the prudent. We do not serve the contentious ones. Let them rave. Let them put forth another king. Yet will Christ remain the eternal King reigning over His believing church. He is the Lord. He will not give His glory to another. He desires incense dedicated to Him. Whosoever shall make such incense unto himself, his soul shall be rooted out from Israel.

None shall succeed who exalts himself to Christ and opposes the truth. They may get their following, but Moses and Aaron will gain the victory. Jannes and Jambres must give way and be shamed. Korah, Dathan, and Abiram may pit themselves against Moses, but they shall perish with all that adhere to them.

A proud Uzziah may rise and take to himself the glory which is not his, but he will be smitten of God. Hophni and Phinehas may for a time make the people to transgress and turn them from the true religion, but they will have their punishment. Let everyone take heed and continue with Christ. Enough of this.

By the grace of God we will also write a little about warfare, that Christians are not allowed to fight with the sword, that we may all of us leave the armor of David to the physical Israelites and the sword of Zerubbabel to those who build the temple of Zerubbabel in Jerusalem, which was a figure of them and a shadow of things to come. For the body itself is in Christ, as Paul says.

Now we should not imagine that the figure of the Old Testament is so applied to the truth of the New Testament that flesh is understood as referring to flesh; for the figure must reflect the reality; the image, the being, and the letter, the Spirit.

If we take this view of it we shall easily understand with what kind of arms Christians should fight, namely, with the Word of God which is a two-edged sword, of which we will by the assistance of God say a few things.

The eternal God has raised His Son Christ a Prophet unto us whom we shall hear; and since Christ testifies of Himself that He is our only Master, therefore it is incontrovertible that we dare not accept any other doctrine but the doctrine of Christ. No strange doctrine which is contrary to the doctrine of Christ and that which the apostles by the Holy Ghost have written and taught us, dare we, I say, accept. For there may be no strange fire offered before God. Christ will not tolerate the leaven of the Pharisees.

Moses had to make the cherubim of pure gold. The words of the Lord are pure words; as silver tried in a furnace of earth, purified seven times.

The Lord will not tolerate it that His teachings are falsified; He punishes all false doctrine, as He spoke concerning Jerusalem; Thy silver is become dross, thy wine mixed with water, and I will turn my hand upon thee and purge away thy dross. Similarly God hates all false doctrine, and therefore the apostles admonish us to abide in God's Word, as John says: Let that therefore abide in you which ye have heard from the beginning. If that which we have heard from the beginning shall remain in you, ye also shall continue in the Son, and in the Father. Paul says that we should beware of those who raise contentions and are offended at the doctrine which he preached, and depart from them. Yes, so strongly does Paul urge his doctrine that he says: If any man preach any other gospel unto you than that ye have received, let him be accursed. Paul teaches in all his epistles to beware of a strange gospel, and to abide in the doctrine which is not his, but of the Holy Ghost, according to the words of Christ: For it is not ye that speak, but the Spirit of your Father which speaketh in you.

Now the Spirit of God speaks thus through Paul: My brethren, be strong in the Lord, and in the power of his might. Put on the whole armor of God, that ye may be able to stand against the wiles of the devil. For we wrestle not against flesh and blood, but against principalities, against powers, against the rulers of the darkness of this world, against spiritual wickedness in high places. Wherefore take unto you the whole armor of God, that ye may be able to withstand in the evil day, and having done all, to stand. Stand, therefore, having your loins girt about with truth, and having on the breastplate of righteousness; and your feet shod with the preparation of the gospel of peace. Above all, taking the shield of faith, wherewith ye shall be able to quench all the fiery darts of the wicked; and take the helmet of salvation, and the sword of the Spirit, which is the word of God. At another place: For the weapons of our warfare are not carnal, but mighty through God to the pulling down of strongholds; casting down imaginations, and every high thing that exalteth itself against the knowledge of God, and bringing into captivity every thought to the obedience of Christ. And having in readiness to revenge all disobedience, when your obedience is fulfilled.

Now he that is not blind will understand with what weapons the Christian is to fight, namely, with the Word of God; with this he should be well armored. For thus speaks the holy church: Behold his bed, which is Solomon's; threescore valiant men are about it, of the valiant of Israel; they all hold swords, being expert in war; every man hath his sword upon his thigh because of fear in the night; that is, each one is armed with the sword of the Spirit against all the wiles of the devil, against all false doctrine. Concerning Christ it is written: Gird thy sword upon thy thigh, O most Mighty, with thy glory and thy majesty. And in thy majesty ride prosperously, because of truth and meekness and righteousness; and thy right hand shall teach thee terrible things. Thine arrows are sharp in the heart of the king's enemies; whereby the people fall under thee.

Here the Scriptures say that Christ shall have a sword. But which sword? He Himself tells us in the Apocalypse in these words, Repent; or else I will come unto thee quickly, and will fight against thee with the sword of my mouth.

If Christ fights His enemies with the sword of His mouth, if He smites the earth with the rod of His mouth, and slays the wicked with the breath of His lips; and if we are to be conformed unto His image, how can we, then, oppose our enemies with any other sword? Does not the Apostle Peter say: For even hereto were ye called, because Christ also suffered for us, leaving us an example, that ye should follow his steps, who did no sin, neither was guile found in his mouth: who, when he was reviled, reviled not again; when he suffered he threatened not; but committed himself to him that judgeth righteously? This agrees with the words of John who says: He that abides in Christ walks as Christ walked. Christ Himself says, Whosoever will come after me, let him deny himself, and take up his cross and follow me. Again, My sheep hear my voice and they follow me. And this is the voice of Christ: Ye have heard that it hath been said, An eye for an eye, and a tooth for a tooth: but I say unto you, that ye resist not evil: but whosoever shall smite thee on thy right cheek, turn to him the other also.

Again, Ye have heard that it was said, Thou shalt love thy neighbor, and hate thine enemy: but I say unto you, Love your enemies, bless them that curse you, do good to them that hate you, and pray for them which despitefully use you, and persecute you; that ye may be the children of your Father which is in heaven, for he maketh his sun to rise on the evil and on the good, and sendeth rain on the just and on the unjust. For if ye love them which love you, what reward have ye? Do not even the publicans the same? And if ye salute your brethren only, what do you more than others? Do not even the publicans so? Be ye therefore perfect, even as your Father which is in heaven is perfect.

Behold, this is the voice of Christ. All those who are His sheep will hear His voice. But those who are not His sheep will not hear His voice, as Christ said unto the Pharisees, Ye believe not because ye are not of my sheep. The Pharisees imagined that since they had Moses and the prophets, they therefore had a halo of holiness; but they did not hear the voice of Christ, therefore it was all to no profit. So it is with all those who do not submit themselves to the commandments of Christ.

Not the leaves of the tree but the fruit is the thing that matters. And which the right kind of fruit is, Paul clearly testifies, saying: The fruit of the Spirit is love, joy, peace, longsuffering, gentleness, goodness, faith, meekness, temperance. Not a word is said about taking up the carnal sword or repaying evil with evil. But rather as Paul says at another place: Recompense to no man evil for evil. Provide things honest in the sight of all men. If it be possible, as much as lieth in you, live peaceably with all men. Dearly beloved, avenge not yourselves; but rather give place to wrath: for it is written, Vengeance is mine; I will repay, saith the Lord. Therefore if thine enemy hunger, feed him; if he thirst, give him drink; for in so doing thou shalt heap coals of fire on his head. Be not overcome of evil, but overcome evil with good. How can Christians fight with the implements of war? Paul plainly said, Let this mind be in you, which was also in Christ Jesus. Now Christ Jesus was minded to suffer; and in the same way all Christians must be minded.

Christ did not want to be defended with Peter's sword. How can a Christian then defend himself with it? Christ wanted to drink the cup which the Father had given Him; how then can a Christian avoid it?

Or does any person expect to be saved by other means than those which Christ has taught us? Is not Christ the way, the truth, and the life? Is He not the door to the fold, so that none can enter into the fold but by Him?

Is not He the Shepherd of His sheep, whom the sheep should follow? Is not He our Lord and Master? And who is it that would be above his Lord? Is it not he that would not suffer as Christ suffered? Who is it that would be above his Master but he that is not satisfied with his Master's doctrine? Let everyone take heed. It is forbidden to us to fight with physical weapons.

Paul says: Put them in mind to be subject to principalities and powers, to obey magistrates, to be ready to every good work, to speak evil of no man, to be no brawlers, but gentle, shewing all meekness unto all men. And the holy apostle James says: Be patient therefore, brethren, unto the coming of the Lord. Behold, the husbandman waiteth for the precious fruit of the earth, and hath long patience for it, until he receive the early and latter rain. Be ye also patient; stablish your heart; for the coming of the Lord draweth nigh. Take, my brethren, the prophets, who have spoken in the name of the Lord, for an example of suffering, affliction, and patience. Behold, we count them happy which endure. We have heard of the patience of Job, and have seen the end of the Lord; that the Lord is very pitiful, and of tender mercy. If we are to be longsuffering until the coming of the Lord, then surely it is forbidden to fight, inasmuch as the Lord is not yet come.

And if we are to take prophets as an example to suffer persecution, then we must put on the apostolic armor, and the armor of David must be laid aside.

How can it be harmonized with the Word of God that one who boasts of being a Christian could lay aside the spiritual weapons and take up the carnal ones, for Paul says: The servant of the Lord must not strive; but be gentle unto all men, apt to teach, patient; in meekness instructing those that oppose themselves; if God peradventure will give them repentance to the acknowledging of the truth. And that they may recover themselves out of the snare of the devil, who are taken captive by him at his will.

All of you who would fight with the sword of David, and also be the servants of the Lord, consider these words, which show how a servant should be minded. If he is not to strive, and quarrel, how then can he fight? If he is to be gentle to all men, how can he then hate and harm them? If he is to be ready to learn, how can he lay aside the apostolic weapons? He will need them. If he is to instruct in meekness those that oppose, how can he destroy them?

If he is to instruct in meekness those that oppose truth, how can he angrily punish them that do not as yet acknowledge the truth? Paul says: if God peradventure will give them repentance. But some do not want to wait for that, and even if they do it with good intentions, they nevertheless with Uzzah lay their hands to the ark of God. Therefore I fear that it will not go unpunished. And even if with Saul they save the best beasts of the Amalekites for sacrifices unto God, yet it will not please the Lord; for it is contrary to His Word. He has pleasure in obedience and not in sacrifice.

But now some say, the Lord wants to punish Babylon, and that by His Christians. They must be His instruments. O God, it would be well if we would leave to the Lord His works, and remember the words of Ecclesiasticus: Seek not out the things that are too hard for thee, neither search the things that are above thy strength. But what is commanded thee, think thereon with reverence; for it is not needful for thee to see with thine eyes the things that are in secret. Be not curious in unnecessary matters.

For many things are shown to men above their understanding, and presumption has caused many to fall, and inclosed their understanding in vanity. It would be well for those who ask with the disciples of the Lord when the kingdom of Israel is to be restored, to observe the answer of the Lord: It is not for you to know the times nor the seasons, which the Father hath put in his own power. But this they forget and cry, God will shortly punish and destroy Babylon. In this the Christians must be His instruments.

With this they deceive the simple; therefore we will oppose this view with Scriptures. It is true that God will punish Babylon, but not by His Christians. For thus speaks Jeremiah: The Lord hath raised up the spirits of the kings of the Medes; for his device is against Babylon to destroy it; because it is the vengeance of the Lord, the vengeance of his temple. Again, Prepare against her the nations, with the kings of the Medes, the captains thereof, and all the rulers thereof, and all the land of his dominion. And the land shall tremble and sorrow: for every purpose of the Lord shall be performed against Babylon, to make the land of Babylon a desolation without an inhabitant.

I am aware that this was fulfilled against Babylon, in the country of the Chaldees, although the Roman Babylon shall not escape the same visitation; but I have quoted this because of the proponents of the sword philosophy who want to prove by this Scripture of Jeremiah that the Christians are to punish Babylon, although the prophet testifies clearly that God has done this by heathen hands, and that it should be done by such, as is shown in Rev. 17:16: The ten horns which thou sawest upon the beast, these shall hate the harlot, and shall make her desolate and naked, and shall eat her flesh, and burn her with fire. For God hath put in their hearts to fulfill his will, and to agree and give their kingdom unto the beast, until the words of God shall be fulfilled.

And so it may be plainly understood that not by Christians is the Babylonian harlot to be destroyed; also that Christians should not exterminate. A Theudas may rise up and cause a disturbance, but he shall not succeed. There may rise up a Judas of Galilee and make a commotion, but he shall perish and all his followers shall perish and be scattered. Therefore let every person beware and observe the Scriptures carefully, and he shall see that the Lord Himself will destroy at His coming and punish all His enemies who would not submit to Him. For Luke says: It came to pass that when he was returned, having received the kingdom, then he commanded these servants to be called unto him, to whom he had given the money, that he might know how much every man had gained by trading; and when his servants had given an account, he said, But those mine enemies which would not that I should reign over them, bring hither, and slay before me.

This Scripture clearly testifies that the Lord Christ must first come again before all His enemies are punished. And how Christ will come again He Himself testifies, saying, For the Son of man shall come in the glory of his Father, with his angels; and then he shall reward every man according to his works. Again, For as the lightning cometh out of the east, and shineth even unto the west, so shall also the coming of the Son of man be. And then shall appear the sign of the Son of man in heaven: and then shall all the tribes of the earth mourn, and they shall see the Son of man coming in the clouds of heaven, with power and great glory. The two angels also testified how Christ would come again, saying, Ye men of Galilee, why stand ye gazing up into heaven? This same Jesus, which is taken up from you into heaven, shall so come in like manner as ye have seen him go into heaven. From this it is plain to everybody how Christ shall come. Therefore when ye shall see Christ come in this manner you may rest assured that all the enemies of God will be punished. And do not suppose that it will be so before His return, for you will find yourself mistaken unless God's Word be false, a thing that is impossible. Luke says that the Lord had received the kingdom.

Of this Daniel says, I saw in the night visions, and, behold, one like the Son of man came with the clouds of heaven, and came to the Ancient of days, and they brought him near before him. And there was given him dominion and glory, and a kingdom, that all people, nations, and languages should serve him: his dominion is an everlasting dominion, which shall not pass away, and his kingdom, that which shall not be destroyed. Here observe of whom Christ receives this kingdom that you may see what abominable deceit it is that some say that John of Leiden would take the kingdom and that when he had taken it, he would give it unto Christ, even as David gave the kingdom unto Solomon.

The evangelist says also that Christ took account of His servants, a thing that will not be until judgment day. Paul says: We must all appear before the judgment seat of Christ; that every one may receive the things done in his body, according to that he hath done, whether it be good or bad. Jesus says: That every idle word that men shall speak, they shall give an account thereof in the day of judgment. Then the faithful servants shall enter into the kingdom of their Lord; then the wicked will be punished, and all whose names are not found written in the book of life will be cast into the lake of fire, seeing that they would not accept Christ as king, but worshiped the beast and his image.

This parable some falsify and say, The enemies of God must be destroyed before the coming of Christ, and therefore we will be the instruments to do it. But they must come to shame; for thus saith the Lord God, the Holy One of Israel: In returning and rest shall ye be saved; in quietness and in confidence shall be your strength; and ye would not. But ye said, No; for we will flee upon horses; therefore shall ye flee; and we will ride upon the swift; therefore shall they that pursue you be swift. Oh, that the advocates of the sword would observe these words! Yes, also those who would be angels to root up the tares! Christ told the parable with a different intent, saying: The good seed are the children of the kingdom; but the tares are the children of the wicked one; the enemy that sowed them is the devil, the harvest is the end of the world; and the reapers are the angels. Inasmuch as the Christians are the good seed, how then can they be the angels or reapers? Or if they be the reapers, how can they be the seed? These two things, the seed and the reapers, are quite different. Its plainness must not be obscured.

Yes, it is true that the Christians are sometimes called angels. But we cannot always when reading of angels refer to believers. There are also other angels of which it is written: Who maketh his angels spirits; his ministers a flaming fire. With these angels Christ will come, as Paul says, The Lord Jesus shall be revealed from heaven with his mighty angels, in flaming fire, taking vengeance on them that know not God, and that obey not the gospel of our Lord Jesus Christ. These angels will be the reapers who at the end of the world, that is in the day of judgment, will root up all tares and cast them into the lake of fire. Until that time the tares will be left among the good seed and the goats with the sheep. Let none think that we should now root up the tares, or that we should now separate the goats from the sheep. For when the Son of Man shall come in his glory and all his holy angels with him, then shall he sit upon the throne of his glory: and before him shall be gathered all nations: and he shall separate them one from another, as a shepherd divideth his sheep from the goats: and he shall set the sheep on his right hand, but the goats on the left.

These words are as clear as the sun, yet some do not understand them, so that we may well say unto them, O foolish Galatians, who hath bewitched you, that ye should not obey the truth, before whose eyes Christ Jesus hath been evidently set forth, crucified among you? This only would I learn of you, whether you are baptized on the sword or on the cross? So foolish are ye, having begun in the Spirit are ye now made perfect by the flesh? Have ye suffered so many things in vain, if it be yet in vain?

What help it that you have left Egypt if you hark back to Egypt, that is to darkness, and leave the true light; desire the flesh of Egypt, that is, human doctrine; and are not satisfied with the bread from heaven?

What does it avail you that you have escaped from Pharaoh, if you are slain by Amalek on account of your disobedience, that is, because you fight against the will of the Lord? What does it profit you that you have gone through the Red Sea with the children of Israel, if you do not enter with Joshua and Caleb into the promised land, by firm faith in God's Word? And how we are to enter into the promised land in the eternal kingdom of God is testified to by Paul and Barnabas who taught the churches that they had to enter into the kingdom through many tribulations.

Christ has not taken His kingdom with the sword, but He entered it through much suffering. Yet they think to take it by the sword! Oh, blindness of man! But thus it must be, that those who will not confess Christ their only Shepherd so that they may be pastured by Him, will have to eat of the pastures which are trampled upon; and that those who will not draw the clear crystal water from the fount of the Saviour, will have to drink the impure water which the false shepherds have stirred up with their feet. And that for the reason that they have done double evil to the children of Israel. They have forsaken the Lord, the living fountain, and have made fountains of their own which appear beautiful but they afford no water.

Therefore I admonish all beloved brethren, yea, I pray you by the mercy of God our Lord Jesus Christ, to give heed to the Word of God, and not to forsake it; for you have seen your master Christ, with the eye of faith, and you have heard His voice, saying, This is the true way, walk upon it, go neither to the right hand nor to the left.

Let every one of you guard against all strange doctrine of swords and resistance and other like things which is nothing short of a fair flower under which lies hidden an evil serpent which has shot his venom into many. Let every one beware.

Let every one behave himself in accordance with the example of the divine Word which he has received from the apostles by faith and love; let every one remember that he has not learned Christ except by suffering. Abide in it. For in Christ is an upright spirit; He is the Light of the world; he who follows Him shall not walk in darkness, but have the light of life. God, the Father of our Lord Jesus Christ, be gracious unto you and enlighten you so that we on earth may acknowledge His way and His salvation among the Gentiles.

All you who have tasted the kindness of the Lord, love Him. The Lord keeps the upright. Be of good cheer, and doubt not; for the Lord will strengthen your souls, all who patiently wait for His coming. The Lord reigneth, let the people tremble; he sitteth between the cherubim; let the earth be moved. This King the Jews scorned, and they were blinded.

# The Spiritual Resurrection

*Van de gheestelicke Verrysenisse*

## c. 1536

*For other foundation can no man
lay than that is laid, which is Jesus Christ.*

I CORINTHIANS 3:11

# Introduction

The first booklet written by Menno Simons after his renunciation of Roman Catholicism was this one on the Spiritual Resurrection. By spiritual resurrection Menno means the new birth which he identifies with the first resurrection mentioned in Revelation 20:6. On the title page, in addition to his beloved I Corinthians 3:11, Menno placed, "Blessed and holy is he that hath part in the first resurrection: on such the second death hath no power." The exact date of writing of this tract is not known, but it is generally assumed that it was 1536, or at the latest 1537.

Menno begins by portraying the sorry spiritual plight of the natural man. He shows that all people stand in need of the new birth, the spiritual resurrection. God graciously effects the image of Jesus in every one of His children, giving them the mind and disposition of Jesus. And the moment one is born into God's family he necessarily enters into a state of warfare with the world, the flesh, and the devil. But God is with the Christian, and enables him to bring forth fruit for Him. Menno wants his readers to look into the image of the Word—and the booklet abounds with Scripture quotations—and thereby ascertain whether or no they have been born anew. If not, let them earnestly turn to God. If they have been spiritually raised with Christ, let them beware of the defilement of sin.

The full title of the booklet is: *The Spiritual Resurrection. A Plain Instruction from the Word of God concerning the Spiritual Resurrection and the New or Heavenly Birth.* In the *Opera Omnia Theologica* of 1681 the tract is found, fol. 177-84, and in the *Complete Works* of 1871, I, 229-37.

J. C. W.

52

# The Spiritual Resurrection

## c. 1536

Awake thou that sleepest, and arise from the dead, and Christ shall give thee light.

The Scriptures teach two resurrections, namely, a bodily resurrection from the dead at the last day, and a spiritual resurrection from sin and death to a new life and a change of heart.

That a man should mortify and bury the body of sin and rise again to a life of righteousness in God is plainly taught in all of the Scriptures.

Paul admonishes saying, Put off concerning the former conversation the old man which is corrupt according to the deceitful lusts, and be renewed in the spirit of your mind, that ye put on the new man, which after God is created in righteousness and true holiness. Put off the old man with his deeds, and put on the new man which is renewed in knowledge after the image of him that created him. Mortify your members that are on the earth.

Now no man rises as to the body unless he has died and that after sickness has gone before and pain and physical anguish, death being bitter to the flesh. Likewise, in a spiritual sense, there can be no resurrection from sin and death unless this body of sin be first destroyed and buried and have sensibly endured pain and the burden of sin, that is, penitence and remorse on account of sin, as is evident from the Scriptures. David says, O Lord, rebuke me not in thy wrath; neither chasten me in thy hot displeasure. For thine arrows stick fast in me, and thy hand presseth me sore. There is no soundness in my flesh because of thine anger, neither is there any rest in my bones because of my sin. For mine iniquities are gone over my head; as a heavy burden they are too heavy for me. My wounds stink and are corrupt because of my foolishness. I am troubled, I am bowed down greatly, I go mourning all the day long. For my loins are filled with a loathsome disease and there is no soundness in my flesh. I am feeble and sore broken; I have roared by reason of the disquietude of my heart. O Lord, all my desire is before thee, and my groaning is not hid from thee. My heart panteth; my strength faileth me; as for the light of mine eyes, it also is gone from me.

Be afflicted and mourn and weep, says James. Let your laughter be turned to mourning and your joy to heaviness. Paul says, Ye were made sorry after a godly manner, to repentance, for godly sorrow worketh repentance to salvation, not to be repented of, but the sorrow of the world worketh death; seeing that ye sorrowed after a godly sort, what carefulness it wrought in you, what clearing of yourselves, yea, what indignation, what fear, vehement desire, and revenge.

Behold, so we must die with Christ unto sin, if we would be made alive with Him. For none can rejoice with Christ unless he first suffer with Him. For this is a sure word, says Paul, If we be dead with him, we shall also live with him; if we suffer, we shall also reign with him.

This resurrection includes the new creature, the spiritual birth and sanctification, without which no one shall see the Lord. This Paul testifies in a word saying, In Christ Jesus neither circumcision availeth anything, nor uncircumcision, but a new creature. Again, If any man be in Christ, he is a new creature; old things are passed away; behold, all things are become new. This is the first resurrection. For if we have been planted together in the likeness of His death, that is, through mortifying the sinful nature of earthly Adam with all his members or wicked lusts, we shall be also in the likeness of His resurrection, knowing this, that our old man is crucified with Him, that the body of sin may be destroyed and the true sabbath be kept in Christ by putting off the sinful body in the flesh, being circumcised with the circumcision of Christ which is done without hands, being buried through baptism in which we have also been raised with Him through faith, wrought by God, ceasing from all works of the flesh, driven by the Spirit, to bring forth the fruits of the Spirit. Henceforth not to serve sin, knowing that it suffices that we have spent our former days after the manner of the Gentiles, when we walked in vanity, wantonness, drunkenness, eating and drinking, and in abominable idolatry. We must spend the remainder of our days not after the lusts of men, but according to the will of God, so that we may say with Paul, I am crucified with Christ; nevertheless I live; yet not I, but Christ liveth in me; and the life which I now live in the flesh I live by the faith of the Son of God who loved me and gave himself for me. For he died for all, that they which live should not henceforth live unto themselves, but unto him which died for them and rose again.

To have a fuller account of this resurrection and regeneration, we must bear in mind that all creatures bring forth after their kind, and every creature partakes of the properties, propensities, and dispositions of that which brought it forth. As Christ says, That which is born of flesh is flesh, and cannot see eternal life; and, that which is born of Spirit is spirit, life and peace, which is eternal life. That which is born of flesh, out of earth through corruptible seed, is carnally minded, earthly and speaks of earthly things, and is desirous after earthly and perishable things. All its thoughts, feelings, and desires are directed toward earthly, temporal, or visible things, such things as those of which it is born or begotten. That which is born of flesh and blood is flesh and blood and is carnally minded, because the carnal mind is enmity against God, for it is not subject to the law of God, neither indeed can it be. Therefore, those who are carnal cannot please God. For they are altogether deaf, blind, and ignorant in divine things. A carnal man cannot comprehend divine things, for his nature is not thus, but to the contrary his mind is adverse and hostile to God. A carnal man cannot understand spiritual things, for he is by nature a child of the devil and not spiritually minded. Hence he comprehends nothing spiritual, for by nature he is hostile and a stranger to God; has nothing of the divine nature dwelling in him, has nothing in common with God, but is much rather possessed of a contrary nature, namely, is unmerciful, unjust, unclean, quarrelsome, contrary, disobedient, without understanding, and irreverent. Thus are all men by nature, tendency, and spirit according to their first birth and origin after the flesh. This is the first or old Adam and is subsumed in the Scriptures in a single word, ungodly or wicked, that is, one without God, a stranger to the divine nature.

This is the nature and property of the earthly and devilish seed, its nature and fruit. For as the seed is, so is the fruit. Whatsoever a man soweth, that shall he also reap; for he that soweth to his flesh, shall of the flesh reap corruption and bring forth fruit unto death. He sins like his father, of and through whose seed he is born, for he is the father of lies and sinned from the beginning, and did not abide in the truth. Therefore, he that sins is of the devil, for sin is not of God but of the devil, and he that sins has not seen or known God. And we know that the Son of God was made manifest to take away sin and destroy the works of the devil, through His death to deprive him of power[1] who had the power of death, that is, the devil, and deliver them who through fear of death were all their lifetime subject to bondage. For by the sin of one man all were made sinners. He that sins is the servant of sin, does the will and works of him whose servant he is and whose spirit leads him. For everyone is a servant to whom he serves, whether of sin unto death, or of obedience unto righteousness; for he that does unrighteousness shall receive according to his works. To them Paul speaks, as quoted above, that they should awaken from the sleep of sin and death, so that the second death might have no power over them, saying, Awake thou that sleepest, and arise from the dead, and Christ shall give thee light.

On the other hand, all those who are born and regenerated from above out of God, through the living Word, are also of the mind and disposition, and have the same aptitude for good that He has of whom they are born and begotten. For what the nature of God or Christ is, we may readily learn from the Scriptures. For Christ has expressly portrayed Himself in His Word, that is, as to the nature which He would have us understand, grasp and follow and emulate, not according to His divine nature, seeing He is the true image of the invisible God, the brightness of His glory, and the express image of His person, who dwells in ineffable light, whom none can approach or see, but according to His life and conversation here on earth, shown forth among men in works and deeds as an example set before us to follow so that we thereby might become partakers of His nature in the spirit, to become like unto Him. So Christ is everywhere represented to us as humble, meek, merciful, just, holy.

[1] A good rendering of the Greek original. *Ed.*

wise, spiritual, long-suffering, patient, peaceable, lovely, obedient, and good, as the perfection of all things; for in Him there is an upright nature. Behold, this is the image of God, of Christ as to the Spirit which we have as an example until we become like it in nature and reveal it by our walk.

All regenerate children of God are thus minded and affected, for they take after Him who has begotten them. And these also are subsumed under one word, namely, godly, or godly persons, having something in common with Him, having the same mind and disposition, the image of God in them as the Scriptures both of the Old and New Testament abundantly show, especially in the epistle of Paul to the Colossians, chapter 3, where he says: Put off the old man with his deeds, and put on the new man which is renewed in knowledge after the image of him that created him. Put on therefore, as the elect of God, holy and beloved, bowels of mercies, kindness, humbleness of mind, meekness, long-suffering; forbearing one another, and forgiving one another: if any man have a quarrel against any, even as Christ forgave you, so also do ye. And above all these things put on charity which is the bond of perfectness. And let the peace of God rule in your hearts to which also ye are called in one body; and be ye thankful. My little children, for whom I travail in birth again until Christ be formed in you, let this mind be in you which was also in Christ Jesus, for Christ is the image of God to whom we must conform. For whom he did foreknow, he also did predestinate to be conformed to the image of his Son. Those, therefore, who have become conformed to the image of Christ Jesus are the truly regenerate children of God, having put off the old man, and having put on the new which is created after God in true righteousness and holiness.

Then when they have conformed to the image of God and have been born of God and also abide in God, they do not sin, for the seed of God remains in them; and they have overcome the world. They are crucified to the world, and the world unto them; they have mortified their flesh and have buried their sinful body with Christ in baptism, with its lusts and desires, and now no longer serve sin unto unrighteousness, but much more righteousness unto sanctification. For they have put on Christ and are purified through the Holy Ghost in their consciences from dead works to serve the living God; bringing forth through the Spirit the fruits of the Spirit, whose end is eternal life. For since they, as was said, have renounced the devil, flesh, and the world, and have quit the service of sin, no longer to live in sin or to serve it, they have as faithful servants voluntarily obligated themselves to God, and as David did, to live henceforth according to His blessed will all their days.

And against these in turn the devil and his accomplices, such as the world and the flesh, being very envious, have declared war and have become their deadly enemies. The regenerate in turn have now become enemies of sin and the devil and have taken the field against all their enemies with the Author and finisher of their faith, under the banner of the crimson cross, armed with the armor of God, surrounded with angels of the Lord, and always watching with great solicitude lest they be overcome by their enemies who never slumber, but go about like roaring lions, seeking whom they may devour, hurt, and harm.

And if they receive a wound, surprised by their enemies, their souls remain uninjured and the wound is not unto death, for they have the anointing of God. They have the true Samaritan and the true physician with them, who can bind up and heal their wounds, for He has compassion over our weakness and frailty. Through His stripes and wounds we are healed. They are not so wholly overcome that they cast aside their weapons and surrender, to become servants of sin again and to be ruled by it. But being strong in the Lord and in the power of His might, they persevere valiantly in battle until they, through Him by whom they can do all things, have gloriously conquered their enemy and say to him, O death, where is thy sting? O grave, where is thy victory? And with Paul they say, Thanks be to God who giveth us the victory through our Lord Jesus Christ. The Lord, says Jeremiah, is with me as a mighty, terrible one; therefore my persecutors shall stumble, and they shall not prevail. They say with David, Blessed be the Lord my strength, which teacheth my hands to war and my fingers to fight. They stand firm until they have disdained their enemies saying, Blessed be the Lord who hath not given us a prey to their teeth; our soul is escaped as a bird out of the snare of the fowler; the snare is broken and we are escaped from our enemies, and out of the hand of those who hate us. The Lord is a rewarder of them that diligently seek, love, and serve Him, as it is written: Behold the Lord cometh, and his reward is with him; yea, his reward and wages, the gift of God, is eternal life through Jesus Christ our Lord. For if you serve the Lord Jesus Christ, you will receive the reward of your inheritance, the crown of life, which God has promised to those who love Him.

As said above, every creature has the nature and disposition of that of which it is born, and is disposed in the same way as is the seed from which it comes. Therefore we will speak a few words concerning the nature, properties, and effects of the seed of the divine Word whereby we are begotten by God from His bride the Holy Church, like unto His image, nature, and being, for where this seed is sown upon good ground into the heart of man, there it grows and produces its like in nature and property. It changes and renews the whole man, that is, from the carnal to the spiritual, the earthly into the heavenly; it transforms from death unto life, from unbelief to belief and makes men happy. For through this seed all nations upon the earth are blessed. Therefore, says James, Lay aside all filthiness and superfluity of naughtiness, and receive with meekness the engrafted word which is able to save your souls. It is also the pure, unadulterated milk whereby the young and newborn children of God are nurtured until they attain to a perfect man, unto the measure of the stature of the fullness of Christ. It is also strong food for the perfect and adult in Christ Jesus. In short, this seed of the divine Word is spiritual food whereby the whole man is nourished inwardly lest he perish and faint in the wild desert of this waste world, as all must do who do not gather daily the bread of the divine

Word to satisfy their starving souls. For man shall not live by bread alone, but by every word that proceedeth out of the mouth of God. Therefore is he blessed who hungers after this heavenly bread and receives the ingrafted word, for it will bring forth after its nature, in due time, an hundredfold. For, says the Lord, As the rain cometh down, and the snow from heaven, and returneth not thither, but watereth the earth, and maketh it bring forth and bud, that it may give seed to the sower and bread to the eater, so shall my word be that goeth forth out of my mouth; it shall not return unto me void, but it shall accomplish that which I please.

Behold this is the nature, property, and effect of the seed of the Word of God. By it man is renewed, regenerated, sanctified, and saved through this incorruptible seed, namely, the living Word of God which abides eternally. He is clothed with the same power from above, baptized with the Holy Ghost, and so united and mingled with God that he becomes a partaker of the divine nature and is made conformable to the image of His Son, who is the first of the born again and of those who rose with Him from the sleep and death of sin, henceforth to serve Him, not in the oldness of the letter, but in the newness of the Spirit.

He that has this genuine renewed nature and disposition has put on Christ Jesus. He is become like unto Him; he has the image of God in himself, is spiritually minded, and is led by the Spirit in his spirit, from whose spiritual body spiritual fruits are brought forth, as a well springing up unto life eternal. For they are in the second birth by the word sown; their hearts begotten by God and born again, bring forth the fruit of life. Whereby they as children born of God are one with the Father, of one mind and disposition, having the divine nature of their Father who has begotten them. Their thoughts are heavenly; their words are truth, well seasoned; their works are holy and good, acceptable to God and man; for they are holy vessels of honor, useful and ready to every good work.

Now Paul exhorts those who are born of the corruptible seed of flesh and blood, who are of the earth, earthy, carnal, without understanding and blind in divine things, yea, children of wrath, that they should mortify and bury the body of sin, namely, the lusts and desires of the first birth in the flesh, and then rise in the power of the heavenly seed from the sleep and death of sin, and be regenerate and walk in newness of life, which is the first resurrection. He says: Awake thou that sleepest and arise from the dead, and Christ shall give thee light. So also does he admonish all newly regenerated children of God who have been changed in mind and disposition through the eternal saving seed of God, and have been regenerated and are risen, that they should be godly, spiritual and heavenly-minded, and yearn for and desire heavenly, incorruptible things. Their hearts should be where their treasure is, and their conversation in heaven as fellow saints of the house of God. He tells them. If then ye be risen with Christ, seek those things which are above, where Christ sitteth at the right hand of God. Set your affections on things above, not on things on the earth. For ye are dead and your life is hid with Christ in God. When Christ, who is our life, shall appear, then shall ye also appear with him in glory.

Here we have an account of how the regenerate children of God who have risen with Christ from the dead and now live with Him, dwell in the heavenly reality and appear to the world no longer to live, for their life is hid in God, as St. John says: Now are we the sons of God, and it doth not yet appear what we shall be; but we know that when he shall appear, we shall be like him; for we shall see him as he is.

With these and the like words too lengthy to copy, the Scriptures admonish the truly regenerated and resurrected ones that they should take heed to their calling and continue perfect in a new, godly walk. For if they have been made partakers of Christ, they should hold to this beginning unto the end, lest they once more depart from the living God through the deceitfulness of sin and an evil heart of unbelief. They must rather remain steadfast and perfect as the chosen children of God, so as to inherit the kingdom of their Father and reign in the heavenlies over sin, death, devil and hell, and all the enemies of the kingdom whom they overcome with Christ as valiant men.

Therefore will they also sit with Christ at the table of the Lord, and eat the bread and drink the wine in the kingdom of heaven, even as Christ overcame and sitteth with His Father in His kingdom which is prepared for them as a city well fortified, free from all danger of their enemies, full of rest and peace, and life and joy. For they eat of the tree of life which is in the midst of Paradise, which garden of pleasure remains closed to the old unregenerate man and to all after the nature of Adam who are still earthly and carnally minded, who still have the nature and veil and partition wall of sin before their hearts as fashioned by Adam. These are they who died with Christ unto sin and have truly risen. These are the newborn to whom the power is given to become the sons of God. These are the redeemed out of all the tongues and nations and peoples. They have on wedding garments for the marriage of the Lamb. They have received the sign TAU in their foreheads by which the servants of God are marked.[2] These are the spiritual bride of Christ, His holy church, His spiritual body, flesh of His flesh, and bone of His bone. These have come to the heavenly Jerusalem, the city of the living God, which came down from heaven. These have come to an innumerable company of angels, to the assembly of the church of the first-born which are written in heaven, and to Jesus the Mediator of the new covenant. They are fellow citizens in the household of God. These have put off the corruptible garment and have put on the incorruptible; have acknowledged the name of God and keep His commandments and the faith of Jesus; the true sheep of Christ, who hear His

[2] The fanatical sects whom Menno opposed firmly referred to their adherents as persons marked with the last letter of the Hebrew alphabet, *Tau*. Some have argued that since Menno also speaks of persons marked with this letter we have evidence that he had at the first belonged to the Münsterites. It is quite as probable that Menno employs the language here found to show what the only tolerable letter *Tau* on the foreheads of men was. *Tr.*

voice alone, knowing no other; the first fruits of His creatures who have the Spirit and quality of Christ. Therefore they know what the will of the Lord is, yes, the chosen generation, the spiritual and royal priesthood, a holy nation, a peculiar people, who in times past were not a people, but are now the people of God, for God had compassion on them. They are the souls of the slain for the Word of God beneath the altar.

In short, with these people old things have passed away; behold, all things are become new; this is all of God who has reconciled us unto Himself through Jesus Christ. These are they who stand before the throne of God with palms in their hands, clothed in white, saying, Blessing and glory and wisdom and thanksgiving and honor and power and might be unto our God forever and ever. Amen.

This is a short instruction concerning the spiritual resurrection or new birth, and the difference between the first and the second birth, between the carnal and the spiritual birth, between the earthly and the heavenly; how everyone is disposed, inclined, and minded according to his birth or origin, and that he is of the same disposition, of the same mind, and of such a nature as that of which he is born or begotten. For the natural man is not spiritual, neither is that which is born of flesh and blood the spiritual birth of God from heaven, but each birth is true to its origin. As the natural man is, so are they who are naturally born. As God is who is a spirit and dwells in heaven, such are also they who are spiritually born of the heavenly being, who far exceed those naturally born of flesh. Here, as in a mirror, one may view and examine himself and judge in his own mind of what birth, mind, disposition, nature, life, and conduct he is. For by this nature a man with but little pains can judge and prove himself. For a man's walk, word, and visage testify concerning a man, and the thoughts of his heart also testify what he is; for no man knows the thoughts of a man save the spirit of man that is in him.

So also all those who find in examining themselves that they are not after their first birth according to the flesh regenerated and renewed in mind, understanding, spirit, and disposition, but are still altogether carnal, earthly, worldly and devilishly minded, and out of their depraved, native tendency prone and inclined to all manner of evil; let these humble themselves before God with Jeremiah saying: Let us examine and prove our ways, and let us turn unto the Lord; let us lift our hands and hearts to God in heaven and say, We have sinned before heaven and in thy sight and have excited thy wrath; let us weep and let our eyes run over with water. Let them say with David, O come, let us worship and bow down; let us kneel before the Lord our Maker. Let us weep before the Lord who made us, praying Him to condescend to remake the work of His hand, to renew that which He has deigned to make. Let them humbly entreat Him for His Spirit who is the great artificer of all this, and say, Lord, send forth Thy Spirit, and we will be created, and Thou wilt renew the face of the earth. Let them continue in prayer[3] and in their desires to God

---

[3] Reading *bidden* (to pray) for *midden* (midst) which makes no good sense. *Tr.*

till they are clothed with the power of the Spirit from on high, remade and renewed in the spirit of their mind, and in astonishment say: This is the change wrought by the right hand of God, the most High.

Similarly those who upon examining themselves find that they are born from above by the grace of God and that they are new creatures in Christ and have become a temple of God; let them take heed to themselves according to the counsel of the Scriptures that being now washed, purified, regenerated, and sanctified, they do not again defile themselves and desecrate and violate the temple of God. For if any man defile the temple of God, him shall God destroy. But let them pray in the Spirit with assured confidence to God their Father, with David, O God, strengthen us and confirm in us that which thou didst work in us. And He will then hear them from His holy temple, according to His promise. For He is faithful who has begun the good work in you; He will also perform it until the day of Jesus Christ. Peter says, Give all diligence to add to your faith, virtue; and to virtue, knowledge; and to knowledge, temperance; and to temperance, patience; and to patience, godliness; and to godliness, brotherly kindness; and to brotherly kindness, charity. For if these things be in you, and abound, they make you that ye shall neither be barron nor unfruitful in the knowledge of our Lord Jesus Christ. But he that lacketh these things is blind, and cannot see afar off, and hath forgotten that he was purged from his old sins. Wherefore, the rather, brethren, give diligence to make your calling and election sure; for if ye do these things ye shall never fall; for so an entrance shall be ministered unto you abundantly into the everlasting kingdom of our Lord and Saviour, Jesus Christ.

May the God of all grace who will in the last resurrection gather the elect into His eternal kingdom grant us such hearts, minds, and dispositions that we, through true faith, and denial of self, may so deny and renounce ourselves that we may have part in the first resurrection of which we have spoken, which resurrection does not take place in the bodily resurrection from the dead, as will be the case in the other resurrection at the last day, but this resurrection consists solely in dying unto, mortifying, and burying the sinful body through putting off and mortifying the old life and in being raised and renewed unto a new and pious conversation. Amen.

## Conclusion

Here, kind reader, you have a brief instruction of the first or spiritual resurrection, the rising from death or sleep of sin henceforth to live a new, godly, pious, unblamable life, according to the example of Jesus Christ, as the Scriptures abundantly instruct us, and as has been related in part. For to this Christ, the Father from heaven directs us, saying, This is my beloved Son, in whom I am well pleased; hear ye him. He says, Hear ye him. Moses also testifies of Him and says, The Lord, thy God, will raise up unto thee a prophet from the midst of thee, of thy brethren, like unto me; unto him ye shall hearken, and every soul which will not hear that Prophet shall be destroyed from among the people.

Therefore we counsel and admonish all in general, let them be of whatever name, rank, class, or condition, to take good heed to the Word of the Lord which we have briefly presented according to our limited gift and simple talent. I hope by the grace of God that you will find nothing in it but the infallible truth of Jesus Christ, for we have not directed you to men, nor to the doctrine nor commandments of men, but to Jesus Christ alone and to His holy Word which He taught and left on earth and sealed with His blood and death, and afterwards had it preached and taught throughout the world by His faithful witnesses and holy apostles.

And we add that all doctrines which do not agree with the doctrine of Jesus Christ and His apostles, let them appear ever so holy, are accursed. For His Word is the truth and His command is eternal life. Therefore our friendly request and kind petition from our inmost soul is that you may read with an understanding heart this our instruction concerning the spiritual resurrection and new creature, and test and prove it with the doctrine of the apostles. If it does not agree with theirs, let it be accursed. For other foundation can no man lay than that is laid, which is Christ Jesus. To Him be praise through all eternity. Amen.

---

# Meditation on the Twenty-fifth Psalm

*Meditatie op den 25. Psalm*

## c. 1537
### Revised 1558

*For other foundation can no man
lay than that is laid, which is Jesus Christ.*

I CORINTHIANS 3:11

---

# Introduction

Soon after his call to the eldership which occurred in the year 1537, perhaps in January, Menno wrote this *Meditation on the Twenty-Fifth Psalm*. The earliest printed edition is that of 1539. In this 1539 edition Menno speaks of not having served the Lord "until now"—words which he eliminated in later printings. The 1558 edition which appeared in the Eastern dialect of the Baltic coastal region was a revision of the 1539 print. All the *Foundation* editions since 1562 contain this work in a Dutch revision. The Latin epilogue is lacking in the *Opera Omnia Theologica* of 1681 but is printed by K. Vos in his *Menno Simons* (Leiden, 1914, p. 281).

The Preface to the *Meditation* is a polemic in which Menno defends his intellectual honesty and declares that he desires only to follow the Word of God. He demands complete liberty of conscience and protests the persecution of religious dissenters.

The Meditation itself is written in the form of a prayer of confession to God, somewhat resembling the *Confessions* of Augustine which were written in the period around A.D. 400. Menno, like Augustine, confesses that he had served the devil from his youth "with diligence." In spite of his continuing struggle with his "unclean flesh" Menno is now an awakened saint of God, however. It was none other than a merciful God who by His Holy Spirit called Menno in sheer grace into His kingdom. Menno pleads eloquently that God may not forsake him and thus allow him to fall back into sin as David and others did in past millenniums. Menno also stresses that God used His Word to awaken him to his dire spiritual need.

Menno protests vigorously against the boasting of grace which many loose-living professing believers were doing. He soberly reminds his readers that it is only the way of the cross which leads to eternal life. Menno was particularly aroused at the memory of the Münsterites whom he does not mention by name, but yet identifies by his references to swords, "adultery," etc.

It should be mentioned that Menno's sinfulness was mostly that of the heart, in contrast with Augustine who abandoned himself to shameful lusts. But Menno confesses that his only reason for abstention was his desire for a good name among men.

In the meditation on the last verse of Psalm 25 Menno prays eloquently for the true church of Christ.

The title given to this work in the original is *A Very Delightful Meditation and Devout Contemplation, Full of Christian Instruction for a Troubled and Anxious Soul under Assault by the World, the Flesh, Hell, Sin, Death and the Devil: On the Twenty-Fifth Psalm. Having the Superscription in Latin, Ad te levavi animam meam* (Unto Thee Do I Lift Up My Soul). *Drawn Up in the Form of a Prayer* by Menno Simons. In the *Opera Omnia Theologica* of 1681 the work is found, fol. 160-76, and in the *Complete Works* of 1871, I, 213-28.                                                      J. C. W.

# Meditation on the Twenty-fifth Psalm

## c. 1537

•-•-•-•-•-•-•-•-•-•-•-•-•-•-•-•-•-•-•-•-•-•-•-•-•-•-•-•-•-•-•-•-•-•-•-•-•-•-•-•-•-•-•-•-•-•-•-•-•-•-•

## *Preface*

It appears, dear reader, that I am being loaded down behind my back with slanders and lies by those who wish me ill; therefore I have expressed my heart, grounds, spirit, faith, doctrine, ambition, etc., following the sentiments of Psalm 24 according to the Latin reckoning, and Psalm 25 according to the Hebrew. I have briefly done this in the form of a prayer, not in words of human wisdom, not in argumentative nor in rhetorical form. But I have done it from the simple and unpretentious reflection of my heart, setting forth the essential difference between a true and a false Christian, together with the entire basis and hope of my faith: what I maintain concerning Christ Jesus, His doctrine, baptism, Holy Supper, ordinances, commands and prohibitions; what is my disposition toward lords, princes, and all who are as yet in the darkness of unbelief and know not the light of truth; and to show that I by the grace of God seek and shall seek nothing upon earth but the unadulterated Word of our Lord Jesus Christ, and that according to Scripture.

Then if I err in some things, which by the grace of God I hope is not the case, I pray everyone for the Lord's sake, lest I be put to shame, that if anyone has stronger and more convincing truth he through brotherly exhortation and instruction might assist me. I desire with my heart to accept it if he is right. Deal with me according to the intention of the Spirit and Word of Christ. If anyone can with Scripture convince me of error and if I will not renounce it, but continue obstinate to the Word of God and brotherly admonition, then practice upon me the tyranny of Nero, Diocletian, or Maxentius as upon an obdurate and ungodly heretic. For this I am ready, although it would be contrary to the usages and doctrines of the first church, for it is evident that they hurt no one for matters of faith, much less did they kill them. But the erring and heretical they faithfully admonished, and those who would not return were then expelled from the church's communion. Afterwards in the time of Arius, they expelled them in misery. Ultimately the bloody tyranny of Antichrist gained the upper hand, and men were interfered with who did not agree with the pope and his abominations. So it still stands as may be seen in many places.

I am called by many, who have neither seen nor heard me, a deceiving heretic. All this I have to hear, for I am no better than the pious fathers who had to hear and suffer not a little. Nevertheless I feel disposed to give my life if it would induce the world rightly to understand my intention, faith, and doctrine, for I know assuredly that I have the Word of God. Do not take it ill of me that I write this. I desire nothing (God who created me knows this) other than to deal plainly with a living voice before everyone, as one overcoming or being willing to be overcome by the Spirit of Christ. For my desire is that I and many will be saved. And it is unnecessary to use the sword against me, for if I do not have the truth I desire with all my heart to be instructed in it, but if I do have it, then men do not persecute me but Him who is the truth, Christ Jesus.

Again I say with the Spirit and Word of Christ, I desire to overcome or to be overcome; in this I appeal to all the world, if you please. But it is in vain. The truth must be throttled and lies defended with the sword. For this is the real disposition and conduct of Antichrist: to employ slander, arrest, torture, fire, and murder against the Spirit and Word of God. But the Lord will see and judge.

I faithfully admonish the reader zealously and earnestly to strive after the kingdom of God and to examine this Psalm with care, word by word, with a submissive humble heart. I hope you will by God's grace find in it consolation in persecution and also the essential difference between a believer and an unbeliever.

May God, the Father of our Lord Jesus Christ, grant the reader a zealous, fervent heart, a sincere, active faith, unfeigned Christian love, and obedience to His Holy Word through Christ Jesus His beloved Son our Lord, to whom be everlasting praise. Amen.

## [THE TWENTY-FIFTH PSALM, EXPOUNDED AS A PRAYER]

*1. Unto thee, O Lord, do I lift up my soul. O my God, I trust in thee: let me not be ashamed.* Sovereign Lord, Lord of heaven and earth, I call Thee Lord though I am not worthy to be called Thy servant; for from my youth I served not Thee, but Thine enemy the devil with diligence. And yet I do not doubt Thy graciousness, for I find in the word of Thy truth that Thou art a bountiful Lord unto all those who call upon Thee. Therefore I call unto Thee, O Lord, hear me, hear me, O Lord! With full confidence have I lifted up neither my head nor my hands as do the hypocrites in the synagogue, but my soul. I had lifted up my heart not to Abraham, for he has not known us, nor to Israel, for he never knew us, but to Thee alone, for Thou art our Lord and Father, Thou art our Redeemer, this is Thy name from of old, as the prophet declares. For this cause, dear Lord, I trust in Thee, for I know truly that Thou art a faithful God over all those who trust in Thee. When I am in darkness Thou art my life; when I am in prison Thou art with me; when I am forsaken Thou art my comfort; when I am in death Thou art my life; when men curse me Thou wilt bless; when they grieve me Thou dost comfort; when they slay me Thou dost raise me up; and even if I walk in the dark valley, Thou wilt ever be with me. It is right, O Lord, that I lift up my grieved and sorrowing soul to Thee, trust in Thy promise, and be not ashamed.

2. *Let not mine enemies triumph over me; yea, let none that wait on thee be ashamed.* O Lord of hosts, Lord of lords, my flesh is weak; my misery and need is great. Nevertheless, I fear not the carnal scoffing of my enemies, but this I fear in ever-increasing measure: to forsake Thy adorably great name and to depart from Thy truth, lest they rejoice because of my weakness and transgression and mock me saying, Where is now thy God? Where is now thy Christ? And so Thy divine honor be reviled through me. O Lord, keep me; keep me, O Lord, for my enemies are strong and many, yea, more than the hairs of my head and the spears of grass in the fields; my unclean flesh never ceases; Satan encompasses me as a roaring lion to devour me. The bloodguilty cruel world seeks my life; it hates, persecutes, burns, and murders those who seek Thy glory. Wretched man that I am, I know not whither to go, whither to turn. Oppression, sorrow, misery, and fear are on every side, strife within and persecution without. Nevertheless I say with King Jehoshaphat, if I know not whither to go, I lift my eyes unto Thee and rely on Thy grace and goodness as did Abraham in Gerar, Jacob in Mesopotamia, Joseph in Egypt, Moses in Midian, Israel in the wilderness, David in the mountains, Hezekiah in Jerusalem, the young men in the fiery furnace, Daniel in the lions' den. Yes, all the pious fathers trusted in Thee, have waited on Thee, and have not been put to shame.

3. *Let them be ashamed which transgress without cause.* O sovereign Lord, even as Thy merciful grace is over all who fear Thee, so also is Thy fierce wrath over all who despise Thee, who walk after the desire of their hearts and with all fools dare to say, there is no God. We have made a covenant with death and an agreement with hell; God knoweth not what we do; thick clouds are upon Him; He observes not the works of men. We will eat and drink, for tomorrow we die; for life is short and full of labor, and there is no consolation when we have gone hence. We will live to the full as long as life lasts, and use created things as it pleases us. We will oppress[1] the poor, defraud the righteous; we will condemn him to a most disgraceful death. O dear Lord, thus does the whole world err. The lusts of the flesh are on every hand, the desire of the eyes and the pride of life; there is nothing but deceit, unrighteousness, and tyranny wherever we turn. Few are they who fear Thy name. Paul says, To be carnally minded is death. The sentence is already passed: If we live according to the flesh we must die. So teach the Scriptures. If we do not repent there is nothing more certain than Thy fierce anger. Therefore, dear Lord, do Thou draw them, rebuke them, and admonish them and teach them so that they may yet repent, acknowledge the truth, and be saved. For are they not the works of Thy hands, created after Thine image,

[1] Reading *verdrucken* (to oppress) for *verdrincken* (to drown). *Tr.*

and dearly bought? Let them not be confounded with Cain, Sodom, Pharaoh, and Antiochus, with all those who have despised without cause.

4. *Shew me thy ways, O Lord; teach me thy paths.* O Lord of hosts, I confess through the word of Thy grace that there is but one way that leadeth to life, strait and narrow, a foot wide, as Esdras has it, surrounded with thorns and dangers all around. It is found by few, and still fewer walk on it. It is like a treasure hid in a field which none can find but he to whom it is shown with the Spirit. Dear Lord, there is no way but Thou alone; all who walk before Thee will find the gate of life. There is another way which seems good to many, very attractive for the flesh, self-seeking as it is, soft, smooth, and broad, planted with roses, pleasant and agreeable to our eye, but its end is death. On this way the whole world walks unconcerned and without fear. Men have preferred things perishable to that which lasts, evil to good, and darkness to light. They all walk on the evil, crooked way, they become faint in the way of unrighteousness, and know not the way of the Lord. It is true, the way of error seems right in the eyes of fools, but I confess through Thy Spirit and Word that it is the certain road to the depth of hell. Therefore, I entreat Thee, dear Lord, be merciful to me a poor sinner; show me Thy paths and teach me Thy ways, for Thy way is the right way, godly, pleasant, humble, chaste, full of peace and of all good. It will lead my soul to life eternal.

5. *Lead me in thy truth, and teach me: for thou art the God of my salvation; on thee do I wait all the day.* O Lord God, my tears, says David, have been my meat day and night, my heart quakes within me, my strength forsakes me, and the light of my eyes almost fails because of the innumerable dangers and snares which are laid for my soul. I am in constant fear lest I be led away from truth by human error or satanic deceit.

O Lord, the subtlety of the learned ones is great. Satan uses his wiles artfully. Some teach merely the doctrine and commandments of men, barren and corrupt trees. Some cry nothing but grace, Spirit, and Christ, but trample daily on Thy grace, grieve Thy Holy Spirit, and crucify Thy Son with their vain, carnal life, as is evident. Some who had in times past escaped Sodom, Egypt, and Babylon and had assumed the yoke and cross of Christ are once more so devoured by the noonday devil, so deceived by the false prophets, as though they had never known Thy Word and will. Yes, seven spirits, worse than the former, have entered into them, and the latter error is worse than the former. Yet they cloak themselves under Thy holy Word and ordinances and pretend that it is Thy pleasure, Word, and will, although Thou didst never think of it, much less desire it. For this I am saddened all along, full of sorrow and heartache, knowing right well that Thy Word of truth is no[2] deceiving lie, as they teach it, but the righteous truth which Thy infallible mouth witnessed here upon earth and teaches in this world. All who are of the truth hear Thy voice as the voice of their only Shepherd, and

---

[2] Reading *niet* (not) for *met* (with) which seems to be a misprint. *Tr.*

of the true Bridegroom, but from the voice of a stranger they flee, always fearing lest they be deceived.

O Lord, remember Thy poor, afflicted servant. Thou art a searcher of hearts, Thou knowest me, that I desire and seek nothing but Thy will. Therefore, dear Lord, direct me in Thy truth and teach me it. For Thou alone art my Lord and God, my Saviour. Besides Thee I acknowledge none other. Thou art my hope, my comfort, my shield, defense, and fortress, upon which I rely with confidence, for whom I wait every day in my fear and sadness and need.

6. *Remember, O Lord, thy tender mercies and thy lovingkindnesses; for they have been ever of old.* O Lord of hosts, when I am buoyed up in the waters of Thy grace, I find that I can neither fathom nor measure them, for Thy mercies are greater than all Thy works. Who, dear Lord, ever came to Thee with a pious heart and was rejected? Who ever sought Thee and found Thee not? Who ever sought help with Thee and did not obtain it? Who ever prayed for Thy grace and did not receive it? Who ever called upon Thee without being heard? Yes, dear Lord, how many didst Thou accept in grace who otherwise by Thy stern justice merited otherwise? Adam departed from Thee and believed the counsel of the serpent; he transgressed Thy commandments and became a child of death before Thee. But Thy fatherly kindness did not reject him, but in grace Thou didst seek him, didst call and reprove him, didst cover his nakedness with coats of skin, and didst graciously comfort him with the promised seed. Paul, Thy chosen vessel, raged like a roaring lion and ranting wolf in Thy holy mountain; nevertheless Thy grace shone about him in his blindness; it illuminated him, called him from heaven and chose him as an apostle and servant in Thy house.

I also, dear Lord, the greatest of all sinners, and the least among all the saints, am not worthy to be called Thy child or servant, for I have sinned against heaven and before Thee. Although I resisted in former times Thy precious Word and Thy holy will with all my powers, and with full understanding contended against Thy manifest truth, taught and lived and sought my own flesh, praise, and honor, more than Thy righteousness, honor, word, and truth; nevertheless Thy fatherly grace did not forsake me, a miserable sinner, but in love received me, converted me to another mind, led me with the right hand, and taught me by the Holy Spirit until of my own choice I declared war upon the world, the flesh, and the devil, and renounced all my ease, peace, glory, desire, and physical prosperity and willingly submitted to the heavy cross of my Lord Jesus Christ that I might inherit the promised kingdom with all the soldiers of God and the disciples of Christ. I repeat, Thy mercies are greater than all Thy works; therefore, dear Lord, assist me, stand by me, comfort me, a poor sinner. My soul is in mortal need, the dangers of hell surround me; help, Lord, and preserve me, keep me, and be not angry. Remember Thy great mercies of which all are made partakers who from of old have waited upon Thy holy name and merciful grace.

*7. Remember not the sins of my youth, nor my transgressions; according to thy mercy remember thou me for thy goodness' sake.* O sovereign Lord, I was shapen in iniquity and in sin did my mother conceive me. I came of sinful flesh. Through Adam corrupt seed has been sown in my heart from which so much misery has sprung. I, a miserable sinner, did not know my infirmities so long as they were not manifest to me by the Spirit. I thought I was a Christian, but when I looked carefully I found myself altogether earthly and carnal and without the Word. My life was darkness, my truth lies, my righteousness sin, my religion open idolatry, and my life certain death. O dear Lord, I did not know myself until I viewed myself in Thy Word. And then I confessed my nakedness and blindness, my sickness, my native depravity, and with Paul I realized that in my flesh dwelt no good thing. I was full of wounds and bruises and putrefying sores from the sole of the foot even to the head. Alack and alas, my gold was dross, my wheat chaff, my services were deceit and lies, to say nothing of my transgressions and flesh. My thoughts were carnal, my words and works without the fear of God. My waking and sleeping were unclean, my prayer hypocrisy. Nothing I did was done without sin. O Lord, remember not the sins of my youth, committed knowingly and unknowingly so oft before Thee, nor my daily transgressions in which because of my great weakness I am alas found daily, but remember me according to Thy great mercy. Blind I am, do Thou enlighten me; naked I am, do Thou clothe me; wounded, do Thou heal me; dead, do Thou quicken me. I know of no light, no physician, no life except Thee. Accept of me in Thy grace and grant me Thy mercy, favor, and faithfulness for Thy goodness' sake, O Lord.

*8. Good and upright is the Lord: therefore will he teach sinners in the way.* O Lord of hosts, although I have walked so unrighteously before Thee from my youth that I am ashamed to lift my eyes to Thee in heaven, nevertheless I appear at Thy mercy seat, for I know that Thou art merciful and kind and desirest not the death of the sinner, but that he may repent and live. Thou didst send forth Thy faithful servant, Moses, who gave Israel the law by the disposition of angels, also Thy servants and prophets who preached the way of repentance and broke the bread of life to the people. Diligently they reproved sin; Thy grace they heralded forth. The right way they taught. Thy sharp piercing sword was in their mouth; their light shone as the golden candlestick; they were as blossoming olive trees, as a sweet smell of costly perfume, yea, as the glorious mountain planted with roses and lilies. Nevertheless, men did not desire them, but they thrust them out cruelly, derided them, persecuted them, and delivered them unto death.

Nor did this exhaust the springs of Thy mercy, but Thou didst send Thy beloved Son, the dearest pledge of Thy grace, who preached Thy Word, fulfilled Thy righteousness, accomplished Thy will, bore our sins, blotted them out with Thy blood, stilled Thy wrath, conquered the devil, hell, sin, and death, and obtained grace, mercy, favor, and peace for all who truly believe on Him. His command is eternal life. He sent out His messengers preaching this peace, His apostles who spread this grace abroad through the whole world, who shone as bright, burning torches before all men, so that they might lead me and all erring sinners into the right way. O Lord, not unto me, but unto Thee be praise and honor. Their words I love, their practices I follow. Thy dear Son, Christ Jesus, whom they preached to me, I believe. His will and way I seek. Thy abundantly great love I acknowledge, not through me but through Thee, for Thou, O Lord, art good, and I am evil; Thou art true and I am deceitful; Thou art righteous and I am unrighteous. Teach me, dear Lord, in the right way; for am I not a sheep of Thy pasture; receive me into Thy care, under the shadow of Thy wings, cover me, for I am greatly tormented; I am poor, wretched, and sorrowful unto death.

*9. The meek will he guide in judgment: and the meek will he teach his way.* O sovereign Lord, Thy divine grace has shone around me, Thy divine Word has taught me, Thy Holy Spirit has urged me until I forsook the seat of the scornful, the counsel of sinners, and the way of scorners. I was wicked and carried the banner of unrighteousness for many years. I was a leader in all manner of folly. Empty talk, vanity, playing [cards], drinking, eating were my daily pastime. The fear of God was not before my eyes. Moreover, I was a lord and a prince in Babylon. Everyone sought me and desired me. The world loved me and I it. I had the first place at feasts and in synagogues. I was pre-eminent among men, even above aged men. Everyone revered me. When I spoke they were silent. When I beckoned they came. When I waved them away they went. What I desired they did. My word was final in all matters. The desire of my heart was granted.

But as soon as I with Solomon saw that all was vanity and with Paul I esteemed all as nothingness, as soon as I renounced the proud ungodliness of this world and sought Thee and Thy kingdom which will abide forever, then I found everywhere the counterpart and reverse. Heretofore I was honored; now debased. Once there was pleasantness, now sorrow. Once I was a friend, now I pass for an enemy. Then I was considered wise, now a fool. Then pious, now wicked; then a Christian, now a heretic, yes, an abomination and an evildoer to all.

O Lord, comfort me, preserve Thy sorrowful servant, for I am exceedingly poor and wretched. My sins rise up against me, the world hates and reviles me; lords and princes persecute me, the learned ones curse and abuse me, my dearest friends forsake me, and those who were near to me stand afar. Who will have mercy on me and receive me? Miserable am I, dear Lord. Have mercy on me and receive me with honor. There verily is none that can preserve me, but Thou alone. Therefore, I entreat Thee, dear Lord, incline Thine ear to my supplication, lead me by Thy right hand. Lead me in the right way lest I stumble upon the dark mountains.

I see that the children of men neither teach nor do the right; deceiving and false is all flesh. The deceiving sects are great and many. Every one urges his matter as if it were built upon a rock, yet they have not the truth. Therefore, dear, dear Lord, teach me Thy truth and cast me not off from Thy presence, for I am miserable. I am in the midst of lions and bears which seek to destroy my soul and thrust it from the way of truth. O Lord, strengthen me; O Lord, keep me so that I may continue in the way, for I know assuredly that it is the infallible truth and the sure way of peace.

10. *All the paths of the Lord are mercy and truth unto such as keep his covenant and his testimonies.* O Lord of hosts, all men boast of Thy grace and favor although they in all their works show themselves to be children of wrath. They lie and cheat, eat and drink to excess, they harlot and fornicate, they rake and scrape, curse and swear without measure, and cover all with Thy grace and the blood of Christ. Everyone sings and shouts: The mercy of the Lord is great; Christ died for us sinners; our labor is sin and unrighteousness. Dear Lord, it is true, of course, but I know that they have no part in Thee, that their hope is vain, their labor without fruit, and their work useless. Yes, their hope is like thistledown before the wind.

They will have no part in Thy kingdom, for they remain impenitent and believe not Thy truth. Alas, they confess not that Thy mercy is everlasting over those who fear Thee and keep Thy covenant. Thy goodness, says David, is extended to the saints, and Thy care is over Thine elect. Thine eyes are upon the righteous, and Thine ears are open to their cries, but Thy face is against them that do evil, to cut off the remembrance of them from the earth. I am Thy friend if I do what Thou hast commanded. It is true, dear Lord, that Christ was given to us, and that He died for us, yet not to such an end that we may now live according to our sinful desires and will, but according to Thy good will, word, and command.

I know, dear Lord, that Thou art no less righteous than kind, that Thou hatest the evil and lovest the good; to the good Thou art kind, but to the wicked Thou wilt in due time appear as a righteous Judge. What did the pure blood of the eternal covenant benefit Cain and Judas seeing they have despised Thy grace and by their traitorous murder have excluded themselves from the merits of Thy Son? What did it profit Pilate, Herod, Annas, and Caiaphas to have seen Thy fountain of grace, Jesus Christ; yes, to have touched Him, seeing they have condemned Him, though innocent, to the accursed death of the cross, the spotless Lamb, the King of Glory? But they who keep Thy covenant and preserve Thy testimony as did Abel, Enoch, Noah, Abraham, Isaac, and Jacob, to them Thy ways are peace and joy, yea, altogether mercy, kindness, and faithfulness.

11. *For thy name's sake, O Lord, pardon mine iniquity; for it is great.* O Lord God, I pray Thee with holy David, Rebuke me not in Thine anger, neither chasten me in Thy hot displeasure, for my wounds are sore and putrefying, and my sins have borne me down; there is no peace in my bones. From the bottom of my heart I confess with the dear Daniel: O dear Lord, O Thou great and terrible God, I have sinned and done unjustly before

Thee; I have walked ungodly, have wandered away from Thee, have walked not in Thy commandments and statutes. Thy proffered grace I have rejected. Thy holy Word I have thrust from me. Thy beloved Son I have crucified. Thy Holy Spirit I have grieved. Unrighteous have I been in all my doings. O Lord, the multitude of my sins frighten me. I know of no evil that I have not committed. I was as envious as Cain, proud and unchaste as Sodom, unmerciful as Pharaoh, refractory as Korah, lascivious as Shimri, disobedient as Saul, idolatrous as Jeroboam, false as Joab, haughty as Nebuchadnezzar, covetous as Balaam, drunken as Nabal, boastful as Sennacherib, blasphemous as Rabshakeh, bloodthirsty as Herod, lying as Ananias. Yes, I say with King Manasseh, that my sins are more numerous than the sands of the seashore and the stars in the heavens. By day and by night they vex me, and no good dwells in my flesh. All that I seek and bring forth is unrighteousness and sin. Not that which I would, but that which I would not, that I do. I, miserable man, know not whither to go. If I betake me to myself I find great faults, impure desires, a vessel of sin. If I go to my neighbor he has nothing with which to help me, no herb or poultice avails; Thy Word alone can heal. The wages of sin, says Paul, is death, but Thy grace is eternal life.

This grace I seek and desire, for this is the only poultice which can heal my soul. The sinful woman availed herself of this as soon as she saw her sores and felt her pain. David availed himself of this when he had disgraced Bathsheba and had slain the pious Uriah. Great was his distress. He saw his wickedness and said, I have sinned against the Lord. He desired balm. O God, said he, according unto the multitude of Thy tender mercies blot out my transgressions, wash me thoroughly from mine iniquity, and cleanse me from my sin. Psalm 51:1, 2. At once the word of the prophet, rich in grace, sounded: The Lord also hath put away thy sin. His troubled heart was quieted; he praised Thy name, proclaimed Thy mercy, and exalted Thy grace above all Thy works. O Lord, dear Lord, I a sorrowing sinner, am aware of the same disease, I desire the same balm, and do not exclude myself from the medication of Thy mercy. I seek no comfort save with Thee, O Lord, for Thy holy name's sake. Help me, so that I may eternally thank and praise Thee. Erase my sin and be merciful to me in all my transgressions, for they are great.

12. *What man is he that feareth the Lord? him shall he teach in the way that he shall choose.* O sovereign Lord, Thy path is the pathway of peace. Blessed is he that walketh therein, for we find mercy, love, righteousness, humility, obedience, and patience in her ways. She clothes the naked, feeds the hungry, gives drink to the thirsty, entertains the needy, reproves, threatens, comforts, and admonishes. She is sober, honest, chaste, and upright in all her ways; becomes all things to all men; none is offended at her; her goings forth are to eternal life—but few alas there be that find her. Yea, I fear, dear Lord, that there are scarcely ten of a thousand that find her, scarcely five who walk in her.

It continues as it was from the beginning when there were but four persons on the earth of whom the Scriptures testify that two were disobedient and a third slew his brother. There were eight righteous ones when the world was drowned and one of them mocked his father. In Sodom and Gomorrah with the adjacent country, there were four righteous persons; one looked back and was changed into a pillar of salt. More than six hundred thousand valiant men left Egypt and only two of them entered the promised land. Not, dear Lord, that all were damned who died on the way, but they did not on account of their unbelief inherit the promised Canaan. So now also, dear Lord, is the eternal land promised to us all if we walk in the way which Thou hast chosen for us. But now they walk the crooked way of death, and therefore, even as those did not inherit the temporal, so will also these not inherit the eternal Canaan.

O Lord, well may I sigh and say, Where is he that fears the Lord? Where is he who has understanding? Where is he who seeks God? They are all gone out of the way, they are together become unprofitable. There is none that doeth good, no, not one. Their throat is an open sepulchre; with their tongues they have used deceit; the poison of asps is under their lips; their feet are swift to shed blood; destruction and misery are in their ways, and the way of peace they have not known: there is no fear of God before their eyes. Rom. 3:12-18. All we see with them is lies. They despise and blaspheme Thy righteousness, yet they sing and speak much of Thy truth, and glory in Thy great name, although there is not one ripe grape on their vine, nor any proper fruit to be found with them.

But those who fear Thee, O Lord, depart from all iniquity. For Thy fear, says Sirach, dispels sin and is the beginning of wisdom. Thine eyes are upon those who fear Thee, Thy Holy Spirit leads them, Thy gracious hand preserves them. They will not fear nor tremble, for Thou art the protector and shelter against noonday heat. Thou art the pardon of their debt, the recovery of their fall. Thou dost enlighten their eyes, makest glad their souls, givest them grace, blessing, and richest peace. He that fears Thee, walks uprightly in all his ways, for Thou teachest him in the way that he has chosen.

*13. His soul shall dwell at ease; and his seed shall inherit the earth.* O Lord of hosts, this is the final reward for those who know Thee. Their souls shall inherit that which is good in the paradise of their God upon Mount Zion, in the heavenly Jerusalem, in the church of the living God, in the congregation of the righteous whose names are written in heaven. They are delivered from hell, sin, death, and the devil, and they serve before Thee in peace and joy of heart all their days. They sleep without fear, for Thou art their strength and shield. They rest under the shadow of Thy wings, for they are Thine. They fear not, for Thou dost warm them with the rays of Thy love. They hunger not, for Thou feedest them with the bread of life. They thirst not, for Thou givest them to drink of the waters of Thy Holy Spirit. They want not, for Thou art their treasure and wealth. They dwell in the house of

Thy peace, in the tabernacles of righteousness, and in sure peace. They have pleasure in Thy law and speak, as the prophet says, of Thy Word day and night in the midst of the people. They wash the feet of their souls in the clear waters of Thy truth. They view their consciences in the clear mirror of Thy wisdom. Their thoughts are upright; their words are words of grace, seasoned with salt. Their works are holy, faithful, and true. The light of their piety shines around them. What they seek they find. What they desire they obtain. Their souls dwell in the fullness of Thy wealth. The dew of Thy grace is fallen on them. The fields of their consciences bear wine and oil without measure. And although they must endure in their flesh, for a time, much misery, suffering, and trouble, yet they know well that the way of the cross is the way that leads to life. They are not ashamed of the way of the Lord, His cross and weapon.

With Christ they contend valiantly, running with patience the race set before them until they have seized the prize and have received the promised crown. Nothing can hinder them since they have become partakers of Thy Spirit, and have tasted of Thy sweetness. They neither waver nor turn aside. Their house is firmly built upon a rock. They are as the pillars of the holy temple. They have eaten of the hidden heavenly bread. O Lord, to Thee be praise. Thy fear abides continually before their eyes; they walk in Thy way. Therefore, shall their souls be blessed, and His seed begotten of the Holy Spirit and Word will enjoy the land of the living wherein Thou and Thy chosen ones shall reign in glory endlessly.

14. *The secret of the Lord is with them that fear him; and he will show them his covenant.* O Lord God, the thoughts of my heart terrify me, and my heart trembles within me, because with Ezra I perceive that so many are born to no purpose. What shall I say, dear Lord? Shall I say that Thou hast ordained the wicked to wickedness, as some have said? God forbid. I know, O Lord, that Thou art the eternally Good, and that nothing wicked can be found in Thee. We are the works of Thy hand, created in Christ Jesus to good works that we should walk therein. Water, fire, life, and death hast Thou left to our choice. Thou dost not desire the death of the sinner, but that he should repent and live. Thou art the eternal life; therefore dost Thou hate all darkness in me. Thou desirest not that any should remain lost, but that they might repent, come to the knowledge of Thy truth, and be saved.

O dear Lord, how sadly have they blasphemed Thine unspeakably great goodness, eternal mercy, and almighty Majesty in this matter! They have, O God of all grace and Creator of all things, changed Thee into a cruel devil saying that Thou art the source of all evil, Thou who art called the Father of days and of lights. It is plain that out of good no evil can come, of light no darkness, of life no death, of God no devil. Yet must their stubborn hearts and carnal minds be attributed to Thy will in order that they may continue upon the broad way and have a cover for their sins, and this because they acknowledge neither Thy divine goodness, nor their own native wickedness.

O Lord God, Thou hast loved us with an eternal love. Thou hast chosen us before the foundation of the world, that we should be unblamable and holy before Thee in love, not regarding what we find written by the faithful Paul concerning Esau, Pharaoh, and Israel. He has done all this in our behalf in order that we should give the honor to Thy name, and not to ourselves. What do we, miserable sinners, have of which we may boast? What do we have that we have not received from Thee? All that we have is of Thy fullness. Therefore all who know Thy Word thank Thee. O dear Lord, the mystery of Thy holy Word is by no means revealed to the rich, the noble, or the wise, but to the poor, the simple, the little children. Yes, Father, said Christ, such was Thy good pleasure. Isaiah says, Thou wilt look upon the miserable and those who are of a broken spirit, and who tremble at Thy Word. Therefore, dear Lord, we miserable sinners pray Thee to lead us in Thy truth, to teach us Thy mercies, to make us rightly to know the power of Thy covenant, that Thou art ours and we are Thine, the covenant which Thou hast made with us in Christ without any merit on our part. For Thy mystery will be found with those who fear Thee and Thou shalt make them to know Thy covenant.

*15. Mine eyes are ever toward the Lord; for he shall pluck my feet out of the net.* O sovereign Lord, I pray with the prophet, If thou shouldst mark iniquity, none can stand before Thee. I, a miserable, grievous sinner, have with all my heart turned to all folly, to gold and silver, pride and pomp, to strange and forbidden flesh. I have turned mine eyes to manifest idols, to wood and stone, and have played the harlot with them many years upon every high mountain and under every green tree, as the prophet says. My idols were according to the number of my days. I have bowed my knee before graven and molten images and have said, Save me, for Thou art my God. I sought sight with the blind, life with the dead, and help with those who could not preserve themselves from dust and rust, from thieves and owls. Yes, I have said to a weak, perishing creature that came forth of the earth, that was broken in a mill, that was baked by the fire, that was chewed by my teeth and digested by my stomach, namely, to a mouthful of bread, Thou hast saved me—even as Israel said to the golden calf, These be thy gods, O Israel, which brought thee up out of the land of Egypt. Ex. 22:4. O God, thus have I, a miserable sinner, toyed with the harlot of Babylon for many years, for I supposed that she was a modest, honest, and chaste woman, a queen of righteousness who was glorious, holy, and acceptable before Thine eyes. For I saw her adorned with purple and scarlet, with gold and precious stones, and pearls, a golden cup in her hand, powerful over all kings upon earth. Therefore, I knew not that she was so very full of pocks and sores, that there was in such a splendid cup so much abomination, that she was such an unblushing, impudent harlot and murderess who deceived the world, persecuted the elect, and drank the blood of the saints. But now I have seen her abominations with my eyes, have felt them with my hands, and I quake because I left Thee, the living fountain, so long, and comforted myself with useless cisterns that can give no water; that I gave Thy honor to images and mere creatures, and worshiped the creature more than the Creator, who is blessed forever. This happened, in part, through the deceitfulness of my eyes, because I was bewitched in my heart by the goodly appearance of the afore-mentioned woman. But now, dear Lord, my eyes are constantly directed unto Thee, till Thou hearest me; they are constantly directed to Thy mercy seat till I obtain grace and mercy from Thee, for Thou alone art He who can help me in the time of my temptation, and pluck my feet out of the wicked net of sin.

16. *Turn thee unto me, and have mercy upon me; for I am desolate and afflicted.* O Lord of hosts, my sins and transgressions I do not hide from Thee, but unreservedly confess that I spent my former days after the will of the heathen and walked with them in all manner of ungodly desires, in pride and pomp, in eating and drinking to excess, and in abominable, blind idolatry. I did all that pleased my wicked flesh, I was a child of wrath, even as others. Thy holy name I held in derision; Thy Word was a fable to me; in reliance upon Thy grace I did all manner of evil.

I was as a whited sepulcher. Outwardly before men I was moral, chaste, and liberal, and none reproved my conduct. But inwardly I was full of dead men's bones, stench, and worms. My cup was clean on the outside, but within it was full of robbery and excess. What I did privately is a shame to mention; all my thoughts were unclean, vain, proud, ambitious, and ungodly; my heart was full of disaffection, hatred, envy, vengeance, and enmity. My desire was to all manner of wickedness, I sinned without bounds. I feared neither God nor devil, law nor Gospel, heaven nor hell. There was nothing that could frighten me; I regarded neither Thee nor Thy Word; my course was onward to all wickedness. I sought nothing but the friendship and love of this world; therefore I did not commit adultery, fornication, and such abominable sins before men, merely because I feared to lose their favor and my reputation, and not because I feared Thee. Yet my vanity, my impetuousness, my merriment, my drunkenness, my sinful lusts, open shames, my faultiness, my pride and honor, my idolatry, were called the true religion. Yes, all my conduct, private and public, was not concealed before Thine eyes.

Thus did I, miserable sinner, spend my days and did not, O God of grace, acknowledge Thee as my God, Creator, and Redeemer, till Thy Holy Spirit taught me through Thy Word and made known to me Thy will, and led somewhat into Thy mysteries. Now I know how dishonorably I walked before Thee, not otherwise than if I had spit in Thy face, had struck Thee with the hand, and trampled Thee and derided Thee as foolish.

O Lord, dear Lord, have mercy upon me, for I am desolate and afflicted; my sins are many and great; my conscience troubles me; my thoughts disturb me; my heart laments and sighs because I have sinned so heinously before Thee. My sins have separated me from Thee, have hid Thy countenance from me, have deserved Thy wrath. I have become a fuel for the burning pool. And yet the deeper I am grieved, the more I am consoled by Thy Word, for it teaches me Thy mercy, grace, and favor and the remission of my sins through Christ, Thy beloved Son, our Lord, ignoring the fact that I neither knew nor feared Thee. This promise quiets me. This promise gladdens me; it leads me with the sinful woman to Thy blessed feet with full confidence and clear conscience, knowing that Thou didst not reject Thy returning son although I have spent my paternal inheritance and possessions dishonorably with harlots and rogues in a strange country, devoured it in my unrighteousness. My God, turn the blessed countenance of Thy peace unto me. I have sinned before heaven and in Thy sight, lay Thy hand of grace upon me; have mercy upon me, a poor sinner, for I am desolate and afflicted.

17. *The troubles of my heart are enlarged; O bring thou me out of my distresses.* O Lord God, my heart weeps and sighs, my conscience quakes and trembles, my soul is as a grieved mother bereaved of her only child, who cannot be comforted, seeing that I, a poor, reckless sinner, for so many years never sincerely sought, acknowledged, or appreciated Thy godly love and fatherly kindness. I have lived more disgracefully than the irrational creatures, for they in eating, drinking, and other things of nature do not go beyond their instinctive urges and do not transgress the laws of nature, but I have lived more unfruitfully, intemperately, and unrighteously against the innate laws of nature than my ungodly flesh desired. Usually I acknowledged a little later that the desires of my flesh were death, my spirit warned me of my evil doings, yet my flesh suppressed all warning. I was in all things a bond servant of sin, sworn unto unrighteousness. I drank down sin as water; my delight was in all manner of folly; the outstretched arm of Thy grace I saw not; Thy calling voice I heard not; Thy inviting love I regarded not. In short, Thy knowledge have I hated, and Thy fear have I cast behind me.

And this is not all, dear Lord, that I acted so pitifully in my ignorance, but I find day by day that my righteousness is as filthy rags. When I think I walk, I fall; when I imagine that I stand, I am down; and when I think to be something, then I am nothing. O dear Lord, keep me, for the fear of my heart is very great, yea, greater than I can write or say. At times I am as a woman in travail. My countenance is pale at the fear of Thee, my hands are upon my loins on account of the trouble of my heart, the dangers of hell surround me, the marrow of my bones is dried up. For here neither money nor possessions are involved, neither flesh nor blood, but my poor naked soul, eternal life or eternal death. Therefore I pray, forsake me not, dear Lord, but open the eyes of Thy mercy and behold my great burden. Stand by me and deliver me from all my distresses.

18. *Look upon mine affliction and my pain; and forgive all my sins.* O sovereign Lord, when the righteous call to Thee, Thou answerest. When they draw nigh to Thee, Thou receivest. Thou art nigh to those who are of a broken heart. Thou comfortest those who are of a contrite spirit. The sacrifice that is acceptable to Thee is a contrite spirit; a broken heart Thou dost not despise. Thou hast sent forth Thy beloved Son, anointed with

Thy Holy Spirit, to preach the Gospel to the poor, to heal the brokenhearted, to preach deliverance to the captives, and recovery of sight to the blind, to set at liberty them that are bruised, to proclaim the acceptable year of the Lord; to comfort all that mourn, to appoint unto them that mourn in Zion; to give them beauty for ashes, the oil of joy for mourning, the garment of praise for the spirit of heaviness.

He proclaimed salvation to all who are heavy laden and with faithful hearts come to Him. He invites all the thirsty to the waters of life; all our sins He bore upon the cross in His own body, and our guilt He blotted out with His blood, even as Moses did in types and shadows when he sprinkled unclean Israel with the blood of oxen and rams and with the ashes of the heifer. For under the law nearly all things were purified by the shedding of blood. If the prefigurative blood had such virtue that it could purify the flesh to sanctification, how much more shall the blood of Thy beloved Son, who offered Himself unspotted through the eternal Spirit, purify our consciences from dead works to serve Thee, O ever-living God. Through the merits of Thy blood we receive the remission of our sins according to the riches of Thy grace. Yea, through this blood on the cross He reconciled all upon earth and in heaven above. Therefore, dear Lord, I confess that I have or know no remedy for my sins, no works nor merits, neither baptism nor the Lord's supper (although all sincere Christians use these as a sign of Thy Word and hold them in respect), but the precious blood of Thy beloved Son alone which is bestowed upon me by Thee and has graciously redeemed me, a poor sinner, through mere grace and love, from my former walk.

Therefore, O God of truth, with whom no falsehood is found, remember the words of Thy prophet which he spake in Thy name, namely: If the wicked will turn from his sins that he hath committed and keep all my statutes and do that which is lawful and right, he shall surely live. He shall not die. All his transgressions that he hath committed, they shall not be mentioned unto him. O my God, look not upon me, but upon the eternal Melchisedek, Jesus Christ, whom Thou hast appointed high priest over Thy house, upon the blessed King of Thy righteousness, full of peace, who has neither beginning nor end of days, and is a high priest forever; who did not appropriate honors to Himself, but was called and ordained of Thee as was Aaron. And in the days of His flesh offered up prayers and supplications with strong crying and tears, and was heard in that He feared. For His sake hear me; for His sake accept me; for His sake be merciful to me. Console Thine afflicted servant.

I have no comfort in heaven above, nor upon earth, but in Thee alone. Have mercy upon me in my great distress. My unclean, sinful flesh assaults me; my wicked nature wages war against me. And moreover, for Thy Word's sake I have become an abomination, an offscouring and byword to all men. All who hear of me shake their heads at me. Without and within I have no rest. I say again, my sins assail me; my soul is in sorrow and pain; therefore, dear Lord, I pray Thee not for gold and silver, for they can profit me nothing in the day of vengeance, neither for long life, for it ever seeks to go in wrong ways. But this only I desire of thee from my whole heart: that Thou wouldst look upon me, a miserable sinner, with the gracious eyes of Thy mercy, and that Thou wouldst take pity on me in my need, and comfort me with Thy Holy Spirit, and forgive all my sins.

*19. Consider mine enemies; for they are many; and they hate me with cruel hatred.* O Lord of hosts, when I was one with the world I spake and did as the world, and the world hated me not; but as soon as I had eaten the book that was shown to me, although it was in my mouth sweet as honey, yet it made my belly bitter, for there were written therein lamentations and mourning and woe. While I served the world I received its reward; all men spake well of me, even as the fathers did of the false prophets. But now that I love the world with a godly love, and seek its welfare and happiness; rebuke, admonish, and instruct it with Thy Word, pointing it to Jesus Christ, the crucified, it has become unto me a grievous cross, and as the gall of bitterness. So cruelly am I hated that not only I myself, but all those who show me love, favor, and mercy must in some places look for imprisonment and death. O dear Lord, verily I am considered worse than a notorious thief and murderer, like a lost sheep in the wilderness of the world, chased, tormented, and pursued unto death by ravenous wolves.

Am I not like a derelict in mid-ocean without mast, sail, or rudder, driven by fierce winds and boisterous waves? My flesh had almost said, I am cheated because I find the wicked, reckless masses enjoying riches, honor, and prosperity and in quiet and peace, while the godly must endure so much of hunger, thirst, affliction, and distress. Their habitation is insecure; they must toil in bitterness for their bread; they are accursed, mocked, persecuted, and hated of all men as filth and stench. O blessed Lord, mine enemies are many and great, their heart roars like cruel lions, their words are as deadly arrows, their tongues are ever against me. At one time I am reviled by them as a false seducer, at another reproached as an accursed heretic, although by Thy grace I possess nothing but unyielding truth. I am their mortal enemy because I direct them in the way of righteousness.

O Lord, I am not ashamed of my doctrine before Thee and Thine angels, much less before this rebellious world, for I know assuredly that I teach Thy Word. I have taught nothing all along but true repentance, a dying unto our sinful flesh, and the new life that cometh from God. I have taught a true and genuine faith in Thee and Thy beloved Son; that it must be active through love. I have taught Jesus Christ and Him crucified, true God and man, who in an incomprehensible, inexpressible, and indescribable manner was born of Thee before all time, Thy eternal Word and Wisdom, the brightness of Thy glory and the express image of Thy person. And that in the fullness of time, through the power of Thy Holy Spirit He became, in the womb of the unspotted Virgin Mary, real flesh and blood; a visible, tangible, and mortal man, like unto Adam and his posterity in all things, sin excepted; born of the seed or lineage of Abraham and David; that He died and was buried, arose again, ascended into heaven and so became our only and eternal Advocate before Thee; our Mediator, Intercessor, and Redeemer. If all the prophets, apostles, and evangelists have not taught this with the greatest clearness from the beginning, then I will gladly bear my shame and punishment. I have taught no other baptism, no other supper, no other ordinance than that implied by the unerring mouth of our Lord Jesus Christ, and the manifest example and usage of His holy apostles, to say nothing of the abundant evidence of the historians and the learned ones of both the primitive and the present church.

Since then I urge my doctrine by the evidence of Thy plain ineffable Word and by the ordinance of Thy Son, who can reprove me and show with the argument of truth that I am a seducing teacher? Does not the whole Scripture teach that Christ is the truth and shall remain that forever? Is not the apostolic church the true Christian Church? We know that all human doctrines are froth and chaff, and that Antichrist has spoiled and corrupted the doctrine of Christ. Why then do they hate me, because out of pure zeal I teach and propound in its purity the doctrine of Christ and His apostles? No one indeed hates the opposers of Antichrist but such as are his members. If I did not have the Word of Christ, how gladly would I be taught it, for I seek it with fear and trembling. In this I cannot be deceived, for I have by Thy grace, through the influence of Thy Holy Spirit, believed and accepted Thy holy truth as the sure word of Thy good pleasure. And it in all eternity will never deceive me. Let them boast and rave, twist and wrangle, extirpate, persecute, and kill as they please. Thy Word will triumph and the Lamb will gain the victory. I know of a certainty that with this my doctrine, which is Thy Word, I shall at the coming of Christ judge and sentence not only men, but also angels. And though I and my beloved brethren were totally extirpated and taken from the earth, yet would Thy Word remain the truth forever.

We are no better than our companions who preceded us. Yet will they cause Thy hand to be raised once more, and realize too late probably whom they have pierced. O Lord, with that unjust hatred they hate me; whom have I wronged in a single word? Whom have I shortchanged a penny's worth? Whose gold, silver, cow or cattle, ox or ass have I desired? I have loved them with a pure love, even unto death; Thy Word and will have I taught them, and with earnest diligence I have shown them by Thy grace the way of salvation. Therefore my enemies are so many, and hate me with cruel hatred.

20. *O keep my soul, and deliver me; let me not be ashamed, for I put my trust in thee.* O Lord God, the word of Paul fills me with terror: Let him that standeth take heed lest he fall. For if a man think himself to be something when he is nothing, he deceiveth himself. For all flesh that is

forsaken by Thy Spirit, is blind in divine things, ignorant, entirely false and
unjust, nay, sin and death, as I have seen plainly in David and Peter. For
though David was a great prophet, and a man after Thine own heart, faithful in all his ways, yet when Thy Spirit departed from him, where were his
chastity, his love, humility, and the fear of his God? Did he not become an
open adulterer, murderer, and boaster of his own glory, until Thy Spirit
once more enlightened him by the word of the prophet, and he acknowledged
how mortally he had sinned, how foolishly he had acted before Thee?

In like manner also Peter. He acknowledged Christ Thy beloved Son,
not by flesh and blood, but by the spirit of Thy grace, was called a Rock by
Christ, and was ready to go with Christ into prison and to death. The trial
came, and the Spirit forsook him for a season, and he could not bear one
word of the servant girl. He denied Christ, and swore that he knew Him
not. But as soon as Christ looked upon him and Thy Spirit returned, he
acknowledged his fall, wept bitterly, and publicly preached the name of Jesus
among all nations, paying no regard to his having been strictly forbidden
to do so by imprisonment, stripes, and threats. He frankly answered, We
ought to obey God rather than men.

I beseech Thee, therefore, dear Lord, that Thou wilt keep my soul
which is bought with so dear a price, lest I turn from Thy truth. For though
I might think with Peter that I could give my life for Thee, and with Paul
that neither tribulation, nor distress, nor persecution, nor famine, nor nakedness, nor peril, nor sword, nor life, nor death nor any other creature shall
be able to separate me from Thy love, yet I do not sufficiently know myself.
All my trust is in Thee. I have not yet resisted unto blood. Although I
have drunk a little of the cup of Thy affliction, yet I have not tasted the
dregs, for when prisons and bonds are experienced, when life and death,
fire and sword are placed before us, then will the gold be separated from
the wood, silver from the straw, and pearls from the stubble. Do not forsake
me, gracious Lord, for trees of deepest root are torn up by the roots by the
violence of the storm, and lofty, firm mountains are rent asunder by the force
of the earthquake. Did not Job and Jeremiah, dear men of Thy love, stumble
in temptation, murmur against Thy will? Suffer me not, therefore, gracious
Lord, to be tempted above that I am able to bear, for Thou art faithful and
good, lest my soul be shamed. I pray not for my flesh, being well aware
that it must suffer and die in time, but this alone I ask: Strengthen me in
warfare; assist and keep me; make a way for me to escape in temptation;
deliver me, and let me not be put to shame, for I put my trust in Thee.

*21. Let integrity and uprightness preserve me; for I wait on thee.* O
Sovereign Lord, O God, when the husbandman had sown good seed in his
field, his enemy came while he slept and sowed tares among the wheat. When
the sons of God came to present themselves before the Lord, Satan came also
among them. Wherever Christ is, there will the devil shortly be also, as alas
I have observed recently. Thy saving Word, Thy gracious Gospel, which is

the proper food of my soul, and out of which it lives eternally, which has been trampled upon for so many years by Antichrist as an idle tale, and a useless lie, is once more received, believed, and acknowledged in power by some through Thy gracious favor. And the hellish lion roars now in angry rage and goes about seeking to devour them without rest or repose, knowing well that his kingdom and dominion must decline and be destroyed thereby. Satan makes use of all his cunning and subtlety and transforms himself into an angel of light. Those whom he has lost through Thy Word he has allured again by false doctrine into his snare and net, and has changed the pure, salutary sense of the Scriptures by means of false prophets and unskillful teachers, into a carnal and deceptive sense. He has authorized the sword and weapons and excited a vindictive spirit against the whole world. Moreover he has dressed up open adultery under cover of the custom of Jewish fathers; also a literal king and kingdom, together with many other abuses at which a sincere Christian is astonished and confounded. But all which Thou hast not planted shall come to nought.

O Lord, preserve me pure and simple in Thy truth that I may neither believe nor teach anything that is not in conformity with Thy holy will and Word, a true faith, sincere love, the right baptism and supper, a blameless life, and Scriptural excommunication, of those who cause offense in doctrine and life. Preserve me, gracious Lord, from all error and heresy; preserve me as Thou hast hitherto in Thy mercy preserved me. Grant that I and my beloved brethren may love and fear Thee with all our hearts, and render obedience to the magistracy in all things not contary to the Word of God. For this, says Paul, is good and acceptable in Thy sight. Preserve me from the wiles of the devil who would fain teach us of another king after the spirit, besides the true King of Zion, Jesus Christ, who rules over Thy holy mountain with the holy sceptre of Thy Word, who is King of kings and Lord of lords, is seated at Thy own right hand in the heavenly places, far above all principality and power, and might and dominion and every name that is named, not only in this world, but also in that which is to come; under whose feet all things are put, who hath all power in heaven and on earth, before whom every knee must bow and every tongue confess that He is Lord to the glory of Thy great name. O dear Lord, keep me in simplicity, under Thy cross, that I may not deny Thee and Thy holy Word in the time of temptation, nor conceal Thy divine truth and will under the mask of hypocrisy, lies, equivocal expressions, so that at the appearance of Thy dear Son, my Lord Jesus Christ, I may receive with all saints the promised kingdom, inheritance, and reward which with firm assurance and perfect confidence we daily hope and expect by the gracious promise.

*22. Redeem Israel, O God, out of all his troubles.* O Lord of hosts, now that I have confessed my sins before Thee, prayed for my transgressions, praised Thy mercy, and desired Thy grace, I must with David beseech Thee in behalf of my brethren. For I observe Israel scattered and straying as sheep without a shepherd. I see the pleasant vineyard of the Lord laid waste and trodden down by all men. The chosen seed of Abraham, the house of Jacob, has again become a proper slave or bond servant in the grievous service of Pharaoh in Egypt. I see that the royal line of Judah is carried away into Babylon, together with the holy vessels which are so lamentably abused by Belshazzar and his consorts. I see that Jerusalem, the dear institution[3] of peace which was likened to a dove, is changed into an inhuman guzzler of innocent blood and a rending Lioness. She that was princess among the nations, the city of the great king, is become destitute of kings, citizens, and walls, a dreary waste. The temple of the Lord, the house of prayer in which the true worship ought to be performed, is become a manifest den of robbers, a lair of lions, bears, wolves, basilisks, dragons, and serpents, a house of idols; nay, the unchaste bed of the adulteress Jezebel. The bride of Christ, the glorious church, who was adorned with many presents in honor of the king, is changed completely into a disgraceful harlot. The ark of the Lord, the glory of Israel, is seized by the Philistines and taken into the temple of Dagon. Why make a lengthy lamentation? Judah is changed into Babylon, Canaan into Egypt, and Palestine into Sodom. The King of glory, Christ Jesus, blessed forever, is daily rated a simpleton and despised as a fool. His holy apostles, the dear witnesses of Thy truth, must, as though they lied, give way with their doctrine to all men. His woven robe which the Scriptures do not want torn or rent is torn into four or five pieces. Antichrist rules supreme in all countries through the preaching of lies. And with violence is Thy Word stifled.

If I travel east, west, north, or south, I find in all places nothing but vain obstinacy, perversity, blindness, avarice, pride and pomp, wantonness, strife, envy, and ungodliness. I find violence, false doctrine, and an impure, seductive use of Thy sacraments. I find tyranny mighty and triumphant in the courts of princes. The learned speak as does the beast. They are ambitious, avaricious, gluttonous, earthly and carnally minded, and teach according to the lusts and desires of men. There is scarcely any that seek for truth, and if there is, he must bear Thy cross.

Therefore, tears are on my cheeks day and night; my soul findeth no comfort; neither bread nor drink is sweet to my taste. Like the prophet Micah, I may well go naked, moan as do the dragons and mourn as the ostrich, for the plague of Israel is incurable. In sorrow I may well lament with Esdras, and say, Our sanctuary is laid waste, our altar broken down, our temple destroyed. Our psaltery is laid on the ground, our song is put to silence, our rejoicing is at an end. The light of our candlestick is put out, the ark of our covenant is spoiled, our holy things are defiled. And the name that is called upon us is almost profaned. Our children are put to shame, our priests are burnt, our Levites are gone into captivity; our virgins are defiled, our wives ravished; our righteous men carried away, our little ones destroyed,

[3] Reading *gestichte* (institution) for *gesichte* (visage). *Tr.*

our young men are brought into bondage, and our strong men are become weak. And what is the greatest of all, the seal of Sion hath now lost her honor, for she is delivered into the hands of them that hate us.[4] Redeem Israel, O God, out of his troubles. Look upon our great misery and distress with the eyes of Thy mercy, release us from the iron furnace of Egypt, bring us out of the land of the Chaldees, let the holy city be builded again upon her former place with walls and gates, repair and rebuild Thy fallen temple, the stones of which are trampled upon in every street. Gather together Thy wandering sheep, receive Thy returning spouse who has behaved so perversely with strange lovers.

O God of Israel, create in us a pure heart that longeth for Thy blessed Word and will. Send forth faithful laborers into Thy harvest, who cut and gather the grain in due season, wise builders who lay for us a good foundation, that in the last days Thy house may be glorious and appear above all the hills, that many people may go thither and say, Come, ye, and let us go up to the mountain of the Lord, to the house of the God of Jacob; and He will teach us of His ways, and we will walk in His paths, that we may walk before Thee in peace and liberty of conscience all the days of our lives, under pious magistrates and blameless teachers, with a Christian baptism, true Supper, godly life, and a proper excommunication, that Thou mayest be eternally honored and praised in us as in Thy beloved children through Thy dear Son, Jesus Christ our Lord, to whom with Thee, O Father, and Thy Holy Spirit, be praise and everlasting dominion. Amen.

## LATIN EPILOGUE*

That which I have written, dear brethren, behold, before God, I lie not.

Since I know I am innocent of the many lies hurled after me, as is customary in the case of such as I am, I know not how that with Athanasius I am accused now of having laid violent hands on a woman,[1] now of cutting off the arm of Arsenius with which I practice magic arts. And whether a Timothy is present to speak for the silent one, I know not.[2]

[4] Fourth book of Esdras 10:21-23.

* This epilogue to Menno's *Meditation on the Twenty-fifth Psalm* does not appear in *Opera Omnia Theologica* of 1681. The translation herewith presented was taken from K. Vos, *Menno Simons*, Leiden, 1914, p. 281. Vos in turn reproduced it from the 1539 edition of the *Meditation*. Ed.

[1] Athanasius, the great opponent of the heretical Arians in the fourth century, had so incurred the wrath of the Arians that they invented all sorts of false charges against him. At one time he was accused of having violated a certain woman—a charge which an orthodox presbyter, one Timotheus, easily refuted.

[2] Athanasius was also accused by the Arians of having cut off the arm of one Arsenius, an African bishop of heretical leanings, and then to have used the amputated hand for magic arts. Athanasius finally cleared himself of the charge by having Arsenius step forward and drawing from beneath Arsenius' cloak first one hand and then the other, adding dryly, "Does anyone here believe that God hath given any man more than two hands?"

Thanks be to this king who has written this Psalm which portrays so exactly the image and the picture of my mind. You have therefore my doctrine and thought; from it you may see what I teach and how my way of life is. Let him who is a Christian judge whether it is evangelical, divine, salvation-bringing.

If it is so, why should I not maintain and defend it to the death? If Socrates for the teachings of his religion,[3] if Marcus Curtius, if Marcus Mutius Scevola for the sake of the city of Rome and the good of the state,[4] if the Jew and the Turk for the laws of their fatherland did not feel free to flee from poison and the abyss and did not fear fire and death, why should I not the rather offer my soul for the heavenly wisdom, for the brethren, yes, for the institutions of Jesus Christ?

And if it is not so, then let some Origen come forward and render harmless most quickly and easily this Beryllus, not altogether sane.[5]

Farewell, and may the Lord lead your hearts in the love of God and in the expectation of Jesus Christ. Once more, farewell.

[3] Socrates, the Greek philosopher, was put out of the way with poison. He was accused of doing violence to the ancestral religion.

[4] Marcus Curtius was the name of a legendary hero of ancient Rome. It is said that in the year 362 B.C. a deep crack in the earth opened up in the Forum of Rome. Soothsayers declared that it would not close up again until Rome's most valuable possession had been thrown into it. Marcus Curtius, so goes the legend, convinced that Rome's soldiers were her greatest treasure, rode fully armed into the rift. It closed up and the spot became a marsh, afterwards known as *Lacus Curtius* (Curtius Lake).

Gaius (Menno erroneously called him Marcus) Mutius Scevola, a legendary hero of Rome, was captured as he made an attempt on the life of King Lars Porsena, when the latter besieged Rome. His captors threatened him with torture to make him assist in taking the city. He thereupon thrust his right hand into a burning hearth and held it there until it was consumed. This bravery made such an impression on the heathen king that he withdrew his forces and made peace with Rome. Gaius Marcus was afterwards called *Scaevola,* (the left-handed one).

[5] Beryllus was a bishop in Arabia in the third century. He conceived heretical opinions as to the person of Christ. A large body of assembled bishops, gathered together to convince him of error, were unable to do so; thereupon Origen, although already out of good standing with the church, stepped forward, convinced him of error, and led him back into the church. *Tr.*

# The New Birth

*Van de nieuwe creatuere*

## c. 1537
### Revised 1552
### Edition of 1556

*For other foundation can no man
lay than that is laid, which is Jesus Christ.*

I Corinthians 3:11

# Introduction

Menno Simons wrote *The New Birth* about the year 1537, and "diligently revised and enlarged and corrected" it Anno 1552. The first edition was published in the Eastern dialect of the Baltic coastal region while the latter, which is here translated from the *Opera Omnia Theologica* of Menno, 1681, fol. 121-32, was in Holland Dutch, and appeared in the *Complete Works* of 1871, I, 165-78. The booklet is pervaded with a strong ethical flavor and an evangelistic zeal; perhaps one could say it has the ring of the Old Testament prophets in its stern denunciation of sin, and its demand for heart religion in place of mere outward ceremonies. Menno fairly bristles as he denounces masses, matins, vespers, confessionals, pilgrimages, holy water, and other human inventions. He warns that unless men are born again their portion eternally will be the lake of fire and brimstone. What people need is to die and rise with Christ, to be spiritually circumcised, to receive the baptism of the Holy Spirit, to put on Christ. In strong language, in the midst of which he twice cries, "Help, Lord," Menno depicts the life and behavior of those who are still living an unregenerate life. He also portrays beautifully the heart and behavior of those who really are in Christ: they follow absolutely the life of love, do not retaliate, but feed the hungry, give drink to the thirsty, are children of peace who learn war no longer. So as to be perfectly understood Menno patiently explains the sword, marriage, citizenship, kingdom, and doctrine of those who belong to Christ. He puts emphasis on proper baptism, Lord's Supper, and excommunication. Menno's message is, "Repent without delay! For nothing avails before God except the new creature, a faith which worketh by love, and the keeping of God's commandments."

The full title of the work is: *The New Creature: A Fair and Fundamental Instruction from the Word of the Lord, Urgently Admonishing All Men Who Call Themselves Christians to Seek the Heavenly Birth and the New Creature, Without Which No Man Who Has Come to Years of Understanding Is or Can Be a True Christian.* Diligently Revised and Enlarged and Corrected by Menno Simons. Following the name of Menno Simons on the title page of *The New Birth* in the *Opera* of 1681 is the date, 1556, which was evidently the edition incorporated therein. But it is believed that this was a reprint of an edition of 1552.

*The New Birth* has greater vigor than any of his other writings prior to the *Foundation* of 1539.                                        J. C. W.

# The New Birth

## c. 1537

●-●-●-●-●-●-●-●-●-●-●-●-●-●-●-●-●-●-●-●-●-●-●-●-●-●-●-●-●-●-●-●-●-●-●-●-●-●-●-●-●

Attend to my words, all people, and understand, all ye who think your-selves to be Christians, and with boldness boast of the grace of the Lord, His merits, flesh, blood, cross, kingdom, and death, even though there is found among you neither Christian faith, brotherly love, repentance, the true use of the sacraments of Christ, the pure doctrine, nor the irreproachable, godly life which is of God, to which the Scriptures admonish. Nor do we find the true religion, evangelical disposition or obedience, but everywhere nothing but ugly, erring unbelief and undisciplined carnal life; false doctrine, falsely adorned sacraments, a satanic heart and mind, an accursed, heathenish idolatry under Christ's name; blind, bloodthirsty tyranny, unmerciful cruelty against all the children of God, yes, manifest, perverse disobedience and de-spising of all the words of Christ and His Holy Ghost, as may be very plainly perceived and seen throughout the whole world.

In order that you may comfort yourselves no longer with such false and vain hopes contrary to all Scriptures and to your eternal damnation, and may not vainly boast in the afore-mentioned riches and glory of the children of God in the kingdom of Christ, His grace, merits, flesh, blood, cross, death, and promises, which do not as yet belong to you since you are altogether earthly, carnal, and devilishly minded, reject Christ and do not keep His Spirit, Word, and example, without which no one can be a Christian; therefore I have undertaken through the merciful grace of the Lord as much as is in my power to point out very briefly from the trustworthy, powerful, saving Word of the holy Gospel of Christ and from the pure doctrine of His holy apostles in this my epistle, who are and who are not in possession of the grace of God, the afore-mentioned gifts, merits, and promises of Christ.

Tell me, dearly beloved, where and when did you read in the Scriptures, the true witness of the Holy Ghost and criterion of our consciences, that the unbelieving, disobedient, carnal man, the adulterous, immoral, drunken, avaricious, idolatrous, and pompous man has one single promise of the kingdom of Christ and His church, yes, part or communion in His merits, death, and blood? I tell you the truth, nowhere and never do we read it in the Scriptures. But thus it is written by Paul: For if ye live after the flesh ye shall die. Adulterers, whoremongers, perverts, effeminate, unclean, idolaters, drunkards, proud, avaricious, hateful persons, betrayers, and those who shed innocent blood; thieves, murderers, and those who know no mercy, those disobedient to God and Christ, will not inherit the kingdom of God unless they repent. Yes, their portion will be in the fiery lake which burns with fire and brimstone, which is the second death.

Behold, worthy reader, hear God's irrevocable sentence and judgment as pronounced upon all who live after the flesh, no matter who it is, whether emperor or king, duke or earl, baron, knight or squire, noble or commoner, priest or monk, learned or unlearned, rich or poor, man or woman, bond or free. All who live after the flesh must forever remain under the just sentence and eternal wrath of God; otherwise the whole Scriptures are untrue.

Therefore the poor, ignorant people are comforted in vain with masses, matins, vespers, confessionals, pilgrimages, and holy water, and what is more, with Christ's grace, death, and blood. The Word stands unshaken: For if ye live after the flesh, ye shall die; for to be carnally minded is death. Therefore I advise and entreat you all together to heed Christ Jesus, who is sent to us as a witness of the truth from heaven. For thus says He, Verily I say unto you, Except ye be converted and become as little children, ye shall not enter into the kingdom of heaven. At another place: Verily, verily, I say unto you, Except a man be born again, he cannot see the kingdom of God. Again, Verily, verily, I say unto you, Except a man be born of water and of the Spirit, he cannot enter into the kingdom of God.

Faithful reader, take heed; these words are not invented or instituted by man, nor are they resolved and decreed by any council. But they are the dependable, precious Word which the Son of God, Christ Jesus, brought to us from the mouth of the Father, and declared unto pious Nicodemus, the scribe, with a dual oath. The Word is powerful and clear and has reference not merely to Nicodemus, but to all the children of Adam who have come to the years of understanding. But alas, it is so obscured by the ugly, leavenous dung of human commands, statutes, and glosses, that scarcely one or two is found in a thousand who have caught the true sense and meaning of the heavenly birth, to say nothing of the active nature, power, properties, and fruits of it. Yes, they have pushed it so far with their philosophic cleverness and man-made holiness that the eternal Wisdom of God, Christ Jesus eternally blessed, is banished as a poor, senseless fool out of the house of His honor, which is His church, with His Holy Ghost, Word, baptism, Supper, divine worship, excommunication, and irreproachable example. And the man of sin, the son of perdition, is placed in His stead with his vicious doctrines, idolatrous infant baptism and supper, with his impure purifications and promises, with his churches, convents, priests, monks, masses, matins, vespers, holy water, icons, pilgrimages, purgatory, vigils, confessions, absolutions, etc. All of these are nothing but the doctrines and commands of men, proposed contrary to the Scriptures, an accursed idolatry and abomination, an open corruption of the Lord's death and sacrifice, a despising of the New Testament or the covenant which was sealed by the innocent blood of the Lamb; a rending of the saving ordinances of Christ, of doctrine, baptism, Supper, life, and separation, abundantly testified to in the Scriptures; ordinances which He taught in this world with incontrovertible clearness and power by the commandment of His Father, and left behind for His children in His Word. None other can be in eternity established so as to stand before Him.

In a word, writers and learned ones have little by little so corrupted everything through their counsel, decretals, and statutes, with all the tyranny and violence of the great, that there is (help, Lord) scarcely an article entire of all that Christ and His holy apostles taught. All the afore-mentioned abominations together with the ungodly, carnal life of the world I call to witness. Nevertheless, they want to be called the holy Christian church, and he that admonishes them in sincere pure love with the spirit and Word of the Lord, must be their accursed Anabaptist and heretic. I tell you again, they want to be the Christian church, though it is evident that in all their actions they are not Christians, but carnal, proud, avaricious, gluttonous, lewd, drunken, idolatrous, blind heathen. And what is worse, some of them are unmerciful, murderous, cruel and bloody devils, for many of their works are done according to the will of the devil. We may with propriety complain of this matter, for the righteous judgment is come upon them so that they are utterly past conversion and little that is salutary remains with them.

Oh, how lamentably is the fair vineyard desolated and how sadly are its branches withered, its walls broken down! The destroying foxes have taken over, the clouds are dry and give rain no longer; there is none to prune or dung[1] it, and if there be one he must be devoured by the dragon or slain by the woman of the Apocalypse, drunken with blood. O merciful, gracious Father, how long will this great misery continue? Our rulers are like devouring lions and bears; our fathers betray us. They who pastor us deceive us. And those who pose as pastors are thieves and murderers of our souls. Well may we sigh and lament from the depth of our souls. Our house is left unto us desolate. For that which was once the church and kingdom of Christ is now, alas, the church and kingdom of Antichrist. And that for no other reason, mark you, than that they ungratefully reject the word of grace and will not have the ruling Lord Jesus Christ to rule over them with the righteous sceptre of His holy Word and Spirit.

Nevertheless, this poor, blind generation hopes to obtain the grace and promises of God through their infant baptism, masses, confessions, and similar superstitious ceremonies and idolatries, which they call the true religion, and use it as a remedy for their sins. Ah, no, dear me, no. For,

---

[1] Reading *mester* (one who applies dung to the fields) for *metser*. *Metser* may also be translated "mason"; and this yields a good sense, for vineyards were supplied with stone walls in Bible times. *Tr.*

says the wise man, the hope of the ungodly is like dust that is blown away with the wind. I have said it once, and I say it again, and that from the mouth of the Lord, who can neither lie nor deceive, Except ye be converted, and become as little children, ye shall not enter into the kingdom of heaven. And, Except a man be born again, he cannot see the kingdom of God.

My dearly beloved reader, take heed to the Word of the Lord and learn to know the true God. I warn you faithfully to take it, if you please. He will not save you nor forgive your sins nor show you His mercy and grace except according to His Word; namely, if you repent and if you believe, if you are born of Him, if you do what He has commanded and walk as He walks. For if He could save an unrighteous carnal man without regeneration, faith, and repentance, then He did not teach us the truth. But He is the truth, and there is no falsehood in Him. Therefore, I tell you again that you cannot be reconciled by means of all the masses, matins, vespers, ceremonies, sacraments, councils, statutes, and commandments under the whole heavens, which the popes and their colleges have made from the beginning. For they are abominations and not reconciliations, I warn you. In vain, says Christ, do they honor me, teaching commandments of men.

But if you wish to be saved, by all means and first of all, your earthly, carnal, ungodly life must be reformed. For it is naught but true repentance that the Scriptures teach and enjoin upon us with admonitions, threatenings, reprovings, miracles, examples, ceremonies, and sacraments. If you do not repent there is nothing in heaven or on earth that can help you, for without true repentance we are comforted in vain. The prophet says, O my people, they which lead thee cause thee to err and destroy the way of thy paths. Isa. 3:12. We must be born from above, must be changed and renewed in our hearts, and must be transplanted from the unrighteous and evil nature of Adam into the true and good nature of Christ, or we can never in all eternity be saved by any means, be they human or divine. Wherever true repentance and the new creature are not (I speak of those who are of the age of understanding) there man must be eternally lost; this is incontrovertibly clear. This everyone who does not wish to deceive his soul may very properly store away in the little box of his conscience.

This regeneration of which we write, from which comes the penitent, pious life that has the promise, can only originate in the Word of the Lord, rightly taught and rightly understood and received in the heart by faith through the Holy Ghost.

The first birth of man is out of the first and earthly Adam, and therefore its nature is earthly and Adam-like, that is, carnally minded, unbelieving, disobedient, and blind to divine things; deaf and foolish; whose end, if not renewed by the Word, will be damnation and eternal death. If now you desire to have your wicked nature cleared up, and desire to be free from eternal death and damnation so that you may obtain with all true Christians that which is promised them, then you must be born again. For the regenerate are in grace and have the promise as you have heard.

The regenerate, therefore, lead a penitent and new life, for they are renewed in Christ and have received a new heart and spirit. Once they were earthly-minded, now heavenly; once they were carnal, now spiritual; once they were unrighteous, now righteous; once they were evil, now good, and they live no longer after the old corrupted nature of the first earthly Adam, but after the new upright nature of the new and heavenly Adam, Christ Jesus, even as Paul says: Nevertheless, I live; yet not I, but Christ liveth in me. Their poor, weak life they daily renew more and more, and that after the image of Him who created them. Their minds are like the mind of Christ, they gladly walk as He walked; they crucify and tame their flesh with all its evil lusts.

In baptism they bury their sins in the Lord's death and rise with Him to a new life. They circumcise their hearts with the Word of the Lord; they are baptized with the Holy Ghost into the spotless, holy body of Christ, as obedient members of His church, according to the true ordinance and Word of the Lord. They put on Christ and manifest His spirit, nature, and power in all their conduct. They fear God with all the heart and seek in all their thoughts, words, and works, nothing but the praise of God and the salvation of their beloved brethren.

Hatred and vengeance they do not know, for they love those who hate them; they do good to those who despitefully use them and pray for those who persecute them. Avarice, pride, unchastity, and pomp they hate and oppose; all drunkenness, fornication, adultery, hatred, envy, backbiting, lying, cheating, fighting, quarreling, robbing and plunder, blood, and idolatry, in short, all impure, carnal works, and they resist the world with all its lusts. They meditate upon the law of the Lord by day and by night; they rejoice at good and are grieved at evil. Evil they do not repay with evil, but with good. They do not seek merely their own good but that which is good for their neighbors both as to body and soul. They feed the hungry, give drink to the thirsty. They entertain the needy, release prisoners, visit the sick, comfort the fainthearted, admonish the erring, are ready after their Master's example to give their lives for their brethren.

Again, their thoughts are pure and chaste, their words are true and seasoned with salt, with them it is a yea that is yea and a nay that is nay. And their works are done in the fear of the Lord. Their hearts are heavenly and new; their minds peaceful and joyous. They seek righteousness with all their might. In short, they are so assured in their faith through the Spirit and Word of God that they are victorious by virtue of their faith over all bloody, cruel tyrants, with all their tortures, imprisonments, banishments, plunder, stakes, executions, racks, and wheels. And out of a pure zeal with an innocent, pure, simple yea and nay they are willing to die. The glory of Christ, the sweetness of the Word, and the salvation of their souls are dearer to them than anything under heaven.

You see, worthy reader, all those who are thus born of God with Christ, who thus conform their weak life to the Gospel, thus convert themselves to follow the example of Christ, hear and believe His holy Word, follow His commandments which He in plain words commanded us in the holy Scriptures, these are the holy Christian Church which has the promise; the true children of God, brothers and sisters of Christ. For they are born with Him of one Father, they are the new Eve, the pure chaste bride. They are flesh of Christ's flesh and bone of His bone, the spiritual house of Israel, the spiritual city Jerusalem, the spiritual temple and Mount Zion, the spiritual ark of the Lord in which is hidden the true bread of heaven, Christ Jesus and His blessed Word, the green, blossoming rod of faith, and the spiritual tables of stone with the commandments of the Lord written on them. They are the spiritual seed of Abraham, children of the promise, in covenant with God and partakers of the heavenly blessing.

These regenerated people have a spiritual king over them who rules them by the unbroken sceptre of His mouth, namely, with His Holy Spirit and Word. He clothes them with the garment of righteousness, of pure white silk. He refreshes them with the living water of His Holy Spirit and feeds them with the Bread of Life. His name is Christ Jesus.

They are the children of peace who have beaten their swords into plowshares and their spears into pruning hooks, and know war no more. They give to Caesar the things that are Caesar's and to God the things that are God's.

Their sword is the sword of the Spirit, which they wield in a good conscience through the Holy Ghost.

Their marriage is that of one man and one woman, according to God's own ordinance.

Their kingdom is the kingdom of grace, here in hope and after this in eternal life.

Their citizenship is in heaven, and they use the lower creations such as eating, drinking, clothing, and shelter, with thanksgiving and to the necessary support of their own lives, and to the free service of their neighbor, according to the Word of the Lord.

Their doctrine is the unadulterated Word of God, testified through Moses and the prophets, through Christ and the apostles, upon which they build their faith, which saves our souls. Everything that is contrary thereto, they consider accursed.

Their baptism they administer to the believing according to the commandment of the Lord, in the doctrines and usages of the apostles.

Their Lord's Supper they celebrate as a memorial of the favors and death of their Lord, and an incitement to brotherly love.

Their ban or excommunication descends on all the proud scorners—great and small, rich and poor, without any respect of persons, who once passed under the Word but have now fallen back, those living or teaching offensively in the house of the Lord—until they repent.

They daily sigh and lament over their poor, unsatisfactory evil flesh, over the manifest errors and faults of their weak lives. Their inward and outward war is without ceasing. Their sighing and calling is to the most High. Their fight and struggle is against the devil, world, and flesh all their days, pressing on toward the prize of the high calling that they may obtain it. So they prove by their actions that they believe the Word of the Lord, that they know and possess Christ in power, that they are born of God and have Him as their Father.

Honorable reader, as I said before so I say again, these are the Christians who have the promise and are assured by the Spirit of God that Christ Jesus with all His merits, righteousness, intercession, word, cross, suffering, flesh, blood, death, resurrection, kingdom, and all His benefits are theirs without recourse to merit, graciously given. But what kind of doctrine, faith, life, regeneration, baptism, supper, ban, and religion the churches of the sects have (their name matters not), and what kind of reward is promised them in the Scriptures, I will let the sensible reader ponder with the Spirit and Word of the Lord.

Here I would call on all the high and mighty lords, princes, and rulers, on all the popes, cardinals, bishops, and wise and learned ones, who from the beginning have perverted and darkened the Scriptures, to show us one single word in the whole Bible, I say in the Bible (for we do not regard human fables and lies), saying that an unbelieving, refractory, carnal man without regeneration and true repentance was or can be saved, simply because he boasts of faith and the death of Christ, or hears the masses and service of the priests, as the whole world does. If they can do this, they will have gained the point. But this never has occurred and never will take place to the end of time. If such worthless men could be saved without repentance and regeneration by hearing masses and going to confessionals as their poor children without the warrant of the Scripture expect, then we might of a truth say that the afore-mentioned means were stronger (though they are idolatrous) than the Word of the Lord. For the Word knows no masses but says that the unrepentant must perish in his sins. Otherwise Moses and the prophets, Christ and His apostles, have been false witnesses, and have miserably deceived us poor sheep because they directed us to such a narrow path.

Ah, no! friend, no! beware, I tell you, God will not lie nor deceive you. For He says through the prophet: I am the Lord, I change not. All that He has testified in His holy Word through His prophets, through Christ and His apostles, is His eternal, immutable will. This we may all ponder if we do not wish to deceive our souls. In short, it is all in vain, all this massing, this counseling, this mediating business. The birth from above and true repentance must take place. We must believe Christ and His Word and abide constantly in His Spirit, ordinance, and example, or eternal misery will be our position. This is incontrovertible.

Therefore, I admonish and entreat you, as one who loves your soul, to repent. Repent, I say, and without delay. The ax is laid unto the root of the trees; therefore, every tree which bringeth not forth good fruit is hewn down, and cast into the fire. Matt. 3:10. Be vigilant for your poor souls that have been bought with a precious price, and be no longer comforted with open lies nor fed with husks which swine eat. For, behold, I tell you in Christ, there is nothing under heaven that can or will endure before God but the new creature, faith which works by love, and the keeping of the commandments—let the learned ones clamor and write as long as they please.

My faithful reader, do not believe me, but the Word to which by the grace of God I have with my small talents pointed you. For I tell you, as the Lord liveth, all who teach otherwise than we have shown from the Word of the Lord, whosoever they be, are prophets who deceive you, who place pillows under your arms and cushions under your heads, who daub the wall with deceptive plaster and speak peace to the wicked, but not out of the mouth of the Lord. For as certain as it is that the regenerate and penitent are the true Christians, who have God's truth, the true light, the pardon of their sins, and the sure promise of eternal life; so certain also it is that the sensuous and impenitent are false Christians, have the lies of the serpent, darkness, sin still their own, and the certain promise of eternal death. That this is the truth will be found to be the case in eternity before the great and Almighty God. Of this His sure Word is to me a true witness. Of this I am by His grace wholly certain.

Now perhaps some may answer: Our belief is that Christ is the Son of God, that His Word is truth, and that He purchased us with His blood and truth. We were regenerated in baptism and we received the Holy Ghost; therefore we are the true church and congregation of Christ.

We reply: If your faith is as you say, why do you not do the things which He has commanded you in His Word? His commandment is, Repent and keep the commandments. And it is evident that you grow worse daily; that unrighteousness is your father, wickedness your mother, and that the express commandments of the Lord are folly and foolishness to you. Since you do not do as He commands and desires, but as you please, it is sufficiently proved that you do not believe that Jesus Christ is the Son of God, although you say so. Nor do you believe that His Word is truth, for faith and its fruits are inseparable. This you will all have to confess by the grace of God.

O poor, blind men, be silent and shamed. Let Christ Jesus with His Spirit and Word be your teacher and example, your way and your mirror. Do you think it is enough merely to acknowledge Christ according to the flesh, or to say that you believe on Him, that you are baptized, that you are Christian, that you are purchased with the blood and death of Christ? Ah, no! I have told you often and tell you once more, You must be so born of God. In your life you must be so converted and changed that you become new men in Christ, so that Christ is in you and you are in Christ. Otherwise you can never be Christians, for, If any man be in Christ he is a new creature. II Cor. 5:17.

If you believe rightly in Christ, as you boast, then manifest it by your lives that you believe, for the just shall live out of his faith,[2] as the Scriptures say. This is the truth, as has been fully attested and shown by Abel, Enoch, Noah, Abraham, Isaac, Jacob, Joseph, Moses, Joshua, Caleb, Samuel, David, Matthias, Zacchaeus, Mary Magdalene, Paul, and all the pious children of God who were from the beginning to this day. But how you in your faith behave and how you are minded may be most plainly seen by your excessive lies, fraud, avarice, hoarding, cursing, swearing, pride, and pomp. For your hearts burn in unrighteousness; you fear neither God nor His Word. Nevertheless you boast that you believe in Christ, have Christ's Word, and that you are Christians. I repeat it, Repent, or hold your peace and be ashamed.

You imagine, moreover, that you were born again in your baptism, and that you received the Holy Ghost. Faithful reader, reflect that if it had so happened to you as you say, you would have to acknowledge that your regeneration took place without the hearing of the Word, without the faith and knowledge of Christ, and without all ordinary knowledge and understanding. You would have to acknowledge besides that the afore-mentioned birth and the received Spirit are altogether without effect, wisdom, power, and fruit in you; yes, vain and dead. That you live neither after the Spirit nor in the power of the new birth, I shall let your gross avarice, drunkenness, pride, and idolatrous, carnal lives demonstrate. All you baptized ones may be my witnesses. Yes, my friend, if you were thus born of God in your baptism and had received the Holy Ghost as your comforters assure you, then certainly the new spiritual life and its new spiritual fruits would also be manifest as was the case with the saints from the beginning and still is. For it is clear that the regenerate do not willfully live in sin, but through faith and true repentance were buried by baptism into the death of Christ, and arose with Him to a new life. Also, those who have the Spirit of the Lord bring forth the fruits of the Spirit. That you do not bury your sins, but serve them to the full; and that you do not bring forth the fruits of the Spirit is daily demonstrated (Lord, help) by your vain, idolatrous, carnal lives. My friend, out of true love I warn and admonish and entreat you, awake and observe what the Word of the Lord teaches. For the Spirit of the Lord refuses to dwell in a wicked soul, or in a body enslaved to sin.

In the second place, I say, if you were properly baptized, according to the Word of the Lord as you imagine, then you would have put on Christ, and would live no longer after the native, evil nature of Adam, but after the regenerate, good nature of Christ. But since this is not evident in your case and you are still wholly carnal and earthly, as is evident from all your fruits, therefore it is clear that you are not regenerate, baptized Christians,

[2] Dutch version.

but impenitent, carnal heathen. For your works are mostly done after a heathen will as one may see and hear. Once more I say, Awake and hear what the Word of the Lord says: If you have put on Christ, that is, if Christ be in you, the body is dead because of sin, but the Spirit is life because of righteousness. Rom. 8:10.

In the third place, I say, If you are properly baptized according to the Word of the Lord, then you have become members and companions of the body of Christ, and have the testimony of a good conscience before God. A body is never divided against itself, neither hates nor hurts its members, but each member serves and assists the other. But it is evident that you unmercifully persecute, murder, and exterminate the elect members of Christ who are of your own flesh and blood. Those moreover, whom He has purchased by His death, regenerated by His Word, endowed with the Spirit, chosen as His peculiar people, and who are depending for a new, reborn, and good conscience, not upon human invention, but leaning in true faith solely upon the Lord's grace, righteousness, prayer, merits, death, and blood. You rely on, and comfort yourselves with, the masses of priests and monks, their confessionals, absolution, water, bread, wine, oil, and vigils. Therefore conduct proves that you are not active members of the before-mentioned body, but are much more destroyers and defilers of it; that you have not a firm, joyful, peaceful, and good conscience, but a fearful, condemned, restless, and evil conscience before God. For we see that all those above-named superstitions and the false worship which all regenerate, pious, and good consciences consider mere abominations, are your chief support and comfort, because you neither have nor know Christ. My friend, beware. You are being deceived miserably by your comforters.

The spirit of prophecy says, And unto the angel of the church in Smyrna write; These things, saith the first and the last, which was dead and is alive; I know the blasphemy of them which say they are Jews, and are not; but are the synagogue of Satan. Rev. 2:8, 9. Well may it be said in our day to all the great and comfortable sects, I know the great blasphemy and see the wicked lives of those who say they are regenerate, baptized Christians, and are not, but are Satan's synagogue. For I do not see how they could do worse.

If we come to the rulers and potentates, there we find nothing but haughtiness and pride, nothing but pomp and vaunting, dancing and leaping, harloting, riding and hunting, lancing and fighting, warring, devastating cities and lands, and living to their heart's desire.

Turning to the regents and judges, we find insatiable avarice, treachery, and clever devices to defraud the helpless and god-fearing (I am not referring to the good). They seek gifts and accept bribes; the right of the righteous they pervert; and they willingly accept the gifts to shed innocent blood. They persecute the truth; reject what is right and good. The fear of God is not before their eyes.

If we turn to the divines, whether preachers, priests, or monks, there we find such an idle, lazy, wanton, and carnal life, such a corrupted, anti-Christian doctrine and interpretation of the Scriptures, such hatred, envy, defaming, betraying, lying, and turmoil against all the pious, that I would be ashamed to mention it before the virtuous and honest.

The common people run as a frantic heifer, as the prophet laments. They lie and cheat, curse and swear by the wounds and sacraments of the Lord, by His judgment, hand, power, suffering, death, and blood. I am ashamed that I have to record these blasphemous abominations. They gamble, drink, and fight. In short, the wicked excess of their lives is not to be turned and their great folly cannot be obstructed. Still this must pass that the afore-mentioned lords, judges, learned and common people are the truly regenerate church and baptized congregation of Christ. May the merciful Lord graciously preserve all His chosen children from such a generation, baptism, and church in all eternity.

I testify the truth in Christ Jesus, take heed if you will; Jesus Christ did not from the beginning tolerate such openly impenitent, carnal sinners in His holy city, kingdom, and church. Nor will He ever endure them, this you may believe.

O Almighty God and Lord, how sadly Thy holy, fatherly will, and Thy adorably great name are derided, and how little is Thy saving, precious Word esteemed! What an ugly, idolatrous, cruel, and bloodthirsty devil is made of Thy beloved Son! All their abominations, sins, and abuses they cover with His blessed holy name, Word, death, and blood.

Shame yourselves, O callous, perverted men. Shame yourselves, I say, before God and His angels, that you live so carelessly as wild rebels without restraint, and nevertheless dare to say that you are the true, regenerate congregation and baptized church of Christ. I have told you often and tell you again that all who are born of God, rightly baptized in the Spirit, fire, and water as the Scriptures teach, are heavenly-minded and godly. Their sins they bury. They lead a penitent, pious, virtuous life according to the Word of the Lord. They show the nature and power of Christ which dwells in them by word and work. They bring forth the fruits of the Spirit and suppress the works of the flesh. They are proper members of the body of Christ and labor according to the gift received. In short, they are fruit-bearing twigs of the true vine, and their fruits abide unto eternal life.

But since it is manifest in you that you show the reverse in all your fruits, and they see in your whole life that all is worldly and carnal, therefore it is clear, is it not, that your boast of the new birth, Spirit, baptism, congregation and church is not the truth, but basically vain, untruthful, and false.

The holy Scripures and our common faith teach us that the holy, Christian church is an assembly of the righteous and a communion of saints. He that can see with but half an eye in the Scriptures must confess that your church and assembly are a church and assembly of the unrighteous, the immoral, the impenitent, the sensual, and perverts, yes, of the bloodthirsty wolves, lions, bears, basilisks, serpents, and fiery flying dragons.

Ah, friends, lift your heads and open your eyes! Oh, ye people, look through the whole world what life they lead, they who have received the same baptism with you, who partake of the same sacraments and worship, who indulge in the same boasting of the death and blood of the Lord and say that they are Christ's church and people. For it is clearer than midday that many of you are so foolish, so driven by the spirit of the devil that you hate, envy, bite, and devour one another, so that you ruin provinces, cities, castles, and citadels with your accursed wars and turmoil. You shed human blood like water. The poor citizen and peasant, men of the same faith, you deprive of life and possessions. You burn, rob, plunder, capture, tax, and torture even those who have never harmed you, or given you an evil word. In truth, I know not how the Behemoth of hell could rant in a more devilish and cruel fashion than you or your members who pose as the church of Christ. God preserve us! You violate matrons and maidens; you persecute the pious and God-fearing. You tolerate public brothels, drunken saloons, fencing schools, gambling dens, and the like disgraces. Of idol houses and images there is no end with all false service. I make no mention of your intolerable, blasphemous cursing and swearing, your lying, cheating, drunkenness, harlotry, pomp, splendor, etc. Why talk at length?

I quit, for it seems to me that nobody can be found under the whole heaven who can relate in detail the gross abominations, wicked acts, abuses, and scandals of those who share your faith and baptism. An honest man must be astounded at these great sins. Dear Lord, help us, yes, whosoever does not yet understand that you are not born from above, that you were not baptized properly but contrary to all Scripture, and that all your boasting of the pardon of sins and the mercy of Christ, His grace, merit, flesh, blood, cross, death, church, kingdom, and eternal promise is vain, and without the Scriptures: he must be, I say, a dull and foolish man.

Ah, reader, how little you ponder the Word of the Lord, so highly recommended to you; how little you regard your poor soul, bought with such a precious price, which must either live with God in heaven or perish forever with the devil in hell. Do you think, my friend, that the Lord is a dreamer of dreams, or His Word a fable? Ah, no, not a letter will fall to the ground of all that He spoke. It is high time for you to reflect that God's promise of grace is not given to the unregenerate and impenitent, but to the regenerate and penitent.

Let every one take warning and trust no longer in lies; for instance, that he is a baptized and regenerated Christian, nor trust to long ancient usages, nor in papistic decretals, nor imperial mandates, nor upon the wisdom and glosses of the learned ones, nor upon the invention, council, institution, and wisdom of any man. My counsel, says God through the power of the prophet, shall stand, and I will do all my pleasure. The Word of God is eternal. Neither princes, nor power, nor men's commands with all their imperial edicts, counsels, and decrees determine faith so as to save a man. It is impossible. We must hear and follow that which Christ Jesus, God's first and only begotten Son Himself, brought from heaven and taught from the mouth of His Father, and confirmed by signs and wonders, and finally sealed with His crimson blood. The decretal stands; stands, I say, and can never be demolished or altered by any gates of hell.

By this counsel we are all taught that we must hear Christ, believe in Christ, follow His footsteps, repent, be born from above; become as little children, not in understanding, but in malice; be of the same mind as Christ, walk as He did, deny ourselves, take up His cross and follow Him; and that if we love father, mother, children, or life more than Him, we are not worthy of Him, nor are we His disciples. We are taught in it that adulterers, whoremongers, murderers, drunkards, idolaters, and the like sinners shall not inherit the kingdom of God; that we must not love the world and the things therein, nor conform to the world; that we through faith must die to our evil flesh and conquer the devil, lead an upright, irreproachable, pious life through faith, and in all things act according to the will of the Lord. Also, we are to baptize upon faith and not without it, and celebrate the Lord's Supper in a sincerely penitent congregation, I mean so far as man can judge. We must practice exclusion or the ban, according to the Scriptures. We are to fear, serve, and love the Lord with all the heart and walk in His commandments, and we are to assist our neighbor, comfort and serve him as much as in us is, and the like doctrine and instruction.

You see, worthy reader, here you have in part the immutable, eternal decretal of God, which was sealed in the wise council chamber of His Majesty; and proof that He recognizes no other. Blessed are they who receive this with a firm faith and conform thereto according to their abilities in all weakness, that is, live according to the divine decretal, ordinance, command, and prohibition, according to Christ's Word, and according to the unblamable example of Christ. On the contrary, cursed are they who despise, reject, curse, hate, defame, mock, persecute, and cast it into fire and water, and comfort themselves with human power, institutions, and fables. For they deny the Lord who bought them and reject the Gospel of peace; nor do they believe that Jesus Christ is their Messiah, Saviour, High Priest, and Prophet. Ah, how good it were if these poor people had never been born. May the Lord mercifully grant them converted and renewed hearts so that they may repent and be eternally saved, if possible.

I will now terminate the matter and direct the well-meaning reader to the Scriptures since the whole world with few exceptions depends upon human doctrine, lies, fiction, fables, perverted glosses, simple idolatry, and false worship; comforting themselves in these and boasting of what they neither have nor are. Therefore have I briefly, according to my few talents, in sincere, faithful love shown you in this epistle who, according to the unadulterated

Word, are the true regenerate, repentant, and baptized Christians that have the promise, and who are not, so that all truly hungry and thirsty souls who are zealous for God may be rightly satisfied with the truth unto eternal salvation and may no longer follow the serpent's cursed lie unto their eternal damnation. Yes, that they may all be helped, made whole, and saved who now stand before the eyes of the Lord with their poor, plundered souls so miserable, sick, poor, and naked. The Lord strengthen you. Believe God's reliable Word, reform your sinful lives, pray with confidence, and be obedient to the Gospel of Christ in order that you may receive the eternal promise to your everlasting joy and salvation, with all the saints, which God the merciful Father has promised to all His beloved children through Christ Jesus.

Grace be with all who seek Christ and eternal life with all the heart. Amen.

If you will allow Jesus Christ with His eternal Spirit and Word to be the Judge, then you will acknowledge that the sure foundation of truth has been shown.

# Foundation of Christian Doctrine

*Dat fundament des christelycken leers*

## 1539—40
### Revised 1558

*For other foundation can no man*
*lay than that is laid, which is Jesus Christ.*

I Corinthians 3:11

# Introduction

The best known and loved of Menno Simons' works is his *Foundation of Christian Doctrine*, first published 1539-40 (the title page reads 1539, but the last page bears the date 1540). Menno thoroughly revised it in 1558. The 1539-40 Dutch edition was reprinted in 1967 for the Eighth Mennonite World Conference sessions, held in Amsterdam that year.

Following the Salutation to the Reader, the *Foundation* contains twenty sections which might be roughly outlined as follows:

I. Call to a Biblical Faith
  A. The Day of Grace
  B. Genuine Penitence
  C. Faith
  D. Request to the Magistracy
  E. Baptism
  F. Refutation of the Pedobaptist Arguments
  G. An Admonition to the Pedobaptists

II. Refutation of Roman Catholicism
  A. The Lord's Supper
  B. Perversions of the Holy Supper
  C. The Duty of Shunning Babylon
  D. The Vocation of the Preachers
  E. The Doctrine of the Preachers
  F. The Conduct of the Preachers
  G. Refutation of the Rebuttal of Babylon

III. Appeals for Toleration
  A. Exhortation to Magistrates
  B. To the Learned Ones
  C. To the Common People
  D. To the Corrupt Sects
  E. To the Church of the Lord
  F. Conclusion

The purpose of the *Foundation* was to acquaint the world with the solid Biblical foundation of the Dutch Anabaptist Brethren of which Menno was an elder or bishop. He hoped that this might help to ease or stop the fearful persecution of the Brotherhood, but in this desire Menno was doomed to disappointment. Even more important, undoubtedly, was Menno's desire to indoctrinate his brethren and sisters in a Biblical faith, stripped of the accretions of the long centuries since the Apostolic Age. In this he was eminently successful. The fact that his group today bears Menno's name around the globe is eloquent testimony to the fact that God did use him to bring leadership both theological and ecclesiastical to his church. The most influential literature from Menno's pen was not his *Complete Works;* it was rather this *Foundation* (with seven other treatises) which appeared in German at Lancaster, Pennsylvania, in 1794 (reprint of the European edition of 1575), and enjoyed three English editions before 1871.

The original title of 1539 was, *The Foundation of the Christian Doctrine.* The 1558 Dutch edition has the following lengthy title: *A Foundation and Plain Statement of the Saving Doctrine of Our Lord Jesus Christ, Briefly Summarized from the Word of God: Together with Other Instructive Tracts Drawn Up by the Same Author. Printed Separately before this but now bound together.*

In the *Opera Omnia Theologica* of 1681 this work is found fol. 1 70, and in the *Complete Works* of 1871, I, 11-102.                                      J. C. W.

# Foundation of Christian Doctrine

# 1539

•-•-•-•-•-•-•-•-•-•-•-•-•-•-•-•-•-•-•-•-•-•-•-•-•-•-•-•-•-•-•-•-•-•-•-•-•-•-•-•-•-•-•-•-•-•-•

## *Salutation*

Dear God-fearing reader: I perceive that our work, which I published a few years ago under the title, *Foundation of Christian Doctrine,* has through the grace of God, to whom be eternal praise and thanks, been productive of much good to some. God's holy Word which was obscured for such a long time has through our little talent been brought back to light. Many well-disposed children have affectionately requested me to see it through the press again, diligently to revise and correct the faulty parts, which were abused by the carelessness of the printer, so hiding the sense from the reader. I allowed myself to be prevailed upon. Here and there I made additions, explained that which was vague, corrected what was spoiled, and omitted what was not needed. The style and language I have improved in order to be better suited to aid the kind reader and to make the despised truth known and acceptable to many.

Not that I have changed the original doctrines and contents; by no means. I have not changed them but improved their form, and it seems to me, given them more force and clarity. He who fears God may judge. But the former edition as well as this is God's Word. All that the first teaches, this teaches also. May the almighty merciful Father grant that through His grace our little work, so lightly esteemed, may produce endless fruit in countless thousands. Amen.                    MENNO SIMONS

## *Preface*

To all magistrates and men of whatever condition, class, or rank they may be, Menno Simons wishes the illumination of the Spirit, and the pure knowledge of the kingdom of God, from our heavenly Father, and His Son Jesus Christ, our Lord, who has loved us and washed us from our sins with His blood. To Him be praise, honor, glory, and thanksgiving forever. Amen.

Dear sirs, friends, and brethren: We learn from the Scriptures and from experience that the prediction of the prophets of Christ, and of the apostles concerning the terrible oppression, misery, want, persecution, danger, anxiety, and false doctrine of the last days is being accomplished fully and so violently that unless the merciful Father graciously shortens these days no flesh will be saved.

Therefore, we poor miserable men entreat and admonish everyone through the mercy of the Lord to please read our doctrine carefully and to understand it correctly. We would have you know exactly what kind of doctrine we hold to, what kind of faith we have, what kind of life we lead, and how we are disposed—the things on account of which we have to hear and suffer so much, be imprisoned, exiled, robbed, derided, defamed, and slain as poor, innocent sheep. This we would have you know in order that you may sincerely lament and weep over your former bloody deeds before God and with greater circumspection guard and keep yourselves from such things and from now on be a pious, reasonable, yes, a God-fearing magistracy; not oppressors and destroyers, but fathers and guardians of all miserable and wretched persons; not exterminators but defenders of righteousness; not persecutors but followers of Christ and His Word.

Therefore, anoint your eyes with eyesalve that you may see and understand what the right way, the truth, and the life are, the way which is so strait and narrow and is found of few; the truth which is known to none except those who are taught of the Spirit of the Lord, illuminated and drawn by the Father; the life which is to know God the Father as the only true God, and Jesus Christ whom He has sent. Know this so that you may see Him whom you have so savagely pierced, and that you may with Saint Paul humble yourselves before the Lord with all your heart, with much fasting and weeping; clothing yourselves in sackcloth and tunic of hair, rending your hearts and not your garments so that you may find grace in His sight. For He is long-suffering, gracious, and merciful, and pardons the transgressions of all who sincerely repent and seek His grace. Do not be Jeroboam, Ahab, and Manasseh any longer, but be David, Hezekiah, and Josiah so that you need not because of your office be ashamed in the great and dreadful day of the Lord, in that day which shall burn as an oven, and shall burn up as stubble all who have dealt unrighteously and have used violence upon the earth.

We entreat you for the sake of the merits of Christ to ponder and reflect upon our doctrine, faith, and intention, and not to esteem us worse than you do thieves and murderers whom you do not condemn without having certain knowledge of their case. Our enterprise is not that of robbers, nor does it have to do with perishable possessions, but with God and His Word, our bodies and souls, eternal life or eternal death. Therefore be not intent upon the usages and customs of the fathers, nor upon the worldly wise and the learned ones, for it is deeply hidden from their eyes. They have ever been those who from the beginning have rejected the wisdom of God through their own wisdom and have trampled it in the mire. For the wisdom of God which we teach is a wisdom which none may understand except those who are desirous of living and walking according to the will of God. It is that wisdom which is not to be brought from afar nor taught in colleges. It must be given from above and be learned through the Holy Ghost. As Paul says, Say not in thine heart, Who shall ascend into heaven? (that is, to bring Christ down from above:) Or, Who shall descend into the deep? (that is, to bring up Christ again from the dead.) But what saith it? The word is nigh thee, even in thy mouth, and in thy heart: that is, the word of faith, which we preach; That if thou shalt confess with thy mouth the Lord Jesus, and shalt believe in thine heart that God hath raised him from the dead, thou shalt be saved. Therefore, be intent upon God's Word, the testimony and example of the holy prophets, the Lord Jesus Christ and His apostles. Let these be your doctors and teachers in the matter and not the ambitious preachers of this world. Then you will perceive whether we are in the truth or not. May the almighty and eternal God give you such hearts and minds. To Him be honor, praise and gratitude, dominion, power, and majesty forever. Amen.

Seeing then that Satan can transform himself into an angel of light, and sow tares among the Lord's wheat, such as the sword, polygamy, an external kingdom and king, and other like errors on account of which the innocent have to suffer much, therefore we are forced to publish this our faith and doctrine. And we desire for Jesus' sake that we might obtain at least so much grace that they would not treat and judge us except according to the Word of God, even as is reasonable and just. But if we cannot obtain that much grace, we have to commend it to the Lord who is the only helper of every one in need. We will, nevertheless, through the grace of God, abide in the Word of the Lord, and comfort ourselves with the Scriptures, which say, Thus saith the Lord that created thee, O Jacob, and he that formed thee, O Israel, fear not; for I have redeemed thee, I have called thee by thy name; thou art mine. When thou passest through the waters, I will be with thee; and through the rivers, they shall not overflow thee; when thou walkest through the fire, thou shalt not be burned; neither shall the flame kindle upon thee; for I am the Lord thy God, the Holy one of Israel, thy Saviour. Fear ye not the reproach of men, neither be ye afraid of their revilings; for the moth shall eat them up like a garment and the worm shall eat them like wool. I, even I, am he that comforteth you: who art thou that shouldst be afraid of a man that shall die, and the son of man which shall be made as grass. Christ also said, Fear not them which kill the body, but are not able to kill the soul; but rather fear him which is able to destroy both soul and body in hell. Whosoever therefore shall confess me before men, him will I confess also before my Father which is in heaven; but whosoever shall deny me before men, him will I also deny before my Father which is in heaven. With the heart, says Paul, man believeth unto righteousness; and with the mouth confession is made unto salvation.

Since then the Scripture insists so strongly that we both believe and con-

fess, and so kindly comforts us against the raging and raving of men, therefore we also desire to continue in it until death and we testify before you in
Christ Jesus that we neither have, nor know any other positions, faith, or
doctrine than that which may be plainly read, heard, and understood in the
following from the Word of God. Amen.

## [I. CALL TO A BIBLICAL FAITH]

### [A.] The Day of Grace

In the first place we teach that which Jesus the teacher from heaven, the
mouth and word of the Most High God taught (John 3:2), that now is the
time of grace, a time to awake from the sleep of our ugly sins, and to be of
an upright, converted, renewed, contrite, and penitent heart. Now is the time
sincerely to lament before God our past reckless and willful manner of life,
and in the fear of God to crucify and mortify our wicked, sinful flesh and
nature. Now is the time to arise with Christ in a new, righteous, and penitent existence, even as Christ says, The time is fulfilled, and the kingdom of
God is at hand: repent and believe the gospel.

The time is fulfilled, that is, the promised day of grace approaches; the
time of the appearance of the promised seed, the time of redemption, the time
of the sacrifice by which all things were to be reconciled in heaven and on
earth; the time for the fulfillment of all figurative transactions into a new,
spiritual reality and an abiding truth; the time for which the fathers hoped:
Jacob, Moses, Isaiah, Daniel, David, etc., with all the patriarchs and prophets,
and which they desired with many tears, which through faith they saw from
afar, and in which they comforted themselves. Yes, it was to them such a
high and happy consolation that good old Simeon desired to live no longer
when he beheld that time and had seen the Redeemer. He said, Lord, now
lettest thou thy servant depart in peace, according to thy word, for mine eyes
have seen thy salvation, which thou hast prepared before the face of all people.

The time is fulfilled, the predictions of the prophets and promises of the
fathers are fulfilled gloriously; the vow is accomplished; Israel has received
its King David, its Prince and Chief, who has arisen as a mighty one to
prepare His course. His going forth is from the heavens; the Anointed who
was the desire of all nations has come, girded about His loins with the sword
of the Spirit and prepared for battle.

The Gospel of the kingdom, the Word of His Father, He has proclaimed;
He has taught and left unto His followers an example of pure love, and a
perfect life. He has conquered the mighty one, destroyed the power of the
devil, has borne our sins, abolished death, reconciled the Father. He has
earned for all the chosen children of God, grace, favor, mercy, eternal life,
the kingdom, and peace. And He has been ordained by His eternal and
mighty Father as an omnipotent King over the holy mountain of Zion, as
the Head of the Church, a Provider and Dispenser of heavenly blessings;
yes, an almighty Sovereign over all, in heaven and on earth. This is what

Christ meant when He said, The time is fulfilled, and the kingdom of God is at hand.

Out of sympathy and a sincere heart I exhort you with the holy Paul to take heed to this day of grace, and be mindful of the Word of God which says, I have heard thee in a time accepted and in the day of salvation I have succored thee; behold, now is the accepted time; behold, now is the day of salvation. And let us as Paul give no offense in anything that the ministry be not blamed. But in all things approving ourselves as ministers of God, in much patience, in afflictions, in necessities, in distresses, in stripes, in imprisonments, in tumults (that is, tumults that arise concerning us), in labors, in watchings, in fastings; by pureness, by knowledge, by long-suffering, by kindness, by the Holy Ghost, by love unfeigned, by the word of truth, by the power of God, by the armor of righteousness on the right hand and on the left, by honor and dishonor; by evil report and good report; as deceivers, and yet true; as unknown, and yet well known; as dying, and behold, we live; as chastened and not killed; as sorrowful, yet always rejoicing; as poor, yet making many rich; as having nothing, and yet possessing all things.

Oh, dear sirs, friends and brethren, my mouth is open unto you, my heart is enlarged toward you; for your sakes I am much grieved that you are so altogether careless, and do not even observe of what kind of people these plain and intelligible Scriptures were written. You so completely despise the Word of the Lord, so shamefully let the precious time of grace which God gives to you, and to us all, for the amending of our ways, pass away and regard nothing except to live wholly according to the impure and wicked lusts of your flesh, bowing the knees before dumb idols.

Alas, it is about time to awake! Remember that the angel of Revelation has sworn by the eternal and living God who made heaven and earth that after this time, there shall be time no more. From the Scriptures we cannot conclude but that this is the last festival of the year, the last proclamation of the holy Gospel, the last invitation to the marriage of the Lamb, which is to be celebrated, published, and sanctified before the great and terrible day of the Lord. With it, it seems, the summer will pass away and the winter come forth. They who, like the foolish virgins, neglect to prepare their lamps will come too late, knock in vain, and be excluded. Therefore comfort not one another with senseless comfort and uncertain hope, as some do who think that the Word will yet be taught and observed without the cross. I have in mind those who know the Word of the Lord, but do not live according to it. Oh, no! it is the Word of the cross and will in my opinion remain that unto the end. It has to be declared with much suffering and sealed with blood. The Lamb is slain from the foundation of the world; He did not only suffer in His members, but also by way of the cross and death has entered into that glory which He, for a time, had left for our sakes. If the Head had to suffer such torture, anguish, misery, and pain, how shall His servants, children, and members expect peace and freedom as to their flesh? If they have called the master of the house Beelzebub, why not those of his household? All that will live godly in Christ Jesus, says Paul, shall suffer persecution. Christ says, Ye shall be hated of all men for my name's sake.

Therefore, tear from your hearts the harmful thought that you may hope for another time, lest you be deceived by your vain hopes. I have known some who waited for a time of freedom, but did not live to see it. Had the apostles and fathers waited for it, the Gospel of the kingdom would to this day have been silent, and the Word of the Lord unpreached.

Oh, that you were Christians and the people of God as you boast yourselves to be, then you would be able to say with Paul, Who shall separate us from the love of Christ? For then the flesh, the devil, sin, hell, and death would all have been conquered, and there would then be no desire to remain longer in this bewildered, bad, and bloody world. Then we would boast of nothing save the cross of Christ, and with Paul desire heartily to be delivered from this tabernacle and to dwell in Christ.

I earnestly desire that you might awake, not hoping nor waiting for a different time. If, however, the merciful Father will give us a bit of freedom and peace, that we will gladly receive with all thankfulness from His gracious hand. But if not, His great name shall be praised forever.

We have already received the acceptable time of grace. The day of salvation is here. Now let us not be like ungrateful, disobedient, bloodthirsty Jerusalem which so perversely rejected the divine grace, the heavenly grace, and the merciful calling. But let us awake, be sober, and give ear to the inviting voice, and in this accepted time arise from the deep slumber of our loathsome sin, for the Lord is at hand. The night is far spent, the day is at hand; let us therefore cast off the works of darkness and let us put on the armor of light; let us walk honestly, as in the day; not in rioting and drunkenness, not in chambering and wantonness, not in strife and envying; but put ye on the Lord Jesus Christ and make not provision for the flesh to fulfill the lusts thereof. Let everyone be vigilant, and sleep not. Let him watch in the time which God has graciously given for repentance. *Ecce nunc tempus acceptum, ecce nunc dies salutis* (Behold, now is the accepted time, behold, now is the day of salvation).

### [B.] *Of Genuine Penitence*

In the second place we exhort you with Christ: Repent ye, and believe the Gospel. O faithful Word of grace, O faithful Word of divine love, thou art read in books, sung in hymns, preached with the mouth as to life and death, proclaimed in many countries, but unwanted in thy power. And what is more, all those who rightly teach and receive thee are made free booty for all. Ah, dear sirs, it will not help a fig to be called Christians, boast of the Lord's blood, death, merits, grace, and Gospel, so long as we are not converted from this wicked, immoral, and shameful life. It is in vain that we are called Christians, that Christ died, that we are born in the day of grace, and baptized with water, if we do not walk according to His law, counsel, admonition, will, and command and are not obedient to His Word.

Therefore, awake, and observe how men live everywhere. Verily you see nothing anywhere but unnatural carousing and drinking, pride as that of Lucifer, lying, fraud, grasping avarice, hatred, strife, adultery, fornication, warring, murder; everywhere hypocrisy, patent blasphemy, idolatry, and false worship. In short, nothing but a mighty opposition to all that God teaches and commands. Who can tell the terrible and alarming nature of this present world? Still men want to be called the holy Christian church. Oh, no! They who do such things, saith Paul, shall not inherit the kingdom of God.

Gentlemen, awake and beware, for the mouth of the Lord says, Verily, verily, I say unto you, Except ye be born from above, ye shall not see the kingdom of God. Also, Verily, verily, I say unto thee, Except a man be born of water and the Spirit, he cannot enter into the kingdom of God. Verily, I say unto you, Except ye be converted, and become as little children, ye shall not enter into the kingdom of heaven. What does it profit to speak much of Christ and His Word, if we do not believe Him, and refuse to obey His commandments? Again I say, awake and tear the accursed unbelief with its unrighteousness from your hearts, and commence a pious, penitent life as the Scriptures teach; for Christ says, Except ye repent ye shall all likewise perish. Do not apply this to such repentance as is taught and practiced by a world that has lost its way consisting only in an outward appearance and human righteousness, such as hypocritical fastings, pilgrimages, praying and reading lots of Pater Nosters and Ave Marias, hearing frequent masses, going to confessionals, and like hypocrisies—things of which Christ and His holy apostles did not say a single word and therefore cannot be a propitiatory sacrifice. Such things will be a provocation rather to stir up divine displeasure. These are empty and vain commandments of men, the accursed and magic wine of the Babylonian harlot, which those who have dwelt upon the earth have drunk for so many centuries, through the just anger of God. But we are referring to a penitence possessed of power and works, such as John the Baptist taught, saying: Bring forth therefore fruits meet for repentance, and think not to say within yourselves, we have Abraham to our Father. And now also the axe is laid unto the root of the trees; every tree, therefore, which bringeth not forth good fruit is hewn down and cast into the fire.

Notice, dear reader, such is the penitence which we teach, to die unto sin, and all ungodly works, and to live no longer according to the lusts of the flesh, a penitence as that of David. When he was reproved by the prophet for his adultery, and for numbering the people, he wept bitterly, cried to God, forsook the evil, and committed these sinful abominations no more. Peter erred mortally once, and not again. Matthew, after his call, did not return to his former conversation. Zacchaeus and the sinful woman did not go back to their impure works of darkness. Those who had been wronged by Zacchaeus he reimbursed, and the poor and needy were comforted with the half of his goods. The woman wept very bitterly and washed the feet of the Lord with her tears, and wiped them with the hair of her head; anointed them with precious ointment, and sat humbly at Christ's feet, to listen to His blessed words.

These are the noble fruits of repentance, acceptable to the Lord. Therefore, it was said to David, that the Lord had taken away his sins. To Peter it was announced that the Lord was risen from the dead. Matthew was accepted as an apostle. Zacchaeus was told that he had become a son of Abraham, and Mary Magdalene,[1] that she had chosen that good part which would not be taken away from her. To the adulterous woman Jesus said, Go and sin no more.

Such a repentance we teach and no other, namely, that no one can or may piously glory in the grace of God, the forgiveness of sins, the merit of Christ, unless he has truly repented. It is not enough that we say, we are Abraham's children, that is, that we are known as Christians. We must do the works of Abraham, that is, we must walk as all true children of God are commanded by His Word, as John writes: If we say we have fellowship with him and walk in darkness, we lie, and do not the truth. But if we walk in the light, as he is in the light, we have fellowship one with another, and the blood of Jesus Christ, his Son, cleanseth us from all sins.

I ask all my readers if they have ever read in the Scriptures that an impenitent, obstinate man who fears not God nor His Word, who is earthly-minded, sensual, devilish, and lives according to his lusts, can be called a child of God, and a joint heir of Christ. I believe that you will have to say, no. But he that with all his heart turns from evil and learns to do well, to him the grace of the Lord is proclaimed throughout the whole Scriptures. As the prophet says, Wash you, make you clean; put away the evil of your doings from before mine eyes; cease to do evil; learn to do well; seek judgment, relieve the oppressed, judge the fatherless, plead for the widow. Come now, and let us reason together, saith the Lord. Though your sins be as scarlet, they shall be as white as snow; though they be red like crimson, they shall be as wool. Again, If the wicked will turn from all his sins that he hath committed, and keep my statutes, and do that which is lawful and right, he shall surely live, he shall not die; all his transgressions that he hath committed, they shall not be mentioned unto him. Read and search the whole Scriptures, the true doctrine and testimony of the holy prophets, evangelists, and apostles, and you will discover most clearly that this godly repentance is to be earnestly received and practiced, and that without it no one can receive grace, enter into the kingdom of heaven, nor have any hope forever.

[1] Menno confuses, perhaps absent-mindedly, Mary Magdalene with Mary of Bethany.

In short, this matter we teach from the Word of God as much as in us is, in order to restrain those carnal lusts which war against the soul. We are to crucify the flesh with the affections and lusts, not to conform to this world, to put off the works of darkness and put on the armor of light; not to love the world, neither the things that are in the world. We must put off the old man with his deeds, and put on the new man, which is renewed in knowledge after the image of Him that created him. It requires that we put off the old Adam with his whole nature and deceitful lusts, such as pride, avarice, unchastity, hatred, envyings, gluttony, drinking, idolatry, and put on the new man, which after God is created in righteousness and true holiness, whose fruits are faith, love, hope, righteousness, peace, and joy in the Holy Ghost. We must be patient in suffering, merciful, compassionate, chaste, sincerely hating and rebuking all sin, having a sincere love and zeal for God and His Word. I repeat, this repentance we teach sincerely to be fruitful and acceptable to the Lord, according to the instructions of His Word. He that receives this repentance in sincerity and continues in it to the end, let him rejoice and thank God. The end thereof is eternal life. But he that rejects and detests it, let him take warning, for the end thereof is eternal death.

Beloved sirs, friends, and brethren, do take it to heart what it is and what the consequences will be so willfully to transgress the commandments of the Lord and so haughtily to sin against the Word of God. Adam and Eve ate but once of the forbidden tree, therefore the earth was cursed. In the sweat of his face he was to eat his bread all the days of his life. Eve and her daughters had to bring forth in pain, and be in subjection to their husbands. They were driven from Paradise, and with all their race had to return to the dust from whence they were taken. There was no forgiveness nor consolation of grace to be had unless the eternal Word, God's eternal Son, should come from high heaven, become man, suffer hunger, temptation, misery, torture, the cross and death, as the Scriptures teach.

O Lord, if this single transgression was so great before God, what will happen to those who so proudly all their days despise the holy Word, covenant, will, and commandment of the Lord, who do not once confess their sins and transgressions though they are full of iniquity from the crown of their heads to the soles of their feet? Cain was cursed and became a fugitive upon the earth as long as he lived because he so enviously slew his innocent brother Abel; alas! what about those who daily without compassion or justice so unmercifully persecute, plunder, and murder the pious children of Abel, who with fervent hearts seek Christ and eternal life?

The whole earth perished in the waters of the flood, because the sons of God looked upon the daughters of men that they were fair, and took to themselves wives of all which they chose, and also because they would not be reproved by the Spirit of God, for every imagination and thought of their hearts was evil continually. Reflect upon the lusts with which the marriages of the world at the present time are begun, yes, how men blaspheming and grieving the Holy Ghost are become like unto the horse and mule; how they all walk in the sinful way, the end of which is hell, eternal damnation, and death.

Sodom and Gomorrah, with the surrounding cities were, because of their pride, excesses, cruelty, and abominable crimes, burnt up with the fire of the furious wrath of God and sunk to the depth of hell. Ah, what will befall those miserable men in the great and terrible day when the Lord will appear in His glory, men whose pride and pomp, excess, gluttony, tyranny, blood-thirstiness, adultery, fornication, and papal abominations, no heart can conceive, no tongue express, no pen describe?

Korah, Dathan, and Abiram, though they were of the seed of Abraham and some of them born of Levi, yet because they revolted against Moses and Aaron, and sought to enter into the priestly office without a call, they and all their company were swallowed up alive by the earth. Consider what will ultimately happen to our sons of Korah, whom God never knew, much less sent, and whose office, calling, and service is not from God or His Word, but as the Scriptures teach: from the pit, the dragon, and the beast; from men who mislead so many poor, miserable souls with their seducing doctrines, Babylonian sorceries, and hypocritical lies, and not only despise, but also persecute, crucify, and kill the true Moses and Aaron and Christ.

If Moses, the faithful servant of God, could not enter the promised land because he upon occasion doubted the Word of the Lord, how shall this unbelieving, crooked, and obstinate generation enter the eternal land of promise and glory? For it is a generation that not only disbelieves and despises the Word of the Lord, the blessed Gospel of Christ Jesus, but also bitterly hates and persecutes it, tramples the blood of Christ underfoot, and stops its ears against the truth. It refuses to be taught by any means, whether with the truth, the unblamable lives of the saints, or the innocent blood of the martyrs of Jesus which has been shed liberally as water in many lands.

O wretched man, you who stand so wholly deformed and miserable before your God, take heed to the Word of the Lord, cleanse your bloody hands and your impure and unbelieving hearts, and mock no longer the grace of God with your vain boastings. Say not that Abraham is your father, that you are the children of God; that Christ died for you, or that you will trust in His mercy. Trust ye not in lying words, says Jeremiah, the prophet; say not, This is the temple of the Lord, the temple of the Lord, the temple of the Lord. It avails nothing that Christ died and that we appropriate His name, if we do not have a sincere, regenerating, vigorous faith in Christ Jesus; pure, unfeigned love; willing obedience, and a pious and irreproachable life. God's mercy, says the Scripture, is to His saints, and He cares for His elect; but the hope of the wicked is vain. The eyes of the Lord are upon the righteous, and His ears are open unto their cry. Ye are my friends, says Christ, if ye do whatsoever I command you.

Therefore we pray and exhort you once more to repent. He is still the same unchangeable God. He hates, destroys, and sternly punishes all wickedness. Yes, He is a righteous Judge of all ungodliness and of every evil work. He visits the iniquities of the fathers upon the children unto the third and fourth generation. On the other hand, He is compassionate, kind, and merciful unto all that do right and fear His name; to many thousands who love Him and keep His commandments.

O reader, precious reader, it is a fearful thing to fall into the hands of the living God! The time is fulfilled; now is the accepted time, now is the day of salvation. The kingdom of heaven is at hand. Do you want to inherit it and enter into it? Then you must repent, not only in appearance as the hypocrites do, but as true penitents with all your heart and all your power, and you must bring forth good fruit. Otherwise, you must be cast out, into the fire of His fierce wrath. Except ye repent, ye shall all likewise perish. Luke 13:3.

### [C.] *Faith*

In the third place we teach with Christ and say, Believe the Gospel. That Gospel is the blessed announcement of the favor and grace of God to us, and of forgiveness of sins through Christ Jesus. Faith accepts this Gospel through the Holy Ghost, and does not consider former righteousness or unrighteousness, but hopes against hope (Rom. 4:18), and with the whole heart casts itself upon the grace, Word and promises of the Lord, since it knows that God is true, and that His promises cannot fail. In this the heart is renewed, converted, justified, becomes pious, peaceable, and joyous, is born a child of God, approaches with full confidence the throne of grace, and so becomes a joint heir of Christ and a possessor of eternal life.

Such persons awaken in time. They hear and believe the Word of the Lord. They weep over their past vain lives and conduct. They desire help and aid for their sick souls. To such, Christ who is a comforter for all troubled hearts says, Believe the Gospel, that is, fear not; rejoice and be comforted; I will not punish nor chastise you, but will heal you, comfort you, and give you life. A bruised reed will I not break, and smoking flax will I not quench. I will seek that which was lost and bring back again that which was driven away and will bind up that which was broken and will strengthen that which was sick. I am not come to call the righteous, but sinners to repentance. By the kindness of my heavenly Father, I am come into the world, and by the power of the Holy Ghost, I became a visible, tangible, and dying man; in all points like unto you, sin excepted. I was born of Mary, the unpolluted mother and pure virgin; I descended from heaven, sprang from the mouth of the Most High, the first-born of every creature, the first and last, the beginning and the end, the Son of the Almighty God; anointed with the Holy Ghost to preach the Gospel to the poor, to bind up the brokenhearted, to proclaim liberty to the captives, to give sight to the blind, to open the prison to them that are bound, and to proclaim the acceptable year of the Lord. Believe the Gospel. I am the Lamb that was sacrificed for you all. I take away the sins of the whole world. My Father has made me unto you wisdom, righteousness, sanctification, and redemption. Whosoever believeth on me shall not be ashamed; yea, all that believe that I am He, shall have eternal life.

You see, dear sirs, friends, and brethren, they who believe this are those of whom the Scriptures say, To them gave he power to become the sons of God, even to them that believe on his name, which were born not of blood, nor of the will of the flesh, nor of the will of man, but of God. These are they who are justified by faith and have peace with God, through our Lord Jesus Christ, by whom also we have access by faith into this grace wherein we stand, and rejoice in hope of the glory of God; and all this, as Paul says, of grace and love. All have sinned and come short of the glory of God, being justified freely by his grace, through the redemption that is in Christ Jesus, whom God has set forth to be a propitiation through faith.

There is none that can glory in himself touching this faith, for it is the gift of God. All who receive it from God receive a tree loaded with all manner of good and delicious fruit. Happy is he to whom God gives this gift, for it is more precious than gold, silver, or precious stones. Nothing can be compared with it. He that receives it receives Christ Jesus, forgiveness of sins, a new mind, and eternal life. For true faith which is acceptable before God cannot be barren; it must bring forth fruit and manifest its nature. It works ceaselessly in love, enters willingly into righteousness, mortifies flesh and blood, crucifies the lusts and desires, rejoices in the cross of Christ, renews and regenerates. It makes one active, confident, and joyful in Christ Jesus. Such a faith, I say, is the gift of God by which the righteous according to the Scriptures are to live as did Abel, Enoch, Noah, Abraham, Moses, Rahab, and all the saints. Every good tree bringeth forth good fruit after its kind. Every tree which bringeth not forth good fruit although loaded with leaves, must be subjected to the curse and consumed by fire. A fruitless, impotent faith, the kind the whole world has, and which does not work by love, be it ever so learned, wise, eloquent, fine-appearing, and miraculous, is in the sight of God unclean, dead, and accursed.

Therefore we exhort you with Christ Jesus, Believe the Gospel, that is, believe the joyful news of divine grace through Jesus Christ. Cease from sin; manifest repentance for your past lives; submit obediently to the Word and will of the Lord; and you will become companions, citizens, children, and heirs of the new and heavenly Jerusalem, free from your enemies, hell, death, sin and the devil, if only you walk according to the Spirit and not according to the flesh. Rom. 8:6. That is, he that believeth on the Son of God hath everlasting life.

*[D.] Request to the Magistracy*[2]

We poor, wretched people, left without human help and comfort; we who like innocent shepherdless sheep have become a prey to the lions roaring in the thicket, and the wild beasts of the field; a spectacle and reproach to the whole world, we have to endure daily the tyrannical sword of lords and princes, the inhuman scoff and scorn of the learned ones, the abominable lying and mocking of the common people. We humbly intreat the Imperial Majesty, kings, lords, princes, magistrates, and officers, everyone in his calling, dignity, and rank, and all our dear and gracious rulers by the crimson blood and wounds of our blessed Lord Jesus Christ, that you would at long last lay aside all ill will and bad opinion concerning us. With proper pity be at least somewhat concerned about the inhuman and heavy oppression, misery, distress, cross, and torture of your sad and innocent subjects. For the great Lord before whom we stand, the Searcher of every heart, to whom all things are opened and revealed, knows that we seek nothing upon this earth but that we with a good conscience might live according to His holy commandments, ordinances, Word, and will. But if there are some harmful sects as alas in our day there have been, they will no doubt in due time become manifest.

Therefore condescend to read our writings diligently and ponder them, and that with a God-fearing and unbiased heart, so that you may know with certainty why you are unable to frighten us from our doctrine, faith, and practice by coercion, poverty, misery, persecution, and death. Ponder the truth at some length and let no more innocent blood come upon you. Be pleased to show some natural reasonableness and human charity toward your poor subjects. Call to mind that we poor and forsaken men, as to the flesh, are not of wood and stone. Together with you we are descended from one father, Adam, and from one mother, Eve, created by the same God. Having a common entrance into this mortal life. We are clothed with the same nature, yearning for rest and peace, for wives and children, as well as you, and by nature fearful of death as are all creatures.

Therefore humble yourselves in the name of Jesus, that your poor souls may be excused. Examine, I say, our doctrine, and you will find through the grace of God that it is the pure and unadulterated doctrine of Christ, the holy Word, the Word of eternal peace, the Word of eternal truth, the Word of divine grace, the Word of our salvation, the invincible Word, against which no gates of hell shall ever prevail; the two-edged sword that proceeds out of the mouth of the Lord, the sword of the Spirit by which all must be judged that dwell upon the earth.

O dear sirs, sheathe your sword. For as the Lord liveth you do not fight against flesh and blood, but against Him whose eyes are as a flame of fire; who judgeth and contends in righteousness; who is crowned with

[2] In the Dutch original the full title reads: *An Admonishing Request to the Magistracy.*

many crowns; whose name no one knoweth but Himself; who is clothed with the vesture dipped in blood; whose name is the Word of God; who rules the nations with a rod of iron; who treads the winepress of the fierceness and wrath of almighty God; who hath on His vesture and on His thigh a name written, *King of kings and Lord of lords.*

O illustrious lords and princes, it is against Him that you in this manner contend with your counsel and sword and weapon. Remember what the great prophet of the Lord, Zechariah, said concerning the children of God in this world always suffering: he that touches you touches the apple of mine eye. It is a frightful abomination and raging terror thus miserably to garrote, to kill, and wipe out those who with such ardent hearts seek the Lord and eternal life, and who would not touch a hair of anyone upon the earth. Precious in the sight of the Lord, David says, is the death of His saints. It is Jesus of Nazareth whom ye persecute and not us. Therefore awake, desist, fear God and His Word. For you and we shall all be called to appear before one Judge, before whom neither power, rank, splendor, fine speech, nor talents will count. For righteous sentence will there be passed upon all flesh impartially, and without respect of persons. Then the miserable will have justice, and the Christ put to death in His elect will come out of the power of death and the hands of tyrants, into His promised inheritance, kingdom, and glory.

Seeing then that you carry on unjustly and tyrannically, according to the evil purpose of your heart, without Scripture and without mercy against the helpless and God-fearing, how can you look for any grace and mercy in the day of the Lord when we shall all have to stand before the impartial judgment seat where everyone will be rewarded according to his deeds?

We ask not for mercy as do the evildoers of this world. In this our doctrine and faith we have not sinned, although we have to suffer so much. We merely opposed the doctrine, ordinance, and life of Antichrist and that with the Word of the Lord as the Scriptures direct us. We resist neither the emperor, the king, nor any authority in that to which they are called of God; but we are ready to obey to the death in all things which are not contrary to God and His Word. Right well we know what the Scriptures teach and enjoin concerning this matter. But so much mercy we request that under your gracious protection we may live, teach, conduct ourselves, and serve the Lord according to our consciences so that to you and many with you, the Gospel of Christ may be rightly set forth and the gate of life swing open. Alas! if the learned ones had the Word of God and not we, how gladly would we be taught by them. But since we have it and not they, therefore we pray for Jesus' sake, Do not crowd us from Christ to Antichrist, from truth to error, from life to certain death.

O illustrious lords and princes, you who are appointed of God to be heads and rulers, reconsider and believe the Word of the Lord. For if you will not desist from unrighteousness, fear God, and do right, it would be well if you had never been born. The innocent blood of Abel clamors in heaven and it will be strictly required of you at the last day. We repeat, Awake; fear God's Word. For God the Lord will Himself rule in heaven alone, and in His kingdom alone, that is, in the hearts of men. He will not allow anyone to depose Him from His glory or supersede Him. Lucifer, the fair angel of God, desired to be equal to the Most High, and was cast out of heaven into the depth of hell, and is kept in chains of darkness until the judgment of the last day.

Beloved sirs, receive it in love and do not be offended. The truth must be confessed. Your pride has risen to heaven; look to Christ and His Word, His example, and His life; judge rightly and you will find this to be true. The almighty, eternal Father, through His eternal Wisdom, Christ Jesus, has instituted and commanded according to His divine counsel, will, and wisdom, all things in His kingdom, that is, His church, relating to doctrines, sacraments, and life. But you are the ones who at the counsel and the suggestion of the learned ones by your inhuman and cruel edict have changed, destroyed, and persecuted these, as if the almighty and eternal Word should yield to your command and authority, and as if the divine ordinances of the Son of God could be changed into a more acceptable form and a better use through the wisdom of men. O greatest of all presumptions, folly of all follies, how proud of you, earth and ashes! Acknowledge your superior, Christ Jesus, who is made to you a Prince and a Judge of God Himself. The heavens, even the heavens, are the Lord's, saith David, but the earth hath He given to the children of men. I presume that if any were to revolt against the emperor or king, usurping his kingdom and government, this would not be patiently tolerated or go unpunished. How much less then will poor mortal flesh go unpunished which rises up against the almighty Emperor, the King, Christ Jesus, to hurl Him from the seat of His divine majesty and to deprive Him of His scepter and the crown of His glory, as though Christ Jesus, the eternal wisdom of God, were incompetent and unfit for the heavenly government. Reflect what has become of those haughty and proud hearts from the beginning who wanted to be on a par with God.

Therefore humble yourselves under the mighty hand of God, as Peter teaches. Take as an example the successful, great king Nebuchadnezzar, and observe how fearfully he was punished by God for his pride; how after the punishment he turned to wisdom, feared the Almighty, exalted His wonderful and glorious works, and His great and adorable name.

Beloved sirs, awake, and repent, for it does not become the creature to rise up against the Creator. Christ wishes to remain the head of His church, He alone the teacher in His school, and He alone the King who will judge His kingdom; not with the doctrines or commands of men, nor with executions and murderings, but with His Holy Spirit, power, grace, and Word.

Therefore we pray you, O ye pillars of the earth whom we through the mercy of God acknowledge in all temporal things as our gracious lords, to let the eternal, almighty king Christ Jesus be the only Saviour, Lord, and Sovereign of men's souls, even as He was appointed by His Father. And may you carry on in the earthly and temporal government to which you have been called. For with all our hearts we desire to render unto Caesar the things that are Caesar's and unto God the things that are God's. Be pleased also to consider this our doctrine and instruction concerning baptism, the Lord's Supper, and the shunning of the Babylonian traffic. Compare them well with the Word of the Lord. We expect, through the grace of God, that you will mightily discover that we believe and teach nothing but that which the true mouth of the Lord has commanded us and the holy apostles have taught and testified. Unto this may the great Lord grant you His grace. Amen.

## [E.] Baptism

Christ, after His resurrection, commanded His apostles saying, Go ye therefore, and teach all nations, baptizing them in the name of the Father, and of the Son, and the Holy Ghost; teaching them to observe all things whatsoever I have commanded you; and, lo, I am with you always, even unto the end of the world. Amen.

Here we have the Lord's commandment concerning baptism, as to when according to the ordinance of God it shall be administered and received; namely, that the Gospel must first be preached, and then those baptized who believe it, as Christ says: Go ye into all the world, and preach the gospel to every creature; he that believeth and is baptized shall be saved, but he that believeth not, shall be damned. Thus has the Lord commanded and ordained; therefore, no other baptism may be taught or practiced forever. The Word of God abideth forever.

Young children are without understanding and unteachable; therefore baptism cannot be administered to them without perverting the ordinance of the Lord, misusing His exalted name, and doing violence to His holy Word. In the New Testament no ceremonies for infants are enjoined, for it treats both in doctrines and sacraments with those who have ears to hear and hearts to understand. Even as Christ commanded, so the holy apostles also taught and practiced, as may be plainly perceived in many parts of the New Testament. Peter said, Repent and be baptized every one of you in the name of Jesus Christ for the remission of sins, and ye shall receive the gift of the Holy Ghost. And Philip said to the eunuch, If thou believest with all thine heart, thou mayest. Faith does not follow from baptism, but baptism follows from faith.

In this manner Christ has commanded baptism and received it Himself, as follows: When the time had come and the hour had approached in which He would fulfill the commission given Him to preach the Word and make known His Father's holy name, He came to John to the Jordan and desired to be baptized of him, that He might fulfill all righteousness. He prepared

Himself to meet temptation, misery, the cross, and death, and as a willing, obedient child resigned Himself to the will of His almighty Father, as He Himself said that He came down from heaven, not to do His own will, but the will of Him that sent Him. He was baptized of John, witnessed to by the Holy Ghost, and acknowledged by the Father to be a beloved Son.

Beloved, so runs Christ's command, so Christ was baptized, so the apostles taught and practiced. Who now will confront the Lord and say it shall not be done so? Who will teach and instruct Wisdom? Who will rebuke apostles and evangelists for falsehood? It would be entirely unbecoming for a child, would it not, to command and judge his father, or a servant his master, and it is much more unbecoming for the creature to exalt himself above his Creator. But now it is manifest that the whole world with its unprofitable doctrines and commandments of men, with its anti-Christian customs, usages of long standing, and by its tyrannical, murderous judgment of the sword over Christ and His Word pronounces the truths of Christ lies; His wisdom, foolishness; His light, darkness, and His Gospel a perverted and false sect. In short Christ must be silent and passive.

Probably it will be said that this was necessary in the beginning of the Gospel because at that time there were no believers whose children might be baptized, but now if the parents are believers then are the children also to be baptized, just as when Abraham believed his children were circumcised. Oh, no, this does not follow; for although Abraham believed God only one half of his seed was circumcised, namely, the male children and not the female, though he was the father of the female as well as of the male children, of which by the grace of God, more shall be said below in the reply.

That in the beginning the Gospel was to be preached and that then faith came by hearing, and that baptism was to ensue upon faith, is undeniable, for Scriptures teach this. But that the children of believers should be baptized because Abraham's children were circumcised, can in no wise be sustained by Scripture. But even if it could be, which it cannot, then there would be but few children baptized, for the number of true believers is, sad to say, very small, as anyone may see.

Not all are Christians of whom it is boasted. But those who have the Spirit of Christ are true Christians, though I do not know where one might find very many. Yes, what more shall we say? All who with Abel bring an acceptable sacrifice, all who with Isaac are born of the free woman, and with Jacob have received the birthright and the paternal blessing; these must be slain by bloodthirsty Cain, mocked by Ishmael, and hated by Esau, even as also we may hear and see on every hand.

This then is the Word and will of the Lord, that all who hear and believe the Word of God shall be baptized as related above. Thereby they profess their faith and declare that they will henceforth live not according to their own will, but according to the will of God. For the testimony of Jesus they are prepared to forsake their homes, possessions, lands, and lives and to suffer hunger, affliction, oppression, persecution, the cross and death for the same; yes, they desire to bury the flesh with its lusts and arise with Christ to newness of life, even as Paul says: Know ye not that so many of us as were baptized into Christ Jesus were baptized into his death? Therefore we are buried with him in baptism into death; that like as Christ was raised up from the dead by the glory of the Father, even so we also should walk in newness of life.

Beloved reader, take heed to the Word of the Lord. Paul who did not receive his Gospel from men, but from the Lord Himself, teaches that even as Christ died and was buried, so also ought we to die unto our sins, and be buried with Christ in baptism. Not that we are to do this for the first time after baptism, but we must have begun all this beforehand, as Paul says: For if we have been planted together in the likeness of his death, we shall also be in the likeness of his resurrection. Knowing this that our old man is crucified with him, that the body of sin might be destroyed, that henceforth we should not serve sin. For he that is dead is freed from sin. For even as Christ has died, has taken away sin, and lives unto God, so true Christians die unto sin and live unto God.

Think not that we teach that Christians are to die unto sin to such an extent as to sense it no longer. Not by any means. But they die unto sin so as to be no longer subjects to their impure lusts. As Paul says, Let not sin therefore reign in your mortal body, that ye should obey it in the lusts thereof. Whosoever is born of God doth not commit sin; for his seed remaineth in him; and he cannot sin because he is born of God.

For even as the death of our Lord would not have profited us had He not risen from the power of death to the praise of His Father, so it will not avail us anything to bury our sins in baptism if we do not arise with Christ Jesus from the power of sin unto a new life to the praise of the Lord. For in that he died, he died unto sin once, says Paul; but in that he liveth, he liveth unto God. Likewise, reckon yourselves to be dead indeed unto sin but alive unto God through Christ Jesus. And as ye have yielded your members servants to uncleanness, and iniquity unto iniquity, even so now yield your members servants to righteousness and holiness. For being made free from sin, ye became the servants of righteousness and have your fruit unto holiness and the end everlasting life.

Here you notice, sensible reader, you who desire to know the truth and seek the salvation of your soul, what the great and holy apostle Paul has taught. If you believe his word, doctrine, and testimony to be true, you will no doubt readily perceive from these assertions and from many other passages in his writings that baptism is as much in place in the case of infants as circumcision was in the case of females of the Israelites. For we are no more commanded to baptize infants than Israel was to circumcise female children. It is also impossible for little children to die to sin as long as it has not become alive in them. Neither can they rise to a new life, as long as they are not born of God through faith, and by the Spirit of God led into righteousness. Therefore beware, for the symbolism of baptism is to bury sin, and to rise with Christ in a new life, things which can by no means be said of infants. Therefore consider at length what the Word of the Lord teaches you on this subject.

Paul also calls baptism the washing of regeneration. O dear Lord, how lamentably Thy holy Word is abused! Is it not most lamentable that men attempt with these plain passages to support their idolatrous and invented baptism of infants, asserting that infants are regenerated in baptism, as if regeneration were simply a matter of immersing in water.[3] Oh, no! Regeneration is not such an hypocrisy but it is an inward change which converts a man by the power of God through faith from evil to good, from carnality to spirituality, from unrighteousness to righteousness, out of Adam into Christ. This is a matter which can in no wise take place with infants, for the regenerated live by the power of the new life; they crucify the flesh with its evil lusts; they put off the old Adam with his deeds; they avoid every appearance of evil; they are taught, ruled, and driven by the Holy Ghost.

Behold, this is the true new birth with its fruits, of which the Scriptures speak and which comes forth from the Word of God through faith, without which no one, that is, no one who has come to years of understanding, can be saved. As Christ says, Verily, verily, I say unto you, Except a man be born again, he cannot see the kingdom of God. Yes, it would be all in vain, even if one were baptized by Peter, Paul, or Christ Himself, if he were not baptized from above with the Holy Ghost and with fire. As Paul says, In Christ Jesus neither circumcision availeth anything, nor uncircumcision, but a new creature. All who are so born of God are changed and renewed in the inner man, translated from Adam into Christ. They are ready to obey the Word of the Lord, and say with Saint Paul, Lord, what wilt thou have me to do? They leave self and human wisdom behind, and submit to the Word and ordinances of the Lord without reluctance or opposition. They submit to baptism according to the command of the Lord. They become and manifest themselves as fruitful branches of Christ, the true Vine, and as comrades in the church of the Lord. They receive forgiveness of their sins and the gift of the Holy Ghost. They put on Christ; enter into the ark of Noah; and are secured against the dreadful deluge of the wrath to come which will come like a net upon all them that dwell upon the earth. This, however, not by the power of water alone or the sign, but by the power of the divine Word received through faith. For where there is not faith through love working obedience (again we speak of those who have come to years of understanding) there is no promise. He that believeth not the Son, shall not see life; but the wrath of God abideth on him.

---

[3] *Indruckinge in't Water* (Opera, 1681, fol. 13b). Menno is apparently paraphrasing Titus 3:5. In any case, Menno describes baptism explicitly in the fourth paragraph of Item 7 of the *Foundation* (Opera, 1681, fol. 22b) as being "the recipient of a handful of water," *een handt vol Waters te ontfangen*. See pages 139 and 350. Ed.

The Lord commanded Moses to stretch forth his hand and with the rod smite the sea and the waters should be divided. Moses believed the word of the Lord; stretched forth his hand and smote with the rod. The waters were divided and Israel was redeemed—not by the rod and the stroke, but by the power of the divine Word received by Moses through a genuine and active faith. If Moses had not believed the word of God, and had through disobedience failed to strike the sea, then undoubtedly it would not have gone well with an affrighted and fearful Israel.

Moses also received a commandment in the wilderness to erect a brazen serpent so that when Israel looked upon it they might be healed of the bite of the serpents. Moses believed the word of the Lord. He erected a serpent. Israel looked upon it and was healed—not through the virtue of the image, but through the power of the divine Word received by him through faith. In the same manner there is ascribed to Scriptural baptism the forgiveness of sins, the putting on of Christ, and the immersion into His church—not on account of the water or the administered signs (else the kingdom of God would be bound to elements and signs), but on account of the power and truth of the divine promise which we receive by obedience through faith. For all those who teach to trust in words, elements, and works, do with Aaron make a golden calf and permit the sinful people therewith to fornicate and commit abomination. For in Christ nothing matters but faith working by love, the new creature, and the keeping of the commandments of God.

Dear sirs, friends, and brethren, awake and do not linger. Render to the Most High the praise and honor due Him and give ear to His holy Word, for those who maintain that the baptism of irrational children is a washing of regeneration do violence to the Word of God, resist the Holy Ghost, make Christ a liar and His holy apostles false witnesses. For Christ and His apostles teach that regeneration, as well as faith, comes from God and His Word, which Word is not to be taught to those who are unable to hear or understand, but to those who have the ability both to hear and to understand. This is incontrovertible.

The holy apostle Peter also declares the same and says that even baptism doth also now save us, not the putting away of the filth of the flesh, but the covenant[4] of a good conscience with God by the resurrection of Jesus Christ.

Here Peter teaches us how the inward baptism saves us, by which the inner man is washed, and not the outward baptism by which the flesh is washed. For only this inward baptism, as already stated, is of value in the sight of God, while outward baptism follows as an evidence of obedience which is of faith. For if outward baptism could save without the inward, then the whole Scriptures which speak of the new man would be spoken to no purpose. The kingdom of heaven would be bound to ordinary water; the

---

[4] Menno quotes the Dutch version here, *Verbondt,* agreeing incidentally with the German Bible of Luther (but not with the Swiss Froschouer, 1536, which reads, *certain knowledge—gewüsse kundtschafft*—rather than covenant). *Ed.*

blood of Christ would be shed in vain, and no baptized person could be lost. Oh, no, outward baptism avails nothing so long as we are not inwardly renewed, regenerated, and baptized with the heavenly fire and the Holy Ghost of God. But when we are the recipients of this baptism from above, then we are constrained through the Spirit and Word of God by a good conscience which we obtain thereby, because we believe sincerely in the merits of the death of the Lord and in the power and fruits of His resurrection, and because we are inwardly cleansed by faith. In the spiritual strength which we have received, we henceforth bind ourselves by the outward sign of the covenant in water which is enjoined on all believers by Christ, even as the Lord has bound Himself with us in His grace, through His Word, namely, that we will no longer live according to the evil, unclean lusts of the flesh, but walk according to the witness of a good conscience before Him.

Although these words of Peter are very plain, the learned ones are not ashamed to force a strange meaning upon them by means of their glosses, having a show of truth and their vaunted reason (probably so that they may retain the favor of the world and live comfortably without cross or affliction), teaching that baptism is a sign of grace, which according to my little wisdom it can in no wise be. For our sign of grace is Christ Jesus alone, by whom God's abundant love is freely dispensed and declared unto us. By signs He was formerly given to the ancient patriarchs. He was gloriously prefigured as by the coats of skin to Adam and Eve; by the rainbow to Noah, by circumcision to Abraham, by which signs they were assured of the divine covenant.

But we are assured by God of His divine grace and His eternal peace by this one sign only which is Christ Jesus. The seal in our consciences is the Holy Ghost, but baptism is a sign of obedience, commanded of Christ, by which we testify when we receive it that we believe the Word of the Lord, that we repent of our former life and conduct, that we desire to rise with Christ unto a new life, and that we believe in the forgiveness of sins through Jesus Christ. Not, my beloved, that we believe in the remission of sins through baptism, by no means. Because even as by baptism we cannot obtain faith and repentance, so we can not receive [by baptism] the forgiveness of sins, nor peace, nor liberty of conscience. We testify thereby that we have repented and believe in forgiveness through Christ. With the fathers it was not so, for they received assurance and comfort by means of the signs that the promise would be true and sure. We have this assurance in Christ Jesus alone in whom all the figurative signs take an end, so that we have in this only true sign, Christ, that which the fathers had in many figurative signs. In short, if we had forgiveness of sins and security of conscience through outward signs and elements, then the reality would be eliminated and made to retreat together with His merits.

Behold, this is the only and true position concerning baptism that can be sustained by the Scriptures; no other can. This baptism we teach and practice even though the gates of hell oppose and resist, for we know it is the plain Word of the Lord and a divine ordinance from which we dare not take away nor add to, lest we be found disobedient and false before God who alone is the Lord and God of our consciences. For every Word of the Lord is pure; He is a shield unto them that put their trust in Him.

O God, what are the learned ones and the highly educated masters of this world doing, who try so hard to minimize God's Word and wisdom and so cleverly urge their own foolish reason and wisdom? They will not succeed. For He will not give His honor to another. He is the Lord; that is His name, and beside Him there is no other. Conquering, He will conquer them. He will turn their wisdom to folly and their reason to shame, for He knows the thoughts of the wise that they are vain.

Luther writes that children should be baptized in view of their own faith and adds, If children had no faith, then their baptism would be blaspheming the sacrament. It appears to me to be a great error in this learned man, through whose writings at the outset the Lord effected no little good, that he holds that children without knowledge and understanding have faith, whereas the Scriptures teach so plainly that they know neither good nor evil, that they cannot discern right from wrong. Luther says that faith is dormant and lies hidden in children, even as in a believing person who is asleep, until they come to years of understanding. If Luther writes this as his sincere opinion, then he proves that he has written in vain a great deal concerning faith and its power. But if he writes this to please men, may God have mercy on him, for I know of a truth that it is only human reason and invention of men. It shall not make the Word and ordinance of the Lord to fall. We do not read in Scripture that the apostles baptized a single believer while he was asleep. They baptized those who were awake, and not sleeping ones. Why then do they baptize their children before their sleeping faith awakes and is confessed by them?

Bucer does not follow this explanation, but he defends infant baptism in a different way, namely, not that children have faith, but that they by baptism are incorporated in the church of the Lord so that they may be instructed in His Word. He admits that infant baptism is not expressly commanded by the Lord; nevertheless he maintains that it is proper. O Lord, how lamentably some do err who court the favor and honor of men, and seek not the favor and honor of God. Since infant baptism is not expressly commanded of God as he acknowledges, it cannot be acceptable to the Lord, and consequently no promise can follow. Therefore the reader should know that true Christians ought not to be governed in this matter by the opinions and traditions of men, but by the Word and ordinances of God. For we have but one Lord and Master of our conscience, Jesus Christ, whose word, will, commandment, and ordinance, it becomes us as His willing disciples to follow, even as the bride is ready to obey the bridegroom's voice.

Since we have not a single command in the Scriptures that infants are to be baptized, or that the apostles practiced it, therefore we confess with good sense that infant baptism is nothing but human invention and notion, a perversion of the ordinances of Christ, a manifold abomination standing in the holy place where it ought not to stand.

Dear sirs, how little the Word of the Lord is regarded which says, Ye shall not do after that which is right in your own eyes, but observe whatsoever I command you. Did not the Father testify from heaven and declare, This is my beloved Son in whom I am well pleased; hear ye him? Does not the whole Scripture direct us to Christ? Are we not baptized in His name that we should hear His voice, and be obedient to His Word? Do you not boast to be the apostolic church? Why then do you go from Christ to Antichrist and from the apostolic doctrine and practice to that of the learned ones? Do observe how severely and frequently God has punished the inventions of men which they considered holy transactions and religion!

Nadab and Abihu, because they offered strange fire before the Lord, were suddenly destroyed by fire before the altar, through the wrath of God.

Saul had mercy on Agag, the king of the Amalekites, and prompted by his invention he spared the best and fattest sheep and oxen to sacrifice unto the Lord, contrary to the word of the prophet. That act of would-be mercy and illustrious zeal was punished as a sin of witchcraft and idolatry because he acted according to his own invention and not according to the word of the prophet. He was reproved by the prophet, smitten with pestilence, and his kingdom was taken from him and given to a more faithful man.

Manasseh, the king of Judah, and others in Israel made their children to pass through fire. They built churches and altars in all the high places, also in cities and countries with good intentions; for they wanted to honor the almighty and eternal God, as may be plainly seen. This glorious and holy choice was so offensive before God that Jeremiah was forbidden to intercede for the people. Israel was desolated, Jerusalem and the temple burnt, and the people with the holy vessels were carried into a foreign land. Therefore, saith God by the prophet, Obey my voice, and I will be your God, and ye shall be my people; walk ye in all the ways that I have commanded you; not those of your own choice; that it may be well with you.

What to do then, my beloved friends, with such willful deceivers who so shamelessly violate the expressed Word of the Lord and so sadly falsify the Almighty and Most High God, teaching that it is the Word of God, even though such things He never thought, much less commanded and never will?

How awful thus to sin against God and so grievously to pervert His holy and precious Word! Yea, they shall be severely punished of the Lord with heavy judgment. They shall not escape the vengeance of His fierce wrath if they do not repent and reform, for God is an enemy of all liars. They have neither part nor lot in His kingdom, but their portion is eternal destruction in the lake of fire.

In the second place, it is evident that infant baptism is become an accursed abomination and idol. For all those who receive it—even though their whole life is so completely pagan, undisciplined, reckless, and nothing but dissipation, drinking, fornication, cursings, swearing, etc.—are called Christians nevertheless, and are accounted under the Lord's grace, merits, death and blood, as though the natural water in baptism could beget them and keep them in Christ. Oh, no! Paul declares, He that hath not the Spirit of Christ, is none of his. Yes, the poor, innocent children, although baptized with the blood of the Lord, and having the sure promise of the kingdom of God, if not baptized with this baptism, must as condemned ones be buried outside the cemetery. What shame and blindness! We will say nothing of godfathers, of making the sign of the cross, of breathing on, of rubbing with salt, anointing with oil, and saliva, too, and the lamentable exorcism, all of which is nothing but open blasphemy and shame, and not commanded of God at all. To what an ugly and horrid idol has this thing grown!

In the third place, we are informed by historians, ancient and modern, and also in the decrees, that baptism and the time of administration was changed. In the beginning of the holy church, persons were baptized in common, unexorcised water upon their first profession, and in view of their own faith according to the Scriptures. Afterwards a change was made; they were examined seven times before being baptized; after that they were baptized at two stated periods, at Easter and Whitsuntide. Hyginus, the tenth pope, instituted godfathers about the year 146.[5] Finally, as Luther tells us, in the year 407, Pope Innocent confirmed infant baptism by a decree. And it is to be feared that it will not be abrogated, save at the expense of much innocent blood of the saints and children of God, even as the prophets in their days reproved the accursed abominations and idolatry of the kings, priests, and the people, not by admonition only, but also with their blood as we read in sacred and profane history.

If now infant baptism had been commanded of God in His Word, why did Innocent add his decree? How can baptism as practiced by the world be right since it has been so frequently changed? We beg you for Jesus' sake to reflect that Christ Jesus, and not the learned ones, is the King and Lord of His church, and rules over it with His scepter, Spirit, and Word. As was said before, He is wisdom itself, and none can instruct Him; He appeared in order that He might testify to the truth. If you are of the truth, then hear His voice, believe His Word, and not that of the learned ones. For His Word is truth. But the word of the learned ones in this matter is seduction, for Christ commands that believers should be baptized and has said not a word of infants that are without understanding. But the learned ones say, he who

---

[5] Modern historians would modify this statement slightly. Hyginus is usually rated as the ninth bishop of Rome. He probably died about A.D. 142. Actually, nothing reliable is known about the man. The first Christian writer to mention baptismal sponsors was Tertullian in his book on Baptism. Tertullian flourished in the early third century, dying sometime after 220. *Ed*

does not have his children baptized, and is himself baptized upon his faith (the thing Christ has commanded) is a fanatic, Anabaptist, and a heretic.

We have given you here the principal reason why we oppose infant baptism not only in doctrine, but also with the sacrifice of our lives and possessions. For we know by the grace of God that there is not one iota in the Scriptures with which they can support it. We tell you the truth and lie not. Is there one under heaven who can attest by divine truth that Jesus Christ, Son of the Almighty God, the Eternal Wisdom and Truth, whom alone we acknowledge as the Lawgiver and Teacher of the New Testament, has in a single letter commanded that children should be baptized, or that His holy apostles taught it or practiced it? If so, there is no further need to force us with tyranny and punishment. Only show us the Word of God, and the matter is settled. For God who is omniscient knows that in our weakness we humbly seek to walk according to the divine ordinances, Word, and will. For this we poor, miserable men are grievously reviled, punished, robbed, and slain in many countries like innocent sheep. But (thanks be to the Lord forever) we are esteemed as unworthy of heaven or earth, even as Christ said: They shall deliver you up to be afflicted and shall kill you, and ye shall be hated of all nations for my name's sake.

And we conclude in this matter, as in all matters of conscience, in view of the wrath of Almighty God, that we must not and may not have our eye on lords and princes, nor on doctors and teachers of schools, nor on the councils of the fathers, and customs of long-standing. For against God's Word, neither emperors nor kings, nor doctors, nor licentiates, nor councils, nor proscriptions matter. We dare not be bound by any person, power, wisdom, or times, but we must be governed by the plainly expressed commands of Christ and the pure doctrines and practices of His holy apostles, as was remarked above. For if we do this, we shall neither deceive in this matter nor be deceived. Woe to him, yes, woe to him, who thrusts from this foundation or is thrust from it, whether through his own flesh, by tyranny, or by false doctrine; and who does not testify to the Word of his Lord before this wicked and sinful generation unto death, both in word and in deed.

Observe, all of you who persecute the Word of the Lord and His people: this is our doctrine, position, and belief concerning baptism according to the instruction of the words of Christ; namely, that we must first hear the Word of God, believe it, and then upon our faith be baptized. Not because we seek sedition and want to fight; not because we want to practice polygamy or expect a kingdom on earth.[6] Oh, no, God be eternally praised, we know very well what the Word of the Lord teaches and implies on this matter. The Word of the Lord commands it. We with a sincere heart desire to die to sin, to bury our sins with Christ, and with Him to rise to a new life, even as baptism signifies. We seek to walk humbly and uprightly in Christ Jesus, in the covenant of His grace, in His eternal peace, and to have a pious and peaceful

6 Menno zealously dissociates himself and his brethren from the Münsterites. *Ed.*

conscience before the Lord, even as the mouth of the Lord has commanded, as His example attests, and as the pure doctrines and practices of the apostles teach and indicate.

## [F.] *Refutation of the Pedobaptist Arguments*[7]

Even as we have briefly set forth the Lord's command, the doctrine and practice of the apostles, and the meaning of baptism, and have shown that it is true baptism and will be that to the end of time, so now by the grace of God we wish as a matter of service to state and refute some of the passages of the learned ones, erroneously drawn by them from Scripture to make void the ordinance of the Lord and place their own in its stead.

[i] In the first place, they teach that we are all the children of wrath and of sinful nature; born of the sinful seed of Adam, and that therefore children must be purified and washed from original sin by baptism.

To this we reply with the Word of the Lord. We also believe and confess that we are all born of unclean seed, that we through the first and earthly Adam became wholly depraved and children of death and of hell: with this understanding, however, that even as we fell and became sinners in Adam, so we also believe and confess that through Christ, the second and heavenly Adam, we are graciously helped to our feet again and justified. To this end He appeared upon earth that in and through Him we might have life. Through Him alone we boast to have obtained grace, favor, and the forgiveness of our sins with God our Father, and not by baptism, whether we are children or believers. For if pardon and the washing away of original sin took place by means of baptism and not actually by the blood of Christ, then the sweet smelling sacrifice which is eternally valid would have been in vain and without power—unless there be two remedies for our sins. But ah, no, the Scriptures speak of but one means, Christ and His merits, death, and blood. Therefore he who seeks the remission of his sins through baptism despises the blood of the Lord and makes water his idol. Therefore let every one be careful lest he ascribe the honor and glory due to Christ to ceremonies performed and to creaturely elements.

It is true that Peter says, Repent and be baptized every one of you in the name of Jesus Christ for the remission of sins. But this is not to be understood to mean that we receive the remission of our sins through baptism. Oh, no, for in such a program Christ and His merits are undone. We receive the remission of our sins in baptism as follows: The Lord commanded His Gospel to be preached to every creature so that all who believe and are baptized may be saved. Wherever there is faith, called the gift of God by Paul, there also are the power and fruits of faith. Wherever there is an active, fruitful faith, there is also the promise. But where such a faith does not exist (we speak of adults), there also is no promise. For whoever hears the Word of

[7] *Dutch:* Here Follow the Objections, and Our Reply to Them.

the Lord and believes it with the heart, manifests it by his fruit and faithfully observes all things the Lord has commanded him. This must be done before the just shall live by faith, as Scriptures teach, and the remission of his sins is announced to him as Peter in this passage teaches and instructs.

If Noah and Lot had not believed the word of the Lord, they would have fared ill. If Abraham had not believed, he would not have obtained such glorious promises. But now have they believed and done the right and are become heirs of righteousness.

If Moses and Israel had not believed the word of the Lord but had been disobedient, how could they have survived the sea and the wilderness? But now have they believed, and according to His promise were helped by the mighty hand of the Lord. But those who provoked Him, and believed not His gracious word and the great miracles, perished in the wilderness and entered not into the promised land.

Atonement was also connected with the sacrifices of the Old Testament. Not because smoking sacrifices have value, for it was not possible, says Paul, that the blood of bulls and goats should take away sin. It was all the Lord's that could be sacrificed, "the cattle upon a thousand hills," as David says. But it was because they believed the Word of divine promise to be true and therefore obeyed His command. So now also is the remission of sins preached in baptism, not on account of the water or the ceremonies performed (for Christ, I repeat, is the only means of grace) but because men receive the promises of the Lord by faith and obediently follow His Word and will.

In this representation infants are not included. For in the Scriptures no command is given to baptize them. Therefore, it is not required of them as a sign of obedience. And since infant baptism is unscriptural, therefore it cannot be a ceremony of God, but a seductive superstition of men and open idolatry; and no promise of God can or may be attached to such abominations. It seems to me it is high time to awaken and to give heed to the Scriptures. To innocent and minor children sin is for Jesus' sake not imputed. Life is promised, not through any ceremony, but of pure grace, through the blood of the Lord, as He Himself says: Suffer the little children to come unto me and forbid them not; for of such is the kingdom of heaven. But concerning baptism He did not command anything.

According to my opinion it is a great error, which some defend, that children of the Jews were pleasing to Christ on account of circumcision and that ours are pleasing to Him on account of baptism. Oh, slander and shame! Everywhere Christ, the only means of divine grace, must yield and things must be ascribed to lifeless rites and elements. I would ask all Pedobaptists how they are going to prove that these children blessed by Jesus were all circumcised, and that there were among them no girls. If they were acceptable on account of their circumcision as is urged, then why were not adults who were circumcised acceptable? Although they were circumcised, He nevertheless commanded that adults should be baptized upon their faith. But concerning infants He gave no such command. He took them in His arms, blessed them, laid His hands upon them, ascribed to them the kingdom, and let them go. But He did not baptize them.

So the very Wisdom of God Himself carried on. But the world would be His superior. Christ does not command that infants should be baptized but believers; but the world commands that we should baptize children and not believers. Yes, more than that, if anyone is baptized upon his faith because the Lord has so commanded, and if for conscience' sake he dares not have his children baptized because God does not command it, such a man must bear a hateful name, and torture, misery, and death besides. This is not so much the fault of the rulers as of those who are esteemed teachers and preachers. For what the rulers do they generally do by the counsel and suggestion of the learned ones.

The fruits show who is their father. They must fill up their father's measure. They have always been such, and methinks will remain so, men who with their false doctrine, vicious counsel, and hard hearts have drunk the blood of the righteous, have executed and killed. It is so disgraceful that it is a shame to mention it. For as the sun shines before all and is seen by everyone, so manifest is the inhuman raving tyranny of the learned ones against the Lamb and His elect. God grant that the eyes of these blind, perverted, bloodthirsty teachers with their tyrants may be opened; that they may tire and weary of their false doctrine and bloodshed. Amen.

[ii] In the second place, they teach that the children of Israel under the Old Testament were incorporated into God's covenant and church through circumcision; but that our children are incorporated through baptism. To this, with Scripture we say, no. Whoever reads the Scriptures understandingly will perceive clearly that Abraham was in the covenant of the Lord many years before he was circumcised; also that the children were circumcised on the eighth day, although they were in the covenant before that. For it is evident that we do not become the children of God through any outward rites, but through the fatherly election of grace through Christ Jesus. But an outward sign was required of Abraham as a matter of obedience and a seal of faith. Likewise of his seed, that they should circumcise the male children on the eighth day, no sooner, no later, and not the female children. If now the covenant depended on the sign and not on the assurance of grace, what would have become of the female children and the males that died uncircumcised in the seven days?

Beloved reader, give heed to the Word of God. Although the women and female children were not circumcised, they had the promise in common in the promised seed, the promised land, the kingdom and glory. They were no less the seed of Abraham and subjects to the covenant of God and under the things signified by the sign thereof than were the circumcised men and male children. From which it is plain that the children of Israel were not in the Lord's covenant on account of circumcision as Pedobaptists assert, but through the election of grace.

And even as Abraham and the children of Israel, the female as well as the male, were in covenant not through the sign but through the election, so also are our children in the covenant of God, even though unbaptized. The word of Paul is secure, He has chosen us in Him before the foundation of the world and has ordained us His children through Jesus Christ.

To repeat, to children the kingdom of heaven belongs, and they are under the promise of the grace of God through Christ, as has been said, and therefore we truly believe that they are saved, holy and pure, and pleasing to God, under the covenant and in His church, but by no means through an external sign. There is verily not a word in all the Scriptures whereby to maintain that children should be incorporated into the covenant and the church by such a sign. Besides it is very evident that they cannot be taught or admonished by word or sacrament as long as they are without the ability to hear and to understand.

The signs are to be used for no other purpose than that by which they were instituted and commanded of the Lord. Since Christ has ordained and commanded to baptize believers and did not utter a syllable about infant baptism, we therefore believe and teach that believer's baptism is of God and His Word, and infant baptism of the dragon and the beast [Rev. 12, 13].

All the rites ordained by God, both of the Old and New Testament, are ordained to exercise our faith and to show our obedience. Therefore we should not use and change them at our pleasure, but we should use them as the Lord Himself has ordained and commanded if we would escape being punished by the fierce wrath of God as were Nadab and Abihu.

Since Christ has commanded that believers should be baptized and not infants, and the holy apostles have taught and used it thus in accordance with the instructions of Christ, as may be seen in many places of the New Testament, therefore all reasonable-minded men must admit that infant baptism, although alas practiced by nearly the whole world and maintained by tyranny, is nothing but a ceremony of Antichrist, open blasphemy, a bewitching sin, a molten calf; yes, abomination and idolatry.

I know very well how they apply circumcision as a figure of baptism and adduce the saying of Paul in proof thereof, saying, In whom also ye are circumcised with the circumcision made without hands, etc. He that attempts to justify infant baptism with this passage does violence to the holy Paul, and perverts his testimony. For he does not teach that external circumcision is a figure of baptism, but of inward circumcision. For even as actual circumcision is performed with a knife of stone, so also must our native Adam's nature be cut off with that spiritual knife of stone and circumcised with the circumcision made without hands. The stone is Christ. The knife is the Word of God. It is with this circumcision that believers, not children, are circumcised, as Paul evidently teaches by this Scripture: Ye are circumcised with the circumcision made without hands, in putting off the body of the sins of the flesh by the circumcision of Christ, buried with him in baptism, wherein also ye are risen with him through faith of the operation of God. It appears to me that these words show plainly that Paul used them not of baptism of infants, but of the inner circumcision of believers. Read also what we said above, in connection with Romans 6.

[iii] In the third place, they say that in baptism children are regenerated, put on Christ, and receive the Holy Ghost. To this we reply: To be regenerated, to put on Christ, and to receive the Holy Ghost, is one and the same thing, and according to their power not different. Do you have the one? Then you have the other also. But that does not at all concern infants, for regeneration as well as faith takes place through the Word of God and is a change of heart, or of the inward man, as was said above. To put on Christ is to be transplanted into Christ and to be like-minded with Him. To receive the Holy Ghost is to be a partaker of His gifts and power, to be taught, assured, and influenced by Him, as the Scriptures teach. These cannot occur in infants, for they have no ears to hear the Word of the Lord, and no understanding to comprehend it. For through the Word and the hearing all must follow.

Perhaps it may be asked whether God is not able to work faith in children, because John the Baptist, as yet unborn, leaped for joy in his mother's womb. We reply to this that we are not speaking of the power of God; He made aged and barren Sarah fruitful and caused Balaam's ass to speak. From this it does not follow that all old, barren women will become fruitful and that all asses will speak. He does not at all times do all that He could or might do. We speak only of the precept of the Scriptures, what it has taught and commanded us in this matter.

Since infants do not have the ability to hear, they cannot believe, and because they do not believe, they cannot be born again. Reason teaches us that they cannot understand the Word of God. That they do not believe and are not regenerated is evident from their action. Whether they are baptized or not, the nature in which they are born is prone to evil from their youth. They know no difference between Christ and Satan; between good and evil; between life and death. Whereby then shall we know their faith, regeneration, Christ and Spirit? The regenerating Word must first be heard and believed with a sincere heart before regeneration, the putting on of Christ, and the impulsion of the Holy Ghost can follow.

Behold, this the Word of the Lord teaches. Therefore, he that does not desire the palatable bread of the divine Word on which our souls have to live may satisfy himself with the husks that the swine eat. We cannot prevent it. I hope that the gracious Father may protect and preserve us forever through His great mercy from their anti-Christian doctrines and Pharisaical leaven.

[iv] In the fourth place, they say that although infants are not in baptism washed from original sin to such an extent that it is no more, yet because of baptism it will not be counted to them as sin. To this we reply: So to teach and believe is open blasphemy against Christ and His blood. I have proved

more than once by the Word of the Lord that Christ is the only remedy for our sins and that there is none other forever. If men will not believe the Word of God, neither I nor any other man can help them. But the way or manner in which believer's baptism is associated with the remission of sins is fully explained above, and he that reads it understandingly will give the Lord Jesus the praise due Him and will not ascribe the remission of his sins to rites and elements.

[v] In the fifth place, they say that Christ has cleansed and sanctified His church with the washing of water by the Word. Children, they say, belong to the church; therefore they must be cleansed with the washing of the water by the Word. To this we reply: Paul does not speak of infants but of those who hear and believe the Word of the Lord, and so by faith are sanctified and cleansed in their hearts, for they are cleansed by the washing of water, as the mouth of the Lord has commanded.

Since infants do not have this cleansing, sanctifying faith, nor the means thereto (that is, understanding) and are not commanded in Scripture to be baptized, how then can they be cleansed with the washing of water by the Word, seeing they have no faith in the Word and no washing of water by the Word? Therefore, all Pedobaptists should know that their infant baptism does not only not cleanse and sanctify, but that it is altogether idolatry, without promise, pernicious, and contrary to the Word of the Lord.

We have proved before that the remission of sins or reconciliation was attached to the Jewish sacrifices if performed according to the instructions of Moses. But when they did not perform them in that way, they did not effect reconciliation thereby, but made themselves the more guilty, as was the case with Saul, Uzziah, Nadab, Abihu, and others. In like manner is the church sanctified and cleansed with the washing of water by the Word, if it is done in every respect according to the instructions of the Word. Otherwise, not cleansing but sinning takes place.

And although infants have neither faith nor baptism, think not that they are therefore damned. Oh, no! they are saved; for they have the Lord's own promise of the kingdom of God; not through any elements, ceremonies, and external rites, but solely by grace through Christ Jesus. And therefore we do truly believe that they are in a state of grace, pleasing to God, pure, holy, heirs of God and of eternal life. Yes, on account of this promise all sincere Christian believers may assuredly rejoice and comfort themselves in the salvation of their children.

[vi] In the sixth place, they say that infants are to be baptized on account of the promise related above, although Christ did not baptize the children brought to Him, nor had them baptized. But this they say, that He after His death had this taught and practiced.

To this we reply: This rejoiner is false and without Scriptural warrant and cannot be supported by a single letter in the Scriptures. We rejoice with all our hearts that children have this promise, but that they should on that account be baptized the Scriptures do not teach; and that they were not baptized before Christ's death gives us greater assurance still, and that for this reason. We know for certain that He did not teach with another Word, another doctrine, another baptism, another Spirit, or another promise after His death than He did before it. That He commanded His holy apostles after His death and ascension to teach and practice infant baptism can never be proved by the Word of the Lord.

O human flesh, thou art not ashamed to lay lies upon the Lord Christ and His apostles, and to practice your infant baptism under the semblance of the divine Word as if the Lord had taught it, although He never thought of it. How much you have become like those who say, The Lord saith it; albeit, I have not spoken. Ezek. 13:7.

As often as we are asked why infants are not to be baptized since they are in the church of God, in grace, in covenant, in promise, we answer, Because the Lord neither taught nor commanded it.

[vii] In the seventh place, they say, The Scriptures indicate that the apostles baptized whole families from which we may readily conclude that there were infants among them.

To this we reply first of all: Since they endeavor to justify their position with conjecture, they acknowledge thereby that they have no Scriptural authority for this doctrine.

In the second place, we answer: In things of such importance, we dare not build upon uncertain conjecture but upon the sure Word which is a lamp to our feet and a light to our path.

In the third place, we answer: Four families are mentioned in the Scriptures as having been baptized: namely, that of Cornelius, of the jailer, of Lydia the seller of purple, and of Stephanas. The Scriptures plainly show that three of these were all believers; namely, the family of Cornelius, the jailer, and that of Stephanas. But touching the family of the seller of purple, although the Scriptures say nothing definitely concerning it, the reader should know that it is not usual in Scripture nor the common custom of the world to call the family by the woman's name so long as the husband is living. Since then Luke calls the family by the name of the woman, reason teaches us that Lydia was at that time either a widow or an unmarried woman. As to how rigidly one may press the assertion that there were children in her home, we shall let the pious reader judge.

In the fourth place, we answer: The word *household* or *houses* does not include the minor children as mentioned in the Scriptures, for Paul speaks of vain talkers who subvert whole houses. Now it is incontrovertible that an infant can not be subverted by false doctrine. Therefore by the word *house* or *houses*, no others can be understood than those who have ears to hear and hearts to understand.

[viii] in the last place, they appeal to Origen[8] and Augustine[9] and say that these assert that they have received infant baptism from the apostles.

To this we answer asking, Have Origen and Augustine proved this from the Scriptures? If they have, we would like to hear it, and if not, then we must hear and believe Christ and His apostles, and not Augustine and Origen.

That this is not the case may readily be seen from Cyprian because he left infant baptism optional, if those who for many years past have been preachers at Nördlingen have rightly informed me in their church records and have not deceived me in regard to the word liberum (free or optional).

Cyprian[10] also was a Greek as well as Origen and lived twenty-five years after him. If then infant baptism was the doctrine of the apostles and practiced by them as Origen and Augustine assert, it must first be proved by the Scriptures, and in that case Cyprian must have committed a great sin to make doctrines and practices of the apostles optional. For anything that is apostolic may not be changed by any man. The word of Paul is indisputable: Though we or an angel from heaven, preach any other gospel unto you than that which we have preached, let him be accursed. Otherwise we will be forced to say that the twelve apostles with their doctrine were not the twelve foundations and twelve gates of the new Jerusalem. Rev. 21:12.

If infant baptism is apostolic, why does Tertullian[11] write and say, "They who present themselves for baptism, confess for a considerable time before the church and before the bishop that they renounce the devil, his pomp and the angels, after that they are . . ."?

Rhenanus[12] annotates on this passage and says: It was the custom of the fathers that adults, that is, grown persons, were baptized by the washing of regeneration.

That infant baptism was not apostolic may be distinctly seen from the passage in Rufinus' translation of Eusebius' *Church History*,[13] volume 10, chapter 14.

Remember also how the early writers contended about infant baptism? If it had been apostolic and drawn from the Gospel, why should they have debated about it?

---

[8] Origen (*c.* 185-*c.* 254), church father of Alexandria, Egypt.

[9] Augustine (354-430), bishop and influential Christian writer of North Africa.

[10] Cyprian, bishop of Carthage, North Africa, beheaded in A.D. 258.

[11] Tertullian (*c.* 160-*c.* 230) was an older Christian leader than Origen or Cyprian. *Ed.*

[12] Beatus Rhenanus (1485-1547) was a Humanist scholar of Alsace, a friend of Erasmus.

[13] Eusebius of Caesarea (*c.* 260-*c.* 340) has been called the father of church history. His ten books on church history cover the period to A.D. 324. Menno is here quoting from the Latin translation of Eusebius Greek *Church History*, made by Tyrannius Rufinus (d. 410). The Mennonite Historical Library, Goshen, Ind., has a 1545 German edition of Eusebius' *Church History* containing the Rufinus supplement here quoted by Menno. It relates to the concern of Bishop Athanasius that catechumens be properly instructed in the faith prior to baptism. *Ed.*

Read also Erasmus of Rotterdam[14] in his *Sua Concilion*, Franck's[15] *Chronicle*, Ulrich Zwingli[16] in his book of *Articles*, Martin Cellarius,[17] *De Immensis Operi Dei*, and you will find that infant baptism was not the doctrine and practice of the apostles.

You see, dear reader, I admonish and advise you if you seek God with all your heart, and do not want to be deceived, do not depend upon men and the doctrine of men no matter how venerable, holy, and excellent they may be esteemed. For the experts, ancient as well as modern, are opposed to each other. Put your trust in Christ alone and in His Word, and in the sure instruction and practice of His holy apostles, and by the grace of God you will be safe from all false doctrine and the power of the devil, and will walk with a free and pious mind before God.

## [G.] *An Admonition to the Pedobaptists*[18]

We are aware, dear reader, that there are many mere talkers who acknowledge from the letter of the Scripture that only believers should be baptized, but nevertheless say: Dear me, what good can water do? Anyway, we have been baptized in the name of God, and if we now have the new life, all is well. And so, dear Lord, Thy noble precious Word is everywhere by this reckless world treated as if it were one of Aesop's fables, as if Almighty Majesty, the Eternal Wisdom and Truth, had taught and commanded something to no purpose.

No, my dear reader, no! His name is the sovereign Lord; His Word is His will; His command is eternal life. All things which He has taught and commanded us, He wants us doubtless to obey. If we don't, woe to us. Christ says, Ye are my friends if ye do whatsoever I command you. My counsel, says the prophet, shall stand, and I will do all my pleasure. Therefore, O creature, cease from replying against God. Give ear to Him and obey His voice, for it is His divine counsel, Word, and will. Who are you, that you should sit in judgment with God? Christ's sheep hear His voice. True Christians believe and do. If you are a genuine Christian born of God, then why do you draw back from baptism, which is the least that God has com-

---

[14] Erasmus of Rotterdam, originally Geert Geerts, died 1536, was a Dutch Humanist. He helped prepare the way for the Protestant Reformation of the sixteenth century but ultimately remained with the Catholic Church.

[15] Sebastian Franck (*c.* 1499-1543) was a noteworthy historian in Menno's day, but also a man who put all his stress on the inner realities of Christianity and rejected all church ordinances, etc.

[16] Ulrich Zwingli (1484-1531) was the leading reformer of Zurich, Switzerland, and the man who led Conrad Grebel, the founder of the Swiss Brethren, to an evangelical faith. Menno probably refers to Zwingli's *Uslegen und Gründ der Schlussreden oder Artikel,* 1523.

[17] Martin Cellarius, originally Borrhaus (1497-1564), was a friend of Luther's colleague Melanchthon. He was successively Catholic, Lutheran, and individualist. *Ed.*

[18] The Dutch title reads: *An Admonition to Those Who Despise the Word as it Speaks of Baptism. Ed.*

manded you? It is a weighty and important command to love your enemy, is it not; to do good to those that hate you, to pray in spirit and in truth for those who persecute you; to crucify your wicked and ungodly flesh with its impure lusts and desires; to tear from mouth, heart, and flesh your pretentious pride, your grasping greed, your foul immorality, your bloody hatred, your gluttonous eating and drinking, your accursed idolatry, your jealous slandering, your reckless, hurtful tongue; and to love and fear with all your heart your Lord and God, your Redeemer and Creator, and in all things to govern yourself by His holy will; to serve your neighbor in sincere and unfeigned love with all your powers, with possessions, houses and lands, with your advice, with the fruit of your toil and travail, with your blood if need be; with a sincere heart to suffer misery, disdain, and the oppressive cross of Christ for the Lord's Word, and to confess Christ Jesus before lords and princes, in prison and bonds, by words and deeds unto death.

It seems to me that these and the like commands are more painful and difficult for perverse flesh, naturally so prone to follow its own way everywhere, than to be the recipient of a handful of water.[19] And a sincere Christian must be ready to do all this, must he not? If not, he is not born of God, for the regenerated are one mind with Christ Jesus. All who by the grace of God have been transplanted from Adam into Christ, have become partakers of the divine nature, and are baptized of God with the spirit and fire of heavenly love, will not contend so disrespectfully with the Lord saying, Dear me, what good can water do? But with trembling Paul they will say, Lord, what wilt thou have me to do? And with the penitents on the day of Pentecost, Men and brethren, what shall we do? They have humbled their own wisdom and are ready to obey the Word of the Lord, for they are driven by His Spirit, and through faith with willing, obedient hearts they begin to do all things commanded them of the Lord.

But as long as their minds are not renewed, and they are not of the same mind with Christ; are not washed in the inner man with clean water from the living fountain of God, they may well say, What good can water do? For as long as they are earthly and sensually minded, the whole ocean is not enough to cleanse them.

Faithful reader, do not imagine that we put great stress on elements and rites. I tell you the truth in Christ and lie not. If anyone were to come to me, even the emperor or the king, desiring to be baptized, but walking still in the unclean, ungodly lusts of the flesh, and the unblamable, penitent, and regenerated life were not in evidence, by the grace of God, I would rather die than baptize such an impenitent, carnal person. For where there is no renewing, regenerating faith, leading to obedience, there is no baptism. Even as

---

[19] All the evangelical Anabaptists practiced baptism by affusion: the Swiss Brethren founded by Conrad Grebel, 1525, the Austrian Hutterites founded by Jacob Wiedemann in 1528, and the Dutch Obbenites founded by Obbe Philips in 1534. *Ed.*

Philip said to the eunuch, If thou believest with all thy heart, it may take place.[20] But know this that should the candidate for baptism come with a hypocritical heart, with feigned faith, his hypocrisy would not be counted to the baptizer as sin, but to the dissembler, for no man knows the heart of man save the spirit of man which is in him.

It verily appears to me that you may get the point that we desire no other water than that which the Word of the Lord has commanded. For since we believe that Christ is the true Messiah to whom the law and the prophets point, whom all the righteous fathers and patriarchs desired, that He came from heaven and gave witness to the truth and that His command is eternal life, we must hear His voice and obey His Word. If we do not, we show plainly that we do not believe, but that we reject His counsel and Word, and are ungrateful toward Him for His love.

I know very well that many of you will say, We were baptized once in the name of God, and that suffices. To this we reply: If only you feared God with all your heart, and acknowledged that His Word and ordinances are just and good, you yourselves would need to conclude that you are not baptized in the name of God, but contrary to it. It is true that the adorable, exalted name of God was pronounced over you, but not otherwise than over bells, churches, altars, holy water, tapers, and palms. All anti-Christian idolatry and abominations, alas, are performed under cover of the divine name; nevertheless they are not done in the power of His name but against it, for they are done contrary to His Word and will.

My dear reader, ponder these words and judge them by the Word of God, and you will find that the baptism which you have received is without the command of God's Word; that it crept in through invented self-righteousness, was proposed by man, and therefore must be accursed of God, who wants to reign and rule alone in His church. If now you want to rejoice in the promise and be a comrade in the church of Christ, you must believe the Word of the Lord and obey His counsel, will, and ordinances. But if you despise these and follow your own counsel and will, and not the Lord's, then you cannot comfort yourself with any Scriptural promise; for he that believeth not, says Christ, is condemned already.

Therefore, comfort yourselves no longer with such vain comfort, saying, We have been baptized once. For your heart is still entirely unbelieving, yes, rebellious and unclean. Your whole life is earthly and carnal, your baptism anti-Christian, outside the Word of God. Therefore arouse yourselves, repent; believe Christ; seek, fear, and love God with all your hearts; then the Word of the Lord and His unction will teach you what is most profitable for you to do or not to do in this matter. And do not say as some do, I will renounce the church and idolatry; I will serve my neighbor, etc.; but I do not wish to be baptized.

O you blind men! Do you think that the Lord is pleased with your

20 Dutch translation. *Tr*.

nonattendance at the [state] church, or with your alms, or any such thing, if you reject His counsel and Word? Oh, no, He desires obedience and not sacrifice. He desires the whole heart, the entire man. With Him neither church nor alms matter ultimately; neither words nor deeds, as long as you do not manifest a new heart and life. For in Christ Jesus, says Paul, neither circumcision availeth anything, nor uncircumcision, but faith which worketh by love, a new creature, and the keeping of the commandments of God.

And whosoever is renewed in Christ and born of God, he liveth no more as Paul says, but Christ Jesus liveth in him. In all his ways he conforms to the Word of the Lord, for that powerful, active faith constrains him to all obedience and to every good work. But where this new life is not found, there fair words do verily occur, but actually only unbelief is there, disobedience, self-will, presumption, and perversity.

Herewith I intreat and admonish you, beloved reader, not to be so contrary against the Lord, saying, What good can water do? Reflect that Christ Jesus Himself was baptized, although He was without sin, neither was guile found in His mouth; yes, He who was Himself the righteousness, the way, the truth, and the life. Tell me, what good could water do Christ who was all in all? The disciples also at Ephesus were rebaptized by Paul because they knew nothing of the Holy Ghost although they had been baptized with the baptism of John. If Christ who was without sin had Himself baptized, and others who had been baptized with the baptism of John, which verily was from heaven, were rebaptized by Paul, why do you despise the Lord's baptism, you who are poor miserable sinners, who were baptized without knowledge and faith with the baptism of the dragon and the beast?

Cyprian the martyr with his entire council in Africa resolved that they who had been baptized by heretics should be rebaptized with the baptism of Christ, and for the reason that they judged that the baptism of heretics could not be the baptism of Christ. Reflect a little, kind reader, who they were that baptized you; by whom they were sent; what kind of faith they had; what kind of lives they led; with what doctrine and ritual you were baptized. If you would seriously ponder this, I could hope by the grace of God, if you desire true peace and liberty of conscience, you would soon discover that you have never known either the external or internal baptism, much less received them.

Behold, beloved reader, here you have the true position and Scriptural exposition of the baptism of Christ and an explanation of the baptism of Antichrist. Pray the Lord, the Most High, for a sound and clear understanding, that you may sincerely know the right and blessed truth, may believe and in the fear of the Lord faithfully perform it. Cease from all vain disputation and opposition, for whosoever disputes and opposes, so that he may continue without trouble, brings ruin to his soul and will never walk with a good and sure conscience before his God, and will always find occasion to dispute and wrangle.

Therefore search God's Word, believe and obey with a sincere and devout heart, be not deceived by the appearance of godliness, by fair speeches, and you will doubtlessly get for yourself a sure doctrine of blessed truth and the consoling promise of grace. The Lord Jesus Christ grant you His grace. Amen.

## [II. REFUTATION OF ROMAN CATHOLICISM]

### [A.] The Lord's Supper[21]

You know, dear sirs, friends, and brethren, that everywhere they write, preach, and boast much concerning the Lord's Supper. But with what confession, with what faith, love, peace, unity, usage, and ordinance is it evident? It is true the mouth of the Lord has ordained a breaking of bread or communion in the New Testament, but not in the manner in which you celebrate it. Your Lord's Supper admits all, no matter who or what: the avaricious, the proud, the ostentatious, the drunkards, the hateful, the idolatrous ones, those who frequent houses of ill fame, yes, harlots and scamps. Evidently it is celebrated moreover with offensive pomp and splendor, with hypocrisy and idolatry. And besides, it is dispensed by ministers who really seek nothing but worldly honor, ease, and the belly.

Many of you are much concerned about the Lord's Supper but not according to the Scripture, as you shall hear. For your table may more properly be called the table of the devil than the table of the Lord. Therefore, I ask you for Jesus' sake, in the true fear of God, to reflect with whom, why, and to what end the Lord instituted, ordained, and left this His last Supper to His church. It is so that it may become to you a living and impressive sign, that it might represent and signify the Lord's great and abundant kindness, the heartfelt peace, the love and union of His church, the communion of His flesh and blood; so that you may die to wickedness and pursue righteousness and godliness, fly from the devil's table and sit down at the Lord's table in the church of Christ, with true faith, a pious, penitent, and regenerated life, and with unfeigned, brotherly love.

Thus saith Paul, I have received of the Lord that which I also delivered unto you, that the Lord Jesus the same night in which he was betrayed, took bread; and when he had given thanks, he brake it and said, Take, eat; this is my body, which is broken for you; this do in remembrance of me. After the same manner he took the cup, when he had supped, saying, This cup is the New Testament in my blood; this do ye, as oft as ye drink it, in remembrance of me.

Here you have Paul's explanation of the words of the Holy Supper, instituted by Jesus Christ, concerning which words the learned ones have indeed disputed much; and alas some of them through their idolatrous misconception (to call it that, and not pride) have put much innocent blood to

21 The original title was, Of the Holy Supper of the Lord.

death, so that what the holy Paul says concerning them is fulfilled: Professing themselves to be wise, they became fools. For they disputed mostly about the sign which matters little, but the thing signified for which the sign was instituted, which matters much, they missed. They also pay little attention, it seems to me, as to what kind of guests or communicants they should be who sit with Christ at His table to partake of this holy sacrament[22] with Him.

With not so much as a word are we commanded in Scriptures to dispute concerning the visible and tangible sign, what it really is. The spiritual judge all things spiritually. For of what substance it is, can be felt and seen and tasted. But this we should consider first of all, that we in our weakness must attain, and as much as possible conform ourselves, to the thing signified, to that which is set forth, represented, and taught all true believers by this sign.

On this account we will not burden the good and pious reader with quarrelsome, fruitless disputing concerning the outward sign, as do the learned ones, but we desire by the help and grace of the Lord, by the power of the divine Word, merely to point out correctly for whom and why Christ Jesus left and ordained this Supper, lest we honor the visible sign above the reality and leave the truth for images.

To come to a proper, profitable, and Christian understanding of the holy Lord's Supper, what it is, for whom it was given, why and wherefore, four things in particular should be observed and considered carefully.

[i] In the first place, we must beware not to make the visible, perishable bread and wine the Lord's actual flesh and blood as some do. To believe this is contrary to nature, reason, and Scripture; an open blasphemy of the Son of God; abomination, and idolatry. Israel had to keep the passover annually at the appointed time, according to the commandment of Moses, as a memorial to the fact that the Almighty God, the God of Abraham, of Isaac and Jacob preserved His people from the punishments and plagues when He slew the first-born of the Egyptians, and by His strong hand and outstretched arm so gloriously and wonderfully led them out and redeemed them from the iron furnace of Egypt and the terrible tyranny and power of Pharaoh, according to the word of His promise. Hence the paschal lamb was called the Lord's *pesach,* that is, passover. The sign stood for the reality, for the lamb was not the passover, although it was called that, but it only signified the passover, as was said. So in the Holy Supper the bread is called the body, and the wine the blood of the Lord: the sign signifies the reality. Not that it actually is the flesh and blood of Christ, for with that He ascended into heaven and sitteth at the right hand of His Father, immortal and unchangeable, in eternal majesty and glory; but it is an admonishing sign and memorial to the fact that Christ Jesus the Son of God has delivered us from the power of the devil, from the dominion of hell and eternal death, by the sinless sacrifice of

---

[22] Although Menno rejected the sacramental theory of the Roman Catholic Church, he did not hesitate to use the term "sacrament" in reference to the Lord's Supper. In this he was followed by many other Anabaptist authors. *Ed.*

His innocent flesh and blood, and has led us triumphantly into the kingdom
of His grace, as He Himself says: This do in remembrance of me.

[ii] In the second place, it is to be observed that there is no greater proof
of love than to die for another as Christ says, Greater love hath no man than
this, that a man lay down his life for his friends. Since this holy sign is only
a memorial of the Lord's death, and since death is the greatest proof of love,
as said, we are therefore admonished, when we are at the Lord's table, to
eat His bread and to drink His cup not only earnestly to show forth and
remember His death, but also to remember all the glorious fruits of divine
love manifested toward us in Christ. God in the beginning made man after
His image, incorruptible, placed him in Paradise, and subjected all creatures
to him. Then when he had been beguiled by the serpent, he was gladdened
and comforted at the thought of the coming Conqueror and Saviour Christ.
God sent Moses and the prophets who zealously urged the law and pointed to
the promised Christ and His kingdom. Christ Jesus according to the promise
of the Scripture finally appeared in this world a true man, born of the Virgin
Mary, and in much misery, affliction, and labor, preached the saving and
gracious Word to the house of Israel, that He sought the lost sheep and
brought them to their true shepherd, and by His bitter death and precious
blood, in love reconciled us unto His heavenly Father. As He Himself says,
For God so loved the world, that he gave his only begotten Son, that whosoever believeth in him, should not perish, but have everlasting life.

Oh, wonderful love of God, unsearchable and past finding out! He did
not send into this sad and sorrowful world an angel, a patriarch, or a prophet,
but His eternal Almighty Word, His Eternal Wisdom, the brightness of
His glory, in the form of sinful flesh. He made him to be sin for us, who
knew no sin; that we might be made the righteousness of God in him. II
Cor. 5:21.

My good reader, do not construe this to mean that there was sin in
Christ. God forbid. The Scripture clears Him of all sin. He was the spotless
lamb. He knew no sin, neither was guile found in His mouth. But Paul
calls Him sin in the Hebrew idiom, that is, a sacrifice for sin. As the
prophet says: He was wounded for our transgressions, he was bruised for
our iniquities; the chastisement of our peace was upon him; and with his
stripes we were healed. He gave His life as a sacrifice for sin.

Behold, worthy reader, all those who sincerely believe in this glorious
love of God, this abundant, great blessing of grace in Christ Jesus, manifested
toward us, are progressively renewed through such faith; their hearts are
flooded with joy and peace; they break forth with joyful hearts in all manner of thanksgiving; they praise and glorify God with all their hearts because
they with a certainty of mind have grasped it in the Spirit, have believed
and known that the Father loved us so that He gave us poor, wretched
sinners His own and eternal Son with all His merits as a gift, and eternal
salvation. As Paul says, The grace and love of God, our Saviour, appeared,

not on account of the works of righteousness which we have done, but according to his mercy he saved us by the washing of regeneration and the renewing of the Holy Ghost which he shed on us abundantly through Jesus Christ our Saviour, that being justified by his grace, we should be made heirs according to the hope of eternal life. Titus 3:7.

Here it is proper to recall how the righteous died for the unrighteous, when we were yet sinners and enemies; how the spotless Lamb in the fire of affliction on the tree of the cross was sacrificed for us as an eternal propitiation for us. The Creator of all, through whom all things were made, was completely broken for our sakes. He who was above all the children of men became the most unworthy of all and was counted with evildoers. The innocent One bore the burden of the whole world, blotted out and made atonement with His crimson blood for the guilt of all, as the Scriptures declare, I restored that which I had not taken. In a word we should recall how that Jesus Christ through His obedience undid the disobedience of Adam and all his seed and by His painful death restored life.

The holy Paul acknowledges this great and glorious work of divine love, crying out, Who shall separate us from the love of Christ? shall tribulation, or distress, or persecution, or famine, or nakedness, or peril, or sword? As it is written, For thy sake we are killed all the day long; we are accounted as sheep for the slaughter. Nay, in all these things we are more than conquerors through him that loved us. For I am persuaded, that neither death, nor life, nor angels, nor principalities, nor powers, nor things present, nor things to come, nor height, nor depth, nor any other creature, shall be able to separate us from the love of God which is in Christ Jesus our Lord.

And this is what John says, Let us love Him, for He first loved us. Nature teaches us to love those who love us. And this is the first fruit of the holy sacrament, if rightly participated in.

[iii] In the third place, we have to observe that by the Lord's Supper Christian unity, love, and peace are signified and enjoined, after which all true Christians should seek and strive. For we being many, says Paul, are one bread, and one body; for we are all partakers of that one bread.

Just as natural bread is made of many grains, pulverized by the mill, kneaded with water, and baked by the heat of the fire, so is the church of Christ made up of true believers, broken in their hearts with the mill of the divine Word, baptized with the water of the Holy Ghost, and with the fire of pure, unfeigned love made into one body. Just as there is harmony and peace in the body and all its members, and just as each member naturally performs its function to promote the benefit of the whole body, so it also becomes the true and living members of the body of Christ to be one: one heart, one mind, and one soul. Not contentious, not spiteful and envious, not cruel and hateful, not quarrelsome and disputatious one toward another like the ambitious, covetous, and the proud of this world. But in all things, one toward another, long-suffering, friendly, peaceable, ever ready in true Christian love to serve one's neighbor in all things possible: by exhortation, by reproof, by comforting, by assisting, by counseling, with deed and with possessions, yes, with bitter and hard labor, with body and life, ready to forgive one another as Christ forgives and serves us with His Word, life, and death. As Paul says, Put on therefore, as the elect of God, holy and beloved, bowels of mercy, kindness, humbleness of mind, meekness, longsuffering; forbearing one another and forgiving one another, if any man have a quarrel against any, even as Christ forgave you, so also do ye. And above all things put on charity, which is the bond of perfectness. And let the peace of God rule in your hearts, to the which also ye are called in one body; and be ye thankful.

Likewise, even as in the natural body the more honorable members such as the eye, the ear, and the mouth do not reproach the less honorable members on account of their inferiority; and even as the inferior members do not envy the superior members for their nobility, but every member in its place is peaceable and serves the whole body, be its own functions high or low; so it is also in the church of the Lord. Paul says, Some he appointed apostles; some prophets; some evangelists; some pastors and teachers. Let everyone be mindful that he boast not of what he is, has, or possesses, for it is all the grace and gift of God. Let everyone attend to his duty, for the perfecting of the saints, for the work of the ministry, for the edifying of the body of Christ; till we all come in the unity of the faith, and of the knowledge of the Son of God, unto a perfect man, unto the measure of the stature of the fullness of Christ. This is also set forth in the Holy Supper, but how the world calling itself Christian lives up to this is shown by its fruits and action.

[iv] In the fourth place, we have to observe that the Holy Supper is the communion of the body and blood of Christ. As Paul says: The cup of blessing which we bless, is it not the communion of the blood of Christ? The bread which we break, is it not the communion of the body of Christ? I Cor. 10:16.

Since then it is a communion, as has been said, we should fraternally exhort all of you earnestly to examine yourselves whether you have been made partakers of Christ: whether indeed you are flesh of His flesh and bone of His bone; whether you are in Christ and Christ is in you. For all who eat of this bread and drink of this cup worthily must be changed in the inner man, and converted and renewed in their minds through the power of the divine Word. By faith they must become new creatures, born of God, and transplanted from Adam into Christ; they must be of a Christian disposition, sympathetic, peaceable, merciful, affectionate, of a humble heart, obedient to the Word of the Lord. The proud, ambitious, selfish, and carnal heart must be circumcised; the evil eye must be plucked out; the ear that delights to hear evil must be closed; the unprofitable, backsliding tongue must be tamed; the unclean, bloody hand must be cleansed; the impure, greedy flesh must be restrained. They must battle against the world, the flesh, and the devil. Their loins must be girt about with truth; they must have on the breastplate of righteousness; their feet must be shod with the preparation of the gospel of peace. They must be armed with the shield of faith; with the helmet of salvation, and the Sword of the Spirit. They must be led by the Spirit of God to be sincere Christians, and endeavor with all their powers in their weakness to be like-minded with Christ.

When He instituted and celebrated the Holy Supper with His beloved disciples Christ said, With desire I have desired to eat this passover with you before I suffer. Then he took the bread and brake it, and said, Take, eat; this is my body which is broken for you. Likewise also the wine: This cup is the New Testament in my blood, etc.; this do in remembrance of me. It was as if He wanted to say: Behold, dear children, so far has that love which I have had for you and the whole human race constrained me, and ever shall, that I left the glory of my Father, and came into this sad world as a poor slave to serve you. For I saw that you all belonged to the devil, and that there was none to redeem you; that you had all gone astray like erring sheep, and there was none who cared for you; that you were a prey to devouring wolves, and there was none to save you; that you were wounded unto death, and there was none that could heal you. Therefore did I come from heaven, and became a poor, weak, and dying man, in all things like unto you, sin excepted. In my great love I sought you out with zeal, found you miserable, sorrowful, yes, half dead. The services of my love I have demonstrated so heartily toward you; your sores I bandaged; your blood I wiped away; wine and oil I have poured into your putrid wounds; set you free from the jaws of the hellish beasts; I took you upon my shoulders and led you into the tabernacles of peace. Your nakedness I covered; I had compassion on your misery; the law I have fulfilled for you; your sins I took away. The peace, grace, and favor of my Father I proclaimed to you; His good will I revealed; the way of truth I pointed out; and I have powerfully testified to you by my marvelous signs and great miracles that I am the true Messiah, the promised Prince and Saviour.

Behold, beloved children, until now have I walked with you, with my Father's Word have admonished, reproved, and kept in His name; but now my hour is at hand; this night I shall be betrayed. All that the prophets said of me has been fulfilled. Since I can serve you no longer with my doctrine and life, I will at the end serve you with my painful sufferings, body, blood, cross, and death.

And this is the very reason why I called you to this Supper, so that I might ordain this usage among you so that you might occasionally come together after my death and commemorate the gracious favors of my fervent love so abundantly manifested toward you, and in particular that I loved you so dearly that I sacrificed my body and shed my blood for you. Greater love hath no man than this that a man lay down his life for his friends. I have obtained everlasting reconciliation, grace, mercy, favor, and peace with my Father as I told you, namely, even as the Son of man came not to be ministered unto but to minister, and to give his life a ransom for many.

Dear reader, consider the Word of the Lord and this institution. For wherever this Holy Supper is celebrated with such faith, love, attentiveness, peace, unity of heart and mind, there Jesus Christ is present with His grace, Spirit, and promise, and with the merits of His sufferings, misery, flesh, blood, cross, and death even as He Himself says: Where two or three are gathered together in my name, there am I in the midst of them. But where the true knowledge of Christ, active faith, new life, Christian love, peace, and unity do not exist, there is not the Lord's Supper, but a despising and mocking of the blood and death of Christ occurs; an encouragement for the impenitent, a seductive hypocrisy, a patent blasphemy and idolatry, as alas we know and see with the world.

Oh, delightful assembly and Christian marriage feast, commanded and ordained by the Lord Himself! Here no carnal pleasures, the flesh, and appetites, but the glorious and holy mysteries, by means of the visible signs of bread and wine, are represented to and sought by true believers.

Oh, delightful assembly and Christian marriage feast, where take place no improper and shameful mockery, and no senseless songs; but the pious Christian life, peace, and unity among all the brethren. The joyous word of divine grace moreover, His glorious benefits, favor, love, service, tears, prayers, His cross and death, are set forth, and urged with delightful thanksgiving and devout joy.

Oh, delightful assembly and Christian marriage feast to which the impenitent and proud despisers are, according to Scripture, not invited: the harlots, rogues, adulterers, seducers, robbers, liars, defrauders, tyrants, shedders of blood, idolaters, slanderers, etc., for such are not the people of the Lord. But they are invited who are born of God, true Christians who have buried their sins, and who walk with Christ in a new and godly life. They are invited who crucify the flesh and are driven by the Holy Spirit; who sincerely believe in God, seek, fear, and love Him, and in their weakness willingly serve and obey Him, for they are members of His body, flesh of His flesh, bone of His bone.

Oh, delightful assembly and Christian marriage feast, where no gluttonous eating and drinking are practiced, nor the wicked vanity of pipes and drums is heard; but where the hungry consciences are fed with the heavenly bread of the divine Word, with the wine of the Holy Ghost, and where the peaceful, joyous souls sing and play before the Lord.

Awake, you who sit in darkness and walk in the shadow of death. Awake, I say, and consider that the supper which you have celebrated until now is not the supper of Christ but that of Antichrist; not the table of the Lord but the table of the devil. For it is generally dispensed only by open deceivers and idolaters, and received by a people who are as yet entirely obstinate and carnally minded, wholly disbelieving and rebellious against the Word of God. Moreover they confess it to be the real body and blood of the Lord and celebrate it with such unbecoming pagan pride and pomp. Oh, abomination and idol!

Beloved reader, I declare the truth of Christ and lie not, that the Holy Supper of Christ is not to be dispensed by a deceiver, nor is it to be received by an impenitent and obstinate sinner. It does not ask any such pride, pomp, and dress as is the custom of the world; neither golden vessels, nor hypocritical show of confessions, absolution, kneeling, and chest smiting, but it deserves to be celebrated with a contrite heart, true penitence, a humble mind, with unfeigned, fervent love, and with peace and joy in the Holy Ghost.

Again I say, awake, and reflect upon what I write. God's work is not keeping a dead letter, an imitation, nor is it the sounding of bells and organs and singing; but it is a heavenly power, a vital moving of the Holy Ghost which ignites the hearts and minds of believers; pervades, comforts, anoints, encourages, rouses, and stirs; makes joyful and happy in God. For this is the true nature and power of the Lord's Word if it be rightly preached, and of His Holy Sacraments if rightly used.

But it is surely high time to take heed to the Word of the Lord. For all who are earthly and carnally minded, who are not born of God and His Word, who oppose the Lord's Word; love not their neighbor, nor assist him in love: these are not in communion with God, therefore they cannot be kernels of His loaf or guests at His table. For to be carnally minded is death, says Paul. Those who are not born from above, Christ says, cannot see the kingdom of God. Samuel says, Disobedience is as iniquity and idolatry. John says, He that loveth not his neighbor abides in death. Again, he that loveth not knows not God, for God is love. In brief, without love it is all in vain that we believe, baptize, celebrate the Lord's Supper, prophesy, and suffer.

Therefore we admonish all those who desire to celebrate this Supper that they learn rightly to know what the true Supper is, what it signifies, how and whereunto it is to be used, and who are to be partakers of it. And then also to examine themselves well, as Paul teaches, before they eat of this bread and drink of this cup lest they comfort themselves with the visible sign and come short of the reality represented by the sign. For they who know not Christ and His righteousness, do not believe Him and His Word, nor walk therein, but walk according to the superstitious doctrine and commands of men: when they nevertheless partake of the Lord's table, they eat and drink damnation to themselves.

All who have received the Word of the Lord concerning faith, and have confessed it to be true, and then transgress it again and do not continue in the acknowledged truth, but walk again in the broad way, resume the love of the world, reject Christ and His Word, and depend upon the seductions and glosses and false promises of the learned ones, these have no part in the Lord's table, for they are without God, as John says: Whosoever transgresseth, and abideth not in the doctrine of Christ, hath not God. II John 1:9.

All who walk in the pride of their heart, despise their neighbor on account of poverty, distress, and affliction, knowing not that they themselves are poor mortals, flesh of Adam, food for worms, and a fading flower, yes, earth and ashes, whether they be emperor or king, rich or learned, and any who with such a proud heart seat themselves at the Lord's table eat and drink damnation to themselves.

All who boast of the Lord's Spirit, name, covenant, Word, knowledge, merits, grace, blood, and death, but reject His holy counsel, doctrine, command, ordinance, and His blameless example, these reject and grieve His Holy Spirit, hate, slander, and speak falsely against their neighbor. If these then seat themselves at the Lord's table, they eat and drink damnation to themselves.

All who love houses, lands, possessions, friends, children, the world, favor, physical ease, honor, and this temporal life more than they do Christ and His Word and attend the Lord's table nevertheless, these eat and drink damnation to themselves. Christ says, He that loveth anything more than me is not worthy of me and cannot be my disciple.

And this is the sum of the whole matter: he who would with the disciples and guests of Christ sit at the Lord's table, be he rich or poor, high or low, must be sound in the faith and unblameable in conduct and life. None is excepted, neither emperor nor king, prince nor earl, knight nor nobleman. Yea, as long as they err in doctrine and faith, and are in their lives carnal and blameworthy, they are by no means to be permitted with the pious to partake of the communion of the Holy Supper. For they are not in Christ, and therefore must remain without until they turn to Christ, repent, walk in the ways of the Lord, and so become one in Spirit and faith with Christ and His church. For the Lord's Supper is a communion of the flesh and blood of Christ; not to the wicked and perverse, but to the sincere, penitent believers as a gift of reconciliation.

If anyone has a good appearance before men, and is inwardly proud, avaricious, carnal, and without the Spirit of God, such a one is not judged by the church but by the Lord Himself, the Searcher of men's hearts and reins, as the Scripture says. We therefore admonish all those who would go to the Lord's table to examine themselves before they go to this banquet, for all who eat unworthily of this bread and drink of this wine, eat and drink damnation to themselves. I Cor. 11:29.

You see, dear sirs, friends, and brethren, the bread of the Holy Supper admonishes us: first, as to the bread as the body of Christ which He sacrificed for us, and the cup of the blood of Christ which He shed in great love for the remission of our sins. In the second place, it admonishes us to unity, love, and peace which must be among all true Christians according to the Spirit, doctrine, and example of Christ, for Paul says, We being many are one bread, and one body. In the third place, it admonishes us to a true regeneration which is of God; to all righteousness, thanksgiving, peace, and joy in the Holy Ghost, to a blameless life. For it is a communion of the blood and body of Christ, of which no one is or can be a partaker unless he becomes according to God's Word a humble, peace-loving, pious Christian, dead unto sin, and born of God; unless he is in Christ and Christ is in him, flesh of his flesh and bone of his bone, a true partaker of the body and blood of Christ. As Paul says, We are made partakers of Christ, if we hold the beginning of our confidence steadfast unto the end. Heb. 3:14.

Behold, beloved readers, here you have the true instructions concerning the Lord's Holy Supper with its meaning, its fruit, power, nature, and the guests, as the mouth of the Lord has ordained, and the holy apostles have left to us and taught; and with what knowledge, faith, love, unity, peace, piety, usage, and ordinance it should be celebrated in the church of God.

With this contrast the supper of the world, and you will learn to know of a truth what an abomination Antichrist has made of it, what superstition he practices with it, and how we poor sinners with all our forefathers have, as idolatrous Israel of old, for hundreds of years[23] offered incense unto the brazen serpent and danced before the golden calf. O my faithful reader, fear God, sincerely examine the Scriptures, and believe the truth.

## [B.] *Perversions of the Holy Supper*

### [1. *The Mass*]

As has been said, the entire Scriptures teach that we have no other sacrifice for sin than the body and blood of the Lord. But since the adversary of Christ has been on the throne for so long a time he has altered the laws of the Most High as set forth in Scripture and has instituted his abomination of desolation in their stead. He has also corrupted the Holy Supper with his councils, violence, and false doctrine, till alas, it has retained only the shadow and the mere name.[24] This they have instituted unto the destruction and corruption of the true eternal sacrifice of Christ which alone is effective before God, changing it into a daily sacrifice for sin, as may plainly be read in the canons of the mass. This undoubtedly is an abomination of abominations, for by it Jesus Christ and His effort and eternal sacrifice is altogether violated, and that He is the atonement and Mediator of the New Testament is undone. He is thrust from the throne of His Majesty. His merits, cross, blood, and death are despised. All the Mosaic types and shadows, all the oracles of the prophets, promises of the angels, and the whole New Testament, are in this way denied—things that unanimously point to the one and eternal sacrifice of Christ. In His place we get an unholy, blind, seductive, and carnal idolater with a piece of bread. Dear reader, do not find fault with these words, for what I write is the truth.

It has gone to such lengths with this wicked seduction that they have arrogated to themselves all power in heaven, upon earth, and in hell. Therefore they break the bread into three pieces; with the first, they reconcile God;

---

[23] Both Menno and his brotherhood had come out of Roman Catholicism. *Ed.*
[24] Menno means Catholicism. *Ed.*

with the second, they intercede for the world; and with the third, as they pretend, they pray for the souls in purgatory.

Through this cursed shame they have climbed so high in honor that they are above all the potentates of earth and have made them personal servants. With this sham and magic idolatry they have raked together money, goods, gold, silver, land, fields, cloisters, cities, principalities, and kingdoms because everybody dotes on this proud ritual as a holy, divine negotiation and honors and fears their proud and pompous names as the messengers of God.

By this very clever and crafty magic the Roman Antichrist has gained such respect and authority that even the imperial majesty, the highest sovereignty on earth, whom God Himself commanded us to honor and fear, has to humble himself and kiss his feet. Yes, beyond that, Frederick Barbarossa, an emperor of great deeds and courage, could not be reconciled with Pope Alexander III[25] until the latter before the church at Venice had walked on the valiant hero with his feet.

In this way Antichrist has bewitched the whole world with his sacrifice.

The gracious, merciful Father be praised eternally, He who has through His paternal grace delivered us, distressed children, from this bewitching sacrifice and has pointed us to the only and true sacrifice of His Son, Jesus Christ, who according to the order of Melchisedec, is ordained a high and eternal Priest over the house of God. In the days of His flesh Christ offered up prayers and supplications with strong crying and tears unto Him that was able to save from death, and was heard because He honored God. He I say, has offered an acceptable sacrifice, a sweet-smelling savor of eternal worth, wherewith He appeases the Father's wrath, makes atonement for the race of men, opened heaven, closed hell, made peace with Him who inhabits heaven and earth, and sits henceforth at the right hand of His Father till His enemies be made His footstool. Yes, with this one sacrifice He has perfected forever those who are sanctified. This neither emperor nor king, doctor nor master, angel nor devil, may oppose. His Word stands fast and immovable. With one sacrifice, I say, with one sacrifice He has perfected forever those who are sanctified.

Readers, dear readers, that is, all those who are still without the Spirit of Christ and His Word, take heed what the Word of the Lord teaches you, and observe the true doctrine of Christ, the true teachers, the true sacraments,[26] the true church, and the true Christian life which is of God, so that you may at long last learn to know what kind of shepherds shepherd you, what kind of baptism and supper you partake of, by what kind of sacrifice you are reconciled, what kind of lives you lead, and of what body you are members.

[25] Alexander was pope, A.D. 1159-81. *Ed.*

[26] As true sacraments Menno recognized (believer's) baptism, and the Lord's Supper (given only to those walking in newness of life, what is now called "close communion"). *Ed.*

Oh, how long, says Solomon, will you simple ones love simplicity, and you scorners delight in scorning? How long will you remain under the heavy bondage of sin? How long will you remain in the communion of the devil, and allow yourselves to be dragged down to the abyss of hell in this way by the cords of unbelief? Rouse yourself and save your poor souls! Depart from among them. Flee all false doctrine. Avoid every appearance of evil. Believe in Christ Jesus. Make a repentant and unblamable life your own; follow Christ with a sincere heart. Enter into the house and covenant of His everlasting peace, into the communion of His flesh and blood. Take upon you His easy yoke and light burden, and you will find rest for your souls. Then you may say truthfully that you are Christians, that you have obtained the remission of your sins by the grace of God through the merits of Christ, and that you are heirs of the eternal kingdom. God grant you all His grace and mercy. Amen.

### [2. Transubstantiation]

In the second place, they have made the bread in the Holy Supper into the actual flesh, and the wine into the actual blood, of Christ, and that by virtue of Christ's Word taken literally: Take, eat; this is my body. They fail to notice that John says in John 6 (where he instructs us plainly how we are to eat His flesh and drink His blood) that it is useless to eat His flesh literally and to drink His blood. Nor could it be done, because He was about to ascend to the place where He was before; therefore we are not to understand this eating His flesh and drinking His blood literally but spiritually, as He Himself says, The words that I speak unto you, they are spirit, and they are life. All those who confess this from the Scriptures, by many disdainfully called cursed heretics and profaners of the sacrament, must suffer for it by water, fire, and the sword.

Dear Lord, is not this wicked error and great blindness to teach and to believe that a piece of bread and a mouthful of wine is changed into the real and actual flesh and blood of the Son of God, and that therewith we may be delivered from hell, the devil, sin, and death, and be made children of grace? Oh, unheard of heresy!

O miserable, blind man, do believe the words of Christ, who says that it is useless to eat His literal flesh, and that His words are spirit and life. John 6:63. Believe that He ascended up to heaven and sits at the right hand of His Father, and that therefore He cannot be masticated nor confined in an alimentary tract nor be consumed by time, by fire or worms, as is the case with the visible bread and wine as one can see.

But where the Lord's church, the dear disciples of Christ, have met in Christ's name to partake of the Holy Supper in true faith, love, and obedience, there the outward perishable man eats and drinks perishable bread and wine, and the inner imperishable man of the heart eats in a spiritual sense the imperishable body and blood of Christ which cannot be eaten nor digested, as was said. Like is benefited by like. This is incontrovertible. The visible man is nourished with visible food, and the invisible man is fed with invisible "bread," as we may plainly learn from the words of the Lord in John 6.

All then who are in Christ and with believing, penitent hearts trust in the pure sacrifice of the body and blood of Christ confess that it is the only cleansing and atonement for their sins, the only and eternal means of grace. These really eat the flesh, and really drink the true blood of Christ, not with their mouths, but believingly in the spirit, as was said before.

From these words the reader may readily observe that the bread cannot be flesh, and the wine blood, for if they were flesh and blood as the idolatrous ones teach and make the poor people believe, one of two things must follow: either the perishable, earthly elements,[27] such as bread and wine, are changed into the imperishable and heavenly Son of God, or the Son of God must be changed into bread and wine. This is incontrovertible.

O dear Lord, they are verily more foolish than any heathen ever were. For the heathen have prayed to and honored the sun, moon, and stars which influenced things below. They have worshiped oxen, dragons, serpents, fire, and other creatures; some of which had the breath of life within them. They also worshiped images of wood, stone, gold, and silver, made by the art of the artist who cast them, carved and beautified them in the likeness of man. But those who name themselves by the name of the Lord, worship, honor, and serve a piece of bread and a mouthful of wine as the actual flesh and blood of Christ, who came from heaven for our salvation, became man, and was sacrificed for us on the tree of the cross for sin. Oh, unbearable abomination and shame that the praise of God, the glory of Jesus Christ, should be converted and changed into such an impotent idol which can neither execute vengeance, nor speak, hear, see, stand on its feet, or walk away, which worms eat and time consumes, which has to be locked up, preserved, helped and carried about by the hands of men just like the idols of Babylon as Baruch relates.

O my faithful reader, do learn rightly to confess Christ Jesus. He does not want to be like Proteus,[28] now being the everlasting Almighty Son of the eternal, Omnipotent God, and then being a perishable creature of bread and wine. Oh, no, what He is He remains to all eternity. Neither can He be confined in any house, church, or chamber, in silver or golden vessels. For according to His eternal, divine Being heaven is His throne and the earth His footstool, and after His holy humanity He has ascended into heaven and sits at the right hand of His Father. He is the eternal and almighty Power, Brightness, Word, Truth, Wisdom, and image of God. He has all power in heaven above and on earth below, all things are under Him, at His name every knee shall bow and every tongue shall confess to Him that He is the

---

[27] Dutch: *creatures.*

[28] Proteus, according to the fable, was a sea-god who could change his shape whenever he was grasped. *Tr.*

Lord to the honor and glory of His Father. He will not return again in the flesh except on the clouds of heaven to judge the goats and the sheep. [Matt. 25].

Therefore I say once more, He cannot be masticated nor digested in the body of any man. This thing Augustine[29] plainly acknowledges, saying, Why do you make ready teeth and stomach? Merely believe, and you have "eaten" Him already!

We know right well, dear reader, that Augustine did not write this of the outward eating of the Holy Supper, but of the inward eating that takes place in the spirit by faith. Therefore we adduced it so that the God-fearing reader might distinguish between outward and inward eating, and not employ the one for the other. For the external use of the sign is nothing but a false show and hypocrisy if the thing which is invisibly represented is not present with it. Concerning infant baptism and the Lord's Supper of the world this may be proved even without the Scriptures. But where the mystery is joined to the signs for which purpose they are ordained, there the baptism of Christ and the supper of Christ are present, as the Scriptures teach.

This is hidden from the world. They acknowledge that a supper is taught in Scripture. But what it is essentially, what it symbolizes, and who are to partake of it, this they know not, so completely has the Babylonian harlot deceived and bewitched them in this matter.

The Holy Supper as taught by Christ and His apostles reproves all idolatry and spurious means of atonement, all hatred, discord, and unrighteousness, for it points exclusively to the one sacrifice of Christ which was made once for all by His flesh and blood as related. It symbolizes Christian peace, unity, brotherly love, and a pious, unblamable life, as has been heard.

Therefore they are adverse to the Supper, have forsaken the Lord's Word and ordinances, and have turned away from the Creator to the creature, and from the Reality to the perishable signs, so that the mocking shame of the godless mass must pass for the sacrifice of the Lord, and the bread and wine for His real flesh and blood. For this is the custom and manner of the ungodly because they know not the true God, the God of heaven and earth, and believe not His holy and worthy Word! Therefore they hate true religion and are hostile to it. In God's stead they have a visible creature that they can touch and construct into a service of their own choice. Just so Israel carried on with the golden calf, with Baal and Moloch; Antiochus with his Maosim[30]; the Babylonians with their Bel; the Egyptians with their Isis, etc. From this fountain springs all the hideous idolatry practiced with this abomination, such as carrying the bread in procession, raising it aloft for adoration, praying to it, offering incense to it, requesting it at a given place, and paying divine

---

[29] Augustine, the great church father, lived A.D. 354-430. *Ed.*

[30] Mauzzim (fortresses) occurs in Daniel 11:38 (Maozim in the Douay Bible). Antiochus IV, called Epiphanes, was a cruel Syrian king, 176-164 B.C., who tried to force the Jews to worship Zeus (whom the Romans called Jupiter). See also pages 516 and 663. *Ed.*

honor and service to it—things for which there is not a hint either in letter or in spirit in all the Scriptures. Alas, with the vast majority this is understood in such a way that they say this is the God that has atoned for us upon the cross—just as Israel said to the calf, These be thy gods, O Israel, which brought thee up out of the land of Egypt. Ex. 32:4.

Besides this, the cup is withheld from the people among Catholics. If it were the Lord's Supper as they pretend, it should, should it not, take place according to the ordinance of the Lord in both elements. But this custom shows that it is not the supper of Christ but a bewitching seduction of Antichrist.

Therefore be wise and sane, you who name yourselves after the name of Christ. Spew out the wine of Babylonian fornication which you have drunk. You have danced and burned incense long enough to the golden calf. Give the Almighty the proper praise and honor lest it happen to you as it did to unbelieving, disobedient, and idolatrous Israel. Although the Lord God had graciously redeemed them from the power and tyranny of Pharaoh, yet they had to suffer punishment on account of their faithlessness and rebellion and perished in the wilderness. And so also it is vain to be redeemed by the blood of the Lord in the dominion and power of the devil if we do not repent, if we continue in idolatry, and if we believe not in Jesus and are not obedient, even in our weakness, and do not live according to His Word.

### [3. Sacramentalism]

In the third place, they teach that this bread is dispensed for the remission of sins. My faithful reader, take notice of what I write. Where Jesus Christ, His Word and Spirit are not confessed, nothing but unbelief, idolatry, error, and uncertain wavering consciences may be seen. They one and all seek some remedy for their sins, but the true remedy, Christ, they do not know. Hence they have invented so many remedies that we can neither describe nor relate all of them: such as indulgences, holy water, fastings, confessionals, masses, pilgrimages, infant baptism, bread and wine, etc.

I know not with whom to compare this generation if not with the sick and wounded person who trusts himself to an inexperienced physician that can give him no helpful prescription nor healing poultice. He wastes his money, he suffers pain and anguish, and gets worse instead of better. An expert and experienced physician is pointed out to him, one who not for the sake of money and words, but out of sheer compassion and love would invite him to his own house, bind up his wounds, and cure him. But such a good and kind doctor he does not want. Who can pity such a man since he would rather perish than be healed?

So it is with this perverse generation. They feel at times that they are not well, but they seek help of those who work their baneful medicine, who make them grow worse; and they are not cured of their ills. The experienced heavenly Surgeon and Physician, Jesus Christ, pointed out by all the patriarchs, prophets, apostles, and by the angels, yes, by the Father Himself, Him they refuse; the One who would so gladly visit all those mortally hurt. He offers His services without money and without price; He has aromatic healing salve very able to heal their wounds, namely, His powerful Word with which to instruct, and His crimson blood to make atonement, as has been said. But they desire Him not; they deflect Him away with hand and foot, with every false doctrine, reproach, lying betrayal, turmoil, persecution, and murder, it seems. O dear Lord, what to do with this disobedient, perverse, and blind generation?

O worthy reader, we testify the truth in Christ. Take it to heart. You may believe, seek, carry on, hope where and what you please; but we are sure of this that you will find in the Word of God no other remedy for your sins that is satisfactory to God than the one we have pointed out to you, which is Christ Jesus—if the Scriptures are not spurious and false.

Thus speaks Isaiah: I, even I, am he that blotteth out thy transgressions for my own sake, and will not remember thy sins. Isa. 43:25. The Father hath laid on him the iniquity of us all. Isa. 53:6. The angel said to Joseph, Thou shalt call his name Jesus, for he shall save his people from their sins. Matt. 1:21. This is my blood of the New Testament which is shed for you and for many for the remission of sins. Matt. 26:28. Behold the Lamb of God which taketh away the sins of the world. John 1:29. For he hath made him to be sin for us who knew no sin; that we might be made the righteousness of God in him. II Cor. 5:21. Who his own self bare our sins in his own body on the tree. I Pet. 2:24. The blood of Jesus Christ his Son cleanseth us from all sin. I John 1:7. He loved us, and washed us from our sins in his own blood. Rev. 1:5.

My good readers, beware and do not deceive yourselves. If there were any other remedy for sin than here related, we might properly say that these and similar passages have not directed us correctly. Then the holy Paul also erred not a little when he said, There is one God, and one Mediator between God and men, the man Christ Jesus, who gave himself a ransom for all, to be testified in due time. I Tim. 2:5, 6.

All those then who seek other remedies for their sins, however glorious and holy they may seem, other than this God-provided remedy, these forsake the Lord's death which He died for us, and His innocent blood which He shed for us. They are those of whom the Lord complains through His prophet Jeremiah: My people have committed two evils; they have forsaken me, the fountain of living waters, and have hewn them out cisterns, that can hold no water. Jer. 2:13.

All false doctrine tends to deny the true mercy seat, Jesus Christ, who alone is our righteousness which is acceptable to God; and to erect strange Baals to be worshiped in the place of Christ as has been said.

Behold, beloved sirs, friends, and brethren, here you have the salutary truth and the real doctrine of the Lord's Supper plainly and briefly set before you, what it is, for whom it is ordained, and what it teaches and represents to us with its mysteries and signs.

Likewise you have here in part the supper of Antichrist with its dreadful abomination wherewith it has perverted the Lord's Supper, has established its own kingdom, and has usurped the seat of God. By it many hundreds of thousands of poor souls have been deceived and are deceived still. And many pious hearts who turn away from this wicked idolatry are by the ranting and raving of the learned ones grievously murdered and slain in some cities.

Compare these two, weigh them well with the Spirit, Word, and ordinance of the Lord, and you will detect, if you believe that the Word of God is true, to what frightful idolatry the world has come. You will also see that we have according to our small ability plainly indicated to you the immovable foundation of truth out of the Word of God.

Praise the Most High, all you who fear the Lord, that He has manifested His immeasurably great love and grace toward us poor sinners in this dreadful time of unbelief, that He has permitted the clear light of His holy Gospel, and the true knowledge of His Son Jesus Christ, to shine forth out of the darkness, the light which was concealed for so many centuries in this dark Egypt under the thick clouds of the abominations of Antichrist. Therefore, let us guard it carefully and walk in it diligently, lest it turn into thick, deathly darkness again, as the prophet has it. Jer. 13:16.

O my dear reader, learn rightly to confess Jesus Christ, who has so ordained this Holy Supper and the breaking of bread for His disciples and all Christians. Believe the glorious and unspeakable gifts of His grace. Fear, love, honor, serve, and follow Him. Walk in blessed union, love, and peace with your neighbor, even as this Supper with its symbolism testifies and teaches. Mortify your evil flesh, crucify its unclean lusts, conduct yourself according to the Spirit, Word, and example of the Lord. So shall your Supper redound to His praise, and your souls continue in life everlasting.

### [C.] The Duty of Shunning Babylon

We also teach and admonish from the Word of God that all genuine children of God, born again of the incorruptible living seed of the divine Word, who have according to the Scriptures separated themselves from this idolatrous generation, who have in obedience assumed the yoke and cross of Christ, and who are able to judge between true and false doctrines, between Christ and Antichrist, that these must according to the Scriptures shun all seducing and idolatrous preachers in regard to doctrines, sacraments, and worship. They must avoid all who, of whatever belief, doctrine, sect, or name, are not in the pure doctrine of Christ and in the Scriptural usage of His sacraments. The reason is that these have neither calling, doctrine, nor life conformable to the Word of God, but are sent by Antichrist, and ordained in his employment and service. For they not only do not observe and acknowledge the pure doctrine of Christ, and the proper usages of the sacraments in the apostolic church, but have also changed them into vain confusion, abominations, and open idolatry, as has been stated. They have deceitfully mingled the precious fine gold of the divine Word with the dross of human doctrine, and the pure wine with the polluted water of their foolish wisdom. They revile so woefully, abuse, storm, and cheerfully destroy and burn the city of God, the city of righteousness and eternal peace; the lovely Jerusalem with its sacred temple, the house of prayer, or traffic and rule therein with their spiritual money-changers, Pharisaic regulations, and superstitious business. Like Belshazzar they in Babylonian immorality and drunkenness mercilessly misuse and degrade the precious vessels of the Lord, the noble souls whom He has consecrated with His crimson blood, and by whom the true service of the Lord should be performed. Like Herod, they mock Christ, the eternal Wisdom of God, as a fool arrayed in a fool's garment and they reject and despise the holy apostles and the witnesses of His eternal truth as vain prattlers and vendors of falsehood.

In short, they preach and recite lies for truth before the poor people; darkness for light; death for life; and Antichrist for Christ.

It is therefore improper, is it not, that the bride of Christ who waits to hear the bridegroom's voice, those dear children of God who have their feet washed and their garments cleansed in the blood of the Lamb, who are established upon the immovable foundation of the apostles and prophets, upon the precious cornerstone, Christ Jesus, that these should again hear the voice of the stranger, and once more defile their garments and feet with the doctrine, belief, religion, and life of those who are condemned and consigned to death, unless they repent.

This we teach according to our limited talents, with all earnestness, as much as in us is, not out of contempt, as the Lord knows, nor yet out of self-will, caprice, or stubborn party spirit, as the carnal world accuses. Oh, No! God preserve all that are His from party spirit. But we do it out of the pure fear of the Lord and the burden of our consciences, God's urgent Word, and the deep love for your poor souls. These drive us, as may be seen with greater clarity presently.

### [D.] *The Vocation [Commission] of the Preachers*

According to the Scriptures the mission and vocation of Christian preachers takes place in two ways. Some are called by God alone without any human agent as was the case with the prophets and apostles. Others are called by means of the pious as may be seen from Acts 1:23-26.

We certainly hope no one of a rational mind will be so foolish a man as to deny that the whole Scriptures, both the Old and New Testament, were written for our instruction, admonition, and correction, and that they are the true scepter and rule by which the Lord's kingdom, house, church, and congregation must be ruled and governed. Everything contrary to Scripture, therefore, whether it be in doctrines, beliefs, sacraments, worship, or life, should be measured by this infallible rule and demolished by this just and divine scepter, and destroyed without any respect of persons.

Therefore we, your willing servants, companions, and fellow mortals, humbly admonish each one of you in the office and service and rank to which you are called, in all love to consider the salvation of your immortal souls, and to ponder carefully the vocation or mission, the doctrine and conduct of the bishops, pastors, and preachers of your churches. Examine them by the Spirit of the Lord, and the doctrines and customs of the apostles, seeing you persecute and destroy so many pious God-fearing Christians because of the idol temples of the ungodly or the bloody clamor of the learned ones. We do not doubt that if you do this with a sincere heart you will soon perceive that we miserable men do nothing more in this matter than the Word of God teaches and enjoins, and that your preachers are not the servants of Christ but hirelings, hypocrites, deceivers, and mockers, against whom the Scriptures warn us no end, picturing them and describing them with many terrible names.

Honorable and reasonable reader, let this be a true and certain rule. All who rightly preach Christ and His Word, and with it bring forth children to the Lord, must have been called by one of the afore-mentioned methods. They must have been urged into the vineyard of the Lord through the true and unfeigned love of God and their neighbor, and through the power of the Holy Ghost. They must put to interest the talent of grace which they have received from God, must rebuke sin and teach faith and righteousness without any respect of persons; and must further the Word and praise of the Lord. They must faithfully perform the work and service of the Lord, and so bring the gathered sheaves into the Lord's barn, and the acquired coins into His treasury.

Such a shepherd the faithful Moses was, for when the Lord informed him that Israel had made a molten calf he hastened from the mountain, and when he heard the tumult and saw the multitude playing and dancing, he burned internally in zealous wrath. He broke the tables of stone on which the Lord had written with His own finger. He cared neither for life nor death. He sprang among the idolatrous people and rebuked them with his word and with the sword, because they gave to a molten creature and cursed abomination the honor of Almighty God, who with such faithful love had so gloriously delivered them from Egypt.

When Zechariah, the son of Barachias, a man full of the Holy Ghost, saw the false worship of the people, he risked his life and defended the honor of the Lord. He rebuked his brethren, the erring Israelites, and said, Why transgress ye the commandments of the Lord, that ye cannot prosper? II Chron. 24:20.

So also was the worthy prophet Jeremiah, although burdened with much suffering and cares, because of much distress and cross-bearing (with which his faithful service was not a little burdened). He had determined in his heart to prophesy no more in the name of the Lord, yet when he saw that the people were ungodly, and neither acted nor spoke aright, he said, God's word was in my heart as a burning fire shut up in my bones, so that I all but perished and could hardly bear it.

So also the holy Paul says, Woe is me if I preach not the gospel! For if I do this thing willingly, I have a reward: but if against my will, a dispensation of the gospel is committed unto me. I Cor. 9:16, 17.

You see, my good reader, all they who by such a power are touched in their hearts, are driven by the Holy Ghost, are constrained by love to God and their neighbor, and are called by the Lord Himself or by a church without fault, believing and Christian, rightly to teach in the house of God, that is, to teach in the church of Jesus Christ, with sound doctrine and by a pious and unblamable conduct, to admonish, rebuke or reprove, and comfort, and assist in paternal love, to administer the Lord's holy baptism and Supper rightly, to ward off diligently with God's Word all seducing and false teachers, and to exclude all incurable members from the communion of the godly, etc. To such Christ says, As my Father hath sent me, even so send I you. Without such a vocation no one can ever rightly preach the Gospel, as Paul says, How shall they preach except they be sent?

Yes, it was with this mission and vocation that all the prophets, apostles, and servants of God appeared. They did not appropriate this honor to themselves as do the preachers of this world; but like Aaron they were called of God, or by the spotless church, as has been said. They were driven into this office by the Spirit of God, with pious hearts, and did ever esteem themselves unfit to serve the people of God or to execute such a high and responsible office.

When Moses was called of the Lord to lead the people out, he declined right heartily. He excused himself and complained that he was of a slow tongue; he did not desire the assigned function. Yes, he resisted so long that the Lord was angry with him. Ex. 4:10-15.

Isaiah dreaded to preach the Word of the Lord, and complained that he was of unclean lips until the angel purged them. Jeremiah was called by God and prepared from birth to be a prophet; and yet he said, Ah, Lord God! I am not fit to preach, for I am but a child. Jer. 1:6. Peter was asked three times by the Lord whether he loved Him, before He would give him charge of His sheep. John 21:15. Paul was called from heaven and drafted by the Lord Himself in the service of the Gospel; for the Lord solemnly' foreordained him and counted him suitable for the ministry. Acts 9:3. Matthias was chosen through the zealous prayers of the church, and the lot of the apostles, to be an apostle in the place of Judas. Acts 1:26.

All they who are not so sent by God nor by an unblamable Christian church after the regulations of Christ and the apostles, as has been said, those who are not called by the Holy Ghost, by the pure, unfeigned love of God and their brethren, and with the true and genuine confession and zeal for the divine Word, but seeking man's favor, praise, money, and profit, a soft and easy life: these will never gather fruit in the vineyard of the Lord, no matter how eloquent they may be, how esteemed and equipped. All that they attempt is wasted effort. They will rise too early or go out too late; their harangue is without power; their service is vain, their labor without fruit, yes, it is nothing but sowing by the seashore and reaping the wind. For no one can serve in this high and holy office conformable to God's will, except he whom the Lord of the vineyard has made capable by the Spirit of His grace.

Since then this vocation is the true mission, vocation, and calling taught in the Scriptures, as has been observed, we faithfully counsel the reader in the pure fear of God to consider what kind of people their preachers are; also by whom and in what way and to what end they are called. For it is manifest that a portion of them are useless, haughty, immoral men; some are avaricious, usurers, liars, deceivers; some are drunkards, gamblers, licentious, open seducers, idolaters, etc., concerning whom it is written that they shall not inherit the kingdom of God if they do not repent. I Cor. 6:9, 10. Some also are idle profligates, young and haughty, wholly unlearned in the Scriptures, anointed and shaven by Antichrist, just so they have a smattering of Latin, as if the office of God and cure of souls depended not on piety and the gift of grace, but on linguistic attainment. No, my reader, no, we shall have to look deeper than that.

Besides this, those so chosen desire nothing but a sensual, easy, carnal life, dishonest and shameful gain, and benefices which heretofore Antichrist and his servants have assembled and multiplied by means of sorcery, theft, and robbery.

They are only called by carnal affection, favor, and faction; one has a son, another a brother, a third a favored friend, a fourth buys his way with money and gifts.

They are also installed and ordained in their office in similar spirit; namely, with drinking and feasting, with pompous greeting, choir letters, appellations, presentations, investitures, and such like shams and shames of Antichrist. But by whom are they inducted thus? By the church? Ah, no! Christ's church knows no such callings, customs, practices, and preachers. They are inducted by an assembly of the impenitent, the haughty, avaricious, fornicators, gamblers, drunkards, and idolaters, who know neither God nor His Word, who walk after the lusts of the flesh, and abuse, persecute, and hate all Christian truth.

And to what are they called? To preach the unfalsified Word of God, to go before the poor people with doctrine and conduct in line with the commands of Scripture? Oh, no, but that they may live the doctrines and commandments of men, resist the holy truth, and betray the pious and godly men who dare not walk the broad way to the bloodthirsty, and in this manner assiduously serve and sustain the kingdom of hell.

My beloved reader, why complain so much at that? It is much worse than I can write. The blind call the blind; the one idolater calls the other; one ungodly man calls the other. The saying of the prophet comes true: deceivers, liars, drunkards, and gluttons are good prophets for this people. Micah 2:11.

O carnal preachers, who, for shame, with Korah, Dathan, and Abiram, run uncalled, particularly you who realize somewhat that your calling and traffic are altogether apart from the Word and Spirit of God, direct your hearts for a change to the Word of the Lord, fear His rigorous wrath and solemn sentence, and reflect how frightfully the afore-mentioned persons were slain by the Lord before all Israel for similar fault. Num. 16:32.

No doubt it suits perverted fleshly ease to live in luxury here on earth with bodies fat and sleek and with gloved hands putting on airs; to be greeted as doctor, lord, and master by men. But when the messenger of death shall knock at the door of your souls and say, Give an account; you may no longer be stewards; when you must appear before the throne of the eternal majesty and before the poor miserable souls which you have led off the true highway of Christ with your deceiving, false doctrine, idolatrous witchcraft, and wickedly liberal life; when you must be wrenched from your lying mouths, your blind and infidel hearts, and your sleek and lazy bodies, oh, where will you conceal yourselves then from the wrath of God? Then men will cry, ye mountains, fall on us; and ye hills, cover us. Rev. 6:16. Ah, then you will know what kind of calling you had, what office and life you led, that you served no one but your impotent god, the belly, the devil, and your self-seeking evil flesh, that you came without being called, that you have sought nothing but the milk, wool, and flesh of the sheep, and that the blind have led the blind until you both have fallen into the curse of the eternal wrath of Almighty God and hellish torment.

Ah, dear sirs, awake and fear God, for the hour draws near that your moment of laughter will be changed into an endless lament, this fleeting joy into eternal sorrow, and this moment of ease and luxury into death and endless woe, as Jude says: Woe unto them! for they have gone in the way of Cain, and ran greedily after the error of Balaam for reward, and perished in the gainsaying of Core. Again, To whom is reserved the blackness of darkness for ever. Jude 1:11, 13.

Behold, beloved sirs, friends, and brethren, since we openly declare that the mission and vocation of your preachers are not of God and His Word but of Antichrist, the dragon, and the beast, that they are not called to preach the Word of the Lord by the Spirit of God and the church, but by their bellies, as were the priests of Jeroboam to worship the golden calf; that they do not enter by the right door; therefore we dare with God's Word to testify that they are thieves and robbers.

Since then we have been saved out of the mouths of the lions, and bears of the pit, and out of the snares of concealed thieves and robbers, through the great Shepherd of the sheep, the High Priest of our souls, Christ Jesus, and are now upon the noble and fruitful mountain of Israel and the green and luxuriant pastures of the holy Word (the Lord be eternally thanked) and our hungering souls have been fed with the food of eternal life, therefore it must ever be a cursed folly to forsake such a true Shepherd, and such precious beautiful pastures, and to turn again to the bare and untended heath under the false shepherd who does naught but rob and deprive God of His glory, and ruin and murder our poor miserable souls.

This I have said specifically of the Popish priests. What the vocation and mission of the Lutherans and Zwinglians is, by what spirit they are driven, what they seek, and what fruits of repentance they achieve by their doctrines and sacraments, we willingly leave to the judgment of all who have been taught of God.

### [E.] *The Doctrine of the Preachers*

Even as we have pointed out to the reader the first part, namely, the mission and vocation of a true preacher according to the Word of God, so now through the grace of God we will in like manner present the second part touching doctrine; for ordinarily it lacks but a little that as is the calling so is the doctrine.

Where the Spirit of God constrains to preach, there the Word will be taught unsullied in the power of the Spirit, and genuine children of the Spirit will be begotten thereby. But where flesh and blood constrains, there a carnal doctrine is taught, and carnal disciples are begotten. For that like produces like is incontrovertible. I deem it unnecessary to prove this just now with many Scriptures, for the fact is evident.

The Scriptures teach plainly that a preacher rightly called must teach the Word of God without perverting glosses, without the admixture of leaven, as Peter says: If any man speak, let him speak as the oracles of God. I Pet. 4:11. They who are the children of the Holy Ghost speak the word of the Spirit, as Christ said, It is not ye that speak, but the Spirit of your Father which speaketh in you. Matt. 10:20. For he whom God hath sent speaketh the words of God. John 3:34. To preach the Word correctly and beneficially is the highest and greatest command enjoined upon a preacher by Christ, even as He said, Go ye into all the world, and preach the gospel to every creature. Mark 16:15.

The Gospel, the Word of God, preached without admixture in the power of the Spirit, is the only right and proper Seed from which truly believing and obedient children of God are born.

Just as the wife cannot bear legitimate children to her husband without his procreative seed, so the church cannot bring forth true children to its husband, Christ, except from His seed, that is, His holy Word. If a woman conceives by any other means she is an adulteress and her child a bastard. So also if the church of Christ brings forth children from the doctrine of man and not from God's Word she is not faithful unto Christ and her children are not His seed.

Therefore nothing may be preached in Christ's kingdom, house, and church except her King and husband's own commands and words, according to which the entire household must govern itself.

This command and word, I say, Christ commanded all true messengers and preachers to observe, saying, Preach the gospel. He does not say, Preach the doctrines and commands of men, preach councils and customs, preach glosses and opinions of the learned. He says, Preach the gospel. Teaching them to observe all things whatsoever I have commanded you. Matt. 28:20.

My faithful reader, observe. All the true servants of God in the Old as well as in the New Testament taught nothing but God's Word, as may be seen and read in many and diverse places in the Scriptures.

Moses was found faithful in God's house, and did and taught nothing which God had not commanded him beforehand.

Isaiah and all the other prophets testified in many places what kind of doctrine they taught, and from whom they had received it, saying: Thus saith the Lord your God, who brought you out of the land of Egypt; thus spake the Lord of hosts. Again, The mouth of the Lord has spoken it. Paul did not dare to speak anything which Christ did not do in him. Yes, Christ Himself did not preach His word but the Word of His Father. He said, My doctrine is not mine, but is of him who sent me; all things that I have heard of my Father, I have made known unto you. John 7:16; 15:15.

Since then the true messengers of God taught nothing but the Word of the Lord, which is the only doctrine by which our souls can live forever, as the Lord said, so it is easily determined here what kind of preachers they are who point the poor, careless people to legends, histories, fables, holy days, images, holy water, tapers, palms, confessionals, pilgrimages, masses, matins, and vespers; who teach of purgatory, vigils, times, bulls, offerings, and make satisfaction for souls and sins, who turn a piece of bread and a sip of wine into the actual body and blood of Christ; teaching and saying that when they have but spoken words, *Hoc est corpus meum* [This is my body], the Lord willing or unwilling—let heaven rend asunder or the earth collapse—He must descend and land on their idolatrous hands. Oh, what blasphemy!

O dear Lord! My heart trembles in my body that I must relate and touch on such awful abominations. But since the plain simple people who do not guard themselves against such seducers are blindly bound hand and foot in their conscience, and are rushed into eternal death and a flood of hell by these useless men, therefore I cannot remain silent, but must through undissembled love to God and their souls make this known.

Who knows but God may give grace that you may receive ears to hear, eyes to see, and hearts to understand, so that you might awake to the snares of the devil wherein you are held.

Yes, good reader, out of this cup they have given the lords, princes, and common men to drink. They have so bewitched them with this abomination that all who turn from this shame and refuse to change the honor of their Saviour into a piece of bread, who shun false doctrines and desire the salutary administration of the table of Christ, these will be reviled as men who vilify the sacraments, and that by all men, and they must suffer and flee as vile and accursed heretics.

O blind leaders, you who, as old as you are, have not rightly understood one sentence of the Word of the Lord, nor received one spark of His Spirit, but have trampled the kingdom of God with your feet, and have thrust it from you with your horns, how truly you are companions of those of whom it is written: That they say, we have made a covenant with death, and with hell are we at agreement, and the overflowing scourge shall pass through, it shall not come unto us, for we have made lies our refuge, and under false-hood have we hid ourselves. Isa. 28:15. Or, Woe unto them that call evil good and good evil; that put darkness for light and light for darkness. Isa. 5:20. Woe unto you, for ye shut up the kingdom of heaven against men, as Christ says (Matt. 23:13), and make the poor souls to err from the way. Once more, Woe unto you!

However, it is not surprising that such persons so bluntly teach such shameful doctrine since they have neither known Christ nor His Word, but they hold and teach all things as they were taught from childhood out of the old usages and papal decrees. But that which grieves me most is that those who now are aware in part of the concealed whoredom of the Babylonian harlot and have vomited up some of the abominations they had swallowed, nevertheless so cling to human sophistry that they can neither be convinced nor taught with the powerful Word of God, with the unblamable lives, the courageous confessions, or with the innocent blood of so many godly saints. And this is true, although some of them have on occasion been forced to yield to the truth with stopped mouths and convicted hearts. But still they cease not to revile and defame the plain, clear truth of Christ and the pious chil-dren of God with hostile tongues and slanderous lips before their carnal blind churches, impelled by the same spirit with themselves, as also are their writ-ers, as may, alas, be seen and heard everywhere. I fear that they are not less guilty than the papists[31] in accusing before lords, princes, and magistrates. They charge, revile, cry out, and write quite as much as the popes against the Lamb of God and His elect, stir up persecution, and cause a tumult when-ever men reject their deceiving leaven; particularly the calf worship of their infant baptism and their corrupted supper.[32]

---

[31] Menno is here scoring the Protestant clergy for inciting religious persecution.

[32] These are two of Menno's chief concerns: infant baptism and an undisciplined church which offers the Lord's Supper to open sinners. *Ed.*

Let each one be on his guard and learn to know them rightly. I know of a truth that they are without the Spirit of Christ and the calling of His Word, for I have heard with my ears and felt with my hands how hostile they are toward those who fear the Lord with all their hearts and who would gladly become Christians. In their doctrines and conduct they seek no less than the papists the friendship of men, honor, pomp, incomes, fine houses, and a soft and easy life.

Ah, my good reader, these are not the teachers who lead many to righteousness, and who shall shine as the light of heaven and as the stars now and in eternity. Dan. 12:13. For I know not where churches may be found which they have led with their services and doctrines to repentant lives and the true worship of God. Their loudest noise is against the pope with his cardinals, bishops, priests, and monks: After that [we] must be reviled by them as profaners of the sacraments, as Anabaptists, mutinous fanatics and heretics, [we] who with the Word of God reprove their seductive doctrines, idolatrous sacraments, and frivolous lives, and wish their souls well.

Yes, if they could find a single one who, although now excommunicated, was previously one with the people of God and now fallen into some reproach, they judge all the godly by this one. See, they say, what sort of people they are! For they seek nothing so much as to find occasion for reviling. Therefore they look only at Judas. But Peter, Andrew, and John they do not see. What manner of people they themselves are, and what kind of disciples they have, they do not notice.

They preach nothing but the grace, the favor, the mercy, and the love of God before their covetous, proud, showy, impure, drunken, and impenitent church, little realizing that the whole Scriptures testify that such folk cannot inherit the kingdom of God. They strengthen the hands of the wicked so that no one repents of his wickedness, as the prophet complains.

O good for nothing, fruitless preachers, you who think you bear the vessels of the Lord, to you are these my words. Why do you talk so loudly about faith and love, since their fruit you so dislike and detest? If you have the genuine and unfeigned love and fear of God, then let them appear in your works.

Say, dear preachers, where is your Christian humility, your godly Christian zeal, pleasure, peace, and joy in Christ Jesus? Where is the mercy which you show? Where are the naked whom you have clothed, the hungry whom you have fed, the needy whom you have put up? Where are the lost whom you have sought, the wounded whom you have bound up, and the sick whom you have healed? Where is your unblamable, pious life which is from God? It is mostly make-believe which you preach, agitate, and allow.

Some of you urge to an extent a pious Christian life. You preach much about Christ, His merits, Spirit, and grace, and are yourselves manifestly those who lead a carefree, carnal life, who crucify Christ afresh, grieve His Spirit, and despise His grace, as may be seen.

O preachers, preachers, how aptly has the Holy Ghost likened you to wells without water, clouds without rain, trees without fruit from which no helpful water can be dipped, nor proper fruit picked. I know not to what you may be better compared than to a woman who lives in all manner of shame and wantonness, but likes to talk about modesty and virtue. Shall we not regard her words as mockery and say, What is the idea of her talking of modesty and chastity, seeing she is full of all manner of immodesty and shame?

Yes, we know that you have demolished some of the little idols of Babylon, such as indulgences, invocation of deceased saints, unclean sanctity, distinctions regarding food, and the like self-righteousness, idolatry, and other superstitions. But alas, the fearful blasphemy and abominations are retained, such as accursed unbelief, stiff-necked obstinacy, earthly-mindedness, unscriptural infant baptism, the idolatrous Supper, and the impenitent old life which is of the flesh.

Therefore we assert, and that with the Word, and say that in your present dimensions you are not ambassadors of God, nor Christian teachers. For it is evident that you reject the Word and ordinances of the Lord, carry on unbidden, and pasture yourselves, and under the name and appearance of evangelical shepherds scatter the Lord's sheep, and lead to destruction many hundreds of thousands of souls through your frivolous doctrine, idolatrous sacraments, and easy, carnal lives.

But the shepherds who are sent of God and have been rightly called, teach the Word of God unfalsified, keep in its holy ordinances, live unblamably in their little power, for they are born of God, are taught and moved by His Holy Spirit; they seek neither gold nor possessions, neither an easy life nor praise of men on earth. They perform their assigned duties with all diligence. They fear God from their hearts and seek their fellow men with great fidelity. They are armed with the weapons of righteousness on the right hand and on the left. Rom. 6:7. They deal without respect to persons. The powerful sharp sword of the divine Word cuts from their lips. The shining lanterns are in their hands. They are taught in righteousness, and are full of spiritual wisdom. They divide the good from the evil, the holy from the unholy, and the clean from the unclean. In brief, they shine in doctrine and life, even as from the beginning to the present time it has been written and observed of all true prophets, apostles, and servants of God.

O dear Lord, how lovely are those pastors and teachers who seek nothing but the extension of the kingdom of God; who preach the word of repentance and grace aright, so that they may win many souls, and that at the risk of name and fame, house and property, person and life.

These are they who with Christ the Chief Shepherd gather and feed His sheep. The others are those who scatter, steal, and murder. They are prophets, but not of God; they preach, but not out of the Lord's mouth. They strengthen the hands of the ungodly. They kill the souls who shall live forever, and make alive those who shall die forever, and that for a handful of barley and a slice of bread. They preach peace to the people when there is no peace. Therefore they shall stand ashamed who practice such abominations, even though they want to be unassailed and unashamed. You see, dear reader, they shamefully deprive Christ of His honor and gain, and scatter His sheep; with the sword of their deceiving doctrines they destroy the poor souls who are so greatly loved by the Lord, so earnestly sought, and so dearly purchased. They so war against the Word and ordinances of the Lord that we say and teach with Christ: Let them alone; they be blind leaders of the blind. Guard yourselves against such false prophets, for though they appear outwardly as sheep, they are nevertheless inwardly devouring wolves. They are the strangers whose voice Christ's sheep know not. They are those against whom Paul warns us saying, Now I beseech you, brethren, mark them which cause divisions and offences contrary to the doctrine which you have learned, and avoid them, for they that are such serve not our Lord Jesus Christ, but their own belly; and by good words and fair speeches deceive the hearts of the simple. Rom. 16:17, 18.

John also says, Whosoever transgresseth and abideth not in the doctrine of Christ, hath not God. If there come any unto you, and bring not this doctrine, receive him not into your house, neither bid him godspeed, for he that biddeth him godspeed, is partaker of his evil deeds. We see then that the Word of God abundantly exhorts us that we should leave them and beware of them, shun their voice and depart from them, and not receive them into our houses, as has been said. If we are Christ's sheep, and the children of the Holy Spirit, we must hear Christ's voice, must we not, and follow after and obey these admonitions of the Holy Ghost. Remember also how sincerely the holy Paul admonished the Philippians that they should guard against strife, evildoers, and the concision. He taught the true servants of God that they should shun those who merely failed, it seems, by holding fast to the circumcision which they had received from their fathers and would not admit that it would be abolished in Christ. For this he reproaches them sternly. How much more diligently must we beware of them who mislead the whole world, revile and persecute the godly, crucify all truth, and support and promote all false doctrine, profanation of God's name, idolatry, and abomination!

### [F.] The Conduct of the Preachers

You have heard concerning the ground of the calling and concerning the doctrines of the preachers. We will now proceed by the grace of God to point out with the Scriptures how the true apostles, bishops, preachers, and pastors in the church of Christ should deport themselves in conduct and life. It is not enough that in appearance a man speaks much of the Word of the Lord. It must also be verified by devout and unblamable conduct, as the Scriptures teach.

Therefore Paul says, But I keep under my body and bring it into subjection, lest that by any means, when I have preached to others, I myself should be a castaway. I Cor. 9:27. For if disciples have to lead an unblamable life, how much more the teachers, because they govern and supervise the hearers. As Paul says, Remember them which have the rule over you, who have spoken unto you the word of God; whose faith follow, considering the end of their conversation. Heb. 13:7.

He also admonishes Timothy thereto and says, Let no man despise thy youth, but be thou an example of the believers, in word, in conversation, in charity, in spirit, in faith, in purity. I Tim. 4:12. In all things showing thyself a pattern of good works, in doctrine showing uncorruptness, gravity, sincerity. Titus 2:7. It is undoubtedly proper that if anyone teaches and reproves others he should first himself be rightly taught and blameless, as Paul teaches: If a man desire the office of a bishop he desireth a good work. A bishop then must be blameless, the husband of one wife, vigilant, sober, of good behaviour, given to hospitality, apt to teach; not given to wine, no striker, not greedy of filthy lucre, but patient, not a brawler, not covetous; one that ruleth well his own house, having his children in subjection with all gravity; for if a man know not how to rule his own house, how shall he take care of the church of God? Not a novice, lest being lifted up with pride, he fall into the condemnation of the devil. Moreover he must have a good report of them which are without; lest he fall into reproach and the snare of the devil. He must be sober, just, holy, temperate; holding fast the faithful word as he has been taught, that he may be able by sound doctrine both to exhort and to convince the gainsayers. Even so must their wives be grave, not slanderers, sober, faithful in all things. I Tim. 3:1-11; Titus 1:8, 9.

Behold, dear reader, so should every preacher and teacher be minded who would rightly govern and rule in the church of God. For if anyone were to reproach and teach others and he himself be reproachable and untaught, he will have to hear, Why do you teach others and do not teach yourself first? You teach that the man should not steal, and you steal yourself. You say a man should not commit adultery, and you do it yourself. You abhor idols, and you commit sacrilege. You boast of the law of God, and you dishonor God by breaking the law. Rom. 2:21-23.

All who are called in this way, who are sound in doctrine and blameless in life, may teach, exhort, reprove, root up, and build in the name of the Lord. Their labors will not be fruitless, as may be seen in the case of Moses, Samuel, Elijah, Elisha, Isaiah, Jeremiah, Peter, Paul, John, and all true prophets, apostles, and servants of God who preached the Word unblamably in the power of the Spirit.

Their doctrine cuts like a sharp-edged sword, for it has power, fruit, spirit, and emphasis, as the prophet says: As the rain cometh down and the snow from heaven and returneth not thither, but watereth the earth, and maketh it bring forth and bud that it may give seed to the sower and bread to the eater, so shall my word be that goeth forth out of my mouth; it shall not return unto me void, but it shall accomplish that which I please, and it shall prosper in the thing whereto I sent it. Isa. 55:10, 11.

Yes, all those who enter the vineyard of the Lord with such a mission and vocation, and in such a spirit, doctrine, and life, as has been said, are the shepherds of whom it is written, I will give you shepherds according to mine heart which shall feed you with knowledge and understanding. Jer. 3:15.

They are the teachers who turn many to righteousness and they shall shine as the brightness of the firmament, as the stars forever. Dan. 12:3.

They are the spiritual streams, the rivers which issue from the fountains of the Paradise of God to irrigate and fertilize the whole country.

They are the spiritual posts and pillars in the court of the tabernacle of Moses, with hangings of fine-twined linen.

They are the threescore valiant men of the valiant of Israel who are around Solomon's bed; they all hold swords being expert in war, every man with his sword upon his thigh, because of fear in the night.

They are the seven horns or trumpets of the golden years before whose sound, message, and preachment the walls of Jericho, namely, all false doctrine, must fall; by whom all power and might battling against the true Joshua, Jesus Christ, and His people, must be brought low.

They are the beautiful messengers of peace who preach God's grace, favor, mercy, love, and peace to us poor, miserable, troubled sinners; and teach us good things. Isa. 52:7.

They are seven unmeasured mountains whereon roses and lilies grow in whose scent and beauty all who fear the Lord rejoice.

They are the splendid and elegant crown of twelve stars of the woman, pregnant and in travail. Rev. 12:1, 2.

They are the walls of the new and heavenly Jerusalem resting on the twelve foundations, that is, upon the ground and doctrine of the twelve apostles. Rev. 21:14.

You see, worthy reader, with such and similar glorious figures and comparisons all pious preachers and teachers are honored in the Scriptures, men whom the Holy Ghost has ordained bishops and overseers in His church, congregation, and house.

These may say with the holy Paul, Be ye followers of us as we are of Christ, for our exhortation was not of deceit, nor of uncleanness, nor in guile: but as we were allowed of God to be put in trust with the gospel, even so we speak; not as pleasing men, but God, who trieth our hearts. For neither at any time used we flattering words, as you know, nor a cloak of covetousness; God is witness; nor of men sought we glory. I Thess. 2:3-6.

These, I repeat, are they who with Christ gather again what was scattered, bind up the wounded, and heal the sick. For they are motivated by the Spirit of the Lord and urged by unfeigned love. They watch and wait on their assigned duties. They fight courageously every day with the weapon of righteousness. They tear down, break, and destroy all that which is against the Word of God, not by external force with iron and sword, but by the preaching of the Holy Word in power and in the Spirit of the Word of the Lord. They till, sow, water, and plant. They harvest what is ripe. They gather their grain and sheaves and carry them into the Lord's barn, and their fruits will abide unto eternal life.

Since the Scriptures ask for such teachers, it is necessary to weigh the conduct of your preachers in the balance and standard of the divine Word before your own eyes so that you may discover how much they differ from the pattern of the true bishop, preacher, and pastor mentioned by Paul to Timothy and Titus. In all their lives and actions and conduct they are the very opposite. They are men who for pretense only, without Spirit, Word, work, or truth, receive so much praise of the world.

It is manifest, dear reader, that the humble office of a true bishop, preacher, and pastor is an office of Christian service. If rightly served it is full of labor, poverty, trouble, care, reproach, misery, sorrow, cross, and pain. But it has been changed by your preachers into sinful splendor and princely glory so that they are greatly feared and honored by those whose names are not written in heaven. They parade in splendid robes dressed in shining sham, and are called proud names. There is not a word to be found in Scripture concerning their anointing, crosses, caps, togas, unclean purifications, cloisters, chapels, bells, organs, choral music, masses, offerings, ancient usages, etc.; but under these things the lurking wolf, the earthly, sensual mind, the anti-Christian seductions and bloody abominations are readily perceived. For they seek nothing but the favor of men, honor, pomp, splendor, a delicious lazy life, personal advancement, gold, silver, gluttony, etc. Yet they suffer themselves to be called spiritual ones [clergy], doctors, masters, lords, abbots, guardians, fathers, and friars.

Alas, how vastly different from the office of the prophets and apostles in service, example, usage, ambition, and procedure. How different they are from the men who without purse enter the Lord's harvest; men without money or much clothing; men who have to be made a spectacle to the whole world, refuse, and rubbish; men who are killed all the day long for the sake of the Lord's truth and accounted as sheep for the slaughter, as may be seen from the Scriptures.

But the chests and coffers of these folk are full, rich with the abundance of Babylonian commerce and sorcery. And they have become princes on earth although censurable. Their shameful seduction of women can hardly be described. They are given to excesses; unchaste, unmerciful, malicious, revilers, unfriendly, unrighteous, liars, drunkards. Their tables are full of uncleanness, as Isaiah the prophet says. Their hearts are full of avarice, and they are hateful toward those who will not contribute to their support. They preach that war will ensue, as Micah says. They have eyes full of adultery, are at home with harlots, beget illegitimate children. They are unbelieving, obstinate, proud, vain, disobedient to the Word, bound with the snare of Satan, considered even by many who have not known the truth to be a burden and a shame to the world. Their fearful, ugly fruits testify before the whole world. They fight against Christ and Christ's Word, hate all the pious, rave and rant against all those who seek the Lord and love and fear Him with all their hearts. In a word, it is impossible to relate all their vices, lewdness, godlessness, private and public disgrace, shame, and fearfulness.

O dear Lord, how precisely the opposite of the upright and true bishops, overseers, and pastors have they become, this haughty tribe that boasts that it can bring Christ down from heaven, atone before God, and forgive sins. They say that they are the true pillars of the church, the eyes and the head. And although I have written this especially of the Roman Catholic priests, the reader must know that I do not consider innocent those who make their boast in the Word. By no means. For if men accept open adultery and fornication, also certain idolatrous practices concerning the bread, they differ precious little as a matter of general practice in the seeking of filthy lucre, idolatrous practice, baptism and Supper, obstructing the pious, besmirching and reviling them.

Therefore I fear that all who preach for money and play the hypocrite with the world are the spiritual sorcerers of Egypt, priests of the groves [Asherah],[33] servants of Baal, prophets of Jezebel, destroyers of the Lord's vineyard, defilers of the land, blind watchmen and dumb dogs, spoilers of good pastures, polluters of the clear waters, devourers of souls, false prophets and ravening wolves, devourers of widows' houses, thieves and murderers, enemies of the cross of Christ, whose end is destruction, whose God is their belly, and whose glory is in their shame; who mind earthly things. Phil. 3:18, 19. They are false teachers, founders of sects, cursed children, wandering stars, withered trees without fruit, twice dead, plucked up by the roots; those who foam out their own shame, to whom is reserved the blackness of darkness forever. Jude 13. Yes, antichrists, locusts that rise from the bottomless pit, and men who pervert those who have not the seal of God in their foreheads.

In short, if they will not repent, they are already condemned according to the Scriptures. Titus 3:11; Rev. 21:8.

Not that I would judge anyone, my good reader. I know quite well that it is written, Judge not, that ye be not judged; condemn not lest ye be condemned. But they are judged of Him who says, The word that I have spoken, the same shall judge him in the last day. John 12:48. Those who do these and similar things, says Paul, shall not inherit the kingdom of God. But if anyone shall do the works whereof Paul speaks, he is not judged by me, nor by any other man, but by the Word of the Lord. Therefore we beg you to measure the conduct of your preachers with the Scriptures, and you will find by whom they are judged.

[33] Amorite or Canaanite goddess of fertility the wooden symbol of which seems to have been erected beside the altar of Baal by the idolatrous Israelites. *Ed.*

O miserable preachers, whose blindness we may well lament bitterly, how good were it if you had not been born! For when this, your short, transitory, splendidly lazy life is spent, if you do not repent, as was stated, your portion will be God's eternal wrath, punishment, endless pain of hell, burnings, woe, and death, as the Scriptures warn. Phil. 3:19.

The reason is because you reject Christ and despise His Word, the only food for the soul, upon which we must live eternally. You despise His Word because it rebukes your vain conduct which is basically naught but flesh and body, world and devil as is evident, seeing that you mislead poor souls so sadly. Those who seek your salvation, admonish you in love with the Word of God, and rebuke your seducing doctrine and with a conduct in all reasonableness you hate so thoroughly, revile, slander, betray, and cause to be expelled, dishonored, killed, and exterminated.

O Balaam, Balaam, how long will you so unmercifully kick and cuff the poor ass which has to bear all the reproach, scorn, and disgrace for the sake of the testimony of his master Christ? Will you never listen to how he answers you in a human voice and reproves your great folly and error? Will you not hear that he is encountered by an angel with unsheathed sword, that is, by the Spirit and Word of the Lord, that he can bear you no longer in your ungodly deeds?

Very well, seed of Cain, Korah, and Balaam, prepare for defense. Lie, cheat, revile, blaspheme, hate, betray, violate and murder as much as in you lies. Quote all the councils, authors, and learned teachers there have been for centuries. Appeal to every lord and prince, every emperor, king, and mighty one on the earth. Use all the force, power, art, and cunning there is; it will avail you nothing. The Lamb will conquer and gain the victory; the people of God will triumph, not with external weapons but in patience with the Spirit and Word of God. Jerusalem and the temple will be built, although Azotus and Sanballat may seek to hinder it, [but] not with inanimate stones which are now traveled in every street with unclean feet. Although all the gates of hell bestir themselves, Babylon will be destroyed and laid waste. The ten kings will and must perform the service to which they were called. You will gnaw your tongues for pain, bitterly cry and weep before the torments of Babylon and say, Alas, alas, that great city that was clothed in fine linen and purple and scarlet, and decked with gold and precious stones and pearls, for in one hour so great riches is come to naught, for her sins rose up to heaven and the Lord remembered her wickedness. Rev. 18:16, 17.

The Gospel will be heard; lies will be exposed; and your blind folly will be made known to all men, even if I and my brethren may be called away so that we do not live to see it; yet that which the Holy Ghost has so plainly foretold and taught through that worthy man John will undoubtedly happen at the appointed time.

O stiff-necked and evil generation, how long will you resist the Holy Ghost? How long will truth be reviled by you and lies praised? How long will your hands and hearts drip with the blood of the innocent? Reform your wicked lives, fear God with all your hearts, renounce all your glosses and willful and man-made doctrine. Meet us in the open and deal with us according to the Word of the Lord, so that the Gospel may be rightly preached and verified with a pious and blameless life. Oh, if you would do this, then no innocent blood would be shed and the truth would become evident.

But we are afraid it will go as the prophet said, The wicked shall do wickedly and none of the wicked shall understand; but the wise shall understand. Dan. 12:10. For it is the custom of all the sects who are outside of Christ and His Word to make valid their positions, faith, and conduct with the sword. The Roman Catholics, the Arians,[34] the Circumcellions,[35] the Lutherans, the Zwinglians, and the Münsterites are our witnesses.[36] But Christ, and those who are His, bear and suffer.

Is it not a grievous error that these poor people want to be called Christians who do such wicked abominations as exterminating, robbing, arresting, burning, garroting,[37] murdering, etc., under pretense as if the kingdom of Christ, the glory of the Lord, the Word and truth of God, were to be defended and maintained with such shocking shame? Ah, no, miserable men, no. All who are moved by the Spirit of Christ know of no sword but the Word of the Lord. Their weapons are powerful, fervent prayer, a longsuffering and patient heart, strong, immovable faith, a living hope, and an unblamable life, as was said. With these the Gospel of the kingdom, the Word of peace, is to be propagated and protected against the gates of hell.

Dear reader, take note if you have any fear of God, then learn rightly to know your bishops, prophets, pastors, and preachers. And remember what is written: Come out from among them, and be ye separate, saith the Lord, and touch not the unclean thing; and I will receive you, and I will be a Father unto you, and ye shall be my sons and daughters, saith the Lord Almighty. II Cor. 6:17, 18. Again, Come out of her, my people, that ye be not partakers of her sins, and that ye receive not of her plagues. Rev. 18:4. Recall that the mouth of the Lord has said, Beware of false prophets, which come to you in sheep's clothing, but inwardly they are ravening wolves. Ye shall know them by their fruits. Do men gather grapes of thorns, or figs of thistles? Matt. 7:15, 16.

[34] The Arians were a fourth-century sect which held unsound views on the person of Christ. Modern theological liberalism ("modernism") somewhat resembles Arianism in its view of Christ as being less than God the Father in His attributes.

[35] The Circumcellions were a fourth-century group of ascetics who flourished in Africa who merged with a portion of the schismatic Donatists.

[36] The groups here listed by Menno as "sects" had, in Menno's judgment, this in common that they did not take their stand firmly and exclusively on the Word of God, but established their respective systems of doctrine partly on human authorities.

[37] A mode of execution by strangulation. The victim wore an iron collar which was tightened progressively to a post by a screw until life became extinct.

Menno is vigorously protesting the persecution of his Brotherhood by the state with the full approval, perhaps even the encitement, of the major religious bodies of the sixteenth century, both Catholic and Protestant. Ed.

They are the salt which has lost its savor and is henceforth good for nothing but to be cast out and to be trodden under the foot of men, as the Lord says. Matt. 5:13.

In short, they are those of whom Paul warned and said: This know also, that in the last days perilous times shall come. For men shall be lovers of their own selves, covetous, boasters, proud, blasphemers, disobedient to parents, unthankful, unholy, without natural affection, truce-breakers, false accusers, incontinent, fierce, despisers of those that are good, traitors, heady, high-minded, lovers of pleasure more than lovers of God; having a form of godliness, but denying the power thereof: from such turn away. II Tim. 3:1-5.

Since then you see with your eyes and feel with your hands that your preachers are such persons as here described, and that the Scriptures abundantly admonish and command that we shall forsake them, fear them, and avoid and flee from them, therefore we teach openly that you must not hear their seducing sermons, not use their sacraments, and not let yourselves in with their false worship.

I say, dear friend, what piety can Israel import from Assyria, Egypt, or Babylon? How can the true service be found with priests of Baal? How can you be properly taught unto righteousness by those who are ignorant of divine things? How can you learn Christ from Antichrist, and the Word of God from false prophets? How can you be blessed by those who are cursed and led by those who are blind? How do you expect to draw water from dry fountains and gather fruit from barren trees? How can you be partakers of the Lord's table and of the table of devils? How can you drink both the Lord's cup and the devil's, and be in fellowship with Christ and with Antichrist? II Cor. 10:21.

You cannot serve two masters, the one contrary to the other. You must love the one and hate the other, or hold to the one and forsake the other. You must be for Christ or against Him, gather with Him or disperse in opposition to Him. Matt. 6:24.

Since then we by the grace of God so plainly see your preacher's mission, doctrine, and lives, how they run without being called, falsify the Word of God, lead a willful carnal life, deceive the poor people; and since we are so abundantly admonished by the Scriptures to forsake, avoid, and shun such preachers because they are so bluntly opposed to Christ and His Word; therefore we desire to be obedient to the voice of our Shepherd in this matter as it becomes all pious sheep of Christ. For the kingdom is promised to the obedient, as the Scriptures say: Not everyone that saith unto me, Lord, Lord, shall enter into the kingdom of heaven; but he that doeth the will of my Father. Matt. 7:21.

Therefore we, in keeping with the contents of God's Word, have turned away from their doctrine, sacraments, and service. We testify to this both by word and deed, and with possessions and blood; before lords and princes, in cities and countries, before you and the world as an admonition, doctrine, and instruction, so that you all, both preachers and hearers, might rouse yourselves, reflect on the truth, repent, forsake the kingdom and fellowship of Antichrist, and enter the kingdom and communion of Christ. We do this so that your poor souls might be kept from the snares of unbelief and be eternally saved.

For we prefer to endure misery, poverty, tribulation, hunger, thirst, heat, cold, bonds, and death, in our mortal bodies, and continue in the Word of the Lord, rather than to lead secure, easy lives with the world, and for the sake of a short, transitory life ruin our souls.

We think with the holy Peter that we should obey God rather than man, and with dear chaste Susanna that it is better to fall into the hands of man than into the hands of God. All who fear the Lord may read and judge.

## [G] *Refutation of the Rebuttal of Babylon*[38]

Reasonable reader, we have set forth plainly the difference between true and false preachers, and why we should not hear the latter. I hope that the God-fearing who acknowledge the Word of the Lord to be true may fully comprehend the basis for this and the truth.

We find some among those preachers who realize somewhat that their cause cannot stand the test of Scripture; nevertheless, not being born of God nor fearing Him, but seeking unlawful gain, the world, and ease, they have jerked some passages from Scripture with which they persuade the simple and those who dread the cross of Christ that it is lawful to hear their doctrine and attend their church services, so that they may continue to live at ease and enjoy good times.

[i] They put forth, to begin with, that Christ said: the scribes and Pharisees sit in Moses' seat: all therefore whatsoever they bid you observe, that observe and do; but do not after their works. Matt. 23:2, 3. From which we conclude that even as the scribes and Pharisees sat in the seat with Moses, and even though their leaven against which Christ warned His disciples was by some mixed with the unleavened dough, that He, Christ, nevertheless said: All therefore whatsoever they bid you observe, that observe and do. Similarly they now also sit in Christ's seat, and even though their doctrine and lives are not wholly upright and pure, yet we are to hear them and practice what they preach in God's name, but not to do according to their works.

And to this I reply by asking whether they want to be one with the Pharisees or not. If they answer yes, they must then themselves judge that they are companions of those who crucified Christ, stoned Stephen, beat the apostles, persecuted the saints, and who are so often threatened with eternal woe. Well may they then be afraid and fear the Lord and His judgments. If they answer no, then they cannot prove anything with this passage.

[38] In the Dutch original the title is: *Here Follow the Rebuttals of Babylon.* Menno uses the term "Babylon" to refer to an unscriptural religious system, as in the Revelation, and seems to refer mainly to Roman Catholicism. *Ed.*

Secondly, we reply: If they adduce this passage, *quasi argumentum a simili* [that is, as it were an argument of similarity], they should reflect that to sit in Moses' seat is rightly to preach and practice Moses' law and ceremonies. This did the scribes and Pharisees. They left the law and ceremonies intact and altered nothing therein, although they practiced some superstition in connection with it, as may be seen. If they had altered things, they would not have been sitting in Moses' seat.

Even as the scribes and Pharisees sat in Moses' seat, these will then also have to show that they sit in Christ's seat; that is, they must prove that they preach Christ's Gospel, baptism, Supper, excommunication, and all things correctly, or the *argumentum a simili* cannot stand. But if this is done, then we may consult Scripture as to what it permits touching human additions. But we know very well that nothing will be found.

Thirdly, we reply: Since the scribes and Pharisees were sitting in Moses' seat, taught the law which pointed to Christ, together with its ceremonies, and practiced them, as already related, so therefore Christ directed His disciples and the people at that time to them. For the law was not yet finished. The perfect sacrifice which was to abolish all typical sacrifices was not yet sacrificed; the veil of the temple was not yet rent; the figures and shadows were not yet changed into a new and abiding reality. But after it had all been accomplished according to the Scriptures, and had been made new in Christ, He did not then send out the scribes and Pharisees with Moses' law, but His disciples with His own doctrine, saying: Go ye into all the world and preach the gospel to every creature, teaching them to observe all things whatsoever I have commanded you.

Since then a new being [*wesen*] has been realized in and through Christ, and since the people of Moses were directed to the preachers of Christ prior to His death, men who rightly taught the law and ceremonies, so also we in the New Testament after the death of Christ are directed to those preachers who sit in Christ's seat, teaching His words in their purity and using His sacraments as the Scriptures teach.

But against those who falsify Christ's doctrine, misuse His sacraments, deceive the people, and lead a wild and reckless life, the Scriptures warn continually. We are to shun, avoid, and forsake them, not to admit them into our houses; for they sit in the seat of Antichrist and not of Christ.

[ii] Secondly, they adduce what Paul says: Quench not the Spirit. Despise not prophesyings. Prove all things; hold fast that which is good. Abstain from all appearance of evil. I Thess. 5:19-22.

I answer: Of what spirit and prophecy Paul said this is to my mind indicated by him. For if the opinion of the apostle had been that we should go to Satan's seducers in public idol temples there to prove their spirit and doctrine, then Paul would have contradicted himself when he tells us to shun and flee from them. For we know of a certainty that they corrupt the Word and sacraments of the Lord, and seek nothing but a good living, and are without the spirit and Word of Christ.

Oh, no, Paul did not write this of hireling preachers such as the scribes and Pharisees were, nor of the heathen priests of Egypt and Babylon (don't miss the point),[39] but he said this of the prophets, pastors, and preachers in the church of Christ. We are not to quench their spirit, but prove their doctrine and hold fast to that which is good. And if they teach anything not in accordance with the Scriptures and true faith, we are to avoid it. For if any man prophesy, let him prophesy according to the proportion of faith, Rom. 12:6, and this is that to which John exhorts his disciples: Beloved, believe not every spirit, but try the spirits, whether they are of God. I John 4:1. And this expression, Abstain from all appearance of evil, may be understood as a separate assertion without connection with the preceding.

My good readers, we have examined your preachers, as well as their spirit and doctrine, so that we may with a clear conscience say that they are not of God and His Word, but of the bottomless pit and of the dragon and the beast. Say, dear reader, how shall we acknowledge those to be preachers who so willfully fight against the Word of God? What communion has light with darkness? What concord has Christ with Belial? The greater part of their teaching and action is delusion and hypocrisy. My reader, do not resent these words, for that I write the truth I may testify to the whole world, their very doctrines, lives, and sacraments proving it.

[iii] Thirdly, they ask: Why shall we not listen to them, for the wise men of the East did listen to what Herod said?

I answer, This remark seems to me to be so childish that it is altogether unworthy of reply. For Herod did nothing but what he was taught by the scribes. He pointed out to the Wise Men the town in which the King of the Jews should be born, and that with a bloodthirsty heart, as the following act shows. He sent them to Bethlehem and said, Go and search diligently for the young child, and when you have found him, bring me word again, that I may come and worship him also. Matt. 2:8.

Herod was afraid when he heard that their own king had been born, lest he lose his kingdom and glory. He spoke of pure hypocrisy and slyness with the Wise Men. He was desirous of the child's death, and wished to take timely preventative action. But when he saw that his hypocrisy miscarried, he became very angry and showed his fierce, tyrannical, wicked disposition. He slew all the children, the innocent children that were in Bethlehem, and in all the coasts thereof, from two years old and under, in order that he might also destroy the born king, as may be seen from Matt. 2:16.

O my good reader, how correctly they appeal to this hypocritical, lying, ambitious, and tyrannical Herod; for the greater part of them are of the same spirit and disposition. It grieves them so much that Christ is born again

---

[39] Menno, rather boldly, uses the word *papen*, a word used only of *Catholic* priests otherwise, to designate the Egyptian and Babylonian priests; and he does not want his readers to miss the implications of this bold usage, namely, the implications that the heathen priests and the Catholic priests are pretty well the same. *Tr.*

through His Word. They practice hypocrisy as did Herod. They lie and say that they are sincere and mean well. For they fear their shameful gain, their rich and easy lives may be lost if Christ should begin to rule, just as Herod feared lest he should lose his kingdom. And they want to destroy the pious, as Herod sought the blood of Christ.

Since then they are manifestly hypocritical liars and earthly-minded and some of them also intent upon blood, as may be seen in some places; therefore we will also take for an example in this matter the Wise Men who, being admonished by a heavenly inspiration, did not return to Herod. And we will by the grace of God faithfully observe the Lord's inspiration, counsel, doctrine, and admonition and turn to those who make Christ known in power and teach in the truth according to the Spirit.

[iv] Fourthly, some of them say, If the very devil should preach the Word of God, why not hear him?

In the first place, I reply to these good-for-nothing slander mouths that it would be good for them to learn rightly to distinguish between the spirit and disposition of the devil and the Spirit and nature of Christ before they utter such insipid, ugly words before the poor people.

The devil was a liar from the beginning and will undoubtedly remain that. Since then he is a liar and the lie is his very nature, habit, and work, as the Lord says, how then can he sincerely and rightly teach and preach the Word of God, which is truth, and is flatly opposed to his lying disposition and nature? And even if he did speak the truth and gave Christ his praise, he still would do it insincerely for he is a devil and the truth is not in him. He confessed Christ correctly, as far as words go, when he said: Thou art Christ, the holy one of God; thou art Christ, the Son of God. Yet Christ was not pleased with his confession but reproved him, saying: Hold your peace, and come out of him. For his confession was made with a diabolical heart, as was said.

Secondly, I say, If anybody wants to hear the voice of the devil, he does not have to go far. Alas, he can hear him everywhere. All who speak lies, speak of the devil. In the beginning he spoke through the serpent; in Israel through the false prophets; and now through the mouth of his preachers, in order to deceive the world and turn it from the truth, so that it is never saved.

From the beginning he has been a lying spirit and ever will be an adversary of God, a falsifier of the Scriptures, and a murderer of souls, who can neither teach nor endure any good because he is by nature unclean, unfruitful, and deceptive, the enemy of every good thing. Therefore we will through God's grace stop our ears and turn our backs upon the devil and all lying preachers, as the Scriptures teach. And we will observe with all diligence that the Scriptures point to Christ, to hear Him. Christ points to His disciples and they to such teachers as are blameless in doctrine and life, as has been related. May the merciful and gracious Lord eternally preserve all the pious hearts against this Herodian tribe and against the devil's preachers. Amen.

[v] Fifthly, some also say that we may listen to them, just so we do not let ourselves be deceived by them.

I answer: The reader should in the first place observe how the people of God were already in the days of Abraham a people separated from the world, who especially since the days of Moses have had their own preachers, ceremonies, ordinances, doctrines, and services, as may be abundantly read and seen in all the books of Moses.

Secondly, that Israel was commanded by God that if a false prophet should rise up among them, even if he were to perform miracles and signs, he should die. Deut. 13:4.

Thirdly, Israel was not allowed to learn or take any doctrine or worship from any strange nation round about them, but was to adhere closely to the law and testimonies.

Fourthly, when certain wicked kings arose, such as Jeroboam, Ahab, Manasseh, and other such who loved their own righteousness and idolatry more than the Word and right worship of the Lord; and when the false prophets multiplied, who turned the people from the Lord and His law, then the Lord raised up true prophets: Isaiah, Jeremiah, etc., who reproved the disobedient, idolatrous kings and false prophets and warned the people against them faithfully, saying: Hearken not unto the words of the prophets that prophesy unto you; they make you vain; they speak a vision of their own heart, and not of the mouth of the Lord. Jer. 23:16. These prophets all pointed gloriously to Christ, to His kingdom and reign.

Fifthly, that Christ ordained and appointed in His kingdom, congregation, or church, as did Moses in his, prophets, preachers, doctrines, ceremonies, and ordinances. In these all true Christians are to live and continue forever.

Sixthly, the holy apostles teach, counsel, and admonish us everywhere that we are to separate ourselves in doctrine and in worship from those who do not agree with the Spirit, doctrine, ordinance, and examples of Christ, be they baptized or not.

Seventhly, the whole world with its spirit, doctrine, sacrament, worship, and conduct are quite diverse from Christ's Spirit, Word, sacrament, worship, and example, and are alas nothing but a new Sodom, Egypt, and Babylon. Rev. 11:8.

Eighthly, all who confess God's Word and partake of His Spirit are called to let their light shine, to give light to the world, to reprove all wickedness with word, deed, life, and death, and to confess the Lord's holy name, Word, and will and to confirm it with a pious and unblamable life according to the Scriptures.

Ninthly, it is better to have a millstone hanged about one's neck and to be cast into the sea, than to offend one of the little ones who believe in Christ. Matt. 18:6.

Tenthly, we are to ponder well, why, or for what reason we hear such preachers. For if we hear them to be taught of them, then we desire the truth among lies, and seek life with the dead. But if we do not want to be classed with them, but use them as a sort of "liberty," as they call it, then we must confess that such hearing is no hearing, but trifling and hypocrisy. By it we despise the Spirit, doctrine, ordinance, counsel, admonition, congregation, and church of Christ, and we strengthen the seductions and abominations, idolatry and kingdom of Antichrist. We conform to the world in all appearance of evil, play the hypocrite with the world, grieve many a pious child of God, make him to stumble, cause strife among the pious, and esteem lightly the innocent blood which is shed in many places on this account.

Behold, my readers, all who fear the Lord and rightly examine and judge these ten articles, here briefly stated in the light of the Spirit and Word of the Lord, will not continue in this position, but will faithfully take heed to the counsel and admonition of the Holy Ghost; reproving the world both by works and doctrine, avoiding every appearance of evil, and walking in the house of the Lord perfectly.

[vi] But in regard to the false worship, the frivolous comfort one another saying, One may let his children be baptized, for the child is clean, the water is clean, to wash and to bathe is also clean. We may also receive the supper at the hands of these preachers, for although it takes place in the temple of idols, yet Christians have no idols any more, nor do they eat it except as bread and wine which verily is pure to the pure, for as Paul says, To the pure all things are pure. They point to Naaman, the captain of the king of Assyria, in the house of Rimmon and say, We pay no attention to the idolatry of the priests, but we worship Him who made heaven and earth.

I answer: If a single passage can be adduced from the Scriptures indicating that uncleanness, sin, falsification of the ordinances of God, idolatry, disobedience to the Word, and hypocrisy, are all pure and permissible to the pure, that is, to the true believers; then we might consider a bit. But we know right well it will not happen.

O my reader, if the dear men of God had understood the Scriptures as these poor people do, then the three valiant young men would by no means have suffered themselves to be cast into the fiery furnace. The upright Eleazer, the God-fearing pious mother with her seven sons, the holy prophets, the apostles and pious witnesses of God, would have saved their lives, and would have escaped cruel torture and pain saying, To the pure all things are pure. Gentlemen, we will cheerfully comply!

Oh, no, my good reader, no. The unclean is not to be touched by the clean. Touch not, says the Spirit of God through Isaiah and Paul, the unclean thing. That is, what the Scriptures forbid. What does it help if a man is cleansed after contact with the dead if he touch the corpse again? Is it not folly for a man to wash his clothes and then trample them in the mire again?

The Scriptures plainly teach that the just shall live by faith, and that a good tree brings forth fruit. We certainly know that a plain and humble soul will never show off in gold, pearls, or costly apparel. We know that he who fears the Lord is honest, chaste, sober, and will never drink, talk, sing, and dance with shameless women. For the knowledge, fear, and love of God and His Word forbid him. And if he should, he would have to confess that his light is darkness and his conduct not agreeable to the Scriptures. Even so it is unbecoming to those who want to boast of the Word and to reprove with Scripture the seduction, idolatry, and abomination of the preachers, to yet associate with them in their doctrine, sacraments, and false service. For words without actions do not edify. Have no fellowship with the unfruitful works of darkness, but rather reprove them. Eph. 5:11.

True enough, all things are pure to the pure, that is, to those who are not contrary to the Spirit and Word of God. For none are called pure in the Scriptures but those who conform to the Spirit and Word of the Lord. To all who agree with the Word, all lawful pure things are pure, such as eating, drinking, clothing, house, home, land, gold, silver, wife, children, goods, fish, flesh, waking, sleeping, speaking, silence, and all things which God has created and given to our support. Since they themselves are pure, they will also use all lawful pure things purely: namely, in the fear of God, of necessity, with thanksgiving and moderation, to the praise of the Lord and to the service of their fellow men; to which end these things are created by God and given to the use of men. But all things forbidden by God, such as hypocrisy, getting mixed up with unfruitful works, conforming to the world, living in abundance, splendor, and idolatry; these are impure to the pure, that is, to the believing, obedient children of God. And they may never, according to God's will, be used by the pure, for the Spirit of God and the Word forbid it to them.

Adam was allowed of God to eat of every herb and fruit of the earth for his sustenance except of the tree of knowledge of good and evil. If he should eat of it, he would surely die. All the fruits and creatures were pure to pure Adam by God's permission, but one tree was impure to him through the prohibition of God.[40] He ate thereof, and together with all his seed fell into death.

And even as all things are pure to the pure, so also to the impure all things are impure and tend to evil. For since they are impure they use all the creatures of God impurely. They eat and drink in superfluity, they are dressed in and shod in pride. Their wives they use to satisfy their lust. They rear children in idleness. Their gold, silver, houses, and goods they possess in avarice, and there is nothing they use purely according to the will of God. They are impure, carnal, disobedient to the Word, and earthly-minded, as the Scriptures say.

[vii] Further, it is also an abominable error and shameless seduction that some of them say outward idolatry cannot defile so long as it is not sanctioned by the heart.

---

[40] We read *Verbod* (prohibitory command) instead of *Verbond* (covenant) which makes no sense in the connection in which it stands here. *Tr.*

My good reader, if that were true all the passages would have been spoken to no purpose which say, Flee idolatry; Have no fellowship with the unfruitful works of darkness; Avoid all appearance of evil, etc. Then would also the offense of the cross have ceased. Oh, no, it behooves the true Christian to be pious externally and internally, glorifying God both in body and spirit.

Aaron, a high priest called of God, a type of the Lord Jesus, when he was constrained by the people to make gods for them which should go before them, was overcome through the weakness of the flesh and yielded to the idolaters, making them a golden calf. Aaron did not worship it in his heart, for he knew right well it was not the God who led them through the Red Sea but that it was a creature made of gold. It was nevertheless charged to Aaron, so that Moses said: What did this people unto thee that thou hast brought so great a sin upon them? Ex. 32:21. Yes, the Lord would have destroyed Aaron had not Moses interceded for him. Deut. 9:20.

I could wish that all founders of sects and their erring spirits, who cloak their refusal to bear the cross and their ease and hypocrisy under the semblance of the Word of God, would ponder this story of Aaron. I trust they would no longer cover their nakedness and shame with fig leaves, but would clothe themselves with the true coat of skins prepared by God: Christ Jesus. For by their ungodly practices which they call liberty they encourage and strengthen the poor, reckless people in their idolatry and unbelief. They grieve the pious unto death, weaken and cause to stumble the poor wavering souls of whom it is written: Whoso shall offend one of these little ones which believe in me, it were better for him that a millstone were hanged about his neck, and that he were drowned in the depth of the sea. Matt. 18:6.

But what the liberty of a Christian is, and how it is to be used according to the will of God, is fully explained. Tell us, dear friends, how can men include in Christian liberty that which is committed so evidently against so many passages in the Scriptures, against brotherly and universal love, and contrary to the example of so many saints?

Oh, if they who introduce such flimsy arguments were pure in heart and did not love [other things] above Christ and His Word, how soon would they acknowledge that that which they maintain is contrary to the Spirit and Word of God. But now I fear they are those of whom it is written, There is a generation that are pure in their own eyes and yet is not washed from their filthiness. Prov. 30:12.

But as to the conduct of Naaman, the following passages must be carefully noted: first, Naaman was neither a Jew nor a proselyte, but a foreigner, not included in the doctrine, ceremonies, ordinances, and legal requirements of Israel. For although he wished no longer to serve idols but rather Jehovah, he did not receive the Jewish sign of circumcision.

Secondly, he was his master's servant upon whose arm the king leaned and who therefore had to be present at the service of his master but wished when the king burnt incense in the house of Rimmon to worship none other than the true God who had cleansed him.

Thirdly, we cannot ascertain with certainty, from the answer of the prophet, how far he did or did not comply.

Fourthly, the house of Rimmon and its service are not the same as our temple with its services, for in the house of Rimmon the name of God, His laws, ordinances, and ceremonies were not abused, for they did not know them. But what abuses, disgraces, God-dishonoring speech, abomination, and blasphemy are carried on in our temples in the name of Christ, all reasonable men may judge in the light of Scripture.

Therefore, if anyone says, Why bother about the manipulations of the priests? Worship God as Naaman did!—it sounds to us like saying: Behold, your good father will be often slanderously mocked, insulted, reviled, and much abused; do not let that affect you! Come along, just do not say anything. But of course in your heart, honor your father, etc. Say, friend, what sane and reasonable child could bear to see such great sorrow in his dear father and simply keep silence?

We realize clearly then how grievously they carry on with our eternal Father, who loved us so greatly, in their houses of abomination, and also with His Son Jesus Christ, who bought us with such a precious price. How they quench His Holy Spirit, hate His will, falsify His Word, abuse His sacraments, despise His ordinances and commands, revile and wrong His children, mislead poor souls, and rob Christ of His gain and glory! If we then would betake us to such open enemies of God, play the hypocrite with them, and listen to their wicked seduction and abominations, we would be very ungrateful children and without love. This is beyond dispute.

No, this is not like pious Christians. For even as Christ owns His church, is not ashamed of her, enlightens her with His Holy Spirit and Word, comforts her in all her distresses, strengthens her in sufferings, with power and wisdom enriches her before lords and princes, the wise, and the learned, and before the whole world, so that they altogether have to be silent and ashamed in the presence of a poor humble Christian, and besides, in the day of judgment, acknowledges her before His Father and gives to her the eternal kingdom, so also the Spirit, nature, and love of Christ require of us that we confess before men His divine honor, Word, will, ordinances, and commands, and moreover that we testify to it with our deeds, possessions, blood, life, and death. We must not thoughtlessly frequent houses of abomination where His great and adorable name is miserably reviled and reproached, and where we can hear no truth nor learn any piety, since it is nothing but hypocrisy which they teach, although garnished with the Word of the Lord, as may be evidently observed from the practical results.

They all run, says the prophet, teacher and hearer alike, like a frantic heifer[41]; they all hate reproof and instruction, and live cruelly according to

41 Dutch translation of Hos. 4:16.

their own lusts. God's Word they desire not. Therefore I fear that the chastening rod is already grasped, and the avenging sword of the Lord drawn, so that probably one ungodly man will so bite the other that many of them will be devoured and consumed. For the senseless people want to be punished!

Fifthly, we must point out that now in the New Testament we are directed to the Spirit, Word, counsel, admonition, and usage of Christ. What these allow we are free to do, but what He forbids we are not free to do. To this all true Christians should conform, and not to doubtful histories and obscure passages from which we can draw nothing certain and which teach the very opposite of what the Lord's apostles publicly taught.

I would faithfully admonish the kind reader not to let himself be deceived with such words but by all means to continue in the certain ground which the faithful witnesses of Christ, the holy apostles, have left us in such clear words. For the kind just mentioned seek only to confound the wavering and to escape the cross of Christ.

[viii] But, they will say, we esteem it to be better to do these things occasionally, in order that we may be able to support our wives and children and serve the poor, than that we should turn against the preachers wholly and thereby make all our possessions a prey.

To which we reply in the first place: The first command teaches, Thou shalt love the Lord thy God with all thy heart, and with all the soul, and with all thy mind. Where the name of the Lord is blasphemed and where His Word is violated, there it behooves you to reprove such things with an unblamable life in all love, by the Word of God; and to protect the praise and honor of God as much as in you is. And remember that the Lord says, Whosoever loves father, mother, brother, sister, wife, children, possessions, and life more than me, cannot be my disciple. Luke 14:26.

Secondly, all who believe that God has created heaven and earth, sustained Israel forty years with bread from heaven and water from the rock, sent Elias his necessary food by a raven; gives the birds in the air, the fishes in the water, and the creeping things on earth, their food; these will not doubt the goodness, power, and promise of their Lord Jesus Christ, who says: Seek ye first the kingdom of God and his righteousness, and all these things shall be added unto you. Matt. 6:33. For if His gracious face is in this matter over those who despise Him, how much more over those who fear Him and keep His commandments.

Thirdly, the Almighty, bountiful Lord, God Almighty, is well able to support the poor and needy, apart from any idolatry, hypocrisy, and devil worship. He has no delight in such sacrifices and gifts of unrighteousness, as the prophet says: Behold, to obey is better than sacrifice, and to hearken than the fat of rams. For rebellion is as the sin of witchcraft, and stubbornness is as iniquity and idolatry. I Sam. 15:22, 23.

All therefore who say that they do this for the sake of their wives and children and for the benefit of the poor may know that they love their wives and children more than God. They minimize the arm and power of God and lie unto the Lord; they cover and adorn their indolence, refuse to bear the cross, and show their unbelief, earthly-mindedness, and hypocrisy under such pretense. Let everyone take heed to himself and fear God, who has eyes like flaming fire which penetrate heaven and earth and cannot be blinded with fine words.

[ix] They also take recourse to the fact that Paul purified himself according to the custom of the Jews, and circumcised Timothy. This has a wholly different thrust, for these were things which God had commanded, although they were terminated in Christ. These were matters to which Paul consented so that he might preach the Word more freely to the Jews, even as he said: Unto the Jews I became a Jew, that I might gain the Jews; to them that are under the law, as under the law, that I might gain them that are under the law. I Cor. 9:20.

And since these words had their origin not in Antichrist but in God, things in regard to which Paul gave in to the Jews, as explained, therefore how can we allege by them that we are at liberty to hear false preachers, receive the baptism, and enjoy the supper of Antichrist, and take part with the world in open idolatry and blasphemy? Even if it is done without the heart, it is at least done in appearance. If we are to have such liberty, we must consider the works of the law which were of God to be as unclean and ungodly as the works and abominations of darkness which are of the devil. And we must regard the renunciation of the cross of Christ as highly as the zeal with which Paul undertook to teach the Jews the Gospel of Christ.

Ah, my faithful reader, if you do not want to lose your poor soul, then let your Christ remain unviolated. Seek His praise, follow His Spirit, doctrine, counsel, admonition, and example, and you will never be put to shame. And you will soon realize that the purification of Paul and the circumcision of Timothy are far removed from the traffic, abominations, idolatry, and blasphemy of Antichrist, until now practiced in the name of Christ. May the gracious, merciful God grant you all to come to the knowledge of the truth and to walk in it. Amen.

[x] Finally, they say, we are still in Babylonian captivity and we may therefore in semblance do the works of Babylon, quoting the sayings of Baruch: Ye shall see in Babylon gods of silver, and of gold, and of wood, borne upon shoulders, which causes the nations to fear; beware, therefore, that ye in no wise be like to strangers, neither be ye afraid of them, when ye see the multitude before them and behind them, worshiping them, but say in your hearts, O Lord, we must worship thee. Bar. 6:4, 5.

We must observe first what is meant by Babylonian captivity. When the Israelites did not serve God correctly in their own country, they were scattered according to the prediction of Moses, by the righteous and gracious punishment of God, among the heathen nations, and led captive under the dominion of Babylon. So likewise it is with those who boast themselves the spiritual Israel. For since they have become unfaithful to the Lord, have rejected His Word, and have turned their ears to preachers of lies, the Babylonian "king," Antichrist, has conquered them. He has robbed them of the true doctrine, ceremonies, and services and has led them captive under his dominion. He has bound them miserably with the cords of his error and idolatrous abominations.

But they who are again enlightened by the Spirit and Word of the Lord, who are born of God, who die unto the old life of sin, who forsake all human errors and rightly use the holy sacrament of the Lord, His ordinances and divine services, these are delivered from spiritual Babylon: namely, sin, hell, death, the devil, the doctrines and commands of men, and from all idolatry and abominations. As Paul says, There is therefore now no condemnation to them that are in Christ Jesus, who walk not after the flesh, but after the Spirit. For the law of the Spirit of life in Christ Jesus hath made me free from the law of sin and death. Rom. 8:1, 2.

All those then who say that they are still captives in Babylon declare thereby that they have not been set at liberty from their sins by the true Cyrus, Jesus Christ, and have not escaped from Chaldea to Jerusalem.

Secondly, we should observe that Israel was not commanded in this passage to conform to the Gentiles. But it was commanded that when they saw them carry their idols (even as we see the papistical procession and shame days, even though we are not in their temple) they should worship God only and give Him the honor. If God had commanded them to conform outwardly to the Babylonians in their idolatrous parade, and merely to serve the Lord with their hearts secretly, then Shadrach, Meshach, and Abednego, acted incorrectly in refusing to worship the golden idol of the princes, because of which they got in greatest trouble! Oh, no, the great miracle performed by God in their behalf testifies that they acted correctly. All those then who teach that true believers are not delivered from Babylon thereby go back on the merits, death, and blood of Christ, on faith and its power, the Holy Ghost and His freedoms, and they despise all the innocent blood of the free witnesses, of the free children of God which is shed in various places.

Let everyone take care what he believes and teaches, for I fear that the one who sheds this blood and the one who fails to honor it will be punished in the same way.

My good reader, examine the Scriptures correctly and you will find that to the free children of God there is no liberty promised as to the flesh here on earth, even as Christ says, Ye shall be hated of all nations for my name's sake. Matt. 24:9. Again, If any man will come after me, let him deny himself, and take up his cross, and follow me. Matt. 16:24. Whosoever killeth you will think that he doeth God service. John 16:2. All that will live godly in Christ Jesus, says Paul, must suffer persecution, II Tim. 3:12, and Through much tribulation we must enter into the kingdom of God. Acts 14:22. For the liberty of the Spirit is to be attested to with much misery, tribulation, persecutions, bonds, fear, and death. The disciple is not above his master, nor the servant above his lord. It is enough for the disciple that he be as his master, and the servant as his lord. Matt. 10:24.

Behold, beloved sirs, friends, and brethren, here you have the leading parts and chief articles of a Christian position or system, together with a plain instruction and exposition of the anti-Christian abominations and Babylonian traffic by which the true apostolic truth, because of the long time,[42] was wiped out and demolished. We have also contrasted light with darkness and truth with falsehood, so that our intention, doctrine, and belief, objective and slight achievement may be made manifest.

And I hope by the grace of God that you will grasp it with both hands if you are reasonable, read it with an honest heart, fear God, and consider Christ the right man. You will see that we are grounded on the only eternal cornerstone, and walk, albeit in weakness,[43] in the right way, and have the plain truth, and that there is no other way or truth to be found in the Scriptures that can stand before God, other than this which we have pointed out and which we with so much tribulation verify and defend everywhere.

I have served you all with this small talent as I have received it from my God. I could wish that I could at some time do it with greater and richer grace to the praise of the Lord. For these things I have renounced name and fame, honor and ease, and all, and have willingly assumed the heavy cross of my Lord Jesus Christ which at times assails my poor weak flesh quite grievously. I seek neither gold nor silver (the Lord knows) but am ready with faithful Moses to suffer affliction with the people of God rather than to enjoy the pleasures of sin for a season. I also esteem the reproach of Christ greater riches than the treasures in Egypt, for I know what the Scriptures have promised us. This is my only joy and heart's desire: to extend the kingdom of God, reveal the truth, reprove sin, teach righteousness, feed hungry souls with the Word of the Lord, lead the straying sheep into the right path, and gain many souls to the Lord through His Spirit, power, and grace. So would I carry on in my weakness as He has taught me who purchased me, a miserable sinner, with His crimson blood, and has given me this mind, by the Gospel of His grace, namely, Jesus Christ. To Him be praise and glory and the eternal kingdom. Amen.

---

[42] Menno felt that Anabaptism was a restoration of pure Biblical primitive Christianity. *Ed.*

[43] The Anabaptists believed in personal holiness and in church discipline, but not in perfectionism. *Ed.*

## [III. APPEALS FOR TOLERATION]

### [A.] Exhortation to the Magistrates[44]

We have indicated in the preface, faithful reader, why and wherefore we have published these our writings. It is, namely, on account of the terrible deceptions and manifold dangers in these times, there being so many and various congregations, churches, and sects all calling themselves by the name of the Lord. There are Roman Catholics or papists, Lutherans, Zwinglians, erring sects, and the Christians who are revilingly called Anabaptists. Likewise in former times among the Jews there were the Chasidim, Zadikim, Essenes, Sadducees, Pharisees, etc., as related by Scripture and profane history. Each boasts to be the church of Christ and to have the Word of the Lord, although the greater part of them are not only not in conformity with the Spirit, Word, and example of Christ, but they revile and slander and are basically at variance with it.

It is just as it was from the beginning. The pious everywhere have had to suffer much from the impious, for example, Abel from Cain; Isaac from Ishmael; Jacob from Esau, etc. And this even though they are created by the same God, have one common natural origin, boast the same Christ, and in the day of judgment meet the same Judge. Antichrist rules through hypocrisy and lies, with force and sword, but Christ rules by patience with His Word and Spirit. He has no other sword or saber.

Man, O man, look at the irrational savage creatures and learn wisdom. Roaring lions, fierce bears, and rending wolves keep the peace among their kind. But you, weak and wretched worms, you who are created after God's own image and are called rational beings, born without tusks, claws, and horns and with a frail and feeble nature, born without rationality, speech, and power; yea, unable to walk or stand up, and dependent entirely upon a mother's help—all of which ought to teach you to be peaceable and not contentious. But when you attain to understanding and manhood, you are so turbulent, tyrannical, and cruel, so bloodthirsty and unmerciful, that it is inconceivable and indescribable. Your conduct, known to all, bears testimony to this. And you boast yourselves to be Christians nevertheless. Oh, no, my faithful reader, no. Christ teaches, Peace I leave you, my peace I give unto you. John 14:27. Paul says, Let the peace of God rule in your hearts, to which also ye are called in one body, and be ye thankful. Col. 3:15. Again, The Son of man is not come to destroy men's lives, but to save them. Luke 9:56.

Since you are so numerous and carry on so inhumanly with pious children, as may be seen, therefore we have stated briefly our conduct, position,

---

[44] The full title in the Dutch is: *A Christian and Affectionate Exhortation to all Magistrates, Learned Ones, Common People, and the Sects; also to the Bride of Christ, not a little Scorched by the Heat of the Sun, in all Places.*

faith, and doctrine from the Word of God. We have printed them so that every slanderous evil speaker and bloody persecutor may discover what our proper intention is, what we seek and do, upon what ground the city of God must be built, and which of all the afore-mentioned assemblies or churches is the right and true church of Christ. For just as there was but one Adam and one Eve, one Noah and one ark, one Isaac and one Rebecca, so there is but one church of Christ, which is the body, city, temple, house, and bride of Christ, having but a single Gospel, faith, baptism, Supper and service; traveling on the same road and leading a pious, unblamable life, as the Scriptures teach.

All then who do not have the pure, unmixed Word of God, genuine active faith, together with the Lord's holy baptism and Supper, in spirit and power, and walk the broad road of the flesh: these are not the congregation and church of Christ. Here neither name nor boasting matters. We must be in Christ and Christ in us; we must be moved by His Spirit, and abide in His holy Word outwardly and inwardly. Otherwise we have no God.

Being seed of the pious Abraham could not save the children of Israel if they did not walk in the way of Abraham. Much less will it save us to be called after the name of Christ if we do not seek His glory with all our souls, and sincerely hear and follow and obey His holy will.

It is well known to all pious people that we and our forefathers for many centuries drudged and slaved under the heavy burden and service of Egypt. We were deceived by the false prophets and never heard the book of the law. The holy city and temple lay waste under the tyranny and dominion of Babylon. The merciful Father had compassion on the grievous distress and sorrow of His people and raised up to us the true Moses and Zerubbabel, Christ Jesus, by His Word and Spirit.

Therefore it becomes you, lords and princes, since you boast of the same Christ, Gospel, redemption, and kingdom, no longer by your mandates and powers to obstruct the passage of the people of God to the eternal promised land. Rather you should assist and favor them more and more by your gracious permission, and with the noble and pious Josiah hear and read, with a broken, humble heart, in the true fear of God, the book of the law of Christ so long lost. Rend your hearts and not your garments, for you are not only led off the true path, but are so much bewitched by the man of sin that you persecute the innocent, pious hearts who hurt or harm not a hair of you or of anyone else upon earth.

With the great king Cyrus release the poor captive children from the land of Chaldea, who mourn and weep at the rivers of Babylon. Release them so that they may once more possess the spiritual Canaan and build up the spiritual Jerusalem, restore the altar and the temple in their ancient capital, establish the spiritual priesthood, and participate in the spiritual sacrifice and service according to the instructions of the Word of God. Release them so that they may no longer fear and observe the Babylonian laws, the teachings and commandments of men; but the law of Israel, God's Word and righteousness. For some of you, though few alas, are so far taught through the grace and Word of God that I hope that you know that neither usages nor councils, learnedness nor sword, nor edict can bend or break the truth of the Most High, the Word of truth, the Word of the heavenly witness, the Gospel of the kingdom. For other foundation can not be laid in all eternity than that which is laid, which is Christ Jesus. I Cor. 3:11.

Therefore wisdom cries out: Turn you at my reproof: behold, I will pour out my Spirit unto you, I will make known my words unto you. Prov. 1:23. Love righteousness, ye rulers of the land. Be wise now therefore, O ye kings: be instructed, ye judges of the earth. Serve the Lord with fear, and rejoice with trembling. Ps. 2:10. For the king that honors wisdom shall rule forever.

Therefore, with a humble heart and in the fear of God, examine this our faithful exposition and judge by Christ's own Spirit and Word as much as in you is. Compare it with the doctrine and lives of the apostles; with the piety, love, customs, deeds, misery, cross, and sufferings of the primitive church; and I hope by the grace of God that you may see plainly that our doctrine is the infallible doctrine and position of the Scriptures. Read this our *Foundation* together with the other tracts appended thereto: the book concerning *Faith* and its power; concerning *Regeneration* or the new creature[45]; of the *Cross,* sufferings, and persecution of the saints; of *Excommunication* and ban or exclusion, and other tracts, published now and then. You will find by the grace of God that this doctrine is the pure Gospel which the Lord taught by His own mouth, and which His holy apostles preached through the whole world, and in the power of the Spirit testified to with life and death. Ours is no new doctrine, as the preachers without truth assert and would have you believe. It is the old doctrine which was preached and practiced in the church for more than 1,500 years, the doctrine by which the church was begotten, is being begotten, and will be begotten to the end.

O illustrious lords and princes, turn to the truth of God and embrace reproof and wisdom. For through wisdom kings reign and princes decree justice. Observe how far your spirit, faith, and lives differ from the Lord's Spirit, Word, and life.

Do you suppose, dear sirs, that you were born for nothing but to live in splendor and show, and to lead a vain, carnal life; that you may continue in your self-will and soul-destroying lusts as you please and still be Christians? Oh, no. If any man have not the Spirit of Christ, he is none of his. Rom. 8:9.

Solomon says, As a roaring lion and a raging bear; so is the wicked ruler over the poor people. The prince that wanteth understanding is also a great oppressor. Prov. 28:15. The poet understood this when he said, For that which kings misdo the common people must pay. But a wise king scatters the ungodly.

---

[45] In this volume entitled, *The New Birth. Ed.*

Therefore, dear sirs, take heed; this is the task to which you are called: namely, to chastise and punish, in the true fear of God with fairness and Christian discretion, manifest criminals, such as thieves, murderers, Sodomites, adulterers, seducers, sorcerers, the violent, highwaymen, robbers, etc. Your task is to do justice between a man and his neighbor, to deliver the oppressed out of the hand of the oppressor; also to restrain by reasonable means, that is, without tyranny and bloodshed, manifest deceivers who so miserably lead poor helpless souls by hundreds of thousands into destruction. Whether the deceivers are priests, monks, preachers, baptized or unbaptized, it is your task to restrain them so that they may no longer detract from the power of the almighty majesty of God, our only and eternal Saviour, Christ Jesus, the Holy Ghost, and the Word of grace; nor introduce such ridiculous abuses and idolatry under semblance of truth as has been done until now. In this way, in all love, without force, violence, and blood, you may enlarge, help, and protect the kingdom of God with gracious consent and permission, with wise counsel and a pious, unblamable life.

Dear sirs, this is your calling and assigned task, and not so cruelly to lord it over the children of God and His Word as, alas, many of you have a way of doing, it seems.

Such rulers were Moses, Joshua, David, Hezekiah, Jehoshaphat, Josiah, and Zerubbabel. They discharged their calling with reason, accommodated themselves to the Word of God, protected their subjects with solicitous care, obeyed the commands of the Lord, abolished the false prophets and priests of Baal[46] with their groves, altars, high places, and idolatry. They faithfully kept their people and country in the ordinances of the Lord, His laws and divine service as commanded by Moses. For the fear of God was in their hearts, and the book of the law in their hand. To it they conformed, and in the light of it they judged the people. They always remembered the Lord their God, who made them such great potentates and rulers over His people.

They feared God with all their hearts, praised His name, and humbled themselves mightily, as David did when he was girded with a linen ephod and danced before the ark of the Lord, yea, so that he was despised by his wife Michal. But he said, I will play before the Lord who chose me, and I will humble myself even more in my own eyes.

O highly renowned, noble lords, believe Christ's Word, fear God's wrath, love righteousness, do justice to widows and orphans, judge rightly between a man and his neighbor, fear no man's highness, despise no man's littleness, hate all avarice, punish with reason, allow the Word of God to be taught freely, hinder no one from walking in the truth, bow to the scepter of him who called you to this high service. Then shall your throne stand firm forever.

Now even as the scepter of Christ is a right scepter, one that teaches, judges, and rebukes everyone without respect of persons, so also must I, poor, unlearned man that I am, lay aside my natural modesty and in love take

46 Reading "Baal" for "Babel" (Babylon). *Tr.*

on boldness wherewith I would fain save your poor souls. With Samuel I must reprove Saul, with Abdia reprimand Jeroboam, with Elijah chide Ahab, with Isaiah reprehend Hezekiah, with Nathan and Gad rebuke David for misdeeds and transgressions, and so proclaim my Lord's Spirit, Word, and will. Who knows but there might be someone of them to notice the fidelity and love of his poor servant, hear his well-meaning voice and Christian exhortation, and so depart from his ungodly and evil way; just as some of the aforementioned kings heard the reproving word of the mouths of the prophets with fear and unto repentance, and humbly received the Word.

And even if my faithful service and love should be rewarded with death, as I have reason to think it may,[47] since haughty and proud flesh dislikes to be reproved, but ever uses its evil nature, yet at that it cannot go worse with me than it did with the pious Isaiah at the hand of Manasseh, Zechariah at the hand of Joaz, Urijah at the hand of Jehoiakim, Abimelech and the other priests at the hand of Saul, John at the hand of Herod, Christ at the hand of Pilate and of the scribes, and the apostles and the pious witnesses at the hand of the entire world.

I do not esteem my life more than the beloved men of God did theirs. Only perishable and mortal flesh which must sometime die can be taken from me, a flesh made to return to dust even though I should live half the days of Methuselah. Not a hair can fall from my head without the will of my heavenly Father; and if I lose my life for the sake of Christ and His testimony, and for sincere love for my neighbor, I certainly know that I will save it in life eternal. Therefore I cannot conceal the truth, but I must testify and reveal it without hypocrisy in the fear of God to my dear sirs.

Dear noble lords, learn rightly to know yourselves, whence you are, what you are, and what you will be. All of you, each and every one, be he emperor or king, issues from the same seed as we poor and common people. You came into this sorrowful world as we did, and you are but vapor, frail flesh, a withering flower, dust and ashes, as are we all. Today you are kings and exult in great and high honor; tomorrow you are laid low, and must be food for snails[48] and worms.

Sirs, dear sirs, humble yourselves. Righteous is He who will hear your case, and mighty is He who will sentence. His name is the Ruler of rulers; He is the Almighty, the holy and terrible, the highly adorable and wonderworking God who has created heaven and earth, and grips in the hands of His strength all majesty, power, and dominion. Him learn to know; Him learn to fear. Rouse yourselves; the time is not far off when you will hear, Give an account of your stewardship; for thou mayest no longer be steward. Luke 16:2.

---

[47] Menno's expectation that he might die a martyr's death was never realized. He died a natural death Jan. 31, 1561, twenty-five years after his renunciation of Roman Catholicism, and in the sixty-sixth year of his age. *Ed.*

[48] Reading *slaken* (snails) for *slangen* (snakes). *Tr.*

Therefore do not hear those who are after fat salaries and a lazy life. They deceive you. They teach you according to the lust of your hearts. They implore for the sake of filthy lucre; they preach to you empty inventions out of their own imagination and not out of the mouth of the Lord. They fatten their bodies and have a good time on the fatness of your poor souls (beloved sirs, get what I mean) although they boast much of the Gospel. Hear those rather who are not like the wind-shaken reed, men who with John and Elijah are not so greatly frightened by the wilderness of misery, who suffer daily for the truth's sake, esteem wood as they do gold, praise as reproach, riches as poverty, life as death, men who seek only the honor of Christ and the salvation of their beloved brethren. They preach nothing but the pure, unmixed Word of God, and seal it with spirit, power, and conduct as was commanded by Christ and proclaimed and taught through the whole world by His holy apostles.

I repeat, Do not hear, do not follow, and do not believe the many learned ones who let themselves be called doctors, lords, and masters, for they mind but flesh and blood. But seek and follow those who pass for the spectacle and filth of the earth, the curse and the offscouring from among them, for with them you will find Christ, the Spirit, truth, power, works, and life. You will also through the grace of God presently discover how that you and your teachers' spirit, faith, baptism, Supper, conduct, and church are outside of Christ's Spirit, doctrine, command, prohibition, ordinance, and usage.

O kings and rulers of the land, where indeed is your faith and love with their pious nature? Where is the fear of your God, your burning lamp, your humble heart dead unto sin? Where is your blameless, godly life which is of God? Is it not Simon-pure world and carnality which you seek and protect? We find in your houses and courts nothing but sparkling pomp and showy dress, boldness and presumptuousness of heart, insatiable avarice, hatred and envy, backbiting, betraying, harloting, seduction, gambling, gaming, carousing, dancing, swearing, stabbing, and violence. This is your chivalrous custom and courtly conduct all the days of your lives. You never once reflect through what misery, tribulation, humility, love, and righteousness the Lord of lords and King of kings walked His way before you, what He taught the children of men, and what pattern or example He left them. The pitiful moaning and misery of the wretched men does not reach your ears. The sweat of the poor we find in your houses, and the innocent blood on your hands. Their gifts and presents are received to pervert judgment and you take counsel against the Lord and His anointed. The prophets of Jezebel and the priests of Baal, men who talk to your taste and fawn all over you, these are in big demand and swarm all over you. These are in big demand with you, men who sit on easy cushions and have a fine time.

But those who with Micah announce disaster and proclaim straight truth, these may look for bonds, imprisonment, and death, to be deemed deserving of death and disgrace. Yea, it has come to such a pass (God help) that where

four or five, ten or twenty, have met in the name of the Lord, to speak of the
Word of the Lord and to do His work, men in whose midst Christ is, who
fear the Lord with all their heart, and lead an unblamable life before all the
world, if they are discovered and accused, they must be devoured by fire or
sword, or "swim" in the bottom of the river.

But they who have met in the name of Belial, a meeting of all wickedness, far exceeding Sodom and Gomorrah, where all manner of sexual perversion is practiced, as it is in Spain and Italy and in the cloisters, also public
brothels, play-houses, fencing schools, and the accursed drunken taverns where
men live in open shame and act so crudely, contrary to God's Word, these live
unmolested and undisturbed!

At that I make no mention of the public assemblies, of all manner of
idolatry where the most high, blessed, and precious name of God is so sadly
blasphemed, the blood of Christ despised, the Holy Ghost grieved, the truth
violated, the lie commended, the poor souls deceived, and the blind, ignorant
people not only directed to the water, bread, wine, and the mass, but also to
the dumb idols of wood and stone, as, alas, it may be so witnessed everywhere.

O my dear sirs, what are you doing? Where in the world is the sword
of righteousness, of which you boast, given and entrusted to you? You have
to acknowledge that you have put it in the sheath, and in its stead you have
drawn the sword of unrighteousness. Yes, dear sirs, men carry on so (may
God have pity) that the prophets may well write and exclaim, My princes
are rebellious and companions of thieves; everyone loveth gifts, and followeth
after rewards: they judge not the fatherless, neither doth the cause of the
widow come unto them. Therefore saith the Lord, the Lord of hosts, the
Mighty One of Israel, Ah, I will ease me of mine adversaries, and avenge
me of mine enemies. Isa. 1:23, 24.

Behold, the princes of Israel in thee, everyone according to their power
is bent to shed blood.[49] In the midst of thee have they dealt by oppression
with the stranger; in thee have they vexed the fatherless and the widow.
They are like the devouring wolves to shed blood and to destroy souls for the
sake of their avarice. Behold, therefore, says the Lord, I have smitten mine
hand at thy dishonest gain which thou hast made, and at the blood which hath
been in the midst of thee. Ezek. 22:6, 7, 13.

Woe to them that devise iniquity and work evil upon their beds! when
the morning is light, they practice it, because it is in the power of their hand.
And they covet fields, and take them by violence; and houses, and take them
away: so they oppress a man and his house, even a man and his heritage.
Therefore thus saith the Lord, Behold, against this family do I devise an evil,
from which ye shall not remove your necks; neither shall ye go haughtily:
for the time is evil. Mic. 2:1-3.

Hear, O heads of Jacob, and ye princes of the house of Israel; Is it not
for you to know judgment? Who hate the good and love the evil; who pluck

---

[49] The language in this citation has been clarified by comparison with the RSV. *Ed.*

off their skin from off them, and their flesh from off their bones; who also eat the flesh of my people, and flay their skin from off them; and they break their bones, and chop them in pieces, as for the pot, and as flesh within the caldron. Then shall they cry unto the Lord, but he will not hear them: he will even hide his face from them at that time, as they have behaved themselves ill in their doings. Mic. 3:1-4.

Woe to her that is filthy and polluted, to the oppressing city! She obeyed not the voice; she received not correction; she trusted not in the Lord; she drew not near to her God. Her princes within her are roaring lions; her judges are evening wolves; they gnaw not the bones till the morrow. Her prophets are light and treacherous persons: her priests have polluted the sanctuary, they have done violence to the law. The just Lord is in the midst thereof; he will not do iniquity; every morning doth he bring his judgment to the light, he faileth not; but the unjust knoweth no shame. I have cut off the nations: their towers are desolate; I made their streets waste that none passeth by. Zeph. 3:1-6.

There are but few of you, are there not, I fear scarcely a one, who seeks the Lord with all his heart; fears, loves, and serves Him. Therefore will also the fury of God be poured out upon you like water, and the sword of His wrath will come upon you, as may (God help) be seen daily in many places.

The writer of the Book of Wisdom says, Power is given you of the Lord and sovereignty from the Highest, who shall try your works and search out your counsels; because being ministers of his kingdom, ye have not judged aright, nor kept the law, nor walked after the counsel of God; horribly and speedily shall he come upon you; for a sharp judgment shall he be to them that are in high places. For mercy will soon pardon the meanest; but mighty men shall be mightily tormented. For he who is Lord over all shall fear no man's person, neither shall he stand in awe of any man's greatness; for he hath made the small and great, and careth for all alike. But a sore trial shall come upon the mighty. Wisd. 6:3-8.

Therefore, dear sirs, take heed wisely, rightly to execute your responsible and dangerous office according to the will of God. For alas, I fear that many of you as yet have paid but little attention to it, and as a result Antichrist with his wickedness is exalted, and Christ with His righteousness is rejected. Ponder if only for once that which is written, Keep thee far from a false matter; and the innocent and righteous slay thou not; for I will not justify the wicked, says the Lord. Ex. 23:7.

At this point I know right well that we have to hear of Münster, kingdom, polygamy, sword, plunder, murder, and the like abominations and scandals which you always assert result from baptism. And therefore you persecute everything the mouth of the Lord has commanded, and the holy apostles taught and practiced, and you cite as proof some seditious sects and conspiracies because of which the clamor of the learned ones and your bloodshedding is supposed to be justified.

No, beloved sirs, no! It will not deliver you in the day of the righteousness of God. I tell you the truth in Christ, the rightly baptized disciples of Christ, note well, they who are baptized inwardly with Spirit and fire, and externally with water, according to the Word of the Lord, have no weapons except patience, hope, silence, and God's Word. The weapons of our warfare, says Paul, are not carnal, but mighty through God to the pulling down of strongholds, casting down imaginations and every high thing that exalteth itself against the knowledge of God, and bringing into captivity every thought to the obedience of Christ. II Cor. 10:4, 5.

Our weapons are not weapons with which cities and countries may be destroyed, walls and gates broken down, and human blood shed in torrents like water. But they are weapons with which the spiritual kingdom of the devil is destroyed and the wicked principle in man's soul is broken down, flinty hearts broken, hearts that have never been sprinkled with the heavenly dew of the Holy Word. We have and know no other weapons besides this, the Lord knows, even if we should be torn into a thousand pieces, and if as many false witnesses rose up against us as there are spears of grass in the fields, and grains of sand upon the seashore.

Once more, Christ is our fortress; patience our weapon of defense; the Word of God our sword; and our victory a courageous, firm, unfeigned faith in Jesus Christ. And iron and metal spears and swords we leave to those who, alas, regard human blood and swine's blood about alike. He that is wise let him judge what I mean.

We do acknowledge, dear sirs, that some of the false prophets were baptized with one and the same baptism, and were one with us in appearance; as thieves, murderers, highwaymen, sorcerers, and the like were baptized together with you. But they were not of us, for had they been of us, as John says, they would no doubt have continued with us.

Christ says, There shall arise false Christs, and false prophets, and shall show great signs and wonders; insomuch that, if it were possible, they should deceive the very elect. Behold, I have told you before. Matt. 24:24, 25.

This warning of Christ was not given to the ungodly, hardened despisers, for these are already entangled in the snares of unrighteousness. It was given to those who are of a contrite heart and a willing soul, so that they might learn to know the spirits and not to allow themselves to be led into error. For the devil as a roaring lion walketh about, seeking whom he may devour. I Pet. 5:8.

The craft and subtilty of the devil, who can clothe himself with the radiance of an angel of light, are not known by some. Therefore many have stumbled and strayed, and alas have landed on the crooked path through the instrumentality of the deceivers. But this was not occasioned by baptism, since speechless elements can neither teach nor pervert. It was done through false prophets against whom I say we have been so faithfully warned by the mouth of the Lord.

Dear sirs, fear God, judge rightly. The truth of God can never be changed, can it, into seduction and error because of the lies of the devil. Oh, no! the Word of our God shall stand forever.

Shall the good angels be considered wicked because of Lucifer's pride and be punished with his punishment, and shall all the apostles be called traitors because of Judas? By no means, for everyone shall bear his own burden. The son shall not bear the iniquity of the father, neither shall the father bear the iniquity of the son. The soul that sinneth it shall die. Ezek. 18:20.

How can men blame Christ and the apostolic doctrine for the fact that the father of lies put forth some who in the name of Christ insisted that circumcision was necessary to salvation, that the dead will not rise in the day of judgment, that Philetus and Hymenaeus asserted that the resurrection of the dead had then already taken place, that some made bold to say that the great day of the Lord was at hand?

How could the apostle help it that the Nicolaitanes[50] had their wives in common, as Eusebius relates?[51] That the Ebionites rejected the deity of Christ, and taught that Christ took His origin in Mary; and that the followers of Cerinthus[52] maintained that the world was created by angels, that Christ was no more than a mere man and had not yet risen, but should rise with us in the future, and thereafter reign one thousand years in the flesh with His saints.

All these sects were about in the days of the apostles, yet the Gospel of Christ remained the true Gospel, the doctrine of the apostles, the true doctrine.

The Scriptures teach us to flee and avoid such leaders of sects and heretics; and we hope willingly to obey the injunction all the days of our lives.

Therefore, my dear sirs, pass an impartial and rational judgment in this matter as before your God who will judge you in His day. This we ask of you for Jesus' sake, for we seek nothing else upon earth (this the Lord knows) than the true foundation of the truth, the praise of Christ, and the obedience of His Word; and that with a good conscience, as we testify to the whole world with our writings, speech, possessions, blood, life, and death.

We write the truth in Christ and lie not, that as to the spirit we acknowledge no king either in heaven above or upon the earth beneath, other than the only, eternal, and true king David in the spirit, Christ Jesus, who is Lord of lords and King of kings.

And if anyone declares himself king in the kingdom and dominion of Christ, as John of Leiden did at Münster, he with Adonijah shall not go unpunished, for the true Solomon, Christ Jesus Himself, must possess the kingdom and sit eternally upon the throne of David.

[50] Rev. 2:6, 15.

[51] The statements of the Church Fathers add no real information to that given by the Apostle John. *Ed.*

[52] Unsound teacher, possibly of Syria, in the first century A.D. His followers were called Cerinthians. *Ed.*

But as to the flesh, we teach and exhort to obedience to the emperor, king, lords, magistrates, yea, to all in authority in all temporal affairs, and civil regulations in so far as they are not contrary to the Word of God. Rom. 13:1-3.

We teach and acknowledge no other sword, nor tumult in the kingdom or church of Christ than the sharp sword of the Spirit, God's Word, as has been made quite plain in this and our other writings: a sword which is sharper and more penetrating than any sword, two-edged, and proceeding from the mouth of the Lord. With it we set the father against the son and the son against the father, the mother against the daughter and the daughter against the mother; the daughter-in-law against the mother-in-law. But the civil sword we leave to those to whom it is committed.[53] Let everyone be careful lest he transgress in the matter of the sword, lest he perish with the sword. Matt. 26:52.

We acknowledge, teach, and assent to no other marriage than that which Christ and His apostles publicly and plainly taught in the New Testament, namely, of one man and one woman (Matt. 19:4), and that they may not be divorced except in case of adultery (Matt. 5:32); for the two are one flesh, but if the unbelieving one depart, a sister or brother is not under bondage in that case. I Cor. 7:15.

No other kingdom do we know, teach, and seek, than that of Christ which shall endure forever, which is neither pride nor pomp, gold nor silver, eating nor drinking, but righteousness, peace, and joy in the Holy Ghost. For we confess with Christ that our kingdom is not of this world. We brought nothing into this world; therefore it is evident we cannot take anything out of it, as the Scriptures say. I Tim. 6:7.

Murder is unknown to us, much less inculcated and permitted, for we believe of a truth that a murderer has neither lot nor part in the kingdom of God. Gal. 5:21. O dear sirs, how could we desire the blood of any man since we have to die daily for man's sake before the Lord who created us and knows that we seek nothing but that we might instruct and lead the world with doctrine, life, blood, and death so that they might reflect, rouse themselves, repent, and be saved? For this is the nature of pure love, to pray for persecutors, to render good for evil, to love one's enemies, to heap coals of fire upon their heads, and to leave vengeance to Him who judges rightly. Rom. 12:20.

We know of no thieving, much less do we teach or permit it. But we are prepared before God and man with all our hearts to share our possessions, gold, and all that we have, however little it may be; and to sweat and labor to meet the need of the poor, as the Spirit and Word of the Lord, and true brotherly love teach and imply. We know very well that theft is expressly forbidden in the Scriptures (Eph. 4:28); that according to civil statute and usage it is punishable by hanging, and according to God's law will be punished with eternal death if there is no repentance.

53 An allusion to Rom. 13. *Ed.*

The Almighty, merciful Lord, through His fatherly grace, Spirit, and power, will undoubtedly keep and preserve without offense to the end all the pious, God-fearing hearts that know Him and are diligent, keeping them from all such fearful errors and ungodly abominations.

And in case somewhere there is left (unknown to me) a remnant of such errorists which would launch something that is from the devil, beloved sirs, know that such people were not of us from the beginning and will forever be outside of us except they repent sincerely and become one with the Spirit, doctrine, and example of Christ as the Scriptures teach. May the gracious Lord grant that they may awaken, get eyes to see, learn to know their works, see their own shame, and be extricated from the snares of the devil by which the poor miserable people are so lamentably held captive at his will.

Therefore, dear sirs, beware lest you be like the reckless and the foolish in judgments concerning the faith, men who proceed without any knowledge of the matter, like irrational creatures in their willfulness and arbitrariness, reviling the good and praising the evil, persecuting and condemning what they understand not. Again I say, Be not like those bloodthirsty, violent, and cruel men. But examine the Scriptures with trembling. With Solomon pray for wisdom. Look to the Spirit, Word, conduct, and example of Christ, and pass an impartial, righteous sentence according to the truth, even as all princes and judges are commanded in the Scriptures, as has been heard.

O dear sirs, observe. If our faith, doctrine, sacraments, conduct, and practice are not of God, as is slanderously said of us everywhere, then we are the most miserable of all men on earth. We pass for every man's deceiver, heretic, Anabaptist, knave, footstool, and prey, and endure the stake, gallows, wheels, sword, fire, water and everything else. In that case see our poor souls become the property of the devil and hell-fire even though in our weakness we so fervently seek the Lord and have such good intentions as may be seen. Oh, no! my beloved sirs, no! The Spirit, doctrine, and life of Christ will not deceive us, for His Word is truth and His commandments eternal life. God's promises stand fast and immovable and will nevermore fail the pious.

Therefore, we pray and admonish you; yes, we counsel and request you, to contrast our desire with your desire, our spirit with your spirit, our doctrine with the doctrine of the learned, our conduct with your conduct, our poverty with your abundance, our disgrace and reproach with your selfish ambition, our affliction and sorrow with your ease and luxurious life, our patience with your tyranny, our cruel bonds and shameful death with your merciless fury and fierce cruelty (I speak of the guilty), and if then you should discover that your doctrine, faith, life, ambition, and conduct are in harmony with the Spirit, Word, and life of the Lord, and are better than ours, then instruct us with a fatherly spirit. We desire so fervently to fear and obey; for the truth we desire to obey unto death.

But if you cannot reprove us with Scripture, and acknowledge our [doctrine and conduct] to be best, then it would be heathenish, yes, ungodly and tyrannical, would it not, to crowd us out of life into death, from heaven into hell, with the sword and violence! This you will have to acknowledge and confess. But so much decency I fear will not be shown us wretched children: to weigh the matter in the balance of the Holy Word, and to measure it with the standard of Christ.

But the reviling, betraying, and agitation of the priests and your unmerciful mandates and edicts must be our scriptures, and your rackers, hangmen, wrath, torture chambers, water and stake, fire and sword (O God) must be our instructors and teachers, to whom we sorrowful children must listen in many places, and finally make good with our possessions and lifeblood. How this is to be harmonized with the Spirit, doctrine, and conduct of Christ, and with Christian kindness, love, and friendly spirit, you, my dear sirs, may ponder at some length. This I know for certain, that all bloodthirsty preachers and all rulers who propose and practice these things are not Christ's disciples. The hour of accounting when you depart this life will teach you the truth. It is verily wholly improper, says Cyprian, that such lionlike raving and wolflike fury should dwell in a Christian heart. Oh, how good it would be for some of you, yes, how good if you had never been born, for many of you regard neither law nor Gospel, heaven nor hell, God nor the devil. But evil flesh will have its way and proceed in accordance with its native tendency.

Do you suppose, dear sirs, that the Almighty God and Lord who holds heaven and earth in the hollow of His hand, who kills and makes alive, the king who rules over all, and upholds all things by the Word of His power, who raises up and brings low, the consuming fire before whose presence the hills must melt like wax, that He will yield and give place to carnal minds and earthly hearts? No, no! Before Him, the great and the commoner are alike, the rich and the poor, the strong and the weak, the learned and the unlearned, the wise and the foolish. With Him is no respect of persons; all who do not fear Him, do not conform to His counsel, doctrine, spirit, and example, whether emperor, king, doctor, or licentiate, he must bear His punishment eternally and be subject to His judgment and wrath.

Dear sirs, fear God, do right, learn wisdom and truth, cleanse your hands which are wet, and which drip with innocent blood, and reflect how the righteous God will in due time punish all unrighteousness, cruelty, and violence, and how severely He from the beginning avenged and visited upon bloodthirsty tyrants the innocent blood, torture, and death of His saints.

The bloodthirsty Cain had to be an accursed, fleeing exile in the land all the days of his life, because he had so hatefully murdered his innocent brother Abel.

The unmerciful, cruel murderer, Pharaoh, with his entire host, was destroyed in the Red Sea by the righteous judgment of God on account of the merciless and cruel tyranny which he visited upon the children of Jacob, God's people.

Joash was slain by his own servants to avenge the innocent blood of pious Zachariah, whom he slew between the temple and the altar.

Manasseh was led away captive because of his great abomination and the idolatry which he practiced, and on account of the innocent blood with which he had filled Jerusalem.

Ahab was shot through with an arrow and his blood was licked up by the dogs at the waters of Samaria. His wife, Jezebel, was thrust out of the window and trodden underfoot of horses. Her flesh was eaten of dogs in punishment for her wicked conduct and the blood of Naboth, according to the word of the Lord which He spoke by Elijah the Tishbite.

Sennacherib had to draw away from Jerusalem in disgrace because of his blasphemous boasting by which he offended the Most High. The angel of the Lord slew in one night one hundred and eighty-five thousand men in his camp, and Sennacherib was thrust through with the sword of his own children in the temple of his god, Nisroch.

Nebuchadnezzar, on account of his pride, was thrust forth by the people for the space of seven times or years. He became like unto the brute beasts, he ate grass like oxen, his body was wet with the dew of heaven, his hairs were grown like eagles' feathers, and his nails like birds' claws.

Belshazzar caroused with his mighty men, princes, wives, and concubines. They were merry, drank out of the holy vessels which Nebuchadnezzar, his father, had plundered out of the temple at Jerusalem, and, while at the height of their merrymaking and joy, praising their gods of gold, silver, brass, iron, and stone, the impenitent and proud tyrant was punished of God in that very night, without mercy, so that he at one stroke lost land and people, life and limb.

Antiochus the Great, a most wicked king and prince, a tyrant of tyrants, was punished of God with such a plague that maggots crept from his body when he was yet alive, and pieces of flesh sloughed from his body. The stench was so intolerable that no one could remain with him, nor he himself endure. The righteous wrath of God went over him, this ungodly wretch, and with unheard-of pain and sufferings he had to end his proud, bloodthirsty, wicked life and leave this world.

Herod, arrayed in his royal attire, seated upon his throne, because of the flattering applause of his people concerning his eloquence and wisdom, exalted himself in his heart against God, and in that very hour he was smitten by the angel of the Lord, and was eaten of worms. According to Eusebius, he departed this life in such a way that all the proud, haughty tyrants may take a lesson and fear.

In a word, how it commonly went with Pilate, Nero, Domitian, Maximinius, Diocletian, and all malicious, bloodthirsty tyrants, and what kind of death they died, men who rose up against Christ and His saints, may be read both in sacred and profane history.

With what death and conscience some of these bloodguilty ones of our day have departed this life, I will for cause leave unwritten. I will however say this much, that neither emperor nor edicts with which they justified themselves all their life could give them calm nor peace in the hour of their death. But oftentimes with sighs and complaints they have been distressed because of the innocent blood which they had shed in the emperor's name, saying, How will it go with us now, miserable men?

O God, what escape? Dear noble sirs, what escape? How will it stand with your poor souls in the day in which the heavens shall pass away with a great noise and the elements shall melt with fervent heat, and the earth also and the works that are therein shall be burnt up? Then we must all appear before the judgment seat and stand before the righteous judge, where everyone shall be rewarded according to his works. He that keepeth Israel shall neither slumber nor sleep, for yet a little while and he that shall come will come, and will not tarry. Heb. 10:37.

Therefore cease flying in the eyes of the Lord, for he that toucheth His saints toucheth the apple of His eye. Have mercy on your own souls which must atone for it with death eternally, unless you turn to God with all your heart, and cease from the blood of His saints. Daily they call to Him, How long, O Lord, holy and true, dost thou not judge and avenge our blood on them that dwell on the earth? Rev. 6:10. They call, I say, and their cries are entered into the ears of the Lord of Sabaoth. Avenging He will avenge,[54] and require the blood of His servants at your hands.

Do not excuse yourselves, dear sirs, and judges, because you are the servants of the emperor. This will not clear you in the day of vengeance. It did not help Pilate that he crucified Christ in the name of the emperor. Serve the emperor in imperial matters, so far as Scripture permits, and serve God in divine matters. Then you may boast of His grace and have yourselves called after the Lord's name.

Do not usurp the judgment and kingdom of Christ, for He alone is the ruler of the conscience,[55] and besides Him there is none other. Let Him be your emperor in this matter and His holy Word your edict, and you will soon have enough of storming and slaying. You must hearken to God above the emperor, and obey God's Word more than that of the emperor. If not, then you are the judges of whom it is written in Micah, They all lie in wait for blood; they hunt every man his brother with a net. That they may do evil with both hands earnestly, the prince asketh, and the judge asketh for a reward; and the great man, he uttereth his mischievous desire: so they wrap it up. The best of them is as a brier; the most upright is sharper than a thorn hedge: the day of thy watchmen and thy visitation cometh; now shall be their perplexity. Mic. 7:2-4.

Therefore fight no longer against the Lamb and His elect. It will be hard for you to kick against the pricks.

Perhaps you will with all scoffers say in your hearts, Where is the promise of His coming? Ah, dear sirs, be careful. We have known many

[54] A Hebraism meaning, He will surely avenge.
[55] A major emphasis among the Anabaptists. *Ed.*

such people, who made a great show in silk and velvet, with gold and silver, passing sentence upon innocent blood, but now they are no more. We ask after their place and it is not found.

The day will break forth as lightning and the hour shall come upon them like a tempest. Behold and repent. We see plainly that the tree buds, that the summer is nigh at hand, and our Redeemer is hastening, who redeems all the troubled souls from afflictions. He will recompense all the proud scoffers with just recompense.

Yes, the day is coming and it is not far off when the righteous man shall stand in great boldness before the face of such as have afflicted him and made no account of his labors. When they see it they shall be troubled with terrible fear and shall be amazed at the strangeness of his salvation so far beyond all that they had looked for. And they, repenting and groaning for anguish of spirit, shall say to themselves, This was he whom we had sometimes in derision and a proverb of reproach; we fools accounted his life madness and his end to be without honor; how is it he was numbered among the children of God, and his lot is among the saints? Therefore have we erred from the way of truth, and the light of righteousness hath not shined unto us, and the sun of righteousness rose not upon us. We wearied ourselves in the way of wickedness and destruction; yea, we have gone through deserts where there lay no way; but as for the way of the Lord, we have not known it. What hath pride profited us? or what good hath riches with our vaunting brought us? All these things are passed away like a shadow, and as a post that hasteth by. Wisd. 5:1-9.

Thus will the terrible, unbearable judgment pass over all who know not God and who obey not the Gospel of our Lord Jesus Christ. They shall suffer pain and eternal destruction from the presence of the Lord and from the glory of His power when He shall come to be glorified in His saints, and adored in them that believe. And they shall hear, Depart from me, ye cursed, into everlasting fire, prepared for the devil and his angels. Matt. 25:41.

Then shall your laughter be changed into weeping, your joy into sorrow, your abundant earthly life into everlasting death, your luxury into eternal woe, your pride into dust and worms, your violence into suffering, your beauty into ugliness, and your cruel and unmerciful tyranny be rewarded with unquenchable hell-fire.

My dear sirs, with Him nothing will be concealed or forgotten. He is the Judge that searches the hearts and tries the reins, who beholds the heights of heaven and the depth of the abyss, and the length of the earth; who will judge and punish not only evil works but every idle word, also every unclean, carnal thought.

O dear Lord! O Lord of lords! where will be the emperor and his edict, his false prophets and their trumped-up doctrine? Then they will howl and weep and cry in anguish of soul, O ye mountains, fall on us; ye rocks, hide us from the face of Him that sitteth upon the throne, from the wrath of the

Lamb. For you will see that it was nought but lies and wind on which you relied, as has been said.

Dear sirs, wake up, it is yet today. Do not boast that you are of royal blood and are called gracious lords, for it is but smoke, dust, and pride. But boast in this and rejoice if so be you are born of God or have become a chosen generation, a royal priesthood, a holy nation, a peculiar people: that ye should show forth the praises of him who hath called you out of darkness into his marvellous light. I Pet. 2:9.

Do not boast that you are mighty ones upon the earth, and have great power, but boast in this rather if so be you rule your land in the true fear of God with virtuous wisdom and Christian righteousness to the praise of the Lord.

Neither boast that you can compel lords, princes, cities, and countries, but boast in this the rather if so be you subdue your earthly mind, and can overcome carnal temptations in the power of faith, and die to ungodliness, triumph through Christ and with all the pious soldiers of God, take the kingdom of honor and receive the promised crown at the hand of the Lord. For if you are such kings, then you are not only kings according to the flesh, but also according to the spirit; those who love the Prince of all kings, who are cleansed of sin by His blood, and have been made to be kings and priests of God His Father, to reign with all the children of God, conquer the world, flesh, blood, sin, death, devil, false doctrine, and all the gates of hell. They rejoice not because their names are enrolled in the registers of the kings of this world; but in the book of life which is in heaven.

O illustrious, noble lords and princes, be pleased to receive in love and humility the simple, plain, but nevertheless true, instruction of your poor servant. Do not despise that wherewith I have so thoroughly and well meaningly admonished your worthy highnesses.

Do not dwell on my weakness nor on my unlearnedness, but look intently at Christ, His Word, Spirit, and example which I have here set forth and taught in good faith to you and to all men according to my small gift.

Repent sincerely with a repentance acceptable to God, wail and weep with David, put on sackcloth and raiments of hair, scatter ashes upon your head; humble yourselves with the king of Nineveh, confess your sins with Manasseh; die unto your ambitious flesh and pride. Fear the Lord your God with all your powers; judge in all wisdom with fear and trembling; help the oppressed; grieve not the distressed; promote the cause of widows and orphans in their right; protect the good; punish the evil in a Christian manner; perform your God-given duties correctly; seek the kingdom and country that will endure forever, and remember that here on earth you are but pilgrims and sojourners in a strange land, no matter how much held in honor.

Hear, believe, fear, love, serve, and follow your Lord and Saviour, Jesus Christ, for He it is before whom every knee shall bow: God's eternal Word, Wisdom, Truth, and Son. Seek His honor and praise in all your thoughts, words, and actions, and you shall reign forever.

## [B.] *To the Learned Ones*

With this I leave all lords and princes in the Lord's hand together with all the magistracy and rulers below them. And I turn to you, O learned ones, you who think that you have the keys of heaven and are the eyes and the light of the people. I will speak with you as with those whose salvation I seek with all my heart because I see plainly that both you and those you teach run confidently into the eternal destruction of your poor souls. Nevertheless you boast that you are the commissioned teachers, and your churches the churches of Christ. And I wish to admonish you in faithful brotherly spirit one and all, Roman Catholics, Lutherans, and Zwinglians, concerning the following articles.

Notice in the first place that your office and service are not of God and His Word but issue from the bottomless pit. For it is evident that you blaspheme and persecute Christ's Word, ordinances, and commands, and teach and promote the word, ordinances, and commands of Antichrist. You violate the temple of God, building and honoring temples of stone. You break the living images in which the Spirit of God dwells, making and adorning images of gold, silver, and wood. You hate a pious, blameless life, encouraging and defending by your frivolous example an unchecked wild life of the flesh. Dear sirs, where is there a single letter in the Scriptures enjoining all your ritual and worship, your masses, infant baptism, auricular confession, etc? Is not all you do and promote deception, hypocrisy, blasphemy, abomination, and idolatry? Whence do your offices and services come and of whom are they? I would advise you in true love to reflect in the light of the Scriptures, and in the true fear of God.

Secondly, consider what you are really seeking in this your office and service. You and I heretofore occupied the same calling, office, and service. I acknowledge without reservation that in all my studies from my youth, in preaching and chanting, I sought only an empty, lazy, soft life; praise and favor of men, yes, simply flesh and belly, till the great and gracious Lord granted me His gracious Spirit and opened the eyes of my heart so that I acknowledged with the preacher Solomon that all my ambition, life, and conduct was vanity and the end thereof certain death and hell.

But that you continue to seek these things is too evident to be denied. For if there were no prebends[56] and cloisters, preachers, priests, and monks would be few. This I know of a certainty. So long as these exist, the world will never lack deceivers and hypocrites.

Dear me, what is your entire ambition and conduct if not world, carnality, belly, and a life of luxury? Who can fathom and describe your earthly mind and carnal life? Some of you parade in ermine, in silk and velvet, others live in headlong revelry, others are avaricious and hoard; some disgrace virgins and young women, others defile the bed of their neighbor, the chastity of

---

[56] Menno is accusing the clergy of avarice. *Ed.*

others is like the chastity of Sodom. The doctrine of all of you is deceiving, your sacraments are superstitious, your piety is mostly wickedness, and your divine service is an open abomination and idolatry. Some of you fear neither God nor the devil. The name of God you blaspheme, His holy Word you falsify, His children and servants you persecute, and in response to His grace, you do all manner of evil. Just so you can lead a carefree life and have a good time, then all is fine. Tell me, is it not so? Worthy men, is it not so? This is, is it not, your chief ambition and striving, great and small. You must acknowledge and grant it, for the fruit is manifest through all the world and cannot be longer hid.

Gentlemen, beware! If men could enter into life on this broad way which you teach and travel, and keep their souls in God, then we may well lament and say that the prophets, apostles, and all the witnesses of God and even Christ Jesus Himself did not act wisely. Neither did they deal honestly with us when they travailed with so much anguish, oppression, sadness, and pain in this sorrowful vale of tears, nor when they directed us miserable weak children to such a way.

Oh, no, dear friends, no. Truth will remain truth forever. If you are not converted to a better and a Christian mind, if you do not die to your error and also to your vain, carnal life, if you do not repent and become like innocent, simple children, you cannot enter into the kingdom of heaven. For to be carnally minded, says Paul, is death.

Teach, clamor, hope, and boast how and what you please; if you wish to be saved, you must walk in the way of the Lord, hear His Word, and obey it. For nothing avails in heaven nor on earth unto salvation: neither baptism nor the Lord's Supper, neither eloquence nor erudition, neither councils nor usages, neither emperors nor edicts, nor even Christ with His grace, merit, blood, and death, if we are not born of God (that is, those who have ears to hear and minds to understand),[57] if we do not believe His Word sincerely, and if we do not walk in the light and do right, as John says: This then is the message which we have heard of him, and declare unto you, that God is light, and in him is no darkness at all. If we say that we have fellowship with him, and walk in darkness, we lie, and do not the truth: but if we walk in the light, as he is in the light, we have fellowship one with another, and the blood of Jesus Christ, his Son, cleanseth us from all sin. I John 1:5-7.

O transgressors, transgressors, examine your hearts; give heed to my words and learn wisdom. You live in luxury and sit in safety, you say in your hearts, We are the people, besides us there is no other; what we command shall be heard, and what we speak will be valid upon earth; we cannot err in the Scriptures, mistake or fail in counsel, nor teach anything amiss. Oh, dear! Oh, dear! Your boasted wisdom leads you astray, and the pride of your hearts causes you to stumble. Return! you are walking on slippery places and your path leads to the abyss of hell.

[57] Menno here excepts children who are saved in Christ without act or ceremony. *Ed.*

Worthy men, do learn to know what God's own and eternal Son, Christ Jesus, suffered upon earth, what He taught, and what example He left you. He sought His Father's glory and the salvation of our poor souls. His doctrine was His Father's Word, and His progress a sure way to the kingdom of God. Who, being in the form of God, says Paul, thought it not robbery to be equal with God: but made himself of no reputation, and took upon him the form of a servant, Phil. 2:6, 7; and came into this sorrowful world, poor and miserable. There was no room for Him in the inn when He was born; nothing whereon to lay His head during His ministry; nor in His death wherewith to quench His thirst. Yet He was the one through whom the almighty, all-bountiful Father provides for all His created beings, place of dwelling, cover, meat and drink, as Paul says: For ye know the grace of our Lord Jesus Christ, that though he was rich, yet for your sakes he became poor, that ye through his poverty might be rich. II Cor. 8:9.

If now you have any fear of God, and do not desire to lead not only your own soul but also those of your poor people into death, then contrast your desire with Christ's, your doctrine with Christ's, your spirit with Christ's, and your life with Christ's. Then you will discover whether you are in or out of Christ, who is your God, what Lord you serve, and of what kind of spirit and kingdom you are the children.

Thirdly, observe what fruits and profits your office and service brings forth. For what is your doctrine but a vain and impotent sowing of the wind which has neither spirit nor power? Your sacraments are an encouragement to the impenitent and your lives examples of wickedness. Where are the greedy whom you have made liberal, the drunkards you have made temperate, the impure you have made chaste, the proud whom you have humbled? How will you teach others, being yourselves untaught, and beget unto Christ a well-pleasing church, as long as you yourselves are the servants of Antichrist and the children of Belial? You must confess, must you not, that you and your followers, both high and low, men and women, are all dead bodies not having the Spirit of God. For with you we do not find contrite hearts, true knowledge of Christ, true love, an earnest desire after the kingdom of God, dying to earthly things, true humility, righteousness, friendliness, mercy, chastity, obedience, wisdom, truth, and peace. But everywhere we find hatred, envy, hard and cruel hearts, a loathing aversion and disdain for the divine Word, love and desire of this world, haughtiness, pride, pomp, lies, trickery, shame, adultery, fornication, robbery, burning, slaying, cursing, and all manner of wickedness.

You see, O barren trees and careless shepherds, these are the fruits you bring forth and the sheep you pasture. These are the churches and disciples you comfort with the blood of the Lord, to whom you announce grace and peace, and to whom you dispense baptism and the Lord's Supper. If I write erroneously, then reprove me.

O dear sirs, so entirely have you lost all Christian reasonableness and understanding; moreover, the light and the Scriptures. You hold captive in ungodliness, under the power of hell, the poor, ignorant people; whole kingdoms, cities, and countries; yes, the whole wide world. And that, O God, for such small hire, namely, for a handful of barley and a bit of bread, as the prophet says. Oh, that I were speaking lies and not the truth, but sunshine is clear, and clearer still the truth which I write.

And this is not enough, O men, that you so miserably deceive the poor wretched souls. Besides this you also revile, defame, slander and shame, betray and liquidate all those who seek and fear God with all their hearts, who rebuke all unrighteousness with doctrine and life, and so willingly walk in Christ. You do this in order that you may continue in honor among the people, unassailed in your conduct, and unhindered in your improper gain and in your easy and opulent life to the end of your days.

Oh, how correctly you are depicted by the Wisdom of God which says, Woe unto you, scribes and Pharisees, hypocrites, for ye shut up the kingdom of heaven against men: for ye neither go in yourselves [mark this], neither suffer ye them that are entering to go in. Matt. 23:13.

What I think I write, and do not dissemble. I fear, worthy sirs, that there are many of you so ungodly and so set on improper gain, indolent life, and the praise of men, that you would rather see all God-fearing men put through the stake than lose a guilder of your incomes, or hear a hard word from the magistracy because of the truth.

O harlot's forehead, when will you be ashamed? Ye diamonds, when will you be softened, and ye Ethiopians, when will you become white? I suppose never, for how can you do anything good, because you have learned evil and are used to it from the cradle?

Alas, my soul must grieve and painfully mourn because of you, that you err so sadly; moreover, that you cover all your disgrace under the Word and name of Christ, and do not notice, O men, that to you are promised in the Scriptures and threatened by the Spirit of the Lord, nothing but punishment, wrath, damnation and the blackness of darkness, the flaming lake and eternal gnashing of teeth, weeping, wailing, fire, woe, and death.

The hour is nigh when you will hear, Give an account, etc. Ah, if it were permitted us when that day comes to walk a thousand years on burning coals, in glowing armor of fire, we should be happy. But now it is hidden from your eyes through your pride and avarice and the ease of a moment.

Perhaps I will be smitten on the cheek by some of you, and with Micaiah be compelled to hear from Zedekiah: Which way went the Spirit of the Lord from me to speak unto you? II Chron. 18:23. Ah, my friend, fear God and understand the truth. You direct the poor careless souls to the subtlety and philosophy of the learned ones, to the many councils, to customs and usages of long standing, to imperial edicts, to the doctrines and commandments of men which are nothing but shifting sands, which cannot save the house from the tempest. I, on the other hand, with Moses, the prophets, the apostles and angels, and the Father Himself, direct you to Christ Jesus to whom all the emperors, kings, councils, usages, and the learned ones will have to yield, for His Word is truth and His commandments are eternal life. To Him every knee must bow, of things in heaven and things in earth, and things under the earth. Phil. 2:10. All who reject Him reject the Father that sent Him.

These things I teach you. To His Spirit, Word, life, commandment, prohibition, ordinance, and usage I point you as to a sure and immovable foundation laid in Zion, to a smooth and certain path prepared by God, who according to His sure promises will lead all true and penitent Christ-believing persons into eternal life.

Dear sirs, observe: there were four hundred false prophets in the days of Ahab, king of Israel, who with one voice predicted good fortune and prosperity, telling Ahab to proceed, for God would give the enemies of the king into his hands. But there was but one Micaiah who spoke the real truth and predicted calamity in the name of the Lord. II Chron. 18:6, 7.

There were also four hundred and fifty prophets of Baal and four hundred prophets of the groves,[58] all of whom did eat at Jezebel's table. There was only one Elijah, a man of God and a prophet of the Lord, who was zealous for the law of his God, and sought His honor. I Kings 19.

Joash, with all the princes, priests, and common people, agreed as to the groves and false worship which they had chosen after the death of Jehoiada, the high priest. There was only the one Zechariah who scored the ungodly abominations and warned against the wrath and punishment of his God. II Chron. 24.

Those renowned and worthy men of God, and they but few, reproved wickedness with their high and glorious talent, with pure and holy zeal in the power of the Spirit, and by the law of God faithfully admonished all the disobedient and idolatrous kings, princes, priests, and the common people, without respect of persons. In return they endured disdain, misery, tribulation, bonds, and death as we may abundantly read and see in the Scriptures and in history. So also I in this matter, with my small talents, with similar intent and cause, testify openly to the truth because I see with my eyes and feel with my hands that you one and all play the hypocrite, flatter lords and princes, and humor the world. Because there is, alas, nobody who opposes this ungodliness with the Word of the Lord, nor reproves the wickedness of the world, I must therefore hear and bear not a little, as did they, although I have such good intentions, such a solid foundation.

O worthy men, check yourselves and ponder the matter. Consider the end and ponder the outcome. You rely on human invention, but we on the Word and truth of God; you rely on the world, we on heaven; you rely on the present, we on the future; you rely on the emperor and force, we on Christ and His promises, until we all appear before Him who will come in

[58] See note on page 173.

the clouds of heaven to requite all flesh. Then you will see what you have lived for, what office you filled, what deeds you have done, for what hire you served, whose word you promoted, whose counsel you despised, and whom, O men, you have so hatefully stabbed.

Herewith I commend you to the Lord, learned ones and preachers, and pray you for God's sake, to the good of your souls, to accept with gratitude and love this my faithful warning, written to you with a sincere and Christian intention; to read it with an understanding heart; to ponder and reread it with fear and trembling. I certainly know you will find nothing in it but kindness, love, seriousness, and a true and sure foundation of the only and invincible truth.

And if some of you think I reprove too severely, then know that I have not done so without the instruction, counsel, and doctrine of the holy prophets, of Christ and the apostles. I have named no names outside of Scripture. Let him that is innocent thank God and rejoice; he that is guilty is not reproved by me, but by the Spirit and Word of God.

Ah, excellent friends, fear God and His judgment; reform your earthly carnal life; say farewell to all your deceptions, blindness, seducements, and the abominations in which you have hitherto been immersed. Seek the right truth with all your powers; pray to God for wisdom; warn everyone; deal and act unblamably. Then you will not be included in those hard and dreadful names of the Scriptures, and you will not inherit punishment and wrath, but grace, mercy, and life as the prophet says: But if the wicked will turn from his sins that he hath committed, and keep all my statutes, and do that which is lawful and right, he shall surely live, he shall not die. All his transgressions that he hath committed, they shall not be mentioned unto him. Ezek. 18:21, 22. The gracious and dear Lord grant you all His grace, knowledge, Spirit, wisdom, light, and truth, that you may be sincerely warned, may repent and be eternally saved. Amen.

### [C.] *To the Common People*

Give ear, ye people, and lend the ear, all you who trust in lies and boast that you are Christians; tear your bands asunder and suffer yourselves no longer to be led as asses bound under a heavy burden of sin by these aforementioned drivers, for they deceive you. They preach to you according to their own opinion and not out of the mouth of the Lord. They comfort you in your wicked ways; they proclaim only grace and peace, although all is displeasure and judgment, as the prophet says: The priests and prophets teach a false worship and comfort my people in their calamity, that they shall esteem it lightly saying, Peace, peace, when there is no peace. They are the blind leaders who lead you and themselves straight into the pit, blind watchmen who do not guard the city of God. They are thieves and murderers, who with the sword of their false doctrine slay your poor souls and steal from you the Word and kingdom of the Lord; greedy shepherds who seek your wool, milk, and flesh, and not your souls. In short, they are those by whom the kingdom of Christ is wholly corrupted, and the kingdom of Antichrist is held in honor, and spread throughout the whole world, men who always assure and strengthen you, poor children, in your wild abominations and your obdurate, blind life, so that alas, none turns sincerely to the Lord; none laments his sins, saying, What am I doing?

Ah, worthy children and brethren, my heart quakes and troubles me when I reflect that such a numberless multitude of men are born to futility, who unless they repent will have to endure the wrath and judgment of the Lord eternally and never find grace.

Dear children, take heed; thus Christ Jesus teaches you. Verily I say unto you, Except ye be converted and become as little children, ye shall not enter into the kingdom of heaven. Matt. 18:3. O dear sirs, this is asserted by God's eternal truth, which cannot lie. And how wickedly you poor ignorant people live, and how far you are from the innocence of children, your fruits testify. For you despise God and His Word; you hate all righteousness and truth; many of you live as the irrational creatures; others go to law and fight, curse, swear, rake, scrape, practice usury, lie, cheat, hurt and defraud one another. Fidelity and piety are seldom found among you; faithlessness and trickery alas are everywhere. It is gambling, gaming, drinking, and carousing that are pastimes among you; to violate women and girls is called gallantry and love; he who can get the best of another, swindle, and rob, this you call clever and keen. Giants are you when it comes to beer, and soldiers when it comes to wine; unrighteousness and destruction are in all your ways. The poor and weak you oppress, and you revile the afflicted, the God-fearing and pious; you think and ponder nothing but evil; you are without understanding, and run, says the prophet, as a frantic heifer.[59] To fix up gorgeously you call the fashion and custom of the country. The one lies in wait for the other's honor, property, and life, and seeks his destruction, as the prophet says. Your faith is hypocrisy, your worship idolatry, your whole life is world and flesh, as may be seen. And then you say, to live without serious reflection is to live correctly—as though ignorance, blindness, despising the truth, and wickedness were a pious, humble, and plain life. Dear children, shame on you for your ugly willfulness and accursed folly.

Do you count Christ a liar and His Word a fable? Oh, no! His declaration stands immovable and shall never be altered. If you live in pride, avarice, greed, unchastity, and in carnal lusts; if you do not believe Christ and His Word; if you continue to be earthly-minded and are not born of God, you must die eternally, unless the Spirit of God is untrue and false.

Say, beloved, why extol the apostles and prophets, seeing you revile their doctrine as heresy and their lives as madness? Why allow yourselves to be called Christians, seeing you hate and oppose Christ's Word and example so heartily?

59 Dutch translation of Hos. 4:16.

You say, we are inexpert, unlearned, and know not the Scriptures. I reply: The Word is plain and needs no interpretation: namely, Thou shalt love the Lord thy God with all thy heart, and with all thy soul, and with all thy strength, and thy neighbor as thyself. Matt. 22:37, 39. Again, You shall give bread to the hungry and entertain the needy. Isa. 58:7. If you live according to the flesh you shall die, for to be carnally minded is death. The avaricious, drunkards, and the proud shall not inherit the kingdom of God. God will condemn adulterers and fornicators. Rom. 8; I Cor. 6, and many like passages. All who do not understand such passages are more like irrational creatures than men, more like clods than Christians.

Ah, my children, my dear children, do not deceive your own souls; seek wisdom and understanding, even as you do your daily food, and you shall find great riches. For the kingdom of heaven suffers violence. Strive, says Christ, to enter in at the strait gate; ask and you shall receive; seek and ye shall find; knock and it shall be opened unto you. The Almighty great God will not be satisfied with a bare name. He desires a true, sincere faith; unfeigned, ardent love; a new, changed, converted heart; true humility, mercy, purity, patience, righteousness, and peace. He desires the whole man: heart mouth, and deed; men who delight in the Word of the Lord, speak the truth from the heart, crucify their flesh; men who will give, if need be, their goods and blood for the Word of the Lord.

You see, dear children, this is the way in which we will have to walk if we desire to be saved. Therefore rouse yourselves and learn wisdom. Hear the inviting voice of God, open unto Him and grant Him entry, lest He complain of you as He did formerly through His prophets of obstinate and hardened Judah and Jerusalem. I have nourished, says he, and brought up children, and they have rebelled against me; the ox knoweth his owner, and the ass his master's crib; but Israel doth not know, my people doth not consider. Ah, sinful nation, a people laden with iniquity, a seed of evildoers, children that are corrupters: they have forsaken the Lord, they have provoked the Holy One of Israel unto anger, they are gone away backward. Isa. 1:4.

Jeremiah says, Every one turned to his course, as the horse rusheth into the battle. Yea, the stork in the heaven knoweth her appointed times; and the turtle and the crane and the swallow observe the time of their coming; but my people know not the judgment of the Lord. Jer. 8:6, 7.

Remember, dear children, how greatly Jesus Christ was concerned at the obstinacy and blindness of the Jews when He said: Jerusalem, Jerusalem, how often would I have gathered thy children together, even as a hen gathereth her chickens, and ye would not. He wept and said, If thou hadst known, even thou, at least in this thy day, the things which belong unto thy peace! But now are they hid from thine eyes. Luke 19:42.

Wherefore lay apart all filthiness and superfluity of naughtiness, and receive with meekness the ingrafted word, which is able to save your souls. Jas. 1:21. Seek God with all your heart, repent sincerely, cleanse yourselves inwardly before the Lord, forsake the world, flesh, false doctrine, and everything contrary to the honor, will, and Word of God. Hear, believe, and follow Jesus Christ, the only and true Shepherd of your souls, who sought you in such great love, and purchased you with such a precious price. Then you may properly boast that you are the people of God and the church of Jesus Christ. To the same dear Lord and Saviour Jesus Christ, be praise and the eternal kingdom. Amen.

## [D] *To the Corrupt Sects*[60]

Christ says, False Christs and false prophets shall arise, and shall show signs and wonders, to seduce, if it were possible, even the elect. But take ye heed: behold, I have foretold you all things. Mark 13:22, 23. O you apostate, erring children, notice that if you had taken to heart this faithful warning of our Lord and Saviour Christ, had acknowledged His Spirit, doctrine, and holy life as a perfect Spirit, doctrine, and life, and had acknowledged Him as the true Prophet, promised in Scripture; if you had received Him as the true and living Son of God, then you would never have allowed yourselves to be led so far from His ways, nor would you have given in to such frightful errors. But, O Lord, I fear that some of you are so far bewitched that you will nevermore come to Christ, the true Shepherd, for you defend as just and right the abominable works of ungodliness which are not only contrary to the Spirit, Word, and will of Christ, but also to reasonable modesty, nature, and reason. And you sustain them with a perverted and obscure interpretation of the Scriptures.

Is it not a grievous error that you suffer yourselves to be so woefully seduced by such worthless persons, and so sadly misled from one unclean sect to another: first to that of Münster, next to Batenburg, now Davidian; then from Beelzebub to Lucifer, and from Belial to Behemoth? You are ever learning but never able to come to the knowledge of the real truth. You suffer yourselves to be led about by every wind of doctrine. You choose out a way for yourselves as do also the priests and monks, and hold not to the head, Christ, from which all the body, fitly joined together, cometh unto a perfect man, unto the measure of the stature of the fullness of Christ.

All this I fear is punishment for your sins, for you are earthly and carnally minded, for which cause you thrust from you the pure knowledge of God and hate the cross of Christ, contrary to all the admonition of the Scriptures. Against the trustworthy example of Christ and His saints you conform yourselves to the pride and pomp, eating and drinking, folly, hypocrisy, and false worship of this proud, useless, vain, and idolatrous world, which

[60] As early as the first edition of the *Foundation*, 1539-40, Menno divided the Christendom of Europe into five blocks: "Papists," Lutherans, Zwinglians, corrupt sects, and the (Anabaptist) group to which he belonged. By the corrupt sects he meant Münsterites, Batenburgers, and Davidians. *Ed.*

you should, by right, instruct and admonish by a pious, humble, sober, and godly walk.

O apostate children, consider how grievously you disgrace the holy Moses, who teaches and speaks to you out of the mouth of God. He says, I will raise them up a prophet from among their brethren, like unto thee, and will put my words in his mouth; and he shall speak unto them all that I shall command him. And it shall come to pass, that whosoever will not hearken unto my words which he shall speak in my name, I will require it of him. Deut. 18:18, 19. This is repeated by Peter and Stephen.

How do you dispose of all the great prophets of God such as David, Isaiah, Jeremiah, and Ezekiel, who, in so many places, with such plain words, through the inspiration of the Holy Spirit, direct us to Christ and His Word? They must verily speak falsely or your prophets must be deceivers and false teachers. This is incontrovertible.

Did not holy Paul say, But though we, or an angel from heaven, preach any other gospel unto you than that which we have preached unto you, let him be accursed? Gal. 1:8. That your prophets with their king, dominion, polygamy, sword, etc., do not agree with Paul and the doctrine and Gospel of the apostles you are all forced to acknowledge and admit. From which follows mightily that they with their doctrine and conduct are accursed and anathema.

Tell me, dear friends, what do you do with the revealed and infallible Word and testimony of the Almighty Father, which He Himself has testified of His Son, and said, This is my beloved Son, in whom I am well pleased; hear ye him? Matt. 17:5. Get this, Hear ye him! But you reject His Spirit, Word, and example, and follow and listen to those who with their spirit, doctrine, and conduct are from the bottomless pit, yes, patent antichrists and false prophets.

Have you forgotten that the Son of God has Himself commanded us that we should observe all that He has enjoined, and that He will be with us until the end of the world?

Do you mean to say that the doctrine of Christ and His apostles was incomplete and that your teachers bring forth the perfect instruction? I answer that to teach and believe this is the most horrible blasphemy, the most irreverent contradiction that can be uttered against the Most High. For you declare thereby that Christ is not the true Son of the true God, the perfect Teacher, and the genuine example of righteousness. You forsake the whole Scripture; you reject the testimony of Moses and of all the prophets who pointed to the only and true Christ, as has been shown. You despise the Word of the Father and reject Christ Jesus with His Spirit, Word, kingdom, and spiritual government. You direct your heart and hope to untruthful mortal flesh and to earthly carnal things which as the Scriptures teach must be dispersed like dust before the wind. Whether this is not a gross blasphemy against the Almighty you may ponder in the light of Scripture and in the fear of God.

Deceived children, where is there a letter in the whole doctrine of Christ and the apostles, according to whose Spirit, doctrine, conduct, and example all Scripture must be understood, by which you can prove and establish a single one of your erring articles?

If you want to appeal to the literal understanding and transactions of Moses and the prophets, then must you also become Jews, accept circumcision, possess the land of Canaan literally, erect the Jewish kingdom again, build the city and temple, and offer sacrifices and perform the ritual as required in the law. And you must declare that Christ the promised Saviour has not yet come, He who has changed the literal and sensual ceremonies into new, spiritual, and abiding realities.

O miserable, erring sheep, notice that in the preceding I have pointed out to the magistrates that the kingdom of Christ is not of this visible, tangible, transitory world, but that it is an eternal, spiritual, and abiding kingdom which is not eating and drinking, but righteousness, peace, and joy in the Holy Ghost. In it no king reigns except the true King of Zion, Christ Jesus. He is the King of righteousness, the King of kings, who has all power in heaven above, and on earth beneath, before whom every knee must bow and all tongues praise. The true King David in the spirit who through His righteousness, merits, and crimson blood has delivered the sheep from the mouth of the hellish lions and bears, has slain the great and terrible Goliath, and obtained for the spiritual Israel of God eternal welfare and peace. Neither this King nor His servants bear any sword but the sword of the Spirit, which pierces even to the dividing asunder of soul and spirit. With the Word of God, which He bears, He defends the kingdom against the gates of hell, and graciously keeps and guards its supremacy in the midst of heavy cross and trial. And this He does not with iron or steel, as the untamed, cruel world does, for His kingdom and dominion is spirit and not letter, as has been shown.

I have likewise asserted that in this kingdom and under this King no other marriage is in effect save that between one man and one woman as God in the beginning ordained in the case of Adam and Eve, and as Christ has once more formulated it that these two shall be one flesh, and that they shall not divorce except for the cause of fornication. Matt. 5:32.

This kingdom is not a kingdom in which they parade in gold, silver, pearls, silk, velvet, and costly finery, as is done by the haughty, proud world; matters which your leaders defend and allow with this meaningless provision; just so you do not desire these things and live for them in your heart. In this way Satan can defend his pride and make pure and good the desire of his eyes. But in the kingdom of all humility (I declare) not the outward adorning of the body, but the inward adorning of the spirit is sought with zeal and diligence, with a broken and a contrite heart.

Here no lying is known, no eating, drinking, or hypocrisy; here none conforms himself to a drunken, abundant, idle, and idolatrous world. Nor

does anyone lay aside the cross of Christ[61] as you do, but here the requirement is to be upright and pious in heart and deed, to speak the truth from
the heart, to lead a circumspect, sober life; to shun all idolatry and false doctrine from within and from without, to abstain from all appearance of evil, to
perform the true worship of the heart; to abide firmly in the Word and ordinances of Christ, to lead an unblamable life before the whole world, and to
testify of Jesus Christ with the mouth, conduct, possessions, and blood, if
divine honor requires it.

Here that confession of sins which some of you propose is unknown, for
here we confess to the true God only,[62] before whom we have sinned, and
to our neighbor against whom we have trespassed.

Here we teach and practice modesty, virtue, and honesty; not immodesty,
shame, and disgrace. I think you understand what I am thinking of.

In short, here the Spirit, Word, will, commandments, prohibitions, ordinances, usages, and example of Christ, to which all Scripture refers us, are
taught; not the inventions of false prophets, high-sounding words, bewitching
make-believe, big talk, dreaming visions, and lying miracles against which the
Spirit of God and the Scriptures everywhere warn and counsel.

Dear children, turn over a new leaf! Everyone who teaches you otherwise than is here testified by the Word of the Lord, even though he were
one who could dry up the bottom of the sea and hurl the stars down from
heaven, he would nevertheless be accursed and his doctrine be deceptive and
erroneous. For to all eternity no other foundation may be laid than that
which is laid, Christ Jesus. He is the cornerstone and foundation in Zion;
every building reared on Him in accordance with His will, Spirit, and Word
becomes a holy house and temple of the Lord.

Ah, apostate children, hear the Word of God and fall in line, for your
way is in darkness and your paths lead to death. Embrace the truth and learn
wisdom, for those who urge you on lead you astray and render uneven the
way in which you must go. Münster and Amsterdam may well be to you an
eternal warning and example. When a prophet, said Moses, speaks in the
name of the Lord, if the thing follow not, nor come to pass, that is not the
thing which the Lord hath spoken.

O dear Lord! How many innocent hearts have they deceived? How
many poor souls have they misled? What great reproach have they caused
the Word of the Lord? What crude abominations have some of them committed unto the appearance of good? How great an occasion for the shedding
of innocent blood by the poor, blind magistrates have they occasioned, magistrates who also have no great knowledge of Holy Writ.

I think it is time you should see and learn to know your lying, faithless,
and deceiving prophets. They are the foxes which destroy the vineyard of the
Lord. These are the thieves and murderers of your souls, false prophets who

[61] Menno refers here to the believer's cross, what it costs a disciple to follow Christ. *Ed.*
[62] Menno excludes auricular confession to a priest. *Ed.*

deny the Lord that bought them, who have directed you, poor erring sheep, by their own lying visions, dreams, and imaginations and have led you, against all the Scriptures, upon a false and loose foundation.

How like have you become to those of whom Eusebius[63] writes, who interpret the prophet according to their own fancy, who deny Paul and the New Testament, and who have carried with them a book which they boasted fell from heaven as a present to them.

So it is also with you, madmen that you are (pardon me, it is the truth which I write). The prophets you read according to the Jewish understanding.[64] The doctrine of Christ and the apostles is a thing of the past, you say, and you contend that another dispensation is beginning and you do not perceive that you thereby deny the Son of God, deny the Scriptures, and comfort yourselves with mere lies, just as disobedient Israel in their time used to do.

O dear Lord! How long shall this sore visitation continue? How long shall the name of the Lord be blasphemed and His Holy Word violated?

Is it not a grievous error and raving madness that Christ the Son of the living God, who achieved eternal righteousness, reconciled heaven and earth by the blood of His cross, with His Word of truth, and with His commandments of eternal life, should be rejected from your hearts, hearts which He has bought at such a price, and which should properly be the dwelling place of Christ; and that poor sinful flesh and mortal men, descended from Adam, full of all unrighteousness, boastful speeches, lies, and open deception, are received by you and placed in Christ's stead?

Oh, dear children, what are you doing? Are you so thoroughly bewitched that you have lost all reason, intelligence, and Scripture moreover, and everything, so that you cannot see at all? Then may God be merciful to you! Good children, observe that not a letter of the law of Moses could be changed till the new Moses came, Christ Jesus, who was promised in the law and the prophets. If then the word of the literal law was so strong, effective, and firm, and in its time unchangeable, although given only through a servant and sealed by perishable blood, how much more powerful, effectual, firm, and unchangeable is the free law of the Spirit, given by the Son Himself and confirmed by the blood of the eternal covenant!

All who taught anything contrary to the word of Moses were false prophets. For nothing was to be taken therefrom, nor added thereto, but they had to decide all matters in the light of the law and testimony. So also all the prophets of the present day are false who teach contrary to the Spirit, Word, commands, prohibitions, ordinations, and example of Christ, even though holier than John, more zealous (apparently) than Elijah, and greater miracle workers than Moses.

But when they persuade you that the doctrine of the apostles was but in

---

[63] Church historian, theologian, and scholar who became bishop of Caesarea *c.* 314, wrote a 10-volume church history, and died *c.* A.D. 340.

[64] Menno is alluding to their Millenarianism. *Ed.*

part and that they now teach that which is perfect, then this is a deception above all deceptions, as said earlier, for thereby the creature is honored above the Creator. Paul does not refer to some other and better doctrine when he refers to future perfection; he refers to the one and only abiding reality announced in the doctrine of the apostles, which in the resurrection of the righteous we shall receive in eternal clarity when all doctrine shall have an end, according to God's dependable promise. If not, Paul would be inconsistent, and the true reality would not be in Christ.

Do you say with the Jews and scribes that Elijah must come before the great and terrible day, and so wait for something new? Then I answer with Christ's own words: All the prophets and the law prophesied until John. And if ye will receive it, this is Elias, which was for to come. Matt. 11:13, 14. Secondly, even though Elijah himself were to come, he would not have anything to teach contrary to the foundation and doctrine of Christ and the apostles. But he must teach and preach in harmony with them if he would execute the office of the true preacher, for by the Spirit, Word, actions, and example of Christ, all must be judged until the last judgment. Otherwise the whole Scriptures are false.

Therefore, one of two things must follow: either we are not going to have any Elijah any more, since John was the Elijah who was to come; or if an Elijah should still come, he must propose and teach us nothing but the foundation and Word of Christ according to the Scriptures. For Christ is the man who sits upon David's throne and shall reign forever in the kingdom, house, and congregation of Jacob.

I would then herewith sincerely admonish you all to weigh and prove all spirits, doctrine, faith, and conduct with the Spirit of Christ; and that ye be sane. All spirits which accord therewith are from God, but those which are contrary are from him who from the beginning has turned Adam and his race from God and has led them by lies into death.

If you will not hear, but continually turn your ears to lies, and believe the deceiving creature more than the infallible Creator; if you set your feet upon slippery places; if you neither fear nor regard Scriptural admonitions, nor the power and punishment of God, but despise all these as idle and useless, and suffer yourselves always to be comforted with falsehoods, visions, dreams, fine appearance, and false interpretations, and if you continue without the cross on the broad way; then will the righteous God send to you mockers and deceivers in droves, and by His righteous judgment allow you to be led from one wicked error to another as may be seen.

You shall be filled with lies, wind, folly, and hypocrisy. You will reap the fruits of your frivolousness, and at last, with all false prophets and lying wonder workers, you shall hear the words: Depart from me, all ye workers of iniquity; I never knew you. Luke 13:27.

Herewith be eternally warned and faithfully admonished of God. Beware, the day approaches, repent and reform. The Word of God is true. If there is anyone among you who fears God, let him reflect on what I write here. Let him search the Scriptures and believe the truth, for God hates all liars. Eternal woe and gnashing of teeth will be the portion and reward of the hypocrite. Whosoever transgresseth and abideth not in the doctrine of Christ, hath not God. II John 1:9.

O ye miserable, deluded children, return. If ye knew what it is to forsake the living fountain of Christ and dig for yourselves dry wells which can yield no water, how soon would you turn your back on false prophets and their hypocritical lives, surrender yourselves to the true Shepherd of your souls,[65] Christ Jesus, and follow and obey His sure counsel, teaching, admonition, ordinance, and holy example in weakness. But alas, deluding blindness has obscured your understanding. The beloved, merciful Lord grant you eyes to see and hearts to understand: this is our sincere wish. Amen.

### [E.] To the Church of the Lord[66]

The Bridegroom, Christ Jesus, through Solomon addresses His bride, the church, saying, Rise up, my love, my fair one, and come away. For, lo, the winter is past, the rain is over and gone; the flowers appear on the earth; the time of the singing of birds is come, and the voice of the turtle [dove] is heard in our land; the fig tree putteth forth her green figs, and the vines with the tender grape give a good smell. Arise, by love, my fair one, and come away. S. of Sol. 2:10-13.

Elect, faithful children, you who with me are called to a like grace, inheritance, portion, and kingdom, and are named after the Lord's name, oh, hear the voice of Christ, our King; hear the voice of your Bridegroom, O thou bride of God, thou friend of the Lord. Arise and adorn thyself to honor thy King and Bridegroom. Although thou art pure, make thyself purer still; although thou art holy, make thyself holier still; although thou art righteous, make thyself more righteous still. Adorn thyself with the white silken robe of righteousness; hang about thy neck the golden chain of every piety; gird thyself with the fair girdle of brotherly love; put on the wedding ring of a true faith; cover thyself with the precious fair gold of the divine Word; beautify thyself with the pearls of many virtues; wash thyself with the clear waters of grace and anoint thyself with the oil of the Holy Ghost; wash thy feet in the clear, sparkling flood of Almighty God. Let your whole body be pure and immaculate, for thy lover hates all wrinkles and spots. So will he desire thy beauty and will praise thee and say: How fair is thy love, my sister, my spouse! how much better is thy love than wine! and the smell of thine ointments than all spices! Thy lips, O my spouse, drop as the honeycomb; honey and milk are under thy tongue. S. of Sol. 4:10, 11.

[65] Reading *herder* (shepherd) for *herodes* (Herod) which the original has by a typesetter's error no doubt. *Tr.*

[66] The Dutch original reads: *To the Bride, Kingdom, City, Body and Church of the Lord, to Whom Be Grace and Peace. Ed.*

Rejoice, O thou bride of the Lord, for your beloved is fairer than all the children of men, the chiefest among ten thousand. His head is as the most fine gold, his locks are bushy, and as black as a raven. His eyes are as the eyes of doves by the rivers of waters, washed with milk, and fitly set. His cheeks are as a bed of spices, as sweet flowers; his lips like lilies, dropping sweet-smelling myrrh. His hands are as gold rings set with beryl; his belly is as bright ivory overlaid with sapphires. His legs are as pillars of marble, set upon sockets of fine gold: his countenance is as Lebanon, excellent as the cedars. His mouth is most sweet, yea, he is altogether lovely. S. of Sol. 5:10-16. Cry out and say: Hearken, O daughter, and consider, and incline thine ear; forget also thine own people, and thy father's house; so shall the king greatly desire thy beauty. Ps. 45:10, 11.

Advance, O queen, thou well favored and fairest of all women; with Esther bow 'neath his powerful sceptre; hear his word and fear his judgment; acknowledge his great love, for he has greatly humbled himself toward thee. Thy birth and thy nativity is of the land of Canaan; thy father was an Amorite and thy mother an Hittite, and as for thy nativity, in the day thou wast born thy navel was not cut, neither wast thou washed in water to supple thee; thou wast not salted at all, nor swaddled at all. Ezek. 16:3, 4. Thou wast polluted in thy blood, behold so despised were your souls, as the prophet lamented. But he has had compassion on thee, has promised thee life, nurtured thee and covered thy shame. He has purified thee from thy uncleanness, has washed away thy blood, anointed thee with balm, clothed thee with spiritual clothes; he has adorned thee with bracelets, earrings, and a beautiful crown, has taken thee as his bride, and has made an everlasting covenant with thee. He has fed thee with oil, honey, and the finest of the wheat; he has led thee to the chamber of his love and kissed thee with the mouth of his peace.

How lovely and gracious a bridegroom and king is this who has chosen his poor, diseased and despised, unesteemed, yes, unchaste servant, to be such an exalted spouse and advanced her to be such a glorious queen! He has spared neither labor, pains, nor expense until he has made her the fairest, purest, worthiest, and noblest among women.

Arise, make haste, adorn and beautify yourself, extol and praise Him who has created you, and called you to such a high honor through the Word of His grace.

The winter is past, the rain is over and gone, the flowers appear on the earth, and the voice of the turtle [dove] is heard in our land. There is nothing more which can harm or hinder. Hell, sin, the devil, death, the world, flesh, fire, and sword are already vanquished by the children of God. All their wisdom is Christ Jesus; the object of their desire is the pure apostolic doctrine and the pious, unblamable life which is from God.

Praises be to the Most High who has silenced the lie and has made the truth to resound in every street. Antichrist goes down in shame and Christ rises to higher honor. Verily the unfruitful, cold winter is swallowed up, and the fruiting, delightful May has come in the land. The lovely, fair flowers spring forth everywhere; the turtledove drops his liquid note. The blessed holy Word, the word of repentance, the word of grace and eternal peace, is proclaimed with word, writings, life, and death in many a land.

Arise, my love, my fair one, come to the garden and vineyard of your beloved to see the fig tree as it buds, and the vineyard as it perfumes the air. Faith is budding forth, love is in bloom, the sun makes tender each twig, and the truth for so long a time barren and drear is coming into view. And although you must now for a short time bear the heat of the sun, yet you know right well that the kingdom of honor in eternal joy is promised and prepared.

Rejoice and watch; swarthy art thou but altogether lovely as the tents of Kedar, as the curtains of Solomon. Thou art the spice garden of the beloved, across which play the north wind and the south so that thine herbs drip with dew.

Fear not, little flock, for it is the Father's good pleasure to give you the kingdom. Not the perishing kingdom of Assyria, of the Medes, of Macedonia, nor of Rome, but the kingdom of the saints, the kingdom of the great King, of David, the kingdom of peace, of grace, and eternal peace, that shall never pass away but abide and stand forever. Therefore hear him and obey, lest you be thrust out with a haughty, disobedient Vashti. Rather with the humble, pious Esther live in endless glory, before Christ the true Ahasuerus, and abide with Him forever.

Glance up, daughter of Zion, and behold what is promised thee, O Jerusalem. Although thou as one without comfort sittest captive for a while, lashed by all manner of storms and hail, yet will your helper in need arrive at the appointed time, who will as the morning bring forth thy righteousness and be thy shelter from every wind and storm. For thus saith He who has loved thee: Behold, I will lay thy stones with fair colors, and thy foundations with sapphires. And I will make thy windows of agates, and thy gates of carbuncles, and all thy borders of pleasant stones. And all thy children shall be taught of the Lord; and great shall be the peace of thy children. In righteousness shalt thou be established; thou shalt be far from oppression. Isa. 54:11-14.

Behold, thy walls are planted upon twelve foundations, thy gates are of pearl, the city is of pure gold, the river of living waters proceeding from the throne of God, and the Lamb is in the midst of you, the tree of life is on either side; its leaves are for the healing of the nations. Holy and happy is he who has part in this city.

Therefore cleanse yourselves, you who seek the Lord. Circumcise the foreskin of your hearts, for this high and holy city may be inhabited by no uncircumcised person; its golden streets are trodden by no unclean feet; its limpid waters are drunk by none that is unclean. The fruit of life is not eaten by any of the ungodly forever, for without are dogs and sorcerers, and whoremongers, and murderers, and idolaters, and whosoever loveth and maketh a lie. Rev. 22:15.

Be like-minded all of you with Christ Jesus; be zealous to hold the unity of the Spirit through the bond of peace, for indeed you are all one single temple, house, city, mountain, body and church of Christ Jesus.

Your light, set it on a candlestick; your city, build it on a high mountain; live without reproach; behave as Christians in all things; fear God in all your ways; praise Him in all your works; great is the grace which has appeared. Prove yourselves in all things, as those who are born of God; shun all false doctrine; render not evil with evil, but return the evil with good. Pray without ceasing; in patience possess your souls; conform all your thoughts to Christ's thoughts, your words to Christ's words, your life to Christ's life. So shall you never be deceived.

Walk worthy of the calling whereby you have been called. Let them tyrannize, revile, defame, and rage, all they that hate the Lord and His Word. They persecute not you but Christ Jesus, who will in His own time judge them, and if they repent not, return it into their bosom.

Strive and struggle valiantly in order that the crown may not be taken from you. Fly to the mountain of refuge, Christ Jesus. Gird yourselves with the weapons of righteousness, confess God's Word confidently, neither falter nor fail. God is your leader; be faithful unto death, so shall you inherit the crown of life.

Whosoever overcomes will be clothed with white clothing and his name shall not be erased from the book of life. And although we appear to the unwise to die, and to have departed from the right way, our souls are nevertheless in surest hope and peace.

It is a faithful saying, says Paul, if we are dead with Christ, we shall also live with him; if we suffer with him, we shall also reign with him; but if we deny him, he will also deny us. II Tim. 2:11, 12.

Therefore fear your God from the heart, watch and pray, and with Jeremiah commend your affairs to Him who has chosen you to be His precious bride, His children and members. He has called you to the kingdom of His grace, and the inheritance of His glory, and has bought you with the spotless blood of Christ Jesus.

Grace be with you and the Spirit, power, and grace of our Lord Jesus Christ, my fellow laborers, brethren and sisters, companions in the faith unto life everlasting. Amen.

### [F.] Conclusion

Dear sirs, friends, and brethren, we have indicated briefly on what foundation and Scriptures we rest, what we seek and intend, and how with the Word of the Lord we rebuke all abominations, sects, and wickedness of the whole world with both great and small, without any respect of persons, and point out to everyone the pure and blessed truth. Let the God-fearing read and judge.

I have not done this as though the cross of Christ[67] may thereby be avoided; in no wise. For I know and am persuaded that the lamb will never be at peace with the wolf, the dove with the eagle, and Christ with Belial. Truth will be hated, even if spoken by Christ Himself from heaven. And neither Scripture nor piety, neither Christ nor apostle, neither prophet nor saint, neither life nor property, will prevail upon men. All those who rebuke in pure and honest zeal this haughty, avaricious, proud, idolatrous, blood-drunken world, all who diligently seek their happiness and eternal welfare, must suffer and tread the winepress.

You shall be hated of all men for my name's sake, says Christ. Through much tribulation you must enter into the kingdom of God. Christ Himself had to suffer and so enter into His glory.

But I have written in order that the noble, pure truth might be revealed; this or that man be won thereby; the blind pointed to the right way; the hungry fed with the Word of God; the erring directed to Christ their Shepherd; the ignorant taught; God's kingdom extended, and His holy name magnified and praised. And all this together with our innocence shall testify on the day of judgment against all bloodthirsty tyrants, against all deceivers, false prophets, and all the proud and impenitent, that to them the truth has been declared. But if you refuse to hear, then your sins will be upon you. God's Spirit, Word, truth, ordinance, and will I have declared unto you, according to my small gifts, and have pointed out to you righteousness. Whosoever has ears to hear, let him hear; and whosoever has understanding, let him perceive.

I confess my Saviour openly; I confess Him and dissemble not. If you repent not, and are not born of God, and become not one with Christ in Spirit, faith, life, and worship, then is the sentence of your condemnation on your poor souls already finished and prepared.

All who teach you otherwise than we have here taught and confessed from the Scriptures deceive you. This is the narrow way through which we all must walk and must enter the strait gate, if we would be saved. Neither emperor nor king, duke nor count, knight nor nobleman, doctor nor licentiate, rich nor poor, man nor woman, is excepted. Whosoever boasts that he is a Christian, the same must walk as Christ walked. If any man have not the Spirit of Christ, he is none of His. Whosoever transgresseth and abideth not in the doctrine of Christ, hath not God. II John 1:9. He that committeth sin is of the devil. I John 3:8. Here neither baptism, Lord's Supper, confession, nor absolution will avail anything. These and other Scriptures stand immovable and judge all those who live outside the Spirit and Word of Christ and who mind earthly and carnal things. They shall never be overthrown, perverted, nor weakened by angel or devil.

If with rebellious Israel you say, We will not hear the word which you have preached to us in the name of the Lord, but we will do as our fathers,

[67] The believer's cross of suffering which true discipleship to Christ entails. *Ed.*

our kings and princes have done for many years until the present time, then I answer with holy Jeremiah and say: Since you have pleasure in lies and do such abominations, therefore the Lord has taken your wickedness to heart and sent you one hard punishment after another. He has sent hunger, pestilence, storms, grief, misery, and the cruel, consuming sword, so that your land is turned to a waste, an amazement and a curse, as one may see in many places. This is because you perform strange worship, despise the Lord your God, reject His Word, shed innocent blood, walk according to your own wills, sin against God and walk not in His law, ordinance, and commands, as the mouth of the Lord has commanded.

And I say that the unprofitable and rebellious world is commonly warned and rebuked against its will, so that the majority of the prophets and the true servants of God are condemned and killed by the princes and magistrates as seditious mutinists, and persecuted by the priests and common people as deceivers and heretics. Therefore we have prepared ourselves both to teach and to suffer, expecting that we will fare no better in this matter than did they. But we do say with Ezekiel, that when that which will come has come, you will discover that the undissembled, pure Word of the Lord has been presented and taught among you.

The merciful, gracious Father, through His loving Son, Christ Jesus, our Lord, grant to you all the gift and grace of His Holy Spirit, so that you may hear and read these our Christian labors and service of true love, with such hearts that you may strive for, confess, believe, and follow after the pure truth with all your soul, and be eternally saved. Amen.

Dear noble lords, grant to your poor servants that we may fear the Lord from the heart and may preach the Word of God and do right. This we pray you for Jesus' sake.

O Lord, Father of all grace, be pleased to open the eyes of the blind so that they may see Thy way, Word, truth, and will, and walk therein with faithful hearts. Amen.

By me, M. S.

# Christian Baptism

*Verclaringhe des christelycken doopsels*

# 1539

*For other foundation can no man
lay than that is laid, which is Jesus Christ.*

I Corinthians 3:11

# Introduction

This book, *Christian Baptism,* was first published by Menno Simons in 1539. Of the first edition only one perfect copy is known; it is in the library of Juniata College, Huntingdon, Pennsylvania. The book begins with a Latin salutation, and ends with a brief Latin address also. The longer preface which follows the Latin salutation is a vigorous repudiation of the charge of heresy, a theme to which Menno returns again and again in the main body of the book. Indeed the main truths are stated over and over again in the book, undoubtedly by deliberate design, so that by constant hammering the truth may demolish the wrong ideas in the minds of many readers.

The book itself has three main themes by Menno's own analysis: The Teaching of Jesus, The Teaching of the Apostles, and The Practice of the Apostles: on Water Baptism. But before launching into the first main subject, Menno starts out with his Explanation of Christian Baptism, telling of the persecution which his Anabaptist brethren were enduring, and attempting to set forth clearly why his group practiced believer's baptism: namely, because they wished to follow the revealed Word of God. The section on Christ's teaching on baptism is rather brief, the one on apostolic practice is somewhat longer, and the most lengthy section is on the teaching of the apostles on water baptism.

In brief, Menno's thesis is that salvation is a pure gift of God, as is the faith which receives salvation. All that Christians enjoy comes by grace through faith. No ceremonies ever did or ever will bring justification. It is therefore a gross abomination to link the salvation of infants—a point on which Menno is entirely certain—with the ceremony of baptism. Only believers can properly observe a ceremony like baptism, which is but an external witness to the faith which saves the soul. Sacramentalism is a dreadful heresy, supported not by Scripture but by the appeal to learned church fathers and to long-standing custom. Infants are therefore saved by Christ's universal atonement; they are the objects of the love and mercy and favor of God. But infants are nowhere in Scripture commanded to be baptized, and they are incapable of the commitments which baptism calls for. Furthermore an awful consequence follows from linking regeneration or salvation with infant baptism: multitudes of people comfort themselves with the hope of heaven when they are actually lost sinners without Christ or the Holy Spirit or the new birth.

The book closes with a touching appeal for toleration.

The original title was: *An Explanation of Christian Baptism in Water as Derived from the Word of God.* By Menno Simons. *In What Manner it was Commanded by Christ Jesus, Taught and Practiced by His Holy Apostles.* In the *Opera Omnia Theologica* of 1681 this work appears, fol. 393-433, and in the *Complete Works* of 1871, II, 189-231. J. C. W.

# Christian Baptism

## 1539

•-•-•-•-•-•-•-•-•-•-•-•-•-•-•-•-•-•-•-•-•-•-•-•-•-•-•-•-•-•-•-•-•-•-•-•-•-•-•-•-•-•-•-•

### *Salutation to Latin Readers*

Read and reread the words which I speak, O ye learned ones who seem to excel others in wisdom and learning. I have added this my little Dutch work concerning the rite of baptism. For I am not well able to treat this matter in Latin, and even if I were able, I should not want to, lest my labor should perish in the hands of my opponents. For I desire that it might become known to every Christian, and yield the greater fruit. For you may see here for yourselves that there are in this work no falsifications of Scripture, no satires, no falsehoods; judge for yourself. Moreover I know it is not the spirit of a Christian to deal deceitfully in any matter, but especially not in a matter so serious.

It becomes the evangelical teacher to set before himself nothing except the most illustrious precepts of the Gospel—such as faith, charity, patience, spirituality, gentleness, peace, mildness, truth, moderation, etc., so that no one will be able with justice to thrust any aspersions against him with any taint of baseness. He must teach not only by word, but also by example, following the teachings of Paul who says, I keep under my body, and bring it into subjection; lest that by any means, when I have preached to others, I myself should be a castaway. I Cor. 9:27. And elsewhere, Having your conversation honest among the Gentiles; that, whereas they speak against you as evil doers, they may be ashamed that falsely accuse your good conversation in Christ. I Pet. 2:12; 3:16. In view of such things it behooves one to repress such ignorance and stupidities lest that saying of the Saviour be turned against us which says, Cast out first the beam out of thine own eye. Luke 6:42. For how can I induce others to become Christian when I myself am not a Christian?

Read therefore, and if anything be found in this work that has not the flavor of evangelical purity and spirit, I will be confounded, not you. For I have written from a sense of pious affection, not that I may injure any one, but for the benefit of all men. Yet what kind of thanks I shall have for service rendered you, I hardly know, unless it be that with my most holy master, Christ, I get all sorts of evil, ignominy, and cross, instead of the deserved reward. And no wonder. Why should they spare me, as I seek the truth and declare openly the offered sacrifice, when almost all teachers of righteousness, who were from the beginning, have been handed over to death in the same way? This is indeed the kind of gratitude which the world displays toward God's servants. Would that in very truth they were Christian who assure themselves that they are Christians. May grace abound with all who love the Lord Jesus with sincerity.

# *Preface*

Beloved readers, in our first publication concerning baptism[1] we have with Christian truth satisfied the desire of every pious Christian. Yet there are some frivolous, rebellious, and carnal persons who, without cause and Scripture, and in every respect without the fear of God, teach, write, admonish, and cry out against us, saying, It is heresy and deceit; for it is written and taught contrary to the learned, and against the doctrine of the holy, Christian church. I had not intended to reply to such perverse, rebellious, disobedient, and contentious persons, according to the Word of the Lord (Matt. 7); but solely to write to the humble, meek, pious, and penitent. For the wise will hear wisdom, will love it, and become wiser; but the fool will hear folly, praise it, persist in it, and die in it. Yet of such contenders and gainsayers, who rail against the Word of God, I would ask two questions, and request them to examine and ponder them well, and to make a polite, honorable reply. In the first place, Who are the real heretics and deceivers? Secondly, Who are they that admonish and teach contrary to the doctrine of the holy church? If they answer these questions fairly, they must themselves pronounce the sentence, that with us the upright truth of Jesus Christ is found and not with them. And on the other hand, that not with us (the wicked sects[2] do not involve us), but with them all sorts of heresy, error, and false doctrine are liberally taught and practiced.

Which of the two parties then are heretics and impostors, I will leave to the judgment of the reader. For *hereticus* means: one who sorts out, one who chooses, one who gleans. For Bede[3] in his work on the Acts of the Apostles says, Heresy means one who selects. If then they are truly heretics who, without Scripture, make themselves a faith, then I truly do not know where to find more miserable and more deplorable heretics than those who daily combat, upbraid, betray as damnable heretics, and persecute us poor, scattered, and rejected Christians. For there is no uglier, nor more abominable heresy under heaven than is found among our opponents, for they shamefully change and pervert the Word and the perfect ordinance and institution of our beloved Lord Jesus Christ. For they baptize such things which God has neither commanded nor ordained to be baptized, namely, little, unconscious children, and bells. They do not baptize those whom God has commanded to be baptized, namely, those who believe. They worship and honor a

[1] Menno's biographers are not agreed on whether the reference is to a booklet now lost (Vos), or to earlier writings as in the Foundation in which he discussed baptism (Krahn), *Ed.*

[2] Münsterites, Davidians, Batenburgers. *Ed.*

[3] The Venerable Bede, *c.* 673-735, was an English monk, theologian, and scholar. The work Menno cites, *Super Acta Apostolorum,* was spurious, however. *Ed.*

231

mouthful of bread and a sip of wine as the Son of God. They ascribe to themselves, without the Word of God, the power of life and death. They place in Christ's stead that man of sin, a child of perdition, whose natural pride, pomp, greed, cruelty, uncleanness, and idolatry are beyond description. II Thess. 2:4.

Truly, I do not know how a worse heresy could be invented, notwithstanding that these miserable men cruelly cry against us, saying, Heretics! heretics! Drown them, slay them, and burn them! And this for no other reason than that we teach the new life, baptism on confession of faith, and the Supper in both elements[4] in an unblamable church, according to the holy Gospel of Christ Jesus. They do this because we rebuke all false doctrine, idolatry, and the damnable carnal life, and point to the blessed Christ Jesus alone, and to no other means of salvation, neither in heaven nor on earth.

If this be heresy, beloved reader, then indeed the true Being is not in Christ; then He is not the true way, the truth, and the life. John 14:6. Be not frightened by their railing and ranting; for from the beginning it has been the case that the unbelieving hate, slander, and persecute the believing; the wicked, the good; the unrighteous, the righteous; the carnal, the spiritual; the heretics, the Christians. It was the case with Cain and Abel, Ishmael and Isaac, Esau and Jacob, the false prophets and the true prophets; as Christ Jesus has told us before, namely: Ye will be hated of all nations, for my name's sake. Matt. 24:9. If they were the true disciples of Christ Jesus, as they boast of themselves, they would persecute, betray, or murder no one for their faith; but with Christ Jesus they would diligently seek to reclaim that which was lost (Matt. 18:11), if we were lost, as they claim. If they were the bride of Christ they would not be hateful, cruel, and bloodthirsty, but meek, gentle, and merciful, minded as is the good and faithful bridegroom, Christ Jesus. But they plainly manifest themselves by their works not to be the bride of Jesus Christ, but rather the bride of him who from the beginning was a murderer, that is, the devil. John 8:44.

If they were the body of Christ they would not crucify and persecute anyone for the sake of the truth of the Lord, but would themselves, with Christ Jesus and His church, be crucified and persecuted for the sake of these things. Matt. 5:11; John 16:1, 2; II Tim. 3:12. For the innocent Lamb does not kill, but from the beginning was killed. Behold, kind readers, what miserable, bloody, tyrannical, and murderous heretics our opponents and persecutors are found to be before God, in all their teachings, abominations, instructions, life, and tyranny. But this they do not acknowledge. If they did, how then could they crucify and persecute the elect children of God, the children of the kingdom and of promise, the brethren and sisters of Jesus Christ, the messengers of peace, and the children of the eternal, imperishable life?

[4] The Catholic Church has withheld the cup from the laity ever since the Middle Ages, especially from the twelfth century. *Ed.*

But now they are so darkened in their minds, their eyes are so blinded, their ears are so closed up that they cannot understand it. For their evildoing and wickedness have obscured and blinded them. The table of the divine Word is to them a snare, and a trap, and a stumbling block, and a recompense. Rom. 11:9. God's stern judgment and awful wrath is come upon them, because they so industriously seek falsehood, and so obstinately combat and reject the lovely truth of Jesus Christ. Prov. 1:11.

Christ Jesus says, They which hunger and thirst after righteousness shall be filled. Matt. 5:6. But these hunger and thirst after unrighteousness, with which they according to Paul are abundantly filled. II Thess. 2:12.

Christ Jesus says, Everyone that asketh receiveth; and he that seeketh, findeth; and to him that knocketh it shall be opened. Luke 11:9. But these seek diligently, night and day, not after the right way, but after the wrong; hoping to find something either in God's Word or in our lives which may be so twisted, bent, broken, or applied as to trample upon and nullify the right, evangelical truth, as if the blessed Jesus had declared and taught the spoken truth with two tongues. If they can find an error in our walk, as alas they often can (for we are all of the sinful, failing flesh of Adam)[5]; then they rejoice that the evangelical truth is all deceit, and has no power over the flesh. Inasmuch as they so assiduously strive against God's righteousness, and delight in falsehood, therefore God smites them with such great blindness that they can neither comprehend nor judge of the teachings of God. Yet they desire so to clothe their cause, however shameful it be, with the cloak of the Scriptures that they may under this Scriptural, holy appearance the better deceive the foolish, ignorant people that likes to be deceived and misled. And thus they remain, both teacher and disciple, in the service of their perishable flesh which they have chosen as their God. Phil. 3:18; Rom. 16:17. Enough said of this.

Again, kind reader, they cry and snarl with rage against us, saying that we write against all the doctors and against the teachings of the holy Christian church. That we write against the greater part of the doctors or the learned men, I sweetly and gladly acknowledge. For whenever they write, admonish, and teach contrary to the Word, ordinances, statutes, and institutions of Jesus Christ, we do not consider their illustrious names, and have nothing to do with their human philosophy. But if they should teach rightly we would not contradict nor write against them.

I trust, by the most merciful grace of our Lord Jesus Christ, that the oldest, most pious, most upright, truest, and most able doctors of the church of Jesus Christ who were long before all other doctors, are received and believed by me and my beloved brethren in every word and doctrine, such as Moses, Isaiah, Jeremiah, David, etc., Christ Jesus, Matthew, Mark, Luke, John, Paul, Peter, James, Jude, etc. Let somebody show me a word in all my writings that I have taught or written contrary to the doctrine of these

[5] Note Menno's express repudiation of Perfectionism. *Ed.*

doctors, then I am willing to be humble, instructed, and taught; but I hope that it may never be truthfully done. If I should write and teach against these pious, irreproachable doctors, then my writing and teaching would be against the teachings and admonitions of the Christian assembly, congregation, or holy church.

I know very well that as to some articles, I admonish, teach, instruct, and write contrary to the instructions and teachings of some assemblies and churches, such as the papists, Lutherans, and the corrupt sects; but not contrary to the teachings of the holy, Christian church. May the merciful Father, whose divine will I industriously seek to obey, save me from teaching, instructing, and writing contrary to the doctrine of the holy church, lest woe be unto my soul forever.

Lest you be alarmed by the word *holy church,* you must learn and know from the Word of God that the holy, Christian church is no assembly of unbelievers, carnal or brazen sinners, even if they falsely appropriate the name of Christ Jesus, and think themselves to be the true Christian church. No, kind readers, no. They are not all Abraham's seed who are born of Abraham. Only the children of the promise are counted for the seed. Rom. 9:8. So, also, the holy, Christian church must be a spiritual seed, an assembly of the righteous, and a community of the saints; which church is begotten of God, of the living seed of the divine Word, and not of the teachings, institutions, and fictions of man. Yes, they are those who are regenerated, renewed, and converted; who hear, believe, and keep all the commandments and will of God; who have crucified the flesh with the affections and lusts (Gal. 5:24); who have put on Christ Jesus, and reflect Him, and become like unto Him (Rom. 8:17); and are heavenly and spiritually minded. Col. 3:10; Phil. 2:4.

These are the holy, Christian church, the congregation of God, the body and bride of Christ whom He has espoused, cleansed, and sanctified. I Cor. 6:19. But they who are carnally minded, never. Rom. 8:8. This holy, Christian church has a spiritual Prince over her who rules her with the unbroken rod of His divine Word (Ps. 2:9); a Master or Teacher who teaches the commandments of eternal life; and a Bridegroom whose voice she is ever ready to hear, that is, Christ Jesus. John 3:29.

If now I contend against His scepter, trample upon His commandments, and teach or write aught against His heavenly doctrine, then I teach and write against the doctrine of the holy, Christian church. For this holy, Christian church has but one doctrine which is fruitful and godly, which is the limpid, pure, and unmixed word of God, the lovely Gospel of the grace of our beloved Lord Jesus Christ. Matt. 28:19; Mark 16:15; I Pet. 1:25. All teachings and decrees which do not accord with the doctrine of Christ are but teachings and commandments of men, be they teachings and opinions of doctors, decrees of popes, councils, or anything else. They are doctrines of man (Matt. 15:9); of the devil (I Tim. 4:11); and anathema (Gal. 1:8). Since we write and teach nothing but the pure, heavenly Word, and the perfect ordinances of the holy Gospel of Jesus Christ and of His apostles, therefore we do not teach and write against the teachings of the holy church, but in favor of them.

Beloved reader, let the frivolous run their course to the end, which is certain death. They will nevermore concede the truth however powerfully they are vanquished, but they will ever delight in hatred, bickering, discord, and disputation, and never tire of them, for they will not go into the straight way of the Spirit, taught of Jesus Christ and His holy apostles. Notwithstanding, although without obedience they want to be considered the children and the church of God. Do not be that way, good reader. Always remember that there is no holy church of Christ other than the assembly of the righteous, and the church of the saints, which ever acts in harmony with the Word and ordinances of the Lord, and with no other doctrine. To eternity, she neither will nor can accept any other doctrine or ordinance in divine matters.

Dear brethren, because the divine ordinance of baptism in water has been perverted for many centuries, and because a strange baptism has been practiced contrary to the true doctrine of the holy, Christian church, namely, contrary to the Word of God, from which evil custom so much false doctrine, unbelief, and fruitless, carnal life have resulted; therefore I have once more pointed out from the holy Gospel how we should practice the true, Scriptural, Christian baptism, in order that the hearts and faith of the wise may be established and assured, the mouths of the fools may be stopped, and that God may have the glory in His holy Word. Read and see if we have not rightly taught and written according to the meaning of Christ Jesus. And because the whole wide world so shamefully blasphemes and opposes the Word of God, and despises His commandments and ceremonies as useless, saying, What good can water do us? without ever considering that the kingdom of God and the will of God do not consist in external ceremonies, but in the willing obedience to the Word of God—therefore we have in the following writings so extensively shown from the holy Scriptures who they are who should be baptized according to the Word of God, namely, the believing (Mark 16:16); or the regenerate (John 3:3; Titus 3:5).

Besides we have also shown how very weak, useless, and groundless all the arguments of the world are, by which they defend infant baptism, so that the before-mentioned despisers of God may know and understand that they are not baptized according to the evangelical commandment of our beloved Lord Jesus Christ. It follows that they are not in obedience to the divine Word, and if they are not in the obedience which has the promise (I speak of those who have come to years of discretion), then they cannot inherit nor obtain the promise, so long as they do not believe the Word of God and obediently fulfill it in all respects. Let every one consider carefully and save his own soul; for our God is a consuming fire.

May the merciful Father, through His blessed Son, Jesus Christ our Lord, grant you a true knowledge and His grace unto betterment of life. Amen.

## [I.] EXPLANATION OF CHRISTIAN BAPTISM

Hear ye now, O illustrious, noble, wise lords and princes! Listen, all judges of the land, where the sword of God is given to the destruction of evildoers, to the protection of the good, and to the punishment of the wicked. Hear, ye wise and prudent who think that you bear the vessels of the Lord. Hear, all ye people of whatever state, condition, trade, or class, who call yourselves Christian, and who boast of His bitter death and precious blood.

### [A. Baptism Occasions Our Being Persecuted]

Since we, for the sake of baptism, are so miserably abused, slandered, and persecuted by all men, and since we are ever suspicioned because of the' ungodly sects (which are to you very harmful, perilous, and abominable, as may be plainly seen) ; therefore we say and testify in Christ Jesus, before God, before His holy angels, before you, and before the whole world, that we are driven only by a God-fearing faith which we have in the Word of God to baptize and to be baptized, and by nothing else; nor will it be found otherwise, neither in this life, nor in death, nor in the last judgment of God.

My dear sirs, we seek nothing in this baptism other than to obey our beloved Lord Jesus Christ, who has taught and commanded us this with His own blessed mouth. Matt. 28:19; Mark 16:16. Consider, we pray you, that we cannot possibly seek carnal profit in this our conduct; neither gold, nor silver, nor honor, nor ease, nor long life on earth. For you may plainly see that we are made a prey to the world on account of it. But we are driven solely by the love of God, by an upright, fruitful faith, which faith studiously examines all the words of Christ, giving ourselves in willing obedience to God; knowing of a certainty that if we oppose, and do not obey that which our Lord has commanded, we can never receive nor inherit the heavenly blessing and divine promise. For through obedience everything is received, as has been mentioned in the preface.

How could Abraham, Isaac, and Jacob together with all the dear fathers and patriarchs have obtained the comforting promise of God, if they had not done, be it ever so little, that which God had commanded them through His holy Word? But they heard the Word of God, firmly believed and carefully obeyed it; and therefore they became joint heirs of righteousness. Heb. 11 :8.

On the other hand, however, all those who did not obey God undoubtedly have had to bear the punishment of the Lord, such as Adam and Eve; Nadab and Abihu; Korah, Dathan, and Abiram; as Saul; as the man of God who reproved Jeroboam the king for his idolatry and was deceived by the old prophet in Bethel, and other instances which may be read of in Moses and other Scriptural writings.

Since we are so sadly opposed by all men in regard to our doctrine and practice of Christian baptism, and since they do not realize that their opposition tends to eternal death, for they oppose Christ and His Word; therefore I will again briefly show from God's Word to them and all persons who shall read, see, or hear these my writings, how wonderfully, powerfully; nay, how incontrovertibly this our doctrine and practice is contained and founded on the holy Gospel of Jesus Christ—although we have fully shown and proved this before in our writings on baptism.

## [B. Why We Practice Believer's Baptism]

Beloved, that our faith accepts this baptism under such a heavy cross and distress is because it is driven to it by three considerations. First, because of the divine commandment of our beloved Lord Jesus Christ, a commandment which can never be broken. Second, because of the teachings of the holy apostles. Third, because of the practice of these same apostles.

## [II. THE TEACHING OF JESUS]

And first, of the commandment: After Christ Jesus had risen from the power of death and was about to ascend to His heavenly Father, He commanded His disciples, saying, Go ye therefore, and teach all nations, baptizing them in the name of the Father, and of the Son, and of the Holy Spirit. Matt. 28:19. Again, at another place, Go ye into all the world and preach the gospel to every creature; he that believeth, and is baptized, shall be saved. Now since Jesus Christ, the eternal Wisdom who cannot err, the eternal Truth who cannot lie, has commanded this, namely, that we shall first preach the Gospel, from the hearing of which comes faith (Rom. 10), and that we shall baptize those who believe—who will or who may turn this divine commandment otherwise, or make it better than the eternal, wise, perfect, blessed Christ Jesus has made it and has commanded it?

Brethren, it was not allowed to change one single word of the Mosaic ceremonies from what they were contained in the Law, for the Almighty God does not want us to follow our own inclinations with regard to the ceremonies which He has commanded us, but desires us to observe His good will and pleasure. For that purpose He has commanded them. In the outward ceremonies as such God takes no pleasure; but He has commanded them because He ever requires of us faithful obedience. His wrath has often come upon those who changed the ceremonies, as in the case of Nadab and Abihu and many others. For He demands, yes, demands, us not to follow our own opinion, but to hear, believe, and obey His voice. Jer. 7:5-7.

If God would have His ceremonies under the law—which were in part attended with trouble, and difficult and quite numerous, and which He commanded not through Christ, His Son, but through His servant Moses—if God wanted these ceremonies kept thus strictly and unchanged until the time of

Christ; how much more so does He want the few ceremonies, but two in number, of the New Testament kept strictly and unchanged: [namely,] baptism and the Supper, which He has commanded, not through His servant but through His only begotten Son, Jesus Christ; and which are neither attended with trouble nor difficulty.

Consider how troublous and difficult it was for the Israelites to travel a long distance over hill and dale, to appear two or three times a year before the Lord at Jerusalem with their offerings of bullocks, rams, goats, and tithes which they had to sacrifice of all their goods. But the Christian ceremonies of the New Testament, baptism and Supper, which are commanded us of God, are not at all attended with trouble or difficulty, although the effect or the thing symbolized by the ceremonies to true believers is attended with great vexation to the flesh. This, however, is not caused by the ceremonies themselves, but by the faith which leads us to these ceremonies, out of love and obedience to the divine Word.

Most beloved, since the ordinance of Jesus Christ is unchangeable, and is the only one that counts with the Father; and since He has commanded that we shall first preach the Gospel, and then baptize those who believe, it follows that all those who baptize and are baptized without the teaching of the Gospel, and without faith, baptize and are baptized on their own opinion, without the doctrine and the ordinance of Jesus Christ. And therefore it is idolatry, useless, and vain. For had Israel circumcised their females because it was not expressly forbidden, then would they still have circumcised without the ordinance of God, for He had commanded that the males were to be circumcised. Gen. 17:10. So also in this instance, if we baptize the irrational children, although Scripture has not expressly forbidden it, just as it was not forbidden to circumcise the females, they nevertheless are baptized without the ordinance of Jesus Christ; for He commanded to baptize those who should hear and believe His holy Gospel. Matt. 28:19; Mark 16:16.

It avails nothing to say as some do that by these words of Matthew and Mark, the holy church is extended to the Gentiles and that thereby the baptism of infants is not excluded.

Dear reader, it is true that by this commandment the holy church is extended to the Gentiles, to the fulfillment of the prophetic Scriptures which long before had seen this through the Spirit, as Paul proves. Rom. 15. Yet the Word stands firmly with regard to both Jews and Gentiles, namely, whosoever believeth and is baptized shall be saved. Faith precedes baptism. For faith is the beginning of all righteousness which avails before God, from which faith baptism issues as a sign and token of obedience. If now children have faith, their baptism is not forbidden by the alleged words of Matthew and Mark.

Again it does not avail anything that some allege and say that the resurrection of the dead was not expressly written in the books of Moses, but was implied as Christ Jesus proved to the Sadducees from Ex. 3:6, namely: I am the God of Abraham, of Isaac, and of Jacob. Even as in these words of Moses the resurrection is not expressly stated, but is implied, since God is not a God of the dead but of the living, as Christ teaches (Matt. 22:32); therefore they say, infant baptism is not expressly stated in the Gospel, yet it is implied.

To this we reply that the resurrection of the dead is no outward ceremony which God has commanded us to do; but it is something which God Himself will accomplish in us by His almighty power. Therefore it is an invisible consolation in the hearts of all believers, which is comprehended by faith alone. But the baptism of little children is an outward ceremony. If now it is an ordinance and Word of God which has promise, then it must be plainly expressed in the Scriptures. If not, it cannot be called a ceremony of Christ.

Neither does that avail which some allege, saying, Although the believing women have no express word of invitation to the Lord's Supper, neither were they at the celebration of the Last Supper of the Lord, yet they are, for good reasons, admitted to the Supper. So also with little children. Even if there is no express commandment for their baptism, neither were they baptized by the Lord or His disciples so far as we can learn from Scriptures, yet they are for good reason admitted to baptism, exactly as believing women are admitted to the Supper.

Kind reader, this is a very crafty argument to deceive the simple and ignorant, for it rides quite high in subtlety, but it is not at all according to the example of Christ Jesus. The Holy Supper represents the death of the Lord Jesus Christ and the love of our neighbors, both of which are grasped and known and practiced by believing women as well as by believing men. If then the unconscious children have that which is represented by baptism, namely, death unto sin, the new life (Rom. 6:4), the new birth (John 3), the putting on of Christ (Gal. 3:27), the moving, quickening Spirit by which we are baptized into the body of Christ (I Cor. 12:13), and a good conscience (I Pet. 3:16), even as believing women have of what is represented in the Holy Supper, then they should be baptized for the same reason that believing women are admitted to the Supper. But this will nor can ever be found in irrational children.

In the fourth place, it avails nothing to quote from Ecclesiasticus that, To fear the Lord is the beginning of wisdom: and it was created with the faithful in the womb, and will be with the chosen women. They say, If then the fear of the Lord is created with the believing ones in the mother's womb, which fear is a fruit of faith, and since the fruit cannot be before the tree, therefore the children from their mother's womb have a fruitful faith. And if they have faith, then their baptism may not be obstructed according to the Scriptures.

Not so, beloved reader, but judge everything according to the Word of God and His Spirit. For I do not doubt but that you will confess that the faith that counts with God is a gift of God, from whence all righteousness proceeds and comes by the hearing of the divine Word. Rom. 10:10. If now it comes by hearing the divine Word, as Paul teaches, how will it be found in little children? For it is plain that they cannot be taught, admonished, or instructed. And many have less sense at birth than do irrational creatures— so without rationality that they cannot be taught anything about carnal things until their hearing, comprehension, and understanding have begun to develop. If they cannot be made to understand anything visible, how can they then prematurely, that is, before they can comprehend things, be taught and instructed in invisible, celestial matters of the Spirit?

Secondly, you know and acknowledge that where true faith is, there is true knowledge of the difference between good and evil, the fear of God, the love of God and also of our neighbor, and the obedience to God and the desire after righteousness. It cannot be otherwise than that a good tree bringeth forth good fruit. Matt. 7:18. Faith works all manner of righteousness, as it is written, The just lives by his faith, and faith is the substance of things hoped for, the evidence of things not seen. Heb. 11:1.

Dear reader, if faith always brings forth good fruits, all manner of righteousness, and is the substance of things hoped for, the evidence of things not seen, what fruits and righteousness which are evidence of faith do our little children bring forth? All they do is nurse, drink, laugh, cry, warm themselves, play, etc., as has been the nature of children from the beginning. Besides, they often show, as they grow, the evil seed of Adam; and as they get a little older, they manifest it still more; but the fruits of faith, or of the new birth, they do not show, as may be plainly observed. And if you do not believe this from your daily experience, then believe the Word of God which never will deceive you. Moses says, Your children, which in that day had no knowledge between good and evil. Deut. 1:39. They had not knowledge between good and evil, as it appears—where then is their faith which has knowledge?

Thirdly, you will acknowledge that all righteousness issues from faith, as our critics themselves allege, and in their opposition quote Rom. 4:5. Without faith there is no godly righteousness; therefore Paul says to the Hebrews[6] (speaking of those who are of years of discretion), Without faith it is impossible to please God. Heb. 11:6. Since children have no faith by which they can realize that God is, and that He is a rewarder of both good and evil, as they plainly show by their fruits, therefore they have not the fear of God, and consequently they have nothing upon which they should be baptized. Yet they have the promise of everlasting life, out of pure grace.[6a] With this the Scriptures move on, and no more is said about them in God's Word, as will become evident below.

[6] Menno accepts the Pauline authorship of Hebrews, a view which gained acceptance in the ancient church for the most part after A.D. 325. *Ed.*

[6a] Note Menno's firm confidence on this point. *Ed.*

Since faith must precede the fruits which come by faith, such as the fear of God, the love of God, etc., which fruits do not appear in little children, as has been said; therefore we must presume that Ecclesiasticus does not teach that the fear of God is in little children from birth; but he teaches that the fear of God is granted to the believers from their mother's womb and that it would be given them in due season because God with His eyes as of flaming fire, which observe all things from beginning to end, foresaw while they were as yet in their mother's womb that they would at the appointed time hear His holy voice, believe with the heart, and through the same faith fear God and be justified. For true faith cannot be without its fruits, as has been often proved.

If then faith were in the little, innocent children from conception, as our opponents say, it would be a fruitless faith, for they do not bring forth fruits; and then preaching is vain. For if that were the case, faith would come by the first creation of the pious beginnings, and not by preaching of the divine Word. Not so, beloved reader. You must consider this a sure, eternal, unchanging, and a permanent principle of divine truth in order to fulfill all righteousness, namely: First, to preach the holy Gospel of Jesus Christ. Second, to hear eagerly and to understand. Third, heartily to believe this Gospel and to bring forth fruit. This being the case, it follows relentlessly that little, innocent children have no faith, for they cannot hear nor learn. If they have no faith, they cannot have the fear of God. Therefore our opponents cannot prove the propriety of the baptism of little children from this passage of Ecclesiasticus.

Little ones must wait according to God's Word until they can understand the holy Gospel of grace and sincerely confess it; and then, and then only is it time, no matter how young or how old,[7] for them to receive Christian baptism as the infallible Word of our beloved Lord Jesus Christ has taught and commanded all true believers in His holy Gospel. Matt. 28:19; Mark 16:16. If they die before coming to years of discretion, that is, in childhood, before they have come to years of understanding and before they have faith, then they die under the promise of God, and that by no other means than the generous promise of grace given through Christ Jesus. Luke 18:16. And if they come to years of discretion and have faith, then they should be baptized. But if they do not accept or believe the Word when they shall have arrived at the years of discretion, no matter whether they are baptized or not, they will be damned, as Christ Himself teaches. Mark 16:16.

I know there are a great many who will ask why I, an unlearned man, am not satisfied in regard to this matter with the doctrine of Martin Luther[8]

[7] Menno recognizes that the age of accountability does not come at a uniform point in the maturation of children. *Ed.*

[8] Luther was about thirteen years Menno's senior. Luther tacked up his theses when Menno was about twenty-one years of age, and over eighteen years before Menno renounced Roman Catholicism. Menno also seems to sincerely recognize the great personal gifts and the genuine spiritual stature of Luther. Yet he was bitterly critical of what he

and other renowned doctors, who are versed in the Scriptures and many languages and sciences, who teach, and particularly Luther, that faith lies dormant in a sleeping believer.

To this I answer: In the first place, if there were such dormant faith in little children (which, however, is nothing but an invention), then it would not be proper to baptize such children, so long as they would not confess this fruit with their mouth, and show it in their fruits and their deeds. For the holy apostles did not baptize any believers while they were asleep, as we have shown in our former writings.

I acknowledge and also solemnly confess before you and the whole world that they and many others are well gifted with learning, eloquence, subtlety, languages, and science, and that I, poor, ignorant man, in comparison with them, am less than a fly is to an elephant. Therefore I am heartily ashamed to write and speak against them with my dull pen and awkward speech. Yet every reader should know that however learned the before-mentioned scholars are, and however ignorant I am, yet our opinions are all worth about equally much before God, for without the command of the holy Scripture nothing righteous can be done and nothing pleasing to God can be practiced, let him be whosoever he may. The holy Scriptures do not refer us to them nor to any other learned person, but to Christ Jesus alone. Matt. 17:46. Whenever such highly renowned men by their subtle acuteness and clever philosophy try to take from us and pervert the plain ordinances of Christ Jesus and His apostles, we must consider their doctrine in that respect the doctrine of men and false; for Christ Jesus is not below them, but above them. Neither has He received His holy doctrine from them, but from the wise Father. John 7:24.

Since by their philosophy they dream of dormant faith in little children, all patently contrary to Scripture and truth, and that the children should be baptized on the basis of such human phantasy, now judge for yourselves, you who oppose me, which of the two is better—to obey the holy Word and ordinance of Jesus Christ, to whom the Father, together with all the prophets have pointed me, or to hear the learned ones, who against the holy Word and ordinance would make me to believe their opinion, perverting the Scriptures. Eradicate from your hearts all partiality and rebellion, so that a true judgment in spiritual matters may be heard of you. God grant that all the learned ones and those who are taught of them may acknowledge and teach truth, and fulfill it in their works. Amen.

Inasmuch as Christ Jesus has commanded His holy apostles that they should first teach the holy Gospel of grace, and then baptize those who should believe; we are in the first place urged by the love of God to teach this Christian baptism according to the Word of God, even though the whole wide world opposes, and afterwards obediently to receive it, and by the grace of God, to preserve it to the honor of God, both in life and death.

felt was the evil sophistry of the state churchmen, defending as they did institutions such as infant baptism, and failing to practice a Scriptural church discipline. *Ed.*

## [III.] THE TEACHINGS OF THE HOLY APOSTLES CONCERNING BAPTISM BY WATER

We are urged by the pure, chaste teaching of the holy apostle diligently to teach and accept this Christian baptism. First, because it is written, Now when they heard this, they were pricked in their hearts, and said unto Peter, Men and brethren, what shall we do? Then Peter said unto them, Repent and be baptized, every one of you, in the name of Jesus Christ for the remission of sins, and ye shall receive the gift of the Holy Ghost. Acts 2:37, 38.

Dearest friends, impress this upon yourselves both now and all the days of your lives, not only concerning baptism, but concerning all doctrine you may hear, lest you be deceived by false teachers. Namely, that even as all the true prophets of God, who were between Moses and Christ, conformed their teachings to the doctrine of Moses, so the holy apostles have conformed their teaching to the doctrine of Christ Jesus, as He had commanded them, saying, Teaching them to observe all things whatsoever I have commanded you. Matt. 28:20.

Therefore consider and ponder well that which shall be taught you by the grace of the Lord, from the Word of God, and you will perceive from the words of Peter how the words of Jesus to Nicodemus, concerning the new birth, should be understood: Verily, verily, I say unto thee, Except a man be born of water and of the Spirit, he cannot enter into the kingdom of God. John 3:5. Dear brethren, the new birth is effected by the Word of God. I Pet. 1:3; Jas. 1:19. When this selfsame Word was taught by Peter at Jerusalem on the day of Pentecost, and the multitudes heard it from his mouth and from the mouth of the other apostles, their hearts were pierced. For by faith they accepted these words, and therefore they said, Men and brethren, what shall we do? Then Peter said unto them, Repent of your former life and be baptized every one of you in the name of Jesus Christ for the remission of sins, and ye shall receive the gift of the Holy Ghost. Christ had said to Nicodemus in this same vein when He first taught of the birth from above: Verily, verily, I say unto thee, Except a man be born of water and of the Spirit, he cannot enter into the kingdom of heaven. John 3:5.

Observe, my elect brethren, how harmonious are both Master and disciples in their teaching, namely, first the birth from above, by which we become children of God (John 1:14); and then the water, by which the obedience of the children of God is signified. Third, the communion of the Holy Ghost, by which we are assured in our hearts of the grace of God, of the remission of sins, and of everlasting life through Christ Jesus our Lord.

Inasmuch as the holy Peter, who is the apostle of God, a true witness sent by Jesus Christ with the words of everlasting life, and who was enlightened and taught by the Holy Ghost, has thus taught and commanded us, namely, that we shall have ourselves baptized, seeing that we believe according to the commandment of the Lord; and in the name of Christ for the remission of sins: therefore we must receive this baptism, even as it is commanded us in the holy Scriptures. Otherwise we cannot obtain remission of our sins nor the Holy Ghost. For who has ever received remission of sins contrary to the Word of God? Surely we cannot take the remission of sins and the Holy Ghost from God as by force. If then we desire the remission of our sins and the Holy Ghost, we must do and fulfill all that which God the Almighty Father has taught in all spiritual things and commanded us through Christ Jesus His beloved Son, and through His holy apostles.

Here it avails nothing that some teach and say, contrary to the holy Scriptures, that the little children are born of Adam, with a sinful or wicked nature, and that therefore they should be washed of their original guilt and sin by baptism. To teach and believe thus, my brethren, is first of all a dangerous idolatry and an abominable blasphemy against the blood of Christ. There is no remedy in heaven nor on earth for our sins, whether original or actual,[9] other than the blood of Christ, as we have shown in our first writings. I Pet. 1:19; I John 1:7; Eph. 1:7. If we ascribe the remission of sins to baptism and not to the blood of Christ, then we mold a golden calf and place it in the stead of Christ. For if we could be washed or cleansed by baptism, then Christ Jesus and His merits would have to abdicate, unless we are prepared to admit that there are two means for the remission of sins, first, baptism; and second, the blood of Christ. This can never be. For the most holy and precious blood of our beloved Lord Jesus Christ must and shall have the praise, as has been so clearly declared and testified by all the true prophets and apostles, throughout the Scriptures.

Those who believe receive remission of sins, not through baptism but in baptism, and in this manner. Since they now sincerely believe the blessed Gospel of Jesus Christ which has been preached and taught to them, the glad tidings of grace; namely, of the remission of sin, of grace, of peace, of favor, of mercy, and of eternal life through Jesus Christ our Lord; so they become a new mind, deny themselves, bitterly lament their old corrupted life, and look diligently to the Word of God, who has shown them such great love, to fulfill all that which He has taught and commanded them in His holy Gospel; trusting firmly in the word of grace, in the remission of their sins through the crimson blood and through the merits of our beloved Lord Jesus Christ.

They therefore receive the holy baptism as a token of obedience which proceeds from faith, as proof before God and His church that they firmly believe in the remission of their sins through Jesus Christ as it was preached and taught them from the Word of God. Therefore they receive remission of their sins in baptism, as the blessed promise of grace proclaims and repre-

---

[9] The original has *wereltlijck* (worldly) which is no doubt a misprint for *werckelijk* (actual), seeing that the word stands as a complement of *erffelijck* (hereditary, or in theological language, original). *Tr.*

sents; and just as Israel after the flesh received remission of their sins by their sacrifices. In case we seek outward baptism only and trust in the literal rite and continue in our old, corrupted life, then indeed our baptism is vain, even as it was in such cases a vain sacrifice among the wicked and carnal Israelites. For the Lord of Hosts complained through His holy prophets that their sacrifice was not pleasing to Him, that it was nothing but a corrupt abomination and a revolting scene before His holy eyes; inasmuch as they despised the law, the love, and the commandments of God, and lived according to the lusts of their flesh. Isa. 66:4, 5, and other passages.

Second, we are not cleansed in baptism of our inherited sinful nature which is in our flesh, so that it is entirely destroyed in us, for it remains with us after baptism. But since the merciful Father, from whom descend all good and perfect gifts, has graciously given us the most holy faith, through His holy Word; therefore we declare in the baptism we receive that we desire to die unto the inherent, sinful nature, and destroy it, so that it will no longer be master in our mortal bodies (Rom. 6:12), even though such true believers are often overcome by sin. As John observes, Whosoever is born of God doth not commit sin; for his seed remaineth in him; and he cannot sin, because he is born of God. I John 3:9.

I repeat, the Israelites received remission of their sins through the promise with which their sacrifices were associated when they offered them with contrite hearts. Not through the sacrifice itself, for then it would be merit, but only through the Word of promise. For it is grace and not merit. Just so we receive remission of our sins when we are true believers and are washed and cleansed in baptism. Through the promise, I say, not through the washing of water, for it is not merit, but through the promise. For it is grace, with which promise the Holy Spirit of God has associated the baptism of believers in the Gospel. As Paul teaches, saying, Christ also loved the church, and gave himself for it; that he might sanctify and cleanse it with the washing of water by the word, that he might present it to himself a glorious church. Eph. 5:25-27.

Observe, dear friends, here is the whole matter. We are not cleansed by the washing of the water, but by the Word of the Lord, as the holy Paul clearly teaches us in the before-mentioned words. Since little children, by reason of their inability to hear and understand the preaching of the holy Gospel, by which comes faith (Rom. 10:17), the faith by which God purifies our hearts, and not by the outward baptism, as has been said before, and since the express commandment and Word of God, which attaches the promise to baptism, refers to those who are begotten by this same Word, and are thus cleansed in their hearts by faith: therefore it follows rigorously that these little children, notwithstanding they are baptized under a false pretense and sham of the divine Word, are not cleansed thereby—if unclean they were, which is not the case.[10] Why? Because the promise is not associated with

[10] Menno is firm in the confidence that infants are justified before God by virtue of Christ's shed blood. They stand in need of no ceremony to insure their salvation. *Ed.*

their baptism. Therefore their baptism is not done according to the Word, but in every respect contrary to the Word. For the Word requires faith, and they have no faith. Therefore the baptism of our opponents is without doubt a baptism of their own choice, without God, without promise, yes, idolatrous, useless, and vain.

Whosoever now wants to balk at this, and refuses to believe the ordinance and Word of God, let him take heed to what he does. For by the baptism of infants he destroys the commandment of the Lord, tramples upon His crimson blood (for he seeks a kind of righteousness in this baptism), and he establishes contrary to the immutable ordinance of God, out of his own carnal choice, a false baptism which God never commanded. Therefore it is not His holy will, as has been said above, and as will be shown much more extensively below.

The Apostle Peter writes that as Noah, in his day, was saved in the ark from the waters of the deluge, so even baptism doth now save us (not by a baptism that puts away the filth of the flesh, but the answer of a good conscience toward God), by the resurrection of Jesus Christ. I Pet. 3:21. By this passage of Peter, the baptism of believers is again clearly affirmed, and the baptism of infants repudiated. For it is clearly impossible that anyone can have a good conscience except he who believes and whose heart is regenerate and converted; who acknowledges the divine Word which teaches that God the Almighty Father, whose enemies we were before, is now again reconciled to us through Christ Jesus, His beloved Son; so that henceforth through the merits of our beloved Lord, neither hell, devil, past sins, eternal death, nor the wrath of God will hurt, harm, or hinder us. All those who truly believe this shall receive and obtain a joyous mind and a good conscience by the resurrection of Christ Jesus, as Peter says, because He has so victoriously triumphed over all His enemies, visible and invisible, to our profit, and has taken His session in the heavenly being by seating Himself at the right hand of His Father. Such persons are first inwardly baptized with the Spirit and fire, according to the Word of God, are taught in their hearts by His Spirit, and are led in all divine truth, righteousness, obedience, and evangelical fruits and works. They are inwardly fired by this fire of love, having become conscious by the Word of God that such great grace, I repeat it, grace, has been bestowed on them through Jesus Christ that they neither regard nor see lords, princes, learned men, councils, long usages, nor their wives, children, flesh, blood, placards,[11] or any other threats; not even life or death. They embrace without reservation continuing glad in the Holy Spirit, not only the outward baptism, but also all the works of love and the fruits of righteousness which the true mouth of the Lord Jesus Christ has taught and commanded us in His holy Gospel, either Himself or through His holy apostles.

[11] An imperial edict was later issued against Menno by Charles V on Dec. 7, 1542, promising pardon to criminals who would deliver Menno over to the authorities. *Ed.*

In this manner baptism saves us, as Peter teaches; not the outward, literal baptism, but the inward, spiritual baptism, which as obedient children of God has led us through the power of faith to the outward, literal baptism. For the outward, literal baptism is nothing more than obedience to the divine Word, and is a seal or proof of the righteousness from whence the true, fruitful faith comes; just as the literal circumcision was to the believing and obedient Abraham. Rom. 4:10.

Since Christ Jesus has commanded that we should baptize the believing ones (Mark 16:16), therefore the holy Peter followed the commandment in his teachings; and has taught baptism to be a work of faith, namely, the answer of a good conscience toward God, which none can have save those who have faith, there being but one literal baptism taught in the holy Scripture. This baptism shows and is proof of the good conscience toward God, as Peter teaches, and so by this Scripture of Peter infant baptism is prohibited, for [infants] cannot have this consciousness as believers have it.

Therefore you should take heed, good reader, whoever you are, lest you sin against God. For all those who lamentably oppose this evangelical believer's baptism (so strictly commanded by Christ Jesus, and taught and practiced by His holy apostles), either by doctrine, by word, or by the sword, verily confess and acknowledge that they were hitherto neither orthodox, regenerate, obedient, nor inwardly baptized with the Spirit and fire. Again, let every one of you beware and take heed, for it does not concern bread and butter, but your poor, naked souls which have been so dearly bought and redeemed by such a precious treasure.

Dear children in the Lord, no matter how incontrovertibly our cause is confirmed and founded in the Word of God, yet some are not ashamed persistently and continually to write, talk, and slander against us; recommending and inciting persecution, slaughter, and bloodshed against us. In part, I presume, from ignorance, and in part out of partiality; in part because they are enemies of the cross of Christ, and in part because they do not desire the blessed, spiritual life which is of God. They say, Although infants have not the answer of a good conscience, as the believing have, yet this should not at all obstruct their baptism, but they ought to be baptized in order that they may be the better instructed in the Word and commandments of God.

Dearest brethren, when an idolatrous, refractory, and disobedient person has not the Word of God wherewith to defend his cause, he yet knows how to invent something wherewith he can so beautify and adorn his invention and carnal righteousness with a semblance of piety and holiness that it seems quite right, just, spiritual, holy, divine, and unblamable to those who are not versed in spiritual matters. The more so because their unchristian hearts and carnal minds are inclined to trust in outward works, yes, through their own notion and opinion, as I understand it. If I teach erroneously, then rebuke me with the Word of God; for the greater part of them have always sought righteousness in ceremonies, and not in Christ.

Even now, as in the days of the apostles and immediately thereafter, the foolish teachers and bishops have adopted the custom of baptizing little children, not in keeping with the divine commandment nor with the doctrine and ordinance of the holy apostles. This may be readily gathered from the book of Tertullian, called *Corona Militis*.[12] He writes that among the ancients most adults were baptized by the washing of regeneration. Understand me well, brethren. Tertullian lived one hundred and eight years after Christ, some say one hundred and forty years.[13] Already in the days of these ancient writers, the true, evangelical baptism which was commanded by Christ and taught and practiced by His holy apostles had degenerated with many, which baptism He clearly testifies the ancients commonly administered to adults. Even if it appears, brethren, that they baptized children in the days of Tertullian's ancestors before him (as it appears, we agree, since he says most, and as the Strasburg scholars indicate from another passage in the same work where Tertullian says that children and adults were being baptized in the same font), it is still true that infant baptism was no apostolic institution nor usage, nor a divine command. For if Christ had commanded it, and the holy apostles had taught and practiced it, then the ancestors of Tertullian would not have baptized some infants but all the infants of true believing parents, without question.

That it is no divine command nor apostolic institution was well known by the dear, old father Alexander,[14] bishop of Alexandria, who was a particular opponent of the Arians; for he, so long after the days of the apostles, did not yet baptize the infants of his church, as may be plainly gathered from Rufinus' translation of the church history of Eusebius, Vol. 10, chap. 14, entitled "Children Play," by Athanasius. Therefore (according to Sebastian Franck) the very wise and learned Erasmus of Rotterdam, a man who has read and understood all the worth-while writers of the world, says that the ancient fathers disputed about infant baptism but never settled it.

Kind reader, since the ancients from the beginning were not unanimous in this matter, and since they did not all practice infant baptism, as appears from the ancestors of Tertullian and also from Bishop Alexander; and since those who practiced infant baptism have always, as may be seen by their writings, sought righteousness therein; therefore we will not build on that which is uncertain, but upon that which is certain, which is Christ's Word. Neither will we seek our righteousness in the outward baptism nor in any other ritual as does the world, but in Christ Jesus, as all the Scriptures teach us. Herewith we desire to appeal our cause to the consideration and judg-

---

[12] Written soon after A.D. 200.

[13] He was born around A.D. 160 and died about A.D. 230. *Ed.*

[14] Lived *c.* 293-373. In the Rufinus paragraph to which Menno refers Athanasius was concerned about the catechetical instruction of the children prior to baptism. Rufinus reports that those receiving instructions were called *catechumens.* Rufinus was a Latin presbyter and theologian who lived *c.* A.D. 345-410. He made Latin translations of various Greek works. *Ed.*

ment of all the world and let them tell whether they have ever read in the Word of God, I say in the Word of God or in His Gospel, that Christ Jesus and His holy apostles taught two different baptisms in water; namely, one baptism that should be administered to the believing, a baptism which represents death unto sin, resurrection to a new life, the answer of a good conscience toward God, and the washing of regeneration (Rom. 6:12; Col. 2:12; I Pet. 3:21; Titus 3:5); and that the other baptism should be administered to infants, signifying nothing but that they should be outwardly washed with water!

Brethren, judge rightly and do not deceive your souls. We know that they say infants are cleansed of their original sin, and that therefore their baptism is not in vain. To this we reply with the Word of God: that such belief is an abominable idolatry, for only the blood of Christ avails, and not the outward baptism, as has been shown above.

In the second place they say that thereby they are accepted into the covenant of God. And we reply, that is not because of baptism, but only through the gracious election of grace (Eph. 1:6); for it is grace and not merit (Rom. 11:6).

In the third place they say that children should be baptized in order that they might the better be trained in the Word of God and His commandments. We reply that we desire to know where such is expressed and written in the holy Scriptures. Give a polite answer, we pray, you who assert infant baptism to be right, just, and necessary, and who so lamentably slander and wrong us on account of baptism, so that we may no longer be deceived in our hearts; but that we may assuredly know by the Word of God where to find this infant baptism. For however industriously we may search day and night, we find but one baptism in water, pleasing to God, which is expressed and contained in His Word, namely, baptism on the confession of faith, commanded by Christ Jesus, taught and administered by His holy apostles; a baptism administered and received for the forgiveness and remission of sins in such a manner as we have fully proved above by the words of Peter. Acts 2:38. But this other baptism, that is, infant baptism, we do not find.

Because this infant baptism is nowhere commanded nor implied in the divine Word, therefore we testify before you and all the world that we have no regard for it, but believe and proclaim it to be idolatrous, useless, and empty, and we do this, not only with words, but also at the cost of our lives, as has been proved by events in many Germanic lands. The reason is this. It is administered without the Word and commandment of God; righteousness is sought therein; and because of this infant baptism the true baptism of Jesus Christ, that is, believer's baptism, is so lamentably rejected and trampled upon by all men as an heretical baptism, as far as the name of Christ is mentioned.

Therefore, brethren, it is verily nothing but opinion and human righteousness to teach without the Word of God that infants should be baptized

that they may be the better trained in the Word of God and His commandments. We find to the contrary that although these parents have their infants
baptized, yet they from youth on are trained by these same parents in keeping
with the nature of Adam unto all manner of pride, pomp, avarice, vanity,
falsehood, cursing, swearing, dancing, singing, foolishness, hatred, enmity,
revengefulness, and to the accursed life of this world; just as the heathen
who have never known God have always done.

What does such baptism as they have received profit them? Is it not a
simon-pure foolishness, deceit, mockery, and shame in the sight of God? Certainly. Take care, if you please, for no greater hypocrisy, mockery, or blasphemy in His sight can in all eternity be found. Inasmuch as the hidden
frightfulness which is hidden in infant baptism is perhaps not yet rightly understood by you, therefore I will briefly illustrate the matter, that you may
the better distinguish between truth and falsehood. I will present to you that
which for many centuries, as all may have seen, has been of daily occurrence
and which alas still occurs daily.[15]

In the first place, we will imagine an extremely corrupt, ungodly, carnal
scoundrel, called a priest however by men, a pastor, vicar, or prebendary.
This same unchaste man full of all manner of tricks and deceit, covers his
damnable knavery with such a fine exterior that no one thinks evil of him,
just as the ravening wolf was covered with the harmless pelt of a sheep.
Matt. 7:5. His head is carefully shaven, as proof perhaps that in a similar
way he desires by all means to shave off and destroy all lusts and desires of
his wicked, sinful flesh. His robe reaches to the floor, as Christ says (Luke
20:46,) as if he were pious, holy, and of honorable conduct. He reads his
prayers with folded hands and uncovered head, with clocklike regularity, as
if he were very ardent and fervent in spirit. He kneels and burns incense before blocks of stone and wood, which he calls Peter, Paul, Mary, and before
the worthy crucifix of the Lord. I tell you this verily, without facetiousness,
of which God is my witness. Judge now whether this is not the way it goes.

Moreover he buys a hundred wafers for a nickel, takes one at a time,
consecrates it as he says, and that mentally without saying a word; he nods
to it, he worships it, he prays to it, and he eats it and digests it. And this
same thing he believes and teaches to be the true flesh and blood of our beloved Lord Jesus Christ, the Son of the Almighty and Living God. Besides
he must be so pure and chaste in his conduct that he is not allowed to marry
a wife, although the holy Scriptures allow it.[16] But the pope has forbidden it.
All these and other abominations he calls a very holy religion, the most holy

[15] As a former priest (1524-36) Menno is able to portray the activity of priests with
accuracy, and also critically. *Ed.*

[16] Menno married a woman named Gertrude from his home village of Witmarsum in
Friesland about 1537. Gertrude and their son John died before Menno's death. Two daugh-
ters are known to have survived him. One of them was interviewed several times by
P. J. Twisck (1565-1636), a Frisian Mennonite bishop and the chief author of the
Confession of Thirty-Three Articles first published in 1617. *Ed.*

Christian faith, etc. And these fruits are begotten and produced by this evil tree, by the faith which is in him. After he has performed his man-made holiness in an orderly, illustrious, and careful way, then he reveals his real self by seeking the best wine, women, and beer; and he drinks, and vomits, he sings, he dances, he laughs, he weeps, he quarrels, he fights, he curses, he swears, he brags, he flirts, he fornicates, whether with his own mistress or with his neighbor's daughter, or wife whose own husband is away from home at another place to earn his living at his trade.

In this way scoundrel and harlot live in shameful adultery and fornication, until the natural result makes it impossible to hide the matter longer. Then if it concerns his mistress or the neighbor's daughter, then the poor child has to go on a pilgrimage, you see; or the blame is ascribed to the janitor or to the neighbor, or neighbor's son maybe. If a married woman is involved, then the wronged husband, ignorant of the wicked shame, the adultery and the duplicity of his wife, must be father of such an illegitimate child of adultery. What a mess!

And brethren, both of them, the scoundrel as well as the harlot, of whom such illegitimate children are born, have been baptized in their infancy, and they claim therefore to be Christians. They boast of Jesus Christ and of His crimson blood, but we may see by their fruits what kind of Christians they are and what kind of faith they have.

### ["Christian" Parents]

Therefore I admonish you, good reader, that you may know what kind of Christian parents they are and what kind of faith they have of whom some children are born, who are nevertheless carried to the baptismal font and baptized on the faith of their fine parents, and therefore called Christians. Oh, what fearful mockery!

In the second place, I find that in many places throughout the world, numbers of vain and abandoned characters, some of them married, some not, some claiming nobility in the world's proud way, some of large means, some of average means, some poor, in short, of all classes, who in the same manner live in all manner of excess, vanity, drunkenness, and impurity, according to their shameful, improper lusts and devilish desires. In all manner of fornication and adultery they seduce and disgrace one girl after the other, notwithstanding that they are baptized. And when they by their lack of restraint have done all this, have brought such shame and dishonor upon simple and unsuspecting souls who are also born of Adam, and who are perhaps deceived by false promises and gifts, and led thereto by their accursed actions, then it must nevertheless among those of their class and social standing be considered a great honor and respectability, as the prophet says. Yet notwithstanding all this, these same persons carry the children who are thus illegitimately born of such seducers, such immoral rascals and abandoned women, to the baptism, that they may be called Christians and be trained up in the same works and fruits as their unchristian, adulterous parents, in whom and by whom they are conceived and begotten in accursed and damnable adultery. Oh, what unbelievers!

In the third place, I find almost generally among men and women of whatever class or condition they may be who are of this ilk, noble or commoner, rich or poor, citizen or yeoman, who were all baptized in infancy, and on that account are called Christians, leading such sinful lives that we can form no idea thereof. Their pride, unchastity, avarice, crookedness in buying and selling, quarreling, hatred, unrighteousness, unmercifulness toward the laborer and the poor, their cursing, swearing, lying, cheating, love of show, debauchery, drinking, their pride and pomp, their dissipation and drinking, their vanity and empty talk, their bloodthirstiness, cruelty, hardheartedness, dissimulation, tyranny, transgression, idolatry, and all manner of wickedness know no bounds. If there are some who are not guilty of all the before-mentioned vices on account of their natural reasonableness, it must be admitted that there is not one in a thousand who industriously seeks and desires to walk according to the commandments of God, or to live according to His blessed will. Nor do they once ask concerning the right way to eternal life that they might be saved, yet they must be called the true, Christian church. God, the righteous judge, has so obscured the understanding and natural intellect of those who reject His holy Word, and who make and honor things of their own choice as an idol. Notwithstanding the heathenish life of both father and mother, yet their infants which are born of them must without the Word of God and merely because of their own invention, be conjured, exorcised,[17] blessed, rubbed with spittle, anointed, crucified, and baptized. And after this has been done in keeping with the tradition of their parents, although contrary to the commandment of God, then they are called believing, Christian people, no matter how wicked, bestial, or devilish a life they lead; and they are admitted and received into the church as full and proper members.

O Lord and Father, how very broad, soft, and pleasing to the flesh is the entrance into this miserable, carnal church; for in her this takes place, no matter who or what or how he is. It is all right if he has only been exorcised before a font, and washed and baptized by a magic-dealing idolater. But how wonderfully narrow, O Lord, is Thy way, and how very strait is the gate which leadeth into Thy poor and holy church. So narrow that on its doorposts are made to hang gold and goods, flesh and blood, all the lust and inclinations of those who desire and sincerely seek to enter in at this narrow gate; and so by Thy grace to rest and remain forever in Thy holy church.

Good reader, I have pointed this out in this manner, first in order that you may the better conceive and understand what kind of Christians they are, what kind of faith they have, and what kind of life they lead, to whom

---

[17] Exorcism is the Roman Catholic ceremony of expelling demons prior to baptism. Luther and Melanchthon defended the practice but the Protestants ultimately discontinued it. *Ed.*

infant baptism has been administered and who now have it administered to their children. I do this so that the true, divine knowledge may increase in you, that you may rightly comprehend by the Word of God how abominably men mock the Almighty God in the matter of infant baptism, and that you may know that there is no fruitful, pleasing, and powerful baptism before God other than the baptism which is administered and received according to the commandment of Christ (Mark 16:16); namely, the baptism upon the confession of faith, as has been said frequently above.

## [Godfathers or Sponsors]

Secondly, I must refer you in the same manner to how wonderfully far the custom of the godfathers who raise the children at the font and answer to their confession of faith, is at variance with the spirit, commandment, and Word of Christ. I do this in order that all this tradition, falsehood, unbelief, abuse, and satanic imposture may appear to you as such and be demolished; and that, on the other hand, truth, faith, the right practice, and the divine good pleasure might spring forth and become known in the hearts of all God-fearing men.

Since then Christ has commanded that the candidates for baptism should first believe (Mark 16:16), before baptism should be administered (Acts 8:38), and since men knew very well that infants had no faith; and since they notwithstanding this wanted to have them baptized (since human righteousness ever has looked upon, profaned, persecuted, despised, and rejected the righteousness of God as useless, imperfect, and foolish), therefore the ninth or the tenth pope, named Hyginus,[18] without any commandment of God, hit upon a happy device with which the world has hitherto been very well satisfied, and by means of which they baptized their infants. But some who feared God more, and therefore took the Word of God more seriously, were for the greater part for this matter excommunicated as heretics, rejected and crushed. The device was this. That some should be chosen from the church whom they called godfathers[19] who should present the children at the font to be baptized, and who should care for and answer for the faith of the child.

Dearest reader, it is true this matter has a fine appearance and show, but it is not in accordance with Christ's Spirit and intention, because the practice of godfathers is a human institution, as history plainly shows. Therefore I am at a loss to know why it is that all the scholars of the upper and eastern countries still use this institution of godfathers, since they have so bravely and incessantly written, taught, and battled with the Word of God against all human institutions and teachings. For nowhere in the divine Word are godfathers so much as mentioned. Everywhere in the Scriptures where

---

18 Hyginus was the ninth bishop of Rome according to Roman Catholic scholars. He lived about A.D. 140. Eusebius stated that he served four years. *Ed.*

19 Menno's source is in error. There is no proof that Hyginus instituted baptismal sponsors. The first father to mention them was Tertullian in his book, *De baptismo,* chap. 18, about A.D. 200. *Ed.*

baptism is mentioned it is shown in very plain characters that the candidate for baptism must believe for himself, must confess it in word and deed, and desire and receive baptism as a commandment of God. Mark 16:16; Acts 2:38; 8:36; 10:48; 16:33, and other passages.

And even if the institution of godfathers were in accordance with the Word of God or the commandment of Christ (which it is not), oh, how, and with what great care we should have to search in city and country for a suitable person to discharge the duties of such an office! For how can one blind man lead another? How can one fool make another wise? How can one poor person be surety for another? (Understand what I write.) In the same manner, one unbelieving person can be no surety for the faith of another. For every man shall bear his own burden. Gal. 6:5. He can neither teach the faith, nor intercede for the faith of another, so long as he himself has not true, Christian faith. For whatever I am to teach another I must understand myself, and prayer must be the prayer of faith (Jas. 5:16), in spirit and in truth. John 4:24.

Since then an unbelieving man cannot be surety before God for the faith of another, nor teach him faith, nor intercede for it, therefore (even if the institution of godfathers were founded on the ordinance of God, which how-ever it is not) it must be acknowledged and admitted that the practice of godfathers in infant baptism is entirely vain, useless, and empty. I will leave it to every intelligent Christian to judge what kind of faith there is in the godfathers themselves.

I know that I will be asked if there are no good, believing godfathers who with good consciences can present the children for baptism. To this I answer quite unequivocally: No. For in the first place, it is human righteous-ness, contrary to the Word of God and without the ordinance of Christ; and therefore it cannot be practiced with a good conscience. In the second place, I admit that there are godfathers who are honorable and virtuous, but truly I do not know that they believe correctly; for if they did, it would be im-possible for them ever to be led to practice such abominable shame with in-fants, without the Word of Christ. For there is no word to be found in all apostolic Scriptures which in any manner teaches and commands us such a thing. I say nothing about the impurity, avarice, pomp, ignorance concern-ing divine matters, idolatry, foolish talk, vanity, refractoriness against God and His blessed Word, and of the accursed, carnal life of most of those who are called to this office by the church, in order that the faith of the parents and of the godfathers alike on the basis of which they baptize these infants and through which these infants are thought to acquire faith themselves may be transferred to them; as we have too often seen that the one adulterous knave calls upon the other; one drunkard upon the other; one proud person upon the other, etc. By their works they show plainly that it is not of God, but that it is deceit, devilish hypocrisy, human righteousness, blasphemy, mockery, destruction of the ordinances of Christ, and in every respect con-trary to the blessed Word of God.

Behold, worthy brethren, in the course of time they have thus subtly perverted and changed the heavenly doctrine and blessed ordinance of our beloved Lord Jesus Christ into such unclean mockery, abuse, and shameful practice. O Lord, Father of all grace, let this fearful and abominable snare and dishonesty to our miserable souls be destroyed. Amen.

## [The Priests]

In the third place, even as we have shown you the faith and life of the parents, the command, faith, and life of the godfathers; so we will now point out what kind of men they are whose office it is to baptize these infants and so to make Christian people out of them. And we point you, faithful reader, to your own pastor, vicar, prebendary, or chaplain as you call him. Yea, to all the priests round about you, that you may closely scrutinize them according to the Word of God, and see if there is among them one, I say one, however many there may be, who is called of an irreproachable Christian church, who is moved by the Holy Spirit, who is unblamable in doctrine and life. O brother, not one, no, not one, however far you travel and however diligently you may search. Their calling is without exception of the dragon and of the beast. There is nothing which leads them to this office but their lazy, greedy, avaricious, proud, and gluttonous flesh. Their teaching for the most part is mere deceit; their worship is all idolatry, spiritual magic out of the bottomless pit, and a cause for the shedding of innocent blood. Besides their daily walk is so shameful, unclean, Sodom-like, adulterous, sensuous, greedy, avaricious, loquacious, vengeful, unmerciful, deceitful, ambitious, blind, godless, misleading, and so abominable that all reasonable men, the angels of God, and the heavens themselves, must be astounded and ashamed thereat.

Say, kind reader, is it not so? Have you ever found greater pride, avarice, gluttony, adultery, fornication, spitefulness, hypocrisy, mockery, and shame than is found among them? I am aware that they are not all equally unchaste and shameful in their daily conduct; yet there is not one among them, however finely he appears before the world, but his commission, his threatenings, and his entire life is of the flesh, of the devil, and contrary to God and His blessed Word.

My dear worthy brethren, he who knoweth all things knows that I do not write this with hatred or with bad intentions. Therefore, judge for yourselves all things according to the Word of God and according to your rational, natural understanding; since you may daily perceive these things before your eyes. You will without doubt acknowledge that I have revealed and presented to you nothing but the truth, out of love for your salvation. Have I done wrong in revealing and presenting unto you the hidden and harmful devices of a thief or murderer? Pluck from your eyes this accursed and abominable blindness, and look upon the truth of your God; root out all unbelief from your darkened hearts and believe the Word of God. The holy apostle says not to keep company, if any man that is called a brother, be a fornicator, or covetous, or an idolater, or a railer, or a drunkard, or an extortioner; with such a one no not to eat. A proof that, although they call themselves brethren or Christians, they are not in the church of Christ on account of their disreputable life. For the church of Christ is a holy, pure, and unblamable church. In another place Paul teaches that such shall not inherit the kingdom of God. Rom. 1:32; I Cor. 5:11; Gal. 5:22; Eph. 5:6.

Now if they are not in the congregation of Christ, and if they cannot inherit the kingdom of God, tell me what things divine or Christian can then be served or practiced by them in the house of the Lord, that is, in the church of Christ? In spite of the fact that we should not keep the company of such, nor eat with them, and in spite of the fact that they according to Paul do not have the promise of salvation because of their unbelief and their fearful, wicked, beastly life, the world is nevertheless so blinded by them and so estranged from God that they look upon, honor, and accept them as true shepherds, teachers, and pastors who have power from God to do anything they please just so they only make their pretensions under the false cover of Christianity and of the holy Christian church, as they call it. What blindness!

These are they, O men, who to this day are allowed to mislead the whole world by their false doctrine, and uselessly to address, to exorcise, and to baptize infants, without the Word or command of God, no matter how sternly and clearly the most holy Gospel of Jesus Christ opposes and rebukes such things. As these spiritual fathers or teachers are, so also are their children who are begotten of them, that is, those whom they teach and baptize, as they plainly prove and verify by their fruits. Brethren, by no other means than by these afore-mentioned teachers and baptizers of infants, the church of Christ is converted into such a work of hypocrisy, such shame, mockery, deceit, apostasy, knavery, and into a very detestable brothel. Oh, the sadness of it!

And so you have presented to you, first, the parents of whom the children are born, with their unbelief and carnal life; secondly, the godfathers, together with their abuses, unbelief, and evil fruits, those who present the children at the font for baptism and answer for their confession; and thirdly, the teachers or baptizers together with their calling, doctrine, idolatry, unbelief, and ungodly works, who baptize the infants as they say, to cleanse and wash them of their original sin. And now all three of these, namely, parents, godfathers, and baptizers, do not themselves know in their hearts either knowledge or faith, or truth, or love, or fear of God, or Gospel, or Christian fruits, or obedience, or remission of sins, or peace of mind, or prayer, or promise, or God, or Christ, or Spirit, or eternal life; but are only Christian in name and boast. These presume to make a Christian out of a child just born, which can neither stand nor walk, hear nor speak, understand nor comprehend, for lack of understanding, as irrational as the animals, unable to distinguish between good and bad, without the Word and without faith, by no other means than by crucifixes, breathings, by salt, oil, chrisms, candles, cloths, empty questions and answers, blessings, exorcisms, baptizings, offerings, and such like abominations. And when this loquacious, idolatrous sham has been practiced upon the infants, then they are Christian people as the nurses tell the mother after these things have been performed saying, We have received from you a heathen but a Christian we return and deliver to you again.

The next thing in order is the setting of the table. Victuals and drink are prepared, the neighbors and friends partake thereof, and the parents are well satisfied with their baptized infant. And from that hour it is trained in all manner of foolishness, unbelief, vanity, sin, shame, folly, idolatry, and all manner of carnal and devilish works in such a way that neither knowledge, faith, fear and love of God, evangelical truth and life can ever take root in it. And should anything Christian spring up in it, then it will have to suffer much and bear the cross of Christ. I repeat, because it is baptized, it is henceforth considered a Christian person, no matter how it acts. You see, dear brother, this is the holy church as they boast it these days, and in this manner one of these "Christians" begets the other, until the world is full of them.

Honored reader, please understand correctly what I have written to you, for I have treated so extensively of this matter that you may know what a secret, hidden snare of soul and what a terrible, fearful idol infant baptism is; and how very useless and idolatrous it is to teach that infants should be baptized in order that they may be the better trained in the Word and commandments of God. In this way human doctrine wears a fine and holy cloak, but in reality it is verily nothing but hypocrisy, falsehood, and a deadly venom for men's souls.

Those who do not rely on this anti-Christian infant baptism, but seek the true Christian baptism which was commanded of Christ Jesus and taught and practiced by His holy apostles, take care of the salvation of their children. Therefore they train them in the fear of God by teaching, admonishing, and chastising them, and with an example of an irreproachable life, in order that when they come to years of discretion they may themselves hear, believe, and accept the most holy Gospel of Jesus Christ, and receive the holy Christian baptism as Jesus and His holy apostles have taught all believers in many a place of the New Testament.

In the third place, Paul also teaches us, Know ye not that so many of us as were baptized into Christ Jesus, were baptized into his death? Therefore we are buried with him by baptism into death; that like as Christ was raised up from the dead by the glory of the Father, even so we also should walk in newness of life. Rom. 6:3, 4. Here the baptism of believers is again powerfully confirmed, and infant baptism denied as emphatically. For as Christ Jesus commanded that we should baptize the believing ones (Mark 16:16), so also it is evident from these words of Paul that baptism represents and signifies something which none can realize but those who believe, namely, it represents death unto sin, or a burying of the old life, and a resurrection into newness of life.

Since Paul says that Christian baptism is such a death unto sin, and a raising again unto a new life, therefore they must confess and admit that none can die unto his shameful lusts and desires and bury his wicked, carnal, ungodly life and that none can rise to a pious, unblamable, godly life but those alone who as dear obedient children of God are edified, taught, and regenerated by the Word of God, which spiritual death and resurrection are represented in holy baptism. At another place Paul calls it the spiritual circumcision, saying, Ye are circumcised with the circumcision made without hands, in putting off the body of the sins of the flesh by the circumcision of Christ; buried with him in baptism, wherein also ye are risen with him through the faith of the operation of God, who hath raised him from the dead. Col. 2:11, 12.

Since then it is clear that only the believers die unto their sins and bury them, and with Christ are raised up unto the new, godly life; and since little children cannot do this, because they have no faith by which God operates in children: therefore it must be acknowledged and admitted, whether men are willing or not, that the baptism of infants is not commanded by the Lord Jesus Christ, nor taught or implied in the apostolic doctrine.

Good reader, it is sometimes alleged that other apostles left Scriptures behind, which Scriptures Pope Gelasius[20] has expurgated, and that perhaps infant baptism was expressed and implied in them.

Dear reader, if our opponents build their cause upon the expurgated Scriptures of the apostles and have no certainty concerning them, but only presume that infant baptism may have been expressed in them, then we would politely reply and ask: Since they refer to the apostolic Scriptures which we do not have, therefore we would like to have a report of them as to what these apostles have taught and commanded concerning infant baptism?

Secondly, since they seek to establish their doctrine by imaginary "scriptures" which they do not have, and that only on presumption, they show thereby that they are unable to verify their doctrine at all by the apostolic Scriptures which we do have.

Thirdly, we say that we should not teach and practice the ceremonies of the Lord, namely, the holy baptism, upon presumption and surmise, but on certainties.

Fourthly, we say that the apostles have all written, taught, and preached in one Spirit. Inasmuch as Christ Jesus had commanded baptism upon the confession of faith, and since Peter, Paul, and Philip taught and practiced the baptism of believers, and not of infants, according to the commandment of Christ, therefore you may conclude from this that it was not taught and practiced differently by the other apostles whose Scriptures we do not have, even if they had written and published six hundred volumes. For if infant baptism were an apostolic institution it would be evident in their writings. Nor would Tertullian, who lived not long after the days of the apostles, have

[20] This silly and untrue claim evidently refers to Gelasius I who was the Roman bishop, A.D. 492-96. *Ed.*

written that among his ancestors, generally speaking, adults were baptized, as has been said above. And Alexander, bishop of Alexandria, would have baptized the infants of his church; and the ancients would not have disputed about it, since all those who feared God would act according to the Scriptures and not deviate therefrom. For what God-fearing person would dare to despise, oppose, or in any manner contradict an apostolic institution?

Those who did not rightly confess Christ, but sought their righteousness and placed their trust in outward ceremonies, got the upper hand in the world; and therefore it was not necessary that this infant baptism should be confirmed by any papal decree or council, since it gradually and of its own accord worked its way into all nations and tongues and became dominant. For the whole church, after the death of the apostles, through the foolish teachings of the bishops, gradually degenerated from the truth in Christ Jesus to the trust in outward ceremonies,[21] as may be plainly seen.

Again, brethren, however plain the passage of Paul in Romans 6 is, and applies to the believers, yet the learned ones of this unfruitful world have inverted and explained it as confirming and assenting to infant baptism. They say that infants should be baptized in order that they may become partakers of the death and holy blood of Christ Jesus, so that when they become of age they may die unto sin and walk righteously before God.

Dear children in Christ, if it would do of our own choice and fancy thus to twist, bend, and mutilate the plain truth and will of God and the most holy and glorious Gospel of our beloved Lord Jesus, then verily I know of no abomination or false religion which we could not thus lightly adorn and beautify so as to give it a good face in the sight of the ignorant. No, most beloved, no. The eternal, omnipotent, and saving Word of God must be taught, explained, and understood according to the true meaning of the Holy Spirit. For they baptize before the thing which is represented by baptism, namely, faith, is found in us. This is as logical as to place the cart before the horse, to sow before we have plowed, to build before we have the lumber at hand, or to seal a letter before it is written. Tell me, would not this be ridiculed by all the world as foolishness? Yes, certainly.

Therefore the Holy Spirit of God did not speak [even] vaguely of infant baptism in this afore-mentioned Scripture of Paul. Children are partakers of the death and blood of Christ by the gracious promise which was given of God through Christ Jesus our Lord, and not by baptism. Luke 18:16. But this passage of Paul speaks and teaches of those who, in their baptism, through their new birth from above and through their fruitful, active faith have died unto their old sinful life and have buried it, even as Christ Jesus died in His flesh and was buried. For whosoever has died with Christ is already justified from his sins, and is victoriously raised up with Christ from the power of sin to the praise of the Lord, in a new, just, godly, and irreproachable

[21] Here Menno touches the heart of the historical problem: the substitution of sacramentalism for the saving Gospel of Christ. *Ed.*

life, by no other means than through God's Word alone, accepted and believed by them through faith, as has been alleged above. Ye are circumcised with the circumcision made without hands, in putting off the body of
the sins of the flesh by the circumcision of Christ; buried with him in baptism, wherein also ye are raised with him through the faith of the operation
of God, who hath raised him from the dead. Col. 2:11,12.

O beloved brethren, do open the eyes of your hearts and understanding,
and take heed; for he who will not willfully battle against his God, or His
holy Word, certainly cannot mistake these plain words of Paul. Yet Henry
Bullinger[22] and many others, on the strength of this epistle to the Colossians,
have taught baptism to have taken the place of the Israelitish circumcision,
without good reason and without Scriptures, yet not without terrible blasphemy and vituperation. For what reason they have done so, I do not know,
unless it be because Paul has placed so closely together and has so intimately
connected spiritual circumcision and the baptism of the believing or true
Christians.

O Lord, Thy divine, blessed Word is ever made to be a shelter and a
defense for all manner of false doctrine, heresy, and practice, so that the
Bible is called by some, the book of heresy. But no matter how ardently
they oppose and how shrewdly they lie and speculate, yet the eternal truth
of God will prevail and triumph in the elect children of God who sincerely
desire and seek the same.

I repeat it; I am heartily ashamed to write or speak one single word
against such highly renowned and learned men. But what shall we do? I
may not allow myself to be robbed by these learned men, may I, of God's
eternal truth which leads to eternal life, and which was so plainly taught us
by Jesus Christ our Lord, and by His holy apostles. For verily, I nowhere
find that we should follow and obey these learned men rather than Christ
and His holy apostles. If it should be said that they are wise, then I reply
that Christ is the wisest; and if it should be said that they are pious, then I
am sure that Christ is the most pious; and if it be said that they are versed
in many languages, I say curtly that the Spirit of the Lord Jesus Christ is not
bound by languages and learning. Therefore the most holy and invincible
truth of God must be defended and maintained by us, not only against them,
but against all the gates of hell, by the most holy Word of God, as God has
bestowed His grace on us, His mercy and knowledge.

For this reason I will hold before my readers the quoted Col. 2:11 with
which they try to prove their point, and humbly beseech them to judge impartially whether we find in this or any other divine Scripture that the circumcision of the Israelites was the prototype of infant baptism. It is incontrovertible that Paul, in this passage and also in Rom. 2:29, teaches that the
literal circumcision was a figure of the spiritual circumcision, but not of infant

---

[22] Henry Bullinger (1504-75), Zurich Reformer, was Ulrich Zwingli's successor in the
Reformed Church of German Switzerland. *Ed.*

baptism. This circumcision cannot be applied to any but the believing, as may be plainly inferred from the figure of the literal practice. For the literal circumcision was to be performed with stone knives[23] on the foreskin. Josh. 5:2, 3; Gen. 17:23. This spiritual Rock is Christ Jesus. I Cor. 10:4. The knife with which the believers are circumcised is the holy Word. Brethren, understand it well. If we wish to remain with the believing circumcised Abraham in the covenant with God (into which covenant we are all graciously accepted, young and old, male and female, through Christ Jesus, and not through any sign), then our earthly, carnal birth which is of the earthly carnal Adam must be circumcised with this same stone knife, which is Christ Jesus and His holy Word. Therefore examine the before-mentioned words of Paul to the Colossians, and judge whether they refer to believers or to infants. Tell me, who is it that is circumcised by the circumcision of Christ? Is it not the believer? Who is it that has put off the body of sin by the circumcision of Christ? Is it not the believer? Who is it that is buried in baptism with Christ? Is it not the believer? Who is it that is raised up into the new life by the faith of the operation of God? Once more, is it not the believer? Yes, these are they who hear the Word of God and believe it, and not, eternally not, little immature children.

Kind reader, since the defenders of infant baptism seek to prove their case by the promise and circumcision of Abraham, therefore observe and ponder how unreasonably they make this assertion; and observe and ponder also that which will be briefly taught and presented by us from Scriptural truth.

In the first place, as we said before, we are all accepted into the covenant with God, not by any signs but by grace, and have obtained the promise by it, if we accept by faith and walk according to the will of the Giver; as Abraham was accepted of God by grace from among the nations, and was made glad with the promises of grace. For he accepted it by faith and walked according to the will of Him who had accepted him, as the Scriptures say. He believed in the Lord, and it was counted to him for righteousness. Gen. 15:6; Rom. 4:3; Gal. 3:6; Jas. 2:23.

To all those who are thus by faith graciously accepted of God into the covenant of peace with Abraham, God has given His ceremonies and figurative signs as a test of the genuineness of their faith. Not that they should thereby be justified (for if it were by the signs, it would not be by grace, Rom. 11:6), but because they were justified by faith, were children of God, children of the promise, in God's covenant, etc., and that they therefore should show their obedience to the commandments of God who had graciously called, accepted, and by His promise comforted them. For those that are obedient unto God are His friends. John 15.

Beloved brethren, this is one reason why God commanded His cere-

---

23 In the Dutch Bible, Josh. 5:2 speaks of "stone knives" where the Authorized Version has rendered "sharp knives." *Tr.*

monies, as is plainly shown in the case of Abraham. For Abraham was already in the covenant with God before he was circumcised. Paul shows that his faith was already counted for righteousness when he was yet uncircumcised. Because he was in the covenant with God, justified by faith, therefore God commanded him the circumcision. It was a useless and dishonorable ceremony in itself, quite useless because it did not benefit anybody else. Secondly, it was dishonorable, for it is performed upon the most dishonorable member of the body. And it was commanded him that the believing father, Abraham, should deny himself, and live not according to his own desires, but only according to the will of Him who by grace had accepted him and chosen him from among the nations. And thus he sealed by this performance, which was dishonorable in itself, that his faith was true and fruitful before God. Gen. 17:12. Why these ceremonies were commanded a second time will be shown hereafter, God willing.

Behold, kind reader, in this manner Abraham was circumcised, and we baptized, because it is thus commanded by God. Whosoever disobeys and opposes the voice of the Lord commanding these ceremonies, and despises the performance of them because of their uselessness and triviality, not observing that it was commanded by God, excludes himself from the precious covenant of grace by his disobedience; neither does he prove his faith to be fruitful and living, but on the contrary he proves that it is unfruitful and dead before God. For he obeys not the voice of his lord, does not live it, but despises it as powerless, vain, and useless.

Therefore, observe and know that we are not accepted into the covenant by an outward sign, but only by grace through Christ Jesus. And because we are in the covenant by grace, therefore He has given and commanded us His signs that we shall perform them upon those upon whom He has commanded them to be performed, namely, upon believers. For if we could come into the covenant with God by any signs or ceremonies, then the merits of Christ were vain and grace were ended. No. Abraham was already chosen, accepted and justified by God through faith before he was circumcised; and because he was faithful and justified through faith, therefore the circumcision was commanded him of God that he should thereby seal his faith. Again, even as Abraham and all his seed born of Isaac, together with others, were already included in the covenant with God, women as well as men, and since the promise was given to both sexes, yet it was not commanded that the females should be circumcised, but the males only.

Observe well, beloved reader, had they obtained the covenant with God by the sign and not by the grace, then the females must have been excluded and without the promise. If not, then it was by grace. It is by grace still, and it will ever be by grace. If they had been disobedient to the Word of God, and had not circumcised their males on the appointed day; or if they had done otherwise than they were commanded of God and had circumcised their females, then they would have had to bear the punishment of their disobedience in their children. Gen. 17:14. They would have excluded them from the covenant of the Lord and would not have obtained the gift of His grace. For God, the Almighty Father, whose voice, will, and commandment all creatures both in heaven and earth should obey, will have the commanded ceremonies performed as it pleases Him, and as He has commanded them to be performed, for therefore He has commanded them. If we do not perform them, or if we perform them differently, we have by our disobedience neither covenant nor promise. This is the right, Scriptural meaning of Abraham's covenant, circumcision and promise. Whosoever teaches you differently deceives your soul, for he points you to merits and works, and not to Christ Jesus through whom alone are received the eternal covenant of peace and the promise of grace, given by God.

Brethren, brethren, how long will you oppose the Holy Ghost? Give the Word of God its due praise, and observe that little irrational infants are in baptism not buried with Christ, nor are they raised unto newness of life; for if they did die, and if they were buried in baptism, then sin would be so destroyed in them that it would never more vanquish their spirit. Since then sin, even after their baptism, so powerfully and so abundantly flourishes in them when they begin to come to years of discretion, as may be plainly seen, therefore the proponents of infant baptism must acknowledge and confess that they bury the children alive, which should not be done; or else that they baptize them all without faith, and contrary to the ordinance of Christ, which is useless and vain.

For this reason do learn, dear reader, that infant baptism is not of God nor through Him. But whosoever rightly acknowledges the love of God for himself through Christ Jesus, and is baptized upon his own faith and through true love of God, according to the doctrine of Christ, Peter, Paul, and Philip, he is rightly circumcised in his heart with the circumcision of Christ, as Paul teaches. He is buried with Christ Jesus; he has died unto sin and is again raised up by a fruitful faith with Christ Jesus unto a new life. Rom. 6:4; Col. 2:12.

The advocates of infant baptism have still another reply, saying, Because Paul in this passage has not forbidden infant baptism, therefore it is proper. To this we reply by asking whether infant baptism is commanded in this or any other Scripture. They must confess the truth and answer, No. If it is not commanded of God, then it is not His ordinance, and therefore it has no promise. To repeat, if it is not commanded of God, then it is not His ordinance; and if it is not His ordinance, then it has no promise; and if it has no promise, than it is doubtlessly useless and vain.

Again, we ask them where in the Word of God it is expressly forbidden to baptize bells. They must own the truth and answer, Nowhere. If it is then not expressly forbidden to baptize bells, does it follow that bell baptism is just and right? No, not at all.

Thirdly, Israel was not forbidden to circumcise the females. Would they have done right if they had circumcised their females? Far from it. For the Scriptures commanded that the males should be circumcised, therefore they considered that it was forbidden to circumcise their females.

In the same manner, Christ Jesus commanded us to baptize those who believe, and that which is represented by baptism is only found in those who believe, as may be plainly seen from Peter and Paul. Therefore we judge that infant baptism is sufficiently forbidden. For they have neither faith nor that thing which is symbolized in baptism.

I repeat, if the advocates of infant baptism assert that by this Scripture of Paul infant baptism is not forbidden, and that therefore it is right, then I say it is not expressly forbidden in the holy Scriptures to bless (as they call it) holy water, candles, palms, goblets, and robes; to read mass and other ceremonies. Yet we say decidedly that it is wrong. First, because men put their trust in it. Secondly, because it is done without the ordinance of God, for He has not commanded us a word of all this; and there is no ordinance, is there, in which His holy, blessed Word is not expressed and implied either in spirit or letter.

Since Christ Jesus has commanded baptism upon the confession of faith, and since the apostles have so taught and practiced it, and since the meaning of baptism according to Rom. 6:3; Col. 2:12; Titus 3:5; Gal. 3:27; I Cor. 12:13, and I Pet. 3:21, cannot be construed except of believers, therefore it is sufficiently forbidden by this divine ordinance to baptize infants. For they do not have faith nor the things symbolized in baptism. Even if infant baptism was begun by some as soon as the apostles were dead, or perhaps even in their time, and was practiced many centuries, length of time does not prevail against the Word of God, as we have shown the pious, God-fearing reader above.

Fourthly, the holy apostle Paul says, The kindness and love of God our Saviour toward man appeared, not by works of righteousness which we have done, but according to his mercy he saved us, by the washing of regeneration, and renewing of the Holy Ghost. Titus 3:4, 5.

Dearest brethren, if we rightly and thoroughly examine this passage of Paul with spiritual eyes, and weigh it with the Scriptures, then the proponents of infant baptism by force of the Scriptures must acknowledge that the Christian baptism which is commanded by God pertains only to believers, according to the commandment of Christ (Mark 16:16), and not to those who in the course of nature are as yet unable to hear, speak, and understand, namely, infants. For it is a washing of regeneration, as the holy Paul has taught and testified by the above words.

Good brethren, because holy Christian baptism is a washing of regeneration, according to the doctrine of Paul, therefore none can be washed therewith to the pleasure and will of God save those who are regenerated through the Word of God. For we are not regenerated because we are baptized, as may be perceived in the infants who have been baptized; but we are baptized because we are regenerated by faith in God's Word. For regeneration is not the result of baptism, but baptism the result of regeneration. This may not be controverted by any man on the basis of Scriptures. Therefore all the learned ones must be shamed before this passage of Paul, let them be ever so learned, who so shamefully teach and make the simple to believe that infants are regenerated in baptism. Beloved reader, such teaching and belief is verily nothing but fraud and deceit. For if the infants were regenerated as the learned ones say, then their whole course would be humility, long-suffering, mercy, pure and chaste love, true faith, certain knowledge, sure hope, obedience to God, spiritual joy, inward peace, and an unblamable life; for these are the true and natural fruits of the new, heavenly birth; but what fruits are found in infants every intelligent reader may judge from everyday experience.

Do you suppose, dear friends, that the new birth consists in nothing but in that which the miserable world hitherto has thought that it consists in, namely, to be plunged into the water; or in the saying, I baptize thee in the name of the Father, and of the Son, and of the Holy Ghost? No, dear brother, no. The new birth consists, verily, not in water nor in words; but it is the heavenly, living, and quickening power of God in our hearts which flows forth from God, and which by the preaching of the divine Word, if we accept it by faith, quickens, renews, pierces, and converts our hearts, so that we are changed and converted from unbelief to faith, from unrighteousness to righteousness, from evil to good, from carnality to spirituality, from the earthly to the heavenly, from the wicked nature of Adam to the good nature of Jesus Christ. Of such people Paul speaks in the quoted Scripture.

Behold, those who are thus minded are the truly regenerate children of God. These are the beloved brethren and sisters of Jesus Christ, who are born with Him from above of one Father, namely, of God. John 1:13; Heb. 2:13. And these regenerate ones are those to whom alone He has taught and commanded the holy, Christian baptism as a seal of faith (Matt. 28:19; Mark 16:15), by which they receive remission of sin (Acts 2:38), and not the irrational infants, as has been frequently shown above from the Word of God. Therefore the holy apostle Paul teaches us by this Scripture that God saves the regenerate by the baptism of regeneration. They are regenerated by the Word of God, and therefore they deny themselves by the power of their regeneration and have obediently taken upon themselves all that which God, the Almighty Father, in His holy Word, has taught and commanded His chosen children through His beloved Son, Jesus Christ our Lord, and through all His true servants and messengers. Therefore I repeat that the baptism by which God sanctifies us belongs to the believing or regenerated, as Paul teaches, and in this manner: First, there must be the preaching of the Gospel of Christ (Matt. 28:19); then, the hearing of the divine Word (Rom. 10:17); thirdly, faith by hearing the Word (Rom. 10:17); fourthly, there must be the new birth by faith; fifthly, baptism out of the new birth (Titus 3:5), in obedience to God's Word; and then follows lastly the promise.

If we do not desire willfully to oppose the Holy Ghost and reject the grace of God, it is impossible to believe that a true faith can be without regeneration and without obedience, and that this obedience can be without promise. For the eternal truth, the blessed Christ Jesus, will never fail nor deceive in His holy Word; and He it is who taught us: first, to preach the holy Gospel, saying, Go ye into all the world, and preach the gospel to every creature. Upon this follows, and whosoever shall believe. After faith comes baptism, and be baptized; and from these things follows the promise, saying, shall be saved. Mark 16.

Since the ordinance of Jesus Christ reads thus, since the one follows from the other, therefore Paul teaches us that God sanctifies us by the washing of regeneration and the renewing of the Holy Ghost; for if true faith and obedience are separated from each other (as they sometimes are, for instance, in the case of those who grieve the Holy Ghost and sin against Him), then such faith does not profit us, for it has no promise because of disobedience, and is useless and dead before God. Jas. 2.

To all those who, by their own invention and without Scriptural warrant, argue for the regeneration of infants because they are baptized, notwithstanding there are no fruits in them as may be plainly seen, to them I reply: First, that they do not know what the new birth is. Second, with the same propriety and reasonability, bells are baptized. God in His Word has no more commanded the one than the other, for according to their nature, there is as little faith and fruits in the one as there are in the other. O Lord, when will this seductive abomination have an end? When will those who now call themselves Christians be Christians? Yes, when will the blessed Lord Jesus Christ be acknowledged to be wise, true, and perfect in His holy Word? I fear, never. For false teaching, unbelief, and opinion is esteemed and loved by these miserable, carnal men, far above the trustworthy doctrine of Jesus Christ and His holy apostles. Notwithstanding we say in Christ Jesus, let them baptize their infants as long as they will; let them teach it as long and as emphatically as they will, and let them bravely defend it on the strength of the garbled Scriptures of learned men, and of long usage. Yet it is all vain and useless before God, for the regeneration of infants cannot be maintained by virtue of the Word of God.

Elect brethren, let them rail and rant against us freely, calling us heretics, let them quote all doctors and learned men who have lived centuries ago, let them comfort themselves with long usage even from the apostles' time. Yet where there is no new birth there can be no baptism administered in accordance with the commandment of Jesus, for baptism is the washing of regeneration (Titus 3); which regeneration none have but the believing only, as we have shown our readers before.

Therefore I would admonish in the Lord all my beloved readers not to heed the flighty philosophy of the learned ones, nor to look at the long usage, but at the plain and unmixed Word of God; and they will surely find by this

Scripture of Paul and others that, according to the commandment of Christ, Christian baptism may not be administered to any except to those who by grace have become believing and regenerate through the Word of God. As long as baptism is administered to infants, it is no washing of regeneration. For the new birth is of the Word of God as has been said, which Word infants, because of their nonage, cannot hear and understand. Therefore they cannot be born again as long as they have the mind of a child. All that which the Father has not planted shall according to God's Word be plucked from the heart of the true believer. Matt. 15. God's Word shall stand forever, and according to the divine Word every pious Christian shall and must build the structure of his faith, if his work is to be pleasing before God, and he shall not build it according to his own pleasure. For God, the Almighty Father, who ruled all things by His Word, will not be honored by human doctrine and commandments. Isa. 29:19; Matt. 15:9; Mark 7:7; Col. 2:22; Jer. 29:8.

In the fifth place, the holy Paul teaches us saying, For we are all children of God by faith in Christ Jesus. For as many of you as have been baptized into Christ, have put on Christ. Gal. 3:27; Rom. 6:3.

My beloved children in Christ Jesus, you are aware that all the world by its blind and foolish unbelief has hitherto followed adulterously after outward works and ceremonies. Yet you should not do likewise. You should know that the righteousness which avails before God consists not in any ceremony and outward work, but exclusively in a true, pious, and fruitful faith, and in this manner. Faith which comes by the Word of God cannot be without fruit except in those who grieve the Holy Ghost, as said above. But it leads into all manner of righteousness, causes men willingly to submit in all obedience, and it gives willingness cheerfully to comply not only with baptism, but with all the words and ceremonies which God, the gracious Father, through His blessed Son, has so clearly taught and commanded in His holy Gospel.

Therefore true faith is the fullness of righteousness (Rom. 3 and 5); yes, it is the mother which bears all Christian virtues, and by reason of this, the Word of God ascribes everything to it, such as righteousness (Rom. 3:23 and 5:1), blessing (Gal. 3:14), salvation (Mark 16:16), and life everlasting (John 3:36; 17:4). It does not ascribe these to ceremonies. If the ceremonies are ascribed to it [faith] then it is not because of these ceremonies, but it is because of the faith which compels us to observe these ceremonies, since they are commanded of God. Therefore know, kind reader, that when the ceremonies in God's Word are coupled with the promise, as the Israelitish sacrifices in the Law, and baptism under the Gospel, then it is not because of ceremony but it is by virtue of faith, which obediently and in love fulfills not only the commanded ceremonies, but also all that which God has commanded, as has been said above.

For this reason the holy apostle Paul taught the Galatians that they were become the children of God through faith (and not by baptism), saying, Ye are all the children of God by faith in Christ Jesus. And again, because they were the children of God by faith, they showed obedience to His Word, and therefore Paul said unto them, As many of you as have been baptized into Christ, have put on Christ. Therefore the principal thing is faith, and not works. But this godly, fruitful faith in which all consists, together with its Christian fruits, is not known to many. For that reason they always seek their righteousness in outward ceremonies. Also in the useless ceremonies of human invention, which are neither taught nor commanded of God, but which they have practiced these many centuries in baptizing infants.

Read what we told you above about the parents, godfathers, and baptizers and you will acknowledge that all the world is by infant baptism led into a false confidence, has been estranged from God, and is blinded in regard to all Christian conduct. And to give their false pretensions a beautiful, holy, and divine appearance, they mutilate and twist the precious Word of God to suit them, as they show clearly in this case; for by this Scripture of Paul and other garbled Scriptures they have fooled and deceived the poor, ignorant people these many years, teaching them that infants put on Christ in baptism. They show plainly by such doctrine that they do not know what regeneration is, nor what it is to put on Christ Jesus.

Most beloved brethren, verily it is the nature of all heresies to tear a fragment from the holy Scriptures and thereby to defend their adopted worship. They do not regard that which is written before or after, by which we may ascertain the right meaning,[24] as in this instance they have plainly shown. For this sentence: As many of you as are baptized have put on Christ, they pick out to give their infant baptism an appearance. But the foregoing sentence, Ye are all the children of God because ye believed on Christ Jesus, from which, as we have shown above, all the rest must follow, that they seemed not to have noticed; and in this way they seek merit in ceremonies, and not through faith in Christ Jesus.

Besides, inasmuch as they are not clothed with Christ nor have put Him on, either actively or passively, and have not tasted His heavenly, spiritual nature and Spirit because they are carnally minded; therefore they do not understand, however much they write and teach, what it means to put on Christ Jesus, I repeat, either actively or passively.

That we may satisfy all gainsayers with the Word of the Lord, and that we may ourselves neither stumble nor err in these words, therefore I would refer all my readers to the Apostle Paul who shows who they are that put on Christ, and what fruits they manifest, by which we may know that they have put on Christ, saying, If Christ be in you, the body is dead because of sin; but the spirit is life because of righteousness. Rom. 8:10; 6:5.

Kind reader, however cleverly the scribes and proponents of infant

---

[24] Menno is asserting the importance of the context for the correct interpretation of any Scriptural statement. *Ed.*

baptism may under a false semblance of the divine Word oppose themselves, yet none can deny that Christ dwells in those who have put on Christ. Since the properly baptized have put on Christ Jesus, He is in them; and if He is in them, then the body is dead unto sin, and the spirit is life because of righteousness. This being the case, I again call on all reasonable persons to judge impartially for themselves, whether it is found in true believers or in infants. If they say, In the believers, their judgment is right; for Christ Jesus dwells in the hearts of the believers. Eph. 3:17. But if they say, In infants, then I would again ask by what means we may find this out, inasmuch as in these infants the death unto sin and the spiritual life are not shown nor found. For all of them, from infancy as long as they do not believe the Word of God, even if they are baptized, are inclined not only to evil, but also to disobedience, as daily experience openly shows in the case of all those baptized of this world.

Therefore I conclude from this Scripture of Paul and say, If those who practice infant baptism remain constant in their un-Biblical opinion and belief, that by their baptism infants put on Christ, then they must come to the conclusion by virtue of the Word of God that Christ Jesus is unbelieving, proud, ambitious, envious, vain, drunk, adulterous, refractory, and disobedient to the Word of God. For whosoever has put on Christ Jesus does not live himself, but Christ lives in him. If they then have put on Christ by their baptism as they say, Christ lives in them and must impel them, according to Paul's teaching. They nevertheless being found to continue still in every manner of carnal and godless conduct, it must follow that they have not put on Jesus Christ nor He does not work in them. They can also consent that Christ Jesus is inoperative in them. Or they may say that the above damnable things are done in them by the Christ whom they have put on.

No, verily, no. For Christ Jesus cannot be without fruits, but whosoever has put on the humble, patient, merciful, lovely, peaceable, sober, chaste, and obedient Christ, in such a one the before-mentioned accursed works are not found; for whosoever has put on Christ is dead unto sin and lives unto righteousness. Rom. 8. He is led by the Holy Spirit, he is with Christ born from above of the Father, and therefore he lives according to the will of the Father, and cannot sin because he is born of God. I John 3:9; 5:18.

Inasmuch as all those who are baptized without faith prove the contrary by their life and do not manifest the nature and virtues of Christ whom they, as they falsely claim, have put on; but they manifest in their entire conduct the nature and vices of the flesh and of Satan; therefore it proves clearly that they have not put on Christ who is from heaven; but that they have put on the devil who is from hell; for it is he who drives and impels and leads them at will, as may be plainly seen. Their inward thoughts and outward works of the flesh and of Satan are the natural fruits which are found in all men the world over, no matter of what state, trade, condition, class, or sect they are.

Dear reader, you will acknowledge of course that every tree brings forth fruit after its own kind, and that by the fruit we may know the tree. Matt. 7:20; 12:33. And so without fail where Christ Jesus is, there are the good fruits of life everlasting; but where the devil is, there are the wicked fruits of eternal death. Whosoever has put on Christ, in him the devil has no place. On the other hand, where the devil is, there Christ has no place. The one must give place to the other; for these are two princes so very different that it is impossible for them to dwell in one heart, or for the two to be received and contained in one human heart. Matt. 6:24; Eph. 2:2.

For this reason I would admonish all God-fearing Christians in the Lord to ponder long and well these words of Paul, and to understand them according to the plain truth. Then they will see plainly that Paul teaches in this Scripture exactly the same thing which Christ has commanded. Mark 16:16. Only believers put on Christ Jesus in their baptism, and they only bring forth true fruits, and not irrational infants, as we have shown to all pious and true believers here and also in our first writings sufficiently well.

Most beloved brethren, let the adherents of infant baptism scornfully ridicule such plain Scriptures to their own condemnation, and let them subtly garble and twist them as much as they please, yet this Scripture will remain forever unbroken before them. It will remain so firm and binding that they will stumble at it, be ashamed by it, and will have to retreat before it, notwithstanding all their glosses. If they would only look into the matter rightly and then judge according to the Word of God what it means and what it implies, according to Paul, to put on Christ (whether spoken in the active or the passive voice, for all those who are not content with the active may apply the passive to Romans 13, although it is in the active by Paul, according to the translation of Erasmus. They would soon perceive that it makes no difference in this matter whether it be taken in the active or in the passive)! But what will it help? If the learned have nothing wherewith to obscure the truth, they invert and twist things before the ignorant, simple people by unknown languages, false explanations, lies, and high-sounding philosophical argument. Oh, how justly Christ said unto the Pharisees, Woe unto you, scribes and Pharisees, hypocrites! for ye shut up the kingdom of heaven against men; for ye neither go in yourselves, neither suffer ye them that are entering to go in. Matt. 23:13.

In the sixth place, Paul teaches, saying, For by one Spirit are we all baptized into one body, whether we be Jews or Gentiles, whether we be bond or free; and have been all made to drink into one Spirit. I Cor. 12:13. By these words of Paul believer's baptism is once more plainly taught and confirmed. On the other hand, anti-Christian infant baptism is rejected and denied because God the merciful Father in His holy Gospel through Jesus Christ points us to faith alone, and to the new birth. Since the believing or regenerate act rightly before God and diligently seek after and fulfill His holy will according to the grace they have received, therefore we must confess that we cannot be led to this godly gift of faith and of regeneration otherwise than by the Word of God through His Holy Spirit. It is verily altogether vain and empty to read, to call, to teach, if the Holy Spirit of God, the true teacher of all righteousness, does not quicken, pierce, and turn the hearts of the believers or hearers by the only God-given means to this end, which is the Word.

Since we have been baptized by one Spirit into one body, according to the teachings of Paul, and since this same Spirit must quicken and turn the hearts by the Word of God, therefore it inevitably follows, does it not, that none should be piously baptized but those only whose hearts are quickened and turned by this Spirit through the Word of God.

All those therefore who hear the holy Gospel of Jesus Christ, and sincerely believe it, and are thus inwardly quickened and stirred by the Holy Spirit, no matter of what nationality or speech they may be, whether Frisians or Dutchmen, German or Walloon,[25] Jews or Gentiles, men or women, all are baptized by this quickening Spirit into one holy, spiritual body, of which Christ is the head, that is, into the church. Col. 1:18. And thus Paul has taught by this Scripture in conformity to the command of Christ. Mark 16:16.

Dear reader, since those who should be baptized are roused by faith and impelled by the Spirit, as Paul teaches, so I will again leave it to your judgment who they are that are led and impelled by the Spirit, whether believers or irrational infants. If you say believers, then your answer is right. For these die unto their flesh, lusts, and desires. Gal. 5:24. They put off the old man and all his works. Eph. 4:23. They seek Christ Jesus in purity of heart. They bring forth the precious fruits of the Spirit which is in them and show outwardly and inwardly in all their actions that they are taught, led, and impelled by the Holy Spirit. Gal. 5:18; Rom. 8:14. But if you answer, the infants, then I would ask you, Where are their spiritual fruits since nothing appears in a child but childish conduct, as we have said above? And yet men baptize them and call them Christians without commandment, without doctrine, without faith. From this it follows that in all the baptized people of the world nothing is found but abominable blindness, idolatry, sham holiness, evil thoughts, vain words, madness against the truth, disobedience, blasphemy, sorcery, and a very wicked life contrary to God and His blessed Word.

I know very well, brethren, that children have *spiritum vitalem* (that is, the spirit of life which God breathed into Adam and into all flesh that they might live, Gen. 2:7), but they do not have the *spiritum justificantem aut innovantem* (that is, the spirit which justifies or regenerates). For if the latter were in them, it would surely be manifested in the fruits. It is impossible that the Holy Spirit of God, which of Himself is living and fruitful, and by

---

[25] In Menno's experience there were three kinds of people: (1) Germanic, (2) Frisians (who were always considered—probably correctly—of other stock); and (3) French-speaking Walloons. Hence in the northern areas the division into Frisian and Dutchman was common, and in the southern provinces the division into Germanic and Walloon. *Tr.*

whom all true Christians are justified, taught, led, and driven, should be idle, dormant, and futile in those in whom He dwells.

Let those who hold to infant baptism speak against this as long as they like, no matter whether they be old, learned, or of high renown, yet it will never be to all eternity proved by the Word of God that the Holy Spirit of God is ever idle, ineffectual, and without fruits. I am aware that one may stumble, notwithstanding he has the Spirit of God, as is shown in the case of the pride, adultery, and manslaughter of David, the hypocrisy of Peter, and the quarrel of Paul and Barnabas. But he will not long continue therein, but will be immediately admonished to repentance, either by the kind admonition of the brethren or by the Spirit. For it is impossible that those in whom the Spirit of the love and the fear of God is could long continue in a shameful sin and transgression. If now the baptized infants have the Holy Spirit, as the adherents of infant baptism affirm, then they must admit that it is a dead, futile, and powerless spirit which can beget neither love, faith, fear of God, obedience, nor any evangelical divine righteousness in these children.

Because they have by human invention contrary to all Scriptural truth, and by self-righteousness, taught infant baptism, therefore they subtly seek to clothe and adorn it with a garbled form of the divine Word in order that the adulterous, enchanting wine which is in the goblet of the Babylonian whore, may be swallowed with great satisfaction as good and pure wine. They say that by baptism children are incorporated into the body of Christ and so become partakers of the Holy Spirit, etc. So to teach is verily nothing but open deceit, lies, garbling of the Scriptures, and a deception of Satan. For in all the baptized of the world we find the very contrary in their fruits all through their lives, as every intelligent Christian plainly sees.

Beloved brethren in the Lord, never give place to such shameful and abominable lies, but examine all things rightly and according to the Word of God, that you may rightly understand all evangelical truth. For thus to adorn infant baptism with excellencies and the illustrious Scriptures which belong only to believer's baptism is just as reasonable as it is to clothe an ape in purple and silk as the common saying of the learned has it, *Simia semper manet simia, etiamsi induatur purpura* [an ape remains an ape though he be clothed in purple]. In the same manner infant baptism will remain a horrid stench and abomination before God, however finely it be adorned by the learned ones with garbled Scriptures. For an infant so long as it is in its infancy will remain ignorant, simple, childish, and disposed to evil, even though it be baptized a hundred times and its baptism be still more subtly asserted by six times a hundred garbled Scriptures. It is plain to an intelligent person that with infants are found neither doctrine, faith, spirit, nor fruits of the divine commandment. Therefore they should not be baptized forever; that is, if we believe that the Word of God is true and will ever remain true, as we have abundantly proved here and in our first writings concerning baptism.

O kind reader, verily if it were not that this bitter, corroding, alkaline spittle of false doctrine and long usage had so been spit into the eyes of your mind, you would acknowledge at once that this massive church in the days of infancy was not incorporated into the pure, chaste, pious, and irreproachable body of Jesus Christ, but rather into the adulterous, idolatrous, and blameworthy body of Antichrist, by the official services of an unclean and anti-Christian spirit.

For if they had been incorporated into the most holy body of Jesus Christ, as they persistently boast, then their works should prove this that they are proper, faithful, and fruitful members of that body into which they are incorporated. For we see plainly that there is no member of the human body created but for some use and purpose, be it ever so small and dishonorable. It is in its way profitable and useful to the body to which it belongs. But how useful the before-mentioned infants are to the body of Christ Jesus will be perceived by all those who are taught of the Spirit.

From this the following follows without question. If they are the body of Christ as they boast, and if Christ is the head of His church, then Christ is the head of the unbelieving, the avaricious, perjurers, gamblers, drunkards, adulterers, fornicators, perverts, thieves, murderers, liars, idolaters, disobedient, bloodthirsty, traitors, tyrants, proud, and of all scamps, harlots, and knaves. For where is there one in the whole congregation of those who were baptized in infancy that walks unblamably in all the commandments of our beloved Lord Jesus Christ, and who either inwardly or openly is not guilty before God of some or many of the before-mentioned crimes. No, good reader, no. The most holy and glorious body of Jesus Christ is wonderfully different from such a cruel, wicked, refractory, disobedient, carnal, bloody, and idolatrous body.

Brethren, since they are such transgressors, blasphemers, and willful sinners, judge for yourselves from these and other Scriptural passages of what body they are members; by whose doctrine, commandment, and practice and by what spirit they were and are yet daily incorporated into this very horrible body, a body that has neither Gospel, faith, Christian baptism, Supper, nor Christian life. Therefore it has neither God, prayer, promise, nor eternal life, but only false doctrine, false faith, false sacraments, false promise, wicked life, and eternal death. O Lord, save all Thy beloved children from such an abominable, bloody body.

However, in the most holy body of Jesus Christ is a true and orderly state of things according to the Word of God, such as the true doctrine, faith, baptism, Supper, love, life, worship, the true excommunication, etc.; and therefore also grace, favor, mercy, remission of sins, prayer, God's promise, and eternal life. Behold, brethren, where these are, there also is the true body of which Christ Jesus is the head. These are the true brethren of Jesus Christ who with Him are born of God the Father; the spiritual Mount Zion which will never be moved; the spiritual house of Israel which is wisely ruled by Christ Jesus our only King, according to the Spirit, with the unbroken scepter of His divine Word; the spiritual Jerusalem in which the great King, the blessed Christ Jesus, has placed the glorious, kingly throne of His honor; the spiritual temple of the Lord in which His holy name is sincerely glorified; the spiritual ark of the covenant with its heavenly bread, blossoming rod, and stone tables upon which the mercy seat,[26] the blessed Christ Jesus, is found under the two cherubims of His testaments according to His promise; the lovely bride of Jesus Christ; flesh of His flesh, and bone of His bone (Eph. 5:30), which He placed in His chamber, and kissed with the mouth of His eternal peace.

Therefore no one can be a profitable member in this most holy, glorious, and pure body of Christ who is not believing, regenerate, converted, changed, and renewed; who is not kind, generous, merciful, pitying, chaste, sober, humble, patient, long-suffering, just, constant, heavenly and spiritually minded with Christ. It is impossible according to the Scriptures that Christ Jesus will or may be a Prince or head of those who do not conform themselves to Him, that is, those who do not sincerely seek, hear, believe, and serve Him, but trample upon Him, blaspheme, and resist.

But those who hear and believe the Word of God are those who by the Holy Spirit have been taught, begotten, and enlightened, baptized into the body of Christ on their own faith, according to the commandment of Christ. These are regenerated of the Word of God. These bury their sins and are raised up with Christ into newness of life. These have a good conscience, receive remission of sins, put on Christ Jesus, become true members of the most holy body of Jesus Christ. These are fruitful, useful, and serviceable according to their strength. On all such are the affectionate eyes of the Lord, the heavenly blessing, and the merciful disposition, attention, and care of the eternal Father, because they have sincerely and fully denied themselves, and have obediently followed the will of God to live according to the will of Him who has graciously called them, Christ Jesus.

Dear reader, since infants are not so disposed and since the Holy Spirit does not operate nor reveal Himself to be in them, and since they cannot serve in the body of Christ as is required by the Word of God (as is plain to all intelligent persons), therefore they should not be baptized. For without the impelling Spirit of God none should be baptized, as we have abundantly proved to all the pious children of God and from God's Word.

Therefore I conclude in regard to this matter of baptism with these plain words: Inasmuch as Christ Jesus, the true Teacher, sent of the Father, has commanded us to baptize believers, and since the dear holy apostles have in the above adduced Scriptures explained that that which is represented by baptism pertains to none but to the believing, and since infant baptism is no

---

[26] The Greek word translated *propitiation* in Rom. 3:25 is the same word which is employed in the Greek version of the Old Testament for the mercy seat. Some versions also render it mercy seat in Romans. *Ed.*

such baptism because it is evident that children have neither faith nor its fruits, which faith and fruits are the things symbolized by baptism, therefore we are forced by the Word of the Lord, by faith, and by the love of God diligently to teach and to receive believer's baptism, to defend it at such a price to the praise of the Lord before lords, princes, and the whole world as true witnesses of Jesus Christ.

## [IV.] THE PRACTICE OF THE HOLY APOSTLES IN REGARD TO BAPTISM WITH WATER

In the last place we are forced to defend believer's baptism even at such a price for the reason that the holy apostles of God have baptized none but those only who desired to be baptized, even as Christ had so expressly commanded them saying, Go ye into all the world and preach the gospel to every creature; he that believeth and is baptized shall be saved. Mark 16:16. This commandment the apostles received from the mouth of the Lord and they have proclaimed the holy Gospel, the glad tidings of grace, throughout the world. Rom. 10. They have preached it to every creature which was under heaven. Col. 1. They baptized all who accepted this Gospel by faith, and none others, as is shown in many Scriptures treating of the Acts of the apostles. Some of these Scriptures I shall place before the reader by which all the rest of the Scriptures will be easily explained.

When Philip was led by the angel of the Lord to the chariot of the eunuch who was come from the land of Ethiopia, and was reading the Gospel of Jesus Christ from Isaiah the prophet, they came unto a certain water and the eunuch said, See here is water; what doth hinder me to be baptized? And Philip said, If thou believest with all thine heart, thou mayest. And he answered and said, I believe that Jesus Christ is the Son of God. Acts 8:35.

Elect brethren, if all the earth were full of learned speakers and highly renowned doctors, and these were by sharp subtlety and human philosophy exalted as high as heaven; yet by the grace of God the word will never be snatched from us, namely, this: That where there is no faith, no baptism should be administered according to the Word of God. Or else we must admit first that the commandment of Christ Jesus is wrong. Or, that the holy apostles have taught erroneously. Or, that the holy Philip here asked a wrong question. Or, that more was required of the eunuch than of all the rest of men. Matt. 28:19; Mark 16:15.

Kind reader, no. But even as Peter and Paul together with all the pious witnesses of Christ always had their eyes fixed upon the commandment of the Lord Jesus Christ and did not act without it or against it, so also the holy Philip, the true servant of God, who preached and taught with the same spirit, would not baptize until the illustrious and famous man had sincerely confessed his faith. So it had been commanded him of Christ Jesus, his true Master, our Redeemer and Saviour.

Since then the holy apostles had their custom that converts had to make confession of faith before baptism, therefore I ask you, beloved reader, How can we require a confession of faith of infants before they are baptized, and who shall confess for them? If you say the godfathers, then I would reply that the godfathers were invented by Pope Hyginus, as we have shown above. Since they came up in Hyginus' day,[27] and since infant baptism has been practiced ever since the time of the apostles, as Origen and Augustine wrote,[28] and as I believe, because those who do not rightly know Christ always seek their righteousness in transacted ceremonies even though it was no divine command nor apostolic usage, as may be proved particularly by the holy Scriptures and also by Tertullian[29] and Rufinus[30] and others—therefore I verily do not see who has answered for them in their baptism which were baptized during the period between the apostles and Pope Hyginus, inasmuch as the godfathers were introduced by Hyginus who was the ninth or tenth pope.[31] The infants which were before him were as little able to know, hear, and speak as the children of the present day are, as the fruits plainly prove.

Observe, kind reader, that all their transactions with children, such as catechism, godfathers, baptism, chrism, and the like, are nothing but patent pretense, human righteousness, idolatry, useless fancy, and opinion.

Inasmuch as Christ Jesus has commanded but one baptism, namely, believer's baptism, and since the apostles have taught and practiced it; therefore those who defend infant baptism must consent and admit, driven by the Word of God, that infant baptism is not by the commandment of Christ, not by the teaching and practice of the holy apostles, but by the doctrine of Antichrist and by the practice of his preachers.

I repeat that the holy apostles baptized none but those who desired it, or those who confessed the most holy faith either by word of mouth, or proved it by their conduct, as did holy Peter. Although he was previously informed by a heavenly vision that he might go to the Gentiles and teach them the Gospel, yet he refused to baptize the pious, noble, and godly centurion and his associates, so long as he did not see that the Holy Spirit was descended upon them so that they spoke with tongues and glorified God. When Peter saw plainly that they were true believers, and that the divine power was descended on them, then he said, Can any man forbid water, that these should not be baptized which have received the Holy Ghost as well as we? And he commanded them to be baptized in the name of the Lord. Acts 10:47, 48.

[27] Hyginus was a bishop of Rome about A.D. 140. He is said to have served four years.

[28] Such was the claim of Origen (c. 185-254) and Augustine (354-430), but it was probably a bit exaggerated.

[29] Tertullian (c. 160-c. 230) was a presbyter in Carthage, North Africa, a great church father.

[30] Tyrannius Rufinus (c. 345-410) was a Latin presbyter and theologian. Spent part of his life as a monk in Egypt and in Palestine.

[31] Hyginus is now reckoned as the ninth bishop of Rome by church historians. *Ed.*

You see, kind reader, here you are plainly taught that Peter commanded that those only should be baptized who had received the Holy Ghost, who spoke with tongues and glorified God, which only pertains to the believing, and not to minor children. Thus the practice of Peter was in accordance with the commandment of Christ. Mark 16:16. Peter did not command infant baptism because the Holy Ghost does not operate in them, as may be plainly seen. This may also be understood from another passage of the holy Luke, for he says, When they believed Philip preaching the things concerning the kingdom of God, and the name of Jesus Christ, then were they baptized both men and women. Acts 8:12. Observe that nothing is said about infants.

Paul, a preacher and apostle in faith and truth, followed the same practice. He required faith of such quality and excellence before baptism that he regarded the baptism of the most holy John the Baptist as useless and vain among the disciples at Ephesus because they knew not the Holy Ghost. He said, Unto what then were you baptized? And they said, Unto John's baptism. Then said Paul, John verily baptized with the baptism of repentance saying unto the people that they should believe on him which should come after him, that is, on Christ Jesus. When they heard this, they were baptized in the name of the Lord Jesus. And when Paul had laid his hands upon them, the Holy Ghost came upon them, and they spake with tongues and prophesied; and all the men were about twelve. Acts 19:3-7.

Now listen, dear readers, for I would here present to you and to all the world three points, which you should impartially consider and judge according to the Word of God. First, was the baptism of John of God? I know you will give an affirmative reply. If now the baptism of John is of God, as it indeed is, and if Paul still considered this baptism which was from above as insufficient and imperfect in these disciples because they did not know the Holy Ghost, and if he after preaching Christ to them, baptized them again with the baptism of Christ Jesus, as is mentioned in Luke, then what must we think of the baptism of children who are naturally unable to understand the divine Word and therefore acknowledge neither Father, Son, nor Holy Ghost, and cannot distinguish between truth and lies, righteousness and sinfulness, good and evil, right and wrong? Does not this prove infant baptism to be useless, vain, and futile as administered and received without the ordinance of God? And if we acknowledge this by the Word of God through faith, then does it not become incumbent upon us to be baptized with the baptism of Jesus Christ, as Christ has commanded it, and as Paul has administered it to these disciples? I say verily that if we do not receive such baptism, there is according to the Word of God neither faith, regeneration, obedience, nor Spirit in us, and therefore no eternal life, as we have frequently shown above.

Let all learned men garble this invincible Scripture and practice of Paul as subtlely as they please, yet to eternity it will never be shown otherwise from the Word of God than that these disciples notwithstanding that they were baptized with the baptism of John were baptized again after they were

taught by Paul, with the baptism of Jesus Christ; because they knew not
that there was a Holy Ghost—at least if baptism is in God's Word to be
and to remain baptism. But, brethren, the preaching of the cross is to them
that perish foolishness. I Cor. 1:18.

In the second place, judge for yourselves, kind readers, since Christ Jesus
Himself and also the holy apostles, Peter, Paul, and Philip, have commanded
and taught no other baptism in all the Scriptures of the New Testament
than baptism on confession of faith and in witness of it, and since the whole
world nevertheless teaches and practices a different baptism; one which is
neither based on the commandment of Christ, nor on the teaching and practices of the holy apostles, namely, infant baptism; and since the world supports it, not by the Word of God but solely by the opinion of the learned
ones and by long usage and by the bloody and cruel sword; therefore judge,
I ask, which of the two we should follow. Shall we follow the divine truth
of Christ Jesus, or the lies of the ungodly world? If you answer that we
should follow Christ, then your judgment is right; but the result for the flesh
will be anxiety, confiscation, arrest, banishment, poverty, water, fire, sword,
the wheel, shame, cross, suffering, and temporal death; in the end, however,
eternal life. But if you answer that we should follow the world, then you
verily judge erroneously, even if the consequence for the flesh will be honor,
peace, ease, liberty, this temporal life, and similar perishable advantages; yet
the end however is eternal death.

Thirdly and finally, judge whether the ordinance of Jesus Christ which
He commanded in His church and which the holy apostles learned and administered as from His blessed mouth, can ever be changed and broken by
human wisdom or dignity. If you answer in the affirmative, you must prove
it by the divine and evangelical Scriptures or else we should not believe you.
But if you answer in the negative, as you should, then you must acknowledge
that they (no matter who they are, whether they lived at the time of the
apostles and were even their disciples), who say that the apostles baptized
infants err shamefully and ascribe falsehood to the apostles, yes, speak their
own opinions and not the Word of God. For the most holy apostles, the
true witnesses of Christian truth, have never taught two different baptisms
in water, neither did they act contrary to the command and ordinance of
Christ nor administer it contrary to their own doctrine.

Oh, had the wise and famous Origen, Augustine, Jerome,[32] Lactantius,[33]
and others not soared so high in their wisdom and philosophy, and had
they been satisfied with the clear, chaste, and plain doctrine of Christ Jesus
and His apostles and restrained their great intellects and subtle wisdom
by the Word of the Lord, then the heavenly doctrine and unchangeable ordinance of our beloved Lord Jesus Christ would not have been subjected to

[32] Jerome, called in Latin Eusebius Hieronymus (c. 340-420), was a great scholar,
translator of the Latin Vulgate.
[33] Christian writer and teacher of the early fourth century. Ed.

such harm and shame! The great Origen especially, by his philosophy and
self-deceit, dealt so shamefully with the Holy Scriptures that Martin Luther
in his book *Servum arbitrium* calls him *Spercissimus scripturarum interpres*
(that is, the falsest explainer of the Scriptures). And besides, it is said
in the notes in Luther's New Testament that this Origen is the great star
which fell from heaven, burning like a lamp, and that his name is Worm-
wood.[34] Rev. 8:11. We will leave it to God who and what he is, but even
though he has treated the Word of God so shamefully and has erred so
sadly, yet, because he pleases the world in regard to infant baptism, therefore
the holy doctrine of Christ Jesus and the apostles must yield, and Origen
is heeded, accepted, and followed as a sure testimony to this idolatrous ceremony. What terrible blindness! What shameful folly that we should not
believe the sure Word of our Lord Jesus Christ, the Word of truth and the
true witnesses who are sent by Him, but we would rather follow to the loss
of our souls those who teach to please us, notwithstanding it is plain from
their writings that they have so often stumbled and erred, and have been mistaken in regard to the truth of Almighty God.

Therefore I ask all my dear brethren in the Lord by the mercy of God
to open the eyes of your mind that ye may be no longer deceived and that
ye may perceive, you who are made uneasy by the writings of the learned
ones, that all the writers both ancient and modern have ever sought righteousness in performed ceremonies,[35] which righteousness we should only seek in
Christ Jesus. And know also that because they have not the Word of God
on their side they do not agree in regard to this matter, and neither speak
of one accord nor write unanimously. Their writings show that some seek
the washing away of original sin; others that children should be baptized
on account of their own latent faith. Or, to train them in the Word and
commandments of God. Still others, to have them included into the covenant
of God. And others again, to incorporate them into the church of Christ.
Kind readers, in this way each of the before-mentioned writers follows his
own and not a common course. If they were supported by the Word of God
in regard to this matter, they would be unanimous. But because they have not
the Word of God, each one follows his own notions, thinking that he can
under the cloak of Scripture defend pernicious falsehood as though it were
the truth. He humors himself so long with garbled Scriptures, so darkens
his mind, that he does not notice nor acknowledge that he teaches and follows
accursed falsehood, but takes it for the blessed truth of God.

And so, dear children, because the learned ones have always sought
righteousness in infant baptism and still seek it, therefore you can easily
surmise that these proponents of infant baptism have because of this consideration gained entrance. With the earliest ancients it was not the common
practice, I say common practice, as may be learned from Tertullian, Rufinus,

[34] This is a fair sample of sixteenth-century polemical writing.
[35] Menno again strikes a blow at sacramentalism. *Ed.*

and others; but as appears, immediately after the demise of the apostles, or perhaps while they were still alive,[36] men began to abuse the true Christian baptism which belongs to believers only, even as some of the Corinthians already in the days of Paul suffered themselves to be baptized for the dead. I Cor. 15:29. So also through the false doctrine and opinions of foolish bishops, the abominable serpent of infant baptism crept in and was so confirmed by long usage that at last it was accepted by all men as an apostolic institution because of the righteousness which men seek therein. Wherefore you must acknowledge, beloved brethren, although infant baptism is ancient, it is nevertheless not by the commandment of Christ Jesus, and by the teaching and practice of the holy apostles, and as a result is idolatrous, useless, and vain.

And because the true, Christian baptism has such great promise, namely, the remission of sins and other promises (Acts 2:38; Mark 16:16; I Cor. 12:13; I Pet. 3:21; Eph. 4:5), therefore the pedobaptists[37] apply the same baptism to infants. They fail to notice that the before-mentioned promises are solely to those who show obedience to the Word of God, for Jesus Christ has so commanded it. Inasmuch as pedobaptism is not commanded, therefore it is not required of children as a matter of obedience. For where there are no commandments there are no transgressions. Again, if baptism is not commanded to infants by God, then they have no promise in their baptism, from which it follows that infant baptism is idolatrous, vain, useless, and void before God, as was said before. For God the Lord has no pleasure in ceremonies unless they are ministered according to His divine and blessed Word.

But little children and particularly those of Christian parentage have a peculiar promise which was given them of God without any ceremony, but out of pure and generous grace, through Christ Jesus our Lord, who says, Suffer little children, and forbid them not, to come unto me; for of such is the kingdom of heaven. Matt. 19:14; Mark 10:14; Luke 18:16. This promise makes glad and assures all the chosen saints of God in regard to their children or infants. By it they are assured that the true word of our beloved Lord Jesus Christ could never fail. Inasmuch as He has shown such great mercy toward the children that were brought to Him that He took them up in His blessed arms, blessed them, laid His hands upon them, promised them the kingdom of heaven and has done no more with them; therefore such parents have in their hearts a sure and firm faith in the grace of God concerning their beloved children, namely, that they are children of the kingdom, of grace, and of the promise of eternal life through Jesus Christ our Lord, to whom alone be the glory, and not by any ceremony. Yes, by such promise they were assured that their dear children, as long as they are mere children,

[36] There is some evidence that infants were sometimes baptized in the second century of the Christian era. *Ed.*

[37] Those who baptize infants are called pedobaptists.

are clean, holy, saved, and pleasing unto God, be they alive or dead. Therefore they give thanks to the eternal Father through Jesus Christ our Lord for His inexpressibly great love to their dear children, and they train them in the love of God and in wisdom by correcting, chastising, teaching, and admonishing them, and by the example of an irreproachable life, until these children are able to hear the Word of God, to believe it, and to fulfill it in their works. Then is the time and not until then, of whatever age they may be, that they should receive Christian baptism, which Christ Jesus has commanded in obedience to His Word to all Christians, and which His apostles have practiced and taught.

Behold, brethren, if now they say that we rob the children of the promise and of the grace of God, you will observe that they contradict us out of hatred and envy, and do not tell the truth. Tell me, who has the strongest ground and hope for the salvation of his children? Is it he who places his hopes on an outward sign, or is it he who bases his hopes upon the promises of grace, given and promised of Christ Jesus? And yet the evangelical truth must in all respects be blasphemed and slandered by the ignorant and frivolous. But notwithstanding this, the just and impartial Judge, Christ Jesus, will at one time pass and execute true sentence between them and us, even if they do not fear it now. I fear it will be tardily acknowledged by many that they did not believe and follow the truth of Christ Jesus but the falsehood of Antichrist. Take heed and watch.

Pedobaptists object quite foolishly, saying that the apostles baptized whole households, as the household of Cornelius (Acts 10:48); the household of Stephanas (I Cor. 1:13); the household of Lydia, and of the jailer (Acts 16:15, 33); included in which they say it may be presumed that there were also small children. From this argument, beloved brethren, they show unwittingly that they cannot produce Scriptures to prove that infants should be baptized. For wherever mere presumption is followed, there evidently no proof is available.

To this objection I would reply in plain language thus: The first three households, namely, of Cornelius, Stephanas, and the jailer, were all believing. Of the first household it is written, There was a certain man in Caesarea, called Cornelius, a centurion of the band called the Italian band; a devout man and one that feared God with all his house, which gave much alms to the people, and prayed to God alway. Acts 10:1, 2. If they all served and feared God, as Luke writes, then they were not baptized without faith, as is plainly shown in the same chapter; for Peter commanded that those should be baptized who had received the Holy Ghost, who spoke with tongues and glorified God, which are all fruits of faith, as every intelligent person will admit.

Again, of the household of Stephanas it is written, I beseech you, brethren, you know the household of Stephanas, that it is the firstfruits of Achaia, and that they have addicted themselves to the ministry of the saints;

that ye submit yourselves unto such, and to every one that helpeth with us, and laboreth. I Cor. 16:15, 16. I repeat it, to serve the saints is a work of faith. Since the house of Stephanas served the saints, as Paul writes, therefore they showed by their fruits that they had faith.

Again, of the house of the jailer it is written that Paul and Silas spake unto him and said, Believe on the Lord Jesus Christ and thou shalt be saved and thy house; and they spake unto him the word of the Lord, and to all that were in his house. And he, the jailer, took them the same hour of the night, and washed their stripes; and he was baptized, he and all his, straightway. And when he had brought them into his house, he set meat before them and rejoiced with all his house. Acts 16:31-34. Or, as Erasmus translates, He rejoiced because he believed in God with all his house. Beloved reader, observe first that they spake unto him the Word of the Lord and to all that were in his house. Secondly, he rejoiced with all his house. To hear the Word is something which pertains to those of understanding minds, and spiritual rejoicing is a fruit of the believing or of the spiritual. Gal. 5:18. Inasmuch as they all heard the Word and rejoiced in God, therefore it follows incontrovertibly that the holy apostles did not baptize them without faith.

In the fourth place, in regard to the house of Lydia, I reply: Because the world tries to establish its cause on presumption, therefore we would say first that presumption ought not to establish faith. And even if mere presumption could count before God, then still the presumption in the case of the house of Lydia would not be in favor of the world but against it. It is the custom in the holy Scriptures and also with the world that a house is named after the man and not after the woman so long as the husband lives, because the husband is the head of his wife and household. Since in this case the house is named after the woman and since there is no mention made of the man, therefore it follows that she at the time was not married. If she was a young woman or a widow as it appears, then the presumption of the world must be given up, for it is more probable that she had no infants since she at that time had no husband.

We continue, even if Lydia had minor children they would not be counted among the baptized of the house. Christ commanded that believers should be baptized and the holy apostles taught and practiced accordingly. From this it may be safely deducted that when the holy Scriptures speak of houses being baptized or houses being subverted, it has reference to those who are of age and may be taught or subverted, even as Paul shows in another Scripture that some subvert whole houses, teaching things which they ought not for filthy lucre's sake. Titus 1:11. If you take the term "whole house" to apply also to infants, then since whole houses were subverted as Paul says, it would follow that infants were subverted by false doctrine. No, beloved reader, no. An infant without understanding can be neither taught nor subverted; therefore they are not counted among the number of those baptized or subverted. The holy Scripture teaches and admonishes both by words and so-called sacraments, those only who have ears to hear and minds to understand, as we have frequently shown above.

If anyone would like to have more information about the ceremony of baptism and about the objections made to it, let him read our first treatise on baptism which we published; and by the grace of the Lord he will be enlightened upon the subject from the Word of God.

Brethren, I conclude this treatise on baptism in water with these words. Inasmuch as God the merciful Father has graciously sent to this miserable, blind, and erring world His chosen, beloved Son, Christ Jesus, who has taught us the holy will of His Father in great clearness; and since He has in His great love offered up His precious and most holy flesh and blood for us, and since to Him the eternal Father has not only pointed us through His holy prophets, but also from high heaven, saying, This is my beloved Son in whom I am well pleased; hear ye him (Matt. 17:5); therefore we say and testify that we should hear this Christ Jesus; that we should believe in Him and follow Him in all things which He has taught and commanded us. We should also hear and follow His holy apostles who by His own divine command were sent out with the most precious Word of grace, namely, with the holy Gospel—or else we have neither God, promise, nor eternal life, as all men may learn from the New Testament.

Christ Jesus has given us this express and incontrovertible command in this wise: First to teach the Gospel and then they who believe shall be saved. Mark 16:16; Matt. 28:19; Acts 19:5; 2:38; 10:48; 16:33. The holy apostles have taught and used no other baptism than baptism upon confession of faith, according to the commandment of Christ as shown and proved by many reasons. Therefore we declare again before you, before all the world, and before God, that we are prompted by nothing but by the fear of God, being so taught by His Word thus to teach this Christian baptism and thus to receive it upon the confession of faith for the remission of sins (Acts 2:38); as I said before. In this way we are baptized with the washing of water by the word (Eph. 5:26), and by the Holy Spirit which quickens our hearts into one body (I Cor. 12:13), of which body Christ Jesus is the head (Col. 1:18; Eph. 1:22). Nor do we know of any other baptism of which God is witness than this baptism of which by the grace of God we have written and taught at such length.

Herewith I beseech you, kind reader, not to be like the insane, blind, and bloody world which judges everything from an envious, rebellious, refractory, and raving heart before it has read and understood; which rejects all good Christian doctrine and usage, sometimes because of habit, sometimes because of the cross, and sometimes because of the plainness of the person. Do not act this way, but judge this and all our writings according to the Spirit and the holy Word of the Lord, and you will see plainly whether we have written and taught you truth or falsehood, whether we teach two baptisms or one, whether we seek to save your souls or to destroy them, whether we seek the honor or the dishonor of the Lord. I trust by God's grace if you are desirous of your own salvation, and if you peruse what we have written and judge it with spiritual discernment, that you will find in it nothing but the teaching which is of God, the eternal, heavenly true and saving will of God, and the very strait and narrow way of truth which the ever blessed Jesus Christ and His apostles have in the most holy Gospel taught and shown to all mankind.

### [Appeal for Toleration]

Take heed, ye illustrious, noble, and reverend sirs. Take heed, ye who enforce the laws in the country against whom it is that your cruel, bloody sword is sometimes sharpened and drawn. I tell you in Christ Jesus that we seek nothing but what we have urged here, as you may clearly see by many, namely, that there is not a false syllable nor deceitful word heard from our mouths or found in us. But we are forced and led by you to the sword, to fire, and to water, as poor, innocent sheep to the slaughter.

And if you should point me to the abominable actions of the corrupt sects, and say that you must therefore oppose baptism by the sword in order that such ungodly doings may be checked and hindered, then I would reply, as follows. Christian baptism is not a corrupt sect. It is the Word of God. Secondly, the holy, Christian baptism does not cause mutiny nor shameful actions, but false teachers and false prophets do, those who boast themselves to be baptized Christians and yet before God are not that. Thirdly, there is nothing under heaven at which I am more amazed and alarmed than I am at the wicked nature of the false, corrupt sects. They frighten me more than death, for I know that all men must die. Heb. 9:27. They frighten me more than the tyrannical sword, for if they take my body, then there is nothing more that they can do. Matt. 10:28. They frighten me more than Satan, for in Christ he is vanquished for me. But if the terrible doctrine of the corrupt sects is found in me, then I would verily be lost already; eternal woe would be to my poor soul. Therefore I would rather die the death (the omniscient One knows) than to eat, drink, to have fellowship or conversation with such, if I knew that they would not be helped by my conversation or admonition. For it is emphatically forbidden in the Word of Christ to keep the company of such. Matt. 7:15; I Cor. 5:11; II Thess. 3:14; Phil. 3. And by the grace of God, I do firmly confess that they are not in the house of the Lord, in the church of the living God, and in the body of Jesus Christ.

Therefore I say, if you find in me or in my teachings which is the Word of God, or among those who are taught by me or by my colleagues any thievery, murder, perjury, sedition, rebellion, or any other criminal act, as were and are found among the corrupt sects—then punish all of us. We would be deserving of punishment if this were the case. I repeat, if we are disobedient to God in regard to religious matters, we are willing to be instructed and corrected by the Word of God, for we seek diligently to do and fulfill His most holy will. Or if we are disobedient to the emperor in matters to which he is called and ordained of God, I say matters to which he is called, then we will willingly submit to such punishment as you may see fit to inflict upon us. But if we sincerely fear and seek our Lord and God, as I trust we do, and if we are obedient unto the emperor in temporal matters as we should be according to the Word of God (Matt. 22:21; Rom. 13:7; I Pet. 2:13; Titus 3:1), and if then we have to suffer and be persecuted and crucified for the sake of the truth of the Lord, then we should consider that the disciple is not above his Master nor the servant above his lord. If they have called the master of the house Beelzebub, how much more shall they call them of his household. Matt. 10:24, 25.

Yet you should know and acknowledge, O dear noble, illustrious lords, ye judges and officers of the law, that as often as you take, condemn, and put to the sword such people, that you thrust your tyrannical sword into the blessed flesh of the Lord Jesus Christ, that you break the bones of His holy body, for they are flesh of His flesh and bone of His bone. Eph. 5:30. They are His chosen, beloved brethren and sisters, who are together with Him, born from above of one Father. John 1:13. They are His dearly beloved children who are born of the seed of His holy Word. They are His spotless, holy, and pure bride whom He in His great love has wed.

Why? Because they have by the operation of their faith and led by the Holy Spirit heartily committed themselves to the service of our beloved Lord Jesus Christ. They do not live any more according to their lusts but in conformity to the will of God alone as indicated in His holy, blessed Word. They would rather surrender everything which they possess and suffer envy, slander, scourging, persecution, agony, famine, thirst, nakedness, cold, heat, poverty, imprisonment, banishment, water, fire, and sword, or any other punishment than to forsake the Gospel of grace and the confession of God and be separated from the love which is in Christ Jesus. Rom. 8:35. But they are averse to the vain doctrine and commandments of men.

Therefore we pray you, as our beloved and gracious rulers according to the flesh, by the mercy of God, to consider and realize if there be reasonableness in you, in what great anxiety and anguish we poor, miserable people are placed. If we abandon Christ Jesus and His holy Word, we fall into the wrath of God. And if we remain firm in His holy Word, then we are put to your cruel sword. O Lord, if it were true that this vast church were Thy holy church, bride, and body as they boast it to be, then we might truthfully assert that Thou art the prince, bridegroom, and head of an abominable, detestable band of murderers who seek after the innocent blood of those who sincerely seek, fear, love, and serve God. For the ignorant, blind people go about like a backsliding heifer, as the prophet says, seeking nothing but the persecution, imprisonment, and destruction of God's saints and children.

All the priests and monks, clerics and Baal-priests who seek and respect nothing but their gluttonous, greedy, and foul belly, and their avaricious, pompous flesh, these do nothing but vilify, slander, lie, and accuse. The judges and magistrates who seek to live of the bloody labor of the miserable take them and deliver them into the hands of the tyrants that they may be in good graces with the rulers, as the prophet says. Mic. 7. What the prince desires the judge declares in order that he may do him further service. The lords and keepers of the law are generally after nothing but favor and friendship of their prince to whom they are sworn—after authority and good wages, sought with great avarice. These are they who torture, banish, confiscate, and murder, as the prophet says, Her princes within her are roaring lions; her judges are evening wolves; they gnaw at the bones till the morrow. Zeph. 3:3. At another place, Her princes in the midst thereof are like wolves ravening the prey, to shed blood, and to destroy souls, to get dishonest gain. Ezek. 22. Oh, how true was the revelation of the holy John, when he saw that the Babylonian whore was drunken with the blood of the saints and of the martyrs of Jesus. Rev. 17:6.

O beloved lords and judges of the land, observe how all the righteous, the prophets, Christ Jesus Himself, together with His holy apostles and servants have been treated from the beginning. And to this day you mistreat similarly those who in purity of heart seek the truth and life eternal. We must run the risk. If you do not fear God, and do not sheathe your murderous sword against Christ Jesus and against His holy church, then we esteem it better to fall into the hands of worldly princes and judges, than to fall into the hands of God. Dan. 6:13. I repeat, take heed, awake, and be converted, so that the innocent blood of the pious children of God which calls for vengeance in heaven may no more be found on your hands forever.

Take heed, also, ye wise and learned ones! Ye common people likewise! For such a people are they, and such is their doctrine and faith whom you daily ridicule and mock as fools, whom you slander as heretics and deceivers, whom you take and deliver and murder in your hearts as thieves, murderers, and criminals. Yet God's Word shall never be broken. I Pet. 1:24. O ye men, to what have ye come that ye are not ashamed daily to mock and to ridicule the blessed Christ Jesus, to trample upon Him and thus like wolves to tear His holy and glorious body, notwithstanding you boast His holy name, Word, death, grace, mercy, and blood.

Say, dearly beloved, if you are the church of Christ, why are you not obedient unto Him? If ye are the body of Christ, why do you destroy its holy members? If ye are the children of God, why do ye trample upon your brethren? If ye are the servants of Christ, why do you not do the things He has commanded? If you are the bride of Christ, why do you not hear His holy voice? If you are the truly regenerate, then where are the fruits? If ye are the true disciples of Christ, where is your love? If ye are the true Christians, where are your Christian ordinances of baptism, Supper, diaconate, ban, and Christian life, as commanded in His Word? If ye are the truly baptized ones of Christ, where is your faith, your new birth, your death unto sin, your irreproachable life, your good conscience, your Christian body into which you were baptized, and your Christ whom you have put on?

O beloved brethren, men have erred long enough. Christ Jesus will no longer be mocked by you as a fool. I tell you as truly as the Lord lives that so long as you are thus earthly minded, carnal, and devilish; so long as you oppose God and His holy Word; so long as you live without the fear of God according to the damnable lusts of your flesh; so long you are not the true church of Christ even if you were using the sacraments rightly, which however is far from being the case.

Beloved brethren, first we must be cleansed inwardly and after that outwardly, or else it is hypocrisy before the eyes of God. I repeat, so long as you live such an accursed, godless life as you have done hitherto, then Christ Jesus was born in vain, He died in vain, He arose and ascended altogether in vain. For He is no Lord, Deliverer, or Saviour of the willful, obdurate, unrepenting, and disobedient sinners. But He is a Lord, Deliverer, and Saviour of those who eagerly hear His divine Word, who sincerely renounce evil and walk according to His holy commandment diligently, all the days of their lives.

May God, the gracious Father, who lives in mercy forever, grant you all true knowledge to comprehend all divine truth, and a heart, mind, and will ready to fulfill that which you now confess by faith from the Word of God through Christ Jesus our beloved Lord. To Him be the honor, praise, kingdom, power, and glory forever and ever. Amen.

## LATIN EPILOGUE
### Let the bride of Christ rejoice.

Here you have, most pious reader, how baptism ought to be practiced in the church of God, the baptism that by lengthy deterioration was corrupted, but now by the generous gift of God restored. Let the rulers oppose as they will. Let the learned doctors by their wisdom do as they may. Let the whole world by every means available to it resist. This is the one and only manner of baptism which Christ Jesus has instituted and the apostles taught and practiced. Truth will remain forever unconquered, no matter how violently many fight against her. Whoever reads with Christian discernment, and judges properly, will welcome this heavenly truth of Christ, for so many ages lost and now regained, and rightly because of its benefit. Let him thank fervently the good and great God. Farewell. Humble yourself, read, receive, believe, and live accordingly, and God will be with you.

# Why I Do Not Cease Teaching and Writing

*Die oorsake van M. S. leeren ende schryven*

## 1539

*For other foundation can no man*
*lay than that is laid, which is Jesus Christ.*

# Introduction

This little explanation of Menno as to his reason for teaching and writing was published in 1539 and bound in one volume with the preceding work of this collection, *Christian Baptism*. As was noted in the introduction to *Christian Baptism*, Juniata College, Huntingdon, Pennsylvania, possesses a perfect copy of this composite volume which is actually made up of three works: *Christian Baptism, Why I Do Not Cease Teaching and Writing*, and *The True Christian Faith*.

As in his earlier works Menno again protests time and again in this book against the fearful persecution of the little brotherhood of nonresistant Christians in which he was an elder and leader. In earnest and pathetic pleas he calls for a cessation of bloodshed for religious dissenters whose only "heresy" is that they were strict Biblicists, insisting only on what the Bible demanded, and discarding all rites, practices, and doctrines which were not taught in Scripture.

Menno stresses also the depravity and wickedness of the human race, for as he looks back over history he sees a long trail of apostasy and sin. This is a race which not only wishes to walk in sin, but which also resists every effort to induce it to live a holy life. The mass of men are simply furious against true prophets and teachers of God who attempt to direct them to repentance, faith, and obedience to God.

This brings Menno to his reason for teaching and writing. In brief it is this: God Himself constrains Menno by the love He has instilled in his heart for lost men and women to speak out in the name of the Lord, calling upon an apostate and erring Christendom to return to the Lord and His authoritative Word. As a servant of the Lord and His Gospel Menno calls upon all people to turn from sin to Christ the Saviour.

In connection with his teaching and preaching Menno feels it advisable to set forth his program and platform as a Christian minister. He wants ministers of the Gospel who walk in the obedience of the faith. He wants a message which rings absolutely true to God's holy Word. He wants a Christian life which is molded after the example and teaching of the Lord Jesus and His inspired apostles. He wants a baptism which is administered only to those who have already turned to Jesus and who have been baptized with the Holy Spirit of God. He wants a Lord's Supper which is offered only to those who are walking in newness of life. He demands the abolition of all extra-Biblical ceremonies and institutions such as auricular confession, holy water, matins, vespers, images, altars, etc. He calls upon rulers to mind their proper business of maintaining law and order, encouraging the good and punishing the evil, but keeping hands off Christ's sincere disciples who insist on following the Bible rather than current custom and practice in an apostate Christendom. In general Menno calls upon all men to follow the law of absolute love as taught by the Saviour, the Prince of Peace. In short, if any man wants to be a Christian, let him follow without reservation the Bible itself, God's holy Word, nothing more and nothing less. Men ought not long for visions or ecstasies: they ought to obey Christ.

As in all his writings, there is a strong ethical flavor pervading all of the book. Menno simply cannot discuss doctrine as a detached theological system: for him it has to be related to holiness and obedience. Much of this book is also permeated with a powerful evangelistic appeal. Let the wicked turn to Christ now, for when He appears on the judgment day it will then be too late to accept His offer of salvation. On that great day when Jesus appears as Judge those who lived unprepared will be able only to cry for the mountains and the hills to cover them and hide them from the face of Him who sits upon the throne.

In the Dutch, the title of this book reads: *The Reason Why I, Menno Simons, Do Not Cease Teaching and Writing.* In the *Opera Omnia Theologica* of 1681 this work appears, fol. 435-55, and in the *Complete Works* of 1871, II, 233-55. J. C. W.

# Why I Do Not Cease Teaching and Writing

## 1539

For Zion's sake will I not hold my peace, and for Jerusalem's sake I will not rest until the righteousness thereof go forth as brightness and the salvation thereof as a lamp that burneth; and the Gentiles shall see thy righteousness, and all kings thy glory. Isa. 62:1, 2.

I am well aware, most beloved readers, that we because of our teaching and writing are cursed, loathed, hated, reviled, persecuted, and eagerly condemned to death by innumerable persons of both high and low estate. The roaring lions gnash their teeth at us. Lords, princes, learned and ignorant people alike rage against us in unspeakable tyranny, as may at all times be seen; not only against us but also against all those who accept and fulfill in deed this our doctrine with believing, faithful, obedient hearts. Not that it is our doctrine, understand this. It is the eternal, heavenly, and unchangeable doctrine of our dear Lord Jesus Christ, which He Himself has brought from high heaven, from the bosom of His Father to earth with His own blessed mouth which cannot lie; which He has taught and heralded to the world by His faithful witnesses, the holy apostles, chosen for that purpose.

Whosoever does not believe that our doctrine is the pure, undefiled, and saving doctrine of Jesus Christ may piously examine the extant Scriptures of the New Testament and he will notice and acknowledge that our doctrine is the pure doctrine, testimony, and Scripture of Christ Jesus, however much his reluctant, lazy, rebellious, refractory, selfish, and disobedient flesh may oppose, become affrighted, tremble, and be awed thereat. Although our cause appears incontrovertible, so much so that it cannot be refuted by Scriptures, yet this ignorant, blind world pursues it as an abominable crime and reviles it as deadly heresy. The prophet says, I have written to them the great things of my law, but they are counted as a strange thing. Hos. 8:12.

Worthy reader, if you would consider and realize how earnestly the righteous God insists upon His holy Word, and how terribly His wrath has always burned against those who did not abide in His divine Word, then you would without doubt, not being in the Word of God, tremble in your inmost soul before God on account of your disobedience. You have read, have you not, how the first parents of all mankind, Adam and Eve, by the power of the divine Word created by God Himself, were punished by Him on account of their disobedience. They were expelled from Paradise, subjected to physical labor, the earthly labor accursed in them, their daughters suffering pain in perilous travail; not to mention that they would have had to die eternal death if the new Man of grace, the blessed Christ Jesus, had not by His grace prevented this. And why all this? Because men did not abide in the true Word of the living God, but lived as they pleased, contrary to the Word of God, trusting in the deceit of the lying serpent rather than in the loving admonition of the true God who by grace had created them wise, righteous, and good, and had made them lords of all creatures. Gen. 2:26.

Do you not know that all the creatures under heaven, both rational and irrational, were destroyed by water, by the righteous judgment of God, save only those that were in the ark with Noah, because they corrupted themselves and lived in sensuous excess, and I think because they did not acknowledge the Spirit of the Lord as their judge?[1] Gen. 6:7, 8. Do consider these things and then you will no doubt sincerely fear your God and abide in His holy Word.

You must have often heard and perchance read for yourselves of Sodom and Gomorrah; of Er and Onan; of the idolaters; of the man who gathered sticks on the Sabbath day; of Korah, Dathan, and Abiram; of the murmurers; of Zimri and the other adulterers; of Nadab and Abihu; of those who hid the accursed things; of Jeroboam, Manasseh, and the other kings, priests, and prophets. These did not continue in the true worship and in obedience to the divine Word, which was given through Moses, but they taught and practiced more or less or otherwise than the law of God required. How terribly and in how many different ways they and their followers were punished and smitten by God, who desires to have His will obeyed! Some were scorched,[2] some suddenly died, some were pierced with the sword, some were stoned, some were swallowed up by the earth, some were bitten by serpents, some were hanged, some were consumed by fire, Saul's kingdom was taken from him, and he died by the sword; the house of Jeroboam and Ahab were extirpated; the eyes of Zedekiah were put out; Manasseh was captured; and all Israel was taken captive to foreign countries, as to Assyria, Babylonia, and Egypt as recorded in Chronicles, Kings, and the prophets.

I repeat, why did all this happen? Because they did not obey the Law of their God. Whether out of self-will or disdain for the Law they transgressed it, establishing without the command of God images, temples, and altars in every city and land, on many mountains and under large trees. Notwithstanding as the prophets have related it in detail, they regarded it not that Moses so strenuously commanded them and their fathers saying, What thing so ever I command you, observe to do it; thou shalt not add thereto

---

[1] Compare the various modern versions of Gen. 6:3. The Luther version states, "The people will no longer permit my Spirit to punish [strafen] them." Ed.

[2] The original has verzonken, which probably is a form of the verb verzengen meaning "to scorch or burn." Reference is to those who perished with the cities of the plain. Tr.

nor diminish therefrom. Deut. 12:32. At another place it is promised that on all those who do not abide by the Word of the covenant, which is written in the Book, all the plagues will come, and on the contrary all the blessings will be to those who abide therein. Deut. 28:58, 59.

All this happened because the children of Israel did not continue in the express commanding Word of Him who had by His powerful hand brought them out of the land of Egypt. But they allowed themselves to be misled by ungodly princes and false prophets, and chose for themselves without the divine commandment places for divine worship; carved for themselves images, and built themselves temples. All this they did willfully, and not by divine command, in a religion of their own construction. This the Holy Spirit has in many Scriptures called shameful whoredom, infidelity, accursed idolatry, and defection from God. The prophet says, Woe unto them, for they have departed from me; destruction upon them, because they have transgressed against me; I would redeem them if they had not taught idolatry against me.[3]

And when Israel deviated from the Law of their God in this way and committed themselves to the willful service of Baal, not being content with the Law, doctrine, and service which God had commanded them through Moses—which Baal with his altars they erected to the service of the living God however, as it appears; then God in His generous grace and paternal love which He bore to Israel for the sake of their fathers sent His faithful servants the prophets, Isaiah, Jeremiah, Elijah, Ezekiel, and others, who warningly reproved out of the mouth of God the apostate princes, false prophets, and the sorrowful, confused people, and brought them back to the true worship and ceremonies of the Law which God had commanded and which they had forsaken.

Moreover, [these prophets] predicted famine, pestilence, failures, drought, war, conflagration, plunderings, imprisonment, and destruction, as visitations on account of their sins and disobedience. They also spoke of divine mercy and grace, salvation, deliverance, peace, mercy, and the eternal glory which in the latter days would so gloriously appear unto all the world through Jesus Christ our Lord, who is the only promised prophet, the truly anointed of the Lord; the spiritual King David who establishes His kingdom by judgment and righteousness; the true Shepherd who leads us into the pastures of eternal life, whose name is Immanuel, that is, God With Us; and The Lord Our Righteousness, who shall reign over the house of Jacob forever. This was the special work of the holy prophets who were graciously sent of God the Lord to the carnal Israel.

But what did it avail, dear reader? They preached both woe and weal, punishment and grace, judgment and mercy; yet it was all in vain, as God plainly proclaimed by these same prophets, saying, I have spread out my hands all the day unto a rebellious people, which walketh in a way that is not good, after their own thoughts.

[3] Dutch translation of Hos. 7:13. *Tr.*

Again, proclaim all these words in the cities of Judah and in the streets of Jerusalem, saying, Obey my voice. Yet they obeyed not, nor inclined their ear, but walked every one in the imagination of his evil heart; therefore I will bring upon them all the words of this covenant which I commanded them to do; but they did not do them. Again, O Ephraim, thou committest whoredom and Israel is defiled; they will not frame their doings to turn unto their God, for the spirit of whoredoms is in the midst of them and they have not known the Lord. Again, the Lord has testified against Israel and against Judah by all the prophets and by all the seers saying, Turn ye from your evil ways, and keep my commandments, and my statutes, according to all the law, which I commanded unto your fathers, which I sent to you by my servants, the prophets. But they would not hear, but hardened their necks like the neck of their fathers that did not believe in the Lord their God. Again, Thus speaketh the Lord of hosts, saying, Execute true judgment, and show mercy and compassion every man to his brother; and oppress not the widow, nor the fatherless, the stranger, nor the poor, and let none of you imagine evil against his brother in your heart; but they refused to hearken, and pulled away their shoulder and stopped their ears that they should not hear. Yea, they made their hearts as an adamant stone, lest they should hear the law, and the words which the Lord of hosts hath sent in his Spirit by the former prophets; therefore came a great wrath from the Lord of hosts.

Beloved reader, they have so stopped their ears and so hardened their hearts that they not only refuse to hear but all together—and particularly the kings, princes, prophets, and priests—have consciously thirsted after the innocent blood of the true witnesses of God who by an inextinguishable fire of love fraternally reproached them for their sins, called them to repentance and turned them to God, and proclaimed and taught the way of the Lord in righteousness.

And in this way the mad, blind world has repaid and rewarded the faithful servants of God, the true prophets and true teachers of divine truth who have sincerely sought their salvation: by vituperation, arrest, beatings, banishings, and death. The rebellious, senseless, whoring, refractory people will not be reproved, as may be read in the fourth chapter of Hosea, and as the men of Anathoth said to Jeremiah, Prophesy not in the name of the Lord that thou die not by our hand. And as for the word which thou hast spoken unto us in the name of the Lord, we will not hearken unto thee. The selfish and time-serving teachers will not be reproved or admonished; they boast of their wisdom and say, We are supported by the Holy Scriptures; although all that the scribes say and teach is falsehood.

Above all, the proud, carnal, worldly, idolatrous, and tyrannical princes, who do not acknowledge God (I speak of the evil princes), who justify all their mandates, regulations, and intentions, no matter how much they may be at variance with God and His blessed Word; as though the Almighty Father, the Creator of all things, who holds heaven and earth in His hand, who rules all things by the Word of His power, had given them permission not only to command, rule, and legislate at will in temporal affairs, but also in the heavenly kingdom of Jesus Christ. Oh, no, dear me, no. This is not the intention of God. It is a great abomination in His blessed sight when mortal man puts himself in His stead. And when He raised up and sent His dear servants, the prophets, who reproved and admonished all the princes, prophets, priests, and common people from the mouth of God; then the princes destroyed them as seditious persons, and the learned ones and the common people as deceivers and heretics. So it was with Zechariah, the son of Berechiah; with Isaiah, Jeremiah, Urijah, Kiriathaim, and others, as may be read in the history.

No matter how wolflike the princes and the learned ones tyrannized and opposed the Law and those who kept it, yet the Law and Word of God remained unchanged until Christ Jesus, so that everyone who desired to be saved had to regulate and conform himself to the Law and its testimony, if he would see the dawn. For God is an eternal God and His will can never be changed by man. Neither prince nor learned man avails anything. God alone has dominion over the souls of men. He will keep it unto all eternity. This is fast and sure.

Therefore all things which they instituted and practiced as holy worship without the commandment of God, or against it (even though it was said to be done in honor of the living God who had so gloriously led their fathers and them from the land of Egypt) were nothing less than open idolatry, spiritual adultery, infidelity, apostasy, blasphemy, and a lamentable abomination, as we have briefly shown from the prophetic Scriptures. God is a God who does not need our labors and sacrifices, because He has made all things. Mine, He says, are the cattle upon a thousand hills. What then can I offer? He will take no other sacrifices than those alone which are commanded in His holy Word, as Samuel spake unto Saul, Behold, to obey is better than sacrifice. I Sam. 15:22. The Lord God of Israel spake through Jeremiah saying, Obey my voice and do according to all that I have commanded you, so shall ye be my people, and I will be your God. Jer. 11:4; II Cor. 6:17.

Beloved reader, all who sought a different way of salvation than the one which God had commanded, either did not think God wise enough to teach the right way, or they thought that He would deceive them by His Word. They despised the commanding voice of their God; they honored and exalted their own opinions and deceitful wisdom far above the wisdom of God. They transgressed the good and precious covenant which God in sheer grace and mercy had made with them and their fathers. The most grievous wickedness and the greatest disrespect of God is not to continue in His divine Word. As the Scriptures say, They transgressed the covenant like Adam, and there they dealt treacherously against me. Hos. 6:7.[4]

Oh, that Israel had acknowledged the most glorious promise of grace

4 Dutch translation. *Tr.*

which was given them and their fathers in regard to the promise of the seed, land, kingdom, and glory! And that they had considered the blessings of God so abundantly shown to them and their fathers when He miraculously led them from the land of Egypt and let them pass through the Red Sea (Ex. 14:22); when He went before them by day in a pillar of a cloud and led the way; and by night in a pillar of fire (Ex. 13:21); when He gave them bread from heaven (Ex. 16:4); when He gave them to drink from the rock (Ex. 17:6); when their clothes nor their shoes waxed old (Deut. 29:5); when He scattered the giants from before them; when He led them into the promised land flowing with oil, milk, and honey; when He gave them fortified cities and well-built houses full of gold and silver, which they had not built; and vineyards which they had not planted (Deut. 6:11); when He gave them these not for their righteousness' sake but out of grace, and because He would fulfill His promise which He had sworn to Abraham, Isaac, and Jacob. Yes, He gave it as a permanent possession, if they should abide in His holy Word and walk in His divine commandments, statutes, and righteousness, as Moses the faithful servant had repeatedly taught and commanded them. Besides, He gave them grain, oil, wine, peace, freedom, religion, and a fame above all the people round about; for there was no people under the heavens which was like unto them. Deut. 4. He led them by the hand as a young child; carried them in His blessed arms; and girded Himself round about them as a girdle, as Jeremiah has it, raising up among them His righteous men and prophets who spoke unto them the words of the Lord, kindly reproving all disobedient transgressors, and gently comforting the pious hearts with the gracious promise of life both temporal and eternal.

Oh, that the children of Israel had sincerely acknowledged all these and many other favors. Then they would never have departed so shamefully from the Word, law, will, and commandments of God their Saviour and Deliverer, who dealt with them in such a fatherly way. But because they did not acknowledge the gracious benefits which the Lord showed to them, and because they did not fear the righteous judgments against them, therefore the wicked, blind flesh and the adulterous spirit of idolatry so misled them, and so estranged them from God, and made them so drunk and mad that they acted worse than the Gentiles which were before them, whom God had on account of their sinfulness rejected and scattered, as the holy prophets in many Scriptures proclaim.

Oh, dreadful wrath of God! It cannot fail: if we reject grace, light, truth, righteousness, salvation, true religion, life, heaven, and the benediction and God Himself, we must by His righteous judgment, without fail, fall heir to wrath, darkness, falsehood, unrighteousness, and idolatry, and at the end eternal damnation, death, hell, the curse, and the devil himself.

Dearly beloved readers, God knows that I love you with pure love in Christ Jesus. I find in all the Scriptures how severely God has always from the beginning of the creation punished all transgression of His divine Word

and all disobedience, as every intelligent reader may clearly understand from
the history of Israel. I clearly see that the whole wide world, from east to
west, from south to north, in the course of time has been misled by ignorant
teachers and preachers, who sought nothing but temporal things, aided by
unfaithful lords and princes. I see that they have left the knowledge of our
beloved Lord Jesus Christ; and faith in Him, the ever blessed Saviour; His
holy Gospel and sacraments; the true religion; and the pious, unblamable
life which is of God. They have been falsely led under the name of Christ to
put faith in a man of proud, unclean, idolatrous, and ungodly flesh (do not
miss the point); in useless fables, doctrine, and human commandments; in
idolatrous baptism and Supper; in images, wood, stone, gold, silver, water,
bread, and wine; in a shameful idolatry; in empty, false, and useless promises. It has gone so far among those who boast of the name of Christ that
there is nothing left them, neither in regard to faith, love, sacraments, nor
in their life, of which it can truthfully be said that it agrees with the life and
doctrine of Christ. Judge for yourselves whether or not I write the truth.

And although some these days boast of the holy Gospel of Christ, yet
there is nothing preached but an ugly vanity, and no stronger than the temporal lords and princes allow and consent. As the princes are, so are the
preachers; and as the preachers are, so are the people. This game has gone
so far that Christ and His holy apostles must be first put down in their doctrine, and we are asked to attach ourselves to the princes and the learned
ones if we do not want to be tortured or burned at their hands, or be murdered by some other tyrannical means. As if the preachers were sent by the
princes rather than by Christ!

Therefore for the sake of the chosen ones of Zion and of Jerusalem, I
can no longer hold my tongue, the truth must be told, so that its righteousness may go forth as a light and its salvation burn as a torch, and that all
men may know the righteousness of the Lord and all tongues, generations, and
people confess His glory. I have sometimes with Jeremiah thought not to
teach any more in the name of the Lord, because so many seek my life. Yet,
I can no longer hold my tongue, for I am with the prophet very much troubled at heart; my heart trembles in me; all my joints shake and quake when
I consider that the whole world, lords, princes, learned and unlearned people, men and women, bond and free are so estranged from Christ Jesus and
from evangelical truth and from life eternal.

When I think to find a magistrate who fears God, who performs his
office correctly and uses his sword properly, then verily I find as a general
rule nothing but a Lucifer, an Antiochus,[5] or a Nero,[6] for they place themselves in Christ's stead so that their edicts must be respected above the Word
of God. Whosoever does not regulate himself according to them and does

---

[5] Antiochus Epiphanes (d. 163 B.C.) was a Syrian king who cruelly persecuted the Jews.

[6] Nero (A.D. 37-68) was a Roman emperor renowned for his evil life and his cruelty.
Ed.

not serve Bel; but maintains the ceremonies of Christ and lives according to the Word of God, such a one is arrested as a hoodlum, made to suffer, his property confiscated, and the poor innocent orphans who have now lost their faithful parents because of the testimony of the Lord must be cast out and find their way begging through the land.[7] But the public idolaters, deceivers of souls, harlots, knaves, adulterers, gamblers, blasphemers, cursers, swearers, drunkards, and similar trangressors are not persecuted, but can live at liberty and peace under their protection (I do not now speak of the good magistrates who are a few, but of the evil ones which are numerous). Besides we have their unreasonable pomp, pride, greed, uncleanness, lying, robbing, stealing, burning, hatred, envy, avarice, and idolatry. Yet they want to be called Christian princes and gracious lords. O Lord! Of what little benefit will these hypocritical, lying titles and false boastings be to them before Christ when He shall appear.

When I think to find true teachers such as are sent of God, quickened by the Holy Spirit, who sincerely seek the salvation of their brethren, who are not earthly minded, but preach the saving, wholesome Word of our beloved Lord Jesus Christ in purity of heart, and who are quite unblamable in their doctrine and life, then I do not know where to find them. Instead I find all over the world and among most of the sects, nothing but robbers of God and murderers of souls; deceivers, blind watchman, dumb dogs, masters of sects who are carnally minded, earthly, and devilish; enemies of the cross of Christ, serving their bellies instead of God; false prophets, idolaters, sycophants, liars, and conjurers. If any person does not believe my words, let him test their walk by the Word of the Lord; let him compare their doctrine, sacraments, spirit, ideals, conversation, and conduct with those of Christ, and common sense will teach you, even without the Word of God, of whom they are sent: how, what, and why they teach, and what fruits their teachings bear.

In the third place, when I think to find an irreproachable church without spot and without wrinkle, one which serves the Lord with all its power and which conforms itself to His Word, then verily I find such an ungodly, awful, corrupted, and confused people, so carnal, idolatrous, immoral, cruel, wicked, unbelieving, ignorant, bloody, unmerciful, drunken, pompous, luxurious, proud, avaricious, greedy, envious, adulterous, false, deceitful, perverted, refractory, disobedient, rebellious, vain, and so devilish that a God-fearing soul must stand dumbfounded and be ashamed. Yet they pride themselves to be the true bride, the believing congregation or church of Christ.

Oh, no, dear reader, no. Christ Jesus does not own such a bride or church. His bride is flesh of His flesh and bone of His bone; she conforms to Him; is made after His image; partakes of His nature; is minded as He is; seeks nothing but heavenly things where Christ Jesus is sitting at the right hand of His Father. Yes, in God's church nothing is heard, seen, or

[7] About 2,000 Dutch Mennonites were martyred in the sixteenth century. *Ed.*

found but the true doctrine of our beloved Lord Jesus Christ and His holy apostles, according to the holy Scripture.

But in the before-mentioned churches it is mostly doctrines, glosses, comments, councils, and commandments of men. Here is faith, there unbelief; here truth, there falsehood; here obedience, there disobedience; here believer's baptism according to God's Word, there infant baptism without Scriptural warrant; here brotherly love, there hatred, envy, tyranny, cruelty, and plentiful bloodshed; here a delightful service of others, there a much wrangling, legal action, gossip, cheating, and in some cases, also theft, robbery, and murder. Here we see instruction, admonition, consolation, reproof in righteousness; there we hear only hurt, accusations, of heresies, vituperation, and slander; here is blessing, praise, thanksgiving; there, cursing and swearing by the passion and wounds of Christ, by the sacraments, flesh and blood, and judgment; here is patience, there anger; here humility, there haughtiness; here pity, there abuse; here true service of God, there idolatry; here spirit, there flesh; here spiritual wisdom, there folly. Here men pray in the Spirit and in truth, there they mock in a flood of empty words; here men pray for God's truth, there they persecute God's righteousness; here is trust in Christ, there in idolatrous rites. In fine, here is Christ and God, and there is Antichrist and the devil. Yes, dearly beloved brethren, the pure, chaste, and spotless bride of our Lord Jesus Christ (judge for yourselves) is quite different from this carnal, unclean, adulterous, and shameful affair.

They verily are not the true congregation of Christ who merely boast of His name. But they are the true congregation of Christ who are truly converted, who are born from above of God, who are of a regenerate mind by the operation of the Holy Spirit through the hearing of the divine Word, and have become the children of God, have entered into obedience to Him, and live unblamably in His holy commandments, and according to His holy will all their days, or from the moment of their call.

And since the worldly church is no such amiable, obedient bride but one who has left her lawful husband, Christ, and follows after strange lovers, as may be plainly seen, and all this through the blindness, ignorance, and the deceit of their doctrines—therefore I seek to accomplish nothing by my writing and teaching (according to the talent God has pleased to give me) but to reclaim this adulterous bride, the erring church, from her adulterous actions, and return her to her first husband to whom she was so unfaithful, notwithstanding he did her such great service. We point out to all sects, nations, and individuals who desire to read or hear our doctrine, writings, and admonitions, not by glosses and human opinion but by the express Word of God which only avails, that there is no salvation on earth or in heaven other than in Christ Jesus, that is, in His doctrine, faith, sacraments, obedience, and walk.

All doctrine which is contrary to His Word or without His command is vain. We refer to such things as purgatory, false vows, differentiations as to places, victuals, and days, to pilgrimages, false sacrifices, etc. Or in the German churches this matter of working in us both good and bad,[8] infant baptism, etc. Again, with the corrupt sects the third David[9]; the carnal kingdom; the notion that to the pure all things are pure so that it is permissible to show outward reverence toward images, to baptize children, and also the matter of polygamy, shameless confession of sins to each other, who know no shame of nakedness; to deny the existence of angels and of the devil, that a more perfect doctrine than that of Jesus Christ, of Paul and the apostles is yet to appear, and similar atrocious ideas. We have in mind also such things as sacraments not set forth in Christ's Word, such as the idolatrous infant baptism and in the false sacrament of the Lord's Supper in a congregation that neither seeks, knows, fears, nor loves God. For it is believed that the visible bread is actually and physically flesh, and the visible wine actually and physically blood. Also holy confirmation, and holy oil as they call it. Also all the items which were not taught by Christ and His apostles, nor enjoined, such as holy water, cups,[10] altars, icons, masses, vigils, indulgences, invocation of deceased saints, vows taken by monks and Beguins, pilgrimages, etc.

We refer here also to the outward and secret life which does not comport with the spirit and life of Jesus Christ, such as unclean and lascivious thoughts, evil lusts, unbecoming shameful words, uncleanness, adultery, fornication, drinking to excess, hatred, envy, the shedding of blood contrary to the ordinance of God, avarice, pride, lying, cheating, backbiting, jesting, theft, usury, murder, swearing, and fighting. All these matters and articles such as doctrine, sacrament, worship, and conduct, which are here noted and others which are not, every reader can easily understand—by the inward unction of God—since they are not implied, expressed, nor commanded in the Word and in the wholesome doctrine of our Lord Jesus Christ (most of them being diametrically contrary to the Word), that therefore we deem them, in the light of Holy Scripture, to be nothing else than false doctrine, deceit, and deception, and nothing but false and perverted, idolatrous sacraments, abominable idolatry, spiritual adultery, apostasy, and carnality; an earthly life. The Holy Spirit of God has abundantly testified through Paul and John that those who commit these things shall not inherit the kingdom of God. Rom. 1:22; I Cor. 6:8; Gal. 5:21; Eph. 3:5; Rev. 22:5.

If the literal Israel was so severely punished and humbled by God because they did not abide by the law, commandments, statues, and righteousness of their God, and because they did not hear and receive the reproving admonition and teachings of their faithful prophets who spoke to them through

---

[8] Luther was in his earliest period, especially, an ardent predestinarian and his opponents very soon hurled the stock objection against him that he taught that God works in us all good—and therefore the evil also. Tr.

[9] Menno is here describing the followers of David Joris, the Davidians. Ed.

[10] The original has Kercken (churches); we read Kelcken (cups). Tr.

the inspiration of God, but stoned them, put them to sword, killed them, reviled and blasphemed them, following a worship of their own choice, as has been shown above, then what must we expect from God if we do not abide in the wholesome doctrine of grace, the faithful use of the holy sacraments, and the works of love which are pleasing to God, and in the pious, unblamable life which no Moses, prophet, angel, nor creature has taught us, but which the eternal Son of God, the eternal wisdom and truth, the eternal love and mercy, the blessed Christ Jesus has taught us by His own blessed mouth, by the commandment of His Almighty Father, which commandment is eternally fast and unchangeable, whose love for us cannot be measured nor fathomed, who has confirmed it by miracles, and at last sealed it with His precious blood, and has proclaimed the same to all the world by His faithful witness of His holy apostles, in the incomprehensible power of the Spirit. This doctrine is nothing else nor will it ever be anything else than the precious Gospel of peace, the glad tidings of grace, of remission of sin, the victory over death, hell, and the devil; moreover, grace, peace, mercy, and access to the Father. And all this out of love and grace—not by works or merit of our own but by means of Jesus Christ alone.

And these are the sacraments which Christ Jesus has instituted and taught. First, the holy baptism of believers in which we bury our sinful flesh and take unto ourselves a new life, seal and confess our faith, testify to the new birth and a good conscience, and enter into the obedience of Jesus Christ who has taught and commanded this Himself and also in His Holy Spirit through His disciples. Second, the Holy Supper in which is represented the death of the Lord who died for us in His great love, and in which is represented true, brotherly love and also the righteous, unblamable Christian life which must be lived inwardly and outwardly in full measure of death unto sin and unfeigned love, comfortable to the Word of God.

My good reader, the whole wide world, all tongues, races, and people have in the righteous judgment of God deserted the one God-pleasing position as to doctrine, sacraments, and life. For they have desired the lie more than the truth, and evil more than good. They have gone over in all false instruction and doctrine, false sacraments, and in such a miserably carnal life that the majority might better be called beasts than men, or rather devils than Christians, as any sensible person led by his natural reasonableness, even apart from God's Word, can easily see and perceive. The learned ones and the preachers who should reprove such things are themselves committed to such false doctrine, unbelief, and even more abominable idolatry and hellish life. Yes, these learned people diligently lead and drive all men to idolatry, unbelief, transgression, and accursed life, both by their teaching and their example, as most of the learned have done from the beginning. They are usually earthly, carnal, and devilish, and they always reject the spiritual and heavenly wisdom and will of Jesus Christ in their life, which restrains carnal lusts as loathsome and fearful. Therefore, since I clearly see this awful despising of the Word of God, and the condemnation of innumerable thousands of souls whom Christ Jesus has so dearly bought and ransomed by His crimson blood, there being no salvation outside of the obedience to the divine Word, therefore I cannot be silent because of the honor and praise of my Lord and God and the salvation of our poor, erring brother, even though it may cost my life.

Who knows, perhaps through me and through my beloved brethren who are and who shall be, God has chosen a means thereto and provided in His grace that some of those who now unwittingly err may yet acknowledge and confess the right way, doctrine, truth, and life, and walk unblamably in Christ before God and before all the world all the days of their lives. O Lord, let it be so. Amen.

Beloved reader, the Babylonian king, namely, the Antichrist, has through his servant, that is, through the false prophets and teachers, demolished the disobedient Jerusalem, the temple of the Lord, and so has imprisoned Israel these many years. Therefore I and my brethren in the Lord desire nothing, God is witness, than that we may to the honor of God so labor with His fallen city and temple and captive people according to the talent received of Him, that we may rebuild that which is demolished, repair that which is damaged, and free those who are captives with the Word of God by the power of the Holy Spirit. And we would bring it back to its earlier estate, that is, in the freedom of the Spirit to the doctrine, sacraments, ceremonies, love and life of Christ Jesus and His holy apostles.

For this reason I am not ashamed to write down, publish, and proclaim loudly my faith, doctrine, intention, and desire before all men who will hear, no matter who they are. Yes, I do not doubt but if those could see my inmost heart who now assiduously seek my life, then their hatred against me and my brethren would change into love and friendliness.

In the first place, we desire according to the Word of God that no bishop, pastor, or minister shall be admitted into the church of the Lord, to teach and administer the sacraments of the Lord, other than those who are comprised in the doctrine, ordinance, and life of our Lord Jesus Christ, and unblamable in all things. I Tim. 3:2; Titus 1:6; Lev. 21:7; Ezek. 44:21. For the Word of the Lord is truth; it is Spirit and life. These things cannot be administered by the carnally minded, by children of death, nor by liars; but by the truthful, by the spiritually minded, and by those who rightly confess Christ Jesus, who feel surely the life eternal in their hearts and who live unblamably before God and walk in Christ Jesus, so that they may truthfully say with Paul, Be ye followers of me, even as I also am of Christ.

In the second place, we desire with ardent hearts even at the cost of life and blood that the holy Gospel of Jesus Christ and His apostles, which only is the true doctrine and will remain so until Jesus Christ comes again upon the clouds, may be taught and preached through all the world as the Lord Jesus Christ commanded His disciples as a last word to them while He was on earth. Matt. 28:19; Mark 16:15.

In the third place, we seek, teach, and desire a true faith and Christian life conformable to the doctrine of Jesus Christ and His apostles, for the doctrine of the preachers is all vain and useless if the Word which is preached is not accepted by faith (Heb. 4:2); and faith is vain and dead before God when it does not work by love (Jas. 2:20).

In the fourth place, we teach, seek, and desire a right Christian baptism; first, with Spirit and fire( Luke 3:16); and afterwards in water, a matter of the obedience of faith, because Jesus Christ has commanded it thus to all the believing, and the holy apostles have thus taught and administered it.

In the fifth place, we teach, seek, and desire such a Supper as Christ Jesus Himself has instituted and administered (Matt. 26:19; Mark 14:22; Luke 22:19), namely, to the church which is outwardly without spot and blemish, that is, without any evident transgression and wickedness, for the church can only judge as to the visible things. What is inwardly wicked and not outwardly apparent to the church, such as the betrayal of Judas, of that God is to judge, for He alone tries the hearts and reins and not the church. Secondly, in both forms, namely, bread and wine. Thirdly, for remembrance of the Lord's death. Fourthly, as a means for inciting to and a demonstration of brotherly love, even as this supper was also called among the ancients, a brotherly Supper, as Tertullian[11] writes.

In the sixth place, we seek and desire that all strange ceremonies and manners of worship which are contrary to the Word of God, or instituted contrary thereto, and which tend to abominable idolatry, may be abolished, such as holy water, auricular confession, infant baptism, masses, matins, vespers, images, altars, false vows, and like ceremonies. These are to be abolished, not by force of arms, but peaceably by the Word of God, so that the poor, ignorant people may no longer be deceived by such vain works which are nothing short of idolatry; but that they may put their faith in the living God and in the merits of our ever blessed Lord Jesus Christ, and they may cordially walk in His divine commandments, not varying to the right or to the left. For in Him is life everlasting, and in none other.

In the seventh place, we seek, desire, teach, and preach that all magistrates, emperors, kings, dukes, counts, barons, mayors, knights, junkers, and burgomasters may be so taught and trained by the Spirit and Word of God that they may sincerely seek, honor, fear, and serve Christ Jesus, the true head of all lords and potentates; so that they may rightly administer and prosecute their office and use the sword given them of God in His fear and in brotherly love to the praise of God, to the protection of the good, and to the punishment of the evil according to the Word of God (Rom. 13:3; I Pet. 2:13) as did the dear men of God, such as Moses, Joshua, David, Ezekiel, Josiah, and others. Read also Deut. 17:2, 3, and you will clearly understand what God has commanded all magistrates.

Besides, we teach the true love and fear of God, the true love of our neigh-

[11] Tertullian was a Latin church father who lived c. 160-c. 230 A.D. Ed.

bor—to aid and assist all men and to injure none; to crucify the flesh and its lusts; to circumcise the heart, mouth, and the whole body with the knife of the divine Word; to exscind all unclean thoughts, unbecoming words, and improper actions.

Now consider whether these things are not the will of God, the true doctrine of Jesus Christ, the true ministering of the sacraments, and the true life which is of God, although the gates of hell willfully oppose them.

Behold, dear brethren, against these doctrines, sacraments, and life imperial decrees mean nothing, nor papal bulls, nor councils of the learned ones, no long usage, no human philosophy, no Origen, Augustine, Luther, Bucer,[12] imprisonment, banishment, or murder. For it is the eternal, imperishable Word of God; it is, I repeat, the eternal Word of God, and will remain that forever. *Etiamsi rumpantur ilia Codro.*[13] Anyone who wishes nevertheless to oppose the war against these things, either with heart, word, or sword, such a one does not war against flesh and blood, that is, against man, but he wars against the Lamb, against Him who has all power, the One who by a word created heaven and earth and the fullness thereof. Yes, against Him who lifts up His hand and says, I live forever.

Very well, if this is the true doctrine of Jesus Christ which alone leads to life eternal, and there is none other, I might be asked by the reader why it is that so very few men sincerely believe and fulfill it in works. In my opinion there are four reasons for this. First, because all lords, preachers, and common people have their hearts set on carnal, earthly, and temporal things, and therefore they cannot admit and accept the blessed doctrine of the Holy Ghost. Second, because they are drunk and full of the enchanting wine of the Babylonian harlot, exceeding rich and not in want of anything. Third, because they do not fear the awful judgment and fearful wrath of God against all disobedience and transgression. Yes, they so utterly disregard the Word of God as if the Holy Ghost were merely jesting when threatening temporal or eternal punishment. Fourth, because they do not acknowledge the great kindness of God toward them in Christ Jesus.

For they do not acknowledge the works of the divine love toward them, namely, that God has created heaven and earth and all the fullness thereof for their benefit. They do not remember that He formed them after His own image from the dust of the earth; placed them at the head of all creation; gave them gold, silver, land, house and home, a cow and calf, fish and flesh, water and wine, beer and bread, cloth and clothing, to supply their needs. They do not remember that He gave them His divine Word: first, the law of nature, then Moses and the prophets, and afterwards His only be-

[12] Martin Kuhhorn, known as Butzer (1491-1551), was a Protestant Reformer of Strasburg. *Ed.*

[13] "Even if the belly of Codrus should burst." This is an adaptation, probably by Menno himself, of a line from Virgil (Seventh Eclogue, line 26), where he speaks of music so sweet that it would burst the vitals of Codrus, a rival poet who was fiercely critical of Virgil. *Tr.*

gotten Son, His wisdom, His power, Christ Jesus, who has taught them the will of His Father in great clearness; opened heaven and closed hell for them; vanquished death, sin, and the devil on the cross; fulfilled the demands and threats of the law and acquired for them grace, favor, mercy, peace, freedom, deliverance, remission of sins and eternal life with the Father if they believe, seek, and desire it, besides calling them daily to repentance, regeneration, and the glory of the chosen children of God; desiring to draw them forth from the darkness of the world and to deliver them into the kingdom of His beloved Son; not letting His righteous judgment come upon them as it came upon Sodom and Gomorrah. If they would remember these things, and that He gives them day and night, sun and moon, rain and drought; and blesses them with wisdom and understanding, with wife, children, labor, and fruits; if they would deep down in their hearts acknowledge these rich gifts of His abundant grace, then all the tyrants under heaven would not separate them from the doctrine, love, sacraments, life and confession of Christ Jesus even if it were possible for them to testify to it by a thousand deaths. Yes, they would say with the Apostle Paul, Who shall separate us from the love of Christ? Shall tribulation, or distress, or persecution, or famine, or nakedness, or peril, or sword? Rom. 8:35.

Because men do not acknowledge the God of all grace in His divine Word, judgment, and beneficences; and do not acknowledge the Spirit, power, will, and life which was in Christ Jesus whom we should follow according to the Word of God; therefore they so wrongfully oppose and persecute the heavenly doctrine of Jesus Christ, and diligently follow, teach, and promote all manner of falsehood, deceit, fraud, and idolatry. I repeat, if they rightly acknowledged and believed the paternal heart, mind and love, protection, favor, will, solicitude and affection of the Almighty God in Christ Jesus, they would no doubt accept, and from the heart fulfill, His blessed Word and admonition. But since they do not rightly acknowledge Christ Jesus and His Father, therefore the Saviour's words are fulfilled, God so loved the world, that he gave his only begotten Son, that whosoever believeth in him should not perish, but have everlasting life. For God sent not his Son into the world to condemn the world; but that the world through him might be saved. He that believeth on him is not condemned; but he that believeth not is condemned already, because he hath not believed in the name of the only begotten Son of God. And this is the condemnation, that light is come into the world and men loved darkness rather than light because their deeds were evil. John 3:16-19.

Take heed, O miserable, erring men! Here the eternal wisdom of the blessed Christ Jesus has declared why you do not believe His precious Word, and do not fulfill His divine will: because you prefer the damnable darkness to the saving light. Once more I repeat, if you sincerely accepted and believed the divine goodness, mercy, and the boundless love of our beloved Lord Jesus Christ toward you, namely, that by His burning love, He became a humble mortal man for you; came down from high heaven into these lower parts of the earth; in love taught and preached unto you the eternal kingdom of God; in love performed miracles, in love prayed, suffered tribulation, anxiety, arrest in prison; in love was beaten, mocked, derided, spit upon, scourged, crowned with thorns, drank gall and vinegar, was blasphemed, crucified, dead and buried for you; in love was raised up, has ascended to heaven, is seated at the right hand of the Father, and by His crimson blood became your faithful servant, Intercessor, Atoner, Saviour, Mediator, and Advocate; if you believe that by love He sent to you and to the whole world His faithful servants, His holy apostles, with the Word of grace—if you believed all this, you would doubtlessly love Him in return, Him who has shown you such great love and grace without any merit on your part. And if you would return the love with which He has loved you and yet loves you, you would, believe me, not tire of seeking and following Him, so that you might live unblamably according to His blessed will, and walk all your life in His divine commandments. As He Himself says, He that hath my commandments, and keepeth them, he it is that loveth me.

Behold, beloved reader, in this way true faith or true knowledge begets love, and love begets obedience to the commandments of God. Therefore Christ Jesus says, He that believeth on him is not condemned. Again at another place, Verily, verily, I say unto you, He that heareth my word, and believeth on him that sent me, hath everlasting life, and shall not come into condemnation; but is passed from death unto life. John 5:24. For true evangelical faith is of such a nature that it cannot lie dormant, but manifests itself in all righteousness and works of love; it dies unto the flesh and blood; it destroys all forbidden lusts and desires; it seeks and serves and fears God; it clothes the naked; it feeds the hungry; it comforts the sorrowful; it shelters the destitute; it aids and consoles the sad; it returns good for evil; it serves those that harm it; it prays for those that persecute it; teaches, admonishes, and reproves with the Word of the Lord; it seeks that which is lost; it binds up that which is wounded; it heals that which is diseased and it saves that which is sound; it has become all things to all men.[14] The persecution, suffering, and anguish which befalls it for the sake of the truth of the Lord is to it a glorious joy and consolation.

All those who have such a faith, a faith that yearns to walk in the commandments of the Lord, to do the will of the Lord; these press on to all righteousness, love, and obedience. These prove that the Word and will of our beloved Lord Jesus Christ is true wisdom, truth, and love, is unchangeable and immutable until Christ Jesus shall come again in the clouds of heaven at the judgment day. These will not make light of God's Word as does the ignorant world, saying, What good can water do me? But they diligently try to obey the Word of Christ in every particular, even if it leads to death for the body.

14 For *al is't alleen geworden* we have read: *al is't allen geworden. Tr.*

You see, dearest brethren, I speak frankly with a certain and sure conviction, not by some revelation or heavenly inspiration, but by the express, definite Word of the Lord. From my inmost heart I am convinced that this doctrine is not our doctrine, but the doctrine of Him who sent us, that is, Christ Jesus. All those who are desirous to do His will, will acknowledge that this doctrine is of God and that we do not declare our own invention, dreams, or visions. But those who do not fear God, do not believe on Christ Jesus, who trample upon His Word, and do not do His will; those who love darkness rather than light; by them all evangelical truth must be cursed as damnable heresy and considered and treated as deadly treason. And yet the Word of God shall remain unbroken until the judgment day.

Woe unto those in whom are lost the abundant gifts of grace, the heavenly Word of peace, the gentle admonitions, the hard and bitter labor, the precious treasure which is the crimson blood and bitter death of our Lord Jesus Christ. Woe unto them! For we can never be saved without faith, love, and obedience to our Lord Jesus Christ. (I speak of those who have come to an understanding age.) Paul says, Without faith, it is impossible to please God. Heb. 11:6. He that believeth not is condemned. John 3:18.

The literal law of Moses could not at any time be changed by the tyranny of princes, by the profundity of the learned, or by the raging of the masses. Nothing could be added to it nor taken from it; it had to remain unchanged as it had been given by God through Moses until the coming of Christ. And as all who did not abide in this law were the children of wrath and of death, just so it is today. Even if all the deceased apostles should be raised up and should teach us otherwise than they did at the time of their service; and if, beside these, Moses and the prophets and the angels of heaven and as many eloquent, boasting, and miracle-working prophets as we have hairs on our heads should appear, and if, besides these, all the princes should roar like devouring lions and ravening wolves, and if every tongue of the learned ones should cut as a sharp razor, it would still be impossible that any could be saved who do not abide by the wholesome doctrine, sacraments, obedience, and life of Jesus Christ. They are the children of wrath, curse, and of eternal death. Even as Christ Jesus Himself said, Not every one that saith unto me, Lord, Lord, shall enter into the kingdom of heaven; but he that doeth the will of my Father which is in heaven. Matt. 7:21. At another place He says, If ye continue in my word, then are ye my disciples indeed; and ye shall know the truth, and the truth shall make you free. John 8:31, 32. From this follows the counterpart, beloved brethren, that if we do not abide in Christ's Word, we cannot be His disciples; that we do not know the truth. And if we do not know the truth, how then can we be made free by it? And if we are not freed by truth, woe unto us that we were born, for then we are as yet in sin, under curse and wrath, and are children of hell, of the devil, and of eternal death. Alas, alas, fear with all your heart, faithful reader, for this will never be found otherwise.

If the bloodthirsty, tyrannical lords and princes had from the beginning acknowledged this, and would now acknowledge it, namely, that Christ's Word is eternal, and will remain unchangeable, and that it cannot be changed by human greatness, never would they have oppressed and murdered those who confessed the divine Word.

If the bishop of Rome and his learned college had taken this matter to heart, he would never have taken Italy from its emperor, and from Christ Jesus the spiritual reign. But he would doubtlessly have said farewell to his worldly glory, pomp, luxury, idolatry, false doctrine, easy life, garbled sacraments, Sodom-like uncleanness, his councils, statutes, and decretals. He would have contented himself with the immutable, heavenly doctrine of the only true Shepherd, Teacher, and Bishop of our souls, Christ Jesus.

Since then the sum of our salvation is included and comprised in Christ Jesus and in His holy Word, and in no one else, nor in any other doctrine; therefore I warn every God-fearing soul by the Word of God, driven by nothing but brotherly love, not to be frightened and misled, neither by the exalted position of the man, nor by the antiquity of a name, nor by learning, eloquence, appearance of ritual, by dreams, prophecies, visions, signs, and powers.

For there can never be a wiser, truer, more diligent, more righteous, God-fearing, unblamable, powerful, perfect, higher, or holier Prophet than the ever blessed Christ Jesus. Everything, too, has testified this of Him, both in heaven and upon earth. In the first place, God testified this to Adam; afterwards to Moses, David, Isaiah, Jeremiah, Ezekiel, Hosea, Zechariah, and to most of the prophets; to the angel Gabriel; to the angels at His birth; by the star of heaven; by the Wise Men from the East; the learned ones at Jerusalem, and John the Baptist. It was testified also at His baptism by the Father and the Holy Ghost; afterward by the multitudes, by the very devils; by the healing, the raising up of the dead; by changing water into wine, commanding the storm to cease; by the loaves and fishes, the fig tree, and the children on Palm Sunday; and at His death by the murderers; the firmament of heaven, the whole earth, the veil of the temple, the stones, the deceased dead, and the centurion under the cross. Say, what is there that has not testified to Christ Jesus? Yes, He is the One, as He Himself says, who after His resurrection ascended to heaven and to whom all power is given of the Father both in heaven and on earth. Matt. 28.

Therefore it is just and right, is it not, yes, it is absolutely required if they do not want to be lost, that all magistrates bow themselves under His scepter; all reason and intellect place itself under His heavenly wisdom; all flesh prostrate itself at His feet; and every tongue confess that He is the Lord to the honor and praise of His Father. I pray all God-fearing readers in the Lord, by the merits of our blessed Lord Jesus Christ, to whom be the kingdom, the praise and the honor, not to consider me, a poor, miserable sinner, to be more than a mere humble servant of Jesus Christ, and a dispenser of His mysteries according to the faith given me of Him, miserable sinner that I am, on account of my unclean, greedy, proud, vain, idolatrous, and carnal life which I formerly led, who still to this day am found sinful, defective, and faulty before my God, not worthy to be the least and humblest servant in the house of my Lord. Yet by God's grace I am what I am.

Brethren, I tell you the truth and lie not. I am no Enoch, I am no Elias, I am not one who sees visions, I am no prophet who can teach and prophesy otherwise than what is written in the Word of God and understood in the Spirit. (Whosoever tries to teach something else will soon leave the track and be deceived.) I do not doubt that the merciful Father will keep me in His Word so that I shall write or speak nothing but that which I can prove by Moses, the prophets, the evangelists and other apostolic Scriptures and doctrines, explained in the true sense, Spirit, and intent of Christ. Judge ye that are spiritually minded.

Once more, I have no visions nor angelic inspirations. Neither do I desire such lest I be deceived. The Word of Christ alone is sufficient for me. If I do not follow His testimony, then verily all that I do is useless, and even if I had such visions and inspirations, which is not the case, even then it would have to be conformable to the Word and Spirit of Christ, or else it would be mere imagination, deceit, and satanic temptation. For Paul says, Let us prophesy according to the proportion of faith. Rom. 12:6.

Nor am I a third David as some have boasted and do even now boast. There are but two Davids contained in the Word of God. The first, a literal and figurative David, namely, the son of Jesse; and the second, the spiritual David, the only begotten Son of God, Christ Jesus. Whosoever poses as a third is a falsifier and a blasphemer against Christ. Let every soul take heed, lest he err in his faith.

According to my natural birth I am nothing but unclean slime and dust of the earth, conceived and born in sin from my mother's womb, trained all my life in all manner of ignorance, sin, and blindness until the clear light of grace and knowledge appeared unto me from high heaven. This has given me such a heart, will, and desire that I willingly seek after that which is good and strive with the holy Paul to follow after, if that I may apprehend that for which also I am apprehended of Christ Jesus. Phil 3:12.

O dearest reader, I repeat that I have formerly acted shamefully against God and my neighbors; and I still do sometimes think, speak, and act recklessly, which, however, I sincerely hate. What am I that I should boast, seek, and teach anything else than the ever blessed Christ Jesus alone, His Word, sacraments, obedience, and His God-pleasing, virtuous, and unblamable life. He is the only one of whom it is written that He was begotten of the Holy Ghost; that He knew no sin; that guile was not found in His mouth; and that His doctrine, Word, will, and commandments are life eternal.

Therefore take heed and watch over your soul. Every Christian must be thus minded in regard to Christ Jesus his Saviour and in regard to His holy Word; nor must he think himself more exalted no matter what gifts he has received, if he would not rob Christ Jesus of His glory. He must remain in a humble walk before God in the true measure of his faith, as it becomes him in Christ. Let no man deceive himself. Let spiritual pride and vain boasting be far from you, For God resisteth the proud, and giveth grace to the humble. I Pet. 5:5.

I see the perils which have daily surrounded us from the beginning. So many souls are deceived by false prophecies, smooth words, sham holiness, faked power, the boasting and the false promises of the Antichrists and the false prophets who are intent upon their own honor, fame, and gain under a semblance of God's Word. Such was the case with the popes of Rome, with John of Leiden, with those of Münster, and others. Therefore I deem it necessary, sincerely to warn and admonish all beloved readers in the Lord not to accept my doctrine as the Gospel of Jesus Christ until they have weighed it in the balance of the Spirit and Word of the Lord, that they may not place their faith in me nor in any teacher or writer, but solely in Christ Jesus. For if they should accept it for my sake and should not first compare it with the Word of the Lord, and so depend upon me or any other man, and not upon Christ Jesus, they would be like unto the culpable Corinthians whom Paul reproved severely because there were dissensions among them, as they boasted in this or that teacher, rather than boasting exclusively in the One set forth by these teachers. I Cor. 1. They would be like unto those of whom it is written, Cursed be the man that trusteth in man, and maketh flesh his arm. Jer. 17:5.

If I should by my teaching gain disciples for myself and not for Christ Jesus, seeking my own gain, praise, and honor, then indeed woe unto my soul. No, brethren, no. The Lord be blessed, I seek not that which Judas the Galilean and Theudas sought. By the grace of God I am not minded like those who, in their imagination, soar above the clouds and want to be like unto the Most High. But I repeat,[15] I am a poor, miserable sinner who must daily fight with this flesh, the world, and the devil, and daily seek the mercy of the Lord, and who with the holy Paul boasts of nothing but Christ Jesus alone and that He was crucified for us. I Cor. 2:2.

My writing and preaching is nothing else than Jesus Christ. I seek and desire nothing (this the Omniscient One knows) but that the most glorious name, the divine will, and the glory of our beloved Lord Jesus Christ may be acknowledged throughout the world. I desire and seek sincere teachers, true doctrines, true faith, true sacraments, true worship, and an unblamable life. For this I must pay dearly with so much oppression, discomfort, trouble, labor, sleeplessness, fear, anxiety, care, envy, shame, heat and cold, and perhaps at last with torture, yes, with my blood and death. My reward according to the flesh must not be otherwise than that of Him

---

[15] Note how true to the Word of God Menno remains in his insistence on depravity and grace. Ed.

who from the beginning has sought the salvation of the world. I say with holy John the Baptist, Christ Jesus must increase but I must decrease. John 3:30. He lives forever and ever, but I shall return to the dust from whence I came, as will all the children of men.

Therefore I beseech you again by the mercy of God and for the salvation of your souls that you may weigh my doctrine and the doctrine of all men who have written from the times of the apostles, and write now, with the Gospel of Jesus Christ and the doctrine of His holy apostles, lest you be deceived by me or by some other man, no matter whether he be a prince, learned or unlearned, holy in appearance or miraculous. Is it the Word of God which I teach? Let those who are spiritual judge. In that case they must accept it in the name of the Lord if they would not be lost. But if it be human doctrine, then let it be accursed of God. For other foundation can no man lay than that is laid by the apostles which is Christ Jesus. I Cor. 3:11.

No doctrine is profitable or serviceable to our salvation but the doctrine of Christ Jesus and His holy apostles as He Himself says, Teach them to observe all things whatsoever I have commanded you. Matt. 28:19.

All Scripture both of the Old and New Testament rightly explained according to the intent of Christ Jesus and His holy apostles is profitable for doctrine, for reproof, for correction, for instruction in righteousness. II Tim. 3:16. But whatever is taught contrary to the Spirit and doctrine of Jesus is accursed of God. Gal. 1.

There is but one cornerstone laid of God the Almighty Father in the foundation of Zion, which is Christ Jesus. Isa. 28:16; Rom. 9:33; I Pet. 2:6. Upon Him alone we should build according to His Word, and upon none other. The whole world, however, has built upon strange foundations such as popes, councils, doctors, doctrines, and commandments of men; upon wrong practices of long standing. Some, alas, still continue to build upon pretending prophets and thus shamefully reject the only noble and proper cornerstone, the ever blessed Christ Jesus. Therefore I cannot be restrained but must warn all God-fearing souls in the Lord by my writings wherever they shall be read or heard that from this moment they may awaken if they desire to be saved (even if I die by so doing), and that they may without delay enter into the wholesome doctrine, sacraments, obedience, and life of our beloved Lord Jesus Christ. For in Him alone is life eternal, as has been frequently said above.

Dear reader, verily I cannot marvel enough at the daring, the deafness, and the blindness of the world. Men are not ashamed to bear the name of Christ and to boast of His merits, blood, and death while nothing is found among them at all by which they prove the good will and nature of Christ Jesus. O ye vain boasters, are you the true Christians in whom God is pleased, as you pretend? Where then is your faith that brings with it God's righteousness? Where is your Christian baptism in which you have buried your sins and put on the new life? Where is your true Supper in which you proclaim the death of the Lord and show your brotherly love? Where is your love and fear of God? your love of your neighbors? your sadness of heart? your mercifulness toward the needy? your obedience to the commandments of God? your new birth from above, from which results a new life which should be unblamable before God and before all the world? Where is the true religion, namely, to visit widows and orphans in their distress and to keep yourself unspotted from the world? Where is the living, holy, and pleasing sacrifice of your own body which you should ever be ready to present for the sake of the Lord's truth? Verily, we find nothing with you but unbelief and its evil fruits: an anti-Christian baptism, an idolatrous supper, the unclean love of the flesh, unmercifulness, pride, avarice, disobedience in all divine matters, a carnal birth altogether earthly, and the old censurable life, led according to the will of him who from the beginning was a proud, false, deceitful, cruel, and bloody murderer.

We find with you no worship but only an external invented set of rites which are pleasing to the flesh, such as bells, organs, singing, celebration, ornamented churches, beautiful icons, differentiations in victuals and in days, false purity and vows, many psalms and *pater nosters*[16] recited with the mouth and not spiritually, corrupted sacraments, falsification, and abuse of all that which Christ has taught and commanded in His holy Gospel. All of these are verily no works of regenerated Christians, but rather the works of Satan or of the foolish, blind, and ignorant flesh. By these works neither the Word or righteousness of God is taught; no flesh is crucified; no neighbors are served; and above all they are not pleasing to God. And they cannot according to Scripture be considered services of God but rather an abominable, fearful, and terrible service of idols. By such means the ignorant, trusting populace is led away from the true faith and trust in Christ Jesus and is led into a false trust in ceremonies, yes, in such ceremonies as the eternal Wisdom, the blessed Christ Jesus, has never commanded with so much as a word. By these ceremonies they plainly show that they believe at heart that Christ Jesus is imperfect, foolish, and unclean. For if they believed Him to be wise and perfect, how could they thus shamefully adulterate, break, despise, and garble His perfect evangelical Word and ordinances? If they acknowledged Him to be spotless, why do they seek their salvation in such impure and strange means, and not in the only pure sacrifice which is Christ Jesus?

But because true religion opposes your carnal sensuousness, pride, avarice, uncleanness, vanity, ease, and the lusts of your flesh, therefore you have chosen for yourselves a vain and strange religion by which you think to be saved, although you do not live according to the Word and will of God. No, dear reader, I repeat. If all creatures under heaven were devouring swords, fire, and water; if all men were cruel and bloody tyrants; and if the profundity of the learned ones ruled all the people, yet all would be in

---

[16] Latin designation of the Lord's Prayer which is much used in Catholic piety. *Ed.*

vain. If you would enter into life, you must be born again (John 3:5); you must be converted, and in malice you should be children (I Cor. 14:20). You must keep the commandments which were taught and commanded by Jesus Christ. There is no other way, for there will never be a way of salvation other than Christ Jesus.

It is the rashest blindness to think that we could be saved and at the same time be avaricious, spiteful, envious, proud, adulterous, and idolatrous. All the Scriptures show plainly and teach that such shall not inherit the kingdom of God. Did you ever find falsehood with God? I think not! The holy Paul says that God is one that cannot lie. Jesus Christ says, Thy word is truth. And if He then is a God that cannot lie and His holy Word is truth, oh, dear, then all is lost with you, for His doctrine and truth is that the unbelieving, contrary, disobedient, avaricious, vain, lying, adulterous, greedy, bold, idolatrous, unfaithful, ambitious, bloodthirsty, and carnal man shall not enter into the kingdom of heaven, but his portion shall be everlasting destruction in darkness and death.

Since you are such ungodly, hardened, and willful sinners, therefore you are, according to the Word of Christ which cannot lie, and according to the doctrine of the apostles who spoke in like Spirit, deprived of the glorious revelation of the children of God and of the future life, and must remain forever, by the wrath of God, in the lake which burns with fire and brimstone. Rev. 21:8.

And if you still trust to be saved while you do not sincerely repent of your old life, then verily your trust is vain. By such confidence you make God a liar because you trust to acquire life contrary to His Word.

What do you think, perverse men, that we shall surprise, blind, and bribe the Almighty, wise, and just God? Do you think that the eternal truth shall become falsehood for your sake? No, dear reader, no. The sure sentence of God was passed with utter finality more than 1500 years ago. If ye live after the flesh, ye shall die. Rom. 8:13. This word is sure and firm.

O world, world, that you should despise as vain and useless, the calling and inviting voice of your God who is as faithful to you as a faithful Father to His beloved children; and that you speak in your hearts with beautiful Tyre, I am of perfect beauty (Ezek. 27:3); and with proud Babylon, I am clean forever and none else besides me; I shall not sit as a widow, neither shall I know the loss of children (Isa. 47:8). Although you now say as do the ignorant, it is peace and freedom, yet I tell you as Ezekiel said unto Tyre, Nothing thou art, and nothing shalt thou forever be. Isaiah said unto Babylon, Thou shalt fall and not rise again. Paul says that the day of the Lord so cometh as a thief in the night, and, As travail upon a woman with child; and they shall not escape. I Thess. 5:2, 3. Although you may now with Capernaum be exalted unto heaven, yet you will unexpectedly be brought down to hell. Matt. 11:23. You eat, drink, dress up, grab, hoard, and scrape, whether legally or illegally. You act in all your transactions as if you would ever remain in this tabernacle of clay; and you never reflect that soon the word will be heard by all of us, Give an account of your stewardship; for thou mayest no longer be steward.

The precious Word of grace and of eternal peace, which is the most holy Gospel of Jesus Christ, you think to be nothing but an invented fable, nay, a damnable heresy, for you drown, burn, persecute, and murder those who teach, admonish, and reprove you by this Word, and who by a strong power of the Spirit are sent to you of God by grace, just as the mad synagogue of the Jews did, so that they did not only persecute and destroy the chosen children of God, the holy prophets, but also the only begotten Son of God Himself, who by the ineffable love of the merciful Father was sent to them for their eternal salvation. What did they say? This is the heir; come, let us kill him, and let us seize on his inheritance. Matt. 21:38.

How long will you continue in your damnable blindness, your wicked stubbornness, and your pernicious madness? Reflect on the abundant marvelous works of grace which Christ Jesus has shown you. If His great love cannot move you to forsake your idolatry, disobedience, and accursed life, then remember His stern judgment which from the beginning of the creation came upon all those who did not abide in His blessed Word and obedience, that you may be moved by such fear, since you are not moved by His love to be drawn away from all evil.

Behold the weeping eyes, miserable world, and hear the tender voice of our beloved Lord Jesus Christ, how He wept for impenitent Jerusalem and said unto her, If thou hadst known, even thou, at least in this thy day, the things which belong unto thy peace! But now they are hid from thine eyes. Luke 19:42. At another place, Behold, I send unto you prophets and wise men and scribes; and some of them ye shall kill and crucify; and some of them ye shall scourge in your synagogues, and persecute them from city to city: that upon you may come all the righteous blood shed upon the earth; from the blood of the righteous Abel unto the blood of Zacharias, son of Barachias, whom ye slew between the temple and the altar. Verily, I say unto you, All these things shall come upon this generation. O Jerusalem, Jerusalem, thou that killest the prophets, and stonest them that are sent unto thee, how often would I have gathered thy children together, even as a hen gathereth her chicks under her wings, and ye would not! Behold, your house is left desolate. Matt. 23:34-38.

Beloved readers, in case you would sincerely take to heart these words of Christ, your bones would become dry by fear. They would shake and tremble. For the fate of Jerusalem and Judah will be yours. You willfully deny that Jesus Christ is your Lord. The true knowledge of His ways you want nothing of. You desire to do as all the heathen have done from the beginning, namely, worship wood, stone, gold, silver, bread, wine, and the works of your own hands. Besides, there is your earthly, carnal, and corrupt life, which may be said not to conform in the least with the Word and the will of Him who by grace created you to His glory.

You have verily so completely rejected Christ Jesus and cast Him from you in derision that there is no doctrine, sacrament, or anything left to you which conforms to His Word. But you have instituted invented doctrines, sacraments, ceremonies, and commandments, as if Christ Jesus the only begotten Son and Wisdom of the Almighty Father, were not the true Messenger. And all those who in brotherly fashion admonish you in your damnable and mortal error, and gently reprove you, and seek to return you to Christ and to His blessed Word, must be arrested and made to suffer as rebellious heretics in all cities and countries.

Good reader, since you have ever been and still are so unthankful for His paternal grace, therefore God has shut up His mercy from you and has brought His just judgment upon you, so that there is neither right, pious, God-fearing truth, nor true teachers, nor deacons, nor Gospel, nor faith, nor Christian baptism, nor Christian Supper, nor Christian life, nor knowledge, nor truth, nor spiritual wisdom, nor judgment, nor ban, nor love, nor piety left on the earth.

Thus the house of which Christ Jesus has spoken is destroyed and the well-prepared vineyard of the Lord is without fruit and is become useless. As the prophet says, Now will I sing to my well beloved a song of my beloved touching his vineyard. My well beloved hath a vineyard in a very fruitful hill; and he fenced it and gathered out the stones thereof, and planted it with the choicest vine, and built a tower in the midst of it, and also made a winepress therein; and he looked that it should bring forth grapes, and it brought forth wild grapes. And now, O inhabitants of Jerusalem, and men of Judah, judge, I pray you, betwixt me and my vineyard. What could have been done more to my vineyard, that I have not done in it? wherefore, when I looked that it should bring forth grapes, brought it forth wild grapes? And now, go to; I will tell you what I will do to my vineyard. I will take away the hedge thereof, and it shall be eaten up; and break down the wall thereof, and it shall be trodden down; and I will lay it waste; it shall not be pruned nor digged; but there shall come up briers and thorns: I will also command the clouds that they rain no rain upon it. For the vineyard of the Lord of hosts is the house of Israel, and the men of Judah his pleasant plant; and he looked for judgment, but behold oppression; for righteousness, but behold a cry. Isa. 5:1-7.

Dear brethren, even as this judgment came first upon Israel, so it also has come upon us. For all flesh has corrupted its ways, from the greatest to the least. The heavens are iron and the earth is metal. There are found neither dew nor moisture in the vineyard of the Lord, nor ripe fruits. There is none to dig, none to prune, none to tend. Everywhere it is accursed. The walls and hedges are trampled down. It is laid waste, to be trampled upon by all men. Strangers have dominion thereof. The heathen have entered into the sanctuary and have spoiled the temple of the Lord. Our princes are rending lions; our fathers betray us; our pastors deceive us; our shepherds are wolves; our watchmen are thieves and murderers of our souls. We find nothing but thistles and thorns. All is plundered and robbed. All is torn up and broken down wherever we turn. And all this is on account of our sins. This we must confess before our God.

Yes, dearest reader, see how much worse we are than those of Sodom and Gomorrah and the other cities which God has destroyed on account of their sinfulness. If we consider rightly, we shall conceive of no sinfulness greater than that of our time; no matter how great a sin it is, such as pride, avarice, fornication, adultery, idolatry, backbiting, hatred, envy, greediness, treason, murder, disobedience to God, contrariness, lying, stealing, hypocrisy, or any other ungodliness, as may be plainly seen.

Besides, flesh passes for Spirit; falsehood for truth; sin for righteousness. Satan is Christ with this miserable, blind, erring world! Antichrist is seated in the temple of God. Pharaoh arms himself against Israel. The powerful miracles and beseeching voice of the Lord are neither seen nor heeded. Thus has this abominable darkness covered the whole land of Egypt.

I repeat, the fearful judgment of God is come upon us because of our sinfulness. As the prophet says: Your iniquities have separated between you and your God, and your sins have hid his face from you, that he will not hear. For your hands are defiled with blood and your fingers with iniquity. Your lips have spoken lies; your tongue has muttered perverseness. None calleth for justice, nor any pleadeth for truth; they trust in vanity and speak lies; they conceive mischief, and bring forth iniquity. They hatch cockatrice' eggs and weave the spider's web: he that eateth of their eggs dieth, and that which is crushed breaketh out into a viper. Their webs shall not become garments, neither shall they cover themselves with their works; their works are works of iniquity, and the act of violence is in their hands. Their feet run to evil, and they make haste to shed innocent blood; their thoughts are thoughts of iniquity, wasting and destruction are in their paths. The way of peace they know not; and there is no judgment in their goings; they have made them crooked paths: whoever goeth therein shall not know peace.

Therefore is judgment far from us, neither doth justice overtake us. We wait for light but behold obscurity; for brightness, but we walk in darkness. We grope for the wall like the blind, and we grope as if we had no eyes; we stumble at noonday as in the night; we are in desolate places as dead men. We roar all like bears and mourn sore like doves; we look for judgment but there is none; for salvation, but it is far from us. For our transgressions are multiplied before thee, and our sins testify against us; for our transgressions are with us; and as for our iniquities we know them in transgressing and lying against the Lord, and departing away from our God, speaking oppression and revolt, conceiving and uttering from the heart words of falsehood. And judgment is turned away backward and justice standeth afar off; truth is fallen in the street and equity cannot enter. Yea, truth faileth, and he that departeth from evil maketh himself a prey.

And the Lord saw it, and it displeased him that there was no judgment. And he saw that there was no man, and wondered that there was no intercessor. Isa. 59:2-16.

Dear friends, God, the just Judge, has sent His fearful judgment into this wicked world, although you do not feel it. For inasmuch as you trample upon the Son of God, deem the blood of the New Testament as unclean, and grieve the Holy Spirit of grace; therefore you are under the terrible judgment and have fallen into the hands of the living God, so that you prefer falsehood to truth, obscurity to light, death to life; and therefore God has sent you error and deprived you of His holy Word, faith, knowledge, and truth, so that you have in this world neither light nor way, nor spiritual wisdom, nor prayer, nor God, nor Christ, nor promise, nor righteousness, nor peace, nor freedom of conscience, nor inward joy, nor hope; notwithstanding you boast the name, mercy, merits, death, and blood of the Lord. Since you say that you acknowledge God, and yet do not honor and thank Him as God, therefore He has suffered you to be deceived by your sensual thoughts and your foolish heart is become obscured. You deem it but mockery to acknowledge God, therefore God has delivered you to a perverse mind, to do the things that are not convenient. Being filled with all unrighteousness, fornication, wickedness, covetousness, maliciousness; full of envy, murder, debate, deceit, malignity; whisperers, backbiters, haters of God, despiteful, proud, boasters, inventors of evil things, disobedient to parents, without understanding, covenant-breakers, without natural affection, implacable, unmerciful. Rom. 1:29-31.

You see, dear reader, God punishes mysteriously by His righteous judgment. God the mighty Lord visits this world in many different ways on account of its sins, as with imprisonment, war, bloodshed, drought, famine, pestilence, and many diseases, at which plagues and chastisements the world is amazed and frightened. Above all, the most terrible wrath of God is the removal of His divine Word. The afore-mentioned plagues, such as pestilence, famine, sword, etc., only punish us according to the flesh, and are chastisements for our correction, as the prophet says, which He inflicts in order that His children may learn wisdom. But when He deprives us of His Word, all is lost. For if we have not the Word, we verily have nothing but unbelief, blindness, error, disobedience, conceit, bitterness, an unclean, foolish, and adulterous spirit, and eternal death. How few, yes, how very few are horror-stricken at these plagues, however abundantly they have come upon them.

If someone should desire to put out a man's eyes, cut off his ears, take his life, or take from him the inheritance of his natural father, would not such a man use all his reason, wit, and wisdom to prevent such pain, shame, danger, and damage? And yet today the world is wholly blind, stone deaf. It lives but is dead. And above all it is bereft of the eternal inheritance of the merciful Father—and does not sense it. Oh, if it acknowledged its own misfortune, how diligently would it seek Him who gives sight to the blind, hearing to the deaf, and true wisdom to the foolish: Christ Jesus Himself.

The harlot adorned in fine apparel has so enchanted you, and the spirit of spiritual adultery has so kept you in its power, that I fear that your abominable unbelief, darkness, blindness, falsehood, and madness will nevermore be taken from your hearts, but that the wrath of God will remain upon you to the end. In this earthly life you will err, without any piety, from one unclean thing to another until the time that we shall be placed before the just Judge, where everyone shall receive his reward according to his works. Then, too late, your blind eyes will be opened, with sighs and empty remorse, acknowledging that you have not walked in the ways of righteousness to eternal life, but in the ways of darkness to eternal death. Ah, where will you then hide yourself from the wrath of God? Then you will cry out in terror, Mountains, fall on us, and hills, cover us. Rev. 6:16. For then there can be no more prayer, no mercy, nor repentance for the sinner. The awful sentence of a just God against all wicked, unbelieving, sinful, disobedient sinners will then begin, Depart from me, ye cursed, into everlasting fire, prepared for the devil and his angels. Matt. 25:41. It would be well for such if they had never been born.

Therefore I will not cease while I live, both verbally and by writing, as far as God the merciful Father, by His boundless kindness, gives me knowledge, spirit, grace, and wisdom, to teach and admonish all those that seek the truth, that they may rouse themselves while it is time and seek the Lord while He may be found, and call upon Him while He is near, that their righteousness may go forth as a light, and their salvation burn like a torch. This consists of nothing but to cast off the works of darkness and to put on the armor of light, to renounce all false doctrine, sacraments, false religion, and the unbecoming, dishonest, carnal life, and again to enter into the divine doctrine, the evangelical sacraments, the services and works of love, and the sincere Christian life as it was taught, instituted, and practiced by Christ Jesus, our only Deliverer and Shepherd Himself, according to the will of the Father.

Thus I labor and strive, according to the small talent given me of God, after nothing, God is my witness, than that the Day-star, the blessed Christ Jesus, the ever-shining Light, may arise in your hearts and enlighten you in all divine truth, knowledge, spiritual understanding, and wisdom, unto life eternal. Amen. II Pet. 1:19.

Dear reader, herewith I beseech you all, whether you be lord, prince, learned or unlearned, whoever you may be, to peruse these and all my writings with a pious mind. I have no doubt but you will then discover that our doctrine, which is the doctrine of Jesus Christ and His holy apostles, does not tend to sedition, discord, treason, and turmoil; but rather, yea altogether, to true Christian love, unity, and peace. Christ Jesus whom we preach is the true prince of eternal peace and not of discord. Isa. 9. Tell me, whom have we wronged? whom injured? We sincerely seek nothing but that we may serve to the salvation of all men. Not only at the cost of our chattels, shelter, gold, silver, and labor, but also, understand it in an evangelical sense, at the cost of our lifeblood.

Verily, verily, I say, If all lords and princes and their subjects who boast of the name of Christ would acknowledge the before-mentioned doctrine of Jesus Christ to be right and true, and were disposed as the doctrine, life, and Spirit of Christ require, then it would not be necessary to fortify cities and towns; to keep cavalry and infantry, nor to manufacture deadly weapons such as guns, swords, and spears. (I do not here speak of the sword of justice which is given as a punishment to the wicked and protection of the good.) The words of the prophet would then be fulfilled, They shall beat their swords into plowshares and their spears into pruning-hooks; nation shall not lift up sword against nation, neither shall they learn war any more. But they shall sit every man under his vine and under his fig tree. Isa. 2:4; Mic. 4:3, 4. It is impossible that those who have committed themselves to the doctrine, life, body, and church of Jesus Christ and remain therein, should seek or desire anything but divine love, peace, and unity; to suppress all evil and protect all good as becomes us in Christ Jesus. We will have nothing of the false prophets of the corrupt sects[17] which in many actions transgress the doctrines, rule, and measure of Christ.

Herewith we commend you to the Lord, O faithful reader. Judge for yourselves according to the Word of the Lord whether or not I have by His grace pointed out to you the truth of our beloved Lord Jesus Christ. Grace, peace, mercy, true knowledge, and life eternal be to all who in truth love Christ Jesus. Amen. Do not hide the praise of God. But let it be read and heard by all who diligently seek and desire it.

Beloved brethren, do not depart from the doctrine and the life of Christ.

[17] Menno refers to the Münsterites, Davidians, and Batenburgers who advocated various evil and unsound practices and doctrines such as polygamy. *Ed.*

# The True Christian Faith

*Van dat rechte christen ghelooue*

## c. 1541
### Revised 1556

*For other foundation can no man*
*lay than that is laid, which is Jesus Christ.*

I Corinthians 3:11

# Introduction

Menno wrote *The True Christian Faith* about the year 1541 and revised it in 1556. The 1556 edition "differs largely" from the first edition, as John Horsch reports (*Menno Simons,* 1916, p. 61). Menno himself reveals what his purpose was in the writing of this book: it was to clear his brotherhood of the charge of legalism, and to show that he and his brethren held evangelical views of faith and justification.

A brief outline of the book follows:

1. God's Marvelous Grace
2. The Roman Catholic Faith
3. The Lutheran Faith
4. The Reformed Faith
5. The True Christian Faith
6. Ten Studies in Persons of True Faith
    (1) Noah
    (2) Abraham
    (3) Moses
    (4) Joshua & Caleb
    (5) Josiah
    (6) The Centurion
    (7) Zacchaeus
    (8) The Penitent Thief
    (9) The Sinful Woman
    (10) The Syrophoenician Woman
7. A Call to Repentance and True Faith
8. Conclusion

The first section is not only a testimony to the great grace of God. It is also another eloquent plea for cessation of persecution, for religious toleration: a theme to which Menno returns again in various books. The comments on Catholicism, Lutheranism, and Zwinglianism are brief and incomplete. Lutherans would be inclined to feel that Menno had a point in his attack on the Christology of Micron (see *The Lutheran Cyclopedia,* Scribners, 1899, art. "Christology"). As to Menno's acceptance of the Melchiorite view of the incarnation—a view which the Swiss Brethren and Hutterites never accepted, and which the Dutch Mennonites soon discarded—more will be said in the introductions to Menno's fuller treatments on the subject. It may be remarked here that Menno wrote in a day when science was but poorly advanced as to understanding the role of the female in reproduction.

Through all of Menno's works there runs a strong evangelistic note. Menno looks out upon society and sees a vast host of lost sinners living in the illusion that they are going to be saved on the judgment day when Christ returns: for are they not baptized, and do they not receive the sacrament? Do not their priests and ministers comfort them with the promises of the

Gospel? Menno cries out against this false hope of heaven, sternly informing his readers from the Word of God that nothing avails before God except genuine repentance and true faith which results in a transformed life. Love for lost souls makes Menno give this witness at the risk of life and limb, the torture chamber and the rack, the sword and the stake.

The full title of this work in the Dutch is: *Of the True Christian Faith; The Faith which Converts and Changes Men's Hearts; Makes Them Pious, Sincere, New, Happy and Blessed; Together with a Discussion of the Characteristics, the Nature, Operations and Powers of Faith. Carefully Revised and Put in Better Form in the Year 1556.* In the *Opera Omnia Theologica* of 1681 this work is found, fol. 71-120 and in the *Complete Works* of 1871, I, 103-64.　　　　　　　　　　　　　　　　　　　　　　　　　　　J. C. W.

# The True Christian Faith

# 1541

••••••••••••••••••••••••••••••••••••••••••••••••••••••••••••••••••••••••••••••••••••••••••••••••••••••••

## [I.] GOD'S MARVELOUS GRACE

To all elect children of God, beloved brethren and sisters in Christ, we wish an increase of faith, grace, peace, spiritual joy, perfect righteousness, and eternal life from God our heavenly Father through Jesus Christ His only begotten Son, our Lord, who loved us and washed us from our sins in His blood. To Him be praise, honor, glory, kingdom, power, and majesty from eternity to eternity. Amen.

Dear chosen children, brothers and sisters in Christ: We are, O God, so rigorously prevented by this foolish, blind world from teaching the true Gospel of our Lord and Saviour Jesus Christ to everyone by word of mouth; and by the cruel, bloody tyranny, the agitation of our useless, wicked priests and preachers, the truth is cruelly restrained against Christ and His Word. (Those poor children seek and love dross more than gold, chaff more than wheat, lies more than truth, and darkness more than light.) Yet will God's only invincible truth, which always triumphs through the Holy Ghost, in the true children of God, bear its crown. And this in spite of the fact that it is bitten so miserably in the heel by the vanquished serpent and his seed--the proud despisers, liars, and blood-shedders—that it can scarcely stand or carry on in obedience to the Lord Jesus Christ. Nevertheless, no matter how fiercely they rave, yet this selfsame, hateful, and bloody seed and serpent must with bruised head lie quite powerless under their feet; for through the power of the Spirit and the Gospel truth in Christ Jesus he is wholly vanquished and beaten.

Since then this old crooked serpent, which from the beginning has been proud and arrogant and false, a cruel murderer, has been put under the feet of Christ and His church, and must endure and see his lying seed destroyed and trampled underfoot through the revealed truth; therefore he gnashes his teeth and breathes out the accursed, infernal breath of heresy through his prophets and preachers in the most frightful manner. He casts out of his mouth the terrible streams of his tyranny, by means of the rulers and mighty ones of the earth, at the glorious woman pregnant with the Word of the Lord, in hope of exterminating and destroying her seed. But God be eternally praised, who has protected her against the red dragon and has prepared a place in the wilderness for her.

Since then for reasons stated I cannot teach publicly, I will serve you nevertheless in writing as long as the Lord will permit me and I live, with my small talent, which the gracious Father has granted me through Christ out of the abundant treasury of His heavenly riches. I say with Paul, to serve is my desire, not with exalted words of human wisdom, for I possess and know them not. I let those seek them who desire them. My boasting, however, is with Paul to know Christ and Him crucified, for to us the knowledge of Him is eternal life. Therefore God cannot endow us with better wisdom than with this, even if it be such rank folly to the world, for she is more precious than gold and silver, pearls and precious stones; there is nothing under heaven to be compared with her. Her ways are ways of pleasantness and her paths are peace; she is a tree of life to them that lay hold upon her, and happy is every one that retaineth her.

Yes, dear brethren, everyone who is rightly taught of God in this wisdom (for it alone is the wisdom of the saints) may for the grace given him boast above all graduate doctors, theologians, jurists, orators, and poets, even though the hands of such a one cannot write nor his tongue speak, and he were the most helpless Irus[1] upon the earth. But all those who do not become acquainted with this wisdom from God, though they were as glorious as Solomon and victorious as Alexander, as rich as Croesus, as strong as Hercules, as learned as Plato, as subtle as Aristotle, as eloquent as Demosthenes and Cicero, and as expert in language as Mithridates; yes, in so great demand that the like were not seen from the beginning, nevertheless they are fools in the eyes of the Lord: this must be confessed and granted.

With this wisdom—so much as the gracious Father, the Giver of every perfect gift, has given me through His Son Jesus Christ—I desire with all my heart to serve not only our brethren and sisters but the whole world. I desire this in order that the hungry and thirsty souls who would gladly live according to the Lord's will (the Lord who created them to His honor and bought them with the blood of His Son), may be clothed from above with this heavenly wisdom and may learn to know God through His Son and Word in the Spirit: the God who says: Let not the wise man glory in his wisdom, neither let the mighty man glory in his might, let not the rich man glory in his riches: but let him that glorieth, glory in this, that he understandeth and knoweth me, that I am the Lord which exercises lovingkindness, judgment, and righteousness in the earth: for in these things I delight, saith the Lord. Jer. 9:23, 24.

Ah, dear children, you who are born of the Word of the Lord through the Spirit, ponder how incomprehensibly great the heavenly goodness and grace have been, which have been manifest unto us through Christ and have been given us of the Father. He has graciously bestowed upon us, miserable sinners, in our awful blindness, the glorious and divine gift of His wisdom. Yes,

---

[1] In Greek mythology Irus was a beggar. *Ed.*

and this He did when we knew neither God nor Christ, were strangers to the life that is of God, children of wrath and of eternal death; knowing not the word of peace, and straying like sheep who knew no shepherd. Recall that He has so graciously permitted us to find through His Spirit this great treasure, the true knowledge of the kingdom of God; the treasure which lies buried in the field and has made known to us the mystery of His good pleasure, and the true regenerating knowledge of His holy Gospel which cannot be taught in schools, nor purchased at any price, nor imported from foreign lands, nor earned by any good works. Recall that He has opened to us with the key of His Word and Spirit the saving Truth, and has closed it to all emperors, kings, lords, princes, the wise and the learned ones of the whole world. Recall that He redeemed us from the power of darkness, and according to His will and good pleasure led us into the kingdom of His dear Son. Yea, He has made us kings and priests so that we might be a chosen and holy people, a people that will serve Him in love and be His own, a people that is to publish His power, and show forth that He has called us out of darkness to His marvelous light, as Peter says. Marvelous grace and love!

Dearest brethren, rejoice in the Lord always. With Paul I say: Again I say, rejoice. The greatest of all emperors, Christ Jesus, who has all power in heaven and on earth, has manifested such grace toward us that He has called you, poor, unesteemed children, to high honor: you who are the reproach, disgrace, and shame of the whole world. He has anointed you kings and priests, kings, I say, who have been anointed with the oil of grace through the Holy Ghost, crowned with the crown of honor, clothed with the garment of righteousness, and who are reigning by Christ your emperor. You are not reigning with the weapons of death, such as muskets, spears, swords, horses, cavalrymen, and foot soldiers as the kings of this world do, but with the invincible and eternal scepter of the power of God, namely, with the sharp-cleaving sword of the holy Word, over gold, silver, cities, countries, lords, princes, flesh, blood, apprehensions, banishments, sword, stake, water, fire, hunger, thirst, nakedness, hell, sin, the law, fear, death, and the devil. You triumph gloriously by the conquering power of your faith both in life and in death, over all your foes, visible and invisible, who would fain deprive you, yes, steal from you the promised kingdom through the counsel of the serpent and his seed. The dominion and government of the spiritual king are spiritual, therefore they cannot be mortally hurt by tyranny, false doctrine, or evil lusts. For the spiritual can do all things through Christ who strengthens them, who also is their helper and redeemer, whose shield and sword is their glory.

Similarly you are also priests, sanctified of God, not with the external oil of Aaron and his sons, nor with the perishable blood of oxen and sheep, nor with any beautifully wrought garments of gold, silk, or precious stones as the law required. But you are anointed, sprinkled, and beautified with the oil of the Holy Ghost, the blood of Christ, and the garment of righteousness; ordained and called thereunto by God. Not to slay the sacrificial victims daily with a knife of steel, and not to sacrifice them upon constructed altars and literal temples of stone, or tabernacles made by hands, as Moses commanded the priests in the law; but to slay human beings all their lives with the knife of the divine Word (spiritually, of course) together with your own contrary flesh and blood. That is, you are to teach and reprove them and yourselves with the Spirit and Word of the Lord, that you and they may die to your unrighteousness and evil lusts, destroy them, and thus offer in your spiritual house or temple, not made with hands, upon the only and eternal altar of our reconciliation, Christ Jesus.

You are not the kind of priests who of your own self-righteousness sacrifice bread and wine for the sins and transgressions of the people, or for the souls of the deceased. Neither are you to sing nor read masses; nor adore, worship, or burn incense to images of gold, silver, wood, or stone, as do the poor, ignorant priests of the world. But you are holy priests who purify and sanctify your own bodies daily and in time of need; priests who sacrifice them willingly as a sweet-smelling sacrifice for the sake of the Lord's truth, together with your fervent prayers and joyful thanksgiving. This you do out of a believing, converted, pure heart, for such offerings are well-pleasing to the Lord.

Would to God that all who pose as priests were changed into such priests. Ah, how much innocent blood would remain unshed, how gloriously the truth would spread, and what a noble, Christian, precious world there would be.

Dear brethren, who can comprehend this grace in full, or relate these benefits aright? Let me repeat. We all strayed as lost sheep heretofore, as sheep who have no shepherd. We walked according to the lusts of our evil flesh, even as they all do who do not know the way of the Father. We were unbelievers and blind in regard to divine things; without understanding, full of bruises and putrefying sores from the sole of the foot to the crown of the head; and by nature children of wrath like others. But blessed be the Lord, Now we are washed, now we are sanctified, now we are justified in the name of our Lord Jesus Christ, through the Spirit of our God. I Cor. 6:11. In a word, we are converted to the true Shepherd and Bishop of our souls, Jesus Christ, who pastures us now in the rich pastures of His truth, feeds us with the bread of His Word, sustains us with the tree of life, and quenches our thirst with the water of the Spirit once more. Who can comprehend and relate this grace?

Besides this, when we were yet ungodly and enemies, He did not punish us as He did the angels that sinned, nor as the first depraved world, nor as Sodom and Gomorrah, nor as those who worshiped the calf, nor as those in the day of provocation, nor as the rebellious and adulterers, nor as those in the wilderness who acted contrary to His will and Word; for He destroyed all these. But us He spared through His great mercy, led us by His right hand, drew us by His goodness, renewed us by His Word, begat us by the

Holy Ghost, and enlightened us by the clear light of His truth. Thus by His grace we bade farewell to the world, flesh, devil, and all and freely entered upon the path of peace, beneath the easy yoke of the Gospel. Methinks this is grace, if ever there was any.

Dearest children, take heed. If now the gracious Father, according to His great mercy, has dealt so kindly with us and has manifested His love toward us without any merit on our part, then it is right and proper for us to love in return; to fear, praise, honor, and serve such a benevolent Lord, and merciful Father with all our powers; to be obedient to Him according to our little power.

Since then He has manifested unspeakable love and grace to us miserable sinners, as has been said, a love and grace which cannot be rightly grasped and understood with the blind eyes and the foolish wisdom of the flesh, it must be grasped and understood with the inward eyes of the mind and through the unction of the Holy Ghost; that is, with a sincere, sure, immovable, confident, vigorous, unfeigned, and pure faith as the Scriptures teach. Since then it requires such an unfeigned love, as has been mentioned, and since we find in the Word of the Lord that all the entire substance of genuine Christianity—such as the new birth or creature, true repentance, the dying unto sin, a new life, true righteousness, obedience, salvation, and eternal life—depends upon a sincere, active faith, according to all the Scriptures, as may be seen and read in many passages; therefore I have through the grace of the Lord conceived a plan to show to all lovers of eternal truth, by divine testimony, from the Word of the Lord, which is the true faith that avails before God and has the promise in the Scriptures; namely, which has drive, power, effect, and fruit, agreeing with the Gospel of Christ and the doctrine of the apostles. I do this in order that all those who see, read, or hear these our writings may know with clarity that the faulty, fruitless faith of the world is useless, vain, and dead, yes, eternally condemned and accursed of God. For its fruits are nothing but hypocrisy, commands of men, idolatry, and false service. It regenerates nobody, it is earthly and carnal, it hates and persecutes the truth. For this faith knows neither Christ nor Christ's Word, as may be evidently seen through the whole world. And God's Word knows of no other faith than that which has power and fruit, that which regenerates the heart, converts and renews, as the Scriptures say: The just shall live by faith.

It is all in vain to boast of faith where the godly new fruits and works of faith are not in evidence.

Therefore we exhort all the God-fearing readers in the Lord, and beg them one and all to impress it on their souls and to write it on the fleshly tables of their hearts, that our holy and Christian faith is not a dead or old opinion as the world in general thinks. Nor is it only a boasted formulation as we find among the great and persecution-free sects. It is an effective gift, the power of God; a living heavenly calling in a heart or conscience that has been opened. It firmly believes and lays hold upon and acknowledges every word of God, the threatening Law as well as the comforting Gospel, to be dependable and true. Whereby in turn the heart is pierced and moved through the Holy Ghost with an unusual regenerating, renewing, vivifying power, which produces first of all the fear of God. For it acknowledges the judgment and wrath of the Lord over all transgressions and sins which are committed against His will and Word. It becomes affrighted, fears, and is amazed before God and therefore dares not do, counsel, or agree to anything which it acknowledges through the Word, in Spirit, that God, the righteous Judge, hates in His soul and has forbidden in His holy Word.

Next, faith also produces the love of God whereby we love Him. For faith knows from the testimony of the Holy Scriptures, rightly understood in spirit, the unsearchably great riches of grace which our merciful good Father, through Christ, has so graciously granted us. Therefore it loves in return, loving God, being moved by the manifest benefit of the aforesaid grace. It is thus freely urged, through the constraining power of love issuing from such unfeigned faith, to obedience to all the commandments of God. As Christ says, If a man love me, he will keep my words. John 14:23.

Behold, this is the faith which we treat in the following composition. For it is the only faith which has the promise in Scripture of salvation and eternal life through Christ, who is the only begotten and first-born Son of God. To Him be praise, eternally. Amen.

If anyone wishes to build a good house or a high and solid tower, a solid foundation is first laid to support the heavy superstructure, lest the work begun at such expense collapse and fall down with great disgrace and loss. So also true Christians should proceed. They must have in their hearts such a sure foundation that they may stand unshaken in the building of their faith, against all the raging tempests, rains, and floods which will try them not a little; so that they may successfully bring to completion, by the help of the Lord, their undertaken work and building; lest they, with everlasting shame and loss to their poor souls, slip from the right road. Paul says, If any man draw back, my soul shall have no pleasure in him.

Faithful brethren, take heed. This precious and well-cut cornerstone, ground, and foundation in Zion, prepared for us by the Father; the foundation on which the entire edifice of our faith must be placed, is Christ Jesus alone. All who are built upon this ground will not be consumed by the fire of tribulation, for they are living stones in the temple of the Lord. They are like gold, silver, and precious stones and can never be made to collapse by such gates of hell as false doctrine, flesh, blood, the world, sin, the devil, water, fire, sword, or by any other means, no matter how sorely they are tried. For they are founded on Christ, confirmed in the faith, and assured in the Word through the Holy Ghost that they cannot be deflected from the pure and wholesome doctrine of Christ by all the furious and bloody Neros under heaven, with all their cruel tyranny.[2] They are not to be diverted from an un-

---

[2] Menno is stressing the Christian's security in Christ.

blamable and pious life which is of God, as we have seen in many places for more than twenty years past,[3] for they are as immovable as Mount Zion, like firm pillars, brave knights and pious, valiant witnesses of Christ. They have fought unto death and do so daily still (God be praised eternally). I speak of those who have the Spirit and Word of the Lord.

Yes, that stone rests so securely in their hearts and is so sealed in them by faith, that in their extremity they regard neither father nor mother, wife nor child, money nor possessions, life nor death. For they are so constrained by loving fear of God in their hearts that they do not dare, as one may see, to speak a false word in order to escape the hands of the bloodthirsty and the dangers of death. For Christ has said, He who does not confess me before men, him will I not confess before my Father, but whosoever confesses me, him will I confess in return.

But I fear very greatly, yes, indeed, it is found to be the case, that the greater part of all those who revile these poor, innocent sheep as accursed heretics, who betray, catch, banish, and take their lives and possessions; are not ashamed nor tremble before their God, who hates all lies, for the value of a nickel to call yea nay and nay yea, but make bold to boast of Christ and to call themselves after His name. If they are such liars and so unfaithful in small things, what they would do in greater things when life and possessions are involved, as is the case with these poor sheep, may be readily imagined.

O reader, reflect! If the old crooked serpent with all his deception, falsehood, and lies lived in the hearts of Christians as he does in the hearts of those who persecute them, their goods would remain unconfiscated and their blood unshed. And they would not only conceal the truth, but they would with all the children of the devil hate and oppose it. All who are born of the truth hate the lie. Conversely, all who are born of falsehood hate the truth. If they hate the truth, how could they speak it, especially when life and possessions are at stake? If our rulers and judges wish to be assured of this difference, let them call before them some of their evildoers who are guilty of death according to their decision and let them question them, without resorting to torture however, to see whether these confess their guilt, for which they are to die, as willingly as these innocent children do their faith. Yes, what is more, let your most highly renowned monks be as sternly examined, touching their profession and caps; your most accomplished priests, touching their terms and masses; as you examine these concerning their faith, and we will see how they will get along with their professions, caps, terms, and masses. The common proverb is, The wolf will manage to get his hide through the forest, but the sheep will be forced to give up his pelt.

Since then these selfsame sheep are born of the truth and have Christ together with His truth, and therefore His Spirit, dwelling in their hearts; nothing but the honest, plain truth of Christ, by which they were born unto righteousness, and converted, will be found in them. Yet it is manifest that

[3] Menno entered the Brotherhood in January, 1536; this was written in 1556. *Ed.*

no matter how piously and unblamably they live, our lying, adulterous, lewd, idolatrous, drunken priests and monks openly rob God of His glory and arrogantly murder those whom Christ purchased with His precious blood. They defame them before the whole world, betray them, and bring them to the stake. This they do for no other reason than that these sheep are compelled through the revealed truth, accompanied by their strong faith, and through the Spirit and fear of the Lord, to renounce their leaven; vain, false doctrine and idolatrous sacraments; and with all their hearts to live according to the will of God. O Lord, thus they carry on over against those who seek and fear Thee with all their hearts.

Dear sirs, when will these foul traitors, this murderous bloody seed with their Judas-like[4] betrayals, be motioned aside and turned down by you?

When will you turn your backs to their deceiving lies and face up to Christ?

When will your deadly and cruel sword be finally wiped clean of innocent blood and put back in the sheath?

When will you hear and fear God more than you do lords and princes?

When will the abominations of Antichrist be grubbed out of your heart and the doctrine of Christ planted in its place?

When will you let yourselves be put to silence by unblamable lives and have enough of the blood of innocent saints?

When will Christ Jesus with His Word, Spirit, and life be conceived in you through faith and in very deed be born in you? Never, I fear; for your heart is so earthly and carnally minded, the eyes of your understanding so darkened, that you desire the world far above heaven, lies above the truth, sin above righteousness, the honor and praise of man above the honor and praise of God.

Yes, dear sirs, why use so many words? You carry on precisely as do the priests and preachers who through the instruction of Scripture acknowledge the truth to an extent; yet because they love their poor cross-fleeing belly more than they do their God, they preach and teach only as much and as far as the mandates and decrees of the princes permit and allow, so that they may not incur the displeasure of the world and be ejected out of their worldly honor and their easy life. So it goes with you also, my dear lords. For although many of you acknowledge that the teaching, ceremonies, religion, and life of your priests and preachers are untrue, deceptive, idolatrous, false, and carnal, and that ours are the doctrine and ceremonies of the Lord, according to the Scripture; yet in order to retain the friendship of the emperor and your incomes (I refer to those who are guilty of blood), you let Christ Jesus with His innocent lambs, without any mercy, be apprehended, banished, robbed, and condemned to death if the mandates are enforced, as the worst of all rogues and scamps, deserving of all torture and shame. And then you put it this way: It is the emperor's edicts which judge you!

---

[4] Reading *Judische* (Judas-like) for *Joodische* (Jew-like). *Tr.*

Dear lords, look out, the hour is fast approaching that the Almighty, the great and terrible God, the impartial, righteous Judge of all our affairs will judge and give sentence; then you will discover too late whom you have persecuted and pierced. Therefore, rouse yourselves in time, fear God, reflect, and reform while it is still called today.

I entreat you, my reader, do not let it annoy you that I have digressed so far; for it was not done without a cause. But now, in the name of the Lord, we will go on in the thing we have undertaken. We will treat and teach as much of it as the merciful Father grants us grace and aid, so that we may modestly show to all God-fearing consciences who seek the truth from their hearts, the real difference between belief and unbelief, between the fruits of faith and the fruits of unbelief. We desire that they may thus grow in the true Christian faith, until the gracious Father, out of the abundance of His glory, strengthens them with strength in the inner man through the Spirit; and till Christ dwells in their hearts through faith, so that they, rooted and grounded in love, may be able to comprehend with all the saints what is the breadth and length and depth and height and to know the abundant love of Christ which passes knowledge, and be filled with all the fullness of God. And besides, that they may discover that it is all hatred and lying which the scribes teach and invent touching the matter of our faith, and also concerning all other matters such as the sword, sedition, polygamy, etc. I refer to that which I and my beloved colleagues preach and teach, verbally and in writing, publicly or privately, to all well-meaning hearts.

Cordially, beloved brethren: when we can with spiritual eyes discern the impure, ugly doctrine concerning faith, with all the fearful unbelief and bewildered evil life resulting from the awful doctrine of those who make their boast of Christ, then we may rightly be grieved to death at their great blindness and grievous errors. For no matter how hatefully and cruelly they carry on, they dare nevertheless to call it the holy Christian faith.

## [II.] THE FAITH OF THE PAPISTS

It is true enough that the papists teach and believe that Jesus Christ is the Son of God, that He sacrificed His flesh and shed His blood for us. But they also say that if we wish to partake thereof and share in it we must obey the pope and belong to his church, hear mass, receive the holy water, go on pilgrimages, call upon the mother of the Lord and the deceased saints, go to confessional at least twice a year, receive papistic absolution, have our children baptized, and keep the holy days and fast days in Lent.[5] The priests must vow "chastity"; the bread in their mass must be called the flesh of Christ, and the wine the blood of Christ; and they must do all their other idolatry and abominations, besides, which are daily practiced by them, as may be witnessed.

[5] Menno himself had been a priest, 1524-36. *Ed.*

And all this the poor, ignorant people call the most holy Christian faith and the institution of the holy Christian church. Although actually it is nothing but human invention, self-chosen righteousness, open seduction of souls, manifest deception of the soul, an intolerable make-a-living and gain of the lazy priests, an accursed abomination, provocation of God, shameful blasphemy, an unworthy despising of the blood of Christ, invented notions, and a disobedient refusal to bow to the holy Word of God. In short, a false, offensive religion and open idolatry, things concerning which Jesus Christ, to whom the Father points, has not left nor commanded us a single letter.

And this is not yet enough, that they practice such abominations. But they proceed also to despise as vain and useless all the true fruits of faith, commanded by the Son of God Himself: the genuine, pure love and fear of God, the love and service of our neighbors, and the true sacraments and worship. They also revile them as damnable and heretical, and exterminate and persecute them. I think this may by all means be rightly considered a sect!

## [III.] THE FAITH OF THE LUTHERANS

The Lutherans teach and believe that faith alone saves, without any assistance by works. They emphasize this doctrine so as to make it appear as though works were not even necessary; yes, that faith is of such a nature that it cannot tolerate any works alongside of it. And therefore the important and earnest epistle of James (because he reproves such a frivolous, vain doctrine and faith) is esteemed and treated as a "strawy epistle."[6] What bold folly! If the doctrine is straw, then the chosen apostle, the faithful servant and witness of Christ who wrote and taught it, must also have been a strawy man; this is as clear as the noonday sun. For the doctrine shows the character of the man.

Let everyone take heed how he teaches. For with this same doctrine they have led the reckless and ignorant people, great and small, city dweller and cottager alike, into such a fruitless, unregenerate life, and have given them such a free rein, that one would scarcely find such an ungodly and abominable life among Turks and Tartars as among these people. Their open deeds bear testimony, for the abundant eating and drinking; the excessive pomp and splendor; the fornicating, lying, cheating, cursing; the swearing by the wounds of the Lord, by the sacraments and the sufferings of the Lord; the shedding of blood, the fightings, etc., which are found among many of them have neither measure nor bounds. Preacher and disciple are as alike as two peas in a pod in regard to many carnal deeds. What I know I write, and what I have heard and seen I testify, and I know that I testify the truth.

All they ask is that men say, Bah, what dishonorable knaves and scamps these confounded priests and monks are! The devil take them, the rascal pope with his shorn crew have deceived us long enough with their purgatory, confes-

[6] Written by Luther in 1522 (Erlangen ed., vol. 63, p. 115). But in the preface to James in his Bible of 1534 Luther omitted this phrase. *Ed.*

sion, and fasting. We now eat whenever we get hungry, fish or flesh as we
please, for every creature of God is good, says Paul, and nothing to be rejected.
But what follows in Paul's statement they do not understand: namely, them
which believe and know the truth and partake with thanksgiving. They say further, How miserably the priests have had us poor people by the nose, robbing
us of the blood of the Lord, and directing us to their peddling and superstitious
transactions. God be praised, we caught on that all our works avail nothing,
but that the blood and death of Christ alone must cancel and pay for our sins.
They strike up a Psalm, *Der Strick ist entzwei und wir sind frei*, etc.[7]
(Snapped is the cord, now we are free, praise the Lord) while beer and
wine verily run from their drunken mouths and noses. Anyone who can but
recite this on his thumb, no matter how carnally he lives, is a good evangelical
man and a precious brother. If someone steps up in true and sincere love to
admonish or reprove them for this, and points them to Christ Jesus rightly,
to His doctrine, sacraments, and unblamable example, and to show that it is
not right for a Christian so to boast and drink, revile and curse; then he must
hear from that hour that he is one who believes in salvation by good works,
is a heaven stormer, a sectarian agitator, a rabble rouser, a make-believe
Christian, a disdainer of the sacraments, or an Anabaptist!

Behold in this way does the righteous Lord permit those to err and grow
callous in their hearts who make the precious death and the most holy flesh
and blood of our Lord Jesus Christ, the Son of God, together with His saving
and reverent Word, a device for luxury, and make them an occasion for their
unclean and sinful flesh. It seems to me this verily may also be called a sect,
free and easy!

## [IV.] THE FAITH OF THE ENGLISHMEN [ZWINGLIANS]

The Englishmen,[8] or Zwinglians, believe and confess that there are two
sons in Christ Jesus; the one is God's Son, without mother, and not subject
to suffering, and the other is the son of Mary, or the son of man, without
father, and subject to suffering. And in this son of Mary, subject to suffering,
the Son of God, not subject to suffering, dwelt; so that the son of Mary, who
was crucified and died for us, was not the Son of God. So one of their principal
preachers, Martin Micron[9] by name, contended before me; also one Hermes

[7] The German hymn to which Menno refers was an adaptation of Psalm 124:7. It was
used to celebrate the release from Rome and the accompanying freedom to worship in an
evangelical way with government approval, a situation that in Menno's mind was hardly
consistent with fidelity to Christ's Gospel. *Tr.*

[8] These people called Englishmen by Menno were Dutch Protestants who had fled to
England where under Edward VI they enjoyed religious liberty. With the accession of
Bloody Mary they had to flee and after much suffering en route they finally came to Emden
where Menno and his followers met them. *Tr.*

[9] Martin Micron (1522-59)—his real name being Martin de Cleyne—was a Zwinglian
reformer in London, Frankfurt a.M., and East Friesland. *Ed.*

of Ronsen (if I recollect his name correctly) two or three times in a large assembly in the year 1554.

Further, the said Micron, when I questioned him concerning the seed of the woman, a matter about which we had had some words in our first conference, acknowledged and said: I will have to grant that a woman has no procreative seed but only a menstrual flux. Before God it is the truth that I write. He also wrote in a tract printed in England of the congealing of this menstrual flux in the womb of Mary (those are his words). If such congealing took place as the tract says, and since he grants that a woman has no more than a menstrual flux, as stated, then it is evident that they believe (if they agree with him) that their Saviour is not God's first-born and only begotten Son, but has His origin in the unclean, loathsome catamenial flux.

John a Lasco[10] also writes that Christ assumed no other flesh than that which was subject to sin in order that He might be subject to temptation and to death. He states in the same book, If He is holy, why was He sentenced in the Father's judgment for the sake of sin, a matter which I cannot understand otherwise before God, than that he believes that the man Christ Jesus was a sinful Christ and guilty of death. Read his defense of the incarnation made against me; there his position may be read.

May God watch over all true hearts that they may never believe such intolerably great abominations. I am filled with loathing and shame surges in my soul that I must broach these things before men, for they are too offensive. But these people defame and slander us daily before all men, by word of mouth and in writing, saying what a very detestable view and doctrine of Christ we have because we confess with the Scriptures that it was the first and only begotten Son of God who died for us. Since they recite these unspeakably ugly things before the poor, sinful people as related, and deceive them so miserably therewith, therefore I am constrained in my conscience, to the honor of God and to the warning of all God-fearing souls, to write this and present it to the reader to ponder, whose mind is held captive by them. For I verily do not know how we could believe more disrespectfully concerning Christ; teach, feel, think, or speak than to say, it was not the Son of God who died for us, but it was an unclean catamenial flux, a man of sin and death.

And if they should want to go back on me and say that I have gone beyond their representations, it was stated so repeatedly and before so many pious hearts that they cannot go back on me. It will in the day of righteous judgment be found before the eyes of the great and eternal Majesty to be as I have related it here. What an abominable sect!

## [V.] THE TRUE CHRISTIAN FAITH

We teach and believe, and this is the thrust of the whole Scriptures, that the whole Christ is from head to foot, both inside and outside, visible and

---

10 John à Lasco (1499-1560) was a Zwinglian Reformer, a native of Poland. *Ed.*

invisible, God's first-born and only begotten Son; the incomprehensible, eternal Word, by whom all things were created, the first-born of every creature. We teach and believe that He became a true man in Mary, the pure virgin, through the power of the Almighty, eternal Father, beyond the comprehension and knowledge of man. He was sent and given unto us by the Father out of mere grace and mercy; the express image of the invisible God and the brightness of His glory. We teach and believe that the first-born and only begotten Son of God, Jesus Christ, is our only and eternal Messiah, prophet, teacher, and high priest. He has fulfilled the requirements of the law for all His believers,[11] inasmuch as they could not do it on account of the weakness of their flesh. He taught us the will and good pleasure of His Father, went before us in an unblamable example, and freely offered Himself upon the cross for our sins. He was a sweet-smelling sacrifice to the Father, the one through whom all we who sincerely believe have received the pardon for our sins; and grace, favor, mercy, liberty, peace, life eternal, a reconciled Father, and free access to God in the Spirit; and all this through His merits, righteousness, intercession, and blood, and not through our own works. Behold, this is in reality the summary of our belief concerning Christ, our Saviour, the Son of God.

All who can believe this as certain and true are sealed through the Word of God in their spirit, are inwardly changed, and receive the fear and love of God. They bring forth out of their faith righteousness, fruit, power, an unblamable life, and a new being, as Paul says: With the heart man believeth unto righteousness. Through faith, says Paul, God cleanses our hearts. And so the fruits of righteousness follow out of an upright, unfeigned, pious Christian faith. Take note carefully.

All those who sincerely believe the righteous judgment of God and His eternal wrath over all sin and wickedness, and do not in their spirit doubt it, these are mindful of the fallen angels, of the first depraved world, of Sodom and Gomorrah, of disobedient, rebellious Israel. They take particular notice of how God humbled His innocent Son who knew no sin, and in whose mouth no guile was found; humbled Him, and made Him the most miserable among men because of our sins. Yes, He was so flogged and mocked that, hanging on the cross, He, the innocent One, complained to His Father saying, My God, my God, why hast thou forsaken me? Matt. 27:45. All, I say, who truly believe this will flee from all unrighteousness as from the fangs of the serpent. They will turn away from all sins, and avoid them more than a burning fire or a piercing sword, for their whole mind and conscience testifies to them that if they knowingly and willfully sin against the law and Word of God, and do not receive Christ in a pure and good conscience; if they live according to the flesh and despise the pleading voice of God, they will fall under the dreadful, eternal sentence and wrath of God.

This the pious and aged scribe Eleazar believed; and the God-fearing,

---

[11] Theologians refer to this as Christ's active obedience. His passive obedience culminated in His death on Golgotha's cross. *Ed.*

virtuous mother with her seven sons (II Macc. 7:1) ; the three faithful young men in the fiery furnace; the beloved Daniel, and the fair, virtuous Susanna, the honorable pattern of all pious women. They considered it preferable to endure for a season the wrath and fury of tyrants than to sin and so provoke the eternal anger and wrath of God.

The just shall live by faith, say the Scriptures. For the true evangelical faith which makes the heart upright and pious before God, moves, changes, urges, and constrains a man so that he will always hate the evil and gladly do the things which are right and good. Just as it is unnecessary to admonish or warn a man of understanding not to cut his own throat or to drink poison, not to jump from a high tower or into deep water; for he knows very well that if he does he cannot escape death; so also it is unnecessary to admonish or warn those who sincerely believe that the wages of sin is death, that drunkards, liars, fornicators, adulterers, the avaricious, idolators, those who despise God, hate, shed blood, swear falsely, steal, etc., shall not inherit the kingdom of Christ. It is unnecessary to warn such not to get drunk, nor to commit fornication, etc. The divine fear proceeds from such a faith; warns, exhorts, disciplines, urges, and deters them so that they will nevermore consent to such carnal, ungodly works, much less do them. For their faith, which is sealed unto them by the Spirit, through the Word, teaches them that the end thereof is death.

You see in this way we must believe with the heart, as Paul says. That is, we must so adhere to the Word, so receive and impress it upon our hearts, that we never turn from it or let ourselves be turned from it. But we allow it to root ever deeper in our hearts so that by its power we fear God with all our hearts, and sincerely repent of our sins. Honest, unfeigned fear drives out sin, for it is impossible to become righteous without the fear of God.

Observe what an excellent, pleasing fruit of faith the fear of the Lord is. It really is the power which expels, buries, slays, crushes, and destroys the sins of believers, and is the first part of true repentance, as we are taught and admonished by the baptism of believers. The fear of the Lord is the beginning of wisdom; a good understanding have they that do his commandments; his praise endureth forever. Ps. 111:10.

Further, all who comprehend with a sincere, unwavering, believing heart, the great solicitude and diligence of God for us (I speak humanly of Him) and His unbounded kindness, mercy, and love, as paternally manifested toward us through Christ Jesus; that He did not spare His eternal Son by whom He created the heavens and the earth, the seas and the fullness thereof, His incomprehensible, eternal Word, power, and wisdom; but for our sakes gave Him over, humbled Him, suffered Him to endure hunger and thirst, to be reviled, apprehended, mocked, His holy face spit upon, to be scourged, crowned with a crown of thorns, condemned, crucified, and slain, so that we through His weakness and stripes might attain to health; through His poverty to wealth, through His humiliation to glory, through His cursing to blessing, through

His punishment to grace, through His blood to pardon, through His sacrifice to reconciliation, and through His death to eternal life—I say, all who believe that He also created every living creature for our use and made them subject to us by the Word; that He serves and provides and aids us with winter and summer, heat and cold, night and day, rain and drought; that He sent His holy apostles with His Word, endowed us with His Spirit, enlightens, governs, admonishes, reproves, and comforts us; has given us the necessary shelter and food to supply our wants, and keeps and sustains us by His grace in the midst of a crooked and ferocious generation; these I say, who can believe this with all their hearts, grasp and apprehend it, can never be prevented, neither by angels nor devil, neither by life nor death, from loving this gracious Father most heartily, who has manifested so great love and mercy toward us grievous sinners; yes, praise, honor, thank, serve, and obey Him all the days of their life.

For this is the greatest delight and joy of believers: that they in their weakness may walk and live according to the will and Word of the Lord. For it cannot fail that where the unfeigned, pure love of God dwells, there must also be the willing, ready service of that love, the keeping of His commandments. The book of Wisdom says, They that put their trust in him shall understand the truth, and such as are faithful in love shall abide with him. Wisd. 3:9. This is what Paul says, in Jesus Christ neither circumcision availeth anything, nor uncircumcision; but faith, which worketh by love. Gal. 5:6.

That love is of such an effective power and nature may be seen in natural love. We do not have to admonish reasonable parents to provide their children with necessary food and clothing, for natural love will admonish them to these things. Similarly, a husband and wife who sincerely love each other count it no hardship willingly to serve each other and do things together as is proper, they being one flesh. So is also the nature and property of holy, divine love. For all those who by faith are one with the Father and with His Son Christ Jesus in love and spirit, through the true and genuine knowledge of the afore-mentioned favor, these do not have to be admonished to serve the Lord, to seek the kingdom of God, to use baptism and the Lord's Supper according to the ordinance of Scripture, to exercise control over heart and tongue, to ponder the law and will of God with all earnestness, to obey Christ and follow Him; and not to love gold and silver, money and possessions, wife and children, life and death above Christ and His Word. For the natural result of the ardent love of God, which is of a pure heart, good conscience, and unfeigned faith, urges and constrains, moves and operates in their hearts so effectively that they are prepared with body, soul, possession, and blood, to do what He has commanded and to leave undone that which He has forbidden as we may see (God be praised) and hear in great plainness and power daily in many pious hearts.

And hereby it is evident that if we wish to love God and walk in obedience to His commandments we must believe, have an eye for His favors, and with the heart cling closely to the Word of His promise, as has been said. For love which is sincere is a noble, precious fruit, it is a branch and plant of faith from which the second part of true repentance issues, namely, the unblamable new life, represented to us by baptism, as related above, out of the fear of the Lord. Without this love all eloquence, all tongues, all knowledge and understanding, all boasting of faith, knowledge, miracles, prophesying, alms, persecution, cross, and suffering are vain before God, yes, barren and dead.

He that loveth is born of God and knoweth God, for God is love. In such a one all things proceed according to the nature and Word of the Lord, for it is the fulfilling of the Law, the obedience to His commands, the bond of perfection and peace, prefigured by the splendid girdle of Aaron and his sons.

Love, says Solomon, is as strong as death; jealousy is as cruel as the grave. The coals thereof are coals of fire, which have a most vehement flame; many waters cannot quench love. Yes, so firm and strong and ardent is love that it surpasses everything, conquers and consumes what is opposed to Christ and His Word, be it world or flesh, tyrant or devil, sin or death, or whatever we may think of or name; and this is all through the power and Spirit of Jesus Christ from whom it originates.

Moses went before with fear, and Christ followed with love. First, the terrifying law, and afterwards the comforting Gospel. Wrath is first experienced in our consciences, and after that grace; first disquiet, then peace; first sorrow, then joy. In short, first the letter which killeth, then the Spirit which maketh alive.

Behold, my reader, such a faith as mentioned is the true Christian faith which praises, honors, magnifies, and extols God the Father and His Son Jesus Christ through loving fear and fearing love, for it recognizes the good will of the Father toward us through Christ. It recognizes, I say, that all the promises to the fathers, the expectation of the patriarchs, the whole figurative law, and all the prophecies of the prophets are fulfilled in Christ, with Christ, and through Christ. It acknowledges that Christ is our King, Prince, Lord, Messiah, the promised David, the Lion of the tribe of Judah, the strong One, the Prince of Peace, and the Father of the age to be; God's almighty, incomprehensible, eternal Word and Wisdom, the firstborn of every creature, the Light of the world, the Sun of Righteousness, the True Vine, the Fountain of Life, the true Door and Shepherd of the sheep, the true Foundation and the precious Cornerstone in Zion, the right Way, the Truth and Life, the promised Prophet, our Master and Teacher, our Redeemer, Saviour, Friend, and Bridegroom. In short, our only and eternal Mediator, Advocate, High Priest, Propitiator, and Intercessor; our Head and Brother.

And since faith confesses all this, therefore, I say, it also observes His Word aright, hears His voice, and faithfully follows His example and counsel, and departs from ungodliness. For the heart is changed, the mind is renewed, and with Moses it clings to the promises as if they were in sight. It patiently waits for them with pious Abraham until with all the elect it occupies and inherits them in the true and eternal reality.

Now faith, says Paul, is the substance of things hoped for, the evidence of things not seen. Heb. 11:1. He says, further, But hope that is seen is not hope, for God, Christ Himself says, is a Spirit; His Word and grace are spiritual; the promise of the New Testament is spiritual; His kingdom and dominion likewise; and therefore we have to judge and evaluate all things through an upright, pure, and sure faith with a candid heart, and judge and see with spiritual eyes. But we may well say with Paul, that faith is not every man's possession.

All those who stop their ears to the rebuking, threatening, and slaying Law and refuse to fear God; all who reject the gracious promise of Christ, refuse to love God, shut their eyes to the light of righteousness, and will neither see nor walk the straight way, but harden their hearts, and will not acknowledge the just judgments, the wrath and displeasure of God, His mercy and favor and His great grace, these are unbelievers. For they reject Christ Jesus, walking boldly on the way of wickedness. They choose for themselves righteousness and a means of salvation contrary to the Word of God; the wisdom of the Lord they consider folly, His truth they hold to be lies, His Gospel a delusion; the virtuous Christian life passes for madness; and the true use of His sacraments for heresy. Open idolatry, human commandments, superstitions, and ugly lies are their greatest comfort and truest worship. Their belly is their God; they love the world more than they do heaven. All their delight is in raking and scraping, in pride and pomp, gold and silver, money and goods. Their buying and selling take place with cheating and tricking. Drinking, gambling, cursing, swearing, hatred, strife, and fighting are the order of the day. They follow the flesh and its lusts. They defame and seek their neighbor's hurt, dishonor, disgrace, and shame. In short, with the fool they say in their hearts, There is no God. Ps. 14:1.

Although they boast of God with the mouth, praise His name with their lips, bow their knees outwardly before Him, and say that they are redeemed with the death and blood of Christ, it is nevertheless all hypocrisy. For they do it mechanically from habit and in appearance; not inwardly through faith, in power and truth. They are those of whom it is written: They profess that they know God, but in works they deny him; being abominable and disobedient, and unto every good work reprobate. Titus 1:16. And all this because they do not believe Christ and His Word. Their end is death. As He says, He that believeth not shall be damned, yes, is already condemned.

What Paul says is true: Without faith it is impossible to please him; for he that cometh to God must believe that he is, and that he is a rewarder of them that diligently seek him. Heb. 11:6. Oh, what an open heart, what profound understanding! Yes, if we grasp these words aright we have reason to be astonished at His wisdom and understanding. For if we ponder the matter rightly, we must confess before the Lord who tries our reins and hearts that we never believed with the heart that God is, and hence we have led a vain, ungodly life. For it cannot be otherwise than that if anyone believes with all his heart that God is, he will also believe that His Word is true, that the wages of sin is death, that all things are open to His eyes, and that there is nothing concealed before Him, and that we must give an account of all our thoughts, words, and deeds before His judgment seat in the day of His coming. Believing all this, we begin to tremble before such an omniscient and righteous Judge, yes, to fear from the inmost heart and tremble greatly.

Again, I say, all who believe with the heart that God is, also believe that He is true, and that therefore none can be saved contrary to His Word. For He is the God of truth, and in Him there is no untruth. His uttered Word abides; it can neither be bent nor broken. Believing this men begin to fear His righteousness and cast behind them all trumped-up consolation, all false promises, all the bolsters and cushions of the false prophets, and they seek the Lord who has bought them. They become small in their own eyes, for the heart is humbled. They sigh and weep, pray and lament, knock and clamor before the throne of grace until they are heard and encouraged by the word of His peace, comforted and raised up with the promise of His grace, and anointed with the Holy Ghost.

Moreover, all who believe that God is also believe that He is gracious and merciful, that He has sent and given His only Son, that He has taught us the right way, fulfilled the Law for us, reconciled us to the Father, and redeemed us by His blood and bitter death. He has conquered hell, the devil, sin, and death, and has obtained grace, favor, mercy, and eternal life. And so the sorrowful, afflicted hearts are refreshed which previously saw only the terrible threatening law, nothing but the wrath of God, and eternal death. They become confident, satisfied, and joyful in the Holy Ghost. They get a joyful spirit, and so are made to belong to their Head and Saviour, united and made one with Him, ingrafted through the Spirit of God and pure, unfeigned love. They are of one heart, one soul, and one spirit with Him; they think, speak, and live, in their weakness, as He has taught and commanded them in His Word. They renounce and avoid all false doctrine, all unbelief, all false sacraments, and all idolatry, together with the spotted garment of sin, which is the evil perverted life, which is of the flesh.

They seek the doctrines and sacraments commanded them of Christ, that religion which is taught in the Scriptures, and that pious and blameless life which is from God. For by faith they are changed in the inner man, converted and renewed, and have a sealed and assured conscience which bears witness to them that God is, that He is righteous and true, gracious and merciful. And therewith they desire and seek and do nothing, either inwardly or outwardly, but that which they know through the Word that Christ Jesus with His holy apostles has commanded and taught them.

Behold, my brethren, now you see what is the real nature of a true Christian faith, and what a great mystery it is, what a mighty meaning,[12] spirit, and power are contained in these simple words: He must believe that

---

[12] *Bediedinge* (meaning) for *bedieninge* (administration). *Tr.*

God is. Whosoever believeth in him has eternal life. John 3:15. He that believeth and is baptized shall be saved. Mark 16:16. Whosoever believeth on Him shall not be ashamed (Rom. 10), and like passages. For it will never fail. Where there is a true Christian faith, there also will be a man dead to sin, a new creature, true repentance, a sincere, regenerated, and unblamable Christian. We no longer live according to the lusts of sin, but according to the will of Him who has purchased us with His blood, has drawn us by His Spirit, and begotten us by His Word, namely, Christ Jesus.

But as surely as faith is in the mouth only, so certainly, no righteousness, no change, no renewed spirit, no penitent life follows; no, nothing but unbelief, hypocrisy, and lies. No matter how much we may talk or argue about the Scriptures, this rule will remain firm and can never be broken: If ye live after the flesh, ye shall die. Rom. 8:13. All therefore who live in pomp and splendor, in eating and drinking, in adultery, fornication, avarice, hatred, envy, gluttony, fraud, and such sins; who defame the Lord's holy and high name, Word, will, and also His church; who slander their neighbors, deprive them of their honor, name, welfare, body, and goods; who curse and swear by the Lord's sufferings, wounds, sacraments, cross, and death, are unbelieving heathen and not believing Christians. This is as clear as the light of day. For their fruits testify before the whole world that they are not the true olive tree and vine from which we may pluck or gather the true, ripe fruits. For where men seek help in the doctrines and commandments of men, use a strange baptism, Lord's Supper, and divine worship, one which Christ has not taught; where they seek the remission of sins by foreign means, such as holy water, masses, confessionals, pilgrimages, etc., there they walk in a perverted Christian path. Christ and His Word are not believed. This all must confess who have only natural discernment and understanding. But all who acknowledge Christ to be the Son of God, and His Word the truth, acknowledge that His commandments are eternal life. These seek no other worship, Word, sacraments, or means of reconcilation, nor any other way of life than that which Christ, God's own Son, presented and taught them by the Word of His truth.

In this it is evident that where sincere and true faith exists, the faith which avails before God and is a gift of God, which comes from hearing the holy Word, there through the blossoming tree of life all manner of precious fruits of righteousness are present, such as the fear and love of God, mercy, friendship, chastity, temperance, humility, confidence, truth, peace, and joy in the Holy Ghost. For where a sincere, evangelical, pious faith is, there also are the genuine evangelical fruits in keeping with the Gospel.

I say evangelical fruits. For the strange fruits such as infant baptism, masses, matins, vespers, caps, crucifixes, chapels, altars, bells, etc., the Gospel knows not. For God has not commanded them, neither through Christ His Son nor through the apostles and prophets. For which reason they are abominations and not believing fruits, even as the golden calf was with Israel, the worship of Baal, the high places, altars and churches, and the rite of making their children pass through fire.

The true evangelical faith sees and considers only the doctrine, ceremonies, commands, prohibitions, and the perfect example of Christ, and strives to conform thereto with all its power. For as fire in its nature can produce nothing but fire and flame, the sun nothing but light and heat, the water yields moistness, and a good tree good fruit after its implanted nature, so also genuine, evangelical faith produces true evangelical fruit and that after its true, good, evangelical nature. Yes, as an honest, virtuous bride, by virtue of the nature of natural love, is ever ready to hear and obey the voice of her bridegroom, and from the sincere, pious heart, good will, and love, which she has for him, will ever so conduct herself before him as before her most faithful friend and beloved husband, whom she respects and loves with all her heart, always willing for his sake to endure whatever may at any time befall her; so also it is with a sincere, regenerate, believing soul who has been espoused to Christ by grace through faith, and become one with Christ through His ardent love. She is ever willing and prepared to do His bidding and will, be it bitter or sweet, for the sake of His holy name; to endure whatever may come his way in evil as well as in good report, be it joy or tribulation, enough or hunger, refreshing drink or thirst, honor or dishonor, in good report or bad, in prison or at liberty, in exile or at home, in comfort or in discomfort, in life or in death. Such a soul partaking of her bridegroom's nature and disposition is pious in heart and thought, true in words, and well seasoned. All her ways are righteousness, piety, serpentlike wisdom, dovelike innocence, a genuine, pious disposition, faithfulness, zeal, peace, fervent prayer, unblamable conduct, a sincere, pure, brotherly love, and voluntary obedience to Christ and His holy Word. For the righteous live by faith, as the following examples from Holy Writ plainly show by the grace of God. Amen.

## [VI. TEN STUDIES IN PERSONS OF TRUE FAITH]

### [A.] The Faith of Noah

The Scripture testifies concerning Noah, the son of Lamech, that he found grace before the Lord, that he was a righteous man, unwavering, and that he led a godly life in his generation. Peter calls him a preacher of righteousness. High and glorious is the testimony given in Scripture concerning this man.

When all the world was depraved before God, and the earth was full of wickedness, the sons of God looked upon the daughters of men that they were fair, and they took them wives of all whom they chose, and would not allow themselves to be reproved by the Spirit of God. Then the Lord said, I will yet give them respite for a hundred twenty years. And He gave Noah a com-

mand that he should make a ship or ark by which he and his house might be
saved from the coming deluge, for God the Lord was about to destroy the whole
world with water.

With all his heart Noah believed the Word of his Lord concerning the
punishment. He kept it in mind as if he saw it before him with his eyes. He
began building as he had been commanded, for he believed with his whole
heart that the threatened punishment would come.

When the afore-mentioned years were past, and the disobedient, wicked
world repented not, the Word of God was ready to be fulfilled. Noah and his
family entered the ark with all clean and unclean creatures, as God had commanded. And on the same day that he entered the ark, the fountains of the
great deep were broken up and the windows of heaven were opened. It rained
forty days and forty nights, till all the high mountains upon the face of the
whole earth were covered fifteen cubits deep, and all creatures upon the earth
that had in them the breath of life: human beings, birds, beasts, and creeping
things were destroyed and drowned. Only Noah and his family, together with
the animals which were with him in the ark, were saved. For he was preserved by means of the ark, by the power and grace of Almighty God, in whom
he had trusted with all his heart.

Through faith, says Paul, Noah honored God. He prepared the ark for
the salvation of his house when he received a divine commandment of things
which were not yet seen, by which he condemned the world, and became heir
of the righteousness which is by faith.

Lovely example, glorious pattern of a firm, unshaken faith! For because
he believed his God, he was upright and unwavering. He believed the threatened punishment as firmly as though it were already present. I repeat, as
though it were already present before his very eyes. Therefore he labored
so many years and through the Spirit of Christ which is eternal he warned
the unbelieving, disobedient spirits of men led captive by sin to repent and
reform. He feared the Word of the Lord, for he doubted not that it would
happen as the Lord had spoken, for he knew full well that the Word of the
Lord would surely come to pass. As Esdras has it, O Lord, thou spakest
from the beginning of the creation, and saidst thus, Let heaven and earth be
made; and thy word was a perfect work. II Esd. 6:38.

And when he had preached and built forty years, eighty, a hundred (the
Scriptures do not say how long he was engaged in the building) he did not
become weak in faith by the long delay, for he well knew that the punishment
of God would come upon the impenitent, because He had formerly told him
so. He also believed that he and his family would be preserved by the mercy
and grace of Him who promised, for He is the God of truth and no lie is found
in Him.

The Lord God warned the pious Noah and said, The end of all flesh is
come before me, for the earth is filled with violence through them, and behold,
I will destroy them with the earth. Gen. 6:13. So also has He now through

His own blessed Son, through His holy prophets and apostles, with His holy Word, truthfully warned us and said: If ye repent not, and are not born of God, do not believe in Christ, walk not in His commandments, do not reform your wicked lives, but serve strange gods, and continue haughty, proud, ambitious, adulterous, bloodthirsty, malicious, unjust, idle, earthly, fleshly, and devilish, you will die in your sins, and will not enter into the kingdom of heaven. You shall be condemned and shall be cast into the fiery pool. You must inherit eternal woe and pain with all the accursed and devils. You may have no part nor communion in the kingdom of Christ to all eternity.

My reader, take heed. If we with the upright and godly Noah observe the faithful warnings of Christ and His Holy Spirit and believe with the whole heart, believe, I say, the Word of God to be true and unchangeable, and that the threatened punishment must come in time, even though it should be delayed a thousand years (I advise every one to watch, for all who die in their sins have already received their punishment, for the time of grace is then already expired), then we would undoubtedly fear and tremble to the inmost of our souls at the wrath and punishment threatened in the Scriptures against all the impenitent, and which will be eternal in its duration. We would pray to God for grace, would clothe ourselves in sackcloth and hairy tunics, would truly repent, reform the wicked life, follow after righteousness, and with our new and spiritual Noah, Christ Jesus, enter into the new and spiritual ark which is His church, ever watching lest the deluge of the coming wrath of God overtake us unexpectedly, with all the unbelieving and impenitent who know neither God nor Christ, neither Spirit nor Word, as it overtook the corrupt antediluvian world, as has been said. Yes, we would sincerely watch for the coming of the Lord, give heed to the time of grace, and preserve our wedding garment. We would have oil in our lamps, that our house be not unseasonably broken through, and we would not with the guest who had not a wedding garment be cast forth from the Lord's wedding into outer darkness to remain eternally outside.

But alas, because we do not believe the threats, punishments, wrath, and judgment of the Lord and pay little attention to the example of Scripture, therefore we say with the mockers, Pshaw, where is the promise of His coming? Do not all things continue as they were from the beginning since the fathers fell asleep? It will, I fear, go with us as it did with the unbelievers and disobedient in the time of Noah and Lot. Sudden punishment came upon them, and as one may plainly see and read concerning the coming of the Lord. I say once more, that because we do not believe the threats, judgments, and wrath of the Lord, but disregard them, therefore do we lead such a reckless, unbridled life, and therefore do all the wicked fleshly desires. We eat and drink, build, sow, reap, and marry without any fear or care. We rake and scrape, amass money, property, gold, silver, and say in our hearts boldly, There is peace and freedom, till swift destruction overtake us.

Again I say, Let everyone take care and watch. The messenger with his

peremptory summons is already at the door and will say, Render an account;
thou mayest be no longer steward. But if we with the unwavering and pious
Noah firmly believed the coming endless wrath and punishment, if we really
believed that which is promised as a future reality to all true children of God,
we would undoubtedly not be found so inattentive, drowsy, and indifferent.
But with deep seriousness, without delay, we would rise from our ugly sin,
separate ourselves from our grievous errors, and that as much as we would
shun the roaring, hungry lion or a bloodthirsty enemy. We would also watch
with open eyes all our days lest the Good Man of the house overtake us sleeping, and that without a watch, or find us striking our fellow servants, or eating
and drinking with gluttons, and so give us our portion and lot with the hypocrites. Concerning this watching read Matt. 24; Mark 13:37.

### [B.] *Abraham's Faith and Obedience*

Abraham, the highly renowned patriarch, was without an equal in honor,
as Sirach has it, because he believed God, and with his whole heart relied on
His Word. Therefore he showed obedience and power in his faith. The Lord
commanded him and said: Get thee out of thy country and from thy kindred,
and from thy father's house, unto a land that I will show thee: and I will make
of thee a great nation, and I will bless thee, and make thy name great; and
thou shalt be a blessing: and I will bless them that bless thee, and curse them
that curse thee: and in thee shall all families of the earth be blessed. Gen.
12:1-3. When Abraham heard the command he believed his God and consulted neither with physical comfort nor with reason. But he humbled himself,
and did not strive nor dispute with God in whom he trusted, and by whose
command he went forth. He did not ask to know beforehand to what land
he should go. He believed his God with his whole heart, was obedient, and
went forth at once with Sarah his wife, as God had commanded, not knowing where he should go. He reposed upon the promise of God, firmly believing that He would not deceive him, for he well knew that He was a God who
was true, dependable in all His words, and would therefore bring him into such
a country as He had promised him.

Behold how simple and plain, obedient and full of confidence is true Christian faith, as may be seen in this patriarch! Compare your faith and its fruits
with Abraham's faith and its fruits, and I presume you will discover that you
have not yet become his faithful seed and children. For it is manifest that
you are stubborn and unbelieving, so fleshly and earthly minded that you would
not surrender a clay hut, a paltry bed, a cow, or a horse, for the sake of the
testimony of the Lord, nor endure a hard word, not to mention forsaking father
or mother, friend or fatherland, for the sake of your faith, and with Abraham
travel with wife and children to a strange land.

Cursed unbelief keeps the whole world from the truth, for how many say,
We know that you have the truth, but what shall we do? We are poor and

along in years; we can no longer labor and earn; we have a house full of children and cannot earn our bread in other lands, and we fear at times that the Lord might not care for us, as He did for Abraham, etc. Others say, We have much property, we are young in years and may live long, father and mother are against it; the wife says, My husband opposes me, and the husband says, My wife is against me—and the like unbelieving fleshly excuses and anxieties. They never take to heart nor understand that the mouth of the trustworthy Christ has richly promised shelter, food, clothing, and every necessity, if only they continue in His Word. David says, I have been young, and now I am old; yet have I not seen the righteous forsaken, nor his seed begging bread. Ps. 37:25.

Faithful readers, observe. If we had as firm a faith and as sure a confidence as this godly man, and dared trust from the heart the living God, oh, how little should we trouble ourselves with such cares as the Gentiles have concerning shelter, food, drink, clothing, and shoes. For we well know that Christ, God's own Son, has promised that if only we seek the kingdom of heaven and His righteousness, and make an honest attempt to earn our livelihood, He will not forsake us to all eternity, but will supply all our necessities, for He cares for us.

Second, observe his faith. When it was reported that Lot, his brother's son, was taken to Sodom by Chedorlaomer the king of Elam and his confederate kings, Abraham rose up with three hundred and eighteen of his servants and followed after the afore-mentioned king. He overtook them in the night, and slew them, and retook all their goods, together with Lot, the prisoners, and their wives. Gen. 14:16.

Here the faithful father showed his love out of his faith, fearing not the power of four kings. He trusted in the living God, he risked his own life and that of his servants, confidently, in order that he might rescue his oppressed kinsman from the hands of his enemies. This is an example to all the spiritual children of Abraham that they should so love their brethren who are with them, born of the incorruptible seed of the holy divine Word, that they will not only assist them with money and goods, but also in an evangelical manner, risk and give their lives for them in time of need. I say, in an evangelical manner, for to aid with the sword is forbidden to all true Christians.[13] In the New Testament all true believers should suffer patiently and not fight and do battle with swords and muskets. But if we wish to save or gain our neighbor's soul by the help of the Spirit and Word of our Lord, or if we see our brethren in need or peril, driven forth for the Word of the Lord, then we should not close our doors to them, but receive them in our houses and share with them our food, aid them, comfort them, and assist them in their tribulations, etc. In such a manner we should risk our lives for our brethren, even if we know beforehand that it will be at the cost of our lives. This example we have in Christ,

---

[13] In common with the Swiss Brethren and the Hutterian Brethren, Menno and the Dutch Anabaptists held to the Biblical doctrine of absolute love and nonresistance. *Ed.*

who for our sakes did not spare Himself, but willingly yielded His life, that we through Him might live.

In the third place, observe that when to Abraham the promise was given that his seed should be as numerous as the stars of heaven and that they should be strangers in a strange land, that they should be compelled to serve and be cruelly treated four hundred years, etc., he believed; believed, I say, and his faith was reckoned to him for righteousness. He waited with patience and it was fulfilled in its time; he murmured not nor disputed with God because his seed was to suffer so greatly for so many years.

This is an admonition to all true Christians to cling to the Word of the Lord with all the heart, and to hold firmly to His promise. For God is a God who cannot forget or break His Word. Heaven and earth shall pass away, but His Word shall abide forever. All who trust in it, to them it shall be counted for righteousness, as it was counted to Abraham.

Through faith he saw the promise from afar, he saw it and comforted himself therewith. So also in our case. The promise of the future eternal life is given us through Christ and we are informed at the same time that for His name's sake we must suffer much from this perverted and wicked generation. This promise is seen from afar, and all who sincerely believe it and comfort themselves therewith will doubtlessly receive it in due time, however hard and long they may be persecuted and tormented by this evil Egyptian people. For although the children of Abraham were grieved with much sorrow and pain for some hundreds of years, yet did the Lord, according to His promise, lead them forth victoriously, and gave them the promised land. So it will be with us if we doubt not the promises, but cling to them with a firm faith as did Abraham, and through faith fear the Lord who gave them.

If we honor Him, thank Him, serve Him, and walk in His commandments, possessing our souls in patience, no matter how lamentably we are persecuted, oppressed, smitten, robbed, and murdered by the hellish Pharaoh and his fierce, unmerciful servants, burned at the stake or drowned in the water, yet shall the day of our release arrive, and all our tears shall be wiped from our eyes. We shall be gorgeously arrayed in the white silken robes of righteousness and follow the Lamb and sit down in the kingdom of God with Abraham, Isaac, and Jacob, possessing that noble and pleasant land of endless eternal joy. Praise God, ye who suffer for Christ's sake, and lift up your heads, for the time is near when ye shall hear, Come, ye blessed, and ye shall rejoice with Him forever.

Notice in the fourth place that Abraham received a command from God that he and also his male children of eight days old should be circumcised, with all his servants, those who were born in his house, and those who were bought: and that this should be a covenant sign between God and him. He did not become vexed nor rebellious against God, neither did he complain nor murmur against Him on account of the great pain he had to suffer in his old age: such a dishonorable and disgraceful ceremony, whereby he could neither praise God nor help or serve his neighbor. But he obeyed and believed the Word of the Lord, and submissively accomplished it without delay, knowing full well that no grace or blessing would be his unless he believed God's Word and did as he was commanded; for obedience inherits the promise.

Once more, the simple, plain submission and willing obedience of Abraham's faith are made manifest by its fruits. For if he had followed flesh and blood or taken counsel with it, he undoubtedly would not have obeyed, but he would have lodged charges against God, or at the least have said, No, Lord, it shall not be so, for this sign will profit me nothing, for Thou art not praised thereby nor my neighbor served. And all the heathen who know not Thy name will mock at it as a foolish work from the very nature of the ceremony. Oh, no! He did not reply against the Lord, but he believed it and performed it, and it was reckoned to him for righteousness, and he was called the friend of God.

This is for the encouragement of all the pious, that they should believe and submissively follow the Word of the Lord, however heretical and ridiculous it may appear to them, not murmuring against the Lord why He has so commanded it. It is enough that they should know that He has commanded them, and in what manner He has commanded.

Again, it puts to shame all haughty despisers and unbelieving mockers who so presumptuously open their blasphemous, wicked mouths against Christ and say, Pshaw, what can baptism profit us? Or, Why does God demand so much water? It is enough if we are inwardly pious men, regard the commands of love, and lead a pious, virtuous life; and such like hypocritical words. For these poor hypocrites do not know that when the inward man, of which they boast, has become upright and pious in God through faith, through the grace, Word, and Spirit of the Lord, then he dare not depart one hair's breadth from the Word and ways of the Lord, but willingly does all things whatsoever the Lord has commanded him, let it be what it will.

Since it is more than clear that Christ Jesus has commanded water baptism upon the confession of our faith, that He received it Himself, that the holy apostles did not teach nor practice any other, that their signification and effect have no other meaning, and so many glorious promises are attached thereto, as may plainly be seen and read (understand me rightly, not by virtue of the wrought sign itself, but because we receive Christ in whom the Father gave the promise through faith, and because we are ready to live according to His Word), therefore, tell me, how shall one obtain the accompanying promise if he does not do what is commanded?

But what is the actual situation? All who do not believe the Lord's Word would rather have money, property, body, and life than Christ. These are earthly and carnally minded. They are those who strive against Christ, disobey the Scriptures, dispute and say, What can water benefit us? If they with Abraham believed the Word of the Lord from the heart, and had become new and changed men in Christ Jesus through the power of the same faith; if they were able to love their enemies, do good to those who ill-treat them, pray for those by whom they are persecuted; if they were ready to forsake possessions and all that they have and are for the glory of the Lord, and if they were ready to give it for needed service of their neighbors; if they were prepared, not to reject the cross of the Lord but were dead unto flesh and blood; if they feared God and His judgments and loved Him for His kindness; then they would undoubtedly not murmur so and dispute against God. They would be ready with Abraham to seal their faith by its fruits, to receive the commanded baptism, to accommodate themselves to all obedience, and according to their weakness walk in the Lord's commandments, as His Word teaches all true Christians.

Since they do not believe Christ and His Word, neither fear nor love Him, therefore they revile, blaspheme, despise His holy doctrines, Spirit, commandments, prohibitions, ordinances, and usages as deceiving heresy, and obedience to Him as an open abomination. O reader, beware! God the Lord is a God who adheres to His Word so firmly that He brought calamity upon Adam and Eve and their posterity on account of the forbidden fruit. For a small transgression Uzzah was punished with death. II Sam. 6:7. On account of one transgression, the faithful Moses was not permitted to enter the promised land. Whoever received not the bloody sign of circumcision was to be cut off from among the people. From this it may be plainly seen that He wants His Word and will to be obeyed if we wish to be saved. For He is the God who has made heaven and earth and the fullness thereof; the Almighty, terrible God, who lives forever in His majesty and glory, a mighty Lord and ruler over all. Woe to him who speaks against Him and despises His Word and will! The works of such a one testify plainly that he does not believe in Christ, and whosoever believeth not, as Christ Himself declares, is condemned already. Therefore it is all in vain to make excuses, or to attempt evasions. How anyone who is so unbelieving and rebellious that he refuses God a handful of water[14] can get himself to love his enemies, to mortify the flesh, to serve his neighbor, and to take up the cross of Christ, I will leave the serious reader to reflect in the fear of his God.

I know for certain that all their disputation, excuses, and evasions are nothing but fig leaves, and their lives nothing but hypocrisy.

In the fifth place, observe when the Lord had spoken to Abraham that at the end of the year he would return, and that Sarah his wife should have a son whom he should call Isaac, and that he would make His eternal covenant with him and his seed after him, though he was nearly a hundred years old, and Sarah ninety, nevertheless he doubted not. He did not consider his own senility and the barrenness of Sarah, but firm and strong in faith he trusted the promise of his God and praised Him for His grace. For he knew that God was able to perform that which He had promised. Therefore, from this same Abraham, because he believed the Word of God, came descendants as many as the sand which is by the sea or the stars in heaven. Gen. 22:17.

[14] All the Mennonites, Dutch and Swiss, practiced baptism by affusion, not by immersion, in the first century of their history. *Ed.*

Behold, most beloved, how an upright, genuine Christian faith regards God as almighty and true, who can and will do all that He has promised. And therefore Abraham looked not upon the senility of himself and Sarah. He doubted not the promised words but believed without wavering, for he knew well that the same God who created heaven and earth, and the fullness thereof through His Word, who had spread forth the heavens and had given the rushing, surging sea its bounds, whose Word sustains the earth in the midst of the water, who rules all with the word of His strength and gives life to the dead, could undoubtedly, if He chose, render fruitful the aged body of a woman which before was barren.

Since then such a promise was given to him of God, he neither doubted nor questioned God's power, but hoped for that which by nature was not to be expected in his case, and especially not in that of Sarah. Through faith in God he received that which was promised to him, namely, his son Isaac, born of the aged and barren Sarah. In like manner it is with us in spiritual matters. If we believe with the whole heart the promised Word of grace, which is the Gospel of peace, whereby the redemption from our sins through the blood of the Lord is made known, then our dead conscience is revived and made to blossom. We receive the spiritual Isaac, Christ Jesus, eternally blessed and bring Him forth in conduct. As Christ said, My mother and my brethren are those who hear the Word and will of God, and do accordingly; but whosoever believeth not this "Isaac," receives not Christ, but the wrath of God abides upon him.

In the sixth place, observe how severely the Lord tried the faith of Abraham when He said, Take now thy son, thine only son, Isaac, whom thou lovest, and get thee into the land of Moriah, and offer him there for a burnt offering upon one of the mountains which I shall tell thee of. Gen. 22:2. Abraham obeyed the Word of the Lord and complied. He took his son with him and went to the place which the Lord had commanded him, and when they had arrived there, Isaac said, Father, behold here is fire and wood, but where is the lamb that shall be offered? Abraham answered his son and said, My son, God will provide him a lamb for a burnt offering.

Ah, beloved, ponder this, this conduct and conversation of Abraham and his son Isaac! I suppose reason will teach you how full of trouble and grief the mind of the father was on account of his darling son, since Abraham was flesh and blood no less than we are. To think that that chosen child, miraculously born to him in his old age through the promise and gift of God, his only son of a free woman, the desire, the joy, and the peace of his heart, the staff of his age, in whom he received the comforting promise, had to be slain and burnt with fire!

No matter how hard and sorely his flesh was assailed, yet he did not oppose God with a single word, nor did he say, Why hast Thou given me a son since he must die? Neither did he reprove the Lord, saying that He was making His own words untrue, seeing that it was through Isaac that the promise was made. But he trusted his God with his whole heart and he humbled his reason and wisdom, and did not follow sense nor flesh. He spared not his beloved son for the Lord's sake. Loving his God far above his child, he refused not to offer him willingly as a burnt sacrifice to Him from whom he had received him. He bound him and lifted him upon the wood and raised his hand and knife to slay him. He believed that God could raise him again from the dead. He proceeded to obey the command which he had received, when an angel spake from heaven saying, Lay not thine hand upon the lad, neither do thou any thing unto him, for now I know that thou fearest God; seeing thou hast not withheld thy son, thine only son from me. Gen. 22:12. And so the obedient, believing Abraham received his son as a type of the resurrection. The word of James is true: Abraham believed God, and it was imputed unto him for righteousness, and he was called the friend of God. Jas. 2:23.

Dearest children, take notice. We must, must we not, when we compare our weak faith and its little fruit with the faith of Abraham, bow our heads in shame. He refused not to travel in unknown lands as soon as he was commanded. He was a man full of peace and sought not his own interest, but he released Lot out of the hands of his enemies. He believed the promise concerning the promised land and the promised seed, never murmuring on account of the long time nor of the oppression of his seed. He suffered himself to be circumcised in advanced age. He believed the Lord's promise concerning Isaac and taught all his servants and children that they should follow the way of the Lord and do that which was right. He was willing to offer Isaac as the Lord had commanded him. Methinks this may truly be called faith.

So entirely was this pious man dead to himself that he denied all his desires, his will and mind, and loved his God alone. He trusted, feared, loved, and honored his God with all his heart and so walked according to His commandments, as is evidenced by his conduct from many passages of Scripture.

But what kind of faith our false and popular Christians possess, who pose as the seed of Abraham, I will let their fruits make out. For they rake and scrape, curse and swear, lie and cheat, primp and parade, eat and drink to excess, commit fornication and adultery, fight, rob, steal, swindle and trick, being full of idolatry and wickedness. Those who have a little light refuse to remove from one village to another, or from one city to another, for the sake of the Word and truth of the Lord. They seek their own advantage and have little use for brotherly love. They are earthly minded and therefore evade the cross of Christ. The promise and goodness of the Lord they do not love, they fear not His coming judgment and punishment, and they love the creature more than the Creator whose name is blessed forever. Amen.

In short, I know not what it is in which they do not live to themselves, doing with it as their god orders.[15] Nevertheless they boast themselves to be Abraham's children and heirs of Abraham's promise. Ah, no, my friends! Your prophets mislead you, and your false hopes deceive you. As the Lord

[15] That is, their carnality or their belly. *Tr.*

lives, I tell you, if you believe not His Word with the whole heart, nor through the power of the same faith walk in His ways, if you bring not forth the Christian fruits of righteousness and do not follow the obedient footsteps of this pious patriarch, then you are not his seed and children, neither have you his faith nor his promise. But all who impress Christ in their hearts through faith, and receive and bear Him by faith, and in faith cling to His Word and obey it, these are the spiritual children of Abraham and heirs of his promise. For they are reckoned to be his seed.

### [C.] *Moses' Faith and Faithfulness*

Similarly Moses, a servant and messenger of God, was also found faithful, alert, living his faith, and active in it. He was called of the Lord to lead Israel out of Egypt. He did not pride himself that he should be a great ruler, but humbled himself before God with all his heart and said, Send, Lord, whom thou wilt, but what am I that I should go to Pharaoh and lead forth Israel? Besides I am slow in speech, heretofore, as well as since thou hast spoken unto thy servant. He refused until the Lord became angry. With fear and trembling he at last took upon himself the assigned task, and surrendered himself to his God in whom he trusted.

Confidently he appeared before the cruel Pharaoh and performed great signs and wonders before him and all his servants. He delivered the people through the outstretched arm and strong hand of God. He divided the Red Sea, and passed with Israel unharmed through the deep. Ex. 14:21, 22. He received the tables of stone on which were written the commandments of the Lord and by the ministry of angels. He caused bread to rain from heaven, and water to flow from the flinty rock. He prepared the tent or tabernacle of the testimony, as it was shown to him upon the mount. He ordained the literal priesthood with all its duties, sacrifices, sanctifications, attire, etc., according to the commandment of the Lord.

He went with the people, pitched the tent and took it down again at the command of the Lord. He gave the people commandments and statutes of the Lord. He stood as a faithful mediator between God and the people when they had sinned, and he turned God's wrath from Israel. Sternly he punished idolaters, fornicators, and the rebellious. He slew Sihon, the king of the Amorites, and Og, the king of Bashan. The Lord was with him in all his ways.

By faith, says Paul, he refused to be called the son of Pharaoh's daughter; choosing rather to suffer affliction with the people of God, than to enjoy the pleasures of sin for a season; esteeming the reproach of Christ greater riches than the treasure in Egypt: for he had respect unto the recompense of the reward. By faith he forsook Egypt, not fearing the wrath of the king; for he endured, as seeing him who is invisible. Through faith he kept the passover, and the sprinkling of blood, lest he that destroyed the firstborn should touch them. Heb. 11:24-28.

Good reader, note carefully the Word of the Lord. When we with spiritual eyes examine such holy examples, and contrast them with the unbearable pride, haughtiness, avarice, idolatry, disobedience, and unfaithfulness of the rulers of the whole world; and with the blind, mad, deluded unbelief of the common people; then we must acknowledge that they are still far from the obedience and active faith of Moses. Yes, they are unbelieving heathen, and not Christians.

Moses believed his God, and therefore he acted rightly in all his affairs. He was kind, diligent, and solicitous for the welfare of the people entrusted to him. He was the meekest of men, and served neither for gift nor reward. He obeyed the voice and Word of the Lord, was faithful in all his house, and faithfully performed his duties in the fear of the Lord. He faithfully commanded in God's name and in upright love, admonishing the people that they and their descendants from generation to generation should heed the voice of the Lord, the God of their fathers, and should follow no other customs, commandments, righteousness, or worship than that which he had taught or commanded them until the new prophet, the teacher of righteousness, the blessed seed of Abraham, Christ Jesus, should come.

But if we should go to our rulers, lords, princes, bishops, priests, monks, and preachers, and all those who boast of the name and faith of Christ, and compare their faith and obedience with the Word of the Lord, the thing that matters, to see if there are any who sincerely seek Christ from the heart; who fear, love, believe, and trust Him; who teach and practice rightly the ordinances, commandments, sacraments, and true worship of God; who conform their whole lives, both inwardly and outwardly, to the Word and example of the Lord; and who in love perform the service laid upon them as did this faithful Moses in all his affairs, then I fear we would have to go far and search long and find but few. And if there are some, they must be, alas, given as a prey to the bloodthirsty, and bear the cross of the Lord.

I confess the truth in Christ and lie not. All fail to hear the voice of Christ who do not believe His holy Word, do not follow His pure, unblamable life from the whole heart, in all humility, patience, meekness, obedience, and love. These do not have the working and living faith of Moses, but these are, after the contents of his doctrines, already judged. Ah, reader, take care! Neither money, name, nor boasting will avail you, but power and deeds, if you wish to be saved and not condemned.

### [D.] The Faith of Joshua and Caleb

It was also through faith that Joshua and Caleb crossed the Jordan and entered the promised land. When Moses sent out the twelve spies to view the land, he said: Get you up this way southward, and go up into the mountain: and see the land, what it is; and the people that dwell therein, whether it be strong or weak, few or many; and what the land is that they dwell in, whether it be good or bad; and what cities they be that they dwell in, whether in tents, or in strong holds; and what the land is, whether it be fat or lean, whether there be wood therein, or not. And be ye of good courage, and bring the fruit of the land. Now the time was the time of the first ripe grapes. Num. 13:17-20.

They went up and spied out the land, even as Moses had commanded them from the mouth of the Lord, and after forty days they came to Moses and Aaron and to the whole congregation in the wilderness of Paran to Kadesh, carrying with them grapes, pomegranates, and figs, saying: We came unto the land whither thou sentest us, and surely it floweth with milk and honey; and this is the fruit of it. Moreover, we saw the children of Anak there. Caleb stilled the people before Moses and said, Let us go up at once and possess it, for we are well able to overcome it. But the men that went up with him said, We be not able to go up against the people; for they are stronger than we. And they brought up an evil report of the land which they had searched unto the children of Israel, saying, The land through which we have gone to search it, is a land that eateth up the inhabitants thereof, and all the people that we saw in it are men of great stature. And there we saw the giants, the sons of Anak, which come of the giants: and we were in our own sight as grasshoppers, and so were we in their sight. Num. 13:27-33.

And all the congregation lifted up their voice, and cried, and the people wept that night. And all the children of Israel murmured against Moses and against Aaron: and the whole congregation said unto them, Would to God that we had died in the land of Egypt! Or would to God that we had died in the wilderness! And wherefore hath the Lord brought us unto this land, to fall by the sword, that our wives and our children should be a prey? Were it not better for us to return into Egypt? And they said one to another, Let us make a captain, and let us return unto Egypt. Then Moses and Aaron fell on their faces before all the assembly of the congregation of the children of Israel. And Joshua and Caleb rent their clothes, and they spake unto all the company of the children of Israel saying, The land which we passed through to search it, is an exceeding good land. If the Lord delight in us, then he will bring us into this land and give it us, a land which floweth with milk and honey. Only rebel not ye against the Lord, neither fear ye the people of the land; for they are bread for us: their defence is departed from them, and the Lord is with us: fear them not. But all the congregation bade stone them with stones. Num. 14:1-10.

Worthy reader, these two faithful men believed the Word and promise of God with all their hearts, as if they had already obtained them, and trusted firmly in His almighty power, paternal mercy, and great works. They saw the awful unbelief, and heard the bitter murmuring of their brethren; they saw that it detracted from the Almighty Majesty, as if He were unable to fulfill His promises unto them, and as though He had deceived them by His word of promise. They were very sorrowful and sad and rent their clothes, as has been said. And therefore they were the only two persons of the six hundred thousand that had come with Moses out of Egypt, who entered into the promised land. All the rest died in the wilderness during the time of forty years, and did not reach the promised land because they did not believe in the Almighty God, the God of their fathers, Abraham, Isaac, and Jacob; the God who with such marvelous signs and wonders had led them through the Red Sea and had so graciously sustained and kept them in the wilderness.

Thus also it is with some at the present day. They have spied out the pleasant land, have seen and tasted its precious fruits, have been enlightened by the Word of the Lord, have tasted the heavenly gifts, have partaken of the Holy Spirit, have tasted of the sweet Word of God, and the power of the world to come, and have beheld the kindliness of the Lord. But they do not reckon with the Lord but with their own sinful, disobedient, evil flesh, which always seeks its own pleasure, and will not willingly bear the cross of the Lord. Therefore they behold with carnal eyes that many powerful tyrants and fenced cities are arrayed against them; that they have to pass through a howling wilderness and must ascend many high mountains; that they must give as a prey, honor, money, possessions, wife, child, body, and life; hence they murmur against Moses and Aaron and seek to stone Joshua and Caleb. They cause their poor teachers and leaders who with true love point them to the Word and example of Christ, and preach the pure truth, intolerable suffering and trouble. They slander and defame beyond measure and choose for themselves here and there a leader, false prophet, or teacher, who with fair words and under false pretense leads them back to Egypt. They prefer temporal to eternal things; they fear perishing man more than the immortal, eternal God, the Lord and Creator of all things. With unbelieving, carnal Israel they say in their hearts, We are not strong enough to go up against this great and strong people, and are not able to obey the doctrine, ordinances, and example of Christ, for all the world is against us, all the lords and princes persecute us, all preachers and priests revile and defame us, and we must become a byword and a derision to all the world. We are much too weak to bear such great misery.

Therefore they want to lay it upon the Lord. This they think, and in so doing err, for their unbelieving carnal hearts have blinded them that they know not the righteous judgment of God. They have no hope that a holy life will be rewarded, and esteem not the honor which will be the portion of an unblamable soul.

Dear reader, take care! For as the Lord lives, I tell you, all those who reject the Word of the Lord in this way become unbelievers once more, and become so earthly and carnal minded that they fear those whom they ought not to fear, and fear not those whom they should fear. They think more of the perishable things, such as home, land, gold, silver, wife, children, life, and limb, than of the everlasting God and His eternal kingdom. They have a greater desire to enjoy physical peace for a year or two, the dark Egypt of this ungodly world; than to inherit the pleasant fruitful land in endless peace with God. They forget that such shall all perish in the wilderness, and unless they repent shall never enter into His rest. Heb. 4:1.

But those who with Joshua and Caleb cling to the Word of the Lord, who firmly believe on Christ, as the Scriptures say, who are firmly assured in their hearts by the Holy Ghost that God will not fail in a single word, but that He will in His time give all that He has promised to those who do not allow themselves to be vanquished by the gates of hell, nor deceived by the subtle lies and philosophy of the learned ones, nor frightened by the tyranny of the bloodthirsty, nor vanquished by carnal lusts, nor enchanted by the fine appearance of false prophets, but walk humbly in the King's highway, follow Christ, their Shepherd and Leader, and govern all their ways by His Spirit, Word, and perfect example; who turn not aside neither to the right hand, nor to the left, behold, these are they who will enter victoriously into the spiritual promised land, the eternal rest and peace, God's eternal kingdom and glory, with all the saints and believers, through grace, eternally inheriting it with Christ, as Joshua and Caleb inherited the literal land through faith, and with their children inherited it. O children, believe it! All things, says Christ, are possible to him that believeth. Mark 9:23.

## [E.] *The Faith of Pious King Josiah*

Josiah, an illustrious and pious king in all his works, did that which was pleasing to the Lord, and walked in all the ways of his father David, and departed not therefrom, neither to the right hand nor to the left. When he was yet a child he began to seek the God of David, his father. In the eighteenth year of his age he sent Shaphan, the scribe, and Hilkiah, the high priest, to give money to those who worked at the house of the Lord. And Hilkiah said to Shaphan, I have found the book of the Law in the house of the Lord, and Hilkiah gave the book to Shaphan, and he brought it to the king.

And when the king heard the words which were written in the book, he rent his clothes as one affrighted before his God. He believed the Word of the Lord, and feared the coming wrath which was threatened in the book which was found. At once he sent Hilkiah, Ahikam, Achbor, Asahiah, and Shaphan, saying: Go ye, inquire of the Lord for me, for the people, and for all Judah, concerning the words of this book that is found: for great is the wrath of the Lord that is kindled against us, because our fathers have not hearkened unto the words of this book, to do according unto all that is written concerning us. II Kings 22:13.

So they went to Huldah, a prophetess, the wife of Shallum, and asked her as Josiah had commanded them. The woman answered them, Thus saith the Lord God of Israel: Tell the man who hath sent you unto me: Thus saith the Lord, behold, I will bring evil upon this place, and upon the inhabitants thereof, even all the words of the book which the king of Judah hath read, because they have forsaken me, and have burned incense unto other gods, that they might provoke me to anger, with all the works of their hands; therefore, my wrath shall be kindled against this place and shall not be quenched. But to the king of Judah which sent you to inquire of the Lord, shall you say thus: Thus saith the Lord God of Israel, as touching the words which thou hast heard, because thine heart was tender and thou hast humbled thyself before the Lord when thou heardest what I spake against this place and against the inhabitants thereof, that they should become a desolation and a curse, and because thou hast rent thy clothes and wept before me, I also have heard thee, saith the Lord. Behold, therefore, I will gather thee unto thy fathers, and thou shalt be gathered into thy grave in peace, and thine eyes shall not see all the evil which I will bring upon this place. And they brought the king word again.

Now when the king heard these words, he sent and gathered unto him all the elders of Judah and Jerusalem. And the king went up into the house of the Lord, and all the men of Judah and all the inhabitants of Jerusalem with him, and the priests, and the prophets, and all the people, both small and great: and he read in their ears all the words of the book of the covenant which was found in the house of the Lord. The king stood by a pillar and made a covenant before the Lord to walk after the Lord and to keep his commandments and his testimonies and his statutes with all their heart and all their soul, to perform the words of this covenant that were written in this book. And all the people stood to the covenant. And Josiah caused all who were to be found in Israel to serve the Lord, and they departed not from Him as long as Josiah lived.

Observe, dear reader, what kind of faith Josiah had, and what the fruits thereof were. He heard the Word of the Lord and believed it. He rent his clothes, inquired of the Lord, and renewed the covenant. For he heard what God had commanded in the same book: that they should not do according to their own thoughts, that they should not follow after strange gods, nor the abominations of the Canaanites and the other heathen which were dispersed before them, but that they should serve the Lord alone and cleave to Him and keep His commandments, statutes, and ordinances as he directed them. He was strong in the Lord, with manly courage, and acted valiantly in all his doings. For he believed and trusted God with all his strength, and with earnest zeal he tore down all that his forefathers and the former kings out of their own imaginations and choice had introduced and established as holy service.

He burned all the vessels of Baal and tore down all the groves,[16] high places, and altars in the land of Judea and Samaria. He defiled Topheth in the valley of the children of Hinnom. He destroyed the horses sacred to the sun, and burnt the chariots of fire. He broke down the altar of Bethel after

[16] The "groves" of Israel were properly *Asherah,* a goddess of fertility, to whom the Jews set up wooden poles or masts for idolatrous purposes. *Ed.*

he had sacrificed the idol priests and dead bones thereon, as the man of God had proclaimed against this altar in earlier times. He destroyed all that was opposed to and contrary to the Law of God. He kept the Passover of the Lord as it was written in the book of the covenant in such a glorious manner as no judge or king had kept it before. He also swept away all soothsayers and necromancers, all images and idols, and all the abominations that were seen in the land of Judah and Jerusalem, in order that they might perform the words of the Lord which were written in the book that Hilkiah, the high priest, had found in the house of the Lord. There was no king like unto him that turned to the Lord with all his heart, and with all his soul and with all his might, according to all the Law of Moses; neither after him arose there any like him. II Kings 23:24, 25.

Hearken now, O mighty princes and kings, and all those who suffer themselves to think that they are believing rulers and Christian princes. To you is my admonition. If you have any fear of God, any love to Christ or His blessed Word, or any reasonable nature—you who have understanding —then acknowledge that you are not gods from heaven, but poor mortal men of the impure, mortal seed of Adam. Humble yourselves under the almighty hand of God, and compare this Josiah and his faith and works with yours, in order that you may learn to know how far you are from the Spirit and Word of Christ, and that you bear nothing but a vain and empty name.

When Josiah was still a child and young in years, he feared God and manifested a mature mind and understanding in all his works. But you, my dear lords, fear neither God nor the devil. Cursed unbelief is your mother, and Belial-like unrighteousness your sister. In divine things you are blind, deaf and dumb, foolish as irrational children.

Josiah was eight years old when he was made king, and in the eighth year of his reign, he began to seek the God of his father David. But your seeking from the cradle on is nothing but pomp and splendor, bold haughtiness of heart, gluttony, immorality, adultery, riding, hunting, fencing, enlargement of your domains, increase of patronage and treasure, fighting, warring, taxing, and fleecing, to afflict the destitute and poor; to domineer over one another, and to live with all your might according to the lusts of the flesh, freely and carelessly. The open deed testifies that I write the truth.

Josiah began in the twelfth year of his reign to cleanse Judah and Jerusalem in the high places, groves, idols, and molten images. But you build them up in every city, village, street, and alley, upon every high mountain and in every deep valley. And whoever dares to admonish you about this with the Spirit and Word of Christ must be a heretic and must tread the press of sorrow.

Josiah cared for the house of the Lord, and appointed and paid craftsmen to labor thereat. But you break down, and by your wicked, cruel mandates, tyranny, and the sword, hinder the house and dwelling of Christ, which is His church, which He has sanctified by His Spirit, cleansed by His blood, and adorned with the Word, ordinances, and sacraments of His Father, lest it be begun again in its apostolic clearness, and finished in its doctrines, sacraments, and conduct, according to the command of Christ and His holy Word.

Josiah swept out all necromancers and soothsayers. He sacrificed the idolatrous priests upon their idolatrous altars and burned the dead bones, etc. But the bones of the man of God from Judah and of the prophets of Samaria he burned not. But you sustain and protect as shepherds of the flock of Christ and keepers of your souls, false prophets and deceiving priests, largely public drunkards, seducers, and idolaters, full of unrighteousness, with hearts shot through with covetousness; men whose belly is their God, blind watchmen and dumb dogs, thieves of God's honor; murderers of poor, miserable souls. You have them in preference at your courts, and give them the foremost seats at your tables. They are honored with high names and great titles, as lords and masters. You present them with splendid dwellings, big incomes and possessions, and say, They who serve the Gospel must live by the Gospel, although they do nothing but place soft pillows and cushions under you, and preach according to the itching of your ears.

But the true, pious teachers and faithful servants of Christ who sincerely seek your salvation, and that of the whole world, who direct you to Christ, who rightly use His sacraments and ordinances, who direct you and all men to the right way, who walk unblamably: these must without mercy or Christian decency be persecuted by you, sentenced to fire and water, and be subjected to the mockery and shame of all the world.

Josiah made a covenant with the Lord and with all the elders, priests, prophets, and common people, that they should serve the Lord as long as they lived. But you have covenanted with Antichrist and with all your preachers, priests, monks, judges, and rulers, to walk the long and crooked way, to follow and to teach the doctrines and institutions of men instead of the true service of God, to give no place to the people of Christ, nor to the commands, Spirit, Supper, life, and separation, but to take the life or the property of any man who acts or speaks contrary to your abominations.

Josiah heard the Word of the Lord and softened his heart; he rent his clothes and wept before the Lord; he feared the coming wrath, because they and their forefathers had rejected the Word of God. But you, my dear lords, are so hardened and blinded, so bound by your sins and lusts of the flesh, through cursed unbelief; so bewitched by the false prophets, that you cannot in the least be moved to penitence, neither by the threatening Law of the Lord, nor by His awful wrath and terrible judgment, neither by the devouring flames of hell and eternal death, nor by the peaceful Gospel of grace, neither by the precious blood of Christ, nor by the pious, unblamable life of all the saints, who with their simple yea and nay[17] are daily murdered before your eyes as innocent sheep on account of their faith and piety. It is about time that you roused yourselves and took notice how you and we

[17] Following New Testament prohibitions the Mennonites do not swear oaths. *Ed.*

with our forefathers have by your ugly, carnal sins and grievous idolatry so abundantly merited the righteous punishment and wrath of God. May the merciful Lord grant you eyes to see.

Josiah turned to the Lord with his whole heart, soul, and might; but you dare proudly to disdain the God who has created you, the Lord who has purchased you. You take recourse to dumb idols, to wood, stone, gold and silver images, to water, bread and wine, to the unprofitable doctrines and commandments of men, yes, to open abominations and idolatry, not observing that it is written: Idolaters shall have their part in the lake which burneth with fire and brimstone. Rev. 21:8.

Behold, dear sirs, that the above is true I may prove by the glaring fact of your proud harloting and carnal life, and by the spoiled, burnt, ruined countries and cities, and the excessively great number of churches, cloisters, priests and monks, matins, vespers, and every other false worship.

Besides, when we, on account of the multitude of our sins, are visited with pestilence, hard times, war, and with other dangerous strange sicknesses and plagues, then your best and loftiest remedies to appease the wrath of God and to quench the burning fire of His anger, are to hear idolatrous masses, processions, as they are called, with dead men's bones; icons, crosses, banners; to carry the horrid abominations of the priests, I mean; and to follow after them with uncovered heads, folded hands, and burning wax candles, things with which you do not turn aside the fierce wrath, but kindle it more and more. For the Lord will not give His divine honor to works of men's hands, inventions, nor anything cultivated or faked, nor does He accept any such masses, processions, crosses, images, and abominations, nor has He ever thought of them, as the prophet says.

Dear sirs, repent. The Lawbook of Christ is entirely lost to you. Christ and His truth, sacraments, Spirit, and life, you have never known, much less possessed. You serve strange gods. You hear, follow, and use the doctrine, sacraments, ordinances, and commandments of Antichrist; you lead an unclean, ungodly, and carnal life. Ah, sirs, take warning, your sins have reached to heaven!

And although it is so little regarded by you (God help), yet this book of Christ, by the grace of God, has been found again by some. The pure, unfalsified truth has come to light through the pure, undiluted Gospel, and is plainly read in your ears; it is expounded before your eyes with a godly, virtuous life, with a confident confession, and with much of the property and blood of the saints. Yet your hearts continue so stony and hard that they cannot be converted or moved, neither by grace nor by wrath, neither by sweet nor by sour, as we have said. Behold, thus has the blindness of Sodom, the darkness of Egypt, the stubbornness of Pharaoh, come upon our miserable kings, princes, lords, and rulers through the righteous judgment of God.

Dear sirs, awake and make haste; the trumpet is sounding, prepare yourselves! Your mortal sickness and festering filthy wounds are pointed out to you. I counsel you to let yourselves be helped. You possess neither Christ nor His Word, I tell you. You battle against the Lamb and His elect. Your way is in darkness and it leads to the abyss of hell. The wrath of the Lord is over you in your land, for your conduct is more carnal and evil than can be imagined or described.

O my dear sirs, reform! Repent with a penitence that can stand before God. Cleanse your hands and hearts before the Lord; change your pride into humility, and your mirth and frivolous joy into sorrow. Rend your hardened hearts and not your garments; hear and seek Christ and not Antichrist; obey Christ's Spirit, doctrine, sacraments, commands, and non-failing example, and not the vain doctrines and commandments of men, for they corrupt rather than improve.

Put away from among you all offenses, abominations, and idolatry, all masses, altars, infant baptism, the idolatrous bread or Supper (I mean as it is used by the world), images, confessions, the wanton Sodom-like impurity of the papistic priests and monks; sweep away all accursed, heathen shames such as brothels, gambling dens, public drunken inns, together with idolatrous temples, high places, groves, churches, and cloisters which were so abundantly built by our forefathers through simon-pure blindness and ignorance, contrary to Scripture.

Help us to obstruct seductive teachers and false sects, great and small, who oppose the Spirit, ordinances, Word, and life of Christ; not with violence, tyranny, or sword, as, alas, it is the custom with you; but with the Spirit of Christ, with doctrine, exhortation, and the like proper services and kind means, so that they may turn from evil and hear and follow Christ.

Permit all faithful messengers and servants of God to preach Christ, to use His sacraments and ordinances according to the Scriptures, to lead a penitent and irreproachable life according to the Scriptures, and so to gather unto Christ a glorious church with the Spirit and grace of God; to bring unto Christ an unspotted, pure virgin.

Again I say, reform! too long you have erred; too long you have mocked God; too long you have worshiped Antichrist instead of Christ; too long you have walked in the perverse and broad way of death. Awaken, it is yet today. Behold, the true book of the Law, the saving, pure Gospel of Christ which was hid for so many centuries by the abominations of Antichrist, has been found!

Hear and read carefully, believe it, and observe it faithfully. It is the Word of the Lord God which Christ Jesus, the first-born and only begotten Son of the Almighty Father, brought from heaven and taught us with His truth-loving mouth. Bow to His righteous scepter. Fear, love, serve, honor, and follow Him with all your heart, with all your soul, and with all your powers, as did the pious Josiah. For the Lord our God is Lord of lords, and God of gods, mighty and terrible, without respect of persons or fear of men.

Yes, dear sirs, if you could thus convert yourselves with all your heart;

if you could change yourselves and humble yourselves before God, could deny yourselves and seek and follow Christ and His righteousness; if you could renounce the world and flesh with all its lusts, as you have heard, then you would be kings and priests not only in natural things, but also in spiritual. You would possess your souls in peace, rule your land in Christian wisdom, in the pure fear of God; then you would be victorious against all the harmful enemies of our souls, live in grace, die in grace, and deserve to be called in truth, without hypocrisy, Christian kings and believing princes. The testimony of Peter to all Christians, I say to all Christians, is true. Ye are a chosen generation, a holy nation, a peculiar people. I Pet. 2:9.

But if you refuse this and remain what you are now, preferring perishing, temporal pleasures and glory above the imperishable, eternal joy and glory, then I could desire you would reflect upon what Sirach says, Why are dust and ashes proud? While he lives he is but disgraceful dung; he that is a king today, tomorrow shall die. Sir. 10:9. Yes, what are they all who come of Adam but dust and ashes, a passing wind, a vapor; poor, miserable, mortal flesh, food for worms, yea, men and not God. O sirs, take warning! Awake and reform yourselves. God is the Lord who will judge you. Once more, take warning!

Behold, my kind reader, here you have before you a few examples of true faith, as of Noah and Abraham before the Law and Moses; and Joshua, Caleb, and Josiah under the Law, cited from Scripture. From these you may learn how simple, straightforward, and ordinary, how honest, bold, and obedient, how full of all kinds of virtues and fruits, genuine faith has been from the beginning, as may also be seen in Abel, Enoch, Isaac, Jacob, Joseph, Jephthah, Baruch, Gideon, Samson, Rahab, Samuel, David, Ezekiel, Elijah, Elisha, and others.

Now I will by the grace of God set forth a few examples from the New Testament, from which you may learn most clearly what an abundantly great power, fruit, spirit, life, and force genuine Christian faith by its very nature always includes, so that you may not through an erroneous opinion conform to this unbelieving, foolish world which boasts of fruitless, dead opinion and a historical confession of Christ as though it were genuine, evangelical, Christian faith.

### [F.] The Faith of the Centurion of Capernaum

It happened when the Lord Jesus entered Capernaum that the servant of a centurion whom he loved much lay sick. When he heard that Jesus was there, he gained the help of some of the elders of the Jews and sent them with a request to Jesus that He would come to him and restore his sick servant. And Jesus went with them. And being not far from the house of the centurion, he sent some of his friends to Him saying, Lord, trouble not thyself, for I am not worthy that thou shouldst enter under my roof [notice his humility], and I did not think myself worthy personally to come to thee. But speak the word, and my child shall be healed.

He acknowledged that all must bow to Christ and His Word and said, I also am a man under authority, having soldiers under me, and I say unto one, Go, and he goeth; and to another, Come, and he cometh; and to my servant, Do this, and he doeth it. It was as if he would say to Christ, Behold, Lord, I am but a man, and have to serve the senate at Rome. Nevertheless I have power over my servants that they must do what I command them. But Thou, Lord, art such a Lord that all the mighty have to bow to Thee; all that is in heaven above and on earth beneath must yield to Thee. If Thou but command sickness and death, they will obey Thee and depart from my child. And again, if Thou command health and life, they will return to him. Therefore, it is not necessary that Thou shouldst come into the house of Thy unworthy servant. Lord, speak with a simple word and my child will be restored. When Jesus heard these words, He was amazed and said to the people that followed, Verily I say unto you, I have not found so great faith, no, not in Israel. Matt. 8.

You see, faithful reader, here you have the centurion as a living example by which you may learn how a true Christian faith humbles itself before God, and doubts not His power. Also, how kindly and graciously faith deals with poor servants, be they menservants or maidservants. The centurion was moved with compassion toward his poor servant, and was so concerned for him that he spared no pains to trouble the elders of the Jews to send to Christ and entreat Him to come and heal his sick servant. This is to the disgrace and shame of all false Christians and especially to many rich, some of whom are more merciless and cruel toward poor servants and hirelings than they are to their dogs and animals (pardon the expression). For as soon as they get so ill that they cannot perform mule's labor, then they are unmercifully turned out of doors, and sent to this or that institution, or to their parents and friends who sometimes have scarcely a bite of bread or an old cot in their houses. Again others with great damage to their little earnings have to get a substitute while they are sick. And even if they do serve their time in health with hard and severe labor, some of these unmerciful, cruel, bloody folk put forth efforts to deprive these poor lambs, who have to watch when they sleep, labor when they rest, run when they command, and stand when they sit, of a goodly portion of their grievous toil. Now they complain that a spoon is lost; then it is a dish that is broken; always they have ruined this or that. Yes, some of them would feed them with water and straw, and pay them with the whip and chaff, as they do their laboring oxen and horses, if they were not ashamed before men. They would not be ashamed of such things before God whom alas they know not. Oh, woe upon such heathenish tyranny and unmerciful cruelty!

The centurion called his servant his child, by which he manifested his fatherly love and humility toward his poor servant. Although he was lord and held in high honor, nevertheless he did not exalt himself above his humble servant, knowing well that they were created both of them by one and the same God, that they were born of one stock. But what virtue and love some heathen "Christians" often manifest toward their miserable servants, their actions, alas, openly show.

How mightily some of the poor children are despised by some of them! How many are the abusive words some of them have to hear, how many a blow they have to endure! Cursed quarreling and evil speaking continue from morning till night; some of their servant girls they make into prostitutes. Yea, what shall I say more? These poor children are regarded by them, and especially by the rich, as the poor, despised donkey is regarded by the well-kept horse, and the filthy pebbles by the beautiful pearls. Ah, reader, it is much worse than I can describe; it is high time for them to consider and to reflect more deeply upon love.

The centurion humbled himself before the Lord with all his heart, esteeming himself not worthy that He should come under his roof. But our haughty, proud heathens strut about with puffed-up hearts and extended necks, proud and haughty; one boasts of his family, another of his wealth, a third of his wisdom, a fourth of his skill and beauty, etc. But the innocent and humble Christ who says, Learn of me, for I am meek and lowly in heart; whose name, Word, death, and blood they boast, Him they do not know.

The centurion believed that Christ was able by His Word to do all that he desired, but these miserable, deluded people pay no more attention to it than they do to a fable by Lucian or Aesop. From which it follows that they lead such an impenitent, carnal life, and use such idolatrous sacraments and false worship, and have departed far from the King's highway. Yet they pose as the true apostolic church, and the believing flock of Christ. But just as Christ testifies of the centurion that He had not found such faith in Israel, so we might say of this people, Such reckless, cruel, haughty, proud, and unmerciful unbelief is unknown among the unconverted[18] heathen who have never heard the Word of Christ! Behold, the righteous Lord lets them err, and fall into blindness of heart, make light of His most holy Word, and hate and reject His fatherly grace, goodness, Spirit, knowledge, and faith.

But let it be not so with you, dearly beloved. Take this faithful, pious centurion as an example so that you may resemble him in his faith, love, humility, and virtue. Be as solicitous for your servants as he was for his servant. Teach them, admonish and reprove them with a fatherly spirit as often as they do wrong. Set them an unblamable example in all righteousness and piety. Sympathize with them a bit in their severe and heavy labor. Comfort them in their poverty, comfort them I say, and grieve them not. Give them decent support and their earned pay and do not dock them in their wages. Protect them in all honorable things. Do not chide them without cause lest they become discouraged; do not discharge them before the agreed time but let

[18] Reading *onbekeerdcn* (unconverted ones) for *onbekenden* (unknown ones). *Tr.*

them serve out without loss their time as agreed, lest the name of the Lord be blasphemed. Be friendly toward them at all times. And if they are weak and sick, assist and serve them. Get someone else to serve in their place without loss to them until the Lord takes them or restores them to health. Be sympathetic and compassionate toward them. Assist them in their need. Do not exalt yourselves above them, nor despise them in their humbleness, for they are your brethren according to the flesh. In short, take the attitude toward them that Christ Jesus takes toward us. Always remember that we also have a Lord in heaven before whose judgment seat we must all appear and render an account of all our works.

But if they are willful and obstinate and refuse to hear your word and command, if they do not follow your admonition and counsel, if they want to rule rather than serve, if they waste their time and labor in laziness, if they are unfaithful, rebellious, and troublesome, wickedly corrupting your family and children, etc., then come to an agreement with them as to wages earned, before two or three witnesses, so that the fault may not be on your side, and the Word of the Lord be not disgraced. In this way let them move on, that your conscience be not troubled on their account and your house and children be not ruined. Yes, my brethren, do to your poor servants even as you desire that it should be done to you, if you were called as they are. This is the law and the prophets.

### [G.] *The Faith of Zacchaeus, the Publican*

It happened as Luke says that Jesus entered and passed through Jericho. And, behold, there was a man named Zacchaeus, which was the chief among the publicans, and he was rich. And he sought to see Jesus, who he was; and could not for the press, because he was little of stature. And he ran before, and climbed into a sycamore tree [or as some say, into a wild fig tree] to see him: for he was to pass that way. And when Jesus came to the place, he looked up, and saw him, and said to him, Zacchaeus, make haste, and come down; for today I must abide at thy house. And he made haste, and came down, and received him joyfully. And he said unto the Lord, Behold, Lord, the half of my goods I give to the poor; and if I have taken anything from any man by false accusation, I restore him fourfold. And Jesus said unto him, This day is salvation come to this house, forasmuch as he also is a son of Abraham. Luke 19:1-9.

Paul says, For whatsoever things were written aforetime were written for our learning, for although we know Zacchaeus' faith, joy, mercy, love, and true conversion, this does not help if we do not imitate his faith with its contrite, pious fruits. I therefore entreat all my readers who still live in manifest sin, all the wealthy, avaricious, unrighteous merchants and retailers, all financiers and usurers, all money-mad judges, lawyers, advocates, preachers, priests, and monks, all drunken innkeepers, together with all those who traffic in unlawful gain, I entreat all these by the love of our Lord and Saviour,

Jesus Christ, properly to consider with an understanding heart this history and narrative touching Zacchaeus. And by so doing they may learn that they do not yet have genuine faith, and that Christianity which avails before God; that they have nothing but fruitless, vain boasting of Christ and of faith.

Zacchaeus was chief of the manifest sinners.[19] He received Christ into his house with joy. He believed and was renewed; he reformed his life; he walked no more in his former evil ways. That our open transgressors do not yet reform their old, ungodly lives, and therefore do not have nor desire Christ and His faith, however much they may boast of it, is as clear as the light of day.

Zacchaeus was rich, and one half of his wealth he gave to the poor. But our rich people seek more and more how they may increase their money and possessions, build their houses expensively, and add field to field. They do not care about the needs of the poor and needy; they are unmerciful, proud, avaricious, and given to luxury. They do not remember what is written concerning them: Go to now, ye rich men, weep and howl for your miseries that shall come upon you. Your riches are corrupted; and your garments are motheaten. Your gold and silver is cankered; and the rust of them shall be a witness against you, and shall eat your flesh as it were fire. Jas. 5:1-3. Neither do they recall that David says, I have seen the wicked in great power, and spreading himself like the green bay tree. Yet he passed away, and, lo, he was not: yea, I sought him, and he could not be found. Ps. 37:35, 36. Ah, what a mighty saying the Lord uttered: Woe unto you that are rich, for ye have received your consolation. It is easier for a camel to go through the eye of a needle than for a rich man to enter into the kingdom of God. Matt. 19:24.

Zacchaeus said to the Lord, If I have taken anything from any man by false accusation, I restore him fourfold. But our miserable misers never cease from cheating their neighbors. For the whole wide world, both men and women, pursue improper and shameful gain, so ceaselessly that it cannot be imagined nor told.

Lords and princes daily seek new ways and means to increase their dominions, taxes, tolls, and rents. They tax and toll, grasp and grab, without any mercy or measure; they suck the very marrow from the bones of the poor, and show by their actions that they are companions of those of whom it is written, Thy princes are rebellious, and companions of thieves. Isa. 1:23. Oh, that they knew Christ, would repent, cease to do evil, and would reflect more on love!

Judges, lawyers, and advocates also seek every device to get more money. They all serve for gifts and money, few excepted. If they did not expect to be benefited, I am sure that there would not be a burgomaster and judge in the whole empire. For the sake of gain they sit and judge and they sometimes encourage cases so that they may fleece somebody. Some of them pervert justice

---

[19] Here, and throughout Menno's writings, the Latin term *publicani,* as found in the Latin Bibles, is translated *openbare Sondaren* (public or manifest sinners) instead of taxgatherer, the technical meaning of *publicani. Tr.*

for the sake of a gift, and do not reflect on what Jehoshaphat said to them: Take heed what ye do: for ye judge not for man, but for the Lord, who is with you in the judgment. Wherefore now let the fear of the Lord be upon you; take heed and do it: for there is no iniquity with the Lord our God, nor respect of persons, nor taking of gifts. II Chron. 19:6, 7.

Captains, knights, foot soldiers, and similar bloody men risk body and soul for the sake of gain, and swear with uplifted fingers that they are ready to destroy cities and countries, to take citizens and inhabitants, to kill them and take their possessions, although these have never harmed them nor given them so much as an evil word. O God, what cursed, wicked abomination and traffic! And they call that protecting the country and the people, and assisting in justice!

Priests, monks, and preachers are equally bent upon shameful gain. They have the audacity to make God's only begotten and first-born Son, His eternal, Almighty Word and wisdom, the one and eternal foundation of heaven and earth, Jesus Christ, with His holy apostles, to be false witnesses, heretics, and deluders. For Christ says, He that believeth and is baptized shall be saved. But they say, He that believeth and is baptized is a heretic, and shall be damned. Christ says, But if thou wilt enter into life, keep the commandments. Matt. 19:17. They say, No one can keep God's commandments.

Paul says, If ye live after the flesh ye shall die. Again, the unrighteous (he means drunkards, the avaricious, the haughty, the unchaste, and the like) shall not inherit the kingdom of God. But they say, We are poor sinners. Who can live as the Scriptures teach? Christ died for sinners, did He not? and the like consolations, whereby they forsake Christ and His Word, and encourage the whole world, rich and poor, small and great, in their wayward and wicked life. So that there are few, alas, who truly repent or ask concerning God. They preach what the ignorant, blind, sullen world wants to hear, in order that the reward of Balaam (their cloisters and incomes, I mean) may be enjoyed by them, and that they may lead an Epicurean lazy life therewith, without care. And they, poor creatures, do not know that they are those of whom it is written: Woe unto them, for they have gone in the way of Cain, and ran greedily after the error of Balaam for reward, and perished in the gainsaying of Core (Jude 11); accursed people. I Pet. 2. O God, that they would consider!

The wicked merchants and retailers (I say the wicked, for I do not mean those who are righteous and pious), together with all those who are out to make money and to make their living that way, are so bent on accursed profit that they exclude God wholly from their hearts. They censure what they should properly praise, and praise what they should censure. They lie and swear; they use many vain words, falsify their wares to cheat the people, and strip them of possessions; they sell, lend, and secure the needy at large profit and usury, never seriously reflecting or taking to heart that it is written, Let no man go beyond and defraud his brother in any matter. I Thess. 4:6.

I could wish that they might more seriously take to heart the doctrine of

Sirach: A merchant shall hardly keep himself from doing wrong, and a huckster shall not be freed from sin; many have sinned for a small matter, and he that seeketh for abundance will turn his eyes away. As a nail sticketh fast between the joinings of the stones, so doth sin stick close between buying and selling. Unless a man hold himself diligently in the fear of the Lord, his house shall soon be overthrown. Ecclus. 26:29; 27:1-3.

This I write as a warning to the God-fearing merchants and retailers, lest they be like the ungodly, and be overcome by avarice. But may they be circumspect in dealing and on the alert against moral danger.

For the sake of this accursed thirst for profit, some become thieves, some murderers, some holdup men; others become necromancers, sorcerers, some harlots and brothel keepers; others, gamblers, betrayers, executioners, and tormentors; also persecutors and slayers of the pious, etc., and all this, I say, for the sake of accursed profit. By these things they openly testify, since they walk in such a way and are so intent on unlawful gain, that they are of the devil and not of God, that they have not the faith and Word of Christ, but in every respect hate them.

Yes, good reader, the whole world is so affected and involved in this accursed avarice, fraud, false practice, and unlawful means of support; in this false traffic and merchandise, with this finance, usury, and personal advancement that I do not know how it could get much worse. Yet they continue to be the priests' and preachers' Christians, and then call this earning their bread honestly, and doing justice to all.

Ah, my reader, how very different all this is from the faith, spirit, and converted life of Zacchaeus. For if we had the spirit, faith, and power of Zacchaeus, which we verily should have, if we would be saved, then few lords and princes would continue in their violence and luxurious lives; few knights and soldiers[20] in their wicked service and bloody deeds; few judges, lawyers, and advocates in their courthouses and offices; few rich persons in the unclean use of their riches; few merchants and retailers in their usury and morally dangerous trade; and few preachers, priests, and monks would continue in their salaries, incomes, and cloisters. There would soon be a different and better situation because, it cannot fail, the righteous must live his faith. Yea, they would with a new and joyful heart say with Zacchaeus, The poor we willingly serve with our goods, and if we have defrauded any one we will gladly reimburse him.

All who with Zacchaeus receive Jesus Christ in the house of their consciences, with him rightly believe the Word of Christ and are truly born by it, these are also given the Spirit of Christ and are of the same mind with Him. Therefore it is impossible for them to defraud anyone of so much as a farthing; the disposition and usage of all true believers being to injure none on earth, but as much as in them is, to assist all; to cheat none, but deal fairly with all. As Paul says, Let him that stole steal no more; but rather let him labor, working

20 *Weynigh Ruyteren ende Knechten* could also mean, *few cavalry and foot soldiers. Ed.*

with his hands the thing which is good, that he may have to give to him that needeth. Eph. 4:28.

But why say much? For my part I do not know where to find the mighty and the rich, in what courts to find judges, lawyers, and advocates, in what city and country to find merchants and retailers, or in what cloister and church to find preachers, priests, and monks, who believe and follow Christ, who out of a new and penitent heart spurn all improper practices, fraud, crafty theft, shady business, and wicked gain, and say with Zacchaeus, Those whom we have defrauded we will repay fourfold. The prophet complains that everyone from the least even to the greatest is given to covetousness. Jer. 8:10.

Since then they are so set on accursed, ugly avarice and improper profits, and deal so flatly and plainly contrary to love, and no true repentance is found, therefore it is evident that they are not in the church of Christ. For the church or congregation of Christ is called His body and bride in the Scripture. If the church is His body, it must be flesh of His flesh and bone of His bone, and if it is His bride, she must be of His generation, righteous, holy, meek, chaste, true, lovely, merciful; yes, must hear and be obedient to His voice. Therefore Christ cannot admit any other members to His church but those who are of one heart, spirit, and soul with Him, partakers of His Spirit, who die to all unrighteousness, bury the old evil life of sin, walk by faith, are unblamable in love, receive the truth joyfully, and willingly serve their neighbors as did this believing, regenerated, and renewed Zacchaeus.

He desired to see Christ and received Him with joy. He believed His Word and turned from his ungodly life; he ministered to the poor and satisfied those whom he had defrauded. In short, he proved himself to be a pious, sincere, regenerated child of God in all his actions; therefore, he heard the peaceable, joyful word of divine grace: This day is salvation come to this house, forasmuch as he also is a son of Abraham. Luke 19:9.

Behold, worthy reader, those who are such penitent and renewed Zacchaeuses, who walk in love, these belong to the church and body of the Lord. As Christ Himself says: By this shall all men know that ye are my disciples, if ye have love one to another. They are the living stones of the Lord's temple and the true citizens of Jerusalem, in which neither dogs nor thieves, no unrighteous persons, none who are avaricious, no sorcerers, no immoral wretches, no murderers, no idolaters, nor such as love or make a lie, shall have a place. Yea, as long as Zacchaeus was such a one, he was outside. For such, says Paul, have neither lot nor part in the kingdom of God and of Christ.

But as soon as he believed the Word of the Lord, repented through faith, and turned to love, from that hour he was granted citizenship by Christ Himself. The gateway of life was opened to him, peace was declared to him, salvation bestowed, and he was acknowledged and received as a joint heir of grace and a child of God. As the Lord says: This day is salvation come to this house. For even as Christ is holy, so must also His children, brethren, members, church, and bride be holy, even as it is written: Be ye holy, for I am holy.

## [H.] The Faith of the Malefactor on the Cross

The evangelists teach that there were two thieves or malefactors crucified with Christ, the one on the right hand and the other on the left. One of the malefactors which were hanged railed on Him, saying, If thou be Christ, save thyself and us. But the other answering rebuked him, saying, Dost not thou fear God, seeing thou art in the same condemnation? And we indeed justly, for we receive the due reward of our deeds: but this man hath done nothing amiss. And he said unto Jesus, Lord, remember me when thou comest into thy kingdom. And Jesus said unto him, Verily I say unto thee, Today shalt thou be with me in paradise. Luke 23:39-43.

Good reader, pay attention to what I write. When we consider carefully the confession of this malefactor, we may well be astonished at the great power, the good character, the abundant fruit, spiritual insight, vision, moving affection, and the confident confession of his faith. It is apparent that he was an abandoned, godless wretch, who neither knew nor feared God, lived in all manner of sin, robbing his fellow man and shedding blood. For Matthew and Mark call him a murderer, and Luke calls him a malefactor. It is apparent also from his own acknowledgment that he deserved to die for his misdeeds.

Nevertheless, as soon as this malefactor heard the sweet word of God out of the mouth of the Lord, between Jerusalem and Mount Calvary, and also as he was hanging on the cross in his extremity, it wrought in him so powerfully that his heart within him was touched and changed. He sought from that moment on the salvation of his fellow men, and rebuked his blaspheming companion, saying, Fearest thou not God? He confessed his own sins and wickedness, saying, We receive acording to our deserts, and the poor condemned Jesus (condemned by the chief priests, Pharisees, and scribes), condemned to die on the cross as one of the most wicked evildoers, and denied by the common people, and condemned to death, Him he acknowledged to be just, innocent, pure, and without sin, saying, This one has done no evil. Besides this he also sought grace and mercy with Christ, although it seemed, and reason could come to no other conclusion, that he was himself denied all mercy and every favor both with God and man. For he was at this time the most rejected and despised of all men, as the prophet complains (Isa. 53:6). But the malefactor turned to none other in heaven or upon earth than to this innocent, reviled, cursed, and crucified Jesus, in full confidence drawing near to Him, as to the throne of divine grace, that he might obtain the remission of his sins, saying, Lord, remember me when thou comest into thy kingdom.

I think this may be justly called a true Christian faith, and a truly worthy fruit of penitence and repentance. And it was to the Lord a refreshing of His thirsty soul, a mollifying of His deep wounds, a consolation of His sore distress, and a comfort in His painful sufferings and death. It was so much so that this man forthwith heard the consoling joyful word of divine grace and eternal peace from Christ, namely: Fear not, all thy sins which thou didst commit in thy ignorance are covered. They shall nevermore be remembered by me or my Father. I pledge my innocent blood as security. Therefore, be of good cheer. What thou desirest, thou hast already obtained. Today shalt thou be with me in paradise.

Behold, my reader, here you have in this malefactor another fine example of a genuine Christian faith with its essential attributes, disposition, nature, power, and fruits. With this same malefactor many vain despisers comfort and cajole themselves in their sinful and impenitent lives, thinking and saying to themselves, God is merciful; He knows that we are the children of Adam and do not live altogether as the Scriptures teach and require. Yet we hope by the grace of God to be saved, as was the malefactor on the cross. These poor children do not know that the malefactor will be a sore condemnation for them, seeing they hear the Word of the Lord so often, and do not believe it or obey it. Ah, reader, let us not mock God so. Many I fear will be disappointed in this matter.

Once more I say that all willful despisers who say and think thus in their hearts will be eternally convicted by this thief and confounded. For as soon as he heard the Gospel of grace he received it in pure conscience through faith and became penitent, regenerated, and pious. These men hear it from year to year, see daily many fair fruits, and see it gloriously attested by possessions and blood. Yet they remain unbelieving, and are hardened in sin. For they reject the inviting grace, they resist the operating Spirit, they despise the preached Word, they trample on the proffered gift. I declare, Where is the Scripture wherewith we may comfort such rude, shameful scorners as they face death, or promise and ascribe to them the grace and peace of the Lord?

I fear that they are the barren, unfruitful earth of which Paul speaks, which drinketh in the rain of the holy, divine Word, that cometh oft upon it, and nevertheless bears only thorns and thistles. Therefore are they nigh unto cursing and will finally be burned. They are those of whom Wisdom laments and says, How long, ye simple ones, will you love simplicity? and the scorners delight in their scorning, and the fools hate knowledge? Because I have called and ye have refused; I have stretched out my hand, and no man regarded; but ye have set at naught all my counsel and would none of my reproof: I also will laugh at your calamity; I will mock when your fear cometh; and when distress and anguish cometh upon you. Then shall they call upon me, but I will not answer. Prov. 1:22-28. But because they do not look for light, He will turn it into the shadow of death, and make it gross darkness.

The malefactor believed as soon as he heard. Oh, that they would do likewise, and would ponder David's words, Today, if ye will hear his voice, harden not your hearts as in the provocation.

The malefactor heard but once and believed, and these hear it so often, and yet they believe not. He heard and was changed. But these hear and remain what they are, and harden their hearts yet more and more.

The malefactor reproved his blaspheming companion, and admonished him to fear God, but these blaspheme and revile all faithful hearts that do so, and they love those who hate the truth.

The malefactor boldly confessed his sins and wickedness without hesitation; but these, no matter how avaricious, drunken, proud, impure, hateful, and idolatrous they are, acknowledge neither transgressions nor sins, and when called to repent and reform, they say, And what have we done?

The malefactor acknowledged that Christ's kingdom was not earthly, for he said, When thou comest into thy kingdom. But these have all their pleasures in gold and silver, in eating and drinking, in pomp and pride, and in the perishing, visible riches of this world, regarding not the invisible, eternal riches which Christ out of grace has bestowed upon all His believers, and merited by the shedding of His precious blood.

The malefactor confessed the poor, condemned, crucified Jesus before all the rulers, priests, Pharisees, and before the people, and acknowledged Him to be his Saviour and Lord. But these alas deny His Almighty Majesty, His heavenly origin and glory, and regard not His judgment, Spirit, Word, ordinances, commands, sacraments, and promises, although He has seated Himself as a triumphant and conquering prince at the right hand of His Father and has received from Him all power, both in heaven and upon earth, in eternal glory.

The malefactor sought to receive mercy, favor, and the forgiveness of his sins of Christ; but these seek it of their preachers, priests, and monks, and that through masses, confessionals, absolutions, bread and wine, holy water, and the like superstitions and abominations.

The malefactor because he believed in Christ heard the sweet blessed words, Today thou shalt be with me in paradise. But these because they believe not on Christ, must hear the dreadful, unbearable and awful thunder clap, Depart from me, ye cursed, into everlasting fire. Their faith was different; so also will be the reward. Let all despisers take this to heart.

And so at the last, take heed. This poor penitent sinner will rise up against those who have comforted themselves with him in their sins, and accuse and condemn them before the face of His Majesty. For they have so often heard the sweet sound of the harp and the new song (that is, the divine Word), and have never with joyful gratitude rejoiced in it, nor ever learned or believed it with open and renewed hearts. But this man heard it but once and immediately believed.

Ah, dear children, beware, and seek Christ while He may still be found. And call on Him while He is still near, lest His anger go forth and the fire of His fierce wrath consume you.

Do you think, O perverse foreigners, that you can receive faith, repentance, sorrow for sin, and the grace of God whenever it suits you? Oh, no, the holy Paul says, Even as they did not like to retain God in their knowledge, God gave them over to a reprobate mind. Rom. 1:28. That judgment will overtake all proud despisers. Children, take heed.

Notice this parable. There is a very rich potentate, emperor, or king whom I through great ignorance have hated all my days. He had such compassion on me, because I am such a poor man, that through his faithful servants he offered me not only his good will and friendship, but also a great sum of gold and many precious stones and gems, out of sheer love and compassion. But I am so contrary and ungrateful that the servants of this kind and deserving ruler, who loves me heartily, are not only not fed and entertained by me, but also driven forth with shame and disgrace, pelted with dirt and stones, placed in jail, threatened in life and limb, their gifts taken, and they are locked up in a closet, trampled underfoot, etc. And then I inform the ruler: I do not now desire your presents, but if in after years you should send your servants, perhaps I would change my mind and receive them and thank you for your favors.

Now I will allow you all to judge whether it would be proper for such a prince again to offer his favor, seeing I treated him and his servants with such perfidy. Or, should he not much more turn his favor into displeasure and recompense my ungrateful tyranny and haughty disdain, and severely punish me? I think you would award me his punishment and not his grace.

So with you, O you scorners! The merciful, great Lord whose riches and grace are unmeasured, has graciously pitied us in these last abominable days, in our great blindness and awful destitution, even though we have hated His holy will from the cradle. Through His faithful servants He has made known to us His beloved Son with His holy Word, Spirit, merits, ordinances, and example, has offered us His grace, peace, eternal life, kingdom, inheritance, joy, and glory together with the remission of our sins.

He dug about us barren trees, supplying plant food for many years. He calls and teaches daily through His elect, who willingly sacrifice possession and life for it. He sets the father against the son, and the son against the father; the mother against the daughter, and the daughter against the mother; the family against the family, and friend against friend, etc. Some He suffers to wander in strange countries, in tribulation, in sorrow, in misery, in distress, in want, in great care, in deserts, in mountains, in dens, and in caves of the earth. He gives signs in the sun, moon, and the stars in heaven above; earthquakes, wars, pestilences, strange diseases, famine, and unheard-of wonders on the earth beneath, so as to gather us as a hen gathers her chickens under her wings in His love, and as a faithful shepherd bring us to the true fold of His grace. He would bring us into the chamber of His covenant, kiss us with the lips of His peace, wash us from all our uncleanness, and espouse us as His bride. He would deliver us from the kingdom of hell and death, and lead us into the heavenly kingdom of His eternal life. In short, so that He may release us from the power of darkness and the devil, and receive us and sanctify us as His chosen children and heirs.

But alas, toward you this is altogether in vain. For as has already been said, His proffered grace and Word you reject; His faithful servants and ministers you persecute and kill; the irreproachable, pious life, together with the courageous confession of His saints, you revile and malign. You scoff at His great signs, wonders, and fatherly reproofs; you scoff and make faces like those of the harlots, and make your hearts as diamonds, refusing to repent and be converted. You say with all sinful scorners, Depart from us, for we desire not the knowledge of thy ways. Who is the Almighty that we should serve him? and what profit shall we have if we pray to him? Job 21:14, 15.

But you are so ungrateful to your God, yes, altogether vain and vicious toward Him; the God who has shown to us such great mercy now and from the beginning. You bluntly reject and ignore His eternal admonitions, chastisement, doctrines, commands, the obedience of His holy Word, and the innocent blood of His saints, together with all His great powers and miracles; yes, you consider them mere deception and heresy. You do not regard the day of grace. You trample on Christ and His holy Spirit, Gospel, regeneration, faith, sacraments, death and blood, together with all His other spiritual riches and heavenly gifts. You do not fear, seek, love, honor, thank, nor serve the Almighty, immortal, only and eternal God. Yet in spite of all this you still hope that you will be saved with the murderer! I declare and warn in love while it is yet today that your hopes will fail. For when you think to find Him, He will hide Himself from you. He will turn His countenance upon you in wrath, as the Scriptures say: Then shall they call upon me, and I will not answer; they shall seek me early, but they shall not find me. Prov. 1:28.

Therefore I entreat and exhort my readers in general, hear while you still have ears, and see while you still have eyes, and understand while you still have hearts. Watch and labor while you still have time and opportunity: lest your ears, eyes, hearts, time, and opportunities be taken from you all at once, and you be handed over to a deaf, blind, impenitent, hardened spirit.

Friends, beware! Now it is today; yesterday is past; tomorrow is not promised us. Short is the time; the Judge is at the door. Therefore do not postpone to turn unto the Lord, and do not defer it from day to day, for His wrath will soon overtake you. Late repentance, says Augustine,[21] is seldom genuine; but if genuine, it is never too late. Repent while you enjoy health, and I declare, says he, that you are safe and sure.

Therefore, do as this thief or malefactor did, for the moment he heard, he believed. In a similar way do you hear and believe. For the eyes of the Lord are upon the faithful. Christ says, Those who hunger and thirst after righteousness shall be filled; they who seek shall find; and they who ask shall receive; they who knock, to them it shall be opened. But if they refuse when He seeks them, eager to bestow His grace, then He will also refuse when they seek Him and would fain obtain His grace. They that despise me, saith the Lord, shall be lightly esteemed. I Sam. 2:30.

Therefore, seek while it is day, in order that you may find; ask in order

---

[21] Augustine (354-430) was a North African bishop, an outstanding leader and writer in the ancient church. *Ed.*

that you may receive; hear in order that you may believe; believe in order that you may do; and do in order that you may live, for faith follows upon hearing, obedience upon faith, and the promise upon obedience.

For this reason all things are ascribed to faith in the Scriptures, such as regeneration, true repentance, sanctification of the heart, the righteousness which avails with God, and the blessings of salvation and everlasting life. For faith is the mother and matrix of all good, as has been related at length.

Seeing then that in this matter this is the true and proper position of the Scriptures, as we have briefly declared, therefore you will have to acknowledge that those who willfully reject are put to shame by the malefactor, and that he will be their accuser in the day of the Lord, as the Lord said of the Ninevites and of the Queen of the South.

But all who hear and believe the Word of Christ, who turn to Christ by the power of faith with all their hearts, acknowledge Him openly by an unblamable, pious life before all the world and confidently seek His grace and mercy, to them He is a glorious Comforter, a precious balm and healing ointment in their troubled and wounded consciences, by which they may see and know God's unbounded favor, mercy, and love toward all truly penitent sinners, no matter how long and how grievously they have sinned, so that they by faith may satisfy their souls with Him, not doubting the grace of God on account of their sinful lives in which they formerly walked. For the Lord did not withhold grace, nor did He say, No, evildoer, your sins are too great and numerous, and moreover you have sinned too long. But as soon as He saw his new heart and heard his confessing love, He poured out His grace upon the poor, distressed sinner, and forgave him all his sins, and said, Today thou shalt be with me in paradise. For he that believeth on me hath eternal life. The prophet also says, If the unrighteous turn from his unrighteousness and does righteously, I will not remember his unrighteousness which he did.

### [I.] The Faith of the Woman Who Was a Sinner

Luke says: One of the Pharisees desired Jesus that he would eat with him. And he went into the Pharisee's house and sat down to meat. And, behold, a woman of the city, which was a sinner, when she knew that Jesus sat at meat in the Pharisee's house, brought an alabaster box of ointment and stood at his feet behind him, weeping, and began to wash his feet with tears, and did wipe them with the hairs of her head, and kissed his feet, and anointed them with the ointment. Luke 7:36-38.

In the case of this woman who was a sinner we see once more what kind of heart, disposition, fruit, and life, a sincere, true Christian faith brings with it. She had been possessed of seven devils (if indeed she was that woman, or Mary, of whom the evangelists make mention), and lived, it seems, as she pleased (for she is called a sinner in the Scriptures) so long as the Lord had not called her out of darkness into light, from lies unto truth. But as soon as she heard His Word, she with eagerness received it in a sincere and renewed heart, by which she, who was such a great sinner, became a penitent and pious woman. Her unrighteous, carnal heart was so inspired and touched that her eyes streamed with tears, so that she wet the feet of the Saviour with them. Her beautiful, braided hair she used as a towel with which to wipe His feet. She died to avarice, for she anointed His head and feet with an ointment so precious that it might have been sold for three hundred pence. Her proud heart was humbled, for she did not seek the highest seat at the table, but sat sorrowfully at the feet of the Lord and heard His blessed Word.

When the Pharisee saw this, he murmured. And Christ said to him, Simon, seest thou this woman? I entered into thine house, thou gavest me no water for my feet: but she hath washed my feet with tears, and wiped them with the hairs of her head. Thou gavest me no kiss: but this woman, since the time I came in, hath not ceased to kiss my feet. My head with oil thou didst not anoint: but this woman hath anointed my feet with ointment. Wherefore I say unto thee, her sins, which are many, are forgiven; for she loved much: for to whom little is forgiven the same loveth little. And he said unto her, Thy sins are forgiven; thy faith hath saved thee; go in peace. Luke 7:44-48, 50.

Dear reader, take notice that all the proud, haughty, avaricious, carnal, and adulterous persons who call themselves Christians, but are not such (for they testify by their disposition, heart, mind, and life that they hate Christ), are thoroughly shamed and reproved by this regenerate, penitent sinner; seeing that because she believed, her proud, haughty, and obdurate heart was changed into a humble, contrite, and broken one.

They say that they believe, and yet, alas, there are no limits nor bounds to their accursed haughtiness, foolish pride and pomp; they parade in silks, velvet, costly clothes, gold rings, chains, silver belts, pins and buttons, curiously adorned shirts, shawls, collars, veils, aprons, velvet shoes, slippers, and such like foolish finery. They never regard that the exalted apostles Peter and Paul have in plain and express words forbidden this all to Christian women. And if forbidden to women, how much more to men who are the leaders and heads of their wives! Notwithstanding all this they still want to be called the Christian Church.

Everyone has as much finery as he can afford and sometimes more than that. One wants to surpass another in this cursed folly, and they do not reflect that it is written, Love not the world, neither the things that are in the world. If any man love the world, the love of the Father is not in him. For all that is in the world, the lust of the flesh, and the lust of the eyes, and the pride of life is not of the Father, but is of the world. And the world passes away, and the lust thereof: but he that doeth the will of God abideth forever. I John 2:15-17.

Once more, this sinful woman became a believer, and from that moment she was cleansed of her unclean wicked flesh, for the unclean devil was cast out of it, as you have heard. But what ugly, shameful unchastity, adultery, and fornication is practiced among many men and women who boast that they believe, in many cities and countries, is best known to Him before whose eyes all things are open, and is alas not wholly concealed before men. It is manifest that the world is full of harlots, adulterers, fornicators, sexual perverts, bastards, and illegitimate children, and alas, it has come to such a pass that they live in freedom and liberty, nothwithstanding that God has commanded through Moses that both the adulterer and the adulteress should die (Deut. 22:22), that there were to be neither harlots nor those who patronized them in Israel, and that the illegitimate children even to the tenth generation were not to be admitted into the congregation of the Lord. And further, it was the express command and ordinance of God that if any one in Israel defiled a virgin not betrothed or engaged, and it was discovered, he was compelled to marry her, if her father consented. And he was not to put her away all his days, because he had humiliated her. Ex. 22:16.

Ah, reader, reflect upon what the last command implies. They all boast, however much given to harlotry, that they are the spiritual Israel, that they have the truth, and that they are baptized in the name of Christ. And yet they are not ashamed to turn their poor, weak sisters, who are included with them in the same faith, baptism, holy Supper, and worship, into poor, disgraced, and degraded strumpets against all Scripture and Christian love; even though God's own mouth and the commandment quoted above commands them that if they be deflowered, then they should take them to wife and never forsake them. If they would ponder these things, many a girl would be spared shame whereas now many an honest man's child is cruelly wronged, and many a girl deprived of her honor and virtue.

I write you the truth in Christ, you may believe it if you will. If you are a Christian or would be one, and have seduced a poor child with your sensuous approaches, and if you would not lose your soul, you are required to marry her and not forsake her nor thrust her away. You have humiliated her, as was said. This is the Lord's own Word and law. Everyone, therefore, who knowingly despises this law of God and rejects the one who has been violated and marries another, will have to confess before God that the former is his wife and not the latter. O you violators of feminine chastity, reflect upon these things and learn wisdom.

If you say that this command has reference only to Israel and not to the Christian, then I would ask you in the first place, whether you consider yourself to be a Christian or not. If you say, No, then do as you like, and look for the judgment threatened to all who are outside of Christ. But if you say, Yes, then the matter is already settled. She must be your wife. For a Christian must not so live with his poor sister as to make her a prostitute. Oh, no, the Scriptures teach that Christians are members of Christ, and not harlots and profligates. I verily hope this blunt language will be understood.

In the second place, I ask, Which should be the more holy and virtuous, the literal or the spiritual people of God? If you say the literal, then you have exalted Moses with his people and service above Christ and His people, a thing evidently contrary to all Scripture. But if you say the spiritual, then the matter is again decided that she must be your wife. For if the literal might not make a sister into a prostitute, much less the spiritual, which is the Lord's own body, brother, sister, generation, and bride.

In the third place, I ask whether the command, Thou shalt love thy neighbor as thyself, is not given to Christians as well as to Israel. If you say, No, you have deserted the whole New Testament, which solemnly teaches the love of our neighbor. But if you say, Yes, then I say for the third time that she must be your legitimate wife. For since you have, contrary to the commandment of love, so woefully disgraced her, therefore the Scriptures teach that you are to honor her by taking her to be your wife. Let everyone see to it that the commands of love will never become obsolete. Blessed are they who take heed to them and observe them in spirit.

In the fourth place, I ask whether there is anyone who with a good conscience can transgress and break the command of God. If you say, Yes, then you deny the whole Scriptures which teach that we must walk in the ways of the Lord and keep His commandments. But if you say, No (and no it is), then I tell you the fourth time, that she is and must be your wife. For it is the commandment of God, firmly based upon love, that if you have deflowered a virgin, you must marry her and never forsake her, as has been said.

Behold, my reader, here you are more than plainly taught what the Word of the Lord teaches in regard to this matter. And if you continue so ungodly as to transgress the commandment of the Lord for the sake of your harlotry, disgracing one and marrying the other, then you may read what your end and sentence will be, in case you do not repent.

I do not mean to say that a person who has in days gone by ignorantly done this thing must leave the wife whom he afterwards married and take in her stead the violated one. Not at all, for I doubt not but that the merciful Father will graciously overlook the errors of those who have ignorantly committed them, and who will now fear and gladly do what is right. But I write this that everyone should guard himself against such disgrace, and reflect more profoundly upon the command of the Lord and on love, and observe how Christ is so wholly despised by the world. For alas, they are altogether driven by their accursed lusts, whether they are lords, princes, priests, monks, noble or ignoble, burghers or peasants, with few exceptions. They pursue the improper, devilish shame and accursed adultery with such an avidity as of a hound after a hare. They are, says Jeremiah (5:8), as fed horses in the morning; every one neighed after his neighbor's wife. There is nothing that can frighten or deter them from this accursed abomination: neither natural reason, nor Moses with all his threatenings, neither the prophets, nor the apostles, nor Christ Jesus Himself; neither heaven nor angels, neither hell nor the devil, neither life nor death. If they can only give free rein to their ugly, unchaste lust, then all is fine as far as they are concerned.

They turn every device to this end. Some they seduce with subtle clever words, others with scoundrel promises and gifts; some by giving them wine to drink, with dances and songs of levity; some by lavish spending, by dress and similar devices; yea, some by their seducing sighings and weepings; just so they can accomplish their ungodly designs and gratify their lusts, then all is fine and dandy. But that they thereby incense Almighty God, transgress His holy Word, disgrace their neighbor, violate love, defile the marriage bed, violate young women, call into being illegitimate children, and condemn their own poor souls forever—about all this they are not worried. They say, This is our portion and our lot, and that is all there is to it.

But I say with Moses: Cursed be they of God who do works of iniquity, and all the people shall say, Amen; and with Job, that hell will consume them as drought and heat consume the snow-waters; with Paul, that God will judge them; and with John, that their part is in the lake which burneth with fire and brimstone, which is eternal death. Ah, that these poor people would take heed, believe, and consider the words of the Lord!

In the second place, I write this so that every one might awaken, sincerely repent, and lament before God his past disgraceful conduct, that He cast him not off eternally but that He be gracious to him for the sake of the blood of His Son. I write it that they may no more defile the bed of their neighbor nor violate young women, but live in all honor, each with his own wife; the unmarried keeping free from all immorality, and if he cannot restrain himself, let him seek a good pious wife in the fear of God. He that has transgressed and has not yet taken another, let him honor the disgraced one, and according to Christian love and the Word of God, lift her out of the dung and teach their children and children's children from generation to generation. Even as the pious Tobias did to his dear son saying: Beware of all harlotry, my son, and take not a strange woman, but keep to your own wife.

Know ye not, says Paul, that your bodies are the members of Christ? Shall I then take the members of Christ and make them members of a harlot? God forbid. I Cor. 6:15. Again, he says, For this is the will of God, even your sanctification, that ye should abstain from fornication: that every one of you should know how to possess his vessel (that is, his body) in sanctification and honor; not in the lust of concupiscence, even as the Gentiles which know not God: for God has not called us unto uncleanness, but unto holiness. I Thess. 4:3-7. Yes, good reader, true believers have to lead an honorable and chaste life, so that adultery, fornication, and unchastity are never so much as mentioned, whether in private or in public (except by way of admonition and warning), for thus it becomes the saints to live.

And even as we find many wicked men who shamefully wrong poor, simple hearts, so on the other hand we find many shameless women and girls who are often the first cause that such disgrace is sought and sometimes practiced upon them. And although many are not guilty of the deed, nevertheless they are not guiltless in that they allow such intimacy with other men and companions, with bold face singing, dancing, drinking, kissing, flirting, primping and fixing up, and the like vanity and abominations whereby with some they kindle the fire of base passions which continue till consumed, as may be seen.

Oh, how properly Sirach admonishes us when he says, Meet not with an harlot, lest thou fall into her snares. Use not much the company of a woman that is a singer, lest thou be taken with her attempts. Gaze not on a maid that thou fall not by those things that are precious in her. Give not thy soul unto harlots that thou lose not thine inheritance. Look not round about thee in the streets of the city, nor wander thou in the solitary places thereof. Turn away thine eye from a beautiful woman and look not upon another's beauty; for many have been deceived by the beauty of a woman, for herewith love is kindled as a fire. Sit not at all with another man's wife, nor sit down with her in thine arms, and spend not thy money with her at the wine, lest thine heart incline unto her, and so through thy desire, thou fall into destruction. Sir. 9:3-9.

Now if the afore-mentioned married and unmarried women were true believers as was this sinful woman, if they would only fear the Lord, they would abandon all vanity and ungodly action, and lay snares for none, nor give any occasion for evil. Yes, they would live honorably and modestly, avoiding all unnecessary adornment and pomp and making or desiring no other clothes than those which are necessary, and which our daily toil makes right and proper. Then they would not be seen very often in the idolatrous temple and idle banquets, for which occasion this pompous show is generally gotten up.

The sinful woman adorned her soul inwardly and not her appearance outwardly, for she believed that these adorn their bodies externally and not their souls internally, for they believe not.

The sinful woman sighed and wept and feared the wrath and judgment of the Lord, for she saw that she had done wrong and sinned. But these people laugh and dance, sing and waltz about, and do not see their enormous misdeeds and grievous sins, and therefore do not fear the coming wrath and judgment of the Lord.

This sinful woman was compassionate and merciful, anointing the head and feet of the Lord, and found the true worship. But these people are unmerciful and cruel, and know of no other worship than to go to the churches, receive holy water, offer tapers and wax candles to blind blocks and icons; to hear masses and vespers read, to call upon departed saints for help, to confess once or twice a year to their idolatrous, drunken, harloting priests; to receive their abomination-bread and absolution, and the like superstitions and deceptions.

The sinful woman sought the company of the righteous, but these people seek the company of the unrighteous. They come together to deal in all manner of foolishness, to deprive their neighbors of their good name, to defame and gossip, to speak disgracefully of one another, to talk about costly furniture, houses, goods, and handsome companions, men, and fine clothing. In short, their works openly show that they have not the faith of the sinful woman and are not in the congregation of the righteous.

The sinful woman sat at the feet of Jesus and heard His holy Word, but these people hear teachers who tickle their ears and preach as they like it. But why talk at length about it? It is, O God, so corrupted that we find the whole world filled with sots of both sexes, deaf ears (spiritually, that is), unenlightened hearts; the blind are leading the blind in such a way that they will all together fall into the pit of eternal death unless they get to see the light—if we believe it to be true what the mouth of the Lord has taught us. For it is all false doctrine, false sacraments, false religion, sheer unbelief, and vain, frivolous life no matter where we turn.

Reader, notice how vastly this sinful woman after conversion differs as to faith and conduct from the faith and conduct of the world. They are like the sinful woman before her conversion, but not after it. Whether such people are believers I will let the sensible reader reflect in the light of the Spirit and Word of the Lord.

I know of a certainty that a proud, haughty person is no Christian, no matter who he is. I know of a certainty that an avaricious, selfish person is no Christian, that a drunken, gluttonous person is no Christian, that an impure, fornicating person is no Christian, that a heady, envious person is no Christian, that a disobedient, idolatrous person is no Christian, that a false, untruthful person is no Christian, that an untrustworthy, thieving person is no Christian, that a defaming, slandering person is no Christian, or anybody incompassionate, or cruel even if he is baptized a hundred times and attends the Lord's Supper daily. For it is not the sacraments nor the signs, such as baptism and the Lord's Supper, but a sincere, Christian faith, with its unblamable, pious fruits, represented by the sacraments, that makes a true Christian and has the promise of life, and in many places besides.[22]

Here neither masses, holy water, holy days, rosaries, auricular confession, nor absolution avail, only a believing, contrite, broken heart, spirit, and mind; a penitent, changed, new heart; a pious life, dead unto sin, according to truth. It was such a confession, such a penance, which this sinful woman performed. And she also heard immediately, Thy sins are forgiven. Thy faith has saved thee; go in peace.

But the abominable auricular confession[23] which is so highly rated by the world is nothing but pure hypocrisy, human righteousness and superstition, open delusion of unbelievers, a false hope of the impenitent sinner, a subtlety invented by the avaricious priests whereby they set aside true confession and repentance, and comfort and strengthen the world in its reckless, ungodly life.

[22] The last five words seem to be misplaced in the original. *Tr.*

[23] Literally, confession to the ear (of the priest)—by members of the Roman Catholic Church. *Ed.*

But if you would perform a genuine penance and receive true absolution of your God, then approach Him with a believing, penitent, and changed heart; with a sorrowing, broken, distressed mind; and leave off sinning. Deal justly and fairly with your neighbor; love, aid, serve, reprove, and comfort him; and if you have sinned against him or deceived him, acknowledge it to him and satisfy him. Behold, this is the only true penance which is taught in the Word of your God. The dear Lord grant that you may rightly understand and do in deed.

I, therefore, entreat and desire all women through the mercy of the Lord to take this sorrowful, sorrowing woman as a pattern and follow her faith. Humble yourselves before the Lord and reprove your avarice, pride, impurity, and all manner of evil. Let all your thoughts be pure; let your words be circumspect and seasoned with salt. And whatsoever you do, do that in the name and fear of the Lord Jesus. Do not adorn yourselves with gold, silver, costly pearls and embroidered hair, and expensive, unusual dress. Use such clothing as becomes women professing godliness and which is suitable in your occupation. Be obedient to your husbands in all reasonable things so that those who do not believe may be gained by your upright, pious conversation without the Word, as Peter says.

Remain within your houses and gates unless you have something of importance to regulate, such as to make purchases, to provide in temporal needs, to hear the Word of the Lord, or to receive the holy sacraments, etc. Attend faithfully to your charge, to your children, house, and family, and to all that is entrusted to you, and walk in all things as the sinful woman did after her conversion, in order that you may be true daughters of Sarah, believing women, sisters of Christ, heirs of the life to come (I Pet. 3:6), and that you may hear the gracious words, Thy sins are forgiven. Thy faith hath saved thee; go in peace.

## [J.] The Faith of the Syrophenician Woman

Matthew writes that Jesus was in the land of Gennesaret, and says, Then Jesus went thence and departed into the coasts of Tyre and Sidon. And, behold, a woman of Canaan came out of the same coasts, and cried unto him, saying, Have mercy on me, O Lord, thou son of David; my daughter is grievously vexed with a devil. But he answered her not a word. And his disciples came and besought him, saying, Send her away; for she crieth after us. But he answered and said, I am not sent but unto the lost sheep of the house of Israel. Then she came and worshipped him, saying, Lord, help me. But he answered and said, It is not meet to take the children's bread, and to cast it to dogs. And she said, Truth, Lord; yet the dogs eat of the crumbs which fall from their masters' table. Then Jesus answered and said to her, O woman, great is thy faith: be it unto thee even as thou wilt. And her daughter was made whole from that very hour. Matt. 15:21-28.

Here you have another fine example and pattern of sincere, Christian faith, for when this woman perceived how powerfully Jesus preached grace, and hearing besides that He could do what He desired, that He manifested love and mercy, that He sent none away comfortless; she approached Him without hesitation, and despaired not of His grace, mercy, love, and power, although she was not heard at the first or second request. Unshaken in her faith and prayer her desire was such that she might be as one of the dogs which partake of the spiritual crumbs of His mercy, and obtain relief for her poor daughter who was so sadly vexed by a devil. Yes, she manifested such a faith, constancy, humility, and piety that the Lord said to her, O woman, great is thy faith; be it unto thee even as thou wilt.

Faithful reader, observe. If with spiritual eyes we consider this woman's faith and fruits we will be taught of her, especially in two particulars. For as soon as she heard that the Lord taught mercy, grace, repentance, and reformation, that He preached the kingdom of God, raised the dead, made the blind to see, the deaf to hear, the crippled to walk, the lepers to be cleansed, the sick to be healed, and that He cast out unclean spirits; that He reproved the scribes, Pharisees, and the common people for their unbelief, perverseness, blind hypocrisy, and carnal lives, and testified that He was the prophet and Messiah who was promised in the Law and the Prophets—things whereby all Judea and the adjacent area were greatly moved—her womanly heart and mind were so turned to Him through such testimonies, miracles, doctrines, and deeds of love, that she did not doubt His mercy, power, goodness, and grace. She, therefore, went to Him with a sincere desire, in sure and true faith, trusting with all her heart that He would not deny her humble prayer, but that He would graciously hear and grant it. She also obtained what she desired.

She heard and believed; she saw and confessed. These foolish people imagine that they are Christian, but are to my mind more unbelieving, blinder, more hardened, and worse than Turks, Tartars, or any other faraway heathen. Their works testify that I write the truth. They cannot be moved to hear or obey the truth by godly means and services, neither by doctrine nor exhortation, neither by irreproachable lives, nor the innocent blood of the saints shed daily before their eyes, as has been mentioned before when treating of the faith of the malefactor.

The agitation and doctrine of the holy divine Word we have had in Germanic lands for many years, and daily more abundantly in such power and clearness that it may be felt with the hands that it is the finger and work of the Lord. For the haughty are humbled, the avaricious made ready to contribute to others, the drunkards become sober, the unchaste pure, and men do not dare permit a single thought or word or deed contrary to the Word, will, and Spirit of the Lord. And they receive it with such conviction that they do not fear to sacrifice for it father, mother, husband, wife, children, possessions, and their lifeblood. For many are burned for it, drowned, killed with the sword, imprisoned, banished, and their property confiscated.

Yet all this avails nothing to these obdurate people. If it is but said when an innocent sheep has been slaughtered that he was an Anabaptist, then it is all right. They never inquire what he professed, what Scriptural grounds he had, what his conduct and life were, or whether or not he had harmed anyone. Neither do they reflect that it must be a unique power and work which separates one so wholly from his drinking, harloting, pomp and pride, vanity, ugly lying, carnal life, and from all idolatry; and constrains him to all sobriety, chastity, meekness, piety, truth, and religion; things for which we have to hear excessively much of shame and disgrace, endure so much persecution and misery, and so often suffer the loss of life, as you may see.

If a thief is led to the gallows or a murderer is broken upon the wheel, or if a malefactor is punished with death, everyone inquires what he has done. He is not condemned by the judges as long as they have not grasped fully the basis and truth concerning his evil deed. But if an innocent, contrite Christian, whom the merciful Lord has rescued from the evil, ungodly ways of sin, and has placed in the way of peace, is accused by the priests and preachers, and placed before their court, they consider it not worth their time to investigate what reasons or Scriptures move him so that he refuses to hear his priests and preachers, to have his children baptized, to attend their services, to no longer eat and drink to excess with them, and to serve the devil. Nor do they care to know why he reformed his life and received the baptism of Christ, or what drives him so willingly to suffer, or even to die, for his faith. They only ask, Is he baptized? If he answers in the affirmative, the sentence is already pronounced that he must die.

Many see or hear such miracles of Almighty God that a poor, unlearned man, yes, sometimes poor frail women or girls, are so fortified in God that they fear neither judge nor executioner: that neither fire nor water, halter nor sword, life nor death, can frighten or deter them from their faith. But their persecutors do not even inquire what they did, whether they are traitors to their country or city, whether they have taken the property or life of others, disgraced someone's daughter or wife, or whether they did anything not in accordance with the Word of God, with common decency, and with natural reasonableness. Oh, no, so much decency and love are not to be found. But if a man has and believes the Word of his Lord, and obediently obeys His commands and ordinances, and gladly regulates his poor, weak members by the truth, then he is called a rebel by the lords, a heretic by the learned ones, and is adjudged by the common people as well deserving severe punishments and grievous death.

Behold, thus has the murderous, bloodthirsty devil deceived the whole world, O God, through his priests and preachers. Yes, I fear scarcely one is to be found among a hundred thousand who will lay to heart such a courageous strong faith, obedience, confidence, power, great suffering, and shameful death, so as to reflect upon his ugly unbelief, disgraceful wickedness, and willful carnal life; or to doubt the doctrine of his teachers, their sacraments, their lives and worship. How truly did the prophets say, The righteous perisheth and no man layeth it to heart. Isa. 57:1. Never can there be found under all heaven a more wicked, obdurate unbelief, a more perverse disdain, a more adamant self-will, a more condemnable folly, a more accursedly wicked state of things than that which we have just now related.

If there is a report of war and soldiers, everybody in the whole country is afraid, both great and small, burgher and peasant. Everybody buys defensive armor; they watch and make ready for defense as much as possible. Or if they hear of famine or pestilence, then all sensible people tremble. And if on the contrary there is a time of tranquillity, peace, prosperity, and weal, then all who hear it rejoice. But now the great Lord Christ Jesus causes His trumpets to sound, His drums to roll, warning us in tender love through all His apostles and prophets against the crafty wiles and subtle assaults of the devil, and that all they must die who follow and obey him. Few are to be found however who put on the armor of God; few who guard against the secret encroachment of Satan and put up a defense. Men voluntarily run into his hands, both men and women, and eagerly do things which please him. Those who do not may expect great tribulation and misery.

Besides, it is manifest that the abominable pestilence of false doctrine consumes the whole world, and that the bread of souls for all hungry consciences is very scarce in consequence of the angry cry and falsifying writings of the serpentlike preachers. And alas, there are few who weep and sigh for it. The eternal grace, mercy, favor, glory, kingdom, and peace of Christ are offered to us, but our ears are waxed dull, our hearts are petrified, and our perverse wickedness desires them not.

So this pious Syrophenician woman did not do; she heard, believed, saw His miracles and confessed His power, and therefore prayed with confidence and obtained what she desired. For she believed Christ with all her heart and doubted not His grace.

In the second place, she admonishes all pious parents that they should have a Christian solicitude for the salvation of their children, because she so faithfully entreated for her demon-possessed daughter, not desisting till she was heard. For it cannot be otherwise that if I am a true Christian, all my work before God and my neighbor are works of love, for God out of whose Word a Christian is born, says John, is love. That the Begetter and the begotten are alike, of one mind and heart, is as clear as blessed daylight.

If now I seek the praises of the Lord with all my heart, and if I love the salvation of my neighbors, many of whom I have never seen, how much more should I have at heart the salvation of my dear children whom God has given me; who are out of my loins, and are my natural flesh and blood; so that the mighty Lord may be praised by them and be eternally honored in them.

Yes, I am sure, and what I write I write from a certain testimony of my own conscience before Almighty God before whom I stand. All properly believing parents are thus minded toward their children, that they would a hundred times rather see them jailed in a deep, dark dungeon for the sake of the Lord and His testimony than sitting with the deceiving priests in their idol church or with drunken dolts in taverns, or in company of scorners who despise the name of the Lord and hate His holy Word.

A hundred times rather would they see them, for the sake of the truth of the Lord, bound hands and feet and dragged before lords and princes, than to see them marry rich persons who fear not God, neither walk in the ways of the Lord, and so be feted in dances, song, and play, with pomp and splendor, with pipe and drum, with lutes and cymbals. A hundred times rather would they see them scourged from head to foot for the sake of the glory and holy name of the Lord than to see them adorn themselves with silks, velvets, gold, silver, costly trimmed and tailored clothes, and the like vanity and pomp. Yes, a hundred times rather would they see them exiled, burning at the stake, drowning or attached to a wheel, for righteousness' sake, than to see them live apart from God in all luxury and carnal pleasures, or be emperors and kings and therefore sent to condemnation.

Woe to all who are not so minded concerning their children. For if I so love their flesh that I overlook their sins, if I do not punish the transgressions of the young with a rod and the older with the tongue, if I do not teach them the ways of the Lord, if I do not set them an unblamable example, if I do not direct them at all times to Christ and His Word, ordinances, commands, and example, and if I do not seek their salvation with all my heart and soul, then I will not escape my punishment. For in the day of the Lord their souls and blood, damnation and death, will be laid at my door as a blind and silent watchman.

Christian temperament teaches plainly that all Christian parents should be as sharp, pungent salt, a shining light, and an unblamable, faithful teacher, each in his own home. The high priest Eli was held responsible because he had not reproved his children enough.

If I see my neighbor's ox or ass go astray, I must bring him back to the owner or keep him safe, as Moses teaches. If now it becomes me thus to do with another man's brute beast, how much more should I be concerned for the souls of my children who are so readily misled, and wander so easily from the right way by their willful flesh in which no good dwells.

If I see my neighbor's ox or ass fallen in a pit, or under the weight of a burden, I do not leave until the beast is helped. How much more should I be solicitous for my children whom I see before me, lying beneath the burden of their sins by reason of the poisonous serpent's nature, knowing that unless they are earnestly reproved and instructed in grace, they will fall into the hellish abyss of eternal death.

Once more, if I see my neighbor's house on fire and his goods perishing, it is reasonable that I should exert myself to put out the fire and as far as possible to bring the goods under cover. But it is much more reasonable that I extinguish the fire of base desires in my child with the water of the divine Word, and preserve the heavenly goods as far as I am able.

The Holy Scriptures teach that God purifies the heart by faith, that faith comes by hearing, and justification by faith. Therefore let everyone take heed, if he truly loves his children, that he acquaint them rightly with the Word of the Lord as soon as they have ears to hear and hearts to understand; that he direct them in the way of truth, and zealously watch over all their doings, that they may from youth learn to know the Lord their God, fear, love, honor, thank, and serve Him, lest the inborn nature of sin rule in them or become dominant to the everlasting shame of their poor souls.

Moses taught Israel saying, These words, which I command thee this day, shall be in thine heart: and thou shalt teach them diligently unto thy children, and shalt talk of them when thou sittest in thine house, and when thou walkest by the way, and when thou liest down, and when thou risest up. And thou shalt bind them for a sign upon thine hand, and they shall be as frontlets between thine eyes. And thou shall write them upon the posts of thy house, and on thy gates. That your days may be multiplied, and the days of your children, in the land which the Lord sware unto your fathers to give them, as the days of heaven upon the earth. Deut. 6:6-9; 11:21.

In another place he says, And it shall be when thy son asketh thee in time to come, saying, What is this? That thou shalt say unto him, By strength of hand the Lord brought us out of Egypt, from the house of bondage. Ex. 13:14.

Joshua commanded Israel by the command of the Lord and said, Pass over before the ark of the Lord your God into the midst of Jordan, and take you up every man of you a stone upon his shoulder, according unto the number of the tribes of the children of Israel: that this may be a sign among you, that when your children ask their fathers in time to come, saying, What mean ye by these stones? Then ye shall answer them, The waters of Jordan were cut off before the ark of the covenant of the Lord, when it passed over Jordan, the waters of Jordan were cut off: and these stones shall be a memorial unto the children of Israel forever. Josh. 4:5-7.

Behold, worthy reader, thus the literal Israel was obliged to teach the children from youth and to acquaint them with all the blessings and miracles of the Lord which had happened to them and their fathers, so that they might fear, love, and serve the Lord all their days, and so receive the blessings, and escape the curse, which was contained in the Law.

In like manner we must also do, if we rightly confess Christ, believe His Word, and with our children desire to obtain the worthy and pleasant land, and eternally to inherit it in grace, the things which He has promised His children. Therefore, let us not neglect it, but observe it well, teach our children rightly in the Word, and point out His righteous judgments—awful judgment—so that they may learn to fear the Lord with all their heart and turn from evil.

Let us also keep before them God's unfathomably great mercy, love, and the services of His grace, so that they may love Him for it and walk in

His statutes. Let us imprint on their hearts Jesus Christ, our only and eternal Saviour, with His Holy Spirit, Word, and example, so that they may rightly know Him and follow in His footsteps. And let us set them an example in all wisdom, righteousness, and truth, with a pious and virtuous life, so that they may through the careful admonition and unblamable example of their pious parents be instructed in the kingdom of God, and furnished to all manner of good works.

For all who have such a faith as this woman had, and see that the end of sin is death, will not cease to sigh and lament to God that He would in mercy assist their poor children so to resist and vanquish the impure spirit of the devil that he may not lead them captive at his evil will, to the eternal shame and disgrace of their poor souls. They pray that their children may from their youth rightly learn to know the immortal, eternal God and Father, through Jesus Christ His beloved Son, and in truth serve Him under His cross. So may they recount all the mighty works and miracles of the Lord our God; the great mercy, grace, favor, and love of His Almighty Father, His blessed Word, will, ordinance, and life, with all the merits, power, and fruit of the death and blood of Christ His Blessed Son; also the goodness, wisdom, truth, and gifts of His eternal and Holy Spirit to their children and their children's children, and to all their descendants: even until the Lord Jesus Christ appear in the glorious majesty of His heavenly Father in the clouds of heaven at the final judgment, to reward everyone according to his works, be they good or evil. II Cor. 5:10.

Behold, worthy readers, thus it behooves true Christians to teach, to admonish, to reprove, and to chasten their children; to set them an example in all righteousness, to rear them in the fear of the Lord, and to care for their poor souls lest through their negligence they depart from the true path, die in their sins, and so perish at last in their unbelief.

The Lord testifies concerning Abraham saying, Shall I hide from Abraham that thing which I do; seeing that Abraham shall surely become a great and mighty nation, and all the nations of the earth shall be blessed in him? For I know him, that he will command his children and his household after him, and they shall keep the way of the Lord to do justice and judgment. Gen. 18:17-19.

The good Tobit taught his son and said, My son, obey thy father, serve the Lord in truth and be upright; keep His commandments, and teach thy children to do likewise, that they give alms, fear God always, and love Him and trust Him with all their heart. And when they attain the age of maturity and have not the power of continence (but him that has it, him I would advise with Paul to use it unto the Lord) do not let them keep company with those outside of Christ and His church, be they noble, rich, or handsome, as do the proud, avaricious, and unchaste of this world; but let them keep company with those who fear the Lord, love, seek, honor, and follow, thank and serve Him with the whole heart, be they noble or common, rich or poor, beautiful or plain, for they are holy and children of saints, and therefore it should and must be done in the Lord.

Let everyone beware and conduct himself properly lest the wrath and fearful judgments of God be inflicted upon him on account of his unchastity and evil desires, even as in the days of Noah and Lot when they came upon the first world.

But alas, how few they are who take this to heart and sincerely seek the salvation of their children! If they can but provide for them worldly and temporal things, then their desires are gratified. The priests' ordinances and the churches' services are their only faith, hope, and the foundation of salvation. They neither know nor seek any other.

Their whole life from beginning to end is contrary to the Word of Christ. For as soon as they are born they are carried to the idolatrous, false bath; the holy name of the Lord is abused over them; they are reared in all vanity and blindness, in pomp and pride, in open idolatry and false worship, and in the unfeeling, carefree life of the world. In and out of their houses they hear and see nothing but unrighteousness, malice, wickedness, lying, defrauding, cursing, swearing, infidelity, avarice, quarreling, fighting, intoxication, fornication, and all manner of disgrace. They never learn to know Christ and His Word aright, but they hate the truth and persecute righteousness. In short, they show by their actions that they are full of the evil, unclean spirit, and are led by his will, as may be seen.

For it never fails, as your spirit is, so is also your conduct in life. If the Spirit of Christ, which is holy and pure, is in you, then are also your whole life and fruit pure and holy. Again, if the spirit of the evil one, which is impure and wicked, is in you, then all your ways and fruits will be evil and impure. This is incontrovertible.

Therefore, Paul says, As many as are led by the Spirit of God, they are the sons of God. Again, Those who are led by the spirit of the devil are the sons of the devil. Dear reader, reflect. If these poor people had but a spark of the Spirit of the Lord they would a thousand times sooner be seethed in boiling oil, or enter into the fire, than hear and see such folly, wickedness, and willfulness in their children, to say nothing about teaching or encouraging such things. For it is incontrovertible, according to the tenor of the Scriptures, that if they do not receive Christ, their end will be eternal death.

Therefore, all who fear the Lord, love your children with divine love; seek their salvation with all your hearts even as Abraham, Tobit, and the Maccabean mother did. If they transgress, reprove them sharply. If they err, exhort them paternally. If they are childish, bear them patiently. If they are of teachable age, instruct them in a Christian fashion. Dedicate them to the Lord from youth; watch over their souls as long as they are under your care, lest you lose also your own salvation on their account.[24] Pray

---

[24] The Swiss Mennonites of eastern Pennsylvania used to have a traditional fear that their own salvation would be imperiled or lost if their children went astray. Here Menno teaches the same view. Ed.

without ceasing, as this pious woman did, that the Lord may grant them His grace, that they may resist the devil; subdue their inborn, sinful nature by the Spirit and help of the Lord; and walk from their youth before God and His church in all righteousness, truth, and wisdom, in a firm and sure faith, in unfeigned love and living hope, in an honorable and holy life, unblamable and without offense, in all the fruits of faith unto life eternal. Amen.

## [VII. A CALL TO REPENTANCE AND TRUE FAITH]

Similarly in all the afore-mentioned examples, the diligent reader may also, with pious and good conscience, seriously reflect upon the faith of the spotless, glorious mother Mary; that of Matthew, the aged Simeon and Anna; also of the blind man and such like, and I trust that he will by the grace and help of God fully understand how very simple, plain, and ordinary, how unfeigned, pious, upright, patient, ardent, peaceable, joyous, merciful, amiable, helpful, quiet, humble, zealous, irreproachable, and pious a true regenerating Christian faith is, inwardly in power before God, and outwardly in fruits before one's neighbor.

Yes, that even as a good, fruitful tree of its own accord, without any compulsion, always brings forth its own good fruits, so also the true Christian faith must bring forth it own good fruits. For it is infallible, The righteous must live out of his faith.[25]

If Abraham, Isaac, Jacob, Moses, Joshua, and Samuel, with all the patriarchs and prophets, believed the Word of the Lord, which was declared to them by angels, and were found faithful to it, how much more should we believe and be faithful to that Word which the Prince of angels, God's only begotten Son, the true witness and teacher of righteousness, Christ Jesus, carried from the high heavens out of His Father's heart, and which He taught on earth below.

It is not enough to say with the mouth that Jesus Christ is the Son of God, that He fulfilled the Law for us,[26] that He paid for our sins with His blood, and made reconciliation with the Father by His sacrifice and death. Neither will it suffice to say that His Gospel is true, that His Word is right, that the wages of sin is death, and that grace is eternal life. It must also be grasped in the heart and taken up in the soul, otherwise it will not justify. With the heart, says Paul, man believeth unto righteousness. Rom. 10:10.

All who believe with their whole hearts that Christ Jesus is the righteous branch of David, the righteous, wise King, the true promised Prophet, the right Way and Truth and our only Redeemer,[27] Intercessor, Mediator, and

---

[25] The Biblical expression, "The just shall live by faith," has been variously translated. In Menno's day, and still, the Dutch translations have rendered it: "The just shall live out of his faith." *Tr.*

[26] This is called Christ's active obedience by theologians.

[27] The Dutch *Versoener* means one who atones. *Ed.*

High Priest (Jer. 23:5), do also at the same time believe that all His words are unchangeable, that His sacrifice is sufficient and perfect. They therefore obey His Word, walk in His commandments, bow to His scepter, and quiet their consciences with His grace, atonement, merit, sacrifice, promise, death, and blood. They believe and confess that if they forsake His Word and will, willfully transgress His commandments, and live after the flesh, that God will require it at their hands and punish them eternally with the fire of His wrath, through His righteous judgment. For if those who willfully transgressed the Law of Moses had to die without mercy upon the testimony of two or three witnesses (Heb. 10:28), how much more will they be punished who trample underfoot the Son of God, who esteem the pure blood of the New Testament as impure, and profane the Holy Spirit of grace?

Yes, kind reader, if we truly believed it and acknowledged it in our souls, it would so move our hearts and enkindle them with the fear and love of the Lord, that even if all the tyrants that ever lived stood before us in all their terrible torture and blood shedding, they would not in the least deter or hinder one iota of the Word and way of the Lord. Moreover, all our impure, carnal thoughts, unseasoned words, and useless, ungodly works would soon die, as Sirach says: The fear of the Lord driveth away sins (Ecclus. 1:21), and, It is impossible to be justified without the fear of the Lord.

Seeing then that it is altogether evident that a sincere, Christian faith acknowledges God in His righteousness, therefore trembles before His judgment, and consequently buries sin and forsakes it, as has been related more than once; and seeing that you nevertheless live in all avarice, unchastity, drunkenness, wrath, fornication, blindness, idolatry, and all manner of wickedness; pray where is then your faith, and the word of God of which you boast so much? Do you not know that it is written, If ye live after the flesh ye shall die? Or do you think that you can trifle with God as with a man? Be not deceived, says Paul, God is not mocked.

Ah, reader, take heed, I tell you the truth in Christ. Beware! If you do not repent with all your heart and seek God through Christ, if you do not hear, believe, and fear Him, but remain earthly and carnal and walk after your desires, your sentence of death is already pronounced. As Christ Himself says, I judge no man. The word that I have spoken, the same shall judge you in the last day.

I therefore admonish you as before God, even as I do mine own soul, lay aside quickly all false doctrine, all unbelief, idolatry, and earthly, improper living, in which, alas, you have hitherto walked so carnally, lest the wrath of God overtake you in the sleep of your sins.

Wake up! He is still merciful. Seek and embrace the true doctrine, true faith, true sacraments, the true service, and a godly life, as the Scriptures teach. Then shall the light break forth as the morning, and thine health shall spring forth speedily, and thy righteousness shall go before thee; the glory of the Lord shall be thy rereward. Isa. 58:8.

And I say, If you really believed and rightly grasped that you become by or in Adam's disobedience children of the devil, of wrath, and of eternal death; become subject to the righteous curse and judgment of God; and that now all faults and sins are taken away and reconciled through the stainless blood of Christ, so that you are called from wrath into grace, from cursings to blessings, out of death to life, not to mention the gracious benefits which are daily shown you; then your hearts would blossom forth as the sweet-scented, blooming violet, full of pure love. Yes, they would leap forth as the living fountain, giving forth the sweet and pleasant waters of righteousness, and you would with the holy Paul say from your inmost soul, Who shall separate us from the love of God? It can never be, if I am in the bonds of perfectness with Him, and love Him with a pure heart, a good conscience, and unfeigned faith, that anything could then turn me away or separate me from Him. For it is my only desire and highest joy to hear and speak of His Word, and in my weakness walk as He commanded and taught through His Son; let it cost money and possessions, flesh or blood, if that please Him.

Behold, dear reader, since then it is clearer than clear in the Holy Scriptures that genuine Christian faith through the fear of God dies to sin, and through love does the right though in weakness, I therefore let you judge whether they believe from the heart who with the mouth say that the blood of Christ is the atoning sacrifice for their sin, and nevertheless seek and follow after all kinds of idolatry, such as infant baptism, holy water, absolution, auricular confession, masses; golden, silver, and wooden saints; cultivated and baked Christs,[28] stone churches, and the drunken harloting of priests. Ah, how well it would be for them to reflect!

I say, As surely as the Lord lives, there will in all eternity be found no other remedy for our sins, neither in heaven nor on earth; no works, no merits, no sacraments, even though they are used according to the Scriptures; no oppression, tribulation, innocent blood of saints, no angel, men, nor any other means but only the immaculate, crimson blood of the Lamb of sacrifice which was once shed for the remission of our sins out of pure grace.

Therefore it is incontrovertible that all those who employ such strange, idolatrous remedies for sin do not belong to the believing, grateful church of Christ. Therefore I will produce a few passages from the Gospels and the apostles' writings, and hang them as a mirror before your eyes in which you may view yourselves and see whether or no you are believing Christians.

The Word of the Lord teaches as follows: Verily, verily, I say unto thee, Except a man be born again, he cannot see the kingdom of God. And, verily I say unto you, Except ye be converted and become as little children, ye shall not enter into the kingdom of heaven. Test yourself with these. If you are born of the pure seed of the holy Word, the nature of the seed must

[28] An ironic reference to the Roman Catholic doctrine of transubstantiation which holds that the (baked) wafer of the communion service is actually changed into the body and blood of Christ. *Ed.*

be in you. And if you have become like little children in malice, then pride, unchastity, avarice, hatred, and envy no longer reside in you, for the innocent children know nothing of such sins. But if you continue to live in the old Adam and not in the new nature of Christ, and walk after the base, impure desires of your flesh, then you prove indeed that you are not born of God and have not His faith.

Again the Word of the Lord teaches, Go into all the world and preach the gospel to every creature; he that believeth and is baptized shall be saved. Here prove yourselves again. He that believes and is rightly baptized, truly repents, circumcises his heart, dies to sin, rises in Christ to a new life, etc. But if you now remain impenitent, your heart uncircumcised, not dead to sin, and if you live outside of Christ and His Word, then your deeds witness that you are unbelieving and have not the baptism of Christ.

Once more the Word of the Lord teaches, If thou wilt enter life, keep the commandments. For in Christ, says Paul, neither circumcision nor uncircumcision availeth anything, but the keeping of the commandments of God. And this is His command: Thou shalt love the Lord thy God with all thy heart, and will all thy soul, and with all thy mind, and with all thy strength, and thou shalt love thy neighbor as thyself. Mark 12:30. Now examine yourselves again. If you love God, you will gladly keep His commandments and you will do to your neighbor as you would have him do to you. But if you despise His Word, do not keep His ordinances in doctrine, baptism, Holy Supper, and separation, and if you do not walk according to His holy and godly commands, but slander, cheat, and betray your neighbor; if you take your neighbor's life, disgrace his wife, daughters, or servants, and treat him perfidiously; if you lead the poor, blind souls from the truth, the way, and the obedience of the Lord, be it through persecution or false doctrine; and so rob them of the eternal kingdom, and so lead them to hell, then it is more than clear that you hate the commandment of the Lord and have not His faith.

And again, the Word of the Lord teaches, Enter ye in at the strait gate; for wide is the gate, and broad is the way, that leadeth to destruction, and many there be which go in thereat; because strait is the gate, and narrow is the way, which leadeth unto life; and few there be that find it. Matt. 7:13. At another place it is written, If any man will come after me, let him deny himself, and take up his cross and follow me. He that loveth father and mother, man or wife, son or daughter more than me, is not worthy of me.

Now test yourselves again. Have you such a spirit, such boldness and faith that you in time of need are ready to forsake father, mother, and your all for the sake of God's Word and His testimony, to take up the cross of Christ, to deny yourself wholly; with Christ to walk upon the way of suffering, and so to enter with the poor, small flock at the narrow, strait gate? Then may the Lord strengthen you. But if you live unto yourselves, reject the cross of Christ, and love father, mother, wife, children, property, or life more than Christ, walk on the broad way with the masses, and enter the wide gate, then the mouth of the Lord gives testimony that you are unbelievers, and that your end is damnation.

And further, the Word of the Lord says, And they that are Christ's have crucified the flesh with the affection and lusts. Gal. 5:24. For those who live after the flesh, such as adulterers, whoremongers, perverts, misers, gamblers, the proud, those given to luxurious adornment, the homicides, hateful, slanderers, the bold despisers and idolaters, these all shall die.

Test yourselves again. If your lusts do not reign in you, if you do not walk in any of these, and such like carnal ways, as has been enumerated, but if you can resist them and keep them under through faith, then thank God, fight piously, watch and pray. But if you give in to your lusts, and walk in the impure ways of the flesh, then reform yourselves. For then it is evident that you are not penitent, believing Christians, but impenitent, carnal heathen.

The Word of the Lord teaches, moreover, Therefore take no thought saying, What shall we eat? or What shall we drink? or, Wherewithal shall we be clothed? For after all these things do the Gentiles seek. But seek ye first the kingdom of God, and his righteousness; and all these things shall be added unto you. Matt. 6:31.

Test yourselves once more. If you believe the strong and resourceful God who nourished Israel forty years with bread from heaven and with water from the rock, and kept their clothes and shoes from wearing out, and fed Elijah by a raven, that He will not forsake you in your distress, but will provide for you by His grace; this is a sure sign that you have the Word of the Lord. But if you are so driven by care that you neglect the kingdom of God and His righteousness, seek temporal more than eternal things, and are so anxious, as if God had more concern for the flowers and fowls than for you and your children, then boast not, for you do not believe the promise and the Word of the Lord.

The Word of the Lord also teaches, For God so loved the world, that he gave his only begotten Son, that whosoever believeth in him should not perish but have everlasting life. For God sent not his Son into the world to condemn the world, but that the world through him might be saved. He that believeth on him is not condemned; but he that believeth not is condemned already, because he hath not believed in the name of the only begotten Son of God. John 3:16-18.

Test yourselves once more. If you sincerely believe these words of Christ with the whole heart; that the Almighty Eternal Father so loved you and the whole human race that He sent His incomprehensible, almighty, eternal Word, wisdom, truth, and Son, by whom He created the heavens, the earth, the sea, and the fullness thereof, His eternal glory and honor into this vale of tears; that He let Him become a poor, sad, and miserable man; that He permitted Him for the sake of the sins of us all to suffer and thirst, to be slandered, apprehended, beaten, crowned with thorns, crucified, and killed; then it cannot fail that your old carnal heart must become a regenerated, spiritual heart; your thoughts must become chaste and pure; your words discreet and well seasoned, and your whole life pious and unblamable.

Once more, awaken, walk in the right way, say farewell to all abomination and idolatry, forsake false prophets, preachers, and priests, and seek the true teachers, sacraments, and divine service. For a genuine Christian faith cannot be idle, but it changes, renews, purifies, sanctifies, and justifies more and more. It gives peace and joy, for by faith it knows that hell, the devil, sin, and death are conquered through Christ, and that grace, mercy, pardon from sin, and eternal life are acquired through Him. In full confidence it approaches the Father in the name of Christ, receives the Holy Ghost, becomes partaker of the divine nature, and is renewed after the image of Him who created him. It lives out of the power of Christ which is in it; all its ways are righteousness, godliness, honesty, chastity, truth, wisdom, goodness, kindliness, light, love, peace.

It sanctifies the body and heart as a habitation and temple for Christ and His Holy Ghost; it hates all that is contrary to God and His Word; it honors, praises, and thanks its God with a faithful heart. There is nothing that can dismay it, neither judgment, nor wrath, nor hell, nor devil, nor sin, nor eternal death. For it knows that it has Christ as its Intercessor, Mediator, and Atoner. It acknowledges with holy Paul, There is therefore now no condemnation to them which are in Christ Jesus, who walk not after the flesh, but after the Spirit. Rom. 8:1. The Spirit of the Lord assures it of being a child of God and a joint heir of Christ; therefore it takes itself to be property of its Lord and Saviour, Christ, who called it by His grace, drew it by His Spirit, enlightened it by His Word, and purchased it with His blood.

Behold, such a living faith it is, one which has such a constraint, power, Spirit, fruit, emphasis in life, that it can avail with God, and has the promise in the Scriptures. Happy is he who has it and keeps it intact to the end!

Let me repeat, test yourselves, whether you are in the faith or no, in Christ or outside of Him, penitent or impenitent. For in the mirror presented you may view the whole face of your conscience and life, if you but believe that the Word of the Lord is true and right. Notice how the true, Christian faith, thanks to grace, is the only living fountain whence flows not only the penitent, new life, but also obedience to the evangelical ceremonies, such as baptism and the Lord's Supper, and that they will have to take their origin and come forth, although constrained by the law. For the rod of the taskmaster is broken already by the bold and submissive spirit of love which is out of a Christian nature, prepared unto all good works and obedience to the holy, divine Word.

For all the truly regenerated and spiritually minded conform in all things to the Word and ordinances of the Lord. Not because they think to merit the atonement of their sins and eternal life. By no means. In this matter they depend upon nothing except the true promise of the merciful Father, given in grace to all believers through the blood and merits of Christ, which blood is and ever will be the only and eternal medium of our reconciliation; and not works, baptism, or the Lord's Supper, as said above repeatedly. For if our reconciliation depended on works and ceremonies, then grace would be a thing of the past, and the merits and fruits of the blood of Christ would end. Oh, no, it is grace, and will be grace to all eternity; all that the merciful Father does for us miserable sinners through His beloved Son and Holy Spirit is grace. But reconciliation takes place because men hear the voice of the Lord, believe His Word, and therefore obediently observe and perform, although in weakness, the things represented by both signs under water and bread and wine. For a truly believing Christian is thus minded, that he will not do otherwise than that which the Word of the Lord teaches and enjoins, for he knows that all presumption and disobedience are like sins of witchcraft, the end of which is death.

Yes, good reader, the genuine Christian faith required by the Scriptures is so active, effective, and powerful in all those who have rightly grasped it through the grace of the Lord, that they do not fear to forsake father, mother, wife, children, money, and possessions for the Word and testimony of the Lord, to suffer all manner of scorn and disgrace, hardship and prison, distress and anguish, and at the end to have their poor, weak bodies, which loathe suffering, burned at the stake, as may be seen daily in the pious children and faithful witnesses of Jesus, especially in these our Netherlands.

Ah, how many have I known, and know many still at this moment, both men and women, servants and maids (would to God they be increased to the praise and salvation of all to many hundred thousands), who from the inmost of their souls seek Christ and His Word. In all meekness they lead a pious, unblamable life before God and man, in weakness albeit, sincere and holy in doctrine, full of the fear and love of God, ready to help others, merciful, compassionate, meek, sober, chaste, not refractory nor seditious, but quiet and peaceable, obedient to the magistracy in all things not contrary to God. They have, nevertheless, for a number of years not slept in their own beds, and do not now; for they are so much hated by the world that they have been persecuted, betrayed, arrested, exiled, and slain like highwaymen, thieves, and murderers, and that without mercy. And it is for no other reason than that they out of true fear of God do not dare to take part in the abominable, carnal life and the accursed, disgraceful idolatry of this blind world. They neither hear nor acknowledge the unchaste, drunken, harloting priests, and deceiving, blind preachers as true apostles and teachers sent from God, nor dare to receive the idolatrous bread with the avaricious, envious, proud, drunkards, harlots, and scamps from their hands. They do not carry their children to the anti-Christian bath and baptism. But they seek such preachers and teachers, also such a baptism, Supper, church, and life, as are in accordance with the Scriptures, and as may stand according to the Word of the Lord.

Behold, before God, it is the truth that I write. Indeed they are such a people, if I know them rightly, who, hypocrites excepted, weep more than they laugh, mourn more than they rejoice after the flesh; who would rather give than receive, and who are ready not only to sacrifice possessions and their all, but also life and death and body for the praise of the Lord, and to the necessary service of their neighbors, according to the command of the Scripture, as much as in them is. No matter how much the poor children are tormented they are still so much strengthened in God that they can neither be moved nor affrighted. They possess their souls with patience, waiting for the joy which is promised. Christ says truly, Ye will be hated of all men for my name's sake. Matt. 24:9.

Since then it is evident from all this that the true evangelical faith is of such a nature as has been said, and that it is the only mother and tree, which through the grace of God bears and yields all manner of fruit, therefore it is highly praised in Scripture as the most precious and greatest work. All things are ascribed to faith, such as the doing of miracles, and the power to become the children of God; to be justified, to be blessed and saved, purified and sanctified, and to have eternal life, as we have related somewhat when treating of the malefactor's faith.

Not, dear reader, as though we believe that faith merits this on account of its worth; by no means. But since the good pleasure of God through His Word has attached His promise to true faith, therefore it must also by virtue of that Word follow faith. For the Scriptures plainly teach that all things, visible and invisible, must hear, bow to, serve, and follow the powerful Word of God, as when He said: Let there be heaven and earth. And with that word heaven and earth sprang into existence. For His Word, says Esdras, is a perfect work. God also says to Israel, If thou shalt hearken diligently unto the voice of the Lord thy God, all these blessings shall come upon thee, but if thou wilt not hearken, the curse shall be upon thee; and it also happened as it was told Israel. For God, says Balaam, is not a man, that he should lie; neither the son of man, that he should repent. For these reasons the promise must follow true faith, or else God who is a God of truth must be untrue and faithless. Oh, no, all that He wills comes to pass,[29] and what He promises must be fulfilled, and not otherwise than He has promised. For He alone is true, and all we are liars. Rom. 3. Paul says, If we believe not, yet he abideth faithful; he cannot deny himself.

Since then faith so firmly acknowledges that God cannot break His promise, but must keep it, seeing He is the truth and cannot lie, therefore does it make His children free, joyful, and glad in spirit, even if they are confined in prisons and bonds, and if they have to suffer by water and fire, in chains, and at the stake. For they are assured in the Spirit, through faith, that God will not withdraw His promise, but will fulfill it in His own time.

[29] Menno believed firmly in the sovereignty of God. *Ed.*

For they believe in Christ in whom the promises are sealed, and through Him also acknowledge His grace, Word, and will, notwithstanding that they in former times walked so wickedly and carnally.

With faithful Abraham they hope that which is beyond hope, and adjust themselves to things invisible as though they saw them, and with full confidence adhering to the assurance, truth, faithfulness, and power of the heavenly promise, which is made in His Word of truth, by the infallible and true mouth of our Lord Jesus Christ, the Son of God, without any prevenient work or merit, through the gracious election and will of His merciful Father. And this same regenerating, justifying, converting, penitent, active, and confident faith, which comes from the Father of lights by the hearing of His holy Word, is the only faith that avails with God and is assured of the promise of grace by the Holy Spirit. The Holy Scriptures know of no other faith than this.

I have read recently that they write that there is but one good work which saves us, namely, faith, and but one sin that will damn us, namely, unbelief. I will let this pass without finding fault, for where there is a genuine, true faith, there also are all manner of genuine good fruits. On the other hand, where there is unbelief, there also are all manner of evil fruits. Therefore salvation is properly ascribed to faith, and damnation to unbelief.

Faithful reader, take heed! Since we see with our eyes and feel with our hands that the whole world, papists, Lutherans, Zwinglians, Davidians, libertines, etc., walk the broad road of sin; lead a carnal, vain life; and do not abide by the pure, salutary, perfect doctrine, sacrament, and unblamable, pure example of Christ; therefore they are all witnesses, are they not, that they reject the cornerstone, Jesus Christ, and believe not His Word and truth. For some of them write much of faith and babble a great deal about the Scriptures.

I declare, Did you ever in all your days read in the Scriptures that an orthodox, born-again Christian continued after repentance and conversion to be proud, avaricious, gluttonous, unchaste, greedy, hateful, tyrannical, and idolatrous, and continued to live after base desires of the flesh? You must say No, must you not? If you should want to point to David and Peter, you must observe how short or how long a time their fall lasted, and how they repented. And now turn to the east or west, south or north, and you will find ungodly, vain, pompous, violent actions and conduct with all those who boast of faith. We shall have to say with Christ and John, that they are, barring a few exceptions, of the devil and not of God. For the devil was proud and haughty from the beginning and so are they. He was a liar and so are they; he was a falsifier of the Word of God, and so are they. He was one who opposed God, and so are they. In short, he was a cruel murderer, an abominable, bloodthirsty tyrant, and so are many of them. The way in which they use those who seek Christ sincerely, and believe, fear, follow, serve, and call on Him has been related often enough.

Yes, alas, they are so enflamed with hatred, wrath, and animosity at them that they will scarcely call them by their proper names, but call them Anabaptists, fanatics, seditionists, factionists, bootleg preachers,[30] deceivers, heretics, rebaptizers, new monks, knaves, and miscreants—although, let me say it again, they seek the kingdom of God and His righteousness with all their hearts (God who tries the reins and hearts of men knows it), and wish no evil to anyone upon earth.

All this they do because of the ugly, ignorant, defaming, envious, bloody, lying, crying, and printing of their learned ones, priests, and preachers, who ever since the blasphemous beast of Antichrist ascended into his kingdom and glory have always been the real cause of the tyrannical shedding of innocent blood in the past and present. For they are those who incite the magistracy to murder, and the thoughtless, reckless people to defame and blaspheme, and they will continue to be the cause until the end, I fear.

But the elect will wake up, repent, and obey the voice of the Lord. For idolatrous, bloodthirsty, confused Babylon shall perish and be destroyed, and fair Jerusalem, the city of peace, shall increase, and through the power of Almighty God be built up in glory. Therefore, all who are called to the marriage of the Lamb rejoice, whose names are written in the book of life with God. Here is the understanding, wisdom, faith, and patience of the saints. Let him that has understanding observe that the Word of the Lord is true. Blessed are they who are prepared and wait for the coming of the Lamb.

Behold, such an unbelieving, impenitent, tyrannical, idolatrous, contrary, disobedient, blind, carnal people are they who imagine that they are the believing church and the real and lawful bride of Christ. These poor children do not notice that all under heaven is spoiled, even as the prophet complains that there is no truth, nor mercy, nor knowledge of God in the land. By swearing and lying and killing and stealing and committing adultery, they break out and blood toucheth blood. Hos. 4:1, 2. The world, says John, lieth in wickedness.

Turning to the lords and princes we find such vanity, arrogance, pomp, and pride, such banqueting, eating and drinking to excess; with some such adultery, fornication, and such unreasonable, blind idolatry; and, with many such unmerciful, raging tyranny moreover, that they are in truth more like haughty Nebuchadnezzar, drunken Belshazzar and Nabal, the bloodthirsty, vain Antiochus, Nero, and Maximinus, than Christ-believing lords and princes.

If we turn to the judges and rulers, to each in his station, with some we find only violence and injustice, with some nothing but avarice, and astonishing devices to commit "honest theft" and "rob honorably." They pass sentence for gain and gift; they honor the high and despise the poor; they do not help the poor widow, orphan, and the oppressed stranger in their affairs;

---

[30] The Word *winckel-prediker* had been used for centuries before Menno's day for evangelical preachers who assayed to preach without the sanction of the Roman church. Hence we have rendered it "bootleg preachers." Compare Luther's polemic against the Anabaptists, *Von den Schleichern und Winkelpredigern*, 1532. *Tr.* and *Ed.*

they execute their office and power with rigor, and not in a fraternal spirit. They serve princes and not God, as the prophet laments: What the prince desires, the judge does, so that he will again reward him. Alas, where will we find one who loves God with all his heart, one who hates avarice, seeks the truth, and who will defend the God-fearing and do him justice?

If we come to the priests or monks, there we find such insatiable avarice that they offer to sell prayers, Psalms, matins, vespers, masses, sermons, baptisms, the Lord's Supper, absolutions, and all their church services, together with their own souls. They take rents and assessments from the deceased; they will go from one place to another for a guilder or so; wherever they find the most milk, wool, and meat, there they are the most sentimental toward the sheep; they like to be flattered and honored by men. They have themselves called doctors, lords, masters, abbots, provosts, priors, fathers, guardians, commanders, and presidents; they like to wear long garments, seek to be greeted at the market, take the first seats at the table and in the church, as Christ said of the scribes and Pharisees. Mark 12:39. Besides, the greater part of them live in such harlotry and Sodomic shame that the angels must be astonished and amazed. They violate one matron after another, one virgin after another. They defraud and corrupt the whole world, both temporally and spiritually. They have all their joy in a temporal, carnal life. They ponder day and night how they may pamper their proud, lazy flesh with the least effort. They carouse and dissipate, saying in the words of the prophet, Come, I will fetch wine, and we will fill ourselves with strong drink, and tomorrow shall be as this day, and much more abundant. Isa. 56:12. They betray the faithful, pious hearts who with all their powers seek Christ and eternal life. They warn every one against the truth and those who pursue it, crying, Hear us; we are your teachers and pastors; we will pledge our souls for you in the judgment of God. And so they encourage the wicked, lest by all means they be converted from their wickedness. They promise liberty to others and are themselves servants of corruption.

I do not know how they could behave worse. Nevertheless these shameless men, who according to the Law of Moses should be stoned, and who according to the Scriptures are eternally cursed and condemned, unless they repent, are alas called pastors and teachers of this poor and reckless people. Behold, thus corrupted is the whole world.

If we come to the preachers who boast of the Word, we find that some are open liars, others drunkards, some usurers, some given to pride and pomp, some defamers and slanderers, others persecutors and betrayers of the innocent, if we notice how they live, how they come by their wives, and what kind of wives they have. This I will leave to the Lord and to themselves. They teach adroitly that there are two sons in Christ,[31] the Son of God and the son of Mary, and that He who died for our sins was not the Son of God.

---

[31] Menno is here criticizing Martin Micron, the Zwinglian Reformer, for his Christology. *Ed.*

They also teach and practice a baptism that is not commanded in the Scriptures, and some of them a Supper in which the bread is said to be the body and the wine the blood of Christ. They have and hold no other ban than the gallows and the wheel. They lead a comfortable, soft, and easy life. They live of mere flattery, deceit, and the booty of Antichrist, and preach just as much as the worldly, carnal magistracy desires to hear, promise peace to the poor impenitent, although there is no peace.

Turning to the common people we find such an impossible, carnal, blind, uncircumcised horde, that we are astonished. They know neither God nor His Word. If nature teaches anything reasonable, that is their piety, but of the Spirit of Christ, His Word, ordinances, will, and life they indeed know but very little. In short, it has come to such a pass in the world that we may well lament and say with the holy prophet, Run ye to and fro through the streets of Jerusalem, and see now, and know, and seek in the broad places thereof, if ye can find a man, if there be any that executeth judgment, that seeketh after faith. Jer. 5:1.

Not one stone has remained upon another. All is desolate which Christ and His faithful messengers taught us of faith, love, baptism, Supper, forgiveness, sin, repentance, regeneration, separation, teachers, deacons, and true religion. They are called the church of Christ by their blind priests and preachers, as if Christ and the Father were to be bought off with names, bread, wine, and water.

Ah, no, the church of Christ is God's elect, His saints and beloved, who have washed their clothes in the blood of the Lamb; who are born of God and driven by the Spirit of Christ; who are in Christ and He in them; who hear and believe His Word; who in their weakness obey His commandments, follow in His footsteps with all patience and humility; who hate evil and love the good; who earnestly desire to apprehend Christ as they are apprehended of Him. For all who are in Christ are new creatures, flesh of His flesh, bone of His bone, and members of His body. How you and the rest of mankind resemble all this I will leave to you and all reasonable readers to ponder in fear of God, in the light of reason as well as Scripture.

Since then all things are desolated through the righteous wrath and judgment of God (because as Paul says, they delighted in unrighteousness and lies) by the false prophets and ravening wolves, so that nothing has remained whole according to the true sense and system of Christ and His holy apostles, and since we find nothing in the whole world among the large and easygoing sects but vain boasting, empty names, false doctrine, false sacraments, blunt unbelief, and an impenitent, carnal life, and that under the name and semblance of Christ and His holy church, therefore, I am constrained by true Christian love on the power and ground of the holy Scriptures to set forth herewith, according to my small gift, given me of God, what is the true Christian faith which has the promise, namely, that faith which changes the man that lays hold of it from evil to righteousness, into a godly spirit both inwardly and outwardly, making him holy, righteous, obedient, new, pious, peaceable, and joyful.

I do this in order that all good, pious hearts (who would fain walk in the right way, but who are alas hindered by their blind priests and preachers) may read or hear this my faithful exposition and fraternal instruction, and be thereby instructed in the faith; that the indifferent and drowsy may be awakened; that all hypocrites may be shamed unto reform, and that all who are serious about God may be instructed and taught the more in faith, if at least they acknowledge this to be the sure foundation of God, as it is and will be forever. May the Lord grant that many may read and understand it, and thus receive and obey it in such a way that they may sincerely repent and be saved. Amen.

And I do this out of an honest and pious heart, and do not labor with any other objective, of which the great God, the Searcher of hearts and reins of men, is my witness; than that I may teach repentance to the callous, reckless world which has nothing so little as Christ and His Word, and may I lead them to Christ and His doctrines, sacraments, and example, that in this way many might be saved. We see plainly that many reckless, carnal people have reformed their sinful lives and have begun an upright, penitent, pious life in the fear of the Lord. Therefore it is gross ingratitude, is it not, yes, a cursed, ungodly tyranny, to hate me and my faithful co-workers so fiercely and recompense us so shamefully, we who manifest such fidelity and love toward them in our manifold sufferings and trials.

But so men have treated all the prophets and faithful servants of God from the beginning; the men who preached the Word and will of the Lord to them with great fidelity, reproved their sins, sought their salvation with all their powers, with many tears, watchings, prayers, labors, cares, and sorrows to the point of death. Therefore it is not strange that they treat us so, for Christ says: For so persecuted they the prophets which were before you. Matt. 5:12.

I hereby entreat through the mercy of our Lord Jesus Christ all my readers and hearers in general, of whatever name, office, station, and condition that you may be, not to speak evil nor to reject my labor as long as you have not read it impartially and understandingly and understood it. Therefore differentiate between the doctrine, sacrament, and life of Christ and the apostles; and the doctrine, sacraments, and life of the priests and the preachers. Distinguish between faith and unbelief, spirit and flesh, righteousness and unrighteousness. Seek after the truth. Strive zealously for your salvation. Believe that God is a God of truth, that He will reward the good and punish the evil, that His Word is truth and will forever remain truth. Fear His judgment; love His bounties. Then you will realize by the grace of the Lord that the afore-mentioned is the true Christian faith which avails with God, which has the promise in the Scriptures as we have so abundantly testified and shown to you by the Word of God and with such strong and incontrovertible argument from the Scripture and the examples, without deceit and fraud as it were before God in Christ Jesus.

May the Almighty, eternal, merciful God and Father through His beloved Son, Jesus Christ, lead you all into His holy, divine knowledge and evangelical truth, and make your faith be so fruitful and active that you may with sincere, new hearts, patiently submit to His cross in every trial and affliction. May you walk with unfeigned love, being peaceable and joyful in the spirit, as the unblamable, pious children of God before the Lord and His church all the days of your life, and come away at the end with the final promise of grace, the end of faith; that is, the salvation of your souls. Amen.

## [VIII.] CONCLUSION

To the Christian reader, Greetings:

Honorable readers, here you have my position and doctrine concerning faith with its innate power, operation, nature, and fruit. And I intreat you all as you love Christ and your own salvation, suppress your contrariety, and be not enraged should you find anything opposed to the customs of our forefathers, ancient usages, or the sophistic writings and the shouting of the learned ones. Test it first and examine it well in the light of the Word, Spirit, life, and example of Christ and His holy apostles, to see if it is not the true content, intention, doctrine, and sense of the whole Scriptures. If you find it so you will have to give up the unscriptural usage and the deceptive cry of the learned ones, and hold to the Word of the Lord, if you wish to be saved.

Therefore let your heart be impartial and your judgment sincere according to truth. For the Almighty God and Lord before whom every knee shall bow and every tongue confess will not and cannot yield to any of the learned ones nor to ancient usage or customs. For He is the Lord and we are servants. We must follow Him and not He us. Ah, reader, lay it to heart!

Similarly, if you find that we preach our doctrine unwaveringly, regardless of the dignity of any man, fearing no man's tyranny nor yielding to any of the learned ones, but find that we in true, sincere love, faithfully teach, admonish, and reprove all who do amiss without respect of persons, with the Holy Spirit of the Lord, His Word, example, and ordinance, in all things in which they err, then I entreat you again not to attribute this to carnal pride, but[32] to well-meant boldness and Christian folly.[33] I would so much like to see you all walking rightly and so being saved, the thing on account of which I have to endure not a little tribulation.

I do not refuse to be the whole world's sot and fool, just so that I may make wise in Christ, and with the Holy Spirit of the Lord and His powerful Word lead them to the wisdom of the saints. I know well that Christ

[32] Reading *mer* (but) for *met* (with) which makes no sense.
[33] Menno is using the expression "Christian folly" in the sense of I Cor. 1:21. *Tr.*

and His apostles and the prophets promoted the same "foolishness" and were of the same mind with me in this matter.

If I reprove, they reprove even more; if I threaten with the wrath and judgment of the Lord, they much more. Are they on that account to be considered carnal and proud?[34] Far from it. Yes, my reader, had not the dark-smoke of ear-pleasing preachers, the accursed false doctrine of the fearful, frightful locusts of the abyss risen up; but had the solemn rebuke, the pure, true doctrine, the Scriptural usage of the holy sacraments and the expulsion of the impenitent without respect to persons, continued in the world, never would the pleasing sun have lost his splendor so, nor would the church have come to such a deadly fall. Therefore, with Paul I esteem it to be a little thing to be judged of men in this matter. For I know that I mean well, do rightly, and reprove only with the truth in order that they may be converted.

May the true heavenly light, Jesus Christ, eternally blessed, enlighten all dark, benighted hearts with the clear and lucid ray of His Holy Ghost and eternal truth, so that they may view in unfeigned, pure faith, the unending brightness of Christ, to the praise and honor of His great name and to the salvation of many men. Amen.

[34] John Calvin wrote of Menno, *"Nihil hoc asino posse fingi superbius, nihil petulantius hoc cane"* (Nothing can be more conceited than this donkey, nor more impudent than this dog). Menno was known to Calvin through Micron. *Ed.*

# A Kind Admonition on
# Church Discipline

*Een lieffelijcke vermaninghe van*
*dat schouwen der valscher broederen*

# 1541

*For other foundation can no man*
*lay than that is laid, which is Jesus Christ.*

I Corinthians 3:11

# Introduction

This is the first of Menno's three books on discipline, excommunication, and shunning. The other two are his *A Clear Account of Excommunication*, 1550, and his *Instruction on Excommunication*, 1558. Our *Kind Admonition on Church Discipline* appeared in 1541 before Menno had encountered some of the vexatious questions which so heavily burdened his heart in his later years. It has an excellent tone. Menno writes from a warm heart of love, calling upon his brethren and sisters in the faith to live close to Christ, to trust only in the Lord and His grace, and not in church ceremonies or even in church membership.

When brethren or sisters fall into heresy—such as that of the corrupt sects—or into a life of sin, every effort is to be made through prayer, admonition, and warning, to win them back. But if all is in vain, and no penitence comes, but the individuals give every evidence of no longer being in Christ, the painful and sad duty falls to the brotherhood to excommunicate and shun such apostates. This is not to be done in a proud, pharisaical spirit, but with an earnest desire to win again the brother or sister who has fallen away. Church discipline is to be redemptive, not punitive.

Menno labored in West Friesland several times each year in the first period of his ministry, to the year 1541 especially. God blessed his labors with good success. The authorities in the province finally felt it necessary to do more than execute the Anabaptists whom they could capture. Posting placards against them was also not enough. They must do away with Menno Simons himself, since he was, as they wrote to Mary, regent of the Netherlands, "one of the principal leaders of the aforesaid sect." They proposed that certain captured Anabaptists should be offered pardons if they would betray Menno over to the authorities. Mary approved of the plan, provided it did not result in the pardon of more than two Anabaptists. But the scheme did not work. Menno was not apprehended. Shortly before transferring his base of operations from West Friesland to Amsterdam in 1541 Menno wrote his *Kind Admonition*.

The full title in the original reads: *A Kind Admonition or Instruction from the Word of God as to How a Christian Should be Disposed; Also as to Shunning and Excommunication of False Brethren and Sisters, Whether Deceived by Heretical Doctrine or Living a Carnal and Offensive Life.* In the *Opera Omnia Theologica* of 1681 this work appears, fol. 631-37, and in the *Complete Works* of 1871, II, 441-49.

J. C. W.

# A Kind Admonition on Church Discipline

## 1541

Menno Simons wishes all true brethren and sisters in Christ Jesus grace, and peace of God our heavenly Father, through Jesus Christ His Son, our Lord, who loved us, and cleansed us from all our sins by His blood. To Him be glory, now and forever. Amen.

Hear God's Word, believe God's Word, perform God's Word, and you will have everlasting life.

Do not judge until you have read through and understood this.

Sincerely beloved children in Christ Jesus, you know, do you not, with what great diligence and as from the bottom of my heart I have of late admonished most of you with the Word of the Lord, by many arguments and writings inspired by a loving spirit, as you yourself have witnessed, I seek nothing (God is my witness) but the salvation of your souls; teaching nothing, asking nothing, advising nothing but that your most holy faith and works may be powerful and fruitful before God; and that your life and walk may be found before God, before His angels, and before all the world, holy, pure, sober, chaste, temperate, humble, gentle, kind, liberal, merciful, righteous, unblamable, in conformity with, and obedient to the Gospel of Christ, a shining light, that in all your doings you may reveal Christ Jesus whom you have put on (if ye have put Him on, as I hope) and thus show in your life His divine and heavenly image after which you were created.

You know that I do not desire your money, silver, and carnal gifts, although I am accused of it by the false and lying world. I ask and seek among you with much care, anxiety, tribulation, trouble, weeping, and labor, such faith, love, spirit, conscience, and conduct as can stand before the righteous judgment of God, and that in Christ Jesus.

I do not doubt, most beloved brethren, that you know very well (if you are born with Christ of God the Father of the heavenly seed of the divine Word) that you must be conformed unto Christ in mind, spirit, heart, and will, both in doctrine and life, as Christ Jesus is conformed unto the nature and image of His blessed heavenly Father to which He was begotten so that He did nothing but that which He saw the Father do; that He taught nothing but the word of His Father. In the same manner those who are begotten of the living, saving Word of our beloved Lord Jesus Christ are by virtue of their new birth so joined to Christ, are become so like unto Him, so really

409

implanted into Him, so converted into His heavenly nature, that they do not teach nor believe any doctrine but that which agrees with the doctrine of Christ; they practice no ceremonies but Christ's ceremonies which He has taught and commanded in His holy Gospel. For how can the twig of the vine bear fruit different from that of the vine from which it springs?

Even as there is nothing found in Christ Jesus but holiness, wisdom, brightness, righteousness, power, love, peace, mercy, and truth of the Almighty Father, so also you have in the same manner partaken of His being and goodness, since you are with Him regenerated and renewed of the same Father.

Behold, brethren, such regenerate and godly-minded persons live unblamably, according to the measure of the holy Gospel of Jesus Christ and His apostles. Therefore He kisses them as His beloved chosen ones, with the mouth of His peace, and calls them His church, His bride, flesh of His flesh, and bone of His bone, of which He begets with inexpressible pleasure by His powerful seed, His holy Word, the children of God, the children of promise, the children of righteousness, the children of truth, and the children of life eternal. But never of the Babylonian, Sodomite, harloting, adulterous, idolatrous, bloody, unbelieving, blind, and unclean wench with which they have for centuries fornicated in wood, stone, gold, silver, bread, wine, false doctrine, and of the very vain, accursed works of their own hands, contrary to Jesus Christ and His holy Word.

Therefore I admonish all our beloved brethren and sisters in the Lord, whereas Christ Jesus is dear to you, never to forget to what you were called, taught, and baptized. Remember the covenant of the Most High which you voluntarily desired and accepted, being taught by the Word of God and led by the Holy Spirit. Remember that according to the doctrine of Paul, you have voluntarily buried in baptism all your avarice, uncleanness, pride, hatred, envy, abuse of the sacramental signs,[1] idolatry, gluttony, drunkenness, sensuality, falsehood, deceit, etc., and that you are arisen with Christ Jesus into newness of life (Rom. 6), if so be you are truly risen with Him. This new life is nothing but righteousness, unblamableness, love, mercy, humility, long-suffering, peace, truth; yes, the whole gentle life which is taught by the Gospel and experienced in Christ Jesus.

O brethren, how far some of us, alas, are still distant from the evangelical life which is of God! Notwithstanding that they stay out of the churches and are outwardly baptized with water, yet they are earthly and carnally minded in all things, thinking perhaps that Christianity consists in external baptism and staying away from the churches.[2] Oh, dear, No! I tell you as truly as the Lord lives, before God no outward baptism counts, nor staying away from the churches, nor Lord's Supper, nor persecution, if there is no

---

[1] Menno refers to baptism and the Lord's Supper.

[2] "The churches" refers to the state churches of the period, whether Roman Catholic, Lutheran, or "Zwinglian" (Reformed). *Ed.*

obedience to the commandments of God, and no faith which manifests itself in love, and no new creature. Christ Jesus says, Verily, verily, I say unto you, Except a man be born again, he cannot see the kingdom of God. At another place, Verily I say unto you, Except ye become as little children, ye shall not enter into the kingdom of heaven. But the regenerate and converted, that is, the believing, are rightly baptized in accordance with God's Word, for they bury their sins in baptism and arise with Christ into newness of life. Rom. 6. They are spiritually circumcised with the circumcision of Christ (Col. 2); they put on Christ Jesus; they show by the washing of regeneration that they are born again; for it is a washing of the new birth (Titus 3).

These regenerated ones use the true Supper, for they proclaim the Lord's death until He comes. I Cor. 11. Their pleasure is in the church of the righteous; their works are nothing but brotherly love, one heart, one soul, one spirit; yes, one undivided body, fruitful, serving, and fellowshiping in Christ Jesus which is symbolized by the outward cup and the outward bread. I Cor. 10.

These regenerated ones shun all false doctrine, all idolatry, all improper use of the sacramental signs in the church or out of the church. They seek the true teachers who are unblamable both in doctrine and life; the true religion as taught and expressed in Christ's Word, namely, the dying unto the flesh (Rom. 12; Gal. 5); the service of the afflicted (Matt. 15); and the visiting of the widows and orphans, as James says. They seek to keep themselves unblemished and unspotted from the world. These regenerated ones bear the cross of Christ with gladness of heart, are so established in Christ Jesus that they cannot be separated from the eternal truth and love of God by false doctrine nor by horrible torments; ever remembering their Lord's Word: Whosoever therefore shall confess me before men, him will I confess also before my Father which is in heaven.

All their thoughts are chaste, gentle, peaceful, heavenly, and of the Holy Spirit; all their words are wisdom, truth, doctrine, admonition in grace, well seasoned, the words of God spoken at the right time. (They are spirit and they are life.) In short, all their works are love, mercifulness, righteousness, piety, and are done in the fear of the Lord.

Dear brethren, this is the true nature and mind of the children of God, who are by grace converted in their hearts and with Christ born of God the Father. Therefore I beseech you as my sincerely beloved brethren, by the grace of God—nay, I command you with holy Paul, by the Lord Jesus Christ, who at His coming will judge the living and the dead—diligently to observe each other unto salvation, in all becoming ways teaching, instructing, admonishing, reproving, warning, and consoling each other as occasion requires, not otherwise than in accordance with the Word of God and in unfeigned love, until we increase in God and become united in faith and in the knowledge of the Son of God, into one perfect man and according to the measure of the gift of Jesus Christ. Eph. 4:7.

Therefore take heed. If you see your brother sin, then do not pass him by as one that does not value his soul; but if his fall be curable, from that moment endeavor to raise him up by gentle admonition and brotherly instruction, before you eat, drink, sleep, or do anything else, as one who ardently desires his salvation, lest your poor erring brother harden and be ruined in his fall, and perish in his sin.

Do not act so unfaithfully as you have hitherto acted, not making the transgressions of your dying brother or sister known to those within the church or without. Exhort him, rather, and seek by prayer, by words, and by deeds, to convert him from the error of his way, to save his soul, and to cover the multitude of his transgressions. Jas. 5. Take heed, brethren, take heed that you allow no defamer among you, as Moses taught. Lev. 19. A double, lying, deceiving, and backbiting tongue do not allow at any time, lest you fall into the wrath of God. Let every one take heed how, where, when, and what he speaks, lest his tongue transgress against God and his neighbor. But always remember the words of Ecclesiasticus: Honor and shame is in talk, and the tongue of man is his fall.

But do not have anything to do, as the holy Paul has taught and commanded, and do not eat, with people who being of age and driven by the Spirit were baptized into the body of Jesus Christ with us, that is, the church, but afterwards, whether through false doctrine or a vain and carnal life, reject and separate themselves from the body and fellowship of Christ, no matter whether it be father or mother, sister or brother, man or wife, son or daughter, no matter who he be, for God's Word applies to all alike and there is no respect of persons with God. We say, avoid him if he rejects the admonition of his brethren, done in sighing, tears, and a spirit of compassion and of great love, and if he nevertheless continues in his Jewish doctrine of sword, kingdom, polygamy, and similar deceptions;[3] in the doctrine of shameless confession to each other, of no shame [for shameful acts], of nakedness; as well as a doctrine that contradicts the cross of Christ, as, for example, that impurity is pure to the pure—all fellowship with evil work such as attending the preaching of worldly preachers, infant baptism, worldly Lord's Supper, and similar abominations, as also drunkenness, avarice, fornication, adultery, unseemly conversation, etc.

But if he affectionately receives the admonition of his faithful brethren, confesses his fall, is truly sorry, promises to do better, and brings forth fruits worthy of repentance, then no matter how he has transgressed, receive him as a returning, beloved brother or sister. But let him beware lest he mock his God, for restoration with the brethren does not avail without restoration before God. Let him be sure that his heeding the admonition, his sorrow, his promise of reformation, and his penitence, are sincere before God who searches the hearts and reins and knows all inward thoughts of men. If his heeding the admonition, his sorrow, promise, and penitence, are not sincere and from

---

[3] Menno refers chiefly to the "corrupt sects," as he calls them: Münsterites, Davidians, and Batenburgers. *Ed.*

his heart, but halfhearted, put on, mechanical, and of hypocritical exhibition, just because he does not want to be thrown out of the community of the brethren, he is still excommunicated by Christ, and is a hypocrite in the sight of God. Nor will he be rated or judged by God as anything else. For God the righteous Judge does not judge according to the outward appearance, but according to the inward intention of the heart.

Tell me, beloved, inasmuch as this is the case, what does it avail to go by the mere name of a Christian brother if we have not the inward, evangelical faith, love, and irreproachable life of the true brother of Jesus Christ?

Or what does it profit to eat of the Holy Supper of our Lord Jesus Christ with the brethren if we have not the true symbolized fruits of this Supper, namely, the death of Christ, the love of the brethren, and the peaceful unity of faith in Christ Jesus? Similarly it profits nothing to move about in the outward communion of the brethren if we are not inwardly in the communion of our beloved Lord Jesus Christ.

Wherefore, brethren, understand correctly, no one is excommunicated or expelled by us from the communion of the brethren but those who have already separated and expelled themselves from Christ's communion either by false doctrine or by improper conduct. For we do not want to expel any, but rather to receive; not to amputate, but rather to heal; not to discard, but rather to win back; not to grieve, but rather to comfort; not to condemn, but rather to save. For this is the true nature of a Christian brother. Whoever turns from evil, whether it be false doctrine or vain life, and conforms to the Gospel of Jesus Christ, unto which he was baptized, such a one shall not and may not be expelled or excommunicated by the brethren forever.

But those whom we cannot raise up and repentingly revive by admonition, tears, warning, rebuke, or by any other Christian services and godly means, these we should put forth from us, not without great sadness and anguish of soul, sincerely lamenting the fall and condemnation of such a straying brother; lest we also be deceived and led astray by such false doctrine which eats as does a cancer (II Tim. 2) ; and lest we corrupt our flesh which is inclined to evil by the contagion. Thus we must obey the Word of God which teaches and commands us so to do; and this in order that the excommunicated brother or sister whom we cannot convert by gentle services may by such means be shamed unto repentance and made to acknowledge to what he has come and from what he is fallen. In this way the ban is a great work of love, notwithstanding it is looked upon by the foolish as an act of hatred.

My brethren, this is really the reason why and for what purpose this excommunication or ban is so solemnly taught and enjoined by Christ and His holy apostles in the Scriptures in regard to false doctrine and sinful, carnal life. Also that we should admonish them, that is, those who will take admonition. Therefore take heed and watch your own soul lest you despise the Word of God in this necessary matter of excommunication and trample on His ordinances. But in every respect use it and practice it with godly wisdom, discretion, gentleness, and prudence, toward those who have gone aside from the evangelical doctrine or life, not with austerity nor with cruelty, but rather with gentleness; with many tears because of the diseased and infected members whom we cannot cure, and in whose case pains and labor are lost.

There is nothing better to do with such than to cut them off with the knife of the divine Word, lest the others be corrupted and the ugly scurvy be transmitted to other sheep. It should be done in such a manner that the erring sister or brother may be made ashamed at heart and won back, as was said above. And in case there be any moving of the Spirit, any little spark of life, or any fear of God in such an excommunicated sister or brother, his or her heart will surely quake and tremble, for by the admonition of the Word of God and by the testimony of their own conscience, they will acknowledge that they have cut themselves off from the communion of Jesus Christ by their false doctrine and vain carnal life, that they have returned to the communion of the devil, and that therefore their lot and part shall not be with the blessed souls in heaven, but with the damned in hell unto eternity, unless they become converted.

May God, the merciful Father, save all His chosen children who have entered into His holy covenant and communion from such a fearful fall, obduracy, and excommunication. Amen.

All apostate sisters and brethren who are offended and angry with us on account of this straightforward doctrine and practice of the Christian ban or excommunication, will be offended more and more, for whosoever is impure will be made still more impure as the Holy Spirit of the prophecies teaches. Rev. 22. For the Word of God is unto the reformation, righteousness, and life of the pious and godly; but unto the lost it is unto offense, unrighteousness, and death. What! Be angry with us because we obey Scripture in this matter? Let them rather be angry with themselves for daring to live and teach contrary to God. If they would renounce their false doctrine and reform their ungodly life, the heavenly doctrine of our beloved Lord Jesus Christ would not make them worse and more angry but it would overpower and frighten and convert them.

By their apostasy, rebellious and carnal hatred, they are deprived of grace and the knowledge of God, and become increasingly more wicked, so that they see death in eternal life, and darkness in the heavenly light of divine truth. Therefore we declare before God and His holy angels that we are clear of their damnable false doctrine, of their sins, obduracy, and eternal death if we have done in vain toward them that which the Lord's Word has commanded us in regard to this matter. We desire not to have communion with them, no lot nor part unto eternity, so long as they do not sincerely renounce their false doctrine and reform their miserable, condemnable, earthly, carnal, and devilish life to the praise of the Lord. But if such things are found in them, in good faith, as before God who sees all things, then we say, Welcome, beloved brethren! Welcome, beloved sisters! And we rejoice beyond measure at the sincere conversion of such brethren and sisters as one rejoices at the restoration of an only son who is healed of a critical and deadly disease, or a lost sheep or penny that is found again, or at the appearance of a son who was given up as lost.

You see, brethren, I will let every apostate brother determine why, wherefore, with what kind of spirit, and with what intention this excommunication or ban was so diligently practiced, first by Christ Jesus and His apostles, and afterward by us, who are intent upon recovering again Christian doctrine and practice as may be learned from the quoted Scriptures.

Very well, dear brethren in the Lord, you who are baptized by one Spirit into one body, and have voluntarily entered into the communion of Christ Jesus, and you also who are of a good will, inasmuch as you must shun[4] the apostate in accordance with the Word of God, take heed that while you shun them as diseased, foul, and unprofitable members unfit for the body of Christ, you yourselves may be found to be sound, fit, and profitable members in Christ Jesus. When you shun them as children of darkness and of death, see to it that you yourselves may be children of the light and of eternal life, so that the righteous sentence of God may not reach unto you, lest you who shun others on account of their evil-doing secretly commit worse things in the sight of God. Take heed lest you judge others of what you yourselves are guilty. Behold, brethren, in this way the ban or excommunication should be practiced in the house of the Lord, that is, in God's church. Nor has it any other weapon unto all eternity. Of this I would have written more but defer it to some other time, if it please God.

Now, beloved brethren, take heed. Take heed, brethren. This I advise you—that there may never be any thoughts in your hearts other than such as are pure, holy, chaste, heavenly, and of the Holy Spirit. Blessed are the pure in heart, for they shall see God. Let your mouth speak wisdom and your tongue judgment. Let all your words be as a sworn oath before God and before the world. Let all your actions be wrought of God, by God, and in God. Measure all your thoughts, words, and actions by the rule of the divine Word so that the wretched slanderer who so diligently watches all your words and actions may find nothing which he can fairly lay to your charge, as Paul taught and requested the church in some instances. Eph. 4:1; I Tim. 3; Titus 2.

It is also the nature of those who are in God not to sin, as John says: Whosoever abideth in God sinneth not: whosoever sinneth hath not seen him, neither known him. Little children, let no man deceive you: he that doeth righteousness is righteous, even as he is righteous. He that committeth

---

[4] Philips, who is believed to have baptized Menno and ordained him as an elder in the brotherhood, inaugurated the practice of shunning apostates and unsound teachers and disciples to protect the brotherhood against such corrupt sects as the Münsterites. Shunning means the breaking of all social fellowship with impenitent and expelled persons. *Ed.*

sin is of the devil; for the devil sinneth from the beginning. For this purpose the Son of God was manifested, that he might destroy the works of the devil. Whosoever is born of God doth not commit sin: for his seed remaineth in him: and he cannot sin, because he is born of God.

Therefore I call you and direct you to consider well the nature of the new birth and to examine it in its reality, namely, the divine nature, and the divine image; of whom it is, that is, of God; from whence it is—from heaven; and what is obtained by it—life eternal. For without the new birth all we do is of the nature of the earthly Adam, of sin, evil, blindness, transgression, the devil, and eternal death—I speak in regard to adults. But in whomsoever the new birth is, there all is godly wisdom, goodness, light, righteousness, peace, truth, Spirit, Christ, God, and life eternal. Therefore the eternal truth, Christ Jesus, says in plain words that we must be converted and born again if we would enter into the kingdom of heaven. For the first birth is of the earth, earthy, and earth-bound; but the second birth is of heaven and is heavenly, and heaven-bound. In a word, the birth of earth makes earthly minded, and the birth of heaven makes heavenly minded.

If this good and perfect gift of the new birth be given us of the Father of light, by grace, then we are the chosen children of God. Then we are the true sisters and brethren of Christ. Then we are conformed unto Christ. Then we are created after the image of God. Then we have the sign Tau on our foreheads.[5] Then the kingdom of God is ours. Then we are the bride of Christ, the church of Christ, the body of Christ. Then Christ dwells in our hearts. Then we are led by the Holy Ghost; we are the chosen generation, the royal priesthood, the holy, begotten people, which is God's own. Then we are the temple of the Lord, the spiritual Mount Zion, the new heavenly Jerusalem, the spiritual Israel of God. Then we are of divine mind and nature; we are delivered from the threatenings of the Law, yes, from hell, sin, devil, and eternal death. Then we have Christ Jesus forever blessed, His Word, life, flesh, blood, cross, suffering, bitter death, burial, resurrection, ascension, kingdom, and eternal joy as a gift from God the Father. But if we are not born again (that is, those of understanding age), then we have not such promises.

Therefore, sincerely beloved brethren, partakers of the heavenly calling through Christ Jesus, humble yourselves therefore under the mighty hand

---

[5] The last letter of the Hebrew alphabet, Tau, was a favorite symbol with the turbulent Anabaptists of Menno's day. True believers were, according to Ezek. 9:4-7 as interpreted by these fanatics, marked with the letter Tau on their foreheads and this constituted them the executioners of those who did not bear the mark.

Unsympathetic students of Menno and his writings have seen in his use of the expression "the symbol Tau" evidence that Menno belonged originally to the Melchiorites who staged the Münster episode, etc. It is however quite as likely that Menno uses the expression in order to divest it of a connotation he detested and to give to it a better and more spiritually tolerable meaning.

(Menno uses the expression also in his tract on the Spiritual Resurrection, fol. 183a of the *Opera Omnia*.)  *Tr.*

of God, and sincerely deny yourselves. Fear God in all your thoughts, words, and works; love and serve God and your neighbor; love God above all things created and your neighbor as yourself. Let all your meditations be in the Law of the Lord. Keep the Word of God; I repeat, brethren, keep the Word of God which has been so often taught you in love, both spoken and written.

Let your ardent prayer at all times ascend to God for all men: for emperors, kings, lords, princes, governors, and for all those that are placed in authority, that God may so direct their hearts, if it be His blessed will, that we may lead a peaceful life in all godliness.

Be not angry in your hearts, nor sharp in your speech concerning others, whether they be slanderers, traitors, persecutors, priests, or monks, no matter what, for they shall receive their judgment from God. But always remember the patience of our beloved Lord Jesus Christ. Remember that we also were foolish and unbelieving, erring, serving divers lusts and desires, by nature children of wrath, as they are. Willingly obey all human ordinances if they be not against God. Be liberal in assisting all children of God. Receive each other without murmuring. Let each one work with his own hands, and eat his own bread, if possible. Shun all laziness and worldly pomp. Stand guard over each other with admonitions, as I have admonished you by word of mouth and now in this epistle.

Do wash the feet of your beloved brethren and sisters who are come to you from a distance, tired. Be not ashamed to do the work of the Lord, but humble yourselves with Christ, before your brethren, so that all humility of godly quality may be found in you.

Above all, pray for your poor humble servant whose life is eagerly sought, that God the gracious Father may strengthen him with His Holy Spirit and save him from the hands of those who so unjustly seek his life, if it be His fatherly will; and if not, pray that He may then give him in all tribulation, torture, suffering, oppression, and death, such a heart, mind, wisdom, and strength, that he may steadfastly fulfill the glorious work of God which is begun in us by the Holy Ghost, to the praise of the Lord.

O my dear brethren, fulfill my desire, and finish as obedient children of God that which I have fraternally taught, admonished, and written unto you from the Word of God to your eternal salvation, so that you may be my glorious crown, hope, and joy in the day of the coming of Christ. Be fervent in spirit and alert. Bless God for all His works toward us, and pray Him to guide your way, and let all your counsel be in Him. Walk fearlessly in the commandments of the Lord. Go not in any manner beyond the Gospel of Christ. Be firm in the way of the Lord. Overcome the world, the flesh, and the devil through that most holy faith which is in you. Eagerly serve one another. In patience possess your souls. Be patient in tribulation. Prepare your hearts for the cross of Christ so that when it comes you may not be mortally afraid with those of little faith.

That is all for this time, but watch keenly all the days of your life for the unforeseeable coming of our beloved Lord Jesus Christ who has made us such noble creatures, bought us with His precious blood, graciously called, enlightened, and regenerated us, who will crown us with the crown of glory, array us in the garment of innocence, and give us the gift of eternal life. To Him be eternal praise and glory, now and forever. Amen.

Reflect, holy brethren, word for word on that which I have written unto you. Read it attentively, reflect upon it diligently, understand it wisely, judge it spiritually, and execute it in godly fashion. O brethren, then I will have written and admonished well and you will have read and obeyed well.

I pray you with the holy Paul by the grace of God not to suppress this admonition nor to lay it away in secret, but to read it to all faithful brethren and sisters in the Lord, as also to all the apostates for whom there is still some expectation, that they may be won back. Yea, not merely to these, but to all men in or out of the church who may desire to hear it. The grace of our beloved Lord Jesus Christ be with all true brethren and sisters. Amen.

Once more, pray for me and for all your servants in the Lord.

Beware of all doctrine and works which do not agree with the Gospel of Christ. Beware!

MENNO SIMONS

# Brief Confession on the Incarnation

*Korte belijdinge van der menschwerdinge*

## 1544

*For other foundation can no man*
*lay than that is laid, which is Jesus Christ.*

I Corinthians 3:11

# Introduction

Jan Laski or John a Lasco (1499-1560) was a Polish-born reformer who became an ardent Zwinglian and Calvinist. About 1543 Countess Anna of East Friesland invited a Lasco to become superintendent of the proposed state church of her land. A Lasco consented to accept this post. Encountering a number of Anabaptists in Emden, the capital, a Lasco summoned Menno to an interview which was held January 28-31, 1544 (the date 1543 in the *Opera* is apparently due to Menno's thinking of the new year as beginning with March rather than January. This was common in various lands in the sixteenth century and later). The two men held their disputation in the chapel of the former Franciscan monastery in Emden. They discussed five topics: the incarnation of Christ, baptism, original sin, sanctification, and the calling of ministers. On two subjects they agreed: original sin and sanctification. On the incarnation they disagreed, as well as on baptism and the calling of ministers. Menno was of course a stout contender for believer's baptism, and for an unsalaried ministry by holy men of God who preached out of love and the call of the Spirit. A Lasco was a Pedobaptist, and his ministers were salaried—and fell below the standards of spirituality and holiness demanded by Menno. Part II of Menno's *Brief and Clear Confession* is devoted to the calling of ministers.

The most difficult point to explain, let alone defend, is Menno's view of the incarnation. And yet Menno's view, though not accepted by the Swiss Brethren ever, and though soon discarded by the Dutch Mennonites themselves, is not ridiculous. It was also held by Wolfgang Musculus (1497-1563), the Reformed theologian, and Professor of Theology in Bern after 1549. In brief Menno's view was an attempt to exalt the truth of Christ's having been conceived by the power of the Holy Ghost, and of His having been sinless. Menno rejected any tendency to divide Christ into two parts: a heavenly and divine Being who came down to earth, and a natural man begotten of a human mother. Menno therefore insisted that Jesus was conceived of the Holy Spirit, not begotten of Mary (Menno thought that women produced no seed), and that He became a human being in Mary (but not of Mary). In spite of his announced intention to accept simply what the Bible teaches, and to avoid all philosophical speculations on the subject, Menno did allow himself to become more deeply involved in this theory than was profitable. It also furnished an excellent point on which his theological opponents could harass him—and which they did not fail to seize. Nevertheless Menno states in his *Brief and Clear Confession* that he passed through a period of severe struggle before he accepted this view, that he entered into the discussion of it with a Lasco against his will, that he did not teach it in the church life of his brotherhood, and that there were (Mennonite) Brethren who had never heard of the theory. It is therefore unfortunate that Menno did not stay by his original intention of avoiding speculation on the exact process of the incarnation, for his views proved to be a point of weakness and served to divert attention away from more important points on which Menno was sound as Gibraltar.

The *Brief and Clear Confession* was written in the year 1544, undoubtedly in the spring, for Menno promised a Lasco that he would furnish such a statement within three months of the interview of late January, 1544. A Lasco then published the treatise without Menno's knowledge or consent. The title in full reads as follows: *A Brief and Clear Confession and Scriptural Demonstration Concerning the Incarnation of Our Beloved Lord Jesus Christ; and Secondly How According to the Scriptures the Ministers and the Church of Christ Should be Minded. Written to the Noble and Learned Gentleman John a Lasco and His Assistants at Emden. A.D. 1544.* In the *Opera Omnia Theologica* of 1681 this work is found, fol. 517-42, and in the *Complete Works* of 1871, II, 325-50.

J. C. W.

# Brief Confession on the Incarnation

# 1544

## *Preface*

Menno Simons wishes the noble and learned John a Lasco and his assistants and all the people of East Friesland, of whatever class or condition in life they may be, genuine faith, clear insight, true knowledge of the Holy Spirit, the lovely fear and pure love of the Lord, an unblamable life and the eternal life of God our heavenly Father, through Jesus Christ, His beloved Son, our Lord, who has loved us and washed us in His blood. To Him be the glory, honor, praise, kingdom, power, and majesty for ever and ever. Amen.

Most dearly beloved friends and brethren:

Near the end of January, 1543,[1] I was with you at Emden discussing in friendly fashion with you there for three or four days the controversial articles of our faith, having been invited and summoned to this. We discussed the incarnation of our dear Lord Jesus Christ first of all, a subject to which you know I had been invited and constrained against my will. In the second place, we treated of the baptism of children; and since we did not come to an agreement in these matters, you let me depart in peace and with a friendly farewell. You requested me, however, to send to your highness within the space of three months, a copy of the statement of my faith which I had drawn up so that you might acquaint your God-appointed rulers with our faith, diligence, desire, manner of life (feeble and weak enough, however), and on what foundation, Scripture, and reason our doctrine and life are founded. I hope and trust, by the grace of the Lord, that you have desired and required this of me without any malice or evil intent.

Therefore I promised to heed your friendly request, rejoicing in the Spirit, because that in this way our faith, doctrine, and life could be best explained by you, dear sirs, to the authorities, and to those to whom the carnal sword has been entrusted.[2] And also that in this way the suspicion might be

---

[1] The exact dates seem to have been Jan. 28-31, 1544. *Ed.*

[2] The Anabaptists believed in a basic difference between the Old and New Covenants. The Old Covenant involved a theocracy, a situation in which God's people were both a body of believers and body politic. This latter involved Israel's maintenance of law and

destroyed which is held against us because of the pernicious turmoil and the shameful doctrine and practice of false prophets (that always come up alongside of this Gospel with an appearance of sanctity and of fidelity to Scripture) ; and that it might be removed out of the hearts of the wise and prudent. For before God, who knows our hearts, we are clear and innocent of the fearful doctrine, commotion, sedition, bloodthirstiness, polygamy, and similar abominations. We hate and oppose these things from the bottom of our hearts as patent heresy, as snares for men's souls, as seductions and deceit, as pestilent ideas cursed by every divine Scripture.

For how could the true brethren and sisters of Jesus Christ, the well-disposed children of God, who with Christ Jesus are born of God the Father and the powerful seed of the divine Word in Christ Jesus, who are regenerated by Christ, partake of His Spirit and nature, who have been made like unto Him, are Christian and heavenly minded—how can such people teach or stage turmoil of any kind; people who are ever prepared according to the measure of their faith to do the will of the eternal Prince of Peace who has taught His disciples nothing but patience and eternal peace, saying, Peace I leave with you, my peace I give unto you. Again, Peace be with you. His kingdom is a kingdom of love, of unity, of peace, and of betterment of life; and not of hatred, turmoil, blood, unrest, and destruction. Again, in peace we are called of God. Let the peace of God rule in your hearts, to which also ye are called. Again, Blessed are the peacemakers. Paul says, The hope of God fill you with all joy and peace in believing.

I am aware, my dear friends, that these Scriptures have reference for the most part to the inward peace which comes through Christ. Yet whoever has this inward, Christian peace in his heart will never more be found guilty before God and the world of turmoil, treason, mutiny, murder, theft, or of consenting to or taking part in them. For the Spirit of Christ which is in him seeks not evil, but good; not destruction, but healing; and not harm, but health. Such men seek to live everywhere in peace with all mankind as far as is possible. They follow peace with all men, and holiness, without which no man can see the Lord. Heb. 12:14.

Behold, beloved friends and brethren, by these and other Scriptures we are taught and warned not to take up the literal sword, nor ever to give our

order within the covenant people by the use of force. The sword of Israel did not pass to the church, however, but to the governments of the world. Hence Menno and his Anabaptist brethren at one and the same time call for absolute nonresistance to evil men on the part of the Christian Church, and for the maintenance of law and order on the part of the state. The Christian shall render all honor and obedience to the state but he cannot administer justice in the state; that is not his calling. The Anabaptists believed that the teaching of the New Testament was always in harmony with these understandings. Romans 13 is not placing responsibility for law and order upon the church but upon the state, and calling upon Christians to obey the government. The distinctive ethic of the Christian, however, is found in Romans 12. Christians are to let God take care of evildoers; they themselves are to feed their enemies, and give them drink. They are to overcome evil only by doing good. Compare Matt. 5:38-48; John 18:36; II Cor. 10:3, 4; II Tim. 2:24; I Thess. 5:15; I Pet. 2:21-23; 3:8, 9. *Ed.*

consent thereto (excepting the ordinary sword of the magistrate[3] when it must be used), but to take up the two-edged, powerful, sharp sword of the Spirit, which goes forth from the mouth of God, namely, the Word of God. By it we desire to destroy the kingdom of Satan, to constrain all the world to repentance and salvation, and to bruise, crush, and pierce all hard and obdurate hearts. I say, we desire by the Spirit, by the grace and power of the Lord, to prune all flesh, whether high or low, rich or poor, learned or unlearned, of all pride, vain show, pomp, avarice, usury, of cheating, lies, deceit, robbery, shedding of innocent blood, of hatred, envy, adultery, fornication, unchastity, unnatural desires, gluttony, winebibbing, perversions, of fearful cursing and swearing, unspirituality, vanity, and of the fearful unbecoming idolatry. And we do all this in order that all men, no matter who they are, may by the fear of God, from which comes the sure knowledge of the judgments of God, become first inwardly humble before Him, and then by the sure knowledge of His blessings so abundantly shown to us, be refreshed and comforted by Christ Jesus, and thus willingly renounce by the power of their faith, working by love, their own wisdom, philosophy, sophistry, unwillingness, sloth, evil lusts, unbelief, disobedience, and the very straying, carnal mad life of this world, and rediscover all divine wisdom, truth, love, earnestness, and sobriety; the true sacraments and true service of God, in full obedience to God and Christ, and in all the Christian fruits which follow from a pure heart, good conscience, and unfeigned love.

We do not contend with carnal, but with spiritual weapons, with patience and the Word of God, against all flesh, the world, and the devil, trusting in Christ. Nor shall there ever be found any other weapons with us. Therefore, be not afraid of us (behold in Christ Jesus I lie not); for we do not desire your destruction, but your repentance; not your condemnation, but your everlasting salvation; not your flesh and blood, but your spirit and soul. On account of these things I have suffered these seven years,[4] and still suffer slander and scorn, anxiety, discomfort, persecution, and the great peril of prison.

The more the Word of the Lord is by the grace of God extended to the reformation of some persons (who are few, however), the more hatred and bitterness increases against me, so that to this hour I could not find in all the country (where alas, the mere boasting of the divine Word is a great deal more plentiful than the fear of God), a cabin or hut (the Lord be blessed) in which my poor wife and our little children could put up in safety for a year or two. Oh, cruel, pitiless Christians.

Oh, that all magistrates and princes, as also all the wise and learned,

---

[3] The magistrate may properly use his sword to maintain law and order (but not to destroy or persecute religious nonconformists). The Christian has only the sword of the Spirit. *Ed.*

[4] Menno became a member of the Anabaptist (Obbenite) brotherhood in 1536. He was ordained as an elder in 1537. This work was published in 1544. *Ed.*

might know the intention and desire of my heart, as also of my beloved brethren, who by the grace, Spirit, and Word of God are converted into a new spirit and new birth. If they only understood our teaching and agitation correctly, how soon their hearts and their minds would be changed. But since they are all of them with but few exceptions nothing but earth and flesh, and lack the Spirit of Christ, therefore, alas, we hear nothing from them but raving and slander. Therefore we can expect nothing from them (I mean the evil disposed) but the stake, water, fire, wheel, and sword as a reward of gratitude that we have sought and yet seek salvation and eternal life for ourselves and for all the world with such diligence, care, pains, and labor from our inmost heart. For I strive after nothing (of which God Most High is my witness) but that the God of heaven and earth, through His blessed Son Jesus Christ, might have the glory and praise of His blessed Word, that all men might be saved, roused in this day of grace from the profound sleep of sinfulness, that they might lay by all clinging sin and the damnable works of darkness, that they might put on the armor of light, that they might with us become, by true penitence, faith, baptism, Supper, ban, love, obedience, and life, one holy, Christian church, one body in Christ Jesus. This the whole world today opposes with all its strength, with both shoulders and horns, not willing that Jesus Christ, blessed forever, should reign over them. Luke 19:47. They persecute, banish, burn, murder, and destroy all those who teach and uphold the glory, praise, honor, will, and commandments of the Lord. *De his satis* [Enough of this].

Inasmuch as I comply with your friendly request in this matter by briefly setting forth in writing my doctrine and faith as I did before verbally, a thing which I am ever prepared to do before all men according to the doctrine of Peter, therefore I desire of you, as you hold Christ dear, that you do not look upon this my confession which is the Word of God, with carnal and blind eyes as the mad and foolish world does, the world which wants to have all things taught according to its own fancy and will under the name of Christ. I ask that you do not measure and judge in a carnal way with dialectics and similar human wisdom, but I ask you to examine it and judge it according to the Word and truth of the Lord, as those who understand spiritual matters; as unblamable, regenerate Christians who are full of the knowledge, love, and fear of God, driven by the Holy Spirit, who do not seek human favor, praise, and honor, their own advantage and carnal welfare, but only the honor and glory of God, and the eternal salvation of their brethren. For to such alone belongs the judgment in spiritual matters, and not to the carnally minded. I Cor. 14:29. The Spirit of God teaches, judges, and understands all things. Paul says, What man knoweth the things of a man, save the spirit of man which is in him? Even so the things of God knoweth no man but the Spirit of God. I Cor. 2:11.

Therefore try your intention and inmost heart as before God who seeth all things. Search yourselves thoroughly and open your hearts before the

Lord. In case you still seek carnal liberty, lusts, honor, and profit, then doubtlessly your judgment in spiritual matters (especially as regards the outward confession) will be quite carnal, selfish, partial, unjust, and false. You will garble and pervert the plain testimony of the Holy Scriptures by book logic and sophism (to free yourselves and to please the world). Beware lest you do this and the terrible wrath of the Lord be visited upon you. I know why I write this to you. I fear for your souls greatly. Ponder what I mean. And if your hearts be sincere, pure, and pious before God (as I hope), and if you earnestly seek for the truth, then you will confess by the grace of God that our humble, plain doctrine, our faith, sacraments, and in the majority of cases the conduct, especially the outward conduct, are unblamable, Christian, evangelical, and in conformity with God's Word and Spirit.

Would that God by His loving-kindness might grant you sincerely to acknowledge in your inmost soul that this is the unchangeable Word and will of God, the Spirit and power of God. I pray you therefore by the precious blood of our Lord Jesus Christ to receive this in gladness and gratitude of heart, and to let your ordained rulers examine it, as well as all men, even as your heart, spirit, or conscience testifies concerning our doctrine, faith, sacraments, and lives. Fear no man's greatness, nor despise his humbleness. Go upon the kingly highway, speaking the truth to all men with a clear conscience, lest you teach, judge, or testify contrary to inward judgment and conviction, to your everlasting condemnation. Truly you know that you are taught by the Word of the Lord that whosoever speaketh against the Holy Ghost it shall not be forgiven him, neither in this world nor the world to come. Matt. 12:32; Luke 10:12; Mark 3:28.

Therefore, most beloved brethren, search your spirits carefully. If you are spiritual, then your judgment will no doubt be spiritual, just, and right. If you are not, and judge of God's deeds according to your own will, woe unto you! I speak unto you as unto one whose soul I seek and love with all my strength. Although you are much more learned than I am, yet I teach and admonish you to judge justly in all things without carnality or partiality. For I am afraid that there are not a few, some of them famous men, excelling in learning, who in part seem to fear the Lord for filthy lucre's sake, for worldly honor and the lust of the flesh, who have therefore written, judged, and taught very shamefully contrary to God and His blessed Word, just to please the authorities, and to the despising of the cross of Christ, against their own consciences and better knowledge.

Very well then, let every soul seek pure, Christian truth in purity of heart, and strive after the same with all diligence, and it will be well with him. Jesus says, If ye continue in my word, then are ye my disciples indeed; and ye shall know the truth, and the truth shall make you free. Those who trust in Him shall understand the truth, and the believing shall serve Him in love. Again, The secret of the Lord is with them that fear him; and he shall show them his covenant. Ps. 25:14.

May the Almighty Father, through His blessed Son Jesus Christ, grant you in all things a true understanding and clear vision to judge rightly in all things, to distinguish according to the evangelical truth between that which is holy and that which is unholy, between good and evil, between right and wrong, between the clean and the unclean. May some of you, having renounced gain, honor, and fame for the sake of the Gospel of Jesus Christ, henceforth be taught by the sure and true doctrine of Scripture, be constrained by the Holy Ghost, and enter into all divine wisdom, truth, righteousness, and into obedience unto Him who has taught us by His powerful Word, drawn us by His Spirit, and bought and delivered us by His crimson precious blood, that is, Christ Jesus. Amen.

Judge aright, and confess the truth.


## [I. THE INCARNATION OF CHRIST]*

Dear sirs, friends, and brethren: When this matter of the incarnation of our dear Lord Jesus Christ was first mentioned by the brethren, fearing that I might be in error about it, I was terrified at heart. I feared that I might be found before God in pernicious unbelief. Yes, I was often so troubled at heart, even after my baptism, that many a day I abstained from food and drink by the great anxiety of my soul, beseeching and praying God, with many tears, that the kind Father by His mercy and grace might disclose unto me, poor sinner who (although in extreme weakness) sought after His blessed will and pleasure, the mystery of the incarnation of His blessed Son, in so far as might serve to the glorification of His holy name and to the consolation of my afflicted conscience.

Thus wandering about for days, weeks, and months, I have diligently discussed the opinions or beliefs in the matter which weighed on my mind so heavily with some of you; yet none could instruct me sufficiently to quiet my conscience. I found with them gross misunderstanding of the Scriptures which they alleged as proof for their assertions, and that not only when measured by my opinion but also by the Scriptures. At last, after much fasting, weeping, praying, tribulation, and anxiety, I became by the grace of God comforted and refreshed at heart, firmly acknowledging and believing, assured by the infallibly sure testimony of the Scriptures, understood in the Spirit, that Christ Jesus forever blessed is the Lord from heaven (I Cor. 15:47); the promised spiritual seed of the new and spiritual Eve (Gen. 3:15); namely, the eternal Truth (John 14:16); the mighty Conqueror of the serpent and his seed (Gen. 3:15; Luke 11:21; John 16:33; Heb. 2:14); which promised seed is the eternal Truth and Word of God, and in the fullness

---

*Menno entitles this section: A True Confession and Scriptural Exposition of the Most Holy Incarnation of Our Dear Lord Jesus Christ. Written to John a Lasco and his Assistants at Emden.

of time, was ordained thereto by the Almighty and merciful Father (Gal. 4:4), conceived in the pure virgin (Isa. 7:14), by the Holy Ghost and power of the Most High, when she heard and believed the heavenly message and good pleasure of the Father, a message brought to her by Gabriel. Luke 1:28.

This eternal Word of God is become flesh. It was in the beginning with God and was God (John 1:2); conceived and come forth of the Holy Ghost (Matt. 1:18); nourished and fed in Mary, as a natural child is by its mother; a true Son of God and a true son of man, born of her, truly flesh and blood. He was afflicted, hungry, thirsty, subject to suffering and death, according to the flesh; immortal according to the Spirit, like unto us in all things, sin excepted. Heb. 2:9. Truly God and man, man and God. He was not divided nor separated as being half heavenly and half earthly, half of the seed of man and half of God, as some express it; but an unmixed, whole Christ, namely, spirit, soul, and body, of which, according to Paul, all men are constituted. Who, being in the form of God, thought it not robbery to be equal with God: but he diminished himself (note this well), having no visible form; therefore he took the form of a servant, was made in the form of man, and was found in the fashion of a man. Phil. 2:7. Who was more exalted than the angels, was made a little lower than they, seeing that he had to die since he was of flesh and blood. Heb. 2:9.

I believe and confess that He was thus, without any doubt, that same flesh which had its origin in the Holy Spirit, born of the seed of the tribe of David and Abraham. Matt. 1:20. He was said to be born of a woman, under the law (Gal. 4:4), circumcised the eighth day, obedient unto His parents, increasing in all wisdom, in age and in grace before God and man. Luke 2:40.

This same man, Christ Jesus, preached, was crucified, died, and was buried. He arose and ascended to heaven and is seated at the right hand of the Almighty Father, according to the testimony of all Scripture. From thence He will come to judge the sheep and the goats, the good and the evil, the living and the dead. II Cor. 5:10; II Tim. 4:1.

Thus I believe and confess that the pure Word of God, Christ Jesus, the Creator, who Himself issued commandments to Adam and condemned him, has instituted Himself in Adam's stead, that is, in his condemnation, death, and promised curse, and has, by His great compassion, love, and mercy, taken upon Himself the condemning burden of His erring creatures. I believe He Himself became Adam in the flesh. And thus He has, by His death, restored life by humbling Himself. By His righteousness and obedience He has paid and fulfilled the eternal righteousness of the righteous God, as He speaks through David, I restored that which I took not away, Ps. 69:4.

For God has not reconciled the world unto Himself by Adam's flesh, for by His righteousness it was subject to the wrath and curse. And what can be reconciled by wrath and curse? But He has done so by Himself, by mere grace, by His eternal Word, that is, by His blessed Son, who became like unto the first Adam in all things, unrighteousness, disobedience, and sin excepted, in order that all honor and praise should belong to God and not to us or to Adam. Yes, Christ Jesus is made unto us of God's wisdom, and righteousness, and sanctification, and redemption: that, according as it is written, He that glorieth, let him glory in the Lord. I Cor. 1:30.

Dear sirs, friends, and brethren: In this way I believe that God has sent his own Son in the likeness of sinful flesh, and for sin and by the sin which he conquered, or for which he was sacrificed, he has condemned sin in the flesh; in order that the righteousness of the law might be fulfilled in us, who walk not after the flesh, but after the Spirit. Rom. 8:3, 4. Again, He hath made him to be sin for us, who knew no sin; that we might be made the righteousness of God in him. II Cor. 5:21. And thus He is become our only sacrifice, fulfillment, and payment, by which God the Father is reconciled, by whom His righteousness is fulfilled, the curse removed, the devil, sin and eternal death conquered, eternal life restored. Yea, [through Him we have] grace, favor, mercy, peace, and eternal life. As Paul says, He that spared not his own Son, but delivered him up for us all, how shall he not with him also freely give us all things? Rom. 8:32.

And so I believe and confess that God was made manifest in the flesh (I Tim. 3:16); that God was in Christ reconciling the world unto himself (II Cor. 5:19); that He has blotted out our sins, and has again seated Himself at the right hand of the Majesty on high where all the angels of God worship Him. Heb. 1:6. And with this doctrine of the conception and incarnation of Christ, all Scriptural testimony and truth agree.

To begin with, Paul says, Who is it but he that also descended first into the lower parts of the earth? He that descended is the same as he that ascended far above all heavens, that he might fill all things. Eph. 4:9, 10. Again, Christ Himself says, No man hath ascended up to heaven, but he that came down from heaven, even the Son of man which is in heaven. John 3:13. Again, in the same chapter, He that cometh from above, is above all; he that is of the earth, is earthly, and speaketh of the earth: he that cometh from heaven, is above all, and what he hath seen and heard, that he testifieth; and no man receiveth his testimony. Again, I am the living bread which came down from heaven; if any man eat of this bread, he shall live forever; and the bread that I will give is my flesh, which I will give for the life of the world. John 6:51. Doth this offend you? And what if ye shall see the Son of man ascend up where he was before? Again, I came forth from the Father, and am come into the world; again, I leave the world and go to the Father. John 16:28. Father, glorify me with the glory which I had with thee before the world was. John 17. Again, That which was from the beginning, which we have heard, which we have seen with our eyes, which we have looked upon and our hands have handled, of the word of life (for the life was manifested). I John 1:10. And there are many such passages, especially in John.

All those who by the grace of God clearly and intelligently perceive and confess this doctrine of the incarnation of our beloved Lord Jesus Christ grasp and confess correctly the unspeakable grace, favor, compassion, mercy, and the inexpressibly great love of God the Father expressed and manifest in Christ Jesus. As He Himself says, For God so loved the world that he gave his only begotten Son, that whosoever believeth in him should not perish but have everlasting life. John 3:16. Again, In this was manifested the love of God toward us, because that God sent his only begotten Son into the world, that we might live through him. Herein is love, not that we loved God, but that he loved us, and sent his Son to be the propitiation for our sins. I John 4:9, 10. For how could God show greater fatherly love to us than so to humble His eternal Wisdom and Truth, His pure, powerful Word, His blessed Son, by whom He created all things; who was like unto Him in form, the image of His blessed being, who diminished Himself and became less than the angels, a poor, despised, suffering mortal man or servant, who alone had to bear the trouble, labor, sin, transgression, curse, and death of the whole world. He so humbled Himself that He became the most miserable of men. Isa. 53:6. A worm, and no man; a reproach of men, and despised of the people. Ps. 22:6. And thus the innocent, the true, the wise, the righteous, the obedient, and the pure Christ Jesus had to expunge, blot out, and satisfy the guilt, falsehood, folly, unrighteousness, disobedience, and pollution of all men. Dearest sirs, have you ever heard of greater love?

My dear holy father and brother, this is, before God, my doctrine, faith, and confession of the blessed incarnation of our beloved Lord Jesus Christ, which is, in my opinion, very strong and incontrovertible in the light of the Holy Scriptures. Therefore I may not be convinced by any view of the matter, by any of your reasonings and writings hitherto advanced by you against our doctrine, faith, and confession; since you turn and explain things according to a natural and carnal sense, and not according to the true explanation and sense of the Holy Spirit; which, doubtlessly, should not be done in this matter, since this glorious work of the incarnation of Christ is wrought and accomplished by God through the Holy Spirit, in a manner far above the natural processes, and according to God's good pleasure.

I repeat, this is my confession to those who demand to hear my belief and feeling in regard to this matter. However, I never teach it so profoundly in my common admonitions to the friends and brethren; nor have I, heretofore, ever taught it thus profoundly, as I have told you verbally. But I simply teach that the blessed Christ Jesus is truly God and man, a Son of God, and a son of man, conceived of the Holy Ghost, born of the Virgin Mary, a poor, despised man, like unto us in all things, sin excepted. I teach that it is He who was promised in the Law and the Prophets, that He is our true Messiah, Christ, King David, Prophet, Priest and Bishop, the Deliverer, Saviour, Sacrifice, Reconciliation, Atonement, Shepherd, Teacher, Example, Mediator, Advocate, Ruler, Commander, Bridegroom, Light of the World, the true Door to the fold, the eternal Wisdom, the Image of God, the Father's

Word, the Way, the Truth, and the Life, etc. For I know full well that there are few who can understand this intricate matter, even after it is explained to them.

Therefore, I say, I think there is nothing better for me and for all teachers than in a simple apostolic fashion to teach the incarnation of Christ for the simple congregation, with a view to its edification, love, comfort, and sanctification, and to follow Him in His holy doctrine and life. Would to God that we were all of such mind. But in case one wants to search further and inquire into this matter, if it be proper and his understanding reaches far enough, it will not be hidden from him. If not, it will be said unto him, Do not speculate beyond your powers. Ecclesiasticus 3:21.

Very well then, even though this is our doctrine and understanding in keeping with the testimony of Scriptures, as we can by the grace of God best understand and comprehend it, yet we fear that our explanation from the Word of God will not satisfy and convince you to unite with us in this matter, but that you will persevere in your adopted reasonings and arguments and try to explain it literally, naturally, and humanlike; not observing that Isaiah, Matthew, Luke, and John clearly testify that it was brought about by faith and in a supernatural way in Mary, by the power of the Holy Ghost, as has been said above.

Oh, let us not minimize the Almighty Father in His mercy! Let us not rob the blessed Son of God of His glory. Dear brethren, the Scripture remains eternal and unbroken. Take heed, lest you err. Thus speaks Isaiah, Behold, a virgin shall conceive, and bear a son. Isa. 7:14. Again, the angel of the Lord said unto Joseph, That which is conceived in her is of the Holy Ghost. Matt. 1:20. Again, when Mary asked the angel the manner of the conception, how it should be, he answered: The Holy Ghost shall come upon thee, and the power of the Highest shall overshadow thee: therefore that holy thing that shall be born of thee shall be called the Son of God. Luke 1:35. Again, this is the sure testimony of John the servant of God and of Christ, concerning the incarnation of Jesus Christ. The Word became flesh. John 1:14. He does not say, The word took unto itself flesh.

You see, dear brethren, how incontrovertible these reasons and Scriptures are by which we aim to establish our matter, yet I fear that we, on account of this matter, will be judged and considered sectarian, heretical, and deceitful, notwithstanding there are many among us who fear the Lord from their inmost hearts and have never in their lives heard a word spoken in regard to the mystery of this matter, as was declared above. Neither have they inquired into it, much less understood it. They are satisfied with the Father's favor, manifested through Christ. They obey Christ Jesus in His holy Word; follow His example, love, doctrine, and life; they rejoice solely at that which they have in Him; the remission of sins, the gift of the Spirit, freedom, grace, favor, promise, mercy, and eternal life.

Oh, that all the wise and learned, even all the men of this world, would satisfy themselves with the plain, humble teachings of Jesus Christ and His apostles, not climbing higher nor lingering lower; would seek God, with purity of heart—and firmly believe, fear, love, and obey His blessed Word. Oh, what precious coin and what glorious gain would then, by the grace of God, be gathered into the treasury of the Lord. But, as it is, there are many, alas, whose faith and knowledge is not in their hearts but solely upon their lips (I say this, not to shame the just), who find pleasure in foolish and useless questions and in disputation; who are versed more in the wisdom of man than in the wisdom of God; who are of corrupt minds, who ever learn and never come to the knowledge of the eternal truth. And whoever contradicts and reproves them by the plain word of the holy Gospel of Jesus Christ, from sheer brotherly love, is from that moment considered by them as shameful, a sectarian, or a wicked perverse heretic. (Judge for yourselves whether what I say is not true.) And yet their own unbelieving hearts are quite earthly, carnal, and devilish, and their whole life nothing but flesh, pride, vanity, sloth, avarice, hatred, cruelty, bloodthirstiness, drunkenness, flattery; in short, nothing but sin and shame. Would that I spoke falsely rather than truly!

Nevertheless let them slander and upbraid as much as they please; we will willingly bear it. We will all be judged by one Judge who will in minutest detail examine and try their case and ours, their zeal and ambition and ours, their conduct and ours. Then it will appear who it is that has anxiously sought the everlasting truth of God, the praise and honor of the Lord, and the everlasting salvation of all mankind. Brethren, beware lest you become like these barren disputers! Take heed, if you would save your souls, that you sincerely seek, desire, believe, receive, and practice the saving truth of God. Amen.

## [A.] Objections

Since I have shown and confessed to you our firm position on the incarnation of the Lord, that He did not become flesh of Mary, but in Mary; and since I have also, in part, adduced the reasons and Scripture by which we are led to such belief, therefore I will now briefly reply to your Scriptures and arguments, hitherto advanced, by which you teach and try to prove that He did not simply assume flesh in Mary but of Mary.

[1.] In the first place, you ask, *Is he not the seed of woman?* We answer, Yes. Gen. 3:15.

From this you conclude that if He is the seed of the woman, then He is also man of the woman. We answer by asking, Did not the deceiving serpent have a body? You must answer yes. For God said, Upon thy belly shalt thou go and dust shalt thou eat all the days of thy life. Again, Did not the deceived woman have a body? Doubtlessly so. If the natural and bodily seed of the deceived woman be bodily, then the seed of the serpent must also be natural bodily seed, of which God Himself has spoken and testified in

Genesis. Unless you are prepared to admit and confess that the one should be understood spiritually and the other literally. Not at all, beloved brethren! But the physical serpent represents the spiritual serpent, namely, Satan (Rev. 12:14), and has his spiritual seed, namely, the lie (John 8:44). Likewise, the woman, who is the mother of all mankind, represents Adam, after she had sinned, flesh of his flesh, and bone of his bone; subject to her husband, the image of the new spiritual woman, namely, the church of Christ, which is the image of Christ (Rom. 8:29), flesh of His flesh and bone of His bone, subject to Him (Eph. 5:30). If the woman be spiritual, then the seed must be spiritual, namely, the eternal truth, which truth is Christ Himself. John 14:6. You see, dear sirs, in this way the serpent is spiritual and his seed is spiritual of which he begets all his children of accursed falsehood. Over against this, the woman is spiritual and her seed is spiritual, of which she begets all her children of the saving truth. Between these is endless war, as may be plainly seen. Yet truth triumphs, and falsehood is vanquished, notwithstanding falsehood opposes with all its power. O brethren, understand the Scriptures aright, lest we, through misunderstanding or pernicious obduracy, deceive and mislead ourselves and many souls with us.

If you are not satisfied with the clear explanation of these Scriptures, but still maintain that both the woman and the seed must be taken literally, then we know and confess that this same woman conceived in her womb the afore-mentioned seed, which is God's Word, not from her body nor of her body, but of God, by the power of the Holy Ghost, through faith. Matt. 1:20; Luke 1:34; John 1:1.

[2.] Secondly, you ask, *Is He not called the seed of Abraham?* We answer, Yes. Gal. 3:16.

From this you conclude that He must be descended from the flesh and blood of Abraham. In confirmation you cite the saying of Paul, For verily he took not on him the nature of angels; but he took on him the seed of Abraham; wherefore in all things it behooved him to become like unto his brethren. Heb. 2:16, 17.

To this we reply, Your conclusion is according to the flesh, and not according to the Word of God. John says, The Word was made flesh and dwelt among us; and it is of the Holy Ghost (Matt. 1:25); therefore it was not Abraham's natural flesh and blood. But by grace it was promised the beloved father Abraham, that he, that is, the true blessing of all nations, should not come of the seed of his brethren, nor of the Gentiles nor uncircumcised ones, but of his seed, that is, of his line, as it is written, In thee shall all families of the earth be blessed. Gen. 12:3. In this way Christ Jesus is promised to Abraham and born of his seed, according to the promise, as Christ Himself says, Salvation is of the Jews. John 4:22. And thus He is called the seed and son of Abraham. Gal. 3:16; Matt. 1:1. For He is, doubtlessly, according to His blessed flesh, conceived of the Holy Ghost and come of Abraham's line for the salvation of us all.

Again, the saying of Paul which you quote to sustain your cause was not taught and spoken by the Holy Ghost in such a sense as you claim; but Paul says, Both he that sanctifieth and they that are sanctified are all of one. That is, as you say, Of one Adam. But we say they are one, that is, of one God. For which cause He (the Saviour) is not ashamed to call them (the sanctified ones) His brethren, saying, I will declare thy name unto my brethren; in the midst of the church will I sing praise unto thee. For as Christ Jesus was born from above of the Father, and is therefore called God's Child or Son, having God as Father, so also to all who receive Christ, To them gave he power to become the sons of God. John 1:12. Such as are regenerated, are born together with Christ Jesus, of one God, have one Father. Therefore He calls the sanctified ones who with Him are born of God His brethren, not because of the flesh but because of regeneration.

If it were otherwise you would have to consent and admit that all wicked, unbelieving, and perverse men and women are brethren and sisters of Christ Jesus as well as the believing, sincere, and pious. Oh, no, for Christ Jesus says, Whosoever shall do the will of my Father which is in heaven, the same is my brother and sister, and mother. Matt. 12:50. Read and understand it aright. Paul[5] says further, Behold I and the children which God hath given me. Heb. 2:13. Forasmuch then as the children are partakers of flesh and blood, he also himself partook of the same (that is, became mortal, as a consequence); that through death he might destroy him that had the power of death, that is, the devil, and deliver them who through fear of death were all their lifetime subject to bondage, which was the seed and generation of Abraham, by the terrible threat, subject to the heavy burden and intolerable yoke of the law of Moses. For verily he took not on him the nature of angels (if you understand this as referring to the good angels, then you should know that they did not sin; but if you take it as meaning the evil ones, then you should know that He rejected them and keeps them in bondage of eternal darkness to the great judgment day). Paul says, For verily he took not on him the nature of angels; but he took on him the very oppressed seed of Abraham. Wherefore it behooved him to be made like unto his brethren in all things (to wit: weak and mortal), that he might be a merciful and faithful High Priest in things pertaining to God, to make reconciliation for the sins of the people. For in that he himself hath suffered being tempted, he is able to succor them that are tempted. Heb. 2:16-18. Now, judge for yourselves whether this is not the right reading of this Scripture of Paul.

[3.] In the third place, you say: *Paul teaches plainly that Christ Jesus is born of the seed of David according to the flesh, and is proved to be the Son of God with power, according to the spirit of sanctification. Rom. 1:3. Therefore He is, you conclude, according to the flesh, of the seed or loins of David, and according to the Spirit, born of God.*

To which we reply: That Christ should be born of the seed or loins of

---

[5] Menno believed that Paul had written Hebrews. *Ed.*

David would follow in the ordinary course of nature, but it is not in accordance with the testimony of Scripture. The Scripture teaches that the Word became flesh and that it came forth from the Holy Ghost. John 1:14. Therefore, beloved brethren, this is the true meaning of Paul and the rest.

The consoling promise of the future Saviour was given to Abraham, that Christ should be born of his seed or line. Abraham branched off into Ishmael, Isaac, and the children of Keturah. The promise of the patriarchs was continued to Isaac, not to the others. Isaac divided into Esau and Jacob. Not Esau but Jacob received the promise given to his fathers Abraham and Isaac. Jacob gave rise to twelve tribes. And in order that the promised Saviour might not be looked for from the tribe of Reuben, Dan, Gad, or any of the eleven tribes, therefore the Holy Ghost points to Judah and not to any of the other tribes. With Judah multiplying into many branches and twigs, the promise is renewed in David. II Kings 7:12.

In this way the merciful Father has ever testified and shown beforehand, from one patriarch to another and from one generation to another, that all men might know from which patriarch and generation the promised Saviour and Deliverer of all mankind should be born, according to the flesh. The Jews were aware of this, saying, Hath not the scripture said that Christ cometh of the seed of David, and of the town of Bethlehem? John 7:42. Also, He came unto his own and his own received him not. He is come of the seed or lineage of David, according to the promise; but they did not receive Him.

Yes, the appointed hour is come. Gabriel is sent of God to a virgin named Mary, who was betrothed to a man. Mary believed the word of the Lord; the Holy Ghost overshadowed her, etc. The Word became flesh, in her. John 1:14. It was conceived and derived of the Holy Ghost (Matt. 1:20); and according to this same flesh, or with this same flesh, which was conceived of and brought forth of the Holy Ghost, He was born of Mary, the pure virgin, who was of the seed and lineage of David. David was of Judah; Judah of Jacob; Jacob of Isaac; Isaac of Abraham. And so the divine promise was fulfilled which God through grace alone had promised and given to the above-mentioned patriarchs. And thus He was born, according to the flesh, as was said above, of the seed or lineage of David; and by His saving Spirit He is proved to be the living Son of God. Rom. 1:4. For if He were to prove or declare Himself to be the Son of God, it must, without doubt, be according to His sanctifying Spirit, inasmuch as He could not be such according to the flesh, since He had diminished Himself, and was forsaken of the Father, was weak, despised, hungry, thirsty, suffering, mortal, and like unto us all in all things, yet without sin. Beloved brethren, take heed! the alleged Scripture of Paul is very clear, and everywhere it has the same single stamp.

[4.] In the fourth place, you say, *Christ is called a fruit of the loins of David. Therefore He must be the natural and physical seed of David.*[6]

Answer. These words, according to the letter, were spoken of Solomon

---

[6] For *lieffelijck* (pleasant) we read *leiffelijck* (physical). *Tr.*

and not of Christ; which Solomon was born of the loins of David. Thus Nathan spake unto David, And when thy days be fulfilled, and thou shalt sleep with thy fathers, I will set up thy seed after thee, which shall proceed out of thy loins, and I will establish thy kingdom. He shall build a house for my name, and I will establish the throne of his kingdom forever. I will be his father, and he shall be my son. (Now note of whom it is spoken.) If he commit iniquity, I will chasten him with the rod of men, and with the stripes of the children of men. Now Christ never committed iniquity; for He knew no sin; neither was guile found in His mouth. I Pet. 2:22. Again, in the Psalms, The Lord hath sworn in truth unto David; he will not turn from it; of the fruit of thy body will I set up on thy throne. If thy children will keep my covenant, and my testimony that I shall teach them, their children shall also sit upon thy throne for ever more. That this is spoken of Solomon literally, he himself testifies in plain words. (I Kings 3:6; 8:20). Solomon, without doubt, represented in figure Christ Jesus, as in His glory, wisdom, building of the temple, etc. You see, very dear sirs, we should not take the letter for the spirit, and the spirit for the letter. But that the promise according to the Spirit had reference to Christ is incontrovertible; for this the holy prophets of God plainly show; and particularly, Isa. 9:6; Jer. 23:5; 33:15.

[5.] In the fifth place, you ask, *Is He not a fruit of the womb of Mary? And is He not called that? And if He is a fruit of the womb of Mary, then He is also brought forth of her flesh by the power of the Holy Ghost. For if He were not of her flesh and blood, then He could not be called a fruit of her womb. But because He is of her flesh He is called the fruit of her body, as an apple is called the fruit of a tree, because it grows on the tree, and partakes of its nature, through the fertility of the earth.*

Answer. According to the course of nature your conclusion is in part right, but according to Scriptural testimony it is altogether wrong. For the Scriptures say that Mary the pure virgin by faith conceived the eternal Word of God which in the beginning was with God, and was God, that it became flesh, conceived and descended from the Holy Spirit (Matt. 1:20); that it was nourished in her; and was in due time born as a natural child is born of its mother. In this way Christ Jesus remains the precious blessed fruit of the womb of Mary, according to the words of Elisabeth, conceived not of her womb but in her womb, wrought by the Holy Spirit through faith, of God the omnipotent Father, from high heaven, as we have frequently shown.

You also allege a natural reason concerning the tree and its fruits in proof of your assertion. Inasmuch as you do, I will reply to your reasoning according to nature; namely, I have a well-prepared field, well pulverized and fertilized, bearing abundance of wheat, corn, or rye. I say, Ah, that is a beautiful crop. But this field could not produce of itself, no matter how well tilled and rich, and no matter how much it was induced to do so by the heat of the sun and the moisture of the atmosphere, until the seed was sown in it by the sower. Being sown, and grown up, it is called the fruit of the field, notwithstanding it was first sown thereon. An apple is called the fruit of the tree, although it is produced and grown by the natural qualities of the tree on which it is grown.

In the same manner the heavenly Seed, namely, the Word of God, was sown in Mary, and by her faith, being conceived in her by the Holy Ghost, became flesh, and was nurtured in her body; and thus it is called the fruit of her womb, the same as a natural fruit or offspring is called the fruit of its natural mother. For Christ Jesus, as to His origin, is no earthly man, that is, a fruit of the flesh and blood of Adam. He is a heavenly fruit or man. For His beginning or origin is of the Father (John 16:28), like unto the first Adam, sin excepted. He is given to Adam and his children, if they hear and receive Him in His holy Word, to their everlasting salvation and deliverance, of God the merciful Father, merely through grace and mercy, without price and without any previous merit on our part.

[6] In the sixth place, you say, *God could not suffer. If Christ's flesh were not on earth or of Adam, but from heaven, then He could not have suffered, and consequently could not have died.*

Answer. Be impartial and judge rightly. Your conception is that Christ Jesus as to the Spirit is of the Father, in which Spirit He was, as you say, not subject to suffering and death, but you hold that He was not of the Father, according to the flesh. According to the flesh, in which He suffered and died, you teach that He is of the earth, in order that thus the law enjoined upon man with threat of condemnation might by the earthly man, namely, Christ, be fulfilled; that He (we being in Him, by the oneness of His human nature and blood with ours, whereby He has fulfilled in our flesh the righteousness of the Father) might save us. This foundation is implied in your Latin syllogisms. We will not controvert this by subtle syllogisms nor by acute human cavilings, for we do not have them. But we controvert it by the plain testimony of the Word, which cannot be turned by glosses, nor broken by human reason.

First, we confess and consent before all the world that God, the Almighty, eternal Father is quite beyond suffering and death, for with Him there is no change. Jas. 1:17. I am God, said the prophets, and I change not. But God the Son, the eternal Word, is diminished, has emptied Himself, became less than the angels, miserable, mortal, human flesh. John 1:14.

You say, *God cannot suffer.* But the Scriptures say otherwise, that God, the Son, has suffered. For He Himself says, I am the first and the last, I am he that liveth and was dead, and behold I am alive forevermore. Rev. 1:18; 22:13. The Alpha and Omega was not Adam's flesh, but He who was before every creature, by whom all things were created. Whose goings forth were from the beginning and from eternity. Eph. 3:9. This is the Alpha and Omega; this same one is become flesh. It is He that has suffered, died. It is He that rose again and shall live forever. Take heed, lest you willfully oppose the Scriptures. Christ cannot be divided into two parts, as you think.

I repeat, the Father is immortal, and not subject to suffering; but for our sakes the Son was diminished and became subject to suffering and death, according to the testimony of Scriptures. Phil. 2:7; Heb. 2:14; I Pet. 1:19, and many other passages. Therefore He prayed His dear Father that He might have again the glory that He had with the Father, which He had lost in becoming man. John 17:5. If He remained unchanged in His divine form, and if He suffered only in that which He took of earth, as you say, then tell me, dear sirs, what had He lost that He desired again of His Father? Examine the Scriptures rightly, and pray; and by the grace of God your eyes will be opened to behold the truth of Christ.

Again, in the second place we answer that it was the entire Christ Jesus who went forth from His Father (John 1:14; 3:31; 6:27; 8:42; 14:24; 16:28; 17:8); became flesh in Mary, the Lord Himself from heaven (I Cor. 15:47). It was the entire Christ who was afflicted and oppressed in the flesh, soul, and spirit, according to the testimony of the Scriptures. In the flesh, for He was crucified. In the soul, because He Himself says, My soul is exceeding sorrowful, even unto death. In the spirit, for when He said this, says John, Jesus was troubled in the spirit. The Christ Jesus who suffered the judgment of the unrighteous died according to the flesh, but was made alive according to the Spirit, in order that He might bring us to God.

In the third place, replying to your syllogisms, we say: The commandment was not given to the heavenly Christ, but to the earthly Adam and his seed, through Christ, that is, through the Word. Transgressing, Adam was condemned to death through the Word, Christ. Gen. 3:19. Since then the righteousness of God is unchangeable and eternal, as you yourselves say, therefore disobedient Adam must die according to the immutable righteousness of God. Since Adam was earthly and of the earth, and since because of his disobedience, he was cursed, therefore nothing could be expected from earth but earth, from curse nothing but curse, and from death nothing but death, as Paul plainly shows. Rom. 5:12.

Now when Adam disobeyed the Word that had created him and refused to hearken, and ate, in spite of the Word, he had to enter into the death announced by the Word, he and his seed. Because it is altogether righteous that Adam and his descendants had to die, he having sinned and not having wherewith to pay; therefore it is solely grace, mercy, and love that he should live. But how? Through the righteousness of Adam's own flesh? Not at all; but through the Word which had made Adam a living being, the Word which gave him the commandment and promised him death if he should transgress, as was said above. And since death was rightly due, Truth having said so, God promised the same Word to Adam, saying that It was to become man, in order that even as Adam was deceived by the liar, and therefore, according to the justice of God, had to die, he might again be delivered by the promised Truth, and thus by grace and mercy inherit life eternal. Adam believed and was comforted, and as a sign of the truth of the promised favor and love, God clothed the poor, naked Adam and his wife with coats of skins. Gen. 3:21.

And so not the earthly, guilty, transgressing, accursed, and mortal flesh of Adam has satisfied God's righteousness and appeased His wrath, as you claim, but only the heavenly, innocent, obedient, blessed, and quickened flesh of Christ, as the Scriptures testify. He bare our sins, by his wounds we are healed. Isa. 53:8. For the promised Word, Christ Jesus, is become man and has fulfilled the righteousness required by the law, as Paul says, For what the law could not do, in that it was weak through the flesh, God sending his own Son in the likeness of sinful flesh, and for sin, condemned sin in the flesh. That the righteousness of the law might be fulfilled in us, who walk not after the flesh, but after the Spirit. Rom. 8:3, 4.

It follows unchangeably that all those who are born of Adam and remain his in not receiving by faith the promised Seed (I am speaking of those who have come to years of discretion), must by the immutable righteousness of God inherit the curse of Adam, that is, death and curse as a reward of sin. Christ Himself says, He that believeth not shall be damned. Mark 16:16. Paul, The wages of sin is death. Rom. 6:23. For they have no communion of the most holy flesh and blood of Christ Jesus. Nor can they ever enjoy His deliverance, kindness, merits, and blessings unless they be truly converted from the shameful darkness of unbelief and sin, to the eternal, clear, heavenly light, Christ Jesus. I John 1:7.

But those who with Adam truly receive the promised Seed and are renewed and comforted in God, who are born from above by this same Seed, who are changed or converted from the disobedient nature of Adam to the obedient nature of the Word, Christ Jesus: these He calls flesh of His flesh and bone of His bone. To these He gives Himself by pure grace, and makes them partakers of His righteousness, merits, cross, blood, and bitter death, yes, His whole life, love, and Spirit; for they are one body and one Spirit with Him; so that they willingly fulfill, by this spirit of love which they have received of Him (for God is love), all that which the merciful Father by His saving truth, Christ Jesus, has commanded. As John testifies, We keep his commandments and do those things that are pleasing in his sight. I John 3:22. Again, Paul says, Love is the fulfilling of the law. Rom. 13:10. Again, Christ, He that hath my commandments, and keepeth them, he it is that loveth me. John 14:21.

Besides you say, *That which is born of the Spirit is spirit.* Dear brethren, we do not say Christ is born of the Spirit, but we do say with the Scriptures that He is incarnate and conceived by the Spirit. Now it is different, as you know, to be born of the Spirit and to be incarnate and conceived by the Spirit. Who doubts, moreover, but that to be born of the Spirit is to experience regeneration! I beseech you, therefore, through the Lord, not to seek to sustain your cause with erroneously adduced Scripture, if any you have.

With this, dear sirs, I conclude my confession of the incarnation of the beloved Lord Jesus Christ. I copy this over for you, as requested, and place it before you in all clarity, as one who is not ashamed of his faith. I do not, however, go so deeply into the matter in my admonitions to the brethren, nor have I done so in the past. But, in an apostolic manner with a view to repentance and love. I pray that you may, by the mercy of God, get a proper understanding of who it was that sinned, and who it was that atoned for sin; that we may ascribe to Adam and his descendants their unrighteousness, darkness, sin, and shame; and give to Christ Jesus His righteousness, brightness, praise, and honor. I pray that in this and other matters, you may not follow human wisdom, but the wisdom of God; not reason, but Scripture; not flesh, but Spirit; not the writings and opinions of the learned, but only the testimony of Christ and His apostles, fearing God in purity of heart from your inmost souls, as I also should, that we may not be, and seek to remain, like unto them who are ever learning and never come to the knowledge of the divine truth. Be sure that you do not ask, hear, and answer except out of godly zeal. Before God, knowing and being counts. In all things be prepared to do the will of God and not the will of your slow, slothful, unwilling flesh. For I know how many there are who are disposed to nothing but to search, inquire, and dispute. They have never made acquaintance with the most necessary things, without which none can be saved, namely, the pervading, regenerating, and sanctifying faith, the constraining fear of the Lord, and the burning love of God and the brethren. Please do not be of that kind. But, beloved brethren, seek and strive after true wisdom; open unto her; she stands before your door; behold her beauty; taste of her fruits; search her strength, and you will love, embrace, and gladly receive her. Your flesh will yield, and the Spirit gain the victory, and go before you in the Word and truth of the Lord, until Adam dies in you and Christ prevails. May God give us all His divine grace. Amen.

Take ye heed, watch and pray. Mark 13:33.


## [II. THE CALLING OF MINISTERS[7]]

My dear sirs, friends, and brethren, just as I have disclosed unto you, in keeping with your friendly request, the foundation of my belief concerning the very comforting incarnation of our beloved Lord Jesus Christ (although I, as has been said earlier, do not teach the same so profoundly before the congregation), I will now briefly point out my position as to how the ministers and the church, which can rightly be called Christian, should before God and all the world be disposed, according to the Scriptures, in so far as we can, by the grace of God, comprehend and understand this from His Word. Yet I will not dwell upon the matter at length, lest by my long tract I become tedious.

First, I would adduce this Scripture concerning the preachers: As my Father hath sent me, even so send I you. John 20:21. This Scripture remains unchangeable in the church of God. It means that all true teachers and preachers are sent of Christ Jesus, as He is sent of the Father, therefore we should

---

[7] Menno entitles this section: *An Admonishing Confession and Clear Exposition to the noble and learned John a Lasco, archbishop at Emden, East Friesland, and to his associates, as to how preachers of the divine Word and how the church of Christ should, according to the testimony of Scripture, be disposed.*

consider who and what this Christ Jesus was, how and what He taught when the Father had sent Him. He is doubtlessly the Son and image of God, the Teacher of righteousness who has taught and testified nothing but the truth, namely, the Word of His Father. He taught it in the power of the Spirit and was urged by the Holy Ghost through an unquenchable love to the service of all mankind. Besides, He was the burning, shining light of the world, the true pattern of all virtue. He could truly say, Learn of me, for I am meek and lowly of heart. Matt. 11:29. Again, I have given you an example (John 13:15), and therefore He exulted by the true testimony of the Holy Spirit, saying, I am the good Shepherd.

This same Christ Jesus, the Bishop of bishops, and the Shepherd of shepherds, who was faithful in all things unto which He was sent of His heavenly Father, never sends to His members, children, and sheep to tend and protect them, any other bishops, teachers, shepherds, and laborers in the vineyard, than those who are of one body, spirit, and mind with Him, even as He is one with the Father. He sends men who by the divine Word, which is Christ, are so renewed, converted, and changed that He may truly say of them, Behold, these are the children which God hath given me. Whosoever shall hear you shall hear me. As the Father testified of Christ, saying, This is my beloved Son in whom I am well pleased; hear ye him. Matt. 17:5.

Again, those who are of one spirit with Christ Jesus are members of His holy body, full of love for God and for their brethren, who with Christ Jesus, their Bishop, seek nothing but the eternal gain, honor, glory, and praise of God, and the inward conversion, regeneration, and eternal salvation of those whose brotherly care is entrusted and commended to them of God. Yes, He sends such as are unblamable both in doctrine and life, and are constrained by the Holy Spirit; who sincerely lament, with Christ, about those who do not acknowledge the gracious time of their invitation, who rejoice with all the angels of God at the conversion of a sinner, who thirst after the salvation of all men as a hungry person hungers after bread. They are so solicitous for the word and truth of the Lord that they dare not teach or preach a word other than Christ Jesus Himself has taught, practiced, and commanded, namely, the pure, unadulterated, Biblical Word in the true sense and meaning of Christ and of His holy apostles; who administer the sacramental signs conformable to the Gospel of Christ, namely, the baptism of believers, and not of infants, and the Supper under both forms, in such church as is flesh of Christ's flesh and bone of His bone; such as are outwardly unblamable and inwardly of one heart, spirit, soul, and body in Christ Jesus. He sends such whose doctrine is a salting salt; whose life is a shining light, who are patient, kind, generous, merciful, hospitable, not avaricious nor selfish, not desirous of filthy lucre, not hateful, bloody, or contentious, well spoken of among those who are outside, ruling their own house well, having a virtuous wife, having the gift of purity, and obedient children. Yes, in all things they are chaste, sober, unblamable, having the Spirit, fear, and love of God. They are so minded in

all things that they can truly say with Paul, to their entrusted sheep, Be ye
followers of me, even as I am of Christ and walk as brethren even as ye have
us for an example, men, angels, saints, and servants of God, irreproachable
leaders in word and conduct, love, spirit, faith, and purity. I Tim. 4:12. Examples to the believers in word, in conversation, in charity, in spirit, in faith,
in purity.

Behold, dearest friends, thus the ministers should be minded who serve
the Lord's church, that they may not hear from the obstinate and obdurate,
Why do you teach others and not yourselves? Nor can they teach otherwise
to the glory of God, for the service of the New Testament is a service of the
Spirit and not of the letter. II Cor. 3:6. Therefore Christ never chooses as
laborers in His vineyard, as servants and builders, such as are avaricious and
drunkards; in order that His servants might teach the kingdom of God,
which is spiritual, in purity of heart, shepherding the sheep of Christ, not by
force, but gently, not seeking filthy lucre, but with a kindly disposition, not
as those who seek dominion of others, but as examples to the flock of Christ,
not serving for a certain benefice, pension, or salary as do your teachers, but
solely for the gain of the souls which Christ Jesus has so dearly bought with
His precious blood.

They look wholly to God (who by His grace, created, delivered, regenerated, and sent them to His service) for their daily needs, diligently supporting themselves as much as is possible by the grace of the Lord, from their own
or their rented farm, or from working at their trade; lest they be found selling
the free Word of God which was given them without price, and living on
shameful gain, robbery, and theft. Let all sincere and pious servants of Christ
beware of this, and whatever they cannot earn by due labor and diligence will
doubtlessly be provided for them as needed, not by the impenitent heathen,
the drunkards, the usurers, the fornicators, but by the converted brethren
who fear the Lord, for whom they sow spiritual things. For such teachers are
the oxen which tread out the corn and are not to be muzzled (I Cor. 9:9;
I Tim. 5:18; Deut. 25:4); men who are worthy of double honor, with whom
all things should be shared, and who shall live by the Gospel according to the
Lord's own ordinance, as the priests under the law lived by the altar. These
are the true laborers who are worthy of their hire, as Christ says. Such
teachers we shall acknowledge, honor, and maintain in love. And for their
labors' sake we keep peace with them, as Paul says, For they watch for your
souls as they that must give account. Heb. 13:17.

Beloved sirs, friends, and brethren, thus has God, the merciful Father,
sent His blessed Son, who was similar and like-minded unto Him in all things,
namely, Christ Jesus. He, in turn, has sent such as are of one spirit, soul, and
body with Him, without a staff, purse, or shoes, with but one coat, without
money, gold and silver, that is, without care and avarice. The apostles ordained, at all places where they had begotten churches, such bishops and
teachers as were unblamable both in doctrine and in life, and had never men-

tioned annual wages, benefices, or rents. For they were men of God, servants of Christ, full of the love of God and their beloved brethren, who labored, taught, sought, pastored, and watched only through love, urged by the Spirit, not only for one, two, or three hours a week in the synagogue, but at all hours and places, in synagogues, streets, houses, mountains, and fields.

As they had received the knowledge of the kingdom of God, the truth, love, and Spirit of God, without price, so they were again prepared to dispense it diligently and teach it without price to their needy brethren. And as for the temporal necessities of life, the begotten church was sufficiently driven by love, through the Spirit and Word of God, to give unto such faithful servants of Christ and watchers of their souls all the necessities of life, to assist them and provide for them all such things which they could not obtain by themselves. O brethren, flee from avarice!

Again, those teachers did not go about peddling their services as these do, but they were called and urged of God, as were Aaron, Jeremiah, Isaiah, Zechariah, Paul, and others. Others, born of the unblamable church of Christ, were chosen by lot[8] as was Matthias. Acts 1:26. Being called, they were constrained by the Spirit to teach, to admonish, to console, to reprove, to serve and defend their poor brethren and sisters according to God's holy Word, with all their strength. When they were thus called, and felt in them an urging Spirit, and moved by love, as was said above, they reasonably worked at their trade with all solicitude and diligence, watching day and night for the eternal salvation of their sheep. They entered diligently into the vineyard of the Lord, ruling the people of God with the rod of the Lord. They did not waver, made use of no flattery; but in a good conscience they reproved the great as well as the small, the rich as well as the poor, the learned as well as those that were unlearned. The Word they proclaimed in their congregation,[9] wholesome and unadulterated, at all times and in all places, as was said above, according to the measure of their faith and Spirit which God, by His grace, had given to every one of them.

Dearest friends, do not excuse yourselves because all who boasted themselves as being teachers of the church of Christ, even in the times of Paul, were not sincere, pious, and urged by love, as appears from Phil. 1:15; 2:21; 3:2. I tell you, they boasted of being such, but in truth, before God they were not. For it is not hidden from you what kind of fruits they produced, and how Paul regarded them. As you know, it is not the intention and will of God, nor ever shall it be, that His holy Word should be proclaimed to the erring world and men brought to penitence, neither by drunkards, whoremongers, avaricious, idolaters, despisers of the Scriptures, the gluttons, proud, thieves, bloodthirsty, vain persons, enemies of the cross of Christ, whose belly is their God, who are already condemned by the Word of God, nor by the carnal and

[8] The Mennonite Church has a long tradition of casting lots among nominees for the ministry. *Ed.*
[9] *Gemeynte.* The word refers to the body of believers, not to a church building. *Ed.*

earthly-minded; but only by the truly regenerated, Christian, unblamable men who sincerely seek God from their inmost souls, constrained by the Holy Ghost and driven by love. Christ said unto Peter three times, Lovest thou me? Yea, Lord, answered Peter, thou knowest all things and knowest that I love thee. Then Jesus said unto him, Feed my lambs. John 21:15.

O my dear sirs, consider as to what spirit drives you, what love constrains you, what church calls you, and what things you seek. Do follow the good and not the evil. I tell you in Christ Jesus that my soul is deeply troubled and sad for your sakes. I pray you, beloved brethren, do not take it ill of me. I must speak with you candidly, for as much as I can deduce and understand from my recent experiences, and from your apparent fruits, you are all—no minister in your church is excepted—motivated by your flesh and belly, and are therefore all hirelings and not shepherds. John 10:12. Or, at best, you are such shepherds as seek the wool, milk, and flesh, and do not tend the Lord's sheep. For wherever the fattest benefices are, there are also the best sheep.

O brethren, consider with what the Lord's prophets have so often threatened such. How many are found among you who—I fear none are excepted—for the sake of an earthen house, or for a few guilders, move from one place to another, as if they were not all bought equally dear and at one price? O brethren, if you confess this to be true, then judge for yourselves what you are after, and if you will not confess it, haughtiness or impenitence preventing it, it can not be denied by the right-minded. God has been mocked long enough. Brethren, repent!

As the teachers are serving their bellies, avaricious, desirous of filthy lucre, earthly-minded, as Paul says, not to say proud, lazy, vain, drunken, spiteful, and envious, so also are minded all those who are taught and begotten of them, as may be plainly seen. For both teacher and church live and walk so shamefully that all heaven must be ashamed and astounded thereat. For their avarice, unchastity, pride, pomp, greed, drunkenness, hatred, envy, fornication, adultery, bloodthirstiness, usury, falsehood, fraud, vanity, and all manner of shame have no limits or end. Moreover, we find open fencing schools, gambling houses, houses of ill-fame, and drinking houses. For as the teachers are, so are also their doctrine, sacraments, and church, as it is said, *Qualis Papa, talis Evangelium et omnia* (As is the Pope, so is the Gospel and all else).

Verily, I say, believe it if you choose, Christ does not send such avaricious, selfish, and carnal teachers, nor does He acknowledge such a self-conceited, carnal, and blameworthy church. Those who are sent of Christ Jesus have His Spirit, and crucify the lusts and desires of the flesh, that they, preaching to others, may not be found themselves shameful. They seek only the praise of God and the salvation of their beloved brethren, refusing all gain, presents, and gifts, so long as they have wherewith to maintain themselves, honoring none for the sake of gain. They live blamelessly, teaching the Word whole-

somely, and administering the sacraments according to the commandments
of the Lord, excluding all impenitent and apostate sisters and brethren, pro-
claiming grace to those that repent, having eternal vigilance and care for those
who of the Lord's church are entrusted to them.

Since then you are not such as the Scriptures require, but are as yet in
opposition to the true doctrine, and also blameworthy as to conduct, as is
apparent, therefore I admonish you in all earnestness and fraternal love,
first to become sincere Christians before you undertake to impress and teach
Christ unto others. Let us examine ourselves that we may learn to know our
own failings, and knowing them, die unto them. For before God, neither fair
words nor semblances will avail. My brethren, I must tell you the plain truth
which may be galling and bitter to you because there is found neither Spirit
nor power, nor trust in Christ, nor fear of God, nor love of the brethren with
your ministers, but only a vain calling consisting of words for the sake of a
salary, without any show of Christian fruits. Therefore all your calling is
nothing but sowing on the seashore or reaping the wind. For the pure Word
of God and the teaching of the Holy Spirit cannot be pointed out and taught
by servants who are themselves unclean and carnal. To this all intelligent
persons must, doubtlessly, assent.

Since then you are blamable both in doctrine and in life, and as your
doctrine, such as you have, is sold for salary and without spiritual fruit, and
since no unblamable church is begotten by you, and since the signs of the
Word are abused by you, therefore it is apparent that you are not the true
messengers of God. But you run on your own account, constrained by the
flesh and not by the Spirit; not seeking the salvation of the church, but rather
the temporal profits and incomes, and that with such greed that you are not
ashamed to receive them as a reward and price of your preaching. In ancient
times these were robbed and cleverly taken from the true and legal heirs, as
Peter says, by theft and robbery.

In this way, to begin with, you sell the precious, free Word of God which
by grace was given us of God without price. And secondly, it is paid for by
that which is stolen. Here lies hidden more than I will disclose. He who
lives by theft and robbery is no doubt a thief and robber. Do consider the
matter in a Christian light. Feel and taste your manifest error, unworthiness,
and plain avarice. I speak of your preachers in general, for they all enjoy
such gain. Your doctrine, benefices, pensions, and rents are such an abomination before my eyes, that verily, brethren, I would rather be beheaded, burned,
drowned, or torn into quarters by four horses than to receive for my preaching such benefices, pensions, and incomes. Yes, when stated salaries[10] to
preachers were established, there surely crept into the church of Christ a very
fearful, corrupting pestilence, which has so corrupted, alas, that there are
scarcely any left who have retained the breath of Christ in them. To this you
must verily all consent. What other reason is there that the preachers have

[10] Through much of their history Mennonites have clung to an unsalaried ministry. *Ed.*

sought the temporal gain of their own bellies more than the eternal gain of the souls of Christ?

Since you freely accept and enjoy the before-mentioned shameful gain, and what is still worse, since you diligently seek and desire the same, how can you defend yourselves and say that you are not desirous of filthy lucre (I Tim. 3:3), and that you do not honor the person for filthy lucre's sake? O brethren, I wish you would awaken to consider the matter and that you were all of one mind with us in this matter, for it would doubtlessly be profitable to both the praise and truth of God, and to your poor souls. [You ought] to dispense, without pay, the precious Word of God, the word of eternal salvation and heavenly grace, which can be merited by no works nor paid for by money, even as we, by grace only, received it of God without price. [Oh], that we again might dispense it without pay, merely for the sake of brotherly love, and teach it to hungry consciences! God surely would not forsake us, but would in every necessity care for us and protect us in fatherly fashion. But it cannot be so with you because you are quite devoid of faith and love.

You are all buried to your ears in filthy lucre; earthly and carnally minded in all things; not yet dead unto the flesh by the power of regeneration. You do not yet receive Christ in all His words, and on that account, you are not yet sound in doctrine. You do not conform the administration of the signs[11] to the Word of God. You are blamable in doctrine, as is plain. You have no power, no fruit of the Spirit, no true fear of God, and no brotherly love. You heap the accusation of heresy, you rave and rant upon the teachings and lives of the pious saints and children of God, who for the testimony of their consciences, confirmed by the Word of God, have fled and left their country and kindred; and who for the sake of the testimony are prepared for water, fire, and sword if God so pleases. Moreover, your doctrine is quite powerless and fruitless. The church which you beget is quite earthly, carnal, and contrary to the testimony and fruits of the holy Word of the Lord. Therefore, we repeat, you are not the true messengers of Jesus Christ. Do not get angry, dearly beloved.

It is for the before-mentioned reasons that we will not hear nor attend your preaching, nor partake of your sacrament of the Supper. For we desire never in all eternity to enter into your church and to become one body with you until sincere repentance be found with you, and you embrace a free, Christian doctrine, not hired nor sold for money, but urged by the Holy Spirit through brotherly love, a true use of the sacramental signs, according to the command, doctrine, and usage of Christ and His apostles, and an unblamable life and walk, led in the love and fear of the Lord. Should we do so before these are found with you, we are sure that we would sin against God and His blessed Word, from which may the kind, merciful Father save us. For before God, it does not become us to commit ourselves to such doctrine, admonition, and church, which, to begin with, err in doc-

11 Menno refers to the sacraments, baptism and Lord's Supper. *Ed.*

trine, and secondly, do not in the least show by their lives that they are the truly regenerate children of God, or the true church of Jesus Christ. But, most beloved, it behooves you, since you have not yet the unblamable doctrine and conduct of Jesus Christ, to renounce your doctrine and life and voluntarily to bid adieu to all the lusts of the flesh, to seek the kingdom of God in sincerity of heart, to enter with us into all obedience to our beloved Lord Jesus Christ with all your strength, if you do not desire to err willfully, that we together may become the holy, Christian, and unblamable church —godly, holy, clean, obedient unto God, serving all mankind, powerful in truth, shining forth in righteousness, dead unto sin, living by the Spirit, yes, in all things Christian, heavenly, and unblamable in Christ Jesus.

Do receive my admonishing confession in good nature, and do not think it is too strict, namely, such words as clean, unblamable, and the like. For they are spoken of Christ Jesus Himself, and of His holy apostles to the church of the Lord. John 13:10; Phil. 2:15. Do not understand, most beloved, that we deem ourselves so clean and unblamable as to be without sin.[12] No, not at all, dear brethren, for I know full well that the holy John teaches, saying, If we say that we have no sin, we deceive ourselves, and the truth is not in us. I John 1:8. For as James says, In many things we all offend. Jas. 3:2. Yes, dear brethren, with Paul I find the appetite to commit sin so strong in my flesh at all times that I often think recklessly, speak rashly, and do the evil which I would not.

But the abominable, shameful sins and offenses, such as adultery, fornication, hatred, envy, drunkenness, pomp, splendor, cursing, swearing, gambling, desire of filthy lucre, abuse of the ordinances of Christ, and lying and fraud, I verily detest from the bottom of my heart. And they should never, by the grace of the Lord, be practiced by any sincere, God-fearing Christians, inasmuch as they hate and oppose them. For the spirit which is in true Christians is a deadly enemy to all wickedness and sin (at the same time we often find that we are born of Adam). And their spirit strives and hungers after the truth, righteousness, will, and commandment of God, yet in great weakness; for they are very much retarded in the works, fruits, and fulfillment by the heavy burden of the sinful flesh. Nevertheless, because the good Spirit of God abides in them, they do not cease to fight against their flesh, so often their hindrance. For the life of true Christians is nothing but an endless struggle upon earth. Whosoever shall fight valiantly and overcome, he will be clothed in white raiment and will be fed with the heavenly bread of the tree of life. Rev. 2:17; 3:5.

Behold, very dearly beloved, inasmuch as you and your church have never triumphed in this battle (I judge from what I hear, and from your actions which I see), but still serve the world, the flesh, and the devil without a care; therefore we judge, according to the testimony of the Scriptures, that you vainly and wrongfully boast of the name, grace, deliverance, merits, death,

[12] Menno here clears himself of teaching Perfectionism. *Ed.*

blood, and promises of Christ; since you have not His Word, and by His Word His faith, Spirit, fear, and love, and consequently do not follow them. Therefore, I pray you by the mercy of the Lord to consider what kind of ministers you are, what kind of spirit impels you, what kind of love prompts you, with what intentions and by what motives you teach, what kind of fruits you produce, what kind of ordinances you use, and what kind of church you teach and serve. Judge all things according to the divine testimony, without self-love, flesh, and partiality. I doubt not but if you examine the matter rightly, you will not be surprised that we will not hear your doctrine, nor use your sacraments, and refuse unto death to become members of your church.

For this remains incontrovertible, eternally unchangeable, that as Christ Jesus is of one mind with the Father, and sent of Him, so all teachers who are sent by Him should be of one mind. Those who are one with Christ in Spirit, love, and life, who teach that which was commanded them by Christ, namely, repentance and the peaceable Gospel of grace, which He Himself received of God, and has taught to the world, all those who hear, believe, keep, and fulfill the same in true fear are the church of Christ. They are the rightly believing, Christian church. They are the body and bride of Christ, the ark, the mount and garden of the Lord, the house, people, city, temple of God, the spiritual Eve, flesh of Christ's flesh and bone of His bone, children of God, the chosen generation, the spiritual seed of Abraham, children of the promise, branches and trees of righteousness, sheep of the heavenly pasture, kings and priests, a holy people which is God's own. Besides, they are chosen to proclaim the power of Him who has called them from darkness into His marvelous light.

All those who have not the Spirit, love, and life of Christ, nor sincerely desire them, have no share in the glorious Jerusalem of God, that is, in Christ's church; no matter whether they be teacher or disciple, prince or subject, man or woman. Besides they have no prayer, no God, no Christ, no promise, no remission of sins, no sure comfort unto eternal life, so long as they do not sincerely repent, receive God's Word, and fulfill it in true fear. As Christ Himself says, He that believeth not is condemned already. John 3:18.

Dear brethren, seek whatever counterassertion you please, yet this foundation shall stand forever and will never be changed. The words of Paul shall never be broken, If any man have not the Spirit of Christ, he is none of his. Rom. 8:9. And, where the Spirit is there shall also be the fruits of the Spirit, as it is infallible that if the Spirit is in man, whether evil or good, it will manifest itself by its fruits.

Finally, dearly beloved, if you want to be the true church of Christ which boasts of the truth, grace, Word, Spirit, and blood of the Lord, then first expel all your preachers who are driven by the unclean spirit and flesh, therefore are not of the church of Christ, namely, all those who are desirous of filthy lucre, as was said above. Also, all drunkards, wranglers, flatterers, the proud, the envious, and the avaricious. For all these testify by their evident fruits that they have not the Spirit of Christ. And if they have not the Spirit of Christ, how can they, poor miserable men, teach and impress the Spirit, power, and will of God, the Word of grace, and the Word of eternal life, which they do not themselves possess and confess? Yes, brethren, it is impossible for me to teach the things which I do not know myself. And how shall I serve in the house of the Lord while I myself am an outsider? Judge for yourselves.

After that, cleanse your church, also. Exclude, according to the Word of God, all harlots and fornicators, drunkards, slanderers, swearers, those who lead a shameful and disorderly life, the proud, the avaricious, the idolatrous, and those who are disobedient unto God, adulterers and the like, in order that you may become the holy, Christian church which is without spot or blemish, which is as a city built upon a hill. In case these things are truly observed and found with you, and besides, a free, Christian doctrine, the true ministration of the sacraments of Christ, not according to the opinion of men or the learned, but according to the true doctrine of Christ and His apostles and the fear and love of God, and an unblamable life, according to the testimony of God's Word, then will you ever have us as your brethren. For it is such that we seek. But if you remain as you are, then I say publicly, Better to die than to enter into your doctrine, sacraments, life, and church, as was said above.

Beloved brethren, it is no use to quote the passage about the Pharisees sitting in the seat of Moses, nor that Herod sent for the wise men of the east; nor that some say, If the devil should preach the Word of God, why not hear it? Christ Jesus did not send the Pharisees, the servants of the letter, to preach the Word of the Spirit and of life. Herod did not send the wise with good intentions. Nor has the devil ever sincerely given praise to God, nor does God want the praise of the devil, for Christ says, Hold thy peace, and come out of him. Luke 4:35. Therefore it is useless to adduce such reasons, inasmuch as God, by His mercy and grace, has somewhat opened the eyes of our mind that we surely know that the spiritual service of the New Testament can be administered by none but by the servants of the Spirit impelled in love by the power of the Holy Ghost; for it is and remains a service of the Spirit and not of the letter. II Cor. 3:6. Enough of this.

In short, deny yourselves, be prepared to do the will of God, seek nothing but His honor and praise and the eternal salvation of your brethren, hunger and thirst after the righteousness of God, believe and receive Christ Jesus rightly in His blessed Word, and you will undoubtedly understand and comprehend the true way, the truth and life eternal, to the praise of God and to your own salvation. May God, the kind and merciful Father, grant us all this. Amen.

Since I, dear brethren, have ambitiously rebuked the preachers for accepting filthy lucre, in this my admonishing confession, according to the Word of God, therefore I do not doubt but that there will be some who will bitterly contradict me in a bitter, but not brotherly manner in this matter, and say, Dear Menno, you cannot forbid us the right and privilege which Christ Jesus has given us, as you have alleged from Paul, that those who serve the Gospel shall live by the Gospel. Why do you try to take away that of which we have the privilege?

To those who contradict me thus, I would first reply by asking, Are the teachers to whom this privilege is given by Christ sent by Christ Jesus? They must answer in the affirmative. Then I say again, since they are sent by Christ who enjoy this privilege given by Christ, therefore those who run on their own account, and are not sent of Christ, do not have this privilege.

Again, I ask whether these teachers to whom this privilege is given by the Scriptures were men of the Spirit of love and of truth. Doubtlessly so. Then I reply: If then they were men of the Spirit of love and of truth, to whom this privilege is granted by the Gospel, then those who do not teach and serve by the Spirit, love, and truth, may not appropriate and make use of this privilege. For they are not the teachers to whom it was given and promised by the Word of God.

Thirdly, I ask whether the teachers which were sent of Christ, and according to the Scriptures enjoyed this privilege, led a shameful life after being called. And if they led a shameful life, and were found corrupt before God and His church, whether they then remained longer as teachers in the unblamable church of Christ. They must doubtlessly answer, No. Then, if they answer, No, as is the right answer, then those whose life and walk in the church of Christ are no more pure and useful than the filthy carrion by the roadside, are no teachers in the church of the Lord; such as drunkards, perjurers, fornicators, avaricious, blasphemers, cursers, swearers, the proud, pompous, envious, those who are averse and hostile to Christian truth, the slothful, the sluggards, contentious persons, brawlers, etc. For if the salt have lost its savor, says Christ, it is thenceforth good for nothing, but to be cast out, and to be trodden under the foot of man.

And if the church is to be blameless, and without spot or blemish, how much more so the teachers, as Christ Himself teaches, saying, Ye are the light of the World. Ye are the salt of the earth. Inasmuch as the before-mentioned, carnal teachers are already excluded from the Christian office of teacher, and deprived of it by God's own ordinance and word, since they do not live up to the doctrine and by their apparent unbelief and lawlessness are not in the church of Christ; therefore they cannot enjoy that privilege. For Christ does not have any undisciplined, lazy, drunken, shameful, lying, parading, greedy, avaricious, and carnal rogues, but honest, pious, spiritual, loving, true, blameless, and God-sent ministers.

Fourthly, I ask whether the men of God, the prophets, apostles, and teachers sent of God, were also hired or bought at a stipulated salary to teach and proclaim the free word of grace. I know that the answer must be No. For they did not teach except under the compulsion of the Spirit and love. I say again, Inasmuch as your preachers are hired and bought at a stipulated salary or wage, and do not preach unless they are hired, they must acknowledge that they are hirelings, and not teachers that are sent; for they do not teach by the compulsion of the Spirit and love, but are enticed and drawn on as was Balaam by the promised salary, benefices, and rents. He who denies this will also deny that the sun shines during the daytime.

Fifthly, I ask if the teachers sent of God, men of the Spirit, of love and of truth, enlightened both in doctrine and in life, lived of a stipulated salary, benefice, or rents; or whether they lived by the services or assistance of the brethren, as far as they could not help themselves. They must confess that it was by the assistance of the brethren, and not of certain benefices, pensions, or rents. This I teach and seek and sincerely desire.

Therefore this is my brief conclusion and Christian admonition to all preachers and teachers. Brethren, humble yourselves and become unblamable disciples, that you may thereafter become called ministers. Try your spirit, love, and life before you commence to shepherd and to teach. Do not go on your own account, but wait until you are called of the Lord's church; I say, of the Lord's church, of the Spirit of God, and are constrained by urging love. If this takes place, brethren, then pastor diligently, preach and teach valiantly, cast from you all filthy lucre and booty; rent a farm, milk cows, learn a trade if possible, do manual labor as did Paul, and all that which you then fall short of will doubtlessly be given and provided you by pious brethren, by the grace of God, not in superfluity, but as necessity requires.

Such privilege the holy Gospel grants to the unblamable preachers who are sent of Christ Jesus; this and no more. But the preachers who run on their own account are earthly and carnally minded, are blameworthy in doctrine and in life, whose god is their belly, who on account of their lazy, gluttonous, easy flesh, teach and serve to please the world, as hired servants, at certain wages; such the Scriptures do not know. Therefore I say for once and for all, If they will not do differently, but always say in their hearts —Let things go the way they please, it makes no difference to us as long as we have our stomachs full—then I will leave them in the hands of Him who shall judge them and us according to His most holy Word, and according to His own good pleasure.

You who are gifted with good judgment do not refuse to bid farewell to the flesh, but to live unto the good God in all things.

## Conclusion

Here you have, dear sirs, friends, and brethren, our plain confession of the incarnation of our beloved Lord Jesus Christ, which I sincerely confess and believe; for you requested me to do so, and, I trust, with a good intention. Therefore I have not been silent about my faith. Now judge the matter rightly, if you be spiritually minded, and if, as you think, I err in human fashion (I trust I do not), then do not think that I do so out of obduracy or partiality. But before God my Creator it is because I acknowledge only the firm, immutable foundation of God's Word and truth.

Brethren, do not think of me as one who seeks something contrary to the will of God. Not at all. The eternal truth and Word and will of God I am prepared to do, come whatever may please His fatherly kindness. This I say emphatically and without hesitation.

I say to you, if you have plainer Scriptures concerning this article of the incarnation of Christ; if you have a clearer basis, plainer truth, or clearer proof than we have, then assist us, and I will by the grace of God change my mind in regard to the matter and accept your view. But above all, brethren, I want you to understand that I do not tolerate human doctrines, clever reasonings, nor twisting of the Scriptures, nor glosses, nor imaginations in regard to this matter, but only the plain Scriptures, truth, and immutable testimony; even as we have presented it, in this matter of our confession. Nothing but Scriptural truth and immutable testimony! And if you cannot advance such, then take heed, keep your peace, and in faith leave to us our peace; for dearest brethren, before God, I seek nothing but the pure, unadulterated Word of God and its testimony.

Besides, I have here presented to you, how and in what manner I admonish and teach the simplehearted brethren, and with which doctrine no God-fearing consciences can be afflicted, nor Christian souls deceived. I pray and desire you to do likewise, that you may build and not tear down. Brethren, if you do not do this, then take heed how and what you teach. I beseech and admonish you in love, but it behooves me not to force you, even if I could do so. Every person shall have to render an account of his teaching and doing before God, and not before men.

In the third place, you have my admonishing confession how both teacher and church should be minded according to the Scriptures, and I pray and desire by the mercy of the Lord that you do not evaluate this Scriptural truth in bitterness. For that which I have written is the unchangeable will and Word of God, and will remain so forever. Therefore take heed that you do not become angry with me on account of my writing because it is contrary to your flesh. It verily is not mine, but Christ's doctrine; not my will, but Christ's. If you become angry; you are not angry with me, but with Christ, who has taught and instructed us in His holy Gospel or Word. And in case you fear God, you will doubtless love me the more, because I, by the grace, Spirit, and Word of God, as far as He enables me, open unto you the kingdom of heaven, and show men the right way. Yes, because I, fearlessly, and in true brotherly love, God is my witness, speak unto you and point you to the eternal, immutable truth; because I cut the proud flesh from your festering wounds and do not flatter you; for I seek not your carnal, but your spiritual friendship; not your honor but the honor of God; not your goods and gifts, but the salvation of your souls. For this reason I tell you the pure truth of God and do not spare you. O brethren, receive it in gladness of heart. It is the only Word and will of Christ. If you reject it, you do not reject me, but Jesus Christ who has so dearly bought us all. Therefore take heed to arouse yourself at once, and no longer wander and proceed in darkness and deadly blindness. And let the poor, ignorant people, the poor, innocent souls, no longer err under your name and cover. The whole wide world depends upon you learned ones. As you pipe, so they dance; as you teach, so they believe; as you proceed, so they follow. Therefore, woe unto you if you teach erroneously; if you destroy and do not gather; if you deceive and do not shepherd; if you corrupt and do not convert!

Receive eyes of wisdom, that you may rightly teach and lead others, according to the will of God; lest the word which Christ spoke become applicable to you, If the blind lead the blind, both shall fall into the ditch. Lastly, I shall send you ere long, if it please God, my treatise concerning believer's baptism, with other doctrines, from which you may clearly learn my foundation, doctrine, aim, and purpose; why I labor, for what I strive, by what Scriptures and for what reason we assert the baptism of the believing ones; and consider infant baptism to be useless, idolatrous, and contrary to the Word.

Read it in all sincerity of heart, ponder it, follow exclusively the true sense of the divine Spirit and truth. Let opinions and notions go, let flesh and reason be destroyed. Many have been deceived thereby. This our doctrine concerning the preachers, concerning the purity of the church, concerning believer's baptism, concerning the Supper in a pure assembly, and concerning the exclusion of the impenitent, is doubtlessly the eternal, immutable Word, will, and ordinance of God; therefore, by the grace of God, we will never be reasoned out of it by human wisdom, cleverness, threats, nor tyranny. At all times I am prepared to testify and assert this doctrine before God and my brethren, with the sure testimony of my conscience, at the cost of all anxiety, persecution, blood, and death. Let the merciful, kind Father deal with me and with all those who sincerely seek and fear Him, according to His divine, blessed will. Read discreetly and judge in a Christian way.

This, in brief, is my position and conviction concerning that which takes place in the Christian church; namely, that before God neither baptism, nor Supper, nor any other outward ordinances avail, if partaken of without Spirit and the new creation. But before God, only faith, love, Spirit, and the new creation or regeneration avail, as Paul plainly shows. Gal. 5:6. All those who by the grace of God receive these from above, have themselves baptized according to the commandment of the Lord, and rightly partake of His Supper. Acts 2:38; 9:18; 8:38; Matt. 28:19.

Yes, with ardent desire these commit themselves to the ordinance and doctrine of Jesus Christ, and shall nevermore willfully oppose the holy will and plain testimony of God. For this reason, dearest sirs, my friendly request from the bottom of my heart is not to argue with me or any other person concerning any outward articles and literal ordinances; but first conquer and subject yourselves, that is, your unbelieving, miserable, refractory, obdurate flesh which keeps and hinders you from the truth, faith, knowledge, and righteousness and obedience of God. Rest assured that if that is rightly vanquished, you will understand all the ordinances of God and confess and practice them. But as long as the flesh has control in you and has sway, you will dispute and oppose, and nevermore comprehend, understand, and follow the immutable foundation of eternal truth. I warn you.

That is enough for the time being. Differentiate properly between Christ and yourselves; between His love and yours; His spirit and yours; His love and yours; His purpose and yours; His doctrine and yours; His sacrament and yours; His life and yours. And you will no doubt find wherein you err and fail.

May God, the merciful Father, grant unto you and to us all, true wisdom, understanding, faith, knowledge, and true judgment; a fervent heart, true fear, love, doctrine, life, sacraments, and ordinances, through Christ Jesus, our Saviour and eternal Deliverer of the world. Amen. Enter ye in at the strait gate. Matt. 7:13.

The truth is bitter, says Jerome,[18] and they who preach it, full of bitterness.

[18] Jerome was a Latin church father who died in A.D. 420. He was the author of many books as well as of a Latin version of the Bible known as the Vulgate. *Ed.*

# A Clear Account of Excommunication

*Bericht van der excommunicatie*

# 1550

*For other foundation can no man*
*lay than that is laid, which is Jesus Christ.*

I Corinthians 3:11

# Introduction

Menno's *Kind Admonition on Church Discipline* of 1541 did not settle the question fully in the minds of some of the members of his brotherhood. In the present book Menno reports that "Much strife has been occasioned among some by the ban." To try to align the thinking of every sincere believer with the holy Word of God Menno wrote this *Clear Account of Excommunication* in 1550. Menno's earnest appeal is that every Christian might heed only the Word of Christ and His apostles.

Menno begins with the instruction of Christ in Matthew 18 as to how difficulties among brethren are to be resolved. He makes much of the final word of Christ, "But if he neglect to hear the church, let him be unto thee as a heathen man and a publican." Menno builds much of his thinking on the Latin Vulgate which employs the term *publicani* for publicans. But Menno treats the word as if it meant open or public sinner. He then proceeds to build an elaborate argument out of the statement, seeking to show the force of it for the church. He explains at length that Christ is not referring to the Law of Moses which called for the execution of various offensive sinners, but to the contemporary practice of the Jews in His own day, after the Romans had deprived them of the right of capital punishment.

Menno also seeks to demolish the objection that "shunning" means nothing more than not counting the excommunicated as members of the church —the result being that church members would treat the excommunicated just as those who never were members of the church. This is most unacceptable to Menno in the light of sound Biblical exegesis. He argues stoutly from I Corinthians 5 that one may have social intercourse with worldly people who make no profession of the name of Christian, but that all unnecessary intercourse must be denied the excommunicated; they must be shunned.

Following the main discussion Menno takes up "Some Questions and Answers" on the subject of church discipline. It is said that these questions were submitted to him by the brethren in the province of Groningen. The entire work, main discussion and Questions and Answers, was circulated only in manuscript form until 1597 when it was printed in Amsterdam. But it is evident from the Conclusion which is found at the end of the Questions and Answers that the latter were a part of the *Admonition* from the first. Later on, the Questions and Answers got detached from the main body of the work. They appear in the *Opera Omnia Theologica* of 1681, fol. 473-78, following Menno's work on Justification, and also in the English *Complete Works* of 1871 following the same book, pp. 276-81 of Part II.

In the Dutch the title of the work is: *A Clear Exposition and Scriptural Delineation of Excommunication for the Benefit of all Pious Children of God.* In the *Opera Omnia Theologica* of 1681 the work is found in two parts, fol. 337-50, and 473-78, and in the *Complete Works* of 1871, II, 121-37; II, 276-81.                                              J. C. W.

# A Clear Account of Excomunication*

## 1550

---

Menno Simons wishes all true fellow believers, brethren and sisters in Christ Jesus, grace and peace from God our heavenly Father, through Christ Jesus His dear Son, our Lord, who loved us, and washed us of our sins through His blood. To Him be glory, honor and praise, kingdom, power, and majesty for ever and ever. Amen.

I discover that for some time now much strife has been occasioned among some by the ban, and that so vehemently and recklessly that brotherly love, I fear, is among many destroyed rather than advanced, and Christian peace and unity is decreased rather than increased, as it, sad to say, usually goes, men in their conceit being thirsty and eager for such harmful disputations. For some hold the idea concerning the ban that they want to avoid and shun not the excommunicated themselves but only their false doctrines and offensive lives. They say this and fail to notice how that they are already themselves fallen into false doctrine, for they make null and void the clear ordinance of Christ (Matt. 18:17), Let him be unto you as a heathen man, etc., and the crystal clear words of the holy apostles. Rom. 16:16; I Cor. 5:3; II Thess. 3:14; Titus 3:10. Others think that the ban should not be practiced beyond evangelical transactions, such as the breaking of bread and the kiss of peace. These make it serve their purpose, twist the plain speech of Scripture which says, Have no fellowship with him, With such a one do not eat, Let him be unto you a heathen man and a public sinner, and many other similar expressions.

And there are some who acknowledge the institutions of Christ and the doctrine of the holy apostles concerning excommunication to be good and proper, but they fail to put them to practice nevertheless, some I suppose out of lassitude, some for the sake of the carnal favor and the love which they feel toward the apostate one, or because they are neighbors or friends, etc.

The express ordinance of Christ and His holy apostles is lamentably annulled by the former as well as by the latter, is obscured and twisted, and by the latter is patently violated and dishonored. By the above-mentioned position a door is opened wide for the admission of all kinds of defection. Men act against all love; against the love of God and Christ, since they

---

* The original reads: *A Clear Exposition and Scriptural Delineation of Excommunication.*

457

disobediently disdain His holy Word, will, and ordinance; and against brotherly love, since these are by such contrariness and disdain greatly offended and saddened; against the love of their own soul, since they willfully expose themselves to every danger of corruption; and in the fourth place against love for the excommunicated. For they despise the counsel of the Holy Spirit and they do not seek to shame the offender unto his conversion. In the fifth place also they are against general love, for by such intimacy with the apostate they make those who are outside suspicious, as though we are one people with the apostate and perverse, and so make the blessed Word of God and His holy church slandered and abused by many through their obstinacy and disobedience.

Therefore I have taken pains, out of a genuine Christian mind and brotherly love (of which God is my witness), as a service to all my dear brethren and companions in Christ Jesus, to set forth with godly truth the true basis of the ban, how it is instituted by Christ Jesus, taught and enlarged upon by His holy apostles, and what fruit and usefulness is found therein. But the evaluation of my exposition I wish to leave to those who seek God and fear Him with a whole heart and are taught by the Spirit of God. Let each man have in mind both God and his neighbor and he will acknowledge that our exposition agrees with the foundation, intention, Word, and will of God.

Dearly beloved brethren and sisters in Christ Jesus, I your poor unworthy servant and companion in the faith and the oppression of Christ pray and beg for the sake of the crimson blood of my Lord Jesus Christ, and for the sake of all love, that no one willfully fight against Christ Jesus and His holy Word, nor against his own conscience, defending his own folly, so as not to be shamed before men. For I hope that a genuine Christian will not seek to shame anyone according to the flesh. But true love always seeks to win the erring and straying brother back to Christ again. Similarly when the pious errs he seeks to be back on the straight path again, does he not? When he is fallen, to rise up again? When wounded, to be healed?

And when he is by God's grace delivered by God's Word from his misconception and error he is not ashamed, but he is extremely glad and happy. He thanks his God that he is led from the crooked way to the straight, and from his misconception to the right and good understanding. He then seeks wholeheartedly to release and deliver him whom he has previously led astray and entangled with his error and misconception. For pure love seeks not her own but that which pertains to God and the neighbor. He that hath ears to hear and a heart to understand, let him hear and grasp what the Lord's Word teaches in great clarity concerning excommunication.

Christ Jesus says: If thy brother shall trespass against thee, go and tell him his fault between thee and him alone; if he shall hear thee, thou hast gained thy brother; but if he will not hear thee, then take with thee one or two more, that in the mouth of two or three witnesses every word may be established. And if he shall neglect to hear them, tell it to the church, but if he neglect to hear the church, let him be unto thee a heathen man and a public sinner.[2] Verily I say unto you, Whatsoever ye shall bind on earth shall be bound in heaven and whatsoever ye shall loose on earth shall be loosed in heaven. Matt. 18:15-18.

Here you have, faithful brethren, the unshakable divine foundation, like a firm rock or mountain, against which all they will bruise and hurt themselves who seek to shake it and ignore it: namely, that even as the Jews in Christ's day shunned Gentiles and manifest sinners, so must we shun and avoid the apostate if they disdain the brotherly service and admonition done with faithful heart and after the doctrine of Christ, persisting stubbornly in their error.

Now in the first place, the Jews did not admit to their Passover the uncircumcised heathen, in obedience to the command of the Lord by Moses. Nor did they admit them to their services, as may be seen from the Acts of the Apostles, seeing that the heathen were strangers, and the service of God pertained alone to the commonwealth of Israel.

In the second place, they also shunned their external company so that they considered it unclean to enter into Gentile homes or to eat and drink with them. They had the same policy toward manifest sinners.

Now just as the Jews did not admit said Gentiles and manifest sinners, neither to their spiritual fellowship nor to their everyday or social company, but avoided and shunned them, just so says Christ Jesus are we to loathe the apostate and impenitent brother, as has been said above. And that this is the actual and natural thrust of these words of Christ, the holy Paul proves —of whom more presently.

You see, my brethren in the Lord, all those who would understand and grasp the cited interpretation of the words of Christ, must realize that Christ does not in this matter point us to the Jewish usage with Gentiles and manifest sinners in the days of Moses and the prophets, but to the usage of his own times. These must in the first place distinguish between Gentiles and manifest sinners, must not consider them of a kind, and they must also understand and perceive how the Jews dealt with both of these in the days of Moses and the prophets, before the scepter was taken from them, and they were subjugated to the Romans.

To begin with, it is incontrovertible that the Gentiles were not of the seed of Abraham, Isaac, and Jacob. They were uncircumcised, without God and the service of God, without the Law, etc. Verily, they were a people that were no people, as Moses has it. It is also indisputable that the publicans and sinners were of the Jews. For Luke says: The publicans came to John to be baptized of him. Again, The publicans gave God the glory and

---

[2] Menno renders the *publicani* of the Latin Bible, very literally, "public, or manifest sinners." We know that *publicani* were taxgatherers. Had Menno been mindful of the technical meaning of *publicani* he would not have developed his argument as he does here. *Tr.*

let themselves be baptized with John's baptism. Further, All the publicans and sinners came to Jesus for to hear him. But the Gentiles did not come to John and to Christ. Hence it is evident that the publicans and sinners were no Gentiles but Jews. The same appears from the woman that was a sinner, and from Matthew the publican, who was enrolled by the Lord as an apostle. But no apostles were taken from the Gentiles, as is evident and true.

Since now the Gentiles and the manifest sinners are two distinct groups, as has been said, and we were to turn now to the Law in order to delineate the freedom of the Jews which they had over and above the Gentiles, so must we also delineate with the same Law the conduct of the Jews, how according to the Law they dealt with the manifest sinner. For the one passage is no less valid than is the other, for both were spoken and testified by the mouth of the Eternal Wisdom.

We know very well, dear brethren, that Moses in his Law gave many liberties to outward Israel for dealing with Gentile nations, in buying, taking interest, serving, etc. But we know too that he judges the obstinate, manifest sinner with his Law under two or three witnesses and without mercy, even to death immediately. Deut. 17, quoted by Paul in Heb. 10. If then we should take the afore-mentioned words of Christ in Matthew 18 according to the rigor and tenor of the Law of Moses it would in the first place follow, with power and irresistibility, from the term *Gentile,* that we have liberty to use external means with the apostate, just as Israel had in regard to the Gentiles. And in the second place, out of the term manifest sinners, it would follow that we ought to put to death the apostate, condemned with two or three witnesses! That would not be at all proper, would it—to use great liberties with someone, and also to kill. To kill is also far removed from the nature and disposition of Christ; for the Son of Man came not to destroy souls but to save them.

Everyone has to take care, for if he wants to fasten on the word *heathen* and construe it according to the Law of Moses, but not the word *manifest sinner,* then he abuses not men but the Son of God, and violates Him shamefully in His holy Word and Truth. For He does not say: Let him be to you as a heathen man, merely, but as a heathen man and a publican. Heaven and earth shall pass away, said Christ Jesus, but my words shall not pass away. Therefore everyone is advised not to violate Christ Jesus in His Word; but to silence his carnal reason, to acknowledge the truth, to unstop his ears, to hearken to Christ, to believe, and to be obedient. Then he will be like unto the wise builder; otherwise his house will fall and its fall will be great.

Further, most dearly beloved brethren, it is not unknown to us how that some take these words of Christ to mean that we are not obliged to shun an apostate and impenitent brother beyond the extent that we believers of the Gentiles must shun those who are still "Gentiles," that is, fornicators, adulterers, drunkards, etc., which they probably call manifest sinners.[3] Those who interpret thus I would beseech and admonish from the bottom of my heart that they would, in the first place, consider well before they accept it as a true basis, believe it, and run away with it— as to which people it was to whom Christ Jesus was sent at the outset, and among which people He began to found and build His church. This Christ Himself indicates sufficiently when He says: I was not sent but unto the lost sheep of the house of Israel. Paul also says: I say then that Christ Jesus was a servant of the Circumcision (that is, to the Jew) for the Truth of God, to confirm the promises made unto the fathers.

Since He was then from the beginning sent to the Jews and taught and preached to them, and not the Gentiles, therefore these words of Christ may not be understood to mean that we are to assume that attitude toward an apostate which now a believer of the Gentiles assumes toward an unbelieving Gentile but that which the literal Jew in Christ's time assumed toward such a one. For Christ, I say, preached not to the Gentiles but to the Jews and therefore directed these His words to nothing else than the Jewish ban, namely, how they were to conduct themselves over against Gentiles and manifest sinners in His day.

In the second place, I request that every God-fearing conscience may reflect well what the word Gentile implies, whether it does not refer to all manifest fornicators, oath-breakers, avaricious persons, unbelieving ones, perjured people, idolaters, homicides, drunkards, etc. Yes, Paul says that they are without Christ, have no God, are strangers to the life that is of God, are dead in sins, are children of wrath, etc. Since now all manifest sinners among the heathen are also included in the word Gentile (for the Gentiles that have not Christ are also all manifest sinners and outside of grace) and Christ speaks here of manifest sinners as of Gentiles, and every word of Christ has its own weight and measure, therefore the Word of Christ may not be construed as though the apostate brother and the heathen, who has not heard the Word of the Lord, are in one category.

In the third place, I desire that every honest brother, called after the Lord's name, shall not knowingly and purposely falsify his Lord's Word, but that he give to it its just honor and praise, and acknowledge that the *publicani* and sinners of which the Gospels speak were not of the heathen but of the Jews, as is evident from Matt. 9:10; Mark 2:15; Luke 5:30; 7:34; 15:2, and it has been related sufficiently above. Now since it is beyond debate that the afore-mentioned *publicani* and sinners were of the Jews and had the sentence of death upon them according to the Law, and since Christ refers to both *publicani* and heathen, therefore it follows with great force

---

[3] Menno is no doubt referring here to the Reformed position, namely, that the force of Christ's injunction in Matt. 18:15-18 is that the apostate and impenitent confessor hitherto considered a member of the flock shall because of his obstinacy in sin be now considered outside the covenant fold, just as the Jews had listed the Gentiles and publicans. *Tr.*

that these words may not be made to refer to the times when Israel still exercised its liberty with the heathen, which liberty Moses had granted them in the Law, for at that time manifest sinners convicted by the Law had to pay with their lives, and it would then follow mercilessly that apostates when heard and judged should die at our hands. But oh, no! For we know that such a bloody ban is an abomination before God, and is unknown among Christians, much less practiced.

And if anyone wants to insist that in our times an apostate is to be dealt with as we now deal with a heathen, and to refuse to see this in the frame of Christ's time, as a heathen was then dealt with by the Jews, such a one will have to recover the Jewish race and its Law and religion, and in this way derive out of them the manifest sinner—which, all will agree, is impossible.

Since then this word *heathen* may not be construed as in the times when Israel did not yet so strenuously shun the heathen (for then we shall have to sentence the apostate to death on the basis of the word *manifest sinner*) nor to the present time (for our manifest sinners are not of the Jews), therefore no one may contradict, with God's Truth on his side, that we must let this refer to the times of Christ, in which time manifest sinners were not put to death but both the heathen and the manifest sinners were shunned by them with one and the same ban.

Since then we have with the above reasoning proved sufficiently to the pious and God-fearing how that Christ had His own times in mind and no other when He said these things, therefore we wish now at once to indicate in simple terms the specific reasons why they so carefully shunned the heathen, and then also why they [merely] avoided the manifest sinners, and did not sentence to death as the Law provides.

All Bible readers know that the Lord very faithfully warned Israel not to make a league nor establish friendship with the Canaanites, Hittites, etc., and not to associate with them, lest they be bewildered by them and serve other gods. Deut. 7. For in case you turn about, said Joshua, to cleave to this people, and unite with them so that you frequent them and they you, so shall the Lord no longer drive out these people from among you, but they shall be a snare unto you, and as rods by your side, and as a thorn in your eyes, until he expel you from his good land which the Lord your God gave unto you. Josh. 23:11-13.

Since Israel did not hearken very well to this fatherly warning but made friends with the strange peoples, and became intimate with them, contrary to God's warning, therefore it happened to Israel as the Lord God had threatened by the faithful servants, Moses and Joshua. Frequently they, by alien company, alien wives, and alien idols, with which they became intimate, came to great apostasy, for which they were severely punished by the Lord. Yes, so that even the highly gifted Solomon, whose wisdom was known afar, allowed himself to be so bewitched by the heathen wives that he became unfaithful to his God, who had appeared to him twice, and he inclined his heart to strange gods. It seems to me, dear brethren, that this was certainly a proper reward for such as despise the Lord's counsel.

And since they, deceived by heathen deceit, so frequently sinned against God, and therefore were so often chastised by God's righteous punishments, they finally accepted the afore-mentioned warning of God set forth by Moses and Joshua with greater seriousness than heretofore, and they repudiated their intercourse with the heathen to such an extent, it seems, that some of the liberties permitted by Moses became inoperative, verily, so that to enter into their houses and to eat with them was considered ceremonially unclean, as is evident. And all this as a result of the resolution not to let them lead them astray again as of yore, and turn away from their God. And this is the reason why the Jews so completely avoid and shun all intercourse with Gentiles. Whether the reason was sufficient a genuine theologian may judge with God's Spirit and Word.

Again, the reason why the Jews avoided manifest sinners but did not put them to death is this. The prophecy of the patriarch Jacob that the kingly scepter was to be turned away from Judah, was accomplished by Pompey the Great[4] who assigned it to the Romans in such a way that the Romans had their own officials and governors in Judea, who wielded the scepter. Therefore the Jews no longer pronounced capital sentence to judge willful and manifest trangressors according to their Law, for that belonged to him who had the scepter, at this time in the hands of the Romans. That this was true the Jews themselves asserted before Pilate, when they said, It is not permitted unto us to put anyone to death. According to the Law it was permitted to them, yes, it was sharply enjoined upon them. But the lost scepter now prevented[5] such, for the Roman servants, Herod, Pilate, etc., who at the moment wielded the scepter in the Romans' stead, did not wish to judge according to the Jewish Law but according to the laws and statutes of the Romans, in whose name they ruled, bound by an oath. And when any Jew acted contrary to Moses' Law but not against Roman morality, the afore-mentioned representative of the Jewish Law did not pronounce capital punishment. And since the Jews were not allowed to punish such a one according to the Law, and that for the above reason, therefore they expelled him from their company and thrust him out of the synagogue, and in this way solemnly shunned him.

Now observe, my faithful brethren. For these recited reasons the Jews in Christ's day shunned these two classes of people, namely, both the heathen and the manifest Jewish sinners: the heathen, so that they might not be again seduced and misled; but the manifest sinners because they were worthy of death according to the Law but for lack of the scepter could not be put to death and exterminated.

[4] Pompey the Great (106-48 B.C.) was the Roman general and statesman who annexed Syria and Palestine. *Ed.*

[5] Reading *weerde* (prevent) for *werde* (became). *Tr.*

Perhaps somebody will answer to this by saying, But why then have they flogged the apostles and stoned Stephen, and why then were many saints put to death by Paul, and the church made desolate, if indeed they were unable to sentence any to death?

My reply is that all that was done in these cases was not done without the Romans' knowledge and consent; for they themselves acknowledged before Pilate that it was not allowed to them to put anybody to death. The stoning of Stephen was not done legally but by a mob in a riot. Even as Luke reports plainly enough, saying: *Exclamantes autem voce magna, continuerunt aures suas, et impetum fecerunt unanimiter in eum.* This they of Zurich translate: They cried out, stopping their ears, and went for him as with one mind.[6] They had the same intentions concerning Christ, and Paul likewise.

Likewise when Paul wrought havoc with the church and put so many saints to death, as he relates before Agrippa, anyone can see that this was not without consent of the magistrates. For it is evident and beyond controversy that the scepter includes the right to take life. Therefore they said that they were not allowed to put anybody to death, since the scepter was taken from them and held in the Romans' hand, as stated above. Verily if they had been competent to pronounce capital sentence they would not have delivered Christ into the hands of Pilate. Then Lysias would not have snatched Paul from the mobbing Jews; Herod would not have arrested Peter, and would not have put John the Baptist nor James to death. For that would never do in any secular rule—for one power to usurp the jurisdiction of the other. Such a government and police power would no doubt very soon go to pieces.

We know very well, dear brethren, that there are some who call this Jewish avoidance or ban, to which Christ was referring, a Pharisaic leaven. They say, we do not want to be referred to any such leaven, apart from the Scriptures.

We pray such for the Lord's sake to ponder well what they say, for it seems to me they do not understand their own words. Did not Moses say that God will judge those who do not hearken to the voice of the prophet? And does not Jeremiah say that He will establish justice and equity in the land? Does not the Father declare from high heaven, This is my beloved Son in whom I am well pleased; hear ye him? Does not Paul say that in Christ are hidden all the treasures of knowledge and of wisdom? I anticipate that Christ's Word and instruction constitute Scripture enough for all pious people; and it is *He,* I say He, and not I, who points His believing ones to this usage regarding the ban! *Tu quis es, qui ex adverso respondes Deo?* [Who art thou that repliest against God?]

If now there is any brother, anywhere under heaven, who can point

---

[6] Menno here quotes the Swiss Froschouer version, translated by Leo Judae, Zwingli's assistant. *Ed.*

to any time other than the time of Christ to which these words of Christ may with divine truth be referred, and the Scriptures remain unbroken, then I shall gladly be corrected and open my ears to truth. For I do not want to fight against the truth (the truth that is my witness) but I want to fight for the truth. For the truth's sake I have had to hear and suffer much these many years. And by God's grace I am still ready to testify to His holy truth, even unto death. But I know, and know full well, that they may not be referred to any other time—unless Christ's Word and Scripture is to be forced, even as the pious reader was shown above with abundant reason and Scriptures.

In the second place, I ask, very similarly for God's sake, that my dear brethren will construe from Scripture just what leaven is and how it is understood in Scripture, before they call this afore-mentioned Jewish ban to which Christ refers here, A Pharisaic leaven. First of all it [leaven] stands for the Word and its power, or, if you prefer, for faith and its power. In the second place, it stands for a godless being or man, one that promotes decay. And in the third place, it stands for a doctrine that leads astray and causes decay. Now if the Jewish ban to which Christ refers was a leaven, as some very erroneously would have it, then they are obliged to make plain from Scripture what decay it introduced, affecting the pure Word and the Jewish conscience. For although God the Lord did through Moses allow to Israel certain temporal liberties of policy (for a time, as was said at the outset), yet He did not give them binding orders to deal with the heathen; but He warned against them. Since now they solemnly took to heart the faithful warning of God, having learned through the many dangers, they therefore probably waived some of the liberties granted them, lest by means of such liberties they be ensnared again and caught in their conscience by the heathen. You who are spiritual, judge now whether it is Scripturally right to call that a leaven, seeing that by all this they did not ignore God's Law but left it basically intact and whole, and so guarded against the corrupter!

Dearly beloved brethren, if this Jewish ban or avoidance, to which Christ refers, is to be called a leaven because they by chance waived certain privileges, and that for conscience' sake, seeing that privileges are optional to forego or to observe (otherwise they were no privileges), and since it was not contrary to the commandment but much rather conformed to God's faithful warning, advice, and admonition contained in the Law, then the holy prophet Jeremiah might very properly have accused the Rechabites of being "leaveners" because they would not drink wine, plant vineyards, sow fields, or build houses because of the command of their father Jonadab— although according to God's Law it was by all means permissible to them, for to them and to Israel were the other blessings expressly assigned and promised with the land.

No, sir! It was not reckoned to them as leaven by the Lord. They were highly commended for respecting the words of their father; and they received a promise from the Lord for it.

And I say besides, if it is to be termed leaven when I go aside from my privilege, either for my own conscience or for my brethren's sake, then permission is no longer permission. And then Paul must also have been an impure "leavener" for insisting so vehemently that we must if need be forego our privilege for the brethren's sake.

From all this it is very evident, as far as insight into the Lord's Word has been given me, that it is a very frightful blasphemy, one that a pious Christian cannot own, that we should want to teach and instruct Christ, the eternal Wisdom, how He shall teach us, to what He should point us. That to which He points they call a leaven, although it was a strong and comforting protection against corruption and aberration. And therefore we declare that it was not against the Law but in line with it, for if that leaven had been contrary to the Law, as some try to make out, then Christ Jesus would certainly not have looked upon it favorably, nor pointed to it saying: Let him be unto thee a heathen man and a manifest sinner. For in other passages He has diligently commanded His followers to keep away from the leaven.

Probably some will reply to me saying, When the Jews shunned the heathen, that is, refused to eat with them, even when the food was ceremonially clean, they acted manifestly contrary to the express command of the Law. For Moses had commanded Israel that even the sojourners among them should be invited to the Feast of Weeks and the Feast of Tabernacles, and together with them be joyful before the Lord: servant, maid, Levite, widow, and orphans together. To these I reply as follows. These same strangers had to keep the Sabbath, enjoying the tithes of the third year and the first fruits, together with the Levites, the widows, and the orphans; and the gleanings of the grainfields, olive trees, and vineyards, together with the widows and orphans. They also had, in common with Israel, the same sacrifice for sins committed unwittingly; and the same penalties. With Israel they were[7] to hear the reading of the Law in the year of Jubilee. From all this and similar Scripture passages it follows that these, the strangers in question, had been incorporated into Israel and were therefore not uncircumcised heathen. For they were already among the Israelites, during the wanderings in the wilderness. As Moses said: You stand this day all of you before the Lord your God, your captains of your tribes, your elders, your officers, all those of Israel, your little ones, your wives, your stranger that is in your camp, from the hewer of wood to the drawer of water, that you should enter into the covenant of the Lord your God, and into the oath which the Lord your God makes with you this day.

For I am of the opinion, brethren, that these cited Scriptures are suffi-

[7] Some such expression as *zij moesten* seems to have fallen out of the text here. We have supplied "they were." *Tr.*

cient proof of this. And they[8] were called strangers because they were not of the seed of Israel and had no share in the division of the land. For this cause Moses commanded the Israelites to give them access to the tithe of the third year, to the gleanings of the grainfields, olive trees, and vineyards, and to the first fruits of the field, as we have just now shown from the very chapters of Moses.

In the second place, I will probably be asked, Why should we avoid the apostates since Christ has said: Let him be to you as a heathen man and a manifest sinner—and it is well known that Christ Himself ate with manifest sinners?

I reply by saying: What kind of sinners they were with whom Christ ate the Gospel writers have made plain. For when the Pharisees murmured against Him Jesus said, Those that are whole need not a physician but they that are sick; but go ye and learn what that meaneth, I will have mercy and not sacrifice; I came not to call the righteous but sinners to repentance. What kind of sinner Matthew remained after he had heard Christ, what kind the woman taken in adultery, and Zacchaeus, is not unknown. Matt. 9; Mark 2; Luke 7, 19.

Again, as Luke has it, All the publicans and sinners came to Christ to hear Him. And with this kind of people He ate, saying to the grumbling Pharisees, Which of you having a hundred sheep and losing one of them does not leave the ninety and nine, etc.?

To continue, that He ate with Samaritans need not surprise us, for they received His Word and believed in Him. But that He is said to have sought lodging in a Samaritan city inn results from an improper translation of the Latin text, which reads: *Missit nuncios ante conspectum suum, et euntes intraverunt in civitatem, Samaritanorum ut pararent illi, et non receperunt eum, quia facies ejus erat euntis Hierosolymam.* In our language, this is: He sent messengers before Him and they entered into a Samaritan city to make appointments for Him; and they received Him not seeing that His face was as though He would go to Jerusalem.

What kind of appointments these were, we may, it seems to me, deduce from the action of the seventy-two[9] mentioned in the ensuing chapter, whom He sent ahead two by two, to make preparations in all the cities and places to which He would come—not to arrange for lodging but so that He might preach the kingdom of God. But they did not receive Him. He does not say that the innkeeper refused to receive Him, but *they,* that is, the citizens to whom He had made preparations to preach, received Him not, and that for the reason reported by Luke, that He was disposed to go to Jerusalem. For the Samaritans and the Jews have always had a hard and severe controversy in regard to religion and worship, yes, so that the Samaritans were considered by the Jews to be worthy of the ban. John 4:9.

---

[8] "They" has been supplied by the translator. *Tr.*

[9] Reference to the seventy (some manuscripts of the Gospels speak of seventy-two) of Luke 10:1. *Tr.*

And even if He had sought lodging, then it is still apparent that the Samaritans were commonly considered not Gentiles, but a remnant of the ten tribes transplanted by Shalmanezer; for the Samaritan woman said to Christ, You are surely not greater than our father Jacob. Now it is plain that Jacob was not the father of the Gentiles. She also was expecting the Christ, whom the Gentiles did not know. She said, I know that Messiah cometh who is called Christ.

To continue, Philip, after the stoning of Stephen, came into a city of the Samaritans and preached Christ to them; and at that time they did not yet feel free to preach the Gospel to the Gentiles nor to go in to them. From this it may be seen that the Samaritans, who considered the patriarch Jacob to be their father, expected the Messiah. And they to whom the apostles had already now, before they had been given permission to go to the Gentiles, preached the Gospel, were not Gentiles but a remnant of Israel, as has been said. Therefore it is not strange that He on one occasion sought lodging among them. Moreover He did not say, Let him be to you a Samaritan; but Let him be to you as a Gentile and a manifest sinner.

See, my dear brethren, no matter how they twist and turn these words of Christ, yet they are applicable to no other time than to the time of Christ. Therefore even as the Jews at that time evaluated a Gentile and a manifest sinner, so should we conduct ourselves over against an apostate, who, whether by false and erroneous doctrine or by an unclean and offensive life, dishonors, rejects, or disgraces Christ Jesus and His holy Word.

I could wish, most beloved brethren, seeing that we have given our interpretation of these afore-mentioned words of Christ, that every Christian would diligently examine whether Paul does not (I Cor. 5) understand them in precisely the same way. Yes, indeed, whoever observes carefully will discover that Paul in his doctrine of excommunication adhered carefully to this rule of Christ and governed himself by it.

Paul says: It is commonly reported that there is fornication among you, and such fornication as is unheard of even among the Gentiles, that one should have his father's wife. And you are puffed up, and have not mourned, that he that hath done this deed might be taken away from among you.

In another passage Paul teaches how that Christ loved His church and gave Himself for it, that He might sanctify and cleanse it with the washing of water by the Word, that He might present it to Himself a glorious church, not having spot or wrinkle, or any such thing, but that it should be holy and without blemish. Now if we tolerate those who so openly disgrace (as did this fornicator), and adulterers, drunkards, railers, covetous persons, contentious folk, and idolators, etc., and if we do not shun them, then we must hear, must we not, this reproof of Paul that we are "puffed up" and do not rather mourn, and separate such open transgressors from us. Brethren, brethren! I fear that this admonition of Paul is not taken very seriously by some people at certain places.

Paul says further, For I verily, as absent in body, but present in spirit, have judged already, as though I were present, concerning him that hath so done this deed, in the name of our Lord Jesus Christ, when ye are gathered together, and my spirit, with the power of our Lord Jesus Christ, to deliver such an one unto Satan for the destruction of the flesh, that the spirit may be saved in the day of the Lord Jesus. I Cor. 5:3-5.

These words of the apostle teach us three things. First, the great love which the faithful servant, Paul, had toward his disciples and children; for although he was not present there, yet as present in spirit, he cared for them in fatherly fashion, and always taught, admonished, and advised them the very best things.

Secondly, we learn in whose name, how and by whom this expulsion is to be effected; namely, in the name, that is, by the command and ordinance of our Lord Jesus Christ. For Paul did not presume to do anything that he had not first received of Christ, as he says. Yes, if Christ had not first instructed Paul to do so, he would not have dared to command the Thessalonians, in the name of our Lord Jesus Christ, that they should separate themselves from every brother who walked disorderly, and not according to His ordinances. For this may properly be called doing things in the name of Christ, when it is done in conformity with His holy Word and will.

Also, it is to be done by the church, that is, no one shall ban by himself or at his own pleasure. It shall be done by the congregation of God, after proper admonition; it shall be done in love, diligence, and faithfulness, with the power of Christ, that is, with the binding or closing key of the Word of God and the Holy Spirit. For if it be done without the Word and Spirit, without love and brotherly diligence, but through bitterness, anger, or a false report, not conformable to the Word, or for reasons not deserving the ban, then it is not a work of God, no medicine to the soul, nor fruit of pure love; but a Satanic contention, a corruption and pestilence to the soul, and an evident fruit of the flesh; in short, a curse, abomination, and stench before God. Let every person reflect at length on these words of Paul, and he will by the grace of God see how rigidly this expulsion is commanded in the Scriptures, and how solemnly it should be practiced in the church, with the power of the Word and the Spirit of Christ.

Thirdly, we learn that we should deliver an unrepenting transgressor unto Satan. Not, brethren, that he was not Satan's possession before the expulsion. As soon as he turned his heart away from the Lord and became ungodly, he became the property of Satan, even as a penitent sinner is the property of Christ. But now with audible voice through the church he is told that he is rejected from the communion of Christ and His church, and he is told that he is now Satan's own until he brings forth true fruits of repentance before God and His church. This is done that his adulterous, avaricious, refractory, and idolatrous flesh may be halted, and he may become ashamed and repentant by such declaration and the shunning by the pious; that he may go down and under as to his flesh, that is, his fleshly lusts; so that he may by these means be brought to repentance and his soul saved in the day of the Lord Jesus.

Here the God-fearing reader may observe in these words of Paul, the first reason why the Holy Spirit ordained this ban in the house of God; namely, with a view to repentance and not to destruction. For if the transgressor makes light of all the fraternal services and admonitions of faithful love that are shown to him, and remains impenitent, then, according to the advice of the Holy Spirit, this condemnation shall with sorrow be announced to him in the church, and he shall be expelled from the church, so as to become ashamed unto repentance.

Concerning this shame, the apostle speaks in another place, If any man obey not our word by this epistle, note that man and have no company with him, that he may be ashamed. II Thess. 3:14.

Observe, brethren, that true evangelical excommunication is an express fruit of unfeigned love, and not a rule of hatred as some altogether erroneously complain and pretend.

Ah, faithful brethren, if we were rightly taught of God, enlightened with the Holy Spirit, and if we loved our neighbors with godly love, how diligent we would be to execute the faithful advice of the Holy Spirit in all reasonableness and love, without respect of persons, no matter whether it concerns father, mother, sister, brother, husband, wife, child, or any relative or friend; for one must demonstrate the greater spiritual love toward them. But now a great many do not seek that which is of the spirit, but that which is of the flesh; not their neighbors, but themselves. If they do so through ignorance, then may the merciful Father enlighten them with His Holy Spirit and guide them into all truth. But if they do so through willful perversity, then we know that it is written, To be carnally minded is death.

In the third place, Paul says, Your glorying is not good. Know ye not that a little leaven leaveneth the whole lump? Purge out therefore the old leaven, that ye may be a new lump, as ye are unleavened. For even Christ our Passover is sacrificed for us: therefore let us keep the feast, not with old leaven, neither with the leaven of malice and wickedness, but with the unleavened bread of sincerity and truth. I Cor. 5:7, 8.

Again, with these words Paul reproves the Corinthians and all other churches with them, who glory in being the church of Jesus Christ and the spiritual house of Israel, and nevertheless tolerate such shameful, corrupting leaven as this Corinthian and his ilk, in their communion. For how can we glory in the piety of the church and reprove the outside churches on account of their ungodly doctrine and life, so long as we tolerate the like leaven of doctrine and life among us, and do not expel it? If we are unleavened, why are we not afraid of the leaven, since the apostle tells us that, A little leaven leaveneth the whole lump?

Secondly, he gives us here the outward Israel as an example. For when they kept the Passover, they did not allow leavened bread in their houses for seven days. Yes, if it was found in any house the souls thereof had to be destroyed from among Israel. Not even an uncircumcised or unclean person was to eat thereof. O brethren! If the figure and shadow were to be so pure, how much more the reality? For our Passover is not a four-footed lamb, but the spotless Lamb of God, Christ Jesus. Our Passover does not last seven days, as did the Passover of Israel, but it lasts forever, namely, from the offering of Christ until the last day. Neither is it kept by unleavened bread, baked of flour, but by the unleavened bread of righteousness and the Word of eternal truth.

Therefore, beloved brethren, let us keep this Passover holy and unspotted, to the utmost of our ability. And let us, in the name of our Lord Jesus Christ, put away from us the corrupting leaven, that is, all those that walk in the uncircumcision of their hearts, and all of impure life (understand, open and known transgressors), that we may be the holy Israel of God; sprinkled with the blood of the Lamb, free from the avenging angel of God so that we may rejoice before the Lord in sincerity and truth, and celebrate and serve all the days of our lives.

All the pious may also learn from these words of Paul—Know ye not that a little leaven leaveneth the whole lump?—the second reason why this excommunication is so proper and useful to the house of God, and why it cannot stand without it. This has been shown by the example of Israel. Moses, the faithful servant of God, had strictly commanded the people of God that they should, without mercy, destroy from among them the willful transgressors, when convicted by two or three witnesses. Also, that if any prophets should arise among them, with signs and miracles to lead them to other gods, that they should not hear them, but put them to death. A father should not shield his child, the husband his wife, etc., but their hand should be the first upon them. They had to destroy completely any city which went after other gods, and make it a heap, so that Israel might hear these things, fear God, and plan such evil no more. I think this was a strict ban which was commanded Israel. If they had stood firm and had followed the command, counsel, teaching, and admonition of God, according to the Scriptures, and had they destroyed the false prophets and idolaters, they would never have become so estranged from God, nor have come to such deadly adultery and degeneration (over against the Law, I mean). For the rejection of the counsel and will of God will never go unpunished.

But now the Holy Spirit does not teach us to destroy the wicked, as did Israel, but that we should sorrowfully expel them from the church, and that in the name of the Lord, by the power of Christ and the Holy Spirit, since a little leaven leavens the whole lump. It is a common saying, One scabby sheep mars the whole flock. The lepers were not allowed among the healthy in Israel; they had to stay in segregated places until cured. O brethren in the Lord! The leprosy of the soul is a leprosy above all leprosy, whether it be in doctrine or in life. It eats like a canker, and, as Paul says, leavens the whole lump. Therefore the Holy Spirit has abundantly taught us to separate such from among us; not to hear the words of the false prophets, for they deceive us; to separate from such who, contrary to apostolic doctrine, cause offense and contention; to shun those who are not satisfied with the salutary words and doctrine of our dear Lord Jesus Christ, but are contentious and desirous of quarreling. We are taught to guard against dogs and the concision; to flee the voice of strangers; to shun a heretic or a master of sects, after one or two admonitions; not to greet nor receive in our houses those who do not teach the doctrine of Christ; and to withdraw from every brother who acts disorderly and walks not according to the apostolic doctrine. Would, says Paul, that they were cut off who disturb you!

Methinks, beloved brethren, the Holy Spirit of God has done well, and fully performed the duties of His office, and His faithful service of divine love toward His chosen people, by admonishing, warning, teaching, and commanding, in Moses and the prophets, in Christ and the apostles, in regard to the shunning of heretics and apostates. If we through obstinacy or disobedience still associate with the leprous against the faithful counsel, teaching, and admonition of God, and intermingle with them, then we may expect to be infected with the same disease. It is the recompense of those who know the nature of the disease, and yet neither fear nor avoid it.

Tell me, most beloved, is it not the greatest foolishness and recklessness, willfully and wittingly to run into the hands of murderers, and to open unto them your house and office? What else can you expect in such a case but stealing, robbing, and murdering?

Oh, let the pious reader receive the command, teaching, counsel, and admonition so faithfully given by the Holy Spirit. Shun all heretics (I refer to those who used to be of us) and apostates, according to the Word of the Lord; whether it be father, mother, wife, child, relative, or friend—whatsoever tries to turn you from God and His Word, and tries to corrupt you by doctrine or by life. Whosoever loves anything more than his God, cannot be the disciple of the Lord. Therefore believe Christ Jesus, and sincerely fear Him in His Word, and you will obey His counsel and doctrine. But if you are offended thereat, then await your punishment. For by the grace of God, I know what it is to despise the Word and will of God, and what I have felt with my hands and seen with my eyes in this matter.

In the fourth place, Paul says, I wrote unto you in an epistle not to company with fornicators: yet not altogether with the fornicators of this world, or with the covetous, or extortioners, or with idolaters; for then must ye needs go out of the world. But now I have written unto you not to keep company, if any man that is called a brother be a fornicator, or covetous, or an idolater, or a railer, or a drunkard, or an extortioner; with such an one no not to eat. I Cor. 5:9-11.

From these words of the apostle we learn that he had on a former occasion admonished the Corinthians, in an epistle, that they should shun the fornicators, the covetous, etc., but that they had understood it as referring to the fornicators of this world. Therefore Paul admonishes them in this epistle that this was not his meaning at all; for if they should shun these and avoid them, they must needs go out of the world. But he means those who are called brethren; as he shows in his plain language, saying, If any man that is called a brother be a fornicator, or covetous, etc., with such an one no not to eat— just as the Jews did not eat with the Gentiles and manifest sinners at the time of Christ, nor keep their company. For Christ and Paul are one, and not divided.

I think, brethren, that this text is so plain and clear that it admits of no controversy. Nevertheless, it must suffer attack, mutilation, and violence by some.

They say, Paul had no authority to burden us with any laws when it was not first taught and commanded him by Christ.

To this we answer, Let everyone ponder, divide, and cut correctly the words of Christ, Let him be unto you as a heathen man and a publican, and he will find by the grace of God, whether or not Paul has first received this doctrine from Christ.

Secondly, they say, Since Paul makes mention here of the Jewish Passover, and adds that we should keep the Passover, not in the old leaven, etc., therefore this passage and also his assertion, With such do not company, with such do not eat, must be understood as meaning a spiritual commingling or communion, that is, of the Lord's Supper.

To such we answer, Israel had a Passover of seven days, but we have an eternal Passover. And even though the Lamb of our sacrifice is eternal, and His sacrifice eternal, so we must now ceaselessly sanctify and celebrate it, ceaselessly partake of its flesh, be ceaselessly sprinkled with its blood, and be unendingly diligent in guarding against the ungodly, corrupting leaven of both doctrine and life. If our feast and Passover then is spiritual and not literal, eternal and not temporal, how then can this passage be applicable of the Lord's Supper, an eating which lasts but for an hour or so?

We answer further, If these words were meant of a spiritual communion, then it should read in the Greek text *Choinònia*[10] and in the Latin, *communicatio*, for these signify a spiritual communion, such as Christ shares with us, and the members of Christ with Christ. It is also used of the sharing of property. But we find another word in the Greek text, and in Latin it reads: *Commisceri, sivi* [should be *sive*] *commertium habere*, which does not point to a spiritual communion at all, but to an outward, physical communion. It appears more plainly so from these words of Paul that he speaks of external communion and fellowship, and not of spiritual intimacy, for he prohibits this communion with the apostates and allows it with the world, which has no spiritual communion with us, nor can have. This is incontrovertible. Yes, if

---

[10] The text clearly reads, *Choinònia*, plainly an error for *Koinònia*.

this communion or association with the world were prohibited, then we could not use the world to satisfy our natural needs, but would have to pine away in poverty, destitution, sorrow, and misery.

We reply, moreover, that Paul had reference to common eating, and not to the Lord's Supper; for he calls it in Latin, *cibum capere* (to take food), and not, *panem frangere* (to break bread). It is manifest that the Lord's Supper is nowhere in the Scriptures called *cibum capere*. And if this were spoken of the Lord's Supper, as some very ignorantly assert, then it would incontrovertibly follow that we are at liberty to invite the world to the Lord's Supper, to greet them with the kiss of peace, and to be one body with them; for this intercourse, unclean and prohibited with an apostate brother, is, according to Paul, clean and permissible with the world. Oh, no! But even as the Jews at that time would not eat a common meal with the heathen and publicans, and since Christ had pointed His followers to that usage, so Paul follows the doctrine and command of his Lord and Master, Jesus, and says that we shall not eat with such.

I think that it has been shown clearly enough for the pious that these words of Paul should not be understood of spiritual communion, nor of the Lord's Supper, but only of external association and common eating. And if it is not permissible in outward and carnal things, much less so in inward or spiritual things.

Worthy brethren in the Lord, I would pray and admonish you all in humility to consider well what the proper meaning of this word *commertium* is, of which Paul speaks, and how we should understand it, lest you give too much liberty to the careless conscience, to its own destruction, and lest you bind the sensitive conscience too strictly, since you have no binding word. For I hear and see, and have, alas, seen too much these many years, that some on every hand know no bound nor discretion in this matter, with the result that there is much dispute and trouble about this excommunication. May the Lord grant His divine grace to the peace, unity, and edification of His holy church. Amen.

Inasmuch as I am an unworthy and humble servant, also called in the house of God, and sincerely desire the good of my beloved brethren and companions, therefore I will present my views concerning this communion or contact in a few words, according to my talent; the views with which I desire to appear before the throne of my Lord Jesus Christ at the day of judgment. And I leave it to the judgment of God's Word, and to all those who have been taught of God. My understanding, therefore, of *commisceri* or *commertium habere,* of which Paul speaks here, is that it points to communion, company, walk, intercourse, presence, usage, conversation, and dealings. It does not refer to an occasional word spoken, or to necessary business, such as dividing a legacy, paying debts, and similar incidental matters. Nor does it refer to services rendered in time of need, for the word *commertium* does not have such a strict connotation. Therefore, in my opinion, they err not a little who give the saying, Have no company with them (Not means not, they say!), the same strength which they attach to, Thou shalt not steal, and, Thou shalt not commit adultery, matters of which Paul testifies that those who are guilty of them shall not inherit the kingdom of heaven. Brethren, if this were the situation, who could stand before his God?

Again, if the word *commertium*, which in our language means company or fellowship, is to be pressed so rigidly that we are not to speak a word with an apostate, and not to transact necessary business with him; then the word *commertium* would be violated, many a pious child would be defrauded, and many an unscriptural procedure followed, and the faithful Paul rejected. For he says, Yet count him not as an enemy, but admonish him as a brother. II Thess. 3:15. Besides, it would reflect very unfavorably upon the Gospel of Christ.

It is also incontrovertible that the manifest sinners and also some heathen lived in Judea, such as Herod, Pilate, Philip, Lycanius, Festus, etc., before whom men had to appear upon occasion. The Jews also had to pay tax and toil to the Romans; and were therefore obliged sometimes to exchange a few words with them, and had necessary dealings with them, although they diligently shunned their daily company, conversation, intermingling, eating, etc.

Dear brethren, take heed, and do not become despisers and masters of the Holy Spirit! And do not, through the sentiments of men, make the way narrower nor broader than the Word, Spirit, and example of the Lord define it.

Paul also says, What have I to judge them that are without? Do not ye judge them that are within? But them that are without God judgeth. Here Paul repeats his former assertion that he did not apply the expression in his first epistle to those that are without, for God judges them, and not we. We ought to put away the wicked persons that are among us, and leave the world to God.

Behold, faithful brethren, how unanimously Christ and Paul agree in this matter of shunning the apostate. And also, how earnestly Paul has taught and advocated this expulsion, yes, he has in this short chapter, six times enjoined this ban. (1) Ye are puffed up, and have not rather mourned, that he that hath done this deed might be taken away from among you. (2) To deliver such an one unto Satan. (3) Purge out therefore the old leaven, that ye may be a new lump. (4) Not to company with fornicators. (5) With such an one, not to eat. (6) Therefore put away from among yourselves that wicked person.

All these are found in one short chapter; besides what he has taught, commanded, and admonished in this respect to the Romans, Galatians, Philippians, Thessalonians, Timothy, and Titus! John also has set forth his view of the matter. I verily do not see how a God-fearing heart can oppose in regard to this matter. There are such good fruits and benefits contained in this shunning. But it seems that this vine must always have its harmful worm.

The opposition makes another objection and says, When one is separated from the church it is not necessary any longer to shun him, for he is no longer called a brother.

To such we reply: They should, in the first place, consider that if such a one, who has confessed the Lord's Word and truth, and for a time, has led a pious, evangelical life, and has in this way received baptism, upon confession of his faith, if such a one apostatizes, and then afterwards sincerely repents, he is not rebaptized, for the Scriptures teach but one baptism. But if those come to conversion who are of the world, then they are baptized upon repentance, for before, they neither knew the Word, penitence, faith, righteousness, nor baptism. Therefore, this is a different matter. They will also be more strictly punished by the Lord in the day of judgment on all the world.

We say also that the world esteems them as brethren nevertheless, and many of them are gladly greeted as such. Therefore it is very necessary to shun them, so that the world and they may know and understand that we do not consider them brethren who are so unclean and blamable in doctrine or in life, lest on their account the Word of the Lord and His church be despised by the ignorant world.

We say moreover that Israel did not shun their manifest sinners, nor the Corinthians their fornicators until they were expelled from the church. It is not a custom or usage in the Scriptures to shun anyone as long as he is carried and tolerated in the church. Therefore we should not shun anyone before excommunication, for if we do we practice a ban neither known nor mentioned in the Scriptures.

We say, finally, that if we commune and associate with an apostate, even after excommunication, then we show in fact that we despise the Word, command, judgment, doctrine, and admonition of God, and that we do not seek the profit and Scriptural shame of the apostate, unto his repentance, and that we do not guard against the corruption of our own souls.

I verily hope that this is sufficient to quiet every God-fearing heart, touching the words of Christ in Matt. 18, and the fifth chapter of First Corinthians; and that no more such vain garbling objections and empty excuses may be made, and these passages turned to the lust of the flesh, for they can no more stand than stubble before the fire, and ice before heat.

From these same words of Christ and of Paul it appears clearly how, when, where, with what spirit, by whom, upon whom, and for what purpose this ban should be practiced and used. I think this position to be so powerful that it cannot in any way be broken, neither with Christian reasonableness nor with divine truth. Let every one fear and love his God with all his heart, and he will, doubtlessly, receive the true knowledge of this matter, and will rightly follow the Biblical usage well-pleasing to God.

## [Some Questions and Answers on Church Discipline*]

*Question 1. Is separation commanded, or is it advised by God?*

*Answer.* Let every one weigh the words of Christ and of Paul referred to above and he will discover whether it is a divine commandment, or advice. Everything which Paul says in regard to separation he generally speaks in the imperative mode; that is, in a commanding manner. We are to purge, and to drive out, and to withdraw from, and to flee. Again we have the commandment, I command you, brethren, in the name of our Lord Jesus Christ.

I think, brethren, these Scriptures show that it is a command, and if it were not a command but advice of God, should we not diligently follow such advice? If my spirit despises the counsel of the Holy Spirit, then verily I acknowledge that my spirit is not of God. And to what end many have come who did not follow God's Spirit but their own may be read in many passages of sacred history, and may be seen today in many instances.

*Question 2. If any person should not observe this ban and yet be pious otherwise, should such a one be banned on that account?*

*Answer.* Whoever is pious will show his piety in obedience, and not knowingly or willfully despise and disregard the Word, commandment, will, counsel, admonition, and doctrine of God. For if anyone willfully keeps company with such whose company is forbidden in Scripture, then we must come to the conclusion that he despises the Word of God, and is in open disobedience and rebellion (I speak of those who know and acknowledge but do not do). For rebellion is as the sin of witchcraft and stubbornness is as iniquity and idolatry. The Scriptures admonish and command that we shall not associate with such, nor eat with them, nor greet them, nor receive them into our houses, etc. And yet if somebody should say I will associate with them, I will eat with them, I will greet them in the Lord and receive them into my house, he would plainly prove that he does not fear the commandment and admonition of the Lord, but despises them. He would show that he rejects the Holy Spirit, and that he trusts, honors, and follows his own opinion rather than the Word of God. Now judge for yourself what kind of sin it is, not to be willing to hear and obey God's Word. Paul says, Now we command you, brethren, in the name of our Lord Jesus Christ, that you withdraw yourself from every brother that walketh disorderly, and not after tradition which ye have received of us. Again, And if any man obey not our word by this epistle, note that man, and have no company with him, that he may be ashamed. Inasmuch as the ban was so strictly commanded and enforced by the apostles, and that out of the mouth of the Lord (Matt. 18:17); therefore we must

---

* In the *Opera Omnia* of 1681 (fol. 473) these questions and answers are introduced with the caption: *Here Follow Yet Some Questions with Which They Have Often Troubled Us. Ed.*

also use it and obey it, since we are taught and enlightened by God. Or else we should be shunned by the church of God for our disobedience. This must be acknowledged.

*Question 3. Should husband and wife shun each other on account of the ban,[12] also parents and children?*

*Answer.* First, the rule of the ban is a general rule, and excepts none; neither husband nor wife, neither parent nor child. God's Word judges all flesh with the same judgment and knows no respect of persons. The rule of the ban is general, excepts none, and is no respecter of persons. Therefore it is reasonable to hear and obey the Word of the Lord in this respect, no matter whether it be husband or wife, parents or children. Second, we say that separation must be made by the church, and therefore the husband must consent with the church in the separation of his wife, and the wife in the separation of her husband. If the pious consort must give his consent, then it is also proper that he also shun her with the church. For what use is there in the ban, when the shunning and avoiding are not connected with it?

Third, we say that the ban was instituted to make ashamed unto betterment of life. Do not understand this shame as the world is ashamed, but understand it as in the conscience. And therefore let it be done in all fairness, reasonableness, and love. If then my husband or wife, parent or child has been judged in the church, in the name of Christ and by virtue of Christ, it becomes me (seeing that the evangelical ban is unto betterment of life), according to the counsel of the Holy Spirit, to seek the reformation of my own body, namely, of my spouse and also of my nearest blood relation, parent or child. Spiritual love must be preferred to anything else. Moreover I would care for them and provide the temporal necessities of life as far as it would be in my power.

Fourth, we said the ban was given that we should not be leavened by the leaven of false doctrine or of impure life by the apostate. It is plain that none can corrupt and leaven us more than our own spouses, parents, etc. Therefore the Holy Spirit counsels us to shun them lest they leaven our faith and thus disgrace us before God. If we love husband or wife, parent or child more than Christ Jesus, we cannot possibly be the disciples of Christ.

Some object to this, saying that there is no divorce but by reason of

[12] The problem of shunning applying to husband and wife, "marital avoidance," was a severe one for the early Dutch Mennonites. All during his ministry Menno stood for strict church discipline, and for shunning. But when it came to marital avoidance Menno was a bit more lenient than some other leaders. Not only in the main body of this work, 1550, but again in 1554 and in 1558 he "repeated the same sentiments," as Horsch remarks. Menno says, "The Scriptures teach that we should bear with the weak. Brethren, it is a matter fraught with great danger."

The attitude of Menno is further clarified in the case of Swaen Rutgers, a Mennonite woman of Emden whose husband was excommunicated, and whom she refused to shun in the approved manner. There were those who counseled that she be excommunicated. But not so Menno. "We have never dared to follow such a course," he wrote. "I shall never consent to such a course." Mrs. Rutgers was not disfellowshiped. *Ed.*

ACCOUNT OF EXCOMMUNICATION

adultery. This is just what we say, and therefore we do not speak of divorce but of shunning, and that for the afore-mentioned reasons. To shunning Paul has consented, although this is not always coupled with adultery, but not to divorce. For divorce is not allowed by the Scriptures except for adultery. Therefore we shall not to all eternity consent to it for other reasons.

Therefore our view is that the husband should shun his wife, and the wife her husband, parents their children, and the children their parents, when they become apostate. For the rule of the ban is general. We must consent with the church to their sentence, we must seek their Scriptural shame unto improvement of life, and take care lest they be leavened by them, as was said above.

Beloved in the Lord, I would here sincerely pray you that you would make a difference between commandment and commandment, and not consider all commandments as equally weighty. For adultery, idolatry, shedding of blood, and the like shameful and abominable works of the flesh will be punished more severely than a misunderstanding in regard to the ban, and particularly when not committed willfully and perversely. Therefore beware that in this matter of matrimony you press none farther than he is taught of God and than he and his conscience can bear lest you seethe the kid while it is still unweaned.[13]

On the other hand, the Scriptures teach that we should bear with the weak. Brethren, it is a matter fraught with great danger. I know too well what in my own time has resulted from the length to which some have gone. Therefore I advise you to point all to the sure and certain ground. And those consciences that are then through the Scripture and the Holy Spirit free and unbound will freely and voluntarily, without the constraint of anyone, by the unction of the Holy Spirit, and not by pressure from men, do that which the Holy Spirit advises, teaches, and commands in the holy Scriptures, if it should be that his spouse be banned. For verily I know that whoever obeys the Holy Spirit with faithful heart will never be made ashamed.

*Question 4. Should we greet one that is banned with common secular greeting, or show our respect at his greeting, since John says, If there come any unto you, and bring not this doctrine, receive him not into your house, neither bid him Godspeed: for he that biddeth him Godspeed is partaker of his evil deeds.* II John 10, 11.

*Answer.* Good manners, politeness, respectfulness, and friendliness to all people becomes all Christians. If, then, an apostate should greet me with the common greeting of Good Morning, or Good Day, and I should be silent, if he should be respectful to me and I should turn my face from him and behave austerely and unfriendly toward him, I might well be ashamed of myself, as Sirach says. For how can such a one be convicted, led to repentance, and be moved to do better by such austerity? The ban is not given to destroy but to build up.

If it should be said that John has forbidden such greeting, I myself would

13 Dutch translation of Deut. 14:21. *Tr.*

say that before my God I cannot understand that John said this of the everyday greeting. But he means that if some deceiver should come to us who has left the doctrine of Christ that we should not receive such a one into our house lest he deceive us and that we should not greet him as a brother lest we have communion with him. But not so with the secular greeting. For if the secular greeting has such power in itself that it causes fellowship with the vain walks of those whom I greet, then it must follow that I would have communion with the adultery, fornication, drunkenness, avarice, idolatry, and bloodshed of the world, whenever I should greet a worldly man with the common greeting or return his compliment. Oh, no, the greeting or kiss of peace signifies the communion. Yet if one should have conscientious scruples in this matter, the feeling that he may not do it, with such a one do not dispute. For it is not worth quarreling about. But I would much rather see all scruples in regard to this matter removed and have Christian discretion, love, politeness, and respectfulness practiced for edification and not rudeness, austerity, impoliteness, carelessness, and disrespect to the destruction of our fellow man. Brethren, beware of discord. The Lord grant every God-fearing person a wholesome understanding of His holy Word. Amen.

*Question 5. Are we allowed to show the banned persons needful services, love, and mercy?*

*Answer* Everyone should consider first the exact meaning of the word *commertium* [translated, fellowship, communion, or social intercourse]. Second, we should consider for what reason and purpose the ban was ordained by the Holy Spirit in the Scriptures. Third, of what a true Christian is born and how he is minded. Fourth, how the merciful Father Himself acts toward those who are already worthy of His judgment and wrath.

All those who can rightly see into these things will doubtlessly not deny necessary service, love, and mercy to the banned. For the word *commertium* does not forbid these but it forbids common daily intimacy, conversation, society, and business, as was explained above.[14] The ban is also a work of divine love and not of perverse, unmerciful, heathenish cruelty. A true Christian will serve, love, help, and pity everybody, even his most bitter enemies. Austerity, cruelty, and unmercifulness he sincerely hates. He has a nature like his Father of whom he is born. For he maketh his sun to rise on the evil and on the good, and sendeth rain on the just and on the unjust. If I then be of a different nature, I show that I am not His child!

Therefore I say with our faithful brother, Dirk Philips,[15] that we should not use the ban to the destruction of mankind as the Pharisees did their Sabbath, but to its improvement, and we desire to serve the bodies of the fallen in love, reasonableness, and humility, with our temporal goods when necessary, and their souls with the spiritual goods of the holy Word. We would rather with the good Samaritan show mercy to the wounded than

---

14 In the main body of the book. *Ed.*
15 Dirk Philips (*c.* 1504-68) was a staunch fellow elder of Menno. *Ed.*

to pass him by with the priest and Levite. James says, For he shall have judgment without mercy, that hath showed no mercy, and mercy rejoiceth against judgment. Be ye therefore merciful as your Father also is merciful. Blessed are the merciful; for they shall obtain mercy.

In short, if we understand the true meaning of the word *commertium,* understand for what reason and purpose the ban was instituted; how a true Christian is and must be minded, and conform ourselves to the example of Christ and of God, then the matter is clear. And if we have not this grace we will shamefully err in this ban and be cruel, unmerciful Christians, from which error and abomination may the gracious Father eternally save all His beloved children.

Brethren, I tell the truth and lie not when I say that I sincerely hate this heartlessness. Nor do I wish to be considered a brother of such unmerciful, cruel brethren, if there should be such, unless they desist from such abomination and quietly follow in love and mercy the example of God and Christ. My heart cannot consent to such unmerciful action which exceeds the cruelty of the heathen and Turk. By the grace of God I will fight against it with the sword of the Lord unto death. For it is against the doctrine of the New Testament and contrary to the Spirit, mind, and nature of God and Christ, according to which all the Scriptures of the New Testament should be judged and understood. All those who do not understand it thus are already in great error.

But in case my necessary service, love, and mercy should become a *commertium,* or that my soul should thereby be led into corruption, then we confess, the Lord be praised, that it is forbidden in the Scripture, and that it is better to leave off our necessary service, love, and mercy than to ensnare our souls thereby and lead them into error. The unction of the Holy Spirit will teach us what is best to do in the matter.

*Question 6. Are we allowed to sell to and buy of the apostates, since Paul tells us not to have fellowship with them; yet the disciples bought victuals in Sychar and the Jews did business with the Gentiles?*

*Answer.* That the apostles bought victuals in Sychar proves nothing at all, for many of the Samaritans were a remnant of the ten tribes, as we have sufficiently shown above[16] from the holy Scriptures. We do not deny that the Jews dealt with the Gentiles, yet they shunned their *commertium,* that is, their daily association, company, and conversation, and did not eat nor drink with them, as the Gospels show plainly in many passages.

Since Christ points us to the Jewish ban, namely, that as they shunned Gentiles and sinners, so we should shun an apostate Christian; and since the Jews did do business with them, although they shunned *commertium* with them, therefore we say that we cannot maintain either by the Jewish example to which Christ points, or by any explicit Scripture, that we should not in any manner do business with the apostate. But this does not hold if *commertium*

---

[16] In the main body of this work. *Ed.*

results, for it is stringently forbidden in Scripture. Therefore it is plain that a pious God-fearing Christian would not have an apostate as a regular buyer or partner. Since I have daily to get my cloth, bread, grain, salt, etc., and exchange it for my grain, butter, etc., it cannot fail but that *commertium* will arise. But when trading is conducted without such *commertium,* then it is a different matter.

And although such trading which is carried on without *commertium* cannot be shown to be prohibited by Scripture, as was said, we would nevertheless pray all God-fearing brethren and sisters in the Lord for the sake of God and of love to act in this matter as in all others as reasonable, wide-awake, discreet, wise, and prudent Christians, and not as vain, reckless, willful, proud boasters and braggers. For a true Christian should always strive after that which is the very best and surest, and follow the pure, unfeigned love, lest he abuse the freedom which he seems to have to the injury and hindrance of his own soul, to the affliction and destruction of his beloved brethren, to the proud boasting of the perverse, and to the defaming of the holy Word and the afflicted church of Christ. I pray and desire similarly that none will be offended in the least at his brother, and mistake and judge him by unscriptural judgment, since he has in this case no reproving example among the Jews nor forbidding word in the Scriptures.

O my sincerely beloved brethren, let us sincerely pray for understanding and wisdom that all misunderstanding, error, suspicion, offense, division, and premature reports may be thoroughly exterminated and a wholesome understanding, doctrine, friendship, love, edification, and sane judgment may be restored and made to prevail. Let everyone look with pure eyes and impartial hearts to the example to which Christ points, and to the wholesome, natural meaning of the holy apostles, and let true, Christian love prevail always. Then he will know by the grace of God how he should act in this matter.

*Question 7. Are we allowed to sit with an apostate in a ship or coach or to eat with him at the table of an inn?*

*Answer.* The first part of this question, namely, to be seated with an apostate in a ship or coach when the captain or driver is no apostate, we deem childish and useless since this so often happens without *commertium* and must needs happen. As to the second part, namely, to eat at the table with an apostate while traveling, we can conscientiously point the questioner to no surer position than this: We advise, pray, and admonish every pious Christian as he loves Christ and His Word to fear God sincerely, and follow the most certain way in this matter, that is, not to eat with him, for that is a foolproof solution. However, if perhaps some God-fearing brethren might eat with such a one, then let everyone beware lest he sin against his brother by an unscriptural judgment. For none may judge, unless he have the judging Word on his side.

Whosoever fears God, whosoever desires to follow after His holy Word with all his strength, loves his brother, seeks to avoid all offense, and desires to walk in the house of God in all peace and unity, will act justly in all things and will not offend or afflict his brethren.

*Question 8. Who, according to Scripture, should be banned or excommunicated?*

*Answer.* Christ says, Matt. 18:15-17, If thy brother trespass against thee, etc., and will not hear thee nor the witnesses, nor the church, let him be unto thee as a heathen man and a public sinner. And Paul, If any man that is called a brother, be a fornicator, or covetous, or an idolater, or a railer, or a drunkard, or an extortioner; with such an one no not to eat. To this class belong also perjurers, thieves, violent persons, haters, brawlers, and all those who walk in open, patent, damnable works of the flesh, of which Paul enumerates a great many. Rom. 1:29; Gal. 5:19; I Cor. 6:9; Eph. 5:5. Again all disorderly persons, working not at all, which are busybodies, such as do not abide in the doctrine of Christ and His apostles, and do not walk therein but are disobedient. Also the masters of the sects. Also, those who give offense, cause dispute and discord concerning the doctrine of Christ and of His apostles.

In short, all those who lead a shameful, carnal life, and those who are corrupted by heretical, unclean doctrine (Titus 3:10), and who will not be overcome by the wine and oil of the Holy Spirit, but after they have been admonished and sought in all love and reasonableness remain obdurate in their corrupted walk and opinion. They should at last[17] in the name of our Lord Jesus Christ by the power of the Holy Spirit, that is, by the binding Word of God, be reluctantly but unanimously separated from the church of Christ, and should thereupon in all divine obedience, according to the Scriptures, be shunned until they repent.

## *Conclusion*

Dearest beloved brethren and sisters in the Lord, even as we have set forth in the beginning of this admonition,[18] you are all aware that for some years there has been much useless division and wrangling concerning the ban. By them Christian love has suffered much and suffers still. I see that this is agitated without Scriptural warrant, without reason and discretion, and contrary to the nature of Christ Jesus and His holy Gospel, both by the stringent as well as the lenient, to the ensnarement of many consciences. Everyone asserts and follows his own view as the best. Therefore I have spent much effort to advise all my dear brethren and sisters in the Lord who ardently seek

[17] Menno was opposed to both harshness and rashness in discipline. He reported waiting as long as one or two years, hoping for the best (*Opera*, 292b). *Ed.*

[18] This statement is decisive proof that the questions and answers were originally a part of this book. *Ed.*

the lovely peace and unity, who do not want to be more nor less strict than the Scriptures. And I write this exposition of the ban or separation, compiled with greatest care from the holy Scriptures, unto the promotion of the peace of all the pious children of God. I hope before God to satisfy all humble, peaceable consciences, for behold I seek nothing before God through Christ Jesus, but that these unscriptural agitations and lamentable quarrels concerning the ban, both as to the stringency and leniency, may be ended thereby, and that the noble, glorious peace and unity in Christ Jesus may remain unbroken and undamaged.

I have written this out of pure love, and in the interest of peace, according to the direction of the holy Word, before my God who shall judge me at the last day. I know, however, that by some I will not earn much thanks, for to some what I have written will be too stringent and others too lenient. I must bear this as I have done these fifteen[19] years. Still I would pray you for the sake of the merits of the precious blood of my Lord Jesus Christ, that if any one should find fault with this my treatise, be it on account of mildness or stringency, not to do so except with the authority of the Word, Spirit, and life of the Lord, and not recklessly and thoughtlessly lest he make blunders. Whatsoever any person can advance and prove I will gladly hear and obey; but I dare not go higher nor lower, be more stringent or lenient, than the Scriptures and the Holy Spirit teach me; and that out of great fear and anxiety of my conscience lest I once more burden the God-fearing hearts who now have renounced the commandments of men with more such commandments. Willfulness and human opinions I roundly hate, and do not want them. I know what tribulation and affliction they have caused me for many years.

Sincerely, beloved brethren and sisters in Christ Jesus, do understand my writings aright. And faithfully follow this my advice, explanation, understanding, and admonition, and you will doubtlessly find great happiness and joy (in the matter of separation) and peace among all the brethren. But whoever rejects them, let him take heed, for he will one day meet his Judge.

In short, it is my faith in and out, my position and confession of the separation which I never before wrote up and published with such clearness and detail. But now necessity urges me, and with this faith, position, and confession which I had from the beginning, I desire to die in Christ Jesus and to appear before the throne of God. For I am aware that it is the most certain exposition of separation which can be explained and taught to the God-fearing consciences from the holy Scriptures. Therefore I ask all my brethren and sisters in the Lord to leave me at peace about this matter and not to trouble me further. By the grace of God there will be nothing heard from my lips but that which my writings state and imply.

Let every brother seek the wholesome sense of the Word of Christ and of His apostles in a humble spirit of brotherly love and of Christian peace, and

---

[19] If Menno united with the Dutch Obbenites in January 1536, it must have been late in 1550 when Menno wrote this. *Ed.*

he will doubtlessly oppose all unscriptural dispute and discord and sincerely follow the true God-pleasing unity.

May the Almighty, merciful Father, through His blessed Son Jesus Christ, grant all brethren and sisters the heavenly gift of the Holy Spirit so that there may be an end to this sad quarreling and discord and thus the church may become a sound and healthy body with the perfect bond of unfeigned, Christian love, bound together in proper, stable peace in Christ Jesus. Amen.

Beloved brethren and sisters in the Lord, I pray you by the bloody wounds of my Lord Jesus Christ to avoid dispute and discord, that you may receive this my labor with affectionate hearts, for in true Christian love I have written it to your service as before God in Christ Jesus.

MENNO SIMONS

*A.D. 1550*

# Confession of the Triune God

*Belijdinghe van den drie eenigen God*

# 1550

*For other foundation can no man*
*lay than that is laid, which is Jesus Christ.*

I Corinthians 3:11

# Introduction

The very heart of Menno's doctrine, and that of his brotherhood, was holy obedience to Christ and His Word. Theology was not enough. There had to be regeneration and holiness. As far as doctrine was concerned, the doctrines of the church were to be simply the doctrines of the Bible. No rationalism, no appeal to church councils or church fathers: their doctrinal platform was the Bible interpreted Christologically, that is, according to the teaching of Christ. On the major doctrines of the Christian faith, as found in the so-called Apostles' Creed, for example, there was no significant difference between the Anabaptists and the larger bodies of Christendom.

As may be noted in Harold S. Bender's biography of Menno, there were a number of strong leaders in the Dutch "Mennist" brotherhood in Menno's day. Leonard Bouwens was bishop in Holland, Gillis of Aachen served the Rhineland congregations, Dirk Philips looked after the congregations of Danzig and the Baltic area, and Menno served the "central district from East Friesland to Holstein, and was recognized as the chief among the bishops."

The bishops used to get together to discuss and agree upon matters of mutual concern and responsibility. The meetings of 1547, held in Emden and Goch, attempted to deal with the problem of a bishop who had become unsound. Roelof Martens, better known as Adam Pastor, was a Westphalian priest who had united with the Obbenites, and was ordained a bishop about 1542 by Menno Simons and Dirk Philips. By 1547 Pastor had come to believe that Christ was not the eternal and divine Son of God, although he accepted the Scriptures as God's Word, and believed in redemption through Christ. Jesus Christ was for Pastor, "The only Mediator between his Father and fallen man." Yet he did not accept the true deity of Christ. The other bishops labored with Pastor, attempting to lead him to the orthodox view of Christ, but in vain. Consequently, in Goch in 1547 Dirk and Menno excommunicated Pastor.

The booklet before us, Menno's *Confession of the Triune God*, was written in 1550 to counteract the influence of Pastor, who had a few followers. At first it was circulated in manuscript form, until 1597, when it was first printed. The copy used in 1597 had been made for the brethren in Groningen, and contained a note at the end stating that Menno was unable to make a copy for each congregation. The tract is dated September 9, 1550.

It is an excellent and simple statement of the Biblical truth that the eternal God exists in three persons, Father, Son, and Holy Spirit. Menno does not try to be philosophical and profound; he seeks rather to be plain and Biblical. He warns against speculation in reference to the eternal God who by His very deity is to us poor mortals incomprehensible.

The full title is: *A Solemn Confession of the Triune, Eternal, and True God, Father, Son, and Holy Spirit. In the Opera Omnia Theologica* of 1681 it appears, fol. 383-91, and in the *Complete Works* of 1871, II, 179-88.

J. C. W.

# Confession of the Triune God

# 1550

## *Preface*

Menno Simons wishes all his beloved brethren and sisters in the Lord, grace and peace, an unbroken, sound, and pure faith, genuine brotherly love, a sure and living hope, and a God-pleasing, irreproachable conduct, confession, and life, from God our heavenly Father, through His beloved Son, Christ Jesus, in the power of the Holy Ghost. Amen.

We know, dear brethren and sisters in Christ Jesus, that we are already condemned by the whole world, to fire, water, and sword, for the testimony of Christ and our consciences; that we are the spectacle, the refuse, and the offscouring of all mankind. We know also that the true Prince of Peace, the blessed Christ Jesus, has summoned and incorporated us into the mansion of peace through the Word of His peace; and that He has ascribed and left to His followers a glorious sign by which men may know them to be His disciples, namely, love. Therefore it is reasonable and Christian that we poor, outcast cross-bearers should be united in the perfect bonds of true love, and that we should be bound together as the members of one body. For we are all baptized into one body and made to drink into one Spirit.

But now we see plainly how the prince of darkness who from the beginning was a murderer seeks with all diligence to disturb this same peace in the house of God, to rend this bond in two, and thus to make odious to many the dear Gospel of our Lord Jesus Christ, as well as our cross and confession and all the Christian assembly, and thus thoroughly to destroy it. John 8:44. Since his bold attacks are so well known to us, therefore it is high time to arouse ourselves to repent, to seek each other in true Christian love, to restore that which has been corrupted, and to cure with the oil of the divine Word that which is diseased. For during the last four years, alas, Christian love and peace have become pretty thin with some, on account of much pernicious arguing and bickering about the divinity of Christ and of the Holy Ghost; also, about angels and devils, and about the ban. This has always been the case where such disputes came up (May the Lord not count it as sin against those who have broached these matters). I see this plainly and have been troubled not a little by some about this matter, since by nature I hate such bickerings

489

and disputings (I have these fifteen years[1] never found any use in it), because
I love peace and unity which are in conformity with the Word of God, more
than I do my own life. (I hope that I do not lie.) Because of these things
my heart is very much troubled, mournful, and afflicted, yea, more so than
I can write.

I could wish, God knows, that I could at the cost of my lifeblood help
all afflicted consciences and could lead them to God. For I love nothing more
on earth, nor before God do I seek anything but the glory of my Lord Jesus
Christ, and the everlasting salvation of my beloved brethren. And therefore
I have been diligent, with great heaviness in my poor sick body, to send you
my inmost faith and confession concerning the eternal, Triune God, Father,
Son, and Holy Ghost, derived from the pure Word of God, wherewith I
will, with an unshaken conscience, before my God, live and die, and will therewith in His grace at the day of judgment appear before Him. With this I hope
to make pleasant and worthy to many the noble and desirable peace and unity
in Christ, and to bring back the love now so sadly bewildered.

Brethren, there has been enough of dispute, quarrel, and complaint of one
another. I think it is time to turn away from the disturbers of the peace and
to seek and pursue with the whole heart Scriptural peace and unity. But I
desire no peace outside of Christ. I ardently desire and pray all my beloved
brethren and sisters in the Lord, by all that is holy, to read, hear, and understand this my admonishing confession, without partiality, bitterness, or malice;
with pure, God-fearing hearts, even as I have written it in purity of heart, as
before God in Christ Jesus, without partiality, bitterness, or malice. I doubt
not but that if you do this, brethren (I mean the contentious and the troubled
ones), then disquiet, dispute, and disunion will recede from the peaceful hill of
the Lord; and peace, love, and unity will again move in.

I sincerely desire that it may be in this spirit read and taken to heart,
that the Almighty, eternal Father, with His blessed Son Christ Jesus and
the Holy Spirit, may remain unassailed in their true, divine being; and
that the afflicted, sad, and wavering consciences may find succor, consolation,
and strength. May the beloved Father grant His grace. Amen.

---

[1] Menno had been a member of the brotherhood 1536 through 1550 to September, almost fifteen years at this point. *Ed*

# A Solemn Confession

## of the

## Triune, Eternal, and True God, Father, Son, and Holy Ghost

We believe and confess with the holy Scriptures that there is an only, eternal, and true God, who is a Spirit; the God who created heaven and earth, the sea and all that is therein; the God whom heaven and earth and the heaven of heavens cannot contain, whose throne is heaven and whose footstool is the earth; who measured the waters in the hollow of His hand; who meted out the heaven with a span; who comprehended the dust of the earth in a measure and weighed the mountains in scales and the hills in a balance; who is higher than heaven and deeper than hell, lower than earth and broader than the sea; who only hath immortality, dwelling in the light which no man can approach unto; whom no man hath seen, nor can see; who is an Almighty, powerful, and an ever-ruling King, in the heavens above and on the earth beneath; whose strength and power none can stay; a God above all gods, and a Lord above all lords; there is none like unto Him, mighty, holy, terrible, majestic, wonderful, and a consuming fire; whose kingdom, power, dominion, majesty, and glory is eternal, and shall endure forever. Besides this only, eternal, living, Almighty sovereign God and Lord we know no other; and since He is a Spirit so great, terrible, and invisible, He is also ineffable, incomprehensible, and indescribable, as may be deduced and understood from the Scriptures.

This one and only eternal, omnipotent, incomprehensible, invisible, ineffable, and indescribable God, we believe and confess with the Scriptures to be the eternal, incomprehensible Father with His eternal, incomprehensible Son, and with His eternal, incomprehensible Holy Spirit. The Father we believe and confess to be a true Father, the Son a true Son, and the Holy Spirit a true Holy Spirit; not physical and comprehensible but spiritual and incomprehensible. For Christ says, God is a Spirit. Inasmuch as God is such a Spirit, as it is written, therefore we also believe and confess the eternal, begetting heavenly Father and the eternally begotten Son, Christ Jesus. Brethren, understand my writing well, that they are spiritual and incomprehensible, as is also the Father who begat; for like begets like. This is incontrovertible.

And this same incomprehensible, ineffable, spiritual, eternal, divine Being, which is begotten of the Father, before every creature, divine and incomprehensible, we believe and confess to be Christ Jesus, the first and only begotten Son, the first-born of every creature, the eternal Wisdom, the power of God, the everlasting Light, the eternal Truth, the everlasting Life (John 14:6), the eternal Word (John 1:1). This does not refer to a spoken word, for it is divine and spiritual, and not carnal and literal. A spoken word is but a passing breeze, grasped in the letter, beginning and ceasing. If understood in this sense, then Christ Jesus before His incarnation must have been a literal word. But no, He is the eternal, wise, Almighty, holy, true, living, and incomprehensible Word, which in the beginning was with God, and was God, by whom all things were made, and without whom not anything was made that was made, and who will endure forever. Therefore He says, Before Abraham was I am. Again John the Baptist says, After me cometh one who was before me. Yes, this glory of the divine being He had with the Father before the foundation of the world. He thought it not robbery to be equal with God, His Father. Therefore, we confess with John the Baptist, Nathanael, Martha, and Peter that He is the Son of the living God.

Dearly beloved brethren, understand me correctly when I say He is the eternal Wisdom, the eternal Power. For as we believe and confess that the Father was from eternity and will be unto all eternity; that He is the First and the Last, so we may also freely believe and confess that His wisdom, His power, His light, His truth, His life, His Word, Christ Jesus, has been eternally with Him, in Him, and by Him; yea, that He is the Alpha and the Omega. Or else we must admit this begotten, incomprehensible, true, divine being, Christ Jesus, whom the fathers have called a person, through whom the eternal Father has made all things, has had a beginning as do creatures (which all true Christians consider a terrible blasphemy, curse, and abomination). May the gracious and dear Father ever protect and uphold all His beloved children in the right and true confession of His beloved Son Jesus Christ.

Dear brethren in the Lord, we believe and confess that this same eternal, wise, Almighty, holy, true, living, and incomprehensible Word, Christ Jesus, which was in the beginning with God and which was God, incomprehensible—born of the incomprehensible Father, before every creature—did in the fullness of time become, according to the unchangeable purpose and faithful promise of the Father, a true, visible, suffering, hungry, thirsty, and mortal man in Mary, the pure virgin, through the operation and overshadowing of the Holy Spirit, and so was born of her. We confess that He was like unto us in all things, sin excepted; that He grew up as do other men; that at the appointed time He was baptized and entered upon His preaching task, and office of grace and love which was enjoined upon Him from the Father, and which He obediently fulfilled. He erased the handwriting, that is, the law, which was against us; and has at last, through the eternal Spirit of His heavenly Father, offered Himself in this human flesh, nature, and weakness, in which He sighed, wept, and prayed unto the Father, and sweat water and blood, and thus purified our hearts of dead works that we should serve the true and living God. All who believe on Him have through Him received grace, mercy, forgiveness of sins, and eternal life, and that by means of His crimson blood which He has in His great love sacrificed and shed on the cross for us poor sinners, according to the good pleasure of the Father. And so He has become our only and eternal High Priest, Atoner, Mercy Seat, Mediator, and Advocate with God His Father.

For even as God, the Almighty Father, through His Almighty Word, Christ Jesus, had created Adam and Eve, so also when they and their descendants were seduced by the serpent He restored them so that we should give no one the praise for our salvation, neither in heaven nor on earth, but the only and eternal Father through Christ Jesus, and that through the illumination of the Holy Spirit. This is enough of the incarnation.

To go on, beloved brethren, we believe and confess Christ Jesus to be the true God with the Father; and this because of the divine honor, acts, and attributes which are found in such abundance with Him, as may be clearly deduced and understood from the following Scriptures. Tell me, beloved, is it not the only and true God who has made heaven and earth, and whose kingdom shall endure forever? Doubtlessly, yes. Paul says, Unto the Son he saith, Thy throne, O God, is forever and ever; a scepter of righteousness is the scepter of thy kingdom. Thou hast loved righteousness, and hated iniquity; therefore God, even thy God, hath anointed thee with the oil of gladness, above thy fellows. And, thou, Lord, in the beginning hast laid the foundation of the earth; and the heavens are the works of thine hands.

Is it not the only God who alone is King of kings, and Lord of lords, and who reigns in heaven and on earth? Most assuredly. And the Spirit speaks in Revelation saying that Christ is King of kings and Lord of lords. Christ Himself says, All power is given unto me in heaven and on earth. Paul says, That at the name of Jesus every knee should bow, of things in heaven, and things in earth, and things under the earth, and that every tongue should confess that Jesus Christ is Lord.

Is it not the only God who saith, I the Lord, the first and the last; I am he? And Christ says in Revelation, I am Alpha and Omega; the beginning and the end, saith the Lord, which is, and which was, and which is to come; the Almighty. And, Fear not; I am the first and the last; I am he that liveth and was dead; and behold, I am alive for evermore.

Is not He who trieth the hearts and reins, the one and only God? Without doubt. And Christ says in Revelation, All the churches shall know that I am he which searcheth the reins and hearts; and I will give unto every one of you according to his works.

Is it not the only God whom only we should serve and worship? Yes. And Christ says through John, That all men should honor the Son, even as they honor the Father. Of the divine ministry Paul says, He that in these things serveth Christ, is acceptable to God, and Let a man so account of us as of the ministers of Christ.

Paul, a servant of Christ—so we read in the opening sentence of all his epistles. Of worship Luke says that when Christ had ascended to heaven they worshiped Him and returned to Jerusalem. Also Stephen in his last prayer says, Lord Jesus, receive my spirit. Paul also says, Let all the angels of God worship him. The murderer on the cross prays, Lord, remember me when thou comest into thy kingdom.

Is it not the only God which is true; and every man a liar? Ah, yes. And the prophet says, There was not any deceit found in his mouth. Christ Himself says, I am the truth. To this end was I born, and for this cause came I into the world, that I should bear witness unto the truth.

Can any forgive sins and grant everlasting life except the only and eternal God? Oh, no! Yet Christ says, Know that the Son of man hath power on earth to forgive sins; and to the sinful woman, Thy sins are forgiven. Also, I give unto them eternal life.

Should we believe in any but the one and only God? Not at all. Yet Christ says, He that believeth on me hath everlasting life. Ye believe in God, believe also in me.

Is not the only God judge of all the world who will raise the dead and at the last day sit in judgment? Assuredly. But Christ says, For as the Father raiseth up the dead, and quickeneth them, even so the Son quickeneth whom he will. He was ordained of God to be the judge of the living and the dead. And at His coming He will judge and sentence.

Now then, dear brethren, since the throne of Christ is an eternal throne, and since the Scriptures are not ashamed to confess Him to be God, and also testify that He formed heaven and earth, that He has all power in heaven and on earth, and that He is the first and last; that He tries the hearts and reins; that it is He whom we should serve and worship; that He is the truth, the One who forgives sins and bestows eternal life, in whom we must believe and who at the last day will raise us from the dead and judge us as has been said, so it follows of necessity that Christ Jesus must be true God with the Father. For God does not give His glory to another. These are all glories, honors, works, and attributes which belong to no one in heaven nor upon earth, except to the only eternal and true God. This all those who are taught of God must freely admit and confess.

Dear brethren, we believe and confess Christ Jesus with His heavenly Father to be truly God; and that because of the plain testimony of the holy prophets, evangelists, and apostles, as we may learn from the following and other Scriptures. Isaiah says, Unto us a child is born, unto us a son is given; and the government shall be upon his shoulder; and his name shall be called Wonderful, Counsellor, The mighty God, The everlasting Father, The Prince of Peace. Isa. 9:6. Again, Say unto the cities of Judah, Behold your God! Behold, the Lord God will come with a strong hand, and his arm shall rule for him! Behold, his reward is with him and his work before him; he shall feed his flock like a shepherd; he shall gather the lambs with his arm, and carry them in his bosom, and shall gently lead those that are with young. Isa. 40:9-11. Read also Ezek. 34:11.

Jeremiah said, Behold, the days come, saith the Lord, that I will raise up unto David a righteous Branch, and a king shall reign and prosper, and shall execute judgment and justice in the earth. In his days Judah shall be saved, and Israel shall dwell safely; and this is his name whereby he shall be called, THE LORD (a name of four letters in Hebrew), WHO IS OUR RIGHTEOUSNESS.

Micah says, But thou Bethlehem Ephratah, though thou be little among the thousands of Judah, yet out of thee shall he come forth unto me that is to be ruler in Israel; whose goings forth have been of old, from everlasting. Mic. 5:2. Read also Heb. 7:3, 4; Isa. 44:6; Rev. 1:8; 22:13. John says, In the beginning was the Word, and the Word was God. John 1:1. The Lord said unto Thomas, Reach hither thy finger, and behold my hands; and reach hither thy hand, and thrust it into my side; and be not faithless, but believing. And Thomas answered and said unto him, My Lord, and my God! Jesus said unto him, Thomas, because thou hast seen me, thou hast believed; blessed are they that have not seen, and yet have believed.

Paul says, Take heed therefore unto yourselves, and to all the flock, over which the Holy Ghost hath made you overseers, to feed the church of God, which he hath purchased with his own blood. Whose are the fathers, and of whom, according to the flesh, Christ came, who is over all, God blessed for ever. Again, God was in Christ, reconciling the world unto himself. Read also John 14; Col. 2; I Tim. 3. Again, Who being in the form of God, thought it not robbery to be equal with God. But made himself of no reputation, and took upon him the form of a servant.

John says, We know that the Son of God is come, and hath given us an understanding, that we may know him that is true; and we are in him that is true, even in his Son Jesus Christ. This is the true God and eternal life. Besides, read the whole Gospel of John, and I Cor. 10:15; Eph. 4; Heb. 1:3; 7:11; 12; 13; and you will by the grace of God find a firm and sure foundation.

Brethren, here you have the incomprehensible birth of Christ, His divine glory, operation, and power, and a number of precious and plain testimonies of the holy prophets, evangelists, and apostles, all of whom with an invincible power testify and point out with such clearness the true, incomprehensible deity of our Lord Jesus Christ. I am convinced and doubt not the least that a pious, humble, God-fearing conscience will be satisfied with this and will not pry into this incomprehensible depth any further. And if any one desires to search and dispute further, to him I predict that he will surely search and dispute all his lifetime, and yet never have a settled mind nor a firm foundation. I warn you, dear brethren, beware.

As we have now indicated and confessed our faith in confession of the true deity of Jesus Christ; so we will also by the grace of God set forth in few words our faith and confession of the Holy Ghost. Let the God-fearing judge. We believe and confess the Holy Ghost to be a true, real, and personal Holy Ghost, as the fathers called Him; and that in a divine fashion, even as the Father is a true Father and the Son a true Son. Which Holy Ghost is a mystery to all mankind, incomprehensible, ineffable, and indescribable( as we have shown above of the Father and the Son) ; divine with His divine attributes, proceeding from the Father through the Son, although He ever remains with God and in God, and is never separated from the being of the Father and the Son.

And the reason that we confess Him to be such a true and real Holy Spirit is because we are brought to this by the Scriptures, for He descended upon Christ at the baptism in the bodily shape of a dove, and appeared unto the apostles as cloven tongues like as of fire; because we are baptized in His name as well as in the name of the Father and of the Son; because the prophets have prophesied through Him, performed miracles, had dreams and saw visions; because He is a dispenser of the gifts of God, and that (take note) according to His own will. He moved Zacharias, the son of Barachiah; He moved John the Baptist while yet in his mother's womb, and He said to Simeon, That he should not see death before he had seen the Lord's Christ. The Holy Ghost said, Separate me Barnabas and Paul. And to Peter, Behold, three men seek thee. He guides us into all truth; He justifies us. He cleanses, sanctifies, reconciles, comforts, reproves, cheers, and assures us. He testifies with our spirit that we are the children of God. This Spirit all they receive who believe on Christ. Paul admonishes us not to grieve Him. Whosoever sins against the Spirit, says Christ, unto him it shall not be forgiven. David desired that God might not take from him this Spirit, for all that have not this Spirit are not of Christ.

Dear brethren, from these plain Scriptures, testimonies, and references, and a great many other texts which are too lengthy to mention and which may be found in abundance in the Scriptures, we believe the Holy Spirit to be the true, essential Holy Spirit of God, who adorns us with His heavenly and divine gifts, and through His influence, according to the good pleasure of the Father, frees us from sin, gives us boldness, and makes us cheerful, peaceful, pious, and holy. And so we believe and confess before God, before His angels, before all our brethren, and before all the world, that these three names, activities, and powers, namely, the Father, the Son, and the Holy Ghost (which the fathers called three persons, by which they meant the three, true, divine beings) are one incomprehensible, indescribable, Almighty, holy, only, eternal, and sovereign God. As John says, There are three that bear record in heaven, the Father, the Word, and the Holy Ghost; and these three are one. Read also Matt. 28:19; Mark 1:8; Luke 3:8; John 14:16; 15:26; I Cor. 12:11.

And although they are three, yet in deity, will, power, and works they are one, and can no more be separated from each other than the sun, brightness, and warmth. For the one cannot exist without the other. Yet all is incomprehensible from the incomprehensible Father, even as the brightness and heat of the sun. The one must exist with the other, or else the whole divinity is denied. For all the Father does and has wrought from the beginning, He works through His Son, in the power of the holy and eternal Spirit. This Son does not work without the Father and the Holy Spirit. Neither does the Holy Spirit do anything without the Father and the Son. Therefore the one must remain with the other, or else there must be an imperfect God. For if we deny the deity of Christ, or the true existence of the Holy Ghost, then we fashion a counterfeit God unto ourselves, a God who is without wisdom, power, life, light, truth, Word, and without the Holy Spirit.

Brethren, understand all this in a divine and spiritual sense, and not in a human or carnal manner. Then you will be satisfied with the plain, clear, simple testimony of the prophets, evangelists, and apostles concerning this deep mystery. Let every one see to it with fear and trembling, lest he put his hand to the consuming fire.

Most dearly beloved brethren and sisters in Christ Jesus, mark well the following. Since the eternal God is such a great and terrible God as you have read; since Christ was thus born of the Father as has been said, and since the attributes of God so richly abound in Christ; and since the prophets, evangelists, and apostles so emphatically declare, preach, and teach Him to be God; and since the Scriptures so abundantly teach and testify of the Holy Spirit and confess that the eternal Father with His eternal Son and Holy Spirit in their divine being, power, glory, and sovereignty are incomprehensible, ineffable, and indescribable, as may be plainly understood from the cited Scriptures (for it is all Spirit and God and therefore beyond human wisdom and insight) ; therefore it is that I pray and admonish all my beloved brethren and companions in Christ Jesus, in the name of all that men can pray to, not to allow and consent to glosses, innovations, nor human explanations, no matter by whom, concerning this incomprehensible majesty. Ever fear, ye who seek God, lest with all your powers, by such ambitious thoughts and human conjecture, you make yourselves guilty concerning the incomprehensible God, who makes foolish all human wisdom contrary to Him. Lest through your vain searching and pondering of such unfathomable matters, you fall into His hands, and at the last be consumed by the fire of His wrath.

Brethren, as for me, I confess that I would rather die than to believe and teach my brethren a single word or letter concerning the Father, the Son, and the Holy Ghost (before God I lie not) contrary to the plain testimony of the Word of God which so clearly points out and teaches through the prophets, evangelists, and apostles.

O my pious, God-fearing, faithful brethren. Let us all be thus minded together; then the desolated cities may be rebuilt; the strong may remain firm; the wavering be strengthened; and peace, love, and unity be restored. I know very certainly that if any one wants to go further than we testify and admonish here from the Word of God, he will lose his way, mount too high, deviate to one side. He will miss the road and will act no more intelligently than he who would try to pour the river Rhine or Meuse into a quart bottle. But those who abide simply and humbly by the Word of God—the witnessing, prophetical, evangelical, and apostolic Word—and firmly believe it, although they do not and cannot fully comprehend it; and guard against all human investigation, disputations, glosses, explanations, perversions, and conjecture in these incomprehensible depths; these will in all temptations stand firmly by the grace of God, and walk all their lives before their God with calm, glad hearts.

I sincerely wish that all the brethren were of like mind with me in this respect, for I have been averse to human sophistry and glosses for fifteen years and still am. I expect to remain so, and by the help of God, to take heed not to offer the blood of the Lord together with leaven. I desire to enter into the sanctuary of God, that is, into His holy church, with the unleavened bread of the pure Word of God, spread with the oil of the Spirit.

O brethren, if only all they who are called brethren were thus minded with me, how soon would the sad afflicted hearts find comfort and gladness and the divided restless minds, unity and peace. O Lord Jesus, have mercy upon the poor, afflicted sheep, and let every hungry and thirsty soul find Thy green pastures and clear waters. Amen.

Dear brethren and sisters in Christ Jesus, receive this with the same mind in which I have written it. Read it plainly among the brethren, and understand it in a Christian manner, and beware, beware, yes, beware, of all disputation, discord, and division. This I desire from my inmost soul for the Lord's sake. The sincere, evangelical peace be with all my beloved brethren and sisters in Christ Jesus. Amen.

*September 9, 1550*                                    MENNO SIMONS

*Editorial Note:* Read also the footnotes to the letter on pages 1036, 1037 of this volume: a letter which was evidently written to accompany this tract on the holy Trinity.    J.C.W.

# Confession of the Distressed Christians

*Bekentenisse van der rechtveerdighmakinge*

# 1552

*For other foundation can no man*
*lay than that is laid, which is Jesus Christ.*

I Corinthians 3:11

# Introduction

In the year 1552 Menno Simons made a determined effort once more to attempt to alleviate or terminate the persecution of his brotherhood. He wrote a group of four books, the exact order of which is not known with certainty. His positive work, *Confession of the Distressed Christians,* goes over much of the same ground covered in earlier works: I. Justification; II. On Hearing the Preachers [of the State Churches]; III. Baptism; IV. Infant Baptism; V. The Lord's Supper; VI. The Supper of the Preachers; VII. The Swearing of Oaths; and VIII. Conclusion.

In his new treatment of justification Menno sets forth with great beauty and clarity the grace of God in the salvation of Christian believers. This work ought to settle once for all the queer notion that because the Anabaptists were vigorous in their demands for a life of earnest Christian discipleship, they were therefore unclear on grace and justification.

In the original, the title of this work is: *A Fundamental and Clear Confession of the Poor and Distressed Christians concerning Justification, The Preachers, Baptism, The Lord's Supper, The Swearing of Oaths—Things Because of Which We Are Grievously Hated, Slandered, and Belied—Derived from the Word of God.*

The other three works of 1552 are: *A Pathetic Supplication to All Magistrates, Brief Defense to All Theologians,* and *Reply to False Accusations.* A separate introduction will be prepared for each of these four books of 1552. All four were first published in the Eastern dialect of the Baltic coastal region, and the first three of the four appeared bound as one book: *Confession, Supplication, and Brief Reply,* in 1552.

In the *Opera Omnia Theologica* of 1681 the *Confession* is found fol. 457-73; and in the *Complete Works* of 1871, Part II, pages 257-76.

J. C. W.

# Confession of the Distressed Christians

# 1552

‣•‣•‣•‣•‣•‣•‣•‣•‣•‣•‣•‣•‣•‣•‣•‣•‣•‣•‣•‣•‣•‣•‣•‣•‣•‣•‣•‣•‣•‣•‣•‣•‣•‣•‣•‣•‣•‣•‣•‣•‣•‣•‣•‣•‣•

## *Salutation*

I sincerely wish to all those who shall see, read, or hear this our *Confession* a true knowledge of the divine Word, a sound and fruitful faith in Christ Jesus, an unfeigned and fervent love, a pious and penitent and irreproachable life in God our heavenly Father through Christ Jesus our Lord, who has loved us and cleansed us of our sins with His blood. To Him be the honor, praise, kingdom, power, and glory, forever and ever. Amen.

Christ says, Whosoever heareth these sayings of mine, and doeth them, I will liken him unto a wise man which built his house upon a rock, and the rain descended, and the floods came, and the winds blew, and beat upon that house; and it fell not, for it was founded upon a rock. And every one that heareth these sayings of mine, and doeth them not, shall be likened unto a foolish man, which built his house upon the sand; and the rain descended, and the floods came, and the winds blew, and beat upon that house; and it fell; and great was the fall of it. Matt. 7:24-27.

## *Preface*

Noble reader, the reason for this writing is this. We and our ancestors for many centuries have sought the light with darkness, the truth with falsehood, life with death, and the way with deceivers.[1] We have strayed also like sheep without a shepherd. Alas, there was none who pointed us to the way of life and led us into the pasture of the Lord. The accursed doctrine of Antichrist had drawn the shameful smoke of deceit from the bottomless pit; had obscured the glorious dazzling of the divine Word. The just judgment of God for sin was come upon this reckless world so that alas there was neither true doctrine nor true knowledge of God and Christ, nor faith, nor baptism, nor Supper, nor ban in accordance with God's Word, nor love nor

---

[1] Menno is characterizing Roman Catholicism in terms of his own spiritual darkness which he endured while a priest. *Ed.*

righteousness found among men. Of it very little is found as yet. All over the world we find false teachers, hypocritical deceivers, and enemies of the cross, who diligently serve their own bellies, who by their tantalizing, erring doctrine proclaim peace to those who know of no peace and strengthen the hands of the wicked so that none converts himself from his wickedness, as the prophet complains.

Yea, they have carried on their wrangling, writing, and preaching so far that the Lord's express ordinances of baptism, Supper, and ban as commanded by Him, and as taught, practiced, and testified to by His holy apostles, they not only consider heretical and false, but they hatefully revile and persecute those who keep them, as may be plainly seen. They have instituted a new baptism unknown to Scripture which is not so bitter to the flesh as the baptism of Christ; a new Supper which is a false comfort to the ungodly; also a "ban" which is nothing but the destruction of the pious, and which cannot be harmonized with anything reasonable, not to say with love and truth. But by it if men are not banished from city and country, then they are sentenced to the stake or water. Nor is it practiced sparingly upon the pious in many places.

In short, they have misled the common people from God, have estranged them by their easygoing doctrine and false sacraments, and have led them into such unbelief and heathenish life that all heaven must be sad and ashamed thereat. Tell me, reasonable reader, who can declare the accursed and ungodly pride, pomp, adultery, fornication, idolatry, Roman and Spanish abominations, unfaithfulness, fraud, avarice, usury, unrighteousness, fast living, drunkenness, hatred, envy, murder, thefts, robbery, plunder, the burning at the stake, betrayal, bloodshed; the indecent, obscene words; terrible lying, the swearing by the ills and pains, the suffering and the wounds of Christ, the sacraments, etc., which are found with this wicked, reckless world. Yet they want to be the church of Christ. Everything is in such a condition of ruin that we may well say with the prophet Hosea, There is no truth, nor mercy, nor knowledge of God in the land; but swearing, and lying, and killing, and stealing, and committing adultery; they break out, and blood toucheth blood. With Jeremiah, A wonderful and horrible thing is committed in the land. With John, The whole world lieth in wickedness; and with the Apocalypse that their sins have reached unto heaven. O faithful reader, it is worse than I can express. Any reasonable person may feel this with hands and feet.

The brightness of the sun has not shone for many years; heaven and earth have been as copper and iron; the brooks and springs have not run, nor the dew descended from heaven; the beautiful trees and verdant fields have been dry and wilted—spiritually, I mean. However, in these latter days the gracious, great God by the rich treasures of His love has again opened the windows of heaven and let drop the dew of His divine Word, so that the earth once more as of yore produces its green branches and plants of righteousness which bear fruit unto the Lord and glorify His great and adorable name. The holy Word and sacraments of the Lord rise up again from the ashes by means of which the blasphemous deceit and abominations of the learned ones are made manifest. Therefore all the infernal gates rouse themselves, they rave and rant and with such subtle deceit, blasphemous falsehood, and bloody tyranny that if the strong God did not show forth His gracious power, no man could be saved. But they will never wrest from Him those that are His own.

Since then they so fearfully fight against the truth, weigh out dross for silver and besides lay to our charge all manner of shame, blasphemy, deceit, and violation (as they did from the beginning to all those who fear the Lord), therefore we are forced by the true love of the divine Word and the salvation of your souls to explain briefly to you according to the Word of the Lord the sure divine doctrine and the pure, immutable truth concerning justification, preachers, baptism, the Supper, and swearing of oaths, things for which we are so roundly hated and slandered, and especially by the learned ones. We do this that you may thereby acknowledge what the holy Scriptures teach in regard to these articles and to show whether we distressed people are such good-for-nothing, ungodly people as the learned ones incessantly cry and inform the common people. If you have ears to hear, then hear the Word of the Lord; and if you have understanding hearts, take heed and follow the truth.

## I. JUSTIFICATION

Honorable reader, it is plain and manifest from Scripture that Adam and Eve, our common parents, were in the beginning created after the image of God by God through Christ; pure, good, sinless, righteous, and immortal, as the Scriptures teach. They remained pure and righteous as long as they did not sin against their Creator's word and commandment. God had said unto them, Of the tree of knowledge of good and evil thou shalt not eat; for in the day that thou eatest thereof, thou shalt surely die. This also came true, for as soon as Adam and Eve, deceived by the serpent, ate the forbidden fruit, they became impure, unrighteous, subject to corruption, of a sinful nature, yes, children of death and of the devil. And by their disobedience they lost their sonship and the purity in which they were created. They would forever have remained with all their descendants in sin under the curse and servitude of death and the devil, if God the merciful Father whose love endures forever, had not again comforted and raised them up by the promise of Christ whom He promised to send to overcome the serpent, for whose sake He would be gracious unto them, forgive their transgression, show them mercy and favor, on the condition that they believed this.

When Adam and Eve heard these glad tidings of grace, the Gospel of peace, from the mouth of God, they joyfully accepted and believed it as the immutable truth of God, fondly clung to it, and comforted themselves with it as a sure foundation of salvation. And so Adam and Eve were again accepted of God through Christ Jesus and were justified and delivered from the eternal death and curse. For they according to the promise of God believed and trusted in Him and looked for Him to appear as the Conqueror, Saviour, and means of grace to eternal reconciliation.

Had they despised this means, and had they not accepted it by faith, they would have remained in the power of eternal death. This is incontrovertible, as Christ Himself says, He that believeth not, is condemned already; again, John the Baptist says, He that believeth on the Son, hath everlasting life; and he that believeth not the Son, shall not see life; but the wrath of God abideth on him. John 3:18, 36. Just as Adam and Eve were bitten and poisoned by the Satanic serpent and became of sinful nature, and subject to eternal death if God had not again accepted them in grace through Christ Jesus, so we, their descendants, are also born of sinful nature, poisoned by the serpent, inclined to evil, and by nature children of hell, of the devil, and everlasting death. And we cannot be delivered therefrom (we speak of those who have come to years of discretion and to actual sin) unless we accept Christ Jesus the only and eternal means of grace by true and unfeigned faith, and with the eyes of the Spirit look upon the brazen serpent which is erected for us miserable sinners by God our heavenly Father, as an emblem of salvation. For without Him there is no help for our souls, no reconciliation nor peace; but only condemnation, wrath, and eternal death, as was said before.

Those who accept this announced Christ by a true faith which, according to the doctrine of Paul, was given us of the Father unto wisdom, righteousness, sanctification, and deliverance, are in a state of grace for Christ's sake and have God as their Father; for by faith they are born of Him. He forgives them all their sins; has compassion on all their human shortcomings and weaknesses. He turns them from the curse, wrath, and eternal death. He accepts them as His beloved children, and grants them Christ Jesus together with all His merits, fastings, prayers, tears, sufferings, pain, cross, blood, and death. Besides this, He grants also His Spirit, inheritance, kingdom, glory, joy, and life. And this we say, not by our own merits and works, but by grace through Christ Jesus. As Paul says, God, who is rich in mercy, for his great love wherewith he loved us, even when we were dead in sins, hath quickened us together with Christ (by grace ye are saved); and hath raised us up together, and made us to sit in heavenly places in Christ Jesus; that in the ages to come he might show the exceeding riches of his grace, in his kindness toward us through Christ Jesus. For by grace are ye saved through faith; and that not of yourselves; it is the gift of God; not of works, lest any man should boast. For we are his workmanship, created in Christ Jesus unto good works, which God hath before ordained that we should walk in them. Eph. 2:4-10.

You see, kind reader, we do not seek our salvation in works, words, or sacraments as do the learned ones, although they accuse us of that very thing, but we seek them only in Christ Jesus and in no other means in heaven or on earth. We rejoice exclusively in this only means. We trust by the grace of God to continue thus unto death.

But that we abhor carnal works and desire to conform ourselves to His Word and commandment, according to our weakness, we do because He so taught and commanded us. For whosoever does not walk according to His doctrine, proves in fact that he does not believe on Him or know Him and that he is not in the communion of the saints.

All those who accept this proffered means of divine grace, Jesus Christ, with believing hearts, enclose Him in the treasure box of their minds. They believe and confess that their sins are forgiven for the sake of His sacrifice, death, and blood; that nevermore His wrath and damnation will be upon them; that He accepts them as His dear sons and daughters, and gives them eternal life. All such become joyous and glad in the Spirit and give thanks to God with renewed hearts, for the power of faith quickens and changes them into newness of life, and they walk by the gift of grace in the Holy Spirit in the power of their new faith, according to the measure of their faith, in obedience to their God who has shown them such great love. They diligently watch lest they fall from grace and the favor of God by willfulness and wickedness. They acknowledge by the Scriptures that Adam and Eve, the antediluvian world, Sodom and Gomorrah, and the fathers in the wilderness were severely punished by God on account of their sins; that the wages of sin is death; and that, also, Christ Jesus, the innocent Lamb of God who knew no sin, endured such humiliation and pain because of our sinfulness.

Since then they believe God's Word which says, To be carnally minded is death, If you live after the flesh, ye shall die, and Adulterers, fornicators, drunkards, the avaricious, the proud, and all liars shall not inherit the kingdom of God, and since they believe that He will save none contrary to His Word; that He will judge in accordance with His Word, that He is the truth and cannot lie, as the Scriptures testify; therefore it is that they sincerely fear the Lord, and by that fear die unto their flesh, crucify their lusts and desires, and shun and abhor the unclean, ungodly works which are contrary to the Word of the Lord.

Besides this, they acknowledge the abundant grace, favor, and love of God toward us as shown in Christ Jesus, and therefore they love their God in return, for He first loved us as John says. And they are ready by this love to obey in their weakness His holy Word, will, commandments, counsel, doctrine, and ordinances, according to the talent received. They show indeed that they believe, that they are born of God and are spiritually minded; that they lead a pious, unblamable life before all men. They have themselves baptized according to the commandment of the Lord as proof that they bury their sins in the death of Christ and seek to walk with Him in newness of life. They break the bread of peace with their dear brethren as proof and testimony that they are one in Christ and His holy church, and that they have, or know no other means of grace and remission of their sins, neither in heaven nor on earth than the innocent flesh and blood of our Lord Jesus Christ alone, which He once by His eternal Spirit in obedience to the Father sacrificed and shed upon the cross for us poor sinners. They walk in all love and mercy and serve their neighbors. In short, they regulate themselves in their weakness to all words, commandments, ordinances, Spirit, rule, example, and measure of Christ, as the Scripture teaches; for they are in Christ and Christ is in them; and therefore they live no longer in the old life of sin after the earthly Adam (weakness excepted), but in the new life of righteousness which comes by faith, after the second and heavenly Adam, Christ, as Paul says, I do not now live, but Christ liveth in me; and the life which I now live in the flesh, I live by the faith of the Son of God, who loved me, and gave himself for me. Gal. 2:20. Christ says, He who loves me keeps my commandments. John 14:15.

Think not, beloved reader, that we boast of being perfect and without sins. Not at all. As for me I confess that often my prayer is mixed with sin and my righteousness with unrighteousness; for by the grace of God I feel, if I but observe the anointing which is in me, when I compare my weak nature to Christ and His commandment, what kind of flesh I have inherited from Adam. If God should judge us according to our deserts and not according to His great goodness and mercy, then I confess with the holy David that no man could stand before His judgment. Ps. 143:2. Therefore it should be far from us that we should comfort ourselves with anything but the grace of God through Christ Jesus. For He it is and He alone and none other who has perfectly fulfilled the righteousness required by God. We are also aware by the grace of God that all saints from the beginning have lamented the corruption of their flesh, as may be seen from the writings of Moses, David, Job, Isaiah, Paul, James, and John.

For Christ's sake we are in grace; for His sake we are heard; and for His sake our faults and failings which are committed against our will are remitted. For it is He who stands between His Father and His imperfect children, with His perfect righteousness, and with His innocent blood and death, and intercedes for all those who believe on Him and who strive by faith in the divine Word to turn from evil, follow that which is good, and who sincerely desire with Paul that they may attain the perfection which is in Christ. Phil. 3:12.

Notice, my dear reader, that we do not believe nor teach that we are to be saved by our merits and works as the envious assert without truth. We are to be saved solely by grace through Christ Jesus, as has been said before.

By grace the human race was created through Christ Jesus when as yet it was not.

By grace it was again accepted through Christ when it was lost.

By grace Christ was sent to us of the Father. John 3:34.

By grace He has sought the lost sheep, taught repentance and remission of sins, and died for us when we were yet ungodly and enemies.

By grace it is given us to believe.

By grace the Holy Ghost was given us in the name of Jesus. John 14:16.

In short, by grace eternal life is given us through Christ Jesus.

This, dear reader, is our faith and confession in the matter in hand. We cannot obtain salvation, grace, reconciliation, nor peace of the Father otherwise than through Christ Jesus. As He Himself says, No man cometh unto the Father but by me. Peter also says, There is none other name under heaven given among men, whereby we must be saved, than the name of Jesus; and that all those who accept this grace in Christ, preached by the Gospel and accepted by a firm faith, and cordially adhered to by power of the Holy Spirit through faith, become new men, born of God. Such men are changed in their hearts, renewed and of a different mind; yes, transferred from Adam unto Christ. They walk in newness of life as obedient children in the grace which is manifested unto them. For they are renewed, have become poor in spirit, gentle, merciful, compassionate, peaceful, patient, hungry and thirsty after righteousness. They strive after eternal life and with good works. For they are believing, born of God, are in Christ and Christ in them; they are partakers of His Spirit and nature, and live according to the Word of the Lord by the power of Christ which is in them. This is according to Scripture to be really believing, to be Christian, to be in Christ and Christ in us.

All those who disregard this preached grace and do not accept Christ Jesus by faith; who reject His holy Word, will, commandments, and ordinances; who hate and persecute; who willfully live according to their lusts, these are all through. It will avail them nothing before the Lord to boast of their faith, new creature, Christ's grace, death, and blood; for they do not believe; they remain in their first birth, namely, in their earthly, corrupted nature, impenitent, carnally minded, yes, utterly without the Spirit, Word, and Christ. Therefore they are children of death as Scripture teaches, for they know not Christ in whom is life. As John says, This is the record, that God hath given to us eternal life, and that this life is in his Son. He that hath the Son hath life; and he that hath not the Son of God hath not life. I John 5:11, 12.

Behold, worthy reader, this is our position and confession of justification as you have here read. Judge for yourselves whether the preachers do rightly when they lie so bluntly saying that we expect to be saved by our merits and works; and that we boast to be without sin.

May the Lord forgive them that they so fiendishly invent such shameful lies. Oh, these miserable men! Would that they would take to heart that the backbiters, slanderers, and liars are of the devil and worthy of death; that God abhors all liars; that they shall have no part in His kingdom; and that a lying mouth killeth the soul.

This, I say, is our position, and by the grace of God it will ever remain that. For we know truly and confess that it is the invincible word and truth of the Lord. Therefore we testify before you and all the world that we do not in the first place agree with those who teach and introduce a mere historical faith which is dead, which knows no conversion, spirit, and fruit. In the second place, that we do not agree that we can be saved by our own merits and works, for reasons above stated.

May the merciful, gracious Father, through His beloved Son Jesus Christ our Lord, grant us all the gift of His Holy Spirit, that we may sincerely believe and confess this before-mentioned grace in and through Christ; and that we may walk and abide therein firmly and faithfully unto the end, to the eternal praise and glory of God. Amen.

## II. ON HEARING THE PREACHERS

It is a well-known fact, kind reader, that on account of this article, principally by the learned ones, we are so hated and persecuted that everyone cries against us and complains that we do not want to hear God's Word. Therefore we are forced, since it concerns the praise of God and the salvation of our souls, to indicate the reason according to the Word of God (which we would gladly omit if we were not required by Scripture) why we do not hear them and conscientiously dare not listen to them, on account of which we have to suffer so much pain and tribulation. Jesus said to Nicodemus, Verily, verily, I say unto thee, Except a man be born again, he cannot see the kingdom of God. Paul also said, If any man have not the Spirit of Christ, he is none of his. And John says, Whosoever transgresseth, and abideth not in the doctrine of Christ, hath not God.

Worthy reader, consider the Word of the Lord. That the preachers of the world are not born again, have not the Spirit of Christ, and do not abide in His Word, their fruits abundantly prove; for it is evident that they falsify the Word of the Lord sadly, and walk according to the flesh, as will be clearly shown.

First, I am convinced that you never saw the preachers who are one with their church ever convert an avaricious person from his avarice; a drunkard from his drunkenness, or a proud person from his pride and pomp— plainly works of the flesh, and according to Scripture punishable with eternal death if not repented of. Inasmuch as they convert none, as it appears, therefore it is plain that their doctrine is nothing but vain prattle without point or power. The whole wide world proves this by its bad conduct.

Secondly, the careless people are sustained and strengthened in their unbelief and willful, carnal life by their easygoing doctrine, sacraments, and unrestrained life. They preach and tell you, there are none that can truly believe; we are all sinners, therefore none can rightly keep the commandments of God. In your baptism you became a regenerated Christian and received the Holy Ghost. And all this in spite of the fact that you had not heard the Word, that you had no faith in Christ Jesus, nor knowledge of good or evil, nor had you any change or renewal of heart, nor could you have because you were an innocent child. You hear their absolutions and receive their bread, as if all were well with you; and you do not realize that you are as yet an impenitent, avaricious, proud, drunken, unclean, envious, and idolatrous man. And there are more such false consolations. We will leave it to you to judge whether these are not rightly called preachers of peace who make arm cushions and pillows for the people and preach such things as are pleasing to hear.

Inasmuch as none are made better by their doctrine and sacraments but are more and more comforted in unrighteousness, therefore it must be acknowledged that they strengthen you in your vice, shut unto you the kingdom of heaven, lead you into the ditch, and are robbers and murderers of your souls.

O good reader, they have so bewitched the ignorant people who so gladly walk upon the broad road with their easygoing doctrine that we may well exclaim with Jeremiah, No man repented him of his wickedness, saying, What have I done? Or who bothers about a pious, penitent, or godly life? What is worse, they have gone so far that alas, they must be called merit-men and heaven-stormers who with faithful hearts hear, believe, fear, love, and according to the measure of their faith, obey the Word of the Lord. Behold, thus entirely has the smoke of the pit darkened the sun and sky. Rev. 9:2.

As to their sacraments, it is manifest that they do not have the sacraments of Christ, but invented abominations and idol worship in a semblance of the Lord's sacraments. For they baptize irrational infants of which Christ has not taught nor commanded a single syllable in the whole New Testament. Yet they are called Christians, notwithstanding that such baptized persons generally walk in perverse ways all their lives and not only do not confess Christ Jesus together with His holy Word, but also hate and oppose them.

Again their Supper is said to be the Lord's flesh and blood, while the Scriptures at many places testify that He ascended up to heaven and is seated at the right hand of His Father, while common sense teaches us, to say nothing of the Scriptures, that He cannot be masticated with tooth nor digested by the stomach. Besides it is distributed by some for the remission of sins. Behold, they have so entirely forsaken the Lord who has purchased them with His blood that they have changed His glory and honor into such a weak creature. If this is not rightfully called serving Baal and molding calves you may judge according to the Scriptures.

Lastly, how they conform their lives to the doctrine of Paul you may best deduce from their fruits and life. They do not walk in humility of heart before the Lord; their appearance and names prove that. They suffer themselves to be greeted as lords and masters; notwithstanding it is forbidden by the mouth of the Lord. Tell me, good reader, did you ever hear or read that the holy apostles and prophets aspired to such high, vain names as do the learned ones and the preachers of the world? The word Rabbi or Master was used of the ambitious scribes and Pharisees but not of the apostles and prophets. Nor do we read of Doctor Isaiah or Master Ezekiel or Lord Paul or Lord Peter. No, all those who have taught the Word of the Lord aright were in their time not honored with such high-sounding names. This I write that you may know that such ambitious, proud spirits can never rightly teach you the disdained word of the cross.

Besides also consider their avarice and solicitude for their stomachs. They do not preach nor render services without pay as if preaching and the cure of souls were no more than peddling, working at a trade, or making a living. Jude says, They honor the persons for the sake of profits. Where there are no benefices or incomes, there we find no preachers; but where these are plentiful, there no want of preachers will be experienced.

Some of them are usurers, some fornicators or adulterers, some greedy, liars, wrathful, proud, hateful, sensuous, vain, and lazy, some envious, bitter, cruel, treacherous, and rebellious toward all those who sincerely seek and fear God. In a word, if you know the Lord and His Word, then you must acknowledge that the best and most pious of them are far outside of Christ and His Word in regard to doctrine, sacraments, and also conduct.

Since all of them in doctrine, sacrament, and conduct are so flatly opposed to the Spirit, Word, and walk of the Lord, as appears, and since as Christ says, Every tree is known by its fruit, therefore it is plainly proved that they seek not the kingdom and glory of God, are not of the Lord, and have not God, as was said before.

If they seek not the kingdom of God as Christ speaks, how then can they rightly preach it and teach it to others?

If they have not the Spirit of the Lord and are not of Him, how then can they be true dispensers and servants of the spiritual office?

And if they have not God, how can they then rightly teach and point out His precious Word unto righteousness?

Inasmuch as it is well known to all persons taught of God that they do not know the kingdom of God and His glory; are not of the Lord, and have no God; therefore we conclude and that clearly that their vocation, calling, office, and service is not of God and His Word; but they are of the bottomless pit, and the dragon, and the beast. Rev. 9:2.

We mean this not of this one or that one but of all preachers in general who do not agree with the Word of God, no matter to which denomination or sect they belong. We do not judge according to anybody's boasting and appearance, but truthfully, according to doctrine, sacraments, fruit, and conduct. We are sure that the high and holy office which should be filled in the power of the Spirit can never be fulfilled by the avaricious; nor the proud and unrighteous, nor by the carnal and earthly minded, nor by drunken and sensuous persons whose God is their belly, as Paul says, nor by slanderers, nor by vain prattlers, nor by liars, nor men-pleasers, nor hirelings, nor by those who falsify, hate, and oppose the Spirit, will, Word, ordinance, and commandments of the Lord, and who are ignorant and blind in spiritual and evangelical matters. The Spirit and Word of God do not know such shepherds and teachers, but the Scripture labels them with many terrible names, and calls them rogues, blind watchmen, dumb dogs, blind leaders, consumers of souls, false flatterers, fools who inquire not after the Lord, preachers of peace of whom it is written, The prophets prophesy lies in my name; I sent them not, neither have I commanded them, neither spake I to them; they prophesy unto you false vision and divination, and a thing of nought, and the deceit of their heart. In a word, they are the teachers against whom the Word of the Lord has faithfully warned us. Read here and there in the prophets, particularly Jer. 23:13; Matt. 7:15; 15:14; 16:12; 24:11; Mark 12:38; Luke 12:1; 20:45.

Say, kind reader, did you in all your life ever read in the Scriptures of proud, avaricious, impure, lying, drunken, and idolatrous prophets, apostles, and shepherds who were pleasing unto the Lord? Or of such who to please men have falsified, changed, and abused the Word, ordinances, and commandments of the Lord? Or of such who said to cities, provinces, or towns, If you will provide for our keep, or if you will give us so much money or income, then we are willing to teach you the Word of the Lord. Oh, no, reader, no. This never was nor ever will be the policy of holy prophets, apostles, or servants of Christ. Of this we may be sure.

Teachers and preachers who are sent of God are born of God, are of godly nature, and are driven by the Spirit of the Lord; they are taught in the things of the kingdom of heaven; they are pressed into the vineyard of the Lord by the pure, unfeigned love of God and of their neighbors. They seek not the gifts of Balak, nor the tables of Jezebel. They seek the praise of God, and the salvation of their souls, and commend their physical needs to Him, who according to the word of His promise cares for the needs of all creatures upon earth.

They teach the Word of the law in the power of the Spirit to the exposure of sins and the rebuke of all flesh by the Gospel of grace, to the consolation, peace, and joy of all God-fearing, pious hearts who previously violated the Law, and trembled before the wrath and judgment of the Lord.

They reprove and shun all false doctrine, deceit, abuse, idolatry, and the willful careless life which is of the flesh, and is contrary to the Word of the Lord. They use baptism, Supper, ban, and all the ordinances of God as commanded them by the Word of the Lord, whether the outcome be life or death. They admonish lords and princes, learned or unlearned, men and women, as much as is possible if they are favored with a hearing; for the Word of God excuses neither emperor nor king, doctor nor master, rich nor poor. All must follow the Word of the Lord who would be saved.

Thus they live in the fear of the Lord; they die daily with the holy Paul for the sake of their brethren. They are pointed at by all the world; are slandered, persecuted, and deemed the essence and original substance of all scamps and scoundrels, even though they are ever ready to show their love and faithfulness to all, as was formerly the case with Jeremiah, Ezekiel, Zechariah, the son of Berechiah, John the Baptist, the apostles, and Christ Himself. And how the pious are at the present time thanked and rewarded for their services and love, the burning, the sword, the stake, and the wheel teach you.

The vocation, calling, doctrine, sacraments, and life of the preachers do not conform to this rule, and are therefore not of God, as was said. They, generally speaking, do not enter but to destroy, steal, and murder, as the Lord says. They falsify and pervert the precious Word and the holy sacraments to gratify their appetites. They reject the Word of God and introduce their own. They kill the souls which would have eternal life and promise life to those that will die eternal death. And all this for the sake of a handful of barley and a mouthful of bread, as the prophet says. They rule rather than serve; deceive rather than lead; corrupt rather than teach; destroy rather than cure; scatter rather than gather; shut the kingdom of heaven against men, and freely lead poor souls to hell.

Behold, therefore it is that we do not hear them, neither can we with good conscience hear them. For the Word of the Lord everywhere admonishes and commands us that we should be on our guard against them; flee and shun them, and not hear them, as was said before.

Judge now, kind reader, whether these reasons are not sufficient to turn one away from the preachers. We have not here presented to you philosophical words, garbled glosses, nor falsehood. We have pointed you to such facts as you may daily see and hear of your preachers. This is what our much beloved brethren and sisters in Christ Jesus, fellow partakers of the tribulation, kingdom, and obedience of Christ, the faithful saints and children of God, have for so many years boldly confessed and bravely asserted before this idolatrous, bloody world in great measure of poverty, by preaching and writing at the peril of life, property, blood, prison, banishment, water, fire, chains, gallows, wheels, and stake.

But preachers remain preachers and the world remains the world, and it seems they never change. They adhere to their idolatry so firmly that they do not suffer themselves to be converted.

Honored reader, we pray you for Christ's sake that you will rightly understand this our confession. Do not think that we have written this out of bitter feelings of hatred, inasmuch as it so openly reproves, reveals, and indicates the shame of the preachers. Oh, no. We testify before you and before the Lord who has created us that there is no hatred or bitterness in our hearts. We know and confess that they are works of the flesh and will be rewarded by death. We have written in purity of heart as before Him who tries the hearts and reins. We have done it to the service of you and all mankind no matter whether they may be our opponents or not, learned or unlearned; to the service of all those who seek the truth. We have done this that we may discover the secret of the Babylonian harlot, the hidden snares of the learned ones and such expositions, that you and all God-fearing hearts may have enough of the inhuman abominations and so understand the Word and truth of the Lord and with all your heart seek and obey the same, that you may be saved.

## III. BAPTISM

Concerning baptism we believe and confess that it is the very institution, word, ordinance, and command of the Lord; and therefore a holy, divine sacrament or sign by which faith and its powers, fruits, and mysteries are gloriously represented and portrayed when rightly administered according to the ordinance of God and not after our own fancy, namely: To the believing ones and not to irrational children.

That we teach and administer baptism on confession of faith is because of these reasons. First, because Christ Himself has commanded it thus. For He says, Go ye into all the world and preach the gospel to every creature; he that believeth and is baptized, shall be saved. Mark 16:15; Matt. 28:19.

Second, because the holy apostles have taught and administered it upon confession of faith, according to the commandment of God, and not to infants. Acts 2:38; 8:37; 10:47; 16:15; 18:8; 19:5.

Third, because the thing signified, that is, that which is represented by baptism, is found with the believing ones and not with infants. Rom. 6:4; Col. 2:12; I Cor. 12:13; Eph. 4:4; I Pet. 3:21; Gal. 3:27.

He who himself is Wisdom and Truth has Himself commanded that we should baptize believing ones. His faithful witnesses, the holy apostles, have not taught and administered otherwise than according to the commandment of the Lord. The thing signified is applicable only to the believing ones and not the infants. By the grace of the Lord we acknowledge from the Scriptures that Moses and the prophets, yes, the Father Himself, point us to Christ that we shall hear Him. According to the doctrine of Paul, no other foundation can be laid, no other Gospel preached than that which is preached to us by the apostles. Therefore we teach, receive, assert, and maintain baptism upon the confession of faith, at the cost of so much sorrow and misery, even at the peril of property and life; for we truly confess, and that in accordance with the Scripture, which is the true light of our feet, that it is the institution, word, ordinance, and commandment of the Lord.

## IV. INFANT BAPTISM

In regard to infant baptism we hold and confess, first, that it is an invented rite and human righteousness. For in all the New Testament there is not a word said or broached about baptizing infants by Christ nor by the apostles.

Second, that it is an infraction and perversion of the ordinance of Christ; for He has commanded that the Gospel should be preached and that those should be baptized who believe. Matt. 28:19; Mark 16:15. But here they baptize without divine command, without the preaching of the Word, without knowledge, faith, repentance, new life, and without all intelligence and knowledge, yet it is called by the learned a holy, glorious work and a Christian baptism and sacrament.

Third, that it is a vain comfort and boast to all the unrighteous. For although they do not understand the Word of God, do not know the truth, but lead a willful, carnal life, yet they boast themselves to be baptized Christians.

Since infant baptism is such a harmful superstition that destroys the Lord's baptism completely, and since the poor, blind world suffers itself to be misled and consoled therewith, and since besides there is connected with it such fearful blasphemy, hypocrisy, adjuration, exorcism, and abuse of the glorious name of God that a God-fearing heart may well be astounded thereat, therefore it is that we so strenuously oppose infant baptism and openly confess that it is not of God or of His Word but of Antichrist and of the bottomless pit.

Luther writes in a book on the education of man that that which is not commanded of God in religious matters of faith is by that token forbidden. Again, concerning the twelfth chapter of Genesis he says, That in such transactions we should not proceed without certain reasons from the divine Word.

Daniel writes, Worship without the Word of God is idolatry.

Philip Melanchthon in a book on the jurisdiction and the authority of the church says that all worship which is not instituted of God by His express Word is false and wrong, let it be glossed over ever so much.

Here Luther and Melanchthon have correctly expressed themselves according to the Scripture, although alas, they did not follow their own advice. If we read and consider the Scriptures, then we clearly find how pointedly God has commanded us that we should not institute a religion of our own choice, but that we should do as He has commanded. On account of self-righteousness and an invented religion, Israel was severely visited and punished of the Lord.

Now do not say, beloved reader, as the ignorant do, that we consign our children to condemnation because we do not suffer them to be baptized. Oh, no, for the Scripture does not tie the kingdom to words and water, but to the election and grace of the Father, in the merits of the death and blood of Christ.

Christ has promised the kingdom to small children without baptism. Matt. 19:14; Mark 10:14; Luke 18:16. On account of this promise we rejoice greatly and give thanks unto the Lord for the grace shown our children. Therefore, take heed and mistake not. For to tie the election, grace, favor, and kingdom of God to a few words, works, signs, and elements is quite contrary to the merits, death, blood, and the Word of the Lord; yes, open seduction, abomination, and idolatry.

## V. THE LORD'S SUPPER

Similarly we believe and confess concerning the Lord's holy Supper that it is a holy sacramental sign, instituted of the Lord Himself in bread and wine, and left to His disciples in remembrance of Him. Matt. 26; Mark 14; Luke 22; I Cor. 11. It was also taught and administered as such by the apostles among the brethren, according to the commandment of the Lord, in which in the first place the Lord's death is proclaimed. I Cor. 11. And it also serves as a remembrance how He offered His holy flesh and shed His precious blood for the remission of our sins. Matt. 26:27; Mark 14:24; Luke 22:19.

Second, it is an emblem of Christian love, of unity, and of peace in the church of Christ. Paul says, For we, being many, are one bread and one body; for we are all partakers of that one bread. I Cor. 10:17. For as a loaf being composed of many grains is but one bread; so we also being composed of many members are but one body in Christ. And as the members of a natural body are not disharmonious, but are altogether united and at one among themselves; so it is with all those who are in Spirit and faith true members of the body of Christ. For this reason this same supper was called by Tertullian[2] a brotherly meal or love feast.

Third, it is a communion of the flesh and blood of Christ. As Paul says, The cup of blessing which we bless, is it not the communion of the blood of Christ? The bread which we break, is it not the communion of the body of Christ? I Cor. 10:16. This communion consists in the fact that Christ has accepted us in His great love, and we are become partakers of Him. As Paul says, We are made partakers of Christ, if we hold the beginning of our confidence steadfast unto the end. Heb. 3:14.

Since it is a sign of such force which is left of Christ, that it is to represent and admonish us of His death, the love, peace, and unity of the brethren, and also the communion of His flesh and blood as was said, therefore none can rightly partake of this Supper except he be a disciple of Christ, flesh of His flesh, and bone of His bone, who seeks the forgiveness of sins in no other means than in the merits, sacrifice, death, and blood of Christ alone; who walks in unity, love, and peace with his brethren, and who leads a pious, unblamable life in Christ Jesus, according to the Scriptures.

Here you have the true Supper of our Lord Jesus Christ with its symbolism and mystery briefly stated, which the mouth of the Lord has left and taught you by His holy Word. If you would be a proper guest at the Lord's table and would rightly partake of His bread and wine, then you must also be His true disciple, that is, you must be an upright, pious, and godly Christian. Therefore prove yourself according to the doctrine of Paul before you eat of this bread and drink of this cup, for before God no feigning counts. He did not institute this ceremony as though mere bread, wine, and eating are

---

[2] Latin church father, c. 160—c. 230 A.D. Ed.

pleasing to Him. Oh, no. He has left this sacrament with you in order
that you might by it faithfully observe and carefully conform yourself to the
mystery represented by this sign or sacrament. For not the ceremony itself
but the matter represented by it, if rightly understood and fulfilled in actions,
constitutes a sincere Christian.

## VI. THE SUPPER OF THE PREACHERS

But of the Supper of the preachers we hold and confess, first, that it
is a false and idolatrous consolation and symbol of peace to those who delight
in walking upon the broad way, such as the greedy, avaricious, usurers, the
adulterers, the lying, deceiving, proud, and unrighteous. It is praised to
them by their preachers that the remission of their sins is announced thereby.
Therefore they console themselves and think that if they partake of it, they
are the people of the Lord. Oh, no, the ceremony makes no Christian, for
so long as they do not become converted and do not become new men born
of God, of spiritual mind, all baptizing and partaking of the Lord's Supper
is meaningless, even if it were administered by Peter or Paul. Paul says,
For in Christ Jesus neither circumcision availeth anything, nor uncircumcision; but faith which worketh in love (Gal. 5:6); the new creature, and
the keeping of the commandments of God (I Cor. 7:19).

Second, we declare that it is a hypocrisy, although it is acknowledged
by few. Christ instituted it in remembrance of His death as a sign of Christian
peace, and as a communion of His flesh and blood; yet the common world
partakes of this Supper in sham as if they believed thus and were thus minded,
and yet they seek the remission of their sins and their salvation in infant
baptism, absolutions, and in bread and wine, as is manifest.

Besides, their fruits openly show that they are not of the body of peace,
for they make use of tricks and crookedness among themselves in buying
and selling. Some also fornicate and commit adultery, lie and cheat; the
one slanders, defames, and robs the other, so that it may be truly said of
them that they do not acknowledge the Christian peace which is of God,
that they are not in the communion of Christ, but that they are in the communion of him of whom John says, Little children, let no man deceive you.
He that committeth sin, is of the devil; for the devil sinneth from the beginning.
I John 3:7, 8.

Third, we say that it is a very frightful blasphemy, abomination, and
adultery, yes, a new golden calf and a Maos[3]; for the blind, careless world
sees plainly that it is a perishable fruit of the soil which they have planted,
cut, kneaded, and baked with their own hands, and it returns to the earth
upon use; that it must be guarded by man lest the worms and age consume
it—and yet it is called by many the imperishable precious flesh and blood of

---

[3] A variant spelling for *Maos*, the singular form of *Maozim*, now generally spelled
*Mauzzim*. See pages 155 and 663. *Ed.*

Christ and is worshiped and honored as the true Son of the living God. We also with our ancestors have done this these five hundred years; it is still done in many large kingdoms, principalities, cities, and districts, exactly as it went in ancient Israel for centuries in regard to the brazen serpent, which was afterward broken in pieces by Hezekiah, king of Judah. II Kings 18:4.

Behold, into such gross idolaters and deceivers has the Apocalyptic Apollyon made the scribes of this world that they by their own wisdom, doctrine, and counsel have raised such an impotent, earthly cereal to the true Son of the Almighty and eternal God! So entirely has the noble Sun of righteousness lost its brightness, and the Egyptian darkness covered the entire land. Rev. 9:2; Ex. 10:22.

Faithful reader, by this our exposition and confession of the preachers with their baptism, Supper, and their envious hearts toward all the pious, learn the mystery of the finely attired woman, seated upon the scarlet colored beast. Rev. 17:3. The beast upon which the woman was seated is full of names of blasphemy. Note the spiritual reference. The woman was arrayed in beautiful attire—in church holidays, churches, bells, chants, organs, baptism, and Supper. The cup in her hand was of God; she boasts mightily of the Word of God, but she is filled with abominations and filthiness of her fornication, and she has made all the world drunk therewith; and the name was written upon her forehead and may be read by all who have spiritual eyes and is called, Mystery, Babylon the great, the Mother of Harlots and Abominations of the Earth.

And although she is so finely arrayed that all kings commit fornication with her, yet she is called a harlot by the angel, and is of such an inhuman and wolfish nature that she is drunken with the blood of the saints, and with the blood of the martyrs of Jesus.

John that holy man of God saw this in the Spirit and was astounded thereat. Yea, kind reader, whosoever rightly understands the abominable power, idolatrous array, spiritual enchantment and fornication, inhuman abomination and frightful bloodthirstiness and tyranny of the woman may well with John be astounded thereat. Therefore fear God and learn wisdom. We have by the grace of God seen through her thoroughly, exposed her shame, and diligently have warned you against her.

## VII. THE SWEARING OF OATHS

David says, Who shall ascend into the hill of the Lord? or who shall stand in his holy place? He that hath clean hands, and a pure heart; who hath not lifted up his soul unto vanity, nor sworn deceitfully. He shall receive the blessing from the Lord and righteousness from the God of his salvation. Ps. 24.

These words of David are full of spirit and wisdom. Yet they are not regarded by the world. Everywhere we find guilty hands, unclean hearts, false doctrine, faithlessness, and but little truth. Yes, it has come to this among the children of men, that the precious yea and nay which were commanded of the Lord Himself can no longer be trusted. Nearly everything which is transacted before the magistracy must be affirmed by an oath, although the Lord has so plainly forbidden the swearing of oaths to all Christians. Matt. 5:34.

The Scripture teaches that we should hear Christ, for He is the king in Jacob, the king of righteousness, the Teacher and Prophet promised of God, who has taught us the Word of the Father; and His Word is truth; His commandment, eternal life.

We confess and heartily believe that no emperor or king may rule as superior, nor command contrary to His Word, since He is the Head of all princes, and is the King of all kings, and unto Him every knee shall bow which is in heaven, in earth, or under the earth. He has plainly forbidden us to swear, and pointed us to yea and nay alone. Therefore it is that through fear of God we do not swear, nor dare to swear, though we must hear and suffer much on that account from the world.

Since throughout the world they act so fearlessly, contrary to the Word of God in regard to this matter, and since sometimes some of the God-fearing ones are thereby put into difficulty, therefore I will by the grace of God show the sympathetic reader from the Word of God what the holy Scriptures at given times teach and imply concerning the swearing of oaths.

First, the reader should observe that swearing was not always practiced uniformly among the people of the Lord. Before the Law the holy fathers had a custom of laying their hands upon their thigh and in this way swearing to others. This may be read in the case of Abraham and his servant (Gen. 24:3), and in the case of Jacob and his son, Joseph (Gen. 47:31). Joseph also swore by the life of Pharaoh (Gen. 42) ; and it seems that such swearing was customary among the Egyptians.

Second, the reader should observe that Israel was bound by the law when it concerned a matter of life or death to swear by the name of the Lord and to keep their oath. As Moses says, And ye shall not swear by my name falsely, neither shalt thou profane the name of thy God; I am the Lord. This oath settled all disputes among Israel. Ex. 22:11; Heb. 6:16.

Third, it should be observed that Christ Jesus does not in the New Testament point His disciples to the Law in regard to the matter of swearing —the dispensation of imperfectness which allowed swearing, but He points us now from the Law to yea and nay, as to the dispensation of perfectness, saying, Ye have heard that it hath been said by them of old time (that is, to the fathers under the law by Moses), Thou shalt not forswear thyself, but shalt perform unto the Lord thine oaths (that is, thou shalt swear truly and fulfill thine oath) : but I (Christ) say unto you my disciples, Swear not at all (that is, neither truly nor falsely), neither by heaven, for it is God's throne, nor by the earth, for it is his footstool, neither by Jerusalem, for it is the city of the great King. Neither shalt thou swear by thy head because thou canst not make one hair white or black. But let your communication be yea, yea; nay, nay; for whatsoever is more than these cometh of evil. Here you have Christ's own doctrine and ordinance concerning swearing.

Behold, beloved reader, before these words of Christ all human laws and policies concerning swearing must stand back and cease; such as the *Juramentum Calumniae,* or the *Juramentum de veritate dicenda,* that is, the oath of avoiding slander, or the oath of speaking the truth; however they may be called, no matter how they be performed; be it by word or by raising of the hand, or holding the hand upon the breast or upon a cross, or upon the New Testament, etc. And the truthful yea and nay ordained of the Lord Himself must be restored, if at least magistrates and subjects do not wish willfully to transgress the Word of the Lord and to dispose of it lightly. For whatsoever is more than yea and nay, says Christ, cometh of evil. This the holy James also teaches, Above all things, my brethren, swear not, neither by heaven, neither by the earth, neither by any other oath: that is, not by God's Word, by the Lord's cross, by the salvation of your soul. But let your yea be yea, and your nay, nay, and not, So help me God, By God and all the saints, as is also the custom in many places; lest you fall into condemnation. Jas. 5:12.

We are aware that the magistracy claims and says that we are allowed to swear when justice is on our side. We reply with the Word of the Lord very simply. To swear truly was allowed to the Jews under the Law; but the Gospel forbids this to Christians. Since Christ does not allow us to swear, and since the magistracy, notwithstanding, proceeds according to their policy, although contrary to Scripture, and since the Scriptures may not be set aside by man, what shall the conscientious Christian do? If he swears, he falls into the hand of the Lord. If he swears not, he will have to bear the disfavor and punishment of the magistracy.

O dear sirs! If you had Christian eyes and could see and sincerely acknowledge what according to the righteousness of God, it implies willfully to despise and transgress the Word of God, then you would rather die than weaken or break the precious Gospel of our Lord Jesus Christ, the ordinance of the eternal God, by temporal statutes and policies.

Nor should we think of asking more than yea and nay, particularly of the pious, God-fearing hearts, who by the fear of their God dare not speak anything but the truth; who esteem every word which comes from their mouth as virtually an oath, and keep their yea and nay unto death. But now alas they dare to constrain them to swear to a trifle concerning some temporal goods or something of the kind, even with their fingers raised to heaven, or with their hands upon the New Testament, by the God of heaven and by His living Word.

O dear sirs, how pitiably your teachers and leaders lead you upon the way which tends to damnation, who incessantly assure you by saying that we should obey the magistracy (which is proper in so far as it is not contrary to God's Word) as if just because one is a ruler he may therefore act and rule contrary to the Lord.

O dear sirs, no, we warn you in faithful love: repent, rouse yourself, and look about you. Your preachers deceive you. With God there is no respect of persons. If you do not repent, are not born of God, do not become like unto children in malice, do not in love execute your office and service agreeably to the will of God, do not do justice to the poor and miserable, and do not walk in obedience to the Word of the Lord with pious, humble hearts, you will find your Judge at the judgment day. Beloved lords, take to heart this saying: Mighty men shall be mightily tormented.

Ye learned ones who by your glosses and errors assert and defend this error, how dare you so flatly contradict the eternal wisdom and truth of God and say, You say that we may in no case swear an oath but we say, You may swear when the love, profit, and need of your neighbor require it. We will leave it to your judgment whether this is not to contradict Christ flatly. It is so plain that it was allowed to the Jews under the Law to swear sincerely, but that to us Christians it is forbidden. It is very plain that according to the New Testament no love of neighbors nor father, mother, wife, or child, nor peril of life may bend or break the Word of the Lord. Matt. 10:37; Mark 8:38.

Therefore, worthy reader, if you fear the Lord and if it should happen that you are asked to swear, then pray the Most High for wisdom, courage, and strength. Do not listen to the glosses of the learned ones, for they deceive you. Do not look to numbers lest you follow in their evil ways, as Moses says. Give way to no flesh in this matter, it makes no difference who, what, or where they be, but admonish them in a becoming manner and in love when they ask of you more than Scriptures command. Continue in the Lord's Word which has forbidden you so plainly to swear, and let your yea and nay be your oath as was commanded, whether life or death be your lot, in order that you by your courage and firm truthfulness may admonish and reprove unto righteousness the useless, empty, vain world (which respects nothing less than the Word of the Lord) by your truthful yea and nay; if perchance some might be converted from their unrighteousness and thereby be led more deeply to study the truth and be saved.

Even at that it is better to incur the disfavor, scorn, and slander of man and remain in the truth, than to be the friend of men and sin against God. The good John Hus[4] declared when he was pressed to swear saying, I am pressed on all sides. If I swear, I have eternal death; and if I do not swear, I will fall into your hands. But it is better to fall into your hands without swearing, than to sin in the sight of God. Thus highly did this worthy man evaluate the oath.

Also read Jerome, Theophylact, Chrysostom, Erasmus of Rotterdam in

---

[4] Jan Hus (c. 1369-1415), Bohemian reformer who was influenced by John Wycliffe and who was burned at the stake at Constance July 6, 1415. *Ed.*

his *Annotations,* Philip Melanchthon on the Fifth Chapter of Matthew, Haymo on Revelation 10 and also Origen at a certain place, and you will find that in this matter they agree with our position, faith, doctrine, and confession.

This is our position and understanding in regard to this matter. Inasmuch as the Lord has forbidden us to swear at all (understand in temporal matters) neither sincerely nor falsely, as was said; and has commanded that our yea shall be yea and our nay, nay; and since Paul and James also testify to this, and since we know that no man nor commandment of man may take the place of God and His commandment, therefore it is that we in temporal matters dare not affirm the truth in more than yea or nay as the case may be. For thus the Word of the Lord teaches us.

We say, in temporal matters, and for this reason: Because Christ sometimes in His teachings makes use of the word verily and because Paul called upon the Lord as a witness of his soul. For this some think that swearing is allowable; not observing that Christ and Paul did not do this in regard to temporal matters as in matters of flesh and blood or money or property but in affirmation of the eternal truth to the praise of God and to the salvation and edification of their brethren.

Herewith we pray all lords and magistrates for Jesus' sake to fear the Lord sincerely, to conform their policy in the matter of swearing to the Word of the Lord, and to consider carefully why they require the oath, namely; As an assurance that the thing promised shall be done. Since we deem our yea and nay to be no less than an oath, why afflict us with further affirmation than the Word of the Lord teaches and allows? For by the grace of God we trust that inasmuch as we are partakers of the Lord and adhere to the Word in which yea is Amen, that therefore it will be found with us that yea is yea and nay, nay; much more so than with the world under strong oaths. In case a man's yea and nay is not kept, let him be punished as a perjurer. That yea is Amen with all true Christians is sufficiently shown by those who in our Netherlands are so tyrannically visited with imprisonment, confiscation, and torture; with fire, the stake, and the sword; while with one word they could escape all these if they would but break their yea and nay. But since they are born of the truth, therefore they walk in the truth, and testify to the truth unto death, as may be abundantly seen in Flanders, Brabant, Holland, West Friesland, etc.

## VIII. CONCLUSION

It is manifest, honorable reader, that the world is so apostate that it esteems everything wrong which God teaches, commands, and desires, and hates it, and with envious hearts persecutes and destroys it. On the other hand, all that which God hates, accurses, and considers an abomination, it looks upon as good and diligently asserts and maintains. Yet they want to be the holy, Christian church and the people of God, as if we could be such by lofty claims, by baptizing children, etc., without faith, the new birth and the Spirit, and obedience to God. No, dear reader, take heed. Those who assure you deceive you and corrupt the way that you should go. Isa. 3:11.

Seeing then that the world is so entirely apostate, and since our opponents so shamefully lie and agitate against us that we cannot appear to answer for ourselves as is manifest, therefore we have written this our confession that everyone who may read, hear, or see it may know why and whereby we seek to be saved, why we do not hear the preachers, and why we insist so strenuously upon believer's baptism and oppose infant baptism so sternly; what is represented by the Lord's Supper and what abominations are implied in the baptism of the learned ones; and that it is not allowed to a true Christian to swear in temporal matters but only affirm by yea and nay.

By so doing we have compared truth with falsehood, light with darkness. and white with black, as you will perceive. If you do not want to be willfully blind, you have here a good eyesalve. We have presented it so baldly and plainly that you must acknowledge it to be the truth, or in perverseness reject it, saying, No, I do not want it. What kind of Christian you are then you may consider for yourself.

Kind reader, do not associate with those who say unto God, Depart from me; for we desire not the knowledge of thy ways (Job 21:12), nor with those who are intent upon blood, for their reward will be death (Rom. 1:32; Rev. 21:27).

This is our position as you here have read. If now you are of a pious mind, and not led by the blind spirit of the spiritual adultery, then judge our cause according to the Word and truth of the Lord. If you do not understand it, then fear God and pray. All those who are born of God and inclined to the Word of the Lord must acknowledge that our doctrine is of God and that truth is on our side. Whosoever accepts them and abides in them unto the end has eternal life; But whosoever rejects them does not reject us, but Christ Jesus Himself, who has taught us from the mouth of His Father and sealed it with His own blood. Rev. 1:5; I Pet. 1:19; Acts 20:28.

The gracious Father through His beloved Son Jesus Christ, our Lord, enlighten you and all hungry hearts by the gift of His Holy Spirit and lead you by His strength into His eternal, saving truth. Amen. To the praise of God and the service of all mankind, by me,

MENNO SIMONS

*A. D. 1552*

# A Pathetic Supplication to All Magistrates

*Supplicatie der armen christenen*

# 1552

*For other foundation can no man*
*lay than that is laid, which is Jesus Christ.*

I Corinthians 3:11

# Introduction

Menno's second booklet of 1552 is herewith presented under the title, *A Pathetic Supplication to All Magistrates.* It is an earnest appeal for a cessation of persecution, of the awful shedding of blood, of putting to death those honest and law-abiding citizens whose only "crime" was that they sought to follow only the Word of God. Along with the *Confession,* the *Brief Defense to All Theologians,* and the *Reply to False Accusations,* this *Supplication* was first published in the Eastern dialect of the Baltic coastal region.

The original title reads: *A Very Pathetic Supplication of Poor and Distressed Christians to all pious, benevolent, and proper Magistrates concerning the terrible Accusations, the Abuse, the Slander, and the Commotion whereby the Learned Ones* [the state church clergy] *slander and trouble them so grievously everywhere, as one may hear and see.*

In the *Opera Omnia Theologica* of 1681 this *Supplication* appears fol. 325-30, and in the *Complete Works* of 1871, Part II, pages 107-13.

J. C. W.

# A Pathetic Supplication to All Magistrates

# 1552

•-•··•-•··•-•··•-•··•-•··•-•··•-•··•-•··•-•··•-•··•-•··•-•··•-•··•-•··•-•··•-•··•-•··•-•··•-•··•-•··•-•··•-•··•-•··•-•·•

*To all pious, benevolent, and proper Magistrates, Lords, Princes, Rulers, and Superiors, do we poor, miserable, and dispersed ones wish perpetual prosperity and a happy reign, in all piety, from God our heavenly Father, through Jesus Christ our Lord and Saviour. Amen!*

## A Very Pathetic Supplication

As is commonly known, O noble, honorable, and kind sirs, there are some who are much more diligent concerning the Law of Theodosius (although it was wrung from the good emperor by the bloodthirsty bishops long ago), concerning the Mandate of Charles V, and the Imperial Condemnation decreed in our times concerning the so-called Anabaptists, than they are concerning God's Word. And they fail to see that these things do not issue from any baptism but from the wicked errors committed in doctrine and in practice by baptized people. For if the afore-mentioned Law, Mandate, and Condemnation were aimed at baptism rather than at the evil deeds committed each in his turn by baptized ones, then even Christ Jesus, all the apostles, Cyprian the Martyr, as well as all the African Bishops, the Nicene Council, and also the Apostle Paul, were by it declared public evildoers. This is beyond controversy so.

We strenuously disapprove of the Donatists, the Circumcellions, and of those of Münster, as well as all the contemporary errors, misdeeds, and abominations (at which in former time the Law of Theodosius and now the Emperor's Mandate and the Imperial Condemnation were aimed, as has been said) and have from the inception of our teaching and doctrine disapproved them. And we, before God and His angels, seek nothing on this earth but that we may obey the clear and printed Word of the Lord, His Spirit, His example, His command, prohibition, usage, and ordinance (by which everything in Christ's kingdom and church must be regulated if it is to please Him) according to our weakness in all subjection and obedience. This our grievous tribulation, oppression, misery, anguish, confiscation, and execution testify at all places. Therefore it is before God and man altogether unchristian, yes,

very evident violence and injustice, that we for the matter of baptism alone
(a baptism which we may defend so mightily with God's Word, and the
apostolic doctrine and usage against all philosophy and human wisdom) are
classified and punished together with the Circumcellions (who according to
the testimony of history committed such unheard-of tyrannies) and with those
of Münster who contrary to God's Word and every evangelical Scripture,
also contrary to proper policies, set up a new kingdom, incited turmoil,
introduced polygamy, etc., matters which we oppose vehemently with God's
Word, condemn, and censure, as is evident and patent from all our acts and
public activity.

In the first place therefore we wish humbly to beg your Noble Highnesses, Honorable and Wise Sirs, for Christ's sake, that you would be pleased
to note carefully with pity and paternal care, how very sadly your unhappy
subjects (who nevertheless were created by the selfsame God, were bought
with the selfsame treasure, and will appear at the last before the selfsame
Judge) are slandered by everybody, specially by the preachers, everywhere
and without any fault on their side; are mocked, violated, and in some places
put out of the way without pity or compassion as men dispose of the most
wicked and awful; are given to the fowls of the air, are (as was also our
Captain Christ) attached to wheels and stakes, so that some of us, and not
a few,[1] must naked and plundered wander in foreign lands with our poor,
weak wives and little children, bereft of the fatherland, our inheritance, and
the fruit of our heavy toil.[2] And all this for no other reason, the Lord knows,
than that we do not associate with the preachers, who by their doctrine,
sacraments, and conduct oppose the Word of the Lord; that we make the
proper use of baptism and the Lord's Supper, that we avoid all idolatry, self-
righteousness, and abuses as required by the Scripture, and wish, as far as
our weakness will allow, fervently to fear the Lord and follow after righteousness.

Be pleased, in godly fear, to ponder what it is that God requires of your
Highnesses. It is that without any respect of persons you judge between
a man and his neighbor, protect the wronged from him who does him wrong,
even as the Lord declares, Execute judgment and justice, Assist, against the
violent, him that is robbed, Abuse not the stranger, the widow, the orphan,
Do violence to no man, and shed no innocent blood,[3] so that your despised
servants and unhappy subjects, having escaped the mouth of the lion, may
in your domain and under your paternal care and gracious protection, serve
the Lord in quietness and peace, and piously earn their bread, as the Scripture
requires.

[1] The version of 1681 has *ende die weynigh* which makes no sense. We have therefore
read *ende niet weynigh*. *Tr.*
[2] The text has *zweeringen*. Since this makes no sense we have substituted *zweetigen*
(sweaty).
[3] Menno is quoting the Scripture quite freely, without following the text literally. We
therefore have refrained from quoting the literal words in any version. *Tr.*

Next we request that your Noble Highnesses would examine in the light of God's Word that never leads astray, the living example of Christ, and the blameless piety of all saints, as to what a genuine Christian looks like; for if reading the liturgy, chanting, handling water, bread, wine, name and fame make a man a true Christian there would be a lot of Christians indeed! But no, dear sirs, no. God's Word knows of no Christians other than such as have had the pure doctrine of Christ preached to them in the Spirit's power, who have accepted it in true faith by the operation of the Spirit, have by the living seed of God been born anew in Christ Jesus, and who in the power of that birth have buried in true penitence that erstwhile sinful life, and have been raised again with Christ. They are people who in their weakness desire to obey the Lord's holy will, His Word, His example, His ordinance and commands, and heartily wish to die to all that is contrary thereto. They fight bravely against all vain and erring thoughts and every attacking sin which still spring up out of our inherited Adamic nature, with a sorrowful and broken heart sigh and lament daily before God over their human weaknesses, failures, and transgressions. They are persons who are prepared to take up the cross of Christ[4] and for the testimony of His holy Word to forsake father, mother, husband, wife, children, possession and property, life itself, if the honor of God requires it. In a word, they are such as are Christ-minded, are in Christ, and Christ in them, who are led by His Spirit, and with a true faith, and a firm confidence, and a lively hope in all trial and tribulation, abide unshaken in the Word of the Lord.

Thus it is powerfully manifest that our faithful brothers and sisters in Christ Jesus, those dear companions in tribulation and in the kingdom and patience of Christ (cf. Rev. 1), love and fear the Lord their God so fervently that they would rather surrender, as a prey to the bloodthirsty, their good name and fame, money, property, flesh and blood, and all things that might appeal to human nature, than knowingly and willfully to speak a falsehood or act the hypocrite over against God's Word. This we wish to give your Noble Highnesses to ponder, whether these people are really such harmful and wicked folk as they are, alas, slanderously said by many to be. Yes, dear sirs, in the Word of the Lord is all their pleasure; their mouths flow with words of wisdom; their love has the aroma of the precious ointment on Aaron's head; their prayers are as the noble incense before the ark of God; their lives shine as the golden candlestick in the house of the Lord. And they seek nothing else on this earth than that they might serve the whole wide world unto righteousness, and save many out of the eternal perdition of their souls by the Lord's grace, Spirit, power, and Word. They would win them to Christ and so be permitted by God's gracious help and gift, in Christ Jesus, to improve the short time of this earthly habitation to the praise of their God and the service of their fellows and be saved for all eternity.

And if this be heresy and diabolical seduction, as the preachers loudly

---

[4] The Christian disciple's cross of suffering which results from following Jesus. *Ed.*

assert, then must the Son of God, Christ Jesus, and all the prophets, apostles, and lofty witnesses of God, have been manifest heretics, all! And then the whole Scripture, which teaches naught but moral improvement, and everywhere points us to Christ, must have been naught but deceit and falsehood! This is not to be denied—that they, as much as in them is, in all that they do, act in conformity to the Word of the Lord, His Spirit, life, command, prohibition, and ordinance, even as the manifest deed before the whole world witnesses and attests.

Since then we and they walk in one Spirit, and before God in Christ Jesus, seek nothing than that we desire fervently, in our poor frailty, to be Christians, as has been said; so we hope by the Lord's grace that your Excellences will in all eternity discover nothing else in your humble servants (we refer to such as are of a kind with us in faith and conduct). And so we beg your Noble Excellences again, for Jesus' sake, to lay aside thoroughly all hostile thoughts against your poor orphans. Turn to us a fatherly and a genuinely benevolent heart, and nevermore imagine that we have any other intention, even if we were as numerous as the blades of grass in the meadow, and the grains of sand on the seashore—which will never come to pass, seeing that the way is so narrow and the gate so strait, as Christ Jesus (whose name we bear) taught us with His own mouth and His holy apostles preached throughout the whole world, asserted from the holy Gospel, and declared with their life and death.

In the third place, we request your Noble Highnesses with a heart of wisdom to observe how according to the Scriptures it goes with such as boast themselves in the knowledge of Christ, how mortally sharp the sword of wrath clashes in every direction. Great and grievous is the Lord's vengeance; the fire of His wrath is kindled. If the Lord in His grace does not quench it, both the green and the dry tree may, as the prophet said, be verily consumed. The prophecy of Christ concerning the last days, as well as that of Daniel and of the apostles are being fulfilled in force. The flesh-consuming sword of the Lord glistens everywhere; and His bloody darts wing their way through every land. Kingdom is pitted against kingdom, realm against realm, city against city, neighbor against neighbor, and friend against friend. Some of your subjects are murdered by the sword, some imprisoned; cities and citadels are laid waste and destroyed. The poor people, in large part quite innocent in the matter, are bled white, are abused, are taxed, burned, and completely ruined; countless many are forced to a life of shame and dishonesty. One grave pestilence and epidemic succeeds another; one inflation drives the other forward. On the sea as well as on the land we hear of storms, distress, and trouble. In a word, the persistent and hard chastisement testifies that the Lord is offended, yet the wicked world does not turn over a new leaf but grows worse and worse daily.

Everyone in general boasts himself to be Christian, and that they have the Word of God, even though their total ambition and conduct is contrary to Christ and to Christ's Word. If one addresses himself to the Magistrates, who surely ought to know about the way of the Lord and the Law of God, as Jeremiah has it, then one discovers that they have broken the yoke and have rent the bands asunder. If we go to the preachers we discover a Cain-like disfavor for all who fear the Lord, an incurable money-madness and a Balaam-like avarice, a frivolous and liberal doctrine, idolatrous sacraments, and a sensuous, vain, and lazy life, as anyone can see. If we turn to the common people there we see grasping greed, carousing and drinking, lying and cheating, cursing and swearing, with some also adultery and fornication, with others plunder and pillage, as they steal and slay. Yes, men carry on in such fashion, alas, that one may well sigh and lament, with the saintly Hosea, that neither fidelity and love nor the Word of God is left in the land but that blasphemy, lying, stealing, murder, and adultery have taken over, and blood touches blood. One can agree with Paul that all are gone out of the way and are become unprofitable, and that they have not known the way of peace; and, with the Apocalypse that their sins have reached unto heaven. Dear Lord, how much longer must this terrible great blindness, blasphemy, error, and abomination last, this willfully reckless life?

Do repent, noble sirs, and be penitent, with a penitence acceptable before God. Humble yourself with Nineveh's king; put off the wicked and spotted cloak of sin; betake you to the ashes of humiliation; cry unto the Lord out of a broken spirit; rend your hearts and not your garments, as says the prophet; let the pious Hezekiah be your example, who turned to the Lord with all his heart and soul, mind and strength, as soon as the Law of his God was read to him out of the book recovered.

Dear sirs, seek God; fear God; serve God with all your might; do justice to widows, orphans, strangers, the sad, and the oppressed; wash your hands of blood; rule your lands with wisdom and peace. Train yourselves in thought, word, and deed upon the crucified Christ Jesus, follow in His steps, and then, though your sins be red as blood they shall be white as snow, though they be red as crimson they shall be as wool! For the Lord takes no pleasure in the death of a sinner but therein that he repent and live.

They who boast themselves to be the church are so completely estranged from Christ that they have only the name. The salt (that is, the preachers) has so completely lost its savor that it spoils more than it preserves, seeing they flatter more than they reprove, and seek for temporal gain rather than the glory of God, whereby they all together, preacher and flock alike, walk on the broad way that leads to condemnation. There is none, alas, to turn them out of the way, as the prophet complains. Yet we would so much desire, as God knows, that all men might rouse themselves, fear the Lord, do hearty penance and be saved, so that the fallen city, which is the church, may be built again on its former foundation, namely, on the firm basis of the apostles and the unadulterated doctrine of Christ, and then give witness to it in a godly and penitent life before the whole world according to the Scriptures. It is because of all this that we are hated so by the learned clerics that by their slanderous shouting and agitation we are forced to leave our possessions to robbers, and our flesh to the hangman, and some of us must, because of the anguish, mockery, and slander, wander aimlessly in foreign lands, as has been said.

And so we distressed and sorrowful ones humbly pray your Excellences for the third time for Jesus' sake to reflect carefully on the matter. And be pleased with Christian fidelity to compare us and the preachers with each other according to the tenor of the ensuing writing addressed to them and with the conditions therein stipulated, so that our innocence might at long last be heard, and the truth be established with the Word of God, so that the innocent may not be longer condemned, contrary to the Word of God, and the guilty no longer defended in their unrighteousness. Yes, kind sirs, if this might at long last come to pass, without partiality and in the fear of God, then you would, by God's grace, soon discover and without equivocation on whose side the truth is, and that the clerics' doctrine, sacraments, and conduct are not in accordance with the Scriptures but misleading and contrary to the Word of God.

O dear and noble sirs, please do not despise our proper and Christian request, but accept it in love unsullied. For it concerns the praise of Almighty God, His eternal Word and Truth, and the eternal salvation of the soul of each of us, souls so diligently sought after, so dearly bought by His crimson blood. Alas, the difference is so great between living forever with Christ Jesus in the throne of heaven and with the demons to perish in hell!

Kind sirs, we are in deep distress and anguish, and are terrified from two sides. For if we follow the truth (as we hope by God's grace and help to do all our days), then we become common prey; and if we give in and revert to the broad way (from which may the merciful Father keep us everlastingly), then we fall into the hands of God, and must bear His wrath eternally. The salvation of our poor souls means more to us than all that human eye can see. At one time that gracious, loving word will be heard, Come, ye blessed of my Father, inherit the kingdom prepared for you. Also that fearful word, with which all that disobey Christ are threatened, which if truly believed cuts through one's body and soul: Depart from me, ye cursed, into everlasting fire, prepared for the devil and his angels. Happy is that man who is found watching, his lamp trimmed, and the wedding garment on hand. Yes, blessed are they that are bidden to the supper of the Lamb!

Noble sirs, we are not joking. Nor do we play with words. What we write we mean from the bottom of our hearts, as our grievous trials, heavy chains, life and limb, testify and declare.

May the great and merciful Lord Jesus, who is a Lord of lords and a King of kings, grant your Noble Highnesses and Honorable Excellences, altogether rightly to know the truth, faithfully to walk in it, piously to rule your cities and provinces in happy peace, to the praise of your God and the salvation of many souls! This we wish with all our heart. Amen.

Blessed are the merciful, for they shall obtain mercy. Matt. 5:7. Be merciful even as your Father is merciful.

Verily I say, what you have done to one of the least of my brethren you have done unto me. Matt. 25:40.

Your Noble Highnesses and Honorable Excellences' faithful and obedient subjects, which we are able to be by the will of God and through His grace.

# Brief Defense to All Theologians

*Korte klaeglycke ontschuldinge*

# 1552

*For other foundation can no man*
*lay than that is laid, which is Jesus Christ.*

I Corinthians 3:11

# Introduction

Menno's third booklet of 1552, and the last of a trilogy, which appeared together in the Eastern dialect of the Baltic coastal region, is his *Brief Defense to All Theologians*. It is evident from various writings of Menno that he held the clergy of the state churches to be largely responsible for the severe persecution of the Brethren (commonly called Anabaptists, but already called Menists—now Mennonites—as early as the 1540's). Time and again Menno pleaded with the civil rulers and with the clergy for an opportunity to hold a theological debate with the clergy in order to see if he could not bring about a cessation of persecution by showing the Scriptural character of the faith he believed and taught, and to which his brethren and sisters held. In the tract before us Menno even goes so far as to list ten topics on which he desired a theological discussion provided he would be guaranteed safe conduct to and from the meeting. But in vain. No such opportunity ever came except for the semipublic interview with John a Lasco in 1544. The days of religious toleration had not yet arrived.

The title of this *Defense* in the Dutch folio edition of 1681 is: *A Brief Apology of Distressed Christians and Scattered Exiles addressed to all the Scribes and Clerics of the German Nations, concerning the frightfully bitter Inventions, Slanders, and Invectives which They so hatefully and without a Show of Truth heap upon us. Also a kind Request for a free Discussion of the Scripture even as is required and proper by Christian Love.* In the *Opera Omnia Theologica* of 1681 this work is found fol. 331-35, and in the *Complete Works* of 1871, Part II, pages 115-20.                    J. C. W.

# Brief Defense to All Theologians

# 1552

•=•=•=•=•=•=•=•=•=•=•=•=•=•=•=•=•=•=•=•=•=•=•=•=•=•=•=•=•=•=•=•=•=•=•=•=•=•=•=•=•=•=•=•=•

*We poor, miserable, and much hated Christians, who have to hear and suffer so much for the testimony of the Word of God and of our conscience, wish all clerics known as Evangelical, it matters not who, how, and where they be, in every country, a renewed and penitent heart, a sound and active belief in Christ Jesus, an unfeigned and fervent love, a beneficent doctrine, a sound judgment in truth, and a pious unblamable life in the fear of the Lord, from God our heavenly Father in the operation and power of His Holy Spirit, through Jesus Christ, His dear Son, our Lord and eternal Saviour. Amen!*

## *A Brief Apology of Distressed Christians*

It is well known to all men and brethren how that in our Netherlands, alas, the pure divine Truth is, because of the envious clamor and agitation of the priests, very much hated and innocent blood is shed as water, so that we distressed sons and daughters, driven by extreme necessity, are forced to flee before the tyrannical sword, and in foreign lands with our helpless wives and little children we must look to God for sustenance, and earn our bread in care and want.

It appears that many of you cry very angrily at us (possibly through misconception, with good intent) and move and stir up the Magistrates (of which, no doubt, some are reasonable and honest) to persecution, contrary to natural reasonableness and Christian charity, with patently invented accusation. You warn everyone against us saying we are like-minded with those of Münster, that we wish to capture cities and lands, if only we could, and that we instigate tumults, resort to the sword, steal and pick pockets, practice polygamy, have our wives and possessions in common, refuse to obey the Magistrates, slay our own children physically and spiritually; that we are Anabaptists, Sacrament-profaners and deceivers, hypocrites; that we boast ourselves to be without sin, are heaven-stormers who are saved by their own merits and good works, a godless sect and rabble-rousers, new monks, scamps, and hoodlums, and that we are possessed by the devil. In a word, alas, we are so represented

535

that those who do not know our confession, faith, etc., hold their noses and stop their ears at the sight of us, and are frightened at us, even though, God be thanked forever, we seek nothing on this earth, before God and His angels, than that we in our weakness may conform to God's Word, Spirit, and example, by His grace, even as the entire Scripture teaches and implies.

The great Lord Almighty, who tries every heart, knows that we are innocent and free of all these recited abominations and excesses wherewith we are so ceaselessly and hatefully slandered by you—before the Lord and His judgment as well as before the whole wide world. Yes, if anyone under the whole heaven can prove with valid truth that we and our leaders are guilty of any of these wicked and mortal crimes, or ever were guilty of them, then we are prepared to keep still and be subject, with life and property all our days, to the informant—this one thing excepted, that we refuse to obey the Magistrates when they command contrary to God's Word. Is it not a lamentable thing that we must be abused with such unheard of excesses which we have not even thought, much less committed?

Worthy Gentlemen, if you knew what we aim at, and how by God's grace we are disposed toward you and toward all, then you would not feel as hostile toward us as you have hitherto done, unless you have arrived at an altogether and complete wickedness and perversity, a thing that we do not hope of any of you.

Since then you wrong us so sadly and heap one lie on top of the other, and no verbal defense, alas, is permitted us anywhere, therefore we are forced to submit a good brief written defense. And we wish therewith humbly to pray you and fraternally to admonish you as to four matters.

In the first place, we admonish you that with a sound mind you reflect that lying is of the devil (John 8:55), that the lying mouth killeth the soul (Sap. 1), that a liar has no place in the city of God (Rev. 22:26), that slanderers deserve death (Rom. 1:15), and that they will not dwell in the house of the Lord nor ascend into His holy hill (Ps. 15:3).

Second, your accusations against us are almost all capital offenses. If now we did not fear the Lord but desired strictly to demand our rights by law, and confronted you, where would you finally appear, since you accuse us before the world of such cursed abominations, which neither you nor any human being in all eternity at a single point can make good with plausible argument?

In the third place, this your conduct is flat against all natural reasonableness as well as against all Christian charity and God's Word. For where has there ever been a man of noble nature who has not concerned himself with the lot of the wretched, nor was not grieved over the grief-stricken? The entire Scriptures teach us in love to receive, serve, aid and comfort the wretched and the stranger. And you observe fully how lamentably we wretched people are everywhere hated, despised, banished, fined, and in many places condemned and killed, but your heart is not so much as moved to direct a single kindly word to us in our grievous affliction and awful need, nor to investigate our foundation, faith, and conduct with a paternal spirit according to the Word of God. Instead you pour more and more oil on the fire, as the saying goes, just so we find no rest on the earth. You shout, you write, you fabricate, you vituperate, you agitate, you lay one great affliction on the other, you drag into dungeons and shackles, precisely as though you have never in your lives read a single letter in God's Word with godly wisdom, nor received a little spark of His holy Spirit. Do you call that acting in Christian charity according to apostolic doctrine and usage and after the Spirit of God, His Word, and His example? We leave this to you to judge.

Say, my dear people, where do the holy Scriptures teach that in Christ's kingdom and church we shall proceed with the magistrate, with the sword, and with physical force and tyranny over a man's conscience and faith, things subject to the judgment of God alone? Where have Christ and the apostles acted thus, advised thus, commanded thus? Ah, Christ says merely, Beware of false prophets; and Paul ordains that we shall avoid a heretical person after he has been admonished once or twice. John teaches that we shall not greet nor receive into the house the man who goes onward and does not bring the doctrine of Christ. But they do not write, Away with those heretics, Report them to the authorities, Lock them up, Expel them out of the city and the country, Throw them into the fire, the water, as the Catholics have done for many years, and as is still found to a great extent with you—you who make yourselves believe that you teach the Word of God!

In the fourth place, we beg of you from the bottom of our hearts, for Jesus' sake, to reflect a moment whether your spirit is one with the Lord's Spirit, and your conviction agrees with His holy Word; whether it is the Spirit of the Lord and the love for your neighbor or the thirst for gain and the thought of temporal support that send and drive you into your profession. Do you preach God's Word out of a pure heart without falsification; administer His sacraments correctly, and lead a pious and irreproachable life as the Scriptures teach; and do you verily shun and expel from the fellowship of the Lord public transgressors, primpers, drunkards, lovers of gain, usurers, liars, swindlers, contentious persons, brawlers, adulterers, such as follow after prostitutes, blasphemers, those who take oaths, unrighteous people, etc., and that without fear or favor? For it is a fact, O Lord, that men everywhere live and carry on as though never a prophet nor an apostle, nor a Christ, nor a Word of God had been on the earth! And still you folks call yourselves the holy Christian Church and the sound teachers, precisely as though Christ's activity in His church is no more than a mere reading of liturgy, chanting, shouting, baptizing of babies, breaking of bread, and carrying a name, and as if Spirit, knowledge, faith, love, penitence, righteousness, work, power, and truth are no longer needed!

No, no, worthy sirs, no! This constitutes the church in Christ: rightly to teach Christ's unadulterated Word in the power of the Spirit; to believe

the same with all the heart and to practice it in all obedience; rightly to use
the sacraments, such as baptism and holy communion, according to His own
commandments and ordinance; to seek God from the heart, to fear Him, love
Him, serve Him; to be born of God; to love one's neighbor, to serve him,
comfort him, help and assist him; to avoid all false doctrine and the works
of darkness; to mortify all carnal lusts that war against God's Word; to deny
oneself and the world, to lead a pious, peaceful, chaste, sober, and humble
life in righteousness according to the truth. In fine, to be of the same mind as
was Christ Jesus! For where these are, there Christ's kingdom and church is.
This is beyond dispute. But those who deceive, who hate, who lie, who
slander, who defame others, who stir up sedition, who thirst after blood, who
are covetous, unmerciful, cruel, proud, impenitent, etc., these are of the
evil one, as John declares, and their portion shall be endless gnashing of
teeth, sorrow, hell, Satan, fire, and death.

Brethren, if you should take this our brief exposition to heart, in the pure
fear of God, and should meditate on it with God's Word and Spirit, then you
would no doubt find so great a beam in your own eye that you would pay
little attention to the little sliver that possibly is in your brother's eye (since
we are all descended from Adam). But to know oneself well is wise, and to
conform in all things to the Word and example of the Lord is healthful wisdom
and prudence.

Seeing then that we are, through no fault of ours, so shamelessly weighted
down by you, and you pride yourselves on being the Lord's servants, who
promote His Word and work, therefore we pray you one and all, for the
sake of the crimson blood of Christ wherewith we are sprinkled, that you
consider for a moment how you carry on toward us miserable and saddened
ones, so that you may no longer trangress with such manifest lies and tyrannies
as heretofore but show a kind and fatherly spirit as comports with a divine
vocation and a Christian name. For we testify before Him who knows our
hearts, before you, and before the whole world, with spoken and written
words, with all we have and are, with life and death, that we from the innermost heart in our poor weakness, subject ourselves to the Lord's holy Word
and will. And we stand ready now and always (we having been thus from
the outset), in case anyone can with more powerful spirit than ours, with more
convincing truth than ours, and with more godly life than ours, instruct us,
we wish from the heart to hear and obey. But if none can more correctly
instruct us, we pray once more, for Jesus' sake, then to leave the truth to us,
and do no longer persecute and sadden the pious who walk in the truth.

We hereby serve notice on you all that we are heartily inclined to appear
with you at a public discussion about the Scriptures, at any convenient time
and place, with one or two from our side, whether preachers or no, whether
in open session or before twenty or thirty reasonable and pious witnesses,
if it pleases you, to treat in good conscience of the following points, for it is
in them that our differences manifest themselves, with the Spirit of Christ,

His Word, life or example, command, prohibition, usage, or ordinance. These points are:

1. Concerning the genuine evangelical preachers and teachers, how according to God's Word they should be disposed and prepared before they are able to preach God's Word properly and to administer the sacraments rightly.

2. Of the doctrine of Christ and His apostles, how they are not subject to change but must remain constant until the day of His coming.

3. Of the Christ, whether He be a perfect teacher and His sacrifice a perfect sacrifice.

4. Of regeneration, what it is, whence it comes, and what is its nature and fruit.

5. Of orthodox belief and love, together with its peculiar properties, powers, and actions.

6. Of God's commandments, and the willing obedience to them.

7. Of proper baptism, how commanded by Christ and practiced and taught by the apostles.

8. Of the Holy Supper of the Lord, what it is, for whom it is instituted and preserved, and what it teaches us, with its mystery and imagery.

9. Of the true apostolic ban or excommunication, its proper fruit and usefulness.

10. Of the pious Christian life which is of God.

And if you care to propose any other matter, you may then broach it and allow it to be judged in the light of the Word of God.

You see, men and brethren, this is what we would gladly see take place, if it could take place with a Christian and genuine safe conduct, without any plotting and trickery, as Christian love and the Word of God require with upright and pious heart, even as Origen, Augustine, Hilary, and still others in their day have done with those who were suspected in their doctrine. That we ask safe conduct and liberty must not be held against us, for you see, alas, how they talk about us on every hand, yes, how angry and enraged they are.

If now you are servants of Christ, and if you seek the honor of the Lord and the salvation of your brethren, even as Isaiah, Jeremiah, Peter, and Paul, etc., have done in their time, you will rejoice greatly, and thank the Lord, restore our reputation, now so sadly hurt among the people, and in the future guard yourselves against such slanderous lapses as have been listed. You will reform your ways and approve of the proposed conclave with Christian fidelity, advise it, and promote it, seeing that we do not want even as some do to have these things settled with a reference to human interest, men's own wisdom, philosophy, and imaginations, but by the very Spirit of Christ, by whose name we are named, His Word, command, prohibition, ordinance, usage, and example.

But if you evade this matter and neglect it, and nevertheless persist in your bitterness, your invention, slander, abuse, backbiting, and defamation, as you have done heretofore, then we poor ones leave it to the Lord as has been the case thus far, and possess our souls in patience, offer our backs to the smiters, and comfort ourselves with the saying, Blessed are ye when men shall hate you, expel you, and speak evil of you, and reject your name as bad for the Son of Man's sake. Rejoice and be exceeding glad, for behold your reward is great in the heavens. But fill ye up the measure of your fathers and make yourselves manifest that ye care not for the sheep but only for their milk, their fleece, and their flesh (Ezek. 34:3). You must do one or the other, namely, you must cease from your trumped-up accusations and noisy slander and enter into a discussion with us, or you must acknowledge that you are no sound teachers and bid farewell to your Gospel, reputation, and Christian name.

Herewith we commend you collectively to the Lord and beg that none shall hold this writing against us, for we have done it for no other purpose than for the defense of the Word and for the protection of our honor and to indicate that we are ready and willing now and always to confer, as has been stated, under the aforesaid stipulations.

The dear merciful Lord grant you all an honest and pious heart to love heartily the beneficent and pure truth of Christ, and faithfully to walk therein, to the praise of God and to the saving of your souls. Amen.

Here is the description of a true preacher: A bishop then must be blameless, the husband of but one wife, who has believing children, not noted for greediness or disobedience. For a bishop must be blameless as God's husbandman, not proud, not soon angry, no wine-guzzler, not sharp-tongued, not greedy of filthy lucre, but one who entertains strangers, merciful, polite, righteous, holy, chaste, and holding fast the teachings of the faithful Word in order that he may be able to admonish and rebuke the gainsayers with the saving truth. (Titus 1; I Tim. 3.)

Done by us who are miserable strangers and Christians dispersed for the Word of God and His witness, in the year 1552.

# Reply to False Accusations

*Weemodige ende christelicke ontschuldinge*

## 1552

*For other foundation can no man
lay than that is laid, which is Jesus Christ.*

I Corinthians 3:11

# Introduction

The final effort of Menno in the year 1552 to bring about a cessation of persecution is the work herewith presented under the title, *Reply to False Accusations*. The date 1552 has not been accepted by all scholars. But Menno here speaks of having opposed the Münsterites "with mouth and pen" for over seventeen years. Menno's first booklet against Münster, appeared the spring of 1535, which would incline one to accept 1552 for the present *Reply*. About the middle of the Preface to this *Reply*, Menno refers to what he wrote in the *Confession*—which would seem to mean the Confession of 1552. The *Supplication* and the *Defense* seem to follow the *Confession* in order. It is probable that late in 1552 the *Reply to False Accusations* appeared. It was written at first in the Eastern dialect of the Baltic coastal region. The first Dutch edition appeared in 1576.

Following a salutation, *To the Reader*, and a *preface,* Menno patiently replies to the following accusations: (1) That the brotherhood consisted of Münsterites, (2) that they were disobedient to the magistracy, (3) that they wished to overthrow the government, (4) that they held their property in common, (5) that they practiced polygyny and shameless lust and adultery, (6) that they cut off as apostates without opportunity to repent those who committed sin after baptism, (7) that they were a devilish gang of fanatics who claimed perfection, denied divine grace, etc., and (8) that they did wrong in not coming out into the open to teach their doctrine.

In the Dutch the title reads: *A Humble and Christian Apology and Reply concerning the bitter, vicious Lies and false Accusations by those who oppose us, and on whose Account we are without Compassion and Mercy lamentably Hated, Belied, Slandered, Reviled, and Persecuted unto Death, as it may, alas, be Witnessed Daily in many Cities and Countries.*

The Dutch Mennonites in 1712 published a small English book containing the Dordrecht Confession of Faith of 1632, an appendix containing some historical data, and Menno Simons' *Excusation,* which latter item turns out to be none other than Accusation No. 1 of Menno's *Reply to False Accusations,* together with Menno's reply. The Mennonite ministers of Pennsylvania subscribed to this booklet in 1725: "We the hereunder written Servants of the Word of God, and Elders in the Congregation of the People called *Mennonists,* in the Province of *Pennsilvania,* do acknowledge, and herewith make known, That we do own the afore-going *Confession, Appendix,* and *Menno's* Excusation, to be according to our Opinion: and also, have took the same to be wholly ours. . . ." Sixteen Mennonite ministers from "Shipack," Germantown, "Canastoge," Great-Swamp, and Manatant [now the Chester-Berks district of the Franconia Conference] signed this statement.

Menno's *Reply to False Accusations* is printed in the *Opera Omnia Theologica* of 1681, fol. 491-516, and in the *Complete Works* of 1871, Part II, pages 297-323.　　　　　　　　　　　　　　　　　　　　　J. C. W.

# Reply to False Accusations

## 1552

⚫•⚫••⚫••⚫••⚫••⚫••⚫••⚫••⚫••⚫••⚫••⚫••⚫••⚫••⚫••⚫••⚫••⚫••⚫••⚫••⚫••⚫••⚫••⚫••⚫••⚫••⚫••⚫••⚫••⚫••⚫••⚫••⚫••⚫••⚫••⚫••⚫••⚫••⚫••⚫••⚫•

## *Salutation*

To the reader, I wish much blessing and salvation.

Inasmuch, Christian reader, as we poor, despised strangers and pilgrims are pushed about and despised and considered refuse by all the world, and that because we diligently seek our salvation with all that is in us, therefore the pious and God-fearing heart must tremble and be astounded at the defamation which they unjustly heap upon the righteous, so that some who yearn after the truth hardly dare to join this body of ardent people. Christian reader, this tract is the string with which we shall tie shut this bag of lies. It is a recital of all the slander and abuse, translated out of love and for the reader's benefit and use from the Eastern dialect,[1] not well known here, into Dutch so that every God-fearing person may stop the mouth of the slanderer. The saying is *Jacula previsa minus feriunt* (Spears seen beforehand wound but few). We pray you to accept in love this our labor which we performed for your service. Our sincere desire and ambition is that many may come to the true knowledge of the truth and be saved. Fare ye well.

## *Preface*

Before God, reasonable reader, what we most sincerely desire is that with all our writing, teaching, living, misery, distress, and confiscation of our goods we may one day gain so much mercy from the children of men that we shall be allowed a private discussion with our adversaries before any number of pious, intelligent, and reasonable men who love and fear the Lord and who can distinguish between good and evil, at least if a public meeting is not allowed. Would that their lies and accusations would not be believed until teacher is confronted with teacher, and the accuser before the accused, with equal rights and liberty, as the Word of God, Christian love, and natural reason teach and

---

[1] The language spoken in the Baltic coastal region. It was called *Oostersch*. All of Menno's new books after 1554 were written in this dialect. *Ed.*

543

imply. We desire this so that the ungodly may no longer be protected in his ungodliness, the wicked in his wickedness, and that the pious and righteous might be no more condemned and oppressed; that God's holy Word by which our souls must live may be made manifest, the fearful lying cease, and the unmerciful and cruel bloodshed be stopped somewhat, a matter which in itself is nothing but the manifest work of the infernal serpent, as Christ Himself says. It hides under the cloak of true zeal and love of God and is used mercilessly without fear, thought, or mercy by those who boast of the name, Spirit, Word, death, and blood of Christ against those who with Asaph wash their hands in innocency.

But we fear that a hearing will not be allowed us. For in Scripture as well as in history we read and find that the pure wholesome truth from the beginning of the world has generally been hated, reviled, and persecuted and that it has, as a general thing, only found shelter with a few in dark nooks and corners as a hateful, ungodly abomination. It cannot come out in the open without tribulation and peril of death. The good pious Jeremiah, because he reproved the scribes for their false doctrine and wickedness, admonished the ignorant, confused the evil populace and urged them to repent, and threatened them with future plagues, was called by the scribes a heretic and deceiver, and by the princes a seditionist and troublemaker. He had to bear much hardship although he was chosen of God and a prophet from his mother's womb, and spake from the mouth of the Lord. He had to hear that on his account they had to bear grievous visitations. Ahab, the bloodthirsty and idolatrous king, had the audacity to accuse the pious and spiritual man that it was he who seduced all Israel. I Kings 18:18. Again King Joram thought that Elisha was the cause of the great famine in Samaria. II Kings 6. John, a man sent from God, blessed in his mother's womb, the greatest born of women, a burning, shining light, the messenger of the Lord, a voice crying in the wilderness, the second and spiritual Elijah, was accused that he was possessed of devils and was at last beheaded because he reproved a shameful case of fornication.

Jesus Christ, Himself the eternal Light and Life, was called Beelzebub, a Samaritan and devil-possessed, an insurrectionist, a transgressor of the Law, a blasphemer, a glutton and winebibber, a friend of publicans and sinners. He was considered worse than a murderer; and at the last He was rewarded for all His glorious miracles, kindness, and love shown to them with a mocking robe, a crown of thorns, scourging, cross, nails and death, after they had derided and blasphemed Him. How they treated Stephen, Peter, Paul, James, and the others, the Scriptures show abundantly.

At the time of the first church the Christians were called swine by some; others called them robbers of God's glory, murderers, infanticides, abominable, unchaste persons who committed all manner of abominations with their own mothers and sisters. It was said that they in their worship shed human blood and also offered their children to idols; that they were rebels, and that because of their separation from the Baal worship, and their occasional night meetings to partake of the Lord's Supper.

They were called enemies of the human race, unfruitful, corrupted, useless people because they would not associate with the drinkers, liars, highfliers, etc., but led a sober, godly, humble, and disciplined life in the love and fear of God. They were called enemies of God also, abandoned evildoers and hoodlums because they refrained from their shameful idolatry and suffered themselves to be exiled, and freely gave their goods and lifeblood for the sake of the testimony of the Lord and the true religion and honor of God.

Behold, thus the blind, ungrateful world has always treated those who sought and feared God with all their hearts, with all their souls, and all their powers, as Cyprian in his *Apology,* Tertullian, and other historians testify. Darkness cannot bear the light; nor falsehood, truth. God's Word is an abomination to the ungodly, for it is a treasure of wisdom hidden from them. Christ says, Light is come into the world, and men have loved darkness rather than light, because their deeds are evil. John 3:19. The pious and God-fearing are always an offense and an irritation in their hearts, and they make their eyes to smart. This is the cause that the world, which wants only to live without restraint or rebuke in idolatry, pride, pomp, licentiousness, and lust, has from the beginning so enviously hated, miserably reviled, and tyrannically persecuted the pious and God-fearing.

Good reader, so it is today as you can see on every hand. The whole world is submerged in all manner of wickedness. False doctrine, idolatry, unbelief, willfulness, shame, and blasphemy are in control. They will not be reproved or admonished. They hate all who would in pure love at the cost of their goods and life gladly deliver them from their wicked and undisciplined life, direct and lead them in the way of peace, and save their souls if possible.

The wise and learned ones who have ever plagued and pestered the pious and righteous the most, as was said in our *Confession,* heap one hideous lie upon another, lest their unreasonable and shameful gain and false boasting suffer or be destroyed. They insinuate and cry that we are Münsterites; that we do not want to be subject to the magistracy; that we want to take cities and countries by force; that we have our goods and our women, like the irrational animals, in common; that we say to each other, Sister, my spirit desires your flesh. Also that we claim to be without sin, and that we think to be saved by our own merits and works, and the like unfounded and unhappy lies, that they might lead from the truth all mankind, and particularly (the Lord have pity) the lords, princes, and magistrates to whom they have poured out liberally from their golden cup, that they may embitter and turn them against all the pious children of God. Whoever can rail and rant, quarrel and slander, and lie sufficiently well to move the magistrates (who perhaps would be reasonable, kind, and favorable enough if they were not spurred on and vexed by this ugly generation of vipers) to persecution so that the innocent sheep that would not injure a hair on anyone's head, are without a hearing with a bag full of lies full of abomination and slander, tied about their neck, led captive, and mercilessly exiled from country, city, and town into misery and privation, and chased into the mouth of ravening lions until they are consumed by sweat, heat, rain, and wind—he who can cause this to be done is a fine evangelical preacher, a capable minister, one who has been hitting the books. This, I think, is a case of filling the measure of their ancestors, as Christ said. O Lord, dear Lord, how long will these inhuman tyrannies and fearful abominations continue?

They have so embittered and hardened all lords, princes, regents, potentates, and common people against us by their fearful cry of murder and their slanderous lying that we cannot acquire sufficient mercy by all our prayers, moanings, and groanings, by our innocence, tears, patience, misery, cross, confiscation, and blood, that we might be allowed a public conference and discussion with those who begrudge us our existence. According to civil justice and the Christian name there should be enough of fairness, reasonableness, and decency with the rulers to make them look into the matter and not to seat themselves rashly and carelessly in an unknown matter in the judgment seat of the Most High God to shed innocent blood. We are ceaselessly slandered by their big and clumsy lies, and the truth is reviled by everybody. Therefore we are driven by the urging of the Word of God and the love of our neighbors to publish in writing our *Apology*[2] with pure Christian truth so that by our defense in writing (they being so enraged that we cannot appear publicly to defend ourselves) the God-fearing conscience which not knowingly acts contrary to the will of God, whether of magistrate or citizen, learned or unlearned, may know that by the afore-mentioned abominations we are innocently slandered and reviled by our opponents. We do this also that God might grant that thus the Word and truth of the Lord might become known and manifest, and that the deceit and faked holiness of the learned ones and priests might be open and manifest to all the world.

Honorable reader, we humbly beseech you for the Lord's sake to consider impartially why we so often refer to the preachers, admonishing and reproving them of many things which alas are not to their honor and reputation. We clearly see that they are those who for the sake of shameless gain and avarice falsely assure and support the whole world in its unbelief, idolatry, and impenitent carnal life. They sadly break the truth and trample it underfoot. They miserably murder and strangle the poor souls which are so dearly bought, not with perishable gold and silver, but with the precious blood of Christ. They viciously and scornfully hate, slander, and revile the pious and God-fearing, and take their goods and even their lives. So wholly at variance with the Spirit of the Lord are they that in order that they may continue in their shameful gain, lust, vain and fruitless life without reproach they do not allow themselves to be admonished, taught, and warned by the

---

[2] See the end of the Introduction to this book (page 542) for the full title of this *Apology and Reply. Ed.*

Word of God, by love, long-suffering, piety, and the blood of the saints. Therefore the glory of God and the salvation of your souls require us to write. The Almighty Lord is our testimony that we aim at nothing but that those who are reasonable, fair, and good—and not knowing as yet the mystery of unrighteousness, as Paul calls it (II Thess. 2:9) since they are as yet carnally minded, not born of God, and kept back by the preachers—may learn to know the preachers and teachers by clear and plain exposition, so that they may reflect upon it and become tired of their shameful deceit and seduction; and that all lords and magistrates who dare boast the name of Christ may know what kind of people and teachers they are who slander us and whom they believe and protect and promote by their arms.

## *[Reply to False Accusations]*

*I. In the first place, they complain and accuse us of being Münsterites; and warn all people to beware of us and take an example from those of Münster.*

*Answer.* We do not like to reprove and judge those who are already reproved and judged of God and man; yet since we are assailed so fiercely with this matter and without basis in truth, therefore we would say this much in defense of all of us—that we consider the doctrine and practice of those of Münster in regard to king, sword, rebellion, retaliation, vengeance, polygamy, and the visible kingdom of Christ on earth a new Judaism and a seductive error, doctrine, and abomination, far removed from the Spirit, Word, and example of Christ. Behold, in Christ Jesus, we lie not.

Besides, I can fearlessly challenge anybody that none under heaven can truthfully show that I ever agreed with the Münsterites in regard to these points. From the beginning until the present moment I have opposed them diligently and earnestly, both privately and publicly, with mouth and pen, for over seventeen years,[3] ever since according to my ability I confessed the Word of the Lord and knew and sought His holy name.

I also according to my small talent have faithfully warned everybody against their error and abomination, just as I would want other people to do for my soul. And, in passing, I have pointed and returned several of them to the true way by the grace, assistance, and power of the Lord.

I have never seen Münster nor have I ever been in their fellowship. And I trust that by the grace of God, I shall never eat nor drink with such if there should be any left, even as the Scripture teaches me, unless they sincerely acknowledge their abomination, and truly repent, and follow the truth and the Gospel in a genuine way.

---

[3] Menno's very first booklet, directed against John of Leiden, appeared in the spring of 1535. Hence this present reply is of the year 1552. *Ed.*

Behold, kind reader, this is my understanding and opinion of the Münsterites, and it also is the opinion of all those who are known and accepted of
us as brethren and sisters, that is, those who on account of the false doctrine,
unclean pedobaptism, and Supper of the preachers, are visited with such a
flood of misery, oppression, and anxiety, and who assert and testify unto death
their pure doctrine of baptism and Supper, with a humble confession and a
pious, unblamable life.

But all those who repudiate the cross of Christ,[4] as did the Münsterites,
and turn their backs upon the Word of the Lord; who go back to their worldly
love, howbeit with a pious exterior; who agree with the false religion again
and fellowship with it, walk in pomp, pride, and drunkenness, walk again on
the broad road, even though they may be baptized—these we do not know
nor accept as brethren and fellows, inasmuch as they do not abide in the
Word of the Lord.

Behold, good reader, this is the truth, and it will ever be found so.
The learned may revile and invent as they like, yet they should know that
although they are now held in honor, and their word has weight on earth, as
the psalmist testifies, we shall at the last appear before a Judge who will not
judge according to respect of persons, nor according to complaint, nor according to exteriors, nor according to favor and partiality, but according to
truth.

But if they should say that we are one church with the Münsterites,
because they and we were baptized with the same baptism externally, then
we would reply that if outward baptism has the power to make all those who
are thus baptized with one baptism into one church, and that it causes all
those who are thus baptized to share in the unrighteousness, wickedness, and
corruption of every individual, then our adversaries may well consider what
kind of church or body they have. For it is evident and well known to
everybody that perjurers, murderers, highwaymen, homicides, sorcerers, and
such like, have received the same baptism they have. If we then are Münsterites because of our baptism, they must be perjurers, murderers, highwaymen,
thieves, and scoundrels an account of their baptism. This is not to be ignored
or denied.

No! The Scriptures do not teach that we are baptized into one body
by any mere sign as water, but that we are baptized into one body by one
Spirit. I Cor. 12:13. The prophet says, The son shall not bear the iniquity
of the father, but The soul that sinneth, it shall die. Ezek. 18:20. Paul says,
Everyone shall bear his own burden. And if they should say now that evildoers are punished by the magistracy according to civil law, then we reply
that we also judge and slay them with the sword of the Spirit, according to
the ordinance and institution of God, with the Word of the Lord. That is,
we separate and expel from us all those who turn away from the truth by any
unclean or false doctrine, or by any willful, carnal walk, as has been said.

---

[4] Menno here refers to the cross of suffering which comes to true Christian believers. *Ed.*

In short, we herewith testify and confess before God, before you, and before the whole world that we from our inmost hearts detest the errors of the Münsterites, as well as every other sect which is at variance with the Spirit, Word, and ordinance of the Lord. Before God in Christ Jesus, we neither seek nor desire anything more than that we may turn the whole world which lies in sin from its wickedness to the right way, and that we may by the Word, grace, and power of the Lord deliver many souls from the kingdom of the devil and gain them to the kingdom of Christ; that we may lead a pious, humble, and godly life in Christ Jesus, and that we may glorify His great and glorious name forever. We firmly believe and confess that all false doctrine, idolatry, ungodliness, and sin are of the devil, and that the reward of sin is everlasting death. Therefore we labor diligently and earnestly, and desire, the Lord knows, to be pious and to fear God. And we poor people are so lamentably reviled and frequently and in many places even slain because of this.

II. *In the second place, they say that we will not obey the magistracy.*

*Answer.* The writings which we have published during several years past prove clearly that this accusation against us is untrue and false. We publicly and unequivocally confess that the office of a magistrate is ordained of God, even as we have always confessed, since according to our small talent we have served the Word of the Lord. And moreover, in the meantime, we have obeyed them when not contrary to the Word of God. We intend to do so all our lives. For we are not so stupid as not to know what the Lord's Word commands in this respect. Taxes and tolls we pay as Christ has taught and Himself practiced. We pray for the imperial majesty, kings, lords, princes, and all in authority. We honor and obey them. I Tim. 2:2; Rom. 13:1. And yet they cry that we will not obey the magistrates, in order that they may disturb the hearts of those that have authority and excite them to all unmercifulness, wrath, and bitterness against us, and that by their continual agitation the bloody sword may be used against us without mercy and never be sheathed, as may be seen.

They ceaselessly excite the magistracy by such gross falsehood, and moreover say Yea and Amen to everything the magistracy commands or does, whether it is agreeable to the Scriptures or not. Thus they by their pleasant doctrine lead these souls into destruction and loss. They seek not their salvation but their own enjoyment and gain. Therefore before God, it is the truth; love compels us respectfully and humbly to show all high officials (some of whom would do right if they knew it and had some Hanani to point it out to them, since it is concealed by the preachers) what the Word of the Lord commands them, how they should be minded, and how they should rightfully execute their office to the praise and glory of the Lord.

And it shall be, said Moses, when the king sitteth upon the throne of his kingdom, that he shall take this second law[5] from the priests and Levites

5 The Hebrew word at this point, *Mishneh,* means double, copy, or second. Menno seems

and copy it into a book. And it shall be with him and he shall read therein all the days of his life: that he may learn to fear the Lord his God, to keep all the words of this law and these statutes, to do them (Dear sirs, mark, it reads, To do them). His heart shall not be lifted up above his brethren and he shall not turn aside from the commandments to the right hand or the left. He shall not multiply horses to himself; neither shall he multiply wives to himself, nor silver and gold. Deut. 17:16-20. Concerning rulers, Jethro speaks to Moses, Provide out of all the people able men, such as fear God, men of truth, hating covetousness, and place them over them to be rulers. Ex. 18:21.

Moses says, And I charged your judges at that time saying, Hear the causes between your brethren, and judge righteously between every man and his brother, and the stranger that is with him. Ye shall not respect persons in judgment; but ye shall hear the small as well as the great; ye shall not be afraid of the face of man; for the judgment is God's. Deut. 1:16, 17.

Jehoshaphat, the king of Judah, said to the judges, Take heed what ye do; for ye judge not for man, but for the Lord, who is with you in judgment. Oh, an important and heroic word! Wherefore now let the fear of the Lord be upon you; take heed and do it; for there is no iniquity with the Lord our God, nor respect of person, nor taking of gifts. II Chron. 19:6, 7.

Paul says, Rulers are not a terror to good works, but to evil. (Mark ye, rulers to whom this office pertains.) Wilt thou then not be afraid of the power? Do that which is good, and thou shalt have praise of the same; for he is the minister of God to thee for good. But if thou do that which is evil, be afraid; for he beareth not the sword in vain; for he is the minister of God, a revenger to execute wrath upon him that doeth evil. Rom. 13:3, 4.

Behold, beloved rulers and judges, if you take to heart these Scriptures and diligently ponder them, then you will observe, first, that your office is not your own but God's, so that you may bend your knees before His majesty; fear His great and adorable name, and rightly and reasonably execute your ordained office. Then you will not so freely with your perishable earthly power invade and transgress against Christ, the Lord of lords in His kingdom, power, and jurisdiction, and with your iron sword adjudicate in that which belongs exclusively to the eternal judgment of the Most High God, such as in faith and matters pertaining to faith. In the same vein Luther and others wrote in the beginning, but after they came to greater and higher estate they forgot it all. Dear sirs, observe how very much Moses, Joshua, David, Ezekiel, Josiah, Zerubbabel, and others are praised in the Scriptures because they feared the Lord, and faithfully and diligently kept His commandments, counsel, and word.

If you will lift up your hearts above the mountains and will not hear what the mouth of the Lord commands you, but listen only to the inventions

to follow a version that had chosen the last translation. On the margin we read, "that is, Deuteronomy," which means the second law. Modern interpreters translate *Mishneh* with the word "Copy." *Tr.*

of your flesh; if you will not acknowledge that you are the officers and servants of the Lord, and that of Him you have received country and people, then you cannot possibly avoid the judgment of Him who has made you to be such exalted potentates, commanders, heads, and rulers. (By all means get this.) Before God, Croesus and Irus are worth equally much. Therefore sincerely fear and love your God with all your hearts. Examine the Scriptures, and ponder how the great Lord in His wrath on account of their tyranny, cruelty, pride, blasphemy, disobedience, and idolatry, has without mercy overturned and destroyed the thrones of great and mighty kings and lords, such as Pharaoh, Nebuchadnezzar, Sennacherib, Antiochus, Saul, Jeroboam, Ahab, and others, as may be clearly and plainly read in the Scriptures.

Secondly, you may understand from these Scriptures that you are called of God and ordained to your offices to punish the transgressors and protect the good; to judge rightly between a man and his fellows; to do justice to the widows and orphans, to the poor, despised stranger and pilgrim; to protect them against violence and tyranny; to rule cities and countries justly by a good policy and administration not contrary to God's Word, in peace and quiet, unto the benefit and profit of the common people, to rule well. You should eagerly seek and love the holy Word (by which the soul must live), the name and the glory of God, and in Scriptural fairness promote and maintain the same as much as possible.

You see, dear sirs and rulers, this is really the office to which you are called. Whether you fulfill these requirements piously and faithfully, I will leave to your own consideration. I think with holy Jeremiah that you have all broken the yoke and rent the bands. For you reject and detest as an abomination and a venomous serpent the dear Word which you should introduce in the pure fear of God. The false teachers and prophets who deceive the whole world, and whom according to the Word of God we should shun, are kept in high esteem by you. The poor miserable sheep who in their weakness would sincerely fear and obey the Lord, and who would not speak an evil word to anyone because they dare not do aught against His Word; who lead a pious, penitent life and make the right use of His holy sacraments according to the Scriptures, abhor with mortal fear all false doctrines, sects, and wickedness, these are exiled from city and country and are often sentenced to fire, water, or the sword. Their goods are confiscated; their children, who according to the words of the prophet are not responsible for the transgressions of their fathers (assuming that the fathers were guilty as they assert), these are thrust forth, divested and naked, and the labor and sweat of their parents they must leave in the hands of these avaricious, greedy, unmerciful, and bloodthirsty bandits.

Oh, no, ye beloved lords and judges, we will leave it to your own judgment whether this is to protect the good and punish the evil, to judge justly between man and man; to do justice to the widow, orphan, and stranger, as the Scriptures teach and your office implies. No, dear sirs, the thing is now in reverse gear. The policy is to punish the good and to protect the evil. We see daily that of which the prophets complained. Perjurers, usurers, blasphemers, liars, deceivers, harlots, and adulterers are in no danger of death, but those that fear and love the Lord are every man's prey. The prophet says, Behold, the princes of Israel, every one in thee is mighty to shed blood. In thee have they set light by father and mother; in the midst of thee have they dealt by oppression with the stranger: in thee have they vexed the fatherless and the widow. Ezek. 22. Read the prophetic Scriptures and you will find what terrible threats the holy and faithful men of God have ever prophesied of such evils and abuses.

And if you now despise these our admonitions, they nevertheless are the firm truth; this you must acknowledge in your hearts, it would seem. For it is manifest and undeniable that in our Netherlands the lascivious, bad, and good-for-nothing men whom they call pastors, ministers, masters, and teachers, some of whom wrong one woman or girl after the other, men who live in all manner of willfulness, ungodliness, idolatry, are dead drunk day and night, and do not know a single word of the Lord correctly, these men rob by their shameful trickery many God-fearing people, who before God and His angels seek nothing but to lead a righteous and unblamable life according. to the direction of the Word of God. They rob them of their country, honor, possessions, and even life, while they the deceivers live at liberty and ease.

Inasmuch as the scale of justice is so badly out of balance, and since you are nevertheless chosen and ordained of God to judge without respect of persons and to deliver from the hands of the oppressor all the afflicted and oppressed strangers; therefore we pray you humbly, most beloved rulers and judges, for the sake of Him who has called and chosen you to your office, not to believe these cruel and envious men who according to Peter are born to naught but corruption and torture and who are always publicly and privately making us so obnoxious by their shouting that men do not want to hear or see us. We pray you not to believe them so long as they in our presence do not prove (which we are sure they cannot do) against us that which they every day from their throne of pestilence and mockery so shamelessly proclaim to the world, to the shame and injury of great numbers of pious and God-fearing people. Dear sirs, we beseech you for Christ's sake to fear and love God sincerely, believe His true Word and act justly.

In the third place, you will also observe from the Scriptures that although you are called great and mighty on earth, yet you may not act according to your own opinion and option. You are to love your Lord and God sincerely as your Creator, Deliverer, and Saviour, and to fear and obey Him as your Head, King, Prince, and Judge; ever diligently to follow the directions of His Word; not to lift yourselves above your subjects and brethren, and never to deviate from the ways and commandments of the Lord. Henceforth, beloved rulers, see to it, you who call yourselves Christian, that you may be that also in deed and in word. Water, bread, wine, and name do not make a

Christian, but those are Christian who are born of God, are of a divine spirit and nature, are of the same mind as Christ Jesus, are led by the Spirit of God, crucify their evil and corrupt flesh daily, walk not after the flesh but after the Spirit, love nothing above God's Word; love their neighbors as themselves; lead an unblamable, regenerate, pious life, and willingly walk in the footsteps of Christ; and who are become new, changed, and converted men and creatures in Christ. These the Word of God calls Christians.

Beloved lords, observe that we do not read in the Scriptures of proud, carnal, perjurious, adulterous, drunken, pompous, unrighteous, idolatrous, and bloodthirsty Christians. But we do read that the portion of such shall be eternal weeping and gnashing of teeth, darkness, fire, hell, death, and the devil. Their portion will be in the lake which burneth with fire and brimstone.

Dear sirs, take care and be no longer deceived. For with God there is no respect of persons. This all the Scriptures teach. It is either life everlasting with the angels around the heavenly throne, or everlasting death with the devils in the bottomless pit. For it must all be judged according to the Spirit, example, and Word of God. Therefore if any man be in Christ, he is a new creature. He that saith he abideth in Christ, he, whether he be emperor or king, ought himself also so to walk, even as he walked. I John 2:6.

Beloved lords, this is God's Word. This is the prize and standard after which we should strive. Whosoever does not strive after and conform himself to this standard, cannot be a Christian. Therefore examine your teachers well. Earnestly and diligently consider whether or not they point you to this narrow way. I presume that they teach naught but peace to you; make your pillows soft and agreeable, and that they do not severely reprove your court-manners and practices, such as dancing, drinking, immorality, lancing and carousing, gambling, and debauchery in general. In short, that you build a wall and they daub it with untempered mortar. Ezek. 13:10.

But we, dear sirs, do not do that. We teach and direct you in the right way which you should walk if you wish to be saved. We do not point you to the pope, or to Luther, or Augustine, or Jerome, but with the Scriptures to Christ Jesus: to hear Him, to believe and faithfully follow Him. For He is the Prophet promised of God, the Teacher sent of God, the Light of the world, the true Shepherd of our souls. Whosoever shall hear, believe, and follow Him has eternal life. He calls to emperor, king, and common man, Except ye be converted, and become as little children, ye shall not enter into the kingdom of heaven. If any man will come after me (or whosoever will be a true Christian), let him deny himself, and take up his cross, and follow me. Whosoever loves anything more than me cannot be my disciple and is not worthy of me. And many other such passages.

Rulers, awake, and learn to know Him. He is the Son of the Most High God, the Lord of lords and the King of kings; the eternal power, Word, and wisdom of God. What kind of pomp, ease, and comfort He enjoyed on earth, the Scriptures teach us abundantly. At His birth there was no room for

554  THE COMPLETE WRITINGS

Him in the inn. In His preaching, He had not where to lay His head. His entrance into Jerusalem was not with cavalry, guards, and knights, but on an ass. At His death He had neither water nor wine wherewith to quench His thirst. Why was it all? Was it that we should live a fat and easy life? Oh, no. But according to Peter, it was that we should die unto sin and live in righteousness.

Behold, dear sirs, behold! These are the court manners which the heavenly Prince, Christ Jesus, has taught all His court on earth, namely, all Christians. O narrow way, O strait gate! How few that find, and fewer still that walk therein.

I write this admonition that the princes, regents, and lords may take heed and observe that they are miserably deceived by the preachers since they preach such easy and sweet things, and point to such a broad way, when the Word of God shows us a narrow way. I herewith humbly beseech you, lords, princes, kings, and judges, wherever you be, for the sake of the precious blood of our Lord Jesus Christ, wherewith we are sprinkled, not to hold it against me a poor, miserable, and despised man, that I have thus faithfully shown my sincere love to you. For I would so gladly see the greatest of all good in your poor souls. My admonition is general and I do not mention names. Whosoever is guilty, let him repent; and whosoever is not guilty, let him guard himself. God is my witness that I desire nothing but that you all may actually be what you are acclaimed to be—noble lords and Christian magistrates—that you may stand impartially between us and our opponents, the learned ones, as becomes your office, so that the seductive, deceiving falsehood may go down and be destroyed, and that the unsullied truth which for centuries has been banished may be restored to its place. Dear rulers, the Word of God is truth. Love, embrace, and kiss it. For its riches are immeasurable, its beauty wonderful, its fruits delightful, and its power eternal life.

*III. In the third place, they say that we are seditionists and that we would take cities and countries if we had the power.*

*Answer.* This prophecy is false and will ever remain so; and by the grace of God, time and experience will prove that those who thus prophesy according to the Word of Moses are not of God. Faithful reader, understand what I write.

The Scriptures teach that there are two opposing princes and two opposing kingdoms: the one is the Prince of peace; the other the prince of strife. Each of these princes has his particular kingdom and as the prince is so is also the kingdom. The Prince of peace is Christ Jesus; His kingdom is the kingdom of peace, which is His church; His messengers are the messengers of peace; His Word is the word of peace; His body is the body of peace; His children are the seed of peace; and His inheritance and reward are the inheritance and reward of peace. In short, with this King, and in His kingdom and reign, it is nothing but peace. Everything that is seen, heard, and done is peace.

We have heard the word of peace, namely, the consoling Gospel of peace from the mouth of His messengers of peace. We, by His grace, have believed and accepted it in peace and have committed ourselves to the only, eternal, and true Prince of peace, Christ Jesus, in His kingdom of peace and under His reign, and are thus by the gift of His Holy Spirit, by means of faith, incorporated into His body. And henceforth we look with all the children of His peace for the promised inheritance and reward of peace.

Such exceeding grace of God has appeared unto us poor, miserable sinners that we who were formerly no people at all and who knew of no peace are now called to be such a glorious people of God, a church, kingdom, inheritance, body, and possession of peace. Therefore we desire not to break this peace, but by His great power by which He has called us to this peace and portion, to walk in this grace and peace, unchangeably and unwaveringly unto death.

Peter was commanded to sheathe his sword. All Christians are commanded to love their enemies; to do good unto those who abuse and persecute them; to give the mantle when the cloak is taken, the other cheek when one is struck. Tell me, how can a Christian defend Scripturally retaliation, rebellion, war, striking, slaying, torturing, stealing, robbing and plundering and burning cities, and conquering countries?

The great Lord who has created you and us, who has placed our hearts within us knows, and He only knows that our hearts and hands are clear of all sedition and murderous mutiny. By His grace we will ever remain clear. For we truly confess that all rebellion is of the flesh and of the devil.

O beloved reader, our weapons are not swords and spears, but patience, silence, and hope, and the Word of God. With these we must maintain our heavy warfare and fight our battle. Paul says, The weapons of our warfare are not carnal; but mighty through God. With these we intend and desire to storm the kingdom of the devil; and not with sword, spears, cannon, and coats of mail. For He esteemeth iron as straw, and brass as rotten wood. Thus may we with our Prince, Teacher, and Example Christ Jesus, raise the father against the son, and the son against the father, and may we cast down imagination and every high thing that exalteth itself against the knowledge of God, and bring into captivity every thought in obedience to Christ.

True Christians do not know vengeance, no matter how they are mistreated. In patience they possess their souls. Luke 21:18. And they do not break their peace, even if they should be tempted by bondage, torture, poverty, and besides, by the sword and fire. They do not cry, Vengeance, vengeance, as does the world; but with Christ they supplicate and pray: Father, forgive them; for they know not what they do. Luke 23:34; Acts 7:60.

According to the declaration of the prophets they have beaten their swords into plowshares and their spears into pruning hooks. They shall sit every man under his vine and under his fig-tree, Christ; neither shall they learn war any more. Isa 2:4; Mic. 4:3.

They do not seek your money, goods, injury, nor blood, but they seek the honor and praise of God and the salvation of your souls. They are the children of peace; their hearts overflow with peace; their mouths speak peace, and they walk in the way of peace; they are full of peace. They seek, desire, and know nothing but peace; and are prepared to forsake country, goods, life, and all for the sake of peace. For they are the kingdom, people, congregation, city, property, and body of peace, as has been heard.

Beloved reader, I poor, miserable man (pardon me for writing this), have in my weakness these seventeen years feared the Word of the Lord and served my neighbors. I have without faltering borne scorn and cross with much misery, anxiety, tribulation, and peril. I trust by His grace that I will do so to the end, to testify with a good conscience to His holy Word, will, and ordinance with mouth, pen, life, and death as much as in me is. Is it possible that at heart I am a stormy, rebellious, vengeful, and bloody murderer? The Most High will save His poor servant from that.

Again, in Brabant, Flanders, Friesland, and Gelderland the God-fearing pious hearts are led daily to the slaughter as innocent sheep, and are tyrannically and inhumanly martyred. Their hearts are full of spirit and strength; their mouths flow like rivulets; their conduct savors of holy oil; their doctrine is powerful; and their life is beyond reproach. Neither emperor nor king, fire nor sword, life nor death, can frighten or separate them from the Word of the Lord. And do you suppose that their hearts are even then still ensnared by bitterness, sedition, vengeance, plunder, hatred, and bloodshed? If that were the case, then there has been a lot of suffering for naught.

Oh, no, reader, no! Learn to know what a true Christian is, of whom he is born, how he is minded, what his real intention and ambition is, and you will find that they are not rebels, murderers, and robbers as the learned ones rave, but that they are a God-fearing, pious, peaceable people as the Scriptures teach.

The other prince is the prince of darkness, Antichrist, and Satan. This prince is a prince of all tumult and blood. Raging and murder is his proper nature and policy. His commandments and teachings and his kingdom, body, and church are of the same nature. I John 3. Here we need not much Scripture, for seeing, hearing, and daily experience prove the truth.

Our opponents invent that we are intent upon rebellion; something of which we have never thought. But we say, and that truthfully, that they and their ancestors for more than a thousand years have been that which they make us out to be. Read history and you will be convinced of this. All those who place themselves in opposition to their shamefulness, dishonor, and evil-doing have had to suffer for it. Even so it is today.

For what they have done these last few years by their writings, teachings, and cries, cities and countries prove. How neatly they have placed one ruler against the others saying, Since the sword is placed in your hands you may maintain the Word of the Lord thereby, until they prevailed on them and have shed human blood like water, torn the hearts from each other's bodies, and have made countless harlots, rogues, widows, and orphans. The innocent citizen they have devoured and plundered; cities and lands they have destroyed. In short, they have done as if neither prophet nor Christ nor apostle nor the Word of God had ever been upon the earth. Notwithstanding, they wish to be called the holy, Christian church and body. O dear Lord, how lamentably is Thy holy, worthy Word mocked, and Thy glorious work derided, as if Thy divine and powerful activity in Thy church were nothing but reading, shouting, water, bread, wine, and name; and as if rebellion, warring, robbing, murder, and devilish works were permissible. Dear reader, behold and observe, and learn to know this kingdom and body. For if they with such actions and doings were the kingdom and body of Christ, as the learned ones assure them, then Christ's holy, glorious kingdom, church, and body would be an inhuman, cruel, rebellious, bloody, rapacious, noisy, unmerciful, and unrighteous people. This is incontrovertible. Oh, damnable error, dark blindness!

And it is not enough that they by their light-minded, licentious doctrine lead the whole world into destruction and sorrow and deprive their own members of property, people, prosperity, and possessions. But besides, in their madness they must lay hands upon the innocent, peaceable, and humble kingdom and body of Christ which does not harm the least upon the earth. Incessantly they lie, slander, revile, betray, and incite. Well may one say with the holy Peter that they are born to torture and corruption: for their hearts, mouths, and hands drip and reek with blood.

Oh, how accurately the Holy Spirit has depicted them, saying, I saw the woman drunken with the blood of the saints and with the martyrs of Jesus. And in her was found the blood of the prophets, and of the saints and all that were slain upon the earth. Rev. 17:6; 18:20.

Behold, kind reader, thus you will observe that they fall by their own sword which they drew against us, as the prophet says. For we may with clear consciences appear before the world (eternal praise be to the Lord) and truthfully maintain that we from the time of our confession until the present moment have harmed no one, have desired nobody's property, much less laid hands on it. We have not sought the destruction or blood of any, either by word or deed. By the grace of God we shall never do this. But what they have done by their tumultuous crying, lying, slander, railing, writing, and betraying, we will commend to the judgment of the Lord.

The merciful and gracious Lord grant and give you and them wisdom that you may learn to know of what spirit and kingdom you are the children, what you seek, what prince you serve, what doctrine you maintain, what sacraments you have, what fruits you produce, what life you lead, and in what kingdom, body, and church you are incorporated. This is our sincere wish.

Kind reader, earnestly reflect upon this our brief delineation of the two princes and their kingdoms, and by the grace of God, it will give you no mean insight into the Scriptures.

*IV. In the fourth place, some of them charge that we have our property in common.*

*Answer.* This charge is false and without truth. We do not teach and practice community of goods. But we teach and maintain by the Word of the Lord that all truly believing Christians are members of one body and are baptized by one Spirit into one body (I Cor. 12:13); they are partakers of one bread (I Cor. 10:18); they have one Lord and one God (Eph. 4:5, 6).

Inasmuch as then they are one, therefore it is Christian and reasonable that they piously love one another, and that the one member be solicitous for the welfare of the other, for this both the Scripture and nature teach. The whole Scripture speaks of mercifulness and love, and it is the only sign whereby a true Christian may be known. As the Lord says, By this shall all men know that ye are my disciples (that is, that ye are Christians), if ye love one another. John 13:35.

Beloved reader, it is not customary that an intelligent person clothes and cares for one part of his body and leaves the rest destitute and naked. Oh, no. The intelligent person is solicitous for all his members. Thus it should be with those who are the Lord's church and body. All those who are born of God, who are gifted with the Spirit of the Lord, who are, according to the Scriptures, called into one body and love in Christ Jesus, are prepared by such love to serve their neighbors, not only with money and goods, but also after the example of their Lord and Head, Jesus Christ, in an evangelical manner, with life and blood. They show mercy and love, as much as they can. No one among them is allowed to beg. They take to heart the need of the saints. They entertain those in distress. They take the stranger into their houses. They comfort the afflicted; assist the needy; clothe the naked; feed the hungry; do not turn their face from the poor; do not despise their own flesh. Isa. 58:7, 8.

Behold, such a community we teach. And not that any one should take and possess the land and property of the other, as many falsely charge. Thus Moses says, If there be among you a poor man, of one of thy brethren, within any of thy gates, in thy land which the Lord thy God giveth thee, thou shalt not harden thine heart, nor shut thine hand from thy poor brother. Tobias says, Give of thy bread to the hungry, and of thy garments to them that are naked. Christ says, Be ye therefore merciful, as your Father also is merciful. Blessed are the merciful, for they shall obtain mercy. Paul says, Put on therefore, as the elect of God, holy and beloved, bowels of mercy; etc. For he shall have judgment without mercy, that hath shewed no mercy; and mercy rejoiceth against judgment.

Again, this mercy, love, and community we teach and practice, and have taught and practiced these seventeen years. God be thanked forever that although our property has to a great extent been taken away from us and is still daily taken, and many a pious father and mother are put to the sword or fire, and although we are not allowed the free enjoyment of our homes as is manifest, and besides the times are hard, yet none of those who have joined us nor any of their orphaned children have been forced to beg. If this is not Christian practice, then we may well abandon the whole Gospel of our Lord Jesus Christ, His holy sacraments, and the Christian name, and say that the precious, merciful life of all saints is fantasy and dream. Oh, no. God is love; and he that dwelleth in love dwelleth in God and God in him.

This I write to shame our backbiters because of their envy. They are so blinded that they are not ashamed thus shamefully to slander us and wickedly to convert good into evil. For although we in accordance with all Scripture teach mercy and love, and serve the God-fearing poor by the sweat of our brow, and would not let them suffer for want, yet we must hear that we teach community of goods, and that every person should beware of us; for that we would like to reach into the chests and pockets of others! Full well they know that it is written, He shall have judgment without mercy, that has shewed no mercy; and, He that loveth not his brother, abideth in death. I John 3:14. They also see plainly that we daily and freely sacrifice our goods for the testimony of Jesus Christ and our consciences.

O reader, it would be well for your souls that you would take notice, and learn to know your preachers. For how can they teach you that which is good while they can hear no mercy?

Is it not sad and intolerable hypocrisy that these poor people boast of having the Word of God, of being the true, Christian church, never remembering that they have entirely lost their sign of true Christianity? For although many of them have plenty of everything, go about in silk and velvet, gold and silver, and in all manner of pomp and splendor; ornament their houses with all manner of costly furniture; have their coffers filled, and live in luxury and splendor, yet they suffer many of their own poor, afflicted members (notwithstanding their fellow believers have received one baptism and partaken of the same bread with them) to ask alms; and poor, hungry, suffering, old, lame, blind, and sick people to beg their bread at their doors.

O preachers, dear preachers, where is the power of the Gospel you preach? Where is the thing signified in the Supper you administer? Where are the fruits of the spirit you have received? And where is the righteousness of your faith which you dress up so beautifully before the poor, ignorant people? Is it not all hypocrisy that you preach, maintain, and assert? Shame on you for the easygoing gospel and barren bread-breaking, you who have in so many years been unable to effect enough with your gospel and sacraments so as to remove your needy and distressed members from the streets, even though the Scripture plainly teaches and says, Whoso hath this world's good, and seeth his brother have need, and shutteth up his bowels of compassion for him, how dwelleth the love of God in him? Also Moses, There shall be no beggars among you.

You see, reader, this charge is as false as are the rest. For although we know that the apostolic churches from the beginning have practiced it, as may be seen from the Acts of the Apostles, yet we may notice from their epistles that it went down in their times and (perhaps not without cause) was no longer practiced. Since we find that it was not permanent with the apostles, therefore we leave things as they are and have never taught nor practiced community of goods. But we diligently and earnestly teach and admonish assistance, love, and mercy, as the apostolic Scriptures abundantly teach. Behold in Christ we tell you the truth and lie not.

And even if we did teach and practice community of goods as is falsely reported, we would be but doing that which the holy apostles full of the Holy Spirit did in the previous church at Jerusalem—although as was said they discontinued it.

But the reason why our opponents lay this to our charge may be easily guessed. Often their hearts are filled with avarice, as Peter says, and they know also that their disciples are intent upon the lusts of the flesh, money, and goods. They are all covetous, as the prophet says. And therefore they make the charge that thus the precious Gospel, the pure truth of our Lord Jesus Christ, which, God be praised, now springs up in many places, may become a stench and an abomination to all men. Behold the arts and cleverness of the serpent.

Reader, beware; let not such liars deceive you. Adam and Eve believed the deceiver and thereby so wickedly sinned against their God. Israel was miserably deceived by the false prophets. And what good things they have done in the New Testament and still do their deeds and fruits openly show.

*V. In the fifth place, some of them invent the report that we practice polygamy and that we have our women in common; that we say to each other, Sister, my spirit desires your flesh.*

*Answer.* As to polygamy we would say, the Scriptures show that before the Law some of the patriarchs had many wives, yet they did not have the same liberty under the Law that they had before the Law. For Abraham who was before the Law had his own sister for wife, as he himself testifies before Abimelech, the king, saying, And yet she is my sister; she is the daughter of my father, but not the daughter of my mother. Jacob had two sisters for wives, Leah and Rachel, the daughters of Laban, his mother's brother. These liberties to marry their own sister and to marry two sisters at once were afterwards strictly forbidden Israel under the Law. Lev. 18.

Each era had its own liberty and usage according to the Scriptures, in the matter of marriage. And under the New Testament we are not pointed by the Lord to the usage of the patriarchs before the Law nor under the Law, but to the beginning of creation, to Adam and Eve (which word we sincerely desire to obey). Therefore we teach, practice, and consent to no other arrangement than the one which was in vogue in the beginning with Adam and Eve, namely, one husband and one wife, as the Lord's mouth has ordained. Matt. 19.

We say one husband and one wife and not one husband and two, three, or four wives, and these counted as one as they charge us, alas, without any truth. These two, one husband and one wife, are one flesh and can not be separated from each other to marry again otherwise than for adultery, as the Lord says. Matt. 5:19; Mark 10; Luke 16.

This is our real position, doctrine, and practice concerning marriage, as we here confess with the holy Scriptures. By the grace of God it will ever remain the position of all pious souls, let them lie and slander as they like. We know and confess truly that it is the express ordinance, command, intent, and unchangeable plain word of Christ.

But as to the charge of the shameful immorality of having our wives in common, we reply with Solomon that we should not answer fools in accordance with their folly, lest we become like unto them; yet we have to do it lest they think they are wise and right.

Kind reader, I am heartily ashamed to touch upon such accursed charges of harlotry and wicked abandon before the ears of blushing pious persons. For they are not only in opposition to the Scriptures but also to all reason, sense, and honor. But since they not only make us out to be wretched scoundrels, but also dogs and swine; and in order that the pious, virtuous hearts who, if possible, would rather die ten deaths than commit such abominations, may see how they are spit upon by some shameless slanderers, therefore it is no more than reasonable to defend our reputation in a Christian manner to the praise of the Lord, and to ward off such slander from us as much as we may.

We hereby testify, now and forever, in this place and before God, that we with the angel of the church of Ephesus hate the works of the Nicolaitanes which God also hates. Rev. 2:6.[6] We teach, as from the mouth of the Lord, That whosoever looketh on a woman to lust after her, hath already broken his marriage vow in his heart. And with Paul, That the adulterers and fornicators cannot inherit the kingdom of God. I Cor. 6.

We are plainly taught by the Scriptures and, by the grace of the Lord, we not only believe but also teach others in this way with the authority of the divine Word. And besides, since we are in constant danger of apprehension, prison, and death; are tied to the stake by threes or fours, by sixes and sevens; are garroted, burned, and drowned, and unmercifully murdered and killed, therefore judge whether we would practice such frightful abominations and immorality at which every reasonable person should stand astounded, and which according to many Scriptures are rewarded by everlasting death and eternal, unquenchable hell fire. Oh, what miserable men we should then be! It is a shameful slander! No, no. We trust that in our weakness, by the grace of the Lord and according to our gift, we have made our bodies and members into a temple and dwelling place of the Holy Spirit. We trust by

---

[6] On the margin we read: "So named for Nicolas the deacon of Acts 6 whose followers, according to the historians, had their wives in common." Modern scholarship has another explanation for the origin of the name Nicolaitanes. *Tr.*

the grace and assistance of the Lord that we will never in all our days fellowship again with harlots and immoral wretches—we mean such who do not
repent.

But how our slanderers and revilers are minded, into what body they
have incorporated their bodies and members, and by what kind of spirit they
are led, their intolerable lies and slander plainly show. Christ says, Out of
the abundance of the heart the mouth speaketh. Matt. 2:34. Every tree
beareth fruit after its own kind. Seneca[7] says, As the man, so is his word.
Yet if these vain men were Christians, and if they had but a little of the
Lord's Word and a spark of His Holy Spirit, as they boast of having, they
would never think of such abominable slander against their neighbors who,
as is plain, sincerely seek and fear the Lord. Much less would they mock and
deride them.

O you rude defamers (I mean all those who are guilty of this shamefulness), do you think that we are like dumb and senseless animals and that
there is no rationality left in us? Shame yourselves a bit for your inhuman
lies and slander. This ugly report and shameful reputation is laid upon us
who are innocent, by you, many of whom are guilty of this very thing. If I
write untruthfully, then rebuke me. It is manifest, is it not, and undeniable
that many of your household of faith are up to their ears in filth, for by their
cleverness and honeyed speech, promises and gifts, they seduce many a young
maiden who is by one baptism, faith, and Supper incorporated into one body
with them, and make them harlots and floor mops! In your brotherhood how
many an honorable man's bed is defiled and his daughter ravished, how many
a shameful adulterer is found, how many an unsuspecting soul is deceived,
how many an illegitimate child born. We leave it to the judgment of all pious
persons if that is not a case of having wives in common and of saying, Sister,
my spirit desires your flesh.

Beloved reader, judge the right and know the truth. Is not your church
full of such debauchees, defilers, perjurers, harlots, and scamps? Are there
not some who operate houses of ill fame? Can we not hear and see unchaste
women sing and dance and drink on street and sidewalk with their sensuous
conduct? Do they not live in city and country in open day? Your answer must
be yes, for it cannot be denied. And all these are your companions in faith,
members of your body, grains of your loaf. Oh, vain doctrine and faith,
fruitless baptism and Supper, unclean body and church.

Behold, kind reader, if you are reasonably minded you must admit that
our slanderers are guilty of the things with which they charge us. My friend,
beware lest you transgress against the God-fearing ones with these slanders.
Sirach says, Whoever accustoms himself to evil saying and whoredom will
never reform. For as we hate all abominations which are contrary to the
Word of God and not only reprove them by our teaching but also at the risk
of life, how much more then this abomination which is contrary not only to

---

[7] Seneca (c. 4 B.C.—65 A.D.) was a Roman philosopher. Ed.

God's Word but also to natural reason? O dear Lord, so they are slandered who sincerely glorify Thy name, who walk in Thy ways, and sacrifice property and life for the sake of Thy holy Word.

*VI. In the sixth place, they invent the notion that we deny all penance and grace to those who after confession of faith and baptism fall into sin.*

*Answer.* This charge if true would be a fine excuse for willful people to persecute the truth. But it is as false and contrary to fact as are their other charges, and can never be substantiated.

But since we are saddled with this accusation and since there might be some among the pious who are not at home in these things, therefore I will present my position and confession as taken from the Word of the Lord concerning classification of sins which are pardonable and which are not. And I present it to the pious and godly reader to ponder it diligently and then to judge.

The Scriptures as I see it speak of different kinds of sin. The first kind is the corrupt, sinful nature, namely, the lust or desire of our flesh contrary to God's Law, and contrary to the original righteousness; sin which is inherited at birth by all descendants and children of corrupt, sinful Adam, and is not inaptly called original sin. Of this sin David says, Behold, I was shapen in iniquity; and in sin did my mother conceive me. The Lord said unto Noah, The imagination of man's heart is evil from his youth. Again, Paul says, We were, by nature, children of wrath, even as others.

Yes, readers, since we all partake of this evil, therefore we would all have continued in death if the righteousness, intercession, death, and blood of Christ Jesus were not given us as a reconciliation to God our heavenly Father. Rom. 5:8. But now for Christ's sake, it is not counted as sin unto us. Rom. 3:5-8.

The second kind of sins are the fruits of this first sin and are not inaptly called actual sin by theologians. They are these: adultery, fornication, avarice, dissipation, drunkenness, hatred, envy, lying, theft, murder, and idolatry. These are also called works of the flesh by Paul (Gal. 5); and that because they have their origin in the flesh which is born of Adam, corrupt and sinful. Rom. 5; Eph. 5.

Wherever original sin, which is the mother, and actual sin, which is the fruit, are connected together, there is no forgiveness nor promise of life; but there wrath and death abide unless these sins are repented of, as the Scriptures testify.

If now the power of original sin is to be broken, and actual sin forgiven, then we must believe the Word of the Lord, be born again by faith and by virtue of the new birth, and by true repentance resist original sin and die unto actual sin if we are to be pious. For as the natural birth which is of Adam is unclean and sinful, and begets all evil and unrighteousness unto death according to the will of the devil, so on the other hand the heavenly birth which is of God is clean and pure, and begets all righteousness and piety unto life according to the will of God. Rom. 5; I John 3:5.

The third kind of sins are human frailties, errors, and stumblings which are still found daily among saints and regenerate ones, such as careless thoughts, careless words, and unpremeditated lapses in conduct. These, although they spring from those sins mentioned above, as do the sins of the unbelieving and impenitent, yet are they not identical with them. There is this difference. The unbelieving ones which are as yet unchanged in their first birth commit sin with relish and boldness,.and without hesitation. Because of the blindness of their corrupt nature, they do not know the ugliness of their sins and besides many of their sins they do not consider to be such, since because of their unbelief the Law has not yet made known unto them their sinfulness.

But those who are born from above are fearful of all sin. They know by the Law that all which is contrary to the original righteousness is sin, be it inward or outward, important or trifling. Therefore they fight daily with their weak flesh in the Spirit and in faith. They sigh and lament about their errors, which they with Paul sincerely abhor and to which they do not consent. They know them to be contrary to original righteousness and God's law, and are therefore sinful. They approach the throne of grace daily with contrite hearts and pray, Holy Father, forgive us our trespasses as we forgive those that trespass against us. They are not rejected by the Lord on account of such lapses, even though they are sinful lapses, which are not committed willfully and intentionally but contrary to their will, out of mere thoughtlessness and weakness—we have as an instance, Peter, who thrice denied the Lord—for they are under grace and not under the Law, as Paul says. The seed of God, faith in Christ Jesus, the birth which is of God, and the anointing of the Holy Spirit remain in them. They exercise themselves in a constant and unending battle; they crucify their lusts as long as they live; they watch and pray incessantly; and although they are such poor, imperfect children, they nevertheless rejoice in the sure trust of the merits of Christ, and praise the Father for His grace.

Behold this defective and weak nature the saints have always lamented. Therefore John says, If we say that we have no sin, we deceive ourselves, and the truth is not in us; if we confess our sins, he is faithful and just to forgive us our sins, and to cleanse us from all unrighteousness. I John 1:8, 9.

The fourth kind of sin is this. After one is enlightened in his heart by the heavenly luster of the everlasting truth, has received the true knowledge of Christ and His holy Word, has tasted the heavenly gifts, the kindness of the Lord, and the power of the world to be, has partaken of the Holy Ghost and is born of God; but in downright wickedness, malice, and willfulness, contrary to his heart and mind and the Spirit which is in him, renounces all knowledge and grace, rejects the Spirit and Word of God; ejects the sweet, new wine which he had drunk; hates and blasphemes and reviles all truth, consciously and willingly with the Pharisees and scribes, ascribing it to the devil, notwithstanding his conscience convinces him that it is the will, Word, power, and work of God; and he then returns to the broad way, and says in his heart with all evil minds, I refuse to be subjected. What kind of sin this is I will leave to the Word of the Lord to make out. Num. 15; Matt. 12; Mark 3; Luke 12; I John 5; Heb. 6.

Dear reader, do not misunderstand. I do not speak of remnants of the old nature even though they are as great as the fall of David (from which may the great Lord eternally save His own) who was so miserably deceived by the lusts of the flesh. But I speak of those who out of downright wickedness, willfully and of set purpose trample upon the Son of God, deem the blood of the New Testament unclean, and profane the Spirit of grace.

O reader, kind reader, take heed and remember that it is written, It is a fearful thing to fall into the hands of the living God. Heb. 10:31.

And although such willful blasphemy and sin had no offering in Israel (Num. 15), and although for sin against the Holy Spirit there is no forgiveness as Christ says (Matt. 12; Mark 3; Luke 12), yet I would beg and advise all the God-fearing ones, as far as I am able, that if any should revert to the patent works of the flesh and of death after his confession and baptism, wisely to consider the matter and not to make a mistake in such a case by premature and unseasonable judgment. For the Lord to whom nothing is concealed knows what sin he has committed, whether he has sinned against the Holy Ghost or not. But let them admonish such a one according to the Word of the Lord. If he repents heartily, if he shows true fruits of repentance according to the Scriptures, if he receives a broken, contrite, and penitent heart once more, and a peaceable, joyful, and cheerful mind, then it is manifest that he did not sin against the Holy Ghost. But if he remains impenitent, continues in his willfulness, and unto the end willfully despises Christ and His Word, then his conduct shows what sin he has committed, and that his end and reward will be death. Rom. 1:8; I Cor. 6; Gal. 5; Eph. 5; I John 3:5; Rev. 21:22.

Behold, kind reader, thus we believe that all sins both outward and inward have their reconciliation in the merit and power of the blood of the Lord, if truly repented of according to the Scriptures.

Let everyone take heed that he walk in the fear of the Lord and accept the grace lest he be delivered to the wrong spirit, fall into the judgment of the Lord, and the penance which avails before God be refused him. For Christ says, Whosoever committeth sin is the servant of sin. Peter says, Of whom a man is overcome, of the same he is brought in bondage. Let therefore none be overcome of sin, lest he be the servant of sin. This is incontrovertible.

I think that this our confession, and also the ban or separation which is laid down in Scripture and which we practice, by which we seek the Scriptural mortification of the apostate unto their repentance, show that in this matter also we are vilified by our opponents. We testify before the Lord and before you that we desire nothing upon earth more ardently than that we may return a poor, erring sinner to the right way.

But this we say, That the promises of God of eternal salvation as preached by the Gospel are not made to the unrepentant sinners, the hypocrites, the avaricious, earthly-minded, mockers, the perverse. They are made to those who with all their heart hear, truly believe the dear Word of our Lord Jesus Christ, and by it become new men, born of God, who die unto this frightful mad world with its ungodly pride, pomp, vanity, and lust. For some would boast of the Scriptures and comfort themselves with it, and their life is contrary thereto and is an open blasphemy and enmity of God. Christ says, If ye continue in my word, then are ye my disciples indeed. John 8:31. Ye are my friends, if ye do whatsoever I command you (John 15:14); for the vine bears after its own kind.

*VII. In the seventh place, they slander us and say that we are vagabonds, sneak-thieves, seductive ones, new monks and hypocrites; that we boast of being without sin, that we are heaven-stormers and merit-men who want to be saved by our own merits and works, an ungodly sect and conspiracy, murderers of infants' souls, Anabaptists, profaners of the sacraments, and men possessed of the devil.*

*Answer.* These and like slanders Christ Jesus together with the holy apostles, prophets, and saints of the first church had to hear many times, as was said in the preface. If they have called the master of the house Beelzebub, how much more them of his household? The disciple is not above his master, nor the servant above his lord. Yet we trust that it is known to all honorable, pious, and reasonable men that all this abuse and slander is spoken against us by our opponents without any truth out of simon-pure hatred and envy, in order that they may in this way hinder and oppose the course of the word and bring distress upon the innocent. Matt. 10:24, 25.

a. As to being vagabonds: Vagabonds are scamps, culprits, lazy rascals, and evildoers, who on account of their worthlessness wander from place to place and do not stay put. But we are poor miserable pilgrims, and according to the flesh sorrowful strangers, who not on account of any wickedness or crime, but for the testimony of Jesus Christ and our consciences, must flee for our lives with our poor wives and little children from before the tyrannical, bloody sword, and as a result have to earn our bread in foreign lands, in anxiety, and must hear many scornful and abusive words; we who should be received in love and provided for and protected according to the Scripture and not unmercifully kicked about, ruined, and besmirched as we are at present on every hand.

b. As to the ugly and vicious slander of being sneak-thieves:[8] Sneak-thieves are thieves and murderers who secretly enter houses for the purpose of taking the property or lives of others, also adulterers and seducers who are

---

[8] When Menno wrote this those who dissented from the prevailing religiosities were forced to have their religious meetings under cover of darkness and in out-of-the-way places. This led to the accusation that they were sneak-thieves, men whose activities could not stand the light of day. *Tr.*

intent upon defiling the houses of their neighbors. Such wait for the darkness, says Job, and say, No eye shall see me. In the dark they break into houses. But we are not of that kind. But it has come to such a pass, by the lying and raving and ranting of the learned ones, that sad to say, one cannot publicly let out a peep about the Word of the Lord, although it is the only bread whereby our souls must live. Moreover we learn from the Scriptures that Moses and all Israel ate the Passover at night; that Jesus admonished Nicodemus at night; that the church assembled at night to pray; that Paul taught the Word of the Lord all night; and that the first church assembled at night to break the bread of the Lord, as the historians report. Therefore we confess that we must practice and promote the Word of the Lord at night as well as in daytime to the praise of the Lord. And so we assemble at times in the fear of God without hinder or harm to any man, the Lord knows, at night as well as in the daytime, in a Christian manner to teach the Word of the Lord and to admonish and reprove in all godliness; also to pray and administer the sacraments as the Word of the Lord teaches.

c. As to being seductive people and deceivers: Those who call impenitent, carnal persons Christians and strengthen them in their blindness, avarice, pride, pomp, splendor, drunkenness, and idolatry, these are deceivers and seductive people who with absolutions, bread, wine, and ceremonies mislead people; who shamefully pervert the Word and sacraments of God and lead the poor, miserable souls into death for the sake of a stomach full of bread or a handful of barley. Of these things before the Lord we are innocent by His grace. For we teach the unfalsified Word of the Lord with a good conscience, without respect of persons. We seek the salvation of every soul and not their favor and gifts. We use the Lord's baptism and Supper according to the direction of His holy Word. And although we are poor, weak, miserable, clothed with wicked flesh, and bruised sinners, yet we would gladly in our weakness act rightly and be pious and live unblamably before the world.

We seek and desire by the grace and assistance of the Lord according to our small talent to raise up that which is fallen; make the rough places plain; seek that which is lost; humble the high-minded; **direct the hungry** into the right pasture, the thirsty to the true fountains, and the blind to the right way, in order that we may thereby sow the Gospel of our Lord Jesus Christ in many hearts to the praise of our God and publish His great and adorable name.

d. As to being new monks: We list those as new monks who formerly established churches, cloisters, human statutes, and the easy Epicurean life under the cloak of a zeal which they have abandoned and have together fallen into a still more sensuous, pompous, and carnal life without change of heart, continuing in their sins and having placed the basis of their faith, hope, and salvation upon human choice and opinion and flattery and glosses from the beginning. It is the manner and custom of monks to follow human statutes, commands, and institutions and not the Word of God. They have their abbots, priors, and pursers or procurators and are called Augustinians, Franciscans, Dominicans, Bernardines, and Jacobins for their founders and masters.

Not so with us. We trust by the grace and mercy of the Lord that we are children of God and disciples of Christ. We know no other Abbot than Him on whom all true Christians call in spirit and truth and say, Abba, Father. Our head or prior is Christ Jesus. Our procurator or purser and dispenser who distributes His gifts to everyone is the Holy Spirit. Our profession is the sincere, frank, and fearless confession of faith. Our statutes and laws are the express commandments of the Lord. Our cap and cloak are the garments of righteousness with which we would gladly clothe ourselves. Our cloisters are the assembly of the saints, the city of the living God, the heavenly Jerusalem. Our soft and easy monks' life and pleasures are the daily expectation of prison and fetters, fire and water, or exile with our wives and children, to suffer hunger, care, discomfort, anguish, sorrow, pain, and tears on our cheeks.

Behold, kind reader, this is the monkhood which we confess to and practice, and none other. By the grace and power of the Lord, we also hope to abide therein unchangeably all our lives. O you rude revilers and defamers!

e. As to being hypocrites: According to the Scriptures hypocrites are those who put on an external holy appearance by words and gestures such as the scribes and Pharisees; a people who are inwardly chock-full of unrighteousness, avarice, hatred, and deceit as our opponents are, who pretend to be Christians, have a lot to say about the Word of the Lord, boast much of the Gospel and the Christian name, claim that they practice the true doctrine of Christ, and that they are His holy church, while at the same time they falsify the Word of God, call the wholesome administration of the sacraments heresy; hate all the pious, and practice the works of the flesh openly, as may be seen. We will let all intelligent persons judge whether such are not the companions and fellows of the scribes and Pharisees.

The reason they throw the ugly word of hypocrite at us and lyingly say that we boast of being without sin is because we teach penitence according to the Scriptures, because we testify with the holy Paul that adulterers, idolaters, drunkards, avaricious, liars, and the unrighteous shall not inherit the kingdom of God; that those who are carnally minded shall die; and with John that those who sin willfully and of set purpose are of the devil and that we therefore even in our weakness have an aversion to such works, although with Moses we have often confessed with tongue and pen and ever will confess that none is clear before God because of innate sin. We say with Isaiah that we are all as the unclean; with David, that there is no living man righteous before God; with Paul, that nothing good dwells in our flesh; with John, that if we say that we are without sin we deceive ourselves and no truth is in us; and with James, that in many things we all offend.

Behold, kind reader, this is why the preachers call us hypocrites who claim to be without sin. Such abominable lies are told by those who make themselves believe that they preach the Word of God.

f. As to being heaven-stormers: Because we teach from the mouth of the Lord that if we would enter into life, we must keep the commandments; that in Christ, neither circumcision nor uncircumcision avails anything but the keeping of the commandments of God, and that the love of God is that we keep His commandments, and His commandments are not grievous; therefore the preachers have to call us heaven-stormers and merit-men, saying that we want to be saved by our own merits even though we have always confessed, and by the grace of God ever will, that we cannot be saved by means of anything in heaven or on earth other than by the merits, intercession, death, and blood of Christ, as has been amply demonstrated above.

Behold in this way the best that there is must by these perverse people be changed into the very worst that there is. And they do not notice that the Scripture in its entirety condemns to death all willful, bold despisers and transgressors of the commandments of God who prove plainly by their deeds that they do not confess the saving grace of God, do not believe in Christ Jesus, and according to Scripture abide in damnation, wrath, and death. For whoso doeth unrighteously showeth by his works whose disciple he is.

g. As to the bitter slander, Ungodly sects and conspiracy: As far as the bitter, envious slander and charge that we are a perverse, ungodly sect and conspiracy is concerned, we answer: If we were allowed an impartial hearing with our opponents before a tribunal of persons who understand the Word of God, we would soon be cleared of the infamous charge, and they would be found guilty. For what kind of conspiracy they are, this Scripture testifies: There is a conspiracy (mark, a conspiracy) of her prophets in the midst thereof like a roaring lion, ravening the prey; they have devoured souls; they have taken the treasure and precious things; they have made her many widows in the midst thereof. Ezek. 22:25.

All may find a place in their sect who will but keep their ceremonies, and acknowledge them to be the true preachers and messengers, no matter how they live, just so they keep out of the hands of the executioner. No drunkard, no avaricious or pompous person, no defiler of women, no cheat or liar, no thief, robber, or shedder of blood (I mean in the conduct of warfare), no curser or swearer so great and ungodly but he must be called a Christian. If he but say, I am sorry, then all is ascribed to his weakness and imperfection and he is admitted to the Lord's Supper, for, say they, he is saved by grace and not by merits. He remains a member of their church even though he is an impenitent and hardened godless heathen; today as yesterday and tomorrow as today, notwithstanding that the Scriptures so plainly testify that such shall not inherit the kingdom of God, for they are of the devil.

Preachers, preachers, learn to know your own sect and conspiracy for a change, we pray you for Christ's sake. You boast that you are the true Christian church, but we fear that you are a new Sodom, Egypt, and Babylon. Ah, for many years we have drunk the same goblet with you and walked in the same spirit; we have received one chrism and anointing with you; we know you in and out.[9] But we have received mercy and have spewed out the abomination we had swallowed, and have willingly entered into the lovely communion of His saints, into the house, kingdom, and body of Christ— those who hate all ungodliness and sinfulness, and with all their strength strive after and desire righteousness and godliness. Although they are called by you and all the world an ungodly sect and conspiracy, yet are they peaceable and joyous in the spirit, and are assured in their consciences that truth is on their side and that they are not an ungodly sect and conspiracy, but God's own peculiar people, church, and body. O Lord, how lamentably and sadly Thy small flock is ever slandered, now and always!

h. As to the ugly smear of being murderers of infants' souls: That same thing we must often hear from these poor, blind people who seek the salvation of their children in the baptism of their preachers—that we murder the souls of our infants—because we believe the Word of the Lord that the kingdom is promised them by grace, by the election of God our heavenly Father through the merits of Jesus Christ, as He says: Suffer little children and forbid them not to come unto me, for of such is the kingdom of heaven. Therefore we do not have them baptized with the baptism of Antichrist. For not the baptism of Antichrist but the promise of Jesus Christ assures us of the salvation of our little ones if they die in infancy. But if the good Father lets them grow up and grants them His grace, then we hope to bring them up in the nurture and admonition of the Lord as much as we are able. When they can understand God's Word, and when they believe it, the Scripture directs them to be baptized. But those who carry on in such manifest hypocrisy and anti-Christian fashion expel the devil[10] from the innocent vessels which are cleansed with the blood of the Lord; they conjure, salt, anoint, and consecrate them and baptize them on the faith of others, although they find not a single word to command such monkeyshine and mockery in all the Scriptures.

They comfort the parents with the thought that by this transaction they are now Christians, and in this way they are from the cradle on raised in all manner of blindness, pomp, boldness, and idolatry, without the fear of God, so that when they come to the years of discretion they have as yet no knowledge of the Word of God and they walk all their lives, trusting in infant baptism, upon a dark and crooked way without confession, without faith and new birth, without Spirit, Word, and Christ. What such people do to the souls of their little children, I leave to their own consideration and to the sentence of the Word of the Lord.

i. As to the inane slur, Anabaptist: The learned ones call us Anabaptists because we baptize upon confession of faith as Christ commanded His disciples to do, and as the holy apostles taught and practiced; also the worthy martyr Cyprian,[11] all of the African bishops; and besides because we with

---

[9] Menno had been a Roman Catholic priest, 1524-35. *Ed.*
[10] The Roman Catholic and Protestant sixteenth-century practice of exorcism. *Ed.*
[11] Cyprian, bishop of Carthage in North Africa, was beheaded in A.D. 258. *Ed.*

the Nicene Council cannot accept the heretical baptism which is of Antichrist as Christian baptism. We are informed by the Scriptures that Saint Paul rebaptized some of those who were baptized with the baptism of John which was from heaven, because they did not know of the Holy Ghost. Acts 19:3. We do not baptize except according to the commandment of Christ, and according to the teaching and practice of the holy apostles; nor do any more than Cyprian did, together with the Council of Carthage and Nicea in this matter (although we assert that we do not believe in all their doctrine). We rebaptize those who are not baptized with the divine baptism as were those who were baptized of John, but with the baptism of Antichrist; persons who at the time of their baptism had no [spiritual] need, as did those mentioned, but were incapable of any Christian response, as both nature and the Scriptures teach, since they were as yet unconscious infants. If for this reason we are to be called Anabaptists by the learned ones, then verily Christ and His apostles, Cyprian and his bishops, the Nicene Council and the holy apostle Paul must verily also have been Anabaptists.

j. As to the blind charge that we are profaners of the sacraments: Some of the learned ones also call us profaners of the sacraments because we do not believe that the bread and wine of their Supper is the actual real flesh and blood of the Lord; or as some have it, because we do not believe that we through the wine and bread actually partake of the actual flesh and blood of the Lord; although we reverentially administer the Supper to those who (as far as man can judge) are penitent as a figure or sacramental sign with fear and trembling, also with thanksgiving and joy according to the Scripture and according to the practice of the fathers such as Gregory, Augustine, Chrysostom, Tertullian, Cyril, Eusebius, etc. And in our weakness we diligently strive rightly to commemorate and to fulfill the holy glorious mystery, the Lord's death; the love, peace, and unity of His church, and the communion of His holy flesh and blood which by this sign of bread and wine are symbolized to all true Christians. The poor slanderers do not notice how woefully they profane the sacraments of the Lord, if we call them sacraments which they administer, although they believe that they distribute the actual flesh and blood of the Lord. Yet they esteem it so little that they distribute it to evident drunkards, liars, avaricious and impenitent ones, as if the Lord's Supper were to be partaken of by the penitent and impenitent alike. Whether this is not a matter of profaning the sacraments, you may ponder in the light of the Scriptures.

k. As to the Pharisaic slur that we are possessed of the devil: We consider those possessed of the devil who speak the devil's words, who teach the devil's falsehood instead of truth, steal God's glory from Him, and sadly deceive souls. But we trust by the grace of God (eternal thanks to God) that we hate the word of the devil from our inmost souls, and that we are very desirous for the words of eternal truth, and for the fruits of the Spirit according to the talent received. This is an evident sign that we are not possessed of the spirit of the devil but of that of the Lord. If we were of the devil as we are reviled, we would walk upon a broader road and be befriended by the world and not so resignedly offer our property and blood for the cause of the Word of the Lord. Yet it is but just that the disciple be not above the master. The Master of the house Himself had to hear that He was of the devil. John 8:48. The Pharisees and scribes had to manifest their nature and spirit, for if they cannot with their foolish wisdom stand before the power and truth of the Lord (for the spirit of Belial must give way to the Spirit of the Lord), then they break forth in madness, heap falsehood upon falsehood, revile and lie with all their might, and ascribe that truth to the devil, although their consciences testify and accuse them that it is the Spirit and power of the Lord. By what kind of spirit such people are urged their words and works sufficiently testify.

You see, good reader, here you have our reply to the principal slanderous charges with which we are always greeted by our revilers, opponents, and persecutors. With such slander their writings are filled and their mouths overflow. We are pictured in such colors (the Lord forgive them) that we are quite likely to be considered a perverse, ungodly people by the great mass who walk upon the broad way, so long as the world shall stand. Oh, perverseness! Generation of vipers, says Christ, how can ye being evil speak good things. Matt. 12:34.

I fear that they are really members of the terrible beast which arose from the sea, which was like unto a leopard, whose feet were as the feet of a bear, and whose mouth as the mouth of a lion, and which opened his mouth to blaspheme the name of God, and His tabernacle and them that dwell in heaven. Rev. 13:2, 6. For what is there which is holy and right according to the Scripture which they do not trample with their feet, and blaspheme with their tongue as an ungodly, accursed abomination? O dear Lord, save all Thy beloved children from this lying, deceiving generation forever.

*VIII. In the eighth place, and finally, they say, Very well, if truth is on their side, let them come out in the open.*

*Answer.* We would faithfully admonish the reader to consider well from what motive and with what intention they say this. For most of them do so from motives of mere ill will and bloodthirstiness, we are sure, thinking that if we would do so it would soon bring the matter to an end. Others perhaps do it through simplicity and ignorance, thinking that we hardly satisfy the Scripture in the matter since Christ and His apostles as also the prophets generally preached in public before the people, and were also sent for that purpose.

To those who say this from motives of bloodthirstiness, we would say that they with the Pharisees and scribes have loaded upon themselves the blood of the innocent and are counted as murderers. Matt. 23:34; John 10:16; Luke 11:49.

But to those who speak thus in simplicity (if there be a few such as we hope) we would advise in all love diligently to search all the Scriptures to see if they will find any passages to show that the apostles and prophets went forth publicly to preach when they were sure beforehand that it would cost them their lives, as we know to be the case if we would without permission come out in the open. No. If I remember, they always avoided places and cities where they were sure men would seek their lives or else they kept themselves concealed, as did Baruch and Jeremiah when King Jehoiakim had commanded that they should be taken. Jer. 36:19.

They have all feared death and fled from it however much they were gifted with the Spirit of the Lord. Moses cried unto the Lord in terror saying, What shall I do unto this people? They are almost ready to stone me. Ex. 17:4. Jeremiah said, O my lord the king, let my supplication, I pray thee, be accepted before theee; that thou cause me not to return to the house of Jonathan the scribe, lest I die there. Jer. 37:20. David fled from Saul from one mountain to the other, and from one wilderness to the other. Urijah of Kirjath-jearim, a prophet of the Lord, fled from before the sword of the king of Judah into the land of Egypt. Jer. 26:20. Elijah, the spiritual man of God, fled to the wilderness before the threats of Jezebel. I Kings 19:3. From fear of those of Nineveh, Jonah wanted to flee into Tarshish. Paul knew that they were lying in wait for him and then he was let down by the wall in a basket by night. Acts 9:24.

Behold, kind reader, thus great men of God have feared death, and did not usually go where they feared violence until they were admonished to do so by an oracle or by a revelation from angels, if my memory serves me.

It is also evident from the case of Elijah who appeared before King Ahab after the long drought and famine. I Kings 18. The apostles freely spoke the Word of the Lord in the temple after they were led from prison by an angel. Paul preached at Corinth one year and a half after the Lord in a vision spake unto him, Be not afraid but speak and hold not thy peace, for I am with thee and no man shall set on thee to hurt thee, for I have much people in this city. And there are other like Scriptures. We are aware, beloved reader, that God has the power to save His own if it be His will. For He smote the Syrians with blindness who wanted to take Elisha. Jonah in the whale He sent through the turbulent waves to Nineveh. He took from the fire its power and shut the lions' mouths. He delivered the apostles by the aid of angels; Peter twice. He is the Lord who lives unchangeable in His power and glory.

These are unusual miracles of God which are not shown to everyone, and no Scripture directs us to go where we know beforehand that we will die or be in prison for life, but we are admonished in plain words to flee from tyrants.

The faithful men and servants of God, filled with the Holy Spirit, have fled. Therefore we say simply and with a good conscience that we will not now nor at any future time publicly go forth unless it is proved to us in sincerity of heart by Scripture (which we know is impossible) that we should do so, before we are urged as were the apostles and prophets by the power of the Lord, be it by revelation from the angels or by the prompting of the Holy Spirit. In that case we are at all times prepared to do the will of the Lord, and publicly to teach His holy Word, and administer the sacraments, come what may.

It is well known to the honorable reader and to all who are acquainted with us that we are called seditionists and troublemakers everywhere by the learned ones, notwithstanding that we are quiet and act decently with all men and if we now should publicly teach the Word of the Lord in the face of the revilings of the learned ones in spite of the mandate of the rulers and of the frenzy of the common people, some of them would cry, Troublemakers, although we are, thank the Lord, clear of all rebellion and bloodshed, as has been heard.

Others would say, and not unjustly, that we deprive ourselves of life by our unrestrained zeal since we know very well what in every place is resolved against us, and we nevertheless in the face of it all publicly teach our doctrine.

Moreover, we desire the reasonable reader to take into consideration that a true teacher who preaches the Word of the Lord unblamably is not permitted at the present time as far as our knowledge goes to dwell in any kingdom, country, or city under heaven, if he be known. If he is not allowed to live in a given place, how can he preach and teach there?

Besides, we see plainly that the innocent sheep must suffer and are delivered up to death, although they are no preachers. And shall the preachers then who are blamed for it all and who with Christ are hated above all evildoers go before the public in these mad and terrible times of evil and tyranny? It would be foolishness. It is not advisable either in the light of Scripture or of common sense.

And although we do not teach at public meetings where all men meet, yet the truth is not hushed up, but is preached here and there both by day and by night, in cities and country, with tongue and pen, at the peril of life, as judges, executioners, prisons, fetters, water, fire, sword, and stake testify.

Flanders, Brabant, Holland, Gelderland, etc., will have to confess at the last judgment that the Word was preached to them in power, for they on account of the preached Word have shed innocent blood like water. It is preached enough in these countries so that we may well say with the holy Paul, If our gospel be hid, it is hid to them that are lost; in whom the god of this world hath blinded the minds of them who believe not. II Cor. 4:3.

Besides, I have about the year of 1545 or 1546 asked of the preachers of Bonn a public meeting and discussion under Archbishop Herman of Cologne on condition of safe conduct. I have also asked this twice in writing of those of Emden, and once of those of Wesel on the same condition. But although those of Bonn and those of Wesel had suggested this to some of the brethren, still when they found that I was willing to do so, it was under a false pretense refused by those of Bonn and also by those of Emden. Those of Wesel wished that the hangman might treat with me. I have also offered the same thing publicly in print years ago, but it was not accepted.

Kind reader, in this way we have from the beginning of our service been prepared and ready to give an account of our faith to every person who desired it in good faith no matter whether he were ruler or subject, learned or unlearned, rich or poor, man or woman. We are ready today to do so as far as possible, for we are not ashamed of the Gospel of the glory of Christ. If anyone desires to hear from us, we are prepared to teach. If anyone desires to know our position, we sincerely desire to explain it clearly if our writings do not suffice. If anyone desires to discuss with us, no matter who he be (except those who have had Scriptural proof enough but have left our camp), in sincerity of heart about the matter of our faith, without philosophy, glossing, and twisting, and according to the unfalsified evangelical doctrine and truth, commandments, prohibitions, usage, Spirit, and example of Christ and His disciples, and that without trickery, deceit, and cleverness, even as Hilary and Augustine and others have done in their day with some who were suspect in their doctrine, then by the grace of the Lord we will not refuse to do so if we possibly can before a public meeting, or before twenty or thirty fair and reasonable witnesses. For our most ardent desire is that the truth may be made manifest. But the bloody, Antichrist-like murder must be omitted, for it is devilish and unbecoming in a Christian, I tell you.

Our adversaries and opponents make our life and doctrine suspicious with many by saying that if the truth be on our side we should come out in the open, although they do so out of pure ill will, for they know very well that it cannot be done since there are tyrants and men who would shed blood everywhere. Therefore we have given them this discreet answer.

If the truth be on the side of our opponents and not with us as they claim, and they can freely go abroad before the whole world (understand as representatives of their peculiar sect to preach their doctrine and faith and life, but we have to be subjected daily to suffering and torture), therefore they should show enough of fairness and love toward us, poor creatures, to obtain liberty from us from the magistrates whom they have by their crying and slander against us caused to be so bitterly opposed to us (something which does not become reasonable men, not to say Christians) so that we may in their presence before a public assembly or before twenty or thirty impartial reasonable witnesses cause our position, doctrine, and faith for which we are persecuted, to be heard and explained according to the sure and true testimony of the holy Scriptures. Then if they have anything to reply against our position, doctrine, and faith, let them speak in the name of the Lord. Truth will be victorious. If not, let them lay their hands upon their mouths and keep silent and nevermore blaspheme and defame that which is right and just.

Good reader, if this could be arranged, many a pathetic execution could be averted, many miserable souls which are now kept by them in such accursed blindness would be delivered from the snares of hell and of death. And the noble, glorious truth now so very much hated and despised by the world would appear in greater splendor and beauty. But so much decency has not been found to the present time.

Since we are not allowed a public discussion in a Christian manner as we have eagerly and at different times asked of them, and since the ignorant and inexpert cry, If they are right, why do they not come out in the open? therefore we will leave it to the consideration and judgment of the intelligent reader, from what motives they cry thus, what kind of faith, love, gospel, and truth they have, and by what kind of spirit they are led. For whosoever has the truth will never come to shame. For truth is great, stronger than wine, kings, and women.

## Conclusion

Here, dear reader, you have our defense and fair reply to the bitter, hateful falsehood and slanders of those who detest us. By it we will live or die and appear before our God at the judgment day. For it I shall not perhaps be thanked by many. But since they on every hand by such inhuman falsehoods and slanders behind our backs rob us of our honor and reputation; so lamentably falsify and suppress the precious, worthy Word of our Lord Jesus Christ; maintain and uphold all the earth in its impenitent, ungodly condition; and cause so much misery to many a precious child; therefore it was needful for us to write this exoneration and Christian defense and a truthful exposition of the eternal, divine truth. We do this so that thereby all intelligent and reasonable readers who cannot hear our spoken defense may judge rightly between us and our opponents, may see the innocence of us all, and may learn to confess the poor, despised truth which is so lamentably stolen from them by their preachers. We desire also to place in the hands of the Lord this and all other shameless charges and accusations which are published against us so viciously and leave them and the whole matter to Him in the judgment of the last day.

Let them demonstrate the nature of their father and fill the measure of their bloodthirstiness, for they do not want it otherwise. We trust by the grace of the Lord to possess our souls in patience, and not to turn our faces from those who spit at us until the coming of Him who shall come. Then they shall see Him whom they have pierced. Rev. 1. And I pray those who read or hear, be they high or low, learned or unlearned, for Christ's sake to accept this my labor in love and to ascribe it to good motives. For I have performed it for no other purpose than to the praise of my God and the service of all right-minded persons, and with a fond hope that the rulers (I mean those who are reasonably minded and would not willfully act contrary to the will of God) may be warned against supporting this ungodly situation and heaping upon themselves innocent blood. May the preachers who err unwittingly by this exposition be led to desist from their lying, slander, reviling, and misleading and no longer serve and protect the kingdom of hell by their godless doctrine, sacraments, and lives. May the common people place their trust in the Word of the Lord, seek the right way, fear the Lord, die unto their sins, and reform their sinful life.

Much beloved reader, do not let it make you angry if this should taste a bit bitter to your flesh. Behold in Christ it is the simple truth, to which we have here testified. There will never be found any other foundation, doctrine, way, light, and truth.

I desire that this shall not be kept away from any reasonable person but that it may be read or heard by everyone, no matter who or where he be, if there is a chance that it might bear fruit and they are not people who plan anyone's destruction or seek his possessions, so that by it the saving truth of Christ Jesus may be extended and the damnable falsehood of Antichrist be destroyed.

May the Almighty, eternal Father, the creator of all things, the God of heaven and earth, grant all my hearers and readers the heavenly gift and the power of His Holy Spirit, that they may hear and read this my humble treatise in the true fear of God, and with pure, impartial hearts may wisely examine, understand, and accept it in true faith, and humbly fulfill it in willing obedience to the praise of their God and the salvation of their souls by His beloved Son, Jesus Christ, our Lord. To Him be honor, praise, kingdom, power, and glory forever and ever. Amen.

Lying lips are abomination to the Lord; but they that deal truly are his delight. Prov. 12:22; 6:17.

Devise not a lie against thy brother; neither do the like to thy friend. Use not to make it any manner of lie, for the custom thereof is not good. Ecclus. 7:12, 13.

MENNO SIMONS

# The Cross of the Saints

*Van dat cruyze der heyligen*


# c. 1554



*For other foundation can no man
lay than that is laid, which is Jesus Christ.*

I Corinthians 3:11

# Introduction

About the year 1554 Menno Simons wrote the booklet before us, *The Cross of the Saints*. The purpose of the booklet seems to be to encourage the brethren, especially the young and immature, to press forward valiantly in spite of the timidity of the flesh. Neither fire nor sword are to be an excuse for being fearful or for losing heart. The saints of God have no choice but to stand true to Christ, for they are by God enabled to undergo even martyrdom should God permit earthly tyrants to put them to death.

The booklet is divided into six parts of unequal length. Following the Preface and a brief introduction, Menno takes up his first topic, Who the persecutors are: what their spirit and nature are, etc. In the second place he raises the question, Why do they persecute true Christians? Third, in an extensive discussion, about a third of the tract, Menno shows that persecution has always been the lot of the people of God, not only the saints of the Old and New Testaments, but of our Lord Himself. Finally, Menno comments briefly on the severe persecution of his own brotherhood in the sixteenth century. The fourth section of Menno's booklet is a fivefold analysis and refutation of the excuses of the persecutors: (1) that the Anabaptists were seditious, comparable with the Münsterites; (2) that they were unteachable; (3) that they misled people; and (4) that they were sectarian separatists. (5) Finally, Menno replies to the excuse that it was not the state churches which persecuted the Anabaptists: it was done by the state on authorization of the emperor. The fifth section of the booklet is a treatise on the blessings of bearing the cross for Christ's sake. Finally, in a brief sixth section Menno cites some promises which those who take up the cross may claim. Although the tract contains little that is new, when compared with the earlier writings of Menno, it is nevertheless one of the finest writings of this man of God. His sharp differentiation between the true children of God and those who were Christians only by profession is Menno at his best. The tract also contains some very tender paragraphs on the love and mercy and faithfulness of God.

In the Dutch original the full title reads: *A Comforting Admonition Concerning the Sufferings, the Cross, and the Persecution of the Saints Because of the Word of God and His Testimony*. This is followed by Matt. 5:11, and Menno's beloved I Cor. 3:11 which appears on all his title pages.

In the *Opera Omnia Theologica* of 1681 *The Cross of the Saints* is printed fol. 133-59, and the folio line reads, "Of the Cross of Christ." The work is found on pages 179-212 of Part I of the *Complete Works* of 1871, also under the folio line, "The Cross of Christ." It is also so entitled in the revised edition of this booklet issued by Mennonite Publishing House in 1946.

J. C. W.

# The Cross of the Saints

## c. 1554

*Preface*

Grace and peace, an open vision of the Lord, and an unruffled spirit in the midst of all temptations do I, Menno Simons, wish with all my heart for all true children of God, from God our heavenly Father through His Son Jesus Christ our Lord, in the power of His Holy Spirit, to the edification and the salvation of us all. Amen.

Most dearly beloved brethren and sisters in the Lord, the most merciful God and Father, through His unfathomable grace and goodness, has again, in these last days of unbelief and abominations, of sin and idolatries, in this frightfully wanton, this reckless, this bad and bloody world, set forth before the eyes and consciences of some His blessed, His holy, and eternal Son Jesus Christ, who was unknown for so many centuries. He has once more opened the book of the divine assertions and of eternal truth, the book which had been closed for so many centuries. He has raised from the vile and putrid graves of their unbelief and unrighteousness some who had lain dead as to the spirit, not for a mere four days as was the case with Lazarus, but for all of twenty or thirty years, yes, all their lives, in all sin and wickedness, and has called them to a new and blameless life. Yes, He is calling certain poor, distressed, straying, lean, and starved sheep by the preaching of His Word of salvation, in the power of His Holy Spirit, out of the hands of the faithless shepherds, out of the jaws of ravening wolves, and is leading them out of the dry, parched pastures of human teachings and commandments into the lush green pastures of the mountain of Israel, giving them unto the care and custody of their only and eternal shepherd, Jesus Christ, who by His precious crimson blood has taken them to be His own freed possession and has cleansed them and purchased them.

Therefore there is consternation in hell's gate; Herod is extremely disturbed, and all the city with him, because they have heard of the wise men, taught of God that the King of the Jews is born. The great dragon, the old crooked serpent who was cast out of heaven and whose head and power are now bruised and broken by the promised Seed of the woman, who is overcome because of the blood of the Lamb and for the Word of His testimony,

burns with anger, knowing full well that his time is short. He therefore presses
forward his work and tyranny through his children and servants of unbelief
with great wrath and raving against those who have been sprinkled with the
blood of the Lamb. Ananias and Caiaphas, together with all the scribes,
conspire to the death of Christ; Judas and all false apostles and teachers betray
Him and deliver Him up; Herod, with all his lords and princes, scorns and
mocks Him. The common people cry out, Crucify, crucify! Pilate and all
those to whom the service of the sword pertains sentence Him to the stake,
to fire, to sword, and to the water. The servants seize Him, spit upon Him,
scourge Him, crown and crucify Him. The centurion pierces His side. The
others mock, blaspheme, and revile Him! Who verily is there that does not
persecute, kill, and violate (whether with heart, word, or hand) the poor, innocent, peace-loving, defenseless Lamb? Verily, in the ungodly Cain has the
bloody, murderous tyranny had its origin and has masterfully shown its essence, its fruit, and its true nature toward the pious and godly Abel.

The afore-mentioned Lamb has from the beginning of the wrath of the
serpent been slandered, persecuted, and slain, and it seems that (as the
Scriptures also say) this persecution will not cease so long as there are
righteous and unrighteous people on the earth together. In our days especially
the cross of Christ on every hand evinces itself as in the days of our first
ancestors, in the case of devout children of God who are as to the inner man
born again of the powerful seed of the Holy Word. Therefore I cannot neglect
it, I must admonish in some small way, my beloved brethren and sisters, companions in faith and affliction, with the Word of the Lord, concerning the suffering, the cross, and the persecution of the saints as it is abundantly related
in the Scriptures and as it was abundantly demonstrated to our fathers, both
of the Old and the New Testaments, and also to many pious witnesses of our
own days—actually and unmistakably. I do this so that they, according to
the example of these same fathers, may with all patience, with calmness and
strength, courage and steadfastness, continue the assigned contest through
the power of their faith and in Jesus Christ, and so receive the promised
crown. To this end may the Father of every good and perfect gift through
His beloved Son Jesus Christ our Lord grant us His rich grace in the power
of His Holy Spirit. Amen.

## [THE CROSS OF THE SAINTS]

Blessed are they which are persecuted for righteousness' sake, for theirs
is the kingdom of heaven. So spake Jesus.

I presume, worthy brethren and sisters in the Lord, that the true laborers
and servants of the Lord, who have with diligence planted and watered among
you according to the gifts which they had received, have begotten you with the

living Word of the Gospel of Jesus Christ; they have built you up in a godly manner upon Christ, the firm and immovable cornerstone, have taught you the holy Word, will, and ordinances of God according to His good pleasure, have joined you in all love as a good, obedient, chaste bride to your bridegroom, Christ Jesus. I presume that they have in all earnestness shown you the straight, the narrow, the despised way; have preached the cross, and have pointed out and admonished you touching the difficulty and the expense of this godly building project.

For it can never be otherwise, as you well know, than that all who wish to obey and follow Jesus Christ and go in by the right door, Christ Jesus, and walk upon the proper highway to eternal life, the light of Christ, must first deny themselves wholeheartedly and then sacrifice all that they have. They must take upon themselves the heavy cross of all poverty, distress, disdain, sorrow, sadness, and must so follow the rejected, the outcast, the bleeding and crucified Christ. As He Himself said: If any man will come after me, let him deny himself and take up his cross and follow me.

Yes, any man who is not ready for this hated and scorned life of the cross and sorrow, and who does not hate father and mother, son and daughter, husband and wife, houses and lands, money and goods, and his life moreover, cannot be the Lord's disciple. My faithful brethren, this is a true and certain word.

For the eternal truth, Christ Jesus, has in many places of the Scriptures said it and testified to it in great clarity. Behold, He said, I send you forth as sheep in the midst of wolves. Be ye therefore wise as serpents and harmless as doves. But beware of men, for they will deliver you up to the councils and they will scourge you in their synagogues, and ye shall be brought before governors and kings for my sake for a testimony against them and the Gentiles. Again, the brother shall deliver up the brother to death, and the father the child, and the children shall rise up against their parents and shall cause them to be put to death, and ye shall be hated of all men for my name's sake. Again, the disciple is not above his master nor the servant above his lord. It is enough for the disciple that he be as his master and the servant as his lord. If they have called the master of the house Beelzebub, how much more shall they call them of his household?

Again, he that loveth father or mother more than me is not worthy of me, and he that loveth son or daughter more than me is not worthy of me, and he that taketh not his cross and followeth after me is not worthy of me. He that findeth his life shall lose it; he that loseth his life for my sake shall find it. Again, then shall they deliver you up to be afflicted and shall kill you and ye shall be hated of all men and nations for my name's sake. Again, they shall put you out of the synagogues.

Yes, the time cometh that whosoever killeth you will think that he doeth God a service. (Read also Matt. 16:34; Mark 8:34; 13:9.)

Again, we must through much tribulation enter into the kingdom of God.

All that will live godly in Christ Jesus shall suffer persecution. If we be dead with him, we shall also live with him. If we suffer, we shall also reign with him.

Yes, of these indicated anguishes, expulsions, smitings, reproachings, slanders, betrayals, apprehensions, plunderings, of this shameful death and this cross of the saints, the whole Scriptures are full—as they are with admonitions, examples, and accounts everywhere.

From the beginning of the world genuine righteousness and devout piety have been in this way miserably hated, persecuted, cast out and killed, as has been abundantly shown in the case of the early pious fathers, and may be seen and found also in these last times as we have said. Therefore I think it necessary and beneficial to show from the Word of the Lord to our youthful, weak, and untried Christians what such persons are who persecute us and inflict upon us this oppression and sorrow, as well as why they do it and by what means they justify their tyranny and bloody deeds.

In order that we may be made ready and prepared for such trials I also want to show what profit comes to us from the cross, and what is promised to all of those who through the power of their faith overcome assault and distresses and maintain the conflict through Christ Jesus. I do this so that they may be armed with the armor of righteousness, the helmet of salvation, the shield of faith, and that they may be girded with the sharp, piercing sword of the Spirit in all humility, meekness, and patience, with ardent prayers and supplications to the Lord. It is so that when any certain surging storm shall rise against us, it may not overtake us unawares, that an unexpected windstorm and cloudburst may not cast down our house; the heat of the sun may not scorch the growing plant, the heat and power of the fire may not burn the erected work to ashes, and that we be not startled and frightened to a deadly apostasy by their threats, their uproar, and their tyranny.

Therefore, my beloved, read and understand in all love, for out of pure love have I written this for the benefit of my dear brethren, according to my talent received. This the Lord knoweth.

## [I. WHO THE PERSECUTORS ARE]

In the first place, dear brethren, I think it very necessary that every pious child of God and soldier under the cross of Christ seeking for encouragement in his oppression and sufferings, which he endures for the sake of the testimony of God and his conscience, consider carefully and earnestly who and what they are that so madly persecute, oppress, and afflict him, of what disposition and nature they are, upon what way they walk, and of what father, according to the Spirit, they are born.

All who carefully observe all this and test it by the Scriptures will find, according to my opinion, that these are not Christians but an unbelieving, carnal, earthly, wanton, blind, hardened, lying, idolatrous, perverted, malicious,

cruel, unmerciful, frightful, and murderous people, who by their actions and
fruits show that they neither know Christ nor His Father, even though they
so highly praise His holy name with their mouth and extol it with their lips.
This is a people that walk in slippery, crooked, and perverted paths, that know
nothing of Christian love and peace, that bathe their hearts and hands in blood
and are born to seize and to kill. They are children and accomplices of him
who from the beginning was a murderer and a liar. The whole Scriptures
testify that they shall forever bear the intolerable curse and malediction of
the righteous judgment of God, and the devouring flames of hell, unless they
awake from the deep and deadly sleep of their ugly sins, sincerely repent, believe with the whole heart the joyous Gospel of Jesus Christ, put on Christ,
and in this way show by their whole lives and conduct that they seek their
God with all their might, fear and love Him— no matter if they are emperor,
king, doctor, licentiate, noble or peasant, man or woman. For with God, says
Paul, there is no respect of persons, but whosoever committeth sin he shall
bear it.

Worthy and faithful brethren in the Lord, note well—such a blind, naked,
poor, miserable, and senseless people it is (in divine things) who so bitterly
persecute and destroy you without mercy on account of your faith. Therefore
the true and chosen children of God must not, no matter how heavily the
cross may be laid on them by these people, be angry over them, but sincerely
pity them and sigh sorely for their poor souls with all meekness and fervor
after the example of Christ and Stephen, praying over their raging and cursed
folly and blindness—for they know not what they do. Who knows whether
God may not give them eyes and hearts to see and know their blindness and
unbelief, to see what an impure life they have led, what kind of people they
have persecuted, and whom they have pierced.

O my beloved brethren, observe and ponder well your own former life.
We have all in former times had the same master, one lord, and wore the same
cloth, as the saying goes. But what we now are we are not of ourselves, but
of God by grace through Christ Jesus. The mighty God who according to
His great mercy has called us out of our accursed darkness into His marvelous
light lives forever. His ears are not stopped nor is His hand shortened; He
can also hear and help them as He helped us—without a doubt. And if they
then never repent but continue with wicked, impenitent hearts in all ungodliness, bloodthirstiness, wantonness, and tyranny, and so take their end, then
we know what the Scriptures testify concerning them, that they shall not
inherit the kingdom of heaven, but that their portion shall be in the fiery lake
which burns with fire and brimstone—and that fire will be an everlasting fire.

Every one then who realizes this thoroughly, namely, that his persecutors
are so wholly blind and destitute of understanding in spiritual matters, as has
been said above, and that their lot shall be like that of the angel of the bottomless pit—with the unbearable wrath of God, death, and hell, which shall last
forever—and he who perceives that the sufferings which we have to endure

from them for the testimony of Jesus are but temporary and for a time, will, through grace, by this means have his heart free from all wrath, malice, and vengeance toward them, and will pray fervently for them, commending his affairs to God in all humility, long-suffering, and peace—for He is our only help in need—and will preserve his spirit unbroken among prisons, fire, and water.

## [II. WHY THEY PERSECUTE THE SAINTS]

In the second place, I consider it a fine, mollifying ointment, and an easing of our misery and griefs, if we will but reflect upon the real reason why our persecutors hate us so and deprive us so grievously of name and fame, of prosperity, property, and life. Namely, it is because the revealed grace of God through Christ has shed its beams upon us and because we have believed and preached the Gospel with simplicity of heart, and have ceased from our blind, careless life and deadly works. It is because we have pressed for the true righteousness of faith, and because we seek to acknowledge and confess the ever-blessed Jesus alone as our Redeemer, Mediator, Intercessor, Saviour, spiritual King, Example, Shepherd, wholly dependable Teacher, and Master. It is because we judge and try all spirits, doctrines, counsels, ordinances, statutes, and ceremonies, in so far as they concern the spirit and the faith, with the Spirit, the doctrine, the ordinances, and the commandments of Christ, and so consider the commands and ceremonies of men which are contrary to the commands and ceremonies of Christ not only as vain and useless but also as accursed and idolatrous in the light of Scripture. It is because we regard and honor God more than man, value highly His glorious and truthful Word; because we, in keeping with the Scriptures, dare not listen to the unclean, unsound, idolatrous, deceitful, and bloodthirsty preachers; because we, as far as we can and may, admonish and set an example to the whole world in all love with the Word and sacraments of God and with humble, meek lives (although in weakness) according to our own gift. It is because we rebuke and shame (though always for their good) their deceiving doctrine, their idolatrous sacraments, and their wanton, earthly, and carnal life. In short, it is because we in good faith set forth before them the sure and infallible truth of God, the true light and the highway to eternal life, and in this way warn and frighten them as much as we may, with doctrine and life, from eternal death in hell and the wrath of God.

Observe, my faithful brethren, it is for the reasons here related that the whole wide world lies, writes, declares, preaches, and raves at the pious, and burns with such inhuman rage as may be seen, so that the fierce, ravening wolves and roaring lions when compared with them cease to be wolves and lions, but seem to be tame animals and gentle lambs. So does the fiery and bloodthirsty spirit of their father drive them that they regard neither the law of God and Christ, which is love, nor reason and discretion, nor the inwardly written law of nature by which every reasonable man should properly according to the good pleasure of God deal with his fellow man in love, bear him, admonish him, serve him, honor him, and care for him—yes, so much so that sometimes the natural father delivers up his own son to death and the son his father, the mother daughter, and the daughter her mother, and one brother delivers the other—on account of his faith, as Christ says.

Behold, so boldly without any restraint or fear do they invade the jurisdiction of God and the office of the Holy Ghost. They banish Christ Jesus, the head of all princes and powers who has all power in heaven and upon earth, from the throne of His divine majesty, and judge with their iron sword after their own blind pleasure and carnal intent the chosen, God-fearing, pious hearts, enlightened in God through Jesus Christ, over whom no literal sword may ever pass judgment—for they are spiritual and contend for God and His holy Word even unto death.

Behold, so malicious and haughty is the human heart and so very cruel and hostile is satanic hatred that there is no fear to fight against the most High with the murdering sword, to pierce Christ Jesus, and to persecute with all their power God's Holy Spirit, His gifts, words, and truth, and all that He commands and desires.

Oh, that God might grant that the blind watchmen of this world, I mean the preachers and the scribes, might pitch their pipes to the right tune, and sound them at the right moment, or else let them hang on the peg, in order that they might not therewith make the deadly murder cry to resound so tyrannically, nor deceive the carnal, blind world any longer, nor set the rulers and magistrates to the destruction and murder of the saints as hounds are set on a deer. Would that God might grant that the people might become heartily sick of and troubled by their leaven and husks, yes, their spiritual stealing and murdering. Would that all rulers and magistrates might tear the bridle from their mouths and pitch their awful mounts from their back and no longer allow themselves like bridled asses to be driven by them any longer. This in my opinion would be good and desirable for their poor souls before God. But I fear that the lying, murderous serpent will continue to be the bitterly biting serpent and that the embattled woman, the new Eve and her children, will have to endure to the end in all patience and long-suffering that daily biting and gnawing in the heel.

## [III. BIBLICAL EXAMPLES]

Even as I have herewith pointed out to you, beloved, in a few words the quality, the spirit, and the nature of those who destroy you and seek your property and life, and also the principal reasons which impel them to do so, so I will now present to my brethren some accounts and examples from the Holy Scriptures for the comfort and refreshment of all miserable, afflicted, and troubled hearts who suffer oppression and misery in the flesh for righteousness' sake, in which accounts and examples these things already mentioned may be clearly found and traced.

In the first place, when Eve, the mother of us all, had brought forth her first two sons, Cain and Abel, then Abel became a shepherd and Cain a tiller of the ground. In the process of time it came to pass, as Genesis has it, that Cain brought an offering to the Lord from the fruits of the field, and Abel brought one from the firstlings of his sheep and of their fat. The Lord regarded Abel and his gifts, but He regarded not Cain and his gifts. Therefore Cain was very angry and his countenance fell through great wrath, even as is always the case with the ungodly toward the pious, because the Lord regards the pious and loves their sacrifices. Cain spoke deceitfully to his pious, humble brother Abel, who did not know the malicious, bloody heart of his brother, saying, Let us go out.[1] And when they were in the field, Cain's hot and vengeful spirit could no longer be restrained, and his bloodthirsty vengeful spirit could no longer be hid. That which lay concealed in the heart had to reveal itself in action. He rose up against his innocent brother, and in his fearsome wrath slew him and took his life. Why did he do this? Because Cain was of the evil one, and his works were evil, and his brother's works were righteous, even as John has it.

It seems to me, dear brethren, that this is a good example and a fair indication as to the way the righteous have always been offscourings and a prey to the unrighteous, and how they will continue to be that, even as the Scriptures testify sufficiently and as daily experience plainly teaches.

In the second place, God blessed the patriarch Isaac and gave him two sons at once. The elder was called Esau and the younger Jacob. Esau was an husbandman and a stalker of game, and he loved to hunt. One day when he came home very tired, he sold his birthright to Jacob, his brother, for some food. After this it came to pass that Jacob, through the craft and cleverness of his mother, obtained the blessing of his aged father, Isaac, by posing as his brother Esau. (But this was the intention and will of God as a figure of the literal synagogue and the church of Christ, according to His word to Rebekah while she was expectant; namely, two nations are in thy womb and two manner of peoples shall be separated from thy bowels. And the one people shall be stronger than the other people, and the elder shall serve the younger.) And when Esau became aware of this, he wept bitterly and said: Right properly is he called Jacob, for he has supplanted me twice. Esau sought the blessing but did not obtain it, for God willed it otherwise, as we have indicated earlier. Esau became very angry with his brother Jacob on account of the blessing with which his father had blessed him. His malicious bitter wrath broke forth and he said: The time is at hand when my father shall mourn; for I shall slay my brother Jacob. Then the blessed Jacob had to flee from his dear father and mother, from the face of his wrathful brother, to a distant country. And he had to become a servant for twenty years in the house of Laban, who also did not deal with him according to equity and love. He dared not go

---

[1] Gen. 4:8 (Latin Vulgate). *Ed.*

back to the land of his birth until the Lord said unto him, Return unto the land of thy fathers, and to thy kindred, and I will be with thee.

My dear brethren, observe. Just as the patriarch Jacob, for his external birthright and blessing, was hated and persecuted by his unspiritual, fierce, and adulterous brother Esau, so also is it at the present time with all those who after the Spirit are called after the name of Jacob, namely, the true Christians, those who in the power of the Holy Ghost through the medium of faith tread upon the devil, the world, the flesh, and blood. Thus it is with those who obtain the birthright recorded in heaven and are blessed through our true Isaac, Christ Jesus, with spiritual blessings in heavenly things unto eternal glory. They are angrily hated and persecuted unto death by their unspiritual, wild, and adulterous brothers, and must therefore flee from country to country, from city to city, under great oppression, want, and discomfort, in prison, in bonds; with hunger, with stripes, with water, fire, and sword, all the days of their lives, as may be seen.

In this way the carnal Esau tyrannizes the spiritual Jacob on account of the spiritual birthright and blessing, even though they are both of them born of the same father, Adam, and of the same mother, Eve, and are created after the image of God.

In the third place, Saul, the first king of Israel, was on account of his stubbornness and disobedience rejected of the Lord. David, the son of Jesse, the Bethlehemite, was thereupon taken, according to the command of God, from the flock and was anointed by Samuel in his stead, although he did not get the government during the life of Saul. The Lord was with David and strengthened his hands. He did great works in the name of the Lord. He delivered the sheep out of the mouth of the lion and the bear; he slew the terribly great Goliath; he got him two hundred foreskins of the Philistines; he acted prudently in all things, properly and valiantly, for the Lord was with him. But it happened, when Saul returned from the slaughter of the Philistines, that the women out of all the cities of Israel came to meet the king, singing and rejoicing with all manner of stringed instruments and tambours, having a fine time among themselves. And they said, Saul hath slain his thousands, but David his tens of thousands. Then Saul became very angry, and the saying offended him, and he said: They have given David ten thousand and me but a thousand! What does he lack save the kingdom itself? From that day on David had no favor with Saul, but Saul sought his life secretly and openly, and with great diligence and craftiness, although Saul knew very well the piety of David and that the Lord was with him. Yes, Saul's heart burned with such ill will, envy, revenge, and bloodthirstiness that when David escaped, the good Ahimelech and the priests of the Lord were put to death, and the whole city of Nob was laid in ruins for David's sake.

Saul regarded neither the piety nor the kindness, the fidelity nor the good deeds of David toward him and all Israel, nor the grace, the works, and the will of God. He became so insane and drunken in his wrath and envy that the enemies and betrayers of David, such as Doeg the Edomite and the Ziphites, were highly regarded and honored by him. But the peacemakers and those who advised for good, such as his own son Jonathan, were hated by him and considered suspect. In short, David had to take to his heels and for some years flee from one land to another, and from one wilderness to another, and from one mountain to another, until Saul was vanquished on Mount Gilboa by the Philistines, and there through utter despair and gloom he plunged the sword, which he had drawn against the righteous and the innocent, into his own heart, taking his own life.

In this way the Almighty Lord and Ruler of all things punishes the haughty, bloodthirsty tyrants, each one in his own time—those that bear the sword of their office against God and His elect, as may be seen here of Saul and in other parts of the Scriptures of Pharaoh, Antipas, Ahab, Jezebel, Herod, and others. On the other hand, He can guard His elect and help them out of all distresses, no matter how they may be pressed, even as He has clearly shown and demonstrated to all Israel at the Red Sea, to David in the present case, to Elijah and Elisha, to Daniel in the lions' den, to the young men in the furnace, and to many others with great power.

And this is another clear example, in the case of Saul and David, how the proud, arrogant, self-willed, and carnal princes everywhere, even though they wish to be called Christian princes and gracious lords, act and proceed against the true David, Christ Jesus, and against all His saints whom He has anointed with the oil of His Holy Spirit—the people who have power from on high with Him, in Him, and through Him to overcome the fearful hellish lion and bear, and Goliath, yes, hell, sin, death, devil, malediction, and the wrath of God. These can have peace nowhere with this evil-intentioned Saul, no matter how innocent, Godfearing, and pious they may be. Here no manner of innocence or piety, praying nor tears, words nor Christ avails. As with David, everything must be twisted and construed for the worse. This has everywhere been the case, and according to my opinion will remain so to the end.

Nevertheless, my brethren, do not fear, for all your persecutors and enemies will become old like a garment no matter how mighty, how glorious and great, they may be esteemed. All flesh is as grass and all the goodliness thereof is as the flower of the field. But ye shall flourish and increase in God, and your fruit shall never wilt, for the kingdom of Jerusalem is given to you and the glorious Lord will be honored in you and He will give you, no matter how Saul may rage, the eternal habitation which He has prepared and set apart from all eternity for you and for all the elect.

In the fourth place, Jeremiah, the son of Hilkiah, a priest of the priests of Anathoth, a man sanctified from his mother's womb, who was chosen of God to be a prophet and a seer from his youth—this man rebuked Judah and Benjamin most sternly for their disobedience, their stubbornness, all manner of transgressions, false worship, idolatry, and bloodshed, out of the mouth of

God and His law. He preached repentance and reform and prophesied the promised Messiah, whom he called the righteous Branch and Root of David. He preached the coming judgment and wrath of God, namely, the captivity and downfall of the king, the destruction of the city and the temple, and the captivity of the people for seventy years, etc.

And these his predictions, faithful warnings, visions, and rebukes out of the mouth of the Lord became to him as sharp piercing thorns. Men cast aside his word and admonitions and would have nothing of them. The pious prophet and true servant of God they made out to be a faithless traitor, a rebel, and a heretic. The Word of the Lord was the occasion of daily mockery. He was often apprehended and beaten and thrown into vile and evil-smelling pits. They plotted his death. He was so pressed and weighed down with the cross that he at one time resolved in his heart to preach no more in the name of the Lord. Yes, he cursed the day of his birth and the man who brought the message to his father that a man-child was born to him. In this way the worthy man of God had to bear the heavy bag of sand for many years for the sake of the Word and the truth of his Lord. He had to give his ear to all who reproach, and his back to all who strike, until the waters of affliction rose in the mouths of the haughty, rebellious, and unbelieving people, and they saw, alas too late, that Jeremiah was God's true messenger and a true prophet. And on top of all this he had to bring his life to a close in Egypt under the stones with which he had been stoned to death as a sign of appreciation for his great love and his difficult, bitter work.

My dear brethren in the Lord, with this I will cut short the narratives from the Old Testament, for time will not allow to relate it all—for what reason the pious Joseph also was grievously hated by his brethren and by them cast into a pit, drawn out again and sold to the Ishmaelites, was accused to be a faithless philanderer by the unchaste wife of his lord, and although innocent had to suffer his lord's wrath, imprisonment, and bonds; likewise, for what reason the noble and noted prophet and evangelist, Isaiah, under the bloody and idolatrous Manasseh, was cut in two with the saw, as the account has it;[2] why the dear and spiritual prophet Ezekiel was stoned by those who remained of Dan and Gad; why Urijah of Kirjath-Jearim was slain with the sword of Jehoiakim, the king of Judah; why Zacharias, the son of Berechiah, was stoned between the temple and the altar; why the powerful wonder-working prophet Elijah had to retreat before the idolatrous Jezebel drunk with blood; why the three youths, Shadrach, Meshach, and Abednego, were cast into the red-hot furnace, and Daniel into the lion's den; why the venerable, pious, old scribe Eleazar and his worthy, pious wife with their seven sons were so inhumanly and barbarously treated by the terrible godless wolf of a man, Antiochus, and were tortured, roasted, killed, and murdered.[3]

You see, brethren, every Christian should be prepared for this. For this

[2] According to Jewish tradition, not the Old Testament. *Ed.*
[3] II Macc. 6:18-31. *Ed.*

is the real reward and crown of this world with which it has paid off, rewarded, and honored all true servants of God who have set before them in pure love the kingdom, the Word, and the will of God. Thus it has rewarded those who have called to repentance and reformation; those who have rendered many kindnesses, services, and favors; those who with every kind of holiness, righteousness, truth, and the fear and love of God, have like the golden candlestick thrown off light in the Lord's tabernacle, and have flourished and blossomed like a fruitful olive tree in the house of God. Everyone who ponders well these and similar histories and narratives of the pious men of God will undoubtedly not lose courage, but in all his miseries, crosses, and sufferings, will by God's grace surely remain standing, and will abide pious and strong to the end.

Even as I have now referred to some histories from the Old Scriptures, stories by which it is plainly seen that true righteousness has everywhere suffered, has been rooted out and crucified, as well before the law as under it, so I will now, by the grace of God, present some examples out of the New Testament. By these each may be sufficiently taught in his own heart to say with Paul that all those who will live godly in Christ Jesus shall suffer persecution.

In the first place take John, the man who baptized Christ—a man sent of God as the evangelists testify; a burning and a shining light as Christ says. Of him Isaiah had prophesied a long time before saying, The voice of one crying in the wilderness, Prepare ye the way of the Lord, make his paths straight. Malachi called him the messenger of the Lord. His birth, greatness, holiness, office, doctrine, and fear were announced by Gabriel, the heavenly messenger, to Zacharias his father. He was the man who was filled with the Holy Ghost already in his mother's womb. He preached repentance to all Judah and pointed out Christ Jesus the Saviour of the whole world, the eternal Redeemer, saying, Behold the Lamb of God, which taketh away the sin of the world. The Son of God Himself gave testimony that John was no wavering reed, that he was not clothed in soft raiment, that he was greater than a prophet, that he was the coming Elias, that he came in the way of righteousness, and that it was he of whom it was said that among all that were born of women there had not arisen a man greater than he. The people also held him to be a prophet, although they did say, He hath a devil. Yet he was cast forth by Herod, the king, as a profligate and vile vagrant, and he had to forfeit some days afterward, like a shameful evildoer, his honey-flowing mouth, and let his head fall under the hand of the hangman—this gloriously chosen holy man and friend of God—and this at the hand of a harlot! His head moreover was fixed up like a fancy dish by a proud and vain dancing girl and an adulterous woman and put on exhibition to the drunken good-for-nothing guests of Herod.

O Lord, so lamentably and grievously have the righteous been destroyed on account of their piety by this abominable, bloody, murderous world; and no one takes it to heart! Yes, they are so treated and dealt with that it seems to the foolish as if the godly were to God an offense and a stench, banished and cursed of God, persons who may to all eternity neither hope for nor find comfort or grace with God. But, ah no, the Lord be blessed. Even though their lives may appear to the senseless world to be nothing but frenzy and their end without honor, yet we know that they are the people and children of the Lord, the apple of His eye, and that their blood and death are dear to Him. We know that after they have for a little while suffered and had trouble they will be recompensed with much good. The kingdom of heaven belongs to them. They will not be touched with the pains of eternal death, but their noble souls will be in eternal rest and peace. Yes, my brethren, every Christian may therefore trust and rejoice in the Lord in every trial and need.

In the second place consider Stephen, the crowned of God,[4] a man full of faith, power, and the Holy Ghost, who did great signs and wonders among the people, as Luke writes, a man endued of God with such wisdom and spirit, according to the promises of Christ, that all who contradicted him, such as the Libertines, the Cyrenians, the Alexandrians, etc., were forced to silence and shame before him. When they saw this, the spirit of their father displayed itself, even as it has done from the beginning: consuming envy could not but use its tricks—Stephen had to be accused of something! Justice and equity were suppressed. Men of Belial were employed to smite the pious Stephen with their lying and murderous tongues, saying, We have heard him speak blasphemous words against Moses and also against God, and that Jesus of Nazareth shall destroy this place and shall change laws which Moses delivered unto us. In this way the lies of the serpent have overcome justice wherever men have counseled to exterminate the saints.

Stephen's own enemies saw his countenance as the countenance of an angel of God. He spoke the Word of the Lord without fear. He rebuked the false dependence on the law and the temple. He testified of Jesus Christ in great power as the one of whom Moses and the prophets had prophsied. Finally he grew very sharp and ardent in his speech to the multitude because they had ungratefully rejected the mercifully seeking God in His proffered grace and goodness. Ye stiffnecked, he said, and uncircumcised in heart and ears, you do always resist the Holy Ghost; as your fathers did, so also do ye. Which of the prophets have not your fathers persecuted? They have killed them which showed before the coming of the just One of whom you have become the murderers and the betrayers; you who have received the law through the disposition of angels and have not kept it. And when they heard these reproving and sharp sounding words, they could no longer endure it, for they were cut to the heart and gnashed their teeth at him.

But Stephen, being full of the Holy Ghost, looked up steadfastly into heaven and saw the glory of God and Jesus standing on the right hand of

[4] Menno is referring to the fact that Stephanus in Greek means "crowned." *Tr.*

God and said, I see the heaven open and the Son of man standing on the right hand of God. Then they shouted and stopped their ears as if they could no longer endure such blasphemous words—that the wicked heretic spoke so highly of himself, and that he gave such honor to Christ. They rushed upon him with one accord and cast him out of the city and stoned him in wrath and frenzy. But Saul kept the witnesses' clothing. Stephen called out, Lord Jesus, receive my spirit. He knelt down and called with a loud voice, after the example of his Master on the cross, Lord, lay not this sin to their charge, for they know not what they do. So the pious martyr fell asleep in the Lord and received the crown of life which God has promised to all those who fear Him, love Him, and seek Him from the heart in all truth.

Note well, God-fearing reader, and learn from such examples how that all those who believe the Word of the Lord with true hearts, who have become partakers of the Holy Ghost, who are clothed with power from on high, and out of whose mouths pour grace and wisdom, who rebuke the world's shame and sin—how these must with Stephen be cast out of the city and get a taste of flying stones.

Dear brethren, pray fervently and prepare yourselves, for through much oppression we must enter into the kingdom of heaven. Here is the patience and the faith of the saints. Oh, my brethren, watch.

In the third place take Paul, a servant of God and an apostle of Jesus Christ, a chosen vessel, a prince of the holy Word, an apostle and teacher of the Gentiles. He was not called to the service of the Gospel by men on earth, but by God Himself from heaven. He was a man mighty and zealous in his teaching and unblamable in his life, one who labored more than all the other apostles. He cast out devils in the name of the Lord, raised the dead Eutychus back to life, restored health to the sick with his handkerchief. The serpent clinging to his hand did not hurt him at all. As a true prophet he foretold many things which were to come to pass in the last days. He was taken up into the third heaven and led into the Paradise of God and saw visions of which no man was able to declare, He was an infallible leader in all righteousness, holiness, piety, and virtue, one who sought and loved not himself, but God and his neighbor with his whole heart. He had nothing of which he could be accused. He regarded all gain as loss that he might win Christ alone, yes, he dared not speak of anything but that which Christ had wrought in him. Yet all this did not help. How holy, how unblamable, zealous, how highly called, and how miracle-working or devout he was, was of no consequence. With Simon the Cyrenian he had to help Christ bear His cross, for as soon as he had been called from heaven, had been taught and baptized by Ananias, had ceased from his tyranny, and had preached Christ in Damascus, he had to be let down over the wall in a basket to escape the snares of the bloodthirsty and flee away.

Many a time was he imprisoned, thrice was he scourged with rods, he was stoned once, in Ephesus he was cast to wild beasts, Then at last after inconceivably many travelings and afflictions from one land to another, after much endured nakedness, cold, heat, thirst, hunger, labor, watchings, cares, dangers, and anguishes, he was seized by the Jews at Jerusalem and was scourged, and accused before the judges. Men vowed to take his life. He was captured in Caesarea, and after his appeal he arrived, after many experiences and ship-wreck, at Rome. There he was brought before the emperor, and at last under Nero, the most bloodthirsty of tyrants, he was executed by the sword and was compelled to yield up his soul and surrender his life.

In like manner were the apostles imprisoned and scourged in Jerusalem, the church dispersed and persecuted, James put to death with the sword under Herod, etc. Anyone who wishes to know still more narratives than are here drawn from the Holy Scriptures, let him read the church history by Eusebius[5] and he will find more such inhuman abominations, tyranny, cruelty, and wicked falsehoods against the innocent. Also, such extraordinary strange inventions of torture to martyr, kill, extirpate, and murder Christians that a natural man, to say nothing of a spiritual one, must in his heart be awe-stricken and amazed.

My most beloved brethren in Christ, be of good cheer and be comforted in the Lord, you who have freely and voluntarily used your shoulders and your back under the cross of Jesus Christ, because you may see and observe from the Scriptures in the above examples from the Old and New Testaments how all pious men and children of God, all the righteous and the prophets, all apostles and true witnesses of Christ, yes, Christ Himself as we have still to hear, have pressed into the true and promised land and into eternal glory through this lonely wilderness, through this narrow, shameful, and bloody way of all miseries and crosses and sufferings.

Yes, this is and remains the only strait and narrow way and door through which we must enter and pass, and through no other may we seek to enter with the saints into eternal life, rest, and peace, even as Christ Himself said: Whosoever will follow after me must deny himself and take up his cross and follow me. Therefore, dear brethren, you who have sought the Lord, have feared and loved Him, and therefore must suffer and take much from this wicked and idolatrous generation, fear not those who take your earthly goods from you—Christ and heaven they cannot take. Nor fear those who can kill the body—they cannot kill your soul. But fear with all your heart Him who has power to cast both soul and body eternally into hell. Yes, my brethren, if you would be the people and disciples of the Lord, then you must bear the cross of Christ. This is undoubted and true.

In the fourth place, now that we have set forth to the kind reader striking narratives from the Holy Scriptures, accounts in which are clearly represented and traced the tyrannical nature, the angry, wolfish tearing and rending, the wicked animal-like torturing and bloodshedding of this godless world against the righteous, we shall now and finally, by God's grace, notice briefly not only

---

[5] The church history of Eusebius (c. 260-c. 340) extends to A.D. 324. Ed.

how the servants of whom we have spoken suffered, but also how the Lord and Prince Himself had to endure much, and so return to His glory.

The apostles testify abundantly how that the Lamb of God, the ever-blessed Christ Jesus, the real Head of all true believers, not only suffered from the beginning in those who were His own, as was related above, but how that He had to suffer in His own flesh in these last times, even though He was the victor over the serpent who was promised to Adam and Eve, the blessing unto all people, the true Shiloh, the Messiah, and the Emanuel,[6] the true plant of David, the Lord who justifies us, the Prince of Peace, yes, the true Son of the Almighty and living God whom all the righteous and prophets of God had desired with great desire.

When He had now, according to the promises given to the fathers, become man, and had preached the penitent and new life in the full power of the Spirit, and when He had in all love, humility, righteousness, peace, and obedience announced the stern and terrible judgment of God over the impenitent, and on the other hand the eternal kingdom, the eternal grace, mercy, kindly favor, and love of His heavenly Father over the penitent, He was Himself that definitive Word in all righteousness. He was God blessed forever, the infallible example, the eternal wisdom, love, and truth, the brightness of the divine glory, the express image of His being, after whom the first man was patterned and created (I mean as to his innermost being), the eternal power of God, the Almighty Word through which all things were created, are governed, and in whom all things must exist. He who knew no sin, in whose mouth no guile was found, the true Light of life, the same was by the darkness that is in the world so hated that He was considered the most despised of men, was blasphemed, persecuted, despised, and trampled upon. The King of kings, the Lord of lords, became poorer than the foxes or the birds, for He had not where to lay His blessed head. On the day of His birth He found no room in the inn, but the manger of oxen was His couch. And as soon as He was born, He had to flee by night to the land of Egypt.

In the time of His ministry He made the blind to see, the deaf to hear, the dumb to speak, the lepers to be clean, the palsied and feeble to be sound. He cast out devils, restored the dead, twice fed thousands with a few loaves and fishes and showed to them all the works and services of pure love. Moreover none could find any fault with Him in His speech or in His life. Nevertheless their bloodthirsty envious hearts were so enraged at Him that they desired that rascal murderer, Barabbas, whom the law had sentenced to death, to live and to have the eternal Life Himself, the Creator and Sustainer of all creatures, to die.

That pure heavenly body of all virtue was by scourging so transformed, that glorious countenance and head of all honor was so disfigured with blood, spittle, and thorns, and so mocked with a mocking garment that even the heathen judge, Pilate, deplored it and said, Behold, what manner of man.

6 The text has "Samuel," in all probability a corruption of *Emanuel*. *Tr.*

Yes, worthy brethren, nothing helped; no pain, no torture, no misery was enough. They would not be satisfied till He was taken away from their sight and condemned to the most shameful death, was stretched out upon the cross like the string on a bow, His hands and feet pierced with cruel nails, His side with a spear, and He was nailed to the cross as if He were a prince and leader of the vicious, and was counted among the murderers. Thus they thanked Him for His incomprehensibly fervent love and beneficence—in His parching thirst in the last hour of His dying He could not obtain a drop of water, but had to be satisfied with vinegar and gall. In short, so was He dealt with that He cried on the tree of the cross with a loud voice to His Father: My God, my God, why hast thou forsaken me? that He lamented through the prophet, I am a worm and no man, a reproach of men and despised of the people. He might well have sighed and lamented with Jeremiah or with Jerusalem saying, All ye that pass by, behold and see if there be any sorrow like unto my sorrow. Thus were the eternal riches for our sakes made poverty. Thus was the eternal Glory dishonored, the eternal Righteousness persecuted, eternal Truth blasphemed, eternal Salvation rejected, eternal Blessing cursed, and eternal Life put to death with the most shameful death.

Most beloved brethren in the Lord, ponder it well. If the laborers have not spared their Master's Son, but have cast Him out of the vineyard and slain Him, how much more His servants? If they have called the Master of the house Beelzebub, how much more shall they call them of His household? As Christ Himself said, If they have persecuted me, they will also persecute you; and further, If the world hate you, you know that it hated me before it hated you, for the disciple is not greater than his master nor the servant than his lord. It is enough for the disciple to be as his master and the servant to be as his lord. Such passages may be found in Scripture in abundance.

I trust, worthy brethren, that from these recited examples the pious consciences may have been shown sufficiently what kind of people they have always been, from what father they are born, and by what spirit they are moved, who from the beginning until the present day have rejected and persecuted Christ, the lovely, peaceful, innocent, and obedient Lamb, and His holy members, and who have plundered, slandered, imprisoned, tortured, racked, stoned, beheaded, drowned, roasted, strangled, slain, and murdered them. According to my understanding of the Word of the Lord, this tyranny will not cease until the rejected, murdered, and crucified Christ Jesus with all His saints shall appear in the clouds as an Almighty Sovereign, a conqueror, and a glorious king before all the tribes and peoples, unto the last judgment.

The fearful tyranny of this blind world has always lain upon the neck of the children of God and still lies there, and as has been said, probably always will lie there. For no way leads nor can lead through the door of life other than this only rocky and thorny way of the cross (I mean according to the flesh, for according to the spirit it is broad and pleasing) even as the Scriptures testify. Therefore have your feet shod with the Gospel of peace, with the precious promises of God, with the pure knowledge of Christ, with the denial of yourselves, with the patience and faith of the saints, and with the sure hope of the kingdom of God. [Arm yourselves] so that the hard stones and the sharp piercing thorns of trial, by which all the pious are tried, may not terrify you and lead you to the broad easy way of the flesh. Lay aside every weight and the sin which does so easily beset you, the cursed works of darkness, all avarice, needless cares, love of home, goods, gold, silver, pomp and splendor, and all that is perishable, all drunkenness and excess, all idolatry and vanity, all uncircumcised and carnal speech, and all manner of wickedness, so that they may not drive you from your course, and you be led off the only narrow and kingly highway to crooked and unmarked byways, even as we, alas, have sometimes seen it happen in our days.

Therefore, my very precious brethren and sisters in the Lord, do take the crucified Jesus as your example and the righteous apostles and prophets of God. Learn through them how they all crept in at this very narrow gate and have left all things hanging at the entrance, for they had their hearts trained there and they were so endowed and drawn by God that they knew nothing, sought nothing, loved and desired nothing save the eternal, heavenly, and imperishable treasure and existence, that is, God and eternal life. They were so grounded in love and driven by love, and were so firm and immovable, that neither life nor death, angels nor empires nor rulers; neither hunger nor sword nor any other torture, pain, or means, could frighten them away from the love which is in Christ Jesus. Their thoughts, their words, their acts, their life, and their death were Christ's. Their kingdom and rest they sought not upon this earth, for they were spiritually, heavenly minded, and all their fruit was righteousness, light, and truth. Their whole lives were pure love, chastity, humility, obedience, and peace. The transient wicked world with all its works was to them an offense and an abomination. They loved their God with all their soul, and therefore they rebuked all that was against His holy will, His honor, and His Word. They loved their neighbors as themselves, and therefore they admonished and rebuked them in love, served them, pointed out and taught God's pure will, Word, and truth with all diligence, and sought their salvation with all their power and at a great cost to their own name and life. And for this cause has the foolish, envious, unthankful world which wades in blood up to its ears so grievously hated, persecuted, and rewarded them with death.

My dear brethren, this happened not only to the prophets, apostles, and those of former times, as the Scriptures relate, but we have in these last times abundantly witnessed the same with our own eyes. How many a pious child of God have we known in the space of a few years (and we know some still, the Lord be praised), who sought Jesus Christ and the imperishable, eternal life, and continue to seek these with a faithful and pure heart. These persons' hearts blossomed in the Lord's Word and love; their mouths flowered forth in power, spirit, and wisdom; their whole life was repentance and piety.

They hated, shunned, and rebuked all abominations, all sin, and all wickedness. There was none that could reproach their conduct with the Word of God. They opposed the idle, carnal, ungodly life of this world (as we still do, and by the grace of God will continue to do) and refused to listen to the words of the deceiving prophets. They dared not entrust their precious souls to the spiritual thieves and murderers and would not serve nor honor the wooden, the stone, and the silver gods. They dared not partake of the unscriptural, idolatrously embellished sacraments, etc. In a word, they heard only the true and living God, believed, feared, served, and loved Him. Therefore the lying seed of the serpent has opened its mouth and has spewed forth so many false, vile, yes, inhuman lies into the face of the pious. It has from the seat of its pestilence defamed and depicted them in frightful colors and shape, and has caused its blind disciples to herald these things forth so that the righteous have become such a curse and offense to the whole world that all men close their mouths and noses before them and flee from them in horror. Yes, any person who can but slander and defame one poor God-fearing Christian is the world's favorite preacher and an esteemed teacher.

No lie is so beastly and crude that they dare not utter it against the godly. Now they accuse us of wishing to take cities and countries; then, we seek to destroy the whole world. Today we are adulterers; tomorrow, thieves and murderers. Now they say that we teach that there is no repentance left to the sinner, and anon, we are said to reject the New Testament and Christ. In short, any man who does not rave and rant about the godly is not a Christian in the world's eye! O Lord, how pure and free nevertheless are all the saints in heart and conscience before their God, from these and similar defamations and lies!

And this unchristian, hellish lying is not enough for the world, but they who know Christ and seek to live after His Word must endure something worse still, as we can see before our very eyes. For how many pious children of God have we not seen during the space of a few years deprived of their homes and possessions for the testimony of God and their conscience; their poverty and sustenance written off to the emperor's insatiable coffers. How many have they betrayed, driven out of city and country, put to the stocks and torture? How many poor orphans and children have they turned out without a farthing? Some have they hanged, some have they punished with inhuman tyranny and afterward garroted them with cords, tied to a post. Some they have roasted and burned alive. Some, holding their own entrails in their hands, have powerfully confessed the Word of God still. Some they beheaded and gave as food to the fowls of the air. Some have they consigned to the fish. They have torn down the houses of some. Some have they thrust into muddy bogs. They have cut off the feet of some, one of whom I have seen and spoken to. Others wander aimlessly hither and yon in want, misery, and discomfort, in the mountains, in deserts, holes, and clefts of the earth, as Paul says. They must take to their heels and flee away with their wives and little children, from one country to another, from one city to another—hated by all men, abused, slandered, mocked, defamed, trampled upon, styled "heretics." Their names are read from pulpits and town halls; they are kept from their livelihood, driven out into the cold winter, bereft of bread, pointed at with fingers. Yes, whoever can wrong a poor oppressed Christian thinks he has done God a service thereby, even as Christ says.

Notice, dear brethren, how far the whole world indeed is from God and His Word, how swift their feet are to shed blood, how bitterly they hate the light, and how fiercely they persecute, defame, and destroy the eternal, saving truth, the pure immaculate Gospel of Jesus Christ, the pious godly life of all saints. This is so not only among papists and Turks, but also among those who boast of the holy Word, although at the first they wrote much concerning faith, namely, that it is a gift of God which must not be pressed upon man, not with any iron sword, but only with the Word (seeing that it is a matter of accepting with heart and will). But this same doctrine the scholars have some years back pulled back again. It appears to me that they have stricken it from their books, for since that time they have drawn lords and princes, cities and countries into their easy and carnal doctrine. They have widely proclaimed the contrary, as is evident from their writings and spokesmen. And they thrust many pious hearts into the hangman's hands by their seditious writings—hearts that gainsay, reprove, and admonish them by the clear Word of God, and point out to them the true principle of the Gospel; namely, faith working mightily in love, a penitent new life, obedience to God and Christ, and the true evangelical construction of baptism, the Lord's Supper, and excommunication, even as Christ Himself instituted and commanded and His holy apostles practiced and taught.

Everyone who does these things out of pure love must pass for a cursed Anabaptist, a rebel, a deceiver, and a heretic—all who fear God had better anticipate it. Nevertheless, all of them together—lords, princes, preachers, scribes, common people (whether papists, Lutherans, or Zwinglians)—wish to pass for the Christian community and the holy church. They do not even take notice of their ungodly, impure, and impenitent lives, that they are basically earthly, carnal, and contrary to the Word of God, that there are some whose hands are wet and drip with the blood of Christians, and that all their affair is so clearly and flatly contrary to the Spirit, the Word, and the example of the Lord. Oh, if only these poor, blind, hardened hearts could know and truly perceive the real nature, character, and spirit of a true Christian! Then they would be ashamed before God and sincerely lament that they so miserably abuse His glorious name, His blessed Word, His divine grace, and so shamefully abuse His precious crimson blood, boast so falsely of it, and use it so shamefully for a covering of all their wantonness, shame, and wickedness.

For a genuine Christian is a man that is born of God after the Spirit; one who has become a new creature in Christ, who has crucified his flesh with its lusts, and who hates all ungodliness and sin. All his works are righteousness, patience, truth, obedience, humility, chastity, love, and peace. He is driven by the Spirit of the Lord, and always his delight is in the law of the Lord, and he speaks of them by day and by night. All his words are in grace, seasoned with salt; he sincerely strives for the pious life which is from God, and he fears his God from the depths of his soul. In short, he is after his received gift of one mind and one nature with Christ Jesus.

If now these miserable people could only see that a Christian is so minded as we have indicated, that he is an amiable and peaceable being and child of God; and if they then had the grace to be so minded also, seeing that they pride themselves that they are Christians, then they would hate none, but would be hated; would slander none, but be slandered; they would defraud none, but be defrauded; they would betray none, but be betrayed; they would rob none, but be robbed; they would not murder, but be murdered; they would not devour the lamb, but be themselves torn of wolves; they would not pounce upon the dove, but be themselves torn by the falcon and devoured, as may be clearly seen.

If then they who persecute us are Christians, as they think, why then are they not of God, and why are they not born of His Word? Why are they then still the old accursed creature, living according to the lusts of the flesh? Why do they let themselves be driven by the spirit of the devil? Why have they their thoughts still fixed upon perishable and temporal things, being concerned therewith day and night? Why does their mouth still overflow with unchastity, vanity, lying, cursing, and swearing? Why do they then not fear God and His Word? Why are they still inwardly like the old deceitful serpent, and why are they obedient to him, and why are they then still such terrible, ravenous wolves, such lions, eagles, and birds of prey, and not innocent lambs and doves as the Scriptures teach?

Ah, dear brethren, let them boast as they will. Christ Jesus does not recognize such wanton, carnal, frightful, and bloodthirsty Christians. He knows only those that have His Spirit; men who sincerely believe and are obedient to Him, persons who are flesh of His flesh and bone of His bones, pious, holy, and pure of heart, who confess Christ Jesus in word and deed before this wicked and evil generation, men who deny themselves and take up the cross of Christ and follow Him, men who say with the holy Paul: Who shall separate us from the love of Christ? They glory in nothing but in the cross of our Lord Jesus Christ, by which they are crucified to the world and the world to them. All they who are thus minded are God's anointed, the saints and Christians. Not so the impenitent, carnal, bloody boasters. Every one does well to remember this, unless indeed the whole Scriptures are falsehood and lies!

It appears to me, dear brethren, that the pious reader may now understand sufficiently what kind of people they are who so shamefully trample upon you with their feet, strike at you with their fists, burden you with lies, and dispossess you of possessions and life. Also, the reason they do so: namely, on account of your sure and dependable testimony of God and your consciences. May you also understand how all they from the beginning, with few exceptions, who have sought God, feared and loved Him, walked according to His divine will and Word, and have reproved and admonished the confused and erring world concerning evil, and that for its good—how these have trod this winepress and have been every man's refuse, every man's heretic, every man's plunder.

## [IV. EXCUSES OF THE PERSECUTORS]

We will now proceed in the name of the Lord to show with few words what feeble and unbecoming excuses are advanced by those who persecute us, excuses which cannot stand before God any more than stubble and sulphur before fire, but wherewith they think to excuse themselves and prove that they are doing right in so molesting and harming the pious. For all sins are of such a character that they seek their own cover and excuse. No matter how shamefully one carries on, he does not want to be considered wicked—but righteous, pious, and genuinely Christian.

In the first place, those who persecute us say that we are like those of Münster were and that we are not obedient to the magistrates.

We reply first of all that we agree that the Münsterites were seditious and acted contrary to the Word of God in many things. But we deny that we are of a piece with them, seeing that we hate and oppose with all our souls their seditious abominations, such as kings, earthly power, the sword, etc., also polygamy, making a deal with the world, and similar shame and abomination. We do not want to eat, drink, or have any communion with them, according to the doctrine of Christ and Paul, unless they renounce their errors and become sound and sensible in the doctrine of salvation.

Even as the papists and the Lutherans are not alike, but different, so are we basically different—even more so—from the Münsterites and certain other sects which sprang from them. That this is the truth we have shown in writing, by our own life, and by oral testimony before lords, princes, and the whole world. It has moreover, been proved by the blood of many pious Christians which flowed like water in many countries for many years to the present time.

That the world will not believe this we cannot help. But we testify that our hearts and consciences are pure and free before God of all sedition, hatred, vengeance, thirst for blood. And we earnestly try to live as much as possible in peace with all men, according to the doctrine of Paul, and if it is not possible for us to keep peace with them, then we still do not desire to avenge ourselves, but we commit it to him who says, Vengeance is mine; I will repay; and we commit to Him alone all our concerns just as Jeremiah and all the pious have done since the beginning.

In the second place we reply, why do they so indiscreetly accuse us of such sedition, seeing that we are so completely free and innocent of sedition, as has been said, and since they do not even notice their own devouring, bloody, murderous seditions, which alas have neither measure nor end, as one can see? O dear Lord, how many principalities, cities, and countries have they destroyed to the ground? How many fires have they set? How many hundred thousands have they dispatched? How they have robbed, skinned, and plucked of his goods the poor peasant who would have gladly kept the peace and was entirely innocent of the contentions of the princes! How many noblemen's wives and virgins have they disgraced? What beastly, inhuman, hellish tyranny did they commit and continue daily to commit? And all of this they do not notice. Yes, it must be styled right and finely done. Dear me, how well does this conform with the doctrine, the nature, and spirit of Christ? How beautifully this accords with the disposition of innocent children whom Christians must resemble in malice; or, with defenseless lambs and innocent doves to which the Scriptures direct us! If the temporal rulers do not have the disposition and Spirit of Christ, then all must acknowledge that they are no Christians.

I am well aware that these tyrants who boast themselves to be Christians justify and make good their abominable warring, their sedition and bloodshed, with a reference to Moses, Joshua, etc. But they do not reflect that Moses and his successors have served their day with their sword of iron, and that Christ has now given us a new commandment and has girded us with another sword (I am not speaking of the sword of justice, for that is a different matter, but I speak respecting war and sedition). Nor do they reflect that that selfsame cross, the sword, which they wield contrary to the evangelical Scriptures, is used by them to stab their own brethren; namely, those who are of the same faith, who have received the same baptism, and who eat the same bread with them, and who therefore are the members of one and the same body. Alas, what a strange, bloody stir the Lutherans have made for several years in order to introduce or substantiate their doctrine, I will leave to them to reflect upon.

Nevertheless, we, although we are innocent, must be called the seditious heretics; and they the pious, peaceable Christians. Behold, so sadly is the understanding of this world darkened! Well, then, let them deal with us as they like. The merciful, gracious Father will surely preserve us from such abominable disturbances as the Münsterites have caused, and which alas are still in vogue among our mixed Christians. For we have, by the grace of God that has appeared to us, beaten our swords into plowshares, and our spears into pruning hooks, and we shall sit under the true vine, that is, Christ, under the Prince of Eternal Peace, and will never more study outward conflict and the war of blood.

In the third place, we reply that we know and use no other sword than that which Christ Himself brought to earth from heaven, and which the apostles used and plied with the power of the Spirit; namely, the one that proceeds from the mouth of the Lord. This sword of the Spirit is sharper than any two-edged sword, piercing even to the dividing asunder of soul and spirit, joints and marrow, and is the discerner of the thoughts and intents of the heart. With this sword and with no other do we desire to destroy the kingdom of the devil, to reprove all wickedness, to plant all righteousness, to set the father against the son and the son against the father, the mother against the daughter and the daughter against the mother, etc., to the extent to which Christ Jesus and His holy apostles have done it in this world. I am not here referring to the prophets Elijah and Samuel (understand me rightly), who also used the external sword, but I mean the prophets Isaiah, Jeremiah, Zechariah, Amos, etc., who only rebuked with doctrine and nothing else.

This same sword we bear and we will lay it down for no emperor or king, magistrate or mayor; for Peter says we ought to obey God rather than men. For the praise and service of Him who has girded us with it we are bound to use it, whether it is our fortune to live or to die, if that should please God.

That the world seeks to change this faithful service of pure love into sedition, this we will have to accept and bear with patience as did our forefathers. Art thou he, said Ahab to Elijah, that troubleth Israel? The prophet answered, I have not troubled Israel, but thou and thy father's house. Jeremiah, on account of his faithful warning and salutary admonition, had to pass for a rebel and a heretic. Christ Jesus had to hang on the cross. Paul and the apostles had to be clapped into prison as deceivers and conspirators, and in the end had to suffer martyrdom. If now the world could pass a true sentence, then it would acknowledge how that not Christ and His followers were seditious toward the world, but that the world was seditious toward Christ and His followers. It would acknowledge that we do not rise against anyone in mutiny, but that the whole world rises up against us in mutiny, tyranny, and "holy war," as may be seen.

Similarly, that we are disobedient to the magistracy in things to which they are ordained of God, this will never be found to be true—I mean in matters pertaining to dikes, roads, waterways, tax, toll, tribute, etc. But if they wish to rule and lord it above Christ Jesus, or contrary to Christ Jesus in our consciences, according to their whim, this we do not grant them. We would rather sacrifice possessions and life than knowingly to sin against Jesus Christ and His holy Word for the sake of any man, be he emperor or king.

That in so doing we do not misbehave but do right, the Scriptures abundantly testify; and therefore with pious Susanna we deem it much better to obey God and so fall into the hands of men than to obey men and so fall into the hands of God.[7] May the gracious Father, through His blessed Son Jesus Christ, grant to this deaf, blind world ears with which to hear and eyes with which to see, that they may be converted and may be saved eternally.

In the second place, we are with great severity but without cause accused by those who persecute us of being headstrong, self-willed, and impossible persons who consistently refuse to be taught or instructed.

To this we reply first, that even if this accusation were true and proper (which it is not), it is still not right for those who persecute us to exterminate

7 This statement is recorded in the Jewish apocryphal passage, Dan. 13:23. *Ed.*

or harm us, since they call themselves Christians, seeing that the punishment of unbelief will be eternal, as the Scriptures testify.

Faith, says Paul, is not every man's possession, but it is a gift of God. Now, if it is a gift it may not be thrust upon a man by external force or by the sword; it must put in its appearance only through the pure doctrine of the holy Word and with a humble fervent prayer in God's grace through the Holy Spirit.

Moreover, it is not the will of the husbandman that the tares should be rooted up as long as the time of harvest has not yet come, as the evangelical parable shows in great clarity.[8] Now if our persecutors were Christians, as they think, and if they considered the Word of the Lord to be true, why then do they not hear and follow the Word and commandment of Christ? Why do they pluck out before the time? Why are they not afraid lest they pluck up the good wheat and not the tares? Why do they invade the province of the angels, who then will bind the tares in bundles and cast them into the furnace of everlasting fire?

Justice would require that since our belief or unbelief (if indeed it is to be called unbelief, as they assert) harms no man upon earth a hair's breadth they should commit us with our belief or unbelief to the Lord alone and to His judgment, who in His own time will judge all things in righteousness, and not like wild and frenzied heathen pursue us with the consuming sword. It is the proper disposition of a true and pious Christian to seek to lead poor, wandering sinners to repentance, and not to destroy them as these men do. All those then who evince a contrary spirit should know plainly of what father they are born. This any sensible Christian can determine with the Bible before him.

In the second place, we reply that we are prepared in every way, even unto death, to receive all sound doctrine, admonition, instruction, and rebuke, in righteousness. We spare no labor, no pains, no expense, if only we can have faithful stewards dispense bread to us in proper season, for our souls hunger after the living Bread, and our spirits thirst for the living Water. All who break it properly and pour it out correctly—these we desire to hear with faithful hearts, and to be obedient to their doctrine.

But we have no appetite for the leaven of the Pharisees and the Sadducees, the lies and the deceiving of the false prophets, the stealings and killings of thieves and murderers. Let whatever God permits happen to us for this. God be praised; we have tasted the heavenly bread! Therefore we have become quite tired of the leaven and the swine husks of the learned ones. We have drunk the clear water, and we let them keep the impure for themselves. The truth has gained entrance with us, and the lie will have to stay out. The light has shone in upon us; there is no room any more for darkness. In short, we have found Christ, the true Messiah, and His saving Word, His pure ordi-

---

[8] An appeal to Matt. 13:29, 30 in support of religious toleration. (The leading reformers appealed to this passage to condemn the church discipline of the Anabaptists.) *Ed.*

nance, and His holy and blameless life (we mean according to the gift received). Therefore we have turned our backs to Antichrist, and hope never again to listen to his teachers, to practice his ordinance in infant baptism and idolatrous supper, nor ever to make our peace with the vile, carnal, wicked life.

If in this matter we sin and do wrong before God and His church, as they think, then the fathers and the Scriptures have fooled us miserably. But ah, no! the Word of God is truth and will always remain the truth, even if all who live on earth are offended at it.

And because we dare not again get mixed up in their false doctrine and their fabricated sacraments, their idolatry and false worship, and their shameful, impure, and bad life, and because we by the Spirit of God and the Scriptures and the witness of our own consciences have turned away from such, therefore we have to pass for headstrong, self-willed, and unconvertible; and, alas, have to be every man's heretic, derision, and plunder.

I do verily hope, dear brethren, that absurd accusations may never dismay the hearts of the pious, nor make them faint, inasmuch as they lack all plausibility, and we on the contrary have on our side the whole of Scripture, together with the prophets, apostles, saints, yes, Christ Jesus Himself—all of whom have remained steadfast and immovable, to the death, against false doctrine, torture, and tyranny. They did not in a single word agree with wickedness, neither in heart, speech, nor behavior.

Shall we then reject the heavenly light again and embrace the cursed darkness? Forsake eternal truth and everlasting life to follow after lies, and pursue death for the sake of some perishable goods and temporal life of half-an-hour? It would be better for us never to have been born. From such a mortal fall may God keep us by His boundless love!

In the third place, we answer that we sincerely detest and hate such teachings and conversion with which those who persecute us teach and convert us, for their end reaches unto death, according to the testimony of all Scripture. The reason? Their doctrine is false and deceptive; their sacraments are idolatrous and without basis in the Word of God; their worship is sheer idolatry; and their whole life is earthly, carnal, and contrary to the Word of God, as may be seen. Yes, they are such a people that one could with justice turn back upon them that which they hurl at us, that is, the assertion that we are a stiff-necked, seditious, impenitent people, whose hearts are harder than the diamond; a people who know not our God. As the prophet has said of Israel, The ox knoweth his owner and the ass his master's crib, but Israel doth not know; my people doth not consider.

Woe to the sinful nation; a people of heavy iniquity; a seed of evildoers; children that are corrupters who forsake the Lord, provoke the Holy One of Israel to anger, and go backward. They hold fast deceit, says Jeremiah. They refuse to return. I hearkened and heard, but they spake not aright. No man repented him of his wickedness, saying, What have I done? Every one turned to his course, as the horse rusheth into the battle. Yes, the stork in the heaven knoweth her appointed time, and the turtle [dove] and the crane and the swallow observe the time of their coming, but my people know not the judgments of the Lord. And there are more passages of similar nature.

With John the Baptist one might well rebuke them and say, Bring forth fruits meet for repentance; and say not that you are Christians, even as the Pharisees said that they have Abraham for their father, for such perverse carnal Christians God does not know. The ax is laid at the root of the tree. Therefore every tree that bringeth not forth good fruit is hewn down and cast into the fire. Neither drunkards, nor covetous, envious, proud, idolaters, adulterers, nor fornicators shall inherit the kingdom of God. We may, therefore, with hearts of compassion, say to those who persecute us, who verily are still such, Repent! For they, alas, with all the rest, lords and princes, learned and unlearned, noblemen and peasants, man and woman, all on every hand, walk in the accursed conduct of bold wickedness. God and His Word they reject; the Holy Spirit they grieve; all righteousness and piety they crucify; God's fear and love they hate. And yet they say to those who do walk in the way of truth, who die unto flesh and blood, who are heavenly and spiritually minded, who with faithful hearts seek Christ Jesus and the everlasting eternal life, Repent; allow yourselves to be instructed, and similar expressions, just as if we had the lies and they the truth, in spite of the fact that according to the gift given to us we love and seek the Lord sincerely. But what they do I leave to any intelligent Christian to judge.

Moreover, they themselves must testify that our ardor, our love, and our conduct far exceed and surpass theirs; nevertheless we have to pass for deceived, headstrong, self-willed, and unconvertible heretics, and they for the real Spirit, the anointed Christians, the true children of God!

My dear brethren, you may judge how powerless and trivial is the world's attempt to vindicate itself in this bloody program and how indiscreetly and childishly we are accused by them. We wish all those who persecute us the grace of the Lord unto repentance, for it is high time that they awake and turn to the Lord.

In the third place, those who persecute us try to justify themselves by saying that it is right that we are persecuted since we mislead many people sadly, and lead them to destruction.

To this we reply, that if one looks at it and judges it from a carnal point of view, then it does indeed appear that many are miserably deceived by us. For all those who desire with obedience and power to follow this our doctrine, this faith, this life and confession, must bring into jeopardy all that which they have received from God—their reputation or good name, farm or soil, gold or silver, father or mother, sister or brother, husband or wife, son or daughter, yes, life and limb. They are pointed at with scornful fingers by all men. They are trampled on, hated by men, slandered and wronged, betrayed and delivered up unto death, gallows, wheels, pits, stakes, and swords, hunger and thirst also. Moreover, want, toil, suffering, distress, cares, nakedness, sorrow, tears, buffetings, prison, shackles, must be their part and portion here upon this earth. No man is allowed without danger to help or befriend them. The father may not receive and assist his son, nor the son his father. In short, they are looked upon by the world as unworthy either of heaven or hell. Moreover, they shun as much as possible all pomp and splendor, eating and drinking to excess, and the frivolous soft life, etc., on which the world dotes and people go for. And over against this they teach humility, sobriety, and a humble, despised life in the fear of the Lord, things which the world hates and rejects. It is therefore verily no wonder, in my opinion, that the erring, blind world which does not have or know the Holy Spirit, as Christ put it, which seeks, understands, and judges earthly things, should consider this imposture and deception and hate it.

But those who are taught of God, who from the old life of sin have risen with Christ to newness of life, who are made partakers of the Holy Spirit and who are spiritually minded, who see things in the light of the Spirit, these do not consider it a deception and an imposture. But they love it above all gold and silver, above all knowledge and wisdom, above all power and honor, above all adornment and beauty, and above all that may be named under heaven; for they know from their hearts that by this one doctrine eternal and everlasting life is laid hold of. Therefore they do not look at the things which are transitory, but at that which is imperishable. They seek and gather a treasure and an inheritance that abideth in heaven, but earthly[9] treasure they care not for. They seek the wisdom that is eternal; and for this they must be the whole world's fools. They adorn themselves with the inner garment of righteousness and despise the external moth-eaten garment of pride. They strive for that kingdom and crown of honor that will abide forever; and the earthly kingdom with its glory they leave to such as take delight in it.

Therefore it is needful, dearly beloved, to judge all things spiritually, for the world is come to such a pass that the pure doctrine of Jesus Christ and His holy apostles is styled heresy. To preach Christ Jesus, His Spirit and life, His pure Word, His will and ordinances, to turn the people from ungodliness to piety, is made to pass for imposture and deception. You see, so blind and senseless in divine things are those who persecute us, they who so miserably oppress and murder us for the sake of the truth. Yes, my brethren, here is the patience and faith of the saints: all those who in their hearts believe this and as it has been related here, will possess their souls in peace, no matter how they are opposed, and they will pray for their enemies with all their power.

In the fourth place, those who persecute us also accuse us with great bitterness because we separate ourselves from their doctrines, sacraments, church service, and from the carnal life, and in such things do not feel free to have to do with them. They say that by so doing we condemn them and consign them to hell.

9 We read *aartsche* (earthly) instead of *gantsche* (total) because the latter makes no suitable sense. *Tr.*

To this we reply in the first place that we do not feel free by word or by deed to approve of their preachers, their sacraments, their church service, their impure carnal life. The reason? They are openly contrary to God and His Word. The preachers go without having been sent. Their doctrine is false, deceptive, and contrary to the saving doctrine of truth. Their life is altogether subject to reproach. They serve for fixed wages. They cater to the world as they please. The foundation of their faith and their religion is emperors, kings, princes, and potentates. What these command they teach, and what these forbid, that they omit. Their infant baptism is without Scripture, and their Lord's Supper is idolatrous and impure, and is administered and received by the impure. Their church service is contrary to the doctrine of the apostles, and their daily conduct is for the most part so carnal and wicked that all the children of God are amazed and frightened.

Seeing then that their doctrines, sacraments, church service, and life are so manifestly contrary to the Word of God, how could we once more make common cause with them in such abominations? That we separate ourselves from them is the express Word and will of God; for what communion, says Paul, hath light with darkness, and what concord hath Christ with Belial? What part hath he that believeth with an infidel, and what agreement hath the temple of God with idols? For ye are the temple of the living God, as God hath said, I will dwell in them and walk in them, and I will be their God and they shall be my people. Wherefore, come out from among them and be separate, saith the Lord, and touch not the unclean thing, and I will receive you and will be a Father unto you, and ye shall be my sons and daughters, saith the Almighty.

These words of Paul are plain and intelligible, and it is therefore utterly impossible that those who have, through the gift of God, received from on high the true light, Christ Jesus, and have received godly righteousness and that powerful effective faith, who have become a fit temple of the Lord, who are driven by the Holy Spirit, who are chosen and adopted to be the children of God—that these should once more be at one with darkness, with Belial, with unrighteousness, with infidels and idolaters. For, seeing that you, by the grace of God, know definitely that their doctrines, sacraments, church service, and life are fundamentally false and spurious (if you indeed have a true zeal for God, count all things but dross that you may with Paul win Christ, if you according to the Scriptures cleave to that which is good and hate the evil, if you have washed your robes in the blood of the Lamb, and in all your thoughts, words, and actions allow yourselves to be judged by the standards of the holy Word and the example of Christ) how can you again be joined to them and say yes to their abominations? We cannot serve two masters at once, can we? We cannot at the same time hold communion with Christ and the devil, can we? We cannot be children and servants of God and also of Satan, can we? If we love the good, then we must hate the evil. If we embrace the truth, we must forsake the lie. Similar arguments in Scriptures there are a great many.

And because we make such a separation from them, and testify by word and deed even unto death that their works are evil, therefore the drive wheel of their hearts impels them to inhuman wrath and indignation, and they say with heart and mouth, as all the ungodly have done from the beginning, Let us lie in wait for the righteous, because he is not for our turn, and he is clean contrary to our doings. He upbraideth us with our offending the law and objecteth to our infamy, the transgressions of our education, etc. He exposeth our secret designs and cunning devices. He is grievous unto us, even to behold, for his life is not like other men's. His ways are of another fashion. We are esteemed of him as counterfeits. He abstaineth from our ways as from filthiness. He pronounceth the end of the just to be blest. Let us condemn him with a shameful death, as the writer of Wisdom puts it.[10]

My dearly beloved brethren, here the Holy Spirit touches the very nerve of the matter, for[11] this our actual confession, that is to say, our separation from them is the real reason why the blind, bloody world raves over us so fearfully, and why we have to hear and suffer so much—just as Peter also says: They think it more strange that you run not with them to the same excess of riot, speaking evil of you. Yes, for this reason Isaiah, Jeremiah, Zechariah, Shadrach, Meshach, and Abednego, Daniel, Eleazar, the mother with the seven sons, Christ Jesus, and all the pious had to die and bear the cross—because they earnestly reproved the world and its doctrines, ceremonies, and conduct, and opposed them to the death.

These things are even unto this day the only motivating cause and essentially the same one (even though those who persecute us allege many, as we have shown), why we are made to pass for the world's Anabaptists, heretics, knaves, and deceivers, seditionists, and we must fall heir to water, fire, gallows, and wheels. But, God be blessed, we know why it is that we suffer! We know also that He who called us in this grace, in whom we trust, will bring our affairs to a good conclusion, and that He will stand by and save His poor harassed children in every time of need and trial, to His eternal praise and glory!

Although those who persecute us say that it is because of sheer wickedness and contrariness on our part, yet their declaration is false and unjust before God, who knoweth the hearts of all men, because our separation proceeds from no other cause or consideration than this—that we desire to observe in our weakness with all our heart the Word and commandment of God, and that we in pure love testify to the world also by our deeds that they all lie in wickedness, yes, that they lie outside of God and His Word; to the end that they might, while they may, awake and turn from iniquity. For how can one teach others gentleness, chastity, humility, or any other virtue as long as he himself is full of all avarice, adultery, pride, and every manner of vice? It would be the height of folly, would it not, for a person to point others to the

---

[10] These quotations are from *The Book of Wisdom* (an Apocryphal work), chap. 2. *Ed.*
[11] We read *want* (for) instead of *wat* (what) because the latter yields no sense. *Tr.*

right way, to warn them of robbers and murderers, and to himself walk a winding unfrequented road, purposely walking right into the net of thieves and robbers? My brethren may reflect on what I mean.

It is not enough for a genuine Christian merely to speak the truth. He must also verify and pursue in power and in deed that which he speaks, or he will have to hear with the Pharisees: You say and do not, as Paul also in Romans says of the Jews: Thou that preachest that a man should not steal, dost thou steal? Thou that sayest a man should not commit adultery, dost thou commit adultery? Thou that abhorrest idols, dost thou commit sacrilege? Thou that makest thy boast of the law, by breaking the law dishonorest thou God? In short, a Christian teaches and acts, professes and practices, believes and obeys, shows the way and walks in it, yes, his heart, his word, his deeds agree. If not, he is a hypocrite and no Christian, just as, alas, there are plenty of them in circulation—men who boast highly of knowledge and wisdom, though in power they are fruitless and vain.

In the second place, we reply that those who persecute us accuse us unjustly and violently of condemning them and consigning them to hell. Ah, no, far be it from us to condemn any man under heaven before his time, no matter how wicked he may be, for we know very well that the Scriptures say: Condemn not, lest ye be condemned. There is One who in His own time will judge every man according to his works, namely, He to whom the Father has committed all judgment; and the man who usurps His judgment shall not go unpunished. Moreover, we know not what grace the sinner may yet receive before his death. Therefore, we are clear and innocent before God of condemning others. Nevertheless, we do make bold to speak decisively by the Word of God as follows: If a covetous man does not turn from his covetousness, a fornicator from his fornications, a drunkard from his drunkenness, an idolater from his idolatry, and does not with a pious, penitent life turn to the true and living God with sorrow and anguish of heart in an active faith in Jesus Christ, then he is no Christian at all and shall not inherit the kingdom of God. If sentence is passed in this way, it is not we that judge, but the Scriptures, as Christ says: He that rejecteth me and receiveth not my words hath one that judgeth him; the word that I have spoken, the same shall judge him in the last day. We know very well that God neither saves nor can save any man contrary to His Word, for He is truth and knows no lie. So then, where there is no faith, no newness of mind, no repentance or sorrow of heart, etc., upon such, alas, Christ Jesus has already passed sentence, saying: If ye believe not that I am he, ye shall die in your sins. Except ye repent, ye shall all likewise perish, and many similar expressions.

You see, my brethren, in this way we judge no man with our word, before the time, as you well know, but we leave it all to Jesus Christ and His Word. He will judge them in His own time. We do not condemn them by our separation, as they complain, but we teach and admonish them by word and deed with all diligence and fidelity to cease from evil, to do that which is good, to conduct themselves correctly, to seek and fear God in a good conscience lest they die in sin and unbelief and remain forever under the wrath and judgment of God. Nevertheless, men insist on turning the pure love and faithful service of the pious into evil and construe it to their disgrace.

In the fifth place, many cover their tyranny and bloodthirstiness with an ineffective fig leaf and say: We do not judge you, but the emperor's mandate [passes sentence on you].

To this we reply, if those who persecute us are Christians and know Christ, as they think, then we desire in all meekness, for God's sake, that they draw a comparison between the emperor and Christ and note well whether the emperor and Christ are like-minded and whether he walks as Christ taught and demonstrated to His disciples. We also ask that they lay the mandate of the emperor next to the Gospel of Christ. If then they discover that the emperor does not agree with Christ in spirit and life, and that his mandate by which they judge is contrary to the Gospel, then they must acknowledge, must they not, that the emperor is no Christian, and that his mandate is prescribed and accursed before God.

It is a very sad and lamentable blindness that they fear and honor the poor earthly emperor so much more than Christ Jesus; and count his bloody and cruel mandate above the precious Gospel. They desire to be considered Christians, nevertheless. Oh, that the emperor and his aides were Christians, as we so earnestly wish! Then much innocent blood would be spared; blood which is now spilt like water, contrary to all Scripture, reasonableness, and love.

Look here, all you who are guilty of innocent blood and who excuse yourselves with the mandate of the emperor, where have you read a single letter in the whole activity of Christ that men should punish to the blood for the sake of faith, and execute with the sword? Where have the apostles ever taught or practiced such? Must not matters of the Spirit (meaning matters of faith) be reserved unto the judgment of the Spirit? Why do the emperor and you place yourselves in God's stead to judge things which you do not understand and which are not given into your care? Do you not recall what befell Pharaoh, Antiochus, Herod, and many others because they feared not the most High and raged against His people? Consider, O you tyrants and men of blood, that the emperor is not the head of Christ, but that Christ is the head of the emperor; that the emperor shall not rule and judge the Christ, but Christ the emperor. Worthy gentlemen, how can you be so rough and bold against Him who created you? So you think that the Scripture mocks us and does not speak the truth? Or, do you hope that your hourglass will last forever and never run out?

Stand in awe of Him who encloses the heavens and the earth in the palm of His hand, who sends forth the fiery shafts of His lightning, the blasts of the tempests, and makes the mountains to shake, who rules all things with the Word of His power, before whom every knee shall bow of things in heaven and things in earth and things under the earth, and to whom every tongue shall confess that He is the Lord. When He calls, you must come to court (*citat enim peremptorie*),[12] no matter who you are, how, or where. In that place there will be no escaping by flight, no counsel, no excuse. When He calls, you have to be there and give an account, for you may be steward no longer. It will be but a little while and the wicked is no more, though his throne seems now to be exalted into the clouds of heaven and his dominion extends to the ends of the earth; yet in a short time he shall be sought and shall not be found.

Therefore, dear children and brethren who are in the Lord, be of good cheer and full of consolation in Christ Jesus, for all who persecute you shall be as grass, and all their power and glory as the flower of the field. Therefore be not afraid of a mortal man, but fear the Lord who has chosen you, for all the children of men shall wither as the grass, vanish as a mist, and wax old as does a garment, but you shall abide forever, as the Scripture testifies, and your souls shall live eternally.

Yes, dear brethren, the desirable day of your release is at hand; the day in which you shall stand with great constancy against those who have afflicted you, and have taken away your sweat and your toil, yes, your blood and your life. Then shall all those who pursue us be as ashes under the souls of our feet and they shall acknowledge too late that emperor, king, duke, prince, crown, scepter, majesty, power, sword, and mandate, were nothing but earth, dust, wind, and smoke.

With this day in view, all afflicted and oppressed Christians who now labor under the cross of Christ are comforted in the firm hope of the life to come; and they leave all tyrants with their heathenish mandates to God and His judgment. But they continue unmovable with Christ Jesus and His holy Word, and they construe all their doctrine, faith, sacraments, and life accordingly; and not in all eternity according to any other doctrine or mandate, even as the Father has commanded it from heaven and as Christ Jesus together with His holy apostles taught in all clarity and bequeathed it to all devout and pious children of God.

I judge, beloved brethren, that it has herewith been made sufficiently evident how that the self-justification of the tyrants with which they make right and proper their tyrannical murders is nothing and heathenish, and that their accusation against us has no foundation or truth. It is openly against Christ and Christ's Word, yes, contrary to reasonableness, righteousness, and love. May the Father of mercies grant unto all who suffer for His truth's sake a sane and sound insight into His Word and truth, and freedom of mind in the face of temptations. Amen.

---

[12] This Latin legal term which Menno inserted in parentheses at this point means: *The summons is peremptory. Tr.*

## [V. THE BLESSINGS OF CROSS-BEARING]

But now we wish by the grace of God to show in a few words how that it serves a good purpose that we are assailed and tempted in the flesh with many oppressions and tribuations here upon earth.

When we consider, worthy brethren, our very weak and sinful nature, how that we are prone to evil from our youth, how that in our flesh no good thing dwelleth, and how that we drink unrighteousness and sin like water, even as Eliphaz the Temanite said to Job, and when we consider how that we have a tendency at all times (although we do seek and fear God) to mind earthly and perishable things, then we see that the gracious God and Father, who through His eternal love always cares for His children, has left behind in His house an excellent remedy against all this, namely, the pressing cross of Christ. Thus we who now through Christ Jesus are taken up to eternal grace to the glory of the Father, who with a pure heart believe on Christ Jesus whom we love in our weakness, may, through the aforesaid cross, that is, through much oppression, tribulation, anxiety, apprehension, bonds, seizure, and so forth, let go of all the transitory things of earth, and that which delights the eyes. And so we die unto the world and unto the flesh, love God alone, and seek the things that are above where Christ sitteth at the right hand of God, as Peter also says, For as much then as Christ hath suffered for us in the flesh, arm yourselves likewise with the same mind, for he that hath suffered in the flesh hath ceased from sin, that he no longer should live the rest of his time in the flesh to the lusts of men, but to the will of God.

Methinks it quite impossible, worthy brethren, that they who voluntarily bow their necks to the Word and will of God, who are willing and prepared to obey the Word in all things, and for these things are constantly persecuted, afflicted, slandered, seized, robbed, and killed, that they should turn their hearts to the love of temporal things and to the vain lusts of earthly existence. For what have we to do with money and possessions, if we but believe that we have a better treasure in heaven, and that the here and the now can neither save us nor help us, and that it will fall into the hands of the plunderers? Oh why should we gratify our flesh in the lusts thereof, when at any moment we look for and expect nothing but to be seized by the officers and be treated by the executioner after his manner; that is, be racked, tortured, drowned, burned, and murdered? How indeed can the world appeal to us, seeing we pass for the world's seducers, heretics, scorners, and fools?

Forasmuch then as the eternal wisdom knows very well our poor weakness, and since earthly ease, peace, and prosperity would so much like to overthrow us before our God and destroy us, make us careless, contrary, lazy, and drowsy, therefore He has appointed the cross to serve as a rod that keeps watch over His own, by which He as a faithful Father keeps His dear children in discipline and piety, rouses them, and makes them go forward. Even as Paul had it,[18] My son, despise not the chastening of the Lord, neither be weary of his correction, for whom the Lord loveth he correcteth, even as a father the son in whom he delighteth. If ye endure chastening, God dealeth with you as with sons, for what son is he whom the father chasteneth not? But if ye be without chastisement, whereof all are partakers, then are ye bastards and not sons. Furthermore, we have had fathers of our flesh which corrected us and we gave them reverence. Shall we not much rather be in subjection unto the Father of spirits and live? For they verily for a few days chastened us after their own pleasure, but he for our profit, that we might be partakers of his holiness.

You see, my brethren, these words of the apostle are surpassingly precious and full of consolation to all those who have to bear the cross of Christ. For, just as a faithful and well-intentioned father does sometimes indeed reprove with a firm hand, chastises and punishes, albeit of pure, unsullied, paternal love, to the instruction and benefit of his dear children, even though it does smart them in the flesh, in order that they may not despise their father's will, command, and voice, but may gladly obey it, and learn, and practice honor, piety, and instruction, so also does our heavenly Father oftentimes chasten His elect children with His paternal rod to the end that they may hear and obey Him in His holy Word, will, and commandments, may put into practice devout instruction and piety, may fear God with sincerity of heart, may not allow themselves to conform to this world, may no longer live unto flesh and blood, and may in this way as obedient and disciplined children of God at the end be made partakers of the promised kingdom and inheritance. But if they refuse the chastening rod, thrust the cross of Christ from them, and through their Father's kind chastening become more and more spoiled and rebellious, if they reject their Father's will and Word, and proceed to act according to their own inclination, then they must at last be cast off and be counted not as legitimate children, but as ignoble bastards.

Therefore, holy brethren, do not refuse the chastening rod of your dear Father. It is employed to your benefit, namely, in order that you may lay aside every weight and the sins which so easily beset you, and in all things without exception fear, love, and obey your Father. You see, in this way this selfsame cross of Christ is nothing but benevolence and love; not indignation and heartlessness, as one can see and judge according to the Word and Spirit of God, and not according to the flesh.

For such reasons as here related did God oftentimes permit His people Israel to be punished by the Philistines, the Assyrians, the Chaldeans, etc., whenever they forgot their God and rebelled against Him, in order that by such scourges and punishments they might once more seek their God, heed His law, cease from evil, and in all things do justly and properly. However, the paternal stroke was for the most part in vain in the case of Israel, even as

---

[18] This quotation from Hebrews is by Menno, in keeping with the common view in his day, ascribed to Paul. *Tr.*

the prophet says: He hath often reproved, but what did it avail? The rod amendeth not the children, saith the Lord God. Or, in another place: Behold, famine and plague, sorrow and anguish are sent as scourges for amendment, but for all these things they shall not turn from their wickedness nor be always mindful of the scourges. Or, again: Thou hast stricken them, but they have not grieved. Thou hast consumed them, but they have refused to receive correction. They have made their faces harder than a rock; they have refused to return. The foregoing words of the prophet show plainly why the Israelites were so often punished and stricken of the Lord, namely, in order that they might turn and repent. But it was all in vain, as the dear prophets lament and declare in the words quoted.

Beloved brethren, let this be an admonition to you, lest you become like disobedient and hardhearted Israel in this matter. Rather may you submit yourselves willingly to the merciful chastening of your Father, and recall that it is written that when we are judged we are chastened of the Lord in order that we should not be condemned with the world.

For this cause, dear brethren and sisters in the Lord, do not reject the chastening and instruction of your dear Father, but receive the admonition of His faithful love with great joy. Thank Him that through His fatherly goodness He has chosen you to be His dear children in Christ Jesus, and has called you by His powerful Word. Thank Him that He has enlightened you with the Holy Spirit in order that through the medicine and remedy of the cross of Christ He may restore to health your poor, weak, mortal flesh, subject to so many harmful and destructive ailments of concupiscence, and has diverted it from the lusts and loves of the world in order that you in this way may be made partakers of the burden of Christ and conformed unto His death, and so attain unto the resurrection of the dead. Even as Paul in a certain place instructs saying: We are troubled on every side, yet not distressed; we are perplexed, but not in despair; persecuted, but not forsaken; cast down, but not destroyed; always bearing about in the body the dying of the Lord Jesus, that the life also of Jesus may be made manifest in our body. But we who live are given up to death daily (are we not?) for Jesus' sake, in order that the life of Jesus might be made manifest in our mortal flesh.

Behold, for this reason He teaches, admonishes, rebukes, threatens, and chastises, in order that we should deny ungodliness and worldly lusts, die entirely unto the world, the flesh, and the devil, and seek our treasure, our portion, and our inheritance in heaven; believe and love only the eternal, true, and living God; and so wait patiently for that blessed hope and the glorious appearing of our Lord and Saviour Jesus Christ, who gave Himself for us that He might redeem us from all iniquity and purify unto Himself a peculiar people serving Him in righteousness and godliness all the days of our lives.

And for this reason, James says: My brethren, count it all joy when you fall into divers temptations, knowing this, that the trying of your faith worketh patience; but let patience have her perfect work, that ye may be perfect and entire, wanting nothing. For even as gold through the fire's heat separates itself from the dross and by the flames becomes more and more pure, so the man of God who is susceptible to it is humbled, purified, and cleansed in the oven and fire of tribulation in order that he may be an everlasting praise, honor, and glory to Christ and His Father, and may with a faithful heart, unhindered by anything, fear this God, and love, honor, and serve Him.

And this is the word that is written in the Book of Wisdom: Having been a little chastised they shall be greatly rewarded, for God proved them and found them worthy for himself. As gold in the furnace hath he tried them and received them as a burnt offering. And in the time of their visitation they shall shine and run to and fro like sparks among the stubble. They shall judge the nations and have dominion over the people and their Lord shall reign forever.[14]

Therefore, dear brethren, be comforted in the Lord and bear your tribulation calmly as pious knights of Christ in order that you may please Him who has called you and chosen you as soldiers. Paul says: If a man also strive for mastery, yet is he not crowned except he strive lawfully. Fight the fight courageously and your king will look with favor upon you. But if ye become fearful, if ye throw down your weapons and your swords and forsake the battle, ye shall receive no crown; for Christ says: He that endureth to the end shall be saved.

I fear that some may be found among our young and inexperienced brethren who allow themselves to be terrified by the fleeting thought, Why do the wicked prosper so, and why do the righteous have to suffer so much? Yes, it appears in the eyes of the imprudent as if the ungodly were born to every good fortune, for they grow and increase as green things do. They marry and are given in marriage. They sow and mow. They gather the grain into their barns, and the money into their chests. Their dwellings are magnificent, full, and well adorned. They cover themselves with gold and silver, with silk and velvet; they nourish their hearts as in a day of slaughter. Their fields and their meadows flourish abundantly. Their cattle are healthy and prolific. Their children are lusty and gay and carefree before their eyes. They play on organs and timbrels, on viol and lute. They sing and dance and say to their souls: Rejoice, and have a good time while you may.

Their preachers confirm and console them, and their worship is a fine thing, above all that is fine. In a word, it looks as if they are loved and blessed of God with an unusual love, and that the righteous, on the contrary, are accursed and hated of God with a special hatred, for they are like a meager thicket in a barren earth, like a poor and outcast night bird pecked at by every fowl, like a pelican in the wilderness, and a sparrow alone on a housetop; all who look upon them mock them; all who know them despise them; no kingdom or realm, no city or state is large enough to endure and

[14] Another quotation from the Jewish Apocryphal *Book of Wisdom* (Chap. 4). *Ed.*

suffer a poor rejected Christian! All who violate him, slander him, and make it hard for him, think they do God a service.

Brethren, if we were to judge after the manner of men we would doubtlessly have to complain with holy Jeremiah, Righteous art thou, O Lord, when I plead with thee. Yet let me talk with thee of the judgments. Wherefore doth the way of the wicked prosper? Wherefore are all they happy that deal very treacherously? Or with Habakkuk, Wherefore lookest thou upon them that deal treacherously and holdest thy tongue when the wicked devours the man that is more righteous than he? Or with Ezra, Are they of Babylon better than they of Zion? Asaph's feet were almost gone; his steps had well-nigh slipped, because he saw the prosperity of the wicked, and observed the opposition and tribulation of the righteous.

All who are assailed with such thoughts I advise and admonish to turn their hearts and eyes unto the Word of the Lord and note well that which is written concerning the end and the issue of both of these: of the ungodly first of all.

Job declares, They spend their days in wealth and in a moment go down to the grave; again David says, Fret not thyself because of evildoers. Neither be thou envious against the workers of iniquity, for they shall soon be cut down like the grass and wither as the green herb. Again, if ye live after the flesh, as Paul says, ye shall die. To be carnally minded is death, and many similar sayings.

But the end of the righteous is as it is written: The souls of the righteous are in the hand of God and there shall no torment touch them. In the sight of the unwise they seem to die and their departure is taken for misery and their going from us to be utter destruction, but they are in peace. Similarly, many are the afflictions of the righteous, but the Lord delivereth him out of them all. Or again, Blessed are ye when men shall revile you and persecute you and shall say all manner of evil against you falsely for my sake. Rejoice and be exceeding glad, for great is your reward in heaven. And again, Seeing it is a righteous thing with God to recompense tribulation to them that trouble you; and to you who are troubled, rest with us, when the Lord Jesus shall be revealed from heaven with his mighty angels, in flaming fire taking vengeance on them that know not God and that obey not the gospel of our Lord Jesus Christ, who shall be punished with everlasting destruction from the presence of the Lord and from the glory of his power, when he shall come to be glorified in his saints and to be admired in all them that believe.

Yes, all who read the Scriptures aright believe and understand, and so have correct insight into the vastly dissimilar end and issue of both. These will not envy them their brief prosperity, their gladness and felicity, but will by the grace of God find consolation and comfort in their own misery, oppression, and cross.

We know very well, dear brethren, how that this cross seems to the flesh grievous, harsh, and severe, and in the present is not considered a matter of joy, but rather of sorrow, even as Paul says. But since it contains within itself so much of profit and delight, in that it constantly adds to the piety of the pious, turns them away from the world and the flesh, makes them revere God and His Word, as was said above, and since it is also the Father's holy will that by it the saints should be approved, and the pretender exposed in his hypocrisy, therefore all the true children of God are prepared to love, to do the will of the Father, rejoicing in it. As Paul says, God forbid that I should glory save in the cross of our Lord Jesus Christ by whom the world is crucified unto me and I unto the world. Similarly, the apostles departed from the presence of the council rejoicing that they were counted worthy to suffer for His name.

We well know that the cross galls and pierces our poor weak flesh, as we see it in the case of Job, Jeremiah, Elijah, and others, and that in a very similar way the Lord Himself desired that if it were possible the cup might pass from Him. Yes, that in the excess of agony He trembled, quaked, and sweat, as it were, great drops of blood, so that an angel from heaven had to comfort Him. Therefore our best counsel is that in faith and humility of heart we fly for refuge to our God alone, even as all pious bearers of the cross have done from the beginning, and seek in full confidence His grace, His aid, His assistance, and consolation. For who has trusted in Him only to be forsaken, and who has called upon Him to find that He did not hear? He is our God and Father. He is our Lord and King. He is our Helper and Protector, our Strength and Fortress, our Comfort and Refuge in time of trouble. He is the Horn of our salvation and the Shade against the heat. By my God, says David, will I leap over a wall. If God is for us, who can be against us? We can do all things through Christ who strengtheneth us. To Him commit your cause. He works in His saints as it pleases Him. Some He has delivered out of the hand of tyrants. Some He has preserved in the midst of the fire. For others He has stopped the mouths of fierce and ravening lions. These He released from prison and confinement; and for them He thrust the fear of death under their feet, and they triumphed gloriously over hunger, thirst, derision, shame, nakedness, stripes, seizures, anguish, gallows, wheels, garrotings, torture, water, fire, life, death, etc. For they were driven by the constraining mighty love of the Lord that turns the bitter into the sweet, and the horrible into that which is much to be desired. Love, says Solomon, is stronger than death. Many waters cannot quench it, many floods cannot choke it. All who have really taken hold of it say with the holy Paul, Who shall separate us from the love of Christ? Shall tribulation, or distress, or persecution, or famine, or nakedness, or peril, or sword? As it is written, for thy sake we are killed all the day long, we are accounted as sheep for the slaughter. Nay, in all these things we are more than conquerors through him that loved us; for I am persuaded that neither death nor life, . . . shall be able to separate us from the love of God which is in Christ Jesus our Lord.

Therefore, dear brethren, you who sigh under the cross of the Lord, acknowledge your God, fear and love your God, believe and trust your God, serve and live unto your God, and that with hearts full and pure, after the example of all the saints and of Christ. And the merciful and the faithful Father according to His great love will not forsake you, but will care for you as for the apple of His eye. In all faithfulness He will stand by you in every grief and need, reach you His hand, and guard and sustain you whether in life or in death, as seems good to Him, to His glory and to the salvation of your souls. For He is so gracious and faithful that He cannot allow you to be tempted above your strength, but will in His great compassion grant a gracious way out, if you believe His Word firmly and surely, and count Him your faithful Father.

You see, my worthy brethren, if you conduct yourselves after this manner in your oppression and trials, if you drink with patience the cup of the Lord, give testimony to Christ Jesus and His holy Word in word and deed, if you allow yourselves as meek lambs for the testimony of Christ to be led with perfect constancy to the slaughter, then in you the name of God will be praised and made holy and glorious, the name of the saints will be revealed, the kingdom of heaven extended, the Word of God made known, and your poor weak brethren in the Lord will be strengthened and taught by your courage.

Yes, my brethren, in the manner here related the sacrifice and blood of Abel speaks to this day; as do the faith and obedience of Abraham, Isaac, and Jacob, the chastity of Joseph, the patience of Job and Tobit, the excellent manly confession of Eleazar, the mother and her seven sons,[15] the courageous constancy, the piety of all the saints who have been before us, and the true and genuine love, the humility, peace, righteousness, and freewill offering of Christ, who according to the promise of God was sent from heaven in everlasting love by God our heavenly Father to be an everlasting example and trustworthy teacher.

Most dearly beloved brethren and sisters in Christ Jesus dispersed abroad in every land, for whose benefit I have out of pure Christian love assembled and transcribed this exhortation, I want to bring the matter to an end. I entreat you in all humility to consider well in the first place what manner of folk they are who so hatefully persecute you and deprive you of life and property. Second, consider for what reason they persecute you and cause you so much grief. Third, note how that all saints, Christ Jesus Himself also, have suffered these persecutions, and how that all the pious must suffer them still, as may be seen. Fourth, hear how feeble all their arguments are with which they try to clear themselves of their bloodguiltiness and accuse us as if they did right in doing so, and as if we deserved every manner of disgrace and punishment. Fifth, how profitable and advantageous that cross is to us, the cross which we must pick up and bear daily for the sake of the

[15] Another reference to II Mac., this time to Chapter 7. *Ed.*

Word of the Lord; moreover, how we should desire to hear, believe, and obey Christ Jesus. For if you ponder these five matters calmly according to the Scriptures, looking into them with purity of heart, I do not doubt that it will be to you a strong and invincible strength, an armor and a shield against all tribulation, persecution, and distress, when distress comes upon you.

## [VI. PROMISES FOR THOSE BEARING THE CROSS]

Finally, I beseech and exhort you, consider with all diligence what it is that is promised to all soldiers and conquerors in Christ in the world to come; namely, an eternal kingdom that does not pass, the crown of honor, and the life that will remain forever. Therefore, O ye people of God, gird yourselves and make ready for battle; not with external weapon and armor as the bloody, mad world is wont to do, but only with a firm confidence, a quiet patience, and a fervent prayer. It can and may not be otherwise—this battle of the cross will have to be fought, this winepress of sorrow trod. O thou bride and sister of Christ, be calm. The thorny crown must pierce your head and the nails your hands and feet. Your body must be scourged and your face spit upon. Gird yourself and be prepared, for you must go forth with your Lord and bridegroom outside the city, bearing His reproach. On Golgotha you must pause and bring your sacrifice. Watch and pray, for your enemies are more numerous than the hairs on your head and the sands of the sea. Even though their hearts, their hands, their feet, and swords are exceedingly red and bloody, be not dismayed, for God is your captain. Your life is but an incessant warfare on earth. Contend valiantly and you will receive the crown promised. To him that overcometh I will give to eat of the tree of life which is in the midst of the paradise of God, and of the hidden and heavenly manna.

Him that overcometh will God make a pillar in his temple and will write upon him his name, the name of the new Jerusalem. He that overcometh shall not be hurt by the second death. He that overcometh, the same shall be clothed in white raiment and his name shall not be blotted out of the book of life, but Christ Jesus will confess his name before his heavenly Father and before his angels. He that overcometh shall sit with Christ in his throne, even as Christ overcame and is set down with his Father on his throne.

O soldiers of God, prepare yourselves and fear not! This winepress you must tread. This narrow way you must walk, and through this narrow gate you must enter into life. The Lord is your strength, your comfort and refuge; He sits with you in prisons and dungeons; He flies with you to foreign lands; He accompanies you through fire and water; He will never leave you nor forsake you. Yes, He will come quickly and His great reward will be with Him. Blessed are they which are persecuted for righteousness' sake, for theirs is the kingdom of heaven. Do not sorrow for that you are black; you are nonetheless comely and pleasing to the King. As a rose you must grow up among the thorns and endure lacerations. Rejoice, for the King delights in your comeliness. For even though in His first appearance He was sacrificed as an innocent lamb, and opened not His mouth, nevertheless the time will come when He will appear as a triumphant prince and a victorious king to bring judgment. Then will those who persecute us look upon Him whom they have pierced. Then will they cry aloud and exclaim: Mountains, fall on us, and hills, cover us. But you will leap and dance for joy like fatted calves of the stalls. Joy and exultation will never forsake you, for your king, your bridegroom and redeemer, Christ Jesus, will remain with you forever. God shall wipe away all tears from your eyes and there shall be no more death, neither sorrow nor crying. Neither shall there be any more pain. God's praise, thanksgiving, and glory shall flow from your mouth eternally. Let me say it once more. Do battle! The crown of glory is prepared for you! Shrink not, neither draw back; for yet a little while and He that shall come will come and not tarry. Now the just shall live by faith, but if any man draw back, my soul shall have no pleasure in him. Take heed and watch lest the fire of the cross consume you as wood, hay, and stubble, lest the floods and storms of persecution overthrow the house, lest the heat of the sun wither the grass, lest like the dog you turn again to your vomit, lest your garments and your feet which you have washed become unclean again, and seven worse spirits take up their abode in you, and so the last error be worse than the first!

Therefore, dear brethren and sisters in the Lord, fear your God with all your heart and with all your souls, and seek Him with all your might. Watch by night and by day. Knock at the throne of His grace, so that with His Fatherly hand He may support you in every affliction, stand by you in all trouble and distress, and faithfully keep you in His way, His Word, and His truth. Thus may you not dash your foot against the stone and so fail in your profession and your life, be broken and disgraced; so may you keep the treasure entrusted to your care, pure and untarnished against that Day, and so with all pious saints obtain the promised land, the inheritance, the kingdom, the life, the crown. This may the merciful dear Father grant you and us all through His blessed Son Jesus Christ in the power of His eternal and Holy Spirit to His everlasting praise and glory. Amen.

# Reply to Gellius Faber

*Beantwoordige over een schrift Gelii Fabri*

# 1554

*For other foundation can no man
lay than that is laid, which is Jesus Christ.*

I Corinthians 3 :11

# Introduction

Jelle Smit, better known as Gellius Faber, first served as a Roman Catholic priest at Jelsum near Leeuwarden in the Netherlands. For twenty years, 1516-36, Gellius is said to have frequently preached Lutheran doctrine from his pulpit. But eventually he became a Protestant in name also, and had to flee. He became a pastor in Emden, East Friesland, where the noted John a Lasco was serving as superintendent of the new Protestant state church. When a Lasco summoned Menno to the capital for a discussion which was held Jan. 28-31, 1544, Gellius Faber was one of the ministers who sat in the meeting which was a sort of semipublic interview. In the year 1552 Faber was much irritated by an Anabaptist letter which fell into his hands, and which explained the position of the Anabaptists in their being unable to unite with the Lutheran state church. Thereupon (1552) Faber published a 78-page book of reply, bitterly attacking the Anabaptists. Menno Simons knew nothing of the Anabaptist letter but felt obligated to reply to Faber. The result is the largest of Menno's writings, but by no means the most significant. What is really significant in this work of Menno is his extended account of his own conversion, renunciation of the church of Rome, and call to the ministry. The book was in press by February 15, 1554 (p. 856).

The book may be outlined as follows:

I. Reply to Seven Selected General Statements of Gellius
II. The Mission or Vocation of the Preachers [Nine Sections]
   Menno's autobiographical account is in the seventh selection.
III. Baptism [Twenty-two Sections]
   Replies to selections from the attack of Gellius
IV. The Lord's Supper [Four Selections]
   In three major discussions Menno replies to Four Points.
V. Excommunication [Eleven Selections Refuted]
VI. The Church
   Menno discusses: A. Differentiation of Christ's Church from that of Antichrist; B. The Recognizable Signs of Each Church; and C. Reply to 14 Statements of Gellius.
VII. Refutation of Six Accusations of Gellius
VIII. Essay: Critique of the Christology of the Clergy
IX. Seven Further Accusations of Gellius, and Menno's Replies
   Conclusion

This reply to Faber was published in 1554. In the Dutch original the title reads: *A Plain Reply to a Publication by Gellius Faber, Minister at Emden, Which in 1552 (if I Do Not Mistake) He, Sad to Say, Put to Press to the Disgrace of the Pious Children of God, to the Increase of their Cross, to the Ensnarement of the Simple, and to the Comfort and Strengthening of the Impenitent.*

In the *Opera Omnia Theologica* of 1681 this *Reply to Faber* is printed fol. 225-324, and in the *Complete Works* of 1871, Part II, pages 1-105. JCW

# Reply to Gellius Faber

# 1554

•-•··•-•··•-•··•-•··•-•··•-•··•-•··•-•··•-•··•-•··•-•··•-•··•-•··•-•··•-•··•-•··•-•··•-•··•-•··•-•··•-•··•-•··•-•··•-•··•-•··•-•··•-•··•-•··•

*To all pious and well-intentioned people, whether of high or low estate, who seek diligently the firm position of God, and who may read or hear my much-needed reply, do we wish a clear, spiritual vision, a sound mind, and an honest judgment in the truth, from God our heavenly Father through His dear Son, Jesus Christ our Lord, in the grace and illumination of His eternal and Holy Spirit. Amen.*

## *Preface*

Paul writes to Timothy saying, This know also, that in the last days perilous times shall come. For men shall be lovers of their own selves, covetous, boasters, proud, blasphemers, disobedient to parents, unthankful, unholy, without natural affection, trucebreakers, false accusers, incontinent, fierce, despisers of those that are good, traitors, heady, highminded, lovers of pleasure more than lovers of God; having a form of godliness, but denying the power thereof: from such turn away. II Tim. 3:1-5.

He says further, I charge thee therefore before God, and the Lord Jesus Christ, who shall judge the quick and the dead at his appearing and his kingdom; preach the word; be instant in season, out of season; reprove, rebuke, exhort, with all longsuffering and doctrine. For the time will come when they will not endure sound doctrine; but after their own lusts shall they heap to themselves teachers, having itching ears; and they shall turn away their ears from the truth, and shall be turned unto fables. II Tim. 4:1-4.

Similarly Daniel says, There shall be a time of trouble, such as never was since there was a nation. Dan. 12:1.

Honorable reader, if you will observe thoughtfully the purposes, teaching, and conduct of the preachers of the present day, and the deplorable status of the common people, you will see plainly that the teachers of whom Paul speaks are here in great numbers and that the abominable time has come. O my reader, take heed! It is such a time that if Sodom were still in existence, it would be considered pious and righteous in comparison with the present, awful world. Yet through the just punishment and fierce wrath

625

of God it was thrust into the depths of hell and bears the vengeance of eternal fire. Jude 1 :7.

Behold, says the prophet, this was the iniquity of thy sister Sodom, pride, fulness of bread, abundance of idleness was in her, and in her daughters, neither did she strengthen the hand of the poor and needy. And they were haughty, and committed abomination before me; therefore I took them away as I saw good. Ezek. 16 :49, 50.

But now alas! men live as if they were born to nothing but ungodliness and the satisfaction of passion, and as if God were a dreamer and His Word a fable. Tell me, is it not so? My good reader, is it not so? Where is he that fears God from the heart and seeks after the truth? Wherever we turn we see nothing but unrighteousness, idolatry, deceit, and despising of God. And then all this is dressed up with the holy name of Christ, His Word, death and blood; besides with human weakness to prevent offense (as they put it), and with false freedom. O Lord, as if Christ were the redeemer of all the impenitent, and the atoner of all perverse sinners! No, my reader, no! Let everyone watch out. Paul says, If ye live after the flesh, ye shall die.

Since then everything is so corrupt on every hand that it has become a second Sodom, yes, a confused Babel or a pitch-dark Egypt, under the pretense and name of Christian churches, and since the merciful and great God has, in these last days of unrighteousness, once more allowed the noble and worthy Word of His divine grace to be known again to some in pure, Christian understanding, and since He has placed it as a pure light in the midst of darkness, the means whereby He in everlasting love will assemble unto Himself for the great and dark day an obedient and willing church through the revelation of His holy Word and the enlightenment of His eternal Spirit, and since He has chosen them as His own peculiar people from the assembly of Antichrist, by true repentance and a virtuous walk (although in weakness), under the cross of Christ, together with a sound use of the sacramental signs according to the ordinances of Christ and His apostles, and through a free and honest confession in the declaration of the blood; therefore all the gates of hell bestir themselves and rave, so that, alas, a true Christian can find but little rest upon earth, it seems.

The magistrates banish and persecute, drag into prisons and dungeons, torture and rob, and in many places deprive them most grievously of their prosperity, possessions, honor, life, and limb.

This perverse and reckless people reviles and dubs us Anabaptists no end, and heaps one vulgar lie upon another; points at us with a finger as though we carried on in a way to make fire and sword too merciful a punishment for our bodies, and eternal hell-fire too merciful a punishment for our souls.

The preachers and the learned ones rave aloud and right hatefully, they revile and slander mightily, as the prophet says. And although we testify by so many tribulations that we, in our poor weakness, sincerely desire to fear and follow the Lord, and that we seek the welfare of all men, yet they reproach without measure. They stir up lords and rulers of cities and countries everywhere, peddling the idea that we are an ungodly sect and Anabaptists; that we seduce the people; that we plan to raise turmoil and rebellion, and more such turbulent inventions and slander, in order that they may thus obscure and extirpate and restrain the noble Word of God, the word of true repentance, the joyful Gospel of grace, the true and powerful faith in Christ Jesus, the pious unblamable life, required by the Scriptures, the glorious kingdom of Christ and His righteousness, so that their cause and unfaithfulness may not be made manifest to the world even as is evident from their fruits; and so that on the other hand the evil working kingdom of Antichrist, the kingdom of this world, may be preserved and maintained in its impenitence, open idolatry, and carnal easy life and unity of unrighteousness, according to the desires of the old serpent, and may continue to the end in the place of the truth.

Behold in this way the prince of darkness who rules in the air, prosecutes his program in the children of disobedience, as alas may be plainly seen in this Gellius Faber, if we in the light of the Lord's Word and Spirit, consider his writing, slanders, revilings, bitter disdainful words and printed accusations, his vain boasting and mighty violations of Scripture.

Since then it is well known to many thousands of honest and reasonable people, as I suppose, that we seek nothing on earth but that we may in our weakness willingly walk in the footsteps of Christ, in obedience to His Word, at the expense of ourselves; that we would so much like to re-light the extinguished lamp of truth, teach many unto righteousnesness, and save our souls by the help and grace of the Lord; things for which we fear one must endure much sorrow, misery, anxiety, cross, and persecution everywhere. And this is so in spite of this above-mentioned Gellius who in this case should be our defense and father (for he calls himself a minister of the holy Word) but who still continually increases our trials and sore persecution and the hatred and bitterness against us by the unscriptural arguments and rebuttal to our position, and by the doctrine put forth by him, with his neatly covered complaints to the magistracy and with his foul slanders. Since he does not hesitate to set forth in his writings in print before all men, to the dishonor of God and His holy Word, and to the shame and disgrace of all the pious, to the confirmation of his own heavy condemnations, and to the deception of the simple, therefore, no well-disposed person can think it ill of me that I, by an open reply, with the Spirit and Word of my Lord, defend to the best of my ability, to the honor of God, the salvation of my brethren, the foundation of my faith, and the praise of Christ my Lord, whose service I unworthily entered by His grace and calling and according to His divine will.

I hope with the gracious help of God to do this with such power and clarity, with so many plain reasons and Scriptures, that not only the learned and the theologians, but also all reasonable and impartial readers and hearers will, by the grace of God, clearly understand that he and the preachers of his group possess the deceiving lies, and we, through the grace of God, the sure foundation of truth.

Herewith, therefore, I humbly beseech and faithfully admonish all my readers, friends, and enemies, to read attentively, to examine diligently, and to judge according to Scripture this my forcibly extracted reply and defense, not with the senses spoiled by partisanship, not drowsily or spitefully, but with wide-awake eyes of the soul. This matter concerns us all, namely, the praise of God and of Christ, and the salvation of our poor souls. Let none imagine that he is not included. There is but one road and gate that leads to life, which is narrow and strait; also, but one doctrine. If we would enter with Christ into the kingdom of His glory, we must all walk the strait way and enter in at the narrow gate, and be obedient to His Word. Of this let every one be aware.

Since, then, it is evident that the doctrine and position of Gellius, and of the learned ones, their sacraments, doctrine, and system are based mainly on human wisdom, and ours upon God's Word, that he and his followers walk upon the broad road, and our followers upon the strait road, and on the one hand, that he is not persecuted, but persecutes by his writings; and on the other hand, that we are persecuted and do not persecute: therefore all right-minded persons must admit, must they not, that the truth and the church is not with them but with us. For it cannot fail, as God's Word and the example of all the pious show, that where the true church is, there is and must be the saving doctrine, true sacraments, unfeigned love, a pious, godly life, and the excommunication of the impenitent and perverse, according to the Word of God; as may be clearly seen and heard by the grace of God in the following reply.

To this end I would earnestly pray all the pious for God's sake, that they would come to my assistance with their fervent prayers to the most High, that He would bestow upon me, unworthy and not too capable a man, together with my beloved brethren and faithful servants in the Lord, the gift of His grace and the fountain of His wisdom to such an extent that we may stop the mouth of all opponents with the power of a true doctrine and unblamable walk, and defend to the end the house of our God, in pure, godly zeal and Christian love, to the honor of His great name. To Him be praise and the eternal kingdom. Amen.

## [I. REPLY TO SEVEN SELECTED GENERAL STATEMENTS OF GELLIUS]

Pure and clear is wisdom; strong and powerful is truth; simple and desirable is righteousness; happy is he who possesses them, for his heart rejoices in the Lord, his mouth speaks what is right, and his feet are placed upon the pathway of peace.

[1] *First of all Gellius quotes the saying of Christ, as a warning to all his readers, against us, Beware of false prophets who come to you in sheep's clothing, but inwardly they are ravening wolves. Matt. 7:15.*

*Reply.* If the reader can rightly distinguish, according to the Spirit and Word of God, between the sheep and the wolves, and know what sheep's clothing is, with which the ravening wolves are covered, then the saying would undoubtedly not be applied to us, but to our opponents; for in what kind of clothing he appears here, with which he keeps the simple in condemnation, and grasps their poor souls, the following reply will, by the grace of God, reveal to all pious and godly readers, if they compare it to his writing.

[2] *In the second place he quotes Paul and says, Now I beseech you, brethren, by the name of our Lord Jesus Christ, that ye all speak the same thing, that there be no divisions among you; but that ye be perfectly joined together in the same mind and in the same judgment. I Cor. 1:10.*

*Reply.* If we consider this saying aright, we find that it admonishes all true Christians not to live carnally nor to be sectarian; that the one should not boast of this man and another of that. It points us to the only and true Shepherd and Saviour of our souls, Jesus Christ, who was crucified for us and in whose name we were baptized. The things of Paul's appeal we in our weakness gladly and earnestly do by the grace of God, as our tribulation, misery, sorrow, blood, and death abundantly testify in many places.

But Gellius uses these words to keep his readers from the unity of the Spirit, Word, house, and body of Christ, and to keep them, through his deceitful doctrine, unscriptural infant baptism, etc., in the unity of the spirit, word, house, and body of Antichrist, and on the broad way, unmoved and unchanged.

[3] *In the third place Gellius has dedicated his writing to a nobleman, as is customary with the learned ones; thinking perhaps that by this means their aim will be more easily attained, through the favor and support of such dignitaries; a thing which the pious witnesses, prophets, and teachers, especially of the New Testament, never desired and much less sought or employed concerning God's truth and Word. [4] In the fourth place Gellius gives two main reasons why he published his writing. The first is, he says, Because I see that these Anabaptists are daily slipping into this country, secretly, from the imperial domain, where they can do and also do the most damage, and not only seek to sow their pernicious seed by night preaching, but also by publications and letters, which we must stop and silence, lest the simple be*

*deceived, and that we may yet redeem some of them who have not yet become revilers.*

*Reply.* These very derogatory words, such as Anabaptists, night preachers, sowers of tares, plainly show also the nature of the man who penned them. Yes, my readers, Gellius knows as well as I do what Christ has commanded concerning baptism, and how the holy apostles practiced it. He knows also how Paul rebaptized some who were baptized by John, although John's baptism was from heaven, because of the defect that they were not informed concerning the Holy Ghost. He knows also that the worthy martyr Cyprian[1] and the African bishops, together with the council of Nicea, did not acknowledge the baptism of heretics, seeing that heretics are outside of Christ's church and without His Spirit and Word.

Notwithstanding all this, we must be called Anabaptists by him in disregard of the fact that we in our infancy were baptized, not only without Spirit, Word, faith, or divine command, but also without all reason and understanding, as may be seen in the children; with an open, anti-Christian baptism administered by such as he and the learned ones of his kind, themselves called anti-Christians, apostates, heretics, and deceivers; men who neither rightly understand God nor His Word; who live in open idolatry; who bend their knees before wood and stone; who put their trust in vain doctrines of men; who willfully walk according to the lust of their flesh, and who worship and honor a creature of God, namely, a bit of bread, as the only and eternal Son of God, etc.

And although we have before us a pattern, Christ's plain Word and the salutary doctrine and open practice of the apostles, besides Paul and both the councils, as has been heard, yet, alas, the bitter revilings and this Anabaptisting against us poor people have alas no measure nor end with him. If we were to return evil with evil we might very well with more justice call them child-baptizers, than for them to call us Anabaptists, for we have the whole Scripture on our side, but they have neither Word nor example.

But his saying, that we can and do the most damage in the imperial dominion, shows, alas, his stupidity and blindness. All Scriptures teach us that idolaters and carnally minded men are worthy of death, and he knows very well that in these countries, according to their religion, an open idolatry and gross abomination obtains. Their life, generally speaking, is nothing but a reckless, impenitent, and carnal life, also at Emden and everywhere. Yet he dares to write that there they do most damage. And this for no other reason than that they storm the kingdom of hell with the Lord's Spirit, Word, and power; rebuke open idolatry; teach the true worship; confess Christ rightly, and point this perverse and carnal people to the right way. And if this is doing damage, as Gellius calls it, then the Scriptures which speak so overly much of the true religion, and an unblamable, pious life, have sadly deceived us. This you must admit. Oh, what perverted judgment!

[1] Cyprian was martyred in A.D. 258. *Ed.*

Behold, in this way does the god of this world blind such rebellious and contentious spirits, who so willfully contend against the Word of God, and who keep the truth in unrighteousness, that they become such obdurate and perverse minds as to call the glorious gain of Christ, brought about by His grace, Spirit, and power, a damage; calling good evil, and evil good. Woe unto such. Isa. 5:20.

I would say further, that he also says in other places that we are the only ones who obstruct their impenitent and wicked teaching by our doctrine (which is not ours but the blessed doctrine of Christ) and by our weak conduct in the fear of God, a walk which results from our doctrine through faith. And he intimates that we are the cause in this way, that they are not so highly esteemed as before and that they do not have the success that they would like to have. Therefore he complains that we do the most damage there. But we say it is because that in carnal passion they serve the world under the semblance of the Gospel, and fondle the rulers in order that they may take over for their use cloisters and churches which were given as alms to the honor of God (although by misconception). It is because they say that they are permitted to advance the Gospel of Christ by the force of arms, etc., telling the people that Christ has paid for our sins, that faith is all that matters, that we are poor weak sinners who cannot keep the commandments of God anyway, and similar easygoing consolations. Thus everybody seeks his benefits and the freedom of his flesh in these things, singing and shouting, The cord is broken and we are free. They turn the grace of God into lasciviousness, as Jude has it, because they continue unchanged in the old state of sinfulness without any fear of God, as if they never in their lives have heard one syllable of the Word of God, and as if God would not punish ungodliness and unrighteousness. We say, therefore, the just Lord who judges all things rightly once more takes from them the knowledge which they may have had, because of their ingratitude (for they teach and proclaim the Gospel of His grace according to the lusts of the flesh) and He gives it to people who will bring forth fruit, as Christ spoke to the Pharisees. Matt. 21:43.

Likewise to the unwarranted and offensive word, *secretly invade*, I reply: Moses and Christ, the apostles and prophets, as also native reasonableness, unanimously teach that we should receive, comfort, defend, help, assist, or serve the miserable, afflicted, and needy stranger. And it is a fact well known to Gellius that these poor children whom he assails so sorely have fled not for any misdemeanor or offense, but because of the testimony of God and their consciences. They fled to a foreign land with their weak women and little children before the bloody, tyrannical sword, for necessary protection, even as pursued doves flee before the hawk. Through the grace of God they place themselves under the protection of a merciful and kindhearted ruler here or there. For the love of divine truth they are bereft of their fatherland, inheritance, and the fruit of every toil, so that they may, through God's grace, support themselves somewhat according to the Scriptures. If he were what he pretends to be, namely, a preacher of the holy Word, then his inmost soul would be moved to compassion, would it not, toward these afflicted orphans and innocent hearts. He would be kind to them and assist them as much as is in his power. He would intercede for them before the magistracy, since he observes in them such a moving spirit and burning zeal that they risk their possessions and blood for the praise of their God, as may be openly witnessed. But now this pitiful misery and sore affliction, namely, that in flight from the gaping lion's mouth and from fire and sword they must seek more merciful countries, this must be called by him *secretly invading.* O Lord!

What kind of preacher and Christian he is; how he acts according to love; and how he walks according to the Word of the Lord in this matter, all reasonable persons who see with but half an eye may judge from these, his writings, together with his similar daily cries of the same kind.

To the slanderous sentence *sowing tares,* I reply: Every seed bringeth forth fruit after its own kind. Gen. 1:11. My dear reader, take heed to what I write. God's Word, on every hand, insists upon a pure heart, a new mind, and a mortified Christian life. John the Baptist says, Bring forth therefore fruits meet for repentance. Jesus says, Repent, for the kingdom of heaven is at hand. Matt. 4:17. Again, I am come to call sinners to repentance (Matt. 9:13), and many similar sayings.

The Scriptures on every hand require of us true repentance, and the sacramental signs, such as baptism and the Holy Supper, signify, represent, and teach to all true Christian believers a penitent, unblamable life. According to the Scriptures, no one can be a true Christian without true repentance, and every kind of seed brings forth fruit after its own kind, as already said; namely, lies, children of lies; and truth, children of truth. It is a fact well known to many reasonable persons that God has, through us and our fellow servants, by His great power and infinite grace, turned unto the true and living God, many a proud, avaricious, unchaste, cruel, lying, carnal, and idolatrous heart, and has so humbled, moved, renewed, and changed them that they would rather die than act hypocritically, or willingly speak or countenance any falsehood against the well-being of their neighbors, as is testified openly in our Netherlands by the precious blood of so many pious saints. But the fruits of Gellius' seed, that is, his followers, remain so entirely impenitent in their lives and unchanged in their hearts that they live in pomp and splendor, dressed in silk and velvet, show off in gold and silver, live in all manner of avarice, unrighteousness, carousing, hatred, and envy. In short, they live according to the unclean lusts of the flesh, and would for the sake of a penny, falsely swear by the Lord or by their soul, etc. Therefore we will let all reasonable and intelligent persons judge who of us sow the tares from which bad fruits come, Gellius and his followers, or we and ours. Whoever sincerely seeks and loves the truth, let him read and ponder.

O dear Lord! in this way Thy holy and precious Word, the Word of Thy grace, the Word of Thy love, by the power and grace of which we will live with Thee eternally, is called by this man and by others also, alas! deceit and pernicious seed. And their open lies, obvious error, and unreasonable adulteration of Scripture (of which more will be said below) is called the true doctrine of Christ and the holy Word of God. If it be willful slander and perverseness, then, alas, it is too much already. But if it be ignorant blindness or error, then may the gracious Father grant them eyes to see. This is my sincere wish, as the Lord knows.

*Moreover he writes that we sow anew our pernicious seed, not only by secret preaching at night, but also by publications, letters, etc.*

*Reply.* I reply with holy David: We believe, therefore we speak, and consequently we must suffer tribulation. For since God, the merciful Father, has given us, poor creatures, the gift of His grace, has bestowed upon us the Spirit of His love from on high, through His Son Jesus Christ, and has dripped into our hearts the heavenly dew of His love; has opened the seven seals of the book of His knowledge; has disclosed the mystery of His divine Word and pleasure; has roused us from the dead and led us into life, has given us a new heart, mind, and disposition, and has nourished us with the bread of life so that we by His grace have found the precious pearl, the rich treasure, and eternal abiding peace, which we could not possibly acquire through the deceiving doctrine, clever sophistry, and false consolations of the learned ones; therefore it is that we would teach, proclaim, and impress on all men to the best of our ability, this revealed grace of His great love toward us in order that they may enjoy with us the same joy and renewal of spirit, and know and taste with all saints how sweet, how good, and how kind that Lord is to whom we have come.

Therefore, we preach, as much as is possible, both by day and by night, in houses and in fields, in forests and wastes, hither and yon, at home or abroad, in prisons and in dungeons, in water and in fire, on the scaffold and on the wheel, before lords and princes, through mouth and pen, with possessions and blood, with life and death. We have done this these many years, and we are not ashamed of the Gospel of the glory of Christ. Rom. 1:16. For we feel His living fruit and moving power in our hearts, as may be seen in many places by the lovely patience and willing sacrifices of our faithful brethren and companions in Christ Jesus.

We could wish that we might save all mankind from the jaws of hell, free them from the chains of their sins, and by the gracious help of God add them to Christ by the Gospel of His peace. For this is the true nature of the love which is of God.

[5] *He accuses us of preaching at night and says in another place that we sneak into cities and towns out of dread of the cross, sit with closed doors, and deal with the simple, not to make them true Christians but apostate Anabaptists.*

*Reply.* To this I reply in the first place, that we sometimes do have to prosecute the Lord's Word and work at night. This is largely due, I fear, to Gellius and the learned ones. For they have so embittered and still embitter all lords, princes, rulers, and magistrates against us by their hateful, unmerited revilings, slanderings, and defamings that we cannot, alas, move them sufficiently with Scriptures, supplications, tears, misery, sorrow, loss of possessions, blood, or life, and so that we cannot secure a promise of safe conduct to face these evident enemies of the cross of Christ to defend the doctrine of God, the blessed truth. But we must (we preachers, that is) regularly conceal ourselves, in shops and secret places, from the persecutors and the bloodthirsty, if we do not wish, all of us, to be rent into pieces and devoured by the terrible beasts which come up out of the sea.

Dear readers, observe well what I write. Gellius accuses us of preaching at night. And it was in the year of 1543,[2] if my memory serves me, that a decree was read throughout all West Friesland that criminals and man-slayers were promised pardon, imperial grace, and repatriation, besides one hundred imperial guilders, if they would betray me and deliver me into the hands of the executioner.

About the year 1539, a householder who was a very pious man, named Tjaert Reynerdson, was seized in my stead, because out of compassion and love he had received me in his house secretly. He was a few days later put on the wheel after a free confession of faith, as a valiant knight of Christ, after the example of his Lord, although even his enemies testified that he was a pious man without reproach.

Also, in 1546, at a place where they boast of the Word, a four-room house was confiscated, because the owner had rented one of the rooms for a short time, unknown to anybody, to my poor sick wife and her little ones.

What edicts have been read against some of us in some cities and countries, and what fines stipulated, what imperial mandates and condemnations of the Roman Empire have been resolved against us, and how we are treated everywhere is not unknown to Gellius and to the preachers of his class. That they are the real cause and instigators of these things, I write and testify without hesitation.

Behold, thus they hate all those who rightly teach God's Word. Notwithstanding, this said Gellius and others are not ashamed to tell people that we, out of fear of the cross, secretly enter cities, doors, etc., as if we were stones and blocks of wood which neither have nor can have fear of death. Although it is well known to him and his kind that the chosen men of God, Abraham, Isaac, Jacob, Moses, and Aaron, the prophets and apostles moreover, nay, even Christ Himself, so feared death that they sometimes fled before it.

In the second place, I say, that so long as I, unworthy man, have served the pious with my small talent, I have taught more, much more, in daytime

[2] The imperial decree to which Menno refers was dated Dec. 7, 1542. *Ed.*

than at night. The Lord is my witness and I write the truth. Yet, this must be reviled as night preaching, shop sermons, etc., as if the Word of God could not be taught anywhere but in their houses of abomination, unknown to Scriptures, and as if God were not a God of the night as well as of the day. Oh, perverseness!

Say, reader, was not the night holy and pure to faithful Moses, and all Israel to eat the Passover? Ex. 12:3-8. Did Christ think it wrong to exhort Nicodemus at night? John 3:2. Did He not partake, with His disciples, of the Holy Supper at night, when He was about to suffer? Matt. 26:26; Luke 22:19; I Cor. 11:23. Did not the church assemble at night, when Peter was delivered from the hands of the tyrant by the help of an angel? Acts 12:7. Did not the holy Paul preach the Word all night hidden in an upper chamber at Troas, and did he not break the bread with the disciples just before his taking leave? Acts. 20:7. Did not the saints of the first church sometimes meet at night to break the Lord's bread and drink the holy cup? for which they became objects of suspicion, and had to hear not a little, and bear such ugly names? Does not Hilarius write that the apostles met in halls and secret places, and that they traversed many countries and nations by water and by land against the prohibitions and decrees of the rulers?

You see, my readers, if it was allowed and permitted to Moses, Israel, Christ, and the apostles, and to the entire first church to preach and practice the Lord's Word at night, then whether it is free to us, especially in these grievous and gruesome times of tyranny, we will let the intelligent reader judge according to Scripture in the fear of his God.

O Lord! Thus men seek causes, accusations, and complaints to insult Thy poor children more and more, and to load them down with the cross, so that they may with a semblance of right persecute and kill them. For these are contrary to their works and they are a smarting to their eyes.

In the third place, I say that I have long since twice requested to treat with them, on Scripture, in public, under safe conduct, before twenty or thirty witnesses or before a popular meeting. But what kind of answer I received, their handwriting, which I still possess, testifies. Afterwards, in the times of Archbishop Herman, the Elector of Cologne, of blessed memory, I offered this same thing at their request to the learned men of Bonn, but my offer was rejected because these good sirs were dissuaded by John a Lasco and A. H.; by their three invented falsehoods, matters which I never thought of, much less said or advised, and which I, for good reasons, will leave unmentioned now: for all of which I have the witness of a preacher named Henry, and a document written in his own hand. But what their intentions were, in regard to this matter, I will leave to Him who knows all things. Also, the preachers of Wesel, in the land of Cleve, made our people believe that they would furnish me safe conduct and treat with me, etc., but when I signified my willingness in writing, I received an answer that they would let the executioner treat with me, and other tyrannical and unchristian words.

I will make no mention of what I asked in my *Foundation* and in my *Preface to the Twenty-fifth Psalm* many years ago; also in my *Excuse,*[3] and in the *Supplication to the Magistracy,* and also in my *Message to the Learned and Preachers of the German Nations,*[4] who boast of the Word, concerning a free discussion in writing, published in the year 1552. And I am still willing and prepared, at all times, as long as I have breath or sense, and can sit on a wagon or lie in a ship, to appear before Gellius or anybody, verbally to defend the foundation of our faith, and to testify to the truth of Jesus Christ, just so it takes place under safe conduct, in good faith, and in Christian fidelity, to the praise of our God, to the extension of His church, to the promulgation of His holy Word, and to the salvation of our neighbors. This is the main desire of my heart, my joy and desire, to preach and publish His great, adorable name, teach His Word, seek His gain, honor, and praise to the best of my humble ability.

Since it is manifest that the world is so embittered against us, that men, alas, do not want to hear or see us, and since so many innocent, pious sheep, who are not teachers, are led about to be slaughtered unmercifully, or mercilessly killed and murdered, and since we distressed teachers are not allowed a hog house (to put it thus) in which to live safely under heaven (nothing is knowingly put at our disposition); and since we through open mandates, are already judged before we are delivered, and condemned before we are convicted (something which in the time of the apostles, as far as we know, was not done), therefore, I pray all my readers, for God's sake, that they would, in the fear of God, thoughtfully consider what gross wrong and violence Gellius and his followers do us, with such wicked and bitter words as *night preaching, shop preaching, conspiracy, secretly sneaking in, etc.,* although it is not and cannot be otherwise, as may be seen. Besides, we have on our side Moses and Christ, the apostles, and also mightily on our side the example of the first church, who prosecuted the Lord's work at night as well as in the daytime, as has been said already. We are also prepared at all times to render an account of our faith and to defend the truth, if we can do so in good Christian faith, without deceit and shedding of blood, as has been said already.

I say further: It is much more praiseworthy to teach the pure, saving truth at night, in a secret shop, when we cannot meet openly in the daytime, than in the daytime to shout deceiving lies and a powerless doctrine of impenitence from the pulpit, as has, alas, been openly done these many years before the whole world. This must verily be acknowledged and granted, for the disorderly state of affairs and the impenitent life of this world testify to it. Jer. 23:3.

*As to his saying that we should be kept out and silenced, lest the simple be misled,* as he calls it, I reply: A better and surer way than the one we

---

[3] This is probably a reference to Menno's *Reply to False Accusations,* 1552. *Ed.*
[4] Entitled in this compilation, *Brief Defense to all Theologians. Ed.*

have by the grace of God, nobody can point out; of this we are convinced from the attestation of our consciences and spirit. For we confess and feel that we have the Word of God. Nevertheless, we will always freely accept, and willingly follow, the instruction of any pious person, who can, in the fear of God, convince us by the Spirit, Word, example, commands, ordinances, prohibitions, and usages of the Lord (by which all things in Christ's church must be judged whether they can stand before the throne of His majesty, and not by tyranny, the power of the magistrate), who in the fear of God can teach anything that would be more useful and better, to greater honor of God and to the edification of His church, than what we have had and confessed during several years of revealed truth, and to which we have unwaveringly testified in so exceedingly much anxiety, misery, tribulation, and persecution. I trust those who seek and sincerely fear the Lord will agree with me in this respect.

But with this writing of Gellius this can surely not be done; for it is full of invective, abuse, defamation, false accusations, secret tyranny, wrong explanations, and very shabby grounds (if I am wrong rebuke me); so that it does not shut the mouths of the pious as he thinks but opens them wider still, and it will probably be the cause of strengthening in wholesome doctrine and truth and so be the cause of loss where he had intended gain. For I trust that by God's grace, when his and my writings are compared, a glorious, clear light will appear in the church of Christ, in a great luster, when it shows to the plain and humble (whom he intends by it to dissuade from our doctrine) what his own nature, works, writings, and fruits are. And by comparing them with Christ's plain Word, Spirit, example, ordinances, and usages I trust it will show to them how earthly and carnal minded he and his fellows are, how he exercises his office, what he really seeks, what the fruits of his doctrine are, what sacraments he uses, what ban he practices, and what kind of church he teaches and defends.

I would, therefore, faithfully admonish and pray him, not to undertake more than he can accomplish; and not to kick against the pricks so stubbornly, for he will find out that it is more than he can do. But let him remember that many a learned man (not that I esteem a man's learning as anything, as long as he opposes Christ in any way) has in these past times put forth great effort in this direction, even as he does; but what has been accomplished by it, the fruits testify openly. For some of them have become such zealots against us poor people, that they have alas made themselves guilty of innocent blood, and have grossly wronged and condemned to the judgment of the devil, many pious and faithful hearts, who through fear and love of their God, dared not to walk with them on the broad road. They have moreover written and contended so urgently for the idea that their church was the only church, that they have brought the poor, reckless people to such a state of wild disorder that they alas, usually lead such a fruitless impenitent life as if neither prophetic or apostolic writings, nor God's Word, nor Christ, nor Spirit had been on earth.

If now they had wisely, obediently, and humbly grasped, heeded, and followed the Word and ordinance of the Lord, the usage and example of the apostles; if they had sincerely feared their God, and had not acted hypocritically with lords and princes, and the world; but if they had taught the true doctrine in true zeal without any respect of persons or favors; if they had rebuked unto the death the sins of all men, high and low, alike, with doctrine and with life; if they had in such obedience dealt with God's work and Gospel, with which they might have gathered and built up unto the Lord a truly penitent people, that is, a true church, according to the example of the apostles; if they had not sought their own profit and ease; and if they had also left the pious and godly uncriticized and unreviled by their crying and writing: then the precious Word, Christ's glorious Gospel of grace, would never have come to such a shameful superficiality; nor the poor, simple people to such untamed abomination as, alas, may be witnessed in all parts of the world; also in parts where men boast God's Word. Thus, I fear, it will go with Gellius; for of what use he has been these many years, with his preaching and services, toward bringing about a pious, penitent life in the fear of God, I will leave to his disciples who are the fruits of his seed, to make out and decide.

Oh, that he would at last take heed, and leave God's holy and precious Word unbroken, and the pious and godly who testify to it with their heart, mouth, life, and death, unslandered; and would that he might learn to know his own hostile, impure, and bitter heart, his deceiving, slanderous, and defaming doctrine, and self-seeking, ambitious flesh; that he might humble himself under the mighty hand of God, as the Scriptures teach. For then he might be helped. But now I fear that his grievous slandering and condemning of all the pious, together with his desire for improper gain, favor, and honor of men, and an easy carefree life, do so blind the eyes of his heart, and bewilder his senses, that he will not know nor desire the glorious brightness of Christ, nor the wisdom which is of God. God grant that what I expect may not come true, and that he may receive mercy. This is my sincere wish for him and all our opponents. Amen.

[6] *Gellius says further, that he has published his writings so that some of our followers who have not yet become slanderers (these are his words) might be corrected. And he says also at another place that some have been delivered through their faithful services, who now with united hearts and in oneness of spirit, adore, praise, and thank their Lord and God, in the assemblies of the public church of God and Christ (these are his words), because they have been delivered from death and damnation, and now have a taste for Christ, and penitence and peace in their hearts.*

*Reply.* To rebuke or reprove in true Christian zeal and unfeigned love, their false doctrine, deceiving, unscriptural sacraments, and their willful and carnal life, with the Spirit, Word, and life of Christ, and to point them to the glorious example of the prophets, of the apostles of Christ, and of all the true servants of God—this he calls slandering. So that our work of love is verily given the worst possible meaning. This is, alas, the way it goes. If we write and speak mournfully, it is called sighing and groaning; if we reprove sharply, it is called invective slander. If we pipe, they do not dance. If we mourn, they do not lament, as Christ said. It is wrongly spoken, no matter what we say to the perverse. Although they commit abomination, yet they are not ashamed, neither do they blush. Jer. 8:12.

If such reproof of open sin, in true Christian love, according to the Word of God, is to be called slandering, as Gellius has it, then it is incontrovertible that all the saints of God, the apostles and prophets, Jesus Christ Himself moreover, were slanderers; as before the world they called the false prophets and preachers, false teachers, deceivers, dumb dogs, blind guides, hypocrites, thieves, murderers, wolves, useless laborers, enemies of the cross, servants of their bellies, children of damnation, dry clouds, dead trees, locusts, etc. But no. Openly to reprove deceit, transgressions, blasphemy of God or His Word, sin and shame, is not slander, as Gellius, through perverseness of heart, alleges against the innocent. But it is the fruit of faithful love of those who would gladly avert evil and promote good in all.

I will leave it to the judgment of all pious and reasonable persons if he is not a downright profaner of the church, a reviler and a slanderer, and a shedder of innocent blood who calls the church of God a harmful conspiracy; the regenerated children of God, apostate Anabaptists; the pure doctrine of Christ, attested to by faith, power, and deed, sectarianism and rabble-rousing fanaticism: who slanders and condemns the baptism which Christ commanded, and the apostles taught and practiced, as a heretical baptism, and maintains and raises before the poor, ignorant people, the baptism of Antichrist, with many high-sounding words and phrases: who promises grace and peace to the proud, obdurate, avaricious, carnal, and impenitent boasters, whom all Scriptures, alas, condemn to death; because they can, in such fine appearance, talk a little about the Scriptures, although without Spirit, power, or change of heart: who without proper cause with all sorts of invective, invention, shame, evil suspicions, and hearsay incriminate and condemn the poor orphans and afflicted Christians who sincerely seek and fear the Lord; and so deliver them to the magistracy to be put in dungeons, and to the executioner to be killed.

But as to his boasting, that some of our brethren have again associated with them, and that others may by his writings yet be made to associate, etc., I answer in the first place: Christ says, Wide is the gate, and broad is the way that leadeth to destruction, and many there be which go in thereat: because strait is the gate, and narrow is the way which leadeth unto life, and few there be that find it. Matt. 7:13, 14. My reader, observe that all who leave the broad way and wish to enter upon the narrow one, and enter in at the strait gate, must forsake themselves, take up the cross and follow Christ Jesus; must become regenerate and mortified Christians; must crucify their flesh and subdue their lusts; must through the power of faith put under their feet all visible and perishable things such as gold and silver, home and goods, yes, wife and children; together with all they are and have, if necessity and the honor of Christ require it. They must be prepared to endure reproach, hunger, misery, pillage, persecution, bonds, and death for the sake of the testimony of God and their consciences. They must adhere to the Word of God with constant prayer and watchful eyes. For all those who are yet laden with the burden of unrighteousness and an evil conscience, such as avarice, ungodly desires, works of the flesh, etc., or who feel at all doubtful concerning the Word and promise of the Lord, cannot pass through the narrow way and the strait gate. Let every one be aware of this. Matt. 7:13.

In the second place I say that the edification and the faith of true Christians is tried in many and various ways, as both Scripture and experience clearly teach and testify. Now they are tempted by flesh and blood, which has neither time nor schedule, then by the lust of the world, and the lust of the eyes which invitingly tempt the self-seeking flesh in which no good dwells. Again by the cross and tribulation which often press heavily; and lastly, by the pleasant preaching of peace and the fondling doctrine of the preachers who constantly cry, Peace, peace, as the prophet says, by means of which they strengthen and give boldness in their faithlessness and disobedience to God to those who draw back from the cross and to whom the way of the Lord is too narrow and who want to enjoy the lusts of the world. It is as Peter says, While they promise them liberty, they themselves are the servants of corruption. II Pet. 2:19. For this reason, some of the seed which is sown by the wayside is picked up by the fowls of the air; some is sown on the stony places, where there is not much earth, and although it grows somewhat, yet it cannot stand the scorching sun of persecution since the soil on which it is sown is rocky; and some is choked by the thistles and thorns, and so does not come to ripe ears. Matt. 13:4-7.

Behold, the real reason why some fearful, frivolous, carnal, corrupt, and self-willed spirits who were so much more earthly than heavenly minded, and with whom we could never live in peace and the unity of the Spirit, have again associated themselves with them is this: The way was too narrow and the gate too strait for them, and the flesh was too urgent; the smiles of the world too inviting, and the tyranny so very great. The thousand expert agents of Satan utilize his mastery without interruption, as every pious person knows by experience. They refused to be thus subjected, as the prophet laments (Jer. 2:17), but would follow their own inclinations in all things, and walk on the broad way of the flesh without the cross and with the world. But it was certainly not because of the writings and services of Gellius, as he boasts [that some of our professed members united with his church].

Behold, these people of whom he boasts so highly, were such (we regret to have to say it) as, with Demas, loved the present world, and who so lived with us for some time that we, according to the divine Word, dared no longer to eat and drink with them.[5] Nor are they bettered as Gellius pretends, but they are corrupted in their faith, and play the hypocrite with the world, with earthly-minded hearts under the pretense of prayer. They have not forsaken the broad way which leads to death but the narrow way which leads to life. They have not gained a taste for Christ, but have lost it. They have found rest and comfort for their flesh, but not for their souls, as Gellius thinks. For facts prove whose cause is right, theirs or ours; whose actions are hypocritical, and whose are not; for our people sacrifice possessions, blood, and even life for the cause; but what theirs do is well known.

My conclusion as to his first reason for publishing his writings is that even as the angel of darkness can transform himself into an angel of light, as Paul says; can feign love beautifully and make great promises, can imitate true confession of Christ and can use Scriptures in a masterly way, so also can his servants, as may be seen. For Gellius says that he published his writings so that he might win some who err from the way and protect the simple from deceit; might silence the Anabaptists, as he calls them; to prevent the entry of pernicious weeds, to serve the church of Christ, to keep the weak ones in the Netherlands in the right understanding of evangelical doctrine and the right use of the holy sacraments, etc. But if we rightly consider it, and judge it by the Spirit, Word, and example of Christ, by the usage of the holy apostles and the first apostolic churches, we find it to be basically nothing but a defense of the flesh; an encouragement to the impenitent, a beautiful occasion for the broad way; a defense of the churches of Antichrist; a confusing and blinding of the simple, a secret agitation to turmoil against the pious, a destroying of the church of Christ, a clever restraint of the godly, an unreasonable, envious defamation of the saints, a falsification of the holy Word; yes, an open support in unrighteousness, impenitence, and carnal liberty.

Behold, this is the effect, fruit, and result of his writings, although he adorns and covers it with such a semblance of good and make-believe of love. If I should not be able to sustain these assertions by fruits and with the power of the Scripture if I meet him sometime, then I will be willing to recant and bear my shame; for I trust that I, through the grace of God, know of what I write.

[7] *Another reason, says Gellius, for publishing his writings is that the nobleman, to whom he dedicates it, offered to bear the expense of printing it, etc.*

*Reply.* Zeal is good and I praise it highly, if it is good and tending to the glory of God. But let every one consider how, why, and to what end he is zealous; lest he make himself guilty of innocent blood, which is the greatest sin, next to sinning against the Holy Ghost.

If His Honor[6] has done this in sincere zeal and with good intentions,

[5] Menno and the Dutch Mennonites practiced the "shunning" of professing members who reverted to a life of gross sin, or turned to heretical doctrine. *Ed.*

[6] That is, the Nobleman who offered to bear the expense of printing the attack of Gellius on Menno. *Ed.*

as Paul did before his conversion, and meant it to be to the honor of God and to the salvation of his neighbors, then I hope that God will give him more light, and make truth more manifest to him. But if he has done it for the sake of an idle name or fame, or for the sake of profit and a pillow for the flesh, a thing which the learned ones very cleverly adjust for such important personages; or if he contends against the people of God with a bitter zeal (a thing that I do not hope), as does Gellius and the preachers in general, then his action might become such a gross sin and blindness that I fear he will never come to the knowledge of Christ.

I would therefore cordially admonish His Honor, and beseech him in Christian love, not again to load himself with the sin of others; for he and everybody else will have burden enough of his own at the day of judgment. All misleading of the miserable souls, all unbelief and idolatry, all frivolity and carnal license, together with all turmoil and tyranny which will probably result from this his writing, will be required in the day of Christ at his hands, no less than the hands of the preachers, if no repentance takes place, because he assists and supports the abomination, with his advice and assistance, with money and material, as much as they do.

Therefore, in my opinion, His Honor would have done better if he had pondered the matter well and had turned his contribution to the support, assistance, consolation, nourishment, and clothing of the needy, especially in these hard times of hunger, and not for the occasion of deceiving many simple hearts and to the greater distress and persecution of the pious.

And so also the fact that Gellius has published his writing under the permission of said nobleman, seems to indicate that he is one of those who honor and esteem a person for the sake of benefit. But for what reason he has done so, or what his object is, and how his heart is, I will leave to the Lord who knows all things.

Experience teaches sufficiently of what disposition the rich are, how proudhearted, ambitious, and covetous of honor. God's wisdom did not say without a cause, Verily, I say unto you, It is easier for a camel to go through the eye of a needle, than for a rich man to enter into the kingdom of God. Matt. 19:24. James also says, Go to now, ye rich men, weep and howl for your miseries that shall come upon you. Your riches are corrupted and your garments are moth-eaten; your gold and silver is cankered; and the rust of them shall be a witness unto you, and shall eat your flesh as it were fire. Jas. 5:1-3. Again, Paul says, For ye see your calling, brethren, how that not many wise men after the flesh, not many mighty, not many noble, are called. I Cor. 1:26.

The mouth of the Lord, as also His faithful servants, James and Paul, have plainly pointed out the dangers of the rich and of those of high standing, and experience teaches how high their hearts climb, as their high titles, houses, emblems, clothes, servants, horses, and dogs make plain. Christ says, Verily I say unto you, Except ye be converted and become as little children, ye shall not enter into the kingdom of heaven. Matt. 18:3. Therefore it would be more in accordance with evangelical righteousness if Gellius would instead diligently urge such proud hearts and high persons to the humility of Christ so that they might learn to forsake themselves, to know themselves, of what they come, and what they are, and what they will be; so that they might die unto their excessive pomp and pride, luxury and ungodliness, might fear God in all sincerity, and walk in His ways, might faithfully serve their neighbors out of their abundance in true humility of heart, and might not kindle the fire of pride, fleshly security, and frivolousness by their fondling or by high-sounding and supplicating phrases; seeing that the inborn, proud nature of the flesh of Adam's children is, alas, already too apt to live in such things, without the encouragement and prompting of flattery and smooth words.

I would, therefore, faithfully admonish all to fear God, to strive after truth, and to love their neighbors. For the time is coming and is not far off when we shall hear each one at his time, Give an account of thy stewardship, for thou mayest be no longer steward. Luke 16:2. I do not dedicate this my reply and defense to this or that one, as is the custom of the learned one, but in Christian humility, To the Pious Reader, and desire to subject it to the judgment of all the godly and pious.

If any one under the entire heaven can teach me with plainer Scriptures or with more powerful truths, whether he be learned or unlearned, man or woman, I will gladly accept such instruction and obey. But by the grace of God, we know we have the sure and true way which Christ has prepared for us. Blessed are we if we walk in it and enter in at the strait gate. Let all of understanding minds, who, in true zeal and in the fear of God, seek the praise of their Lord, read and judge that which follows.

## [II.] THE MISSION OR VOCATION OF THE PREACHERS

[1] *Gellius complains very much of a bitter and derogatory letter by the Anabaptists, as he calls them, in which they are said to have given five special reasons, as I understand from his writing, why they cannot conscientiously listen to the preachers as true and unblamable, and cannot partake of their sacraments as true and Scriptural ordinances, etc. Of these five reasons the first is: The vocation or calling of preachers. Concerning this Gellius assiduously asserts that his is Christian and Scriptural and ours sectarian and unscriptural.*

*Reply.* How bitter and derogatory the said epistle may have been I do not know, for it has never come into my hands. But I surmise that it was not so bitter as Gellius complains; and I surmise that it was a reproof of his condemnations, deceptions, and unscriptural impenitent sacraments—a thing which he invariably calls reviling and invective, and which must be called by horrid names.

Seeing then that I did not read the letter, I will not undertake to defend every word of it. But as to the five articles in which the preachers are rebuked and accused (things which Gellius wants to justify and defend) these I have made my care for the sake of the office of the divine Word, seeing that I also am not very honorably reproached and reviled. And I hope, by the gracious help of God, to defend these articles with such power and clearness of Scripture that all impartial and reasonable readers, on comparing our writings, will, by the grace of God, behold as in a mirror that he and all the worldly preachers are not the called preachers and teachers of the church of Christ, to whom the Scriptures point; but manifest preachers and teachers of the world, or members of the church of Antichrist against whom the Scriptures by all means warn us, and in many passages cause us to recoil from. He that has ears, let him hear what the Word of the Lord teaches.

*Gellius points out a difference between the vocation or mission of the prophets of Christ and the apostles on the one hand, and the calling of the bishops, pastors, and other servants of the church on the other hand, and says, That the mission of the prophets of Christ and the apostles took place without human mediation, solely of God; but that the mission of the pastors and bishops is done by God through human agents.*

*Reply.* We do not contradict this, but acknowledge it to be true and right. But we deny that the vocation which he boasts took place in accordance with the apostolic doctrine and usage. And we say that we should note carefully these five following points or articles, according to the Scriptures; namely, by whom they are called; [of] what [character] they are that are called; to what they are called; what fruit the called ones bring forth; and what the genuine desire and ambition of the called ones is.

[a] In the first place, I say that the calling which took place in the first apostolic church, by means of man, was not done by the world, but by the true Christians and obedient disciples of the Lord and His Word. For Luke writes, And when they had ordained them elders in every church, and had prayed with fasting, they commended them to the Lord, on whom they believed. Therefore, Paul says to Titus, For this cause left I thee in Crete, that thou shouldst set in order the things that are wanting and ordain elders in every city, as I have appointed thee. Titus 1:5. Read also I Tim. 3:12.

Since then the preachers boast of such a vocation, issuing from God, by means of man, as has been said, therefore I would ask without any facetiousness who is the Paul, or Barnabas, or Timothy, or Titus that has called and ordained Gellius and his colleagues to their services. If they answer, the magistracy, then I would ask in the second place, if the magistracy who appropriates this matter to itself has the Spirit, calling or ministry, ordinance and power of Paul, Barnabas, Titus, and Timothy. If they say yes, then I would like to see this proved by Scripture. If they say, because they are part of the church, as Gellius suggests, then I would ask in the third place, whether then they are led by the Spirit of God, whether they have crucified the flesh with its lusts, and in their weakness walk blamelessly as Christians, even as Christ Jesus and His followers have led and taught; whether they have become new creatures; whether they are in Christ and Christ is in them, etc. And if they say that God knows, and not we, then I would ask in the fourth place, are they then such trees that we cannot see their fruits, and such lights that we cannot see their brightness? My reader, ponder well these questions that I have put.

Scripture teaches openly that there is no Christian save he who is in Christ and has His Spirit. Rom. 8:9. It is evident that the magistracy does not conform itself to the example and Spirit of the Lord, as may, alas, be detected on every hand by their fruits. For they live in every matter according to the lusts of the flesh, seek vain honor, greed, elegant living, etc. They are earthly and not heavenly minded; and we may well consult the Word of the Lord whether it belongs to such people to ordain preachers, pastors, and servants in the church of Christ since their fruits testify that they are as yet themselves without Christ's Spirit, kingdom, church, and Word, as has been said.

If they should say that they are not called by the magistracy, but by the church, then I would ask in the fifth place, whether the church which has called them is flesh of Christ's flesh and bone of His bone, that is, a church which sincerely seeks and fears God; that walks in obedience to His Word; loves and serves its neighbor; restrains its ungodly lusts; strives after truth with all its heart; leads an unblamable, pious life, and is prepared for the sake of the will and Word of the Lord to abandon money, goods, blood, and life, yes, father and mother, husband and wife, children and everything else, if the honor of God requires it. If they answer no, as no it is, then it is already proved that they are not the church and people of the Lord; for the church of Christ must in the unity of Spirit be one with Christ, as has already been heard. If then they are not Christ's church, how then can they call preachers in the church of Christ, as did Paul, Barnabas, Timothy, and Titus, and the first church? If, on the other hand, they answer yes, then I say again their manifest unrighteousness, slander, wickedness, avarice, pomp, drunkenness, luxury, unchastity, hatred, envy, unmercifulness, violence, etc., testify before the whole world that the answer is no.

Seeing then that it is manifest that both the magistracy and the subjects are directly contrary to the Spirit and Word of Jesus Christ, to His walk and have not a single letter which in this matter conforms with the Spirit and actions of Paul, Barnabas, Timothy, and Titus, or of the first church, therefore I am very much surprised that he can be so foolish and rash, or so very proud and bold as to boast, in these gracious times of revealed truth, that he and similar preachers were called and ordained by God and by the means of man, as were the elders of the first church, by Paul, Barnabas, Timothy, and Titus.

Oh, that God would grant that he might consider, so as not to compare the faithful men and dear servants of God, as well as the zealous, regenerate congregation and pious children of the first churches, with this impenitent, reckless and wild world which wishes to be considered the true church; and would not blind the poor, simple hearts, who regard the holy Word but little, with such a semblance and unwarranted reference to the Scripture. It would be useful and good for his poor, miserable soul at the time of his departure.

I would leave it to the reflection of all intelligent readers, how the vocation of which the preachers boast can stand the test of the Scriptures, since those who did the calling are found to be not only no regenerated, pious Christians, but also open despisers and impenitent opponents of God and His Word, as may, alas, be seen on every hand.

[b] In the second place, we should notice of what disposition, doctrine, and conduct the called servants of the Word should be, according to the testimony of the Scriptures: namely, Blameless, the husband of one wife, vigilant, sober, of good behavior, given to hospitality, apt to teach, not given to wine, no striker, not greedy of filthy lucre; but patient, not a brawler, not covetous; one that ruleth well his own house, having his children in subjection with all gravity; not a novice. He must be holy, just, temperate, etc., holding fast the faithful word as he hath been taught; that he may be able, by sound doctrine, both to exhort and to convince the gainsayers. Moreover he must have a good report of them which are without; lest he fall into reproach and the snare of the devil, etc. Even so must their wives be grave, not slanderers, sober, faithful in all things. I Tim. 3; Titus 1.

My dear reader, observe. This is not my word but that of the Holy Ghost, which sets before you the true example of a genuine preacher, bishop, pastor, teacher, and servant who will serve fruitfully in the church of Christ, bringing forth fruit which will remain. John 15:16.

To such teachers the Holy Ghost points us to obey and follow. Paul says, Obey them that have the rule over you, and submit yourselves, for they watch for your souls, as they that must give account, that they may do it with joy and not with grief. Heb. 13:17. In another place he says, We beseech you, brethren, to know them which labor among you, and are over you in the Lord and admonish you, and to esteem them very highly in love for their work's sake, and be at peace among yourselves. I Thess. 5:12, 13.

Such teachers are compared in the Scriptures with oxen that tread out the grain, which must not be muzzled. They are the elders worthy of double honor, and the faithful laborers, worthy of their hire. Deut. 25:4; Matt. 10:10. But how it stands with Gellius and all the preachers of the Germanic nations, whom he esteems as faithful servants, this I leave to the impartial reader to judge according to the Word of the Lord.

My faithful reader, consider well that which I write. They boast that they are called in accordance with Scriptures, as you may hear; although you may see with your eyes, and feel with your hands, that most of them lead the life portrayed by Peter and Jude. Many of them are, alas, so fallen in the fullness of Bacchus that they live day and night as swine in complete complacency; their tables are full of vomit and filthiness, as the prophet says. Isa. 28:8. They fearlessly walk after their own lusts, as Jude has it, and they esteem as solid joy the temporal life of luxury, as Peter says. They are spots and blemishes, sporting themselves with their own deceivings while they feast with you.

Some of them also have been caught in open fornication and seduction of women. How their wives, as a general thing, behave according to Scriptures may be seen in their fruits. Others are so avaricious that they have become open usurers. They drag the filthy dung together in such piles (money and possessions) that I can truthfully say that they, through the easy doctrine of their Gospel, have become lords upon the earth; although most of them are still loved by the world, and highly esteemed by the ignorant. Their pomp, laziness, ease, vanity, frivolousness, and pride are greater than can be described, to say nothing of their tyranny, lying, reviling, slander, betrayals, and agitation against all who seek and fear the Lord.

Reader, it is verily as I write. Oh, how gladly would I silence and cover this, if the honor of God and His Word, and the love for your souls did not compel me. But now necessity compels me to touch upon their ugly shame. Their abominations are so gross and terrible that my soul shrinks back at the thought of them, to say nothing of mentioning or writing them. How their conduct agrees with the description by Paul, who teaches us that they shall be blameless, having but one wife, not given to wine, not avaricious, not covetous of filthy lucre; that they shall be temperate, modest, good, and amiable, and have a good report of those that are without: this I will leave to all pious hearts to judge in the fear of God, according to the Scriptures. You see, my reader, since it is manifest that they are quite contrary to the Word of the Lord in their walk, therefore it is in fact nothing but vain hypocrisy to call such unfruitful, monkey business, evangelical edification and vocation.

But Gellius tries to clear himself of this, and to lay the blame on those who, according to his writings, lead an unchristian life after the lusts of their flesh, and not after the ordinance of the apostles, saying that they cannot by their impenitence weaken the call of the pious. Then I would answer saying, in the first place, since he complains of them so much in his book and says that they would do better as pastors of swine than of the sheep of Christ, and wishes that they would be deposed from office, etc., and since these constitute the majority of them as may be openly seen, therefore Gellius should admit, should he not, that according to the Scripture, we should not hear such, nor partake of their sacraments, even if they were the true sacraments, which they are not, for he himself admits that they are good for nothing, and wishes that they were deposed.

In the second place I ask: Since Gellius admits that they are unfit for their offices, and since he and they are in one communion and calling and pastoral service, why does he tolerate them in their offices and why does he not, by the authority of his calling, excommunicate and depose them with the advice and consent of his church? For they are a harmful hindrance to the church and a reproach and disgrace to Gellius and his fellow preachers, whom I could wish were themselves pious and unblamable.

If he says that the magistrates are to blame, then he admits that those magistrates are not true servants and members of Christ, since they admit such offensive people as adulterers, gluttons, covetous persons, etc., as are met with on every hand, to be preachers, ruining the souls of the poor miserable people by their wicked, offensive lives, to say nothing of their doctrine; all of which they might prevent with a single word, without bloodshed. And what is more, Gellius himself is a faithless shepherd and dumb watchman who does not admonish nor rebuke the magistracy, who are his own electors and members of his church, for the pitiful ruination of the church. And why does he not expel them from the sacraments and the fellowship of his churches in case they refuse to hear?

In the third place, I say, it would be proper for Gellius, first, to learn from Scripture to know the nature of Christ and His church together with the true church servants, pastors, and preachers; to judge all things by the Spirit, Word, and example of the Lord and therewith to compare himself, his fellow preachers, and his church, before contending so bitterly against the pious, and accusing them before the whole world.

I say further, since, if I understand him correctly, he excuses us from hearkening to adulterers, drinkers, strikers, etc., and from partaking of their sacraments (and does so probably to make his cause have a good appearance with some); therefore we are forced to view in the Scriptural light, how he according to Paul's doctrine can stand as a pastor in the church and a servant of Christ.

Paul says a bishop must be blameless, a matter wherein all that is proper in a true preacher and shepherd is contained; and it is obvious that Gellius is not unblamable, but blamable in many respects. That he is a friend of the world, who seeks to please the world, contrary to the Word of God and the example of Christ, the apostles, and the prophets, is evident, otherwise he would not be without persecution (II Tim. 3:12), nor would he have exercised his service in comfort for so long a time, as is testified by the example of Christ, the apostles, and all true witnesses.

He is a hireling, moreover, one who has hired himself out, as a servant at certain wages and a stipend, contrary to the example of Christ and the example of all the true messengers who have been sent by Him. He not only does not suffer persecution for the sake of the testimony of Jesus, but he himself persecutes the godly, pious hearts who have neither injured nor harmed him, nor anybody else; namely, by his advice, word and writings, will and sentiments, contrary to the example of Christ and all the elect, as may, alas, be seen by these writings. Besides this, his doctrine is erroneous, seductive. He is a reviler, condemner, defamer, and a backbiter of the innocent who sincerely fear God and are zealous for His Word; yes, who seal it with their blood, something which he does not do. This his writing does, alas, demonstrate abundantly; in which he without just cause accuses and condemns before the world the God-fearing, pious hearts as apostate Anabaptists, conspirers, secret infiltrationists, sowers of pernicious seed, excommunicated sects, apostles of the devil and his tools; so making them the object of suspicion, although they sincerely seek the Lord and daily risk possessions and blood for the sake of His holy Word.

Besides, he is a proponent and defender of the kingdom of Antichrist, a falsifier of the Scriptures, an abuser of the sacraments, a strengthener of the impenitent, a teller of lies, etc., as will be plainly shown by the grace of God, each in its own place.

[c] In the third place, it should be observed for what purpose the true preachers are called; namely, that they should teach the Word of the Lord correctly, rightly use their sacraments, lead and rule aright the church of God, gather together with Christ and not scatter, console the bereaved, admonish the irregular, seek the lost, bind up the wounded, ban those that are incurable, without any respect of persons whether great or small; and solemnly watch over the vineyard, house, and city of God, as the Scriptures teach.

Behold, my reader, these are really the reasons why the Holy Ghost has ordained in the house of the Lord bishops, pastors, and teachers, according to the precept of Paul who says, He gave some apostles, and some prophets, and some evangelists, and some pastors and teachers; for the perfecting of the saints, for the work of the ministry, for the edifying of the body of Christ; till we all come in the unity of the faith, and of the knowledge of the Son of God, unto a perfect man, unto the measure of the stature of the fulness of Christ. Eph. 4:11-13.

But for what purpose Gellius and all the preachers of the world are called may be determined from their doctrine and work; namely, to preach as the magistrates and the world like it. Also, so that they may sacrifice to the two golden calves of Dan and Bethel (understand what I mean); to keep the church of Antichrist without penance and regeneration in the unity and peace of the flesh, on the perverted and crooked road of darkness and death, under the name and semblance of the Word, contrary to the Spirit, doctrine, and example of Christ; to console the willful, reckless world (which without regeneration, wishes to pass for the church of Christ, in its impenitent and ungodly nature) with the death and blood, baptism and Supper of the Lord; to ban Jesus Christ and His Word and Spirit, so that the world may live on in its unrighteousness and old nature unrebuked, so that the preachers may continue in their improper gain and carefree life, and the poor ignorant people, both rich and poor, may live on in the lusts of their eyes, their pomp and splendor, drinking, carousing, in avariciousness and hoarding, in short, may continue unreproved in the broad and easy way of the flesh. This is, alas, too manifest to be denied; yet men undertake to adorn their cause with the Scriptures; they talk much about it; boast greatly of the grace and favor of God; they use baptism and Supper under the appearance of truth exactly as if they were the church of Christ, although, in fact, they are nothing but a selfish, refractory, impenitent, earthly, and carnal people, as is obvious by their fruits. If I do not write the truth, reprove me.

Since then it is clearer than broad daylight that they are not called to defend the church of Christ, which is of God and of a divine nature, with salutary doctrines, Scriptural sacraments, an unblamable life, earnest punishment (and not with flattery and respect of persons), with faithful admonition, and if necessary, separation; but since under false pretenses of the name and church of Christ, they are servants of the world, highly rewarded by it, honored and loved by it; since they speak of it and please it, and it seeks and loves to hear them; since they are of the world, as John says, therefore, it is in the third place, an irrefutable evidence, that they, alas, are not the called servants of the church of Christ, as they falsely pretend, but the servants and proponents of the kingdom of Antichrist, as may be clearly learned from their doctrine, walk, and fruits if we examine them carefully.

[d] In the fourth place, we should observe what kind of fruits they bring forth, for Christ says, I have chosen you and ordained you, that ye should go and bring forth fruit, and that your fruit should remain. John 15:16. We confess with holy Isaiah, as does Gellius also, that the doctrine of the holy Gospel, if preached in the power of the Spirit, according to the Spirit of Christ, cannot fail to bring forth fruit. For as the rain cometh down, and the snow from heaven, and returneth not thither, but watereth the earth, and maketh it bring forth and bud, so also is the word that goeth forth out of the mouth of the Lord. Isa. 55:10.

But Gellius, and we also, should consider that these sowers should first by the power of true faith and the co-operation of the Holy Spirit be changed into the Spirit and nature of Christ, and then should teach or present to the people the pure, unadulterated seed, which is the Word, without all abuse, leaven, and hypocrisy, for where there are such sowers, there will fruit be and increase. The word of the prophet, which the mouth of the Lord has spoken, must be true and firm. But where there are no such sowers there they arise too early or go forth too late; and labor and pains will be in vain; for God does not work unto repentance, except through those who are of His Spirit.

Since then the word of true preachers does not remain fruitless, as we have seen, and since we clearly see that the seed of the preachers of the world brings forth no fruit unto repentance, but only generates hypocrites, therefore it is an indisputable fact, is it not, that they have not the Word of the Lord in power, but that they are useless workers and not true preachers, unless the word of the prophet be false, which says, If they had stood in my counsel, and had caused my people to hear my words, then they should have turned them from their evil way, and from the evil of their doings. Jer. 23:22.

Preachers are known by their fruits, and Gellius and his fellow preachers have preached their doctrine and sacraments many years to the whole world (a thing which they can do without fear, seeing they do not oppose the reckless, impenitent world in its hyprocrisy and carefree life, but rather strengthen and encourage it). Yet they do not convert a usurer from his usury, nor a miser from his avarice; they do not bring their disciples beyond a profession in name and appearance, remaining unchanged in their hearts, hating and opposing true righteousness, walking on the broad way, and earnestly pursuing the world's flesh, money, and possessions. The pompous remain pompous; the proud remain proud; and liars remain liars, as is manifest. Therefore this their fruitless preaching, vain doctrine, and church service prove mightily that their office is not of God and His Word, but of the son of the abyss, Antichrist, and of the world, however much they beautify, adorn, and boast of their cause. The Word of God will and must remain true. Isa. 55:11.

[e] But now Gellius appeals to his fruits, and says, *Is not the preaching of the truth and the light of the holy Gospel, which we studiously promulgate both by teaching and writing, a good fruit and glorious testimony that our calling is of God and not of the devil; a ministry by which the kingdom of the devil is destroyed and by which the papistical abominations, idolatry, masses, vigils, tonsures and caps, etc., have, praise God, become an odor of death?*

*Reply.* If the silver were not mixed with the dross and wine with water, that is, if they would preach the truth without falsehood, and the light without darkness, clear and pure, in the power of the Spirit, and if they would testify before the whole world by a pious and irreproachable life, then we would agree with them that it is a glorious light and a noble fruit. But since they play the game incorrectly, and transform truth into lies, the true apostolic baptism into the baptism of heretics, the church of Christ into pernicious sectarianism and conspiracy, etc., and on the other hand, transform lies into truth and the anti-Christian baptism into Christian baptism, and the reckless, wild world into the Lord's church, etc., therefore, we say that their doctrine is deceiving, bad, and wrong, and not the doctrine in truth, as Gellius boasts and pretends.

Yes, my reader, they preach the Word of the Lord in such a way that unrighteousness and abuse remain intact. They teach the truth in such a way that in many matters false doctrine, lying, and deceiving is not weakened nor destroyed. They use and practice religion in such a way that the high places are honored, and idolatry is not avoided; they preach of a Christian church in such a way that the church of Antichrist remains in full power, as is openly manifest to the whole world, both by their work and their tyranny. In a word, it is manifest that they preach and promulgate the Gospel in such a way that no repentance follows, but every one alas, remains as he is; yes, what is worse, the people are not only not improved, but are daily growing worse. Here neither glosses nor syllogisms avail, nor any clever excuse; their fruit testifies that their doctrine is faithless and false, as said before. Jer. 23.

The serpent spoke the truth all right when he said, God doth know that in the day ye eat thereof, then your eyes shall be opened; and ye shall be as God, knowing good and evil, Gen. 3:5. But that which he promised earlier, Ye shall not surely die, this he lied. Adam and Eve were deceived thereby. Thus, also, do those who teach the serpent's word. The impenitent, carnal people are so pointed to the Lord's death by their unscriptural, impenitent sacraments, and so consoled in their willful Adamic nature and life, by false promises (although they do sometimes speak the truth, as did the serpent; produce Scriptures, reprove sin in part, and praise virtue), that there is nobody who is truly sorry for his sins, who sincerely repents of his wickedness, or ceases from it, saying, What am I doing? Behold, says the prophet, so they practice falsehood and strengthen the wicked, but none repent of their wickedness. Jer. 23:22.

But that some of them have so weakened the papistical abominations, for this they and we should thank the Lord. But what does it avail if they expel the pope if they themselves step in his place? It is true indeed that many branches of the tree of antichrist are hewn off, but the roots and trunk still remain. And although they have destroyed some high places, yet they walk in the ways of Jeroboam and have not come to Jerusalem to engage in true worship.

Yes, good reader, if the learned ones had firmly hoped in the living God, had faithfully adhered to His Word, had not played the hypocrite with the world, and had themselves in power and deeds faithfully practiced, without fear of the cross and the disfavor of the magistracy, that which they have in some of their writings pointed out, oh, what a noble and clear light would have appeared on the world which now, alas, has become such a pernicious darkness and bewilderment and a broad way through the fear of the cross, through hyprocrisy, self-seeking, desire of ease, ambition, and favor of men.

[2] *In the second place he says, Is the whole Bible translated into the German language by Dr. Martin, of blessed memory, a fruit to be despised? Are the songs or hymns composed by Luther and many others a contemptible fruit? Is not the constancy which with fear of life and limb is seen in these days of opposition, and in the beginning of the Gospel, a noble and genuine fruit of our calling? But these fruits are of no account in their sight or else they will not see them; although they are the surest and best, etc. But the fruits of the outward life and dealings with men (although often done of mere hypocrisy) are the only ones they have an eye for.*

*Reply.* The deceased, with their translations, writings, and hymns, we will leave undiscussed, for they have already found their Lord and Judge. But we will turn to the living with whom we have to speak. His saying that writing, translating, and composing are the surest and best fruits, is, in my opinion, a very senseless assertion, seeing that such things can be done through learning and knowledge of languages, without regeneration and change of heart, as he himself well knows. Yes, even as the Bible or the Scriptures are read by the greater part of the world with impure, carnal hearts, so also can they undoubtedly be translated with a carnal heart without regeneration from one language into another, through knowledge and skill in languages.

And even as the hymns are generally sung thoughtlessly in God's house or temple, and with great frivolousness at banquets, in the streets and in riotous taverns, here and there, so also may they be composed by a frivolous heart without spirit or regeneration. Therefore, these are not the surest and best fruits, as Gellius proposes; they do not abide. (But all that some in bygone times may have written, in true zeal, which is Scriptural or conformable to Scripture and useful to the betterment of the pious, this we should properly praise and value.)

However, the surest and best fruits are so to preach the Word of God in power that many are born of God by it, are turned to God, are led to fear and love Him, to serve their neighbors, to restrain flesh and blood, to believe on Jesus Christ with all the heart, and tremble at His Word; doing nothing contrary to it, truly worshiping God and conforming their whole life or walk to His Spirit, word, and example; for such fruits remain.

I would also say, since he boasts of the danger and the constancy (as he calls it) of some of their number, who now in these times of war (which he calls days of assault, if we understand him correctly) can no longer uphold and advance their cause by force of arms, and since he considers this a noble fruit, although they have probably not been tried unto blood, as happens daily to our people, why does he so crudely attack and condemn our cause, which the Lord knows we desire to maintain without recourse to sword or any other deadly weapon, something which cannot be truthfully refuted? We have patiently walked according to the example of Christ, have sacrificed our possessions and blood which might have been saved by a single hypocritical word, and at all times enter willingly and in great numbers in constancy that cannot be conquered, into death by sword, water, and fire; defenseless and without any resistance.

But we give praise to God that some of them have bared their necks for the sake of the testimony which they had, and have given their blood. With James we count them blessed, yes, our companions in the sufferings of Christ, for their deeds have proved that they sought God and were faithful in that in which they had been enlightened. But what will that help these men, seeing they close their hearts to the light of truth; resist the Spirit, Word, and will of God; preach lies, pervert and abuse the sacraments, and console and encourage the wicked, wild world in its impenitent, reckless life—things which the faithful heroes to whom they refer so approvingly did not do? For they were faithful in everything which they acknowledged as the truth. If they had known more, they would doubtlessly have died for that also, as well as for that which they did at the time acknowledge right and good. If now our opponents are of the same spirit, then they may boast because of them. But their fruits show plainly that they are, alas, very different.

So also in regard to his contention that the fruits of an outward life are the only things that matter in our sight, etc. Do not our sore oppression, heavy trials, great tribulation, our misery, possessions, and blood, our open and frank confession, moreover, openly testify that he makes this assertion against all truth? Yes, that he openly wrongs and abuses us? *O malitiosam calumniam ac perversitatem* (O malicious calumny and perverseness).

My kind reader, observe that all Scripture and the power of the true faith constrain us zealously to teach an upright, pious, godly, and penitent life. For Jesus Christ says, Let your light so shine before men, that they may see your good works. Paul also teaches that we must be sincere and without offense till the day of Christ, walking worthy of the Lord and His Gospel. Peter says that we must have our conversation honest among the Gentiles, and John says that we should walk even as Christ walked. Matt. 5:6; Phil. 1:10; Col. 1:10; I Pet. 2:12; I John 2:6.

Since Scripture then, on every hand, enjoins upon us a pious life, as has been heard, therefore, it is reasonable and just, is it not, if we believe the Word of God, that we zealously follow, in our weakness, that which the Spirit of the Lord has so clearly taught and enjoined in His holy Word.

But this assertion, that such fruits alone matter in our sight, is written, alas, from an impure heart. For I presume he knows very well that we plainly teach that we cannot be saved by outward works, however great and glorious they may appear, or that we can thus entirely please God; for works are always mixed with imperfection and weakness, are they not, and therefore through the obstacle of our corrupted flesh we cannot attain wholly to the original righteousness required in the commandments. Therefore we point to Christ Jesus alone, who is our only and eternal righteousness, reconciliation, and propitiation with the Father, and we do not, eternally not, put any confidence in our good works. My reader, I write the truth in Christ Jesus and lie not.

Oh, that Gellius would omit his loose talk, and write no more than that which is true, for a liar is a disgrace and shall not inherit the kingdom of God. Ah, that he could taste what a true Christian faith is; what is required in its nature and what it asks and implies in nature and power. Then he would know what it is that brings forth such a pious, penitent, and precious life which he has lately so disgracefully slandered and hatefully called devilish fruits, hypocrisy, and a new monkdom; and as appears he would still slander if the experience of many and the great quantity of innocent blood did not stand in his way.

Behold, dear reader, now you can see how they adorn and deck their ugly hypocrisy, fruitless and impenitent church services with writing, translations, singing, etc.; although for the most part done without repentance and regeneration, as has been heard, and how they wrongly construe and explain the sincere, pious fruits of true faith to which all the Scriptures, ceremonies, and sacraments tend; so that they may daub the wall with untempered mortar, and console the poor, miserable people so that they disregard the Word of the Lord. But when the Lord's hurricane, flood, and great hailstones shall come with a great noise, then the wall which they have daubed with untempered mortar will be demolished and leveled to the ground so that the foundation thereof shall be discovered.

[3] *In the third place, Gellius writes that the office of a preacher consists of two parts, namely, in uprooting, hindering, and destroying; also planting and building, etc. And he boasts that their fruits thus far, especially pertaining to the first part, cannot in many kingdoms and principalities be ignored. And he says that the Lord Jesus Christ (so he writes) has, by their services, planted sincere repentance and such true Christian faith in many hearts, that the small community at Emden (comforted, so he says), in sure anticipation of the heavenly treasure, willingly supports poor people by the hundreds, etc.*

*Reply.* We admit that the first part of a preacher's office consists in uprooting, hindering, and destroying, and that the other part consists of planting and building. And this constitutes sure proof for us that they are not the preachers to render such services. For although they have in many cities and countries taught people to know better in regard to certain abuses and idolatries (which were so gross that they might without Scripture be known to be abominations) things for which we all thank the Lord forever, yet the essence of all deception, namely, false doctrine and unscriptural sacraments, with which they comfort the world and sustain it in its impenitence and natural state, is left intact, as well as the source of all wickedness, the depraved Adamic heart, which is the source of all unrighteousness, as alas, may be seen on every hand by the fruits.

If then they are the true preachers as they pretend, let them perform the first part, namely, let them pulverize with the hard hammer of the divine Word, the proud, obdurate hearts, the avaricious, impure hearts, the blood-guilty, tyrannical hearts, etc., of whom it is written that they are worthy of death. Let them humble them by the eternal judgment and punishment of Almighty God; let them uncover their wicked and corrupt nature and flesh by the force of the commandments, so that they may learn to know themselves, may see their shame, and then with broken and sorrowing hearts, in view of the coming wrath and eternal punishment of the just and great God, with fear and trembling, repent and die unto their sins, crucify their flesh, restrain their lusts, and so walk before their God with broken and humbled hearts. Behold, this is the best and most important uprooting, destroying, and breaking down of which the Scriptures speak, and to which the true preachers are called.

Then let them point such moved and broken hearts, such penitent and sighing sinners. who with Peter and Magdalene are broken of heart, weep bitterly, with David confess their guilt, to the only and eternal throne of grace, Christ Jesus. Let them teach them the eternal mercy, love, favor, and grace of God, according to the Scriptures; console them with the Gospel of His peace; pour the lovely, mollifying oil of the promises of Christ, so rich in joy, into their wounds carefully after the smarting of the wine poured therein, so that they may thus, grasped by faith, arise with Christ from the deep death of their shameful sins into the new life of all virtue; that they may in true faith, in pure unfeigned love, ever walk without offense after the example of Christ and all the pious, and give thanks to the Lord for His love. Behold, thus do all true preachers plant and build, those who are called by the Spirit of the Lord and are fit for His service.

Reader, observe. Since it is certain that Gellius and the preachers are not such destroyers and builders, uprooters and planters, but they are those who destroy that which is good, and build up that which is bad, they root out truth with their bad doctrine, and plant falsehood with their false sacraments and comfortable life; therefore our position and teaching, that they are not the servants of Christ nor His true messengers, remain unvanquished.

*He writes that the Lord by their service has planted sincere repentance and such a true Christian faith in many hearts that the small congregation at Emden is comforted in anticipation of a heavenly treasure, etc.*

*Reply.* If this were actually so, as he writes, it should be attested to by the fruits and manifested by the works. For Paul says, The kingdom of God is not in word, but in power. Let nobody boast against the truth; we will be judged by one before whom nothing is hidden. Nobody knows what true Christian faith and true repentance are except he who has actually received them, and has felt their power. If God then plants such repentance in many hearts, as he would have us believe, why then are he and similar preachers still so impenitent themselves, so adverse and hostile to truth, and so contrary and blamable as to wholesome doctrine? If those of whom he speaks at this point are of the same mind with him (which we do not hope), then he has not written the truth; this is too certain to be denied.

Those hearts in which God has planted the true repentance and a true Christian faith cannot, especially in these times of revealed truth, be long hidden or remain without the cross which the holy Scriptures predict even if they should be persecuted by their own preachers or relatives. For if they would testify their faith by a proper confession, life, and works, which is true and ardent faith in action, then they would soon experience that with Christ they do not long remain without the cross. Let Gellius put it as he pleases, and let him give it whatever color he likes; the Word of Christ remains and is the word of the cross; all who accept it in power and truth must be prepared for the cross. This both Scriptures and experience teach abundantly.

This had to be said here lest we console any with a false boast and notion, and lest the Word of the Lord, spoken to the false prophets, be applicable to us: Ye promised life to those souls to whom you should not have promised it, by your lying to my people that hear your lies. Ezek. 13:19. Read also Jer. 8:23.

Nevertheless many are tolerated in their churches who willfully live in pride and pomp, in carousing, drunkenness, avarice, and the lusts and works of the flesh, etc. This the service of a true and faithful preacher through which God works mightily does not tolerate if the evangelical Scriptures and apostolic ordinances and doctrines are to come to their own and be true.

But as to the alms and support of the poor, I would say that it is a good and praiseworthy work, and I heartily approve of it. Many pious heathen philosophers, such as Aristotle, Plato, etc., have also considered it right and just. But that sincere and true repentance, or the true kernel and basis of sincere love which is a fruit of true faith, consists therein, this we deny; for we may give in hypocrisy, as well as in love, as may be witnessed in the scribes and Pharisees, by manifest heathen, and daily still in the case of the papists.

Paul also agrees with this, saying, And though I bestow all my goods to feed the poor, and though I give my body to be burned, and have not charity, it profiteth me nothing. I Cor. 13:3. Therefore let every one take heed as to the purpose and mind with which he gives alms. For the love which is of God and is of a divine nature, hates all boasting and hypocrisy, and does not know them. Of this I am sure.

If Gellius points to the support and service of the poor, which I say is praiseworthy, as a fruit of true repentance, then I ask in the first place, whether he finds a lack of alms with our church, although we are exiled to foreign countries, and are living in poverty and misery, and are partly robbed of our possessions.

In the second place, I say that if he wants to boast of true repentance, he should commence with the repentance of such a faith as brings forth the love and fear of God, and not with the alms for the poor. For the Lord's own mouth says that love is the keeping of His commandments; yes, the greatest commandment. Deut. 6:5; Matt. 22:36.

My dear reader, if he and his could fully comprehend sincere, true repentance and true Christian faith, which he imagines has been planted in their hearts, oh, how heartily would they fear their God, and love and thank Him for His grace and favor, and how willingly would they follow and heed His holy Word! But how they love and thank Him for His grace and love, and how they hear and obey His Word, their actions and fruits, alas, show too plainly.

If they actually love God, and if a true, living faith and a genuine repentance has been implanted in their hearts, as he boasts, why then do they still walk after the manner of heathen in pomp and pride, in the lusts of their eyes, show an adornment of their houses, in avariciousness, carousing, drinking, etc.? Why do they not heed the words of Paul, If ye live after the flesh, ye shall die? Rom. 8:13. If indeed they love their neighbors as the Scriptures command and as true repentance implies, why then do they practice usury, and why do they scrape so over against each other, and why are they so perfidious with each other? Why do they go to law and plead? Hatred, envy, lying, deceit, backbiting, and defamation are verily still prevalent among his followers everywhere, besides cursing, swearing, quarreling, fighting, warring, robbery, and plunder, and with some adultery and fornicaton; to say nothing about their sad reviling, profaning, and defamation of all those who seek and fear the Lord. What kind of repentance and faith this is, the thing of which he boasts so loudly, you may consider in the fear of God.

O my dear reader, observe. It never fails that where true faith is, there also is the righteousness of faith; where there is unfeigned, Christian love, there also is obedience to the holy Word; and where there is true sincere repentance, there also is an irreproachable life, according to the truth. This is incontrovertible.

Is it not a false assertion to say that the giving of alms shows true repentance, since we do not know whether it is done in sincerity of heart or in hypocrisy and vanity, while he can plainly see that most of those who give alms are nothing but world and flesh, yes, without the new creature, repentance, and regeneration?

It would be good if he could take to heart what is written: The gifts of the ungodly do not please the most High; and sins are not remitted by many sacrifices. He who sacrifices of the possessions of the poor (notice this) carries on as he that slaughters the son in the sight of the father. But to keep God's commandments is a rich sacrifice, and to respect the command (notice this) is a sacrifice that helps. To depart from wickedness is a religious activity (notice this) pleasing to the Lord, and to forsake unrighteousness is a propitiation. Again, To obey is better than sacrifice, and to hearken, than the fat of rams.

I would say further that I am inclined to think that I know that the before-mentioned alms, of which he boasts, are not the two mites or pennies of the widow's necessity, but only a small crumb of their abundance, riches, and luxury. This I frankly assert, and I have not the least doubt that if they would apply to the support of the poor their silk, damask, the abundance of their clothes in which many of them go about so gloriously, the great and beautiful ornamentations of their houses, the golden and silver necklaces, the useless, costly leggings, gold chains, earrings, silver- and gold-plated swords, besides the booty of the distressed which probably may be found in the houses of some, then the poor would not suffer in the least from want. Ah, my reader, this must nevertheless be called true repentance by him and a highly praised work. If such boasting of outward works was heard from our side, how soon would we hear that we are merit religionists, and that we want to be saved by our own merits!

O Lord! Dear Lord! thus the ignorant people are deceived and consoled in their impenitent reckless life with achieved works and merits. I think that such preachers are with justice reproached as peace preachers, pillow placers, and false daubers by the Spirit of the Lord, since they praise such a carnal people as penitent and blessed, according to the prophetic word, even though they are still quite earthly and carnal, as their daily walk openly testifies before the whole world.

My faithful reader, observe the Word of the Lord, and take heed to yourself, for it is not always a true Christian faith nor sincere repentance which the children of the world, who like to walk upon the broad way, sometimes teach and represent as true faith and sincere repentance. But this is true faith: that which cordially accepts all the words of God, the threatening commands as well as the consoling Gospel, and trusts in them as the true and sure Word of God, etc. From such faith, which Paul calls a gift of God, springs the fear of God which drives out sin, and the true love which gladdens, enlivens, and cheers the heart, and leads it into the obedience of the Word. John 14:16, 17.

Now where there is such a faith which brings forth a new, converted, and changed mind; which dies unto sin and strives after a new life, transplants us from Adam to Christ, puts off the old man with all his works, and puts on the new man with his works, and thus conforms all his thoughts, words, and works to the Spirit, Word, and ways of the Lord; behold, there is that true repentance to which the holy prophets, John the Baptist, and Jesus Christ, together with all the apostles and pious servants, have so earnestly pointed and so faithfully admonished us.

All those who will rightly preach this faith and this genuine repentance, and bring forth fruits by it, must themselves first truly believe and sincerely repent. This is too obvious to be denied. And that Gellius and similar preachers do not yet in power and truth believe and sincerely repent thus, this I will leave to be judged by their own writings and fruits, both here on earth and before the throne of God and Christ.

[4] *Gellius further writes, Even if many of our audience turn the preaching of the holy Gospel to lasciviousness, as Jude has it, and that such fruits of life are not altogether prevalent as the result of our preaching (although so many pious and penitent hearts do show them that we can never grant it), what would this be but the old lament of the prophet Isaiah, Who hath believed our report, etc? He also points to the saying of Christ, If they have kept my word, they will also keep your word; with which he doubtlessly means to say, Gellius writes, that even as the world has not kept my doctrine, neither have they kept yours. He also refers to the parable of the four kinds of seed or soils in Matt. 13.*

*Reply.* It has never, from the beginning, been God's usage to preach repentance through the impenitent. Thorns do not bring forth grapes, neither do thistles yield figs, God's own mouth and wisdom declares. Since it is clear that Gellius and similar preachers are still so earthly and carnal and are driven by such an unmerciful, tyrannical, and reviling spirit (which is really the native spirit, nature, and fruit of the old serpent), how then can they rightly preach the penitent, pious life and the fruitful, merciful, lovely spirit, nature, and disposition of Christ, which they not only do not acknowledge but revile as hypocrisy and which they sincerely hate in all the pious?

In the second place, I say, that the peace-preaching and the cushion-making of those learned ones as done here, will, I fear, make few truly repentant persons. For although the world is so wicked and wild that one may well be terrified at its great wickedness, nevertheless they are so comforted and consoled by their preachers, with their pedobaptism, Supper, alms, and with the merits, grace, death, and blood of the Lord, that they make themselves believe that they are the Lord's chosen holy church and people.

In the third place, I would say, since he speaks doubtfully, saying, *Even if many of our audience turn the preaching to lasciviousness, and little fruit were brought forth by it, which we however do not admit, etc.,* the reader should mark well how mightily they defend the world and promote the church of Antichrist, saying, If it were true, etc. And yet the whole Germanic nation has nevertheless come to such a wild and reckless freedom by the preaching of their free Gospel that if we politely admonish and reprove them for their open unchastity, carousing, drinking, pomp and splendor, cursing and swearing, lascivious, unchaste, and foul words, we must immediately hear that we are conspirators, vagabonds, fanatics, heaven-stormers, Anabaptists, and other impolite terms of reproach.

But as to the complaint of Isaiah and the saying of Christ, If they have kept my saying, etc. (John 15:20), with which he wishes to cover and adorn his unscriptural practices and doctrine of impenitence, I would ask him whether Christ and the apostles received as disciples those who lived after the flesh, those who drank to excess, cursed, took usury, the avaricious, those who patronized houses of ill fame, violated marriage vows, etc., so long as they had not sincerely repented.

If he says yes, then he speaks contrary to all Scripture. For Paul says that we shall not eat with such, if they call themselves brethren (I Cor. 5:11), and that they shall not inherit the kingdom of God. I Cor. 6:11; Gal. 5:22. If he says no, then I ask in reply, Why do they then receive them as disciples, seeing they are not disciples of Christ, but according to His own words, disciples of the world?

If he answers that they do not do that, then I ask him, Why then do they baptize their children before they extend to them the Supper? Why do they not rather separate them according to the Scriptures from the communion of those whom he esteems pious? If he answers that he does not know who they are (which he can by no means truthfully say), then I ask finally whether he does not know a tree by its fruits, whether he cannot see a light (for that is what the Scriptures call them) that shines in darkness, nor a city which is built upon a high mountain. Matt. 5:14.

Since Gellius and all the preachers admit and tolerate such impenitent persons, whom he himself calls worldly, as has been heard, into the communion of their churches, against the doctrine and practice of Christ and of the apostles, therefore, they must acknowledge, must they not, that Christ's church is the world, or the world is Christ's church. They must acknowledge that they, contrary to the apostolic doctrine, ordinance, and example, dispense the sacraments to the world also, sacraments which according to the Scripture belong only to the penitent who have placed themselves in the obedience of the Word in the church of Christ. They in so doing include the penitent (if any there be) in the fellowship of the impenitent; and they are manifest sycophants and enemies of the cross of Christ, who fawn upon influential people, wheedle the world, and so (in order to continue in their ease) transgress the Lord's Word and ordinance out of sheer disobedience, for the sake of their own poor bellies, rejecting it as powerless and unnecessary.[7]

So also as to his reference to the Lord's parable, I could wish that he would examine it more carefully, so as not to console himself therewith. For it has reference to the true preachers and disciples who had been put to the trial and the cross of Christ, in obedience to the Word; not to the cross-fleeing preachers and the world, as may be learned not only from the Scriptures but also from experience.

For some reject the received and known truth, and the sown seed is picked up by the fowls of the air and it does not bring forth fruit. Some become weak and tired, they wither and dry up by the heat of the sun (the cross, oppression, and misery), proving themselves to be wood, hay, and stubble. I Cor. 3:12.

Some are smothered by the cares of this world, by deceitful riches and the lusts of the flesh, so that the received knowledge dies in them, and the lusts and love of this world get the upper hand, which in our times, as in the times of the first church, is seen alas, more than too often in the case of men who with Demas, once more grasped the love of the world.

But the last-named kind receive it in a sincere, pious heart and bring forth fruit with patience. Although they are sorely tempted by all kinds of assaults, anxiety, oppression, and mortal perils, yet they are, by the gracious help of God, so armed with a true faith, love, hope, and patience or long-suffering, so confirmed in God, that no fire of tribulation can consume them (for they are gold, silver, precious stones), nor sword and pain frighten nor keep them from the ways of the Lord.

That the before-mentioned parable has reference to such Christians

---

[7] Reading *onnoodig* (unnecessary) instead of *onmoedig* (not courageous). *Tr.*

and not to the world and its preachers, is too clear to be controverted or
denied. And so Gellius and similar preachers of the world remain defenders
of unrighteousness, comforters of the impenitent, and servants of the kingdom of Antichrist, who sadly deceive not only their own souls but also those
of their church, and stay and strengthen them in their gross abominations
and impenitent carnal lives to eternal destruction by their twisted Scripture
and powerless consolations.

In the fifth place it should be observed what the preachers' desire and
seeking is. The Scriptures teach that Moses and Jeremiah emphatically refused their task and office, but were, nevertheless, called by God and sent,
as Jeremiah lamented when the cross bore heavily upon him. Jer. 20:8.

It must be observed that all the prophets, apostles, and faithful servants
of God sought and desired nothing but that they might proclaim the name of
their God and might point their neighbors to the way of peace. Money,
property, honor, and an easy life they have not sought, but they executed
their assigned office (a thing alas not weighed by these heedless people)
with many sore trials, miseries, anxieties, sorrows, beatings, poverty, bonds,
martyrdom, and death, as the Scripture and history in many examples teach.
But how the preachers of the world have hitherto refused the service, and
even now refuse it, and what they seek in so doing, experience and the Holy
Spirit plainly teach us, saying, that they promise death to the pious and life
to the wicked for a handful of barley or a piece of bread; that they seek the
fat and the wool, milk and the flesh; that they pasture themselves, but not
the Lord's sheep; that they preach peace whenever their bellies are filled (that
is, whenever they are well paid) and mobilize for war whenever men do not
thrust food into their mouths!

That this is true, that they do not seek souls, but a carefree, easy life,
this the open facts witness; for we never in all our life have seen preachers
living where there were no revenues or incomes. Also, that Gellius does not
seek the salvation of his sheep, but the revenues, this he has shown recently
when he left those of Norden, where he was called by the same calling, and
moved to Emden where the annual income was greater, a thing which the
fathers in times gone by, in their councils and decretals, considered unjust,
and which they punished with the ban.

If he sought the salvation of their souls, and not the revenues, as belongs
to a good and faithful shepherd, after the example of his Lord Christ and
of all faithful servants; why then did he cancel his first calling, which was,
according to his representation, divine? Why leave the first sheep who were
no less delivered through the death of the Lord, and bought with His precious
blood, than the last, of which he now has the charge? Oh, hypocrisy and
carnal covering!

[5] *As to what Gellius writes concerning the support of the preachers,
how the congregation (of which the magistracy is a part, as he writes) supplies and cares for their necessities, how they need to worry but little, since it*

*is enough and certain, since they serve the Gospel (so he writes) that they also eat of the Gospel and live by it, quoting Matt. 10:10; Luke 10:7; I Tim. 5:18.*

We reply as follows: If Gellius and the preachers were such laborers as are referred to in these chapters, then it is plain that the sustenance of the Gospel is theirs by right and by promise. But if anybody should go into the service and uselessly spend and scatter his Lord's goods, if he were faithless and sought himself in all things, and did the things which are contrary to the will, benefit, and honor of his Lord, should such a faithless servant receive the support and sustenance which is due to the faithful and industrious laborer? I think you will say no, and that he should the rather meet the displeasure and punishment of his Lord. And so the Lord speaks, When the Lord therefore of the vineyard cometh, what will he do unto these husbandmen? They said, *Malos male perdet et vineam suam aliis locabit Agricolis* (Matt. 21:41) (that is, He will miserably destroy those wicked men and will let out his vineyard unto other husbandmen).

We acknowledge that sustenance has been promised by the Scriptures to the true and faithful servants. But since Gellius and similar preachers are unfaithful servants, who waste the Lord's goods, steal the gain; scatter, not gather, His sheep; who, alas, without fear or hesitation lead to hell in great numbers his precious jewels, that is, the poor, miserable souls, even as those truly regenerated persons can see by the testimony of their open deeds in the light of the Word of the Lord, therefore their sustenance is not the sustenance of true preachers, is it, but an unreasonable, shameful gain; an improper livelihood, and the reward of the deceived souls. This, all of sound understanding must acknowledge and grant.

O my faithful reader, ponder this. As long as the world distributes splendid houses and such large incomes to their preachers, the false prophets and deceivers will be there by droves.

All heresy, seduction, idolatry, tyranny, drunkenness, pomp, pride, and hypocrisy can by their methods be defended with Scripture; as also their improper and scandalous belly-serving and carefree life, which the ignorant and blind world believes to be right.

But I testify openly, I testify and do not keep silent, that the preachers of the world, one and all, are Balaamites, who love the reward of unrighteousness and serve for the sake of a handful of barley and a piece of bread, whereby they profane the name of God. Ezek. 13:19. Prophets of Jezebel who eat at her table are they, servants and defenders of Maoz who are honored with great rewards of Antiochus, that is, Antichrist; Ahabites, who, for the sake of a field, stone the pious Naboth, that is, advise and instigate by their speeches, writings, backbiting, accusations, will, or permission, the killing of many an innocent, pious child of God.

In similar vein, they are priests of Jeroboam, who contrary to the example of Christ and His holy apostles, hire themselves out for money or yearly salary to an open service of impenitence, out of keeping with the evangelical writing and example; without power or divine operation, without moral improvement and regeneration, as may be openly seen, by which their service is useless labor and make-believe, and an improper peddling moreover.

Oh, how clearly has the Holy Ghost portrayed them before our eyes, if we would but see, saying, And through covetousness shall they, with feigned words, make merchandise of you, having men's persons in admiration because of advantage (II Pet. 2:3; Jude 16), and other similar sayings. For that they have sought unreasonable gain and an easy, lazy life from youth, and still seek it, is so obvious that it cannot possibly be denied.

Besides, their benefices and properties have been formerly boot-legged in by clever ruses, the thieving witchcraft, the spiritual robbery of Antichrist, and they still are made available every day by such persons who walk upon the broad way without repentance and who find, alas, little pleasure in the Lord's holy Word.

These men act the hypocrite and coddle the magistrates and those of influence. They comfort the impenitent and persecute the pious; they falsify the plain Word, sacraments, and ordinances of Jesus Christ by which the church should be gathered and maintained. They preach to suit and please the world so that they may receive with honor under the semblance of the Gospel the reward of blood of the poor, miserable souls, a thing they seek so diligently, in order that they may possess it in peace, and enjoy good times with all. And then they console themselves with the idea that they serve the Gospel and should therefore live of the Gospel. Behold, thus they give a Scriptural shape to all kinds of false affairs and works, and give a fine appearance to all kinds of hypocrisy.

My faithful reader, I warn you in sincere love, take heed. Once more I say unto you, the true and faithful servants of Jesus in the apostolic churches had nothing to do with such annual stipends, rents, and property, but the greater part earned their bread by their own labor. They served the church of Christ, nevertheless, in all love and humility, and walked before Him with true doctrines and an unblamable life. They have diligently guarded the Lord's house, city, and vineyard; have protected it against all evil and deceiving spirits with the Word of the Lord; have admonished the disorderly, consoled the afflicted, reproved the transgressors, excommunicated the disobedient and refractory; they have served reasonably. For them the world was the world, and the world's cross they have patiently borne. They have made their own way, and whatever necessities they needed above that they received not of the world, but at the hands of their pious disciples in humility, without avariciousness or desire of filthy lucre, seeing that the Scriptures allow them this, as said above, for they pastured the Lord's sheep aright, they tended the vineyard faithfully, tilled the field of the Lord industriously, and stored the sheaves and fruits in the Lord's barn, as the example of the prophets and apostles indicates and the Spirit and Word of the Lord command and enjoin upon all faithful servants.

I would conclude my remarks in regard to the calling of the preachers saying, since the Scriptures teach that the servants of the holy Word shall be duly called either by the Lord Himself, or by means of the pious, as has been heard; that they shall be unblamable; that they must rule the Lord's church correctly, bring forth abiding fruits, destroy and build up, seeking not filthy lucre, but the honor and praise of God and the salvation of their neighbors, etc.; and since we see with our eyes and feel with our hands that they, alas, are one and all called of such as we would wish had the Spirit of Christ; moreover that they are themselves blamable in all things, for they are of an unmerciful, tyrannical disposition, and of an earthly, carnal conduct; therefore we conclude that they pervert the Gospel and do not teach it in power and true repentance. They use the sacrament wrongly without power, spirit, and moral improvement, and dispense it to those who are no disciples of Christ. They deceive the people, do not bring forth permanent fruits, plant that which is evil, and root out that which is good; they do not really seek the honor and praise of God, but their own profit and gain, the favor of the world, and an easy, carefree life (I will let their doctrine, sacraments, fruits, and life testify to this). Therefore I say, without equivocation, that they are not the called preachers and servants of the church of Christ, whom we must, according to the Scriptures, obey, accept, and follow; but they are belly-preachers, servants of Antichrist, against whom we are consistently warned in the Word of God. We are not to hear or follow them nor their doctrines but to flee from and avoid them as deceivers, false prophets, wicked men, and faithless servants.

Yes, my reader, why should they talk at length about their calling, preaching, church service? It is, briefly stated, not possible, according to the sure promise and prophecy of Jesus Christ and the prophets, that a true and faithful preacher, witness, or teacher, especially in these evil times and in this wicked and most tyrannical world, should faithfully teach and proclaim, without respect of persons, the pure Gospel of Jesus Christ, without being driven forth, proscribed or killed. Much less is it possible that he shall enjoy life at ease and liberty, as these do, without persecution, yes, receive a big annual salary of the world and be highly honored and praised by all men!

Read the entire holy Scriptures and see if you can find that Christ Jesus, with His holy apostles, true witnesses, and followers, fared as they do and received as they do; or whether persecution, cross, tribulation, anxiety, prison, and death were not generally promised, and in most part, also delivered. Besides experience teaches this abundantly every day still.

If then the preachers acted rightly, if they walked according to the example of Christ and His apostles; if their teachings and dealings were right, as they pretend them to be, it is incontrovertible that all the Scriptures would have to be wrong, the word of the cross would have come to an end, and Christ and His prophecies would be proved false.

Therefore, alas, all their boasting and artful construction, concerning their calling, office, doctrine, and church service, together with their defense are, in fact, erroneous, puerile, hypocritical, false, and without truth. For all seek their own and not the things which are Jesus Christ's, their own ease, and not the salvation of their neighbor. They are enemies of the cross; they serve their own bellies. If they would rightly reprove all the ungodliness, idolatry, abuse, pride, pomp, splendor, hypocrisy, and the unfaithfulness of this world, without respect of persons, whether high or low, with the same earnestness, fervor, heart, mind, etc., as did Christ with His holy apostles and true witnesses, if they would proceed boldly, if they loathed all the unrighteousness of the world as Christ Jesus and His apostles did, then they would not long remain at ease in their elegant houses; nor would they receive such incomes, and they would have little prestige in this reckless, wild world. Of this I am sure.

But now they proceed to follow another policy. They make the garment to fit the man, as the saying is, and they teach and act in such a way that the world may like them, and put up with them, and that they may be friends of the world, so that they may sit secure in their ease, enjoying good times. This is something evident to all, and a sure proof that their mission and calling, together with their doctrine and church service, are in every particular without the ordinance, Spirit, and Word of God, as was said above.

Now Gellius has the reply to his article on the calling of the preachers. I would earnestly beseech him and all the preachers to reflect a little in the fear of God, for before the flaming eyes of the Lord, which penetrate heaven and earth, nothing wrong will remain hidden, however artfully it may be covered before man's eyes, and decked and adorned with smooth words.

[6] *Next Gellius attacks our calling and says: Before we grant to our preachers that they have the Word, and let them pass for people who bring forth fruit, they must first be properly called by a church of God, and not by an assembly of people that have been misled by false prophets; and they must first step out into the open to preach, or actually show that Christ acted incorrectly when He did not prefer to preach in secret so as to avoid the cross (as he says is the case with us) rather than in public.*

*Reply.* The mission or vocation of Moses, of Christ, of Paul, of the apostles and prophets, was not left unvilified by the perverse. Moses had to hear that he had killed the Lord's people and that he had led them into the wilderness so that they might perish through want and misery. Christ Jesus was called a winebibber, a blasphemer, and one possessed of the devil. Paul was called mutinous and an apostate Jew, etc. Behold, thus in their time the mission of the faithful servants of the Lord, nay, of the Lord and Messiah Himself, was despised, although bolstered by many miracles. How much more then shall we be despised, who are such weak and insignificant instruments, and come to a sevenfold more wicked and evil world than theirs was.

Inasmuch then as we are reviled by our opponents, the learned ones, that we are not called of a church of God, but of false prophets, or a false church, therefore I would briefly admonish the reader to weigh well with the Scriptures who, how, and what the church of God is. It is not a collection of the proud, avaricious, usurers, pompous, drunkards, and impenitent as the church of the world is, of whom the learned ones are called, but a gathering or congregation of saints, as the Holy Scriptures and the Nicene Creed clearly teach and present, namely, those who through true faith are regenerated by God unto Christ Jesus and are of a divine nature, who would gladly regulate their lives according to the Spirit, Word, and example of the Lord, men who are actuated by His Spirit, and are willing and ready patiently to bear the cross of their Lord Jesus Christ.

Behold, dear reader, such were the churches which the apostles and faithful servants won unto Christ Jesus and added to with His Spirit and Word. The Scripture knows no other in all eternity. From such and of such with fasting and prayer have the pious and unblamable pastors and teachers been chosen and called unto the Lord's service; and not of the world, as has been heard.

Since then the preachers of the world and their congregations are not the church of Christ but are such preachers and churches, who by their spirit, words, and deeds inside and out are of the world, as is plain; and since the merciful, great Lord in these last days of all abominations, graciously gathers together, by His Word and Spirit, many faithful hearts from all unscriptural sects, both great and small, and from different nations and tongues into one faith, and places them as an admonition to sincere repentance, with their doctrine, life, goods, and blood before the whole world, before lords and princes, the learned and the unlearned, men and women, as a light and a candlestick: therefore these must be the Lord's church and people. Or else the Word of God, which is the truth, must be erroneous and false. And now that some from among these and by these are chosen with tears and care, with fasting and prayer, and after the example and doctrine of the apostolic church ordained to the service of the Lord by the laying on of hands, although unknown to the world, now all men of sound mind may judge whether according to Scriptures such calling or choosing is consistent with Scripture and according to the usage of the first church; and whether it can stand before the Lord and His church as divine, holy, and just.

Moreover it is well known to me that the preachers tell the simple (which Gellius' writings, if properly read, also imply) that I have received my faith, doctrine, and calling from a deceiving, tumultuous, and corrupt sect by which (as he writes) the Lord has undertaken to purge His church. And so I am forced briefly to explain the transaction, of which I would otherwise, for the sake of modesty, remain silent; namely, how I came to the knowledge of my Lord and Saviour Jesus Christ; and how I afterward, unworthily, became one of His servants.[8] And I hereby beseech all my readers, for God's sake, to consider well this my narration, and that they will

8 Menno means a minister of the Gospel. *Ed.*

not think hard of me for it, nor consider it as vain boasting that I tell it here. For the honor of my God and the love for His church compel me. Let each man judge as he pleases. He who has created me and has to this day graciously delivered me from my enemies, knows me; He knows what I seek in this life and what my greatest desire is.

### [Menno's Conversion, Call, and Testimony[9]]

My reader, I write you the truth in Christ and lie not. It happened in the year 1524, my age then being twenty-eight,[10] that I assumed the duties of a priest in my paternal village called Pingjum. Two others of about my age also officiated in the same functions. The one was my pastor, fairly well educated. The other was below me. Both had read the Scriptures a little, but I had never touched them, for I feared if I should read them, I would be misled. Behold, such an ignorant preacher was I for nearly two years.

In the year following it occurred to me, as often as I handled the bread and wine in the Mass, that they were not the flesh and blood of the Lord. I thought that the devil was suggesting this so that he might separate me from my faith. I confessed it often, sighed, and prayed; yet I could not come clear of the idea.

The two young men mentioned earlier and I spent our time emptily in playing [cards] together, drinking, and in diversions as, alas, is the fashion and usage of such useless people. And when we touched upon the Scriptures I could not speak a word with them without being scoffed at, for I did not know what I was driving at, so concealed was the Word of God from my eyes.

Finally, I got the idea to examine the New Testament diligently. I had not gone very far when I discovered that we were deceived, and my conscience, troubled on account of the aforementioned bread, was quickly relieved, even without any instructions. I was in so far helped by Luther,[11] however: that human injunctions cannot bind unto eternal death.

Through the illumination and grace of the Lord I increased in knowledge of the Scriptures daily, and was presently considered by some (not correctly however) to be an evangelical preacher. Everyone sought and desired me; the world loved me and I loved the world. It was said that I preached the Word of God and was a good fellow.

Afterwards it happened, before I had ever heard of the existence of brethren, that a God-fearing, pious hero named Sicke Snijder was beheaded at Leeuwarden for being rebaptized. It sounded very strange to me to hear of a second baptism. I examined the Scriptures diligently and pondered them earnestly, but could find no report of infant baptism.

9 The section dealing with Menno's conversion, renunciation of Roman Catholicism, and calling as an elder in the Obbenite brotherhood, etc., was early made a separate tract. It has often been printed in Dutch, German, and English. *Ed.*

10 Menno was therefore born about 1496.

11 Menno was helped by Luther's writings, not by an interview. *Ed.*

After I had noticed this I discussed it with my pastor and after much talk he had to admit that there was no basis for infant baptism in Scripture. Still I dared not trust my own understanding but consulted several ancient authors. They taught me that children are by baptism cleansed from their original sin. I compared this idea with the Scriptures and found that it did violence to the blood of Christ.

Afterwards I consulted Luther. For I sought for the basis of baptism. He taught me that children were to be baptized on account of their own faith. I perceived that this also was not in accordance with the Word of God.

Thirdly I consulted Bucer. He taught that infants are to be baptized so that they might be the more carefully nurtured in the way of the Lord. I perceived that this doctrine also was without foundation.

Fourthly I consulted Bullinger. He pointed to the covenant and to circumcision. This I found likewise to be incapable of Scriptural proof.

When I noticed from all these that writers varied so greatly among themselves, each following his own wisdom, then I realized that we were deceived in regard to infant baptism.

Shortly thereafter I was transferred to the village in which I was born, called Witmarsum,[12] led thither by covetousness and the desire to obtain a great name. There I spoke much concerning the Word of the Lord, without spirituality or love, as all hypocrites do, and by this means I made disciples of my own kind, vain boasters and frivolous babblers, who, alas, like myself did not take these matters too seriously.

Although I had now acquired considerable knowledge of the Scriptures, yet I wasted that knowledge through the lusts of my youth in an impure, sensual, unprofitable life, and sought nothing but gain, ease, favor of men, splendor, name and fame, as all generally do who sail that ship.[13]

And so, my reader, I obtained a view of baptism and the Lord's Supper through the illumination of the Holy Ghost, through much reading and pondering of the Scriptures, and by the gracious favor and gift of God; not by the instrumentality of the erring sects as it is reported of me. I hope that I write the truth and do not seek vain glory. But if some have contributed and have assisted me somewhat, then I render thanks to the Lord forever for this.

Meanwhile it happened, when I had resided there about a year, that several launched adult baptism. When the innovators came, or where they were from, or who they really were, is to this hour unknown to me, neither have I ever seen them.

Next in order the sect of Münster made its appearance, by whom many pious hearts in our quarter were deceived. My soul was much troubled, for I perceived that though they were zealous they erred in doctrine. I did what

---

[12] In Friesland.

[13] Compare Menno's confessions in his *Meditation on the Twenty-fifth Psalm. Ed.*

I could to oppose them by preaching and exhortations, as much as in me was. I conferred twice with one of their leaders, once in private, and once in public, but my admonitions did not help, because I myself still did that which I knew was not right.

The report spread that I could silence these persons beautifully. Everybody defended himself by a reference to me, no matter who. I saw plainly that I was the stay and defense of the impenitent who all leaned on me. This gave me no little qualm of conscience. I sighed and prayed: Lord, help me, lest I become responsible for other men's sins. My soul was troubled and I reflected upon the outcome, that if I should gain the whole world and live a thousand years, and at last have to endure the wrath of God, what would I have gained?

Afterwards the poor straying sheep who wandered as sheep without a proper shepherd, after many cruel edicts, garrotings, and slaughters, assembled at a place near my place of residence called Oude Klooster.[14] And, alas! through the ungodly doctrines of Münster, and in opposition to the Spirit, Word, and example of Christ, they drew the sword to defend themselves, the sword which the Lord commanded Peter to put up in its sheath.

After this had transpired the blood of these people, although misled, fell so hot on my heart that I could not stand it, nor find rest in my soul. I reflected upon my unclean, carnal life, also the hypocritical doctrine and idolatry which I still practiced daily in appearance of godliness, but without relish. I saw that these zealous children, although in error, willingly gave their lives and their estates for their doctrine and faith. And I was one of those who had disclosed to some of them the abominations of the papal system. But I myself was continuing in my comfortable life and acknowledged abominations simply in order that I might enjoy physical comfort and escape the cross of Christ.

Pondering these things my conscience tormented me so that I could no longer endure it. I thought to myself—I, miserable man, what am I doing? If I continue in this way, and do not live agreeably to the Word of the Lord, according to the knowledge of the truth which I have obtained; if I do not censure to the best of my little talent the hypocrisy, the impenitent, carnal life, the erroneous baptism, the Lord's Supper in the false service of God which the learned ones teach; if I through bodily fear do not lay bare the foundations of the truth, nor use all my powers to direct the wandering flock who would gladly do their duty if they knew it, to the true pastures of Christ—oh, how shall their shed blood, shed in the midst of transgression, rise against me at the judgment of the Almighty and pronounce sentence against my poor, miserable soul!

14 A group of radical Anabaptists, evidently former Melchiorites, who were not nonresistant in doctrine and life. In March, 1535, three hundred of these "Old Cloisterites" seized an old Monastery ("Cloister") near Bolsward, and were destroyed by the authorities. They did not accept such offensive ideas of the Münsterites as polygamy, however. Ed.

My heart trembled within me. I prayed to God with sighs and tears that He would give to me, a sorrowing sinner, the gift of His grace, create within me a clean heart, and graciously through the merits of the crimson blood of Christ forgive my unclean walk and frivolous easy life and bestow upon me wisdom, Spirit, courage, and a manly spirit so that I might preach His exalted and adorable name and holy Word in purity, and make known His truth to His glory.

I began in the name of the Lord to preach publicly from the pulpit the word of true repentance, to point the people to the narrow path, and in the power of the Scripture openly to reprove all sin and wickedness, all idolatry and false worship, and to present the true worship; also the true baptism and the Lord's Supper, according to the doctrine of Christ, to the extent that I had at that time received from God the grace.

I also faithfully warned everyone against the abominations of Münster, condemning king, polygamy, kingdom, sword, etc. After about nine months or so, the gracious Lord granted me His fatherly Spirit, help, and hand. Then I, without constraint, of a sudden, renounced all my worldly reputation, name and fame, my unchristian abominations, my masses, infant baptism, and my easy life, and I willingly submitted to distress and poverty under the heavy cross of Christ.[15] In my weakness I feared God; I sought out the pious and though they were few in number I found some who were zealous and maintained the truth. I dealt with the erring, and through the help and power of God with His Word, reclaimed them from the snares of damnation and gained them to Christ. The hardened and rebellious I left to the Lord.

And so you see, my reader, in this way the merciful Lord through the liberal goodness of His abounding grace took notice of me, a poor sinner, stirred in my heart at the outset, produced in me a new mind, humbled me in His fear, taught me to know myself in part, turned me from the way of death and graciously called me into the narrow pathway of life and the communion of His saints. To Him be praise forevermore. Amen.

It happened about one year after this while I was secretly exercising myself in the Word of God by reading and writing that some six, seven, or eight persons came to me who were of one heart and one soul with me, beyond reproach as far as man can judge in doctrine and life, separated from the world after the witness of Scripture and under the cross, men who sincerely abhorred not only the sect of Münster, but the cursed abominations of all other worldly sects. In the name of those pious souls who were of the same mind and spirit both with themselves and with me, they prayerfully requested me to make the great sufferings and need of the poor oppressed souls my concern, seeing that the hunger was very great and the faithful stewards altogether few. They urged me to put to good use the talents which I, though unworthy, had received from the Lord.

---

[15] Menno's renunciation of Roman Catholicism occurred late in January, 1536. *Ed.*

When I heard this my heart was greatly troubled. Trouble and fear were on every side. On the one hand I was sensible of my limited talents, my unlearnedness, my weak nature, the timidity of my spirit, the exceedingly great wickedness, perversity, and tyranny of the world, the great and powerful sects, the subtlety of many minds, and the woefully heavy cross that would weigh on me not a little should I comply. On the other hand I saw the pitifully great hunger and need of these God-fearing, pious children, for I saw plainly that they erred as do harmless sheep which have no shepherd.

At last, after much prayer, before the Lord and His church I gave these conditions: that we should pray earnestly to the Lord for a season. Then if it should be pleasing to His holy will that I could or should labor to His praise, He would give me such a mind and heart as would say to me with Paul, Woe is me, if I preach not the Gospel. And if not, that He might employ means so that nothing would come of it. For Christ says, If two or three shall agree on earth as touching anything that they shall ask, it shall be done for them of my Father which is in heaven. For where two or three are gathered together in my name, there am I in the midst of them.

In this way, my reader, I was not called by the Münsterites nor any other seditious sect as it is falsely reported concerning me, but I have been called, though unworthy, to this office[16] by the people who had subjected themselves to Christ and His Word, led a penitent life in the fear of God, served their neighbors in love, bore the cross, sought the welfare and the weal of all men, loved righteousness and truth, and abhorred wickedness and unrighteousness. These things show pointedly, do they not, that these people were not such a perverted sect as they are made out to be, but true Christians, though unknown to the world; if at least we believe that Christ's Word is true, and His unblamable, holy life and example, infallible and right.

And so I, a miserable sinner, was enlightened of the Lord, was converted to a new mind, fled from Babel, entered into Jerusalem, and finally, though unworthy, was called to His high and heavy service.

When the persons before mentioned did not desist from their supplications and my own conscience made me somewhat uneasy even in my weakness, because I saw the great hunger and need referred to, then I surrendered myself soul and body to the Lord, and committed myself to His grace, and commenced in due time, according to the contents of His holy Word, to teach and to baptize, to till the vineyard of the Lord with my little talent, to build up His holy city and temple and to repair the tumble-down walls.[17] The great and mighty God has made known the word of true repentance, the word of His grace and power, and the salutary use of His holy sacraments, through our humble service, doctrine, and unlearned writings, together with the diligent service, labor and help of our faithful brethren in many towns and

16 The office of elder or bishop of the Obbenites, now called Mennonites. *Ed.*

17 Menno was ordained as an elder by the Dutch Anabaptist, Obbe Philips, who later defected. Obbe reports that the service was held in Groningen. *Ed.*

countries. It has been made known to such an extent, and He has made the fashion of His churches so glorious, and has bestowed upon them such unconquerable power that many proud and lofty hearts not only have become humble; the impure, chaste; the drunken, sober; the avaricious, benevolent; the cruel, kind; and the ungodly, pious; but they also faithfully left their possessions and blood, life and limb with the blessed testimony they had, as it may be seen daily still. These are not the fruit and evidence of false doctrine in which God does not operate. Neither could these people endure so long under such dire distress and cross were it not the power and word of the Almighty which moves them.

What is more, the Lord gives them such grace and wisdom in their trials, even as Christ has promised to all His children, that all the worldly-wise and famous teachers, together with the bloodguilty and bold tyrants who, O God, boast that they are Christians, have been vanquished and put to shame by these invincible knights and pious witnesses of Christ. These tyrants know of no other weapon or recourse than banishment, arrest, torture, burning, murder, and killing, even as the custom of the old serpent from the beginning has been, and as may still alas be witnessed daily in many places in our Netherlands.

Now this is our calling, this our doctrine, and the fruit of our labor, on account of which we are so horribly slandered and so hatefully persecuted. Whether or not all the prophets, apostles, and faithful servants of God have endured similar sufferings on account of their faithfulness, we willingly leave to all the pious to judge.

But as to my poor, weak, and imperfect life, I freely confess that I am a poor, miserable sinner, conceived in sin, of sinful seed, and sinfully brought forth. I can say with David that my sins are ever before me. My thoughts, words, and actions convict me. With the holy Paul I observe that in me, that is, in my flesh, dwelleth no good thing. Rom. 7:18. Nevertheless, I may boast this much in my weakness, that if this wicked, violent world could only hear our doctrine with patience (not ours, but Christ's) and in the true fear of God follow it submissively, then this would undoubtedly be a more Christian world and a better one than, alas, it is now.

I thank my God who made me willing with the holy Paul to hate the evil and to follow the good. And I could wish that I could with my own blood deliver this wicked world from its ungodly and evil nature and gain it to Christ, to fear the Lord with all the heart, to love, seek, and serve Him, to do right before Him, and to be an unblamable pious Christian. This is by His grace my only desire.

I hope through the mercy and assistance of the Lord that no one upon earth may with truth accuse me of an avaricious and luxurious life. Money and riches I do not have. Nor do I desire them, although some alas, from a perverted heart, say that I eat more roasted than they do seethed; and that I drink more wine than they do beer. My Lord and Master, Jesus Christ, was also called a winebibber and a glutton by the perverse. I trust that through the grace of the Lord I am innocent in this matter, and stand acquitted before God.

He who purchased me with the blood of His love, and called me, who am unworthy, to His service, knows me, and He knows that I seek not wealth, nor possessions, nor luxury, nor ease, but only the praise of the Lord, my salvation, and the salvation of many souls. Because of this, I with my poor, weak wife and children have for eighteen years[18] endured excessive anxiety, oppression, affliction, misery, and persecution. At the peril of my life I have been compelled everywhere to drag out an existence in fear. Yes, when the preachers repose on easy beds and soft pillows, we generally have to hide ourselves in out-of-the-way corners. When they at weddings and baptismal banquets revel with pipe, trumpet, and lute; we have to be on our guard when a dog barks for fear the arresting officer has arrived. When they are greeted as doctors, lords, and teachers by everyone, we have to hear that we are Anabaptists, bootleg preachers,[19]deceivers, and heretics, and be saluted in the devil's name. In short, while they are gloriously rewarded for their services with large incomes and good times, our recompense and portion must be fire, sword, and death.

Behold, my faithful readers, in such fear, poverty, misery, and danger of death have I, wretched man, performed to this hour, without alteration, the service of the Lord. And I hope through His grace to perform it to His glory as long as I linger in this tabernacle. What I and my faithful colleagues have sought or could have sought in performing these our heavy and dangerous duties is apparent to all well-disposed people, who may readily judge from the works and their reward.

Herewith I humbly entreat the reader for Jesus' sake to accept in love this my forced confession concerning my illumination, conversion, and calling and to receive it in a good spirit. I have made it out of great necessity so that the pious reader may know how it went, seeing that I am slandered by the preachers and am accused without foundation of truth of being called and ordained to this service by a seditious and heretical sect. He that feareth God let him read and judge.[20]

Again, that Gellius wants to force us out into the open with our doctrine has, I hope, been answered sufficiently above in connection with the matter of night preaching. Yet I would append these three questions.

[18] From 1536 to 1554 Menno was a hounded "hedge preacher." Soon after his becoming an Obbenite he married. Thereafter his wife, and later his children, suffered with him. *Ed.*

[19] The original has *Winckel-predikers,* a name used for centuries before Menno's time to designate persons who preached without sanction of the Catholic Church. The word *Hage-preeker* (usually, but incorrectly, translated "hedge-preacher") has the same connotation, *hage* being an old word meaning "unauthorized." *Tr.*

[20] Herewith ends the account of Menno's conversion which has often been lifted out and printed as a separate tract. *Ed.*

In the first place, whether a person who would persuade somebody by loose talk or force him into deep water, or to take poison, would not be a homicide, if he knew beforehand that death would result.

In the second place, since Gellius boasts to be a called preacher and preaches in public, I would ask: Why is he not moved to love and compassion for his own fatherland? Why does he not enter into Catholic territory? Why does he not hold forth his faith, sacraments, and doctrines contrary to the emperor's decree, tyranny, persecution, and permission—the things he demands of us?

Thirdly, since he will admit, as I suppose, and must admit according to Scriptures, that the avaricious, the proud, the haughty, the drunkards, the showy, the usurers, liars, and unrighteous persons cannot inherit the kingdom of God, and therefore are not Christians, therefore, I would ask him, Why does he not ignore the fear of the cross (a matter for which he blames us) and expel without all respect of person the impenitent ones of his church from the communion of his sacraments according to the doctrine and ordinance of the Holy Ghost, since it is God's express Word and ordinance? He would have us preach publicly, notwithstanding that he well knows that we can no more do so without the loss of life, than walk on water without sinking, or take poison without dying. For he and the learned ones have brought about such a state of affairs by their disgraceful slanders and preaching, that we are, alas, already tried and sentenced before we are apprehended. At the same time he praises the magistracy for obstructing us! And he knows very well how about ten years ago he treated one of our people who would gladly proclaim to the people from the pulpit the testimony he had in sincerity of heart. And he knows how he refused me a discussion of Scripture twice, as has been heard. And yet he writes that if we are true teachers, we should preach in public, while he himself, for the sake of a livelihood and and fear of the cross, does not preach his doctrine (however big or small it may be) in his own land, but has moved to another and freer country and there, although he can freely practice his doctrine and sacraments, neglects expulsion, Scriptural reproof, and the ordinances of God for fear of the cross. Now let the reasonable reader conclude from all this what kind of Christian, let alone preacher, he is, since he assigns to us miserable ones that which he himself does not touch with his little finger, as you may see.

If Gellius could take these three questions to heart and would consider them in a Scriptural light, and in the fear of God, he would be ashamed all his life that he so rudely attacks us, contrary to all love, reasonableness, sense, and Scripture, and that he under such a semblance so tyrannically strives after the ruin, blood, and death of the pious.

But to his writing that the prophetic and apostolic doctrine and sacraments should not be taught and dispensed in shops and corners, but in public, I would reply: We admit that Christ Jesus for the most part preached in public; however with such discretion that He sometimes avoided the raving,

storming crowd and walked no more among them, after they had resolved
upon His death; except when the time of His suffering had arrived (which
time was known to Him beforehand) and the prophecies were to be fulfilled.
Luke 21:32.

Similarly, although Jesus Christ sent His disciples to preach the Gospel to all people, to Gentiles as well as to Jews, He did not say nor ask
that they should serve nor dispense His sacraments, namely, baptism and
the Supper, before the eyes of the enemies of His Word. Therefore it is
obvious that Gellius accuses us of this without any truth or foundation of
Scripture. He accuses and reproaches not only us, but also Christ Jesus,
God's eternal Word and Wisdom Himself; for He celebrated His Holy
Supper at night in a secret place with a separated people. He also accuses
and reproaches Paul and the first apostolic church, which often held its brotherly meetings at night, in private gatherings, as has been said more than
sufficiently above. Do observe how openly he speaks against God's Word!

[7] *He writes further that our calling is not testified to by anything,
except that we not only fill the hearts of many with a mad and irreconcilable
hatred of all true servants of the church, no matter how pious they are, as
well as of all church ordinances, but inspire them with a contentious spirit and
a hostile mood.*

*Reply.* If hostile bitterness had not so entirely blinded the eyes of his
mind, and if but a small spark of the true Christian spirit were in him, then he
would soon acknowledge the precious fruits of true repentance. But now he
has fallen into such a blind mood, alas, that he calls the glorious fruits of the
Holy Spirit the fruits of the devil and new monkdom; and the heavy, pressing
cross of so many pious saints he terms a[21] cross of evildoers or heretics, matters which in my opinion are a grievous sin and gross slander.

The Pharisees said, This fellow doth not cast out devils, but by Beelzebub, the prince of devils, although they perceived mightily in their hearts
that it was the finger and power of God. Christ said that it was blaspheming
against the Holy Ghost. But what Gellius does against us I will leave to the
Lord.

God knows that I wish that I might deliver him and all the preachers
from their sore damnation, and that I would do it at the risk of my own life.
Behold, thus I "hate" him and all those who seek my life; even though we
must hear so much evil. And, I trust, by God's grace, that all who fear the
Word of the Lord will be of one mind with me. Notwithstanding this, he
writes that we hate with an irreconcilable hatred (which may God forbid);
and this for no other reason than that we in sincere and faithful love earnestly reprove the patent deceivers who walk in hypocritical sham, whom he calls
the true and pious servants of the church, and that we call false and unscriptural the use of infant baptism, together with all abuses which he calls church
ordinances, not only by the Spirit and Word of the Lord, but also by our

21 Reading *een* (one or a) instead of *en* (and) which does not make sense. *Tr.*

possessions and blood, and because we point to the crucified Christ Jesus, to His Spirit, Word, ordinances and to the doctrine and usage of his holy apostles.

I verily believe that a spiteful, envious person has no part in God's city. And if we, who are daily killed for our love, are still living in hatred and envy, then much suffering is done in vain.

I trust that I write the truth when I say that I am frightened at hatred and envy more than at fire and sword. Yet we must hear that we hate.

Behold, thus good is ever given the worst possible construction, and love is declared to be hatred. What sentence the Scriptures pronounce against such people may be seen from Isaiah 5.

[8] *He also accuses us saying that we do not agree, but quarrel among ourselves in regard to many articles of the Christian religion; namely, in regard to the fulfillment and abrogation of the Law, the justification of man, the deity and incarnation of Christ, the power of the magistrates, etc.*

*Reply.* I hope that I may write confidently, that we who are grains of one loaf are also of one mind in Christ Jesus. But even as in the times of the apostles, false teachers arose in the apostolic church, men who introduced and taught false doctrine, as may be read in their writings in many passages, false teachers who were after many admonitions separated from the communion of their church, if they did not repent; so also in our times. Satan never sits still. Paul says, There must be also heresies among you, that they who are approved may be made manifest among you. And if such close their ears to truth, reject admonitions, and start perverse sects, then they may no longer be our brethren, as the Scriptures teach. And so long as we do this in obedience to the holy Word, and in the true fear of God, we are sure in our consciences that we will be free of all sects, as also of all slander and evil, even though we must hear such charges from the world.

Since it is a fact well known to Gellius and his fellow preachers that peacebreakers and sect makers have absolutely no fellowship with us, but are and must be outside, unanimously expelled from us according to apostolic doctrine and usage, therefore it is very wrong of him, is it not, to revile so many pious persons (who hate discord and strife and disunity, and seek nothing but that they may humbly follow the crucified Jesus in the peace of their hearts), calling them troublemakers and so making them suspect with the world, with such an evil report and bad name.

If he should say that he counts them as being of us because they have at one time received the same baptism with us, then I would reply that then Peter, and Simon the sorcerer, Paul, and Phygellus, etc., would by that token also be all one. Then all papists, Lutherans, and Zwinglians, besides all thieves, murderers, sorcerers, perverts, fornicators, and scoundrels are one, for they have also received one baptism. This is incontrovertible.

Again, in regard to his accusation that we dispute among ourselves in regard to the fulfillment of the Law, the justification of man, the power of the magistracy, etc., I may say I hope that I can testify before the Lord and His church with a clear conscience, that I to my knowledge have disputed, or as Gellius calls it quarreled, with but one person in regard to the justification of man, and this one has already run to ruin. Nor have I ever discussed the fulfillment of the Law, or the power of the magistracy other than by way of brotherly instruction. What our confession and grounds are concerning the before-mentioned articles may be clearly seen in our writings.

O dear Lord, would that Gellius might recall his own words when he writes that the calling of the pious should not be weakened on account of the impious, and would that he had sufficient fear of God in him to draw back from the lies, violence, and injustice which he so wrongfully practices on us. For what does he do but purposely, and probably against his own sense of right, rob the pious of their good name so that he may obstruct the Word, and may make good his cause by making ours false and suspicious with open lies, lest his Pharisaic faithlessness be made manifest. Yes, he carries on as though he would say: Judas was a traitor and thief; therefore all the other apostles were traitors and thieves. Again, Simon the sorcerer was a scoundrel; therefore all the members of the apostolic churches were scoundrels, etc. He knows very well that we do not, and may not, allow sect makers, peacebreakers, and unscriptural agitators in the fellowship of the peaceful and pious, as has been said.

Oh, that he would leave the peace-loving unreviled, and that he could rightly discern the plentiful quarreling, bitter hatred, grievous division, rupture, and bickerings of all those who uphold infant baptism, could see how pathetically they are divided among themselves, that they are also so inflamed by envious zeal one against another that they not only call each other fanatics, violators of the sacraments; not only violate and blaspheme and send each other to hell, but they also, as is the custom with sects, reach for the sword against each other, destroying countries and peoples, cities and citizens, contrary to the meek nature, doctrine, and example of Christ Jesus and His apostles, as is evident.

Besides their learned men are so divided among themselves that we can scarcely find five or six in the whole country who agree in doctrine.

One includes everything in the providence and predestination of God, *quasi necessarium* (as if by necessity). Another denies it.

The third encloses Christ's flesh and blood in the bread and wine; the fourth takes it spiritually.

The fifth baptizes the children on their own faith; the sixth on the covenant with Abraham and its promise.

The seventh says that it is proper to persecute for the faith; the eighth denies it vigorously.

The ninth praises faith even where fruits or works are absent; the tenth says that faith must be active in love.

The eleventh says that the sacraments may be dispensed by the impenitent and perverse; the twelfth denies it. And many other like schisms exist among them.

Notwithstanding they call the godly, pious hearts and peaceable children of God who are zealous for God and His righteousness, as much as is in their power, who are bent on His Word and who know not of quarreling, a contentious sect and ungodly, deceiving conspirators, while they on the contrary are called peaceable, unanimous teachers; and the impenitent wicked world, the church and the people of God!

Behold, so plainly does the Lord let the wisdom of the wise become folly that to them Christ Jesus is Belial, and Belial Christ Jesus; light darkness, and darkness light; that they, alas, fail to notice the doctrine, life, power, confession, life and limb of the elect of God, but driven by contrariness, malice, hostility, and partisanship they give everything its worst possible thrust seeking all kinds of excuses to assail the pious, to blaspheme the truth, and to uphold unrighteousness, lest any be converted, repent, and sincerely seek and follow the Word of the Lord. O Lord! grant that they may be exposed.

[9] *He further writes: Nor is it the desirable fruit, but a shameful disgrace that they, contrary to the example of the prophets, of Christ, and of the apostles, constitute themselves a church, desecrate the Lord's Sabbath, forsake the public assemblies and worship, hate and upbraid the servants, and not only fail to examine the solicitous labors and prophecies of the ministers, contrary to the Holy Spirit's command and doctrine, but also boldly despise them, as well as the Sabbath commandment.*

*Reply.* Observe, reader, how beautifully they adorn lies, and how fearfully they suppress and despise truth under cover of virtue. The entire evangelical Scriptures teach us that the church of Christ was and is, in doctrine, life, and worship, a people separated from the world. Acts 2:42. It was that also in the Old Testament. And since the church always was and must be a separate people, as has been heard, and since it is as clear as the noonday sun that for many centuries no difference has been visible between the church and the world, but that they have without differentiation run together in baptism, Supper, life, and worship; a matter that although done in ignorance was plainly contrary to all Scripture, therefore we are constrained by the Spirit and Word of God, not of ourselves, to gather together to the praise of Christ Jesus, and to the service and salvation of our neighbors, not unto ourselves, but unto the Lord, a pious and penitent congregation or church out of all impure and deceiving sects of the whole world: not contrary to the doctrine and example of Christ Jesus and the apostles, as Gellius falsely accuses, but according to the Spirit, doctrine, and example of Jesus Christ (since He has manifested to us His Word and truth). We are constrained to gather them under the cross of misery in spite of all the violence and gates of hell, in patience, and not by force of arms and turmoil (as is the custom of the sects), and to separate them from the world, as the Scriptures teach, so that they may be an admonition, example, and Christian reproach to this reckless, impenitent generation, as has been heard already.

They keep and sanctify the Lord's Sabbath (which is now no longer literal, but spiritual,[22] and never terminating with the true Christians) not by wearing fine clothes, not by carousing, drinking, vanity, and idleness, as the unthinking world does on its external Sabbath and holy days, but by the fear of God, by a clear conscience and unblamable life, in love to God and their neighbors (which is the true religion) keeping and sanctifying it to the Lord eternally. They do not attend the public gatherings (which are, alas, not consecrated to Christ, but to Antichrist in all manner of vanity and hypocrisy, in pomp and splendor, held on their Sabbath and holy days in their impenitent church service, which tend to nothing but deception) in order that they may, out of a pure heart and fear of their God, in the gathering of the saints and the true service, convince the erring and thus make manifest the truth and true doctrine to the benefit and betterment of all mankind.

They do not hate and detest the open deceivers and false preachers who so miserably deceive the poor people, as Gellius makes bold to say they do, but they earnestly reprove them in love according to God's Spirit and Word, in order that they may repent and be converted, as the Scriptures teach us.

In short, they do not despise the commandment of the Holy Spirit, and the teachings of the Sabbath commandment, nor the painstaking labors and the prophecies of the true and faithful servants of Christ, nor the precious gifts of the Holy Spirit, as he very wrongly complains they do. But they omit at the risk of possessions and life, according to the counsel, doctrine, and admonition of the Holy Spirit and the power of the true Sabbath, the false labors, and the powerless, impenitent, and mercenary prophecies of the servants of Antichrist who do not serve Christ and the church, as they boast, but who serve their bellies and the world. And they do not dare to hear and follow them, as is right and proper according to the Scriptures of eternal truth, since their doctrines and fruits reveal them for what they are.

Their priests, says the Lord, teach for hire, and the prophets divine for money. They rely upon the Lord and say, Is not the Lord amongst us? No evil can betide us; therefore Zion shall be plowed like a field, and Jerusalem shall become heaps. Jer. 26:18; Mic. 3:12.

It is also manifest that Gellius and similar preachers have done the very thing of which he accuses us, for they, long before we did,[23] organized a special church, separated from the papists, as is known to all men and cannot be denied. But that we had to separate from them is their fault, we are sorry to say. For if we had found the right with them, we would have remained with them, but now, alas, we had to leave them at the cost of life and possessions, as may be seen.

Behold, my kind reader, here you have my simple reply to the main articles

---

[22] In agreement with the Christian Church of the first few centuries Menno does not associate the Lord's day with the Jewish Sabbath. *Ed.*

[23] The Dutch Obbenites had been in existence about two years before Menno united them in 1536. *Ed.*

concerning the vocation of the preachers, articles which Gellius so industriously brings forward in the defense of his cause and to the hurt of ours.

I have no doubt but that you, by the grace of God, will find a clear difference, explanation, and foundation in this matter, if you compare his writings with ours and judge according to the Word of the Lord by the manifest fruits on both sides.

This is the principal part of my exposition: that nobody can be a preacher called and well pleasing to God, a servant in the Lord's house and church, without the Holy Spirit which works in all true Christ-believers, nor without regeneration which transforms the heart from earthly to heavenly things through faith, nor without unfeigned love which seeks nothing but the praise of God and the salvation of one's neighbor, nor without the blessed pure Word which cuts and cleaves without respect of person, high or low, nor without the pious, unblamable life which is of God.

## [III.] BAPTISM

Of the baptism of believers I consider it wholly unnecessary to write much here, why we teach that it shall be received and practiced upon faith, for we have explained this matter lately by so many plain Scriptures and reasons to the intelligent reader, that he can plainly see and palpably feel the foundation and truth.

Therefore I will omit this and turn to the main article and arguments with which Gellius undertakes to defend his infant baptism as apostolic and Christian, in order to rebut them with the Scriptures. I hope by the grace of God to do this with such clearness and power that all intelligent readers who read thoughtfully may perceive that Gellius can no more stand before the holy ordinance, Word, and truth of the Lord with his infant baptism, than he can with his view of the vocation of preachers.

Before I take the matter up, I would, not without cause, relate to the kind reader what happened some years ago when I had a discussion with John a Lasco, Gellius, and Hermes. We had a lengthy discussion concerning baptism and they granted that the Scriptures which make mention of the matter speak of adults or believing ones. We at last got to the subject of infant baptism, which according to their opinion (although without Scripture) was also right. At last, after discussion and after many unscriptural assertions put forth by them, I put forth two questions and prayed them for God's sake to answer them Scripturally. The first was: Does a ceremony which is practiced without the command of God, have any promise? They answered, No. Then I asked them in the second place: Is not such a ceremony, which is practiced without the command of God, idolatry? They answered, Yes.

When I heard them answer these questions correctly, I said: Very well, worthy sirs, what then becomes of your infant baptism? They all three simultaneously answered: Yes, dear Menno, if you insist upon a command, then show us where it is commanded that we should baptize believers. When I heard this, I was very much alarmed, for I perceived that in fact they were activated by nothing but partisanship and carnality. I pointed them to the sixteenth chapter of Mark, where the Lord speaks, Go ye into all the world, and preach the gospel to every creature. He that believeth, and is baptized shall be saved. Mark 16:16. But this was no command in their eyes. Then I referred them to the twenty-eighth chapter of Matthew, where the Lord says, Go ye therefore and teach all nations, or as the Hebrew[24] text has it, Make all nations disciples and baptize them (some translations having, baptizing them) in the name of the Father, and the Son and the Holy Ghost. Neither did this satisfy them, for we read, said they, *baptizing,* and not *baptize them,* although, alas, they knew very well that the surest text, namely, the Hebrew, has this in the imperative mood, *and baptize them,* a thing which I had not until then noticed as I read.

Behold, so willfully did they contend against the plain Word and truth of God that they openly denied it to be a command, although they had many times read, also according to the Lutheran translation, that the Lord enjoined it as an express command, saying, *and baptize them.*

When I perceived that they were taking refuge behind a participle, I proposed saying, If I command my servant saying, Go and plow the ground, sowing it with wheat; as the Lord said, Go and teach all nations, baptizing them, etc., then have I not (I ask) commanded my servant to plow the land and to sow it with wheat, although I used the participle sowing, just as the participle baptizing is used in the passage? They answered that this was philosophy and not Scripture. Behold, my reader, thus clumsily they sought to deny the truth!

Seeing that they, although with vanquished hearts, obstinately persevered (as did the Pharisees) in falsehood, and would not yield to the powerful and plain truth, I was much chagrined and said, Ah, men, since I find that you indeed in perversity of heart, reject God's truth, and delight in falsehood, I will be silent and speak not another word with you concerning this matter; for, alas, it is all in vain!

Reader, in the day of the appearance of Jesus Christ, before His impartial and eternal judgment, it will be found true as I write here.

Behold, so dishonestly do they deal with God's precious and eternal truth that they at that time pretended that there was no command to baptize the believers, and now they have an abundance of commands to baptize the unconscious children. O God! thus they play with the souls of men and they know not how to garble, bend, and break the sure foundation of truth so that they may remain on the broad way without the cross, may please the world, and lead a careless life according to the lusts of the flesh.

[1] *Gellius says first of all in regard to this matter, that we blasphemously sin against the holy church because we say that children cannot believe, cannot*

---

[24] Menno here twice writes *"Hebrew,"* perhaps absent-mindedly, when he should have written *"Greek."* Ed.

*repent, and cannot obey the Word of the Lord although they constitute, so he says, a great part of the church and are referred to in plain and clear words by the prophet Joel in the preaching of repentance, etc.*

*Reply.* His beginning is unscriptural and unscriptural will his end be. Observe, the Word of God shall be our judge. Tell me, is it not a great blindness in him to undertake to include unconscious children in the preaching of repentance? And then he himself admits a little later that they cannot because of their immature understanding understand the doctrine, which is a doctrine of penitence. But if they cannot grasp the doctrine, how can they then believe it; and if they do not believe, how can they then repent; and if they do not repent, how can they be included in the preaching of repentance? If they then have neither doctrine, faith, nor repentance, which he admits they cannot have on account of their undeveloped understanding (and which is not necessary since they are God's own while sin has not become alive in them to bring forth fruit), therefore, all of sound judgment must admit, must they not, that he reproves himself and shows that he wrongfully accuses us when he says that we speak blasphemously against the Holy Ghost when we say that little children cannot repent, believe, nor obey. For he himself admits that they, in the immaturity of their understanding, cannot understand the doctrine from which faith, repentance, and obedience must come, as has been said already.

[2] *In the second place, he writes that there is but one church and one faith, in the Old and New Testament, from the time of Adam to the end of the world. And he says that from the time of Abraham, under the Old Testament, there was given the commandment of preaching and circumcising; and in the New Testament, preaching and baptizing, without regard to the age of persons, etc., unto the gathering, edification, growth, and increase of the church.*

*Reply.* I understand it that all those from the time of Adam to the present have had and shall have the Spirit of Christ, who in the power of the same Spirit have walked and shall walk in truth, each in his own time: that these are the Lord's church, kingdom, and people—this I grasp. But Gellius should have added that each dispensation has its own doctrine, ordinance, and usage. From the time of Adam to Abraham no ceremony was practiced on children because the Lord had not commanded it; circumcision was commanded from Abraham to the time of Christ. But now we have Christ, the promised prophet to whom all the Scriptures point. Through Him we hear and obey the eternal Word and wisdom of God. All we who abide in His doctrine walk in the truth (for His Word is truth, and His command is eternal life, John 12:17), and we must obey whatever ordinance this wise Counselor has made concerning the children of the New Testament. What He has enjoined and what He has not enjoined concerning them all pious, faithful hearts may search in His holy Word.

But when Gellius says that in the New Testament preaching and baptizing take place without differentiation as to age, this is in my opinion so flatly contrary to Scripture, common sense, and his own words, that he should properly be ashamed of himself for the assertion. For what can we teach a little, irrational child unto repentance by the Word of God? Christ wants us to preach the Gospel to those who have understanding, and to baptize those who believe it. Nor has He left in His Gospel any other command, ordinance, or example concerning this matter.

Besides, Gellius acknowledges that the children, on account of their lack of understanding, cannot grasp the doctrine, as already heard. Yet he writes in the face of this plain ordinance of the Almighty God, and his own confession, that in the New Testament teaching and baptizing are commanded without respect to age. Behold, thus bluntly do they err who reject the Word of the Lord. Is this not violently expelling Christ and introducing Antichrist in His stead? And is it not manifestly wrong? I must admit that I have never read a word in the Scripture with such a mind.

[3] *In the third place, Gellius writes that a church, according to the command of God which changes not (as he says), is not more severe and wrathful toward our progeny and children (since they are children of the promise), than toward the children born to Israel after the flesh. The church gives to them the seal of the covenant of grace because of the fellowship which they have with the covenant or promise of God, with salvation, the church, and eternal life, according to the words, I will be your God, and the God of your seed. And he asserts that in this way in the assembly of the church, one and the same command, not two different commands, were in force, both as to the preaching and the use of the sacraments.*

*Reply.* Gellius carries on as did all the false prophets who so miserably deceived the people, saying, Thus saith the Lord of lords, although the Lord had not spoken it, as Scripture informs us. Jer. 23:17; Ezek. 13:7. Say, reader, is it not a presumptuous deed and a condemnable audacity to dare to publish to the whole world that God has commanded it, even though the eternal Wisdom has neither commanded it by word nor deed? Read the New Testament through, from beginning to end, and if a word can be found that the mouth of the Lord has commanded it, or that the apostles have anywhere taught or practiced it, then we will, by the grace of God, unanimously admit that he is right.

Inasmuch then as it is clear that nothing has been mentioned concerning it [infant baptism] in all the Holy Scriptures, as has been said, and that he nevertheless dares to write that they do it according to the command of God, therefore the pious reader may observe how sadly he sins against his God, especially since truth is now manifest. How lamentably he deceives the poor souls with open falsehood when he writes that God commanded it; for the Holy Spirit, I say, has not taught of it in a single word, nor manifested it unto the church of God by word or the practice of the true witnesses of Christ.

His assertion that the command is not altered is so baldly and boldly opposed to truth that we may well wonder at it. The Scriptures clearly testify that God promised Abraham the multiplying of his seed, and the land of Canaan as an eternal inheritance, and in this way it was commanded him that he should circumcise himself, his son Ishmael, etc., also all male children of eight days; for it was a covenant in the flesh. And similarly the blood-sign of the circumcision of the foreskin, on the eighth day of their age, of all the male children and not the female children, etc., was commanded to believing Abraham at the promise of the multiplication of his seed and the possession of the land of Canaan. But to us the blood-sign of circumcision is not commanded, but baptism in the water. Note the first difference: not on the eighth day, but when we, through the service of the Spirit, in faith, are born of God, and have become followers of Abraham. Observe the second change: not only the males, but both males and females; they who through the preaching of the holy Word bury the old life of sin and with Christ arise in newness of life; they who are pricked in their hearts; they who circumcise their minds and hearts; they who put on Christ, and who have the testimony of a clear conscience before God. Observe the third change: not to possess a literal kingdom and land, and to become a great people upon the earth, as was promised to Abraham and his seed. Rather, for the sake of the Word and its witness to bear all manner of anxiety, distress, and misery upon earth; to turn the heart away from all visible and perishable things; to die unto pomp, pride, the world, flesh and blood, and thus to walk in our weakness as Christ has walked in His perfection. Notice the fourth change [from prosperity to persecution].

Behold, reader, how openly he falsifies the Scriptures and how mightily he perverts the truth when he writes that the command is unchanged; that in the gathering of the churches under the Old and New Testament one and the same, and not two different, commandments are given, both as to preaching and the use of the sacraments—when it is all changed and renewed, as may be clearly gathered from the foregoing references. I will leave to your reflections if such a thing may not be called perverting truth into falsehood.

And when he says that the church is not more ungracious and stern to our children than to the children, as to the flesh, born of Israel, I understand him to say that if God does not want our children baptized, He is less gracious to them than He was to the children of the circumcision; by which he openly testifies that he attaches the kingdom, grace, and promise of God to that sign. If God is gracious only to such children as have received, or will receive that outward sign, then it must incontrovertibly follow that God has been ungracious and wrathful to all the children before the law of circumcision, as well as to all children under the law who died before the eighth day in the wilderness, as well as to all the girls and women, because they were not circumcised. And then He must also be displeased with all the children under the New Testament, for He has not given any command to baptize them.

Oh, no! To children belongs the kingdom of God, not by virtue of any sign, but by grace alone through Christ Jesus. Matt. 19:14. And as to his calling infant baptism a sealing of the covenant of grace, I would reply, if he can produce a plain passage in all the New Testament where the baptism of the believers is called a sealing of the covenant of grace, then he will have won the

case. But I know of a certainty that he can never do so. If the baptism of the
believers, which is ordained of God Himself, is not called this, how then can
infant baptism which is not ordained of God, be called this; a mere human
invention and fiction of man?

If he should appeal to circumcision, then I would say that there are two
distinct and different signs, that the first is not the same as the second, and that
for these following reasons: First, because all the signs before the law and
under it, given to the patriarchs, such as the coats of skin to Adam, the rainbow
to Noah, the circumcision to Abraham, the yearly offering of the high priests—
all unitedly pointed to Christ who has now appeared, and in whom all the preceding signs are fulfilled. We have now no sealing or assurance through outward signs and symbols, but through the true Sign of all signs, Christ Jesus.
As He Himself says, As Moses lifted up the serpent in the wilderness, even so
must the Son of man be lifted up, that whosoever believeth in him should not
perish, but have eternal life. For God so loved the world that he gave his only
begotten Son. John 3:14-16. Secondly, we are not now a people of the letter,
as was Israel, but a people of the Spirit, who, before they come to the sign, are
already turned to God, through the preaching of repentance; who die unto the
old sinful life; upon whom the light of grace shines in their hearts; who accept
the true Sign of peace, Christ Jesus, through faith; arise with Him into new
life; and are thus sealed in their hearts through the promise of the Holy Ghost
and the eternal covenant of the divine grace. For if we were not sealed in our
hearts before the sign, then we could not truly repent before the sign; nor could
we take upon ourselves the reproach, disgrace, anxiety, tribulation, and misery
of the cross.

But by the sign, which we accept in obedience to the holy Word, we testify
that we, through Christ (who is the true sign of grace, given us by the Father,
made known to us through the Word), have peace with God, and that we are
sealed with the Spirit of His grace.

Behold, my reader, here you may now observe that the signs of the New
Testament do not seal or assure us, as the learned ones teach the poor people;
but that our only eternal surety is Christ Jesus; that the sealing of our hearts
is the Holy Spirit, and that the signs or sacraments are given to the penitent,
sealed, and secured Christians, for no other purpose but to admonish and remind us that we should walk in continual repentance; that we should exercise
our faith by them, and that we should eternally give praise to the Lord for His
inexpressibly great kindness and grace through Christ Jesus.

All who teach you differently, and point you to bread and wine or water
as something by which you are sealed or secured, as Gellius does here—as
though you get something thereby—these point you away from the true reality
to the signs, from Christ back to Moses, and give you a vain hope and a false
security so that you remain impenitent and without Christ all your lifetime.
For you console yourself so much with the signs that you remain without the
signified truth, as may, alas, be plainly seen in the case of the whole world.

For no matter how drunken, covetous, showy, vain, and untruthful they may be, they still boast themselves Christians. They are so consoled with this godless sealing by the idolatrous water (I say godless sealing because it is so flatly contrary to the Word of God), and with the bread and wine of the preachers, that they one and all walk upon the broad way, and remain without the Word of God.

This is the actual fruit and effect of the sealing of Gellius, which he praises so highly and teaches so beautifully.

But as to the saying: I will be your God and the God of your seed after you, from which they conclude that even as the children of Abraham were circumcised with him on account of one and the same promise, so also our children should be baptized, I would reply as follows: To Abraham was the promise given that God would be his God and his children's God after him. In this promise the females were included, no less than the males. This must be admitted. Notwithstanding, Israel did not circumcise the females, although included in the promise, but only the males, and that because God had so ordained it. From which it may be plainly educed that the male children of the seed of Abraham were not circumcised for the sake of the promise but for the sake of the commandment enjoined upon Abraham and his seed. If it had been done on account of the promise, and not because of the commandment, then the females should also have been circumcised, as fellow participants and heirs of the same promise. This is incontrovertible.

In the second place I would say: If Israel had followed the doctrine of Gellius and some other preachers in this matter, then they would also have circumcised the females, notwithstanding they were not commanded to do so; for they were fellow partakers of the covenant of grace, even as our children (a thing for which they want to have them baptized) are joint heirs of the promise.

If they should answer that the ordinance referred to the males and not to the females, although the females were also children of grace, then I would reply that their cause is already lost. For even as the command of circumcision at that time had reference only to the males and not to the females (although the females had the same promise), so also does now the ordinance of baptism have reference to the believing and penitent and not to irrational children, although they are joint heirs of the promise, as has been heard.

If they say further: If infant baptism is not commanded neither is it forbidden, then I would reply: The circumcision of females was neither commanded nor prohibited, even as infant baptism is neither commanded nor prohibited, yet they did not circumcise the females, and that because they were not commanded to do so.

Therefore all who censure us because we do not baptize our children, who are fellow heirs of the promises and are not prohibited from being baptized, these also censure Israel because they did not circumcise their female children, who were fellow heirs of the promises and were not prohibited from being circumcised.

Thirdly, I would say, Since I notice that Gellius includes only the children of believing, and not those of unbelieving parents in baptism, and since he well knows that the proud, avaricious, pompous, envious, bloodguilty, harlotous, and idolatrous persons do not believe, nor according to the Scripture have any promise; therefore I cannot be astounded sufficiently at his inattention, that he, against his own belief and doctrine, still baptizes the children of such parents, whom he must acknowledge to be without God and Christ, and therefore have no promise. If he says that he does not know the faith of every man, then I would reply that he then acknowledges in the first place that his infant baptism has an unstable foundation, if we, according to his own words, are to baptize them upon the promise of their parents, although he does not know whether the parents believe or not.

And in the second place he then acknowledges that such parents are trees without fruit, and lights without glow.

But why talk at length! If Gellius were to tell all his show-offs, drunkards, usurers, and unrighteous people without respect of person that they are without Christ and have no promise, and bar their children from baptism, he would not long remain a preacher at Emden, nor enjoy his easy, carefree life in peace.

*He writes further that Paul asserts that baptism has taken the place of circumcision, that it has one and the same signification, and that it is called the circumcision of Christ, etc.*

*Reply.* In this matter Paul himself will rebuke him for misconstruing his saying. For he says, Beware, lest any man spoil you through philosophy and vain deceit, after the tradition of men, after the rudiments of the world, and not after Christ. For in him dwelleth all the fulness of the Godhead bodily. And ye are complete in him, which is the head of all principality and power: in whom also ye are circumcised with the circumcision made without hands, in putting off the body of the sins of the flesh by the circumcision of Christ: buried with him in baptism, wherein ye are also raised with him through the faith of the operation of God, who hath raised him from the dead. And you, being dead in your sins, and in the uncircumcision of your flesh, hath he quickened together with him, having forgiven you all trespasses. Col. 2:8-13.

My faithful reader, observe the Word of the Lord. The doctrine of the New Testament and His sacraments treat of none but of those who have ears to hear and hearts to understand. For it is a service of the Spirit, and not of the letter, as Paul says. II Cor. 3:6.

Seeing then that the preachers point the poor, simple people to the elements, water, bread, and wine, and teach that baptism seals us, makes fast and sure that we are in the covenant of grace, that God works effectively in His sacraments, etc.; and since we find however that neither the sealing, certainty, nor power are found in their hearts at all, but that they are led by the preachers to a false boast, vain hope, and uncertain certainty under the semblance of the Gospel; therefore, I would faithfully admonish all my readers and hearers with these afore-mentioned words from Paul, not to be deceived by such high-sounding, fair words by the philosophy and deception of men, nor by the hypocrisy and worldly institution of the learned ones, but to follow after the perfect institutor, Christ Jesus, in whom dwells bodily the entire perfection of the Godhead, truth, light, power, righteousness, etc., and who therefore does not point His own to uncertain, deceitful, dark, and unrighteous ways, but in Him all true Christians are complete and full of His grace, love, and power.

He is the head of all principalities, before whom every knee shall bow, and whom all tongues shall confess that He is the Lord, and that besides Him there is no other. Therefore His Word shall avail and His commandment must stand, and not that which the world proposes for His kingdom or church. All regenerate children of Christ, who are of His Spirit, are not now circumcised with hands and knife, as was the case with literal Israel, but with the Word of God, His Spirit and power, in the impure foreskins of their hearts so that they are become in the Spirit a new regenerate Israel and people of God, by dying unto their sinful flesh, and by restraining the old man through the circumcision of Christ which purifies and reverses their hearts through His Word and Spirit. Seeing that the penitent are by baptism buried with Him, die unto the old sinful life, and arise in the new life of righteousness and virtue, by means of faith which God works by the preaching of His powerful Word and the inspiration of His Holy Spirit in all who believe, therefore the faithful God and Father who has raised His Son from the dead, has also shown His power to us miserable sinners, and has graciously resurrected us, who were dead in the circumcision of our sinful flesh in so many gross sins and trespasses, unto the new life with Him; He has called us from darkness unto light, and has placed us in the heavenlies together with Christ Jesus.

Behold, dear reader, this is the real position and meaning of the words of Paul, words by which Gellius tries to prove that baptism has taken the place of circumcision and is called the circumcision of Christ.

Now judge, if you fear God, whether you find a word in Paul that was said of minor children. That this saying of Paul has reference to the believing and penitent ones, and not to irrational children, all reasonable persons, to say nothing about spiritual persons, must acknowledge and grant. And yet he writes that this saying implies that baptism has taken the place of circumcision and is called Christ's circumcision. He does not notice, or will not notice, that the circumcision of Jesus Christ to which Paul refers is done without hands, and that he administers daily with his hands his infant baptism, which he calls the circumcision of Jesus. Behold, thus lamentably does he falsify Paul, and thus violently does he break the Word of God.

If now he wants to seek an evasion or adorn his cause, saying that God works effectively through His sacraments, invisibly in the heart, that which the sign represents, then the deceit will be the more evident. For how will God operate through a sign which is an abomination in His eyes? I say an abomination, because He has not commanded it, and because neither doctrine, confession, faith, nor repentance, the things which these signs represent, go before. Then, also, the sign and the things signified must be one and the same, which never was nor ever will be the case, unless the letter become spirit. This is incontrovertible. Yes, my reader, how the baptized children are circumcised with the circumcision of Christ Jesus in the foreskin of their hearts, the circumcision of the New Testament, that the deeds and the fruits of the whole world, alas, plainly show!

[4] *In the fourth place he writes: As in the Scriptures which testify that women participate in the merits of Christ, and are disciples, a command is implied that the Holy Supper shall be dispensed to them, so also do the Scriptures which testify that children are of the church of Christ and of the kingdom of God, imply the commandment that they should be baptized.*

*Reply.* The words of Gellius prove clearly that women are entitled to the Lord's Supper; for he acknowledges that they are disciples. If they are disciples, as indeed they are, then it is manifest that they hear the Word of God, believe, repent, suffer themselves to be baptized, and that they are partakers of His mysteries, endowed in power with the effective thing of the Holy Supper. Since they are believing and penitent disciples, as has been heard, therefore it is reasonable and right, is it not, that they should employ the sign, whereby this mystery of faith, and of the holy Gospel, are represented to the believing ones and urged upon the repenting. Even as we cannot deny that the believing, repenting women have the reality and the thing signified in the Holy Supper, namely, the remembrance of the sacrifice of the flesh and blood of Christ, the love of God and their neighbors, etc., the very things for which it was instituted by the Lord, therefore they should have a place at the Lord's table, as believing, penitent disciples and guests.

Now Gellius, to make his infant baptism of effect, must prove and show to us by works, Scripture, and truth, that minor children have the reality and signified thing of holy baptism, namely, faith, repentance, obedience to the Word, a bold and peaceful conscience, etc., the very things for which the sign of baptism was instituted by the Lord, even as the believing, penitent women possess the essence of the Holy Supper. But if he cannot do this, then it is sufficiently proved that this his assertion and argument from similarity are not acording to the Scriptures, but deceitful, false, and contrary to God's Word.

He writes further that if such a command to baptize children, as he has adduced from Scripture, is not enough, then he wants us to point out a prohibition in God's Word, proving that it is God's will that we bar children from baptism.

To this I reply: In the first place, Gellius herewith openly shows that he regrets that his reference to the command of infant baptism cannot in his own opinion stand with Scripture. For he turns from the doctrine of commands and wants us to point out a prohibition, never observing that if one wants to partake of anything, namely, of ceremony, he must first adduce and point out the institution or command.

If he wants to defend the infant baptism which he teaches and practices, then let him prove that is it commanded, and not ask us to point out or show where it is prohibited.

We practice baptism in a manner as the mouth of the Lord has commanded, for we know that it is written, What thing soever I command you, observe to do it; thou shalt not add thereto nor diminish from it. Deut. 12:32. Yes, my reader, I offer Gellius and the learned ones the entire Scriptures, if they can find an instance in all the Scriptures where the pious and faithful men of God have changed a letter of all the commands, and ceremonies, and that they have practiced them otherwise than God had commanded them. Then we will reflect further upon the matter. But we know of a certainty that it cannot be done.

The Lord commanded Israel that they should circumcise their male children on the eighth day. There was not a letter that they should not do it on the fifth, sixth, seventh,[25] ninth, or tenth day. They never circumcised a female; nor did they circumcise on the seventh nor the ninth day. For the ordinance and command of the Lord insisted on the eighth day, and the male children; and not on the seventh or ninth day nor the female children, as has been heard.

If now they had circumcised the females, or if they had circumcised the males before or after the eighth day, although it was not expressly forbidden, they would still have committed an abomination, as Nadab and Abihu did with the strange fire, and they would have circumcised without God's Word. By the grace of God, no man can with Scripture take this away from me.

It was also commanded to Israel to eat the paschal lamb in remembrance of their deliverance and departure out of Egypt, on the fourteenth day of the first month, in the evening. It had to be a male lamb, without blemish, of the first year, etc. Ex. 12:5. Israel did so and never offered a ewe lamb, but always a male, although the Lord has not, with a single letter, forbidden the offering of the ewe lamb; for if they had offered a ewe lamb, they would have acted contrary to the command which stipulated that it should be a male.

In the second place I say—appealing to the testimony of the Almighty and great God, who says, This is my beloved Son in whom I am well pleased; hear ye him—If Gellius can point to a single word of divine truth and unadulterated testimony of the Holy Scriptures, that this Son of God so testified to, Christ Jesus, the Father's eternal Truth and Wisdom, has taught or commanded one word concerning infant baptism, or that His holy apostles or heralds have taught it, or that they at any time or place baptized infants, then I will recant, willingly submit to dungeons and bonds, confess my fault, repent, and stand before the whole world conquered and shamed. This I promise in sincerity of heart.

But if he cannot do so, as he never can, and if he still clings to infant bap-

---

[25] The word *eighth* is printed in error and obviously should be deleted. But it appears in the Dutch. *Tr.* and *Ed.*

tism, calling it apostolic and right, thereby forsaking the ordinances of Christ and the apostles' doctrine and usage, consoling the people in their impenitence, then it is manifest, is it not, that he is a deceiver of poor souls and a falsifier of the holy Word, who wants to be wiser than the Son of God Himself. For he says that it [infant baptism] is a sealing of the covenant of grace, an incorporation into the church of Christ, etc. And the great Lord has not at all spoken reproaching the Holy Spirit for failing to mention in the Scriptures this doctrine and usage; nor reproaching the apostles for not divulging unto the pious such an important matter, as he says, and for not testifying thereof in a single word in all their writings, and thus revealing it unto their successors.

In the third place I would refer Gellius and all his preachers to Luther, who writes very clearly that we should renounce not only that which is contrary to the Word of the Lord, but also that which came up alongside of it. And he advises everybody (although, alas, he himself did not follow this advice) to follow certainties and not uncertainties, seeing that the Scriptures admit of no addition nor diminution (a matter by which he has caused no little rupture in popery). If the Scriptures do not tolerate it and we find nowhere a word in Scripture commanding infant baptism, as Luther himself admits in his *Contra Anabaptistas,* then I would leave it to the impartial judgment of all who have understanding, whether infant baptism is not thereby prohibited.

[5] *In the fifth place Gellius writes: Their assertion that children have no ears to hear, and cannot distinguish between good and evil, says he, does not prove that the sacrament of the incorporation into the church does not belong to them; for the children of the Old Testament church had no such ears either, and could as little distinguish between good and evil, as can our children now.*

*Reply.* Just as soon as Gellius has proved the command, ordinance, or usage of the Lord, that we shall incorporate them by such a sign, then we will consider the matter further. But such proof he will lack.

We say with the holy Paul, Blessed be the God and Father of our Lord Jesus Christ, who has blessed us with all spiritual blessings in heavenly places in Christ: according as he hath chosen us in him before the foundation of the world, that we should be holy, and without blame before him in love; having predestinated us unto the adoption of children by Jesus Christ to himself, according to the good pleasure of his will, to the praise of the glory of his grace. Eph. 1:3-6.

My faithful reader, understand well what these words of Paul imply. This paternal adoption unto sonship; this great favor, love, and grace through Christ Jesus; this holy, unblamable life in love, of which Paul speaks here, is preached by the Gospel. All who rightly believe it, and are through faith truly converted, changed, renewed, and born of God, who partake of the Holy Spirit, these are children of the covenant, graciously accepted of God, and blessed with all spiritual blessings in heavenly places in Christ; even before they have come to the sign of baptism.

Behold, thus we are by God's election through faith in Christ Jesus, and by the impulsion and renewal of the Holy Spirit, incorporated into the body of Christ, which is the true church, and we become flesh of His flesh and bone of His bone; and this not through any external sign.

But this rule does not at all apply to minor children. For they have no ears to hear nor hearts to understand. Nevertheless they are in grace, children of the kingdom, heirs of the promise; not through any outward sign I say, but by the adoption of grace in the reconciliation, mediation, and merits of the death and blood of Christ, as the Scriptures teach. The New Testament treats with those of years of discretion, and its sacraments belong to the penitent. Let this be to you a sure and eternal doctrine and principle.

All those who philosophize differently concerning the signs of the New Testament, and who praise and recommend these signs before one has faith, deceive you, however beautifully they may adorn it with borrowed words such as sealing, sign of grace, incorporation, etc., for it is in essence nothing but human wisdom, deception of souls, and hypocrisy against God's Word. If the children under the old covenant were incorporated by circumcision, and the children under the new covenant by baptism, as he says, then I conclude mightily from his own words that the children who died before the eighth day, and those who were left in the wilderness, besides all the females, were not in the Israelitic church, and consequently had no grace, covenant, nor promise. So also our children, who through death are hindered from baptism. Oh, abomination and blasphemy! If that is not binding God's election, grace, favor, love, kingdom, covenant, and salvation to the element water, and to the rite, I will leave to the judgment of all the godly and pious.

[6] *In the sixth place he complains saying we have always received in return for our diligence and clear, convincing explanation of the Scriptures, yes, for our faithful care to bring them back to the right way, naught but revilings. For what do we hear from them, but that we are wolves, bloodhounds, receivers, etc., who run without commission and bring forth no fruit?*

*Reply.* All those who genuinely seek our salvation and rightly teach the Word of the Lord, and walk before us with an unblamable life (understand, according to the doctrine, Spirit, and example of Christ Jesus) are not reproached by us, nor by the Scriptures! but we thank and love them from the heart, and hope by the grace of God never to despise their brotherly diligence and fatherly care, but in pure love and with many thanks we will receive them, and as much as we in our weakness are able to do, follow them. But that Gellius and the preachers are reproachfully called deceivers, false prophets, rending wolves, men guilty of blood, etc., by the Scriptures is not our fault, but theirs; seeing they so lamentably falsify the Scriptures; reject Christ Jesus and His Spirit, Word, and walk; preach according to their own pleasure; seek improper gain; teach and walk to suit the world; rend the poor sheep by their false doctrine and deceiving sham; upbraid, blaspheme, belie, and betray the pious faithful hearts, delivering them to the sword of the magistracy and executioner, as may, alas, be too clearly witnessed at many different places.

Yes, reader, if he is unable to bear to be called certain hard names of which he is guilty according to the Scriptures, let him consider how shamefully he accuses with pen and tongue in his hostile, seditious doctrine of blood, the poor, miserable souls who are quite innocent, calling them godless sects, apostles of the devil, deceived conspirators, bootleg preachers, secret infiltrationists, sowers of tares, etc., before the whole world, thus depriving the innocent of property, welfare, honor, blood, and life; and making the unmerciful, cruel tyrants feel free to rob, imprison, banish, and murder. My faithful reader, reflect, and see if I do not write the truth.

[7] *In the seventh place he writes: The example of the apostles is for us an emphatic command; for the Holy Spirit testifies that the apostles baptized whole households, children not excepted, which surely would have been excepted if it were wrong to baptize them.*

To this I reply, in the first place, that Gellius hereby shows that he has no command for infant baptism; for he grounds his doctrine and faith upon presumption and not upon a commanding word, by which all things are to be judged that are to please the Lord.

In the second place, I say that the Holy Spirit has testified in clear print that the three families of which the Scriptures make mention in particular, saying they were baptized, were all believing persons as may be plainly understood from reading Acts 10:33, 34 as to the household of Cornelius; Acts 16:15, of the household of the jailer; I Cor. 16:15, of the household of Stephanas in good clear report.

But as to the house of Lydia, it is plain that she at that time had no husband; for the house is assigned to her, which is neither the custom of the world nor of the Scriptures if there is a husband. Since the New Testament then makes mention of but four households and three of them were believing, and the fourth, as it appears, had no husband, as has been heard, how much then we should press the idea that there were little children in these households both nature and the Scriptures teach us!

*He further writes that it cannot be gainsaid that the children, all through the Scriptures, are always included in a house, or household; for a house or household includes both young and old; therefore children should also be included when the Scriptures mention that whole households were baptized.*

*Reply.* As soon as Gellius proves to us, with God's Word, that minor children believe, then we would gladly count them among the believing, baptized households and allow them to be baptized. But since he cannot possibly do so, we would faithfully admonish him and all the preachers to take heed how and what they say concerning this matter; for all they philosophize and propose about it is mere deceit. Besides I would ask him if we can cause little irrational children to believe by means of God's Word, or to disbelieve by means of false doctrine. If he says Yes, then his answer is contrary to all the Scriptures, to common sense, and to his own words, for he admits that they, because of their lack of understanding, cannot comprehend the Word. But if he says No, then he admits that by including both old and young as one household, he has gone contrary to Paul. For Paul says (Titus 1:10) that the vain talkers and deceivers subvert whole houses, something which cannot be done to little children, because of their deficient understanding, as he himself admits.

He also says that we too boldly exclude the children, which the Holy Spirit has not excluded, etc. To this I reply: The Holy Spirit has commanded and ordained that we should teach the understanding ones, and baptize the believing ones, and this ordinance we follow. Therefore, it is not boldness, but obedience, when we do as the mouth of the Lord has commanded us. But whether the preachers are not bold against the Holy Spirit, who reject His doctrine, counsel, and ordinance as heretical and sectarian, and institute instead a doctrine and ordinance to suit their own taste, of which we find not a single word in the Scriptures, this I will leave to those who fear God and to His Word, to judge.

As to his appeal to Tertullian, Cyprian, Origen, and Augustine, I would reply: If these writers can support their assertions with the Word and ordinance of God, then we will admit that they are right. But if not, then it is the doctrine of men, and accursed by the Scriptures. Gal. 1:8. In the second place I say, Rhenanus annotates Tertullian[26] saying that it was customary with the ancients to baptize adults with the baptism of regeneration.

Cyprian,[27] the martyr, left infant baptism optional.

Erasmus of Rotterdam[28] writes that the ancients have disputed much concerning infant baptism, and never came to a conclusion.

Zwingli writes: Although we know that the ancients baptized children, yet it was not so general as it is in our time, but they were publicly instructed in the faith, and when they then confessed the faith which was imprinted in their hearts, then they were admitted to the water. This doctrine, he says, I wish to have again brought into practice (Lib. Articulorum).

Bucer[29] writes that the ancients usually baptized adults and not children.

Oecolampadius,[30] in his reply to Balthasar,[31] writes: I do not find Scripture passages which enjoin infant baptism, as far as your humble servant can see.

Luther admits also in his Contra Anabaptistas (if I mistake not) that they have no express command to baptize children.

[26] Tertullian lived c. 160—c. 230 A.D.
[27] Cyprian was beheaded at Carthage in North Africa in A.D. 258.
[28] Geert Geerts, commonly called Erasmus, lived c. 1466-1536. Ed.
[29] Martin Bucer or Butzer (1491-1551), whose real surname was Kuhhorn, was a German Protestant reformer who somewhat mediated between Luther and Zwingli. Ed.
[30] Oecolampadius (1482-1531), whose real name was Johannes Heussgen (sic!) or Hüssgen, was a Zwinglian reformer in Basel, Switzerland. Ed.
[31] Balthasar Hubmaier was an Anabaptist whom John Horsch describes as "the most distinguished defender of believers' baptism and Anabaptist principles in general." (He did not hold to nonresistance, however.) He was burned at the stake in or near Vienna, Austria, in 1528. Ed.

What Martin Cellarius,[32] Otto Brunfels,[33] and others write concerning this matter, is too lengthy to be related here.

Since it is plain that few children were baptized among the ancients, as the above-mentioned Rhenanus, Zwingli, and Bucer show; that Cyprian left infant baptism optional, and that these others acknowledged that there is no express command for it, how then can Gellius truthfully write that they have received infant baptism from the apostles; that it is an incorporation into the church, and a sealing of the covenant of grace? Let the kind reader ponder this in the fear of his God.

Yes, my reader, if the matter of infant baptism stood as Gellius asserts, then the fathers sinned not a little for baptizing so few children, and for leaving optional that which he says the apostles practiced and taught to be an incorporation into the church, a gracious sign and a sealing of the covenant. Ah, what deception and human cleverness!

In the third place I answer: If we consider the confession and the doctrine of the learned ones touching infant baptism, we find it to be such a confused Babel that we must acknowledge that it cannot be of God. For some of the ancients (not the apostles), as it seems, baptized some children but not many. Some say they have received it from the apostles; others deny this. Some have formerly baptized, and still baptize, to wash away original sin; others, because they are children of the covenant. Some baptized them upon the faith of the church; others upon the faith of their parents. Some upon the faith of the godparents; others upon their own faith. And still others, in order that they may be the more piously reared in the Word of God. Behold, thus are the advocates of infant baptism divided among themselves.

Inasmuch then as they do not agree and are not of one mind as to upon what and to what end we shall baptize, therefore it is manifest that they baptize without the Word of God. For if their cause were rooted in Scripture, then they would baptize to the same end, according to the same ordinance, rule, and doctrine. This is incontrovertible.

[8] *In the eighth place he writes that it is nowhere prohibited in Scripture, nor said to be wrong. And that the Lord Jesus Christ testifies that His Word and will is not His but His Father's who is in heaven.*

*Reply.* Read through the entire Scriptures—Moses and the prophets, Christ Jesus and the apostles, and ponder them diligently, and you will find in more than one instance that God was not only not pleased at ceremonies and worship not commanded, but that He has often severely punished them. O dear Lord, what a blind rejoinder. As if man could, with a clear conscience, do this because there is no explicit prohibition, thou shalt not baptize infants!

---

[32] Martin Cellarius (1499-1564) was early influenced by the Zürich Anabaptists, associated much with Capito and Oecolampadius, and finally served as a Reformed Professor of Old Testament in Basel, Switzerland. *Ed.*

[33] Otto Brunfels (*c.* 1488-1534) was a versatile scholar, botanist, theologian, and physician. Brunfels opposed the persecution of "heretics." *Ed.*

Then they may also dedicate holy water, candles, palms, clocks, and priests, read masses, build convents, churches, altars, and become monks and Beguins, go on pilgrimages, and pray for the deceased souls, etc., as just and right! For there is not a word to be found in the Scripture which expressly forbids these things saying, You shall not do these things!

If he should say that the implications of Scripture and the fruits testify that these things are contrary to the Word of God, then I reply: Still clearer do the implications of the Scripture and the fruits testify that infant baptism is contrary to God's Word. For the mouth of the Lord has not spoken of it so much as a letter. All those who practice it abuse the name and ordinance of God and act a hypocrite, and they that receive it console themselves, when they come to years of understanding, that they are baptized Christians, although their whole walk is generally altogether impenitent, ungodly, earthly, and carnal, as may be seen.

In the second place I answer: Christ Jesus has testified saying: Go ye into all the world and preach the gospel to every creature. He that believeth and is baptized shall be saved. Mark 16:16. Behold, this is the express, eternal, and unchangeable ordinance of the Lord, which He has in this matter commanded and left to His church. The apostles have also taught and practiced thus.

If now minor children believe, that is, if they are penitent (Rom. 6); are circumcised in the foreskin of their hearts by the circumcision of Christ (Col. 2:11); if they have a clear conscience before the Lord (I Pet. 3:21); if they have a new mind (Titus 3:1); all of them the outcome of faith and represented by baptism—then baptism cannot be refused them. But since it is plain that they have none of these things, therefore we say that infant baptism is a veritable superstition, an abuse of the glorious and holy name of God, a falsification of the ordinance of Christ, a vain, hypocritical consolation to the impenitent, a sacrament of the church of Antichrist, an open deceit, blasphemy, and idolatry. Notwithstanding all this, this thoughtless man writes that it is the word and will of the Father; and in this way the eternal Father and His beloved Son and Holy Spirit, together with the chosen holy apostles, must be a cover for his deceitful abomination and wicked blasphemy. O Lord!

[9] *In the ninth place he writes that they have the promise that God, the Father, Son, and Holy Ghost, a true and living God, is powerful in connection with His commandment, and is ready to work mightily in the children of the church, to bestow on them His Spirit.*

*Reply.* If he could prove infant baptism by the Word of God, by apostolic doctrine and usage, or by the example of Christ, as he proposes, then we would gladly admit it to be a holy rite and pleasing to God, and sure to have its meaning, admonition, benefit, and fruit and power. For God commands nothing in vain. But since it cannot be proved that it was commanded, and since baptism cannot be integrated with little children, seeing that the signs of the New Testament are given to the penitent, therefore we say again that it is not a God-pleasing ceremony, and, according to all Scripture, it is a cursed blasphemy and abomination, as has already been heard. And how powerfully God works through such abominations may be plainly seen in the cases of Nadab, Abihu, Jeroboam, Uzzah, and others.

The pious reader must know also that the children of the church are not sanctified by means of ceremonies, words, and water, but only by the grace, favor, merits, blood, and death of the Lord, and by no other work or means through all eternity.

But as to his writing that God graciously bestows upon the baptized children His Spirit, we could wish that he would learn to consider more deeply and learn to know what the work of the Spirit is before he teaches such doctrine. Is it not sad and to be regretted that such people dare to take upon themselves the care of souls while they have not yet learned to know what is the nature, fruit, and power of the Holy Spirit? For wherever the Holy Spirit is, there must also be His fruits. This is incontrovertible. And what fruits we find in children when they come to rationality, we may, alas, notice in their words, works, and life.

I say further that if in their baptism the Spirit is graciously bestowed upon children, as he contends, and seeing that the Scriptures teach that the Holy Spirit is given to the believing ones, then it must follow (since the children do not as yet believe) that the Holy Spirit is not given them through faith, but that He is earned through the accomplished ceremony of the preachers. And what is blunter still, such a spirit, which is wholly without knowledge, intelligence, impulsion, power, fruit, and work, as may be seen! Oh, coarse blindness and error!

[10] *In the tenth place he writes: The Lord Jesus Christ commanded the children to be brought to Him (a thing which the Anabaptists never and nowhere do), and that He embraced them, laid His hands upon them and blessed them, that is, baptized them with the Holy Spirit. For all these things done by Christ cannot be without effect.*

*Reply.* I would ask Gellius and all those who practice infant baptism: First, whether all believers brought their children to Christ during the time of His ministry. If they say Yes, then they will be ashamed, for they cannot prove that assertion with Scriptures. But if they say No, then they acknowledge that they are wrong to begin with when they make this to refer to a common presentation, that is, as they take it, in baptism.

In the second place, I ask whether in any part of the Scripture bringing is called baptizing. If they say Yes, then they cannot produce proof. If they say No, then they admit that they also adulterate the Word of God, by explaining and construing bringing to mean baptizing.

In the third place, I ask whether Christ baptized the presented children with water. If they say Yes, then I answer with John, that Christ Himself did not baptize. John 3:5. But if they say No, then they acknowledge in the third place, that to defend infant baptism on the strength of this bringing is erroneous.

In the fourth place, I ask, seeing that he says that Christ baptizes these children with the Holy Spirit, whether this baptism with the Spirit is the same thing as the baptism with water. If they say Yes, then the Spirit must be letter, and letter, Spirit. But if they say No, then they themselves judge that Christ's action with the children does not teach nor imply infant baptism.

In the fifth place, I ask: How are we to understand this presentation— physically or spiritually? If they answer, Physically, then I say that it cannot now take place, seeing that Christ is taken from us, as far as His bodily presence is concerned, and is gone to a place where we cannot go in the body. I Tim. 6:16. But if they answer, Spiritually, then I would ask in reply why Gellius then brands such an ugly mark on the cheeks of the pious, whom he calls Anabaptists, by writing that they never and nowhere bring their children to Christ, a thing that could not have been written out of a pure heart of people who, many of them, are so very solicitously caring for the salvation of their children by teaching, admonishing, and punishing them, having a constant care for them, as God's Word and the love of their children command and teach all Christian parents.

Ah, that God would grant that Gellius and his followers might pay more attention to this spiritual bringing, as I hope that many of our people, by God's grace, do, and that they would let go of the infant baptism which they so much stress. This, I think, would be good. For they usually lead their children, from the cradle on, to the devil, by rearing them in ignorance, blindness, pomp, pride, vanity, and idolatry, as their fruits plainly show to all people of understanding minds.

Behold, my reader, from these questions and answers you may notice how Gellius and the learned ones can come through with their doctrine and the saying, Suffer the little children to come unto me, a passage which they press so and quote so frequently.

Observe, too, that Gellius, by his writing that we never and nowhere bring our children to Christ, not only judges and disgraces us, but also Christ Jesus since He has not commanded such bringing to Him. And he also judges and disgraces the holy apostles who have not testified nor taught us a word in regard to this matter and practice in the whole Scriptures.

[11] *In the eleventh place he writes: Since Luke testifies that John the Baptist was sanctified in his mother's womb, and leaped at the presence of Christ (which he says was doubtlessly caused by a spiritual influence) and also as Jacob, in his mother's womb, etc., therefore it is manifest that God also works in the children of the church, according to their stature through His Holy Spirit, and that the baptism of children has both command and promise.*

*Reply.* If these unusual miracles of God, which were wrought in John and Jacob, are to be a general rule, then these following miracles must also be general rules. Sara and Elisabeth, two barren, old women, gave birth to children in their old age, and Balaam's ass spoke; therefore all aged barren women give birth to children and all asses speak! Oh, no! That such unusual miracles of God were no general rule may be learned from the floating of iron with Elisha, and the passing of the Israelites through the Red Sea with Moses, and the standing still of the sun and moon with Joshua.

I say moreover, if from this motion of John, as Gellius sees it, it should follow that all the children of the church, or of believers, have the Holy Spirit, then the greater part of his fellow believers in Germanic lands (whom he earlier calls faithful servants of the same calling, office, and service) are greatly disrespected in their doctrine, faith, and usage. For he writes that the children of the church have the Holy Spirit, whereas they believe and teach that they have the evil spirit, for before they baptize them, they say: Depart thou evil spirit and make room for the Holy Spirit.[34] So it goes with all who teach and practice this shameful doctrine.

And although they are unanimous in the practice, yet they are so divided in opinions as to why, on what, and unto what they are to baptize, that we are verily forced to say that it is nothing but a senseless hocus-pocus,[35] and devilish mockery. Notwithstanding he writes that infant baptism has both command and promise, although he knows that he cannot produce one plain letter from all the Holy Scriptures to show that the wisdom of God has commanded it, or that the apostles have taught or practiced it; or that the thing signified, which only the penitent have, can be asserted of children. And I say nothing of the fact that the ancient writers state that the first unfallen church did not practice it, as has been heard.

Is not this properly called falsifying the Word of God, breaking the Scriptures, perverting the truth into lies, and stealing the honor and praise of God, killing souls, and defending the church of Antichrist? I say again, as I did before, I have never read a word in the Scriptures with such a thrust [as that infants are to baptized].

[12] *In the twelfth place he writes that baptism was not first instituted by Christ in Matthew's Gospel, for it was commanded before through John and practiced by the disciples of Christ, so that we are not driven, writes he, to make it regulative.*

*Reply.* Let everyone take heed and observe what the Word of the Lord teaches. Gellius is not at all ashamed, alas, to deny the plain Word of God, and writes that we are not obliged to make it regulative in regard to baptism, that Christ did not make it a command to baptize the believers only, nor that His heavenly Father did when He commanded John to baptize, and that the real purpose in the passage was not to indicate what persons may or shall be baptized. Behold, thus lamentably is your Lord's holy Word distorted.

Inasmuch as Gellius respects His Lord's mouth so little, and so lament-

---

[34] Menno has the Lutherans in mind, a wing of the Reformation toward which Gellius and his partners were quite sympathetic, and with whom at the first remnants of the exorcisms of the Catholic ritual survived. We have evidence here that Menno was quite well informed about his contemporaries. *Tr.*

[35] Literally *vain larva*. In the Roman mythology a wicked elf or goblin was called a larva. In Menno's day it seems to have come to stand for malevolent goings on. *Tr.*

ably falsifies His Word, therefore I will place the words of Christ, according to Matthew and Mark, before the reader, so that he may see what rule and law He has made concerning the practice of baptism, and what command He has given. Christ says, All power is given unto me in heaven and in earth. Go ye, therefore, and teach all nations, baptizing them [understand, those whom you have made or make disciples by your doctrine] in the name of the Father, and of the Son, and of the Holy Ghost, teaching them to observe all things whatsoever I have commanded you. Matt. 28. Again, Go ye into all the world, and preach the gospel to every creature. He that believeth [namely, the preached Gospel] and is baptized, shall be saved; but he that believeth not shall be damned. Mark 16:16. Behold, this is the Word and ordinance of the Lord, how we are to baptize and when. I think these words are too plain to be twisted with glosses or changed with subtlety, namely, that we are to preach the Gospel, and baptize those that believe it.

But what John taught and baptized before Christ is evidence in our favor and not against us, for he administered it to those who confessed their sins (Matt. 3:6), and not to irrational children as the disobedient, bad preachers do.

Since John did not before Christ baptize any but the penitent, and since Christ commanded it upon faith, the apostles taught and practiced it thus, and also the first church, as has been heard; therefore the reasonable reader may in the fear of God reflect how miserably and pathetically the poor souls are deceived by these unkind people who so wholly falsify the pointed, clear words of Christ concerning baptism and His pleasing pure ordinance, so turning it to a deceptive meaning and sense.

But when he writes that the apostles in Matthew 28 were commanded to gather unto Christ a church from all nations, and to teach them, not that which Moses, but that which Christ had taught, then we agree. Yet through no other command nor ordinance than to preach the Gospel, make disciples by means of the doctrine, baptize these same disciples, and so gather unto the Lord a peculiar people, who should walk in Christ Jesus in righteousness, truth, and obedience, as the regenerate children of God, and thank His great and glorious name forever. And with such a people that walks in His fear, love, Word, ordinances, and commands, He will always be, even to the end of the world. But of infant baptism there is no thought.

[13] *In the thirteenth place he writes that the apostles, some of whom were baptized by John, and also those who came to him from the villages and from Jerusalem, were indiscriminately baptized by John, not as though they already had quite an exhaustive knowledge of Christ, or a genuine faith with all their hearts at the time of their baptism.*

*Reply.* If I can understand him correctly, he would conclude from this, that even as the baptized disciples were before baptism not fully developed in doctrine, faith, and repentance, but had to exercise themselves in continual repentance, and die unto sin, as baptism represents, so also the children, although they have no faith before baptism, will, after baptism, when they come to rationality, strive after the doctrine, repent, die unto sin, and walk in newness of life, etc.

To which opinion (if at least this is his opinion) I reply: The prophets prophesied of John. His birth was announced by an angel. Christ testified of him that he was the second Elias, a shining light, not clothed in soft raiment, and not like the waving reed; that he was the greatest of all those born of women, etc. From which it may be concluded that he was no frivolous, reckless preacher, but that he earnestly and valiantly executed his office of preaching repentance well-pleasing to God, and that he rightly practiced the commanded baptism according to the ordinance. And, although his disciples were not so thoroughly instructed in all things, yet he did not baptize any but those who confessed their sins, as was said.

But as to his explanation of the words: If thou believest with all thine heart, which Philip spoke to the Ethiopian, that they mean no more than to believe without deceit and sham, a thing he rightly required of the eunuch, and that Luke has recorded this to leave an example to all servants of the church as to how adults should be baptized, seeing he also had come to maturity, we reply that this is right. We desire nothing else of all who baptize, than that they first examine the faith and foundation of the candidate for baptism before they baptize him, lest they, in their work and service, be found to be hypocrites.

I think that this is verily a plain example that the servants of the church should not ask a confession of faith from others, but from those themselves who wish to be baptized as also Otto Brunfels says concerning this: He does not say (writes he), If you believe or promise in your child's stead then it is permitted to baptize.

Since Gellius has brought up the disciples and those baptized by John, and as appears, would thereby show that baptism does not exactly require true faith, and that it makes little difference whether faith comes before or after; and since we pass for Anabaptists with him, therefore I am in my simplicity asking him whether the commandment of Christ, and the example of the eunuch, are not sufficient to show that faith should precede baptism, and that baptism requires true faith, the very reason for which Paul rebaptized the disciples of John who had before been baptized with the baptism of John, although John's baptism was not of men, but from heaven. Matt. 21:25. He cannot Scripturally answer it otherwise, can he, than that it was done because they had never known that there was a Holy Ghost. Inasmuch then as these disciples were once baptized in their years of maturity, with divine baptism, and lacked nothing but that they had not been told about the Holy Ghost, and on that account were rebaptized by Paul; therefore Gellius should consider whether or not true Christian baptism requires genuine faith, and whether he does not wrong us by reproachfully calling us Anabaptists because we repeat the baptism of those who were previously baptized not with a divine baptism, as were the disciples of John, nor because of a defect or omission, but because they were baptized with an anti-Christian baptism, without any knowledge, faith, command, or word, as the reckless, ignorant world can in part judge and see.

If we are Anabaptists because we repeat a baptism instituted by man and administered to those who had no knowledge, how much then was Paul an Anabaptist for rebaptizing those who were of understanding minds, and were then baptized with the baptism which was from heaven and ordained of God!

In the second place, I would ask: Since he calls us Anabaptists, as has been heard, what does he think of Cyprian, together with both the councils—the African and the Nicene—which unanimously resolved that heretics have no baptism, and that therefore those who have been baptized by heretics shall be baptized with the true baptism? If he says that he considers them Scriptural and right, then he admits that he himself has not been baptized with the right baptism, and that we are right in rebaptizing those who have been baptized of such who are not only by Scripture, but also by Luther, Zwingli, and the learned ones, declared to be anti-Christian servants, and the essence of all heresy, before the whole world, as we may see on every hand in their writings.

But if he declares them bad and sectarian, then he thereby asserts in the first place that the church, or at least a great part of it, was at that time bad and sectarian.

In the second place, he asserts that he binds God's Spirit, work, Word, ordinance, and command to the anti-Christian and heretical service and works.

In the third place, he asserts that he is an anti-Christian and a heretic himself, since he was baptized with an anti-Christian and heretical baptism, and still defends it as true baptism.

O my reader, would that Gellius had but half an understanding of the Word of God, and could see but a little of the truth! Then he would all his days lament before God that he has so lamentably profaned the Lord's express command and ordinance given through John, Christ, and the apostles; that he has so hatefully slandered the pious, and that he passes such a thoughtless and ungodly sentence, by his writings, that he not only pronounces us, but also Cyprian, all the African bishops, the Nicene Fathers, besides also the holy Paul himself, open Anabaptists, nay, heretics, as you may see.

[14] *In the fourteenth place he writes that it is with baptism now as it was with circumcision formerly; namely, that even as God began circumcision with Abraham upon foregoing instruction, and it then passed upon Abraham's seed and children as a sure seal of the promise, so also did John the Baptist initiate baptism with adults and it then gradually moved over to the children since it could not occur otherwise because of circumcision.*

*Reply.* That it is with baptism as it was with circumcision before, namely, in this respect, that it was begun upon previous instruction, is altogether in keeping with our ground and doctrine; for Christ Jesus has so ordained it and His holy apostles have so taught and practiced it. But that it should, by the command of Christ, and by the teaching and practice of the apostles, have gradually passed upon the children, is mere conjecture and human opinion, and not Scripture.

For if it stood thus, then the apostles erred. For not in their day did they baptize after the manner of circumcision commanded by God, baptizing at one and the same time the believers and the children (a thing they by no means did). Also, Abraham at God's command circumcised himself and his household, as well as the males of eight days afterward, and not little by little, making circumcision to pass to the children, as Gellius proposes concerning the apostles and their baptism.

But that he writes that it could not be otherwise because of circumcision is ingenuity and not Scripture. For the apostles, and also John, administered to believing ones of the Jews the sign of baptism. Why did they not also administer it to their children then, if God had so ordained and commanded it, as Gellius pretends?

No, no. The command of the Lord concerning circumcision referred expressly first to Abraham and his household and then to the males of eight days old. Gen. 17:14. But this the command concerning baptism did not do, for it applies only to the believing and not to the children who are unable to hear. Matt. 28; Mark 16. Therefore baptism did not gradually pass to children, as Gellius pretends, but it was afterward instituted apart from the Word, ordinance, and command of God, by disobedient and heady men, who, alas, have considered a performed ceremony above the Lord's command and its meaning, as is the custom with the learned and worldly-minded.

Again, as to his writing that *the promise is sealed by baptism and that it belongs not only to the adult but also to the children,* the reader must know that the promise of the grace of God, and of the eternal covenant, is no longer sealed with perishable blood of oxen and rams, nor by any visible water and ceremonies, but once for all by the crimson blood of Christ on the cross. Blessed is he who believes it, and heartily accepts it. This promise is made to the unbaptized children no less than to the baptized believing ones, so long as they are clothed with innocence, and go on in simplicity. But when they come to rationality,[36] and accept the preached Gospel of grace through faith, then the Scriptures teach us to baptize them. Matt. 28:19; Mark 16:15. But if they reject grace, and lead an easy, impenitent life, then neither Christ's blood nor death will avail them; much less word and water. For, He that believeth not [the Scripture refers to those of years of discretion] is condemned already. John 3:18.

[15] *In the fifteenth place he writes they err abominably because they rigidly conclude from the Scriptures and examples which speak of adults that it is a sure ordinance of God that children are not to be baptized, a matter for which there is not a tittle in the whole New Testament. And therefore they err no less than I should err, if I refused to feed my children that ca..not work, because Paul said, He that does not labor shall not eat, which is undeniably spoken in regard to those of mature years, and not of children.*

36 What is now commonly called the age of accountability. *Ed.*

*Reply.* It seems to me that Gellius purposely upholds things contrary to Christ and truth, so that he may execute the office of an anti-Christian preacher, according to the pleasure of the world. For, while he should write that we act rightly according to the Scriptures, and that there is not a tiny tittle in the New Testament that children should be baptized, he actually writes that we err abominably, and that there is not a tittle saying that they should not be baptized.

Since he so violently and willfully contends against the Lord and His truth, and since he in various ways seeks to make his cause plausible by the use of many borrowed words, lies, conjectures, and perversions of the Scriptures, and says that we err abominably, etc., therefore I would briefly tell him this: If he can at any time prove to us by the unadulterated, divine Scripture and truth that John the Baptist mentioned infant baptism anywhere, or that it was commanded by Christ and taught and practiced by the apostles, or that it gradually passed upon the children by the ordinance of the Lord, as he writes, or that bringing is called baptizing and baptizing is called bringing in the Scriptures, or that Christ and the apostles baptized the children that were brought to them, or Christ baptized them with a Spirit that was powerful in works (the Spirit of God is never inoperative), or that small children believe or repent, that they bury their sins and are circumcised through faith, and arise with Christ in newness of life, or that circumcision is called baptism and baptism circumcision, or that they have the answer of a good conscience, or that baptism anywhere in the Scriptures is called a sign of the covenant of grace, a sealing of the promise, and an incorporation into the church, or that minor children speak with tongues as the believing members of the house of Cornelius did, of whom Peter says, Can any man forbid water, and that these should be baptized, which have received the Holy Ghost as well as we, or that the first church which was sound, practiced it by the apostolic doctrine, usage, or command, or that God operates in transactions which He has not ordained, then we will put our pen into the inkwell, repent, and confess before the whole world that our cause in this matter is mere seduction and nothing but falsehood.

But if he cannot do so (as he never can), then I would faithfully admonish and fraternally beseech him to consider earnestly and thoroughly how shamefully he reviles God, the Father, Son, and Holy Spirit, John the Baptist and the apostles, in this matter of infant baptism. How lamentably he falsifies the plain, clear Scriptures, and deceives the poor souls; what clumsy big falsehoods he urges upon the poor people; how deceitfully he crowds in the accursed abomination representing it as a holy, glorious work! Similarly also, how unjustly he accuses us of erring abominably, we who so mightily have on our side Christ's plain Word, the apostolic doctrine and usage, the signification of baptism, and the usage of the first and unfalsified church—and that while he cannot show by a single word of all the Scriptures that his infant baptism has any foundation in the ordinance and command of God. My faithful reader, beware; fear God; do right; search the Scriptures; shun falsehood; and follow the truth!

Again, to introduce the saying of Paul, that if any does not work, neither should he eat, into his argument, it is to his own disadvantage, and is too childish to warrant a reply, for Paul thereby commands idlers and parasites to earn their own bread by honorable labor lest they become an offense and a care to others, a matter that cannot apply to children; therefore such labor is not commanded them. Neither does Paul say, He who does not work, etc., as Gellius writes, but he says, If any refuse to work, neither should he eat. So, too, baptism is not commanded to be administered to irrational children, but to those who believe the Word of the Lord, lead a penitent life, and who have a sound understanding and comprehension of baptism, as has been said several times.

[16] *In the sixteenth place he writes that in Christ Jesus no differentiation of persons or time is made. For the benefit of the kingdom of Christ is not limited to any city, time, or persons; similarly, neither to any age or race.*

*Reply.* Herewith, it seems to me, he contends that although baptism, as he says, has taken the place of circumcision, and the males only were circumcised in Israel, notwithstanding this, both males and females are to be baptized now, be they believers or children, whether born of believing parents or no. If that is his meaning and foundation, then he will know that even as God's grace, favor, love, covenant, and promise in the New Testament extends to both men and women, so also in the Old Testament. For if God had fastened His covenant of grace and all things to signs, whether it be circumcision or baptism, and if those alone were in the church who had received the sign, then the Israelitic women were in an unfavorable situation, and also the children of the first churches, since the former according to the Scriptures were not circumcised, and the latter according to certain ancient authors were not baptized, as has been said.

No, reader, no. Abraham and all his seed, I mean both men and women, young and old, were the Lord's people and church. But the males only were circumcised, not the females, the male children of eight days old and not female children according to the ordinance of God. Nevertheless they were all, both men and women, members of the church, in the covenant of God, and children of the promise; although, I repeat, the males only were circumcised, and not the females.

Similarly in the New Testament. The Gospel is preached, and all who believe it and are baptized, shall be saved; be they men or women. They are members of the church of Christ, in God's covenant and grace. They are joint heirs of the kingdom of God, and children of eternal life. So also the children, although they are not baptized.

For even as God would have His ceremonies under the Old Testament, such as circumcision, Passover, sin offering, burnt offering, etc., performed, just as He had ordained and commanded them through Moses, so also will He have His signs under the New Testament, such as baptism and Supper, performed in no other way than He has commanded and ordained through His Son.

For He says, This is my beloved Son in whom I am well pleased; hear ye him. If now this Son has enjoined infant baptism, then we ought to practice it if we would be His disciples. But since He has not done so, therefore we testify with Scripture that it is accursed, as has been said. Gal. 1 :8.

I say moreover, if now they wish to place the children of both believing and unbelieving parents in the same grace, which according to my opinion would not be altogether contrary to the Scriptures,[37] then they must recall their doctrine by which they previously referred the grace and covenant of God with so many words to the children of believing parents only. And then they must admit that their insistence regarding Abraham and his seed, by which they seek to establish continuity between circumcision and baptism, has no similarity to, nor connection with it at all. For it was not commanded to Abraham to circumcise all the children of the vicinity who were not his seed, but only those who were of his seed, as may be learned from Genesis 17.

[17] *In the seventeenth place he writes: Would to God that they would rightly understand the fifth chapter of Ephesians where Paul describes the church saying, Christ loved the church and gave himself for it that he might sanctify it and cleanse it with the washing of water in the word, or as Erasmus renders it, through the word. Then he goes on saying, This incontrovertibly includes the children along with their parents, does it not, that is, the believers and their seed, nay, the whole church. How then would they be excluded from the expression, He has cleansed the church with the washing of water by the word?*

*Reply.* I trust that we, through the grace and enlightenment of the Lord, shall in our simplicity grasp these words of Paul, not with obscured, but with open vision. We offer Gellius and all the learned ones the entire Scriptures, besides all reason and experience, if they can show one jot in the Holy Scripture, or derive from reason and experience, that we can teach little children the Word of God, from which originates the true cleansing of the heart; or that the Scriptures of the New Testament anywhere deal with them by the Word and sacrament. If they can do this, then we will grant that they are cleansed by water through the Word, or in the Word. But if they cannot do so, then it is already settled that these words of Paul were not written of little children.

It is true, Christ has so loved His church, that He has given Himself for her, and has sanctified her through the power and merits of His innocent blood, and has cleansed her by water, which is a proof and sign of a new and penitent life, but not otherwise than in the Word, or through the Word, preached in the power of the Spirit, accepted in true faith, and followed by the baptism as commanded in His ordinance.

Ye are clean through the word which I have spoken unto you, said Christ. Not, my reader, that they were clean because it was outwardly spoken unto them, but because they believed that which was spoken unto them. For God

---

[37] In other words, Menno regards the children of unbelievers as well as of believers as safe in Christ. *Ed.*

does not cleanse the hearts through any literal water, word, or ceremony, but through belief in the Word (Acts 15:9). Otherwise all who heard the Word externally, and received the sign of the water externally, would be holy and clean. This is incontrovertible.

[18] *In the eighteenth place he advances an argument and syllogism saying, Whatever belongs to the church, belongs also to the members of the church. Baptism belongs to the whole church, old and young, therefore baptism belongs to all the members of the church.*

*Reply.* In my opinion, it would be good for Gellius, since he boasts himself a preacher of the holy Word, to leave his dialectics to the wise ones of the world who, alas, seek their own praise and honor more than they do God's; and if he would satisfy himself with the unfalsified doctrine, foundation, and truth of Christ, and with the plain and simple testimony of Matthew the publican, and of Peter and John the fishermen, so that he might not deceive the unlearned by such wise reasoning, and lead them from the way of truth.

As to his major premise (as he calls it) I would say that if Gellius had asserted it of grace, reconciliation, promise, eternal life, etc., which are bestowed upon the whole church, young as well as old, for Christ's sake, and not of the ordinance of the church, then he would have proceeded correctly, but as it is, he will have to admit that it is wrong, and contrary to the Word of God. For, as regards the ordinances of which he speaks, in which baptism is included, I would say that all the members of the church are not of one and the same calling, service, and work, and are not under one and the same ordinance; for the Lord has ordained apostles, prophets, evangelists, pastors, and ministers in His church; but this does not imply that all are apostles, prophets, evangelists, pastors, and ministers. So also He has given ordinances, together with baptism and the Lord's Supper, in His church, but not that we should administer and give them to the irrational children, but only to the believing and the penitent.

As to his minor premise, I reply, our entire doctrine, belief, foundation, and confession is that our innocent children, as long as they live in their innocence, are through the merits, death, and blood of Christ, in grace, and partakers of the promise, as has already been heard. But the doctrine of the New Testament, which is a doctrine of the Spirit, does not include them with those who are ruled and governed by the Word and sacraments of God, and who are really called the church of Christ in Scripture.

That the children should be considered in the church on account of the promise, to this we consent. But we deny that they should be included in the ordinances of the church, for this is out of keeping with all of Scripture and reason, as Gellius himself will have to say presently.

He also openly reproves Christ and the apostles, together with the Holy Spirit, for he writes that baptism belongs to both old and young, although they have not left us a single example or one word in all the Scriptures whereby it is taught or commanded, as may be seen.

Since both his major and minor premises are not in harmony with the Word and command of God, how then his conclusion that baptism belongs to all the members of the church, can stand the tests of the Word and ordinance of God is by this made sufficiently clear to the kind reader.

I say further that if this his syllogism is right and true (which it is not), then mine also is correct: Whatever belongs to the church belongs also to the members of the church, that is, in Gellius' interpretation, the young as well as the old; and it follows that since doctrine and faith, knowledge of Christ through repentance, a regenerated, new life, the circumcision of the heart, a new and happy conscience, baptism, Lord's Supper, the love of one's neighbor, a living hope, joyful thanksgiving, etc., belong to the church, therefore they belong to all the members, both young and old. If he denies this first premise of mine, then thereby he denies his own, for mine is identical with his. If he denies the second, because children on account of their immaturity cannot as he admits, be preached to and therefore cannot repent or partake of the Supper, etc., then he testifies that the children do not belong to the church which is governed by the Lord's Word and sacraments, and that his whole syllogism, wherewith he includes all the members of the church, both young and old, in one and the same ordinance is wrong and false, yes, without basis in God's Word. This is my answer to the argument of Gellius and his associates. How fine and fast they, according to the Scriptures, stand with this, you may ponder in the fear of your God.

[19]*In the nineteenth place he talks at length about the child who was, according to Mark and Luke, called to Christ; and thinks thereby to prove, I believe, that children believe, or if they do not believe, that they are nevertheless reckoned as believing, be they a day or two, or a month or two old. He writes further that a child of two, three, or four years old may be corrupted by bad examples; and that we are too hesitant because we do not dare to baptize those to whom Christ (so he writes) ascribes faith.*

*Reply.* If Gellius and the learned ones had received but a little of the nature, power, and properties of true faith in their hearts, they would be ashamed all their days for speaking so erroneously of that precious noble faith which is a power and gift of God. Moses says that the children have no understanding of good and evil. The wise man says that they have no understanding. Wis. 12:25. Paul says, Brethren, be not children in understanding. And yet Gellius dares to write that they believe—as though faith were but a fancy that has no motive, power, or work!

Oh, no! True faith, which counts before God, is a living and saving power, which through the preaching of the holy Word is bestowed by God upon the heart; a thing that stirs, changes, and regenerates it to newness of mind; restrains all ungodliness in us; destroys all pride, ambition, and selfishness; makes us like children in malice, etc. Behold, such faith it is to which the Scriptures refer, and not a dead, vain, and unfruitful fancy, as the world dreams. And that such faith is not found in children of two, three, or four years, both the Scriptures and common sense teach us.

O dear Lord! What great blindness, that this rash man does not notice that he and his preachers who read the Scriptures every day in their fashion, some of whom have grown gray already, are still so unbelieving that they for the sake of a stomachful of bread, falsify the plain Word of God; lead the poor, miserable souls to hell in droves; upbraid, slander, and hate all the pious; and heap upon them without their faults, slanderous lies and disgraces; dare to incite the magistracy to tyranny and blood; delighting in pomp and pride, luxury, avarice, etc.—clear proof that they are not only unbelieving, but also wholly earthly and carnal. And then they assert that a child of two or three years of age has faith. Oh, folly and error!

The reason why Christ called unto Himself the child, embraced it, and placed it in the midst of His disciples was that the disciples were contending as to who would be the greatest. He set the child before them as an example, and said, Verily I say unto you, Except ye be converted and become as little children, ye shall not enter into the kingdom of heaven. And so we must receive the kingdom of God as a child (as to malice, that is), as Mark and Luke write. Paul says, In malice be ye children. For whosoever therefore shall humble himself, said Christ, as this little child, the same is greatest in the kingdom of heaven; and whoso shall receive one such little child [that is, one who has humbled himself as this child] in my name, receiveth me. But whoso shall offend one of these little ones which believe in me [he says, which *believe* in me] it were better for him that a millstone were hanged about his neck, and that he were drowned in the depth of the sea. Behold, thus Christ Himself explains to what kind of "children" we should refer this.

As to his writing that children are reckoned as believers, this is merely reason and human opinion which cannot be substantiated by a single word of the Scriptures. Again, as to his assertion that a child two, three, or four years old may be offended, or made worse,[38] I would say first, if we were to apply this saying, Whoso shall offend one of these little ones which believe on me, etc., to young children as Gellius does (to which I, on my part, do not consent), then the whole world might well be astounded at these words, from the inmost of their souls. For how they rear their children of two, three, four, five, six years, and with what ungodly, offensive life they walk before them, their shameless wickedness and rascality, alas, teach us, both in city and country. O reader, would that the world might take to heart a little more the salvation of their children, and would not from the cradle lead them to hell by their doctrine and example. This would be good for their souls at the day of judgment!

Second, if the preachers and magistrates could rightly understand this saying of Christ and believe it and be just and true moreover, then in my opinion, the offensive, deceiving doctrine would soon be at an end, and the tyrannical sword would be put into the sheath, by which, now, alas, so many

---

[38] The Dutch word for "to offend" is *ergeren*, literally, "to make worse." *Tr.*

hundreds of thousands of souls are worsened to everlasting destruction, and enclosed in the kingdom of hell. O Lord! Woe unto the world because of offences, says Christ who is God's mouth and wisdom. Matt. 18:7.

To his writing that we are too hesitant, and that we dare not baptize children, I would say this: The Scriptures teach us that you must not do that which you think proper, but that which I command you. Deut. 4:2; 12:32.

Nadab and Abihu, the two sons of Aaron, brought strange fire before the Lord, which He had not commanded them. And there went out a fire from the Lord and devoured them. Lev. 10:1, 2.

Jeroboam, chosen king of the ten tribes of Israel, instituted a worship not commanded by God, and he had to hear from the prophet that God would extirpate his house as a man sweeps away dung, until it was all over with him. I Kings 14:10.

Uzziah was thrust forth for life because he burned incense upon the altar of incense, to which the Lord had not called him. II Chron. 26:16. And there are many such cases.

Luther writes in his preface to Isaiah, God will not be told how He is to be served. He wishes to teach and lead us. His Word must stand. It must lead and enlighten us, for without His Word all is idolatry and vain falsehood, no matter how fine and pleasing it may appear. And in the third chapter of Daniel [Luther writes], Worship without God's Word is always idolatry.

I would say further, All those who have sought God and have sincerely feared Him, have continued in His ordinance and Word.

Israel never once circumcised a female, nor offered a ewe for the Passover. For God had ordained that the males should be circumcised on the eighth day, and that rams should be offered (Gen. 17:11; Ex. 12:5), as was heard before.

Since we know from the Holy Scriptures that Moses and the prophets, and the Father Himself moreover, so unanimously point to Jesus, who is Wisdom and Truth, to obey Him; and since we, by the grace of God, know right well that He is the true prophet, and perfect Teacher, whose Word is truth, and whose command is eternal life; and since He has not commanded us a single letter about infant baptism, nor have His true witnesses, the holy apostles, taught it, nor left an example; and since we also find that the thing signified is not applicable to children; and since we know besides that the Scriptures do not admit of strange worship, humanly proposed ceremonies, and additions or subtractions, and that God has so often punished such self-chosen righteousness and worship, as was heard; and since we know that the first uncorrupted church did not practice infant baptism, as has often been heard; therefore we are so hesitant (as he puts it) that we dare not baptize our children, because the cited cases together with our unfeigned love of blessed divine truth, the sincere fear of our God, and the power of our faith, although in weakness, prevent us.

O reader, would God but grant that our opponents could rightly understand what frightful abominations they commit on every hand with their infant baptism, and how they press it to the dishonor of God and the destruction of their neighbor. Then I could hope that this matter would soon be improved by the help of God, and turned to a more Scriptural use.

In the first place, they make God and the Holy Scriptures into liars by their infant baptism; for they assert that it is God's ordinance, and there is not a single word or example to be found in all the Scriptures that so much as suggests infant baptism.

In the second place, they destroy the true church of Christ, and thereby establish an anti-Christian one, which bears the name and semblance of the Christian church; although it hates and despises the doctrine, ordinance, and usage taught by the Scriptures.

In the third place, they console the world thereby in its unrighteousness; for no matter how ungodly, adulterous, perjurious, covetous, pompous, hateful, bloodthirsty, gluttonous, drunken, carnal, idolatrous, and false they are, yet they boast that they are baptized Christians.

In the fourth place, they hate and persecute all those who, out of pure, godly zeal, avoid this deceitful abomination, reprove their damnable worship, and point them to Jesus and His Word alone. Yes, they are then called apostate Anabaptists, apostles of the devil, deceived heretics, offscourings, and free booty.

In the fifth place, although they and their writers have in the past condemned unto hell the institutions and commands of men, and have written one volume after another against them, yet they, alas, altogether continue to cling to this rude abomination,[39] because they do not want to assume the cross, nor the reproach of the world. They act the hypocrite in all things, as the world likes it. They heap one abominable error upon another, hang crosses upon the child's breast and forehead, and bless and conjure and ask the godfathers whether they believe, etc. They exorcise [demons from infants] and similar disgraceful things. So we are forced to say, are we not, that all pedobaptists are hypocrites above all hypocrites, and that infant baptism is an open immersion into the church of Antichrist, the beginning of all deceit, and an accursed blasphemy and magic, which is not only contrary to the plain Word and ordinance of the Lord, but also against all reason, nature, and common sense.

For who that has read but half a word of the Lord does not know that a cross made with fingers cannot help or save a child; that the guiltless, pure, little creature, the innocent child which is cleansed by the blood of the Lord is not possessed of any devil; and that one cannot answer for the faith of another since it is a gift of God?

Say, kind reader, what greater mockery and cruder hypocrisy could be invented, than to ask an irrational[40] person in somebody else's name: Do you

---

[39] Menno implies that the governing principle of the Reformation, the rejection of all unscriptural institutions and ceremonies in favor of a wholly Biblical doctrine and practice, was not fully carried through; infant baptism was, for example, wrongly retained. *Ed.*

[40] "Irrational" seems to be required to make sense, although the original reads, "rational." *Tr.*

believe? Do you renounce Satan, etc.? And then upon an affirmative answer, baptize a child that cannot understand and cannot speak, and for whom yes and no, God and the devil, truth and falsehood, life and death, are all the same? Oh, blasphemy and shame!

O Lord! O dear Lord! How long will this misleading deceit and crude abomination be practiced! I should think it were time that the world would take heed, and learn to know such open deceivers and their doctrine, baptism, Supper, life, and fruits, and that it would have more respect for the ordinance, will, Word, ways, and works of the Lord.

[20] *In the twentieth place he accuses us of a false certainty, as he calls it, namely, that we, or our people, say that we are assured in our hearts that they err, and that we have the truth.*

*Reply.* The Lord speaks through Moses, Whosoever will not hearken unto my words which he [that is, Christ] shall speak in my name, I will require it of him. Deut. 18:19.

The Father says, This is my beloved Son, in whom I am well pleased; hear ye him. Matt. 17:5.

Christ says, Teach them to observe all things whatsoever I have commanded you. Matt. 28:29.

Paul says, Though we, or an angel from heaven, preach any other gospel unto you than that which we have preached, let him be accursed. Gal. 1:8.

John says, Whosoever transgresseth, and abideth not in the doctrine of Christ hath not God. He that abideth in the doctrine of Christ, he hath both the Father and the Son. II John 1:9. And similar passages.

Since all the Scriptures point us to the Spirit, Gospel, example, ordinance, and usage of Christ; and since we, in the matter, do not follow fancy, our own opinion, false explanations, and doctrines of men, as was reported, but follow Christ's plain Word and command, the doctrine and usage of the holy apostles in the first, unfalsified church; and since they, our opponents, have no more command to baptize children than Israel had to circumcise females, or to build churches, altars, and places of worship on hills or in valleys, or to allow their children to pass through the fire, and no more command than the papists have to baptize bells; and since they nevertheless insist upon calling the baptism of believers ordained by Christ, a heretical baptism; and since they esteem and practice infant baptism, which was instituted in hypocrisy calling it Christian baptism; and since they boast moreover that they do well in not allowing this usage to be taken from them; therefore I would gladly leave it to the judgment of all reasonable and impartial readers, who of us is most like the Sennacherib, Holophernes, the Pharisees and deceived sects, mentioned by them, in the matter of false certainty.

[21] *He writes further: What else was it that deceived the Anabaptists previously so that they took up the sword, if not just such certainty, that they imagined that as a people of God, marked with the sign of Tau,*[41] *they should*

---

[41] The fanatical sects whom Menno opposed firmly referred to their adherents as per-

*capture the whole world and hang us preachers, who said they knew better, in our own doorways.*

*Reply.* Dear reader, observe. What else does he say here than, Beloved lords, will you still be merciful to such bad people and wicked heretics? Persecute them, capture them, banish them, and extirpate them; they deserve it! Whether the Holy Spirit in Revelation does not call this the sting of scorpions, you may ponder and decide. Rev. 9:10. He says a little farther down that our church began with me (a thing which, as will be shown later, I do not admit) and he knows very well that I never was in the company of those mutinous people, but that I have always reproved their doctrines and abominations with the Word of the Lord, as much as I do those of the preachers. Nevertheless, he casts these ungodly practices and wicked deeds before our feet, in order thereby to make us, who are innocent, suspicioned by all the world, and he passes the sword to the magistrates. I will leave it to the consideration of all the pious and God-fearing, if this is not seeking the blood of the innocent.

Oh, that enough decency were found with him, not to confuse the innocent with the guilty. For what does he seek, but to change Simon Peter into Simon the sorcerer, and John and James into Judas?

Yes, exactly, as though I should say, I have known some pedobaptists who were open adulterers and thieves, therefore Gellius and all pedobaptists are adulterers and thieves. Would not that be wrong in me? O faithful reader, how justly has holy David portrayed such vicious people, saying, The wicked murder the innocent in secret places; their eyes are privily set against the poor. He lieth in wait secretly, as a lion in his den; he lieth in wait to catch the poor. Psalm 10:8, 9. For by such cry of murder it comes about that in some places the pious and faithful hearts, men and women, youths and maidens, the gray-headed, the lame and the halt, are pitilessly and mercilessly, as the world's worst, imprisoned and robbed, their children set on the street, homeless and penniless; some tortured with hot oil, others hanged, racked, pilloried, thrown into the water, strangled, burned, beheaded, and similar heathenish tyranny. Behold, these are, alas, the best and foremost fruits which these blood-preachers produce in some countries by their writings.

Would to God that he and his preachers, together with all the papists and monks, who are guilty of innocent blood, might find mercy and grace before the eyes of the great and Almighty God, in the day when the fearful sound of the last trumpet shall resound, and that the innocent blood of which they are the cause might not be counted against them! This I could wish from the bottom of my heart. But if they continue in their present mood and do not turn from ungodliness, then, says the Spirit of God, the fiery pool will be their reward and part. Rev. 19:21.

sons marked with the last letter of the Hebrew alphabet, *Tau.* Some have argued that since Menno also speaks of persons marked with this letter we have evidence that he had at the first belonged to the Münsterites. It is quite as probable that Menno employs the language here found to show what the only tolerable letter *Tau* on the foreheads of men was. *Tr.*

I say further, just as we hate and reprove in Gellius and all seditious people the bitter and hateful heart, and the bloody and hostile crying and writing, so also do we hate and reprove (in evangelical fashion, that is) those that fight with the sword, steal, rob, or in any manner wrong anyone on earth, be he friend or foe.

Here father, brother,[42] emperor, neighbor, king, friend, great or small, baptized or unbaptized, makes no difference; all those who shed blood against the Word of God, who act contrary to love, who wrong, destroy, or afflict their neighbor, cannot be our brethren, for we know and say truly that they are not Christians.

That the mutinous and their followers at Münster have, alas, in the past, taken up the sword contrary to God's Word, we have to hear continually, as if we were one with them in that abomination, although we are so wholly innocent in the matter. But that they themselves cause whole countries to arm, and so ruin them; that they destroy one principality after another; that they cause all manner of violence, affliction, and sorrow everywhere: this they do not seem to see. Yes, this must, alas, be called right and good at that.

It is manifest that not only France, Italy, Spain, and Burgundy, but also all the German peoples, who boast of the Word, as well as the whole world, are guilty of the same tumult as far as fighting, warring, robbing, and shedding of blood go. Why then do they introduce here the crimes of the seditious, seeing they err so greatly in the matter themselves and are as guilty? Paul says, Therefore thou art inexcusable, O man, whosoever thou art that judgest; for wherein thou judgest another thou condemnest thyself; for thou that judgest, doest the same things. Rom. 2:1.

[22] *Finally he writes: Our eyes, or the eyes of our people, have seen better than the eyes of the Anabaptists, instead of construing it of willful sinning, the thing wherewith they have driven some to despair, and some to suicide. . . .*[42a]

*Reply.* Since he takes this pot shot at us also he shall know that he has outreached himself, writing thus. For I can say and insist with a clear conscience that I never was troubled by the brethren concerning this matter, and that the doctrine has not been held among us in my time.

I have always taught that all sins which are repented of are pardoned in the blood of the Lord, be they what they may. David's adultery and shedding of innocent blood, is to me a sure testimony. Yet everybody should take heed that he sincerely fears God, does the right, and that he does not willfully sin against his God, that he does not pervert falsehood into truth, nor truth into falsehood, as did the scribes. For who knows whether he who thus willfully sins against his God will ever again all his days receive grace and come to true repentance? Christ says, Whosoever committeth sin, is the servant of sin. John 8:34.[43]

---

[42] Menno had himself lost a brother in the insurrection at Oude Klooster. *Tr.*

[42a] This portion of a sentence seems to refer to the supposed severity of the Anabaptists in their preaching against certain sins, and evidently representing them as unpardonable when committed after baptism. *Ed.*

[43] On the margin at this point we read: *Anima, quae per superbiam aliquid commiserit,*

I fear that if his Imperial Highness were to present to me many costly gifts, and I should be ungrateful to his Imperial Highness, and should squander them, or trample upon them, or cast them from me, then his Imperial severity would undoubtedly severely punish me for such ingratitude, and would probably not again offer me such favors and costly presents.

Therefore, take heed not to willfully despise and falsify your Lord's Word, nor proceed too boldly according to the pleasure of a carnal mind; lest the manifested grace be withheld from you all of a sudden, and your mind be turned[44] into an evil and proud direction. He that fears God, let him shun evil.

Even as Gellius solemnly exerts himself by his false doctrine, to make false the Word of the Lord, to bring to nought His precious blood, and to harden and encourage the impenitent, reckless world in its wild and wicked ways under an appearance of the holy Word, so he also exerts himself, in my opinion, in order that he may root out the salutary, pure faith from the earth by all kinds of false and criminal slander and to deliver the pious and godly children into the hands of the executioner.

If I am wrong, rebuke me. Whether he is not more properly called a bird of prey than the gathering mother hen[45] he wants to be, this I will leave to himself and to the Lord.

But the Lord, who is the shield and surety of all oppressed people, turns back the onslaughts of the ungodly. He destroys the liars. He abhors the wicked and deceitful, for there is no faithfulness in their mouth. Their inward part is very wickedness; their throat is an open sepulcher; they flatter with their tongue.

Therefore they shall not stand before the storm; their lamp shall be extinguished, and their glory shall vanish. For the Lord is strong who shall judge them, and He will require the poor, deceived souls and the innocent blood at their hands, and He will give them their reward.

Behold, worthy reader, from this you may realize that the doctrine and confession of the preachers in regard to infant baptism cannot stand according to the Scriptures; that it is founded neither on the Lord's command, nor on the doctrine or practice of the holy apostles as is the baptism of the believers, but merely upon glosses, opinion, conjecture, falsehood, borrowed names, and lengthy custom.

If you are of reasonable bent, then let the infallible and true Word of the Lord, and your impartial heart, judge between us and the learned ones.

I would hereby, for God's sake, ask all my readers not to hold it against me that I reprove falsehood with Scripture, defend truth with truth, point out the right way, seek your souls, controvert the false prophets, expose their deceiv-

*peribit de populo suo* (The soul that doeth ought presumptuously, it shall be cut off from among his people), a quotation, in part, of Num. 15:30, a text that might well be construed so as to occasion the despair, etc., mentioned by Gellius. *Tr.*

44 Reading *ghekeert* (turned) for *gheleert* (taught). *Tr.*

45 On the margin Menno gives the page on which Gellius in his writings speaks of a mother hen *(Litera F, second leaf). Tr.* and *Ed.*

ing, secret snares; and promote the Lord's praise. He that seeks the Lord in sincerity of heart may read and judge.

## [IV.] THE LORD'S SUPPER

We will, for the sake of brevity, omit writing at length about the Lord's Supper, because we have previously published our position and belief of this matter with many Scriptures. Whosoever delights in the truth may read them and reflect on them in the fear of God.

Yet we would, in our simplicity, warn the pious reader in regard to our reply to Gellius, that it is written, For we, being many, are one bread and one body; for we are all partakers of that one bread. I Cor. 10:17. We learn from the Scriptures that the Holy Supper was instituted by the Lord as a sign and testimony and proof, not to the world but to the church of God, that all of us who partake of one bread, are members of one body, namely, of the body of Christ. Since we see with our eyes and feel with our hands that both the dispensers and partakers of the worldly Supper are not true members of the Lord's body because the dispensers are all hirelings, thieves of the honor of God, and murderers of our souls, who sustain the thoughtless, reckless people in all manner of unrighteousness and blindness, and in a free and carnal life, by their promises, philosophy, and invention, deceiving all the world, and hating, reviling, belying, apprehending, banishing, and abusing the pious who depart from evil, follow the Word of the Lord, and regularly eat of His bread; and since the partakers are, speaking generally, an impenitent, willful, and vain people, yes, worldlings, who not only disrespect the Spirit, Word, and knowledge of the Lord, but for the most part trample it underfoot, as may be seen, therefore we abstain from their supper. For the sincere fear in our hearts, impelled by the Word of God, prevents us from partaking of it with such dispensers and partakers, lest we also partake of their deceiving conduct and abominable abuse, and at the day of Christ receive the same reward with them.

He boasts a great deal of his admonition, yet all his admonition is nothing but vain prattle without all power. For how can he and similar preachers rightly teach Christ and admonish others, while they are yet filled from the top of their heads to the soles of their feet, with all manner of unrighteousness, blindness, and shame?

They should reflect upon the words of Sirach, and rightly learn to know themselves, because many of them are as yet such useless people that they are more fit to be swine herders than shepherds of the sheep of Christ, as he writes; also, that Gellius is not only a falsifier of the Scripture and deceiver of souls, but also a very cruel, profane, defaming, and unmerciful man, as may be very clearly learned from his writings.

[1] *He writes that they admonish those who partake, in the first place, that they should be well grounded in the Law and principally in the holy Gospel.*

*Reply.* Wherever the law is rightly preached and taken to heart so that it reveals its nature and power, there we find a broken spirit, a penitent, humble heart, and a conscience which trembles before the Word of its God, which checks and drives out sin, as Sirach says.

This is the real function and end of law: To reveal unto us the will of God, to discover sin unto us, to threaten with the wrath and punishment of the Lord, to announce death and to point us from it to Christ, so that we, crushed in spirit, may before the eyes of God die unto sin, and seek and find the only and eternal medicine and remedy for our souls, Jesus Christ.

So also where the Gospel is preached in true zeal, according to the pleasure of God, and unblameably in the power of the Spirit, so that it penetrates the hearts of the hearers, there we find a converted, changed, and new mind, which joyfully and gratefully gives praises to its God for His inexpressibly great love toward us miserable sinners, in Christ Jesus, and thus it enters into newness of life willingly and voluntarily, by the power of a true faith and a new birth.

If Gellius would hammer at the innermost heart of his followers, and of himself, with the hammer of the law, and zealously kindle fire in them with the zeal of the holy Gospel so that they would in true repentance forsake their unclean, hateful heart and their pagan pride and pomp, in houses, clothes, gold, silver, their luxury, avariciousness, drinking, and carousing; and if they would enter with Christ into newness of life, then I would feel free to admit that that which he has written here concerning the Lord's Supper, did for the most part, sound not so bad.

But now he consoles the poor with an empty purse, puts the shirt over the jacket and the cart before the horse.[45a] For the signs of the New Testament are in themselves quite powerless and vain and useless if the thing signified, namely, the new, penitent life, is not there, as has been said above in connection with baptism.

[2] *He writes further that they in the second and third place, admonish them that it is not enough to know and to understand the doctrine, and have and carry it in their hearts, but that it should also be confessed or practiced at the risk of life and limb, and* [3] *that they must arm themselves for the cross and opposition, patiently and obediently bear it, and follow their bridegroom, for the devil cannot bear such confession; therefore hates and persecutes it.*

*Reply.* Caiaphas said unto the Pharisees and scribes, it is expedient for us that one man should die for the people, and that the whole nation perish not.

His pretentions sounded right, yet his cruel, bloodthirsty heart did not perceive that it was he who, through bitter zeal, sought the life of the king of all glory. I Cor. 2:8.

That Gellius and similar preachers sometimes talk of a pious life according to the Scriptures, and admonish concerning the cross, we do not deny. But how they nevertheless love true righteousness which flows from true doctrine, and how they praise those who confess it may, alas, be seen from their rude and disgraceful writing and crying.

---

45a In the margin we read, "Penitence should precede the Sacrament and not vice versa." *Tr.*

Since he writes that he admonishes them thus as was heard, and since it is plainly manifest that he hates the true righteousness, power, fruit, and obedience which true preaching brings forth, but also loads it, I fear, with the cross by his ugly and disgraceful writing; therefore the godly, pious reader may consider if he is not like unto the scribes and Pharisees, in this respect, who, although they taught the literal Law, yet so hated its righteousness that they, by their hateful counsel and advice, crucified Him who was promised in the Law, the Fulfiller, Jesus Christ!

Dear reader, understand what I write. External preaching, hearing, baptism, and Supper (which are done in appearance) do not count before God. But before Him teaching and believing count, believing and doing, outward baptism and Supper according to the letter, and inwardly according to the Spirit and truth. Behold, this is what God's Word and ordinance teach us.

So long as such impenitent, carnal people are the dispensers, and such good-for-nothing, pompous, covetous, usurers, carousers, and drunkards, the partakers, so long, I say, it is not the true Supper of the Lord, but a meal of the impenitent, an encouragement to the unrighteous, and a superstitious mockery, however much it may be adorned and decked before men with many admonitions. For outside of the church of Christ, which is a gathering of the penitent, there is neither baptism nor Holy Supper.

Once more, understand that which I write: Without penitence, neither water, bread, nor wine, or ceremony, avail in Christ; even if they were administered by the apostles themselves. Before Him avail a new creature, a converted, changed, and broken heart, a sincere fear and love of God, unfeigned love of one's neighbors, a mortified, humble, sober, and peaceful life according to the Word and example of the Lord. Where there is such a new being, there indeed is true baptism and the true Supper. But, once more, to be baptized externally, and to partake of the Supper, merely in the letter and in appearance, not also inwardly before God in Spirit and truth, I repeat, is nothing but to grasp at a shadow, to mimic God's work, yes, to be hypocrites and deceivers.

Is it not lamentable blindness that these poor, straying people attach so much value to the outward, visible sign, and do not notice that they are, with all their heart, hostile to the invisible things signified, for which the visible sign was commanded in the Scriptures? As if God had a special pleasure in mere elements, water, bread, and wine, and not in the thing signified, which is represented, pictured, and urged thereby!

Oh, no, reader, we cannot please nor serve God with mere water, bread, and wine; for by His hand it was all created. But for this reason baptism and the Lord's Supper have been ordained in the Lord's house: that we thereby might declare our faith and obedience, walk in continual and eternal penitence, remember His unspeakably great love and blessings, be admonished that He has offered for us His pure, spotless body, and that He has shed His precious, crimson blood for the atonement of our souls in the burning flame of His eternal love for us; that we ever walk with Him in unity of Spirit and follow in His steps; love, assist, console, reprove, bear, admonish, sustain, and serve each other as members of one body; and prove ourselves unto death, as the newborn children of God in all righteousness, holiness, truth, etc. Behold, dear reader, for this purpose the signs of the New Testament were left us. If Gellius and similar preachers were to use the Holy Supper with such heart and spirit; if the thing signified, the fruit, Spirit, and power, were present; if they and their followers were seen to be in the thing signified, the fruit and the spirit (although in weakness), as it is represented by the sign; then we would, by the grace of God, soon approach each other and dispute but little about this sign and usage. But so long as they teach the broad way, practice and uphold infant baptism, reproach and defame the baptism of believers, as long as they do not separate their disciples and church from the world and teach an unblamable doctrine and life—so long we can never unite with them in doctrine and sacraments, regardless of consequences, as God pleases. For we know of a certainty that we have the Lord's invincible, strong truth and they damnable, weak falsehood.

My faithful reader, reflect on what I write. Our separation from the doctrine and sacraments of the preachers is principally for two reasons. In the first place, because we verily know from Scripture and by their conduct, and are assured in our hearts by the Spirit, that they are not pastors, but deceivers. The entire Scriptures teach us that we are not to hear, but must shun such preachers. For if we are afraid of physical thieves, murderers, and wolves, how much more should we fear those who so miserably rend our poor souls, who keep us in darkness, deprive us of the light of the brightness of Christ, and fearlessly lead us to the frightful, indissoluble darkness of everlasting and infernal torment, for the sake of a stomachful of bread. For God's sake, dear reader, do not take it ill of me. Behold, before God it is true what I write.

The second reason is that we may by such shunning testify to you and to all others, by open deeds, that you are outside of the Spirit, Word, kingdom, and church of Christ, that you are walking on the wrong way, and are allowing yourselves to be miserably deceived by your preachers, so that you may yet be roused in time, may depart from evil, walk in truth, and be saved eternally.

If you are of reasonable minds, then consider well what we seek hereby, and think not that we are so thoroughly deprived of our minds that we walk this narrow way through contentiousness and partisanship. Oh, how gladly would we save our weak bodies, our wives and little children, our possessions and lives, and live peaceably with the world, if we were not constrained by the love of God's honor and the eternal salvation of your and our souls!

But as it is, we must for the two mentioned reasons, risk all, and if the case requires, suffer death in sincere, genuine love. For truth is usually maintained dearly; and sincere, faithful love is crowned with a crown of thorns. O Lord!

[4] *In the last place he writes: From this every pious Christian may easily see how unreasonably these people censure us because of our Lord's Supper, and*

*the gathering of Christ's church, accusing us of dissension, wrath, and enmity, the while themselves quarreling about the articles of faith among themselves, and sowing enmity, contention, wrath, and discord, as has been said: these men who never thoroughly investigated our doctrine and who have scarcely witnessed our partaking of the Supper!*

*Reply.* To this I reply, in the first place: the unrighteousness which shuts us out from the kingdom, church, body, and Supper of Christ, does not consist merely in enmity, contention, wrath, and discord, but also in all other kinds of works of the flesh, such as pomp and pride, avariciousness, drinking and carousing, etc.

Although enmity and discord existing among some are, as he says, by the use of their Supper in part reconciled, yet all the other abominable sins and unrighteousness remain unrepented of, as may be very plainly and publicly seen by their fruits. The heathen also make peace among themselves when they are at variance with each other, yet that does not make them genuine grains of the Lord's bread and the true members of His body. Let every one of sound mind reflect upon what I say.

In the second place I say, he cannot with truth substantiate his charge against us of enmity, contention, and discord.

But even as he and his fellows accuse our Christian doctrine and faith, our sacraments and actions before all; cause trouble and affliction, and we, by the grace of God, do not deal with them in anger and wrath, but with patience, in Christ's Spirit and Word, teaching, reproving, and admonishing them, maintaining truth with truth, and from our inmost heart showing and pointing out to them the right way at the risk of life and blood (a matter for which they hate us so), so also, at times, some rise up among us, as was the case in the apostolic church, who would rather follow their own reason than the Scriptures, who would return to the broad road, seek honor and a name, and make unscriptural assertions. With such we treat and reason, admonishing and reproving them as the Scriptures teach, and I trust we do this reasonably and in love. If they allow themselves to be taught, desist, and strive after peace, then we thank the Lord for His gift. But if they despise fraternal admonition and love, remain stubborn in their ways, and cause contention and discord, then they cannot be our fellows and brethren, until they acknowledge their faults, and return to the Lord's people in peace. If this should be causing contention, enmity, and discord about the articles of faith, or rather keeping uncleanness from the house of the Lord, all right-minded people may judge, both by their common sense and the Scriptures.

In the third place I say, the reason why we have not heard their doctrine, nor seen their partaking of the Supper, as he complains, is that we see and have for a long time seen by their fruits that their doctrine is vain and powerless, and their sacraments out of keeping with the Word. For of what spirit both their preachers and disciples are the children, may best be seen from the dishonest, slanderous, bitter, false, spiteful, and seditious writings of the preachers; and secondly, from the abominable show of clothes, the pretentious building and adorning of houses, and from the superfluous, carnal, easy life of their disciples. What does it help that they make a good show, and argue well with fair words, as long as they in fact forsake the Scriptures and the thing signified, the fruit and power of the holy sacraments, yes, hate and persecute it? If I do not write the truth, then reprove me.

In the fourth place, when Gellius accuses us that we forsake the church of Christ, I reply that we according to the teachings of the Word and ordinance of God, and the example of the holy apostles, forsake the world and their false prophets, and that we, through the Spirit and grace of Christ, free the church of Christ from snares, faithfully admonish her in our weakness, establish and edify her according to the command of the holy Word. What business has this poor, rash man for speaking and boasting of the church of Christ, while she is yet quite unknown to him?

I willingly make myself available. Let them arrange for a free discussion with the preachers, either privately before witnesses, or publicly before a full assembly, and if I cannot prove and maintain by the power and truth that the preachers one and all are deceivers and not pastors, and that their show-offs, graspers, usurers, swearers, and cursers are world and not Christians, then I will publicly acknowledge before all the world that we not only have forsaken the church of Christ, but also rend her and cause many a pious heart much misery, affliction, and trouble.

But if I can sustain these assertions by the power of the truth, why then must we still hear so many evil words? It is more than high time, is it not, that the preachers would cease their deceiving, that they and their disciples, who, where, and what they may be, would wake up, tremble at the wrath and punishment of God, repent, conform themselves according to the Spirit, Word, and example of the Lord, and establish a true Christian church in accordance with the command of the Scriptures, and that they would disclaim and avoid their borrowed names and false pretensions, such as evangelical teachers, faithful shepherds, pastors, preachers of the holy Word, etc., which they, to the dishonor of God and the destruction of their neighbors, put on in sham.

Behold, reader, I write you the truth and lie not. I seek nothing before my God but that I may gain Gellius and all the preachers, in all lands where they are, to Christ, by the Spirit and Word of God; or that I, vanquished by them, may stand abashed before all the world as an open deceiver. If now they are of Christian disposition and preachers of the holy Word who are desirous of godly unity, as they pretend to be, then let them grant me what I desire, namely, a free discussion so that the grounds and doctrines of both sides may be heard, so that thereby the pure saving truth of Christ may move forward and the impure, damnable falsehood of Antichrist may be destroyed.

But in case they refuse this (as they have done twice before) and continue their slanderous defamation and vituperation as heretofore, and accuse us with all manner of accusations before the uninformed people, as he does here—

that we forsake the church of Christ, that we are a misled, deceived people, and that we call good evil—what else can we do but leave them to the Lord and His judgment; submit willingly to the cross as done thus far; possess our souls in patience; and as much as possible admonish those of fair minds thoughtfully to consider what kind of preachers and pastors they have; what great injustice they do us poor, miserable people; how scornfully they reject truth, and defend falsehood; whereas we in all humility and true love, invite them to this free, Christian discussion of the Scriptures, to the praise of Almighty God and His eternal truth, and to the happy refreshment of all the oppressed and afflicted souls? They refuse us this, and besides accuse us by their slanderous publications without fairness and without all foundation and truth; they hatefully accuse us before the whole world, and cause many a pious innocent child to be deprived of possession, honor, and life, as, alas, may be witnessed in many localities of our Netherlands.

## [V.] EXCOMMUNICATION, BAN, EXPULSION

Before I begin a reply to Gellius' excuse as to why they do not have excommunication, ban, or expulsion in their church, I would point out to the kind reader, from Scripture, how that excommunication, ban, or expulsion was not always practiced in the same manner, nor according to the same ordinance, by the Lord's people.

The ban of Moses was to punish the expelled one with death. Deut. 13; Lev. 16:24; Num. 31:16; Josh. 7:26. This ban was in force until the time of the Roman domination. At that time a change was made; for under the Roman scepter they could no longer execute the Law as to extermination because it was involved in the power of the scepter. But they used the ban on those who disobeyed the Law. That is, they ejected them from their synagogues and assemblies, shunned their daily associations, and neither ate nor drank with them, as may be learned from many of the Scriptures of the apostles.

To this shunning, rule, and usage, the doctrine and example of Jesus Christ and the holy apostles unanimously point us, and these two following benefits are derived from them.

In the first place, that we may not be deceived by the erroneous doctrines of the false spirits, and contaminated by their carnal, vain life. Know ye not, says Paul, that a little leaven leaveneth the whole lump? Purge out, therefore, the old leaven.

Yes, my reader, wherever this excommunication, ban, or expulsion is zealously and earnestly taught and practiced in the fear of God, without respect of persons, there doubtlessly the church of the Lord will be maintained inviolate, in salutary, pure doctrine, and in a life without offense. But where this is neglected, there we find nothing but vanity and world, which may be plainly seen in all the churches and sects which are not of us.

Reader, observe. So long as the literal Israel in this respect followed rightly the ordinance of the Lord, and punished those deserving of the ban according to the Word of the Lord they remained upright and pious; but when they neglected it, inclined their ears to falsehood, and gave place to false prophets, then they deviated from the way of life, and fell into all kinds of wickedness and idolatry, as the prophetical Scriptures, on every hand, complain and declare.

It was also the case with the first church. For so long as the pastors and teachers required a godly, pious life, administered baptism and Supper to the penitent only, and rightly practiced expulsion according to the Scriptures, they remained the church and community of Christ. But as soon as they sought an easy, carefree life, and hated the cross of Christ, they laid aside the rod, preached peace to the people, and gradually made the ban less severe, and so established an anti-Christian church, a Babel or world, as may also, alas, be noticed for many centuries now. Yes, my reader, if we had not in our times strictly observed this means ordained by God, then we at this day would have become a reproach and curse to the world, whereas now (I hope) we in our weakness, by the grace of God, are an example and a light to many men, although the wicked world will not acknowledge it. In short, a church without ban or expulsion is like a vineyard without wall or trenches, or a city without walls and gates. For the enemies have free access into it, to sow and plant their pernicious tares unhindered.

In the second place, the fruit is that the wicked, by a proper admonition and expulsion performed by the pious, may become ashamed in their hearts, may humble themselves, and sincerely repent before God and the church. In this way Paul delivered the Corinthian unto Satan for the destruction of the flesh, that the spirit (notice this) might be saved in the day of the Lord Jesus. I Cor. 5:5. He did the same with Hymenaeus and Alexander, that they might no longer blaspheme. I Tim. 1:20. At another place he writes, If any man obey not our word, note that man and have no company with him, that he may be ashamed; yet count him not as an enemy, but admonish him as a brother. II Thess. 3:14, 15.

Behold, reader, here you have briefly stated of whom the ban or separation is ordained in the house and church of God, how, and when to be used. Judge, now, if you fear God, if it is not an essentially noble and necessary work of pure love, ordained by God as a service of love, although the unenlightened and refractory judge and consider it as enmity; although its ultimate design and fruit is that the church may remain sound in doctrine and unblamable in life; that those who err, whether in doctrine or life, may be converted, and return to the pasture and flock of the Lord. But how far, yes, how very far, all the preachers and churches of the world are from this God-pleasing ordinance and very needful practice!

[1] *That expulsion is not practiced in his church is by him excused thus: That the papistical abomination by its abuse has so frightfully destroyed the ordinance of the churches and the right use of the ban, that it cannot be re-established suddenly.*

*Reply.* If we diligently search the writings of the historians and compare the actions of the church reported by them with the Scriptures, then I predict we will not find that there was among all the Germanic nations a true, apostolic Christian church which was sound in doctrine, sacraments, ordinances, and life; but that they were at the outset founded upon the papistic foundation and abominations, and remained there these many years.

Since, then, they are not founded by the apostles upon the foundation of Christ, but by the pope on his own foundation, and since the church is, in every respect, a papistical, and not a Christian church, and since it is wholly evident that it has at this hour neither teachers nor congregation, life nor sacrament in keeping with the ordinance, doctrine, and example of Christ, therefore he can never practice the ban until he bans himself, because he is a falsifier of the Scriptures and deceiver of souls; and then the entire church, because they are one and all impenitent in life and outside of the command, ordinance, and Word of Christ as to doctrine, as may be seen. Consider what I say, He that doeth evil hath not seen God.

[2] *In the second place he writes, We admit that in many churches negligence is found, which we cannot praise; which is caused in some places by the fact that the magistrates are so diligent in punishing all sins and violations that occur publicly, that the pastors feel that little is left for their ban to do.*

*Reply.* In my opinion, it is high time that the preachers would quit their trifling with the souls of men; that they would acknowledge openly that they are not the church of the Lord, but a poor, erring, and carnal flock and world; and then begin earnestly to teach themselves, and next to preach rightly the word of sincere repentance in the power of the Spirit. All those who would accept it in sincerity of heart and truly repent, would then receive the sacraments of the Lord according to the ordinance of God, and those who would scornfully despise it, would by the power of the holy Word be excommunicated without respect of persons, rich or poor. Then they might be able to gather a church unto Christ, and rightly practice the ordinance of the Lord in it, according to the Scriptures.

But as long as they baptize irrational children, and consider Christian all those who are baptized, dispense the bread to the impenitent, and tolerate all the avaricious, the usurers, the pompous, drinkers, and carousers, in the communion of their churches, so long will the world be their church, and their church the world.

In such a state of affairs they may preach and admonish all their days about separation, and the true ordinances, but never introduce them, since it is evident that all their doctrines and sacraments are nothing but a vapor, vain and powerless, for they are not rightly called preachers, their sacraments are not the true sacraments, and their disciples are not the Lord's church and people.

Say, beloved, how shall a house be built as long as there are no workmen, lumber, iron, stone, and mortar? He who is of sound mind may ponder on what I say.

I say further, if Gellius rightly understood Christ and His Word, he would be ashamed all his days for these two reasons: First, because he undertakes to excuse the pastors, by saying that the magistracy punishes open transgressions, as if therefore excommunication were not necessary. I think that hundreds of pastors can be found in Germanic lands, who never in their life have known that the avaricious, drunkards, adulterers, etc., are to be excommunicated. Yes, what is worse, the greater part of them are themselves publicly guilty of such carnal conduct. Seeing then that it is as clear as daylight that he seeks to adorn and cover this ignorance, yes, negligence and shame, with the excuse that the magistracy punishes the transgressors, this is, in my mind, nothing less than willfully to defend falsehood and oppose truth.

Second, he would be ashamed because he complains that the magistracy does not listen to, nor grant authority to the pastors. Say, good reader, where in all the days of your life did you read in the apostolic Scriptures that Christ or the apostles have invoked the authority of the magistracy against those who would not hear their doctrine or obey their words? Yes, reader, I· know for certain that wherever the magistracy is to execute the ban by the sword, there the true knowledge, Spirit, Word, and church of Christ are not. Whether this is not rightly called, with the papists, to invoke the secular arm[46] I will leave it to the judgment of the discreet reader.

Also, observe here his hypocrisy and his harmful flirtation with the great, for where do we find, alas, more ungodliness than among those in authority? Notwithstanding this, he wants the ban to be maintained by them, as if they were the true and faithful members of the church of Christ and the children of His congregation. And he never observes that if the pastors would rightly judge according to the criterion of the holy Word, the magistrates, next to the preachers themselves, would be the first, according to the Scriptures, to be separated and excluded from the communion of the pious, if they would not repent and regulate themselves according to the Spirit and example of the Lord.

Seeing then that he so openly wheedles the magistrates and those of high standing, and so bluntly and contrary to all the Scriptures flatters them, therefore I cannot neglect to admonish all magistrates and rulers, and in faithful love to warn them, to consider how miserably they are deceived by the preachers. Beloved lords, observe. You boast one and all that you are Christians and have the Word of God, although it is manifest that so many of the

---

[46] All through the Middle Ages heretics were tried by the church and if found guilty were handed over to the secular arm (the civil power) for punishment "seeing that the church does not draw blood." Tr.

lords and princes daily shed human blood like water by their wicked warring and tumult; that they rob many innocent people of their homes and property, burn their houses and homes, make many afflicted orphans and helpless children; drink and carouse day and night; abuse the creature of God above measure in wine, beer, victuals, clothing, etc., all of which merit excommunication and cannot stand the test of the Scriptures, as I presume many of the learned ones and preachers themselves know very well. Yet they connive at it, desiring their authority, help, and assistance; they play the hypocrite with them, they talk to their taste and fancy, do not separate and punish, however wickedly they carry on, and dispense to them the bread and wine exactly as though they were members of the body of the Lord and brethren of His church. By this they so comfort and strengthen them in their wickedness that they never stop to inquire about the fear and ways of the Lord. For it is all, Peace, peace, that they preach, even as the prophet complains. Beloved lords, take heed. They lead you straightway to the abyss of hell! Therefore, beware! I tell you the truth in Christ Jesus, they deceive you. Once more I say, Beware, they deceive you.

On the other hand, they hate and upbraid above measure all those who seek the Lord sincerely, who strive after His holy Word in their weakness, and who would gladly lead a godly, pious life in the fear of the Lord; because they, in true godly zeal and brotherly love, reprove and admonish them to their own good concerning their false doctrine, false sacrament, hypocrisy, and comfortable life, according to the teachings of Scripture, and point them to Christ. They hate and revile; yes, we are called apostles of the devil, apostate Anabaptists, conspirators, and sects by them.

Behold, thus they fawn upon and flatter those in authority, although they generally are upon the broad way; and thus ambitiously they shamefully upbraid the innocent who never harmed them, and who would so gladly lead a pious life. Yet they boast that they are evangelical preachers, and that they teach the Word of God.

[3] *In the third place he writes: The disdain for the servants of the church has everywhere become so great through the activities of the devilish conspirators and heretics that but few churches are able to submit themselves to their pastors in unity of spirit, a thing so necessary.*

*Reply.* That the disrespect to the preachers has become so great is due to nothing else but their own exceeding wickedness, deceit, avarice, blasphemy, and shame. As the prophet says, Behold, I will corrupt your seed, and spread dung upon your faces, etc. Ye are departed out of the way; ye have caused many to stumble at the law; ye have corrupted the covenant of Levi, saith the Lord of hosts. Therefore have I also made you contemptible and base before all the people, according as ye have not kept my ways, but have been partial in the law.

Yes, dear reader, they have spread their sin so wide, and have so trafficked in the souls of men, that the just and great God could no longer endure it;

therefore He has graciously inspired some pious hearts with the Spirit of His divine knowledge, by His great love, and has discovered unto them the adorned Babylonian woman, the preachers and their churches, with all their fornication, abomination, and bloodguiltiness, and thus made manifest their inhuman shame. And these, because they warn all in unfeigned love against the deadly enchanting poison of her cup, by doctrine, life, example, blood, and possessions (by which they seek nothing but the praise of God and the salvation of their neighbors), are called devilish conspirators and sects. O Lord! What rude blasphemy! What awful shame!

Ah, my dear reader, if we could come out in the open, how soon would it become evident who the devilish conspirators and perverse sects are! But what does it help? The scribes and Pharisees sat upon exalted seats, but Christ had not whereon to lay His head. Besides He had to hear that He was possessed of the devil and wrought His miracles in the name of Beelzebub.

Is it not sad, perverse hypocrisy that this man undertakes to blame us for their not practicing the ban when it is known and manifest to the whole world that the greater part of the preachers are such heedless, blind, and carnal people that they acknowledge neither God nor His Word, and seek nothing but that they may feed their carefree, lazy flesh in all luxury and have a good time? What kind of Christians their churches or disciples are, what knowledge they have and how they fear God, may, alas, be seen from their words and works in cities and countries.

[4] *In the fourth place he writes: It is a fact well known to the whole community (he refers to Emden) that we have for several years labored diligently to establish the Christian ordinance of the ban once more.*

*Reply.* The world knows no ban except when such a transgression has been committed that the executioner bans them with the sword, noose, or fire, for the sake of their evil-doing. Or, if one sincerely repents and returns to God, lays aside the wicked, sinful life in true fear, and puts on the new life of true repentance, then they, along with the papists in some places deprive such an one of honor, possessions, and life, or exile him and so drive him into the mouth of the gaping lions.

But that they should, according to the Scriptures, shun the misers, drunkards, fornicators, etc., that they should neither eat nor drink with them, this they do not know and cannot do, since they are, as a rule, unchanged in heart, earthly-minded, and full of all manner of avarice, pomp, extravagance, and carnal works.

Therefore I say again, they may admonish all their life concerning the ban and never establish it according to the Word of God. For how can one avaricious person shun the other, one drunkard the other, and one deceiver the other, according to the Scriptures, and separate him from the communion of the church, since they one and all are earthly-minded and outside the communion, Spirit, and Word of the Lord, as has been heard?

[5] *In the fifth place he writes: The example of the Anabaptists frighten*

*us, who practice the ban with discord, hatred, and irreconcilable wrath one against the other so that it tends more to the rending and destruction among them than to edification and the gathering of the church.*

*Reply.* Blinded vision, erroneous judgment, humoring and wheedling those of high standing, vituperation and slandering of the pious, excusing of sins and twisting of Scriptures, is all I read or see with them.

Oh, how little is the fear of God with them, it seems; for here he undertakes to cover up his avoiding the cross and his disobedience by citing the example of others. Reader, remember that the Word of God should teach and govern us. That some rebellious person takes offense at us, we cannot help. We act as the Word of God has commanded us.

All those who enter into the obedience of the Word, and afterwards live or teach contrary to it in an offense-giving way, cannot be our brethren and sisters if they will not hear our admonitions. Here neither greatness nor littleness, riches nor poverty, man nor woman, friend nor foe, makes any difference. With God there is no respect of persons. They must all bow to the Spirit, Word, and scepter of Christ, or they cannot be brethren.

Since it is manifest that the Spirit of the Lord departs again from such as seek the broad way and become desirous of the freedom of the flesh, of money and possessions; such as give offense to the pious by their frivolousness and self-conceit; therefore, since they are at last expelled, no hope remaining for their reformation, the fellowship of the pious, their hand, mouth, and daily association being denied them albeit with tears and sorrow, and they become angry because they hate to bear this shame which is visited upon them in love for no other purpose than for their reformation, and if they slander and cry out loudly, as also the preachers do, because we dare not hear their teaching and partake of their sacraments, then we must leave it to the Lord, for we cannot prevent that some of them become Davidians[47] and Epicureans (as Gellius calls them) in spite of all our faithful admonitions, diligence, labor, and brotherly service.

There is nothing else to be said about it. The seed did not fall on good earth, but by the wayside, on rocky ground and among thorns, it seems.

I repeat. We have used the faithful service of our brotherly love from our inmost hearts; we have admonished and entreated them, and have put up with some of them a whole year or two, ever waiting and hoping the best of them, and have not hastily separated them, as he accuses us without all foundation.

Since we follow and practice the ordinance of the Lord also in this respect, if he feared the Lord he would reasonably commend our action for rightly observing the commands of God at the risk of possessions and life, for proceeding according to the Scriptures, without any respect of persons; he would acknowledge the truth, and confess that not our example frightens them but the fear of the cross. For if they would proceed with kings, dukes, lords, and princes according to the Scriptures, and also with their drunkards, their avari-

47 Followers of David Joris, a leader of one of the "corrupt sects." *Ed.*

cious, showy people, then it would be quite a different thing with them. This I say without reservation and can prove it in truth.

[6] *In the sixth place he writes: If they think that they with their banning have done much good unto edification, then let them point out from the several hundreds which they have banned, not ten but five, whom they have banned in love and helped through brotherly admonition, or whom they have brought to order and have saved by their remedy.*

*Reply.* He seeks all kinds of reasons to blaspheme the Word and work of God so that he may give some good appearance to his cross-fleeing and hypocrisy. Inasmuch as he says that separation tends more to destruction than edification, therefore the reader should know that we daily find by experience that the following benefits result from expulsion among us: First, that we thereby follow and obey God's Word. Second, that we thereby rid the congregation of false doctrine, discord, and offensiveness as has been said. Third, that the disobedient are thereby admonished to reflect, return, and repent. Fourth, that we thereby testify that we do not consent nor agree with the Münsterites and other rebellious sects. Fifth, that we thereby admonish all preachers and their churches that they are also in this matter outside the ordinance and Word of God. Sixth, that thereby the whole world may learn from us that the counsel, doctrine, ordinance, and command of God are to be maintained and obeyed.

Behold, dear brother, these are the fruits which true expulsion daily brings forth by the grace of God. But the preachers, alas, do not regard them. And even if it were true that few are reformed thereby, as he accusingly cries out, they must still admit that these afore-mentioned glorious results are obtained thereby.

Reader, take notice that no matter how we sing to the wicked, it is never done correctly, for if we had disregarded this means and divine ordinance as the preachers do, and had left everybody to follow his own mind (from which may the great Lord ever preserve us), how loudly would they cry that we are all seditionists and Arians. But now that we expel them, according to the Scriptures, from the communion of the church, it is called a ruinous rending and a hasty ban. Behold, thus they seek, on every hand, to destroy truth and uphold falsehood.

[7] *In the seventh place he writes, It is better not to use the ban, than to use it unto the destruction and rending of the church.*

*Reply.* Even if it were as he asserts, then still, a good thing should not be abandoned for the sake of some. If the ban is a destruction and rending of the church, then Christ and the apostles have very much deceived us in this regard, for teaching us this ordinance openly, both by word and example, as may be read in the Scriptures. But what does it help? He might briefly state his point thus: We refuse to expel and ban; for they are, as a general thing, all led by an erroneous spirit, and are members of the body of Antichrist.

[8] *In the eighth place he writes: None have proved a greater difficulty and obstacle in re-establishing the ban than have the Anabaptists who have*

*caused a disturbance in the building of the church of Christ, and in its right course, have brought the ministers into disrepute, and have under semblance of truth drawn many zealous hearts from the church (with whom it might have been begun) and led them into much falsehood.*

*Reply.* If I had not learned to know Gellius from his other writings, this his excuse in regard to the ban would more than clearly teach me what kind of man he is. O dear Lord. It is verily nothing but hypocrisy, falsehood, and deceit that he produces! He writes that we obstruct the ban. Yet, if he would confess the truth, he would have to admit that not we, but his own unbelief, carnal mind, and his cross-fleeing flesh stand in his way.

He writes that we have caused disturbance in the building of the church, although it is manifest that we point all the churches of the world, by doctrine and life, with possessions and blood, to the right way, the true worship and ordinance, and that they themselves are those who, with all their strength, disturb the course of the building of the church of Christ by their frivolous doctrine, false sacraments, and vain life.

He writes that we have brought the ministers into disrepute, because we reprove them in unfeigned love, and point them by doctrine and life to Christ's example, Spirit, and Word, although he acknowledges above that some are more fit to be swineherders than shepherds of the sheep of Christ.

He writes that we have, in semblance of truth, drawn many zealous hearts from the church, persons with whom the ban might have been begun, and have led them into many errors; although the facts show that we do not separate them from the church but from the world and that we led them by the hand and help of God into eternal truth.

I say further: Their doctrine has been preached for over thirty years in Germanic lands and there are whole kingdoms, principalities, and cities where not a single Anabaptist, as he calls them, is to be found. Who is it that obstructs the pastors there in re-establishing the ban? In all the time that they have preached and taught their doctrine, they have never yet banned one fornicator, drunkard, or avaricious person, from the communion of their churches, And still he writes that we obstruct and hinder them. O dear Lord! Thus the pious have to hear it everywhere, although they seek God sincerely, and would gladly see a Christian church true in doctrine, sacraments, ordinances, and life.

[9] *In the ninth place he writes: For two reasons we could not do it so soon (he means establish the ban) as the Anabaptists did. First, because our gatherings are public and consist of many hundreds, all of whom we cannot know well, while their gatherings are secret and consist of but few. Second, because we do not establish sects, as they do, which is a work of the flesh, and befriended by the devil, but we establish an eternal church unto Christ, which the devil bites in the heel, and robs of all good things.*

*Reply.* Above he has partly acknowledged that many of their hearers are of the world. Here he writes that their gatherings consist of many hundreds, and that they gather an abiding church. Yet they never get far enough to separate their disciples and church from the world, and bring them into a divine ordinance. The reason is that they themselves are of the world.

But as to his writing that their assembly is large and kept in public, while ours is small, I will with the Word of God reply in this manner, Wide is the gate, and broad is the way, that leadeth to destruction, and many there be which go in thereat; because strait is the gate, and narrow is the way, which leadeth unto life, and few there be that find it. Matt. 7:13, 14.

Yes, my reader, if you attentively read the Scriptures you will find that the number of the elect was always small and the number of the unrighteous very great. The pure genuine Gospel of Jesus Christ, the true knowledge of eternal truth, never was so common in the world that the true believers could be counted by many hundreds of thousands in any country or city. Christ Jesus and His eternal truth must ever dwell with the few in retired places; but Antichrist can go undisturbed in public with his falsehoods and count his followers by the thousands.

Again, by his writing that they cannot know all on account of their great numbers, he testifies that brotherly love is very thin with them; for where is there a Christian pastor who does not know his sheep? And where is the Christian brother who does not know his Christian brother? If the preachers do not know all, on account of their great number, still one brother should know the other. They should observe, teach, admonish, comfort, and reprove each other, and seek each other's salvation; for this is the Word and unction of God.

Reader, observe. He pretends that they cannot possibly know all, and I, who am most of the time keeping myself in retired places, could point them out in great numbers. Let him travel through city and country where they boast of the Word, and let him listen and look closely, and he will find out how they dare heap one falsehood upon another, and one ungodly act upon another, how they dare to swear by the Lord's holy flesh, blood, death, wounds, and sacraments, and with what beautiful clothes, leggings, vests, chains, and swords they show off. Let them take a view of the wicked, drunken taverns, fencing-schools, and houses of ill fame, and of shooting galleries, of which there is no lack in Germanic lands. Let him examine the courts of kings and princes, and go into the ways of the nobility, and I presume he will find thousands doubly deserving of expulsion. But an earthly mind and perverse heart has, alas, little regard for the ordinance and Word of the Lord.

Again, to his assertion that they do not make sects, as he says we do, and that it is a carnal work, I could wish that Gellius and all the papists, Lutherans, Zwinglians, Davidians, etc., could appreciate this matter, for it is written of heresies and heretics, that they shall not inherit the kingdom of God.

It is a small matter to us to be called sect-makers by the world; for the children of God from apostolic time were called that. Notwithstanding, we in our simplicity would say this in regard to this matter, that we point to Christ Jesus, God's eternal Wisdom, Truth, and Son, for He is the One whom it concerns, and we appeal to His doctrine, ordinance, and usage with confidence. If anyone under heaven can convince us with the infallible Word that we are wrong, and act contrary to His Word, then we will gladly hear it and obey the truth.

But in case they cannot do so, they must confess, must they not, that we are the apostolic Christian church and that they are the deceiving carnal sects.

But that sects have gone out from us, and not from them, is also a strong proof that we are the church, and that they are not. For Paul says, There must be also sects among you, that they which are approved be made manifest among you. I Cor. 11:19. John says, They went out from us, but they were not of us. I John 2:19.

Say, beloved, why should Satan fight with sects against those who are sects already and his adherents? But those that turn to the Lord, these he bites in the heels and seeks to devour. Gen. 3:15; I Pet. 5:8.

[10] *In the tenth place he writes: If they said only that we or our people do not teach concerning the ban, that would be unfair to us and to many teachers and churches, and they might be put to shame because of this, quite readily. But as to the assertion that we neither have practiced nor used* . . . .

*Reply.* In my opinion, it would be well for him not to be sarcastic about these things, but to observe the Word of the Lord somewhat more carefully. Before God the literal teaching with the voice does not matter, but action in power and truth. If they should say that this would cause a disturbance, then I ask what kind of pastors and shepherds they are, if they neglect the will and Word of God on account of the disturbance of the world. Let all the right-minded judge this according to the Scriptures.

[11] *In the last place he writes: Even if we should admit it to be true that this defect exists in all of our churches (although the contrary is true in many of them, for in the Dutch church in London one was banned; and it is not wholly omitted here in Emden), Would the church on account of this defect lose its name and henceforth, as they say, be no longer the church of Christ? Then truly our body, to which the church is likened, would lose the name of body on account of some blemish or wound.*

*Reply.* This is rightly called, as I think, to make lies a refuge. For he says the contrary is true of many churches; yet he can point to only one in the many kingdoms, principalities, cities, and towns, who was banned, namely, at London, England. I have never in all my life heard a more ridiculous argument. How manifestly does the great Lord turn their wisdom to folly and their understanding to nothing. Yet the blind, ignorant world does not see it.

Reader, reflect and see if mockers of which Peter and Jude prophesied have not arrived. The whole Germanic nation or people, yes, all countries are so replete with ungodliness, abomination, and wickedness that one is frightened and shamed. Yes, the righteous who fear the Lord are as scarce as grapes in a vineyard carefully gleaned, and in which few grapes are left to pluck and use, as the prophet laments, and out of so many hundreds of thousands, he points to one who was banned at London that it may be said that they do practice the ban and so give some face to their disobedience.

I think that they will act so clumsily that the whole world must see that it is nothing but hypocrisy, falsehood, and deceit. O Lord, how long will this mockery last?

But to his writing that if the church must lose its name on account of a defect, then also our bodies would lose their name on account of a blemish or wound, I reply: If this were the only defect in their church, then there would yet be hope that things would improve; but their defects and faults are so numerous that they could better be compared to a dead body, that is, one without spirit or life, than to a body that has one blemish or wound as he pretends.

I think that the cunning of the fox which destroys God's vineyard (a passage which he in his writing applies to us) is plainly discernible here. For how cunningly they flee before the power of truth, from one hiding place to another, lest they be caught, may, alas, be clearly gathered from this frivolous excuse concerning the ban.

## [VI.] THE CHURCH

### A. An Instructive Comparison Whereby the Church of Christ and That of Antichrist May Be Known.

Gellius complains that we rend the congregation of God, desert the church, and that we are devilish sects and conspirators; and on the other hand he boasts that they gather an abiding church. Therefore, in my opinion, it is necessary, in the first place, to compare the churches with the requirements of the Scriptures so that the pious reader may know thereby the difference, and see which and what the church of Christ is, and also what the church of Antichrist is; how long they both have existed; by whom they are; of whom they are brought forth; by what means they are begotten; to what end; of what disposition or nature each one is; what fruits they bring forth; and by what signs they may be known: lest he be deceived by the preachers, and revile the church of Christ as a heresy and conspiracy, and call the church of Antichrist the church of Christ.

[1] In the first place it must be said that the community of God, or the church of Christ, is an assembly of the pious, and a community of the saints, as also the Nicene symbol puts it, which from the beginning firmly trusted and believed in the promised Seed of the woman, which is the promised Prophet, Messiah, Shiloh, King, Prince, Immanuel, and Christ; the which will accept and believe to the end His Word in sincerity of heart, follow His example, be led by His Spirit, and trust in His promise, as the Scriptures teach.

These pious people are commonly called Christians or the church of Christ, because they are born of Christ's Word by means of faith, by His Spirit, and are flesh of His flesh and bone of His bone, even as the children of Jacob were on account of their natural birth called the house of Israel. Rom. 9:7-9.

On the other hand it should be observed that the church of Antichrist is a gathering of the ungodly, and a community of the impenitent, who reject the afore-mentioned Seed, Christ, and His Word; and oppose His will; and for that reason are called the anti-Christian community or church, because they, through the intrigue and direction of Antichrist, the real opponent of Christ, teach, believe, act, and establish a strange worship, contrary to the Spirit, Word, example, and ordinance of Christ, all with the appearance of the Word and the name of Christ.

[2] In the second place it should be observed that the church of the pious is from the beginning, although it did not always have the same ordinance, nor the same name in the Scriptures. For, before the exodus out of Egypt, they had no particular written law, yet they feared the great and powerful God, faithfully served Him, offered burnt offerings, and walked in His ways, as may be seen in the case of Abel, Noah, Abraham, Isaac, Jacob, and others; and they were at that time called children of God. Gen. 6:2. Afterward, Abraham received a command to circumcise himself and all his household, and all the males after him, on the eighth day. Gen. 17:10. About four hundred years after that, Moses was given the Law, and from that time they were generally called the people of God, or the house of Jacob and Israel. At last Christ Jesus, our and the whole world's Messiah, appeared, to which all the Scriptures point. All those who hear Him, believe His Word, and follow in His steps, are now called Christians or the church of Christ.

Although each era has its own ordinance and usage, and although the church is called by different names, as has been said, yet all before, under and after the Law, who in sincere, true fear of God, walk and continue to walk according to the Word and will of God, hope in Christ, and will do so to the end, these are one community, church, and body, and will always remain so; for they are all saved by Christ, accepted of God, and enriched with the Spirit of His grace.

It should be observed that the church of the ungodly, which is the church of Antichrist, had its origin with the first ungodly men who were inspired with the spirit of the devil (who is envious of all good thngs), and will be that unto the end. For the counter church has generally existed from the beginning, side by side with the Christian church, and was the most numerous. Until the deluge, it is spoken of in the Scriptures as, the children of men. Gen. 6:2. But from the deluge until the circumcision of Abraham, they are called Gentiles. After the time of the circumcision they are called Gentiles or the uncircumcised.

They have not known the true and living God, but have worshiped and served the handiwork of men, wood, stone, silver, and golden gods, besides dragons, serpents, oxen, fire, the sun, moon, etc., until the apostles preached the Gospel unto all the world, and gathered a church unto Christ; which church has, in the meantime, been so destroyed by Antichrist that the majority have degenerated into open Gentiles and idolaters, although in sham they have themselves called Christians; for they bend their knees before sticks and stones, and ask the assistance of the work of man's hands. Others, the best minded of them, seek comfort and salvation, and perform ceremonies, in water, bread, wine, absolution, etc. So that we are forced to say that they are the church of the impenitent and the church of Antichrist.

[3] In the third place it should be observed that the Christian church is of God. As Paul says, For both he that sanctifieth, and they who are sanctified, are all of one. Heb. 2:11. For even as Christ Jesus, who is the true Saviour, is of God, yes, is God's only begotten and first-born Son, so also are all those who in sincerity of heart believe His words and are given to drink of His Spirit. As John said, But as many as received him, to them gave he power to become the sons of God, even to them that believe on his name; which are born, not of blood, nor of the will of the flesh, nor of the will of man, but of God. Again, Everyone that loveth, is born of God.

On the other hand it should be observed that the church of Antichrist is of the evil one, even as the Lord said unto the Pharisees, Ye are of your father, the devil, and the lusts of your father ye do. He was a murderer from the beginning, and abode not in the truth, because there is no truth in him. When he speaketh a lie, he speaketh of his own; for he is a liar, and the father of it. John 8:44. He that committeth sin, is of the devil; for the devil sinneth from the beginning.

Reader, observe. By these words the spirit of truth has already judged all liars, blood-shedders, avaricious people, perjurers, adulterers, drunkards, pompous, idolaters, together with all the unrighteous, to be of the devil, that is, that they are the devil's congregation. Nevertheless, they boast that they are the church of Christ, as also the Pharisees boasted that they were Abraham's seed and children. John. 8:39-44.

[4] In the fourth place it should be observed that the church of Christ is begotten by sincere, pious preachers and Christians, who are actuated by the Spirit of Christ, and who are, with Moses, Samuel, Isaiah, Jeremiah, Peter, Paul, John, etc., irreproachable in doctrine and life, who in pure and faithful love seek their neighbors, and say with Paul in sincerity, Be ye followers of me, even as I also am of Christ. I Cor. 11:1. They preach the Word in the power of the Spirit, who as shining lights give light before all men, and who with all their strength put their received talent to work and make a great gain therewith to the treasury of the Lord. For thus it was God's way and will from the beginning to proclaim the doctrine of repentance through pious and unblamable servants, as has been sufficiently shown under the heading, *Calling of the Preachers.*

On the other hand it should be observed that the church of Antichrist is brought forth by faithless preachers, who are actuated by the spirit of Antichrist; who with Korah, Dathan, and Abiram seek standing with the people, who with Balaam seek improper gain, and with the prophets of Jezebel seek choice victuals; who with Hananiah speak to men's preferences; who with the false prophets preach nothing but peace; who mind earthly things and are carnal, and seek nothing but world, ease, honor, belly, and gain. Phil. 3:19; Rom. 16:17.

Oh, reader, how the greatest and highest esteemed preachers of our day, men whose names have become famous, have minded the poor, naked, and crucified Christ Jesus, and the souls of men, with their Gospel, may, alas, be seen from the accursed, ungodly splendor of their houses, and from the vain and fancy ornaments, chains, rings, silk, and satin, of their women and children. Notwithstanding, they are called the evangelical theologians, and ministers of the holy Word; alack and alas, of the comfortable and carnal gospel!

[5] In the fifth place it should be observed that the church of Christ is begotten by the Spirit and Word of Christ. For even as an honorable woman can bring forth no legitimate children but from the seed of her lawful husband, so also the bride of Christ, namely, the church, can bring forth no true children but from the legitimate seed of Christ, that is, from the unadulterated and rightly preached Word, through the Holy Spirit, and conceived in the hearts of the believers. Paul says, In Christ Jesus I have begotten you through the gospel. James says, Of his own will he begot us with the word of truth. Read also Romans 10 and I Peter 1.

On the other hand, the church of Antichrist is begotten of deceiving seduction through the spirit of error. Paul says, Now the Spirit speaketh expressly, that in the latter times some shall depart from the faith, giving heed to seducing spirits, and doctrines of devils; speaking lies in hypocrisy. Yes, reader, what else has the church of Christ laid low and the church of Antichrist raised up again, if not the vile, false doctrines of the learned ones, the many mutually contradictory councils, decretals, statutes, doctrines, and commandments of men? What is it that blinds the Germanic peoples today? What keeps them in their ungodliness, if not the frivolous doctrine of the preachers, the miserable infant baptism, the unscriptural, idolatrous Supper, and the neglect of the Lord's ordinance of the ban as practiced by the apostles?

The prophets on every hand complained that Israel inclined its ears to false preachers. Christ Jesus and His holy apostles faithfully warned in many Scriptures against false prophets; for they deceive you, says Christ; they serve their bellies and not the Lord Christ, says Paul; they promise others liberty and are themselves servants of corruption, says Peter. They turn the grace of God unto lasciviousness (Jude 4), and they are of Antichrist. O reader, reflect diligently on what I write.

[6] In the sixth place it should be observed that the church of Christ is begotten for the purpose of hearing the Lord, of fearing, loving, serving, praising, honoring, and thanking God sincerely. As Moses says, And now, Israel, what doth the Lord thy God require of thee, but to fear the Lord thy God, to walk in all his ways, and to love him, and to serve the Lord thy God with all thy heart and with all thy soul; to keep the commandments of the Lord, and his statutes. Deut. 10:12.

Again, Ye shall walk after the Lord your God, and fear him, and keep his commandments, and obey his voice, and ye shall serve him, and cleave unto him. Deut. 13:4. Peter says, Ye are a chosen generation, a royal priesthood, a holy nation, a peculiar people; that ye should show forth the praises of him that hath called you out of darkness into his marvelous light. I Pet. 2:9.

Behold, the church of Christ is begotten to this end, that His great and wondrous works, His Almighty Majesty, His inextinguishable love, and His adorable, high, and holy name may be eternally glorified. But the church of Antichrist despises, hates, and reviles God, as the prophet says. They transgress my covenant as Adam did, by which they despise me, says Hosea (6:12). Yes, all who reject the Lord's will, Word, counsel, admonition, chastening, grace, and love, hate Him, and will not be ruled by Him. Luke 19:14. They do not do His will, but their own; they say in their hearts: Depart from us, we will know nothing of Thy ways. Who is this most High, that we should serve Him? Behold, thus they boldly despise the Almighty, eternal God, who is the Creator, Messiah, and Lord of all the earth. May the dear Lord grant them eyes that they may see their great faults, and hearts to understand them! This is my sincere wish for them. Amen.

[7] In the seventh place it should be observed that the church of Christ, in her weakness, is disposed and minded as Christ Jesus was. For Paul says, If any man be in Chist, he is a new creature. II Cor. 5:17. He is led by the Spirit, and acknowledges through this Spirit that he abides in God and God in him; he partakes of the divine nature. Yes, dear reader, the true church hates that which Christ hates, and loves that which He loves; for she is His bride, flesh of His flesh, and has been made to drink into one Spirit. Therefore she cannot be otherwise minded than Christ, for she is begotten of the Word, and abides in Him, and He in her, over her, and through her. I John 4:12; John 15:4-7.

Place over against this the church of Antichrist, and you will find that it is of like nature with its father, of whom it is begotten, namely, proud, envious, murderous, false, disobedient, self-conceited, earthly and carnally minded, selfish, avaricious, haughty, proud, pompous, luxurious, impure, and altogether contrary to Christ. For all things that Christ forbids, they do; that which He commands, they despise; whatever He hates, they love; and whatever He loves, they hate. And then they boast that they gather an abiding church, as has been heard. He that hath ears to hear and judge whether or not I speak the truth may decide.

[8] In the eighth place it should be observed that the church of Christ also brings forth the fruits of Christ, as He says, I am the vine, ye are the branches. He that abideth in me, and I in him, the same bringeth forth much fruit.

Every tree bears after its own kind. All who are born of God, and partake of the divine nature, these fear, love, serve, and praise God with all their heart; walk unblamably; they teach, admonish, reprove, uphold, and comfort their neighbor in brotherly fashion; they die unto the flesh and its lusts daily; they conform their ways according to the Word of the Lord and continually lament their being such poor, weak, imperfect sinners.

They strive to become conformable unto the death of the Lord, that they may arise from the death of their sins, and that they may attain unto a perfect being in Christ. Not, my reader, that they have already attained or become perfect, by no means; but they strive, with Paul, to follow after, if they might apprehend that for which they have been apprehended of Christ Jesus. Phil. 3:12.

On the other hand, look at the fruits of the church of Antichrist. Their preachers teach falsely, deceive boldly, and live a soft and easy life. The magistracy carries on as though men were born to no other purpose than to make war and tumults, to hang and kill, to destroy cities and countries, to make vain show, drink, carouse, and to live in all manner of luxury. Yea, many act so that they, alas, might better be called roaring lions and howling wolves than human beings and reasonable people, to say nothing of Christians.

The common people drink, carouse, curse, swear, rake and scrape, and cheat. In short, men live, on every hand, as though God were a teller of fables and His Word a fiction. Behold, such are the fruits of those who boldly boast that they are the church of Christ. Oh, would to God that they might see what Christ Jesus, after whom they call themselves, and His holy apostles, have taught them in plain words, and what example they left them, and then they might yet be helped. For as it is, they only play with the letter, cry, and boast; but no Spirit, work, fruit, or power are apparent. Alas!

B. THE SIGNS BY WHICH BOTH CHURCHES MAY BE KNOWN.

Although I surmise, good reader, that the difference between both churches may be fully grasped in the foregoing comparison, I will, nevertheless, for the sake of greater clarity, briefly present the following signs by which the one church may be known from the other so that truth may be fully declared and known.

[1] In the first place, the sign by which the church of Christ may be known is the salutary and unadulterated doctrine of His holy and divine Word. God commanded Israel to abide in the doctrine of the Law and not to deviate therefrom, neither to the right hand nor to the left. Deut. 5:32. Isaiah admonished Israel to conform themselves to the Law and its testimony, or they would have no dawn. Isa. 8:20. Christ commanded His disciples saying, Go ye into all the world, and preach the gospel to every creature, and teach them to observe all things whatsoever I have commanded you. The prophets testify on every hand that they spoke the Word of God. Thus saith the Lord of hosts, they say. Again, the mouth of the Lord says. Again, Thus speaketh the Lord God who has led you out of the land of Egypt—and other like testimonies. Paul also says, But though we, or an angel from heaven, preach any other gospel unto you, than that which we have preached unto you, let him be accursed. Gal. 1:8. In short, where the church of Christ is, there His Word is preached purely and rightly.

But where the church of Antichrist is, there the Word of God is falsified. There we are pointed to an earthly and unclean Christ and to foreign means of salvation which the Scriptures do not know. There we are taught a broad and easy way. There the great are coddled, and truth is perverted into falsehood. There easy things are taught, such as the poor, ignorant people gladly hear. In short, there they are consoled in their predicament so that they may underrate it, and say, Peace, peace, when there is no peace. Jer. 8:11. They promise life to the impenitent, whereas the Scriptures say that they shall not inherit the kingdom of God. I Cor. 6:10; Gal. 5:21.

[2] The second sign is the right and Scriptural use of the sacraments of Christ, namely, the baptism of those who, by faith, are born of God, who sincerely repent, who bury their sins in Christ's death, and arise with Him in newness of life; who circumcise the foreskin of their hearts with the circumcision of Christ, done without hands; who put on Christ, and have a clear conscience: moreover the participation in the Lord's Holy Supper by the penitent, who are flesh of Christ's flesh, and expect grace, reconciliation, and the remission of their sins in the merits of the death and blood of the Lord, who walk with their brethren in love, peace, and unity, who are led by the Spirit of the Lord into all truth and righteousness, and who prove by their fruits that they are the church and people of Christ.

But where they baptize without the command and Word of God, as they do who not only baptize without faith, but also without reason and intelligence; where the power and thing signified in baptism, namely, dying unto sin, the new life, the circumcision of the heart, are not only not practiced but also hated by those who come to years of discretion; and where the bread and wine are dispensed to the avaricious, the showy, and impenitent persons; where salvation is sought in mere elements, words, and ceremonies, and where a life is led contrary to all love, there is the church of Antichrist. This all intelligent persons must admit. For it is manifest that they reject Christ, the Son of God, His Word and ordinance, and place in its stead their own ordinance and performed works, and so establish an abomination and an idolatry.

[3] The third sign is obedience to the holy Word, or the pious, Christian life which is of God. The Lord says, Ye shall be holy, for I, the Lord your God, am holy. Lev. 19:1. Christ says, Let your light shine before men. Paul says, Be blameless and harmless, the sons of God, without rebuke, in the midst of a crooked and perverse nation, among whom ye shine as lights in the world. Phil. 2:15. John says, He that saith he abideth in him, ought himself also so to walk, even as he walked. I John 2:6.

But how holy the church of Antichrist is, how her light shines, how unblamably and purely they walk, and how their life agrees with Christ's life, may, alas, be seen from their words and works on every hand.

[4] The fourth sign is the sincere and unfeigned love of one's neighbor. For Christ says, By this shall all men know that ye are my disciples, if ye love one another. John 13:35. Yes, reader, wherever sincere, brotherly love is found without hypocrisy, with its fruits, there we find the church of Christ.

John says, And everyone that loveth is born of God, and knoweth God, for God is love. I John 4:7, 8.

But where brotherly love is rejected, where they hate, defame, strike, and beat each other, where everyone seeks his own interests, where they treat each other deceitfully and faithlessly, where they curse, swear, and vituperate, where they defile their neighbor's maids, daughters, and wives; deprive each other of honor, possessions, and life; commit all manner of willfulness, abomination, and malice against each other, as may, alas, be seen on every hand: all intelligent persons may judge according to the Scriptures, whether there is not the church of Antichrist.

[5] The fifth sign is that the name, will, Word, and ordinance of Christ are confidently confessed in the face of all cruelty, tyranny, tumult, fire, sword, and violence of the world, and sustained unto the end. Christ says, Whosoever therefore shall confess me before men, him will I confess also before my Father which is in heaven. Matt. 10:32. Whosoever therefore shall be ashamed of me, and of my words, in this adulterous and sinful generation, of him also shall the Son of man be ashamed, when he cometh in the glory of his Father, with his holy angels. Mark 8:38. Paul also says, For with the heart man believeth unto righteousness, and with the mouth confession is made unto salvation. Rom. 10:10.

But where the papists stick with the papists, Lutherans with the Lutherans, Interimists stick with the Interimists,[48] etc., now build up, and anon demolish and act the hypocrite in keeping with the magistracy's wishes, everyone who is enlightened by the truth and taught by the Spirit may judge what kind of church that is.

[6] The sixth sign is the pressing cross of Christ, which is borne for the sake of His testimony and Word. Christ says unto all His disciples, Ye shall be hated of all nations for my name's sake. Matt. 24:9. All that will live godly in Christ Jesus shall suffer persecution. II Tim. 3:12. Sirach says, My son, if thou come to serve the Lord, prepare thy soul for temptation. Set thy heart aright, and constantly endure, and make not haste in time of trouble. Cleave unto him, and depart not away, that thou mayest be increased at thy last end. Whatsoever is brought upon thee, take cheerfully, and be patient when thou art changed to a low estate. For gold is tried in the fire, and acceptable men in the furnace of adversity. Eccl. 1:5. Read also Matt. 5:10; 10:23; 16:24; Mark 13:13; Luke 6:22; John 16:2; Acts 14:18; II Tim. 2; Heb. 11:37; 12:2.

---

[48] After the defeat of the Protestant forces in the Smalcaldian War, soon after Luther's death, the emperor demanded that the Lutherans return basically to Roman Catholicism, but omit certain of the more objectionable features thereof such as withdrawing the cup from the laity. The married clergy were to be permitted to retain their wives in the interim of this intermediate religion until a general council of the Roman Catholic Church could be convened to determine the future of these compromises with Protestantism. The Interim ended when Maurice of Saxony organized a powerful military league against the emperor, compelling him to guarantee the religious liberty of the Lutherans. *Tr.*

This very cross is a sure indicater of the church of Christ, and has been testified not only in olden times by the Scriptures, but also by the example of Jesus Christ, of the holy apostles and prophets, the first and unfalsified church, and also by the present pious, faithful children, especially in these our Netherlands.

On the other hand, the ungodly, heathenish lying; the hating, envying, reviling, blaspheming; the unmerciful apprehending; the exiling, confiscating, and murdering, and the sentencing to water, fire, sword, and stake, seen in various localities, are plain signs of the church of Antichrist. For John saw that the Babylonian woman was drunken with the blood of the saints, and with the blood of the martyrs of Jesus. Rev. 17:6. He also saw that to the beast which arose from the sea, a mouth was given, speaking great things and blaspheming against God and His holy name, and His tabernacle or church, and them that dwell in heaven. And it was given unto him to make war with the saints, and to overcome them. Rev. 13:5, 6. Yes, my reader, this is the very way and work of the church of Antichrist, to hate, persecute, and put to the sword those whom she cannot enchant with the golden cup of her abominations.

O Lord! Dear Lord! Grant that the wrathful dragon may not entirely devour Thy poor little flock, but that we, by Thy grace, may in patience conquer by the sword of Thy mouth; and may leave an abiding seed, which shall keep Thy commandments, preserve Thy testimony, and eternally praise Thy great and glorious name. Amen, dear Lord. Amen.

With this I will terminate the doctrine of the churches, and conclude this subject with the following questions and answers, which I trust, by the grace of God, will give the industrious reader no little gain and bring great clarity.

*Question. What is the church of Christ?*

*Answer.* A community of saints.

*Q. With whom did she originate?*

*A.* With Adam and Eve.

*Q. Of whom is she?*

*A.* Of God through Christ.

*Q. Of what kind of servants is she begotten?*

*A.* Of those who are irreproachable in doctrine and life.

*Q. Whereby do they beget her?*

*A.* By the Spirit and Word of God.

*Q. To what purpose do they beget her?*

*A.* That she may serve, thank, and praise God.

*Q. Of what mind is she?*

*A.* In her weakness, of Christ's mind.

*Q. What kind of fruits does she bring forth?*

*A.* Fruits which are conformable to the Word of God.

*Q. What is the church of Antichrist?*
*A.* A congregation of the unrighteous.
*Q. With whom did she originate?*
*A.* With the first ungodly ones.
*Q. Of whom is she?*
*A.* Of the evil one through Antichrist.
*Q. Of what kind of servants is she begotten?*
*A.* Of such as are blameworthy in doctrine and life.
*Q. Whereby do they beget her?*
*A.* By the spirit and doctrine of Antichrist.
*Q. To what do they beget her?*
*A.* That she may despise, forsake, and hate God.
*Q. Of what mind is she?*
*A.* Of an earthly, carnal, and devilish mind.
*Q. What fruits does she bring forth?*
*A.* Fruits contrary to the Gospel.

*The True Signs by Which the Church of Christ May Be Known.*

I. By an unadulterated, pure doctrine. Deut. 4:6; 5:12; Isa. 8:5; Matt. 28:20; Mark 16:15; John 8:52; Gal. 1.

II. By a Scriptural use of the sacramental signs. Matt. 28:19; Mark 16; Rom. 6:4; Col. 2:12; I Cor. 12:13; Mark 14:22; Luke 22:19; I Cor. 11:22, 23.

III. By obedience to the Word. Matt. 7; Luke 11:28; John 7:18; 15:10; Jas. 1:22.

IV. By unfeigned, brotherly love. John 13:34; Rom. 13:8; I Cor. 13:1; I John 3:18; 4:7, 8.

V. By a bold confession of God and Christ. Matt. 10:32; Mark 8:29; Rom. 10:9; I Tim. 6:13.

VI. By oppression and tribulation for the sake of the Lord's Word. Matt. 5:10; 10:39; 16:24; 24:9; Luke 6:28; John 15:20; II Tim. 2:9; 3:12; I Pet. 1:6; 3:14; 4:13; 5:10; I John 3:13.

*The True Signs by Which the Church of Antichrist May Be Known.*

I. By a frivolous, easy, and false doctrine. Matt. 7:16; 15:9; 16:4; Rom. 16:26; I Tim. 4:2; II Tim. 2:16, 17.

II. By an unscriptural use of the sacramental signs, as infant baptism and the impenitent Supper. I Cor. 11:19, 20.

III By disobedience to the Word. Prov. 1; Titus 1:15, 16; Matt. 7:26; 25:26.

IV. By hatred of the brethren. 1 John 3:15.

V. By hypocrisy and denial of the name of God and Christ. Matt. 10:33; Mark 8:38; Luke 9:26.

VI. By tyranny and persecution against the godly. John 15:20; 16; Rev. 12:13.

Behold, dear reader, we have shown you clearly the foundation of both churches; what they are, of whom, whence, and of what mind they are; what kind of fruits they bring forth, and by what signs they may be known.

Whoever does not err by choice, to him a plain way is here pointed out. If you want to be a true member of the church of Christ, you must be born of the Word of God; be Christian minded; bring forth Christian fruits; walk according to His Word, ordinance, and command; die unto the flesh and the world; lead an irreproachable life in the fear of God; serve and love your neighbors with all your heart; confess the name and glory of Christ, and be prepared for all manner of tribulation, misery, and persecution for the sake of the Word of God and its testimony.

But if you refuse this, and remain unchanged in your first birth, if you lead an impenitent easy life, neglect the Word and ordinance of the Lord, act the hypocrite with the world, and spurn the cross, then you cannot be a member of the church of Christ unless the Word of God be false and fallible. For on every hand the Scriptures teach faith, love, the fear of God, repentance, obedience, dying unto the flesh, denial of self, a new life, and the cross. Therefore, sincerely fear God, deny yourself, search the Scriptures, follow the truth, and take heed lest you be deceived and lose your poor soul for the sake of this short moment and its enjoyments.

Having given a Scriptural explanation of the difference between the two churches, I will now turn to Gellius' arguments by which he would call their church Christian, and ours a sect and conspiracy. And I will dissolve his arguments quite readily, I hope, by the Word of the Lord, so that the impartial reader must clearly see that he seeks with all his power to suppress the salutary and plain Word of God, together with His holy church, and to excuse and uphold as well as he can the lie of the deceiving serpent and their church.

[C. REPLY TO GELLIUS' ARGUMENTS.]

[1] *In the first place he writes: The saints at Corinth and the church at Galatia, whom Paul reproaches for abominably great sins, continued, nevertheless, to hear the Word of God, and to receive the sacraments from their bishops and pastors.*

*Reply*. If Gellius and the preachers were as to their doctrine and life in agreement with Scripture, if they rightly served their sacraments, if they separated their church from the world according to the Scriptures, then we might talk of hearing preachers. But so long as the preachers remain deceivers, use their sacraments contrary to the Word of God, and so long as their disciples are of the world, so long as they practice neither ban nor punishment as the Scriptures require, so long, in my opinion, it is of no use to say much in regard to this. For it is manifest that they are without Christ and His Word.

Reader, understand this matter rightly. Paul did not put up with the ungodly state of affairs in the before-mentioned churches, as the preachers do now, but he rebuked them in severe terms and urged the obedient to expel, and that with solemn language; especially those of Corinth he threatened if they did not reform themselves.

Gellius should do this too and should not console the poor, reckless people with the idea that other people in the past have also sinned, for this is surely what Sirach calls excusing with the example of others. Neither can it help his cause, for these churches were originally constructed rightly. But afterwards some of them were misled by false prophets and heretics, and led into byways. Some of them, as appears, had again given themselves to an easy carnal life, as is generally the case with those who turn their backs upon the truth and delight in new doctrines, discord, and disputation, as experience has sufficiently taught me also more than enough these last years.

Paul calls the disturbers at Corinth contentious and heretics or sect makers, and those of Galatia he calls deceivers. He desires and commands that they be separated from the church, lest the whole lump be leavened by this leaven. I Cor. 5:6; Gal. 5:9.

Since the before-mentioned churches were rightly established in the first place and afterwards made contentious by the heretics and carnal persons who arose among them and were reproved by Paul because they tolerated such contentious persons with their open abominations, how then can Gellius be helped by their example as long as he and his preachers never were the true preachers and their churches never were separated from the world, and therefore not the church of Christ, as has been heard?

[2] *In the second place he writes: Zacharias, Elisabeth, Joseph, Mary, Simeon and Anna, together with other saints, heard the Word of God in the church of the Jews (among whom were the murderers of Christ), and the disciples of the prophets did not separate the murderers of the prophets from the church.*

*Reply*. These words of Gellius show that the Jewish synagogue, although many pious persons were among them, such as Zacharias, Elisabeth, etc., was not the Christian or apostolic church, and that they did not have nor use the ordinance of Christ and His holy apostles. For it can never in all eternity be shown that in the apostolic church, so long as she remained the apostolic church, there were persecutors and murderers of the pious, or that she tolerated such, as was at that time the case with the Jewish synagogue. Therefore [Gellius] answers and judges himself, for he does not boast that their church is the Jewish synagogue in which such abominations were found, but he claims that they are the Christian church, which never thought of such things, much less practiced them.

Again, we should not follow the before-mentioned church in such abominable abuses and sins, but should be thereby admonished how we should according to the doctrine of Paul treat such as always come up among the pious; and that we should not, on account of such, distrust the promises of the Lord, as if we were not the church of Christ. For we are thereby taught that in the church of Christ, which is always being bitten in the heels by her opponents, offenses, blasphemies, and heresies will arise. But we must expel such whenever the case requires it, after proper admonition; whereby the church openly testifies before God and man that she is clear of such offenses and deceivings, a thing which the worldly church does not do. For it tolerates and retains them as members, contrary to the Word and command of God, ordinance of the Holy Spirit, example or usage of the holy apostles, although they know very well that the institution and command of the Lord does not allow it. Yet they willfully do it. Therefore they cannot be Christ's church and community so long as they continue thus; or else the express Word of God must be fallible and false. O reader, weigh this matter carefully.

But from his writing that the disciples of the prophets did not separate any from the church, among whom were the murderers of the prophets, I can only understand that [he proposes that] their church still remains the church of Christ, notwithstanding that numbers of wicked and ungodly persons are found among them, and are allowed to remain among them, so clearly contrary to the evangelical Scriptures and to the usage of the apostolic church. Oh, no, reader! Take care! This cannot be. As long as the transgressors and willful despisers of the holy Word are unknown to the church she is innocent, but when they are known and then not excluded after proper admonition, but allowed to remain in the fellowship of their religion, then, in my opinion, she ceases to be the church of Christ. For she transgresses willfully and does not abide in the doctrine of Christ. She despises the Word and ordinance of God, because she refuses to bear the cross of Christ to the praise of God and to the service of her neighbors, and because she does not want to shoulder the opprobrium of men, so making herself guilty of the sins of others. Therefore she, according to John, has not God in power and in truth. II John 1:1.

[3] *In the third place he writes that they are plainly the church of God and Christ who publicly assemble, hear the Word, accept and preach it; who with open confession and in the holy, divine name, dispense and partake of the sacraments, and who bun the offensive evildoers and obdurate sinners.*

*Reply.* If to meet publicly, although in all manner of vanity, pomp and pride, and splendor, to preach in worldly fashion, to baptize infants, to break the bread with the impenitent, to pray in sham, and exterminate thieves and murderers with the sword, constitutes the church of Christ, then it is incontrovertible that all the papists also, together with the Arians, the monks, etc., were Christ's church; for they all have done these things publicly. Oh, no, by no means; but, where they meet in the name of Christ, where the unadulterated Word of God is preached, be it in secret or in public, where the baptism and Holy Supper are served in accordance with the ordinance of Christ, where not merely gross evildoers who are judged by the law of the emperor, but also drunkards, prostitutes, avaricious, and usurers are excluded from the communion of the pious, according to the doctrine and example of the pious; behold, this is the visible church which is set forth in Scriptures.

[4] *In the fourth place he writes, That she is invisible to the eyes of men, who cannot search the heart, but only before the eyes and judgment of God is the true church of God and of Christ; which is contained in the visible church, that is, in the number of those called; since God, through the preaching of His holy Gospel and through the use of His holy sacraments, works powerfully in her and regenerates many unto life everlasting, who are known only to Him, who knows those who are His own, and who searches the hearts of men; they constitute the true bride of Christ, etc.*

*Reply.* In part I admit this to be right; however, with this understanding: that the visible church, in which the invisible (as he calls it) is contained, must be sound in doctrines, sacraments, and ordinances, and irreproachable in life before the world, so far as man, who is able to judge only that which is visible, can see.

Since it is clearer than clear that Gellius and similar preachers are blameworthy in this thing (for it is plain that they falsify the Word of God, abuse the sacraments, wheedle the world, upbraid the pious, do not separate their church from the world) and since none of their disciples rebuke her for such open transgressions and abuses, but everyone is satisfied with her, with her doctrines and sacraments, follows and maintains them, one and all play the hypocrite, walk upon the broad way, hate the cross of Christ and lay it upon others, therefore I dare not admit that notwithstanding all this, the invisible church should still be among them; and for the reason that I know of a certainty that it cannot fail, that where the true church of Christ is, there she will be made manifest among this wicked and perverse generation by words and work, for she can as little be hid as a city upon a hill, or a candle upon a candlestick.

[5] *In the fifth place he writes that the churches at Rome, Corinth, Ephesus, etc.; and also the strangers dispersed in Pontus, Galatia, Cappadocia, Asia, and Bithynia, are called by Paul and Peter the saints and the elect; for the church (he writes) is called after the better part of its members and is called the church of God or of Christ, holy, pure, irreproachable.*

*Reply.* Think not, kind reader, that all those who lived at Rome, Corinth,

Ephesus, Pontus, Galatia, Cappadocia, etc., were called the church of Christ by Paul and Peter, even as all those who live in Meissen, Düringen, and the German states are called the church of Christ by the preachers. By no means. But they refer to the small number who, begotten by the Word of the divine power, separated themselves from the world, and with open confession willingly placed themselves under Christ and His covenant. If I should write, the chosen children and saints of God at Antwerp, Ghent, Leeuwarden, and the strangers dispersed in the Germanic countries, then I would not mean all those who live in Antwerp, Ghent, Leeuwarden, or the Germanic lands; by no means. For they also live there who persecute and trouble the chosen children of God not a little; but I would refer to those who confess Christ Jesus through true faith and who are obedient to His holy Word.

Behold, reader, if the preachers, in the same manner, would separate their church from the world and would preach the Word of God in purity, and would administer the sacraments in accordance with the Scriptures, and would strive after a pious and Christian life in their churches, then he might truthfully boast that the elect which he (I believe) calls the invisible church, are included in their visible church, as he pretends.

[6] *In the sixth place he writes, If now they say your church is not believing, holy, and without reproach, etc., then I appeal first to the congregation of the Jewish people, from which we may learn that they at the time of Elijah, Jeremiah, Daniel, and all the prophets, of John the Baptist, of Christ and the apostles, not all were holy. This the Scriptures of the prophets and of the apostles teach us plainly. But they, although both people and magistrates were for the most part wicked, were nevertheless the church of God and of Christ and were called that on account of certain pious people, the church to whom God sent His prophets.*

*Reply.* If the preachers would rightly discharge the duties of their office as Elijah, Jeremiah, and the prophets did; and if some were found in their church who followed the Word of the Lord, as was the case in the time of the prophets, then the case of Gellius might be helped. But now they do not happen to be Elijah, Jeremiah, and Daniel nor[49] teachers driven by the Spirit of Christ, but such preachers and teachers as were reproved by Jeremiah in many of his Scriptures, such as were destroyed by Elijah, and against whom we are faithfully warned by Christ and His apostles not to hear them.

I say further: Israel was the literal people, and had the promise for the sake of the fathers on account of their birth after the flesh. The Law was given them that they should serve God, and walk according to His commandment, and even when they transgressed the Law and did not observe that which God had commanded, they still remained the literal people, and God, ever mindful of the covenant made with Abraham, Isaac, and Jacob, put forth His faithful servants, the prophets, and sent them often to reprove them earnestly out of the Word of the Lord, to point them once more to the Law, and boldly

---

[49] Reading *niet* (not) for *met* (with) which yields no suitable sense. *Tr.*

to threaten them with punishment for their sins. Not so with us at present, for we are not the literal race born from the loins of Abraham and Isaac, but of the Word of God through the Spirit. If now we forsake this birth which is of God, if we abide not in the Word of Christ, and enter again into the broad way, then we do not remain Christ's church and people. II John 1:9.

Behold, reader, since it is manifest that Gellius and similar preachers, together with their churches, never were the spiritual people, because they, as appears, are not born of God in truth but are earthly and carnally minded, live according to the lust of the flesh, did not enter in at the right gate, but teach an impure doctrine and use foreign sacraments whereby no abiding church can be gathered unto Christ, as has been heard, and moreover, act altogether contrary to the Spirit, Word, and will of Christ, yes, hate and despise them: how then can they be likened in the matter unto Israel, which was the people and church on account of the fathers; whereas this people and church never were the church of Christ in Spirit, as has been heard.

Finally I say: All the Scriptures, both the Old and the New Testaments, on every hand, point us to Christ Jesus that we are to follow Him. Whosoever does not hear Him, it will be required of him. Therefore take heed. As I have said before, although all the pious from the beginning were one congregation, church, or body, yet at different periods they have had different doctrines, ordinances, and worship. Moses gave the Law and Israel had to obey it until Christ, who was promised, appeared. To His Spirit, Word, and ordinances we are now directed. If it can be proved to us by His Word that His Spirit has allowed drunken, avaricious, pompous, adulterers, blasphemers, tyrants, and murderers (that is, such as do not repent) in the fellowship of the apostolic churches, and also ordained that open deceivers and worldly-minded persons could be bishops and pastors, then I will allow that they are the church of Christ. But if they cannot do so, as is impossible, then they must acknowledge that their church which is full, yes full of such people, is not the church of Christ as they boast, but a willful, contrary, and disobedient people, yes, the church of Antichrist and world, and that their propositions in this matter are nothng but open seduction, falsehood, and deceit. Reader, observe. I testify this unto you in Christ. Believe it if you will. I write the truth unto you.

[7] *In the seventh place he writes: In the second place I appeal to the church of the Corinthians, which Paul reproves on account of their dissensions first, saying, I, brethren, could not speak unto you as unto spiritual but as unto carnal. I Cor. 3:1.*

*Reply.* I have said above that this church was first rightly taught by Paul, and won to Christ; but being deceived by philosophers who despised the doctrine of the cross, and assailed by false apostles, became divided, the matter for which they are reproved and fraternally instructed by Paul and were admonished to expel the impenitent and carnal-minded. For the Scriptures command and instruct us to do this, namely, that such should first be admonished, and if they do not repent, unanimously expelled from the fellowship of the church. Judge now what[50] Gellius can prove by this since he and his colleagues have never been separated from the world, and are not the church of Christ. For, man alive, he merely manifests his cross-fleeing and open disobedience, covers up and defends the great and grievous transgressions of his disciples, however gross they be, with the example of others.

[8] *In the eighth place he writes: In the third place I appeal to the parable of Christ, of John the Baptist, and of Paul. Christ compares the church with a field in which the tares grow together with the wheat until the harvest. Or, with a net in which both good and bad fish are caught. Or, with ten virgins of whom five were wise and five were foolish. Or, with a royal wedding, where the good and evil were gathered together and one was found by the king to be without a wedding garment, etc.*

*Reply.* This first parable is explained by Christ Himself saying, He that soweth the good seed is the Son of man; the field is the world [understand it rightly, Christ says, It is the *world*, and not the *church*, as Gellius claims]; the good seed are the children of the kingdom; but the tares are the children of the evil; the enemy that sowed them is the devil; the harvest is the end of the world; and the reapers are the angels. Matt. 13:37-39.

Reader, understand it rightly. Christ, the Son of man, sows His seed, God's Word, by means of His Spirit, in the world. All who hear it, believe, and obey, are called the children of the kingdom. In the same manner the opponent sows his tares, false doctrine, in the world; and all that hear and follow him are called the children of evil. Both wheat and tares grow together in the same field, namely, in the world. The husbandman does not want the tares to be plucked up before their time, that is, he does not want them destroyed by putting them to death, but wants them left until the harvest, lest the wheat be pulled up for tares.

Ah, reader, if the preachers understood this parable properly and feared God rightly, they would not cry so loudly against us (who, alas, are everywhere called tares, Anabaptists, heretics, and conspirators) : Down with the heretics! even if we were heretics, which may God forbid. Oh! what noble wheat they destroy! But what does it avail? Satan must agitate and murder, for it is his real nature and work, as the Scriptures teach. Gen. 3:4; John 8.

Some of the other parables, as of the net with the good and bad fishes, of the wise and foolish virgins and their lamps, of the royal wedding and of the guests, and of the threshing floor with the wheat and chaff, although the Lord spoke them in allusion to the church, yet they were not spoken for the purpose that the church should knowingly and willingly accept and suffer open transgressors, drunkards, carousers, seducers, avaricious, robbers, gamblers, and usurers in their communion; because then Christ and Paul would differ in doctrine; for Paul says that we should avoid and shun such. But they were spoken because many run along with the Christians in sham, and place them-

---

[50] Reading *wat* (what) for *want* (for) which makes no sense. *Tr.*

selves under the Word and sacraments, people who in fact are no Christians but hypocrites and make-believes before their God. And these are likened unto the bad fish, unto the foolish virgins who had no oil in their lamps, unto the guest without a wedding garment, and unto the chaff which will be cast out by the angels at the day of Christ. For they pretend that they fear God and seek Christ; they receive baptism and the Lord's Supper and put on an external sham; but faith, repentance, true fear, and love of God, Spirit, power, fruit, and work are not found in them.

But as to the two kinds of laborers in the vineyard, and those called to the great supper, the reader should know that they have a different meaning and cannot conform to his sentiments. Whosoever loves truth may examine them, and judge by the Holy Scriptures what their proper meaning is.

Again as to his reference to vessels of dishonor, I let Paul explain his own words; for he says, If a man therefore purge himself from these, he shall be a vessel unto honor, sanctified and meet for the Master's use, and prepared unto every good work. II Tim. 2:21.

Behold, dear reader, here you may notice how miserably he twists the Word of the Lord, that they may verily be the church of Christ, although they knowingly and willingly admit open transgressors to the communion of their church, contrary to the Scriptures. But the flaming eyes of the Lord which search everything are not blinded by such dressed up speech.

[9] *In the ninth place he writes, If now the church is distressed by such evils and must put up with the wicked unto the day of judgment, as some of these parables imply, yes, if she never was so fortunate as to be entirely rid of evil ones and hypocrites, no matter how strictly she used the ban, therefore they err and sin grievously when they say that we neither teach nor have the church of God as did the patriarchs, prophets, and Moses, etc.; and they err grievously when they revile our church (which is founded by our faithful service, upon the true foundation, according to the example of all messengers of God, which is daily increased and built up, upon the elect cornerstone) because of evil persons calling it an unbelieving, unholy, and blameworthy church, against all the Scriptures, so bringing not only our church into disrepute, but also all the churches of the Germanic peoples, yes, of all the Christian world which do not and cannot have a different complexion, only their own church excepted which they call holy, pure, irreproachable, and spotless by virtue of their dreadful ban.*

*Reply.* If he had said that the church is troubled with such evils, and that she must suffer them, meaning it in such a manner that the true church must suffer the enmity, tumult, violence, and tyranny of the wicked, and put up with the wicked actions of the perverse, then he would have written the truth. But since his idea is that even as the church always had hypocrites among her number and that therefore it must have its evil ones, that is, open despisers and transgressors, therefore he writes contrary to the Word of God. For Paul says, Therefore put away from among yourselves that wicked person, that is, separate from the communion of your church him who is wicked. I Cor. 5:13.

Again, to his writing that we grossly sin by saying that they do not have the church of God, and to his boasting that they build their church upon the true cornerstone, I say that his boasting is false. For that they build their church not on the true cornerstone is evident from their frivolous doctrine, false sacraments, reckless life, and his ugly writings. For it is manifest that they are at fault everywhere, they falsify the Word of God and misuse the sacraments, practice no expulsion, and that both teachers and hearers alike for the greater part walk upon the perverse ways. Whether therefore we sin because in faithful love we admonish them for good, and with humble pious hearts show them that they neither have nor can be such a church, this the reader may judge. We know for sure that where there is no pure doctrine, no pure sacraments, no pious Christian life, no true brotherly love, and no orthodox confession, there no Christian church is—let them boast as they please.

Again, in regard to his complaint that we not only condemn and revile them but all the churches of the Germanic nations, nay, of the whole Christian world, calling them unbelieving and unholy, the reader should know that we condemn no one. For He to whom the Father has given it will do that, Christ Jesus. Yet we do say this, and teach it with mouth and pen, that all those who are not born of God and His Word, are not driven by the Spirit of Christ, are not changed into His nature and disposition, however high and fine an appearance and name they may assume, are not Christ's church and congregation. Emperor nor king, doctor nor licentiate, pope nor Luther, makes any difference. All who would be in the church of Christ must be in Christ, must be minded as He was minded, and must walk as He walked, or else Christ Jesus, John, Paul, and all the Scriptures are false. This is too clear to be refuted.

Since he accuses us that we condemn all the churches of the Germanic countries, and of the whole Christian world, as he boasts, therefore I answer with short, plain words that if the German churches and the before-mentioned world were born of God, were minded as Christ was minded, and walked as He walked, then the accusation of Gellius would be right, seeing that we do not acknowledge them to be true churches. Since they prove indeed that they are outside of Christ, walk and act contrary to His Word and will, are quite earthly and carnally minded, therefore they are not judged by men, but by the Word of the Lord, as Christ said, The word that I have spoken, the same shall judge him in the last day. John 12:48.

Further, by his writing that the said churches do not and cannot have a different complexion, he himself rules that they are not the church of Christ. For Christ wants His church to have, keep, and follow His Word, ordinances, and commands, whether it be to the joy or to the pain of the flesh.

You see, dear reader, since it is more than clear that the Scriptures teach,

both by word and example, that open transgressors should be excluded from
the communion of the church, and since those preachers for fear of the cross
which might easily result fear men more than God and serve their bellies
more than the praise of the Lord, therefore their public actions testify that
they are not the bride and sheep of Christ; for they do not hear His voice,
neither do they follow His doctrines and commands.

So also to his writings that we consider our church holy, pure, and irreproachable on account of the cruel ban, this is my simple reply: we do not boast
at all but of the grace of our God through Christ Jesus. Our frailty is great,
our stumblings manifold, and we feel with Paul that nothing good dwells in
our flesh. Notwithstanding, all true members of the church of Christ strive
after the irreproachable, holy existence which is in Christ; they govern their
conduct according to the Word of the Lord; they follow His commands and
ordinances and exclude those whom the Scriptures expel; a matter which he,
alas, calls a fearful ban. O Lord!

O God! Thus the precious, noble Word is esteemed unworthy by this
thoughtless man. For by this abominable, unseasoned blasphemy, not only we,
but also the Son of the Almighty and living God, together with the Spirit of
eternal wisdom, by whom this ban was commanded, and all the apostles and
first church moreover who so diligently taught and earnestly practiced it, are
made to be fools. For if the ordinance is folly, then He who ordained it and
all who teach and practice it, must be foolish. This cannot be denied.

Observe, reader, whether this may not be called hating the Word and will
of God, despising His commandments, and speaking blasphemous things against
the most High, you may reflect upon it and judge by the Scriptures. O reader,
wake up. Beware, and learn to know your preachers, and of what spirit they
are the children.

[10] *In the tenth place he writes, thus they must be given up to a wrong
mind who judge prematurely and without sound sense and leave the church
from motives of spiritual pride and fancied dreamed-up sanctity more than
from honest righteousness, having no other reason than that they, according to
the manner of the Pharisees, would justify themselves by despising others.*

*Reply.* I fear it would weary the reader if I replied to all his invective and
false accusations minutely. Yet I would say, if I could speak with Gellius
before the public, I have no doubt but many, through the grace of God, would
discover that it is not we but they themselves who have been given over to an
evil mind, that they judge *us* prematurely and without decency, remain outside
of the church of Christ for motives of pride, and not only despise us in Pharisaic
fashion, but also often deprive us of possessions and life, as may be witnessed in
various localities. But we must suffer and bear and comfort ourselves with
the saying, Blessed are ye, when men shall revile you, and persecute you, and
shall say all manner of evil against you falsely, for my sake. Rejoice, and be
exceeding glad; for great is your reward in heaven; for so persecuted they the
prophets which were before you. Matt. 5:11, 12.

[11] *In the eleventh place he writes that they will easily dispose of us, saying that if we pose as the church of Christ, we must prove the saying of Christ to be true in our case, The gates of hell shall not prevail against it; and ask where our church then resided, unovercome by the devil, Antichrist, and sects. He writes further, Since the church (which is not bound to any place but is scattered over the whole earth) has this article of faith, and will have it to the end, I believe in one holy, Christian church, the communion of saints, therefore we are forced to acknowledge that God, true to His promise, keeps His church, and has at all times kept it, even though the old serpent, the devil from hell, deceives her by the lusts of the flesh, the glory of the world, and even though the many sects and conspirators, or the rulers of the world persecute and disturb and spoil her, until she becomes inattentive to her affairs, drowsy in her prayers, inattentive to the will of God, ungrateful for His Word, or apostate from Christ, and so stirs up the wrath of God that He takes from her the light of His Word, and lets her fall into grievous error to which idolatry, adultery, fornication, and other uncleanness and sin and disgrace usually attach and follow, so that the church in such case, almost destroyed, ruined, and annihilated, is scarcely worthy of the name.*[51]

*Reply.* I would beseech the faithful reader earnestly to observe how the words of Gellius sound, which I have here quoted at length. He admits that the church, deceived and disturbed by the devil through the lusts of the flesh, the pride of the world, conspirators and potentates, has become drowsy, inattentive, ungrateful, and apostate from Christ; has stirred up the wrath of God, and has fallen into all manner of wickedness and sin. Yet he asserts that she has remained the church of Christ, as if the church could inherit from generation to generation, and as if the church does not consist in faith, Spirit, and power. I know of no clumsier nor blunter argument, as may be heard.

Therefore observe that which I write, and let it be unto you a certain rule —namely, where the Spirit, Word, sacraments, and life of Christ are found, there the Nicene article is pertinent, I believe in one holy, Christian church, the communion of saints, etc. But where the Spirit, Word, sacraments, and life of Christ are not found, but where the spirit, doctrine, sacraments, and life of Antichrist are found, there the church of Antichrist is, and not the church of Christ, although we might boast a thousand times, I believe in one holy, Christian church, etc. For without or against the Spirit of Christ, His Word, sacraments, and life there can in all eternity be no Christian church, twist the matter as you please. The Word stands immutable, Whosoever transgresseth, and abideth not in the doctrine of Christ, hath not God. II John 9.

[12] *In the twelfth place he writes, Since God, in His grace, has in grace made an eternal covenant with His church, and has promised her that the gates of hell (although they may rend and weaken her) will not wholly prevail*

---

[51] The thrust of this lengthy sentence is that if the promise that the gates of hell shall not prevail against Christ's church is valid, then the position of the Anabaptists is untenable, namely, that the church of pre-Reformation times was no longer the church. *Tr.*

*against her, therefore He at all times preserves a shadow of evangelical doc-*
*trine and of His sacraments upon which the church must lean; and also some*
*members, standing upon the true foundation and who will grow up amidst the*
*thistles and thorns, wolves, bears, and lions and be delivered from shipwreck*
*in a violent storm as Noah in the deluge was saved from the great waters, etc.*

*Reply.* Wherever men conform themselves to the Spirit of Christ, His
Word, sacraments, ordinances, commands, prohibitions, usage, and example,
there the holy Christian church is found, as has been heard, and there also the
promise holds that the gates of hell will not prevail against her. For although
she grows as a rose among thorns, as he writes, and dwells in the midst of
bears and lions, and is as a ship cast about by winds and waves, and must
suffer much tribulation, yet she cannot be put down, that is, she cannot be
turned from Christ (who is the true Christian church) ; for she is built upon
a rock.

That this is the truth, the Scriptures and His examples teach us on every
hand. And we have also found it to be so in experience within the last few
years. For however fiercely the lions, bears, and wolves have these past years,
by their frightful mandates, apprehending, torturing, and murdering, roared,
raved, and rent, and no matter how the waves frequently roll up to the clouds,
yet they have to leave the revealed truth to the humble and pious children.
And no matter how sharply the thistles and thorns may pierce, yet this noble
and beautiful rose grows by the day, and eternal praise be to God, increases in
size and strength, whereby it becomes manifest to many reasonable persons
that God's promise to the church stands firm, and that it is the glorious
miracle and mighty power of the most High. For neither death, nor life, nor
angels, nor principalities, nor powers, nor things present, nor things to come,
nor height, nor depth, nor any other creature, shall be able to separate them
from the love of God, which is in Christ Jesus our Lord. Rom. 8:38, 39.

Yet this thoughtless man imagines that they are the true Christian church,
and does not observe that the before-mentioned thistles, thorns, wolves, bears,
and lions (by which the true church has been so much troubled, and still is
troubled) are members of the very church which he claims was and is the true
church of Christ. For they, during the last centuries, have used one and the
same sacrament, and, unseparated, were greeted as the children of grace, and
were admitted and accepted in the communion of these churches.

Besides, he also consoles the poor people as though the Lord has at all
times preserved a shadow of the evangelical doctrine and of His sacraments
upon which the church might lean, as though God were well pleased with such
a dead shadow and false preaching and child baptizing; and as if the church
of Christ, the bride of God and of the Lamb, could be sustained by adulterated
doctrines and unscriptural sacraments. O dear Lord! How long will such
blunt errors continue? He who cannot understand such palpable deceit must
have an excessively obdurate and perverse heart, or he must be a very foolish
and blunt man, I must verily say.

[13] *In the thirteenth place he produces two arguments whereby he proves, as he thinks, that their church is the universal church, as he calls it, wherewith God has dealt thus, etc. And in the first place he writes, In which church Antichrist was seated, according to the prophecy of Paul, where he has placed himself as God, and has exalted himself above God: this is the true church to which God has given the promise, although she was frightfully polluted and miserably distorted. In our church Antichrist has sat, has placed himself as a god, and has exalted himself above all that is called God and religion. Therefore our church is the true church and temple of God to which God's promises are kept. This argument he proves with these words, The first premise is true, for Paul calls the church in which the Antichrist would place himself, The temple of God. The other premise is also too clear to be denied from the prophecies of Paul and the teachings of experience, for in the churches which baptize infants, he has exercised power and sway together with all gruesome tyrannies, has trampled underfoot all religion and worship. Now if both premises are true, then it follows also that the conclusion is true; and he shows the Anabaptists openly in what fearful condition they are for leaving our church and departing from us.*

*Reply.* I will place my syllogism next to his. Where true religion and worship required by the Scriptures are trampled underfoot, there the church of Christ is not. Antichrist has, Gellius testifies, trampled underfoot the true religion and worship required by Scripture, in the church of which Gellius speaks. Therefore the before-mentioned church to which he appeals is not the church of Christ. All Scriptures teach that my first premise is true; for Moses said, Whosoever will not hearken unto my words [he has in mind Christ's words] I will require it of him. Deut. 18:19. Christ says, If ye continue [mark, He says, Continue] in my words, then are ye my disciples indeed. John 8:31. Again, Paul says, If any man preach any other gospel unto you than that ye have received, let him be accursed. Gal. 1:9. John also says, Whosoever transgresseth, and abideth not in the doctrine of Christ, hath not God. II John 1:9.

My second premise, Gellius himself admits to be true, for he says that Antichrist has trampled religion and worship under his feet, as has been heard.

Since then the first premise can be substantiated by the Scriptures and the second is granted by Gellius to be true, therefore my conclusion must be allowed me, namely, that the church to which he refers is not the church of Christ. For she has not accepted the Word of Christ, but a strange gospel, and has not continued in the pure doctrine of His holy apostles. Therefore they have no God in power, and are not the disciples of Christ; or else the quoted assertions must be wrong and false.

As to the first premise of Gellius, Paul testifies in plain words that it is false, for he says, That day shall not come, except there come a falling away first, and that man of sin be revealed. Here Paul teaches in plain polite words that the falling away from the faith would come as it did.

Since Paul openly testifies by the Spirit of God that the falling away would come before the day of the Lord, and also shows through whom it would come, namely, through the man of sin; and since it is clearly visible that this son of perdition has placed himself in the temple of God, that is, in the hearts and consciences of men, or if you prefer, in the stead of God in the before-mentioned church, and has so wholly corrupted it, has deceitfully changed it under the name of Christ from the doctrine and ordinances of God to his own doctrine and ordinances, therefore I would leave it to the attentive reader to judge whether this church, which is so completely occupied, overpowered, and destroyed, can be God's temple. If he judges that it cannot, then he judges rightly according to Scripture. Otherwise many passages of the Scriptures would be fallible and false; and it would follow that both God and the devil, both Christ and Antichrist have sat in one and the same temple and have reigned in one and the same church. But if they judge that it can, then I would say once more that Luther and all his learned ones have gone wrong in bringing about such a disturbance, tribulation, and misery in the world by their doctrine and change, since they, according to Gellius, still remained the church of Christ, even though Antichrist had quite destroyed and demolished the true religion, had trampled it underfoot. Reader, reflect upon this, and judge whether I do not write the truth.

In his second premise he condemns himself, for he writes that Antichrist has sat in their church which baptizes children, has placed himself therein as a god, yes, has trampled underfoot the true religion and worship, etc. He also acknowledges above under the heading of the ban that the papists are no Christians; for he says, Those that leave us would rather become papists again than Christians. Good reader, observe closely what I write. Since it is manifest that the Roman Antichrist has so many years reigned in peace in their church, has given them to drink from the cup of his abomination, has destroyed the true religion, and has instituted his abominations in its place, and since he himself admits that the papists are no Christians, therefore, it is certain and plain that their church was not the universal Christian church and temple of God, to which the promise of God is fulfilled, as he puts it. For it cannot be that they can be not Christ's but Antichrist's disciples and still remain the Christian church and temple.

Now consider whether the pious (whom he calls Anabaptists) act so erroneously by deserting all the anti-Christian abominations, the false, condemned sects and churches; and whether they place themselves in such a frightful position, as he sighingly complains, by humbly submitting themselves to the only, eternal Redeemer, Christ Jesus, and by gladly placing themselves as an example of all obedience and virtue, in their weakness, before all the world's churches and congregations.

[14] *His second argument is this: In and with all churches in which the doctrine and faith is directed toward Christ Jesus, which are not altogether fallen away, which do not altogether reject and profane Christ and His holy*

*Gospel, and which do not altogether trample on or omit the holy sacraments, as under the regime of Mohammed, there remains the name of the holy church. Our church, which has infant baptism as an apostolic ordinance and the doctrine and faith of Jesus Christ as taught by the apostles, never was altogether fallen away, as it was with the Turks; although abominably adulterated and weakened by Antichrist; therefore the name of the church remains with our congregation and true members of the church are in it.*

*Reply.* If his first premise were sound and right according to the Scriptures, then it would also be sound and right to say that the doctrine and faith never was entirely fallen away among the Arians, Circumcellians, Münsterites, and other sects; nor was the Gospel wholly rejected and profaned, and the sacraments altogether trampled upon by them. Therefore, the name of the church remains with the Arians, Circumcellians, Münsterites, etc., and true members of the church are found among them. Then we are also wrongfully called devilish heretics, conspirers, and apostate Anabaptists by him, since we so highly prize the Gospel and the sacraments of our Lord Jesus Christ that we daily sacrifice our possessions and blood for their sake, as may be seen.

If he should say that the before-mentioned sects did not act and teach in accordance with the Scriptures, and that they therefore were not in the communion of the Christian church, then he condemns himself still more patently. For the papistic church to which he appeals did not do this either. And if they taught and carried on rightly, then he very unjustly says that they are not Christians, as has been heard.

Again by his writing, There still remains the name of the holy church, he openly testifies that his assertion is without all foundation in the Scriptures. For he does not appeal to the unfalsified doctrine and to the salutary use of the holy sacraments, nor to the pious irreproachable life which should ever be found in the church of Christ, but to the mere name of the holy church, as if the name could keep the church in God and could bind it to the promise apart from the Spirit, Word, sacraments, faith, and obedience of Christ. No, no, my reader, no. I know, says the First and the Last, the blasphemy of them which say they are Jews and are not, but are the synagogue of Satan. Rev. 2:9. If the mere name constituted the true church, then without controversy all the raving tyrants, enemies of Christian truth, all murderers, perjurers, harlots and prostitutes, avaricious, pompous, and unrighteous people would be members of the church of Christ, for they call themselves after the name of Christ.

And as to his second premise I say in the first place, Since he says their church has infant baptism as an apostolic ordinance, he thereby lays open falsehood upon the holy apostles, the upright, pious witnesses of eternal truth. For he can never in eternity prove by a single word in the Scriptures that they taught or practiced infant baptism, as has been shown above more than sufficiently.

In the second place I would say that the church to which he appeals was not only perverted and weakened as he has it, but has become so estranged from God, that she has worshiped, honored, and shown religious veneration to wood, stone, gold, and silver gods, bread and wine moreover, as has, alas, been seen these many years in all the temples and houses of worship throughout Europe, and as may still be seen daily in many kingdoms, cities, and towns. And Gellius still wants it said that the church was represented here. I have not often heard reasoning much more odd. Therefore, dear reader, beware, and do not listen to the smooth talk of the learned ones, for they deceive you. But hearken unto Him who says, I am the light of the world; he that followeth me shall not walk in darkness, but shall have the light of life. John 8:12. And then you will in all eternity never be deceived.

Reader, understand what I mean. We do not dispute whether or not there are some of God's elect in the before-mentioned churches; for this we, at all times, humbly leave to the just and gracious judgment of God, hoping that He has many thousands unknown to us, as they were to holy Elijah. But our dispute is in regard to what kind of Spirit, doctrine, sacraments, ordinance, and life it is with which Christ has commanded us to gather unto Him an abiding church, and how to keep it in His ways.

Behold, reader, these are his most important arguments with which to maintain his assertion that their church is the true one, namely, because they descend from the papistic churches and baptize their infants, etc. Do hear how strangely he writes. In my opinion, he writes all that comes to his mind, if it has but a little plausibility so as to tickle the ears of the thoughtless people and strengthen them in their impenitent, easy life. If these adduced assertions of his were true, then it could not be otherwise than that hitherto the church of Christ must have been the church of Antichrist; or that of Antichrist, the church of Christ; then also Christ and Antichrist must both have reigned in one and the same church; infant baptism must without any Scripture be apostolic; and the mere name constitutes the church of Christ. Of this, by the grace of God, no one can successfully deprive me, let him twist the matter as cleverly as he pleases.

## [VII.] CONCERNING SOME ACCUSATIONS AGAINST US

[1] *In the first place Gellius accuses us, saying, They (he means us) falsely adorn and deck themselves with the sanctity of the church. For since the Holy Spirit (which sanctifies the church both by the remission of sins, the mortification of the old man with all its lusts, and also by the restraint or annihilation of the sins in the flesh) is given through faith, therefore I cannot see how they can receive the Holy Spirit, together with true sanctification and be the holy church, seeing they angrily contend among themselves about the deity of the Holy Spirit (who, besides other evidence, sufficiently proves His deity in the work of sanctification), as well as about many other principal articles of the faith.*

*Reply.* Zwingli formerly taught[52] that when a thief stole, or a murderer killed, God's will compelled them to it, and that their punishment was also brought about by the will of God; a position which, in my opinion, is an abomination of abominations. If now I conclude that because Zwingli taught this, therefore all preachers teach it, it would be a wrong conclusion. How could Athanasius keep Arius from teaching that the Holy Spirit was a creature of the creature Christ?

Reader, understand my meaning. I never entertained the thought that God's Holy and eternal Spirit was not God in God, and God with God. Yet, Gellius would accuse us, who are not guilty, of denying the sanctification, grace, fruit, and power of the Holy Spirit, because some,[53] who have been expelled by us, have erred in this respect, and probably still err; although he sees with his eyes and feels with his hands the sanctification and power of the Holy Spirit in our people, namely, that they restrain the old man with his lusts and destroy the sins in their flesh, a thing which he calls the sanctification of the Holy Spirit, as has been heard. Behold, thus he reviles those who have not merited it and so he accuses the non-guilty. Whether this is not the Pharisaic, envious, and defaming spirit, which put an evil construction on all that was good in Christ and His disciples, and incited the thoughtless populace against them, this I will leave to him to reflect.

[2] *In the second place he accuses us, saying, They have a proud faith; one half of which is founded upon the merits of Christ, and the other half upon their own merits. For Obbe Philips, who has a great many followers (so he writes), plainly asserts that the justification of man results not from faith alone, but from faith, love, and good works.*

*Reply.* I would, in my simplicity, ask Gellius this question: Does it follow that because Obbe Philips formerly advocated this doctrine, therefore Menno and the others also follow it? If he says Yes, then I would say that he does us an injustice, as alas, he frequently does. For our doctrine and publications abundantly testify that we and the church of God are not thus minded, but that we seek justification in the righteous and crucified Christ Jesus alone.

But if he says No, then I could wish he would exercise enough virtue and decency to make a difference and not mix the innocent with the guilty. And I also wish that he would say no more than the truth; for he writes that the before-mentioned Obbe Philips has a considerable number of followers, and I dare to say that not more than six or ten can be found who believe as he does.

[3] *In the third place he accuses us, saying, How can they be a holy church who disagree among themselves about the Head of the holy church, who do not allow Him to be true God, and thereby revive the old Arian heresy?*

*Reply.* We may thank the most High with loving hearts that He manifests unto us His fatherly grace and marvelous mercy, that even our most

---

[52] Zwingli died over thirty years before Menno wrote this.
[53] Adam Pastor (Roelof Martins) was excommunicated for unsound views of the Trinity. *Ed.*

adroit and clever opponents cannot accuse us but by such puerile and, for the greater part, false reasoning. If he would practice natural honesty, not to mention love and truth, as much as he, alas, practices bitter and envious hostility, how loath would he be to think the thing which he now publishes in writing, without discrimination, saying that we revive the old Arian heresy, although it is known to him and his colleagues that such people do not have, nor may have, part in the communion of our churches, so long as they do not renounce such errors, as has been heard.

O dear Lord, how long will such bitter and envious accusations and false backbitings continue? Would to God that the magistrates feared the Lord a little and pondered their office correctly, and placed party over against party and heard them; then they would learn at long last whom and why they persecute, and what kind of people and teachers they are whom they daily maintain and encourage in their injustice and abominations by their authority.

[4] *In the fourth place he accuses us, saying, If they are the true, holy church, the spiritual bride of Christ, pure, holy, and unblamable, then let them prove the unity of the Spirit, especially concerning the twelve articles of faith, which are the foundation of the church, and let not one be the follower of Menno, the other of Adam Pastor, the third of Obbe, and the fourth of Dirk, etc. For although they ban one another as much they please, it is still evident that they are all Anabaptists and are and remain enemies of pedobaptism, and so do not cease to conspire and agitate against the churches of Christ.*

*Reply.* I hope that we, by the grace of God, are so wedded to our Lord and Bridegroom, Christ Jesus, that we are prepared to sacrifice our lives for the sake of hearing His holy voice. We do not boast of our sanctity and piety, but of our great weakness, although we are slandered thus by Gellius. I trust also that we who are grains of one loaf agree not only as to the twelve articles (as he counts them), but also as to all the articles of the Scriptures, such as regeneration, repentance, baptism, Holy Supper, expulsion, etc., which Christ Jesus (whom we together with Isaiah, Peter, and Paul confess to be the foundation of the churches—and not the twelve articles[54] as he has it) has preached by His own blessed mouth, and left and taught us in clear and plain words.

Neither are we so divided as he says, for the followers of Dirk and we agree, and I trust through the grace of God, we will ever continue so. But that Obbe has become a Demas, and that Adam Pastor has left us is not our fault. Such things also happened in the time of the apostles. May God raise them up again at His will. They have been dismissed, and alas, are no more counted among us, so long as they do not repent.

His writing that we still conspire and agitate against the church of Christ, and other like bitter and taunting words, show that he is so driven by the spirit of hostility that he cannot write or speak a polite and reasonable word about us; but he must call us fanatics, conspirators, shop-preachers, and sneaks.

---

[54] The so-called Apostles' Creed. *Ed.*

And he never observes into how many large and carnal sects the pedobaptists, who boast to be the church of Christ, are divided and differ in doctrine, as has been pointed out before. One party is papistic; the other Lutheran; the third Zwinglian; and the fourth Calvinistic, etc. And although they quarrel violently among themselves, revile, condemn, and ruin each other as much as they please, yet it is still evidently true that they all baptize their children and remain unfriendly to the baptism of Christ, and continue to agitate and conspire against the truth and the church of Christ. O reader, if the world could only learn to know who are the fanatics and conspirators, then we might hope for better times; but now it is hidden from their eyes.

[5] *In the fifth place he accuses us, saying, If they are the holy church, then let them hearken unto the voice of Christ, which says that the word of the holy Gospel and its sacraments should not be preached and dispensed in secret nooks and corners, but in public.*

*Reply.* If we are not the true church of Christ, but if Gellius and his kind are that church, as he represents it, and would yet force us into the open, why has he then twice refused a public discussion under safe conduct (although he knows I have to suffer so much for my faith and doctrine), which I have requested of him so urgently? It would be only fair if we erred in some things (from which may God preserve us) and he could stop my mouth (which God knows I should gladly have stopped with truth, just so I hear stronger Scripture and more powerful truth). It would be fair, I say, for him to confront me, vanquish me, and convince me of my deception and so receive the applause of his fellows (which he, in my opinion, seeks not a little) and save my soul and the souls of many others besides.

If he is a true preacher, and a member of the true church of Christ, why does he then press us to go before the public, although he knows very well that I could not do so without blood and death? I freely offer myself if he can show one plain passage in the Scriptures that the apostles and prophets have publicly taught at such places where they knew that the people had resolved upon their death, as alas, they have everywhere done concerning us; and by the grace of God, we will do it too. But I know of a certainty that he can find no such example or Scripture in the Bible. Yes, dear reader, if he would be straightforward in assigning the reason why he always wants me to preach in public, he would confess that he seeks nothing by this false and empty pretension but to make our cause appear suspicious with the people and his cause good, and that he is not a little thirsty after the blood of the innocent, since he, I say, against all reason, love, and Scriptures, presses us to proclaim our doctrine publicly, well knowing that in all the Germanic peoples, not a place can be found where this can be done without imprisonment, violence, blood, and tumult. If now he actually were what he would like to be considered, namely, an upright, irreproachable preacher, how loath he would be to think of the gross disgrace which he now, alas, dares loudly to proclaim both by speaking and writing. David says, The Lord will abhor the bloody and deceitful man. Psalm 5:7.

[6] *In the sixth place he accuses us, saying, If they want to be the true church of Christ, then let them look around to see how old their origin is and how it agrees with the origin and age of the true church. That their church does not go back to Adam, Abraham, or David is proved by their false notion and abominable error in connection with the incarnation of Christ, whereby they let Him be neither God nor man and rob us of our Messiah, etc. Also, above, under the head, The Vocation, he writes, It is an abominable fruit that they have revived and reintroduced to the world such a disgraceful error in regard to the incarnation of Christ. For if Christ did not have our flesh (which He did not have unless He received it from the woman, according to the promise), then the Law was not satisfied in our flesh; then the righteousness of God is not yet paid, the righteousness which without the Boosegelt[55] and ransom would not let us go free and unpunished.*

*Reply.* The learned ones revile and complain constantly because with the angel Gabriel, with John the Baptist, with Peter, with Martha, with the apostles, and with the eternal Father Himself, we confess the entire Christ, both as to His divinity and as to His humanity, to be the true, only begotten, and first-born Son of God, and dare not teach and believe more nor otherwise than the Word of the Lord teaches us concerning Him. I would therefore beseech all readers and hearers to pay attention to the following brief answers and references. I hope by the grace of God to explain the matter so clearly in a few words that the reader will plainly see that they not only rob us of our Saviour's doctrine, sacraments, Spirit, life, ordinances, and usage, but also of His most holy origin, glory, honor, and person; and that they, by their deceiving glosses and reasoning, make Christ a composite, impure, and impossible Christ, according to nature as well as to Scriptures. Whosoever has ears to hear let him hear, and whosoever has a mind to understand let him grasp.

## [VIII.] THE CONFESSION OF THE LEARNED ONES CONCERNING CHRIST

*The confession of the learned ones concerning Christ is, That the eternal Word, the second person in the Godhead (these are their words), the eternal Son of God, has assumed the human nature of our flesh; yes, that the whole man Christ, who was sacrificed and who died for us, is the natural seed of the woman, of Abraham, and of David. The seed of the woman (they say) according to the ordinance of God (Gen. 3), with which seed, namely, Mary's flesh and blood, the before-mentioned divine person, the eternal Word and eternal Son, has united Himself, so becoming one person, in Christ. Or, that the whole man Christ Jesus, body and soul, is the natural fruit of the flesh and blood of Mary, in which the eternal Word dwelt. The man Christ Jesus died, but the Word remains whole and intact.*

*Reply.* It seems very strange to me that the learned ones never cease to

[55] Cf. the explanatory note on page 856. *Tr.*

revile us with their ugly and derogatory words, and put us in ever greater distress and woe with the bloodthirsty, we who have plainly and incontrovertibly on our side the firm and immutable foundation of the holy apostles and prophets, nay, also the blessed mouth and testimony of Christ Himself; while they have neither reason nor Scripture on their side, as may be seen. For, that all the following grievous and unbearable absurdities and abominable errors result from their confession is clearer than broad daylight.

First, they get a composite or divided Christ, of which one half must have been heavenly and the other earthly; even as some even boldly dare to assert that the person of Christ consisted of two principal parts, namely, God and man.

Second, they get an unclean and sinful Christ, for the *Defensio*[56] says: *Christum non alterius ullius carnis participem factum esse, quam quae et peccato (ut tentaretur) et morti simul obnoxia esset*, etc. (That is, Christ was made to partake of no other flesh than that which was under both sin [so that He might be tempted] and death.) At another place the *Defensio* says in regard to Christ: *Si sanctus quomodo sub peccatum in Patris judicio condemnatur?* (That is, If He is holy, why is He then condemned for sin at the judgment seat of the Father?) This agrees perfectly with the writing of Gellius; that the righteousness of God would not leave us unpunished, without *Boosegelt*[57] or ransom.

Reader, observe, how could they speak more vilely and blasphemously of the most holy humanity of Christ, yes, of the Son of the Almighty and eternal God, than they do here? For if Christ were flesh of our sinful and death-guilty flesh, and if He were thus tempted by His own flesh, then the sin with which He was tempted must have dwelt in His flesh, and then He died in just recompense and not for grace. This is too clear to be refuted. Nor could it be otherwise if we derive Christ's flesh from Adam's sinful and guilty flesh.

Again, if His holy, precious flesh were such a *Boosegelt*[57] and ransom as Gellius blasphemes, how then could the righteousness of God be satisfied and paid thereby, according to the holy will of God? If this may not be rightly called preaching an impure and sinful Christ, and robbing men of our most holy Redeemer and Messiah (something which they would like to lay at our door), I will let all right-minded and reasonable people reflect in the light of Scripture.

Third, they get two persons in Christ, namely, the one the second person of the Godhead, and the other the man of Mary's flesh, in which human person the divine person dwelt. This is an error not only controverted by us but also by Luther, who says, Beware, beware (I say) of the *Alleosi*[58]; it is the devil's imp; for it will ultimately construct such a Christ as I do not want to be called

---

[56] Menno is referring to a tract by that name published by a Lasco. *Tr.*

[57] See explanatory note on page 856.

[58] The Bonosians, followers of Bonosus, bishop of Sardica in the fourth century, held that Christ is God's Son by adoption. *Tr.*

after; namely, that Christ henceforth is no more, and that His suffering achieves no more, than the suffering of a common saint. For if I should believe that human nature alone suffered for me, then Christ would be a very poor Saviour; He would stand in need of a Saviour Himself. In short, it is unspeakable what the devil seeks and intends with this *Alleosi*. We say, God is man and man is God; we cry against them that they divide the person of Christ, as if He were two persons.

For if the *Alleosi* is to stand, as Zwingli teaches it, then Christ must be two persons, one divine, the other human. This he says.

Reader, observe what kind of Christ they teach and propose.

Fourth, they get two sons in Christ, of which the first is the Son of God supposed to have been without a mother, and the second, the son of Mary without a father; in which son of Mary the Son of God is said to have been placed, so uniting into one person, as they claim. Behold, what a strange thing they produce!

Fifth, the man Christ Jesus was then not the first-born and only begotten Son, but the third son of God in order, who was not of God, but created, and woud be as Pomeranus says, the Son of God by adoption, *Quod & Bonosiano-rum sive Monosolitarum hæresis est* (that is, Which also is a heresy of the Bonosians or the Monosolites. I say he would be the third in order. For the first is the Word; the second, the first Adam; and the third, the man of Mary's flesh, who is said to have been adopted as a son of God, as has been heard.

Sixth, then we are not recovered and saved through God's first-born and only begotten Son, but through Mary's son, created of Adam's impure and sinful flesh, as also the *Defensio* and its followers dare to assert in the face of all the Scriptures, saying that the nature carried in the loins of Adam which committed the transgression also had to remove and make restitution according to the righteousness of God.

Seventh, if we are delivered in such fashion through Adam's flesh, as they represent, then we should not only give thanks to the Father for His Word, but also to Adam's flesh, through which our deliverance took place. This all straight-thinking persons must admit.

Eighth, if the man Christ were a created creature of Adam's flesh and we were delivered through him, as the learned ones hold; and since God speaks through the prophet that He will not give His glory to another, and since it is manifest that we honor our Redeemer, Christ, no less than we honor the Father; therefore it must follow that either God did not speak truly through His prophets, or that they are all idolaters because they give divine homage to a creature of Adam's flesh, a thing so strictly forbidden in the Scriptures, and so often severely punished by God. Behold, readers, such an impossible, impure, and divided Christ it is to which the learned ones point and teach you by their sophistic argument and twisted Scriptures: a Christ thrown together of two persons and two sons; one of which dwelt in the other, and one of which suffered and the other not; and the one that suffered not was not God's son but Mary's. I think this may verily be called forsaking the Lord that bought them, and preaching a strange Christ whom the Scriptures never knew.

Ah, reader, dear reader, how very lamentably the deceitfulness of the old serpent robs us, through the subtle reasoning of the learned ones, of this noble, exalted, and precious Saviour. It points us to an impure, sinful, earthly, and created being; never observing that the Holy Spirit openly testifies that the Word of God was made flesh (John 1), and that this same Word become man is our Emmanuel and our God, the Lord who justifies us, the first-born and only begotten, God's own Son descended from heaven, the living bread from heaven which was not His invisible deity as the learned ones say, but His visible flesh as He Himself testifies; come forth from God; the First and the Last; who humbled Himself while He was in the form of God and did not assume the form of a great emperor or king, but of a humble servant; became like unto man; found in the form of man; obedient unto His Father unto death, yes, unto the death of the cross; truly God and man, man and God. God before all times, of God and in God; God's eternal Word, in time, according to the promise made to the patriarchs, become a miserable, suffering, and mortal man in Mary, the pure virgin, who was of the natural seed of Abraham, and espoused to a man of the house of David named Joseph, to which the evangelists carry back their genealogy. Not composite or divided, as the learned ones teach, but an undivided, only Christ and Son of God; pure and spotless, planted of the seed and Word of the Father in Mary by the Holy Spirit of God and conceived by her through faith; fed and nourished in her virgin body and in due time become a genuine man, I say, just as Isaac was brought forth by Sarah, and John by Elisabeth, etc. He was born of her according to the promise; obedient to the Law; a light to the world; a preacher of grace; an example of righteousness; and was at last innocently condemned to death, not for His own sins, for He knew none, but for our sins. He was nailed to the cross; He died, was buried, arose, and ascended to His Father in heaven, where He dwelt before; and He is our only and eternal Mediator, our Advocate, Intercessor, Sacrifice, and atoning High Priest with God His Father. Thus the Almighty and eternal God, our merciful heavenly Father, alone keeps forever the honor and praise through this Christ, our eternal Redeemer, His first-born and only begotten Son and eternal Word, our Lord; and not through the impure and sinful flesh of Adam as the learned ones propose.

Observe, reader, which of these confessions is the most powerful and has the strongest foundation in the Scriptures; and in which of the two the greater love of God, and higher honor to Christ, is detected. Notice whether God had taken a man of the seed or flesh of Adam,[59] as the learned ones teach, or whether He had given His eternal Word, power, wisdom, nay, the heart of His own body (to speak humanly) in death for us, as all the Scriptures teach.

[59] Note the editorial introductions pp. 420 and 784 for comments on Menno's peculiar theory of the incarnation. *Ed.*

Oh, it is a very precious word, God so loved the world that he gave his only begotten Son. Again, In this was manifested the love of God toward us, because that God sent his only begotten Son into the world. And again, Herein is love, not that we loved God, but that he loved us, and sent his Son to be the propitiation for our sins. Notice He has sent His Son, not a man of the seed of Adam without a father. Paul says, He spared not his own Son (Rom. 8:32), and other plain statements.

*Now they urge against this that God in the beginning created man and woman and blessed them saying, Be fruitful and multiply. By this they say, a woman is become as much a contributor to the birth, and supplies as much from her body to the fetus, as the man does. And they conclude that Christ was promised out of the woman, and is called woman's seed, fruit, and son, in the Scriptures, Abraham's seed, a seed and fruit of the loins of David. Therefore He must, as to His humanity, be of Abraham's, David's, and the woman's seed. They refer us to the philosophers, to sensible women, and to creatures. I am heartily ashamed of the fact, the Lord knows, that I have to use such human argumentation (they force me to it) in this glorious and holy transaction of God.*

*Reply.* Seeing they try to sustain the matter with the reference to Gen. 1, appealing to God's and nature's ordinances, therefore they should speak of both husband and wife as they now become one flesh, for the ordinance referred to requires carnal contact for human procreation. This the Jews also assumed when they said of Christ, Is this not Joseph's son, the carpenter, and is not his mother's name Mary?

If now they counter that the Holy Spirit performed the function of a father, then I reply, that Christ's birth did not follow the formula of Genesis 1, and that in that representation the Holy Spirit was the father of Christ.

But if they say that not the Holy Spirit, but the Father Himself functioned in Mary, through the Holy Spirit, then I reply, that they thereby acknowledge once more, as above, that the birth of Christ was not in accordance with God's ordinance in Genesis 1. Also they grant then that the man Christ, who purchased us with His precious blood, is not God's first-born and only begotten Son, but a created creature of Mary's flesh. And how this agrees with the confession of the holy apostles and prophets, I will let their own writings make out.

I say, moreover, that we do not go to the philosophers, nor to the sensible women, who are not agreed, nor to the evidence from the creatures (to which they point us) but to God's grace. We will go to the Lord's own Word, the true fountain of all wisdom, and to the dependable witnesses of the Holy Spirit. And in it we seek diligently how much a natural mother, according to the ordinance of God and Genesis 1, contributes and supplies from her flesh through conception.

That both man and woman are by the saying, Be fruitful and multiply, made competent by God unto procreation is too plain to deny. But each in his own ordained place: the man a sower and the woman as a receptive field,[60] prepared by God unto procreation, without which it is impossible for fruit to be born.

That this is God's ordinance, the Scriptures teach everywhere. Paul says, Even as the woman is of the man, so also is man by the woman. Notice first that he says that the woman is of the man; and then that he is not *of* the woman but *by* [Dutch, *through*] the woman. I Cor. 11:12. At another place he says that Rebecca conceived of Isaac. Ponder what this means. So also Sarah, says he, received power by faith to receive seed (from her husband, that is), to carry it, and that therefore from one (Abraham is meant), and he as good as dead, so many were born. The Lord visited Sarah, Moses writes, as He had promised and she conceived and bare a son to Abraham. Notice carefully, it was Abraham's seed she received, and to Abraham she bore a son; so also Bilhah conceived and bare Jacob a son. A nation and a company of nations (God said this to Jacob) will come of you (note, He says of you) and kings shall come from thy loins (notice again, He says thy loins). Gen. 35:11. Levi, says Paul, was still in the loins of his father Abraham (he does not say in the matrix of the mother) when Melchisedec came to meet him. Heb. 7:10. I also am a mortal man (writes the author of Wisdom) like unto the rest, born of the generation of the first created man, formed in flesh ten months long, congealed in blood of *man's* seed (notice this). Wisd. 7:3. Job says, Hast thou not poured me out as milk and curdled me like cheese? Job 10:10.

I do certainly think that we can gather from these passages that the father is the real origin of his child and the mother the prepared field, as has been related. Even as a field does not receive its own, but the sower's seed, to sprout, feed, and increase it and bring it to fruition so that it is called, although sown upon it, that field's seed (as indeed it is), so also the woman conceives seed, not of her own body but of that of her husband, to nurture it from her own flesh after God's ordinance, to carry it, and at the proper time to bring forth the fruit. The fruit is then called the mother's seed, fruit, and son, no less than the father's from whom she at the first received it, exactly as the before-mentioned sown seed is called the seed and fruit of the field for the reason given.

My reader, in this sense, I believe and confess that Christ Jesus also, God's only begotten and first-born Son and eternal Word, is Mary's or the woman's seed, offspring, generation, fruit, and son, marvelously sown in her virgin body by the Holy Spirit, just as Isaac was a seed, offspring, generation, fruit, and son of Sarah, John of Elisabeth, and Joseph of Rachel.

And I say that if the learned ones' proposal in this matter were correct (a thing which I do not at all grant, nor for the afore-mentioned reasons can grant), then the mother would have ten times as much right concerning the child; for the mother's function, not the father's, is fraught with great distress

---

[60] Menno's generation was ignorant of the contributory role of the woman in conception. Menno is scientifically in error here. *Ed.*

nine or ten months long, she must nourish it of her own body, and give it birth not without danger and peril, and nurse it moreover a year or two with milk from her own body. And yet disregarding all this the jurisdiction over the child is in all the Scriptures assigned, not to the mother, but to the father, as may be seen in the cited passage in all clarity.

My reader, take note. If the position of the learned ones were correct, then half the flesh necessarily of the children of Shelah, the son of Judah, was Canaanite because of the Canaanite woman; of the children of Moses, Midianite because of the Cushite woman; of the children of Joseph, Egyptian because of the Egyptian woman. This is beyond dispute.[61]

Nor could the man Christ Jesus then have been more than half a man, that is, in so far as the woman's part and portion according to the learned ones' representation goes; which half a man, this is too clear to deny, then came not merely from Judah to whom the promise pointed, but also in part from Levi and in part from the Canaanites through Rahab, and in part from the Moabites through Ruth.

Now notice, my reader, how very sadly the learned ones pervert God's ordinance touching the seed, fruit, and son of the woman, and how they vilify the Christ, God's only begotten and first-born Son, asserting that His most holy flesh was of Mary's flesh for the reason that He is called in Scripture seed, son, and fruit of the woman. They do not perceive how emphatically both nature and Scripture teach us that the first origin and seed of the human fruit is originally of the father and not of the mother; a thing that is evident also from the fact that the carnal function of the seed remains intact until senescence, but the maternal function of the field does not extend beyond fifty years or less, as may be seen.

But as to the fruit of David's loins, I say first of all that that promise was made literally not of Christ but of Solomon. Nathan, David, and Solomon are my witnesses. Thus spoke the Lord by Nathan to David, as he was planning to build the Lord's house, saying, When thy days are fulfilled and thou shalt sleep with thy fathers, I will set up thy seed after thee, which shall proceed out of thy loins, and I will establish the throne of his kingdom forever. I will be his father and he shall be my son. If he commit iniquity [a thing that can never be said of Christ], I will chasten him with the rod of men and with the stripes of the children of men. II Sam. 7:12-14. This is literally the way this passage goes. And that David understood these words of the prophet as applying literally to Solomon his own words show plainly. My son, said he to Solomon, it was in my mind to build a house unto the name of the Lord my God, but the word of the Lord came to me saying, Thou hast shed blood abundantly, and hast made great wars; thou shalt not build a house unto my name, because thou hast shed much blood upon the earth in my sight. Behold a son shall be born unto thee, who shall be a man of rest and I shall give him rest from all his enemies round about, for his name shall be Solomon, and I will give peace and

---

[61] And the statements actually are true. *Ed.*

quietness unto Israel in his days. He shall build a house for my name and he shall be my son and I will be his father, and I will establish the throne of his kingdom over Israel forever. I Chron. 22:7-10.

So also Solomon understood the promise, as his message to Hiram shows when he sent him word saying, Thou knowest how that David my father could not build a house unto the name of the Lord his God for the wars which were about him on every side until the Lord put them under the soles of his feet. But now the Lord my God hath given me rest on every side so that there is neither adversary nor evil occurrent. And, behold, I purpose to build a house unto the name of the Lord my God, as the Lord spake unto David my father saying, Thy son, whom I will set upon thy throne in thy room, he shall build a house unto my name. I Kings 5:3-5.

Moreover, in the Psalms it is written, For thy servant David's sake turn not away the face of thine anointed. The Lord hath sworn in truth unto David; he will not turn from it: Of the fruit of thy body will I set upon thy throne. If thy children will keep my covenant and my testimony that I shall teach them, their children shall also sit upon thy throne for evermore. Psalm 132:10-12. Read also Psalm 89.

And so, my reader, these clear, plain passages show plainly that the afore-mentioned promise made to David in the old literal system was not made in reference to Christ, but to Solomon.

I say in the second place, that the prophet Isaiah prophesied of Christ saying, Unto us a child is born, unto us a son is given, and the government shall be upon his shoulders, and his name shall be called Wonderful, Counselor, The mighty God, The everlasting Father, The Prince of Peace. Of the increase of his government and peace there shall be no end upon the throne of David and upon his kingdom to order it and to establish it with judgment and with justice henceforth and even forever. Isa. 9:6, 7.

And the angel said to Mary, And the Lord shall give unto him the throne of his father David, and he shall reign over the house of Jacob forever, and of his kingdom there shall be no end. Luke 1:32, 33.

Faithful reader, take note. Since these two faithful witnesses, Isaiah and Gabriel, assign David's kingdom and throne so clearly to this promised king and Messiah Christ, saying that He shall sit in it and rule over it forever, and since it is evident that in this world He had no kingdom, yes, was poorer in the fleshly things than are the foxes and the birds, and since we know that God's promise made by the mouth of the prophet and the angel is true, there-fore we have to understand this of another rule, kingdom, and throne than that of David; unless we say that the afore-mentioned witnesses erred in regard to their promise and did not speak the truth. If then the promised rule, kingdom, and throne are not David's literal or earthly rule, kingdom, and throne, but if they are spiritual, then verily also the king that is to sit on it and rule it is not David's literal or physical fruit, but a new and spiritual fruit even as the afore-said rule, kingdom, and throne are new and spiritual. Otherwise one half of the throne must be taken literally and the other half spiritually. This is too evident to be denied.

In the third place, I say that the reader must notice that Christ is, in the Scriptures, called the fruit of the loins of David and the seed, fruit, and son of the woman in no other sense than as to the promise and tribe to which He was born as to the flesh, or with the flesh; and, that He is entitled to a real mother according to God's ordinances of Genesis 1. For if He were as to His humanity of Mary's flesh, as the learned ones say, then He would not be the true Son of God nor a genuine son of Mary, for then He would have been made or born as to His whole human substance from Mary's flesh and not come forth originally and born from God His Father—which would not only be against the essential qualities of the terms, father, mother, and son, but also against God's ordinance, against nature, and against all the Scriptures, as was said.[61a]

In this way the promise of the fruit of the loins of David is fulfilled in the old order in Solomon and in the new spiritual order in Christ, a common thing in Scriptures, as can be seen literally in the case of Isaac (Gen. 21:22), David (Psalm 27), and Samson (Judg. 13:5), in a literal sense; but plainly referred to Christ by the apostles and Gospel writers in the new dispensation.

*Second, our opponents use still another argument saying, God can neither suffer nor die. God's Word is God (John 1), therefore that Word can neither suffer nor die.*

That God the Almighty and eternal Father, the source of all good, is not subject to suffering and death is plain. But that His Word became subject to suffering and death the entire Scriptures teach clearly. He who wishes to deny this denies God's great power, first of all, by which He does and will do forever whatsoever pleases Him. In the second place he denies the love of God whereby He so loved us that He gave His only begotten Son. He denies in the third place the testimony of God which He has given by the holy apostles and prophets and the Holy Spirit concerning His dear Son. In a word, he who denies that the Word of God became flesh and who seeks to make Christ a man of Adam's flesh, declares thereby that not the first-born and only begotten Son of God, but an earthly creature of Adam's unclean and earthy flesh is his Messiah, Redeemer, Saviour, Lord, and God.

*Third, they say that the man Christ is conceived in the purest blood of Mary; that the Son of God assumed our flesh; that the Word of God united with human nature and dwelt in our flesh; that He had to satisfy the Law in our flesh; that He is our brother by virtue of His birth from Adam's flesh; that He is flesh of our flesh, and that our flesh is now at the Father's right hand.*

To reply to all, or some, of these statements, I do not consider necessary, for I confess that they constitute an alien gospel of which not a letter is mentioned in the Scripture and which therefore is accursed and anathema. Gal. 1:9.

---

[61a] Menno does not discuss Rom. 1:3, 4. *Ed.*

Nevertheless, we do acknowledge that He is our brother. But not in the sense of the learned ones, seeing they call Him their brother: in the first place, because of the flesh of Adam from which they want to derive Him; a thing we do not do because we say with Scripture that even as He is a true son born of God, and called by Paul a first-born among many brethren, so we also, born with Him of the same Father, must be His brethren. I say His brethren, because He is the first-born, as has been related.

Similarly, I say that He is not flesh of our flesh as they have it, but that the regenerate are flesh of His flesh as the Scripture says. For if He were flesh of our flesh as they assert, then Christ must have been a sinful, accursed, and death-guilty Christ. This, according to God's everlasting righteousness, is too clear to deny.

No, reader, no. But even as the first and earthly Adam testified of Eve, who was taken from his body, that she was flesh of his flesh; so also the second and heavenly Adam. Speaking of the new Eve, the church, made by God to be His bride in the Spirit and made of His most holy and life-giving flesh, the Spirit and the Word testifies that she is flesh of His flesh and bone of His bone. Eph. 5:30. For Eve did not say of Adam that he was flesh of her flesh, but Adam said that of Eve. Gen. 2:24.

I conclude saying and testifying before God and also before the whole world that even as we believe and confess that the entire Christ Jesus is our only and eternal Messiah and Redeemer, God's eternal Word, yes, His only begotten and first-born Son and that God is His Father; so also we believe and confess that He is, according to the promise made to the fathers, the true seed, fruit, and son of Mary His mother according to the ordinance laid by God upon all genuine mothers in the matter of human procreation. For she did her duty and assignment as far as it pertained to her according to the said ordinance imposed by God, except for the fact that she did not conceive him in marital intimacy, but supernaturally, of the seed of God. She received the word according to the angel's announcement by means of faith in a marvelous way, beyond all human understanding, by the Holy Spirit.

Here, then, you have our simple and clear position and belief concerning Christ Jesus, God's only begotten and first-born Son, even as the Lord's infallible Spirit teaches through the witness of His holy Word in unmistakably clear terms. This confession stands (stands, I say) and will by God's grace remain standing against all the gates of hell forever. For it is mightily derived from God's unfalsified, pure Word, immovable and sure—and this article especially, which the learned ones declare, is the cause for our being called neither church nor Christian, but an erring people and wicked heretics, although we have the power of the entire Scripture and the ordinance of God clearly on our side. May God give them eyes to see. Amen.

All who desire further exposition of this article may consult our reply to a Lasco's *Defensio,* and they will by God's grace, I hope, find a good and true exposition, sense, and position of all things.

## [IX. FURTHER ACCUSATIONS OF GELLIUS]

[7] *In the seventh place he accuses us, saying, That their church has not existed since the time of Abraham and that therefore they are not the true church is evident from the fact that they in disobedience to the will of God refuse the seal of the eternal covenant to the children of the church, as it has since the time of Abraham been practiced and maintained in the churches.*

*Reply.* Abraham was commanded by God to leave his fatherland, his kinsmen, and his father's house and go to a land which the Lord would show him. Abraham believed God and departed, as the Lord had commanded him. Gen. 12:4-6.

Again, the Lord commanded him that he should offer Isaac, whom he loved, his only begotten of the free woman, as a burnt offering. Abraham believed God; he was obedient, and prepared to do whatever God commanded. Gen. 22; Rom. 8:32.

In the same manner, he was commanded to circumcise himself, his son Ishmael (Isaac was not yet born), and every man-child of his household, and all the males after him, on the eighth day. Abraham believed God, and did as the Lord commanded him. Gen. 18:10.

Behold, thus Abraham believed his God (believed Him, I say) and it was counted to him for righteousness. Gen. 15:6; Rom. 4:3. In the same way God has spoken unto us in the New Testament, not only by angels and prophets, as He did unto Abraham and the patriarchs, but also by His Son, which Son has commanded that the Gospel should be preached to all peoples, to the Gentiles as well as to the Jews, and that those who believed it should be baptized (Mark 16); even as it was commanded Abraham to circumcise all males. Gen. 17:10-13.

This command we have received from the mouth of Christ, therefore we believe it; even as Abraham did in his day. We believe it, I say, and do it. We teach those of understanding minds and baptize those that believe, not in disobedience, as Gellius slanders, but in obedience to the clear, plain, and expressed ordinance and command of Christ, God's own Son.

Dear reader, observe. The Lord, Christ, thanked His Father, saying, This is life eternal, that they might know thee, the only true God, and Jesus Christ, whom thou hast sent. John 17:3. At another place He says, If ye continue in my word, then are ye my disciples indeed. Notice He says, If ye continue. John 8:31. And now that the merciful and affectionate Father, through His great kindness, has uncovered for us the glorious knowledge, and the wonderful deep mystery of His beloved Son, and has, moreover, given us such a fruit through His Spirit that we dare not willfully and knowingly deviate one hair's breadth from His Word, ordinance, and command, as is testified to the whole world and shown by our tribulation, misery, property, and blood; yet, alas, according to the judgment of Gellius and the learned ones, we are not the believing church, nor the disciples of Christ, as may be seen.

Behold, thus the righteous judgment of the Almighty and great God is come upon the wise and learned of this world: so that the clear and plain signs by which the true disciples and church of Christ may and must be known, are esteemed an abomination and error, and they who have through grace received them from above are not accounted Christians by them, as has been related.

[8] *In the eighth place he accuses us, saying, They must admit that their church has existed but sixteen or seventeen years, that is, since the time Menno Simons commenced preaching. For they do not want to be traced back to those of Münster, Amsterdam, and Oude Klooster, among whom Menno lost a brother, lest they be called seditious or the seed of seditious ones.*

*Reply.* We point to Christ Jesus our only and eternal Prophet and Messiah, sent of the Father, who is the only true Cornerstone in Zion, the true Teacher, Lawgiver, Commander, Intercessor, and Head of His church, together with all His angels, apostles, and prophets, through whom He spoke in former times, and also His Spirit, Word, ordinances, commands, prohibitions, usage, and example. Now if Gellius, or any other person under heaven, whether learned or not, can convince us by divine truth that we teach or maintain anything contrary to His Word and ordinances, then I sincerely desire to desist from the wrong and follow that which is right. This He knows who has purchased me. For I desire greatly to be saved. But if they cannot do this by the truth, but only in appearance of truth, blaspheming the truth out of hostile hearts, as all the perverse do, and if they are forced to leave our testimony unbroken, then it is sufficiently proved that our hated, despised, and small church is the true, prophetic, apostolic, and Christian church, which was begun with the first righteous ones who walked according to the will of God; and not with me, as Gellius, with impure heart, alas, invents.

Secondly I would say, since he repeatedly throws the errors and seductions of the Münsterites at us, errors of which we are clear and always have been, before God and man, therefore I could beseech him to take a look at his own baby-baptizing church, to see how abominably they have, for years, turmoiled among themselves, how they have plunged into sorrow countries and nations with their cursed, wicked wars and have dispatched innumerable human beings together with their poor souls to the prince of hell, and have placed them as an offering upon his altar and table; a thing of which, alas, the learned ones by their seditious writings, together with the priests, monks, and preachers, were the principal cause, as is as clear as day to many reasonable people.

Thirdly I say that I suspect that he so rudely alludes to the mistake of my poor brother (who is now no longer subject to the human punishment which he bore once in the flesh, but is kept to the judgment of his God) exactly as though he cannot control himself for anger and bitterness. By it no man can be helped in the least or taught unto righteousness. Methinks he has done this for one of two reasons: either that he would thereby make me suspicioned with the reader, as though I formerly were of the same feeling as my brother; or, that he would thereby make a blot on my reputation.

If he did this for the former reason, namely, to make me suspicioned, then all those who formerly heard me when still of the papal church and all who have ever heard me until this hour, and also my published writings, will be my testimony that he wrongfully suspects me and makes me suspect; for I never thought of such a thing, much less taught it.

But if he did so for the latter reason, namely, to blemish my reputation, then he should know that I and my people, I hope, have not harmed him nor his a hair's breadth. Also my poor brother, whom he so hatefully brings up, did no greater wrong than that he erroneously, alas, defended his faith with his fist and met the violence committed, just as all the learned ones, preachers, priests, monks, and all the world do. I presume that I have merited it that he so hatefully casts this at my feet, because of my faithful love, because I have in sincerity of heart pointed him and all the preachers to the blessed divine truth, and because I have admonished them to their own well-being. And how this bitter thrust, which cannot possibly have been made out of a good heart, agrees with honor and the fear of God, all reasonable and right-minded readers may judge by the Scriptures and ordinary discipline. May the kind Lord grant that he may rightly learn to know the unclean and carnal heart from which this unmerited abusive stroke comes; so that he may purge it and sincerely repent. This is my one and highest revenge and punishment which I wish to invoke on him!

[9] *In the ninth place he accuses us saying that we cannot prove that infant baptism is an anti-Christian abomination; nor show from the anti-Christian ordinance who was the institutor thereof. It can also be proved, he says, that long before the reign of Antichrist (which was still unknown, or very weak at the time of Augustine), yes, from the time of the apostles on, infant baptism was practiced.*

*Reply.* We teach and practice such a baptism as was commanded by Jesus Christ, God's own Son; as was taught by His faithful witnesses, the apostles, in clear and explicit terms, and as was transmitted to us by their practice; which is believer's baptism. Whosoever now wants to teach and practice any other baptism must show by the Scriptures whether it is commanded. But if they cannot do this, as they never can, then it is already proved that it is not Christ's baptism but Antichrist's. This is too clear to be denied.

But as to his assertion that the reign of Antichrist was as yet unknown, or weak, at the time of Augustine, it is not necessary to answer. Whoever will, let him read history, and he will find in great clarity that Antichrist was in full honor at the time of Augustine and that he ruled in the hearts of men with his doctrine.[62]

[10] *In the tenth place he accuses us, saying, If they were the true messengers of God who are to purge and deliver the church of Christ from such abominable anti-Christian errors, they should not be a separated sect, for*

---

[62] In other words, the fall of the post-apostolic church into all sorts of superstitious and unscriptural practices came long before Augustine's day. *Ed.*

*the prophets and all the faithful servants of God, through whom God has often purged His church, did not separate themselves from the church to establish a church of their own, but they remained with the church and bestowed their faithful labor upon the church at the peril of their lives.*

*Reply.* Let Gellius do as he may and slander as he can. I say once more, for the third time, that we advance Christ Jesus and all His prophets, apostles, Spirit, Word, ordinances, and life. If he can convince us therewith that in any article we go against this or do not agree with it, then I will agree with him that we are a separated sect. But his raving and ranting are not pertinent. But if he cannot do so, as he never can, and still calls us a separated sect, he shows thereby that he is no better judge of the church of Christ than was Tertullus before Felix, and the Jews at Rome before Paul. Acts 24:14.

I say further that if he can prove to us that the faithful prophets joined with the calf worshipers of Jeroboam, with the Baal worship and abominations of Israel which they so vehemently reproved, and remained united with those who disobeyed the Law; and also that the holy apostles admitted the Pharisees and scribes together with other rebellious persons into the communion of their churches, then we admit that he has a good cause to reprove us and to write as he does. If they did not (and they did not), but on the contrary reproved by the power of the Spirit the abominations which had crept in, according to the pure Word and ordinance of God, at the peril of their lives, then he must admit, must he not, that he accuses us without cause, since we do not otherwise than according to the example of the holy apostles and prophets. Thus we reprove all false doctrine, unrighteousness, and abominations with a pure apostolic teaching, spirit, ordinance, and Word of our Lord Jesus Christ, without which no true church of Christ can exist; since we avoid that which is wrong and faithfully in love and purity teach and proclaim the salutary Christian truth with tongue and pen to all the hungry hearts at the peril of life and possessions.

Lastly, I would ask, since he calls us a separated sect because we are not one with them, why have he and his followers seceded from the papistic and Lutheran churches? If he says, Because of the abominations found among them, then I reply that we do it for the very same reason. For they forsake the Son of the true and living God and point us to an earthly creature of the unclean and sinful flesh of Adam as our Saviour, and moreover do not follow the command and ordinance of God in regard to baptism and Holy Supper and expulsion. We will never, come weal or woe, as God may please, desire to be of one church with those who seek reconciliations and salvation in the sinful flesh of Adam, who reject God's testimony of His Son and ignore His ordinance. But we desire to be one church and body with those who give praise to God for His Word, with those who confess the whole Christ to be the only begotten and first-born Son of God, and who abide unchangeably in His holy ordinance, example, Spirit, and Word. Let those of understanding minds understand that which the Word of the Lord teaches.

[11] *In the eleventh place he accuses us, saying, From this it follows that*

*the calling of their doctrine is false, and that their whole church, service, and walk cannot aid to salvation, but can only serve to the corruption and destruction of the true church; and therefore they do not suffer innocently as Christians but as those who will appropriate the office of another (he quotes I Pet. 4); except that they want to suffer for a cause of which they must be doubtful themselves and for which no martyr from the beginning has suffered.*

*Reply.* Even as the Spirit of Christ and of unfeigned love interprets all that is good and godly as right and godly, so also the spirit of Antichrist in bitter envy explains everything that is right and godly as wrong and ungodly. For it is testified to with possessions and life that we dare not willfully and knowingly deviate one hair's breadth from the Word and example of the Lord, but judge everything according to the doctrines and usages of the apostles, so far as the Lord gives grace. We, in our weakness, would gladly conform our poor weak lives to the Scriptures, gladly seek the praise of God and the salvation of our neighbors, at the peril of possessions and life. Yet he dares write that the calling of our doctrine is wrong, and that our walk and actions are not conducive to salvation, that we cause all manner of corruption and disorder, and that we do not suffer as Christians, but as evildoers who are busybodies in other men's matters. Behold, thus all that is good and praiseworthy is ever interpreted as evil, to the hurt of the pious.

O reader, beloved reader, if only the poor, ignorant world would sincerely accept this, our hated and despised doctrine, which is not ours but Christ's, and would faithfully obey it, then they might change their deadly swords into plowshares and their spears into pruning hooks; they would level their gates and walls, and dismiss their executioners and hangmen. For all those who accept our doctrine in its power by the grace of God, will not wish evil to anyone upon earth, not even to their most bitter enemies, much less do evil or harm. For they are the children of the most High, who sincerely love all that is good, and in their weakness avoid that which is evil, yes, hate it and loathe it. Yet we must hear that we suffer erroneously, as has been heard.

But as to his assertion that we suffer for a cause of which we must be doubtful ourselves, and for which no martyr ever suffered, he shall know that if we doubted our faith we would not so deeply impress the seal with our possessions and blood as we do. For a house built upon the sand cannot withstand such floods and hurricanes as come upon us daily. Matt. 7:25.

Neither do we suffer on account of an uncertain cause, as he proposes, but for the sake of the name of the Lord Jesus Christ, for His holy, precious Word and ordinances, for the sake of the sincere confession of God and Christ, obedience to the Scriptures, the things for the sake of which all have suffered from the beginning who have rightly suffered according to the will of God, as may be plainly and clearly learned from history and Scripture.

[12] *In the twelfth place he accuses us, saying, That they are the church, and Jacob [Israel], is false since they pollute the true church of Christ with many errors which they daily produce and bring forward from the abyss of*

*hell. They destroy the true sheep of Christ; they wrongfully adorn themselves with the sanctity of the church; they cause strife and dissension concerning the articles of faith; they are carnal, they sneak about and preach in secret, and they do not agree with the elders of the church, as was said before.*

*Reply.* If the Spirit and truth had taught the writer at this point, the game would have doubtlessly been reversed, for this accusation laid upon us should have been laid upon our opponents. For they still maintain and uphold some gross errors which were formerly brought forward by Antichrist from the abyss of hell (to use his own expression), both by doctrine and force. And thereby they cause the godly much affliction and tribulation, cause many a pious child to be deprived of possessions and life; they falsify the truth, and preach falsehood; they are carnally minded, denying emphatically that the man Christ Jesus is God's only begotten and first-born Son. While we with our small despised band shun and forsake all anti-Christian abomination and errors, build up the church of Christ and place it once more upon the true foundation, publish and proclaim the clear and plain truth to many with tongue and pen at the peril of life. To the displeasure of the world we confess the whole Christ to be the true, only, and first-begotten Son of God, as did the angel to Mary, John the Baptist, Peter, Martha, and the Father from high heaven Himself. And we rightly use His ordinances of baptism, Supper, and ban as all those did from the beginning who rightly knew God and acted according to His will.

Behold, reader; these are the most important and weightiest accusations laid against us by him; and that they in part are hollow inventions, in part false explanations, false suspicions, false storytelling, and partisan gossip, whereby he obstructs the course of divine truth, sustains falsehood, abuses the godly, and consoles the impenitent in their easy life, is fully proved by this our reply.

[13] *In the last place he writes of us, saying, Experience has taught that their teachers and prophets are not such teachers and prophets of God. And that they are not the people of God, I have, perhaps, already proved too powerfully. From which, then, it is clear that our magistrates do right by not letting them proceed in their wicked course but obstructing them diligently. And we might, in pastoral and paternal faithfulness or solicitude for the church of Christ, lest the church be quite destroyed, speak and conclude a bit more sternly concerning them. But then we would be called persecutors and bloodhounds by them.*

*Reply.* Jeremiah, Micah, Elijah, Christ Jesus, and Paul could not pass for the true prophets and servants of God with the perverse; neither can we. But the great Lord shall in due time make it manifest who are the faithful prophets and servants of God and who are not.

Again, to this saying that we are not the people of God, we answer with holy Paul that it is a very small thing that we should be judged with the judgment of men, and especially by men who are so flatly opposed to the ordinance, will, and Word of God as may be seen in the case of Gellius from his writing. Yes, kind reader, if he and similar preachers acknowledged us to be the people of God, they would thereby acknowledge that they are not of that group, a thing which an ambitious carnal person who seeks reputation and fame never will do.

To his assertion that the magistracy does well in obstructing our course, which he calls wicked, I reply, that the longer he writes, the more clumsy and offensive he becomes and the more he manifests his blindness. If he is a preacher called by the Spirit of God, then let him show a single letter in all the New Testament that Christ or the apostles have ever called on the magistrates to defend and protect the true church against the attack of the wicked, as, alas, he calls us. No, no, Christ Jesus and His powerful Word and the Holy Spirit are the protectors and defenders of the church, and not, eternally not, the emperor, king, or any worldly potentate! The kingdom of the Spirit must be protected and defended by the sword of the Spirit, and not by the sword of the world. This, in the light of the doctrine and example of Christ and His apostles, is too plain to be denied.

I would say further, If the magistracy rightly understood Christ and His kingdom, they would in my opinion rather choose death than to meddle with their worldly power and sword in spiritual matters which are reserved not to the judgment of man but to the judgment of the great and Almighty God alone. But they are taught by those who have the care of their souls that they may proscribe, imprison, torture, and slay those who are not obedient to their doctrine, as may, alas, be seen in many different cities and countries.

In short, kind reader, if the merciful Lord did not, in His great love, temper the hearts of some of the magistrates, but if they should proceed according to the partisan instigation and blood-preaching of the learned ones, no pious person could endure. But as it is, some are found who, notwithstanding the railing and writing of the learned ones, suffer and bear with the miserable, and for a time show them mercy, a thing for which we will forever give praise to God, the most High, and express our gratitude to such kind and fair governors.

But to his writing that in paternal and pastoral solicitude and faithfulness they might speak and decide a bit more sternly against us, I reply, If he had entered in at the right door of Christ, who is the Prince and Head of all true pastors, and if he had tasted in his heart the friendly and amiable Spirit, nature, and disposition of Christ, then he would not, by any means, think of such a resolution against the blood of others, much less write and mention it. This I know of a certainty, that the Spirit of Christ is not so inclined.

Reader, observe, the reason that he does not write boldly that the magistracy may very well plunge its sword in us, is that he does not want to be called a bloodhound or persecutor; nevertheless he does make it plain that if they should do so, he would call it a praiseworthy thing. Whoever is not quite destitute of understanding, understands very well what his position is in the matter. Oh, doctrine of blood!

Ah, that he might comprehend the force of the word which the Lord speaks, Ye are of your father, the devil, and the lusts of your father ye will do.

He was a murderer from the beginning. John 8:44. For, since he emboldens the bloodthirsty by such writings, and since I have myself heard from his own mouth recently that it is right to persecute and kill men on account of their faith (understand, such faith as they think to be heretical), he has thereby loaded the innocent blood upon his soul. I say innocent blood, for neither he nor anybody else upon the face of the earth can, by the grace of God, convince us with stable truth that we act or do aught against Christ or His Word, or that we deserve the punishment and sword of the magistracy.

Let him know further that this blood-doctrine of his is not only contrary to Jesus Christ, God's own Son, and that of His servant, Paul, but also contrary to the doctrine of Luther. (See his tract, *De Sublimiori mundi potestate.*) It is also contrary to Jerome, Augustine, Theophylact, Anselm, Remigius, and others, who agree that the heretics should not be killed, but admonished and convinced; and, if they do not repent after admonition, according to the Word of God, expelled from the communion of the church and shunned.

Behold, this stone thrown so high by him might light upon his own head. For what greater and more terrible heresy, deception, and blasphemy can be imagined than to assert that the pure and holy flesh of Christ is a *Boosegelt*[63] and ransom for sin; to adulterate so sadly Christ's ordinance and the apostles' clear and plain doctrine of baptism, to neglect expulsion as required by the Word of God, to slander the pious, and to console and encourage the impenitent and carnal-minded with twisted Scriptures, as he has constantly done in his writings from beginning to end?

If we were thus to resolve against those who are wrong in doctrine or faith, as he proposes, then we would have to begin with him, because he is a protagonist of such great errors, as may be plainly seen by comparing our writings when placed next to each other.

May the merciful, dear Lord grant him and all our opponents eyes wherewith to see the right position of truth, open hearts to understand it rightly, and a willing, free, and new mind to believe and follow it indeed. Amen.

## Conclusion

Here, dear reader, you have my answer, extracted from me, to the insipid, blasphemous writing of Gellius, which he has published and printed, A.D. 1552, against the unadulterated truth of God and His scattered church; a tract whereby he so lamentably falsifies the blessed doctrine of Christ, and so sadly and without their fault accuses the innocent pious hearts before the whole world. I could not omit to reply, being duty bound by my office, to which I was unworthily ordained by God, through the pious. I had to reply to him with the Word of the Lord, and publish it in print, even as he did in the first place

[63] See explanatory note on page 856. *Tr.*

against us, to the praise of God and His truth, to the justification of the innocent, and to the instruction of the humble.

Whoever seeks and strives after truth may find it. It has been shown with great clearness. But whoever despises it, does not despise us, but Christ Jesus who has taught it unto His church through His holy apostles and who has left it to us by the testimony of the Scriptures through His Holy Spirit.

I hereby offer myself to you and to the whole world, if these writings are not sufficient, and if safe conduct is granted, to an open and free discussion with Gellius and the learned ones. If I cannot maintain my doctrine and faith with Scriptures, and if I cannot prove their doctrine and faith to be deceiving, that is, in those matters that keep us apart, then I will not refuse to acknowledge my fault before the whole world, to retract my doctrine, and with my books, to enter into the fire. But if I can do it, then I desire and ask nothing more than that they acknowledge their fault, discontinue to deceive the people, repent, teach the truth to the people, and flee from falsehood. Herewith I commend you to God; may He guide your feet upon the way of peace, and lead you all in the unadulterated, pure knowledge of His eternal, saving truth. Amen. The grace of our Lord Jesus Christ be with all who sincerely seek and fear Him. Amen.

MENNO SIMONS.

# The Incarnation of Our Lord

*Bekentenisse van de menschwerdinge*

## 1554

*For other foundation can no man
lay than that is laid, which is Jesus Christ.*

I Corinthians 3:11

# Introduction

As a background for this volume, one should read the Introduction to Menno's tenth book, a statement of faith prepared by Menno at the request of John a Lasco, entitled *Brief and Clear Confession*. This statement followed a disputation held by Menno and a Lasco in the former Franciscan Monastery in Emden, January 28-31, 1544 (1543 if one thinks of the New Year as beginning with March, as many people did in the sixteenth century and later). On that occasion Menno promised to submit to a Lasco within three months a confession of faith, the result being the *Brief and Clear Confession* of 1544. Without Menno's knowledge or consent a Lasco then proceeded to publish Menno's *Confession,* and the following year he also published his attack on it, entitled *Defensio* (1545). For nine years Menno seems to have made no reply to the Defensio, but early in 1554 he finally got around to writing his rebuttal, the work now before us, entitled *The Incarnation of Our Lord.*

Menno himself divided this work on the *Incarnation* into three parts: I. Reply to Various Charges of John a Lasco; II. Menno's Statement of Belief About the Incarnation of God's Son; and III. His Rebuttal("Confutation") of the Arguments of a Lasco.

As has been noted elsewhere, the Swiss Brethren never shared the view of Menno and the Dutch Mennonites on the Incarnation, and the Dutch Mennonites themselves did not long retain it. Yet this theory of Menno's has long been a point of attack on the part of the opponents of the Mennonites. To a certain extent, modern Mennonites are therefore a bit embarrassed by the peculiar views of Menno on this subject. Yet it should be noted that Menno is not guilty of heresy: and he had only the best of motives, namely, to uphold a high view of the person of Christ, to recognize Him as the eternal Son of God, and to avoid regarding Him as corrupted by the fallen nature of Adam which Menno thought the view of his opponents implied. The only answer to Menno's fears on this last point is to fall back on the miracle of the Holy Spirit conception of our Lord: God miraculously cleansed the seed of Mary of all sinful depravity at the conception of Jesus by the Holy Spirit.

In the *Opera Omnia Theologica* of 1681 this treatise, *The Incarnation of Our Lord,* bears the long and imposing title, *On the Incarnation: A Clear and Irrefutable Confession and Exposition based squarely on the Scriptures, that the entire Christ Jesus, God and man, man and God, is God's only begotten and first-born Son; neither divided nor composite, but a single, undivided Person, Son, and Christ, the Word of God incarnate in Time: Together with a fundamental Confutation and Solution of the Principal Objections offered by John a Lasco in his* DEFENSIO. The title page prints John 6:51 as well as the usual I Cor. 3:11. This work is found in the 1681 Dutch edition, fol. 351-82, and in the *Complete Works* of 1871, Part II, pages 139-77.

J. C. W.

# The Incarnation of Our Lord

# 1554

## *Preface*

To the kind reader, blessing.

I notice dear reader, that books treating of the incarnation of our Lord and written in Latin and in Dutch are in circulation, books which must, it seems to me, make us of such bad reputation that they who hear them or read them must, alas, stop their ears and hold their noses at the sight of us. Therefore I am obliged to reply to some of the accusations which are laid upon me so unfairly, and largely by John a Lasco. In the second place, I add thereto my deep conviction and faith concerning Jesus, the Son of God. And in the third place, I meet with the divine truth and Scriptures, as God gives me grace, the principal objections wherewith he attacks our position and conviction.[1]

I do this not for my own person's sake, for I know very well that my truth will probably remain falsehood in the eyes of the learned ones, and I, with all the holy apostles and prophets on my side, will remain the archheretic—even if Christ Jesus should speak with the same power in me and by means of my unlearned talk as He did of yore in and through the same apostles and prophets.

What I do, I do out of a pure love for my Lord and Saviour and for His holy Word and out of love for my dear brethren ; also out of a kindly feeling which I entertain toward my opponent. I desire that Christ Jesus, the Son of the Almighty and great God, may be known as a true Son of His heavenly Father ; that the Scriptures may remain inviolate ; and the distressed and hungry consciences, so eager to follow what is right, might perceive and know the right and with happy hearts thank the Almighty and eternal Father through His only begotten and first-born Son, Christ Jesus. I do this also so that the pious reader may know through whom he is reconciled to his God, and that he may hold this position with clear and unequivocal Scripture and irrefutable truth.

For this cause have I undertaken this task before I die[2] so that I (who in my weakness and submissiveness wait for my release from this earthly tabernacle)

---

[1] The full title of a Lasco's *Defensio* of 1545 is given in Cornelius Krahn: *Menno Simons* (Karlsruhe i. B., 1936), p. 62, n. 194. *Ed.*

[2] Menno wrote this in 1554; he died in 1561. *Ed.*

may leave behind a sure testimony and a memorial, as to how glorious or inglorious, how high or how low, how great or how little I have in the days of my service considered the Lord Christ, my only and eternal Surety, Comfort, Refuge, Saviour, and Redeemer. For I know right well how they rail and rant concerning us.

Now I have divided this little book into three parts. Part I is a reply to some items and accusations, matters that do not concern the doctrinal matter at issue, which were laid at my door without show of justice by John a Lasco. Part II is a statement of my convictions, sustained by Scripture, concerning the origin of Christ's human nature. Part III contains the principal objections urged against our position, especially by John a Lasco, as well as a powerful reply and sustained argument drawn from God's Word. I divided thus in order that the reader might not become confused as he reads, but by this device have an intelligent grasp and understanding of what we have written.

And I beg my readers, for Jesus' sake, be they learned or unlearned, kindly disposed or otherwise, not to read my report with a perverse mind, but thoughtfully and intelligently; to reread it and fathom it well, to compare it with the Scriptures, and to judge it in their light. I will ask the reader not to believe the long and voluminous writings of the learned ones, their teachings and their glosses, but the Scriptures; to investigate the argument without rancor, and so to believe the most certain truth and to follow in the true fear of God, and to give Him proper praise, as fair and reasonable people, in keeping with the Christian name, should. I am sure that all who read with such attention will very soon discover that our opponents' position, doctrine, and belief concerning Christ, the Son of God, is altogether deceiving and erroneous, and that ours is the position, the testimony, yes, the power and the truth of Scripture.

I beg the reader also not to take it ill of me if occasionally I call a lie, a lie, and am a bit stern with injustice. By God's grace I hope to do it without bitterness and in terms as restrained as possible. I hope the reader will not be irked when I am constrained to relate the same words and substance more than once, and finally that he will not judge me without knowledge of the matter and grow angry. For I only want to clear myself with the truth, as is only fair, to defend my faith and hope with Scripture, to seek to promote the honor and praise of my Saviour—things that it is my duty to do not only in the written and spoken word, but also with my lifeblood if His glory should require it.

May the dear Lord, the true Son of the true and living God, whose honor and praise it alone concerns, grant to every well-disposed and respectful reader an eager mind with which to investigate diligently, and an enlightened and courageous heart wherewith to understand aright. Amen.

## PART I

*First of all John a Lasco writes that I have magnified his name so that I, because of the discussion which I had with him, might gain correspondingly in reputation and honor among "our people," as he calls them.*

*Reply.* It is true that I addressed him as the noble and learned, etc., in my declaration made to him and the other preachers. But I did it out of no other motive than common politeness and that in the simplicity of my heart.

Nor have I given him any such hateful name as he has given me when he called me a doctor or master of the Anabaptists. Neither did I call him by any such high-sounding titles as those he uses of himself when he calls himself, *"Poloniae Baro."* I have not used his name for any such purpose as he, alas, ascribes to me. Thank God, I have come to understand Paul well enough to know that if I should seek to please men, I cannot be Christ's servant. Even if I should derive greater honor from the name of Christ than I can derive from that of any mortal man, even if he were emperor or king, then my affair would still not stand well at the end. For if I seek my own honor, and not God's, then there will be no honor for me. But I hope to seek an honor that abides with me forever. Men may judge me as they see fit and as they wish to acknowledge before their God in the day of Christ. He who has eyes as of flaming fire knows all my ambitions and deeds, my coming in and going out, my rising up and my sitting down. If I were not known of Him beyond the judgments of men, then I might well exclaim: Woe is me that I have been born.

*In the second place he writes that I have abused his name without cause as well as their church and its services.*

*Reply.* That I have written anything beyond the truth about John a Lasco and his colleagues no one will, I hope, be able to prove. But if I have hurt them with the truth, the thing they resent so, let them blame the truth for that and not me. I gladly leave to the judgment of fair and reasonable men whether I wrote rightly or wrongly, too little or too much, in all that I have written about his and his associates' doctrine, sacrament, ritual, churches, or congregations.

If their doctrine and ritual is of God and His Word, why then are not their perverse and reckless disciples converted from their wicked conduct? For according to Scripture it cannot fail; a doctrine and service that is of God must have its effect and influence. Isa. 55:11; Jer. 23:28. But that they are engaged in threshing empty straw is too evident to admit of denial. My conscience testifies only this: that I have dealt fairly and correctly with them and their churches, for I have merely rebuked in them that which all the prophets, apostles, and faithful witnesses of God have rebuked so passionately before me, namely, the impenitent, carnal life that is known to all. If now I have erred so seriously in this matter, then I may go to court against both Moses and the prophets, Christ and the apostles for charging me, poor unworthy man, and all God-fearing preachers, so sternly and solemnly—the reason why we distressed people have to hear and suffer so much in this mad world. Whatever I have done in this matter, I have done in the interest of their poor souls, out of faithful and genuine love, with a view to their improvement. This, the One who created me knows.

*In the third place he says, I have been obliged with the authority of God's Word to deliver our doctrine from your slander, a doctrine which you may be able with your shouting to censure in the eyes of your followers, but which you are unable with the authority of Scripture (of which you always speak so highly) to attack.*

*Reply.* If to rebuke error with God's Spirit and Word may be called slander, then not only I, but Isaiah, Jeremiah, all the prophets, and Christ Jesus and His apostles have slandered, and not a little bit. I have rebuked their affair with the Word of the Lord, and with it, by grace, convicted them that they are not the true messengers of God, nor their congregation the true church. If John a Lasco wants to make out that our doctrine (which is not ours, but the Lord Christ's) and our rebuke drawn from the Holy Scriptures is slander, and if he wants to make out a good case before God, who judges aright, for his own doctrine of the incarnation, pedobaptism, the call of his preachers, his view of excommunication, and the free and careless life of his church, then he will have a hard enough task. Philosophy, rationalization, and glosses, we shall, I greatly fear, have a plenty, but very little of the power of Scripture, its basis and truth. Yes, my good reader, I am sure that if men would refrain from invoking the secular power in their own behalf, as no doubt they should, then it would soon be apparent on whose side Scriptural victory is.

*In the fourth place he says, When we substantiate our doctrine with the power of the divine Word, then the matter itself will make it evident that we have been defamed by you without cause and our common innocence will be praised by it.*

*Reply.* Just as soon as he has so validated his doctrine and sacraments with the authority of the divine Word, as he boastingly asserts, then I myself will acknowledge to them that I have improperly and wrongfully rebuked them. For all they do is to comfort the poor people with falsehood and with imagined promises to keep them on the crooked way. Even if he could demonstrate his doctrine and sacraments to be Scriptural—which, however, he can never do, try as he may—even then the matter would be less than half settled, for doctrine and sacraments are vain where fruitful, active faith and an irreproachable, pious conduct are not in evidence. It is unto this end that doctrine is given and the sacraments ordained. What kind of life is found in their congregation generally, and among most of their preachers as well, they may judge who observe their conduct daily and are versed in Scripture.

*In the fifth place he says, If you had sent us your writings as you had promised, then we could have answered you in private, but now you have disseminated them among your followers before you came to us, etc.*

*Reply.* I am not aware of making any such promise, nor do I understand why I should promise such a thing, for I have nothing of which to write except my own belief and foundation, which I desire to testify, not only with secret writing, but also with my own blood before the whole world, if the Lord will sustain me with His grace.

But when he writes that I disseminated them among my followers, etc., he goes too far. For as soon as I had departed, I took up my abode in a secret place, as I have had to do for many years, for the testimony of Jesus and my own conscience, and I very simply put my belief and position in writing, and without delay sent it to them as agreed upon.[3] This only excepted, that I handed it to that honorable man, the late M. H. G., since he was at that time bailiff and burgomaster. The Lord is my witness that this is so, and since this is the way it went, how then can I have disseminated it among my followers before I delivered it to them, as he charges me here and accuses? And even if I had done that of which he accuses me, in what way would that have wronged him and his associates, it being the position and belief not merely of me but also of us all, as many realize? His own sense has convinced him that it would seem unwarranted to the reader, without cause, to write such a slanderous and bitter book about a person.[4] Therefore he had to trump up something so that his writing about the poor Menno, who because of the great tyranny cannot defend himself before the world, might have a show of cause. But whether it can stand before the impartial judgment seat of Christ will become evident in his declaration. May the dear Lord not reckon it against him as sin, for I know that I am innocent.

*In the sixth place he writes, It is the fault of your people that I have to deal with you publicly, etc. They have verily spread a report in West Friesland and in a large part of Holland, that you and your colleagues are permitted to teach your doctrine in our churches, that we have been worsted in the argument and have nothing with which to reply to you.*

*Reply.* Never in all my days have I heard a word of all this except what I read here. If some of our people have boasted thus (a matter that I cannot entrust to them) as he writes, then it is evident that in that matter they have not spoken truth but sheer falsehood, and this lie is a shameful thing, yes, of the devil and soul-killing. Wisd. 1:12. If then such a report has reached him, it is still not proper for such a man to lend his ear to such detestable agitators and liars, nor to publish it as an everlasting memorial to the whole world without basis in truth, and to the great injury of his neighbor. And if he has invented this and did not hear it from anybody—a thing that I do not suspect him of— then he disgraces his illustrious name and causes his poor soul to fail grievously; for lying is a shameful thing and it shall find no place in the city of God. Rev.

---

[3] Menno and a Lasco held a disputation in Emden, Jan. 28-31, 1544. Menno promised to send a Lasco a statement of his views within three months—his *Brief and Clear Confession*—which a Lasco promptly published. *Ed.*

[4] Menno here refers to a Lasco's *Defensio* of 1545 directed against Menno and his views. *Ed.*

21:22. I say again that I do not suspect him of having invented this. But this I do suspect, that he has been too eager to listen, too quick to believe, too hasty to write. Anyway, whatever be the truth in the matter this I know, that in the matter of his present writing, let him doctor the matter up as he pleases, he has not acted toward me as Christian fairness and love require. The great Lord will in His own good time make it to appear what each man seeks and pretends, defends, teaches, and promotes.

*In the seventh place he accuses me saying that I have ridiculed the two Latin syllogisms which he handed me when I went away; that I despised learning and proficiency in language, disdainfully called them philosophies; referred to myself as a humble theologian, a matter with which I ensnare the untutored and simple folk, and make myself a reputation; but that my simplicity is not simplicity but rather ignorance, etc. Yes, he has portrayed me in such a way that the memory of me will probably continue with men for all time—although, alas, not much to my honor.*

*Reply.* That he has called me by these latter nicknames came about because I had written to him and his collaborators saying, Let us not treat of these things in subtly invented syllogisms nor with any clever human sophistries, for we do not have any of these things. But let us use in our debates only the plain and unequivocal Word that cannot be twisted with glosses, nor broken with human wisdom. These are my words of 1543,[5] written in my *Confession* sent to him and his fellow preachers.

If you are of a pious heart, then judge whether I have hereby deserved such an ugly and bitter attack. But I discern that I have earned this beautiful bouquet, not by the quoted words, but by the poor and despised truth. Understand correctly, dear reader. Learnedness and proficiency in languages I have never disdained, but have honored and coveted them from my youth; although I have, alas, never attained to them. Praise God, I am not so bereft of my sense that I should disdain and despise the knowledge of languages whereby the precious Word of divine grace has come to us. I could wish that I and all pious hearts were at home in them if only we would employ them in genuine humility and to the glory of our God and the service of our fellows. Is it not an ugly shame that they should speak so little truth and forever desire to load me down (although altogether undeserved by me) with such a bag of lies? Yes, dear reader, if I wanted to pay back in kind as the law of nature would teach me, I should like to assemble some of the invented vilifications which they have in part spoken, and in part written of me, things of which neither he nor any other person shall ever convict me with the truth. Whether this may be called right and fair, let any impartial and reasonable heart determine in honorable fairness.

I could beg him and all our adversaries for God's sake and from the bottom of my heart, not to deal otherwise with me than I do with them, unless it is my blood they seek—which I do not hope of some of them. Whatever shortcoming

[5] The year (New Style) is 1544. *Ed.*

I see in them concerning it, I admonish them and rebuke them, as love requires, although they resent it. But that I should lie about them, from this may the great Lord preserve me! I know right well out of what an impure fountain falsehood flows and what its outcome is. I know, too, that this is not the seed from which we beget God's children, and gather a church unto Christ. This, I wish that they would do: admonish me with the truth and reproach me if I should err in human fashion in some matters; argue their case (if they have one, which alas they do not have) with Scripture; and leave it to the seed of the serpent to resort to lies, and to Cain's seed to use force.

As to my unlearnedness, the thing which he so bitterly hurls at me, I am not only ignorant, but altogether unlearned; and not, or only slightly, proficient in languages. Yes, reader, I say with Socrates, very freely, that as far as human wisdom is concerned, I know but one thing, and that is that I do not know. But as to the heavenly wisdom, I am by God's grace in so far taught of God that I confess from the heart that my Saviour and Redeemer, Christ Jesus, is God's only begotten and first-born Son and that he who believes in Him has everlasting life (John 3:18); that a liar is of the devil (John 8:45); that he who hates his brother is a murderer (I John 3:15); that he who does not repent, must die in his sins (Luke 13:4); that the wages of sin is death (Rom. 6:23). And out of this unsung wisdom (eternal thanks to the Lord) I have derived such reverent fear in my poor soul that my earthly mind is converted to a better frame, and I am heartily sorry that I fail to walk in Christ with all my strength according to God's will and be a righteous and blameless Christian; and that I am unable to beget the whole world out of its proud and godless life, unto a new and penitent Christian life, with the Lord's Spirit, power, and Word. For my only joy and my heart's desire is that we might rightly preach Christ, according to His holy Word, magnify His holy name, seek Him, fear Him, love Him, and serve Him; yes, that we might be the city of the living God, the glorious kingdom of His honor, and the temple of His Holy Spirit, etc.

Now this wisdom which effects such power and yields such fruits, I consider to be the very finest that can be named, even if it is taught and recovered by an ignorant teamster or hod carrier; yes, it is the only oil of gladness for my perturbed heart, the only cure for my heavy care; and by God's grace, it will finally also be the glorious adornment and the crown of my glory. Read about this noble, highly learned wisdom and philosophy in the proverbs of Solomon, also Sirach and the Book of Wisdom, and you will discover what is its proper excellence and power.

You see, dear reader, for the sake of the sweetness of this philosophy, its nobility, its virtue, its fruit, its delightfulness, and its beauty, which I have not learned from any famous doctors nor in any institution of higher learning, and in order to delight my poor soul with its living power, I have preferred to be the fool of the world's learned ones, in order that I might be found of God to be wise, rather than to be one of the most famous of the worldly wise, and at the last be a fool in God's sight. And so this is my apology and brief reply to his caustic invective.

Once more I say that I put down those words, *subtle syllogisms,* and, *clever sophisms,* without the least disdain for learning and in the simplicity of my heart. And I have neither despised nor wronged anybody by so doing. I honor learnedness whenever it is properly and reverently employed. But above all things do I praise the simple and virtuous wisdom that is from above; for it will never perish but abide in glorious honor with all the pious in eternal life.

This, then, is the first part of this book. I would have preferred not to mention these things if they had not occasioned the estrangement of some, the obstruction of the Word, and the grieving of God-fearing people. But as it is, I am forced to do this. May the dear Lord grant us all His grace. Amen.


PART II

OUR CONFESSION


The reason we do not grant the learned ones' doctrine in regard to the Lord's incarnation, but oppose it with Scripture and truth, is this. We see with our eyes and feel with our hands that they rob us of Christ, the Son of God, and direct us to an earthly, sinful creature, and a man born of Adam's impure and sinful flesh. Their doctrine and representations in the matter are irreconcilable with God's ordinances (Gen. 1:28), with Scripture, and with the implications of the terms, father, mother, and son. A great many absurdities result inevitably in regard to Christ, such as original sin, condemnation, curse, death, etc.

In their view, Christ would be but half a man, if the woman contributed as much to the fetus as does the man,[6] as they assert. And we get two persons, one divine and the other human, called by them two natures or parts. And we have two sons, one the Son of God without any mother and not subject to suffering, and the other the son of Mary without any father and subject to suffering. Again, if God is to be called the Father of the man Christ, then He must be a Father who makes, rather than a Father who bears His son, and Christ must be a made rather than a born Son of His Father. Then, also, the restoration of Adam and his seed takes place, not by the Word from which it all must come, but by his own guilty and condemned flesh with which the Word clothed itself and in which it abode as long as it was on earth. And there are a great many absurdities besides.

Therefore I considered it good and needful, before I proceed to the confutation and the solutions of the objections, to set forth out of pure and blessed Scripture our faith concerning Christ the Son of God, in order that the reader

[6] Menno's view is scientifically in error. *Ed.*

may thereby realize that the Lord Jesus Christ is not an impure and divided Christ of two persons or sons, but an undivided and pure Christ, a single person, God's own first-born Son and only begotten Son. Whoever is wise and fears God, let him read and judge.

I advance then, in the first place, the ordinance of God, to which John a Lasco himself refers, namely, Be fruitful and multiply—and I gather from this ordinance that human procreation occurs by the marital intimacy of husband and wife, prerequisite to childbearing, but from the man's seed. The new life has its origin not in the father, but comes from the father through the mother, as will be set forth in greater detail presently.

And I take as proof in the first place the case of Sarah, when the Lord said to Abraham, thy wife, Sarah, will I bless, and she shall bear thee a son; and thou shalt call his name Isaac. Gen. 17:19. To understand this passage, as well as God's ordinance of Genesis 1 aright, the reader should recall that Sarah was barren (as she herself declares, Gen. 17:2) and old, and that it had ceased to be with her after the manner of women. Gen. 18:11. And yet, by faith, she received strength to conceive seed from her husband, that is, to carry it and to bear Abraham a son in spite of her age.

Now my simple mind can only understand the blessing of Sarah thus, that the closed womb of Sarah, who had reached her menopause, and was therefore incapable of conceiving, was by the power of God opened by the faith of Abraham and Sarah so that she conceived seed from her husband, carried it, nurtured the fetus, and in due season was able to give it birth. In this way, Isaac was conceived of Abraham's seed, and to Abraham a son was born, after God's ordinance of Gen. 1:28.

Lay next to this the saying of Philo, or, if you prefer, that of the wise Solomon, I am also a mortal man, like all the rest, born of the generation of the first created man, and am fashioned of flesh, congealed in blood ten months long, of a father's seed [notice he speaks of a father's seed], and that by the gratification occasioned by the marital contact. Wisd. 7:1.

Again, the Lord said unto Jacob, Be fruitful and multiply; a nation, and a company of nations shall be of thee; and kings shall come out of thy loins. Gen. 35:11. Or, Levi was still in the loins of his father when Melchisedec met Abraham. Many such clear expressions could be added. For example, Rom. 9, etc.

Now I will let the philosophers speculate and the experts in natural science wrangle as to what and how much a mother contributes to her offspring. God's ordinances and the example of Abraham and Sarah, and the abundant testimony of Scripture are enough for me in the matter. They prove, beyond challenge, that a child takes its origin in the father and not in the mother.

In the second place, I adduce the words of the holy angel Gabriel, when he announced to Mary that she would conceive and bear a son. She asked, How shall that take place, seeing I know no man? The angel replied, The Holy Ghost shall come upon thee, and the power of the Highest overshadow thee; therefore that holy thing that shall be born of thee shall be called God's Son.

Now here you have the testimony of a trustworthy messenger that God is a genuine Father of our Lord Christ. It seems to me that God's own angel has here rebuked the falsehood of those who say that the crucified Christ had no father.

Since then we discover out of God's own ordinances and out of the multitude of Scripture passages that a child takes its origin primarily out of the seed of his father, according to God's ordinance, as has been stated; and since we are instructed so solidly in all Scripture that God the Father is a real Father of His Son, Jesus Christ, therefore we say that we believe and confess that God's eternal Word (also called God's seed in Scripture) descended from above and entered into Mary by the overshadowing of divine power, and beyond the understanding of man and according to the changeless plan of the Almighty and heavenly Father and the gracious promise, and by the operation of the Holy Spirit became in a wonderful way a genuine tangible man, subject to suffering, but not to destruction. All this according to the plain testimony of John in the Gospel as well as in the epistle. A man, I say, like unto us in all things, sin excepted. He did not come as the learned ones without Biblical warrant say, *of Adam's unclean seed, kept clear of sin by God's power.* That which never knew sin is the seed and origin of his flesh. As John testifies, The Word became flesh. Compare also the passages of Scripture that testify that Jesus Christ was God's first-born and only begotten Son and you will discover how sadly they err who say that the human Christ had no father.

Moreover, of Mary, the Lord's mother, we believe and confess that the Almighty and eternal God and Father, by the strong power of His eternal and holy Spirit, graciously prepared her virgin body (as He also prepared the senile body of Sarah) so that it was fit by faith to receive the intangible eternal Word according to the angel's announcement (just as Sarah did by marital contact receive seed of Abraham). And that same Word became flesh, was fed and nourished in truly human fashion in her virgin body by ordinary food and drink (just as Isaac was in Sarah), as a regular child of her flesh and blood to the certain testimony that he was truly human and not a mere phantasm. And so He was born, as the Scriptures say, in due season, an undivided and genuine Son of God and Mary, as an ordinary child of its parents (the only exception being the absence of sexual contact).

And in this sense we believe and confess that He was the seed of the woman, of Abraham, and of David. This was given to her out of special favor and grace, to the salvation and redemption of the whole world and of God the Father, according to the sure word of His promise, the highest assurance and certain proof of His divine love. This woman, ordained of God, conceived Him in Nazareth in the indicated manner as the Saviour of the whole world, according to the saying of the angel, and gave birth to Him in Bethlehem.

Notice, dear reader, that Matthew and Luke did indicate that it was by God through the Holy Spirit that Mary conceived, but that did not indicate clearly enough to satisfy the curious, out of whose seed the conception did primarily occur. In the meantime certain sects arose in the church, such as the Cerinthians and the Ebionites, who, according to historians, introduced grievous heresies in regard to the person of Christ.

Whereupon, John, at the request of the bishops of Asia Minor, wrote very clearly of Christ, the Son of God; not merely of His everlasting deity, as the learned ones say, but also of His holy humanity. This a glance at his writings will show. With unambiguous words and in unmistakable clarity, he indicated who and what He was from eternity; who and what He did in time become; of what seed and by whom Mary (of whom Matthew and Luke had spoken) had conceived; namely, not of the *unclean seed of Adam* but of the pure seed of His Father, God's Word. And he says, The Word became flesh.

He does not say, *The Word assumed a man of our or of Mary's flesh and dwelt in this,* as our opponents say. He indicates, moreover, whence He came, what He taught us, what example He left us, what we have because of Him, whence He ascended again, etc. Now whoever believes John's testimony correctly has eternal life through His name. John 20. But he who does not believe, but rejects it, is not of God, and has neither the Father nor the Son, but is an antichrist and deceiver. This is our plain and simple confession concerning Christ the Son of God.

Now to elucidate our doctrine a little more thoroughly, the reader must know that the Scriptures indicate by all means that God the Almighty Father has created all things by the Word of His power. Gen. 1 :1 ; Psalm 33 :6. By it He rules all things, by it He sustains and keeps all things. Col. 1 :16; Heb. 1 :21. And even as it is plain that Adam was created by that selfsame Word, but because of his disobedience fell into death and condemnation through God's righteousness, together with all his seed; so it is plain that of himself and by himself, he could never rise to his feet again since he was together with all his seed so corrupted in his nature and so condemned by God's righteousness. And God's eternal love constrained Him, lest Adam and his kind be lost forever, to save him out of his fall, condemnation, and curse by that selfsame Word whereby He had created him, so that He might have all the honor and be praised eternally through His Word and Son, Christ Jesus, for His unspeakably great love and grace. For if the restoration had been by any other means than by the Word, then we could properly praise and thank that means.

Notice with our confession and faith the whole Scriptures agree, as you have by God's grace very clearly seen from the passages quoted. John says, In the beginning was the Word, and the Word was with God, and the Word was God, etc. And the Word became flesh and dwelt among us, and we beheld his glory as of the only begotten of the Father, full of grace and truth. This testimony of John we believe to be correct. That is the reason we let it stand unviolated, in order that the entire Christ may continue to be God's Son. For we see plainly that our view in this matter agrees with all the Scriptures and fits.

We truly believe and do not doubt that the Holy Spirit who seeks to lead

His own into all truth did not intend it otherwise than He declares here to His faithful and simple fisherman, John. For if the dear messenger of the holy peace had not so intended it as it is written here, then the churches so troubled by the matter had not been quieted by his writings, but had more than ever before been driven apart, and we poor descendants would be pointed to a very dark and uncertain position. Oh, no! His witness is clear and plain, and clear and plain it will remain: *The Word became flesh.*

Our confession is endorsed by the Lord Himself when He says, I am that living bread that came down from heaven; whoso eateth of this bread shall live forever; and the bread that I shall give is my flesh, which I give for the life of the world. John 6:32.

Reader, consider the Word of your Lord. Christ says that His flesh came from heaven, and the learned ones say that it came of Adam's flesh. Here are flatly opposite positions. What must the God-fearing conscience do now? If it clings to Christ's Word and testimony, then it will pass with the learned ones for a deceiver and a heretic. But if it adheres to the testimony of the learned ones, then it makes Christ a liar. And seeing that we discover the learned ones and Christ so completely at variance with each other, and since we know Christ to be the guileless truth and all men to be liars, we cannot forsake the truth for falsehood, can we? No, we must turn from falsehood to truth. Let men think of us as they please. God's Word abides forever. Isa. 40:8; I Pet. 1:24.

Quite probably our opponents will attempt an evasion at this point and say, Christ speaks of the most worthy element in Him, for His deity is from heaven, and it assumed Adam's flesh, etc. I reply: Let them believe Christ's own Word and testimony, then they will realize how they interpret it according to their own desires and not according to the intention and truth of the Christ. For this is what He says, I am that living bread come down from heaven [notice how He says, come down from heaven] and that bread that I will give is my flesh. Notice He does not say, is my deity, but my flesh which I give for the life of the world. It seems to me that Christ has explained His own words quite sufficiently, and the explanations and glosses of the learned ones are unnecessary. But both Christ and John could not speak more plainly of the origin of His holy flesh than they have done in the above passages.

Therefore let everybody be careful how he glosses, for he who falsifies this clear and solid testimony falsifies not a man's word, but his Lord's. Neither does he reject us, but the Son of God and His Holy Spirit, and the exalted apostle John, who testified with such plain and clear words, preserved for us in such clarity.

Christ endorsed this our confession when He says, Father, glorify me with that glory which I had with thee before the world was. John 17:6. To my mind, this is a clear enough testimony how that Christ humbled Himself, and for our sake laid aside for a time His divine prerogative, right, and glory. For although He was very righteousness and the eternally Blessed One, He did not refuse to became a sacrifice for sin, and a curse for us. But I say, good reader, that if He *in this way continued in His erstwhile estate undiminished and not subject to suffering,* as John a Lasco and his group propose, and if He had only *hung upon Himself a strange tabernacle of the flesh of Mary,* then He had not lost a thing, had He, which He could then desire back again of the Father, seeing that He was not diminished but continued undiminished in His erstwhile estate.

But now it is apparent that the eternal and indescribably glorious Word, that was from all eternity in everlasting glory and brightness, in an incomprehensible way in the Father and with the Father, did in time lay aside His brightness for a season, and in our behalf became a poor, miserable, mortal man and died a bitter death for us. And in this way He desired to have back again His erstwhile brightness which He had with the Father before the world was, and which He had, for a season, for our sakes laid aside, etc. This passage is too clear to be obscured by man-made wisdom. Therefore, believe the Word of your Lord, trust in the truth, and you will not be deceived.

With this our confession the holy Paul also agrees when he says, What is it to ascend but that he first descended into the lowest parts of the earth? He that descended is the same as he that ascended far above the heavens in order that he might fill all things. Eph. 4:10.

To this plain statement of Paul add the testimony of Christ which He testifies of His origin, saying, No man hath ascended up to heaven, but he that came down from heaven, even the Son of man which is in heaven. John 3:13.

Study the above words of Paul carefully. For if he asserted this descending and ascending of His deity only and not of His humanity, how then is to be harmonized the afore-mentioned witness of Christ in which He says, No man hath ascended up to heaven, but he that came down from heaven, even the Son of man which is in heaven. John 3-13; Eph. 4:9. Recall that Christ calls Himself the Son of man, and says that this Son of man descended from heaven. But *the son of Mary, whose flesh is of Mary* did not descend from heaven, did He, but must have *sprung from Adam's flesh,* if the position of the learned ones be correct. No, the Word is descended from heaven! It became flesh or man, here below on earth, and has thereafter ascended again to highest heaven where He was at the first.

Seeing then that in the quoted passage Christ Jesus speaks not merely of His deity, but of His humanity (for He speaks of the Son of man), therefore it is clear, is it not, that the man Christ did not have His origin on earth but in heaven, for He cannot be called the Son of man because of His *eternal Godhead which remained undiminished,* as the learned ones say. Again, He could not when He uttered these things be in heaven, as to His humanity, if that humanity was of Mary rather than from heaven. Therefore we must refer this saying to the entire Christ, both as to His deity and to His humanity.

But then it follows irresistibly that the entire Christ Jesus, both God and man, man and God, has His origin in heaven and not on earth, as John testifies elsewhere, He that is from above is above all; he that is of the earth is earthly, and speaketh of the earth; but he that is from heaven is above all. John 3:31. Similarly, I came forth from the Father, and am come into the world; again, I leave the world and go to the Father. John 16:28.

So then it follows plainly (if at least we accept the words of Christ, of John, and of Paul, as true) that the Word descended from heaven, became flesh in Mary, dwelt among men, fulfilled Scripture, ascended again, was seated at the right hand of His Father, and is adored by the angels of God. Notice, my reader, how mightily these passages fit together, and how Christ, John, and Paul agree. Fast and unmovable is the testimony, The Word became flesh.

Paul explains our confession further and says, The first man is of the earth, earthy; the second man is the Lord from heaven. As is the earthy, such are they also that are earthy; and, as is the heavenly, such are they also that are heavenly. I Cor. 15:47. Reader, observe that although Paul speaks here primarily of the resurrection of the dead, and of the future glory, yet he testifies by this same Scripture the coming again, and the origin of and the difference between the first and second Adam, saying, The first man is of the earth, earthy; and the second man is the Lord from heaven. For as the first man, Adam, is called earthy on acount of his being of the earth; so, also, the second man, Christ, is called heavenly because He is from heaven.

If any one should want to interrupt and say that *Christ is here called heavenly on account of His divinity,* then you may know that Paul rebukes such with his significant words: The second man (he says, The second *man*) is the Lord from heaven. I cannot see how the great witness could express himself more plainly. And since Christ is then such a heavenly Being, and is glorified again of God His heavenly Father, with His eternal glory which He had with Him before the beginning of the world, therefore the holy apostle also calls all His true members, after their resurrection, heavenly. Not that they are from heaven, as Christ is from heaven, but because they, by grace, through the power of God, in the resurrection, will partake of the heavenly glory and of the angelic nature. As Christ also says, Father, I have given them [that is, my disciples] the glory which thou hadst given me.

Again Paul says, Our conversation is in heaven; from whence also we look for the Saviour, the Lord Jesus Christ, who shall change our vile body, that it may be fashioned like unto his glorious body, according to the working whereby he is able even to subdue all things unto himself. Phil 3:20. Read also what Christ says of such. Luke 20; I John 3.

For this reason Paul calls them heavenly and says, As we have borne the image of the earthly, so shall we also bear the image of the heavenly. That is, when this corruptible puts on incorruption and this mortal puts on immortality, then we shall shine forth as the sun in the kingdom of our Father, and as the stars of heaven in brightness forever. Dan. 12:13. Yea, when we shall be like unto the Lord and shall see Him face to face, as He is.

At another place the Scriptures say of Christ, I am the First and the Last, the living One, and I was dead, and behold I live through all eternity. Rev. 1. Here the Holy Spirit brings forward another invincible witness, at which all clever disputers and famous masters of this world must be put to shame. If now they want to pervert this clear and plain Scripture, by their deceitful reasoning, as they do the Scripture of John 1:14, and all the Scriptures, then let them know that we do not follow the glosses of man, but the Word of the Lord. But if they let it stand unviolated, then their cause is already lost. For the Holy Spirit testifies that the First and the Last, and the living One, died.

That *the flesh of Mary* was not the first and the last, all intelligent persons must verily admit. If then *the man Christ was of Mary's flesh,* as the learned ones say, which neither is nor can be the First and Last, and if He had died, then the Spirit of God, which is the Spirit of truth, would not have spoken truly. Yea, neither Christ Himself, who says, I am the First and Last, was dead. I would say further, If indeed *the man Christ Jesus was a natural offspring of Mary's flesh,* and if *the eternal Word only lived therein,* as our opponents put it, and if this same man died, and the Word remained undiminished, then Mary's flesh must be the First and Last. This is too plain to be denied.

Since it is evident that Mary's flesh neither is nor can be the First and Last, as has been heard, and since it is true, according to the testimony of the Holy Spirit, that the First and Last has died, therefore I conclude therefrom that the explanation of our opponents by which they point us to Mary's flesh, is deceitful and false, and that the learned ones are badly mistaken when they say that *the Son of God remained undiminished, and the son of Mary died.* I say again, The Word stands immovable, The Word became flesh.

Again, with this our confession agree all the prophets who have spoken of Christ, the Son of God, through the Holy Spirit. Micah says, But thou Bethlehem Ephratah, though thou be little among the thousands of Judah, yet of thee shall he come forth unto me that is to be ruler in Israel; whose goings forth have been from of old, from everlasting. Mic. 5:2. And Isaiah, Behold a virgin shall conceive and bear a son, and thou shalt call his name Immanuel, God with us. Isa. 7:14; Matt. 1:23. He says further, Unto us a child is born, unto us a son is given, and the government shall be upon his shoulders, and his name shall be called Wonderful, Counselor, The mighty God, The everlasting Father, The Prince of Peace. Isa. 9:6. At another place, Say unto the cities of Judah, Behold your God. And Jeremiah says, Behold, the days come, saith the Lord, that I will raise up unto David a righteous Branch, and a King shall reign and prosper, and shall execute judgment and justice in the earth. In his days Judah shall be saved, and Israel shall dwell safely; and this is his name whereby he shall be called, *The Lord our Righteousness.* Jer. 23:5.

My reader, observe. Since then the going forth of this Prince has thus been from eternity, as has been related, and His name by the Spirit of the Lord

is called Immanuel, The mighty God, The everlasting Father, Our Righteousness, etc.; and since the prophets describe Him with such unmistakable words,
as do also the apostles, whence He is, who, and what; therefore I conclude that
the man Christ Jesus is not of unclean, sinful flesh, but of the unspotted, pure
seed and Word of God, His Father, as John says, The Word became flesh.

This then is our proper faith and confession of Christ, the Son of God,
namely: That we are all created in Adam our father through the supernatural
Word, and that we, by and in the same Adam, have become of a sinful nature
and subject to death; that we also, by means of this eternal, supernatural Word,
and not by means of the sinful flesh of Adam, are graciously accepted of God
and mercifully called unto life everlasting. Even as Christ says, God so loved
the world, that he gave his only begotten Son, that whosoever believeth in
him should not perish, but have everlasting life. Psalm 33:6; Rom. 5:12; I
Cor. 15:3; John 3:16.

That we dare not divide Christ, the Son of God, after the representations
of the learned ones, but confess Him to be entirely the true Son of the true
and living God, is because the entire Scripture constrains us. The angel testified of Christ, the son of Mary, saying, That holy thing which shall be born
of thee, shall be called the Son of God. Luke 1. Again, the Father testified,
This is my beloved Son in whom I am well pleased. Again, John the Baptist
says, He that sent me to baptize with water, the same said unto me, Upon
whom thou shalt see the Spirit descending and remaining on him, the same
is he which baptizeth with the Holy Ghost; and I saw it and bare record that
this is the Son of God. Again, Nathanael saith unto him, Rabbi, thou art the
Son of God, thou art the King of Israel. John 1:49. Again, when Jesus asked
His disciples, Whom say ye that I am? Peter answered and said, Thou art
the Christ, the Son of the living God. Again, Martha said, I believe that thou
art the Christ, the Son of God, which should come into the world. Again, the
disciples, together with the others, said, Verily, thou art the Son of God.
Again, Christ said to the blind man, Dost thou believe on the Son of God?
He answered and said, Who is he, Lord, that I might believe on him; and
Jesus said unto him, Thou hast both seen him and it is he that talketh with
thee. Again, when the centurion saw that He so cried out, and gave up the
ghost, he said, Truly, this man was the Son of God. Mark 15:39. Again, Saul
was with the disciples at Damascus, and preached Christ in the synagogues,
that He is the Son of God. Acts 9. Again, John says, We have seen and do
testify that the Father sent the Son to be the Saviour of the world. Whosoever
shall confess that Jesus is the Son of God, God dwelleth in him, and he in God.
I John 4:9. Besides these, there are many other clear passages.

Inasmuch as the Scriptures so abundantly testify that also the man Christ
is the Son of God, therefore it is manifest that Martin Micron[7] and those of
his mind do fearfully err when they say boldly, *The man Christ was not the*

---

[7] Martin Micron (1523-59) was a Zwinglian (Reformed) Reformer of Norden in East
Friesland. *Ed.*

*Son of God; he had no Father, but there are two sons in Christ—the one the Son of God without mother, and not subject to suffering; and the other the son of mankind, or the son of Mary without father, and subject to suffering.* I think this may be called rejecting the Son of God, together with all these plain Scriptures, and pointing us to a divided Christ, yea, to an unclean, sinful flesh and creature, guilty of death, whom the Scriptures never knew and still less taught. *O detestabilem blasphemiam* (Oh, detestable blasphemy!).

Now he that can believe firmly and grasp correctly that the Word did not take unto itself a man of Mary's flesh, but that, according to the testimony of John, it became flesh, to him is the true insight of Christ thereby opened wide. Such a one will not argue *per Synecdoche, de parte ad totum, neque de toto ad partem* [Latin for, By Synecdoche, from the part to the whole, or neither from the whole to the part]. He will not take recourse to the worthiest part in Christ, nor to the communication or communion of names.[8] Neither will he unite *two persons and sons in one person and son,* as our opponents do. But he will leave the Scriptures unviolated, and acknowledge with John the Baptist, with Matthew, with Martha, and with the whole Scriptures, that Christ Jesus is God's first-begotten and only-begotten Son, a single and undivided Christ, God and man, man and God, a single person and Son, who in His flesh has satisfied the handwriting of the Law (which we, because of our weakness, could not do); and was at the last condemned for the sin of us all and sentenced to the death of the cross as an innocent, spotless Lamb.

So there you have our confession concerning the most holy incarnation of our Lord Jesus Christ, the Son of God and Mary; a confession on account of which we receive such a lashing of our opponents saying that *we are their and the whole world's seducers and heretics.* And for the reason, I say, that we teach together with the entire Scripture that the Lord Jesus Christ is God's own and genuine Son, as has been set forth above.

Very well! Since it may not and cannot be otherwise with them, they had better run their course (we cannot prevent it) until they are met by the angel of the Lord, and rebuked by the ass. Num. 22; II Pet. 2. They had better beware, however, lest they dash their foot too severely on the Rock of offense. Isa. 8; Rom. 9. The time of reckoning will soon be here. As for me, it is a small matter that I be judged of them.[9] I hope to strengthen myself in the Lord who has taken me by the right hand, and who knows intimately all my desires, intentions, and doings. He will verily execute our cause to His honor, for He knows that we do not desire to seek our praise but His. Therefore He will protect His own honor. It might even be, through their writings and slanderings against us, and through their manifestly erring doctrine in regard to Christ the Son of God, that it may become apparent to some

---

[8] The Reformed theologians against whom Menno is writing taught that since Christ's person is a single person but with two natures, a human and a divine, therefore the Scriptures sometimes transfer to Christ's human nature that which if strictly taken belongs only to the divine nature, and vice versa. *Tr.*

[9] cf. I Cor. 4:3. *Ed.*

that they themselves are in double measure what they would like to make us out to be. May the great God grant them grace. Amen.

## PART III

### THE CONFUTATION

Before I proceed to the confutation of the arguments of our opponents, I must first faithfully admonish the kind reader not to deal with the dazzling brightness of the eternal Godhead in such a way as to become guilty, not to undertake audaciously to fathom a depth that is beyond us—lest he, when he thinks that he has fathomed it, blind his eyes and unexpectedly fall down the precipice. For it is manifest that many great and profound geniuses have been gravely mistaken and have made fools of themselves by their pretentious inventions.

The Tritheists taught that there were three Gods. Arius separated the second substance from the first substance as of a lower order. Macedonius said that the third being, namely, the Holy Ghost, was no God, but a servant of God and the Son. Aetius and Eunomius taught that the Father, the Son, and the Holy Ghost were things or beings not of equal rank. The followers of Origen held that the Son could not behold the Father, and the Holy Ghost could not behold the Son. Maximinus feared that the Father was a part of God and each person was one third of the Trinity. The Metangismonites said that the second person was in the first, as a small vessel is in a larger. The Alogi said that John uttered a falsehood when he said that God was the Word, because they could not comprehend the mystery of the Word. The Monarchians such as Praxeas and Victorinus said that the Almighty Father was Jesus Christ, and that He had placed Himself at His own right hand. The Sabellians identified the name and the person of Christ with the name and the person of the Father and are called Patripassians; for they believed that it was the Father that suffered. Behold in such manner do they rave who want to understand things that cannot be grasped, and who want to climb higher than the Scriptures teach.

Erasmus of Rotterdam said, This Word was God. It was Almighty, out of the Almighty, brought forth by the Father, not in time but before all time; coming forth from the heart of the Father, but in such a way as never to become separate from Him. Moreover he says that the Father begot Him from eternity and will beget Him forever. And in his *Ecclesiastae,* Christ is the Word of God, Almighty, who proceeds without beginning and without end from the heart of God. Martin Luther says, The Word is that which God speaks in Himself, and which remains in Him and is never separated from Him.

We do not find fault with the testimony of Erasmus and Luther, but we have cited them to indicate what a diversity of opinion there is. Philip Melanchthon says, The Word is begotten in thought and is called the image of God, for the thing is the image of the thought. Tell me, dear reader, who can or may rest his conscience on such argument and such foundation?

And certain church councils resolved that there were three hypostases in triunity, that is, three substances and these *Homoousioi,* that is, of identical substance. Both these terms became suspect, Erasmus says.[10]

And so men follow their own opinions and inclinations, build upon vapor and wind, look at each other and not at the Word of God, confuse the simple minds not at home in the Scriptures. They agitate for their opinions and not for the Word; and whoever cannot agree and does not follow them is called a deceiver and a heretic.

Therefore, for Jesus' sake, since so many a clever man has been blinded by the radiance and is blinded even now, I pray you not to ascend higher in this impenetrable mystery than your ladder will reach, nor to grasp beyond that which God has revealed. For you cannot grasp more of the indescribable beauty and generation, how, and in what manner this occurred in eternity, than you can of the indescribable Father Himself.

Therefore, let not the opinion and glosses of the learned be the foundation upon which you build your faith. Let the undeceiving plain Word of God and the testimony of St. John be a sure foundation whereon to build—the John who says, In the beginning was the Word, and the Word was with God, and the Word was God. All things were made by him; and without him was not anything made that was made. John 1:1. This same Word, which was from the beginning, and in the course of time became flesh, is called by Paul the Son, Christ Jesus, and the first begotten of all creatures. Col. 1:15.

Yes, good reader, if the learned ones had left intact the testimony of John which he spoke of Christ's eternal deity, and if they had given their minds in subjection to the Word of God, there would never have been such dark confusion in the world concerning Christ, the Son of God.

Therefore I advise you in faithful love, take heed and beware, for the testimony of John is too clear to be obscured by glosses, and too strong to be broken by philosophy. Whosoever would rather drink the precious clear wine of divine truth, than the impure waters of human glosses, let him hold to the Word of his Lord, and let him abandon the unscriptural, destructive explanations, garblings, opinions, and ideas of the learned ones.

This is enough of the eternal and incomprehensible deity of Christ.

Now by the grace of God we will proceed and maintain by the power of the Scriptures that they err abominably who say, *The word is not become flesh, but it has taken unto itself our flesh or a man of our flesh,* as will be briefly and clearly shown in the following:

*In the first place John a Lasco writes, and says, Divine justice requires that that which we ruined in our flesh included in Adam's loins, must be made good by that same flesh. Or, as some say, that the nature which introduced sin, should be punished for that sin, and that that which incurred death should also put death to naught.*

*Answer.* Since he and his followers would uphold their cause with a reference to the justice of God, and declare that the introducer and the institutor should suffer punishment, they should not, by right, use the words, *our flesh and nature,* but *Adam and Eve,* in their writings. For they were the first introducers and institutors, and not the flesh and nature of their descendants, as may be openly seen from Gen. 3:6.

The nature of man was first created pure and good, but was corrupted through Adam's disobedience. And since he was thus corrupted in his nature, all his children were born corrupted. Nevertheless, the children were not the introducers and institutors, but Adam and Eve. If the justice of God requires the punishment of the introducer and institutor, it would according to justice be right that not any of the children should be punished, for they were not the innovators. Adam and Eve should have trodden the press themselves, for they were the ones that had dug and fashioned it.

Oh, no. Adam and his seed were helpless because of the weakness of their flesh. They were guilty above measure and had not a penny wherewith to pay. But their death was canceled for Christ's sake, who, through His eternal love (seeing that Adam and his kind were impotent), appeared in the shape and form of sinful man, and fulfilled the justice of the Father. By the sacrifice of His precious, crimson blood, He tore to pieces the handwriting of the Law, and made good and paid for all that which Adam had incurred by his transgression. Col. 2:3; Eph. 2:15.

Since they make much of the justice of God, I deem it necessary to enlarge on this a little in order that the intelligent reader may learn that this assertion of theirs is quite powerless, nay, in every respect without foundation in the Scripture.

It is manifest, kind reader, that Adam and Eve, misled by the serpent, fell into condemnation, and death lay in their seed by the justice of God. Gen. 3:6. Nothing can be born of them but that which is condemned and guilty of death. Rom. 5:12; I Cor. 15.

Since then Adam, because of his disobedience, was guilty and condemned to death by the eternal justice of God; and since the Lord Christ, according to His holy humanity, was a natural fruit of the flesh of Adam, as they assert, then the man Christ must be condemned and guilty of death, on account of his human birth. This is too clear to admit of denial, or else our opponents must take back their own argument and acknowledge that God's justice is not eternal.

INCARNATION OF OUR LORD                                    805

Oh, no. The flesh of Christ is holy, pure, spotless, it knows no sin, it makes pious and saves. It is a true bread of souls, as is the Word, which in these last days, according to the intention and purpose of the Father, became a true man, able to suffer for the salvation and eternal deliverance of all; and although innocent, died the death for us.

It avails in no manner that they say, *Mary was blessed, and her fruit was saved from sin by the power of God.* We acknowledge that Mary was blessed, and that the fruit of her womb was without sin; but we deny that Mary was without sin in consequence of the blessing. For Paul says, The scripture hath concluded all under sin, that the promise by faith of Christ Jesus might be given to them that believe. Gal. 3:22.

Again, if the man Christ had been flesh in Mary's flesh, then Mary would have been saved through her own flesh, and Adam would have been reconciled through his own flesh. Then the justice of God would have been broken, and our condemnation, curse, and death dissolved and requited through a flesh condemned, cursed, and guilty of death.

Oh, no. The Scriptures teach plainly that we have all become sinners in Adam, and that we have all fallen under the judgment, wrath, and condemnation of God, through sin, and become subject unto death. Rom. 5:6; I Cor. 15:22. And of Christ it testifies that He is the Lamb without spot, that He has not known sin, and in His mouth no guile was found. Since then it is manifest that the Scriptures include Adam and all his descendants in sin, and insist upon the innocence of Christ; therefore the respectful and right-minded reader may conclude that the holy Man, Christ Jesus, is not of the unclean flesh of Adam, but that He is the holy and pure Word of God (John 1); and that this saying of the learned ones, *The justice of God requires, etc.,* is not the sure testimony and Word of God, but merely human embroidery and fiction.

Would that our opponents would ponder what the justice of God, in the language of Scripture, really implies. I could hope that they would then not hold so strongly to their position as they have thus far done. Neither would they say that he who does not accept their doctrine sins against the Holy Ghost. They might, at the very least, ponder once in a while whether they are perhaps in error.

*In the second place a Lasco urges that we must understand the conception of Mary, of which Matthew and Luke report, in this way: that as far as her part in it was concerned, it was nothing unusual.*

*Answer.* It is surprising to me that a man as learned as he is should blunder about so recklessly as to insist that Mary's part in the matter was ordinary; whereas it is clearly shown all through the Scriptures that the conception of Mary was brought about by supernatural causes, a particular miracle of the most High, and a glorious sign of the Lord our God. As Isaiah says, Therefore the Lord himself shall give you a sign: Behold, a virgin shall conceive, and bear a son, and shall call his name Immanuel. Isa. 7:14. Again, Matthew writes concerning the conception of Mary, thus, When Mary, his mother, was espoused to Joseph, before they came together, she was found with child of the Holy Ghost. Then Joseph, her husband, being a just man, and not willing to make her a public example, was minded to put her away privily; but while he thought on these things, behold, the angel of the Lord appeared unto him in a dream, saying, Joseph, thou son of David, fear not to take unto thee Mary thy wife; for that which is conceived in her is of the Holy Ghost. And she shall bring forth a son, and thou shalt call his name Jesus; for he shall save his people from their sins. Matt. 1. Again the angel said to Mary, Thou shalt conceive in thy womb, and bring forth a son, and shalt call his name Jesus; he shall be great, and shall be called the Son of the Highest; and the Lord God shall give unto him the throne of his father David; and he shall reign over the house of Jacob for ever; and of his kingdom there shall be no end. Then said Mary unto the angel, How shall this be, seeing I know not a man? And the angel answered and said unto her, The Holy Ghost shall come upon you, and the power of the Highest shall overshadow you; therefore also that holy thing which is born of you shall be called the Son of God. Luke 1.

From all this it is very evident that the conception of Mary was supernatural and a sign and miracle of the Lord. Therefore it is all to no purpose that the learned ones philosophize about the naturalness of it, for it does not fit the facts.

And if men were to insist in spite of all these plain passages of Scripture that the conception of Mary was, at least in part, natural, then it is still evident from the ordinances of God and from nature that the substance and origin of the child is from the father and not from the mother—as has been sufficiently set forth in the confession above, as well as in the *Reply to Gellius Faber*.

These assertions are nothing but philosophy and human wisdom, without Scripture, and not worthy of an answer. But I have briefly refuted them, and pray you not to despise my references; but let knowledge go before the accusation, lest you make a mistake, as Sirach says.

*They also throw this at us, that the Scripture speaks of the Saviour as the seed of the woman, of Abraham, and the fruit of the loins of David.*

*Answer.* In the first place I say that he who deduces from these Scriptures that the man Christ was flesh of a woman, the natural seed of Abraham and David, who all descended from the unclean flesh of Adam, such a one must also introduce the unrighteousness, curse, and sin of Adam. And if they assert that He was free from the unrighteousness, curse, and sin of Adam, I answer, Then He was not of the natural seed of Adam; for the seed of Adam was unclean, sinful, and accursed—therefore nothing but unclean, sinful, and accursed flesh could be begotten therefrom. Unless it be true that the unclean begets the clean, the sinful the holy, and the accursed the blessed; so that the original pollution was changed to its opposite. This is too plain to admit of controversy.

Yes, reader, if the matter of the incarnation of the Lord stood as our opponents say, then it would be manifest that Christ Jesus was not so pure in His incarnation as was Adam in the original creation. For if they say, as is correct, that Christ was conceived in the pure virgin by the Holy Spirit, then we remind them that Adam also had no other father than God, for which reason Luke calls Him the Son of God. But even at that, Adam was made of pure earth, and that by God. But Christ, if He were Adam's natural seed, had to be made of impure earth, that is, of impure, human, and earthly seed. This is too plain to be denied.

In the second place I say, If the man Christ were a natural fruit and seed of the impure, sinful flesh of Adam, then He would also, because of the unending righteousness of God, be guilty of the judgment and of death itself. And if He were Himself guilty, how could He redeem us? Must it be admitted that God's justice terminated and that the sinful had atoned for sin, the condemned for condemnation, and the guilty for death?

Oh, no. No unclean animal was permitted to be offered as a sacrifice of atonement in Israel, but it had to be without blemish. And if the shadow had to be without blemish, how much more the reality by whom eternal reconciliation is brought about, and by whom all symbolic offerings were fulfilled and finished. Heb. 9:10.

In the third place I would say, Whoever asserts that the man Christ is a natural fruit and seed of Adam, Abraham, David, and of the woman, he also asserts that there are two persons in Christ, two sons; that the Father is no true father, the mother no true mother, and the Son no true son, as has been said before.

In the fourth place I say, If the man Christ were of the flesh and blood of Mary, then it is manifest that He was not God's Son, but a created creature, since He would not be begotten of the Father, but of the flesh and blood of Mary, according to nature, as has been sufficiently shown.

In the fifth place, If the man Christ were of the flesh and blood of Mary, as they propose; and since it is quite evident that the birth of man, according to the ordinance of God, cannot be without father and mother; and since it is also evident that the child does not proceed from the mother, but from the father; therefore if the man Christ came forth without a father from the body of the mother, contrary to the ordinances of God, then a new creation must have taken place in Mary, which creation could not have occurred without the Word. But if such creation did occur, then it is manifest that the one half or part of Christ must be created by the other half; Mary's son by God's Son; and that the two, namely, the Creator and the creature, thus became one person and Son. Dear reader, observe what frightful things they invent!

In the sixth place I say, As all men have both father and mother, and each of these in turn has his parents, so, also, Christ Jesus had both Father and mother. His Father was an incomprehensible Spirit from all eternity, and will remain so to all eternity. Therefore He could have no genealogy on the side of the Father; but the mother who was the true daughter of Adam, Abraham, Isaac, and Jacob, conceived Him in her virgin womb through the Holy Ghost, by His Father's word; and she begat a true man in due time. Her genealogy is stated in the Scriptures; for when He became incarnate in a human being, He had to have a family tree, of which He came. And this is the word which Paul speaks, Born of the seed of David according to the flesh. Not that there were two sons in Christ, the one without father, and the other without mother; one the Son of God, and the other the son of man, as our opponents propose. But He who was God's Son was also the son of man; and He who was the son of man, was also the Son of God. Not two, but a single and undivided Son, as the ordinances of God, and the whole Scriptures teach and imply.

If you cannot understand this, then note this parable: Charles V is a son of Austria; he is also a son of Spain; not that he is, therefore, one son out of two sons—but he is an only and undivided son. On the side of the father he is a son of Austria, and on the side of the mother he is a son of Spain. Thus, also, is Christ Jesus a Son of God and a son of man; the Son of God on the side of His Father, and the son of man on the side of His mother. Not one son out of two sons—but an only and undivided Son, the Son of God and of Mary, as has been shown.

Again, if you are still troubled about the fruit of the loins of David, I would refer you to my *Confession* which I wrote to John a Lasco and his preachers in 1543.[11] In connection therewith, I admonish you to observe how the throne and kingdom of David were promised to Christ by Isaiah and the angel Gabriel; which promise was, however, not literally fulfilled in Christ, but in Solomon, who was a figure and symbol of Christ, as were also Isaac, Moses, Aaron, Joshua, and Joseph. Since the whole Scriptures teach us that His kingdom and throne are not literal but spiritual, therefore we must, in the same manner, judge the fruit and the king who shall sit upon the throne and reign; or else the one word must be understood literally and the other spiritually. This is too plain to be controverted.

Second, observe what Christ asked of the Pharisees in regard to Christ the son of David, and notice how He reacted to their response. Matt. 22:42; Heb. 1:13.

Thirdly, observe that if the man Christ were a natural fruit of the loins of David, then there are implied in Him all the absurdities which we have in part related above and will relate in more detail presently, the Lord willing.

Fourthly, observe that all the attributes of God are equally perfect in Him. Therefore His perfect and eternal love had to meet His perfect and eternal righteousness. As Christ says, God so loved the world, that he gave his only begotten Son, that whosoever believeth in him should not perish, but have everlasting life. John says, Herein is the love of God made manifest, that he sent his only begotten Son into the world that we through him might live. For as He condemned Adam and all his seed unto death by His eternal justice on account of disobedience, so also has He, on account of the obedience of Christ, by His eternal love promised life to all who believe in Him; for as His righteous

[11] Menno wrote 1543 rather than 1544 because he evidently thought of the new year as beginning with March. *Ed.*

punishment of the sins of Adam's descendants who reject Christ lasts forever, so also His paternal love to forgive sin through Christ lasts forever to all those who believe in Christ and accept and obey the word of His grace. John 3:16.

*In the third place it is insinuated that my position is that Christ was born of the Holy Ghost.*

*Answer.* It is very unreasonable that people are always trying to saddle me with things of which I am not guilty. In my first *Confession* I have plainly and clearly shown in Latin letters[12] that I do not believe that Christ was *born* of the Holy Ghost, but that He was *conceived* by the Holy Ghost. Yet I must hear that I teach that Christ was born of the Holy Ghost. Dear Lord, how lamentably I am slandered. What do they do to me other than that which the scribes did unto Jeremiah when they counseled about him, and said, Come, and let us devise devices against him, and not regard his reasoning. I guess I was born to turn my ear to the slanderer, and my back to the scourger. Nevertheless I hope, by the grace of the Lord, that men will live to see the time that some of them will wake up and acknowledge in all humility and with penitent hearts that they have not despised me, but the Word of God, and that they have scorned His Spirit.

*In the fourth place it is insinuated that I teach that the Word was changed into human flesh and blood in the womb of the virgin.*

*Answer.* That I have ever at any place spoken or written so will never, I trust, be proved; yet they dare to say and write so of us. I have said, as the high apostle has taught me, that the Word became flesh. That testimony I leave unbroken; and I leave it to the incomprehensible One, who through His omnipotent power so arranged it for the salvation of us all, as to just what and how much was changed. Yet I would in my simplicity add this. If this witness of John, which I quoted literally, is to be interpreted in such a way as to imply that Menno teaches with John that the Word became flesh, and therefore his position is *that the Word changed into flesh etc.,* then let men remember that change does not alter the basic substance of which a thing consists. Adam was a man created of the earth; and although he was made of earth, yet he remained earth as the Lord said, Dust thou art and unto dust shalt thou return. Gen. 3:19. Again, in the resurrection of the dead, all those who have returned to dust shall through the power of God be resurrected from the dust. It is manifest that we were earth at the outset, then flesh, then earth again, and finally flesh once more, now glorified, as the Scriptures testify. See how the original substance of which a thing consists remains even when it is changed?

Reader, do not misunderstand me. I do not mean by this parable that the Word was changed into flesh and blood, even as the earth of which Adam was made was changed into human flesh. I have presented this parable for the purpose of showing to the reader that even if the Word were changed in becoming incarnate, it still remained the Word. John 1:14; 8:23; I John 1:2; Rev. 19:13.

---

[12] "Latin letters" probably means "emphatically"; for in the 16th century Roman type was used for emphasis, the rest of the text being in Gothic characters. *Tr.*

*In the fifth place he writes, The Lord Christ was a Spirit from the beginning, unchangeable, holy, and eternal. If then He was Spirit and unchangeable, how has He changed His substance or His being to become flesh?*

*Answer.* If I understand him correctly, he says on page five of his folio E, that he has not yet grasped the meaning of my expression, *factum est,* that is, *is become.* If now he has not rightly comprehended me, then I cannot see why he should charge me with a certain interpretation. I have quoted John verbatim. Can it be that he is unable to understand John, unless recourse be taken to glosses and corruptions?

Since they insinuate, both by word of mouth and in writing, that I interpret John's expression in such a way as to imply such change (although they have not heard or read any such thing from me), therefore I beg my readers not to ascribe any doctrine of the change of the eternal Word to me, save as follows, in plain terms: I believe and confess that there is an Almighty, eternal, and incomprehensible God, Father, Word, and Holy Ghost, who has dwelt and shall dwell eternally in everlasting glory. And I believe that this same Almighty, eternal Father, before all creatures, yea, from the beginning and from eternity, begets of Himself this Almighty, eternal Word in a divine and therefore incomprehensible manner; and that His Almighty, eternal Spirit proceeds or flows from Him through the Word or Son. But I do not comprehend it.

I also believe and confess that this Almighty, eternal Father, through His Almighty, eternal Word, which is the Son, has, in the power of His Almighty, eternal Spirit, created heaven and earth with all their fullness, and that He, by this same Word, preserves and maintains all things created. But I do not comprehend it.

I believe and confess further that all human nature shall at the sound of the last trump arise again from the earth with a glorified body, through the power of the Almighty and eternal God. And I believe that the children of God who have walked before Him in firm faith and patience here on earth shall receive the glorious, promised kingdom of honor at the hands of the Lord. I believe, on the other hand, that those who have rejected the Lord and His Word shall be tormented eternally with unquenchable, everlasting fire, with the devil and his angels, under the fearful, unbearable judgment of the Almighty and great God. But I do not comprehend it.

Faithful reader, observe that although I do not comprehend the Almighty, only, and eternal God in His eternal, divine being, in the dominion of His glory, in the creation and preservation of His creatures, in the reward of both the good and the evil, and in many of His works, yet I do truly believe these things, and for this reason: Because the Scripture teaches them. In like manner I cannot comprehend how, or in what manner the incomprehensible, eternal Word became flesh or man in Mary; nevertheless I do truly believe that it became man, because the Scripture teaches it. I know that it is a work that was done by the Lord, and it is a miracle before our eyes, even a work that intellect cannot fathom, nor acuteness comprehend. Truly is it said, Who shall tell of his birth? Isa. 53:10; Acts 8:31.

Inasmuch as I realize that it is an exalted and incomprehensible miracle of the Almighty and great God which the Almighty, eternal Father, through the omnipotence of the power of the Holy Ghost, has wrought in Mary; and inasmuch as I know how very perilous it is for one to enter into the incomprehensible profundity and divine mystery with one's foolish earthly understanding; how dangerous to garble the plain testimonies of the Holy Ghost by distorting glosses and human cleverness; therefore it is that I dare not believe nor teach more nor less of the holy incarnation than the holy prophets of the Lord, Christ Jesus, and also John, Peter, and Paul, teach me on every hand in the Scriptures, with such incontrovertibly clear testimonies, all of which are surer and wiser witnesses to me than all the learned ones who have been, are, or ever shall be on the earth; although I repeat, I cannot comprehend just how it took place—the unfathomable mystery—with my dull, earthly understanding. Sirach says, Inquire not into the things which you cannot bear, and that which is too great or too exalted for you do not search.

*Also, as to the saying of Malachi, I am the Lord, I change not* (Mal. 3:6), *and as to the question of John a Lasco, If He is eternal, how then could He die?*

*Answer.* Malachi is not speaking of God's substance or being, but of His purpose, counsel, will, and decree. From which I confess, and as a consequence of which I confess, that God's purpose, counsel, will, decree, promise, and love are eternal and unchangeable and must therefore come to pass as He wills and has determined in His wisdom.

Inasmuch as it is manifest that the Almighty, eternal, and unchangeable Father rules and does all things according to His eternal, unchangeable purpose, counsel, will, and decree; and since He through His eternal and unchangeable love has provided His eternal holy Word or Son, that He according to His firm and unchangeable promise should become the Paschal Lamb, as Peter says, therefore it had to be that the Word in due time became flesh, although we cannot comprehend it. It was the gracious purpose, counsel, decree, providence, and will of His Almighty and eternal Father, source and fountainhead of all good, whose gracious purpose, counsel, decree, providence, and will stand eternally fast, according to the cited word of the prophet, and can never be changed.

Honored reader, there you have my reply to the afore-mentioned three questions: Is He a Spirit? how could He become flesh? Is He God? how could He change? Is He eternal? how could He die? Before God that is what I believe, and by His grace I hope to continue so to believe unto the end.

I have not taken counsel with nature and human wisdom in the matter, but with the Word of my Lord, which is the true light to my feet, which shows me in plain words that the conqueror, the promised seed of the woman, born as to the flesh from the loins of Abraham, Isaac, Jacob, Judah, and of David's line; who is the world's Benediction, Shiloh, Messiah, Christ, King, Redeemer; was born not of unclean, sinful flesh, but of the pure seed of His heavenly Father, the Word of God conceived of the Holy Ghost, in the Virgin Mary; and in her become flesh, as John says. Christ Himself also says that He is from above, that He is the Bread from heaven, and that He went forth from the Father. John 16. And Paul says that He is the Lord of heaven, descended from above. I Cor. 15; Eph. 4:8. And in the Apocalypse, He is called the Alpha and Omega, our Immanuel. I plainly see that our opponents cannot refute these and similar plain Scriptures, but they garble them by their intellect with many exceptions and glosses, and turn them to another end. Therefore, I repeat, I turn away from the natural wisdom, bind my faith and conscience to the Word of my Lord, and truly and firmly believe and trust that this great miracle of God was thus produced in Mary—although I cannot comprehend just how it took place.

Good reader, he who ascribes any other view to me in the matter of a change in the eternal Word is a liar and does not report truthfully. The testimony to which I take recourse is firm and binding: *The Word became flesh.* But how and whether it was changed and how much, He only knows who in His eternal love has so arranged for it unto the salvation and everlasting redemption of us all. To Him be praises forever. Amen.

At this point I will perhaps be asked, Is not the Father of divine nature? Whence then has Christ derived His humanity? To this I answer: From whence came the abundance of water that flowed from the hard rock? The rock was no water nor watery substance. Was it not produced beyond all human knowledge by the omnipotence of God, to whom nothing is impossible? Similarly, how did the virgin conceive otherwise than through the power of God and the operation of the Holy Spirit, above the comprehension of all philosophers? Yes, above the comprehension of Mary herself, for she said, How shall this be, seeing I know not a man? And the angel replied that with God nothing is impossible, and continued, The Holy Ghost shall come upon thee, and the power of the Highest shall overshadow thee; therefore also that holy thing which shall be born of thee shall be called the Son of God. (He does not say that holy thing which shall come from thy flesh and blood, as our opponents say.)

Perhaps they continue, saying that if the Word became flesh and did not assume our flesh, then it did not remain God's Word either, exactly as when Lot's wife became a pillar of salt, she was no longer man or a woman; and when the water became wine it was no longer water. I would reply: The Scriptures say that Lot's wife became a pillar of salt, and that the water became wine. So say the Scriptures, and so it shall be. But the Scripture does not say that Lot's wife took unto herself a pillar of salt, and that the water took unto itself wine. In the same manner the Scriptures also testify that the Word became flesh; but they do not say that the Word took unto itself our flesh.

And if some Scripture could be produced to prove that becoming means taking unto one's self; or that two persons and sons of different natures and minds can be one person and son; or that there was a true Son from the beginning who did not have both father and mother; or that a son can be his father's son without being his father's seed, then we might ponder the position somewhat more carefully. But since they never do nor can produce such Scripture, and since the Scriptures testify that Jesus Christ is the Son of God, therefore the testimony of John remains firm and immovable, *The Word became flesh.* Let human wisdom rebel against this as much as it pleases [yet it still stands].

I say finally, if the Word did not become flesh, but assumed a man of Mary's flesh, and used it as an instrument for suffering, as our opponents assert, then it is apparent that Jesus Christ was not a Son of His Father in truth, as John has it, or actually in the flesh (*corporatus* as Castellio translates) ; for if He is to suffer Himself, and not somebody in His stead, then He had to come in the flesh, otherwise He would have been unable to suffer, as is too clear to deny. All who deny that, says John, are deceivers and antichrists. II John 1 :7.

*A Lasco says also, If He was holy, how then was He condemned before the Father's judgment as one under sin? At another place, Christ assumed no other flesh than which was under sin (so that He might be tempted) and subject to death.*

*Reply.* If we are to understand his words as they read, then Christ with His holy flesh was subject to sin and death. This is incontrovertible. For he says, If He was holy, why then was He condemned for sin under the judgment of the Father? As if He were unholy and guilty of death and the judgment, and had earned the wrath and punishment of God! But this had to be the case if we are to assert that the flesh of Christ was Mary's flesh. Therefore it is manifest from his words that the sin by which He was tempted dwelt in His flesh ; and that thus He did not die for us out of grace, but as one guilty in Himself. For the wages of sin is death.

O dear Lord! If the poor Menno were to speak of the Son of God thus blasphemously, and were to include Him in sin, oh, what an ugly, bitter song would be sung about him! But whatever the learned ones dream and philosophize, must be accepted as right and good.

This, then, is my brief reply to a Lasco's words just cited. Isaiah and Peter testify of Him that He did not know sin, and that no guile was found in His mouth. Yea, dear reader, He was holy before He became man, and holy in His incarnation. He will also remain holy forever. For such a high priest became us, holy, guiltless, undefiled, and made higher than the heavens. For if He were not innocent and holy, He could not have paid for our sins and guilt, but must have suffered for His own imperfections and guilt. But now the Scriptures testify that He was bruised for our iniquities and was stricken for our transgressions. Isa. 53.

*In the sixth place he writes, The antithesis of Paul whereby* the form of God *is placed over against* the form of man *teaches us that even as that by which we know God to be God is nothing else than His limitless power and the brightness to which none can approach, so also that by which a servant may be known as such is nothing else than our humanity, sold under the servitude to sin by the disobedience of our first parents, Yet in such a way that He assumed our flesh, but not the enslavement of our flesh.*[13]

*Answer.* Now we leave to the reader to choose whether to explain this form of a servant as having reference to a merely servile form, or as John a Lasco thinks, to a sinful form. If it has reference to a merely servile and not to a sinful form, then it does not support the assertion that the Word has assumed our flesh. But if it is explained as John a Lasco explains it, as having reference to a sinful, and not to a merely servile form, then it must necessarily follow that that is also in Christ, on account of which we are called servants, namely, sin. Otherwise, the antithesis breaks down, as you will hereafter, by the grace of God, clearly hear and see.

I deny that I mistranslated the Latin expression *Exinanivit semetipsum,* as John a Lasco accuses me of doing. For at one place I wrote, *He has humbled Himself.* I trust I have not written it wrongly. At another place I wrote, *The Son, the Word, was diminished, went outside Himself, was made lower than the angels.* But nowhere have I written that *He went out from Himself,* as John a Lasco wrongfully accuses me. I will leave it to the judgment of all grammarians whether or not I have written correctly.[14]

Christ surely did humble Himself greatly since He was the Almighty, eternal Word, Wisdom, and Power of God and became such a poor, weak, despised man. He also went outside Himself not a little, since He was in divine form and became such a despised servant. Yea, reader, that Paul speaks of the servile and not of the sinful condition we may well deduce from the following Scriptures. *Behold,* says Isaiah, *my servant, whom I uphold; mine elect, in whom my soul delighteth.* Matthew is my witness that the prophet speaks this of Christ, and He is called the servant of His Father because He has performed the work and service of His Father here on earth for us poor sinners. As He says, *Even as the Son of man came not to be ministered unto, but to minister, and to give his life a ransom for many.* Matt. 20: 28.

I repeat, Paul speaks of the servile and not of the sinful condition which Christ in love took upon Himself for our salvation. For if he here spoke of the sinful and not of the servile condition, then Christ must also have assumed the form of a servant, that is, sin. Otherwise the phrases, the form of a servant, and the form of God, could not be placed over against each other. For as the phrase, form of God, indicates His true divinity, so also the phrase, the form

[13] A Lasco had discussed a problem that presents itself in the Reformed interpretation of Phil. 2:7, namely, whether the human nature which Christ assumed was the original sinless human nature or the fallen human nature. A Lasco asserts the latter but adds that this does not imply a tendency toward sin in Christ. A Lasco makes much of the fact that in the Greek original we read of the *Morphee* (form) of God but of the *Scheema* (form) of man. *Tr.*

[14] A Lasco had written that Menno came to his view of the Incarnation by an erroneous rendering of *inanivit semetipsum.* Menno had translated, said a Lasco, "He went out of Himself." But Menno uses that expression elsewhere for "humbling oneself" (cf. *Opera,* 539B). On the other hand, the fact that Menno had written *exinanivit* instead of the regular *inanivit* seems to imply that a Lasco's criticism was just. *Tr.*

of a servant, must indicate His true servile form. Or it must follow from the argument of John a Lasco that although Christ was in divine form, yet He lacked the divinity, just as He had the form of a servant but not the servitude to sin or the servility.

No, He was in the form of God, and was thereby truly God. Thus He also took upon Himself the form of a true servant, and was therein a true servant; as may be deduced from Isaiah, Matthew, and the words of Christ. And in this sense the antithesis, the form of God, and the form of a servant, exists, and does not require the exception made by John a Lasco. And this is Paul's object in writing to the Philippians about this, that they should not be contentious one with another, nor seek their own vain, carnal honor, or anything selfish, but that they should, after the example of Christ, humble themselves one toward another, and walk in love. For although Christ was in the form of God, yes, equal with God, He made Himself of no reputation and took upon Himself the form of a servant, and not the exalted form of a mighty emperor or king. He came to minister unto us and not to be ministered unto. Matt. 20:28. He was made like unto us in all things, sin excepted. He sought not his own but that which was ours; and for our sakes became obedient unto death, even the death of the cross. Phil. 2:8. Thus the assertion of John a Lasco, that the Word took unto Himself our flesh or a man of our flesh, remains unproved.

But as to a Lasco's point that while Christ was here upon earth He was still also in heaven: that His face shone as the sun, that His raiment was white as the light, and that He healed the sick, raised the dead, and by His word remitted sin, which power belongs to God alone, does not prove that He received His holy flesh from our sinful flesh. It proves rather that He still remained God and His Word, notwithstanding He for a time so humbled Himself and surrendered His divine splendor, attributes, right, and glory for our sakes. Whosoever sincerely fears God, let him consider and judge.

*In the seventh place he asserts it as his position that the Word did not become flesh, but that He took unto Himself our flesh of Mary, and confirms this with the Scripture of Heb. 2:14, which reads thus, Forasmuch then as the children are partakers of flesh and blood, he also himself partook of the same.* He says, The Word was made flesh; *but not that He in any manner changed His first estate or form, but He has taken unto Himself our flesh and has therewith covered His divinity while here upon earth.*

*Answer.* All those who desire a Scriptural and correct understanding of the Scriptures quoted, and also of Christ, the Son of God, should observe well that God, the Almighty, eternal Father, the true Creator, who wills and works, is the only source of all good. He, in an incomprehensible way, before all creatures, begat of Himself His Almighty, eternal, and incomprehensible Word, and has through the same created all things, and thereby governs, maintains, and preserves them. He in His eternal justice, love, and in all His attributes, together with His incomprehensible Word and Holy Spirit, is an eternal and

perfect God, and beside Him there is none other. He is eternal and unchangeable in His counsel, purpose, will, and decree, as was said before.

And this Almighty, eternal Father, through His Almighty, eternal Word,
in the power of His Almighty, eternal Spirit, has, according to His divine
purpose, counsel, will, and decree, created Adam and Eve, the parents of us
all, as righteous, good, and pure creatures and unto eternal life. Yes, after
His own image and likeness, as the Scriptures testify, that He gave unto them
the command of life and death, that they might fear, love, praise, thank, and
serve Him, and live according to His will.

Behold, this is the Creator that created Adam and Eve. It also shows
through what He created them, and how and for what purpose He created
them; what He permitted and what He forbade them to do; what He promised
them if they obeyed and what He threatened if they should disobey. And thus
the glory of God began to shine.

In this piety, holiness, and righteousness, Adam and Eve remained, so
long as they did not deviate from the counsel, Word, will, and command of
God, in which all things have and must have their being. But man was left
in the hands of his will, as Sirach says. And the old serpent, the subtle creature
that envied God and all good, caused the glorious, noble creature of life to
be led from the favor and grace of his Creator into condemnation and death,
and obscured the glory of God. He began with Eve, the weaker vessel, to
tempt her with the desires of appetite. For the woman saw, says Moses, that
the tree was desirable for food and pleasant to the eyes. He falsified the Word
of the Lord, and said, Ye shall not surely die, and made glorious promises, saying, In the day ye eat thereof, then your eyes shall be opened; and ye shall be
as God, knowing good and evil. Adam and Eve disobeyed the command of
their God and Creator, by which alone they must live; and believed the promise
of the serpent. They ate, and through the justice of God fell into the threatened
curse, condemnation, and death. And thus the deceiving serpent established
the kingdom of hell and of death.

There lay the miserable, accursed Adam and his wife, Eve, in the power
of the devil, poisoned from the sole of the foot even unto the head, both within
and without, with his impure, deadly venom. They became subject unto sin
and death. There was now no escape for Adam and all his descendants as far
as God's righteousness goes. For the word of life had been despised; the holy
commandment of God had been transgressed; the venom of the serpent had
been swallowed. Alas, all was lost to them. Their eyes were opened, shame
was acknowledged, the gnawing worm was in the disobedient, self-accusing
conscience; there was nothing but shaking and trembling, sighing and sadness.
They fled before the face of the Lord and knew not where to hide from His
wrath. For the righteousness of God kept urging the saying, For in the day
that thou eatest thereof thou shalt surely die.

The counsel, purpose, will, and decree of the Almighty, eternal God continued unchanged: that He would make manifest His glory and have a man

after His own image and likeness. This was foreseen and decreed by God, as has been said, but with Adam it was all over, as also with all his descendants, he being full of venom, and disgraced before his God. Therefore if the unchangeable will, counsel, and decree of the unchangeable God was to be established, there must be another who was like the corrupted Adam before his fall; for it was upon such a man that God's will was urging; and with Adam all was lost.

Therefore the incomprehensible, eternal Word, by which Adam and Eve were created, in which all things are and must forever exist, the Almighty Power and Wisdom of God, must become man, that He might bruise the head of the deceiving serpent for the salvation of the condemned Adam and all his descendants; that He might be victorious over temptation; that He might fulfill the holy and unchangeable will of the Father; that He might destroy the dominion and power of the devil; and that He might by His willing obedience and spotless sacrifice and by His undeserved death, discharge and put away the guilt and deserved death of Adam.

Behold, the glad Gospel and the glad tidings of divine grace, which God declared to the poor, distressed, and fugitive Adam! He accepted them through faith, comforted himself therewith, and sincerely rejoiced in grace.

And this is the Redeemer who I say was promised to Adam as the seed of the woman, the benediction of all the world, promised to Abraham, Isaac, and Jacob; the glorious Branch, Rod, Plant, and Fruit of David, symbolized in Solomon, the natural fruit of his loins; who was to sit on his throne and reign in Israel forever. All who believe on Him shall receive the mercy, grace, and peace of God. But whosoever does not believe on Him, on him the wrath of God abideth. John 3:36.

From all this it follows that even as Adam was in the beginning created and we in him, through the Word, he and also we are raised up again by God through this same Word, and accepted in grace. John says, In the beginning was the Word, and the Word was with God, and the Word was God; the same was in the beginning with God. All things were made by him, and without him was not any thing made that was made. And the Word was made flesh, and dwelt among us, and we beheld his glory, the glory as of the only begotten of the Father, full of grace and truth. Behold, in such plain words the Spirit of God testifies that both the creation and restoration of Adam and his seed was brought about by no other means than through the Word, as has been heard.

And to explain this more clearly, and to learn to understand how entirely sinful, impure, poisoned, powerless, and weak we all have become in Adam, I would point you with Paul to the Law and the Scriptures. They will depict to you the impure, powerless nature and sinfulness of our flesh so plainly that you will be forced to acknowledge that the holy, glorious, and spotless Redeemer, through whom we are reconciled to God, could not be of such impure, sinful, and accursed seed and flesh as the learned ones teach us, and with their philosophic reasonings declare without basis in Scripture.

Moses says, Thou shalt not lust after, or thou shalt not covet. Dear reader, in these few words is properly represented the first righteousness in which Adam was created in the beginning; and which righteousness is by God still required of his descendants. Consider and consider again these words of Moses and examine yourself carefully before your God who tries the hearts and reins, whether or not you sometimes lust contrary to the Law, and find such forbidden lusts in your flesh.

If you imagine yourself free from these things, you make God a liar (I John 1:10); and thereby you also shame all the righteous ones of God who were from the beginning; for they have all complained to one another of their contrary and wicked flesh, and have, alas, too unanimously shown it in their conduct. The Scriptures testify that I speak the truth.

Yes, reader, if any man born of the sinful flesh of Adam had completely fulfilled the Law, then for such the commanded yearly sin offering, which was offered by the high priest in the holy of holies, was useless and fruitless. Neither would it have been necessary for the Son of the most High, the eternal Word of God, to become man. For such a person could have done all that was needed, and fulfilled the required righteousness. But as it was, there was neither prophet nor any man of God, born of Adam, so holy or so pious, that he did not have to console himself with the promise of God in regard to Christ, symbolized in the sacrificial offering, and with the divine grace, through faith.

But if you find you do not do that which the Law requires, but that you are not only always being attacked by the lusts which dwell in your flesh, but that they are also often contrary to your will too much for you, then you must acknowledge that you are already condemned to death by the law of righteousness. For the Law says, Cursed is he that continueth not in all the words of this law to do them; and all the people shall say, Amen. Deut. 27:26.

Behold, precious reader, if you would rightly know and acknowledge how miserable, naked, powerless, impotent, unclean, sinful, and poisoned all of Adam's seed is become in him, through his transgression, and how his seed is, through the just righteousness of God, fallen into his wrath, judgment, curse, condemnation, and death, then, I say, Search the Law diligently. For it points out to you, first, the obedience to God and righteousness required of you; and also the weakness of your sinful flesh, your impure and evil-disposed nature; and that you are already condemned to death, according to the rigor of the above-mentioned righteousness, since you, through your inherent weak nature and evil-disposed flesh, do not walk in the required righteousness as God has commanded and required of you in His Law. The anointing that is with you, if you will only observe it, will make it plain.

Inasmuch then as Adam and his seed are so entirely corrupted, and the nature in which he was created pure and clean is become so wholly impure and evil disposed, and is therefore under the righteous judgment of God, and since everything has come under sin; therefore, if this venom was to be weakened in its power; if the corrupted nature of Adam was to be delivered from the curse and judgment of sin; if the righteousness of God was to be satisfied; if the power of the devil was to be broken; if curse, wrath, condemnation, and death were to be taken away; if the handwriting of the Law, which required such righteousness of Adam's children, was to be broken in pieces; if the eternal providence, counsel, will, and decree of God were to be fulfilled; if His kingdom and glory were to be revealed; and if there was to be such a man as the counsel, will, and decree of God required: then the everlasting love of God required that there should be another man who, conquering the devil, should disturb his power, fulfill the righteousness of God, make known His glory, offer a pure sacrifice, and in this way out of love and compassion be innocently accursed and condemned to death; not of Adam, but for the ever-lasting salvation of Adam and his seed; that thus the corrupted and condemned Adam, together with his corrupt and condemned seed, should be again accepted in grace, through His name, and be delivered from their great fall.

It could not, I repeat, be a man of Adam's flesh. For the corrupted flesh of Adam could not beget fruit which could fulfill this since it was so thoroughly corrupted and condemned before God. But it must be a man who was free from the deserved curse, condemnation, and death of Adam, and also from all his venom, sin, and unrighteousness, as has been sufficiently heard.

Observe, my faithful reader, and learn to know your God in His grace and love. For although the whole Scriptures conclude Adam and Eve, together with all their descendants, entirely under sin, curse, condemnation, and death, according to justice, yet it does not leave in hell the disquieted, afflicted conscience, which has been so far taught and directed by the Law that it feels its wounds and stripes, and acknowledges that it is deserving of eternal death and condemnation. But the Scriptures show in comforting words and symbols, where and of whom to get the healing medicine, namely, of Christ Jesus. For it is He who with all His righteousness, merit, cross, blood, and death was graciously given of God our heavenly Father to the fallen and condemned Adam and his posterity for their eternal salvation and reconciliation.

I think verily that this is a joyous Gospel, and glad tidings to all afflicted and sorrowing souls (who by the Law have been driven to an acknowledge-ment of their sin and death, and tremble and shake before God's just judgment and severe wrath). The Almighty, eternal God and Father has so loved us miserable, insignificant, and condemned sinners who have wandered away from Him, and according to His righteous judgment are deserving of eternal death, that He sent into this miserable world His Almighty, eternal, and in-comprehensible Word, His only, eternal, and beloved Son, the brightness of His glory. He was like unto Adam before the fall, as a proof and means of His divine grace; and this One has, through His perfect righteousness, willing obedience, and undeserved death, led us from the kingdom and dominion of the devil into the kingdom of His divine grace and eternal peace.

Since then the Scriptures declare the first Adam and all his seed to be such an impure, sinful, accursed, and condemned Adam, and pronounce Christ, the second Adam, free from all impurity, sin, curse, and condemnation; therefore the impartial reader may well deduce therefrom that such a precious, glorious fruit could not be plucked from a noxious alder or thorn bush, but had to be derived from some other source, namely, from Him who is the only cause and eternal source of all good things, as has been said.

That the holy and saving flesh of Christ was not of the sinful and condemned flesh of Adam may be plainly observed from the following passages and figures of the Holy Scriptures. Isaiah says, All we like sheep have gone astray; we have turned everyone to his own way; and the Lord hath laid on him the iniquity of us all. He hath done violence to no one; neither was any deceit in his mouth. Yet it pleased the Lord to bruise him. Isa. 53. I must pay, says the Psalmist, in the person of Christ, that which I had not taken. Psalm 69:5. He bare our sins in his own body on the tree. And by his stripes we are healed. I Pet. 2:24; Isa. 53:12. For he hath made him to be sin for us, who knew no sin; that we might be made the righteousness of God in him. II Cor. 5:21; Rom. 3:9. Again, We are all sinners and come short of the glory of God; but are made righteous, without merit, by His grace, through the deliverance which is in Christ. Or, The scripture hath concluded all under sin, that the promise by faith of Jesus Christ might be given to them that believe. Gal. 3:21. Ye know, says John, that the Son of God was manifested to take away our sins; and in him is no sin. I John 3:5. Read also all these Scriptures: Isa. 7:9 and 40; Jer. 23:33; Mic. 5; John 1, 3, 5, 6, 8, 9, 10, 11, 14, 16, 17; I Cor. 15; Acts 20; Eph. 4; I Tim. 3; I John 1, 2, 3, 4, 5; Heb. 1, 2, 3, 7; Rev. 1:19.

## HERE FOLLOW SOME FIGURATIVE REFERENCES

He is the spiritual Tree of Life in the midst of the Paradise of God, not planted by man but by God Himself. Gen. 2:17; 3:22. All those who shall eat the fruits of this tree, with pure hearts, shall live forever, and the leaves of the tree are for the healing of the nations. Rev. 22:3.

He is the spiritual, brazen serpent, symbolized in the Mosaic serpent (Num. 21:9), which was erected for us miserable sinners in the wilderness of this world by the Father as a healing sign, which had the form of the venomous serpent, yet not its venomous nature. All those who believe on Him are delivered from the curse, condemnation, and death introduced by the serpent. And whosoever does not believe on Him, on him the wrath of God abides, and he must eternally bear and suffer according to God's eternal justice, the assigned curse, death, and condemnation. John 3:36.

He is the spiritual mercy seat which is made, not like the ark, of shittim wood; but of fine, pure gold, from which God graciously hears us and speaks unto us through His Spirit and Word. Ex. 25:10; Rom. 3:24; Heb. 4:13. He is the spiritual Paschal Lamb, which is without spot, and in the sprinkling and sanctification of whose blood the chosen Israel of God was ever graciously saved from the destroying angel, and from the wrath of God, in the midst of the cruel, dark Egypt of this world. Ex. 12:23; Num. 9:16.

He is the true bread from heaven, which is not made of natural grain or wheat (I mean of our sinful flesh) but comes of the dew of the eternal Word and is the only true food for our souls, by which we shall live forever, if we only eat of Him through true faith. Ex. 16:5; Num. 11:18.

He is the Rock which was taken from the mountain without hands (that is, without human collaboration), which Nebuchadnezzar saw in a dream, and which Daniel interpreted as the One who should crush and destroy the kingdoms of iron, clay, silver, and gold; yea, all the kingdoms of the world, for He has all power in heaven and upon earth. He is a powerful King over all; and to His kingdom there shall be no end, nor shall it pass over to any other people. Dan. 2:44.

Kind reader, determine from the above-mentioned Scriptures and figures, if you fear God, whether such doctrine is based upon the Scriptures which assert that this righteous, holy, spotless, obedient, and saving Redeemer was born of the unrighteous, sinful, impure, disobedient, and condemned flesh or seed of Adam, and that He took His humanity from it. Oh, no. This pure, clear water, with which all our spots were to be washed away, could never be drawn from such an impure, stagnant pool. Let every man reflect what the Word of the Lord teaches him.

Now we will, by the grace of the Lord, enlarge upon the Scriptures of Hebrews 2, that we may rightly comprehend the teaching and truth thereof; and that our opponents may not boast that we do not satisfy them. I would refer first to the first chapter of Hebrews and have you observe what is said there of Christ. In the first place it reads, God hath in these last days spoken unto us by his Son, whom he hath appointed heir of all things, by whom also he made the worlds. In the second place it reads that this same Son is the brightness of his glory, and the express image of his being. Third, that He has purged our sins by Himself. Fourth, that He is the first-begotten Son of God, and that all the angels shall worship Him. Fifth, that He is God, and that His kingdom and throne shall endure forever. Sixth, that He laid the foundations of the earth, and the heavens are the work of His hands. I think that if you ponder earnestly these Scriptures and rightly observe them, you will soon perceive from whence Christ came, who and what He is. For these plain evidences teach clearly that the world was made by Him; that He is the brightness of the glory of God; that He has expunged our sins by Himself; that He is the first-begotten Son of God, that He is God, and that He has laid the foundations of the earth. This could not be of Mary's flesh!

If they say that these Scriptures do not refer to the son of Mary, but to the Son of God, then they confess to a divided Son, two persons, two sons. Besides, they are convicted by these very Scriptures that these things are said of the whole Christ. For He has spoken with us as a man, and we are also cleansed of our sins through His human suffering and death, as the Scripture teaches. I John 1:7; I Pet. 1:19.

But if they defend themselves by taking recourse to synecdoche or to communication of names, then I would answer in brief, plain words that the plain, faithful souls, Peter and John the fishermen, Martha, the kitchenmaid, and the simple Nathanael, knew nothing of all such satanic witness and human cleverness; but they have given praise to the visible and tangible Christ, and have confessed that He is the Son of God. Matt. 16:15; John 6:69; 11:27.

This is further explained in the second chapter in these words: What is man, that thou art mindful of him? or the son of man, that thou visitest him? Thou madest him a little lower than the angels; thou crownedst him with glory and honor.

Here I would faithfully admonish the faithful reader to observe that both Erasmus and Jerome, in their Latin translations, have rendered this, Thou madest him a little lower than the angels; and the Hebrew Psalm has it: Thou madest him inferior to God; with praise and honor thou crownedst him.

This agrees with the word of Paul, where he says, Who being in the form of God, thought it not robbery to be equal with him, but made himself of no reputation, and took upon him the form of a servant. Phil. 2:7. At another place he says, Though he was rich, yet for our sakes he became poor. II Cor. 8:9. This also agrees with the word of Christ, Father, glorify me with the glory which I had with thee, before the world was. John 17:5. I think these plain Scriptures and clear testimonies surely prove that the teachings of our opponents are unscriptural and erroneous, when they say that the Son of God remained in His first form and estate, unchanged and unhurt.

This same man who for our sakes was thus humbled and made less than God and the angels, we see is Christ, who by suffering death was crowned with praise and honor. For even as He humbled Himself unto obedience to the lowest extreme in our behalf, therefore He was exalted to the highest by the Father; and that although innocently, He tasted of death for the sake of Adam and all his posterity, by the grace of God; since Adam and his posterity could not in any other way be delivered from the power of death. For it became Him, for whom and by whom are all things, who has brought many children unto glory, to make the Prince and Captain of their salvation perfect through suffering, since both the sanctifying Christ, and those who are sanctified through Him, the regenerate, are all of one, that is, of God.

And so the sanctified ones and He that sanctified them have one Father. As John says, As many as received him, to them gave he power to become the sons of God, even to them that believe on his name; which were born not of blood, but of God. And therefore our Saviour is not ashamed to call them [the sanctified ones] his brethren, saying, I will declare thy name unto my brethren, in the midst of the church will I sing praise unto thee. Yes, dear reader, if the flesh of Christ were of Adam's flesh, and if we were called His brethren on that account, as is the doctrine of the learned ones, then one brother must beget the other. Besides, then all the ungodly, yes, prostitutes and scamps, must all be Christ's brethren and sisters! This is too plain to be controverted.

No! He has Himself plainly declared who His brethren are. Matt. 12:59; Mark 3:35; Luke 8:21. And He not only calls them His brethren, but also His children, and says, Behold, I and the children which God hath given me. They are called His children for the reason that He has begotten them unto God His Father by the word of His grace, through the power of His Holy Spirit, by the sprinkling of His precious blood. At another place He also calls them His mother, bride, flesh, and bones; which they could not be according to the flesh.

Yes, dear reader, if He had received His flesh from the flesh of His children, as John a Lasco and his followers insist, then the children must have begotten the father! Christ, the new Adam, would say to His new Eve: I am flesh of thy flesh—and not, Thou art flesh of my flesh. If you fear God, then reflect and judge. Gen. 2:23.

### [THE IMPORTANT PASSAGE: HEB. 2:14-17]

*Since the children partake of flesh and blood, so He, in the same manner, partook of the same that He might through death take the power from him who had the power of death, that is, the devil, and deliver those who, of necessity, were in servitude all their lives. For He does not accept the seed of angels, but of Abraham; therefore He must become like unto His brethren in all things.*

You see, this is the strongest and most important passage wherewith John a Lasco (in regard to this matter) sets the whole Scriptures against themselves, divides Christ and makes Him into two persons and sons and, as he thinks, brings unity into his whole work, argument, saying, and glosses. And this is his real position: As the children are partakers of flesh and blood, so also has the Word or Son of God received or assumed this flesh and blood from the flesh and blood of the children; and has thus in our flesh vanquished hell, sin, death, and the devil.

Inasmuch as he works the above saying so relentlessly, therefore I have by adducing many Scriptures enlarged upon the inherent, unclean, sinful flesh and nature of the children, and their deserved death and condemnation on the one hand; and the pure, holy flesh and nature of Christ, His undeserved death and judgment on the other, so that the reader might thereby rightly understand and comprehend that the Lord Jesus Christ could not come of such unclean flesh and seed of the children, nor assume human nature from them. For the flesh of the children is unclean and sinful, but the flesh of Christ is pure and holy.

Since His pure flesh could not be of the impure flesh of the children, as has been said, and since our opponents make so much of this Scripture, therefore I will examine it word for word, and by the grace of God give to each word its wholesome and right meaning.

First, observe that the word *children* has reference to none other than those who are called Christ's brethren earlier, namely, those who believe in Him, and who are born of God by the living power of His Spirit and Word, as has been said.

Second, observe that the Scriptural meaning of *having communion with flesh and blood* is not simply having flesh and blood, as some have interpreted it; but it also means to be intimate with flesh and blood, and do things which are forbidden of God, through the lusts of our flesh.

Third, observe that since the said children still have fellowship with sinful flesh and blood and are still subject to such human weakness (although contrary to their will) by which they continually fall and fail—therefore they must have such a High Priest who could have compassion with their human failures, since He was tempted in the same manner, although without sin, as said.

Fourth, observe that the adverb *similiter* [*similarly*] here expresses a true human nature in Christ, it is true, but not a natural conception as John a Lasco claims and argues. For it is manifest all through the Scriptures that the conception of Mary was supernatural, that it was brought about by the Holy Ghost, through faith, as has been abundantly shown.

Fifth, observe that the expression *partaking of flesh and blood* means nothing else than having flesh and blood; since His children and brethren also have flesh and blood, as Sebastian Castellio has rendered it—but with this distinction that His flesh was holy and knew no sin, and therefore experienced no decay; but the flesh of His brethren and children is sinful, and therefore subject to decay. I Cor. 15:53; 5:4.

Sixth, observe that Paul does not at all times use the words *partaking of flesh and blood* in the same sense. In one place he writes, If others be partakers of this power over you, that is, If others have this power over you. Again, He that thresheth in hope should be partaker of his hope (I Cor. 9:12), that is, should receive that which he hopes to get. Again, in the tenth chapter, verses seventeen and twenty-one, of the same epistle, the word is used for enjoying. Inasmuch as the word *partaking* has not everywhere in Scripture the same meaning, therefore, wherever it is found, it should be explained in accordance with the true nature and meaning of the Scriptures, or else the whole Scriptures must be broken because of a word.

Seventh, observe that the word *eorundem* [that is, *of the same*] has reference to the words flesh and blood, but not to the flesh and blood of the children, for that is unclean, sinful, guilty, and condemned. If it had reference to the flesh and blood of the children, as John a Lasco and Martin Micron assert, implying that the Son of God took unto Himself a perfect man, body and soul, of the flesh of the children, then it is incontrovertible that all the following indissoluble inconsistencies must result:

a. An impure, sinful, accursed Christ, and guilty of death, even as the flesh of the children of whom He is said to have taken His flesh is impure, sinful, guilty, etc. For wherever the flesh of the children is, there, also, is the sin and curse of the children. This cannot be controverted unless justice be changed and the curse removed by our own flesh. To which Micron in the first conversation[15] replied, Christ was pure and without sin and that because Mary did not conceive Him by marital intimacy of the seed of man. I answered: I must understand then that sin is because of the marital intimacy, which is an ordinance of God, and not because of the transgression of Adam. He answered: No, it was because of the justice of God that his nature became a corrupted nature. I asked, How? He answered: Because God had said that in the day that thou eatest thereof thou shalt surely die. I then replied, Then God was the cause of the sin in Adam, and the threatened death must not merely be the punishment of sin, but sin itself. I said, Martin, do observe what reasoning you bring forward.

b. A divided Christ of whom one half must be of heaven and the other half of earth.

c. Two persons in Christ, one divine and one human. To this Micron in our second discussion[16] replied that there were not two persons in Christ, but one person; for although the Word was one person from eternity, that was no person which was conceived in Mary. He also said, Although each human being is a person, and although the man Christ was a man as any other man, yet the human Christ by itself was no person. I am ashamed to mention such improper things. Paul justly says, Oh, where is the disputer of this world?[17]

d. Two sons in Christ, the Son of God without mother and not subject to suffering, and the son of man without father and subject to suffering; a thing which Martin Micron, both in our first and also in our second discussion, openly admitted more than once before us all in plain language. O God, what strange things we hear!

e. Not the first-born and only-begotten Son of God, but the fatherless son of Mary of the accursed sinful flesh of Adam died for us—something which is directly contrary to Christ, John, Paul, and the whole Scriptures.

f. The eternal sacrifice of reconciliation, once sacrificed for the sins of the whole world, was not the spotless Lamb, but an unclean, blemished sacrifice which was subject to sin and death, as may also be clearly seen in the writings of a Lasco.

g. The angel Gabriel, Peter, and the Lord Himself acknowledge that the man, Christ Jesus, is the Son of God. Thomas acknowledges Him as his Lord and God. Besides the whole Scripture teaches that He is our Advocate, Reconciler, Mediator, High Priest, Deliverer, and Redeemer; and if He is to be of the unclean sinful flesh and seed of Adam, then it is manifest that a

[15] Menno evidently refers to an exchange between himself and Martin Micron in their eleven-hour meeting of Feb. 6, 1554, in Wismar. *Ed.*

[16] Held in Wismar Feb. 15, 1554. *Ed.*

[17] The classic Reformed conception of the Incarnation, which Micron states repeatedly, is that Christ was one Person, divine, but with two natures, one divine and one human. No new being came into being at Christ's birth; an already existing being assumed human nature by that event. *Tr.*

created creature and a man of the sinful flesh of Adam is our Redeemer, Deliverer, Reconciler, Advocate, High Priest, yea, Lord and God Himself, something which is not only an abomination and idolatry, but also open blasphemy against God.

h. If the Man Christ was of Mary's flesh or of the flesh of the children as our opponents assert, and that without a father, then Mary must have been both father and mother in this case, for God has from the beginning ordained in His wisdom that in the procreation of a man, both the father and mother are needed, as Genesis 1 plainly shows.

i. If the Man Christ were of Mary's flesh, then since God's ordinances do not allow for a woman to bear a human being from her own flesh or body, as has been said; then it would seem that Christ was not a son of His mother, but a monster[18] brought forth by a word indwelling in her contrary to God's ordinance.

j. If the eternal Word by which everything was created had partaken of such a carnal son of the flesh of the children or of Mary, and had thus united Himself in one person and son, then the Creator and the creature, the motherless Son of God, and the fatherless son of Mary, must have become one undivided person and son. This is incontrovertible.

k. If the Word had assumed such flesh of Mary and if it did not become man, then God is not the true Father of Christ, Mary no true mother, and Christ no true Son of both His Father and mother. Moreover, the whole Scriptures are denied which testify that Christ is the Son of God. I think that all these insoluble inconsistencies show sufficiently that John a Lasco has not given the Scriptural meaning to the word *eorundem* [i.e., *of the same.* Heb. 2:14].

Eighth, observe why Christ, the Prince of our salvation, became man, namely, that He might *destroy* [render powerless] the prince of death, the devil, by His undeserved death, and that He might thus deliver and free His poor, enslaved fearful brethren and children from the accusing Law, from the Judgment of sin, and the terror of death.

Ninth, observe that the passage, He takes not on him the nature of angels, but he takes on him the seed of Abraham,[19] should not be understood as having any reference to the taking on of human flesh, as the learned ones explain it, but to the partaking of grace, by which we are accepted. For he uses the word "take" in the present tense and "angels" in the plural number, and says, He takes not on him the nature of angels, but he takes on him the seed of Abraham

[18] Menno has *portentosa creatuer.* The ancients thought that when a creature of unusual shape or character was born this was a portent from heaven. Hence such creatures were (and still are) called monsters from *monstrare,* Latin for "to show." *Tr.*

[19] The Dutch version of Heb. 2:16 is ambiguous. It may mean "He assumes the nature, etc." (as the Authorized Version also has it) or "He accepts the nature, etc." Menno is against the former and chooses the latter. It was Castellio who first proposed to translate the verb with "help" and he is followed by most moderns. Menno has Castellio's rendering on his margin. *Tr.*

—the children of promise (Rom. 9:8) ; the believers (Gal. 3:29) ; His brethren and children. He accepts them in grace to the praise of His Father (Rom. 15:7) ; prays for their faults and weaknesses. Rom. 8:7; Heb. 5:10. For they can never be freed from the inherent, impure, wicked nature of their sinful flesh in this life.

Tenth, that which is like unto a thing is not necessarily the same as it, and therefore it cannot be maintained by this passage, Wherefore in all things it behooved him to be made like unto his brethren, that Christ received His pure and holy flesh from Adam's impure and unholy flesh.

Dear reader, behold, if you examine this explanation of the Scripture of Hebrews 2, and weigh it in the balance of the Scriptures, you will find very plainly that this is the meaning of the above-mentioned passage. That although Christ, the Prince of our salvation, has led us to His glory and accepted us as brethren and children in faith, yet we are in our first birth derived from Adam and so poisoned by the serpent and so corrupted by nature, that we can never-more become free of our unclean flesh so long as we dwell in this tabernacle; but ofttimes (although against our will) mix and soil ourselves therewith and become convinced by the handwriting that according to the eternal justice we are guilty of death.

Since we are entangled by such wicked, sinful, disobedient, and guilty flesh as all the pious children of God have from the beginning dolefully lamented, and since we could not be entirely freed from the sting of the serpent, therefore it is that our Prince, Saviour, Brother, and Father, Christ, in His extremely great love has given Himself according to the counsel, purpose, will, and decree of His everlasting Father, and in accordance therewith partook of flesh and blood; not of the flesh of the children, for they are sinful and unclean, but as John says, The Word became flesh. Yes, He became a despised, afflicted, tempted, and mortal man; and He has boldly come forward to battle for His subjects, His sanctified brethren and children. He has placed Himself heroically in their defense, and has shamed the tempter in his temptation; has van-quished him in his power; has taken his weapons, bruised his head, satisfied and blotted out the handwriting; erased it with His crimson blood; discharged our guilty and deserved death by His innocent and undeserved death to the fulfillment of the prophetic word, O death, I will be thy plagues; O grave, I will be thy destruction! He has thus delivered and freed His chosen, His saints, His brethren and children from servitude and the penalty of the Law, from the judgment of sin, and from the fearful terrors of the threatened death in such a manner that their human weakness and mistakes will, for His sake, no more be counted against them as sin, if they will but walk before Him with penitent believing hearts, and will steadily cling to His Word with firm and sure consciences.

Behold, thus Christ, the Son of God, has accepted the seed of Abraham, to the praise of His Father, has set it free, and has therefore appeared in person and become in all things like unto His poor, weak, afflicted brethren in all

manner of poverty, misery, affliction, distress, fear of death, and mortality;
that thus He might be a compassionate, merciful, and faithful High Priest to
reconcile the sins, defects, and errors of His saints before God His Father. For
He has walked with them in the same temptation, battle, misery, anxiety, and
fear of death. Therefore He can also come to the rescue of all those who are
tempted by the world, hell, sin, devil, and death. This is my reply to the construction which John a Lasco and his associates put upon the Scriptures of
Hebrews 2 so emphatically. If you fear God, then read and judge.

*In the eighth place he explains the testimony of John and says, The Word,
the Son of God, commenced to be of the seed of David, of the Virgin Mary,
flesh, man, Christ, Immanuel, etc. Again, The Word has assumed our flesh.
Again, The Word, which from the beginning was only God, is become* (that
is, it commenced also to be) *flesh* (that is, man), *and has dwelt* (that is, has
taken its abode) *in us* (that is, in our flesh) *through his partaking of it, as
Paul says. These are his words in regard to the Scriptures of John 1.*

I am astounded that he dares to publish such improper explanations in
print, when he well knows that there are so many wise and learned theologians.
O dear Lord! How frightful it is to mix God's clear wine and the high
testimony of the Holy Spirit with such impure water, and thus to corrupt it
by earthly wisdom. He has so treated this plain Scripture that if I had any
doubt of my faith and position (which, thank God, I do not have) he would no
doubt have dispelled it altogether and given me great liberty.

Inasmuch as he belittles so sadly the wonderful, glorious work of divine
grace and love, which the Almighty, eternal Father has so graciously shown
us poor, miserable sinners, through His eternal Word and Son; and since he
would rather break the holy Word and testimony of the Lord than desert his
own clever reasonings, therefore I pray everybody for God's sake not to think
hard of me that I an unlearned man oppose this, and confute his unscriptural
explanations with clear, plain Scriptures and reasoning, and thus lay the foundation of truth.

I trust that no reasonable and impartial person, nor he himself can in any
way blame me for publicly replying to him and defending the praise of the
Lord, since he has publicly written against me and fearfully violated the Word
of my God as I understand it. I would undoubtedly have excused him and
would not have mentioned his name if only he and his associates would leave
the Scripture unbroken and would not so indiscreetly war against the clear,
pure truth, both verbally and in writing. But my conscience and the Word of
God constrain me to defend the praise of my Lord and my faith.

I say first, that he by his explanation has broken the testimony of the
Holy Ghost and has adulterated the Scriptures. For he writes, *The Word,
the Son of God, has of the seed of David, of a woman, of the Virgin Mary,
commenced to be flesh.* But in Rom. 1:3, I read, Born of the seed of David
according to the flesh; Gal. 4, born of a woman; Matt. 1:21, That which is
conceived in her, is of the Holy Spirit. Inasmuch as he has not left the Scrip-

tures in their natural sense, but has garbled and turned them to his own advantage; and, instead of *born of* and *conceived of* he writes, *began to be;* therefore he shows clearly that he cannot prove his explanation by the Scriptures, but merely embellishes it with Scriptures and then presents it as truth.

Second, I say that there is not a letter to be found in all the Scriptures that the Word assumed our flesh, as he keeps repeating; or that the divine nature miraculously united itself with our human nature; or that the Son of God remained unchanged and took on Him the son of Mary; or that the Son of God bestowed all His attributes on the son of man, and that one person was made of two, as John Brenz says; or that the son of man was the chosen Son of God, as Pomeranus says; or that the Word, the Son, assumed a perfect man of the flesh of Mary; or that the blood of Mary was congealed together in her womb, as the ministers of the refugee churches of London say; or that He put on our flesh; or that He dwelt therein; or that He was flesh of our flesh; or that our flesh sits at the right hand of the Father. Therefore I say that they are wrong in all these matters, yes, more than that, that they are anathema! For they are a strange gospel and a new doctrine which is not derived from the Spirit and Word of God, but is invented of flesh and blood.

Third, I say that his explanation is out of shape in every particular. For he says, *The Word began to be man, and he also says that it dwelt in our flesh.* Now if it began to be man, as it truly did, as the testimony of John when not adulterated, clearly shows—how then could it also dwell in the flesh of man? For to begin to be a house and to dwell in a house are widely different. This all reasonable people must admit.

Fourth, I say that this explanation of his is inconsistent with itself. For if the Word began to be, then it did not remain unchanged in its first estate. But if it remained unchanged, then it did not begin to be, but it began to assume a man of our flesh and thus it began to dwell in one of us of our flesh. Let him turn the matter as he pleases. Therefore, I will not let John a Lasco be the expounder but will let the faithful John himself explain his own words. He writes, That which was from the beginning, which we have heard, which we have seen with our eyes, which we have looked upon, and our hands have handled, of the Word of life, for the life was manifested, and we have seen it. I John 1:2.

Since then [John a Lasco's] explanation is inconsistent in itself and contrary to both nature and Scriptures, and since [the apostle] John shows me such a plain position, therefore I will not establish my foundation and faith on such uncertain, dark, and colored glosses, but I will establish them on the clear, certain, and undeceivable testimony of John [the apostle], for I know that his testimony is true, yea, that it is the unbroken truth and the pure Word of God.

Fifth, I say that his explanation of the verb *habitavit* [has dwelt] is false, for he says that the Word and our flesh, or the son of Mary, assumed by the Word, are one person and one Christ. And here he claims that the Word, which is the Son of God, has taken its abode in our flesh, and he refers to Xenophon, etc. From which one or the other must follow, either that Xenophon and his house are one being and thing, even as the Son of God and the son of Mary (according to his explanation, of course) are one person and Christ; or, if Xenophon and his house are two separate things, as they really are, that then also the Son of God and the son of Mary, in whom God's Son is said to have dwelt, are two separate persons and Christs; for that the one who dwells in a house and the house itself are two different things, is too evident to be denied.

I say further, that his explanation of the verb *habitavit* is not at all founded in fact. For the evangelist uses the verb in the past tense and says, *has dwelt;* from which it is evident that John does not here speak of dwelling in our flesh, but of His dwelling among men, as all intelligent translators have rendered it. For if he had spoken it with such a meaning as John a Lasco offers, then he would have said *dwells,* in the present tense, or we will have to acknowledge that the Word did not dwell in the man Christ longer than while He walked here on earth, which to my understanding would be a gross abomination and a great error.

Sixth, I say that the explanation cannot stand, for all the Scriptures in regard to Christ would then be made to contradict themselves. There would be two persons and sons in Christ—a sinful and guilty Messiah—the Father no true father, the mother no true mother, and the Son no true son. The prophets, Gabriel, the angel of the Lord, Jesus Christ, John, and Paul would all be false witnesses, as has been previously heard.

Finally, I say as I have said earlier, that John wrote his Gospel and testimony of Christ, the Son of God, in a very controversial time. If he had not meant just as he wrote, but if he had written it in such a confused and strange sense as John a Lasco explains, then he would not have abated the dispute thereby, but would rather have given it new cause. Oh, no. John has simply, clearly, and plainly given his testimony, foundation, and faith concerning Christ Jesus, the Son of God, and our only and eternal Messiah, and has testified, without ambiguity, that the Word of God, which was from the beginning, became flesh, and that this same incarnate Word has dwelt among us. But he did not add a syllable that He assumed our flesh, or that He dwelt in a man of the flesh of Mary, as alas, John a Lasco, by his human wisdom, obscures the apostle's plain word and clear testimony, and has beclouded, inverted, and twisted it.

Inasmuch as he, in his *Defensio* and explanation, has so sadly broken the Scripture and has so clumsily turned from the truth, as you may plainly see from the above explanations, therefore I felt constrained by the pure love to God and your souls, to cover over his great misunderstanding and gross errors; that the glory of the Lord may be maintained and that you may be led in the right, true confession of your God and of His beloved Son Jesus Christ.

But it is with some hesitation that I mention him by name and expose his errors, although he has given me an ill reputation and hateful name with many by his writing. I leave it to the Lord. Perhaps he thinks that he has done rightly. Whatever I do, I do for conscience' sake to the glory of my Lord and Saviour, Christ; for His glory I love far more than the honor of all creatures—and Him I must seek with all my strength, even at the cost of my life.

I am sure that if John a Lasco seeks the praise of God more than his own, if he loves his neighbor as the Scriptures require, and sincerely seeks after truth, he will not be angry with me, but will love and thank me for not excusing him in this regard, but faithfully showing him his errors, for maintaining my faith and doctrine according to the truth, for warning my fellow men against perdition, and most of all for protecting and defending the Word of my Lord, my Lord's glory and great name, as much as is in my power, according to the testimony of the Scripture and my conscience. But if it be held against me, as it is to be feared it will, then I must commend it to the Lord who, in His great love, has to this hour stood by me in all my needs with His fatherly faithfulness, and who has so graciously helped me in all my temptations.

Behold, dear reader, here you may see how far we differ from our opponents in the confession, doctrine, and faith of Christ, the Son of God. Now judge, if you fear God, which of the two parties has the stronger foundation in Scripture.

If you properly compare the Scriptures which they quote in this controversy, then you must reject the position of our opponents and cling to ours. For they can never, never be construed in the sense which they attach to them. For every intelligent person who will not willfully combat the plain truth and boldly reject the Holy Spirit, must acknowledge that from their doctrine it follows that the Lord, Christ, must be an unclean, sinful, accursed, condemned, and death-guilty Christ; that there are two persons in Christ, the one divine, the other human; two sons, the one the Son of God without mother, and the other the son of Mary, or the son of man, without father; and that not God's first and only-begotten Son, but the son of the unclean flesh of Adam died for us. Besides, all the prophets, Christ, and the apostles must be false witnesses. This is too plain to be broken by writing or twisted by human reason.

But he who understands our foundation and subjects his reasoning to the Word of God; he who believes as true and fast the testimony to which John testifies in his first chapter concerning the incarnation, and does not violate it; he who attributes nothing more to Mary, the mother of our Lord, than that which is attributed to a true mother in Genesis 1; he who leaves God the Father a true father of His Son Christ, Mary a true mother, and Christ a true Son both of His Father and of His mother—to such a one all the Scriptures in this respect are plain. He does not require the glosses of any one, for there is not a sentence in all the Scriptures which contradicts him. He has an undivided, pure, and innocent Christ, the Son of God and the son of Mary; a single person, of all of which, I trust, you have been duly convinced in the foregoing exposition founded on the power of the Scriptures; and which by the grace of God, you will see by the following brief diagram.[20]

[20] In the tract by a Lasco against which Menno is writing the former had submitted

This **Latin summary and diagram** I have submitted for the benefit of the learned. In translation it reads as follows: The eternal Word of God, by which all things were made, which is the Alpha and Omega, was in time and in the town of Nazareth, according to the predestination of God, according to the decree of God, according to the promise of God, conceived by the Virgin Mary (who knew no man) as flesh or man, was born and became flesh. John 1:14. According to which flesh conceived in Mary, through the Holy Spirit, of the Father's eternal Word, He in due time, was born of the seed or lineage of David, of a woman, of the Virgin Mary, in Bethlehem, as an only-begotten Son of God, according to the promise and the lineage of the mother, also of Abraham, of David, and of the seed of the woman, the fruit and son, a Saviour of the world, the Lord Himself from heaven, the bread which came down from heaven, Immanuel, the mighty Prince, our God, the Lord our Righteousness.

Faithful reader, there you have our foundation, doctrine, and confession of Christ, the Son of God; how He is become flesh in Mary, and how He came into the world, as we before our God believe and teach our brethren. And we would hereby pray and faithfully admonish every one gratefully to accept this noble and precious Son of God with a sincere desire to hear, love, and serve Him in gladness of heart and faithfully to follow in His footsteps; to walk without reproach in His Word and ways, freely to proclaim His honor and praise, to glorify His holy name, and humbly and obediently to bend his heart before his Majesty, since the merciful Father has shown us such great love as to give us, poor, miserable sinners, His only, eternal, and beloved Son. For He is the Man who has victoriously led us poor children, through the merits of His cleansing blood and bitter death, according to the gracious plan, counsel, will, and decree of God, His heavenly Father, from the kingdom of hell and from eternal death into the glorious kingdom of His divine honor and eternal peace. Everlasting praise to His illustrious, wonderful, high, and glorious name. Amen.

# *Conclusion*

Christ says, This is eternal life, that they might know thee, the only true God, and Jesus Christ, whom thou hast sent. John 17:3. At another place, If ye believe not that I am he, ye shall die in your sins. John 8:24. John also says, Whosoever shall confess that Jesus is the Son of God, God dwelleth in him, and he in God. I John 4:15. Again, Who is a liar but he that denieth

a diagram setting forth his view of the Incarnation. Therefore Menno also offers a diagram at this point (1681 *Opera*, p. 381). It is in Latin and necessary changes in word order make it quite impossible to translate. The reader does not lose much because the content of Menno's diagram follows in the ensuing paragraph. *Tr.*

that Jesus is the Christ? He is antichrist, and denieth the Father and the Son. Whosoever denieth the Son, the same hath not the Father. I John 2:22.

Oh, that our opponents would rightly take to heart these and the like Scriptures, and would learn to know who and what the Son of God is, and from whence He came. Then they might yet be delivered from the chains of the deceiver and be led into the light of the true doctrine. But as long as they do not know Christ, it will always be wrangling and disputation, changing falsehood into truth and truth into falsehood. Yes, they will be so deluded and blinded that all those who, with the angel Gabriel, with the eternal Father, with John the Baptist, with Peter, Paul, Martha, Christ, and with the whole Scriptures, confess Christ Jesus to be the true Son of the living God, must alas by them be called deceivers and heretics. O dear Lord, how long will this great abomination continue?

Oh, that they might yet awaken in time while it is yet today and give just praise unto Christ; that they might see their accursed hypocrisy, false religion, the lamentable deceit of the poor and miserable people, and the ignorant, reckless life of the wicked; that they might renounce and discontinue it! What a blessing that would be to their poor souls! But I fear that so long as the spiritual Antiochus dispenses idle life so liberally, and Jezebel sets the tables so attractively, the accursed Moaz will retain his sway and the world will not be in want of false teachers and deceivers.

Kind reader, ponder well what I write. I warn you in faithful love, watch, look, and observe well what you believe and what you uphold; for your teachers deceive you. Watch and pray; the Day is at hand, and comes speedily when we must all stand before the impartial judgment seat of our God, who judges without respect of persons, and will reward every one according to his works, be he emperor or king, doctor or professor, rich or poor, man or woman.

In short this is my reply to the *Defensio* of John a Lasco. With this I will not only appear on earth before man, but also in the Day of my Lord Christ, according to the Word of His promise, and in His grace before the eyes of His Majesty. If you are of reasonable disposition and not blinded by the spirit of the envious partisans, nor led away by bitter zeal, then judge between us and our opponents; who of us glorifies Jesus Christ more, the Son of the true and living God; who has used the Scriptures to greater edification, and who has turned them to suit his own position. But beware of judging according to the flesh; but judge in purity of heart, as before your God, according to truth.

From my innermost soul I wish you a true and unfeigned love, a true confession of God and Christ, the compelling fruit and love of God, a pious, penitent, cheerful heart, an irreproachable Christian life, a true understanding, and a good judgment. Amen.

OBSERVE: For God so loved the world, that he gave his only begotten Son, that whosoever believeth in him should not perish, but have everlasting life. For God sent not his Son into the world to condemn the world; but that the world through him might be saved. He that believeth on him is not condemned : but he that believeth not is condemned already, because he hath not believed in the name of the only begotten Son of God.  John 3 :16-17.

MENNO SIMONS

# Reply to Martin Micron

*Antwoordt aan Martinum Micron*

## 1556

*For other foundation can no man
lay than that is laid, which is Jesus Christ.*

I CORINTHIANS 3 :11

# Introduction

The year 1553 found Menno living in Wismar in Mecklenburg, one of the cities of the Hanseatic League. This was the year in which the Zwinglian Protestants of London got into difficulty and had to flee. Two ships carrying these Zwinglian refugees left London for the continent on September 15. They first sailed to Lutheran Denmark, hoping for an asylum. But when King Christian of Denmark learned that they were Zwinglians he ordered them to leave his land. One of the ships arrived at Wismar on December 21 but froze fast in the ice some distance from the shore. The Mennonites of Wismar went to the aid of the refugees, taking to them bread and wine for their refreshment. Poor as they were, the Wismar Mennonites also made up a purse of twenty-four *Thalers* for these people. But the Zwinglian leaders refused the gift, stating that all they wished was opportunity for employment. The Mennonites assisted them so far as it was in their power.

Among the leaders of these refugees were John a Lasco (1499-1560), the Polish reformer, and a certain Hermes Backereel. The latter had a discussion with Menno on various points of doctrine on December 26, 1553. Thereupon the Zwinglians sent a messenger to Norden in East Friesland to bring Martin de Cleyne, called Micron (1523-59), to assist in the debate with Menno. Micron arrived in Wismar January 25, 1554, and ultimately held two debates with Menno: the first on February 6 when the two men discussed baptism, the incarnation of Christ, the oath, divorce, the calling of ministers, and the magistracy. This discussion lasted eleven hours without interruption and was concluded with a common meal. Nine days later the two men met again and disputed over the incarnation in a rather heated manner.

Menno was living in a secret location at this time, but Backereel learned from a child where Menno's home was. Menno granted the Zwinglians an interview on condition that the location of his residence be kept secret. Backereel gave his hand that this would not be divulged. Menno reports bitterly that it was not long after the first disputation before it was known even on the streets of distant Emden where Menno dwelt!

On June 18, 1556, Micron published his *True Account* of part of the discussions which he had had with Menno some two years earlier. Menno promptly wrote the booklet before us, *Reply to Martin Micron,* dated October 7 [1556], as well as his *Epistle to Martin Micron,* dated nine days later. It was Micron, however, who got the last word, for his final book against Menno appeared in 1558, *A Reckoning.*

The whole discussion is tedious and tiresome. While no one can blame Menno for the primitive state of science in his day, yet one cannot but wish that he would have had more good sense than to waddle through the mire as he does in this monotonous and repetitious discussion. As a matter of plain fact, Menno was simply wrong scientifically in his central argument that human generation and inheritance rest with the father only. His aim, which was to uphold a high view of the person of our Lord, was of course laudable. But his arguments are wearisome, and his style is less than courteous; there is no excuse for the sharp polemics of sixteenth-century authors. Section X is perhaps the only edifying section in the entire *Reply*. The average reader may turn to that, and omit the rest of the book, for it is unprofitable.

In the *Opera Omnia Theologica* of 1681 the *Reply to Martin Micron* is printed fol. 543-98. In the *Complete Works* of 1871 it is found in Part II, pages 351-401, though with considerable omissions. The full title in the Dutch (1681) is: *An Altogether Plain and Polite Reply Derived from the Truth and Power of the Holy Scriptures in 1556 and Directed against Martin Micron and his anti-Christian Doctrine and False Account of the Discussion held in 1553 in the Presence of Many Between Him and Me before Many Witnesses and Dealing with the very sacred Incarnation of our Lord Jesus Christ; to which is appended a Hearty but Stern Epistle or Admonition to Him Urging Him to Repent and be Saved.* The title page includes John 17:3, and of course Menno's motto, I Corinthians 3:11.                    J. C. W.

# Reply to Martin Micron

# 1556

•-•-•-•-•-•-•-•-•-•-•-•-•-•-•-•-•-•-•-•-•-•-•-•-•-•-•-•-•-•-•-•-•-•-•-•-•-•-•-•-•-•-•-•-•-•-•-•-•-•-•

## *Preface*

To the well-disposed reader:

It is manifest, honorable reader, that even as Satan, jealous of the divine honor and of our salvation in the beginning of creation, used the serpent as an instrument to lead Adam and Eve off the way of life and thus to lead them into death, as he actually did (Gen. 3:19), so he now uses his false authors and preachers, some of whom he dresses up in fine sheepskin in angelic appearance of garbled Scriptures, philosophies, human reason, a life of civil virtue, and words of human cleverness. With these he ensnares poor captive souls in their great blindness and sin, and robs them by his endless tricks of their only means of salvation, Jesus Christ.

The serpent said unto Eve, Shall you die for that? Ah, no, it shall not be! So now our opponents say, Is Christ the Son of God? No, He is not. The man Christ had no father. From the beginning the devil did not and could not stand the true faith in Christ Jesus, namely, that we should acknowledge Him to be the true Son of God, as may be plainly understood from I John 2:22; 4:3; II John 7. For where Christ is confessed to be the first-born and eternally begotten Son of God, there the world is overcome. I John 3:5. There men are in God and God is in them. I John 4:15. In short, there is life eternal (John 3:36), whereby in turn the power of the devil is broken and his kingdom destroyed. Yes, Christ Himself had to suffer death because He confessed Himself to be the Son of God. Matt. 26:64; Mark 14:62; John 5:18; 19:7. If Satan then was so averse to such faith in the beginning, how shall he put up with it now, since in the righteous judgment of God because of sin he is risen, thanks to Antichrist and his servants, to full dominion and has gained the mastery of the whole earth by his seductive doctrine, explanations, glosses, statutes, commandments, idolatry, tyranny, and violence?

We see clearly, since Christ Jesus by His grace has shown Himself through the clouds sufficiently so that we with Peter and with all the Scriptures confess Him in power and truth to be the Son of the true and living God and submissively seal this faith with the sign of holy baptism, as did the Ethiopian (Acts 8:36), according to His commandment. We do this because we would

838

in our weakness walk according to His commandments and be saved by His grace, no matter how terribly we are reviled, slandered, cursed, persecuted, and murdered by this corrupted, perverse, blind, and carnal generation because of it. Satan has never from the beginning tolerated the true faith in Christ Jesus, nor its seal done in obedience. He will never unto the end put up with it.

Apollyon of the Apocalypse has so corrupted things by the locusts of the bottomless pit that but little truth remains with man. It is manifest that not only the Turks and the papists, but also those of whom one might expect better things, are those who hate the brightness of the most holy birth of Jesus Christ on which true faith depends, as well as the nature, power, fruit, impression, and seal of faith, as may be seen by the writings of our opponents.

Oh, dear, how very little these poor children have and know of the kingdom of God and of the power of His Holy Word, although they may think perhaps that they understand a great deal. For it is very clear that an earthly, carnally minded heart, a vain, proud mind, a hateful, envious person, and an untrue and false tongue are not of God but of the evil one. I John 3:8. It is evident that the writings of our opponents are prompted by an earthly, carnal, hateful, and false heart; that they did not seek the glory, name, and honor of God but their own and that their writings are unfair and untruthful. This can be easily deduced from the fact that from beginning to end they do not speak a kind word about me nor our beloved brethren and that they are quite silent about the favor faithfully rendered them in time of need; that they do not so much as mention that they were so often argued down that they had no further excuses to make, something which I do not mention to our credit but to the praise of the Lord. It is also evident from the fact that they do not in all their writings mention the acknowledgments which they made before us all, that woman has no procreative seed,[1] but only a menstrual flux whereby in fact their whole cause was already lost. Also that there were two natures in Christ and that the one who was crucified was not the Son of God. This does not become an impartial writer who does not seek his own honor but sincerely seeks the honor of God. Nor does it become them to call me altogether ignorant, yes, like unto a foolish cuckoo (as he once called me) which always sings the same song and himself poses as an expert in the Scriptures, while before God and His angels, and before all present it was actually quite different as by the grace of God will be found and clearly seen from my following writings if judged according to divine truth. Very little, alas, have they pondered the Scripture of Paul which says that we should not be desirous of vainglory. Gal. 5:26.

They give such an untrue account of the discussion and so lamentably violate the Father and His Son in their noble, dear, powerful, and true Word and all those who confess them; and they have brought such shame upon our beloved brethren who daily piously suffer and die for the sake of the Lord's Word, insinuating that their whole life and death are but madness and that they forsake possessions and kindred for no other cause than heresy. Therefore

---

[1] Menno was ignorant of the woman's role in procreation. *Ed.*

I am impelled as in duty bound and for the love of my Lord and Saviour, Jesus Christ, and His holy church, faithfully and truthfully to record all that which Micron has willfully suppressed to the dishonor of Christ and His holy Word. I do this not urged by wrath, for I leave this matter to Him who in due time shall judge us all without respect of persons. I leave this to Him. I relate also how slanderously he has blasphemed the Father and the Son, the Word, and those who confess it, and how wrongfully he attacks our faith and doctrine concerning the incarnation of Christ as taught and testified to throughout the Scriptures in incontrovertible power and clearness.

I beseech all readers for the Lord's sake to read this my explanation with impartial hearts, to consider well the position, and to pray the Lord for grace and understanding. I trust to be able with God's help to make such explanation and distinction with such power and clearness of the Holy Scriptures that men will see plainly that anti-Christian deceit is on the side of our opponents and that the clear position of truth is on our side. Therefore I would have the judicial expression applied, *Alteram partem audito* (that is, Hear also the other side). Compare my writings with theirs and do not err through prejudice as do my opponents.

I beseech you also not to take it ill of me that I use such expressions as seed of man, seed of woman, menstrual flux, etc. God knows how unwillingly I do so, but necessity forces me in order that the glory of Christ Jesus may not be obscured with many, and that the heavenly brightness of His holy birth may not remain obscured by the anti-Christian glosses and sophistries of Micron's breath from the pit.

I am amazed at the man's heart and mind that he dares to write down such absurd fables, and that he dares to show himself so ambitious and proud (something from which before God I cannot escape as I consider his writings) for it will doubtlessly be observed by many an intelligent person. For what does he do all through his writings but exalt himself and trample me in the dust as is the nature of all proud people? So much so that I would not have written if it touched me only and not the honor of God, since so many God-fearing, pious people were present who heard the discussion from beginning to end. Moreover it is well known perhaps to thousands, as I presume through my printed writings which are daily read here and there, that I have frequently solicited public discussion at the risk of being burned if I could not maintain my faith and doctrine with Scripture, a request which alas has never been granted.

If now I were so entirely ignorant as his writing reports, it would be very odd that such a discussion should have been so long denied me since he might thereby have gained many a soul, might have put many a child on the right track if we were wrong, and as he might have gained such fame and reputation if he had been successful among those of high standing and also among the whole world. But Micron has not yet forgotten, although he writes so boastingly how he sat there with us.

If Micron and Hermes had feared God as they pretend by their sheep's clothing, they would not have acted so foolishly as they have done by their writings. But I presume that the one who urged Pharaoh to persecute Israel, notwithstanding he had seen such miracles in Egypt by the hands of Moses and Aaron, to meet his punishment in the Red Sea; the one who urged Antiochus to turn Jerusalem into a pit of death to meet his superior and avenger on the way; that that same one has urged Micron and Hermes to write this way so that their covert hypocrisy, their many falsehoods, ambitious partiality (I call things as I judge them before the Lord), shameless ingratitude, undeserved slander, falsification and willful garbling of the Holy, divine Word, their corrupting glosses, sophistical philosophy, miserable deceit of the poor, despised souls, abominable, anti-Christian doctrine, blasphemy of both the Father and His blessed Son, palpable blindness, and their vain, carnal hearts may by this our explanation be made manifest; so that in this way hearts which are bound by their snares through the falsehoods which they publish against us, by the fine appearance they put on, and by the garbled Scriptures which they teach by smooth, flattering words of human wisdom, may be unbound and set free to the glory of the Lord.

I do not know what else to say or think of the matter. For more than two years ago I warned him by a man of considerable name and who believes as he does that if he would put it in print (for I was told that he had this plan) and would not report it as it actually happened, for I observed that he was not saving with falsehood, I would reply to him if I lived and the Lord granted it. But he realized that if he did not falsify he would get but little fame and honor with the world, for it would have left the impression that Micron lost out completely, something that conceited, proud flesh does not like to hear.

Yet I would never in my life have thought that he was of such extremely ambitious, partial, false, slanderous, and shameless mind, if I had not been convinced of it in our discussion and now by this writing of his. I would have thought that reason would have told him, even without the warning of any one, that if he should do as he did while I am still living, it would get him nothing but shame and dishonor with all fair-minded readers. But Micron had to bring forth according to that which was in him.

But perhaps he hoped or thought that I might in the meantime die, and that he might thus continue in fame and honor without rebuke before men. He was also aware that he could not offend the world which gladly accepts and hears such comfortable lies and falsehoods by abusing me. Whosoever can best defame us and rail the loudest and paint me and my brethren in the ugliest colors is with them a great prophet and a fine preacher. But let them run their course until stopped by the Lord. John says, They are of the world, and therefore they speak of the world, and the world hears them. I John 4:5. Let the dear Lord grant them grace if that be possible. Let the reader take due notice of the following reply that he may learn to know Christ, do the right, and be saved.

## [I.] HOW AND WHEN THE PEOPLE CALLED ENGLISHMEN[2] CAME TO US AND WHAT FAITHFUL LOVE OUR BRETHREN SHOWED THEM

In the year 1553, a little before midwinter, it was told the brethren that a shipload of people had arrived from Denmark who on account of their faith were driven from England and that they lay a short distance from the shore, frozen up in the ice with their ship.

When the brethren heard this they were moved by Christian mercy on their account as was proper. They talked it over and concluded to lend them assistance and help them out of the ice and escort them to the city in an orderly way without any commotion as they also did—although they suspected that it might cause trouble with the government as indeed it did.

They met them with wheat bread and wine so that if there should be any sick among them they might strengthen and quicken them therewith. And after they had escorted them into the city, they made a collection of twenty-four *Thalers* out of their poverty and presented it to their leaders to be distributed among the needy if such there should be among them. They refused the money and said they had enough of that but that they would like that labor would be provided for some of their number in which our brethren assisted them as much as they could.

One of our number offered helpfully to take the children of John a Lasco into his house and to do the best he could for them. To which Hermes Backereel answered, No, that will not do, for John a Lasco is a man who has to negotiate frequently with lords, princes, and other high personages, and it might (reader, observe) cause a scandal if his children should stay with such people. On hearing this I observed that we had not met with the true, plain, and humble pilgrims of Jesus Christ.

Behold, these are the details of their arrival, and such faithful love have our brethren shown them. It was, however, not long afterward taken ill of us by the ungrateful Hermes. And Micron out of dislike for the truth and out of dislike for the brethren, it seems, has omitted the item lest someone should ascribe any piety to our group.

## [II.] HOW IT HAPPENED THAT THE ENGLISHMEN HAD A DISCUSSION WITH US

After they had been a few days in the city, Hermes and his followers called some of us together and asked for a discussion, and after many prententious assertions he said unto us, I am a clergyman and would like to have a clergyman put over against me, for I have heard that Menno is in the city.

[2] Micron and his party are called "Englishmen" by Menno because they had spent some time at London and other English cities in the refugee churches there. With the accession of Bloody Mary, an ardent Catholic, they had to flee the country again. They were not permitted to land in Denmark, a Lutheran area. *Tr.*

Therefore I would like to confront him or some other minister. For I have had discussions with hundreds of your people and when they are vanquished, then they invariably appeal to their teachers. Behold thus he spoke.

I might here write a good deal about his false inventions and his ambitions and slippery tongue; also about his unkind and hateful investigations behind my back, seeking if he could not find a splinter about me to magnify into a big beam and to tie this upon my back as a sign of shame. Also how he tried to get from an innocent child the location of my secret dwelling place. But as it cannot teach nor help the reader, therefore I will leave it to the Lord and leave the shame of Hermes untouched that the reader may not think that I wish to reward evil with evil, from which may the Lord forever save me. Yet I could wish that he might be a bit more truthful and less partial, and that he would fear the Lord his God more.

The discussion was agreed upon with Hermes and his followers upon the following condition: that they would tell nobody where the discussion took place since I was a poor, weak man hated of all the world. Upon which they on their part gave our brethren their hand that they would never tell it. But how they have kept their word their deeds have shown. For it was but a short time until men were telling each other in the streets of Emden where Menno lived, and that Micron and his fellows had had a discussion with him. And besides, they have published it in print to all the world. If honorable, pious persons are not bound to respect their word and pledge more, a thing which is considered the same as an oath by reasonable people, then I will leave it to the judgment of all readers, both those for us and those against us. But there are many who think that nothing you can do to us can be wrong.

In the same manner they have not repaid very well the city which showed more nobility toward them than all the east country and Denmark, when in that severe winter they knew not where to find shelter. With their insipid partial writings they have made the city suspect among lords and princes and other cities as though the city harbored and sustained us, although the city knew no more of my sojourning there than they did of the hour of their death.

Lastly, they published the names of some good persons who had not deserved it, that they might be known in all countries to which they might move. If the Lord does not prevent, a price will be placed upon the head of one of them who has shown them such good service or on that of his little children. If they had now in all this considered the unfeigned pure love which wishes, much less does harm to none, common honesty and their word of honor, seeing that their activity instructs none upon the earth nor makes them better before God and looks more like the work of a tattletale than of a pious man, then according to my opinion it would resemble the evangelical Christian character, spirit, discipline, and reasonableness more than it does. The Lord's word is true: The fruit shows what the tree is. Matt. 12:33.

This is the way they acted who pretend to be Christians and say that we are heretics, who call upon God as their witness and judge that they have faithfully described the discussion, while they are well aware that the first sentence they wrote was a falsehood. And how quite untrue it is will by the grace of the Lord be shown by simple truths from the sequel.

## [III.] THE TRUE ACCOUNT OF THE DISCUSSION BETWEEN HERMES AND ME

This is the way Hermes and I came to have a discussion in the winter. It happened when we met for the purpose of discussion that I briefly admonished them in regard to the suffering, oppression, tribulation, persecution, and cross of true Christians. To which he immediately answered: That by this I wish to make his doctrines suspect among our party, a thing that I had not so much as thought of. I desisted and said, Very well, Hermes, I suppose you would like to discuss the question of the incarnation first. He answered, Yes. Then I said, State your conviction. When he had done so, I said, Dear Hermes, look out what you say, for behold all these absurdities follow from your belief and I enumerated eight of them.

And behold when I had finished my speech there was among them a certain Jacob Michiels whose name also appears in Micron's writings, who asked me if I could prove that from Scripture, thinking that I had stated this as my own position. I told him that he might ask that of Hermes, since it was his faith and doctrine. On hearing this he looked down and was silent. I told him three times in succession to get Hermes to prove it to him from the Scriptures. I have yet to receive his answer.

When I noticed this ugly partisan spirit, I was grieved. I said, Dear sirs, are we to treat the Word of the Lord thus? What a pity! When you thought that it was my doctrine, you asked for Scripture; but when you discover that it is Hermes' position, you have Scripture enough. O friend, I said, repent and be ashamed before God, for you do not treat His Word as becomes a true Christian. And this is one of the principal witnesses who listened objectively as Micron boasts, but without truth.

Afterward Hermes found his tongue and said, I will scatter these absurdities as the wind scatters the dust. Dear Hermes, I said, do not speak so proudly. It does not become a Christian. I know you will have to let me keep them. And praise the Lord for His grace, it has come true as I can plainly see by Micron's appendix, even though they have racked their brains about it for more than two years.

The absurdities remain unsolved and about all we heard from him was, He assumed.[8] So at last I said, My dear sir, show me where do you find written that He assumed our flesh or our human nature as you claim? He then answered, Paul teaches us that Christ assumed the form of a servant. Phil. 2:7.

When he was through I asked him whether or not he agreed with John a

[8] Reference is to the classic Reformed formula that Christ *assumed* our flesh and blood. *Tr.*

Lasco in this doctrine. He answered, Yes. I replied: Well, a Lasco has placed these expressions, *in the form of God,* and *in the form of a servant,* over against each other, saying that He was in the form of God and thereby was truly God, and He has similarly taken upon Himself our sinful form and was thereby constituted man; but the sins, he continued, on account of which we are called servants in the Scriptures, He did not have.

From this comparison one of two things result. Either if He had the sinful form and not the sin, then He by virtue of the comparison must also have had the divine form but not the deity. Or if He did have the divine form and also the deity, then He must also have had the sinful form and therewith also sin. Otherwise the comparison breaks down and cannot stand. In this representation there must be accepted either that Christ Jesus was a sinner or else that He was not God. And how such doctrine agrees with the Scriptures I will leave to your own judgment.

Then he replied: The Scriptures testify that He was without sin. True enough, I said. Therefore it is manifest that this comparison of a Lasco is false and that you cannot defend this doctrine. But if the Scripture is to remain unbroken, then this is the true comparison, even as Christ was in the form of God and was thereby truly God, so He humbled Himself and did not take on Himself the form of a potentate, emperor, or king whom we should serve, but the form of a poor servant because He wanted to serve; for as He was truly God in God and with God His Father from eternity, so He became our true servant in due time. Matt. 12:18; 20:28.

With this he abandoned that Scripture and said, There is another one much plainer, which has it that He has taken on Him the seed of Abraham. Heb. 2:16. Not so, Hermes, I said. We should not falsify the Scriptures thus. For it does not read that He has taken on the seed of Abraham but it reads that He takes it on. Which taking on shall last unto the end.

He then took the words of the same chapter and said that Christ has become partaker of the children's flesh and blood and is thus on account of the flesh called our brother.

On hearing this I replied, There you have another falsification of the Scriptures, for it is written that He took upon Himself the flesh and blood but not the flesh and blood of children. Therefore let us get at the meaning of these words at the outset, lest we do violence to the Scriptures. Paul says, He that sanctifieth and they who are sanctified are of one. Now I ask, To whom does this one refer? To God or to Adam? He replied, To Adam. Then it follows inevitably, I said, that all ungodly people and children of the devil, such as thieves, murderers, drunkards, proud detesters, homicides, harlots, and scamps, are Christ's brethren and sisters. He frankly admitted that they were.

It would follow further, if we were Christ's brethren and sisters on account of the flesh, then also we would be His children on account of the flesh; for Paul says, Behold, I and my children. From which it would surely follow that the one brother has generated the other, and the children their father, according to the flesh. And I will leave you to study out how such begetting could be according to the Scriptures and the ordinance of God.

After we had spoken some other words concerning the partaking I asked him if Adam had not partaken of flesh and blood. He answered, Yes. Well, said I, of whose flesh and blood did he partake if we are to understand this partaking as you do? Therefore, beloved Hermes, look out, your learned ones deceive you. Paul says, He that threshes in hope, should be partaker of his hope, that is, that he may obtain that for which he hopes. Again, in the same chapter: If others be partakers of this power over you, are not we rather? That is, if others have this power. Again we are made partakers of Christ, not that we have taken a part or portion of Him, but the whole. Heb. 3:14.

Therefore, beloved Hermes, I warn you to let the Scripture remain Scripture and do not force it to suit. For Paul does not say that the unsanctified ones, such as liars, haters, the proud, adulterers, and children of the devil, are one with Christ, our Saviour, but that the sanctified are one with Him, that is, those who with Him are born of one God. On account of which birth of God and not of Adam, we are His brethren; for the regenerated ones have one Father together with Christ. As He is the first-begotten Son of God, thus He is also the first-born among many brethren. Heb. 1:6; Rom. 8:29.

As the holy Paul then teaches that He is the first-begotten among the brethren, therefore it is very plain that He is not our brother out of Adam, but out of God; for He was not the first-begotten of Adam, therefore the children of Adam must through regeneration by faith also become the children of God (John 1:12), and therefore also Christ's brethren (Matt. 12:50; Mark 3:35; Luke 8:21; Heb. 2:11).

Behold He is not ashamed to call His brother such regenerated and sanctified ones who with Him have one Father (not harlots and scamps and children of the devil), saying, Thy name (He means His Father's name, not Adam's) I will declare unto my brethren. Again, I will trust in Him, namely, in the Father and not in Adam. And again, I and the children which God, not Adam, hath given me. Even as it is very plain that the children are not the carnal but the spiritual children (for He had no carnal children), so His brethren must be spiritual brethren, or else one Scripture must be understood spiritually and the other carnally; then also sister Mary must have begotten her brother Christ in the flesh. This is incontrovertible.

Although now such regenerated persons are His sanctified brethren and sisters, they still have, contrary to their will, fellowship with flesh and blood through the inherent, sinful nature; they sin, stumble, and transgress and so are through the before-mentioned fellowship conscious of guilt because of the law which requires perfect righteousness. And behold, therefore their Saviour, first-begotten Brother and Father, Christ, has in like manner partaken of flesh and blood, not of the children, for it does not read that way. Otherwise, He must have been a sinner of a sinner, and one son of two sons; one of whom was in heaven, eternal and immortal, the other of earth and mortal. But the Word

itself is become flesh, that is, by way of explanation, true mortal man, subject
to suffering in Mary. As John says, The Word is become flesh, like unto His
sanctified brethren in all things, sin excepted, that He might satisfy the Law
in His innocent flesh and not in our guilty flesh, remove its power that He
might conquer the deserved death by His undeserved death, destroy the devil
who had the power of death, bruise the serpent's head, sanctify us unto God
His Father by the virtue of His crimson blood, and assist us in all our temptations and distresses which result from our wicked flesh and the inspirations of
Satan. Behold, this is really the position of Paul. Heb. 2:14. And by such
explanation Christ remains the undivided Son of God, the Scripture remains
unbroken, Christ remains the Sanctifier and we His sanctified ones, brethren
and children. There is not a single Scripture which opposes this. But Hermes'
confession and faith come with many absurdities, as has been heard.

When I mentioned absurdities once more he asked me to confess my faith
as he had done his; and he said he would show more inconsistencies (although
he had not heard it as yet) in my faith than I had shown in his. And when
I had made my confession, he said, This is too long to suit me; I cannot reply
to it. I then subsumed in short, clear terms. But no absurdities were listed,
not one.

Behold, worthy reader, these are the principal points and Scriptures which
Hermes and I discussed concerning the incarnation of Christ. I say the principal ones, for to repeat all the words which passed between us is impossible.

After mealtime we came to the discussion of pedobaptism[4] which he tried
to justify with the assertion that children, as he said, are accounted as believing
by the Scriptures, and that Zacchaeus (he insisted upon Zacchaeus, notwithstanding I told him that it was not Zacchaeus) and his whole house were
baptized.

Kind reader, if I were to give an account of the discussion as it happened
it would seem to some readers as if I did it out of party spirit. To others who
know me, it must seem very foolish of him to challenge us while he did not
know more of Scripture. Therefore I told him a couple of times, Dear Hermes,
you are too much a novice in the matter; you will have to learn a great deal
before you try to defend your cause. What is become of all your proud words
which you spoke at the start? Yet Micron writes that some of their weak
brethren were very much strengthened by Hermes during the discussion. I
will let it go at that. They have to blindfold their reader so that he may not
observe that Hermes acted childishly and to their shame.

I know of a certainty, however, that Micron was summoned immediately
after the discussion, as his own writings imply. For their brethren who were
with us were in great need inwardly and outwardly. What he means by inwardly I will leave to the reader to ponder.

---

4 Commonly called infant baptism. *Ed.*

[IV.] HOW MICRON HAS PARTISANLIKE RELATED OUR
FIRST DISCUSSION, HOW HE HAS OMITTED THE MOST
IMPORTANT MATTERS, AND HOW HE GARBLES MY WORDS,
AND HOW HE DRESSES UP HIS OWN

When we were seated for the discussion I said to Micron, I hear that your name is Martin Micron. You are unknown to me, and I have never in all my days heard a word about you before you came here. But I understand that you have made a reputation at London by your speaking and that you have published some things also, as I hear. Therefore my fraternal admonition and request to you is that if you hear more powerful truths and firmer foundation in this our discussion, than you have heard or learned before this, that you seek not your own fame and honor but the praise and honor of the Lord. To which he replied, Menno, I admonish you the same. I said, I am here for that very purpose and I have suffered for many years because I would gladly have the truth and follow it.

This brotherly admonition given him in faithfulness of heart he sadly changed in the latter part of the discussion; each time he was overtaken in his false anti-Christian doctrine. He said that I had accused him of seeking his own praise and honor by his writing and speaking in London, a thing of which I had never thought, for I did not even know him.

He appealed to his own folk as witnesses, which poor children under his spell all agreed with him. At this I was grieved and said, Is there no fear of God before your eyes? There are now ten of you, all of whom answer as he wants. If there were ten thousand more besides you, you would still not tell the truth in this matter. What would it sound like if I should at the outset confront a man with whom I was not acquainted and of whom I had heard nothing but good and say that he had sought his own honor with his writings?

All our brethren contradicted him and said, Dear Micron, you transgress, for so and so has Menno admonished you and thus you have answered him. Yet it was of no avail. These unkind, bitter, false, and defaming words must alas be published in his book. What kind of spirit this is, how he follows the unfalsified Christian truth, piety, and love, and how faithfully he narrates the matter, I will let the fair and reasonable reader judge, as well as his dishonest falsification of my first words which I spoke to him with such good intention.

We then discussed some articles with which my writings are full, to which it was useless to reply. Finally we came to the matter of the incarnation, the matter for which we are called such abominable heretics and deceivers by them, namely, because we confess with God the Father, with Christ, and with the angel Gabriel, with Peter and with all the Scriptures that Jesus Christ is the Son of God.

His confession and position came down to this, that there are two sons in Christ, the one eternal and not subject to suffering; the other temporal and subject to suffering; and that the one which was crucified for us was not the Son of God. This confession he did not make thoughtlessly by mistake, but with premeditation and a sober mind before us all; and he repeated it at least four or five times. Yet he calls on the Lord to witness that they frequently confessed with us that the Son of God died for us. Sirach very properly says, Many would rather do the worst than to lose their honor; and do it for the sake of the ungodly. Sir. 20:24.

I set before him the absurdities inherent in his belief and after many assertions made at length, I let him read undisturbedly an hour or an hour and a half from the Bible about the seed of woman, the seed of Abraham and of David, and about the fruit of the loins of David. And when he had finished reading I asked what he wanted to assert thereby. I assert thereby, he said, that the man Christ is of the fathers and that the Word did not become flesh as you say. This was the thrust of his words.

I replied, I heartily acknowledge and confess all these Scriptures to be right and good; for they teach us and testify that such a Saviour should come. But now we will see from the Scriptures from whom the human fruit really comes; whether it comes from the father or from the mother. On hearing this, he said, Do you expect to see that? I answered, Yes, for I hope by the grace of God to be able to prove by holy, divine Scripture that the origin of the child is from the father and not from the mother, but through the mother. This, I think, was something new to him, for he said, Dear, Dear, let us hear that. I quoted I Cor. 11:8 where Paul says, Man is not of the woman, but the woman of the man. On hearing this he interrupted me and said, This is spoken of Adam and Eve. Hold on, said I, it continues: even so is the man also by the woman. Was Adam then by Eve? At this he was silent, as one who is beaten. I showed him many plain Scriptures as Gen. 15:4; 17:6; 19:32; Rom. 9:7; Heb. 7:10; 11:12. I also referred him to the genealogy, Matt. 1, and showed him that Christ, according to his position, must have been a Syrian, a Canaanite, a Moabite, and an Ammonite as well.

I also argued from analogies in nature as of the sower, his seed, and the soil; from which Micron tries to make it appear to the reader that I made use of reason rather than Scripture against him. But as men say, Micron's little finger knows full well that the seed of the land and the seed of man are called by the same name in the Scriptures, and that also Abraham cast his seed, [that is,] sowed it (Heb. 11:11); although Micron twists it in his writings and would apply the casting to Sarah as to imply that women have procreative seed. What we are to call such willful falsifiers of the holy divine Word, I will leave to the impartial reader. This is the same cleverness as that which the serpent employed when he led Adam and Eve into death. Gen. 3:1. Good reader, the Scriptures, together with nature, openly testify to us by the ordinance of God that there is seed which is sown, and just so there must be fit soil to be sown, for neither in the unplowed land evidently, nor upon houses, trees, and rocks do we sow. And whether or not my comparison of the husbandman, of his seed, and of his field can stand according to the Scriptures, I will leave not to the calumniating Micron and Hermes, but to the reasonable reader.

When I had finished my argument I said, Behold, Martin, this analogy from nature which I have proposed, you may ponder by yourself at your leisure, but give reply to my Scriptures.

Then he scratched his head as one perplexed and said, Dear me, this philosophy of the seed of the woman! On hearing this, I replied, I have proposed plain Scriptures whereby I have proved that the child is originally of the father and not of the mother, and you want it to be of the mother without the Scriptures. Dear me, which of us two makes use of philosophy, you or I? He made no reply at all.

But now he writes as if he had said thus, The words of Paul (I Cor. 11:7) should be understood as having reference to Adam and Eve; for Paul wanted to humble the men that they should not exalt themselves above women on account of their glory (which in a sense is true, but that is not the point with Paul). Micron desires to apply it to Adam and Eve and Paul said it in reference to all who are born of Adam and Eve. For he says, For as the woman is of the man, even so is the man also through the woman. Notice, he says, through the woman. For if onanism had been practiced consistently, no human progeny would have resulted. The seed must have a proper seedbed or matrix to produce fruit and to generate according to the Word and ordinance of the Lord; and therefore Paul says, Neither is the man without the woman, neither the woman without the man in the Lord. I Cor. 11:11. I trust that such plain Scriptures can be understood.

Again concerning the Scriptures of Wis. 7:2, Micron says, It does not read of man's seed alone. To which I reply, Micron must be a man who esteems the judgment of the Almighty God so lightly that he does not fear to falsify such plain words or to obscure them by his breath from the pit in such an ugly way. It is so plain that the Holy Spirit in plain words here ascribes to the father that which belongs to the father, according to the ordinance of God, and to the mother that which belongs to the mother, namely, the blood in which the seed coagulates. I repeat it that such plain words of the Scriptures are easily understood.

As to my indication that Sarah conceived of Abraham and Rebecca of Isaac (Heb. 11:11; Rom. 9:7), he replies now, although in the discussion he did not refer to it, that Abraham and Isaac are called the originators of their descendants, he says, to exclude other men, and also because woman had lost her prerogative through sin. This is such glossing as one would expect from somebody who has lost both Scripture and his reason. Therefore this is my brief reply, God does not ascribe to any that which He has not given, nor does He demand of any one that which is given Him; for He is a God of reality and not of a mere name. And if the Lord had done so for the reason given by Micron, then God would have had pleasure in the name and not in the reality. He would also have ascribed more to those patriarchs than truthfully belongs to them, and taken from woman what belonged to her. Mark what kind of God the sophistry of Micron posits.

As for the prerogative of which he writes, I would in all love ask him what kind of prerogative this was which woman has lost through sin. Is she perhaps no longer woman and is she become unfit to fulfill her maternal function in the matter of procreation to which she was ordained of God? That she is woman still and capable of performing her function in conjunction with her husband is too clear to need proof. Therefore I do not know what this prerogative might be, as the Scripture says no more than: I will greatly multiply thy sorrow and thy conception; in sorrow thou shalt bring forth children: and thy desire shall be to thy husband and he shall rule over thee. Gen. 3:16. But men must tell the plain reader some fairy tales when glosses with an appearance of Scriptural warrant are no longer available.

Dear me, if we poor folk were to abuse the Scriptures one-twentieth part as much as they do (something from which may the eternal Lord save us) and would pull the wool over the eyes of simple people as does Micron by his glosses, then (help, Lord) how they would turn up their noses at us. They would also have full right to do so. Nevertheless, however they teach and do; it is a welcome gospel to the poor, deceived world, as was commonly the case from the beginning with all false prophets and their followers. Let him break the bones of the Passover lamb and cut off Samson's hair until the time comes that it is ended with him and he has to give an account before the Lord of his seducing.

In this way Micron left us in possession of the Scriptures which say that the origin of the child is to be sought with the father and not with the mother.

After some more discussion we came to their absurd doctrine of an impure Christ; and I asked him if he confessed Mary to be of the impure and sinful seed of Adam. He answered, Yes. But he said she was pure because the angel said unto her, Blessed art thou among women. Luke 1:28. To this I replied, The Lord said unto Abraham, I will bless thee, and I will bless them that bless thee. Again he promised to the obedient parents under the law, Blessed shall be the fruit of thy body. Deut. 28:4. Does that make Abraham, together with all those that bless him and all those who are born of such pious parents, pure and without sin?

He did not reply to this but said, Christ was pure and without sin, and that because He was not born of marital intimacy, nor of the seed of a man. I replied, Out of that representation follows to begin with that the seed of the woman (if she had such, which is not the case) remained pure and sinless, and that it was only the seed of the man that became impure and sinful. In the second place, it follows that the sinfulness comes from the marital intimacy which was given in God's original creation and does not result from Adam's sin!

He then replied, God was the cause that the nature of Adam was corrupted. (I noticed that he was altogether stuck and did not know what to say further.) I asked him, Why? Because, he said, God said, In the day that thou eatest thereof thou shalt surely die. Do I hear you say that God was the cause of the transgression of Adam, together with some other remarks? No, he said, I did not say that. O Micron, I said, consider what absurdities you advance, and what a weak unscriptural position it is which you assert and maintain. He did not reply another word to this, yet he asserts in his writing now that he defended the purity of Christ before us. If that is not seeking one's own honor in giving an untrue account of the discussion, I will leave to the reader to judge.

And how the assertions which he now makes in his writings will stand in the light of the truth, we will show by the Scripture. · He writes, We can conclude nothing under sin but that which the Scriptures conclude under it. Rightly did he write that, but contrary to himself. For the Scriptures include Adam and all his seed under sin. Therefore it must be so with Adam and all his seed, as cannot be denied. He further writes, That which the Scriptures exempt, we should also exempt. Right again, but contrary to himself once more! For the Scripture exempts Christ and therefore we also exempt Him. The reason is that He is from above of God who is pure and not from below of the impure Adam, which Adam, I repeat, according to the Scriptures, is concluded under sin with all his seed, and the Scriptures do not contradict themselves.

He further writes that the apostles and prophets had no need of saying so much about the holiness and purity of Christ if He were from above and not of Adam. This is such a childish gloss that it amazes me. For if Christ were such a pure man of impure Adam as our opponents say, then the Scriptures would contradict themselves or else Adam must have had two seeds of which one was corrupt and the other remained pure, which is not taught thus by Holy Writ. What blind blows they deliver!

Finally, he writes: That which God testifies to be holy, man cannot make common or unholy, and adduces Acts 10:15. Here the most holy holiness of the flesh of Jesus Christ is by him compared to the flesh of the animals which under the law were forbidden to Israel to eat and which are now under the Gospel allowed as clean. As if Adam by a word, even as the animals under the law, was declared unclean and then again by a word (again as these animals) was made clean in this his seed of which according to Micron, Christ should be generated. By this Micron brings no little shame to the most holy holiness of Christ's flesh. Oh, what an ugly gloss!

Behold, dear reader, this is the best foundation upon which Micron can build his assertion of the purity of the flesh of Christ. At the time of the discussion, he did not advance a single word of this, but now after two years he has dug this up. You may consider for yourselves whether he does not make his doctrine suspect by such ugly and impossible glosses.

This matter of the seed of the woman was taken from him by Scriptures. He could find nothing to solve the absurdity. He was in a tight spot. So he proposed the following question, as if he were so confused that he knew not what to say and yet wanted to say something that it might not be said that he had been silenced. Said he, I wonder whether you believe that Mary was a human being. (For God's sake, Hear what he has proposed!)

On hearing this, I grew reckless and answered thoughtlessly, She certainly was not a cow, was she? (What an ugly question was this he asked me!) Now this is the way the reference to a cow got into the story, the cause of which he fails to state but the story he adduces quite strangely and little to my honor.

Some of his group have made of this, as it has been written to me out of Flanders, that I have called one of their ministers a clumsy cow, a thing which I did not do that way.

I confess before him and before all readers that I did not answer him honorably, and I am sorry for it, for I should have given him a patient answer, not to have returned foolishness with foolishness. But to which of us the greater blame should be attributed, to Micron with his surprisingly impolite question or to me with my unseasoned answer, this I would gladly leave to his own consideration if he were impartial.

After this had taken place I had but little desire to discuss with him at that time, for I saw that he so quite partisan-like placed himself against the truth, although he had nothing to advance whereby he could defend his position. So I was led to say: Excuse me, good Martin, but it would be well if you would learn to know yourself better, for you are too young in the Scriptures (I did not mean his youngness in years) to defend the foundation of your doctrine in regard to this matter.

Listen, he said then, I will tell you something else. But as it had no foundation at all and was nothing but senseless sense, and as he went from one thing to another, I answered recklessly: Away with your talk. All you adduce is nothing but anathema.

He then became very angry and cried out thrice: The pope has taught you that. But I answered with the same words three times, Not the pope but Paul has taught me this. Gal. 1:8. For it is a strange gospel, your philosophy about Christ which is not taught us by the apostles nor by the Scriptures. I did not say a word about I Cor. 16:22, although he without any truth, as alas is his habit, says and writes this out of malice to shame me.

Once more I acknowledge that I might have listened to him more patiently than I did. Yet the Son of God has not lost His Sonship and His rights by my reckless answer, nor was Micron's anti-Christian doctrine thereby made the Christian doctrine. I became sick of answering his foolish questions, for I began to observe by what kind of spirit he was prompted.

Besides, he has quite inverted the narration of the discussion, has enlarged his ten words into very many to adorn his cause, has abbreviated mine in many instances to weaken our cause, and has written many things which were never thought of. That by which his position was vanquished, he has not mentioned at all. Yet this audacious man dares to call on God as his witness that he has given a true account. (O Lord!)

Very well, everyone will have to give an account of himself before his God, let him adorn his falsehoods and swear to them as much as he pleases. By the grace of God, I shall affirm my humble truth with yea and nay, as Scripture teaches.[5] Whosoever can believe my writings so put may do so, and those who will not believe them, I cannot prevent. I will appeal to nothing higher. I have suffered much pain and trouble for about twenty-one years for the sake of yea and nay,[6] and have borne it submissively, and I hope by the assistance of the Lord not to desert it in my old age on account of Micron's and all anti-Christians' false doctrines—let Satan portray me by his scribes and servants as he may.

## [V.] WHAT AND HOW MICRON ACKNOWLEDGED IN OUR SECOND DISCUSSION AND HOW WHOLLY UNFAITHFULLY HE HAS REPORTED THE SAME

Micron writes that he proposed another discussion and suggested that we pray. I shall let it go at that, seeing that it can neither harm nor help the matter but I know how it was done.

Now when we were assembled I asked him first of all, You recall, dear Micron, how that in our earlier discussion we talked at length about the matter of the seed of women. You heard my report at the time. What do you think of it? To what conclusion have you come?

He replied before the whole assembly with good plain words, I must acknowledge that with woman there is no procreative seed, but only a menstrual flux.

Of this unambiguous assertion he says not a word in his report which he seals with the Lord's name. The reason is that his whole case was lost in and by it. And what to think or believe of such a faithless reporter, the reader may judge, a reporter who says not a word about the weightiest matter of all, on which the whole matter turns.

Having heard this his acknowledgment I said to the entire gathering, Gentlemen, with this our disputation is really already ended, for Micron acknowledges openly that a woman has no procreative seed. Dear Martin, said I, what becomes now of all you said about this in our first discussion?

Hearing this, Micron shied away so bluntly that I was unable to keep him to his acknowledgment, when he noticed that his whole case was lost by it. For if a woman has no procreative seed as he admitted (as indeed she does not have), then one of two things must follow: either Christ had to come from the menstrual flux, that is all (as Micron acknowledged) that she had to contribute; or He had to be made of one of Mary's extremities, an arm or a leg or by some other creation—which would sound pretty absurd to the reader. Or Micron would have to confess with us that the Word became flesh, a thing which he can hardly do, whether because of his great blindness or because of jealous partisanship.

And although he went back on this and refused to admit it before the

---

[5] See Matt. 5:33-37; 23:16-22; Jas. 5:12.
[6] Menno refers to his refusal to swear an oath. *Ed.*

reader by reason of the great shame, seeing he loves his own honor more than
that of Christ as may be gathered from such conduct, yet it is evident before
God who knows it all, before himself, and before us all who heard it that it
went as I have here related. And from this, one of two things must follow:
either that Micron is an unstable, unsteady, and frivolous man, who is unable
to walk on one single path, or that he is a two-faced and false deceiver who
knows better than he teaches the poor people. It is too bad that we have to
spend our precious God-given time in the fruitless reading of the writing of
such frivolous folk who have neither shame nor the fear of God.

In the second place, I asked him if he admitted the confession which he had
made concerning the two sons in Christ at the time of our first discussion. He
answered, Yes. Then I desired Andrew (whom he calls Cananeus) to write it
down, which he did in Micron's presence. It reads thus: Two sons in Christ:
the first God's eternal Son born of Him before time, without mother and not
subject to suffering. The second, Mary's son or the son of man, born of her
in time without father and subject to suffering. In which son of Mary the Son
of God dwelt so that the man Christ who died for us was not the Son of God,
for He had no father. Behold, this was his confession which we all heard from
his own mouth and which was written down in his presence.

When Andrew had written it down, Micron said, Read it to me. After it
was read I asked him if he had not written it correctly. He replied, Yes. And
now comes this untruthful man and writes that they frequently confessed that
the Son of God died for us, although it happened exactly as related above. And
he repeats it in his writing, and says that He had no father, for on page 32 he
writes: As to the essential origin of the human substance (which human nature
or human substance he called the second son) He had no father according to the
testimony of the Holy Scriptures. And he refers to Isa. 7 and Matt. 1. In this
way the pure Holy Scriptures, because they call Mary a virgin, must be the
cover of his abominably false doctrine, notwithstanding it clearly testifies in
many places that God is His Father, and that He is the Son of God. Luke 1:31;
9:35. Now this is the man who according to his report has so valiantly discussed and so powerfully argued the foundation of his doctrine as he with
simon-pure falsehood makes his followers to believe, and gains such an illustrious wreath upon his head as he claims in his book—to his eternal shame, however. The proverb that honor shames those who seek it is true.

In the third place, I asked him since he says that the man Christ had no
father, whether he did not nevertheless call Him the Son of God. He answered,
Yes. I asked him, For what reason, whether on account of birth or of regeneration or of creation or of adoption? For if He is truthfully called a son it must
be because of one of these four reasons, or else one would speak a falsehood as
often as he would call Him a son. I received this answer: On account of neither
of these four reasons. This is all the answer he gave me, but he sought another
retreat that he might not be caught in the net of truth. This question (unanswered at the time) he now adduces in distorted form saying on page 173, that

He is called the Son of God on acount of the union of the two sons (which he cleverly calls two natures that it may not sound too strange for the plain man), of which union we can not find a letter in all the Scriptures. By this he asserts publicly that the crucified Christ Jesus, who has borne the sins of the world and has reconciled it unto God His Father, was merely one who was called the Son of God and that God is therefore a God of names merely and not the God of truth. Surely this is too much of blasphemy, that the Almighty great God and His blessed, beloved Son must hear from such a man.

In the fourth place, I asked him if he knew that Gellius Faber had issued a publication against us and if he had read it. He answered, Yes. Well, said I, how do you like it? It is an excellent tract, he said, and I have also let our brethren read it.

Ah, Martin, said I, do you extol that wicked shame so full of shameful falsehood in which the Word and ordinances of the Lord are so grievously mutilated and in which the most holy flesh of Christ is called a *boose geld*[7] and ransom? If the Lord helps me he will be answered (for when this happened my production was already to press). Behold, I tell the truth.

Then Micron said, I have spoken to Gellius about the *boose geld* and he claims that it is a mistake of the printer and that it should be *loose geld* (a ransom). Then one of our group said *loos* in this tongue means false or frivolous. Was Christ's flesh perhaps false or frivolous money?[8] On hearing this I said, I have often thought to myself, how is it possible that a man could write so awkwardly? Is it perhaps a misprint? Reflecting on the matter, said I, I remembered that John a Lasco and he saw eye to eye in this doctrine and that a Lasco wrote against me: If Christ was holy, why was He then condemned by the judgment of the Father on account of sin? Again, Christ partook of no other flesh but fallen flesh in order that He might be tempted and might be subject to death. And since these men are agreed, I thought, and since these sayings of a Lasco openly say that Christ was not holy but that He was of a sinful flesh, guilty of death, therefore might in the same manner Gellius[9] write a *boosegeld* and ransom? Behold, thus I answered and not otherwise.

When I related this, Micron asked to read the assertions of a Lasco. This

---

[7] The Dutch word *boose geld*, if there were such a word, would mean "bad or wicked money." But *boose geld* is plainly a misprint for *loose geld* which would mean the same as "ransom" (cf. the German *erlosen*). In the text it actually serves as a synonym for "ransom." That this *boose geld* was a misprint Menno and his associates must have known; but the episode offered an opportunity to twit Micron for his view of the incarnation, a view which Menno considered sub-Christian. *Tr.*

[8] Menno's associate, who was probably from the South, was unaccustomed to the long vowel in *loose geld*, for in his area, as in modern Dutch generally, it was written and pronounced *losgeld*. His remark, not too seriously intended, that *loos* means "false" or "frivolous" was prompted by a possibility which he saw to twit Micron further. Notice that Menno does not take up his associate's suggestion that *loose geld* would still mean "bad money." *Tr.*

[9] All the later editions have: as the learned ones *Geleerden* have written. The earlier edition of 1646 has merely the abbreviation *Gel*—no doubt an abbreviation for Gellius rather than for *Geleerden*. *Tr.*

granted, at last, having studied long enough, he said, It is written a bit obscurely. Obscurely, said I, yes, wickedly. And this discreet reply of mine he has not only suppressed but twisted it lamentably to my shame. Besides he has left the expressions of a Lasco out of the narrative and in this way he blames me for that which others have done. Whether this was done out of the spirit of truth which is without partiality and with true Christian love as if standing before God, I will leave to the all-seeing God and to his own conscience.

Inasmuch as I have found it printed in his book, and since the sayings of a Lasco imply that Christ's flesh as a flesh guilty of death as has been heard, which may rightfully be called *boosegeld* and ransom seeing he deems it to have been sinful, then what (Dear me) have I said, about which to make such a fuss, and so mortally to wound me as he perhaps thinks? The more so since it is their position and the unmistakable result of their doctrine. But now he must by sheer falsehood do Gellius a favor at my expense, although at one time after they had received my reply he spoke quite differently to some preachers at Emden about Gellius and his book.

We took up next the absurdity of including two persons in Christ to which Micron answered, We do not assert that there are two persons in Christ, but we say there was but one person. For although the Word was from eternity a person, yet when it was conceived in Mary it was no person. Dear me, notice what oddities he invents.

He said further, although every man is a person and although the man Christ as man was a person as any other man, yet the man Christ if taken by Himself was no person. Is it not a shame that one has to repeat such foolish words before intelligent persons? Paul truly asks, Where is the disputer of this world? I Cor. 1:20.

When we had finished our arguments in regard to this matter, I said, I understand that some of you say, Menno said recently that the whole Christ was God's Son; but he did not prove it by Scripture. Therefore I desire to do so now, and I will read the Scriptures of the New Testament to you which testify that the whole Christ Jesus inside and out, from head to foot, visible and invisible, is God's only-begotten and first-begotten true Son, if you listen patiently as I did when you were reading. Do so, he said.

I collected about twenty-four or twenty-five strong plain Scriptures to some of which I shall refer here. The first was, The Holy Ghost shall come upon you and the power of the Highest shall overshadow you; therefore also that holy thing which shall be born of you shall be called the Son of God. Luke 1:35. Here the angel of the Lord testifies that Christ Jesus should be the Son of God, and you, Micron, say that He was not that.

The Father Himself says, This is my beloved Son in whom I am well pleased. Matt. 3:17; 17:5; Mark 9:7; Luke 3:21 and 9:35. And you, Micron, dare to contradict and say that He is not that. Again Christ said unto the blind man, Dost thou believe in the Son of God? He answered and said, Who is he,

Lord, that I may believe on him? And Jesus said unto him, Thou hast both seen him, and it is he that speaketh with thee. John 9:35, 36. Here the visible, speaking Christ confesses Himself to be the Son of God, and you, Micron, say He is not that.

Christ says, What and if ye shall see the Son of man ascend up where he was before? John 6:62. Here Christ testifies that the Son of man was from above and that He would return thither again. And you, Micron, say that the son of man is not of heaven but of the earth.

Peter answered Christ, to the question: Who say ye that I am? saying, Thou art the Christ, the Son of the living God (Matt. 16:16); and Christ blessed him for it. And you, Micron, say that the man Christ was not that.

The centurion at the cross confessed Him to be such; he said, Truly this man was the Son of God. Mark 15:39. And you, Micron, controvert it and say that He was not that.

All the apostles confessed Christ to be the Son of God (Matt. 14:32, 33); also, John the Baptist, Nathanael, and Martha (John 1:45; 11:27). And you, Micron, are not ashamed to say that He is not that.

John says, These are written that ye might believe that Jesus is the Christ, the Son of God; and that believing ye might have life through his name. John 20:31. Dear Micron, take heed; all who do not believe that make God a liar, because they do not believe the witness that He gave of His Son. I John 5:10. Yes, it is the spirit of the Antichrist, for they deny both the Father and the Son. I John 2:22. Behold, Micron, what kind of spirit you are, and we will let you judge this by Scripture, the Scripture of John. What is your answer to all those plain Scriptures which I have read?

He scratched his head again as he did during the first discussion when he was stuck on the subject of the seed of the woman. Both he and Hermes became pale, as the brethren told me, for I did not notice it. And Micron said, These Scriptures I confess to be mostly right and just. Not all? I asked. I have not added a single word but merely read from the Bible. Tell me which are not right.

I received no answer at all, but again he asked a strange question three or four times, which I refused to answer, desiring an answer to the Scriptures which I had read. At last he spoke, but merely deceitfully, that he might lead me away from my Scriptures which he could not answer because they were too powerful and plain, and also because he wanted to make a show before his group. It will be an answer, he said. Then go ahead with your questions, said I. Do you believe, he said, that Christ was born of the Father, and seated with the Father from eternity? I let him ask the question again.

Martin, said I, you do not act as becomes a true and pious man. Is that an answer to my Scriptures? Immediately he began to boast that I could not answer his question. I became sad for having begun to discuss with such a perverse man, for I saw clearly that he was not led by the spirit of truth. I said further that I had never read in the Scriptures of such a birth as the one which he inquired about, a birth which implied a sitting with God from all eternity. If you have read of it, I said, then point it out to me.

No, he said, we want to hear the answer from you. Martin, said I, shame yourself that when I want to know the Scriptures you are not willing to show them. He said again that he wanted to get the answer from me. Man, man, said I, by this you show what kind of spirit is in you. What rude contrariness to require of me that which is not found in the Scriptures. Heaven and earth have not stood 6,000 years and the Scriptures say that heaven is God's throne, and the earth His footstool, and that God is an eternal God who has neither beginning nor end. If I should ask you now, what were God's throne and footstool before heaven and earth were created, you would be obliged to answer me, while the Scriptures say nothing about it. I again received the answer: We want to hear the answer from you. Mark with what kind of spirit this man discussed.

Seeing the bait which he threw out to get a certain thing from me, I said to him: Micron, your purpose, seeing that you cannot stand before the truth, I see through. Therefore understand me aright so that you may quote me correctly. Whatever the Scripture testifies concerning the eternal, divine form of Christ, I sincerely believe, although I may not thoroughly comprehend it. That His goings forth have been from of old, from everlasting; that He is the Alpha and the Omega, the eternal Word of the Father, His Wisdom and Son, by whom all things were created; the first-born of every creature, who is before Abraham was, and other like Scriptures I do not comprehend. But that there was a birth from everlasting as you say, I cannot find in the Scriptures.

Inasmuch as I cannot find this in the Scriptures and as I am prepared to obey them unto death, therefore I make you my teacher to show me (seeing you ask such confession of me) where it is written and by the grace of God I will not in the least controvert it. For I was certain that he could not show it. We were told once more: No, we want to have the answer from you. Now judge of the spirit of those who discussed with us.

I will now leave this to the judgment of all impartial, reasonable readers whether Micron has met us in discussion as a godly, humble, kind, and pious Christian to teach me and all of us, or to be taught of us, in the matters pertaining to Christ Jesus through the Spirit and the Word of the Lord, or whether he sat with us and treated with us as a wicked, proud, cruel, and defaming Pharisee.

A ruder and uglier discussion I never heard of. In the first place, because he wanted to hear from us something which is not in the Scriptures. And in the second place, because I desired him to show it to me and he would not for the sake of truth and love do it. But Micron knew that he could not find it in the Scriptures, yet by such tricky argument, after he had lost his position, he tried to make a show among his followers who understood so little about the Scriptures. But he was caught in the net he set for us, as you may clearly see from the following account.

When I observed that he had lost all Christian reasonableness, that no Scripture would avail anything in his case, and that he strove for nothing else but to get the Word from me which he might by false addition peddle about us, I desired of him to elucidate his question a bit, namely, whether he believed that Christ from everlasting was so born of the Father that He was from eternity seated with the Father and next to Him. Three or four times he said, Born.

Born? I said. I do not contradict that, for you have heard my confession clear enough, but explain your question. It was again the same word, Born.

Then I said to Hermes, Do tell us what is your faith? He spoke in his usual, thoughtless manner and frankly said, That He was seated next to the Father.

Very well, Micron, I said, is that your faith also? He answered again, Born. (For the fox was afraid that he should be caught in his own den.)

Micron, said I, say yes or no. We have had enough of your born. Then he said, Yes. Very well, said I, then give attention.

I presume, I said, that you have read that there was a sect in ancient times which was called Tritheists because they worshiped three gods. If you have the same faith concerning the Holy Ghost that you have concerning the Father and the Son, then it is plain that you are a Tritheist, for you separate them as being seated separate one next to the other. He made no reply to this at all.

In the second place, I said, You are aware that Arius[10] was deemed a heretic because he said that Christ had a beginning. He answered, Yes. This is right, I said, but reflect. If Christ was from eternity differentiated from the Father, and seated next to Him as you say, and eternity has neither beginning nor time, then He is not the Father's Son, for in such case He is not born of the Father; and if He be born in such a manner that He was differentiated from the Father and seated next to Him as you have it, then He must have had a beginning, for the begetter must be before the begotten in a sense such as you propose. This is as clear as day. If you then are not Arians, I will leave to your own judgment. (I am yet to be replied to.)

In the third place, I said, Some ancient and recent writers have compared the eternal, divine Being to the sun. That is, they have compared the body to the Father, the brightness to the Word or Son, and the heat to the Holy Ghost. For as these three, the body, the brightness, and the heat, are one sun, thus the Father, His Word, and His Holy Spirit are one true God. And as the brightness cannot be separated from the sun and yet remain brightness, thus the Word cannot be separated from God and still remain the Word, yet the Word is not the Father, nor is the Father the Word. And therefore, you daily sing in your temples *Lumen de lumine,* that is, Light of lights. Paul says, He is the brightness of the glory of God. Heb. 1:3.

Behold, dear Micron, thus the before-mentioned writers have confessed concerning the eternal, divine Being and you have confessed so. I will leave

[10] A Greek churchman of Alexandria, Egypt. He died in A.D. 336. *Ed.*

it to your judgment whether you do not forsake their faith and whether you do not make them false writers by your confession. He did not reply so much as a single word.

In the fourth place, I said, You surely believe that Christ Jesus the Almighty Word, Wisdom, and Power of God was from everlasting. He replied, Yes. Very well, said I, if such a birth then took place as you say, that He was seated, divided, and next to the Father, then the Father must have been seated without wisdom, word, and power from eternity, inasmuch as they were separated as you assert. This is too plain to be controverted. Dear Micron, consider how shamefully you judge of God. Not a word did he reply to this.

But now he comes and says that Christ from eternity was born of the Father although yet remaining in the Father. Mark what a double tongue and unsteady spirit this person is. At the time of the discussion Christ was from everlasting, seated, divided, and next to the Father, and now He remains in the Father. In such a short space of time he has changed his mind on five points concerning the incarnation of Christ as is shown in the admonition written to him. And now he tries to cast upon me the ugly blot of his own unsteadiness, while the merciful Lord has by His grace and power for about twenty-one years[11] kept me steady in one sense and foundation of doctrine, notwithstanding the subtle onslaughts devised against me by so very many crafty spirits, as all must testify who have impartially read my books and heard my admonitions.

I would faithfully admonish all readers in love, and would humbly pray them for God's sake, for none to say or think that I by these four answers to his proposed and explained question would change or forsake my doctrine concerning the birth of Christ, the eternal Word, before every creature. No, not at all. For with all those who with the holy Paul in truth confess Christ Jesus to be the first-born of every creature and that without the intermixture of any human philosophy, with these I hereby confess to agree now and forever.

I declare that if Micron had asked in accordance with the Scriptures whether I confessed Christ as to His eternal, divine Being to be the first-born of every creature, then I would without hesitation have answered him in the affirmative. It would then also have been possible for his questions to be answered. But since his questions were the result of reason and not of the Scriptures and since he would in this way make the Word a separate person, seated next to God from everlasting, of which not a single word is found in Scripture before His ascension, therefore Micron was immediately defeated by the four absurdities concerning the eternal, divine Being, absurdities from which he could not extricate himself at all, as has been said.

Mark also that he has reflected upon the clumsiness of his mind which he without any Scripture used against me, so that he is now ashamed of his

---

[11] Menno's conversion occurred in 1535, and his renunciation of Roman Catholicism in January, 1536. The above was written late in 1556; it is dated Oct. 7. *Ed.*

own confession and words. For he says, If I am correctly informed, he never talked about this being seated next to God. If this is correctly reported, then alas it is too gross a falsehood. He also writes now that he is born of the Father from everlasting, but that he nevertheless remained in Him, as is also the doctrine of the Nicene council, of Athanasius, Erasmus of Rotterdam, Luther, Pomeranus, Melanchthon, Bullinger, and of the most sensible, learned ones, as can be easily deduced from their comparison with the sun and also from the writings of some of them.

Again he uses philosophy and not the Scriptures as was the case in the first matter which he has now retracted. For the spirit of wisdom has not left us a single word concerning the unfathomable, incomprehensible mystery of the eternal birth, whether He became separate from the fatherly Being at His birth before all creatures or whether He remained mysteriously one therewith. For God is a Spirit and we do not understand Him. John 4:24.

Since he again resorts to reason rather than to Scriptures, searching curious reason might ask him in return concerning the word, born. How can one be born and still remain in the one that gives him birth? I do not know where Micron could find a direct answer, wherewith he could stand before the disputer. Therefore I could wish that the unrevealed mystery were left with God. For all who want to follow their own reason in this mysterious depth and impose it upon this matter, these are immediately caught in the snare of the disputer, no matter how they manage.

We see clearly that the Holy Ghost has in the Scriptures hidden this mystery and He has not in any manner revealed it unto us, neither by prophet, apostle, nor by the Son Himself. It is manifest that it cannot be explained by intellect how short or how long, how near or how far He was by this birth removed from the Father since He is a Spirit. We learn from history and find in our own time how many piercing eyes have been blinded by this impenetrable brightness. Therefore I warn all pious hearts that would walk with a good conscience before their God not to speculate about this mysterious and indescribable majesty of the immeasurable, eternal Godhead, not to conclude, assert, teach, or maintain more than the Holy Ghost has revealed and taught in His holy Word, lest they by their human imagination make themselves a God which is not revealed unto them in the Scriptures. For it is sufficient for all godly souls that they have such belief, conviction, and opinion of God as His Word directs and points out, that Christ Jesus is from everlasting the mysterious, eternal Word, wisdom, and power of the Father, the firstborn of every creature, an eternal, true, complete divine Substance or Being, in God and with God, and that this same One by the power of the Almighty, eternal Spirit according to the promise became in time a true mortal man, subject to suffering, in Mary, as the Scriptures teach.

For if we had needed more knowledge and understanding of this mysterious birth, the Holy Spirit of truth who teaches His own unto all godliness, would certainly not have hidden it from us, but would have revealed or explained it to us by some of His holy apostles or prophets or by the Son Himself.

I therefore pray all pious hearts for Jesus' sake to submit their reason to the Word of the Lord, to feel and believe concerning God as the Scriptures command and teach, not to ascend higher nor descend lower and to walk before God and His church with a humble, contrite heart, and he shall find rest for his conscience. Whosoever feareth God, let him reflect upon what I write.

When he was once more hemmed in and held fast, he broke forth with a disturbed mind, as it appeared, and said, Do you perhaps believe that Christ was nourished by Mary? Yes, I said, I sincerely believe so. Fie, he said then, with your impure Christ! For if He was nourished by her, then He must also have become impure. He knew not, as I thought, what to say, so astounded was he.

Dear Micron, I said, control your heart and tongue. We speak of His origin and not of His nourishment. And if nourishment could make Him impure, which it cannot according to Christ's own word (Matt. 15:11; Mark 7:15), how much more the substance taken from such body of which the fruit should have come, as you say and teach. That Mary was born of the impure, sinful seed of Adam of which you derive the flesh or humanity of Christ, this you granted me. Nor can you produce a single Scripture of which you could prove her spotlessness,[12] as I made sufficiently plain in the first discussion.

Behold, honorable reader, here you have the principal foundation of that which Micron and Hermes have suppressed in their narration. It is easy to guess for what purpose and with what intention they have done so. It did not happen otherwise than we have here related, as is well known to the all-seeing God, to Micron and Hermes, as also to their own witnesses and to all of us who were present. He was quite exhausted in the argumentation of the question of the seed of the woman, a matter on which their whole position rests. He has admitted in the latest discussion that the woman has no procreative seed but only a menstrual flux, an admission whereby their whole case was lost, if he had not gone back on his word. He has also admitted that there were two sons in Christ, and that the crucified one was not God's son, whereby he had already relinquished the Son of God. Nor could he prove by the Scriptures the purity of the flesh of Christ, as required by his view of the matter, nor that there were two persons in the one Christ as he professes to believe, nor did he know how he could show the fatherless Christ, as he makes Him, to be the Son of God. He could not reply a single word to all the powerful Scriptures which I produced to prove that the visible, palpable, speaking, and dying Christ Jesus was God's own Son. Lastly, he was so clumsily caught in his unscriptural strange question. He is silent on all these, not even touching upon them and yet he calls upon the name and judgment of the Lord and upon my own conscience that he has faithfully narrated the matter in discussion. Therefore, I will leave it to the judgment of all reasonable, fair readers whether he has

---

[12] Menno knows nothing of any "Immaculate Conception." For him Mary had a sinful nature just as all other descendants of Adam, Christ excepted. (Compare his remarks under his eighteenth point, below.) *Ed.*

written as a true, dependable writer or as a false one; whether he won the discussion or lost it; whether he has done justice to truth and to us or whether he has done wrongfully; whether he sought the honor and glory of God or his own honor and fame; and also whether he could be considered a pious, praiseworthy, honorable, unblamable, true, and beneficial teacher or a wicked, faithless, ungodly, blamable, and lying deceiver and calumniator—seeing that he wrote through envious partiality and carnality without truth. And yet to sustain his falsehood, he has so highly sealed it, alas, as was heard.

When I had answered his last question, they left me and went to the fore part of the house. What he said there, I cannot say for certain, for I was not there myself. But I was told by the brethren that he was still arguing there, notwithstanding the weapons were knocked out of his hands by the force of Scripture. Some of their members about the doors next to the street were too noisy in their talk. For this reason some of the brethren said they had better go and asked them to lead us out of the gates. Of this he so unworthily has made, *thrust* out, that he might thereby make a greater stench and hatred for the pious and true, and make them a bad name.

Justly has the Holy Spirit likened this generation to the fearful locust of the Apocalypse whose shapes were like unto horses prepared unto battle, with crowns on their heads like gold, which however are not gold, of which Micron and Hermes have each placed one on their heads by their writings; their teeth are as the teeth of lions, and they have tails like unto scorpions and there are stings in their tails. Rev. 9. Consider what the Holy Spirit means, as also that the serpent should bruise the heel of the seed of the woman. Gen. 3:15. Methinks that they have not stung a little by this writing of theirs. The Lord forgive them and grant that they may yet, if possible, find His merciful grace.

Had they now been people of contrite hearts as they should be according to the Scriptures, small in their own sight, born of truth, gifted with the power of the Word, they would have thought, What is the use of writing? Our cause is lost, and if we now defame them, we do so out of partisanship and not with truth. For it is manifest that they do not hate us, because they have shown us such faithfulness and love in time of need.[13] But alas there was not so much prudence, honor, reason, thoughtfulness, and love found with them.

Even as we have truthfully and plainly shown all that which Micron has with great subtlety suppressed in his narrative to the dishonor of God and His holy church, so we shall now by the grace of God briefly show to the reader how far we differ from them in regard to this matter in order that thereby truth may be the more clearly distinguished from falsehood and light from darkness.

[13] See the editorial introduction to this book. Menno refers to the kindness shown the Zwinglian refugees by his brethren. *Ed.*

## [VI.] THIRTY-ONE ITEMS AND DIFFERENCES PRESENTED TO SHOW THAT MICRON WITHOUT SCRIPTURE SAYS THIS, AND WE WITH THE SCRIPTURES SAY THAT

1. Micron and Hermes have clearly and publicly confessed before us all that Christ Jesus was so born of the Father from eternity that He was differentiated from the Father and seated next to Him from all eternity. Notice that this being seated next to the Father is without Scriptural warrant.

We confess, and that according to the Scriptures, that Christ Jesus was from eternity the Father's wisdom; His eternal Word by which all things are created; that His goings forth were from the beginning and from the days of eternity; that He was before Abraham was born; that He was before John the Baptist and came after him; that He was the first and the last; the first-born of every creature. But of such a birth which implied session next to God from eternity, as Micron and Hermes acknowledge before us, we do not read in the Scriptures. Consider whether this our confession is not in accordance with the Scriptures.

2. The position and belief of our opponents is that this so differentiated Son of God did in due time assume a real son, body and soul of the flesh and blood of Mary. Note, two sons and a divided Christ.

Our doctrine and belief is that this same Word, Wisdom, and First-born, as we have confessed, in due time descended from heaven, and that He became a true, mortal man subject to suffering and death by the power of the most High and His Holy Spirit, not of Mary but in Mary, above all human comprehension. As John says, The Word became flesh. Notice whether this our confession is not in accordance with the Scriptures.

3. Micron and Hermes have frequently confessed before us all that there were two sons in Christ; the one the eternal Son of God and the other the temporal son of Mary. Notice again, two sons and a divided Christ.

We confessed, as said before, that He who was the Word, Wisdom, and First-born from eternity became the Son of man in time, a single undivided Son, whose Father was God, also from all eternity, and whose mother was Mary in time. Observe if this our confession is not according to the Scriptures.

4. Micron and Hermes have frequently and plainly confessed before us all, and still do so in their narrative many times, that the Son of man had no father, sometimes they say no near father, which is the same as no father. Notice how they disgrace both the Father and His Son, Christ.

We confess with the angel Gabriel; with the heavenly Father, with Christ Himself, with all the apostles, with Peter, with John the Baptist, with Nathanael, with Martha, and with all the Scriptures that God is His Father. Observe whether this confession is not altogether according to the Scriptures.

5. Micron and Hermes have frequently and plainly confessed before us all, and do so still in their narrative, although not so bluntly, that the crucified Jesus who died for us was not the Son of God, and is united into one with the

aforementioned.[14] Observe if this is not forsaking the Lord who has purchased them, as Peter says.

We confess, and that with all the Scriptures, that the crucified Christ Jesus is God's first-born and only-begotten own true Son, whom He has not spared, for our sake, but sent Him to be the propitiation for our sins, by His paternal, divine love; by whose blood we are cleansed and bought; who also in the last extremity confessed God the Father to be His Father, crying, Father, into thy hands I commend my spirit. Notice whether our confession is not altogether in accordance with the Scriptures.

6. Micron makes use of a simile that even as body and soul are an undivided man, thus the Son of God and the son of Mary are an undivided person. Mark for the third time, two sons and a divided Christ.

We say that what the Holy Scriptures and all the world call one, that is one, and that which they call two is two. If there are two sons in Christ which were begotten at different times, the one from eternity, the other in time; of different persons, namely, of God and of Mary, in different forms; the one invisible and not subject to suffering and the other visible and subject to suffering, according to the doctrine of our opponents; then there must also be two persons in Him; otherwise the Word was no real Son of God nor the son of Mary a real son of man; or else the one must be taken away by the other and absorbed. This by the grace of God shall not be taken from us by human reasoning without the Scriptures. Nor is such a parable of body and soul in regard to this matter known to the Scriptures; nor such a Saviour in Christ who was changed from one son into two sons, from one person into two persons of earthly and heavenly, of holy and sinful, of good and evil, of pure and impure, of blessed and accursed, of God and man, united in one Christ. Notice whether this is not in line with the Scriptures.

7. Our opponents hold that since the man Christ was born or begotten of Mary that He, therefore, must be of her flesh and seed, and they quote Matt. 1:16. Notice in the fourth place, two sons and the divided Christ.

We say, Obed was also begotten of Ruth, and Solomon of Bathsheba; yet nevertheless Boaz and David were their fathers who begat Obed of Ruth, and Solomon of Bathsheba. Similarly was the man Christ begotten of Mary, God the heavenly Father being the father who begat Him of Mary. The active voice is used in speaking of the father, the passive voice in speaking of the fruit and that through the mother. Consider whether we do not teach in accordance with the Scriptures.

8. Micron, commenting on Psalm 128:3, says that children come from the substance of the mother just as grapes come from the substance of the vine. Notice how he disgraces the ordinance of God and also the husbands.

We say that if Micron wants to gloss he should do it in such a way as to have some plausibility. For in this way he excludes man completely from the

---

[14] Reference is to the divine nature of Christ, which according to Micron's theology was united with the human nature into one personality. *Tr.*

procreative process as if the creational ordinance in the matter were useless. For it is evident that women do not bear children except from the procreative seed of man as can be learned from nature and can be read in the entire Scriptures; a thing which vines together with all other trees are unable to do seeing that God has not so ordained for them. Observe whether this is not altogether Scriptural.

9. The position and doctrine of our opponents is that the man Christ is of the natural seed of David, because the Scriptures say, Of the fruit of thy body will I set upon thy throne. Mark for the fifth time, two sons and a divided Christ.

We say that the doctrine of the Holy Scriptures is that He is David's supernatural, promised, and given Son, for if He had been David's natural son, as our opponents have it, then He must have been of Joseph's natural seed (for the evangelists count to Joseph), and then the Word did not become flesh. That the woman has no procreative seed is clear as day, and as by God's grace will be shown below from Scripture. Observe whether we do not teach according to the Scriptures.

10. Again, the position of our opponents is that the man Christ was David's seed and they quote Rom. 1:3 and 9:5. Mark for the sixth time, two sons and a divided Christ.

We say that the doctrine of the Holy Scriptures is that the same One, who was God's Almighty eternal Word from eternity, did in time according to the promise become man by God's almighty power in the Virgin Mary who was promised to a man of the lineage of David, called Joseph, to which Joseph the evangelists go back. He was thus in due time born according to the flesh of the same lineage in which He was become flesh, as the Lord had promised unto David. In this way Christ was born of the seed of David, that is, of the lineage of David, but did not become flesh of the seed of David as our opponents assert by garbling the Scripture. Observe whether we do not teach according to the Scriptures.

11. The position and doctrine of our opponents is that the man Christ is flesh of our flesh and bone of our bone and that our flesh is seated at the right hand of the Father. This he advocates in his tract on the doctrine of the church of God. In the seventh place, two sons and a divided Christ.

We say that the position and doctrine of the Holy Scriptures is that the regenerated church of Christ is flesh of His flesh and bone of His bone, even as Adam testifies of his Eve that she was flesh of his flesh and bone of his bone. But Eve was not thereby of Adam. Christ also testifies of His church which He has begotten by virtue of His holy Word in the sprinkling of the most holy blood by faith that she is flesh of His flesh and bone of His bone; but the church is not born of Christ. See whether we do not teach you according to the Scriptures.

12. The doctrine of our opponents is that the man Christ and we are of one Adam and are therefore brethren in the flesh. The foundation of this as-

sertion is that Paul says, He that sanctifieth and they who are sanctified are all
of one (that is of one Adam, as they say). Notice in the eighth place, two sons
and a divided Christ.

We say that the doctrine of the Holy Scriptures is that Christ and His
regenerated church are of one God, that is, those who hear and obey His Word.
Therefore He calls them His brethren and says, I will declare thy name unto
my brethren. For even as He is God's first-born Son, so is He also the first-
born of the brethren. Rom. 8:9. If He were our brother in Adam as our
opponents teach, then He must have been Adam's first-begotten son, for He is
the first-begotten of the brethren, as was heard. Then also all the ungodly of
the whole world who have the devil as their father, must be Christ's brethren
and sisters, as well as the regenerated ones who have God as their Father. See
if we do not teach you rightly according to the Scriptures.

13. The position of our opponents is that Christ has partaken of the flesh
and blood of His children, which cannot be explained or understood otherwise
than that He has received His flesh and blood of the children. Notice in the
ninth place, two sons and a divided Christ.

We say that they thereby violate the Word of the Lord and the ordinance
of creation. For the Scriptures say no more than that He partook of flesh and
blood. Nor was it from the outset God's ordinance that one brother should
beget the other, or children the father, but the fathers the children. If they
should say that the children are spiritual children (as is also the case, seeing
that Christ had no natural children), but that the brethren are nevertheless
carnal brethren, then to begin with they violate the Scripture in explaining
the one word which is so closely connected to the other as being understood
in a spiritual way and the other in a carnal way. Secondly, they create an
absurdity. Consider whether they teach according to the Scriptures.

14. Micron frequently writes that Christ has assumed the seed of Abraham, and refers to Heb. 2:16. For the tenth time, two sons and a divided Christ.

We say, and truthfully, that Micron adulterates the text sadly, for Paul
does not say, has taken, but he says, takes unto himself the seed of Abraham,
that is, the children and descendants of Abraham. Mark how he deals with
Scripture.

15. Micron has acknowledged openly before us all that a woman has no
procreative seed but only a menstrual flux. Yet he tries to derive the man
Christ from Mary's flesh and blood. For the eleventh time, two sons and a
divided Christ.

We say that a woman has no procreative seed but only a menstrual flux,
as she has not, according to Scriptures and Micron's own confession. Yet
if the man Christ came from Mary's flesh and blood, as they say, then He
must have come from unclean blood or from a member of Mary's body as
Eve was made from a rib of Adam. Ponder what is said here and whether we
do not teach according to the Scriptures.

16. Now Micron writes that a woman does have procreative seed of which

the man Christ was then begotten. When he discussed with us she did not have it, and now she does![14a] Observe for the twelfth time, two sons and a divided Christ.

We say that the Scriptures nowhere ascribe procreative seed to woman. but it speaks often enough of children of women, who are called the seed of women, because they conceived them of the man and in due time bore them to their husbands as may be read in Gen. 16:15 and in many other places. Observe whether we do not teach in accordance with the Scriptures.

17. Micron has written, in the tract that he made in England, concerning the doctrine of the church of Christ that the blood of Mary congealed in her virginal womb (I shame myself for writing it) into our flesh. For the thirteenth time, two sons and a divided Christ.

We say, and with God's Word, that the Word which was in the beginning with God, and was God, by which all things were made, according to the testimony of the evangelist John, became flesh in Mary—not her blood thus congealed, as Micron's shameless book teaches. Ponder whether we teach in harmony with Scripture.

18. Micron acknowledged publicly that although Mary was of Adam's impure and sinful flesh, she was nevertheless holy and pure because the angel said unto her, Blessed art thou among women. Consider whether such doctrine can be sustained with Scripture.

We confess with Scripture that since Mary was of Adam's sinful seed even as we are, therefore she was no less under sin than we are, for the Scriptures make no exceptions. If Mary had been pure on account of such a saying, then God might have cleansed the whole world by such a statement, and it would have been unnecessary for His dear Son to be sent into such pitiable form into this wicked world. Oh, no, there had to be someone else who for her, no less than for us, would satisfy the law, pay the debt, and perform the sacrifice of atonement, if we and she were to be saved. Observe whether we teach in Scriptural fashion.

19. Micron also acknowledged that although the man Christ was of Adam's seed he was nevertheless pure and sinless because He was conceived without marital contact from the seed of man. Once again consider whether such teaching can be harmonized with the Word of the Lord.

We confess before God and our readers that if the man Christ came from Adam's sinful seed, as Micron urges and a Lasco's position implies, then He was no less under the curse and sin than we, for the Scriptures, I say, make no exceptions. And in that view sin results from marital intimacy and not from Adam's transgression. Then, too, only the seed of man would have become impure and the seed of woman, if she had such, had remained pure, as was said above. Observe whether we do not teach in accordance with the Scriptures.

---

[14a] We now know from science (if not from Gen. 3:15) that Micron was right. *Ed.*

20. Now Micron writes that we should consider free from sin whatever
the Scripture frees therefrom, and that we should not declare common and
unholy that which God testifies to be holy, and he quotes Acts 10:15.

We confess and say, and that in accordance with the Lord's Word, that
the Scripture exempts none from sin but Him that is free indeed, namely,
Christ Jesus (Isa. 53:12) ; whereby it is plainly shown that He is not of Mary's
flesh, which was also concluded under sin; but that the Father's most glorious
Word, which knew no sin, became flesh. John 1:14. For He is holy and that
in truth, and shall ever remain holy. Therefore in my opinion it is great disrespect for the most holy flesh of Christ which is the true food for our souls,
the living bread given in such great love unto the reconciliation of the sins of
all the world, thus to compare it with the flesh of animals which were forbidden
as food under the law, and were therefore deemed unclean, and which are
now again under the Gospel allowed as clean and free, as was once heard.
See if we do not teach in accordance with Scripture.

21. The doctrine of our opponents is that the Son of God has for us fulfilled the law in our flesh. For the fourteenth time mark, two sons and a divided
Christ.

We say that it is the doctrine of the holy Scripture that none born of the
guilty and sinful flesh of Adam could fulfill the law which was spiritual; for
the seed of Adam was too much corrupted; and was also by the righteous
judgment of God subject to the curse. Deut. 27:26. Inasmuch then, as it became altogether helpless and weak in Adam, and the law continues to accuse
us before God, therefore He in His great love took pity on Adam and all his
seed and did not spare His own Son, but sent Him in the form of sinful flesh.
Rom. 8:3, 32. He fulfilled the law for us, who without guilt Himself died for
us guilty sinners that through Him we might live. And so He became our
holy, innocent, and spotless High Priest, Mediator, Advocate, and Reconciler
with God His Father. The glory remains to God our Almighty Father by His
blessed Word or Son, as the Scriptures teach. Observe whether we do not teach
you in accordance with the Scriptures.

22. The straightforward doctrine of our opponents is that the man Christ
who died for us was not of heaven but of earth. For the fifteenth time, notice
two sons and a divided Christ.

Our doctrine is according to the Scriptures that He was of heaven and not
of earth, as He Himself says, I am the living bread which came down from
heaven, and this bread that I will give is my flesh. John 6:51. Again in verse
62, what and if ye shall see the Son of man [notice, He says the Son of man,
who Micron says was of earth] ascend up where he was before. Again, I am
from above, ye are of this world; he that cometh from above is above all; I
came forth, says Christ, from the Father, and am come into the world. Again,
I leave the world and go to the Father. Paul also says, The first man is of the
earth, earthy; the second man is the Lord from heaven, and many other similar
Scriptures. By the grace of God, we will at the proper time plainly show what

kind of spirits these are who deny these plain Scriptures and direct the poor, ignorant people to a divided, earthly, impure, and sinful creature and Christ, also what abominations they commit by their false doctrine. Observe whether we do not rightly teach in accordance with the Scriptures.

23. Micron says, they testify sufficiently that the name without truth and reality is vain, and that none can be saved by the name unless he have above all the reality of the being, for out of the reality must the name come. Mark how he judges himself here.[15]

We say that he is right, that the name without the reality avails nothing. And yet he confesses in different parts of his writing that the man Christ, as he calls Him, had no father, still he calls Him the Son of God; he calls Him of heaven, yet he says He is of earth; he calls Him pure, yet confesses that He is of the impure seed of Adam, and says other like things. Whether or not Micron has judged himself thereby, that he calls vain and empty names, and does not speak the truth (for according to his doctrine, the Son of God is the son of man and the man Christ is the Son of God) I will let himself and all intelligent persons judge according to his own word.

24. Micron says: Since then the same human nature (he means the whole man of Mary's flesh) in which He suffered, was His own flesh and body, and not that of some other one, therefore it cannot be concluded therefrom that God's Son did not suffer for us. Mark how the mere name and not the reality must avail with him, contrary to his own doctrine.

We say that Micron manages well with his glosses, that they may not be too much concerned on account of his seductive doctrine, for at different places he says that Christ according to His human substance and nature had no father, and that He suffered in this same human substance and nature which had no father. And here he says that this was God's Son and that He suffered for us. What kind of glosses and what kind of writer this Micron is, and what one should think of his position and doctrine, I will let each one judge for himself from Micron's own writings. This is not the simple language of truth as he writes. I know not what greater shame one could invent.

25. Micron writes that the Scriptures say that the Son of God suffered and died for us. This he writes for two reasons. First, to prove the inseparable union of the two natures, the divine and the human in one person, Christ. Secondly, to show that Christ's suffering in His body and flesh could not effect man's salvation otherwise than by such inseparable union of the divine and human natures in one person, Jesus Christ. In the seventeenth place mark, two sons and a divided Christ.

We say Micron generally sings the same tune about the union of the two natures all through his appendix, a matter of which not a single word can be found in all the Scriptures. We ask nothing more than that he shall show us where the Scriptures say: This is the divine nature in Christ, or that is the

---

[15] Micron had asserted that according to Menno's view of the incarnation Christ's humanity was merely an ascribed humanity, a humanity in name and no more. *Tr.*

human nature in Christ, although I confess both these to be in Christ, but not as the doctrine and teaching of our opponents construe it. Or else that he show us where the Scriptures say this is the union of the two natures in one person as he generally dreams and relates; or that he show us where the perfect Son of God is called only of divine nature, and a perfect man, body and soul, is called only a human nature, as he would make the reader believe, in order that we may reflect upon it. If it is not Scriptural, it is anathema. Gal. 1:8. And if it is Scriptural, let it be shown us and the matter will be settled. O God! what crass deceit this is which they falsely teach the poor, ignorant people under semblance of the Scriptures.

I would further say that if it were such an inseparable union, and that the same made His suffering have the power unto salvation, as he says, then it is manifest that also the divine nature suffered. For that which is inseparable cannot be separated. Yet in other places he says that the divine nature did not suffer, whereby he makes the nature separable. Thus he contradicts himself, and lies and falsehood remain, no matter where he turns with his glosses. See if we do not rightly teach you according to the Scriptures.

26. Micron writes: They speak very unwisely of this great and holy mystery of our salvation, who say that Mary's flesh was crucified for us when the man Christ was born of her, for they do not consider that Christ was not only man, but also God. Notice for the seventeenth time[16] two sons and a divided Christ.

We say that Micron makes his glosses worse and worse, so that it must be apparent that he advocates the cause of Antichrist. I leave it to the judgment of all the world if the man Christ (mark what he means by saying the man Christ) were of the seed of Mary, derived from her substance as the wine is of the vine, and the blossom and fruit are of the tree, whether it was then not Mary's flesh and blood that was crucified for us. Although one could not say when Absalom hung in the tree, There hangs David, as he writes, yet one could have truthfully said, There hangs David's flesh and blood. We do not say Mary was crucified, but Mary's flesh and blood (mind, I speak this in the manner of Micron) was crucified; that is, if He were born of the flesh and blood of Mary, or else the whole Scriptures must be wrong which says that we are the seed, children, flesh and blood of Adam, on account of our physical birth. Mark whether we do not rightly teach you in accordance with the Scriptures.

27. Micron says that David confessed Christ to be his Lord, according to His deity, and to be his son according to His humanity. Psalm 110:1; Matt. 22:42. Two sons and a divided Christ, for the eighteenth time!

We say that the prophets call Him, without differentiation as to His divinity or humanity, our Immanuel, The mighty God, The everlasting Father, The Lord our Righteousness. Paul calls Him, Our Lord. Thomas called Him, My Lord and my God. Christ says, All power is given unto me in heaven and in earth. Paul says, That at the name of Jesus every knee should bow, of

[16] So in the text. There is an error in the count. *Tr.*

things in heaven, and things in earth, and things under the earth, and that every tongue should confess that Jesus Christ is Lord. We read also that all things are put under His feet, and that the Father gave Him to be head of all things to the church, and set Him at His own right hand in heavenly places, far above all principality and power and might and dominion and every name that is named, not only in this world, but also in that which is to come; that He is the Judge both of the dead and of the living. Whether He is not also David's Immanuel, the powerful God, Father, Jehovah, Lord, Head, and Judge, all those may reflect in the fear of the Lord, who rightly confess the Lord and His Word. Consider whether we do not rightly teach you according to the Scriptures.

28. Micron writes, If the flesh of Christ were of the substance of the heavenly Father as Menno dreams, then the heavenly Father must also have flesh and blood; or else Christ could have no flesh and blood, but would be only a Spirit, since God is a Spirit. This is blind reason and not faith.

We testify and confess before God and all our readers and that in accordance with the Word of the Lord that the eternal, incomprehensible Word is of the eternal, incomprehensible substance of the Father and has to be if it is to be God. For what can be God, with God, and in God which is not of His substance or being? We confess also that this same Word came down in time and became truly man in Mary by the almighty power of God, beyond human comprehension. Behold, so the Holy Scriptures teach and so we believe, notwithstanding Micron dares to call it dreaming.

The holy angel Gabriel, and the dear evangelist, together with John the Baptist, Peter, and all the apostles, nay, Christ Himself, certainly knew, as well as Micron and the learned ones do, that God the Father was a Spirit and that He was not of flesh and blood; yet they confessed before all the world that the visible, touchable, the eating, drinking, speaking, sleeping, waking, walking, teaching, sighing, weeping, dying, and reviving Christ Jesus was the invisible, eternal, and living Son of God, as may be plainly seen by the steady testimony of the whole New Testament. O God, what abominable snares these are to catch poor souls and to drag them to the pit of destruction!

29. The position and doctrine of our opponents is that the Word was God from the beginning, and therefore could not suffer. They refer to John 1:1. It was flesh, and could, therefore, not become flesh. Reason, notice, and not faith.

We say and confess and that by the strength of the Scriptures that this same Word which was in the beginning with God and was God did in time become man and dwelt among us. For God so loved the world, says Christ Himself, that he gave his only begotten Son. He spared not his own Son, says Paul, but delivered him up for us all. And John says, He sent his Son to be the propitiation for our sins.

All those who deny this forsake the eternal love of God who so loved us that He gave His only-begotten Son, and they deny the promise of truth whereby God promised that the Messiah should be our Immanuel, our God, and the Lord Our Righteousness. They deny the almighty power of God by which He can do whatsoever He plans and purposes. They make Gabriel a false messenger, for he said that nothing was impossible with God. They are in opposition to all the Scriptures which testify without any division that Christ Jesus is the only-begotten and first-born Son of God. They make the Father a liar; for they do not believe the testimony which He has given of His Son. They have neither Father nor Son, for they deny the Son. They remain under the wrath of God, for they believe not in the name of the only begotten Son of God. They ascribe to Christ all the gross absurdities which neither Micron nor any other man can take away from us, as may be clearly seen by his appendix, if any one has spiritual eyes to see. Consider whether we do not rightly teach you in accordance with the Scriptures.

30. Micron and Hermes say that if the Word became flesh and did not assume the flesh of Mary, then there must have been a new creation in Mary. Notice how flatly they oppose the foundation of truth.

We say that if all miracles and powers of God, by which many things were changed into different beings or forms from what they were before, were to be called new creations, then we would find many such new creations in the Scriptures, as when water was changed into wine or turned into blood, Lot's wife was changed into a pillar of salt, the dust of Egypt was changed into lice, and many other miracles. The omnipotence of God was in it acknowledged, yet it was not called a new creation in the Scriptures.

If now our opponents' position be granted (which it nevermore shall be) that the human Christ be derived from the flesh of Mary, then we leave it to the kind and impartial reader to ponder in the light of Scripture whether a new creation did not occur in the case of Christ from Mary, in a manner similar to the derivation of Eve from Adam at the beginning; for Micron himself acknowledges that a woman has no procreative seed, but only a menstrual flux, and God's creational ordinance does not permit a woman to bring forth of herself. And still a complete man, soul and body, was according to their representation derived from Mary's flesh. Notice whether we do not teach in accordance with the Scriptures.

31. Micron writes that we place in the stead of the true Christ a new unknown Christ whom neither the patriarchs, prophets, apostles, nor any of the thousands of martyrs ever confessed.

We say that Micron, as do all false prophets, grieviously slanders the pious patriarchs, prophets, apostles, and witnesses of Christ and that he violates their sure, true testimony, preserved in the Holy Scriptures concerning Christ Jesus, the Son of God. For it is manifest that the prophets confessed Him to be their Immanuel and that He was to be the son of a virgin, who without human seed was to be conceived of the Holy Ghost, for God Himself was to be the Father. They confess Him to be their mighty God, everlasting Father, their Jehovah who would make them and us righteous; that His goings forth were from everlasting; who was to be the Lord and Prince of Israel; that He was the wisdom of God, and was to show Himself on earth and dwell among men. David confessed Him to be his Lord; He was to be the Lord strong and mighty; the Lord of Sabaoth, things which no man of Adam could be. All the holy apostles, the angel of God, the Father Himself, and Christ Himself, John the Baptist, Nathanael, and Martha confessed Him throughout the New Testament to be the true Son of the true and living God, yes, to be His only-begotten and first-born Son without division. I say without division; for that the son of man was the Son of God and that the Son of God was the Son of man Peter plainly confessed, upon which also salvation was promised him of Christ; that the church should be built thereon, and that flesh and blood had not revealed it unto him, but the Father which is in heaven.

And now come these rash people who without Scriptural warrant divide Christ saying that He was not the Son of God as to the flesh but is merely called that for the sake of their invented union. They rob us of both Father and Son. They make false and untrue all the Scriptures together with all the apostles and prophets, yes, also the Father and the Son. They take the innocent apostles, patriarchs, and prophets with whom we agree in all particulars as a mere cover for their falsehood. They point us from the firm foundation of truth to the shifting sands of explanation, perverted Scriptures, and glosses. They build their church upon a man and creature, born of the impure, sinful seed and flesh of Adam without Father. And although they, poor children, are quite earthly and carnal, as may be seen from their writings and works, yet they boast that they rightly teach Christ, which none can do but by the revelation of the Father and the Holy Ghost, as Christ Himself says: No man knoweth the Son, but the Father; neither knoweth any man the Father, save the Son, and he to whomsoever the Son will reveal him. Matt. 11:27.

Observe whether we invent a strange Christ to whom the prophets and apostles have not pointed, as these untruthful people falsely accuse us before all the world.

Oh, that they were intent upon God, that they sought the glory of God and the salvation of their neighbors, and not their own vain honor and glory! How gladly would they confess that we have the pure, saving truth, and they the impure, accursed falsehood; but as it is, it is hid from them by their earthly, carnal vision.

Behold, honorable reader, here you have distinctly presented to view the principal differences between us and our opponents concerning this article. And I will now faithfully show you for further explanation their unscriptural confession, pervertings of the Scriptures, falsifications, together with their principal glosses, of which they make use without Scriptures, or with a false and garbled understanding of them, whereby they quite obscure the brightness of Jesus Christ, the Son of God, break the foundation of truth, ensnare the simple reader, deprive him of the Father and the Son, and so hold him fast in the curse, sin, and death as has been heard.

## [VII.] FORTY-FIVE UNSCRIPTURAL CONFESSIONS, EXPLANATIONS, ERRONEOUS GLOSSES, FALSIFIED AND GARBLED SCRIPTURES, REPRESENTED TO THE READER FOR THE EXPLANATION OF THIS MATTER

1. That Mary who was a natural daughter of the impure and sinful flesh of Adam was without sin and pure, as Micron confessed before us all at the discussion—of this there is not a word in Scripture.

2. That such pure, innocent, spotless, and blessed fruit as was Christ Jesus was born of such impure, sinful, guilty flesh as was the flesh of Mary, since she was a daughter of the impure seed of Adam—of this not a word in Scripture.

3. That Adam had two seeds, of which the one was holy and pure, as was Christ, and the other sinful and impure, as are we, as must be concluded from the doctrine of Micron—of this not a word in Scripture.

4. That Christ was born of the Father from eternity, and had a session apart from the Father and next to the Father from eternity, as Micron and Hermes confessed before us all—of this not a word in Scripture.

5. That the blood of Mary congealed in her virgin womb into our flesh, as Micron's shameless book teaches—of this not a word in Scripture.

6. That Sarah had an ejaculatory seed, as Micron explains the passage contrary to all exegetes and translators—of this not a word in Scripture.

7. That a woman has procreative seed, as Micron says she has—of this not a word in Scripture.

8. That Christ, the Son of God, was made of the seed of woman, as Micron has falsely rendered (Gal. 4:4), so making his Zurich brethren and Luther false translators, for they unanimously render born and not made of a woman—of this not a word in Scripture.

9. That a woman without conceived seed should bring forth of herself, as Micron says that Mary did—of this not a word in Scripture.

10. That Mary is called a virgin in the Scripture because she conceived without the reception of procreative seed, as Micron glosses—of this not a word in Scripture, but rather that she was called that because she knew no man.

11. That the Word or the eternal Son of God without mother (I write according to their position) thus united Himself with the son of man without father, that He assumed or put on the same, that He dwelt therein and so became one person and son, as is the position and doctrine of our opponents—of this not a word in Scripture.

12. That there were two sons in Christ, of which one was visible, subject to suffering and earthly, and the other invisible, not subject to suffering and heavenly, as is the foundation of our opponents—of this not a word in Scripture.

13. That the divine nature thus united itself with the human nature (whereby he means two complete sons) into one person as he so often repeats—of this not a word in Scripture.

14. That such a union of God's Son and Mary's son, as Micron invents, may be compared with the union of body and soul of man—of this not a word in Scripture.

15. That such a divided two-son, two-person, earthly and heavenly, righteous, pure and impure Christ was promised by the prophets and preached by the apostles, as Micron says without any truth—of this not a word in Scripture.

16. That Christ in such a way was God and man in one Person, as Micron teaches—of this not a word in Scripture.

17. That the human Christ who died for us had no father, as Micron blasphemes to the shame of God—of this not a word in Scripture.

18. That the Son of God is called the son of man and the son of man the Son of God, by reason of such union as our opponents assert without any Scripture—of this not a word in Scripture.

19. That from the beginning any complete man of body and soul should have been begotten without father, as our opponents assert of Mary—of this not a word in Scripture.

20. That Christ had a sinful flesh and one guilty of death, as John a Lasco blasphemously teaches and with whom Micron agrees—of this not a word in Scripture.

21. That the Word which from the beginning was God, took its tabernacle, tent, or dwelling in our flesh, as John a Lasco philosophizes—of this not a word in Scripture.

22. That the Son of God thus covered His divinity with humanity so long as He was upon earth, as John a Lasco writes—of this not a word in Scripture.

23. That the one who had transgressed had also to make good in his nature, as is the position of our opponents—of this not a word in Scripture.

24. That the Son of God fulfilled the law and reconciled the Father in our flesh, as is the position of our opponents—of this not a word in Scripture.

25. That we could not have become partakers of His heavenly and spiritual benefits, gifts, treasure, and attributes, for example, His life, holiness, righteousness, merits, etc., if Christ had not had our human nature, essence, and substance, as Micron writes—of this not a word in Scripture.

26. That the son of man who is confessed to be the Son of God by Peter, by John the Baptist, by the angel, and by all the Scriptures, said in any part of the Scriptures: No, I am not the Son of God, but He that dwelleth in me, whom you do not see, is the Son of God and because of Him I am called His Son, as of the doctrine of our opponents—of this not a word in Scripture.

27. That the angel Gabriel told Mary that such a divided son would be conceived in her, as Micron garbles—of this not a word in Scripture.

28. That Jesus Christ was not just as much God's Son according to His most holy humanity, as according to His eternal divinity, as our opponents teach—of this not a word in Scripture.

29. That the human Christ was of earth and was called heavenly only on account of some glorious attributes, as Micron writes—of this not a word in Scripture.

30. That flesh and blood come of the seed of Adam as our opponents say that the flesh of Christ is come, should be the true bread of life on account of some glorious attributes as the very words of Christ are made to say—of this not a word in Scripture.

31. That Abraham and Isaac were called the originators or the authors in the Scriptures lest it should be attributed to other men, as Micron says, without the Scriptures—of this not a word in Scripture.

32. That Christ took on Him our sinful form, as John a Lasco forces Phil. 2:7 to say—of this not a word in Scripture.

33. That Christ took on Him the seed of Abraham, as Micron garbles the text of Heb. 2:16—of this not a word in Scripture.

34. That Christ partook of the flesh and blood of the children by being begotten of it, as our opponents falsely explain the text of Heb. 2:14—of this not a word in Scripture.

35. That God was manifest in our flesh as our opponents explain the Scripture of Paul, II Tim. 3:5—of this not a word in Scripture.

36. That Christ dwelt in our flesh by being born of it, as our opponents explain I John 2:4—of this not a word in Scripture.

37. That the purity of the most holy flesh of Christ is comparable with the cleanness of the animals which were declared clean, as Micron has done in connection with Acts 10:15—of this not a word in Scripture.

38. That the most holy flesh of Christ Jesus was flesh of our impure, sinful flesh, as our opponents make the poor people believe—of this not a word in Scripture.

39. That Christ should be the Immanuel in our flesh, as our opponents propose—of this not a word in Scripture.

40. That Christ and we are brethren as to the flesh, as Micron teaches the unrepentant, gross world without the truth— of this not a word in Scripture.

41. That children of the devil, such as liars, haters, homicides, falsifiers of the Scriptures, defamers, etc., are Christ's brethren and sisters, as well as the children of God, as we must conclude from the teachings of our opponents, yes, our opponents—of this not a word in Scripture.

42. That the Son of God united Himself with human nature, that is, with a complete man of the flesh of Mary and that He ascended with such flesh, as Micron unscripturally twists Eph. 4:10 to say—of this not a word in Scripture.

43. That our flesh is seated at the right hand of the Father, as is the doctrine of our opponents—of this not a word in Scripture.

44. That Christ is our Head and we, His body, members and brethren on account of the flesh, as we must understand from the teachings and position of our opponents—of this not a word in Scripture.

45. That a man of the impure, sinful seed of Adam is our Advocate, Mediator, Reconciler, and High Priest with God the Father; and that we should together with the Father worship, honor, and serve Him as the true and

living God, as our opponents try to make out—of this not a word in Scripture.

Good reader, observe that the whole position and belief of our opponents concerning this article is built upon nothing but human wisdom, philosophy, explanations and glosses, applications and unwarranted and garbled Scriptures, whereby they make it appear as if their anti-Christian doctrine were the doctrine of Christ the Son of God, and whereby they cause themselves to be the true teachers and us the deceivers with the world, which alas knows little of divine matters. But how they will stand at the coming of Christ before His impartial judgment seat, I fear most of them will find out too late.

I will now point out to you by the grace of the Lord the absurdities that must follow with force from their doctrine and faith, in such clearness that you can see and feel that their doctrine is not of the fountain of the eternal wisdom, as Micron dares to boast without any truth, but that is exhaled from the abyss by the locusts of Apollyon. Take heed!

## [VIII.] FOURTEEN MIGHTY ABSURDITIES WHICH MUST FOLLOW FROM THE POSITION OF OUR OPPONENTS

1. It follows irresistibly from their position that there are two sons in Christ, of which one was the eternal Son of God without mother, and not subject to suffering, and the other the son of Mary or the son of man, without father, and subject to suffering. Whether or not such doctrine and faith is an absurdity, I will leave you to judge according to the Scriptures.

2. It follows mightily that there are two persons in Christ, for where there are two complete sons, there must without fail be two persons, unless the one swallows up the other and by their fictitious union quite absorbs him. If this cannot be called an absurdity, you may judge according to the Scriptures.

3. It follows mightily that the eating, drinking, sighing, weeping, suffering, dying, and crucified Christ Jesus was not the Son of God, notwithstanding He is confessed by all the Scriptures to be the first- and only-begotten, own Son of God, for they say that He had no Father. You may judge by the Scriptures whether this may not be called a blasphemous absurdity and open denial of the Son of God.

4. It follows mightily that they lie as often as they call the man Christ the Son of God; for how can He be a Son of God according to their doctrine? For they publicly write and confess that He was not derived from God's substance but from Mary's. You may judge according to the Scriptures whether this is not a blasphemous absurdity which is not conformable to the true God who acts according to truth and does not deal in empty names.

5. It follows mightily that it is a divided Christ who became a Saviour and Jesus Christ, [and that He was] of God and of man, of the heavenly and of the earthly, of the pure and of the impure, of the righteous and of the unrighteous, of the good and of the evil, and of the blessed and of the accursed, as was said before of these diversities. You may judge by the Scriptures whether this may not also rightly be called a blasphemous absurdity.

6. It follows mightily that the eternal sacrifice of atonement once offered for all the world was not the spotless Lamb which the Scriptures confess Him to be, but an impure, sinful, and accursed man of the impure, sinful, and accursed flesh and seed of Adam. You may judge by the Scriptures whether this is not a blasphemous absurdity.

7. It follows mightily that since the holy apostle Thomas acknowledged the crucified and visible Christ to be his Lord and God, and since the entire Scripture witnesses that He is our Atoner, Mediator, Comforter, High Priest, Saviour, and Redeemer, that if He were but a man of Adam's impure and sinful seed, as our opponents assert, it would evidently be that an earthly, unclean, sinful, and condemned creature of Adam's earthly, unclean, sinful, and condemned flesh is our Atoner, Mediator, Comforter, High Priest, Saviour, Redeemed, yes, Lord and God. Whether this is not rightly called a blasphemous absurdity and anti-Christian abomination you may ponder in the light of Scripture.

8. It follows mightily that if Mary begot the human Christ from her flesh, as the learned ones say, that she must have been not only the mother but also the father, for from the beginning it was ordained that in order to procreate there must be both a father and a mother and no child can be born without a father, as can be gathered from the Scriptures and nature. Whether this is not an unheard-of absurdity, judge from Scripture.

9. It follows mightily that since woman cannot of herself beget, seeing she has no procreative seed, as the Scripture asserts, and if the man Christ was nevertheless from Mary's flesh as our opponents imagine, then He must have been born of the Word, as Eve was made of Adam, and then this created Word and the created man of Mary's flesh must have coalesced into one Jesus Christ. Whether this is not a blasphemous absurdity and open shame for Christ judge from Scripture.

10. It also follows mightily that if the man Christ were of Adam's impure seed as our opponents teach, the Scriptures saying we must worship God and Him alone, and the prophet asserting, I will give my honor to none other, and it being clear that the Saviour Christ is adored, honored, and served no less than the Father, then one of two must follow, either that the Scriptures do not rightly teach us, or that we are idolaters who worship, honor, thank, and serve such an earthly, sinful, and guilty Christ as our opponents teach and advocate without Scripture. Judge from Scripture whether this is not an idolatrous absurdity and blasphemy.

11. It follows mightily that if a woman has procreative seed, which she does not have, and the man Christ were of Mary's seed as our opponents hold, then our Saviour Christ was not only of Judah but also of Syria, Canaan, Moab, and Ammon, as Matt. 1 asserts in plain language. Whether this is not properly called an absurdity and blasphemy, judge from Scriptures.

12. It follows mightily, if I am able to understand the writing of Micron, that the eternal Word became the Spirit of man, and that it only took to itself

a tabernacle of Mary's flesh; quoting Peter for such a purpose, I believe, saying He was put to death in the flesh but quickened by the Spirit. I Peter. 3:18.

If now he understands the Spirit of Christ to be the spirit which He commended to the Father, as well as the immortal Son of God with which according to his doctrine He was united, then Peter did not write enough by merely saying, quickened by the Spirit, and not as also by the immortal Son of God with which He was united. Mark what I say.

And if he understands it as having reference merely to the spirit of Christ and not also to the immortal Son as he confesses Him to be, then the Son of God must have become according to his doctrine a spirit of man, or else I do not know for what purpose he adduces this Scripture. You may judge in the light of Scripture whether this is not a clumsy absurdity and crude mask for the poor, ignorant world.

13. It follows rigidly if the doctrine of the learned ones is right, that the Almighty Word whereby heaven and earth are filled must have united itself with such a little body of the flesh of Mary and must have sighed, wept, eaten, drunk, suffered, and died with it and must have lain dead with it in the grave, or else it must have merely sheltered in Christ's spirit and at death departed therefrom and at the resurrection again united therewith the second time. You may judge from Scripture whether this is not rightly called a strange absurdity.

14. It follows mightily that if the Word or the eternal Son of God did so take on Him such a man of Mary's flesh and blood and united Himself therewith into one person and son, as our opponents speculate, then God the Father was not the true father of Christ, Mary not the true mother, Christ not a true Son, and all the Scriptures are thereby denied which confess Christ to be the first- and only-begotten, the true Son of God, without any distinction between divine or human, between flesh and spirit, visible and invisible, immortal and mortal, as we have explained above and below, with the Word of the Lord. You may in the fear of God judge by the Scriptures whether this cannot be rightly called a blasphemous absurdity and an open denial of both the Father and the Son.

Elect readers, such an unscriptural, divided, unclean, sinful, and earthly Saviour and Christ our opponents teach by their anti-Christian, obscure, involved, subtle, and dark words of human wisdom. I place before you in plain and clear words the mirror of their deceit. If you will, you may see clearly how lamentably you are deceived by them.

Their doctrine and faith are really nothing but patent anti-Christian deceit and the seduction of the old serpent, for they speak of taking unto, uniting two into one, divine and human nature, glorious attributes, etc., whatever we read or hear from them, of which we find nothing in the Scriptures. They make these assertions and adorn them with many broken Scriptures, glosses, and false applications. Therefore I say, first in Micron's own language, that all they philosophize and invent does not touch us, since it is not according to Scripture. And secondly, in the language of the holy Paul that it is anathema, since it is

a strange gospel of which not a single word is taught in the Scriptures, neither
by the prophets, nor by Christ, nor by any of His apostles, in such a sense as
our opponents teach it. Take heed!

Next we will by the grace of the Lord present to view in the first place
the basis of the confession and doctrine of our opponents concerning this article,
together with its proper contents, fruit, end, and promise, and in the second
place the foundation of our confession together with its proper contents, fruits,
end, and promise, that you may by such comparison in black and white the
more readily guard against the deceit of the old serpent, and find the sure and
firm foundation of truth, and believe and follow it with a sure conscience without hesitation.

## [IX.] THE DOCTRINE CONCERNING JESUS CHRIST AND ITS IMPLICATIONS AS HELD BY OUR OPPONENTS

Honorable reader, the following is the whole content, conclusion, sense,
basis, and thrust of our opponents concerning the incarnation of our Lord.
It is the occasion for all the hatred toward us and our bad reputation. By their
human wisdom and the cunning of the old serpent they proclaim that all the
glorious promises concerning Christ, the Son of God, contained in Moses and
the prophets, such as grace, mercy, remission of sin, peace of conscience, reconciliation, and eternal life consist in the unclean sinful flesh of Adam which
they without Scripture call clean even though it is Adam's flesh.

They confess publicly (witness their own confession) that there are two
sons in Christ, of which one is the Son of God from everlasting, without
mother and not subject to suffering, and the other the son of Mary or the son
of man, without father, and subject to suffering. Which two they say (but
without Scripture) are united into one person; so that the Man Christ who
walked, ate, drank, sighed, wept, and hung on the cross, and who cried to
His Father, Into thy hands I commend my spirit; and who lay in the tomb
three days, was not the Son of God.

They make the most holy, the ever-blessed Christ Jesus a sinful and
accursed man. One of their number writes publicly: If Christ were holy, why
was He condemned to death by the judgment of the Father on account of sin?
They say that He partook of sinful flesh that He might be tempted and be
subject to or guilty of death. They expect salvation of an earthly, sinful creature of the unclean, sinful flesh of Adam and make Christ Jesus not only of
the sinful and accursed flesh of Adam, Abraham, and David, but also a Gentile
of the Gentiles, namely, a Syrian of the daughters of Bethuel and Laban, a
Canaanite of Rahab, a Moabite of Ruth, and an Ammonite of the mother of
Rehoboam the son of Solomon.

They make a creature of the unclean, sinful flesh and seed of Adam their
throne of grace and atoning sacrifice, their High Priest, Mediator, Advocate,
Intercessor, and Reconciler, and they falsely call Him the Son of God. I say

falsely, for they publicly confess that He had no father. They call Him their Lord and God and yet they say and write that He is of earth and not of heaven. They worship, honor, and serve Him as they do the Father Himself. Oh, horrors!

They dissect and violate the Scriptures because they do not believe the testimony of John that the Word was made flesh; they falsify the plain confession of the angel of God, the Father and the Son Himself, of John the Baptist, of Peter and of all the apostles, of Paul and of all the Scriptures, which unanimously testify that the conceived, born, suffering, entire Christ, outwardly and inwardly from top to bottom, visible and invisible, is the first- and only-begotten Son of God without any divisions.

They dissect and violate the whole Gospel and the noble and precious epistle of John in which he testifies more than sixty times that Christ confessed Himself to be the Son of God and confessed God to be His Father; also frequently that He went forth from the Father and that He was sent and came from heaven.

They twist and abuse the Holy Scriptures quite sadly, heap one ugly and unwarranted explanation upon another. Christ, they say, has assumed our human nature of Mary; now it is two sons and natures combined into one person and son, and then the Son of God has put on the flesh and blood of Mary, has dwelt in it, as in a tent or tabernacle.

One of their learned ones writes, The Son of God has brought all His qualities to the son of man. Another writes that the man Christ was God's adopted and accepted Son. Still another that the one nature in Christ was altogether divine and the other half divine and half human. Some write that the divine nature also suffered. Others write and say that He suffered only in His human nature and not in His divine nature. Micron says that Mary's blood became in her our flesh, that Christ's flesh is of our flesh, and that notwithstanding He is of earth and of Adam's seed, He is still called heavenly on account of certain excellencies, and other like accursed words and odd and willful glosses and abominations of which not a word is found in the Scriptures.

Is it not a pitiful shame, nay, a horrible and grievous thing, to wade in such pure, limpid waters with such filthy feet and thus to obscure the precious and bright Son of righteousness with such infernal exhalations of the anti-Christian doctrine? And that for no other reason than that they do not trust the testimony of John and of the angel, do not believe the almighty power of the Father, but judge everything according to nature and not according to the Scriptures, and attribute more to Mary than belongs to a true mother, according to the ordinance and Word of the Lord.

From which it follows mightily, yes, is evident according to the doctrine and testimony of John, that they alas have neither the Father nor the Son, that the wrath of God abides on them, that they shall not see life: for they do not believe in the name of the only-begotten Son of God. They must die in their sins, for they do not believe it is He; they do not overcome the world;

they are not in God nor God in them; for they do not confess that Jesus is the Son of God. Oh! how well it would be if these poor people would take heed, rightly confess Christ the Son of God, and give Him His due praise and honor.

## [X.] THE DOCTRINE CONCERNING JESUS CHRIST AND ITS IMPLICATIONS AS HELD BY US

Our position is, and that according to the Scriptures in power and truth, that the whole Christ Jesus, visible and invisible, inside and out, mortal and immortal, is the first- and only-begotten Son of God, as the angel, John the Baptist, the apostles, and all the Scriptures confess Him to be; that He is the incomprehensible, eternal Word by which all things are created, supernaturally come from heaven. We hold that by the power of the Holy Ghost He became man in the Virgin Mary who was espoused to a man of the house and lineage of David, named Joseph, above all human understanding. We hold that in this flesh He was begotten in her and in due time born of her, a single undivided person, Son and Christ, God's true and natural Son as to origin and essence, and Mary's supernatural Son as to His conception. I say supernatural, for it was not brought about by the usual marital intimacy. It was promised that He should be born of the lineage of Abraham, Isaac, Jacob, Judah, and David, as it also happened. He is by reason of His mother, Joseph's wife, called in the Scriptures the righteous Branch of David, a rod of the stem of Jesse, the fruit of the loins of David, represented by the literal Solomon. He is Wonderful, Counselor, the mighty God, the everlasting Father, our Immanuel, our God, the Lord our Righteousness, the Wisdom of God, the Lord of David, the Lord strong and mighty, who in the beginning founded the earth and made the heavens, our new and spiritual Solomon, seated upon the new spiritual throne in the new and spiritual kingdom and reign of David; God's true Son, I say, by reason of His Father; Abraham and David's son by reason of His mother: a single, undivided Son of God and Mary come forth from the Father, descended from heaven, conceived in Mary, born of her, a true man, like unto us poor children of Adam in all things, sin excepted. He hungered and ate, thirsted and drank, became tired and rested. He was fashioned in the likeness of men; He has fulfilled the law for us; He sought the lost sheep, taught the kingdom of God, and confirmed His mission by miracles and signs. At the last He died the bitter death innocently for us who were guilty when we were yet ungodly and enemies. He has purchased, sanctified, and cleansed us by His own blood and not by the blood of another; He has reconciled us with God our Father, made us kings and priests. He was delivered and raised from the bonds of death and ascended to His Father where He was before. By His precious crimson blood He became our only and eternal High Priest, Intercessor, Mediator, Advocate, and Reconciler with God His Father. He is our Lord and God, whom we in our weakness should honor and praise because of His infinite love and grace as much as we honor the Father Himself.

We confess that even as the Almighty, eternal Father through mere grace and love has in the beginning created Adam and Eve by Christ His Almighty, eternal Word, so He, now that they together with their entire seed have fallen,[17] has by the same Word, by His almighty power, made man, raised them up again out of pure grace and love, accepted them as His children in order that we should eternally thank and praise God for His grace—through the Word or Son and not through Adam's sinful flesh.

With such a confession the whole Scripture remains in this matter unbroken and unchanged. Not an absurdity or gloss or false assertion is found, as alas they are found on every hand with our opponents.

The Almighty, eternal God retains His glory and honor by His Word or Son. The Father remains the true Father of the whole Christ, the mother the true mother, and the Son the true Son of both His Father and His mother, a Son from above and not from beneath, of heaven and not of earth, pure of the pure God, a single Son and person, the King and Lord of heaven and of earth, a Saviour of all the world, in whom all the present and future promises are contained, by whom they are transmitted and received. Eternal praise be to His adorable, glorious, and exalted name. Amen.

All those who can in this way firmly believe this wondrously high work of the inexpressibly great love of God and who can confess with Peter and all the Scriptures that Christ Jesus is the true Son of the true and living God; they have both the Father and the Son; they overcome the world; they are in God and God is in them; they are saved from the wrath of God and have eternal life; they acknowledge the severe justice and the merited curse which came upon Adam and all his descendants through Adam's disobedience. They, therefore, fear God, bury their sins, and turn from evil. They equally much acknowledge the inexpressible love of God so richly shown us in Christ Jesus; they enter newness of life with Christ, for they believe in the name of the only-begotten Son of God.

Honorable reader, take care! I warn you in sincere and faithful love, for it concerns eternal life or eternal death. If you are not wholly blind, you must notice the dishonesty which Micron has used, and also by these thirty-one differences, forty-five unscriptural confessions, explanations, and unwarranted glosses, falsified and garbled Scriptures, and by these fourteen insolvable, blasphemous absurdities that his inconsistencies, together with the basis of their confession concerning this matter, faithfully and plainly set forth, are nothing but anti-Christian deceit of the old serpent. You will notice also that our position and faith, on account of which we must alas hear and suffer so much, are the firm, immutable, invincible rock and stone of the eternal truth which the holy apostles and prophets, together with all the pious witnesses of God in the

---

[17] The text is ambiguous; the expression "with their entire seed" may be construed either with "fallen" or with "raised." We have chosen the former alternative since it is not likely that Menno would have consented to the universalism implied in the other alternative. *Tr.*

first, uncorrupted church, confessed before the man of sin (who cannot bear this position as may be seen, I John 2:22; 4:3; II John 1:7) entered and was seated in the temple of God.

Not a single Scripture is falsified or broken by us. Not a single gloss is made. To not one absurdity are we driven. It is the plain Scripture and its foundation which we present to the reader, as you may feel with your hands and see with your eyes.

But even though our exposition is more than enough, as it seems to us, yet we wish to point out over and above that, with the power of the Scriptures and with the observable facts and ordinances of creation, that the procreative seed, the matter on which our opponents' entire case rests, is not to be sought with the mother but exclusively with the father. We add certain other articles moreover. By these our opponents' entire position and doctrine must go down in the minds of all pious and sensible people as sophism, impotent and anti-Christian and seductive, ours being evaluated and judged to be evangelical, powerful, beneficial, and godly. He who fears God may consider what we write.

## [XI.] MISCELLANEOUS ITEMS TOUCHING THE INCARNATION

*[A.] Matt. 1:16 and its bearing on the view that procreative seed is found with the father and not with the mother.*

*Of whom was begotten Jesus who is called Christ.* These words Micron takes to be, it seems, the strongest and principal argument of his whole doctrine concerning the incarnation of Christ. He takes them to mean that the Word did not become flesh, as John says, but that it became a complete man of body and soul by the process of begetting (as they beautify it), by assuming it from Mary's flesh and blood in unity of person, as they gloss the passage.

With these few words I wish to reply simply and plainly to his lengthy composition and with this same text in Matthew. Boaz was begotten of Rahab. But by whom? By Salmon, was it not? Obed was also begotten of Ruth. But by whom? By Boaz, was it not? Solomon was begotten of Bathsheba. But by whom? By David, was it not? You must agree, for Matthew is my witness.

In the same way Christ was begotten of Mary, but by whom? Was it not by God? Again you must agree, for the angel of the most High is my witness.

For even as Salmon, Boaz, and David begat Boaz, Obed, and Solomon, from Rahab, Ruth, and Bathsheba respectively; Salmon, Boaz, and David being the fathers who begot them, and Rahab, Ruth, and Bathsheba being the mothers from whom they begot them; just so God the Father begot His Son, now become man, from Mary; God the Father being the one who begot Him, and Mary being the mother by whom He begot Him. Observe that this our position is stronger and clearer than all learned philosophy and garnished glosses under heaven. Ponder whether we do not direct you to Scripture.

It is plain that they build their entire structure on this position—that the man Christ was begotten of Mary's seed, as was said. Out of it and based on it they fashion all their glosses, explanations, perversions of Scripture, and bold claims wherewith they entrance the poor, plain reader. Therefore I hope by the Lord's help and grace to explain to all unbiased and sensible readers with so forcible an argument from Scripture, and also from observable facts of God's ordinances, that men may see with one eye shut that procreative seed of which and by which the human race exists and multiplies is to be sought with the fathers and not with the mothers. Even as Micron openly admitted in plain terms before the assembly but now retracts again like an unstable and unsteady person.

I want to request the honorable and reasonable reader, for God's sake, as I did once before, not to take it ill of me that I am forced to repeat this matter. The extreme necessity of the honor of Christ necessitates me to do so, seeing that it is our opponents' strongest argument in which all their seduction in this matter is contained. They disgrace the Christ, the Son of God, so greatly. They sustain the whole wide world in its great blindness. I am constrained therefore out of love for my Lord and Saviour Christ and for your poor souls to expose this position with fear and trembling so that you may in truth grasp and perceive that their whole position as to this begetting of Mary, about which they make such a noise, is nothing but drifting sand, and cannot stand before God's Word any better than the flax can stand before the fire.

That men have the procreative seed is first of all evident from the story of Onan and his censurable conduct as recorded in Gen. 38:9. Then too it is evident from some of the Mosaic institutions and regulations as recorded in Lev. 15:16; also Wisd. 7:2 is pertinent. Finally, it is also evident in your own body, if you have come to manhood, in the function which God has in His blessing you and all men according to creation.

Therefore you have clear Scripture and your own body teaching you in all clarity that to men has procreative seed been given. Since these things are clear from Scripture and nature, therefore I request Micron and his kind to show by a passage from Scripture that any woman has at any time committed the sin of Onan or was in need of the purification regulations of Moses. Then we will see further. You know very well that they will not be able to do it, but what sort of pollution occurs in women they themselves know best. It is mentioned in Lev. 15:19 and many other places.

In the second place it is evident that procreative seed is present with men and not with women. The patriarch Judah and his brother Simeon had each a Canaanitish wife. Gen. 38:2; Ex. 6:15. Joseph had an Egyptian wife (Gen. 41:45); Moses a Midianitish (Ex. 2:22), and Aaron of the tribe of Levi had a daughter of Judah to wife. Ex. 6:21. Jehoiada the high priest had the daughter of Joram to wife, also of the tribe of Judah. II Chron. 22:11. Now if our opponents' position were correct, which it by no means is, namely, children have their origin as much in the mother as in the father, then the children of Judah were half Canaanites by virtue of their Canaanite mother, Shuah; the children of Simeon also; the children of Joseph half Egyptian by the Egyptian mother; those of Moses half Midianite; and half of the entire priestly tribe first by the wife of Aaron and then by the wife of Jehoiada must have been of the tribe of Judah. But not a letter is found in the Scriptures that priestly dignity did also adhere in the tribe of Judah.

In the third place it is plain that procreative seed is to be sought with men and not with women from the genealogy of Christ given in Matt. 1; for if one takes due cognizance of the foreign women occurring therein, then it must follow that Christ the Son of God was first a Jew of the Jews, then a Syrian of the Syrian Rebecca, in the third place a Syrian again out of the Syrian Leah, in the fourth place a Canaanite of Rahab, in the fifth place a Moabite of Ruth, in the sixth place an Ammonite of Naama, the mother of Rehoboam. In this way five sixths of Christ would be heathen: two parts Syrian, the third Canaanite, the fourth Moabite, the fifth Ammonite, and only the sixth part would remain to Abraham even though he and not the Gentiles had so repeatedly received the promise of the blessed seed, as can be read in Genesis repeatedly.

Now when we restrict the procreative seed to the father, Judah remains Judah, Simeon remains Simeon, Joseph remains Joseph, Moses remains Moses, and the priestly tribe the priestly tribe. Then the promises go on unaffected. The tribe and the name continues in the case of Abraham, Isaac, Israel, Judah, and David, not the foreign strains, although some had married into them, as has been said. It seems to me that all unbiased and reasonable readers would be able to understand such straightforward and untwisted Scriptures.

In the fourth place it appears that men only have the seed of procreation from this plain Scripture. The Lord said to Abraham, This shall not be thine heir, but he that shall come forth out of thine own bowels shall be thine heir. Gen. 15:4. (Notice, it says of thine own bowels.) Also, I will make thee exceeding fruitful and kings shall come out of thee. Gen. 17:6. (Notice, it says out of thee.) Again, Hagar bare Abraham a son, and Abraham called his son's name which Hagar bare, Ishmael. Gen. 16:15. Again, through faith also Sarah received strength to conceive seed [from her husband that is, to carry it, etc.], and therefore sprang there even of one so many descendants as the stars of the sky in multitude, and as the sand which is by the sea innumerable. Heb. 11:11. Again, Sarah conceived and bare Abraham a son in her old age. Gen. 21:2. Again, Levi was still in the loins of his father (notice, it says the loins of his father) when Melchisedec came to meet Abraham. Heb. 7:10. Or, Rebecca had conceived by one (notice this) even our father Isaac. Rom. 9:10. Also, be fruitful and multiply (God said this to Jacob). A nation and a company of nations shall be of thee and kings shall come out of thy loins. Gen. 35:11. To continue, all the souls that came out of the loins of Jacob (notice, out of the loins of Jacob) were seventy souls. Ex. 1:5. And the daughters of Lot took steps to preserve seed of their father (Gen. 19:32), or, if a woman shall have conceived seed and born a man-child. Lev. 12:2. Also, the man is not of the

REPLY TO MICRON                                    889

woman but the woman of the man; as the woman is of the man so also is the man by the woman. I Cor. 11 :8 and 12. Again, congealed in the blood from the seed of man. Wisd. 7 :2.

You see, worthy readers, although our opponents collide as with blind eyes with these and similar passages of which the Bible is full, yet they will have to leave this position to us unviolated, namely, that the origin and substance of the child comes from the father's body or loins, that women come of men, that mothers conceive seed from the fathers, that in the blood of the mother the fruit congeals with the seed of the father, and that in this manner mothers bear children unto the fathers, as is plain enough from the recited Scriptures.

In the fifth place it is evident that the procreative seed is found with men and not with women from a consideration of the mystery or glory which Paul indicates of Christ and His church. Eph. 5 :23. Christ our spiritual Father begets His spiritual children through preaching accompanied by the power of the Holy Spirit and of His spiritual seed, that is, His Word, and of or through His spiritual wife, the church. And this same spiritual wife has no other spiritual seed of spiritual procreation than that which she receives of her spiritual husband. Just so every physical man begat his physical children by or through his physical wife with which he is according to God's ordinance wed and one. He does this by his physical seed that has been given him, for this is God's blessing. The same physical wife has no other seed of procreation than that which she receives of her physical husband, I say, just as the spiritual woman has from her spiritual husband, as may be seen in the entire Scriptures and in the processes of the ordinances of God.

In the sixth place it is plain that procreative seed is found with man and not with woman in the creation of both man and woman, and also from the very word *seed*. For no learned one can deny that the word seed is related to the word sowing. The Greek term is *sperma,* and the Latin *semen.* The Germanic tongue has seed; the same word is used for insemination whether of fields or of the maternal matrix.

Seeing then that it is such seed which is sown, therefore there must be a sower who sows it in suitable fields on which to sow. Now consider carefully the creation and the position of both parties, namely, of men and of women and then you will observe of whom sowing is pertinent and of whom the being sown. In this way you will get a proper understanding of this matter.

And although this position is irrefutable in the comparison of field and sower, and is sustained altogether by Scripture as may be seen, yet Micron cannot leave this position unviolated but asks where this comparison occurs in Scripture so that he may have something wherewith to make me suspect in the eyes of the reader, as though I had urged not Scripture but unsupported reason against him. And the good man has completely forgotten that he has made so very many ugly glosses, perversions, and falsifications of Scripture, explanations, and the union of two persons or natures as glorious qualities, etc. —things which are not mentioned in Scripture so much as a single letter. But how can he refer to my words fairly when he twists and misinterprets the plain and lucid witness of the Almighty Father and of His blessed Son, yes, of the angel and of all the apostles?

Since things pertaining to the procreation of man stand thus according to Scripture as we have explained, therefore it would be well if our opponents would grasp the meaning of the expression, increase and multiply, in Gen. 1:28 a bit more clearly, and ascribe to men what pertains to men, namely, the insemination; and to women, yes, to women what pertains to them, namely, the reception and the bearing, and would not agitate so ignorantly, as though the sowing had been ordained by God to both parties equally much as they alas without Scripture do now.

It would be good also if they took notice that the sower's ability to sow continues as long as he has strength, but that the field, namely, the woman, though sown, ceases to flower at the age of fifty or thereabouts.

In the seventh place it is plain that the seed of procreation is found with men and not with women from the fact that if woman did have procreative seed, of which human fruit can come, as our opponents hold, then it is plain that women could be both fathers and mothers of their children and that the father would be unnecessary since women would have the procreative seed plus also the nurture and everything else from which the human fruit can come, increase, and be born. Let everybody ponder that God's ordinance is not in vain. Once more I hope that such plain and straightforward speech will be understood.

In the eighth place it is plain from the following that procreational seed is to be found with men and not with women. We know that God is a righteous God who wrongs no one and accepts no one's person, be they men or women. With this the Scripture is full. And it is plain that the father's function occurs without distress and not over a lengthy period of time, but the mother's function, to the contrary, after conception must be borne about nine months long with a great deal of bodily distress in the mother; she must nurture and carry and with danger to life bring forth, and even after that must for a long time nurse, tend, and assist. And yet the jurisdiction over the children is throughout Scriptures ascribed to the fathers and not to the mothers. If now the origin of children were as much of the father as of the mother as our opponents hold, then it would seem that God gives less than their due to women, taking from the poor slaves their children; theirs by so much inconvenience, and assigning them to the fathers who have been so little troubled for them.

The ancient writers of jurisprudence seemed to have had a proper insight when they ascribed to the nobility a child born of noble father but of a commoner mother and denied nobility to a child born of a commoner father and a noble mother.

Dear reader, here you have all these precious clear declarations of Holy Writ, all these irrefutable arguments drawn from creation as well as the demonstrable practice in your own bodies, clearly and plainly set before your eyes, showing the procreative seed occurs with men and not with women. If now you still say that you cannot see it, then I say that you are like unto a person who shuts his eyes in broad daylight and asserts that he cannot see that it is day. For I do not know how it could be still more plainly and bluntly said.

This I know of a certainty, that even if all our opponents were sharp tongues, and each of their hairs a clever writer, they would still have to let us retain this our position that procreative seed is found of men and not with women. Firm and immovable is the Word, sealed with the Holy Spirit's own witness, congealed in blood, of man's seed. Wisd. 7:2.

In this it is evident that our opponents are already vanquished with all their glosses, explanations, perversions, their talk of assuming, of union, glorious qualities, etc., and their perverted Scriptures by this our irrefutable exposition. They will have to confess in their hearts that they have cheated the people with this begetting of Mary's seed, and that if the man Christ were of Mary's flesh He would have to be derived from the menstrual flux, or from a drop of blood, or from one of her extremities. In that case He should not be called woman's seed but only woman's blood or member, as is crystal clear.

[B.] *How the expression,* seed of the woman, *is to be understood according to Scripture.*

When Micron says that to woman also procreative seed is ascribed (Gen. 3:15 and Ruth 4:12), this is my cordial reply. Just as it is plain that the seed that the farmer sows cannot attain to fruitfulness otherwise than by means of the proper and God-ordained means thereto, namely, the field, so it is also plain that insemination takes place not of the woman but by her husband and that therefore the seed cannot come to its fruition except by means of the proper and divinely prepared means, namely, the woman.

The fruit of the same sown seed of the farmer comes forth by means of the field and is therefore called the fruit of the field, and that rightly, for the reason that there would not be nor could be according to God's ordinance in nature any fruit except through the field. So also man's children which come from his seed through the wife are called her seed for the reason that there could be no fruiting except through the wife, as is evident.

And that the word seed usually refers to descendants, children, or progeny in the Scriptures is too plain to require many words. So Abraham spoke to the Lord: Thou hast given me no seed. Gen. 15:3. Abraham did not complain of the lack of unborn seed, but his complaint was that God had not given him children of it.

Mary also said (Luke 1:55), As he spoke to our fathers, to Abraham and his seed forever. She said this of Abraham's descendants and not of procreative seed, for Abraham was long since dead.

Paul's position is no different when he asserts that he was born of the seed of David. He meant that he was a descendant of David. For when Paul said that, David had long since returned to the dust from which he had been taken.

At another place Paul says (Heb. 2:16), He took not on him the nature of angels, but he took on him the seed of Abraham, namely, his children and descendants, which will take place to the end of time.

Similarly Nathan said to David: And when the time comes that you shall sleep with your fathers, I will raise up of your seed which shall come from your loins (that is, by means of your son who shall be born to you, for procreation is out of the question in the case of a man deceased). At the time of this promise, Solomon was not born as yet.

Seeing then that it is clear that procreational seed is found with men and not with women and that the word seed commonly refers to children and descendants, therefore it is plain that the expression, the seed of the woman, means no more in Scripture than woman's children, descendants, or progeny which they have borne of seed received according to God's ordinance from their husbands, and in due time brought forth by birth.

Therefore the friends of Boaz said to him when he was about to marry Ruth, May your house be built as was that of Peres whom Tamar bare to Judah of the seed [that is, the children] which the Lord will give you of this woman. The said Tamar when she was about to be capitally punished said, By the man [notice, she says, by the man] whose these are I am with child. Gen. 38:25. And so Tamar has answered Micron's contention which he flings at us about Ruth and the seed of the woman.

And what Micron says of Sarah and his assertion that the common translations of Heb. 11:11 are faulty, I say boldly and bluntly that he is a patent falsifier of the Holy Scriptures, for neither the Scriptures nor the order of nature assert that woman has ejaculatory seed. Read Luther's translation, that of those of Zurich, Erasmus of Rotterdam, Sebastian Castellio, together with all the rest who could teach the languages to either of us for three or four years. Nowhere will you find such a rendering as Micron has out of partisan bias offered. Everything he now or at any time brings up out of the Scriptures concerning the seed of the woman has the same meaning and is hereby refuted already.

[C.] *Concerning Gen. 3:15, I will put enmity between thee and the woman and between thy seed and her seed.*

Micron accuses me with saying that we should not understand the expression, the seed of the woman (Gen. 3:15), in a carnal but in a spiritual sense only. I deny this flatly. For never in my life was it my intention to exclude Christ from this promise. But I have said repeatedly and say now that with this passage the notion that women have procreative seed cannot be established. For as the deceived Eve was a literal woman, so also was the deceiving serpent a literal serpent into which the devil had entered. For the Lord said, Upon thy belly shalt thou go, and dust shalt thou eat all the days of thy life—something which the devil who is a spirit could not do. If now we are to understand the seed of the woman as procreative seed, as Micron does, then also the seed of the serpent must be understood as procreative seed between which two the enmity would exist, for what is said of the one seed must apply also to the other (for one word serves for both). In that sense the literal serpent only would be vanquished by Christ. Understand rightly what I write.

On the other hand, if the serpent be a spiritual serpent, as it indeed is, represented by the deceiving serpent, then the woman must also be a spiritual woman represented by the deceived woman, and so again what is said of the one seed must apply to the other, for if the serpent is spiritual, so also is her seed, which is falsehood, spiritual (John 8:44), of which alas the serpent begets such people as write such deceiving, lying, slanderous, proud, and biased books as Micron and Hermes have done in this instance.

In the same manner as the woman is spiritual (Eph. 5:25; Rev. 12:6; 19:7), so also is her seed spiritual, that is, the truth of which (eternal glory be to God for His grace) she begets such children as walk in the truth, sincerely speak the truth, and for the sake of the truth with yea and nay willingly submit to death.

And behold, between these two, the children of truth and the children of falsehood, there is an eternal enmity. The seed of woman overcomes, and that by sincere firm faith in Christian patience by the Spirit and Word of the Lord; yet it is often bitten in the heel by the vanquished seed of the serpent. For their name is reviled, their doctrine is censured, their life is hated unto death, their chattels are stolen, their flesh is burned, and they are drowned, and they must be on their guard daily against the venomous, murderous seed, as I in my weakness have experienced for more than twenty years, not a little.

Behold if we understand it in such a way as we have here explained then the spiritual things remain spiritual, carnal things carnal, and the Scriptures remain unbroken. But that I should exclude Christ from this promise, may the Lord prevent. For I have been taught by the grace of the Lord to know that Christ is the power, the beginning, the middle, and the end, of the whole promise and will remain such forever. For He is the spiritual husband of this spiritual woman. His Word is the seed of woman, which Word He is Himself, as He says, I am that which I spake unto you. John 8:25.[17a] He spoke and taught the truth and He is the truth; He spoke and taught love and He is love; in short, He spoke of wisdom, righteousness, holiness, and deliverance, and He is Himself Wisdom, Righteousness, Sanctification, and Redemption. I Cor. 1:30.

He alone is the victorious Prince, the triumphant Conqueror who was promised by these words, who has bruised the serpent's head for us, and also we in Him and by Him, as Paul says, In all these things we are more than conquerors through him that loved us (Rom. 8:37), and I can do all things through Christ which strengtheneth me (Phil. 4:13), and Who is he that overcometh the world but he that believeth that Jesus is the Son of God? I John 5:5.

It is manifest from all this that Christ and His Spirit, Word, wisdom,

17a Dutch version. _Tr._

truth, righteousness, sanctification, peace, and deliverance and all that Christ is and has, can in the power of truth never be separated. Where the one is the other must be also. Therefore I will not leave it to the judgment of Micron and Hermes, but to the judgment of the impartial reader, whether I exclude, as Micron reports, the man Christ, in whom our salvation is, from this promise and say that these things must be understood spiritually (although the allegory is spiritual in itself).

It has always been my understanding that He is here promised unto us of a woman, and I have so stated in some of my books, yet I must suffer this abuse from him as alas I must in his writings often. I do not know why I should contradict it, for He is not promised of a man who has procreative seed, but of a woman who does not have it, of a virgin, from which we must deduce that He was not to be the impure seed of mortal man, but the Son of the most High.

Nor can the expression, seed of the woman, help Micron in the least, because in the Scripture it means no more than the child of a woman and not of some unborn seed that can neither overcome nor experience the biting of its heels. And that the seed of woman, her fruit or child, is originally of the father and not of the mother has been so mightily shown from Scripture that all erring scribes and preachers under heaven will have to let us retain it, no matter how subtly they twist the Scriptures or pile up their comments and glosses. The Word stands fast touching the procreation of Adam's children, congealed in blood of the seed of man (Wisd. 7:2), and touching Christ, the Word became flesh (John 1:14).

Here then you have our Scripture—a solid, incontrovertible reply to all the unfounded, wordy, sophistic, and powerless words which Micron and Hermes adduce in their whole account about the seed of woman.

How godly women of which he writes and who he complains should not like this, I do not understand, since I allow to their men or husbands whose honor all virtuous and honorable wives do always gladly maintain and to themselves, each in her assignment or part, honestly according to the criterion of eternal truth that which their God the Lord has allowed them Himself by His Word, by the observable functions of nature, according to His divine pleasure.

I will not say anything about what shame Micron brings upon all honorable women by his insipid writings making them not only women but also men. Railing and ranting are not my interest. It suffices me to defend the foundation of our doctrine to the praise of the Lord. He must stab me now and then in order that he may thereby embitter some hearts against me still more, and make truth still more hated and abhorred as also our name.

[D.] *Micron's confession that Christ is the Son of God and of man.*

Micron writes: Jesus Christ is called the Son of God because He was eternally and supernaturally begotten of God the Father as to His divine essence. Similarly He is called the son of man because He was in the fullness of time begotten of a human being, Mary, as to the flesh or human nature.

I would urge the kind reader earnestly to consider my reply to Micron's confession and to judge it with a frank, unbiased heart. I trust by the grace of God that if he does so he will discover the falsehood and deceit of our opponents in great clarity, and on the other hand he will feel as with his hands that the truth is with us.

In the first place, if we compare the verbal confession which he made to us with his written confession now, he appears to be as slippery as an eel caught by the tail. For at the time of the discussion he confessed repeatedly before us all that the crucified Christ Jesus had no father or near father, and says so still at different places in his writing. Nevertheless he comes back and writes, but without the truth, that they confessed repeatedly before us that the Son of God died for us. It is the same song, but he sings it to the inexpert to a little better tune.

It would sound too bad thus crassly to forsake the crucified Christ Jesus and say that He had no Father, as he did before us.

Verily, I do not know what to say or to think of this man. Now the man Christ is the Son of God, then He is not; now God is His Father, then He had no Father. For he writes plainly that the man Christ who died for us was begotten not of God but of the seed of Mary and that He had no father. If He then was begotten of the seed of Mary and not of God, and if He had no father, as he says, then it is plainly falsehood, lies, and deceit to say that the Son of God died for us. Yes, if we put the very best construction on his exposition, He can be no more than an adopted or nominal son without truth, let him gloss the matter as much as he will. I will leave the impartial reader to consider whether this is a simple and plain reasoning according to the truth, or an equivocal and dark argument of falsehood.

Now observe, first, his equivocation together with the vague, unsteady, frivolous foundation of his doctrine, and his intolerable error to teach that the crucified Christ Jesus was not God's own true Son but merely a nominal Son, as was heard. I do not see what greater blasphemy one could invent. Yet he is a good teacher and writer and that for the reason that he has so finely (but falsely) portrayed the old heretic, Menno!

Secondly, I say that the whole Scripture and the observable function and human creation teach plainly that procreative seed is found with men and not with women. This he acknowledged openly in our latest discussion. Yet he says that the human Christ was of Mary's seed. Notice again his great instability and how grievously he has dishonored and abused the Lord's own Word by which we all must live, and also His unchanging holy ordinance, creation, and the natural order which in this matter is God's own work. He who has sense may ponder what I say.

In the third place, I say that he makes two separate begetters by his confession of which each has in turn begotten a son of his own substance and kind, namely, God and Mary. And in this wise God who is a spirit has from eternity begotten of Himself a Son who is spiritual, invisible, not subject to suffering, and God from all eternity. And Mary who was a human being begot a son in time of her seed, physical, visible, subject to suffering, and temporal. There you have the real thrust and sense of all their glosses and explanations which they make about this matter. But they conceal it from the eyes of the common people with their embellished inventions lest the ugliness and abomination be evident. And therefore we must point out plainly their deceits so that you may perceive aright and be the better able to avoid and guard against them. Whether there are not two distinct sons and persons of which one was divine and the other human, I will leave to unbiased readers the world over, to judge.

These two distinct sons or persons they now not only without, but also against, Scripture combine into one, saying that the Son of God united Himself with the son of man into one person. For the sake of which union the Son of God is now also called the son of man and vice versa. Reason and no Scriptures, you notice!

I reply in plain terms in the first place that as long as they do not negate and undo with Scripture our incontrovertible exposition, argument, and Scripture above related, and so firmly proved with Scripture in God's own ordinance and creation, namely, that the procreative seed is not found with women but with men, but as long as they let us keep this untouched as they must forever, we will say that their talk about this begetting of Mary's seed is basically nothing but lies and deceit, seeing that it is not Scriptural.

If their doctrine of this begetting of Mary's seed were to stand, Matt. 1:16 should read, Mary begot Jesus who is called Christ. For that the father is the one who begets, the mother is the one through whom he begets, and the offspring is that which he begets, is too evident to call for proof.

In the second place, I say that as long as they have not shown from Scripture that a human infant can be begotten of human seed without a father, which they can never do, I say again that all their glosses about this begetting of Mary's seed are lies and deceit because they are without Scriptural warrant.

That Christ Jesus had a true and immediate Father (which Micron as an open contradicter and blasphemer of God, led by the anti-Christian spirit of his blind seductions, to his everlasting shame denies to Him) the angel Gabriel, the Father as well as the Son, together with John the Baptist, Peter, Martha, Nathanael, all the apostles, Paul, yes the entire Scriptures will be my witness.

Thirdly, as long as they do not prove to us by the Scriptures, which they can never do, that the Son of God is called the son of man, and the son of man the Son of God, for the reason that there was a union of the two as they frequently assert without the Scriptures, so long I say they sin against the truth as often as they call the Son of God the son of man, and the son of man the Son of God. For the name is given as Micron himself confesses in truth and fact. And how it is done by him the reader may consider. To mock man is not honorable but to mock God is too abominable and blasphemous.

Fourthly I say, So long as they do not prove to us by the Scriptures that such a union took place as they assert it did, so long it is the lies and deceit of the old serpent, since it is not according to the Scriptures. For it is manifest that it is no union, as they call it, but a fearful division of the most holy and undivided person of Christ whereby he manifestly makes two persons and two sons in Christ which are born of two different persons at two different times in two different forms. He robs the crucified Christ Jesus of His beloved Father, and the Father of His only-begotten, beloved Son. He makes the greater part of the most holy flesh of Christ of Gentile origin. He esteems the man Christ no higher than an adopted or nominal son of God. He points us to an unholy, sinful, accursed sacrifice, to an impure mercy seat, High Priest, Saviour, Advocate, and Christ of the unholy, sinful, accursed, and creaturely flesh of Adam. In fact he makes Mary both the father and mother of Christ, breaks and disputes the whole Scriptures, together with the ordinances of God concerning procreation, and includes so many abominable absurdities in Christ that a noble heart trembles at it whenever the matter is earnestly considered and pondered.

Behold upon such a foundation has Micron built his false doctrine of the union of the Son of God, the falsely so called Son of God which he teaches all through his book in so many smooth sentences and garbled Scriptures. If you have eyes to see, then notice what kind of abomination Babylon, the mother of whoredom, pours from her golden cup and sets before you by her messengers and servants. Woe unto those that drink thereof, for she will so enchant them that they will tumble and fall.

[E.] *How according to Scripture Christ is the Son of God and also the son of Abraham and David.*

If we are to have the proper conception of the son of Abraham and of David and if we are to leave the Scripture intact, then we must observe these three rules: (1) that no procreation can take place without a father; (2) that procreative seed is not found with woman, and (3) that nevertheless the woman is no less necessary in procreation, as was shown with Scripture clearly enough, above.

Seeing that both are necessary for the procreative process and since procreative seed is found with the father and not with the mother, therefore it is clear that Christ Jesus is acknowledged to be not Joseph's but God's Son, and that throughout Scripture. Hence it is easy to see how Christ is called Abraham's or David's son in the Bible; namely, His human birth, out of their lineage, as Paul says. Now to Abraham and his seed were the promises made. He saith not, and to seeds as of many; but as of one which is Christ. Gal. 3:16.

In the same manner we should consider also that both the evangelists, Matthew and Luke, count the genealogy up to Joseph and not to Mary. Luke makes no mention at all of Mary but says, Being as was supposed the son of Joseph, which was the son of Heli. Luke 3:23. The evangelists' position should be noticed. From this it is plain that they do not show the lineage of which according to the promise is born He who is and forever shall be the Jehovah, Immanuel, Saviour, and Lord of the world.

For if such a man as Christ was should have been begotten of human seed as our opponents say He was, one who was to be deliverer of the whole world as Christ Jesus is, then the Scriptures would have indicated the one of whom He was begotten and came, and not the one of whom He was not come. For the Holy Spirit is a Spirit of truth who teaches and instructs rightly. According to the position of the learned ones our salvation would not be attached to the Scriptures but to an uncertain notion. For it is manifest that there is not a word found in them which shows that Mary was of David's lineage. Luke says that she was a cousin to Elisabeth who was a daughter of Aaron.

Now if our opponents want to press us to believe that the man Christ was David's natural son and seed, then let them prove first that there can be a child without a father; then that Mary was David's daughter, and finally that a woman has procreative seed. That they cannot do these things I am quite sure in my soul.

Good reader, get me right. I do not say that Mary was not David's daughter. But the Scriptures do not say that she was. But the point is that inasmuch as our opponents base their whole structure upon the idea that the man Christ was the natural seed and son of David and that by Mary, therefore they must have the sure testimony of the Holy Scriptures whereby they can prove it to be as they assert, before they proceed to such an important thing on which the salvation of all the elect depends as they insist. The mattter rests on mere assumption and not on the sure ground of Scriptures, for it may be that she was a daughter of David, and again maybe she was not, inasmuch as they did not always follow one rule in regard to marriage as may be seen by sacred history. Nor does it make much difference, seeing that a woman does not have procreative seed. In the eyes of the evangelists, it was enough that she was the wife of a son of David so that the promise might be fulfilled in the line to which it was promised as has been frequently said. Therefore I do not contradict it in the least that she was a daughter of David. But I say a sure testimony of the Holy Scriptures on which such a matter of eternal salvation should be built, as our opponents insist, and such a testimony there is not.

Yes, good reader, if the eternal Word or Son of God were really to assume humanity of human seed as our opponents insist, then it would have been much more fitting, would it not, and in accordance with Scripture and creation if He had joined Himself with Joseph's seed in Mary into a single person, seeing that Joseph already had procreative seed and was no less legally qualified than was Mary. Then it could be truly said that the crucified Christ was Abraham's seed and David's son, a thing to which they cannot now arrive except as far as the mother is concerned, a mother who in the tenor of Scripture has no procreative seed—unless the whole nature and the whole Scripture were suspended and inverted in the case of Mary, a thing that did not occur.

If they should say that it had to be a virgin according to the word of the prophet, and that therefore it could not be of the seed of man, then I would answer in plain words that they thereby pronounce their own sentence—that Christ was not the natural seed and son of Abraham and David, but a supernatural and promised and given seed. For He was not begotten of one of Abraham's and David's sons with whom there was procreative seed, but of one of their daughters with whom there was not, being a virgin, who knew no man, but was promised to one of David's sons, begotten of the incomprehensible, eternal Word of the Almighty great God, which she conceived by faith, carried, and brought forth. He was the first- and only-begotten true Son of God as to His eternal Father, and He was the promised, given, and born son of Abraham, Judah, and David as to His mother, who was a daughter of Abraham and the wife of Joseph the son of David as was heard.

I will now leave all the passages of the Holy Scriptures which treat of the seed, fruit, and branch of Abraham and David with the following remarks. The Saviour, King, Prince, Conqueror, and Prophet graciously promised to Abraham, Isaac, Jacob, Judah, and David, was in time born a true man of one of their daughters according to the promise. To Him the kingdom and throne of David were promised before by Isaiah, and again at His conception, when David's throne was a thing of the past, promised by the angel that He was to reign forever therein. This kingdom and throne He did not receive literally but spiritually, for they were already a thing of the past. His kingdom is an everlasting kingdom and shall not be left to other people. He is acknowledged all through the Scriptures to be the first- and only-begotten Son of God which He could not be if He were begotten of impure, human seed as our opponents say, and not of God. Moreover, His house and temple which He carves is not a literal house of literal wood, stone, metal, gold and silver, as was the perishable house of Solomon. But it is built of living, precious stones of the imperishable gold and silver upon the immovable foundation of the holy apostles and prophets, put together by the Holy Ghost. Hereby it is manifest that the promise made to David should be understood in the old literal frame as pointing to Solomon and in the new spiritual frame to Christ, for if we measure the genealogy of His blessed flesh in the line of David most minutely, then we find that He was at best the son of the non-procreating daughter of David, and at that there is not a word in all the Scriptures saying that she was or was not of David's daughters.

Behold such a foundation the big talk of Micron has, a matter that he will not let the gates of hell take from him as he boasts—something which they doubtlessly will not do, for they would rather strengthen and aid him in such a cause. It is the strongest fortification and best artillery of hell, as may be clearly seen by the writings of John. But that which will take it will have to be the gates of heaven, the strong Spirit and Word of the Lord against which neither hell nor the gates of hell, nor the devil himself can prevail.

Whosoever desires to have more information about this matter of David's seed may examine our reply to John a Lasco impartially and by the grace of God he will find the true foundation and meaning thereof.

And behold thus our position and doctrine remain fast and sure, that Jesus Christ is the only first-born and undivided Son of God by whom He has created heaven and earth and the sea with their fullness; and that He is not the impure, sinful, accursed, earthly seed of Abraham and David as our opponents philosophize and make believe.

Truly, He is the new Melchisedec, the King of perfect righteousness and of eternal peace, whose father, mother, and genealogy according to the true foundation of the Holy Scriptures are unknown to the whole world, the glorious Prince and wise Lord, the peace-loving Solomon who is seated upon the new spiritual throne of His father David, prepared for Him by His eternal Father in eternal glory, and He shall reign forever over the house and kingdom of Jacob. Consider whether we do not rightly teach you in accordance with the Holy Scriptures.

[F.] *Concerning the two natures in Christ, rightly and wrongly understood in the light of Scripture.*

Micron replies to the sixth absurdity listed by me and says that when I assert that according to their view, God's Son did not die for us, this is caused by a great misunderstanding whereby I do not or will not understand the union of the two natures, the divine and the human, into one person, Christ; and he says that in both discussions they have repeatedly stated that God's Son died for us.

To which I reply thus: First, that they cannot truthfully say that they stated once during the discussion that the Son of God died for us. For they have distinctly asserted all the time that the man Christ had no father (or as Micron sometimes said, that He had no near father). He still says this in different places in his book as anyone may read and see.

O dear Lord, what a frightful abomination that a mortal man and earthly creature dares so boldly to lie against his own conscience, dares so lamentably to belittle the King of all honor, so calmly to deceive the poor souls, and to commit such great deceit and shame against the Word of the Lord. Oh, that they could see what they are doing!

Secondly, I reply as I did before him, that there cannot be a word found in all the Scriptures about this union of two sons, of God's Son and the son of man, into one person, Christ, which he generally and insidiously calls two natures, and which he compares with the union of the body and soul of man.

That the body and soul of a living man are one person is as clear as the light of the sun. But that such a man, body and soul, which is a complete person, was thus united into one with the Son of God who is eternal, or that the eternal Son of God thus united Himself with the Son of man (which two sons they call two natures without Scripture) may be read in the glosses of Micron but not in the Scriptures. You may consider further what kind of Christ they teach you by comparing this criticism of ours with the Scriptures.

Thirdly, I say that if Micron desired to deal with the readers as a faithful minister he would not deal in such equivocal, veiled, dark reasoning but would express and explain his foundation and meaning without duplicity and say that the eternal, immortal Son of God put on a temporal, mortal son, body and soul, of the flesh and blood of Mary, and that He has thereby delivered us. For in the matter this is the proper meaning, sense, and thrust of all their writing, glosses, and teaching as their public confession before us all clearly testified and implies as has been said.

But now he deals without faith, for he means two actual sons of which one was divine and the other human and yet he calls them two natures so that the simple reader may not be offended at the bluntness. Which nature is but a property of him who possesses it and which is not the one himself who possesses it. For if one sees a man he does not say, That is a human nature, but that is a man, for the property is not the being itself but the being possessor of the property. And if Christ had only the property, namely, the nature, and if He did not have the being itself which are the substances, then He was neither God nor man. For I repeat, the natures are not the being itself but the being possesses the nature. Therefore it would be becoming of Micron to deal unequivocally and not to deceive his readers and hearers by such incomprehensible strange words so that they might comprehend the foundation of his doctrine and understand what he means. For teaching is done in order that men may understand what is being taught.

But it would give the thoughtful reader too much of a jolt bluntly to confess and teach that there are two sons in Christ and say that the crucified Son was not God's Son but a sinful, accursed man of the sinful, accursed flesh or seed of Adam. And therefore they must fix it so as to retain their honor and name with the world and enjoy their salaries and incomes at ease.

Behold, thus we must with Scripture expose the fine cloak of the Babylonian harlot which Micron and the preachers would gladly hide under their glosses, wrong explanations, and falsified Scriptures since they live of her table. We do this so that you may rightly observe and see their monstrous shame, their pox and deadly leprosy (understand it spiritually), that you may in the fear of your God guard against it.

I cordially admit, however, that Christ had two natures; but not in such a sense as Micron believes. I confess it in a Scriptural sense in the following manner. Peter writes of the church of God and says, Ye are partakers of the divine nature (II Pet. 1:4); whereby he clearly testifies that there are two natures in a Christian; the one, the human nature which is born of Adam, and the other, the divine nature of which he partakes by faith in the birth which is of God by the Holy Ghost. If then there are two natures in one Christian as there are, why then not in Christ? For since He is the only and true Son of God, having no other origin than God, therefore He must also have the nature of the one of whom He is. This is too plain to be controverted. That He had the divine nature He has proved by these manifest apparent attributes of a true, divine nature, as by His perfect righteousness, truth, holiness, love, and miracles. And even as He had the divine nature, I say, because of His divine origin, so He also had the unblemished, pure, human nature (like unto the nature of Adam before the fall) and that because of His true humanity. For as truly as He was the Father's Almighty Word from everlasting, so truly did He also in the fullness of time become a true, mortal man. And since He thus became a true man, He must also have had the property of a true man which is a true human nature (though uncorrupted) or else He would not have been a true man. This is incontrovertible.

Although the Scriptures say nothing about the two natures in Christ, yet I admit it in the above sense, for I am sure that one cannot separate the nature from anything any more than he can separate the light from the sun and the heat from fire, or humidity from water.

That He had the true human nature as well as the divine He has shown by the apparent results of a real human nature, such as hungering, thirsting, being weary, sighing, weeping, suffering, and dying.

Behold, in this sense I plainly and openly confess according to the fashion and ordinance of the holy, divine Scriptures that there were two natures in the only, undivided person and Son of God, Christ; and not as Micron does, who without Scripture makes one Son of two sons and one person of two persons, which he calls two natures and which according to his glosses were born at two different times, of two different persons, in two different forms, and which several natures remained distinct and were incomprehensibly united into one person, Christ, according to his writing. Observe which of us best points you to the Scriptures.

It is hardly necessary to reply to some Scripture which he adduces whereby he tries to prove that it was not the Son of God but the son of man (who according to his fable had no father) that suffered. Of these Scriptures in my opinion, the strongest is that Peter says Christ was put to death in the flesh but quickened in the Spirit. I Pet. 3:18. Yet this is too simple to need reply. (For who ever suffered otherwise than in the flesh?) Peter says, Forasmuch then as Christ hath suffered for us in the flesh, arm yourselves likewise with the same mind: for he that hath suffered in the flesh hath ceased from sin. I Pet. 4:1. Notice that Christians also suffer in the flesh as Christ Himself did, yet they are not therefore one son composed of two sons, as Micron says that Christ is.

Nobody can suffer otherwise than in the flesh. As Christ Himself says, Fear not them that kill the body, but are not able to kill the soul. Matt. 10:28; Luke 12:4. Also, to the murderer, Today thou shalt be with me in paradise. Luke 23:43. His flesh hung upon the cross, and was afterward buried, from which it is very plain that it was said in regard to His immortal spirit.

Christ also said, Father, into thy hands I commend my Spirit. He did not cry, Father, into Thy hands I commend Thy Son with whom I have been so long united into one person and which was my Spirit. For one of three conclusions must be drawn from Micron's writings. First, that the indwelling Son of God whom he generally calls the divine nature and the son of Mary whom he generally calls the human nature must have had one spirit or soul together, and this spirit they must at death have commended into the hands of the Father simultaneously. Second, that two entities remained alive at the death of Christ, first, the immortal Son of God which had dwelt in Him and secondly, the spirit or soul which he had received of Mary. Third, that the eternal Son of God must have become the spirit of mortal man which had put on a dwelling place or tabernacle of Mary, which He offered for us—as was said in treating about the absurdities.

From all this it follows that it is mere shifting sand upon which they build their doctrine of two natures or two sons in Christ according to their manner, and that it can stand no better before the power of the divine Word than the stubble can stand before the fire. And so we firmly hold our ground that Christ Jesus is the only undivided and true Son of God and that He is not one Son composed of two different sons as is the anti-Christian false foundation and doctrine of our opponents.

[G.] *That God the Father is the real Father of the whole Christ, His Son, and that the whole Christ is the real Son of God His Father, the position which Micron contradicts in many places and says that it is not so.*

Micron says at some places that the son of man had no father or near father. He said this at the time of the discussion, too, many times. This is so plainly opposed to all Scripture that one must be astounded and ashamed thereat, for who has ever, as old as he is, heard or read of a child that had no father.

Since he so boldly denies Christ Jesus a father as to His humanity, therefore I trust I will show to the reader who is the Father of Christ by a number of Scriptural references. By their power the reader must say, if he be not entirely given to error, that Micron and the learned ones by their writings have deceived him and have taught an essentially anti-Christian position.

Thus spake the angel of the most High to Mary when she wondered whence this fruit should be, seeing she knew not a man: The Holy Ghost shall come upon you, and the power of the Highest shall overshadow you; therefore also that holy thing which shall be born of thee shall be called the Son of God. Luke 1:35. Now note who is the Father.

This plain Scripture Micron has obscured by his smoke from the pit saying: The angel meant to say to Mary that her child should not be man only (he means of her flesh), but also truly God, and His Son according to His eternal, divine being. Not a single word did the angel say to that effect; nor did he make such a division in Christ as Micron does. The angel merely announced that she should conceive and that the fruit should be the Son of God and that God should be the Father of the child. Notice how Micron breaks the testimony of the holy angel which he at God's command bore to Mary from high heaven saying that the holy thing which should be born of her should be the Son of God.

Again the heavenly Father Himself testifies of Christ Jesus saying, This is my beloved Son in whom I am well pleased. Hear ye him. Here the Father proclaims Him to be His beloved Son, without any division. And Micron says that He is not that.

Once more, Christ said unto the blind man, Dost thou believe on the Son of God? He answered and said, Who is he, Lord, that I might believe on him? And Christ said unto him, Thou hast both seen me, and it is he that talketh with thee. John 9:35. Here the tangible, visible Christ who according to the position of Micron was only the son of man, confesses Himself without division to be the Son of God. And Micron says that He is not. At another place Christ says, What and if ye shall see the Son of man [mark, He says the Son of man] ascend up where he was before? Here Christ Himself confesses that the Son of man was from heaven. Micron says that He was of earth, and that He is called heavenly on account of some glorious qualities, as if Christ were a Christ in name merely and not a Christ in truth.

When Christ asked His disciples saying, Whom do men say that I, the Son of man, am? (mark, He asks about the Son of man), then Peter said, Thou art the Christ [without a division], the Son of the living God. And Micron says that the son of man was not the Son of God!

Again, John the Baptist says, He that sent me to baptize with water, the same said unto me, Upon whom thou shalt see the Spirit descending and remaining on him, the same is he which baptizeth with the Holy Ghost. And I saw and bare record that this is the Son of God. Here John confesses the visible Christ (who according to our opponents' position was only the son of man) to be the Son of God. And Micron says that He is not that.

The centurion on Golgotha said, Truly this man [mark, he says, this man] was the Son of God. And Micron says that He is not that. Paul says, God sent forth his Son, made of a woman. Gal. 4:4. And Micron writes, God sent forth His Son who came of a woman. At another place Paul writes, He that spared not his own Son. Mark, he says, His own Son. Also, this, we are reconciled to God by the death of his Son. John says, The blood of Jesus Christ his Son cleanseth us from all sins. At another place, God sent his Son to be the mercy seat[18] or propitiation for our sins, which reconciliation according to Micron's false doctrine, is not brought about by the blood of the Son of God, as John and Paul teach, but by the blood of the son of man, who according to Micron had no father, as has often been heard.

Kind reader, if you will closely observe it, you will find more than sixty instances in the New Testament where Christ Jesus confesses God the heavenly Father to be His Father and Himself to be the Son. From the beginning to the end, you will not find anything about such a division and union as our opponents teach, neither in Christ's words nor in those of any of the holy apostles or evangelists.

[18] The Greek word used by Paul in Rom. 3:25 was actually used of the mercy seat in the Greek version of the Old Testament. *Ed.*

Micron writes at more than one place, If God, the Father, is the Father of the man Christ, then He must also have had flesh and blood. From which it is manifest first that he does not allow the crucified Christ a Father. Whereby the angel of God, the Father and the Son Himself, also John the Baptist, Peter, John, Paul, Nathanael, Martha, and the whole Scriptures are made open liars and false witnesses by him. For they have repeatedly confessed Him to be the true Son of the true and living God.

Secondly, it is manifest that all such writing is not of the living spring of the Holy Spirit; nor of an enlightened, firm believing heart which without wavering trusts, with Joshua and Caleb, in the power and true promises of Almighty God; but that it is solely of human wisdom and an unbelieving, carnal heart which cannot judge but according to the Scripture. And yet, through excessive blindness it destroys the ordinances of this same nature which God established in the first creation, for it speaks of the child without a father.

Kind reader, take heed! The almighty power of God, the incompresensible miracle of His divine love, and the certain sure word of His eternal truth should have more worth than the blind intellect of our corrupted nature if we would rightly learn to know Christ and follow and obey His holy Word.

The dead body of Adam, created of the dust by the breath of God, became a living soul (Gen. 1:27), and water gushed forth from the rock (Ex. 17:6). Yet the earth was no living soul, neither was the rock of watery substance. If they should say that this was done by the power of God in a supernatural way, as is the case, then I would reply, So also was brought about the miraculous incarnation of Jesus Christ in Mary by the omnipotence of God by which He can do anything He pleases. As the angel says, The power of the Highest shall overshadow thee. Luke 1:35. For with God nothing is impossible.

I am of the opinion that all those who believe in power and in truth that God was able in the beginning to create heaven, earth, and sea and the fullness thereof by His mighty word, and now by the same word, rules, directs, and maintains the same, who believe that He is able by the same power to raise Adam and all his descendants at the end from the dust and reclaim them from the lowest parts of the earth and the depths of the sea and place them before the face of His majesty, such a person will also believe that this same God had the power to send His incomprehensible, eternal Word down from heaven and let it become by the power of His Holy Ghost a true mortal man in Mary. As John says, The Word became flesh. I repeat, in Mary, for in the Father or in heaven, He was not flesh, nor outside of Mary before He was conceived, as I have often confessed in plain language and proved conclusively from Scriptures. Notwithstanding this, Micron is not ashamed to garble my words as if I had said that the Word was flesh in the Father or in heaven, a thing which I can say with a good conscience I never thought of in all my life.

I do not see how one can differentiate between the spirit of our opponents and the spirit of the Pharisees and the false prophets. They always garbled the words of the pious prophets and of the Lord Christ, and were always intent upon making them disreputable; and out of mere hatred and envy of the truth, got rid of them by violence, falsehood, and force. And so these men out of mere hatred and envy of the truth deal with me an old, sorrowful man,[19] for alas they have portrayed me all through their book in such colors that I do not see how they could have depicted Behemoth and Beelzebub in uglier colors than they have depicted me. And yet, I have never in my life wished them any harm, and much less done it, but have shown them all Christian faithfulness and discretion by giving them good counsel in their need as the love which is of God teaches all true Christians.

Nevertheless they have written this lying, infamous, and slanderous falsehood against me undeservedly as thanks for my faithfulness whereby they cause me to be tenfold more obnoxious in all countries than I ever was before. And this for no other reason really than that we confess Christ Jesus to be the true Son of the true and living God with the angel Gabriel, with the Father, with Christ Himself, with John the Baptist, with Peter, and with all the Scriptures, and that we in our weakness would gladly hear and obey His Word, commandment, prohibition, ordinance, and unblamable example, and be saved by His grace—things which our opponents utterly hate and dislike. For they publicly avow that the Son of man whom we confess to be the Son of God, according to the Scriptures, was not the Son of God, for He had no father, say they. They contradict His express ordinance of baptism which He taught and commanded us with His own mouth whereby all the regenerate, believing children of God submissively testify before Christ and His church that they are prepared and willing to follow His holy Word and divine will unto death.

Oh, dear, do observe what abominations and poisonous draught it is which men pour out for you from the Babylonian cup. True and immutable remains the testimony of the Father. This is my beloved Son in whom I am well pleased.

*[H.] Of what divine seed and substance God the Father begot His blessed Son Jesus Christ, a true son of Mary.*

You have heard, faithful reader, in all our foregoing incontrovertible Scripture and argument that the origin of a child is of the procreative seed of the father and not of the mother, for she has none, even as Micron acknowledged openly before us all. You have also heard that God the Father is a true Father of the whole Christ and that the whole Christ is the true Son of God His Father. We will now show you by the grace of the Lord with the holy divine Scriptures what kind of divine substance, matter, seed, or essence it was of which this same Son of God and Mary was begotten and brought forth so that you may confess and see the clearness of the human birth of Jesus Christ, according to the Scriptures, the smoke of the bottomless pit being cleared away by the power of the strong Word, and driven away by the wind of the Holy Spirit.

John testifies saying, In the beginning was the Word, and the Word was with God, and the Word was God. The same was in the beginning with God.

---

[19] Menno was then about sixty years of age, but was somewhat crippled physically. *Ed.*

All things were made by him; and without him was not anything made that was made. In him was life, and the life was the light of men. And the Word [which was in the beginning] was made flesh, and dwelt among us, and we beheld his glory, the glory as of the only begotten of the Father, full of grace and truth.

Here John as a faithful witness of truth points out the divine seed, material, or essence (I speak as a man) out of which God the Father brought forth and begot in time the man Christ out of Mary, namely, the incomprehensible, eternal Word.

If you want an immutable, true, and firm foundation of faith, and the true sense of these words of John, and do not want to be deceived by the lying seed of the old serpent, nor robbed of your Saviour by the subtle deceit of Antichrist, you must observe and cling to these two principles.

First, that God the Father is confessed to be the true Father of His Son Christ by the Scriptures, and that no one can really be a father except of that which he has brought forth and begotten of his own substance, that is, of the seed of his own body.

Secondly, that Christ Jesus is confessed to be the true Son of God His Father by all the Scriptures, and that no one can really be somebody's son if he was not brought forth or begotten of his substance or seed.

It is plain that God the heavenly Father is the true Father of Christ His Son and that Christ is a true Son of God His Father, as is testified all through the Scripture. Therefore it is sure and manifest that we should leave unglossed and unbroken the testimony of John when he says, The Word became flesh. For since Christ is God's true Son and God the Father Christ's true Father, the Father must also have had in Himself or with Himself His incomprehensible Word by which all things were made that are made, as was heard.

If our opponents should say that the Word was Spirit from the beginning and could therefore not become flesh, then you may answer, First, if the Word could not become flesh as you say, then the power of the Father is lessened and His arm by which He can do anything He desires or intends is shortened, and the angel has borne false testimony to Mary when he said that there is nothing impossible with God.

Secondly, you may answer, If the Word could not become flesh, as you say, then all the Scriptures deceive us, which testify and teach, without any division, union, or exception as to nature, sons, or persons, that Christ Jesus is God's Son and that God is His Father, as was said.

Thirdly, you may answer, If the Word could not become flesh, as you say, then the Holy Scriptures testify falsely that He is of heaven and not of earth; that He came forth from the Father; that He is the bread and Lord from heaven; that He is the Alpha and Omega, and other like Scriptures.

Fourthly, you may answer, If the Word could not become flesh, as you say, then one or the other of you must be wrong: either you who say that He could not become flesh, or John who says that He did become flesh, as was heard.

If they should say further that the Lord put on His flesh by generation of Mary's seed as they actually do, then you may answer thus, We desire that you show us where it is written in Scripture that a woman has procreative seed, or else we will say that it is the glossing and falsehood of the old serpent and not the Lord's truth.

Secondly, you may answer, By such assuming you rob the Father of His Son and the Son of His Father. You divide Christ into two parts, into good and evil, into righteous and unrighteous, into heavenly and earthly, etc. You point us to a sinful creature and an impure sacrifice. You make Mary contrary to the entire Scripture and the order of nature, to be both father and mother. You commit idolatry with the earthly and sinful flesh of Adam. You make all the pious witnesses of Christ such as John the Baptist, Peter, etc., false and faithless and you make yourselves Antichrist and set the Scriptures against themselves.

In the third place, you may answer, Becoming is becoming and assuming is assuming, nor will it be found otherwise in the Scriptures. When Christ became twelve years of age, He became twelve years of age, counting from the time of His human birth. Christ became a curse (Gal 3:13), and He became such so that He hung between two murderers on the cross. Water was made wine, and it became such. Lot's wife became a pillar of salt, and she became one. For becoming, I say, is becoming, and cannot be explained in any part of the Scriptures as meaning assuming.

If they would still follow their reason and say, If the Word is become flesh, it has lost its first essence by the change, you may answer, John has taught us that it was made flesh and he has not said a word further as to how or to what extent it is changed, something that you inquisitive ones, driven by the spirit of Antichrist, want to know and hear of us.

Secondly, you might answer, Adam was made a living soul (I Cor. 15:45); yet he remained dust, for the Lord said unto him, Dust thou art, and to dust shalt thou return. Gen. 3:19.

Thirdly, you might reply, We are asked to believe with the heart, not to comprehend with the reason. For Paul says that faith is the substance of things hoped for, the evidence of things not seen.

Fourthly, you might reply, Paul says that He is God. And Christ says that He is a Spirit. Zophar the Naamathite says, He is as high as heaven and deeper than hell; longer than the earth; and broader than the sea. Job 11:8, 9. And the prophet says that He comprehended the dust of the earth in a measure. Isa. 40:12. Also, saith the Lord, the heaven is my throne, and the earth is my footstool. Isa. 66:1. But there is no man born of Adam whose reason and intellect is sufficient to measure this God and Spirit or comprehend His being. Therefore it would be well for them to abandon their high, soaring intellect in such incomprehensible depths and to bow themselves humbly under the word of the Lord, to ponder the saying of Solomon: he that investigates deep things will be oppressed by the majesty.

Kind reader, if reason were to decide this incomprehensible, deep matter and not the Scriptures, then I would ask them a rational question concerning their faith, out of which they could scarcely extricate themselves. It would be this: whether or not they believe that the Almighty, incomprehensible Word, of which heaven and earth are full, and which is also the eternal wisdom and power of the Almighty, eternal Father, has confined Himself in such congealed blood, as Micron put it at one place, or in such a little body of Mary's seed as he has it now. I presume they will leave the question unanswered. For if they say that it was so confined, then they get a Father who has divested Himself of His Word, wisdom, and power to confine it in such a human seed or blood. And if they say that it was not so confined, then they make their own foundation untrue and false, for they say and teach that the Son of God which is God's eternal Word, wisdom, and power has put on the son of Mary or of man, that He has united Himself therewith into one person.

I repeat that it would be well for them to leave such unmeasured depths unfathomed, to stay below the clouds, and not to soar above heaven with their earthly foolish reason. For I think that when they have measured the height of the heavens and the depths of the abyss, have weighed the mountains and counted the drops of rain, then they will give me a reasoned answer, fathom and explain how things stand in this matter about which I asked concerning their faith, foundation, and doctrine. I say that I do not at all consult reason in this incomprehensible and lofty matter, but adduce the Word of the Lord, whereby I am plainly taught that Mary, the Lord's mother, conceived in faith the Almighty, eternal Word of the Almighty, eternal Father by which all things were made that are made, and that the same by the great power and operation of His Almighty, eternal Spirit, became a true, visible, tangible, pure, and holy Man, subject to suffering and death, not of her but in her, above the comprehension of all men. He who was already the first-born of every creature and also according to His human form the first- and only-begotten true Son of God was supernaturally born to God His father of Mary, according to the flesh, just as Isaac was naturally born to Abraham by Sarah; Solomon to David by Bathsheba, and John the Baptist unto Zacharias by Elisabeth.

This first- and only-begotten true Son of God thereby became also a son of Abraham, Isaac, Jacob, Judah, and David as to His mother (but in the genealogy of Christ, the son of Joseph) in the fullness of time and according to the promise. He graciously fulfilled the spiritual law,[20] which no flesh of Adam could fulfill, for all the descendants of Adam, in perfect righteousness, trod the winepress of bitter wrath for us. To Him the law and all the prophets point, and in Him all the glorious promises of the inexpressibly great grace and love of God are fulfilled. And after He had performed the service of His divine love He again ascended up where He was before. John 6:62. He has all power in heaven and upon earth and is through the sacrifice of His death and blood our only and eternal mercy seat, Reconciler, High Priest, Mediator, Advocate, and Peacemaker with God His Father.

[20] Menno means that by His "active obedience" Christ kept the Law; and by His obedience the saints are made righteous. Cf. Rom. 5:19. *Ed.*

In this way the most high, most gracious, and most merciful God and Father retains His glory, praise, and honor through His blessed, eternal Word and Son, and not through the unclean, sinful flesh of Adam, as our opponents teach and invent.

Now, beloved reader, notice how our opponents are deceived in this matter by their earthly, carnal reason which would judge this miracle, not according to the Scriptures, but according to nature, and therefore do not believe that the Almighty God had the power to let His eternal Word become flesh in Mary and so beget a true man of her. For which reason they have played this ugly farce about me, although these poor souls are more than doubly that which they would make us out to be, namely, false teachers and perverse heretics.

For they say and teach without any Scripture that the man Christ who died for us was not the Son of God and that He had no Father, and we say that He is God's Son and that God is His Father, according to all the Scriptures.

They say and teach without any Scripture that the Word has put on a whole man of Mary's flesh and seed, and we say and teach according to the plain testimony of John, that the Word was made flesh, not of Mary, but in Mary.

They include two different persons and sons, one divine and the other human, in the one Christ, without Scripture; and we say that there is but one undivided person and son, according to the Scriptures.

They say and teach without Scripture that the visible Christ was earthly of the earth; and we say and teach that He is heavenly, of heaven, according to the Scriptures.

They say and teach without Scripture that He is pure of the impure Adam, and we say and teach that He is pure of the pure God, according to the Scriptures.

They point us without Scripture to an accursed, sinful sacrifice, and we point to a spotless, innocent sacrifice according to the Scriptures.

They worship contrary to all Scriptures the creaturely flesh of Adam, and we the Almighty, eternal Word which became man by the infinite power of God in harmony with the Scriptures.

In short, they place their whole salvation in the unclean, sinful flesh of Adam, that is, in a man who according to their fabulous writing and contrary to the Word and ordinance of God was begotten from the seed or blood of Mary, without Father. And we place ours in the Almighty, eternal Word, become man in the fullness of time, by which all things are made, ruled and consist forever, which was from everlasting the eternal wisdom, power, and glory of God His Father, one with God, His eternal Father and the eternal Holy Ghost, blessed forever. Amen.

Fast and firm remains the word. The Word became flesh. O merciful, gracious Lord, enlighten the eyes of all the blind that they may see Thy heavenly brightness and rightly confess the majesty of Thy honor. Amen, dear Lord, Amen.

# *Conclusion*

Honorable reader, here you have our fundamental explanation and plain reply to the untrue and unfair narrative of Micron and Hermes and to their anti-Christian false doctrine concerning Jesus Christ the son of Mary. I am now and at all times willing and ready to appear before God and His angels, before friend and foe, and before the whole world, unto water, fire, sword and death, and unto the coming judgment.

I would pray you all, kind readers, through Christ as before God to reflect earnestly what kind of spirits and people these are who have written the narration and its appendix and articles concerning us. They have kept quite silent about the kindness so faithfully shown them in their need. They have not said anything about the plain acknowledgments which they made, as above stated, whereby they had already lost the whole point in discussion, nor do they mention that they were pinned down frequently so that they knew not what to say. They have not written a single considerate word about me in their book. From the beginning of the discussion to the end of their writing they have only studied and aimed how they might most expertly defame me and make our doctrine, which is the pure doctrine of Christ, a stench to many.

In several instances they have sadly garbled our words and given them an erroneous thrust. They have added to or subtracted from their own and changed the meaning. The order of the discussion they have changed. They have made many unscriptural glosses, have falsified the Holy Scriptures, made false witnesses of the Father Himself and His blessed Son, of the angel of the Lord, of John the Baptist, and of all the evangelists and apostles, and of all the Scriptures, as may be seen.

How they fill the measure of their fathers, the false prophets, who from the beginning have praised and taught falsehood by hypocrisy, have hated the truth and reviled the faithful servants of God, and defamed them; have turned the faithful service of their love into the worst thing possible, have accused them before lords and princes, have hindered them in the doctrine and true religion, and at last have taken their lives and confiscated their goods!

It is but little to me that they have trampled me into the dirt and have by their lies caused me to be a stench to many, for I am aware that I am worthy of dishonor since I am born of Adam of impure seed, a vile and unworthy sinner, as all those have complained who from the beginning were rightly over-shadowed by the glory of the Lord. But that I am therefore such an unsteady liar and tricky scamp as I am depicted by our opponents, by the slanderous, false, unkind, and bitter spirit of envy—God preserve me! Many pious people of both the Old and the New Testament had to hear this same thing with me. Christ promises us a great reward in heaven, for it is done for His name's sake. That they so sadly shame the Son of God, falsify the Scriptures, and falsely console the poor, unenlightened souls by such an open falsehood and encourage and keep them in their accursed blindness grieves my soul night and day. For which reason I was eagerly ready to write this reply to the praise of the Lord and to your service.

I would that you would earnestly consider what a pure, clear, and unadulterated foundation of truth we have pointed out to you and to all the world concerning Christ.

And on the other hand how plainly and flatly we have discovered and manifested unto you and all reasonable readers the anti-Christian foundation and doctrine of our opponents. Whosoever has but half an eye may see where the deceit is hidden.

We now and at all times willingly volunteer that if they can prove to us by the unbroken and unfalsified Scriptures that Adam had two kinds of seed of which one was pure and the other impure, or that the Scriptures anywhere call that holy, pure, and heavenly which is unholy, impure, and earthly in itself, or that there ever was or can be a human child without father, or that women have procreative seed, or that two sons can be one son, or that the Scriptures anywhere mention such a union as our opponents invent, or that ever anyone was the true son of another without his being begotten of his substance or seed, or that God is a God of falsehood so that He would call the man Christ His Son without His actually being such, then we will gratefully and diligently reconsider the matter in all love. Behold, before God, it is the truth that I write.

And in case they cannot do so, which they surely never can, then our opponents, in so far as they are reasonable men, shall acknowledge that they have the impure, deceitful doctrine of Antichrist and we the wholesome doctrine of Christ in spite of the fact that we must hear and suffer so exceedingly much.

Yes, reader, if we consider the writings of John the evangelist, we clearly find that the spirit and doctrine of our opponents already was abroad in his time. For at that time they denied that Jesus Christ was the Son of God and that He had come into the flesh, something which these also often did in their writings and verbal discussions which they had with us. From which it is manifest that it is the trickery and deceit of the old serpent.

I would therefore humbly beseech all godly, pious hearts who sincerely and diligently seek Christ and eternal life for the Lord's sake first to pray fervently for all our opponents both high and low of state, learned or unlearned, rich or poor, who ignorantly err and who are sustained and strengthened in their impenitent, reckless life by such false teachers and writers as are our opponents; so that the merciful, gracious Lord may give them eyes to see His glorious, exalted origin, and rightly confess His truth, and that that may not be lost with which they are so dearly bought.

And secondly pray that the Lord may grant me and all our fellow laborers of the house of God together with the whole church the Spirit of His wisdom, and may keep us by His grace sound in doctrine, strong in faith, ardent in love, quickened in hope, diligent in the work of the Lord, unblamable in life, and patient in all the oppression and tribulation of which alas we experience not a little by the slanderous, tumultuous, and seditious crying and writing of our opponents; so that we may set a living example to the world that many may see our new Christian walk in the truth and examine it, and repent, and so be saved forever.

I beseech you in the same manner not to leave these writings idle and hidden, but to send them east, west, north, and south into the hands of all men, and to let many read them in order that the bright sun of righteousness which alas has been obscured for so many centuries by the smoke from the bottomless pit of the anti-Christian false doctrine, may shine forth with the power of truth and that our glorious and holy Saviour, the first- and only-begotten true Son of the Almighty, living God, the ever-blessed Jesus Christ, may be rightly confessed by many to His glory.

To this same eternal Saviour, together with the heavenly Father and the Holy Ghost, be praise forever. Amen.

MENNO SIMONS

*October 7.*

# Epistle to Martin Micron

*Sent-brieff aan Martinum Micron*

## 1556

*For other foundation can no man
lay than that is laid, which is Jesus Christ.*

I Corinthians 3:11

# Introduction

For the circumstances which led up to the literary battle between Menno Simons and Martin Micron, see the editorial introduction to the preceding work, *Reply to Martin Micron.* The work before us is dated, October 16 [1556]. In the Dutch (1681) the full title is: *A Hearty but Stern Epistle to Martin Micron Himself, Intended as an Altogether Necessary Reply to his Crude Lies, Abuse and Undeserved Accusations concerning the Magistracy, the Oath, etc., which he has Set before the World to the Shame of the Holy Word of God and His Poor Churches: Also Intended as a Mirror for his Straying Soul so that he may Learn Rightly to Know Himself, and that All Our Readers may Know How Very Wickedly he has with his Writings Dealt with God and Man, so that he may Know himself, Repent, and be Saved.* As usual the title page also contains Menno's beloved I Corinthians 3:11.

In the *Opera Omnia Theologica* of 1681 the *Epistle to Martin Micron* is printed fol. 599-618, and in the *Complete Works* of 1871, Part II, pages 403-24, though in abbreviated form. The most valuable part of the treatise for modern readers is Menno's treatment of the swearing of oaths. In this letter Menno also staunchly asserts that his doctrine and teaching underwent no real change from the beginning of his life in the Anabaptist brotherhood in Holland in 1536 until his writing to Micron in 1556.                    J. C. W.

# Epistle to Martin Micron

# 1556

---

## *Preface*

The pure, true knowledge of Jesus Christ, the Son of God in truth; a wholesome understanding of His holy Word; a new, changed, and understanding heart; a new, fair, pure hand and tongue; a new, godly, unblamable life in the fear and love of God; together with the unfalsified, pure, and good disposition, nature, fruits, and unction of the Holy Ghost do I wish Martin Micron from the inmost of my heart; from Him who is the Giver of every good and perfect gift to the enlightenment of his poor soul, through Jesus Christ His beloved chosen Son, our Lord and eternal Saviour. Amen.

All Scriptures teach and enjoin, honorable Martin, that we should love the Lord our God with all our heart and with all our soul and with all our strength, and our neighbors as ourselves. On these two commandments, says Christ, hang all the law and the prophets.

Love is the total content of Scripture. Everyone that loveth, says John, is born of God and knoweth God. He that loveth not, knoweth not God; for God is love. And he that dwelleth in love, dwelleth in God, and God in him. Without this love, it is all vain, whatever we may know, judge, speak, do, or write. The property and fruit of love is meekness, kindness. Love is not envious, not crafty, not deceitful, not puffed up, nor selfish. In short, where love is, there is a Christian.

We are urged to love by the Scriptures and cannot be Christians without love. Now you do not only call yourself an ordinary Christian, but also a leader and a minister; therefore you have done quite wrong not to have consulted the commandment of love in the fear of God before you published your false, defamatory, proud, bloodguilty, and anti-Christian narration and book.

You have manifested yourself before God and man in such a manner as though you had never in your life felt and confessed the least particle of the pure, unadulterated nature of love as I shall show and explain by the grace of the Lord in an impartial, sincere conscience by this my admonition out of love

917

of the divine honor and the holy Word. Also out of love for your poor soul that you (if there is yet a breath of life and a semblance of reason left in you and you were not so completely blinded by hate and bitterness) may by such instruction written for your own good be led to see your ugly suppurating sores and deadly wounds and be helped by the heavenly medicine of the Lord's Spirit and Word by genuine sincere repentance to the praise of the Lord and the salvation of your soul. If there be any reason left in you, reflect upon what I write.

One. It is manifest and cannot be successfully denied by you nor by any person else that you have by your writing made a liar of the Almighty great God, the God of heaven and of earth, the Father of our Lord Jesus Christ, who can neither lie nor deceive; for He testifies of Christ and says, This is my beloved Son in whom I am well pleased, and you say that He is not, for you have orally confessed to us and you write so still at different places that the man Christ which you call the human nature in Christ had no father.

Observe whether you are not one of the spirits of whom John says, He that believeth not God has made him a liar; because he believeth not the record that God gave of his Son. I John 5:10. Dear Micron, reflect and see if I do not write the truth.

Two. It is manifest that you have also made a liar of Christ, who is the eternal truth, by your writing; for He confesses more than sixty or seventy times in John that He is the Son of God and that God is His Father; that He came from heaven and that He is gone forth from the Father; and that He is the only begotten Son. And you write boldly and publicly that He is not; that He had no father according to His humanity, that He is of the flesh and seed of Mary, of earth and the natural son or seed of Abraham and David.

Observe and see if you are not one of the false teachers and prophets who forsake the Lord that bought them. II Pet. 2:1. Dear Micron, reflect and see if it is not the truth that I write.

Three. It is manifest that by your writing you make false witnesses of the heavenly messenger, the angel of the most High; of the humble plain Nathanael in whom was no guile; of John the Baptist, the holiest born of women; of Martha, the hostess and servant of the Lord; of Peter, the faithful shepherd of the sheep; of John, the apostle whom Jesus loved; and of Paul, the chosen vessel. For they all testify unanimously and that without any division as to humanity and divinity that Christ Jesus is the Son of God; and you publicly proclaim that as to His humanity He is not.

Observe whether you are not the servant of the abominable beast which opened his mouth in blasphemy against God to blaspheme His name and His tabernacle, and them that dwell in heaven. Dear Micron, reflect and see if I do not write the truth.

Four. It is manifest that you have made such witnesses of your own brethren who were present at the discussion and who alas did not know much about the matter; as were those who testified against Christ, Stephen and Naboth (that is, if your brethren agree with your unjust, partial charges, which I hope they do not). For as these testified out of hatred of the truth against the righteous to please Jezebel and the scribes; so also these out of hatred of the truth through your influence testify against me to please you and your ilk (I speak of the guilty ones) who defame me thus. They heard your confession concerning the seed of the woman on which foundation your whole doctrine is built, concerning the two sons in Christ, that the crucified One had no father. They witnessed that you had no argument that held wherewith to defend the doctrine of Christ's purity; that you could make no reply to the Scriptures we read to show that the entire Christ was God's Son; that you took recourse to an unscriptural question which we answered in such a way that all escape was cut off; and that you turned from one thing to another. One would suppose that if they were people of common self-respect who sought the honor of God and your salvation, as we thought when they first arrived, that they would charge you before all men that you have out of mere hatred and envy heaped up unfair, devilish falsehoods, and not the impartial, godly truth, to defame your neighbors and that you have done so to your own eternal shame. But it is an old proverb, As the shepherd goes, the sheep follow. Christ truly says, If the blind lead the blind, both shall fall into the ditch. Dear Micron, reflect and see if I do not write the truth.

Five. It is manifest that you lamentably deceive all your readers and hearers who believe your writing, and that you kill their poor souls. For it is known to the Lord, who has eyes as a flame of fire, to yourself, and to all of us who were present, that in fact your case was lost. Nevertheless you console them with devised lies, as is the way with all false prophets, whereby you rob them according to John of both the Father and the Son; keep them under the wrath and curse, whereby you keep them out of God, and God out of them, so that they do not overcome the world, for they do not believe that Jesus is the Son of God.

Observe and see if you are not one of those who shut up the kingdom of heaven against men, as the Lord says. Dear Micron, reflect and see whether it is not the truth I write.

Six. It is manifest that you have with your writing acted toward some of us and also toward myself personally, not as an honest, virtuous, godly, pious Christian, but much rather as a dishonest, shameless, indiscreet, and bloodthirsty Corycaeus, or informer. For it is a fact that you have without the truth listed a poor, innocent man whom you well knew as a minister, who is no minister, nor apt ever to become one. By this you will perhaps deprive him or his poor children of their whole welfare, yes, a couple of thousands, if the Lord in His providence does not prevent. The Spirit of the Lord does not enjoin you thus to act toward the innocent.

Dear Micron, if you had one pious drop of blood in your body, you would have mercy on the innocent, weak cripple[1] whom you, alas, repay thus before the whole world for his faithful services of love willingly shown you and yours

---

[1] Menno here refers to himself. *Ed.*

with sincere, Christian intentions. In the same manner you have acted toward the others who furnished you with cover, board, and drink; who carefully led your company into the city, furnished them quarters, and showed them all manner of kindness in pure love. Let the Christian reflect and judge according to the Lord's Spirit and Word whether this is the work of honest, Christian love which wishes harm to none, much less does it.

Besides you have practically pointed out my place of abode, which I had enjoyed until that time (information which Hermes had obtained by pumping a poor child), while you are well aware that everywhere they try to take my life out of mere hatred of the truth. By such conduct you surely cannot teach unto righteousness, nor instruct the ignorant. And the work in itself does not indicate the reasonableness and love of a regenerated Christian. It shows rather an unmerciful, cruel, envious, hateful, ravenous, bloodthirsty heart and the bitter mind of an informer as all the reading world must judge and say.

Whether you have done this by the merciful, compassionate, faithful, unadulterated, and pure Spirit of Christ as a pious, virtuous man—or by the unmerciful, tyrannical, faithless, false, and unclean spirit of Antichrist, as an ungodly and shameless spy—to get me an old, afflicted man in trouble, I will leave to the consideration of your own soul as before God who tries the hearts and reins in Christ Jesus.

Observe and see if you are not one of those who say in their hearts, It is hard for us to see him; for his life does not conform to ours. Dear Micron, reflect and see if it is not the truth that I write.

Seven. It is also manifest that you encourage and strengthen the rulers in their impenitent lives not a little by your writing; rulers who are usually quite obdurate, proud, ambitious, puffed up, self-conceited, pompous, selfish, earthly, carnal, and often bloodthirsty. And that you may gain their favor and praise the more therewith I, miserable man, must be your blind and imprisoned Samson as a spectacle and derision, although I never in my life spoke an insulting word against the rulers or against their office and service.

I have from the beginning of my ministry fraternally warned them in my writings in faithful, unadulterated truth from my soul against the destruction of their souls, admonishing them to a godly, penitent, Christian life, pointing them with the Scriptures to the perfect Spirit, Word, commandment, prohibition, ordinance, and example of Christ. And when you proposed your pharisaical, Herod-like question concerning the magistracy, I said nothing more to you than that it would hardly become a true Christian ruler to shed blood.[2] For this reason, If the transgressor should truly repent before his God and be reborn of Him, he would then also be a chosen saint and child of God, a fellow partaker of grace, a spiritual member of the Lord's body, sprinkled with His precious blood and anointed with His Holy Ghost, a living grain of the Bread of Christ and an heir to eternal life; and for such an one to be hanged on the gallows, put

[2] Menno here bravely takes his stand against capital punishment, even when to do so made him still more odious to the theologians and the rulers of his day. *Ed.*

on the wheel, placed on the stake, or in any manner be hurt in body or goods by another Christian, who is of one heart, spirit, and soul with him, would look somewhat strange and unbecoming in the light of the compassionate, merciful, kind nature, disposition, spirit, and example of Christ, the meek Lamb—which example He has commanded all His chosen children to follow.

Again, if he remain impenitent, and his life be taken, one would unmercifully rob him of the time of repentance of which, in case his life were spared, he might yet avail himself. It would be unmerciful to tyrannically offer his poor soul which was purchased with such precious treasure to the devil of hell, under the unbearable judgment, punishment, and wrath of God, so that he would forever have to suffer and bear the tortures of the unquenchable burning, the consuming fire, eternal pain, woe, and death. Never observing that the Son of man says: Learn of me, I have given you an example, Follow me, I am not come to destroy souls, but to save them.

Behold, this was the foundation of my guileless words which I at that time spoke to you in sincerity of heart, according to the style and spirit of the Gospel of Christ. These words you daub with this hateful color before all men saying that I make many pious rulers homicides, that I protect and encourage the hoodlums in their wickedness. I will leave it to your judgment what kind of spirit prompted you thus enviously to write about my plain words. O Micron, you misbehaved too grossly! For what else do you do by your writing but upbraid and blaspheme Christ Himself, whose example I follow in this matter, for pointing unto repentance the adulterous woman who was already adjudged by the law of Moses and letting her go uncondemned. Paul also did not punish the Corinthian further (according to the Mosaic and human law he was deserving of death) than with separation [excommunication] whereby he won him unto God, something which with your putting to death he could not have done. Dear Micron, reflect and see if I do not teach correctly.

I do not doubt in the least but that all reasonable men who shall read my writings, if they have any Scriptural knowledge at all, will say that I have not spoken unreasonably but truly and Christianly, although I have to hear such an ugly greeting from you.

Profane history shows that the Lacedaemonians, who were heathen[3] did not practice capital punishment, but they imprisoned their offenders and put them to work. It happened that when some of them showed natural piety, ability, counsel, deeds, honor, and self-restraint, they raised them to high office. They were not driven by the bloodthirsty spirit of murder as are some of the preachers and writers who dare boast of the crucified Christ and His office or service, who cause to be placarded,[4] and without mercy, out of hatred for the truth (because they according to God's Word refuse to participate in their erring doctrine and false religion), and also thrust them into the hands of the

---

[3] In contrast with the profession of the rulers of Menno's era. *Ed.*

[4] The reference is to public notices calling for the arrest and prosecution of wrongdoers. Emperor Charles V issued an edict against Menno as early as Dec. 7, 1542. *Ed.*

executioner—not merely those who are guilty before civil law, such as thieves, murderers, sorcerers, etc., but also the sincere, faithful children of God who sincerely seek Christ Jesus and His holy truth and walk unblamably before the world—to be tortured, drowned, burned, or put to the sword. O Lord!

My witnesses that I write the truth in regard to this matter are not only the papist and Lutheran writers but also your highly esteemed leaders and brethren, John Calvin, Theodore Beza, and the book of John a Lasco which was ready to be printed but by the contradiction of some people was again recalled.

Beloved Micron, if you and they were born of God and impelled by the Spirit of the Lord, if you had tasted the sweet Word of God and the fruits of the world to be, you would never afflict the pious as you have done by your untrue, false writing, nor would you encourage any in their bloody doings, but point them to the meek Lamb, and let the dead bury the dead. Ponder what I mean.

That the office of the magistrate is of God and His ordinance I freely grant. But him who is a Christian and wants to be one and then does not follow his Prince, Head, and Leader Christ, but covers and clothes his unrighteousness, wickedness, pomp and pride, avarice, plunder, and tyranny with the name of magistrate, I hate. For he who is a Christian must follow the Spirit, Word, and example of Christ, no matter whether he be emperor, king, or whatever he be. For these following admonitions apply to all alike: Let this mind be in you which was also in Christ Jesus. Phil. 2:5. He that saith he abideth in him, ought himself also so to walk, even as he walked. I John 2:6.

Behold, you show by your conduct that you very neatly speak and teach to tickle their ears, and the lusts of their hearts, inasmuch as you point them to the punishing Moses and not to the forbearing Christ. You encourage them in their vain, proud, pompous, and unmerciful carnal life which agrees little with the life of an innocent, contrite, humble, merciful, compassionate, pious, and regenerate Christian whose conversation is in heaven. This indicates that you are a deadly enemy to their poor souls, and that you do not treat them in keeping with the task of a true messenger of God. They build the wall and you daub it with untempered mortar. Ezek. 13:10. You cry, Peace, peace, while there is no peace. Jer. 8:11. Dear Micron, reflect if it is not the truth that I write.

That these things are so your unscriptural glosses concerning the oath make plain. Christ says, Ye have heard that it hath been said by them of old time, Thou shalt not forswear thyself, but shalt perform unto the Lord thine oaths; but I say unto you, Swear not at all; neither by heaven, for it is God's throne: nor by the earth; for it is his footstool. Matt. 5:33-35. And you, Micron, say that nothing but light-minded, false oaths are hereby prohibited, as if Moses allowed Israel to swear light-mindedly and falsely, and that Christ under the New Testament merely forbade these, notwithstanding that all intelligent readers know that it was not merely allowed Israel to swear truly but it was also commanded them to do so. Lev. 19:12; Deut. 10:20.

If the Israelites then, as you hold, had the liberty in this matter that we have, and if it be such a glorious thing and such an honor to God rightly to swear by the name of God, as you make bold to lie against your God, then tell me (Dear me) why Wisdom did not say, You have heard that it hath been said to them of old, Thou shalt not forswear thyself, and I say the same thing. Instead Christ says, Moses commanded not to forswear thyself, but I say unto you, Thou shalt not swear at all. O God, what a grievous pity that such plain words of the Son of God are thus lamentably falsified and plastered over with the vile dung of satanic glosses, merely to suit the rulers who are but dust, as Musculus[5] and you have done! How little you have pondered the Scriptures which say, We ought to obey God rather than men. Acts 5 :29.

It is very plain that Christ Jesus, the teacher of righteousness, points away from the oath of Moses, which was also an oath of truth, and sworn by the name of the Lord, an oath which you practice and recommend to the reader highly. Christ points us to the yea and nay in truth, and since I know of a certainty that His Word is the truth and His commandment life eternal, therefore I am confident and bold to teach it thus, truly believing that He will not deceive us by His doctrine.

It is a great joy to me that such faithful children in truth are found who are prepared to seal the holy commandments and testimony of the Lord with their possessions and blood (although I have to hear your reproach). Nor do I doubt but that they at the day of Christ will be a part of my crown, for they suffer as a testimony against you and all the world; suffer for reproving in love your deceiving, lying hearts and tongues so that you may be brought to reflect, even though they alas are called such detestable people by you.

If they were no more faithful to truth than Hermes[6] and you have shown yourselves in your writing and speech to be, then they would not so gallantly adhere unto death to their yea and nay in truth. Of this we are convinced.

They so faithfully adhere to their dependable yea and nay which Christ has commanded us, that they would forsake their possessions and life rather than transgress this commandment. Their whole mind and life conform to this yea and nay, always spoken truthfully before God and man. These people are in distress on that account; therefore I will leave it to the consideration of all impartial, reasonable readers as also to yourselves whether I and our beloved brethren are deserving of such innocent bloodshed because we have led them by the assistance and power of the Lord, in the power of the Word, in the Holy Spirit, from falsehood unto truth, from unrighteousness unto righteousness, from darkness to light, and from the old, sinful life of ungodliness to the penitent, new life of godliness to which Moses and Christ, together with all the prophets, apostles, sacrifices, commandments, prohibitions, ceremonies, and sacraments, unanimously point. [I will leave it to them to judge] whether perhaps you deserve to be called deceivers, you and your kind who say what men like to hear and write so as to incite to blood, who denounce the powerful

---

[5] Prof. Wolfgang Musculus (1497-1563) was a Reformed scholar who taught in the Swiss University of Berne. Ed.

[6] See the Introduction to Menno's *Reply to Martin Micron. Ed.*

doctrine as taught from the lips of the Lord, and also denounce as erring folk the valiant witnesses and saints of Christ who would rather die than willfully transgress the Word of the Lord, or confirm aught further than by yea and nay. By so doing you open the doors wide to the rapacious rulers to rob such pious souls and to the bloodthirsty to murder them.

Worthy Micron, if you were one of the true messengers and servants of Christ, as alas, you boldly boast, you would point the magistracy who usually have high and proud hearts and are quite carnal in their life, to the true, sincere repentance which can stand before God, and teach them the Spirit, mind, nature, and Word of the Lord, if you had such. Then the unction itself[7] would teach them without any man's assistance how they should conduct themselves in regard to such weighty matters as bloodshed, the oath, and other matters. But now alas things have to be turned upside down so that there may be something wherewith to charge us before the blind world and to cry that we are unfit to live. O Martin, your scorpion's sting and lion's teeth are too sharp and vicious, for your venomous, deadly stings and bites are alas too numerous.

Tell me, who is wronged because we for conscience' sake (the mouth of the Lord having forbidden it) do not dare to take an oath when we testify the genuine truth when this is called for and do it without guile? The oath serves no other purpose than to make men testify truly. Can the truth not be told without oaths? Do all testify to the truth even when under oath? To the first question you must say yes, and to the last no. Is the oath the truth itself to which one testifies, or does the truth depend upon the man who takes the oath? Why does not the magistracy then accept the testimony confirmed by yea and nay as commanded of God instead of that confirmed by that which is forbidden? For it can punish those who are found false in their yea and nay as well as those who swear falsely.

I trust that no person is so confused as not to know that the ordinances of God which are of heaven should not give way to the ordinances of men which are of earth, but that the earthly ordinances of men should give way to God's ordinances if they would be Christians and proceed according to the truth.

Therefore it would be well for you to observe that by your writing concerning the oath you make foolish or false teachers of Christ, the Son of God, and of the holy apostle James. For Christ's position and doctrine is that Moses has commanded not to swear falsely, but that under the New Testament one should not swear at all. James says that we should not swear, neither by heaven, neither by the earth, neither by any other thing (Jas. 5:12), and you gloss this as did the serpent saying that it is not so, but that we may swear to the truth, etc. And thus the eternal Wisdom Himself and His holy witness James, alas, must be your pupils and flunkies.

Consider also that you condemn the innocent, and clear the ungodly, both of which are an abomination in the sight of the Lord. Prov. 17:15. In this way you strengthen the hands of the evildoers and daub the wall with untempered

7 Cf. II Cor. 1:21; I Thess. 4:9; I John 2:20, 27. *Ed.*

mortar, as was said before. Dear me, reflect and see if you are not one of those whose mouths speak great swelling words, having men's persons in admiration because of advantage. Jude 16.

And remember that you cause great distress to the pious hearts who are born of the truth, and faithfully walk in it, and seal it with yea and nay, and you load the innocent blood upon yourself.

John saw the finely attired harlot upon the scarlet-colored beast, drunk with the blood of the saints and with the blood of the witnesses of Jesus. And whether or not you in your heart have drunk or do drink such a draught of blood with her, I will leave to the omniscient Judge, and to yourself. Dear Micron, reflect and see if I do not rightly point out your sores.

You did not fear but diligently exerted yourself to falsify, obscure, and break the Lord's express Word for the purpose of pleasing the magistracy. You have also alas exerted yourself to garble my words, as if I had cited the words of David (who did not delight in false doctrine neither has sworn deceitfully, Psalm 24:4) in my article concerning swearing for the purpose of proving that under the New Testament we should not swear, although I adduced these words for no other purpose (as my words plainly show) than to show that but little attention alas is given these days to the piety exhibited in the words of said Psalm, as is plainly shown by your false, defaming tongue and hand (although you call yourself a preacher of the holy Word) toward me, poor man, who alas has or finds but little consolation from the children of men.

Besides I had written a note in the margin saying in plain words that it was spoken by David in a legal sense, and that under the New Testament we were to use yea and nay instead. You have drawn back from nothing to make me ridiculous and obnoxious to the reader.

In the same manner you have not avoided to call me inconsistent because I wrote that we should not swear at all in regard to temporal matters, because Christ did not use the word verily in worldly matters, but only in connection with His doctrine, etc. I know of nothing that I wrote which you did not wrongly explain and garble! I wish that you would consider in the fear of God what kind of spirit it is that has taught you thus. My saying that one should not swear at all in worldly dealings was taught me not by this or that gloss of the old serpent, but by the Word of the Lord. Matt. 5:37; Jas. 5:12.

I specified an exception in regard to doctrine to aid the reader, for the purpose of showing that Paul and Christ did not make use of the terms, *Verily* and *God is my witness* (which the learned ones would construe into an oath for the purpose of establishing their position), in treating of temporal matters, but in connection with their teachings only.

If this matter is weighed in the balance of the holy, divine Word carefully in such a manner as to keep the unity of the Scripture, then it should be observed that the oath and certain affirmations do not have the same form in the Scriptures. It is manifest that an oath was and is still always sworn by the Deity, or by something else. This is not the case with an affirmation such as Paul and Christ used in their teaching.

Abraham said unto his servant, Put, I pray thee, thy hand under my thigh; and I will make thee swear by the Lord, the God of heaven, and the God of the earth. Gen. 24:2. Joseph said to his brethren, By the life of Pharaoh ye are spies. Moses said, Thou shalt fear the Lord thy God; him shalt thou serve, and to him shalt thou cleave, and swear by his name. Again, Christ says, Neither by heaven, nor by earth, neither by Jerusalem, neither by thy head, nor by the temple, nor by the altar (and one might add, neither with the world, nor by God, nor by the Gospel, nor by a cross, etc.).

And so you see an oath is always sworn by something. This is not the case with an affirmation which is made without an oath.

Affirmations occur without an oath, but an oath cannot be made without an affirmation. And so Christ and Paul often affirmed their words with high affirmations, but they did not swear to them. For nowhere did they say, This we swear or affirm by the truth, or by God, or by our soul. They said simply, *Verily,* or *God is my witness,* and other like affirming words.

I abide by the holy Word, commandment, and prohibition of the Lord, simply and truly, and point my neighbors who would fear God without guile to yea and nay, as the mouth of Truth has commanded me and all true Christians to do. I sincerely strive to instruct according to my small talent, the poor, blind world in the true, divine knowledge through Jesus Christ without any respect of persons, and to point out the falsehood of Antichrist and the old serpent according to the truth, thus to lead men to the vision of eternal peace by His grace. This doctrine shows its power in many, as may be seen. Therefore it is that they are so enraged at me that no Turk or Tartar, no tyrant or monster under the whole heavens, no matter how ungodly he be, is hated as I, miserable man, am. [I am] hated of the world because of this defaming, false, bloodthirsty writing and shouting of the learned ones, who for the sake of their poor bellies teach the broad, easy way with all the false prophets. He who created me knows what kindly disposition and love I bear to you and all my enemies and slanderers. If I could serve you with my life unto righteousness I would at all times be willing and prepared to do so by the grace of God. This I write with a good conscience as before God in Christ Jesus.

Dear Micron, do consider how crudely you out of hatred for the truth treat me, a sad old man, quite contrary to all truth, to the dishonor of the Almighty God, and contrary to the virtuous, pious nature of the divine Christian love which does not want to defraud or harm anyone. But what will help? The innocent, defenseless Lamb must be hated and murdered in His members.

I will, since you do not want it any other way, let you teach and counsel your church, the world, to fight and retaliate as did Moses and the patriarchs, according to your manner; teach them to punish, scatter, imprison, and destroy their enemies, depriving them of life and property, to sentence criminals regardless of whether they repent or not, as you write; teach them also to swear and be sworn after the manner that Moses commanded his Israelites. But I shall and will by the grace of God faithfully teach and counsel all true, regenerate children of God, and followers of Christ, rulers and otherwise, with the sure word of the holy Gospel, to use no other sword than the one Christ Jesus and His apostles used, to be merciful and sympathetic to penitent sinners, even as Christ is merciful unto us; mercifully to punish the impenitent and to admonish them in love as Christ admonished us; and scrupulously to stand by their yea and nay, as the true teacher and finisher of the New Testament, the ever-blessed Christ Jesus, Himself, has distinctly commanded and taught us with His guileless mouth; no matter what the consequences to my person may be. Dear Micron, reflect and see if I have not rightly pointed to the Scriptures, and consider also by what spirit you have abused me. True is the wise man's word, Who is able to stand before envy? Prov. 27:4.

Eight. It is also manifest that throughout your book you have labored with all your might to make the truth of Christ, taught by us to the measure of our talent, obnoxious and hateful to the reader and hearer, together with my person, and to make the falsehood of Antichrist taught by you pleasant and glorious, together with your person. You have so conducted the matter, but alas not with God's Spirit, that if I had been a mere beginner of three or four months in the church, I would probably have carried on (according to you in your untrue, partial writing) as I have done.

But thus the righteous Lord makes manifest unto the simple and plain the impure spirit, the heart, bitterness, ambition, hatred, envy, falsehood, and unbecoming defamation. Also the false doctrine of all such people who so cover up their wolf's heart with a fair sheepskin, as you wear, so that the simple can scarcely perceive it. The venomous, deadly arrows and lies shot at me show to the whole world what kind of spirit is in you. Now it is Menno's great inconstancy; then it is his gross ignorance or ignorant wisdom, or clever trickiness, Menno's lies, etc. And you even declare that I have changed my doctrine. In short, I do not know what you wrote that was not to the dishonor of God, of the saints, of the truth, of the church, and of me.

I thank my God with joyful heart that by His grace He has kept me these twenty-one years in one doctrine and foundation of faith without any change,[8] notwithstanding I was unworthy, called to my unbearably hard service in such perilous, dark, erring times, as all those will admit who have walked with me in Christ Jesus during the time of my pilgrimage and have from the beginning read my plain works and books and heard my admonitions.

It may be that I am a grossly unlearned and a not too brainy person as you have described me. I have never in my life boasted of great intellectuality, learning, cleverness, and brains. But I do boast that I in my weakness seek the praise of the Lord and the salvation of my soul, and that I have learned so much in the school of God by His grace, that I know that the whole, undivided Christ is God's first- and only-begotten and true Son, and that those who contradict this are the spirits of Antichrist; that all blasphemers against God, defamers of the saints, falsifiers of the Scriptures, willful liars, public slanderers,

[8] From the beginning of 1536 through 1556. *Ed.*

enviers of the pious, ambitious, bloodthirsty men are ungodly persons, and not Christians. On the other hand I know that all those who hear and follow Christ, and submissively, obediently, and conscientiously follow His Word, ordinances, and unblamable example in faith, by virtue of the new birth, are the children of God, and they shall forever inherit the kingdom of honor. I trust that I shall stand before the throne of the High Majesty in His grace with this my gross ignorance, which is wisdom in the sight of God, but hidden from the world, while all the pretentious and proud who are so wise and clever in their own sight, shall hear, Depart from me, ye that work iniquity; I have never known you. Friend Micron, take heed.

I trust that I shall be found innocent before the Lord and His judgment of the charge *clever trickiness* which you prefer against me, for I have dealt with you with no more clever and tricky heart than those do who daily for the sake of the testimony of Christ and of their consciences, die right along,[9] with a glad and joyous mind. Notwithstanding this I have to hear from you this unkind, false charge made before all the world. But the Lord will be our judge.

As to my lies, of which you accuse me, this is my plain answer, I am also included in the word, All men are liars. Psalm 116:11; Rom. 3:4. Yet I would rather die than lie willfully, be it slightly or grossly. I hated falsehood even before I knew of whose seed it was. I shall also in my old age by the grace of God avoid it so far as possible, now that I know its origin and father.

O Micron, Micron, how you deal with me exactly as did the false prophets and stiff-necked Jews out of mere hatred of the truth treat the good Jeremiah saying, Come and let us devise devices against Jeremiah and pay no attention to his words. John the Baptist had to hear from the Pharisees and scribes that he was possessed with the devil. And Jesus Christ was called by them a wine-bibber and glutton. Matt. 11:19. He had to hear that He cast out devils in the name of Beelzebub (Luke 11:15), and all this so that by these means they might frighten the ignorant, reckless people from the truth, and keep them in their leaven and vain, false doctrine. Just so you carry on toward me, afflicted man, out of mere hatred of the truth. For if you could only daub me with so much filthy falsehood that they would be affrightened at me, then you would hope that the cause of Christ was already lost. So utterly blind is poor, foolish flesh which is not overshadowed by the brightness of the Lord.

You may fill the measure of your fathers until God arrests you. Yet I am assured in my heart, by the grace of the Lord, that as Jeremiah, John, and Christ remained Jeremiah, John, and Christ, however much they were slandered by those who wished them ill and persecuted them out of hatred against the truth, so I also by the merciful grace and power of God will remain the same Menno Simons in Christ which I was in my weakness for more than twenty years, no matter how wrongly they lie about me and depict or portray me out of hatred against the truth. The false prophets, scribes, and Pharisees were

---

[9] In the Dutch Mennonite brotherhood about two thousand brethren and sisters were executed in the sixteenth century, one fourth of them being women and girls. *Ed.*

enemies of the truth and bloodthirsty, and therefore they died without God; so you also are without God and His grace, and you together with all false hypocrites will receive your reward unless you sincerely repent, something that I don't look for in you because you so willfully suppress the truth in regard to our discussion, tell so many falsehoods, knowingly falsify the Scriptures, and act so deceitfully against your neighbor in his absence, a thing which no regenerate Christian will or can do. For the Word remains the truth. Reflect and see if I do not put my finger on the sore spot.

Nine. It is manifest moreover that you have committed against yourself and your soul which was ransomed at such a precious price the grossest kind of shame and injury for these reasons: because by your writing you have made yourself an open accuser, corrector, reprover, yes, a teacher and instructor of God the Father, of Christ the Son, of Gabriel the angel, and of all the apostles and saints of the New Testament. The Father confesses Christ Jesus to be His beloved Son with any divisions; Christ confesses the Father to be His Father, and the angel and the apostles together with all the other witnesses, unanimously testify the same in regard to the visible, tangible, dying, and rising Christ. And you boldly say and write that He is not. I will leave you to consider in the fear of God whether you are not such an one as I have written.

You prove yourself to be an open corrupter of the Holy Scriptures. For you write that Christ is of David's seed, that He is of a woman, whereas the unfalsified texts have it: Born of the seed, that is, of the lineage, of David. Born of a woman, as may be seen by the Lutheran and Zurich translations.

You write that Christ has partaken of the flesh and blood of the children (Heb. 2:14), and the text says nothing more than flesh and blood without the addition *of the children;* if we accept the Scriptural meaning of the pronoun *eorundem,* which means *of the same.*

You write at different places that Christ has assumed Abraham's seed in the *preterite,* that is, in the past tense, while the text says, He takes on him (in the present tense). Whoever does not believe it may read the text of Heb. 2:16.

You say that Sarah put forth procreative seed of which Isaac was born, so excluding Abraham from the procreative process, although the Scriptures and nature make it plain that man only has procreative seed and not the woman, as was made very plain above.

It is manifest that you have of set purpose falsified the holy, divine Scriptures and made yourself a translation and scripture (as Tatian made himself a gospel, as you write) in order that you may the better maintain your anti-Christian doctrine before simple and unlearned people. Therefore I will leave it to the judgment of the impartial, reasonable reader of the world what kind of preacher and writer you are.

O dear Micron, consider to what you have already come. It looks as if you have just about lost both the Scriptures and reason by the deadly disease of your ambitious and envious partiality. If you should defame his Imperial

Majesty and his son Philip, as you have defamed the heavenly Father and His blessed Son Christ, in your writing, and should say plainly, No, King Philip is not the son of the emperor; he is the son of another person and is only called the son of the emperor; if you should, moreover, falsify their public mandates, sentences, and commandments as you have done the adduced Scriptures and plain ordinances, Word and commandments of Christ concerning baptism and the oath; and moreover, if you should mock, malign, scorn, and belie their oath-bound retinue and faithful servants because they honored and respected the emperor as the true father of Philip, and Philip as the true son of the emperor, and because they faithfully respected and obeyed their mandates, sentences, and policies, (Lord help us) what capers they would cut and what war songs would be sung. What you now deserve and must expect in due time from God the Lord because you so lamentably blaspheme the Ruler of rulers, the God of heaven and earth, and His blessed Son Christ Jesus, because you falsify and abuse their heavenly mandates, ordinances, and explicit and plain commandments, and because you so lamentably slander, malign, belie, hate, and persecute their faithful servants by your mean and ugly writings—and consequent distress and care—this I will leave to the Almighty God in His judgment. Dear friend, ponder upon what is said here.

You have made yourself an open, perjuring liar, for you call God as witness (which you, I believe, consider the same as an oath) that you have given a true account of the discussion, and the first thing you wrote in your book is a bald lie. For you write, *A true narration,* and how quite untrue it is God knows, as also you yourself, and we. We have touched on this part in the above description of the discussion.

As to my very first words and brotherly admonition, If you should hear more powerful truths and surer foundation from us than you have held hitherto, then you ought not to seek your own praise and honor; but cordially to seek the honor and praise of the Lord, etc. This you have quoted in your book coupled with a gross falsehood. You represent it as though I had said reprovingly that you have sought your own honor and praise by your writing in England. Something which at that time I had never thought about, for I knew you no more than if you had never been born. Yet you tie this shame around my neck. I will leave you to judge whether it was the spirit of truth and of godly, faithful love, or the spirit of impure falsehood and faithless envy which inspired you to write thus.

You write that Hermes Backereel had already proved to me that Mary was a daughter of David. He must have a Bible and Scripture different from ours, for it cannot be found in our Bible and Scripture. I have not pressed you nor Hermes for proof, since it was irrelevant, seeing that procreative seed is not found with women. And now you make it appear that I said that she was not David's daughter, and that Hermes proved to me that she was. I have enough of this hideous lying!

You write that you frequently confessed before us that the Son of God died for us, while I dare say and testify with a good conscience that you never touched upon it during the whole discussion. But when I asked you at the last discussion[10] whether you did not still call the man Christ, who you said had no father, the Son of God, you answered yes. When I asked again why you called Him that, seeing that in your view He had no father, what kind of answer I received has been related above. Yet you dared to falsely write down that you frequently confessed it to us.

Though you were not ashamed of gross and ugly falsehood against us before men, because you are aware that you cannot sufficiently transgress against us despised ones in the sight of the world, which is your church; yet one would reasonably expect that you would be ashamed to do so before your God who tries the hearts and reins, and that you would remember that it is written, A thief is not so bad as a man accustomed to lying, for he can never attain to honor; that the lying mouth killeth the soul; that God will destroy the liars, and that their part will be in the lake which burns with fire and brimstone.

You maintained the purity of your Christ against us, you say, and that procreative seed is found with women, but before the Lord, before you, and before us all, it did not occur otherwise than I related in the narration of the first discussion concerning the absurdity that you had an impure Christ. You were so stuck with your notion of the seed of the woman that in the latest discussion you acknowledged openly that women have no procreative seed but only a menstrual flux. What shall I say more? When I began to read your book I made a beginning of noting the lies on the margin, but I found so many that at last I let it go, being astonished at the spirit of falsehood which drove you to write such a perverted and false account.

I was also surprised at the fact that there was not sufficient common sense left in you to consider that you might go to such lengths with your biased writing and clumsy falsehoods, that many of the readers, particularly of those present at the discussion, might suspect you of writing falsehoods out of mere partiality and thereupon leave your church. But the spirit of wisdom alas has not kissed the dwelling place of your soul, nor greeted it with the friendly lips of its truth.

You have also made yourself a very unsteady, wavering, and inconstant person, one whom we cannot overtake on one position and doctrine. For at one time of the discussion you confessed that Christ from everlasting was born of the Father, and had His session, differentiated from the Father, and next to Him. Now you have changed your position and write that He remained in the Father. Notice your first change. Secondly, you confess two sons in Christ and now you say but one Son, yet in fact two if we consider your doctrine without partisan bias. Thirdly, you confessed that the crucified Christ who died for us was not God's Son, and now you write that you frequently confessed that He was. Notice your second and third changes. And yet you write that He had

10 The two discussions were held Feb. 6 and 15, 1554 (Old Style, 1553, as Menno always writes it). *Ed.*

no Father. Is this what you mean by *Simplex veritates oratio,* as you write, The word of truth is plain? This I will leave to you to consider. It must be admitted that if one cannot see frivolous inconstancy and false duplicity in this, he must be quite unintelligent and blind. Fourthly, you confessed that Christ should not be worshiped according to His human nature, and now you say that He should be. Notice your fourth change. Yet you confess that He was an earthly man of earth, who was born of Adam's seed. (If this is not idolatry, we may truly say that the Scriptures deceive us.) In the fifth place you acknowledge that woman does not have procreative seed. And now you write that she has. And that in spite of the fact that you wrote years ago that the blood of Mary (at that time you did not speak of the seed of Mary) congealed in her to become our flesh and blood, as is reported above.

Whether so many confessions and retractions are consistent with a sincere, pious, constant, and well-founded preacher and writer (as you like to be called) who out of ambition denies and covers it all, this will I herewith leave to all impartial readers to judge.

In the fifth place you have made yourself before all intelligent persons a very proud, self-conceited, bold, and ambitious boaster because you sing such great triumphs, and brag in your book, while it is manifest to God, to yourself, and to all who were present that you had already lost the whole point in discussion. It would also be manifest to the whole world if you had but honestly reported as it happened, for you confessed two sons in Christ, and that the crucified one was not God's Son, as you in fact still do, and that women have no procreative seed, whereby you had already finished the discussion. You could not answer a word to all the Scriptures I read whereby I testified unto you that the Son of man, the visible, tangible, eating, drinking, suffering, dying, and rising Christ, was God's own, true Son, nor could you reply a word to my four convincing answers with which I overcame your unscriptural question concerning the birth from everlasting, the session next to the Father, etc., all of which you have left out of your narration!

Neither did you in the discussion say anything about the union of the two sons, which are generally called two natures, which is now your strongest Scripture, although in fact it is not found in the whole Bible. For if you had, you would by the help of the Lord have received an answer. You have told such abominable falsehoods, you have changed the order of the discussion, twisted my words, misinterpreted them, abbreviated or added to them at pleasure, and dressed up your own words, whereby it is manifest before God and man that your discussion of us, and particularly the account thereof, was not prompted by a humble, converted, and contrite heart, nor by the spirit and love of Christ, but by an ambitious, self-conceited, proud, lofty flesh and spirit. I will leave it to the all-knowing God and to yourself who knows your ambitions the best, and also to the pious reader who walks in the truth, whether this which I say is not the truth. O friend, teach yourself before you undertake to teach others! Behold yourself inwardly and outwardly in the clear mirror of Christ and His holy Word, that you may realize what an ignorant preacher and contrary Christian you are before God.

In the sixth place you have also made yourself a false prophet and preacher, a deceiver of men, a patent hypocrite and ravening wolf in sheep's clothing. Do not take it amiss that I call you these things and tell the truth. For how can you teach a more false doctrine than to teach that God the Father is not the true Father of the whole Christ; and that the whole Christ is not the true Son of God; to make the angel of God, John the Baptist, and all the apostles of God false witnesses; to make Christ, the eternal truth, a false teacher; for He says that we are not to swear at all, and you say that we are allowed to swear to the truth; to make the baptism which was commanded by Christ and taught and practiced by His holy apostles a deviating baptism, and to want to teach a different doctrine and practice of which not a word is found in all the Scriptures.

Yes, worthy Micron, if you want to follow good advice, you would quit your writing, for try as you may, it is certain that you by your strongest arguments and best points do nothing in fact but assume the role of teacher over the eternal wisdom, Christ Jesus, the Son of God, and His Holy Ghost, together with the apostles of Christ. You change their words, doctrine, commandments, institutions, ordinances, and practice as though they in themselves were not good enough and right, yes, you make them powerless and vain and useless. And thereby you show that you are their teacher and master. Beloved Micron, take heed. The more you write, the more manifest you make your own shame and false doctrine, and the greater you make the guilt of your deceit. My friend, be warned.

You console the poor, blind people with falsehood, deprive them of both the Father and the Son, falsify the Word of the Lord most lamentably, from which it is very plain that you forsake the Lord who has purchased us, that you are prompted by the spirit of Antichrist, that you are anathema, for you teach a gospel which was not taught us by the apostles of Christ. You rob God of His honor; you are a murderer of souls which Christ Jesus has purchased at such a great price, a messenger of darkness who transforms himself into an angel of light.

Once more, do not take it amiss that I write the truth. I repeat, a ravening wolf are you in sheep's clothing who devours the souls of men by a false explanation of the Scriptures under a fictitious semblance of truth, robs them of the truth, and thus sacrifices them and leads them to the prince of hell for the sake of a yard of wool and a loaf of bread. I do not mention that you cause so much grievous trouble to many a chosen saint of God, deprive him of possession and even of life by your false doctrine because you falsely charge, slander, defame, and trample underfoot the doctrine which is the clear, pure, unadulterated, powerful, saving, and regenerating doctrine of Christ. You call these heresy and deceit, and the faithful children which are thereby converted from unrighteousness unto righteousness and from the dumb idols unto the living God you call deceitful, sectarian people before the erring, blind, and carnal world of blasphemers, blood preachers, messengers of the devil, blood-thirsty tyrants, and covetous robbers.

Ah, Micron, my friend, how good it were if you, unless it be that you repent, had never been born. To what have you let yourself be brought by your proud, conceited, and turbulent flesh, by your writings for a little puff of empty honor which you can enjoy for so brief a time in this insane and troubled world, to bring such grievous blasphemy upon the Almighty, eternal, and good God, such disgrace and shame upon His holy apostles and faithful witnesses, such great disgrace upon the Word of the Lord, such fatal deceit to the people, such great grief to the pious, and such unspeakably ugly sin upon your own soul. For your whole book is nothing but a plain declaration and manifestation of your own shame and anti-Christian doctrine, both for the present and the future world. It discovers, proclaims, and publishes aloud your abominably great abuse and error unto all men who seek the Lord. Friend Micron, reflect and see if I do not rightly point out your very dangerous wounds and deadly sores according to the Scriptures.

Finally, you have made yourself a shame and dishonor to all the rest of the preachers who are your fellows in doctrine and in service in the sight of all the pious world. You migrated from Flanders to England, from England to Friesland for the sake of the Gospel, as it is represented. You do much writing and disputing. You lead a reasonable and publicly correct life before the world. You are not exactly considered an adulterer, a drunkard, or a braggart, as I hear. In short you are clothed in sheep's clothing, etc. Perhaps you are looked upon and considered a leader, a great light, or at least an outstanding man by the people. And yet you are in truth found to be before God and all intelligent persons such a one as we have somewhat shown you to be in this letter from your own writings. Now we will let the reader consider in the fear of God what we are to think of the others who are not thus covered with sheep's clothing, but who covet, grasp, gormandize and guzzle, boast and brag, lead a careless, easy, and carnal life, who fear neither God nor the devil, who sell the souls of men for a trifle and are eager for big incomes and an easy life but are in the same doctrine, vocation, and service with you. And how we should conduct ourselves in regard to attending the preaching of both you and them (a matter on account of which they bite their tongues for madness), I will let everyone judge who cordially seeks God according to the Word of the Lord.

I am very much surprised that the other preachers, part of whom although they do not want to be upon the narrow way with Christ and His chosen ones, are nevertheless to an extent of reasonable nature, do not reprove you and stop your slanderous writings, it being a shame to them as well as to yourself, for never was their anti-Christian position and doctrine concerning Christ, the Son of God, so bluntly and crudely, so coarsely and plainly revealed as it was by your bold assertions and blindness and by my necessary reply thereto. Anyone who has eyes to see may see what terrible unbelief and abominable position and doctrine you have. But then you will remain good teachers in the sight of the world, for it is such that they seek and desire. John truly says, They are of the world; therefore speak they of the world, and the world heareth them. I John 4:5.

You see, honorable Micron, I have placed the clear mirror of truth before the eyes of your conscience and have properly cut asunder the invisible members of your soul. Now open your eyes and you will see what kind of man you are and with how great a malady you are afflicted as to the soul, from which malady spring all these obnoxious exhalations such as lying, vituperation, defamation, false explanations and falsifications of the Scriptures, and twisted glosses. Just as by the law the knowledge of sin is, so this epistle will discover unto you how wholly and mortally you are bitten by the serpent, and how he has corrupted you before God by the damnable venom of his evil nature, and made your whole life unclean.

If the merciful Lord, by His loving-kindness, should by this means make you feel and know the coarse and blunt shame which you have committed against God and man by your slanderous writing, which I fear you have until now by your great blindness, hatred, ambition, and self-love noticed but little, then do not tarry if you would not die in your ungodliness; come before the throne of grace, to the ever-blessed Christ Jesus with a broken, contrite, repentant spirit in an unfalsified faith, with a changed, pentitent, and new heart. For He is the spiritual, brazen serpent, raised up unto all Adam's children who are poisoned in Adam, as a healing sign. He is the man who can help and heal you of all the deep wounds of your sick soul. He is the physician in Israel. Of Him alone is found the ointment and medicine of eternal life. And if you would commit yourself to Him and follow His advice, so as to find help and health for your diseased soul, you must give yourself up to Him, obey His Word, will, commandments, and prohibitions; and deny your selfish, ambitious, pretentious, partial, envious, vain, wrathful flesh which leads you to this abominably false writing. You must become little in your own sight; lay a better and Christian foundation in your heart; relinquish your glossing and falsification of the Scriptures, idolatrous sacraments, and all hypocrisy; seek and fear the Lord in His holy Word with sincerity of heart. With tears you must reconcile yourself with your neighbors whom you have wronged with pernicious falsehood, in sincere brotherly love and by other writings published to the world confessing that through mere hatred against the truth you have without cause defamed their name still more, a name already hated too much for truth's sake. I fear you will hardly do so unless you become a more godly, penitent, and pious Micron than you, alas, have been thus far.

So long as you do not do this, it is manifest that you hate your neighbor without cause, and are hostile to him out of hatred of the truth, and are therefore separate from Christ and counted with murderers. O friend, reflect and repent. Take diligent heed lest you destroy forever your precious soul for the sake of a little temporary and vain praise. But a little while and Micron is no more! O the sentence, Depart from me, ye cursed, into the everlasting fire! What a sentence!

Friend Micron, in faithful love I warn you. Take heed, I pray you. I have in our times known several persons who were prompted by a like spirit of bitter zeal against the Lamb and His chosen ones, and who were judged and punished before the eyes of men by the Lord, who does justly and properly reward the unjust.

It is about eighteen or nineteen years ago that a highly esteemed man who was much respected by the world (whose name and country I will not mention) wickedly advised that they should destroy me together with the pious. His words and ungodly thoughts were hardly finished when the avenging hand of the Lord was laid upon him. He slumped down at the table and in a moment his bloodthirsty, impenitent, ungodly life was ended in a terrible way. Oh, fearful judgment!

And about the same time it happened to another man who thought that he would set his trap in such a way that I could not escape, that he at the very meal he was eating when he said this, was suddenly pierced by an arrow from the Lord, stricken with a severe disease, and thus had to give an account before the Lord. He was buried within eight days.

Another who was to become an officer to the emperor at a certain place thought that he would destroy this people as long as the emperor was the emperor. He came to the place where he was to be located and perform his function. And four or five days thereafter the bell was tolled for him and the requiem sung over him. Behold thus God the Lord annihilates the designs of the ungodly who storm this holy mount and destroys those who hate His truth and are hostile thereto.

It happened in the year 1554 that three of our brethren were at Wisbuy in Gothland for the purpose of earning a livelihood. A preacher of the city named Laurentius who was of the spirit of his father cried after them in the street and abused them as much as he could and said that they should not do business there if it were to cost him all that was enclosed by his jacket, meaning his body and his soul. A few days afterwards he conversed with one of these brethren, in the presence of another preacher who was not unreasonably minded. He reviled and carried on terribly. The great Lord in the presence of both of them checked him so that he lost his voice all of a sudden and within twenty-four hours he was a corpse. Oh, terrible punishment and judgment of God!

A case almost similar occurred the same year at Wismar. A town crier named Smedesteet had been engaged. He said that he would rather have a hatful of our blood than a hatful of gold. He persuaded the magistracy, who gladly have and hear such flatterers, to proclaim just before the bitterly cold winter to the poor people to clear the place before St. Martin's day or else they would be put where they would not like to go. Smedesteet was very joyous that he had accomplished the fulfillment of his heart's desire. But to his own condemnation! For the same day the Almighty, great Lord laid the hands of His wrath upon him and within seven days the Lord took him away by a severe illness. Yet the blind, hardened world does not observe these things.

In the year 1555 in the same city there was a preacher named Vincentius who lives there still. He never tired of his godless railing and slandering. On the day they call the Ascension day and on which they preach on the Scripture, He that believeth, and is baptized, shall be saved (Mark 16:16), he said he would revile and slander us as long as his mouth would open. The same hour the strong Lord closed it and bound his tongue. He fell down in the pulpit and was carried by all fours to his house by some of those present, as one punished of God, a dumb man. So God can punish those who touch the apple of His eye and harm it. If I were to relate all the incidents which in my time befell the enemies of the saints, it would require a separate volume and chronicle.

Therefore I advise you in sincerity of heart no longer to oppose such a strong and avenging God and Lord. I tell you in Christ that it will be too hard, yes, too hard for you to kick against the pricks. Acts 9:5. For His name is Sovereign Lord, Mighty Prince. Isa. 9:6. Who is like unto thee, glorious in holiness, fearful in praises, doing wonders? Ex. 15:11. His arrows never miss and when He calls we must appear. None can escape from Him and avoid His wrath. O Micron, take heed.

Yes, good friend Micron, if your battle were merely against me as you perhaps think, you would already have won it. For the whole world is on your side in this matter, yes, the serpent himself, and against me; for this position is the only weapon according to the doctrine of John which is to conquer his kingdom, the world. But the battle is not against me but against the truth itself, against the Father and His blessed Son, against the whole Scriptures, and against those who dwell in heaven. Therefore take heed. For although the reckless, coarse world may say Amen to your cause, yet you will not have your way with the most High, whose glory, honor, truth, and testimony I according to my small talent uphold by His grace and power.

And if you have already deprived me of my honor, good name and fame, body and life (things which I have already long ago surrendered and deem of little consequence for Christ's sake) in the sight of the world, which is not covered by Christ's prayer (John 17:9), yet, thank God, I have never harmed you nor wished you any harm. Nevertheless, God the Father will remain the true Father of Christ, and Christ the true Son of God; and you will have to turn from your impure, anti-Christian doctrine to the unfalsified pure doctrine of Christ, or you will be one of those of whom it is written, He that believeth not is condemned already, because he hath not believed in the name of the only begotten Son of God. John 3:18.

Neither partisan agitation nor disputing will prevail against God and His Word. He is the one who will win out, and His Word is the doctrine which will remain the truth. If you do not believe that Jesus Christ is the Son of God, that His testimony and Word are true, and that His ordinances are the true ordinances; if you are not born of God, do not become of divine disposition and nature; are not urged and possessed of the Holy Spirit, do not sincerely repent; if you are not in Christ, nor Christ in you, then, according to the doctrine of John, you are one of those who have no God. I John 2:22.

But if you have Christ, if you actually believe that He is the true Son of God, then you have both the Father and the Son (I John 2:24) ; and you will walk as He walked; you will not willfully tell a falsehood, for you were born of the truth; you will not hate; you will not defame; you will not inform against your neighbors; you will wrong no person; you will seek the salvation of others, and not their destruction; you will reprove their sins; you will rightly teach; and you will deceive none, for the spirit of love which does rightly before God and man will dwell in you and will prompt you.

If you have Christ in power, you will walk in the light. John 3:21; 8:12. You will follow the true Shepherd and will enter in at the right door. John 10:2. You will walk upon the true road, remain in the truth, in the true vine (John 15:1) ; build upon the true rock (Eph. 2:20; I Pet. 2:5) ; you will not falsify the Word of God, for your spirit is one with the Spirit of Christ, your faith will be one with His word, and your life, though in weakness, one with His life.

You will seek the praise and honor of the Lord and not your own; you will confess Christ as your Saviour in life or death before all the world. All your pleasure will be in the law of the Lord, and your whole life in His fear. Your thoughts will be pure and all your words seasoned with salt. Your daily combat will be against the world, the devil, and your own evil flesh. And you will by your honest, virtuous life set an example to all the world. The cross taken upon you for the sake of the Lord's Word and testimony you will patiently bear. And if you should be overtaken to think, say, or do anything wrong, you will sincerely lament it. In short you will prove by all your actions that you are a chosen child of God, born of the heavenly seed of the holy Word, and that you are become a living member of the body of the Lord.

Dear Micron, such penitence and reformation I sincerely wish you, and I would like to see it truly manifested in you in power and truth, and I then for the sake of the testimony of Jesus, together with you, would make a sacrifice of my blood to the praise of the Lord and to the edification of our neighbors. I repeat, Repent, so that the precious treasure given for us be not lost in your case.

Herewith I commend you to the Almighty God. Let Him bestow upon you according to His great grace what I would like to see you have. This is my last word to you. Do as you please in speech and writing, unless you are converted into a better mind, for I constrained and urged you to do so by the God-fearing ones.

Nor shall I hereafter ask or solicit a public discussion with any person and that for these reasons: first, because I have these many years desired it by numerous written and verbal requests and have never been granted it. From which it is manifest that they care but little about the glory of God and the souls of men.

Secondly, because your principal teachers and leaders such as John a Lasco, Calvin, and Theodore Beza whom you confess to be your most worthy and most beloved brethren are men of blood.[11] That this is the case is testified by their own books, and also by old Servetus of Geneva,[12] and Joris of Paris who was burned in England.

Thirdly, because your brethren, the Walloon church, as they are called, have at Frankfort in their publications vowed against us, which two things we did not know so clearly heretofore as we do now.

Since I plainly see that there is nothing but deceit, faithlessness, bloodthirstiness, and perverseness found among the children of men wherever one may turn himself, and since nothing counts or can count for so little on earth as the praise of Christ and the salvation of souls, therefore I will let Babylon, with its false preachers, impure doctrine, idolatrous baptism and Supper, together with its false religion, and impenitent, vain, easy life, be Babylon; and will with the holy prophet Habakkuk, stand upon my watch and set me upon the tower to which I have been called, although so unworthy, and clearly sound the trumpet of the holy divine Word from the walls and gates of Jerusalem, according to my small talent, and faithfully awaken the citizens of the eternal peace, joyfully to sing the lovely hallelujah through the streets with grateful, joyous hearts to the honor of God (Heb. 2:1); to attire themselves before God and the world in the shining, white raiment of the saints in sincerity of heart and purity of doctrine. I will faithfully admonish them with careful, pious Esdras and say, My people, hear my word, and prepare yourselves for the battle and evil things. With holy Paul, Take unto you the whole armor of God, that you may be able to withstand in the evil day (Eph. 6:13), and with Christ Himself, Watch and pray (Matt. 24:42). For the prince of darkness with his whole force and kingdom besieges the city of God, storms by night and day, makes many assaults with flesh and blood, as falsehood and false doctrine, the lust of the eye, with imprisonment, banishment, confiscation, bloodshed, tyranny, and violence. Whoever does not pray without ceasing and keep himself in the fear of the Lord cannot stand.

Once more, I will let Babylon be Babylon. Those who are piously inclined will leave off their ungodliness and betake themselves to the marriage feast of Christ, for truth is revealed and the repast is prepared. Blessed is he who enters in with sincerity of heart, and saves his wedding garment. I would sincerely warn all the chosen children of God, the sincere faithful brethren and sisters of Christ, with beloved John, our most beloved brother and fellow in tribulation, in the kingdom and in the patience of Christ Jesus, and

---

[11] That is, men who favor the use of force and bloodshed with religious nonconformists. Ed.

[12] Burned at the stake in Geneva, Switzerland, Oct. 27, 1553. John Calvin served as his formal accuser in court. Ed.

would say, Children, love not the world, neither the things that are in the world, for all that is in the world, the lust of the flesh, and the lust of the eyes, and the pride of life, is not of the Father, but is of the world; and the world passeth away and the lust thereof; but he that doeth the will of God abideth forever. I John 2:15-17. Friend Micron, once more be warned, repent, pray to God for grace, earnestly reflect upon that which I have written.

And do not be angry because I have so sharply reproved you. I have done so with the truth to the honor of God, and to the benefit of the reader, just as I reprove the whole world without respect of persons, in order that you might rightly learn the brightness of Christ, see and feel your foul sores, be healed by the Lord's medicine, sincerely repent, and be eternally saved.

I herewith commend you to the gracious, merciful God and Father for the enlightenment of your blind soul and the reformation of your sinful life by His blessed, first-born, and only true Son, Christ Jesus, by the enlightenment and the impulsion of His eternal and Holy Spirit unto more righteousness.

Open rebuke is better than secret love. Faithful are the wounds of a friend; but the kisses of an enemy are deceitful. Prov. 27:5, 6.

By me, MENNO SIMONS

*October 16*

## A FRIENDLY REQUEST TO THE READER

It is an old proverb, honorable reader, So many men, so many minds. Every person generally judges according to his own ideas, whereby many an unjust and wicked sentence is rendered especially where blind and perverse partiality has sway.

Since I find that our opponents with their false doctrine cannot stand before the power of the holy, divine Word, and since they diligently try to defame and calumniate us, and so to garble our words that we with truth on our side are rejected by the world, and they with falsehood on their side are honored by the world; therefore I pray all impartial readers not to be offended at it if they should say, Menno has not truthfully reported at this point.

In accordance with the doctrine of Christ, I hope to rejoice in being called a liar by those who hate the truth. I trust that those who are born of the truth will not charge me with falsehood, for I have chosen truth for a mother more than twenty-one years ago.[13] I also desire in my weakness to walk in her ways as an obedient, faithful child, without looking back and without offense so long as I remain on earth. Of this my hand and mouth, my humble life, together with my tribulation, poverty, privation, misery, cross, and death, shall be witness against my enemies at the judgment of Christ. Take heed.

I deem it impossible word for word to describe this just as it transpired (those parts of the discussion which Micron has suppressed or misinterpreted). Nor have the holy apostles and evangelists who described the actions and

---

[13] Menno was converted about April 1535. He wrote this in October 1556. *Ed.*

doctrine of Christ, by the inspiration of the Holy Ghost, done so. For the one describes the same occurrence this way and the other that way. It sufficed them to show the foundation of truth; so it does us. I do not desire to wrangle about a word. I only care to show to the reader that the crucified Christ Jesus is God's first-born and only-begotten, true Son, and to show that Micron has given quite an untrue account of the discussion and that he has deceived his readers by open falsehood.

I pray them not to take it amiss that I also referred to John a Lasco. It was not done through hatred nor dislike, but through zeal for the glory of God and of Christ His Son, and for the honor of eternal truth, and for the sincerely desired salvation of your souls. These have urged me to do so, because Micron acknowledges that they are of one mind in doctrine, and I do not see that one could believe, teach, write, speak, hold, or feel more abominably concerning the crucified Christ than a Lasco does in his *Defensio* against me. Besides, I hear that he also is become a man of blood, notwithstanding he said to me that none should be harmed on account of the faith.

But now as I hear, it is not on account of faith but on account of disobedience! Just as the foundation is shifting sand, so are their assertions. Let the rulers command us things in keeping with the Gospel of Christ and neighborly love, and if we then refuse to obey them, then let them punish us justly. I will leave it to the judgment of all reasonable rulers as before God in Christ, whether it is in accordance with or contrary to the Scriptures to expel the poor souls because they fear God; confess the crucified Christ to be God's Son; receive the holy baptism according to the commandment of the Lord and the doctrine of the apostles; affirm their testimony by yea or nay in accordance with Christ's command, and because they lead a penitent, pious life in righteousness.

I am aware that there are many unsuspecting hearts who look very much more to John a Lasco and to the learned ones than they do to Christ and His apostles; therefore I have also referred to his errors in regard to this matter so that all God-fearing readers may see what kind of writers and teachers they are who are so highly esteemed and whose names are held in such honor.

I pray that none will accept my saying that I will no longer solicit a public discussion in such a sense as meaning that I have no courage. This is not the meaning I wish to impart. But I do not desire to discuss publicly nor privately with such people as those to whom I referred in my epistle; nor with such as dishonestly falsify, change, break, and misinterpret my words and testimony, and slander us as did Micron from the beginning to the end of his writing. For I generally find myself deceived by them on all sides. It is a variety which likes to lead an easy life and does not like to take up the cross of the Lord.

But if any rulers should be troubled at heart concerning the Scriptures and begin to suspect their preachers and teachers, and would ask me to a public discussion for the sake of finding out the truth, it would be as glad a tiding to me as I could hear on earth. Nor would I, I trust, be dissuaded nor prevented by the God-fearing to whose hands and counsel I always willingly commend myself. For we are sure that we have the Scriptures and truth on our side.

I pray them not to take this for railing and slandering, that I sometimes handle Micron roughly according to the truth. It was done for no other purpose than that he and his followers may acknowledge their deceiving, lying spirit, through such earnest admonitions which are in keeping with the foundation of Scripture, that they may take a dislike to their abominable doings and renounce their evil ways. Also that all the unsuspecting good hearts which are bound by their snares of unrighteousness may be delivered to the praise of the Lord.

It was done in the same spirit which actuated the holy apostles and prophets, and which actuated Christ Himself in their several reproaches. If anyone should reprove me for my severity, let him reproach Christ and His messengers first. For it is they who have in the Holy Scriptures taught me and all teachers who follow and uphold the truth.

All those who have a Scriptural understanding know that where we find mention made in the Scriptures of the despising and blaspheming against God we also find added the sentence and sharp rebuke of the Holy Ghost.

It is manifest that Micron is not ashamed to tack one falsehood to another, to make a translation to suit himself, to deny the testimony of God the Father, of Christ Jesus His blessed Son, of the angel Gabriel, together with that of all the other witnesses of the New Testament, to flatter the rulers, to seek the favor of men, and to deceive the poor souls for which the Lord's blood was shed; therefore it surely is not wrong to call him by such names as are applied to him in the Scriptures by the Holy Ghost. Truth must have its straight course. It does not turn for emperor nor king; much less for false prophet or teacher who speaks the language of the serpent, perverts the testimony of God into falsehood for the sake of vain honor, and who for fleshly appetite strengthens the ungodly and troubles the saints. Whosoever has sound judgment and knows the way of the Holy Ghost in the Scriptures must say that I am right.

I pray that no person will think that I write this way to render Micron evil for evil. Ah, no. I leave vengeance to Him who is Judge of all the world. I have done this to the service of Micron and all the erring ones so that they may be converted and give becoming praise and honor to Christ, the Son of God. The truth is set before them by the grace of God in such power and clearness that no man can undo it with the Scriptures nor contradict it with reason. Therefore it would be well if our opponents would see more clearly so that they may with all the saints flee from the future judgment and that they may in the day of His appearance stand before the throne of His Majesty in eternal joy.

If they do not, but refuse; if they remain obdurate and partisan minded;

if they repay good with evil and love with hatred; if they seek assistance from the worldly powers since they are too weak in the Scriptures, and lie in wait for the corruption and misfortune of the pious by falsehood and beautiful inventions, as has alas been the case hitherto with many, then we must leave it to the Lord, possess our souls in patience, and remember the saying of Christ: For so persecuted they the prophets which are before you. Matt. 5:12.

Finally, I warn in faithfulness all my readers both great and small, rich and poor, kindly disposed and otherwise, as before God, and sincerely pray them in Christ Jesus to read in fairness this our incontrovertible, thorough answer and explanation, and rightly to weigh it in the balance of the holy, divine Word, and compare it with the erroneous position and doctrine of our opponents, so that they enlightened by the truth may find the true way to life.

Let none believe me, but the truth which I have, according to my small talent, placed before you in invincible power and clearness, according to the pure doctrine of the holy apostles, evangelists, prophets, and of Christ Himself. In Christ, be warned. Your poor souls are sadly deceived by the doctrine of our opponents, for it is the smoke from the bottomless pit which obscures the bright Sun, Christ Jesus, and the air of His holy Word. It is the falsehood of the old serpent, its egg and progeny; he that eateth it dieth and that which is crushed breaketh out into a viper. Isa. 59:5. It is the spiritual dung with which Ezekiel had to bake his bread. Ezek. 4:12. In short it is the horrible, abominable draught of the golden cup of the Babylonian harlot, drunken with the blood of the saints, with which he has made drunk all who dwell in the earth.

Their doctrine and confession stand clear and manifest that the crucified Christ Jesus was not the true Son of God, for they say He had no father, and is only called so on account of their invented union. They reject the baptism of Christ; they rage and blaspheme against it and institute a different baptism which is neither taught nor commanded them by the Scriptures. The difference between the oath of Christ and Moses they deny and say we are allowed to swear to the truth, that it is a holy thing, etc. Matt. 5:34. Let him who is intelligent understand what we have explained in both our book and epistle.

John says, The Word was made flesh. John 1:14. Paul says, Great is the mystery of godliness. God was manifest in the flesh, justified in the Spirit, seen of angels, preached unto the Gentiles, believed on in the world, received up into glory. I Tim. 3:16. We sincerely confess this testimony to be true and right, as do also all others which confess the visible, tangible, crucified Christ to be the Son of God; therefore we must alas be called by the world, sectarians and heretics. It is time to look out. Kind reader, take heed. God grant you His grace. Amen. Read attentively and judge without partiality Amen.

# The Nurture of Children

*Kindertucht*

## c. 1557

*For other foundation can no man*
*lay than that is laid, which is Jesus Christ.*

I Corinthians 3:11

# Introduction

About the year 1557 Menno wrote the brief tract herewith presented as *The Nurture of Children*. He begins with the truth that children all inherit a sinful nature from Adam, and therefore they stand in need of discipline and Christian nurture. As a pastor who traveled much in the congregations of the brotherhood, Menno often observed children who obviously were not being brought up in the Lord's nurture and discipline. He therefore became concerned to do what he could to help Christian parents to an awareness of their solemn responsibilities and duties. Children, said Menno, should be taught to read and write, and should also learn such handcrafts [as would be serviceable in an economic manner later on]. The main point, however, was not economic but spiritual: children must be brought up to fear God and to obey His Word. Any punishment given was to be "with discretion and moderation, without anger"—insights not yet fully appreciated by many parents. Another point stressed is that of keeping children away from corrupting associations, from children who would teach them to lie, swear, and engage in mischief. Menno was a bit sensitive to the possible charge that he was trying to "run the affairs" of others, but he earnestly insists that he is concerned only with the upbuilding of the Christian Church.

The original Dutch title reads: *A Sound Instruction and Doctrine as to How all Pious Parents are, According to the Scriptures, Required to Govern, Chastise and Educate their Children, and to Nurture them in a Pious, Virtuous, and Godly Life.* The title page contains Prov. 23:13, 14; 29:17, 15; as well as the usual I Cor. 3:11.

In the *Opera Omnia Theologica* of 1681 *The Nurture of Children* is printed fol. 215-22, and in the *Complete Works* of 1871, Part I, pages 269-76.

J. C. W.

# The Nurture of Children

## c. 1557

*Preface*

To the elders in all churches, chosen by God in Christ Jesus; my beloved brethren in the Lord, mercy and peace be unto you from God our Father through the merits of our Lord Jesus Christ, in the power and co-operation of the Holy Spirit, which He poured out upon us abundantly through the same Jesus Christ our Saviour; in order that being justified by His grace we should be made heirs of eternal life. To Him be praise for ever and ever. Amen.

My dearly beloved brethren in the Lord, we thank the Lord always for you in all our prayers, and pray without ceasing unto our kind Father, in the name of His Son Jesus Christ, that He would strengthen you with the gift of His Holy Spirit, so that you might be filled with all knowledge, wisdom, discretion, and power, and be able rightly to serve the church of Christ, the simple, pious hearts, with the Word of God, according to your gift and calling. Conduct yourselves according to the calling wherewith you are called and chosen by God and His holy church, as shepherds and teachers, to the end that the saints may be edified by the common service, to the edification of the body of Christ.

Take diligent care of your sheep and watch your flock, at all times earnestly exhorting them to love, to good works, as did Paul, to the pure fruits and love of the Lord, to a godly, unblamable conduct, in all humility, righteousness, love, peace, unity, mercy, and obedience to every word of God. Warn them diligently against all false doctrine and the sword of evil tongues; for he who does not bridle his tongue, that man's religion is vain. Let them also take heed in their whole walk and conversation to circumcise their hearts, season their words, and perform all their actions in the fear of the Lord, that they may make a good name for the Gospel of Christ and for His holy church, may obey His Word and will, and so be saved.

Beware of all innovations and doctrines not contained in the Word of Christ and His apostles, nor consistent therewith. At all times point to Christ and His Word. Let all those who would introduce anything other than what Christ teaches in His Word be anathema. For other foundation can no man lay than that is laid, which is Jesus Christ. He is the precious cornerstone in Zion and will remain that forever. Hear Him, believe Him, trust Him, follow Him, hope in Him, and abide in Him; press diligently after Him, conforming yourselves to His Spirit, Word, and life, and you shall neither deceive nor be deceived.

My dearly beloved brethren in the Lord, I beseech and admonish you, not to neglect the service of your brotherly love, but to attend faithfully to it. Take heed unto yourselves and the entire congregation over which the Holy Ghost has made you overseers, to rule the church of God which He has purchased with His own blood. Again, with Peter, I who also am an elder, exhort the elders, feed the flock of God which is among you, not by constraint, but willingly, being obedient to the church of Christ in all matters that are proper and right, as Paul directed Titus, saying, In all things showing thyself a pattern of good works; in doctrine, showing uncorruptness, gravity, sincerity, sound speech that cannot be condemned; that he that is of the contrary part may be ashamed, having no evil thing to say of you. So watch in all things, endure afflictions, do the work of an evangelist. Do all in the fear of the Lord faithfully, and with obedient and perfect hearts. For to this end were you made watchmen and placed over all the servants of the house and all that shall be done therein. Therefore be diligent to show yourselves honest workmen, obedient, blameless, that need not be ashamed, rightly dividing the word of truth. Therefore I wish and desire of you to be earnest in this, so that they who believe in God may be made zealous to excel in good works, which is good and profitable unto all men. Instruct, reprove, rebuke, exhort, and console, as occasion may require; and forsake not the fraternal assembly and institutions of the Lord. Strengthen one another pleasantly with the Word of the Lord, so that you may increase in faith, love, and righteousness, and come unto a perfect man, unto the measure of the stature of the fullness of Christ.

With this, dear brethren, I will commit you to the Almighty Lord, and beg you to acquaint all the brethren with this brief admonition, concerning the education of children, in order that every one may comply and in the nurture and instruction of his children observe and obey the same. The Lord Jesus Christ be with my dear and beloved brethren in all eternity. Amen.

## THE NURTURE OF CHILDREN

To all the elders and companions in the faith of Christ: Grace be unto you and peace from God, our heavenly Father, through His beloved Son, Jesus Christ, our Lord and Saviour, by the power and co-operation of the Holy Spirit, to His eternal praise and glory, and to our edification and salvation. Amen.

You are aware, beloved brethren and sisters in Christ Jesus, that we all, no matter who or what, are born with an evil and sinful flesh from Adam. Yes, and all our desires from our youth are always inclined to the worst, as

Moses writes. We know, do we not, that we find nothing in ourselves from the heritage of our first birth but blindness, unrighteousness, sin, and death. If now the power of this native disposition is to be broken, suppressed, and destroyed, it must be accomplished by the pure fear of the Lord, which proceeds from a true faith through the Word of the Lord, and from a certain knowledge of the righteous judgment and terrible wrath of God, which will burn eternally against all impenitent sinners. For the fear of the Lord is the beginning of wisdom. It drives out sin and makes genuinely pious children, as we learn from Jesus [ben Sirach].

Since then the merciful Father of our Lord Jesus Christ, the Almighty great Lord, has shone about us with the light of His grace, and has aroused us through faith in Jesus Christ from iniquity and ungodliness to a life of righteousness, therefore, let us diligently follow the glorious example of the true love of Matthew, the publican, who was not satisfied with enjoying the heavenly calling and grace himself alone, but went and invited other publicans and sinners to it, so that they might also be saved and obtain the like Spirit, grace, and mercy from the Lord, For such is the nature and disposition of Christ.

Put out, therefore, to interest the talent given you from on high and feel genuinely for your unbelieving, blind father and mother, sister, brother, husband, wife, servants, and neighbors. Do not conceal from them the gift, grace, Word, and will of God; for their feet are in the way of death. Who knows whether they may not free themselves from the snares of unrighteousness in which they are bound and entangled, and turn themselves to the Lord with all their hearts. My dear brethren, I am referring to those who are reasonable and decent folk. Ah, brethren in Christ, if we should see any such in danger of water or fire, or in any mortal danger, and if there was a prospect that we could render them assistance, would not our inmost souls be moved with compassion toward them to help them if we could? Undoubtedly. And now we see with our own eyes, if only we believe the Lord's Word, that they are walking in the shadow of eternal death, are already buried in hell and due to be consumed forever by the eternal, unquenchable fire, in so far as they do not turn unto Christ and His Word, repent, and become new men, as the Scriptures teach. Therefore consider seriously the fearful misery and wretchedness of their poor souls which must live forever, and study diligently and faithfully whether they may not in some way by your faithful ministry of pure love, and by the direction and instruction of the divine Word, be rescued and delivered from everlasting destruction, and be saved. For genuine charity is of such a nature that it is constantly hungering and thirsting after the glory of God and the salvation of all men, even of those who are strangers to us according to the flesh.

Beloved brethren and sisters in Christ Jesus, forasmuch as we are now constrained by the good will and interest of kindly love, and confess through the unction of the Spirit and Word of God, that the nature of man is completely corrupted in Adam and is rebellious against the Word of the Lord from childhood, therefore let us be mindful and solicitous of our own children, and let us display unto them a still greater degree of spiritual love than with others; for they are by nature born of us, of our flesh and blood, and are so solemnly committed to our special care by God. Therefore be sure that you instruct them from their youth in the way of the Lord, that they fear and love God, walk in all decency and discipline, are well mannered, quiet, obedient to their father and mother, reverent where that is proper, after their speech honest, not loud, not stubborn, nor self-willed; for such is not becoming to children of saints.

The world desires for its children that which is earthly and perishable, money, honor, fame, and wealth. From the cradle they rear them to wickedness, pride, and idolatry. But let it be otherwise with you, who are born of God, for it behooves you to seek something else for your children, namely, that which is heavenly and eternal so that you may bring them up in the nurture and admonition of the Lord, as Paul teaches.

Moses commanded Israel to teach their children the law and commandments of the Lord, to talk of them when they sat down in their houses and when they walked by the way, when they lay down and when they rose up. Now since we are the chosen generation, the royal priesthood, the holy nation, the peculiar people, that we should show forth the praises of Him who hath called us out of darkness into His marvelous light, therefore we ought to be patterns and examples in all righteousness and blamelessness, and to manifest this to the whole world as we are called to this. For if we do not keep a strict watch over our own children, but let them follow their evil and corrupt nature; if we do not correct and chastise them according to the Word of the Lord, then we may verily lay our hands upon our mouths and keep still. For why should we teach those not of our household, seeing we do not take care of our own family in the love and fear of God? Paul says, If any provide not for his own, and specially for those of his own house, he hath denied the faith, and is worse than an infidel.

Dearly beloved brethren and sisters in Christ Jesus, take heed that you do not spoil your children through natural love, that you do not offend, do not rear them in wickedness, lest in the day of judgment their soul be required at your hands, and it happen unto you, on account of your children, as it did unto Eli, the high priest, who was punished by the hand of the Almighty, on account of his sons. But imitate carefully the witness declared by the angel of the Lord concerning pious Abraham. I know him, says He, that he will command his children and his household after him, and they shall keep the way of the Lord, to do justice and judgment. For this is the chief and principal care of the saints, that their children may fear God, do right, and be saved. Even as the God-fearing Tobias admonished his grandchildren, saying, My son, hearken unto thy father; serve the Lord in truth, and follow him in uprightness, be diligent to do that which is well-pleasing to him and what he has commanded, teach this to thy children that they give alms, fear God all their days, and trust in him with their whole hearts.

My beloved brethren and sisters in Christ, you who sincerely love the Word of the Lord, instruct your children thus, from youth up, and daily admonish them with the Word of the Lord, setting a good example. Teach and admonish them, I say, to the extent of their understanding. Constrain and punish them with discretion and moderation, without anger or bitterness, lest they be discouraged. Do not spare the rod if necessity require it, and reflect on what is written: He that loveth his son causeth him oft to feel the rod that he may have joy of him in the end. But he that is too lenient with his child, takes his side, and is frightened whenever he hears a cry. A child unrestrained becomes headstrong as an untamed horse. Give him no liberty in his youth, and wink not at his follies. Bow down his neck while he is young, lest he wax stubborn and be disobedient to thee. Correct thy son, and keep him from idleness, lest thou be made ashamed on his account.

Dearly beloved brethren and sisters in the Lord, if all parents who boast the name of the Lord would heed the words of Sirach, and would inscribe them on the tablets of their souls, oh, how virtuous, pious, and devout would many children be reared, who now, alas! run around wild and unrestrained, bring no honor to their parents, nor to the church and the Gospel of Christ. An evil-nurtured son, says Sirach, is the dishonor of his father. Again says he, though they multiply, rejoice not in them, except the fear of God be with them; for one that is just, is better than a thousand; and better it is to die without children, than to have them that are ungodly.

My dear brethren, ponder these words well and digest them. Necessity compels me to write; for some, alas! carry on so with their children that one is constrained to write and reprove. I write and admonish you once more: Take heed, lest the blood and condemnation of your children be upon you. If you love your children with a godly love, then teach them, instruct them in God, lest the Word, blood, and death of the Lord remain in vain in their case, and the Lord's name and church be blasphemed by the foolish because of them.

Beloved brethren in Christ, if you rightly know God and His Word, and believe that the end of the righteous is everlasting life, and the end of the wicked eternal death, then study to the utmost of your power, to lead your children on the way of life and to keep them from the way of death, as much as in you is. Pray to Almighty God for the gift of His grace, that in His great mercy He may lead and keep them in the straight path, and keep them there, leading them by His Holy Spirit. Watch over their salvation as over your own souls. Teach them, and instruct them, admonish them, threaten, correct, and chastise them, as circumstances require. Keep them away from good-for-nothing children, from whom they hear and learn nothing but lying, cursing, swearing, fighting, and mischief. Direct them to reading and writing. Teach them to spin and other handicrafts suitable, useful, and proper to their years and persons. If you do this, you shall live to see much honor and joy in your children. But if you do not do it, heaviness of heart shall consume you at the last. For a child left to himself, without reproof, is not only the shame of his father, but he disgraces his mother also.

This brief little admonition I have written to my beloved, out of hearty love, and that not without reason. For in the course of my ministry, I have, which is too bad, observed more than enough how disorderly, improperly, yes, heathenish, many parents carry on with their children. The bad love of the flesh is so very great with some, and they are so blinded by the natural affection for their children that they can neither see nor perceive any evil, error, or defect in them at all, notwithstanding they are frequently full of mischievous tricks and wickedness, are disobedient to father and mother, lie right and left, quarrel and fight with other people's children, and mock people as they pass by, crying after them and calling them names.

Brethren in Christ, to ignore, by reason of blind, carnal love, and to excuse these and similar disgraceful tricks of children is a love not to be applauded, but much rather to be shunned and avoided; for it is earthly, sensual, devilish. Since we are the salt of the earth, the light of the world, the holy nation, the chosen generation, yes, the bride of Christ, it by no means becomes us, to have, or to bear such carnal love or foolish regard toward our children. But it is our duty, as far as in us is, diligently to instruct, govern, and rule our children and household as well as ourselves, in conformity with the honor and virtue that is pleasing to God, and in keeping with the Word of God.

With this I want to clear my soul before the Lord and His church. And I desire for the Lord's sake that this epistle may not be resented. Let the elders read it aloud to all the brethren so that the innocent may avoid these things and those that are guilty of them, of these faults and failings, may reform, without thinking that I want to run their affairs. Ah, no! Before God, I desire nothing in this, but that in all things, you may conform yourselves to the Scriptures and to Christian decency, and that all things in the Lord's church may be conducted according to the divine will and good pleasure. He that searches hearts and reins knows that I lie not. Therefore, receive it in love, for in faithfulness have I written.

With this, beloved brethren and sisters, I commend you to God and to the word of His grace, which is able to build you up, and to give you an inheritance among all them which are sanctified.

The very God of peace sanctify you wholly, that your whole spirit, soul, and body be preserved without spot, and blameless, unto the coming of our Lord Jesus Christ. Faithful is He who called you. May the merciful Father, through His beloved Son, Jesus Christ, our Lord, strengthen you all with the precious gift of His Holy Spirit. Amen.

# Meditations and Prayers for Mealtime

*Een christelijcke benedictie voor, een gracias na den eeten*

## c. 1557

*For other foundation can no man
lay than that is laid, which is Jesus Christ.*

I CORINTHIANS 3:11

# Introduction

About the year 1557 Menno produced another small tract herewith entitled *Table Prayers for Mealtime*. It is divided into two main parts: a meditation and prayer to be used before partaking of food, and a meditation and prayer of thanksgiving to be used after the meal. The entire meditation is saturated with Scripture quotations in the usual style of Menno Simons. The purpose of the little work is evidently to establish table prayers firmly in the lives of the saints of God, and to kindle in their hearts a spirit of gratitude and thanksgiving toward the heavenly Father. He is a loving Sovereign who ever looks after the needs of His earthly creatures including His children. Menno's heart is especially tender as he thinks of his brethren and sisters undergoing persecution as followers of Christ Jesus the Lord.

Since this tract is missing in the *Opera Omnia Theologica* of 1681, it was also omitted in the *Complete Works* of 1871. K. Vos reprinted the original Dutch in his *Menno Simons* (Leiden: E. J. Brill, 1914), pages 282-88, from which it was translated into English for this edition of Menno's writings. We may indeed be thankful that this little jewel has not been permitted to perish.

It may be remarked that even to the present generation, the Mennonites of eastern Pennsylvania, also Europe, often have prayer both before and after eating (the latter is spoken of as "returning thanks") on formal occasions, as for instance when a Mennonite minister is being entertained, though it is by no means confined to such occasions.

J. C. W.

# Meditations and Prayers for Mealtime

## c. 1557

●-●-●-●-●-●-●-●-●-●-●-●-●-●-●-●-●-●-●-●-●-●-●-●-●-●-●-●-●-●-●-●-●-●-●-●-●-●-●-●-●-●-●-●-●-●-●-●-●-●-●-●-●

*This Is a Christian Grace Before Meals, Together with a Prayer of Thanksgiving After Meals—Intended for All Genuinely God-fearing Folk, and Moreover Intended to Be Taught to Their Children from Childhood on, in Order That They May Learn to Fear the Lord, May Learn to Know Him, and to Walk in His Commandments All Their Days, to the Praise and Glory of the Lord and to the Salvation of Their Souls. Amen.*

Man shall not live by bread alone, but by every word that proceedeth out of the mouth of God.

## I. A CHRISTIAN GRACE BEFORE MEALS

O give thanks unto the Lord, said David, for He is good. For His goodness and mercy endureth forever. O taste and see that the Lord is good; blessed is the man that trusteth in Him. O fear the Lord, ye His saints, for there is no want to them that fear Him. The rich He sends away empty, but they that fear the Lord shall have lack of nothing. He giveth food to those that fear Him. He remembers His covenant forever.

Thou shalt eat the labor of thy hands; happy shalt thou be and it shall be well with thee. Thy wife shall be as a fruitful vine in the innermost part of thy house; thy children like olive plants round about thy table. Behold, thus shall the man be blest that feareth the Lord.

I have been young and now I am old, says David, and have never seen the righteous forsaken nor his seed begging bread, even as Thou hast, O Lord, demonstrated to the children of Israel. Thou hast given them bread from heaven and water out of the flinty rock in the wilderness forty years long. O Lord, Thou hast fed Elijah with flesh and with bread by the ravens morning and evening—also by the widow of Zarephath in that the meal did not diminish in the jar nor the oil in the cruse for a long time, according to the word spoken by the Prophet Elijah, the Tishbite—and by the angel of the Lord, with bread and with water under the juniper bush when he fled before Jezebel. O Lord, Thou hast fed Daniel in the den of lions in Babylon by the angel of the Lord, and by the Prophet Habakkuk with the victuals which he had prepared for his reapers. Habakkuk spoke saying, Daniel, Daniel, take of the food which God has sent to you. And Daniel spoke saying, And, Lord, Thou art ever mindful of me and dost not forsake those that call upon Thee and love Thee. And he rose up and ate.[1] O Lord, Thou hast so wonderfully, and unexpectedly, and, according to the Word of the Lord spoken by Elisha the prophet of the Lord, fed those of Samaria when the hunger was so great that the women (by nature quite pitiful, as Lamentations has it) did sod and eat their own children, even as at Jerusalem.

O Lord, Thou hast with five barley loaves and two fishes fed about five thousand men, not counting women and children—twelve basketfuls remaining—by the power of Thy prayer of blessing and thanksgiving. What is impossible with men is possible with God. This, Lord, Thou Thyself hast declared.

Therefore, Thou hast in the Gospel taught Thy children that fear Thee saying, Take no thought for thy life, what ye shall eat and what ye shall drink, nor for the body what ye shall put on. Is not the life more than food and the body than raiment? Consider the birds of the heaven. They sow not, neither do they reap, nor do they gather into barns, and your heavenly Father feeds them nevertheless. Are you not much more than they? Which of you can add one cubit to his stature by being careful for it? And why do you take thought for raiment? Consider the lilies of the field how they grow. They toil not, neither do they spin—I say unto you that even Solomon in all his glory was not arrayed like one of these. If God so clothe the grass of the field, which today is and tomorrow is cast into the oven, would He not much more do such for you, O ye of little faith! Therefore, do not be filled with care saying, What shall we eat? or, What shall we drink? or, Wherewithal shall we be clothed? After these things do the Gentiles seek, but your Father knows that ye have need of all these things. Seek ye first the kingdom of God and His righteousness and all these things shall be added unto you. Be not therefore anxious for tomorrow, for tomorrow will be anxious for itself. It is enough that every day carries it own burdens, as Christ says.

But godliness with contentment is great gain, for we brought nothing into the world; and neither can we carry anything out. But having food and covering we shall be therewith content, etc. For God has created meat, says Paul, to be received with thanksgiving by them that believe and know the truth. For every creature of God is good and nothing is to be rejected if it be received with thanksgiving, for it is sanctified through the Word of God and prayer.

For this reason let us pray: Our Father which art in heaven, hallowed be Thy name. Thy kingdom come, Thy will be done on earth, as it is in

---

[1] This account of Daniel and Habakkuk is found in the Apocryphal book called *Bel and the Dragon*. *Tr.*

heaven. Give us this day our daily bread and forgive us our debts as we forgive our debtors. And lead us not into temptation, but deliver us from the evil [one], for Thine is the kingdom, and the power, and the glory forever. Amen.

How lovingly do the eyes of the Lord behold the righteous. His ears are open to their prayers. And if there is any lack among His people, He fills it with every good gift. Their daily bread comes to them unexpectedly out of the hand of the Lord their God.

The heavens are the Lord's, says David, and all that is in them; the earth, and the fields, and all that on them is. Therefore, humble yourselves wholly before the mighty hand of God and fear the Lord, the Almighty God.

Therefore, eat and drink at this time, friends, together, for this food is given of God, our heavenly Father. Therefore, to Him be praise, honor, glory, and thanksgiving from eternity to eternity. Amen.

## II. A CHRISTIAN GRACE OR PRAYER OF THANKSGIVING AFTER MEALS

We thank Thee, Lord God and Father, Creator of heaven and earth, for all Thy good gifts which we, O Father of lights, have received of Thee, and receive daily out of Thy liberal hand through Jesus Christ, Thy dearly beloved Son, our Lord, Thou who hast clothed our bodies with the needed covering and hast satisfied them with the natural bread.

We pray Thee humbly, as our dearly beloved Father, to look upon us, Thy children, persecuted for the sake of Thy holy Gospel, and earnestly desirous, in our weakness, to live devoutly in this world. Be pleased to keep us in Thy Word in fatherly fashion, in order that to the end of our days we may remain constant in Thy Word and Gospel, revealed by Thee to the plain and simple, and hidden to the wise ones of this world. Look upon us with Thine eye of pity, as Thou didst upon the prodigal son, upon Mary Magdalene, upon the woman of Canaan, the centurion, the thief on the cross, Zacchaeus, and upon all those who have with tears desired Thy grace.

And feed our souls in like fashion with that heavenly bread, Thy holy Word, by which our poor souls may live, and give us to drink of that living water, the Holy Spirit, who can lead us into all truth, whom the world cannot receive because it knows Him not, nor sees Him, even as Thou Thyself, O Lord, hast said. For the world lieth in wickedness, said John, and will perish with all that is therein; but he that doeth the will of God abideth forever.

Therefore we pray Thy Fatherly mercy, with sorrowful hearts, and out of the depth of our souls, for all men, for kings, and for all magistrates, in order that we may live a quiet and peaceful life in all godliness and gravity. For, said Paul, this is good and acceptable in the sight of God our Saviour, who would have all men to be saved and come to the knowledge of the truth.

O Lord, be pleased to enlighten them with Thy grace, those that are still in darkness and who walk in the ways of death and err unwittingly; and receive all those who with a firm trust come to Thee seeking Thy grace and mercy, confessing that they know not, and that henceforth they would live after the will of God, to reform their lives, do penance, be converted, be born again, believe the Gospel and obey it, confess it before the world, and live it. This we pray, O holy Father, for Thy great name's sake.

We also pray, dear Lord, especially for all those who confess Thy holy Word aright and who seek to live according to it in their poor weakness. Be pleased to guard them against all false doctrine and carnality of life; against the wiles of Satan, who, according to the holy Paul, transforms himself into an angel of light. Keep them also from temptation, and from the love and friendship of this world which according to the holy James is enmity with God, lest Thy Holy Spirit be grieved and Thy holy Gospel be blasphemed among the foolish and the perverse.[2]

This we pray, O eternal Father of lights from whom all good and perfect gifts come forth, even as James says, and for the sake of Jesus Christ, Thy dearly beloved Son, our Lord, in whom Thou art well pleased and at whose name every knee should bow, of things in heaven and things on earth, and things under the earth, and before whom all tongues must confess that Jesus Christ is Lord to the glory of God His Father; and, as the holy Paul teaches, through Him in whose name we must all be saved and of pure grace. And we believe, moreover, that there is no other name under heaven given among men by which we must be saved, other than in the name of our Lord Jesus Christ, even as Peter testified before the Council at Jerusalem, to whose high and holy and altogether adorable name be praise and honor, power and majesty, from eternity to eternity. Amen.

---

[2] The text has come down to us with the expression *den onverstandigen en verkiezen;* but this makes no sense and we have therefore read *verkeerden* (the perverse) instead of *verkiezen. Tr.*

# Instruction on Excommunication

*Onderwijs van de excommunicatie*

## 1558

*For other foundation can no man*
*lay than that is laid, which is Jesus Christ.*

I Corinthians 3:11

# Introduction

This is the third treatise of Menno on excommunication and shunning, the other two having appeared about 1541 and 1550. It is Menno's second-last book. This *Instruction on Excommunication* appeared in the year 1558, being dated June 11 of that year. Menno wrote to ground the church, especially its ordained leaders, more firmly in the doctrine and practice of the ban. Some elders were too severe, others too lenient. Menno was concerned because he knew the deceitfulness of Satan and of his servants who made a profession of being genuine children of God. Menno was also concerned because he had observed the sad consequences of being too lax in the shunning of excommunicated apostates. He says that he himself knew of about three hundred cases where a believing man or wife failed to shun the unbelieving spouse, and was thereby ultimately lost to Christ and His church. The tract portrays eloquently the awful condition of those who are cut off from the body of Christ, the church. Menno warns sharply about the need of immediate action in the case of open sinners, adulterers, and the like. Such people are not to be given two or three warnings, but are to be forthwith excommunicated. And those who live in offensive sins of the flesh are not to be immediately restored on the basis of an easy statement that they are sorry; it is better to first see genuine evidences of new life in Christ. On the other hand, a sharp distinction should be made between an unpremeditated fall, as in the case of Peter denying his Lord, and an unrestrained living in sin as was the case with the incestuous man at Corinth.

The full title of the work in Dutch is: *A basic Instruction or Report concerning Excommunication, Ban, Expulsion, or Separation from the Church of Christ: Its Nature, What Persons it takes in, The Reasons and Design for which it was Taught, Enjoined and Left to us by the Apostles in His Holy Word, Faithfully Set Forth from Sacred Scriptures for the Use of All Lovers of the Doctrine of Eternal Truth, to Serve the Cause of Holy Christian Peace without Partisan Preferences.* In addition to I Cor. 3:11 the title page also contains Phil. 2:3.

In the *Opera Omnia Theologica* of 1681 this work is found, fol. 185-214, and in the *Complete Works* of 1871, Part I, 239-68.

J. C. W.

# Instruction on Excommunication

# 1558

●━●••●••●••●••●••●•●••●•●••●•●••●•●••●•●••●•●••●•●••●•●••●•●••●•●••●•●••●•●••●•●••●•●••●•●••●•●••●•●••●•●••●•●••●●●●

## Preface

Brethren and sisters in Christ Jesus, it is known to all true children of God who are enlightened by His Holy Spirit that human reason is in Adam so depraved through the bite of the old crooked serpent that it has kept but little which is conducive to godliness. Yes, it has become so perverse, haughty, ignorant, and blind that it dares to alter, bend, break, gainsay, judge, and lord it over the Word of the Lord God. Nobody's spirit or gift yields; it insists that it is right, and it calls all it does or says God's Word. Whereby the saving truth is often violated and lovely peace and peaceful love made to endure much injury, infamy, and disgrace, as may be seen.

In the second place, it is evident that also the bewitching spirit of Antichrist has made the whole world so drunk with the cup of his abominations, has so rejected the doctrine of Christ and His holy prophets and His holy apostles, their sacraments, spirit, life, ordinances, usages, example, and true religion, that but little that is of a salutary nature is left among men, so that it is difficult to restore that which has fallen into decay to its proper usage to which the Lord had ordained it.

In the third place, it is evident that the old master, Satan, the archenemy of God and of our souls, is always about us as a roaring lion, seeking whom he may devour, as Peter says. He assails us in divers ways; now with the unclean, wicked nature of our depraved flesh, and anon with some bewitching false doctrine and honeyed word; now by persecution, cross, and oppression, then with a carefree worldly life and freedom of the flesh; now with riches and abundance, then with want and poverty. In short, his fiery darts take no vacation; they fly by day and by night, in private and in public. He that does not zealously continue in the fear of God cannot withstand the manifold assaults of his temptations. Yes, when we think the victory is attained, then we are assailed the most violently. Some he incites to quarreling and wrangling under the semblance of truth. Such are called by Paul men of corrupt mind and destitute of the truth. The fruits of this are solely abominable envy, disgraceful defamation, slanderous revilings, unclean, troubled spirits, a lamentable infraction of the holy peace of God, a grievous annulment of pure Christian love, a mighty hindrance to the saving doctrine, a fruitful mother of contending sects, and a paved way to ruin, as we have alas seen frequently in the days of the revealed truth.

O brethren, beware; I repeat, beware and watch. For James says that such wisdom is not from above, but that it is earthly, sensual, devilish. For the wisdom which is from above, says he, is first pure, then peaceable, gentle; notice again, easy to be entreated; notice once more, full of mercy and good fruit without partiality; note yet again, and without hypocrisy. Yes, my brethren, where there is no such peace, friendly, teachable, and impartial wisdom, there is nothing but a faked appearance of good; promiseless, impure, and sinful prayer, an unsteady wavering mind, and a restless and troubled spirit full of strife and dissension, no matter how much we may boast of the truth. The Lord grant us eyes to see it.

In the fourth place, it is evident that the congregation or church cannot continue in the saving doctrine, in an unblamable and pious life, without the proper use of excommunication. For as a city without walls and gates, or a field without trenches and fences, and a house without walls and doors, so is also a church which has not the true apostolic exclusion or ban. For it stands wide open to every seductive spirit, to all abominations and for proud despisers, to all idolatrous and willfully wicked sinners, yes, to all lewd, unchaste wretches, sodomites, harlots, and knaves, as may be seen in all the large sects of the world (which however pose improperly as the church of Christ). Why talk at length? According to my opinion, it is the distinguished usage, honor, and prosperity of a sincere church if it with Christian discretion teaches the true apostolic separation, and observes it carefully in solicitous love, according to the ordinance of the holy, sacred Scriptures. It is more than evident that if we had not been zealous in this matter these days, we would be considered and called by every man the companions of the sect of Münster and all perverted sects. Now, however, thank God for His grace, by the proper use of this means of the sacred ban, it is well known among many thousands of honorable, reasonable persons, in different principalities, cities, and countries, that we are innocent of and free from all godless abominations and all perverted sects, as we also make known and announce very deliberately to the whole world, not only by our doctrines and walk, but with our possessions and blood in evident deed.

We see all this and observe that now the bright light of the holy Gospel of Christ shines again in undimmed splendor in these latest awful times of anti-Christian abominations. God's only-begotten and first-born Son, Jesus Christ, is gloriously revealed; His gracious will and holy Word concerning faith, regeneration, repentance, baptism, the Lord's Supper, and the whole saving doctrine, life, and ordinance has again come to light through much seeking and prayer; through action, reading, teaching, and writing. Now all things (God be praised for His grace) proceed according to the true apostolic rule and criterion in the church, by which the kingdom of Christ comes to honor and the kingdom of Antichrist is going down in shame. Therefore the archenemy of our souls violently opposes and uses his ancient wiles and arts most subtly againt it; himself becoming a Christian, it seems. Do not misunderstand how this is meant. He proudly boasts of the faith, rebukes, yes, rejects all the Babylonian traffic; he is baptized, seats himself among the saints at the Lord's Supper, praises the lives of the pious, hears exhortation, gives alms, receives the poor, washes the saints' feet, says that Christ is the Son of God. In short, he plays the part of an unblamable, regenerate, penitent, and true Christian.

But in the meantime he watches where he may assail us most easily and injure us the most. He invades eagerly our depraved and bewitched souls, some of whom it seems as yet know little about the nature and disposition of the Holy Ghost. He presses them skillfully, for he knows beautifully how to clothe his cause with the letter of the Scriptures. He speaks orthodoxly, says that whatever he does he does out of pure fear of God and love to the church, and with the Word and truth of the Lord. He begins as though in the anxiety of a distressed conscience to argue and dispute with some, principally concerning the separation which he can tolerate and endure so little. Here and there he uncovers his clever but pernicious questions and answers, whereby he so incites and inflames the perverted and bewitched minds against each other that some of them when they cannot stand before the power of the truth from mere partisan spirit born of the tainted flesh, leave the pleasant Jerusalem of peace and return again to unclean, blind Babylon, or build up a seceding sect of their own, as I have with much sorrow seen literally two or three times in my day.

Behold, this is the treasure which the old deceiver seeks with his wranglings. For whether we stay away from the idolatrous church or not, whether baptized or not, is immaterial to him, just so he can inflame our hearts with hatred and envy one toward another, corrupt our minds, terminate our love and disturb our peace. If he can sow discord, defamation, suspicion, lies, enmity, and backbiting which generally, as he knows, arise from such finespun disputes; if he can but do this, then he has gained his end. Ah, dear brethren, beware, for it is more than clear that all those who have not the meek, friendly, peaceful, and peace-loving spirit of Christ, but have their eye set on debate, disputation, rupture, and division, are not of God. Take it to heart.

Inasmuch then as we know that he did from the beginning of the clarified Gospel to the present moment cause us so very much pain and sorrow of heart with his cunning agitation, unfruitful, contentious questions and answers, and many pernicious disputations, therefore I do most affectionately and sincerely entreat all who would desire to walk peaceably and quietly before the Lord and His church, in the fear of God with a good conscience, that they would one and all as before God in Christ Jesus, lay this sincerely to heart; how faithfully the Holy Spirit of Christ warns us against all unprofitable, foolish questions, answers, disputations, and quarrels which He hates right heartily. For He is the Spirit of love and peace and therefore teaches it to all His children, and writes it upon the tablets of our hearts with the gracious finger of His heavenly flame. Ah! do reflect upon what we teach; also that His holy kingdom and Word are a kingdom and word of peace, not of strife; that His messengers and servants are messengers and servants of peace, in order that you who call yourselves after His holy name, who alone has graciously called you into His kingdom of peace, through the Word of His peace, that you may escape the snares of the devil, and that you may so conduct yourselves toward all men in all your ways after the will and pleasure of Christ, and promote His holy Word and ordinance, that you may plant and tend that true righteousness required of God, such as faith, love, repentance, regeneration, piety, and peace, together with all other fruits of the Holy Ghost, that you may gladden the hearts of all the sorrowful of heart, together with the young and tender souls in Christ Jesus, and strengthen, console, and encourage them in all their imminent trials, temptations, tribulations, and anguish so that the most holy city and temple which lay demolished for so many centuries may again be rebuilt at its former site, and all its sacrifice and service be restored in proper order. Yes, that the saving light of the true Gospel of Christ may joyfully progress among all nations, kindreds, and tongues in its clearness and power, and that the accursed lie of Antichrist may vanish and go down.

Seeing then that the powerful Word of the Lord is more and more miraculously breaking forth, and that therefore all true hearts would gladly see and have unanimity in this matter of the ban, whereby they are some-times so greatly troubled and perplexed, as has been related; that they might all proceed observing one rule according to the Scriptures, as is Christian and right; seeing that I, an unworthy person, the weakest of all the saints, have been severely assailed in this matter by many different spirits for twenty-two years and have suffered many an attack whereby others not only were taught of me, but I of others (the Giver of all good gifts be praised in His church), and seeing that I have acquired more knowledge in some things through length of time and through many cases, therefore I was fraternally requested and besought by several pious hearts who would gladly see the right in all things that I would make it a point before the close of my life[1] to set forth in orderly fashion the ground and meaning of the true apostolic ban or separation in writing formally, and to let the elders and ministers of the church examine it, as well as all those desiring peace, so that if anyone after my departure (for I am now quite weak and gradually becoming an old man) might cause any trouble, strife, or dissension among the quiet and peaceful under pretense that he heard this or that from me at any time, or concluded from some of my writings which have never set forth so plainly

[1] Menno wrote this in June, 1558; died in January, 1561. *Ed.*

concerning husband and wife,[2] and of open, offensive, carnal sinners as is done here, that then men may refer them to my final position with which I fell asleep in God and made my departure from the flesh. The request was also made so that the pious uncertain conscience might thereby be helped so that it might attain an assurance of confidence in men's minds.

To this request although altogether Christian and good I have acquiesced with hesitation, and that especially because I know very well that they are not all brethren and sisters in truth and power who will read, hear, and see it. And where the attitude is not pure nor true love, there the understanding is generally partial and the interpretation unjust, as alas I have often experienced in my days. Ah, that some of them might obtain grace. Besides, I know that preferences, judgments, affections, and minds are varied, and that the consistent grasp of the truth and the fear, the Spirit, and the unction of the Lord are not possessed by everyone in the same fullness; therefore, I fear that try as I may not all will be satisfied nor follow it as the firm foundation of the truth. If only we all had the eyes of understanding, those of us who think we see, it would according to my opinion soon come to a more solid basis and foundation.

Yet I confidently expect that those who in the fear of God sincerely seek unity and peace among the pious and are desirous for certainty will not despise and vilify this my careful and brotherly labor in the interest of holy peace and the explanation of eternal truth accepted by me in true Christian faith, but that they will receive it with gladness and give the praise to God for His grace. For it appears to me, although it may possibly be foolish in me, that no more certain way to the truth will be found with which we may stand before God and man than that which I have impartially and according to my limited talents pointed out and explained hereafter as before God in Christ Jesus, in accordance with our small talent on the basis of Holy Writ.

The stiff-necked, bold, and perverse scorners I do not serve. Neither the inflexible partisans or embittered agitators. But those I serve who with an impartial, renewed, and Christian mind allow themselves to be instructed by the Holy Spirit, the fear of God and pure love, men who have received the Lord's holy Word and truth in pure mind, who obediently follow it through the received unction, and so are free from all bitter partisanship, vain honor, hatred, and envy. For with such we find the lovely spirit of peace, a pious and sincere disposition, an unleavened, pure heart and love, and therefore also an upright and pure mind, and an unspoiled, saving position and exposition. These live no more unto their self-seeking flesh, but unto Christ and their neighbors. They subject themselves to all men, are humble, opposed to all unscriptural contention and strife; they readily acknowledge their shortcomings wherein they have erred. They make peace with their

[2] The question referred to at this point is that of "marital avoidance," i.e., must married partners cease cohabiting when one of them is excommunicated from the church? *Ed.*

neighbors whom they have grieved, regarding neither honor nor dishonor; they heap fiery coals upon the heads of their adversaries; they walk unblamably in order that they may stir them again unto truth with love, lead them from the way of error and bring them unto Christ and save them eternally. Behold, these are they, I say, whom I serve with these my writings, for they possess Christ in power with His Spirit, Word, and love, and thus with Him, in Him, and through Him[3] they possess true Christianity which will stand before God, which is a useful, cheerful, peaceful, and joyful matter. Ah, children, be admonished, learn rightly to know the depths of the devil, and beware of discord. May the merciful Father grant unto us the wise Spirit of His grace. Amen.

## I. JUST WHAT IS THE APOSTOLIC BAN

Sincerely faithful children in the Lord, whom my soul loves in truth, since I have undertaken in fatherly faithfulness this very risky task for the benefit of you and all the pious (I say risky task, for I am well aware that it has caused much grief among the humble for a long time, and I fear that all is not over yet[4]), therefore, I entreat you one and all, both the involved and the uninvolved, by the deep crimson wounds of Jesus, and that from the bottom of my heart, all of you who with me bow your knees before the Almighty, great God. I admonish you by the righteous judgment of His coming which He will hold in the clouds of heaven in flaming fire with His angel host, not to judge this my difficult task by natural standards according to likes or dislikes; but with an impartial and pure heart of peace, reading it article by article, yes, word by word, with sincere Christian love and according to the rule and position of truth. Observe in the first place what excommunication from the church of Christ basically is, which was left behind and taught us in the Word by the Lord's holy apostles, so that you despise none ignorantly, nor say with scorners, Let them ban, their ban is not fatal, and similar insipid expressions. I tell the truth in Christ and lie not that I would rather allow myself to be cut into pieces until the day of judgment if that were possible, than to allow myself to be excommunicated according to the Scriptures, by the servants of the Lord, from His church. O brethren, take this seriously.

All that was anathematized in Israel in the ordinances of the law, whether man or beast, had to die, and the accursed goods had to be burned with fire. A dreadful and severe ban was this. But in the kingdom and government of Christ, if we grasp its true character, no repentance following, a still more dreadful ban obtains, for it is not now a physical extermination or

---

[3] Reading *door hem* (through him) for *voor hem* which does not make good sense. *Tr.*
[4] This is an understatement; most of the trouble came later. *Ed.*

the death of our flesh, as Moses' ban, nor an exclusion from a stone temple or synagogue as was the excommunication of the Jews and is to this day, but it is a valid declaration of the eternal death of our soul, announced by the faithful servants of Christ on the basis of Scripture against all offensive, carnal sinners and confirmed schismatics. It is a delivering over to Satan, yes, a public expulsion, excommunication, or separation from the congregation, church, body, and kingdom of Christ, and that in the name of Christ, with the binding power of His Holy Ghost and powerful Word.

Since then this ban is such a dreadful and severe ban, as has been related, therefore let one take care to conduct himself before God and His church so as never in all eternity to be smitten with such a curse by Christ or by His church as to be placed outside the holy congregation, body, city, temple, church, kingdom, and house of Christ. For it is incontrovertible that all who are outside of the congregation and church of Christ must be in that of Antichrist. And what the reward of such persons will be, if they do not repent, is spelled out in plain letters. Ah, children, beware, be extremely careful, watch out, pray fervently, and be on guard! God's judgments are terrible, and it is a fearful thing to fall into His hands.


## II. OVER WHOM THIS APOSTOLIC BAN IS TO BE USED

We find in many places in the Holy Scriptures that the rightly believing church is the spiritual body, the bride, army, city, and temple of Jesus Christ, our only spiritual head, bridegroom, king, and high priest, prefigured by the literal Eve, Rebecca, and the camp, city, and temple of Israel. In the political state of Israel no leper, none that had an issue, nor those who were defiled by the dead, were allowed in the camp as long as they were not healed and purified according to the law, nor were they allowed to ease themselves within the camp. No uncircumcised, nor unclean person was admitted to the Passover. Moreover, all those (observe the details of Israel's ban) had to die without mercy on the testimony of two or three witnesses, who despised the Word of the Lord and set aside His commandments, those who committed abominations in Israel and served strange gods. For, says Moses, they were to be a holy people to the Lord.

And so it is in the new reality of Christ, for His church is a congregation of saints and an assembly of the righteous, even as the Nicene fathers have for centuries confessed with us. Even as Adam had but one Eve, who was flesh of his flesh and bone of his bone, even as Isaac had but one Rebecca who was of his own tribe, and even as Christ had but one body which was heavenly and from heaven, and was righteous and holy in all its members, so also He has but one Eve in the spirit, but one new Rebecca, who is His spiritual body, spouse, church, and bride, namely, those who are believers, the regenerate, the meek, merciful, mortified, righteous, peaceable, lovely, and obedient children in the kingdom and house of His peace; pure, chaste virgins in the spirit, holy souls, who are of His divine family and holy flesh of His flesh, and bone of His bone.

From all this, according to the doctrine of the holy apostles, it is plain that the obstinate schismatic or sectary who causes offense and discord contrary to the doctrine of godliness, and those who do not abide in the doctrine of Christ, who lead an offensive life, or greedy people who lead a soft and easy life at the expense of others,[5] shall not be allowed a place in the holy house, camp, city, temple, church, and body of Christ, the church, but that we with common voice must exclude and shun and avoid them according to the Scriptures, unto the salvation of our own souls, and unto their reformation. Faithful children, be warned. Terrible is the word which John utters, Whosoever transgresseth and abideth not in the doctrine of Christ, hath not God. And in another place, He that committeth sin is of the devil. Once more, be warned.

## III. THE REASON WHY THIS BAN IS COMMANDED IN THE SCRIPTURES

John teaches and says that God is love. Since then God is love, He also manifests the nature of that which He is, namely, love. That this is the truth may be readily perceived in the creation and preservation of all His creatures, the restoration of Adam and Eve, the preservation of Noah and his sons with the ark in the flood, the blessing of Abraham, Isaac, and Jacob, the deliverance of Israel from Egypt, in the sending of Moses and the prophets; and most of all in the holy incarnation of our Lord Jesus Christ, the Son of God, in His gracious and powerful doctrine, His miracles, prayers, weeping, cross, blood, and death; also in the revelation of the Holy Spirit, and in the commission of His holy apostles.

Since then it is evident that in this way God is love and will be that forever, and that from the beginning He manifested the glorious fruit of love toward His children, so also now does He conduct Himself this expulsion, although it is terrible and severe, and notwithstanding that it has such a terrible consequence with the stubborn and unconverted sinner, as has been heard. For He is the wise and omniscient God who with His flaming eyes sees through the hearts and reins of men, who judges their ways and knows in detail His creatures and handiwork, what weak vessels we are; yes, that some of us can scarcely withstand a gentle breeze of deception, but allow ourselves to be led away immediately, or to be polluted with the pernicious, ugly life of the wicked. Therefore He has by His paternal love and boundless mercy given us, His poor, weak children, this countermeasure of expulsion, and has approved it by the Holy Spirit and the Word, and has commanded it to this end that we should expel the turbulent, stubborn

[5] Reading *cupieuse* (greedy) for *curieuse* (curious) which does not make good sense. *Tr.*

schismatics, together with the offensive, carnal, scandal makers, from His holy congregation, church, and house of peace, and according to the Scriptures, avoid and shun them until the day of their conversion, lest they through fair but vicious words tear us away from the confident hope we have in the truth of Christ, their false doctrine eating as doth a canker, as Paul puts it, and to preclude that these awful people with their impure carnal life should pervert us and give us a bad name among those who are without. This is the first reason for the ban, the matter because of which the Spirit of God has so earnestly commanded and taught it in His holy Word. Whether this reason is not an unusually great work of the faithful love of Christ, which is of great usefulness, service, power, and fruit to all the pious, I will let all the faithful consider in the fear of their God.

The second reason is that all those who once more forsake the holy Word and the true way, and revert to the world, to despise the holy covenant, make void their received baptism and promise of righteousness, and once more hear the false prophets, and accept the love of the world, walk the broad way of the flesh or cause contentions, schisms, and sects and perverse things among the pious, may be frightened by this ban and so brought to repentance, to seek union and peace and so to be set free before the Lord and His church from the satanic snares of their strife, or from their wicked life. Behold, this is the second reason why the Spirit of the Lord has so earnestly recommended and taught the ban in His holy Word. And whether this is not also a special good and great work of His love, and of like power, usefulness, service, and fruit to the wicked (if they, that is, observe it in fear) as the first is to the pious, this will I leave to the faithful [to decide] in the fear of God. Whoever can rightly understand and see the afore-mentioned reasons, according to the Scriptures, has to my mind already found the true ground of the holy excommunication.

Since then we know that this our ban or expulsion is commanded us in the Scriptures, and that it has two such highly important reasons, as has been related, therefore we have reason enough, if we rightly carry the Christian name, carefully to teach the blunt and direct command, doctrine, and ordinance of the Lord and His holy apostles as a worthy, proper, and good word of their great love, and obediently to follow it. Similarly, it is also evident that they sin grievously against the Word of the holy apostles, and their great love, and against the fidelity and love of the church, and most of all against their own souls, who revile this beneficent, divine ordinance, led by the perverseness of their lazy, disobedient, sinful flesh, a devilish contention, and trample it in the mire so shamefully under the vile and dirty feet of their wicked blasphemy. Bold is that man who would rebuke his God, or gainsay and censure His Word. Ponder what we say.

## IV. THE TRUE APOSTOLIC BAN MAKES NO EXCEPTIONS

Undoubtedly it is well known to us all, dear brethren, that the first commandment of the second table is an unusually strong and solemn commandment, Honor thy father and thy mother. We know that all they had to die according to the law of Moses, who cursed, struck, or disobeyed father or mother. We know too that the bond of undefiled, honorable matrimony is so firm and fast in the kingdom and government of Christ, that no man may leave his wife, nor a wife her husband, and marry another (understand arightly what Christ says), except it be for adultery. Paul also holds the same doctrine that they shall be so bound to each other that the man has not power over his own body, nor the woman over hers.

But these regulations, the first concerning parents and the second concerning wedlock, stand fast and firm and cannot nor may not be altered or broken by any man so long as we can in God and with God, in a good conscience, observe and keep them, as the afore-mentioned regulations require, without transgressing the holy Word. But it is incontrovertible that if this cannot be, then the spiritual must not make way for the carnal, but the carnal must make way for the spiritual.

Therefore, I entreat all the pious for the Lord's sake, who are sanctified with us unto Christ Jesus, through the Spirit of peace, together with faith in His precious blood, that they may impartially and spiritually examine these following grounds or reasons (things about which we are sore troubled) with God-fearing and understanding hearts, and learn that we would fain proclaim this position with Christian discretion to such of our fellow believers whose lot it may be to be involved in these things (may God spare them the experience) and declare it in faithful love to the salvation of their souls, without giving offense to the young and tender minds. All who fear God may judge what we set forth.

The first reason is that we truly recognize through the Spirit and Word of God that the heavenly marriage bond between Christ and our souls, through the interposition of His innocent death and precious blood, and contracted in the soul by faith, must be kept unbroken in willing obedience to the only and eternal bridegroom. Therefore, a man may not in deference to father, mother, son, daughter, husband, or wife, life or death, yield or compromise in any disobedience to His Word, even in the smallest matter; for God the Lord will, shall, and must be the God of our consciences and remain the only Lord of our souls, and not our father, mother, husband or wife, as we may see in plain print.

The next reason is that the faithful apostles, John and Paul, teach us so firmly that we are, in the first place, to shun the apostates, lest they infect us with the impure, seductive doctrine, and involve us in their ungodly, carnal lives, as has already been said in connection with the reasons for the ban. We see with our eyes and feel with our hands that none can more easily infect us than our own fathers, mothers, husbands, wives, or children, if they are corrupted, especially because of the daily association with them and the natural love for them, and what is more still, since husband and wife are of one flesh. Therefore I verily do not know how they will escape the snares of death if they do not diligently observe the holy Word and faithful counsel of the Lord in this matter. For now they pray and plead, and presently they bicker and strike. Now they revile and vituperate, and presently they weep and lament. Ah, children, take warning: their tears are nothing but crocodile tears, and their tongues are set on fire from hell, as James says. I omit to say that some of them run after idolatry and false prophets, heatedly reviling the holy Word, sacraments, and ordinances of Christ, and highly recommending the abominations of Antichrist. Besides, the conduct of some of them is nothing but rake and scrape, pride and pomp, booze and carouse; and how immorally some of them live with their poor wives, especially when they are drunk, I will leave to the Lord to judge. And whether anyone could nevertheless live with such wanton, vicious, ungodly wretches, without being hurt in his faith, love, and unction, and associate with such ugly, unclean, sticky tar pots without being polluted in his conscience, I will leave all who are conversant with the holy Word to reflect with the anointing of the Spirit.

The third reason is that Paul teaches us that we are, in the second place, to shun the apostate so that he may be led to reflect and to repent of his wicked life or sectarian doctrine through the shame of such shunning. Knowing then that this is the position and purpose of the Holy Spirit in regard to the ban as has been related, therefore it is verily right and according to the Scriptures proper that we, in this matter, follow His divine counsel, love, doctrine, good will, and solemn commands, and not less but more carefully in faithful love toward our most beloved father, mother, husband, wife, and children than toward others, because I say, they are our dearest friends, yes, our own flesh and blood, and we cannot by any other holy means lead them from evil, and turn them to the way of the saints. Ponder what we teach.

The fourth reason is that we truly confess that there is but one single ban in Scriptures, a ban which does not have reference merely to the spiritual communion such as the Lord's Supper, and the handshake, and the kiss of peace, but it extends also to natural contacts, such as eating, drinking, daily affairs, and conduct. If the father is to shun his son, or the son his father, the husband his wife, or the wife her husband, in the spiritual communion only and not in natural communion, then there must be two bans in the Scriptures, the one extending to the spiritual communion and the other both to the spiritual and the natural. This is clearer than daylight. Once more, reflect upon what we teach you.

The fifth reason is that pious parents as well as the church must assent to the excommunication of the apostate children, and their pious children must assent to the excommunication of the apostate parents, and the pious husband must assent to the excommunication of the apostate wife, and the pious wife to the excommunication of her apostate husband, and they must agree that justice is being done them according to the Scriptures. And if now they would shun them only in spiritual communion, they would make void their own sentence which they in common with the church have pronounced, and they would not seek the salvation of their dearest friend with that spiritual love and zeal with which the Word and Spirit of the Lord command them. And moreover, they would continue in the great danger of infection, the very thing against which, so that they might evade it easily, the ban is given to the pious by God's Word, without exception of husband or wife, parent or child, in a clear and plain commandment, as has been stated. Again I say, reflect upon what we teach you.

The sixth reason is that I have known not much less than three hundred spouses in my day who did not observe between them and their mates the ordinance, counsel, doctrine, will, and command of the Lord and His apostles concerning shunning, and have so run together into perdition. O God, we are alarmed at the thought that such a touching loss may in part be, due to our abashed silence. We would, therefore, in the future conduct ourselves so, since the care of the church is entrusted to us unworthy though we be, so as to prevent, as we may and somewhat more in line with apostolic teaching and counsel, all corruption and apostasy; and deliberately, purely, and plainly teach and maintain the ordinance of the ban, as well between parents and children, man and wife, as among others; to all our brethren, if occasion, time, person, and situation require, in order that in the first place we may clear our own souls and so stand acquitted before God and His saints in the great day of Christ, and secondly, so that no one to whom the matter becomes actual, may plead innocent, saying, It was never told me.

Behold, elect brethren in the Lord, these are the most important articles and principal reasons which weigh upon us eagerly to teach this position and make it prevalent. Is there a man under heaven, no matter who, learned or unlearned, young or old, without us or within, man or woman, who can instruct us with the Word of truth that the spiritual marriage bond made with Christ through faith, may yield to the external marriage bond, made in the flesh with man? Consider whether a husband can deceive or corrupt his wife, or a woman her husband? Or whether a pious man is not bound to seek the salvation of his unconverted wife according to the counsel and command of Holy Writ, or the wife, the salvation of her unconverted husband? Consider whether there are two bans in the Scriptures, one of them extending to the spiritual fellowship merely and the other both to the spiritual and temporal? Consider too whether the pious mate is not obliged to vote with the church to exclude his impenitent spouse? Ponder too whether in the whole Scriptures any exception of man or wife, parents or children, is made in this matter? Ponder whether spiritual love has to yield to carnal love? If so, then we desire with all the heart to abandon this our doctrine, to acknowledge our error, and with great earnestness to teach the contrary before the whole world, as is Christian and right. For we regard neither slander nor praise, honor nor disgrace. But we are solicitous for the honor of God and Christ and the eternal salvation of your souls; the matter on account of which we are considered by many as the offscourings, refuse, and filth of the world, as may be seen.

But if this cannot be done, as it never can, then in the first place my sincere prayer and fraternal admonition to all who might have erroneous views of this matter is not to sin with slanderous invectives against the stone and the builders because of an unclean, infected mind, nor through error to sustain or comfort any in disobedience to the Word, nor in the danger of apostasy and defilement, lest they make themselves guilty of other men's sins, but that they would give the good will and ordinance of the Lord due honor and praise in this matter, plucking out the offending eye of folly and passing a sound judgment according to truth; averting sin from the congregation, and so putting in practice the incontrovertibly clear Word, counsel, and command of the Lord, with all the pious, and assisting with all devoutness to maintain it.

Secondly, I entreat all who might be concerned about the slanders of the ignorant, to view the matter impartially in a divine light, and to consider that not only this matter is hated by the world, but also all the Christian transactions, such as the true evangelical baptism, Lord's Supper, life, and the true service; yes, that they are considered as an abomination, a scandal and a disgrace, and that they, out of mere hatred of truth, are not ashamed to label all the pious as accursed heretics, Anabaptists, agitators, harlots, and knaves, and in many places to deprive them of possessions and life, as may be seen. However, the pious are so much honored of God that He acknowledges and adopts them as His chosen children, as His sons and daughters, the apple of His eye, His bride and spouse, and grants them the gift of eternal life. For there is nothing under heaven that they love more than their God, or as much, as they plainly testify and demonstrate by their actions. And so also in this matter, for how can there ever be a greater love for God and how can there be a more praiseworthy confession than that one should be willing and ready not only to give up his temporal goods, ease, honor, and prosperity, but also to shun his dearest friend upon earth, while in full health, out of sincere regard for Christ, in obedience to His eternal and holy truth? Your confession of God, together with genuine obedience to His most holy Word, does not give birth to ugly slander or disgrace. Ah, take this to heart.

Thirdly, I entreat all dear brethren in general that they would always consider with wise and sober minds to what end they have assumed the gentle yoke of the living and Almighty God, so that they may act and walk in a becoming manner, in the most holy covenant of grace before Him and all mankind, and live and walk with their life's partner in such piety, love, union, and peace, and with such fidelity and care, that from now on we need never again to hear of this miserable ban or expulsion, but of sincere Christian piety, of delight and godly joy. Reflect on what we teach you.

Fourthly, I entreat all those whose lot it should be at any time to be involved in this sorry business to take diligent care in the pure fear of God, not to seek the selfish, lazy, and idle flesh above Christ, nor to cover it with fig leaves, lest the wrath of the Lord who hates all lies, hypocrisy, and subtle trickery, punish them with blindness and perverseness, and assign them their portion with hypocrites, but that they might by virtue of true faith (seeing it will no doubt be difficult and hard for them) valiantly overcome themselves in Christ, and so in obedience steadfastly obey that which the Holy Spirit of the love of Christ has commanded and taught by His holy Word in this matter. Ah, let us reflect on this.

Finally, I entreat all elders, teachers, ministers, and deacons in the love of Christ, not to teach this whole difficult matter recklessly, sternly, and unwisely, but in the full fear of God, and with Christian prudence and paternal care, in a true, apostolic manner, not too hastily or too slowly, not too rigidly or too leniently, lest they seethe the young and tender kid while it is still unweaned, but that they take the first green ears of their land and dry and harden them first by the heavenly fire of pure, unfeigned love, and beat them into pieces in the mortar of the holy Word, and pour upon them the oil of the Holy Ghost, which makes us willingly obedient unto Christ, and lay upon it the sweet-smelling frankincense of a sincere and firm faith, from which all must come, and which is such a fragrant odor in the Lord's nostrils, and so bring to Him an acceptable meat offering in His holy temple. Lay it to heart in true love, the ground of my admonition.

## V. THAT KNOWN CARNAL SINNERS BANNED BY GOD ARE TO BE EXPELLED FROM GOD'S CHURCH AND SO, WITH SCRIPTURE, DIRECTED TO TRUE REPENTANCE

Before I proceed to explain this article, I would earnestly admonish the reader that about eighteen years ago, I published a little admonition in which I made no distinction of sins but through my inexperience spoke without differentiation of three admonitions. I say inexperience, for to the best of my knowledge I had neither heard nor known at that time of any fornication, adultery, and such like among the brethren. It appeared to me impossible that those who had entered with us upon the paths of righteousness should have any desire or will to such gross abominations. Therefore, I did not seriously reflect upon the matter. Behold, before God it is the truth which I write.

In the same vein I wrote a little book in 1549 in reply to those who would apply excommunication only to the spiritual fellowship and were charging us on all sides with slanderous words saying that we practiced a rigid, cruel, unmerciful, and Pharisaic ban.

Finally, I wrote similarly in a few words against Gellius Faber. To this day I have made no clear-cut differentiation in my writings. Nor could I have made them as I acknowledged openly. For my information of things was too limited, so long as the matter had not become an issue with some and so had not come to my attention. But when I had grasped the essence of the dispute and had carefully weighed all the circumstances in the balance of the holy divine Word with great care, the six following reasons gave me a powerful assurance in the matter. (The Helper of all distressed souls be praised for His grace.)

We are, in the power of the holy Word, to exclude from the holy church of the Lord, all offensively carnal sinners, such as fornicators, adulterers, drunkards, etc., and that without foregoing public admonition which adds to the mortification and public rebuke of their sins and godless conduct, so inciting them to do penance. I say in the power of the Word, for it is evident in the first place, as Paul teaches, that neither fornicators, nor idolaters, nor adulterers, nor effeminate, nor abusers of themselves with mankind, nor thieves, nor covetous, nor drunkards, nor revilers, nor extortioners, shall inherit the kingdom of God (I Cor. 6:10), but that their portion will be eternal death in the lake of fire.

We see then that it is clear that the condemnation of God is already pronounced against them by His eternal Spirit and powerful Word, both in heaven and on earth; that they exclude themselves, and by their ungodly works, forsake the church; that they are no longer flesh of Christ's flesh, and members of His holy body, seeing they are so carnal and devilish that they have made themselves into dogs and swine and are the bond servants of sin. If we would now admonish them who are the children of the devil, and on the strength of a mere promise, even without any evidence of a genuine repentance, and consider them as dear brethren still, greeting them with the peace of the Lord, what would this be but to make void and of none effect the righteous judgment of the Almighty and great God, declared by His own Spirit and Word through the apostles concerning such ugly defilers? Consider such blunt and bold blasphemers as children of God still and members of Christ? I would that we might all impartially, and in the fear of God, ponder how such a great despising of Christ and His righteous judgment is to be harmonized with Scripture.

In the second place, it is evident that all those who despise us are eager to find a mote in us (they hate us so for the truth's sake) in order that they may magnify it into a beam and defame us grossly. If we are to acknowledge such open manifest scoundrels, and receive as our dear brethren such God-cursed wretches, without any fruit of sincere repentance, on a mere promise, perhaps more the result of natural shame and hypocrisy than the fear of God, and if we were to break with them the peaceable, blessed bread of the Lord's holy Supper and so by our deeds confess that they are fellow members of our church; then we would undoubtedly represent the fair bride, the honored of Christ, to all the ungodly as a disgrace and scoff to all of our enemies. May the gracious Lord preserve us from now on from thinking these things. Much more, from doing them. Ah, take note.

In the third place, it is evident that with these three admonitions concerning gross offensive miscreants we would make many great hypocrites. For I fear that there have been some of late who have carried on their ugly tricks and shame in secret, till time and outcome could no longer conceal them. Yes, I understand that if some of them had not been detected by great adroitness, they would, I fear, have continued in their old course to this hour. But as soon as it was disclosed, wailing and weeping could be heard. For who could verily be so far gone by God that when he has disgraced his neighbor's wife, daughter, or servant girl, or robbed him of his money or wallet, and if caught, accused and admonished would not say, I am so sorry that I did it. Since experience teaches us progressively, as has been said, therefore it is also right and according to the Scriptures proper not to hobnob longer with such filthy sots, nor feather their nests, nor put up with them longer in their wicked conduct and wicked nature as with false prophets, but put them where the Holy Spirit of God puts them in Scripture, namely, outside the church, so as not to minimize the Lord's sentence pronounced against such people in His Word, and so as to preserve the community of grace, the unleavened lump of Christ, the anointed kings and priests of God, so that they may continue in their lovely aroma and honor, and so that the transgressors may, by these means, be brought to repent sincerely before God and the church, and so present their offering and gift with a clean, pure, new conscience as truly sanctified saints of Christ on the altar of reconciliation in His holy temple. Now reflect upon what we teach!

In the fourth place, it is evident that Paul teaches us that a schismatic or a heretic admonished once or twice, and not submitting, is to be avoided. Since then, we are not required by the Holy Spirit to reprove a man more than once or twice, some of them being externally quite pious still, and some of them perhaps not knowing better, but thinking they are in the right, tell me how then are we to admonish thrice those who are not ashamed to sin against God's plain words, but also against the law of native and reasonable nature, men who deliberately violate their neighbor's wife, daughter, or servant girl? And who frequent riotous taverns and houses of ill fame? Or purposely falsify in their business dealings? In short, such as are already sent to eternal death by the Spirit and Word of the Lord, if they do not repent, as has been heard?

It would verily, according to my opinion, be altogether improper, if we rightly reflect upon it, to run after such immoral wretches any longer with three admonitions before expulsion—men who are already excluded by Christ with His own key from heaven. It would be improper, if they refuse the first and second admonition, to consider them brethren in the church till the third time. And if they would, even then, say that they were sorry let them remain brethren, and if not, to tell them before the church out of the Word of God that they have no more fellowship with Christ, but are condemned persons according to the Scriptures. All who are taught of God may judge impartially how such doctrine and policy could stand before the justice and Word of the Lord.

In the fifth place, it is evident, as far as I in my simplicity can judge, that the holy Paul wrote in this vein in the fifth chapter of his first epistle to the Corinthians; for he says that they should not associate nor eat with fornicators, or covetous persons, or idolaters, or drunkards. He does not even mention an admonition, to say nothing of two or three, but he says that a little leaven will leaven the whole lump, which is undoubtedly true, for how sour the pious are, because of such scoundrels, made to smell, although they would otherwise be in good odor, experience has alas shown too plainly.

In the sixth place, it is evident that Paul did not only teach this doctrine thus, but also showed it by an open example in the case of the unclean Corinthian who was keeping house with his stepmother in a very unbecoming manner; for without any previous admonition he judged him according to his ungodly deed, and expelled him by the Word and Spirit of the Lord from the church, and delivered or consigned him to Satan, into whose hands he had already fallen through his unnatural, ugly immorality, in order that through this severe sentence and open shame, he might mortify and bury his unclean, shameful flesh, with its carnal lusts, and that his soul might be saved in the day of the Lord. Nor was he received again until a year or more, as history informs us, when they saw such penitence in him that they feared lest he might be swallowed up with overmuch sorrow.

And it would, according to my opinion, be good even now, not so soon to readmit such carnal defilers and grievous sinners who have beyond measure defamed the holy Word and who have brought such great sorrow upon the pious with their ungodly, abominable disgrace, on the basis of a word of regret or a promise, but it were well to attend closely for a time the fruits of their repentance. For it is not always repentance when men say, I have sinned. But repentance is a converted, changed, pious, and new heart, a broken and contrite, sad and sorrowful spirit, from which come the sorrowful tear and lamenting mouth, a genuine forsaking of the evil in which we were held, an earnest and hearty hatred of sin, and an unblamable pious Christian life; a repentance that will stand before God. I entreat you to learn rightly to know both repentance and sin. Take heed thereto.

Behold, faithful brethren, here you have my weightiest Scriptures and considerations, and reasons which move me more deeply to reflect upon this matter in the fear of God. I say again, as I did above, in speaking of the separation of husband and wife: if there is one under heaven, no matter who or where, who can show me with firm divine proof that a known fornicator, adulterer, drunkard, known or unknown, is a member of the holy body of the Lord until he has been admonished two or three times; if there is anyone who can show that the sentence of the Holy Spirit pronounced by Paul, by the entire Scriptures against such mortal violators is contingent upon two or three admonitions; if any can show that we have no cause to fear that the pious would be exposed to vilification if we have no more than an oral promise to do better; if there is any who can show that we may, by the power of the keys, retain those whom God has already excluded by the Word of His truth; if there is any who can show that the church may judge uncertainties with the Holy Spirit and the word of Christ (I mean where there is no evidently genuine repentance); that the church may retain hypocrites, as well as the truly repentant, in such a case and greet them as brethren; if there is any that can show that the church may also with truth and power proclaim the grace, mercy, and peace of God, and eternal life, by the authority of the Scriptures, to those who are under His displeasure, curse, wrath, and sentence of eternal death, on account of their condemnably wicked deeds; if there is any who can show that it is not the committed sin or abomination, but the excommunication which leads sinners to death; if there is any who can show that it is not the Spirit of grace through a sincere faith and true repentance, which avails before God, but the outward association with the church that brings the transgressor the promise of life; if there is any, I say, that can convince us of all this, then we desire cordially to follow him, and to change and renounce our views.

But if this cannot be done, as it never can be, I entreat all who are troubled over the matter, not to make themselves like the vain comforters and the false prophets, who strengthen the hands of the wicked, daub the wall with imitation mortar, and teach, Peace, peace where there is no peace, but I beg them to leave unbroken the sentence of the Lord which poured from the bosom of His divine righteousness; and I beg them to tear the deceptive bolsters and pillows from under the heads and arms of the ungodly, and to keep clean and pure the holy vineyard of Christ, His city, house, temple, body, and church, as much as in them is; to build upon a certainty, and so with Scripture point the impenitent sinners to repentance, as has been heard. Be faithful, reflect, and learn wisdom.

## VI. OF SECRET SINNERS WHO, ONCE MORE INWARDLY ADMONISHED BY THE HOLY GHOST, ARE CONVERTED TO GENUINE REPENTANCE

The full desire of my heart is to the Lord constantly, that each one of us would so fear and know God as to say in spirit and truth with David, Whither shall I go from thy Spirit? Or whither shall I flee from thy presence? If I ascend up into heaven, thou art there; if I make my bed in hell, behold, thou art there; if I take the wings of the morning, and dwell in the uttermost parts of the sea, even there shall thy hand lead me, and thy right hand shall hold me; if I say, Surely the darkness shall cover me; even the night shall be light about me; yea, the darkness hideth not from thee; but the night shineth as the day; the darkness and the light are both alike to thee; for thou hast possessed my reins; thou hast covered me in my mother's womb. And with Isaiah, Woe unto them that seek deep to hide their counsel from the Lord, and their works are in the dark, and they say, Who seeth us? And who knoweth us? Note that he says, Woe!

Chosen brethren, take heed. No one under heaven can so conceal himself in a corner of the earth that he cannot be seen by the flaming eyes of the Lord, nor that he cannot be found in his sin by the avenging hand of His wrath. Yes, no thought lies hidden in our hearts which is not open to the eyes of the Lord. I therefore warn all in general, that with all your powers you guard against sins, whether secret or open. If not sincerely repented of, their outcome will be eternal death. Let all bold and heedless sinners take note.

I write this to all faithful brethren as a Christian warning so that you may fear the Lord's judgment, both openly and privately, and studiously avoid sin. For although we may not be reproved or seen of men here, yet we cannot escape the eyes and punishment of God. Ah! that we all understood this.

For verily, if at any time one should in a carnal abomination sin against God in private (from which may His power preserve us all), and should the Spirit of the grace of Christ, which alone works genuine repentance in us, once more take hold of our heart and grant genuine repentance, in this matter we are not so to judge; for it is a matter between a man and his God. For since it is evident that we seek our righteousness and salvation, the remission of our sins, satisfaction, reconciliation, and eternal life, not in or through the ban, but solely in the righteousness, intercession, merits, death, and blood of Christ, therefore, since the two objectives for which the ban is commanded in the Scriptures have no legitimate function in this case (in the first place, because the sin is private and no infection can for that reason be occasioned, and in the second place, because his heart is already touched, and his life penitent, and consequently no mortification and regret are necessary), therefore, we have no binding key of Christ nor any commandment wherewith to punish him yet more, or bind or shame him before the church. Ponder what we say.

## VII. WHAT IS THE TRUE SENSE OF CHRIST'S SAYING (MATT. 18:15), IF THY BROTHER SHALL TRESPASS AGAINST THEE

Our only and eternal High Priest and Teacher Jesus Christ undoubtedly knew our poor, imperfect, and feeble nature from which (if we are not extremely careful) many transgressions against our neighbor result. Therefore, He teaches, saying, If thy brother shall trespass against thee, go and tell him his fault between thee and him alone; if he shall hear thee, thou hast gained thy brother. But if he will not hear thee, then take with thee one or two more, that in the mouth of two or three witnesses every word may be established. And if he shall neglect to hear them, tell it unto the church, but if he neglect to hear the church, let him be unto thee as a heathen man and a publican. Whereupon Peter asked Him, How often shall my brother sin against me, and I forgive him? Till seven times? Jesus saith unto him, I say not unto thee, Until seven times; but, Until seventy times seven.

These words of Christ teach, in the first place, that if anyone sins against his brother through negligence, infirmity, thoughtlessness, inexperience, or any mistake, that the latter should not hate him in his heart for it, nor copy his transgression. But out of genuinely brotherly faithfulness he should admonish, and in love reprove him, lest his dear brother fall into greater error and perish; but in this way be restored; and he, as Moses says, be not guilty for his sake. It is the nature and anointing of all true Christians, not to hate any for wrong done, but to seek with all their hearts how they may teach the wrongdoer and lead him on the straight path of love. Therefore, a true Christian is a stranger to hatred.

In the second place, these words teach us that he who has transgressed should receive the admonition of his brother in love and be reconciled. Even as He teaches at another place saying, Therefore, if thou bring thy gift to the altar, and there remember that thy brother hath aught against thee; leave there thy gift before the altar, and go thy way; first be reconciled to thy brother. Yes, no less is it the nature and disposition of true believers that those who are born of the holy seed of divine faith, when they trespass against a brother, have neither peace nor rest in their hearts as long as they are not reconciled by a sincere reconciliation with him in Christ Jesus. For they are a seed and generation of peace, children of love, who manifest their Christianity effectively, and testify by deeds that they know God. But those who do not do so have the words of Jesus to judge them. Although the first transgression may not of itself be so fatal, yet it causes the transgressor, if he regard not love, to become estranged and carnal, so that he must bear severe punishment on account of his contrariness. For it is evident that he wrongs his brother, rejects the admonition of love, acts contrary to Christian charity, despises the church of God, rejects the Word of the Lord, and that he would rather continue unreproved in his transgression through his stubbornness, would rather walk in the crooked paths of wrong; yes, forsake the kingdom and people of Christ, than to humble his stubborn, proud flesh and be reconciled in love, according to the Word of the Lord, with his brother against whom he has transgressed. Paul rightly observes that to be carnally minded is death. Observe this.

In the third place, these words teach us if the transgressing brother will receive in love the brotherly admonition of his wronged brother, be humbly reconciled, and so repudiate his wrongdoing, then he must no more remember, but sincerely forgive him, even if he has sinned against him more grievously than is the case. Even as God, for Jesus' sake, forgives all of our sins; so must we also in Christ forgive our neighbor all his transgressions which he has committed against us, small and great. And we should not under any circumstance indulge in hatred or vengeance against him, even though he should never reform. A true example of this we have in Christ and in Stephen, His witness. And it is also the nature and disposition of all who are born of God, that they possess their souls in peace and patience, keep their conscience pure and unsoiled, their prayers unhindered, their love unbroken, their faith sound and true, their minds firm and unwavering, no matter how men behave toward them.

From all of which it is more than clear that these three several admonitions of which Christ speaks (first, between him and you alone; secondly, before witnesses, and thirdly, before the church) must not be understood of all the offensive, carnal sinners, upon whom the eternal sentence of death is already pronounced, but of the transgression of brother against brother. And that for the following reasons:

First, because He says, If thy brother trespass against thee. Note that He says, against *thee,* and does not say, against God; for all the sins he committed against you, you may forgive him, as far as you are concerned, but not those that he commits against God.

Secondly, because He says, Tell him his faults between *thee* and *him* alone. Notice that He says between thee and him *alone.* A public violation or sin calls for a public, not a private rebuke. I hope all who know Sacred Writ will grant me this.

Thirdly, because He says that in the mouth of two or three witnesses every word may be established. Notice that He says, two or three. And that an open transgression requires no witnesses, but is itself its own accuser and witness, is as clear as the noonday sun.

Fourthly, because He says, Then tell it unto the church. Notice, unto the church. For us to announce an open, well-known disgrace to those who already know it, is quite useless, and all who have any sense or understanding will grant it.

Fifthly, because He also says in Luke 17, And if he trespass against thee seven times in a day. Notice He says, trespass against *thee.* Now no true Christian sins mortally against his brother seven times in a day, not to say seventy times seven, much less against his God. Ah, take note.

Sixthly, because He says, And seven times in a day turn again to thee, saying, I repent. Notice that He says, turn to thee seven times in a day. I imagine that if any one were to come to us but two or three times in a year, not to say in a day, to pilfer our chests or purses or to disgrace our wives, daughters, or servant girls, and each time say, Ah, brother, I repent, he would soon be told that he is a confounded scamp and an ungodly specimen of scoundrel. I say, take note.

Seventhly, because He says, Thou shalt forgive him. And the entire Scriptures teach plainly that none can forgive sins (these are the hundred thousand talents which we owe to the King) but God alone. We can only forgive the hundred pence that our poor brother owes in his poverty, as the Lord's own simple parable teaches in all plainness. Do ponder this.

Observe that in this construction the Holy Scripture remains whole and unbroken and travels in a straight line; in an offense of brother against brother use three admonitions before excommunication, in the case of a heretic or sectary use one or two, and in the case of an open, offensive, sensual sinner who is already condemned by the Word of God use none at all, as has been heard. I Cor. 5; II Cor. 13.

Without partiality and with faithful love ponder what the position of the Holy Word is!

## VIII. THAT WITH DAVID'S SIN, REPENTANCE, AND FORGIVENESS, WE ARE NOT TO PERVERT THE TRUTH, BUT TO UNDERSTAND IT CORRECTLY, ACCORDING TO SCRIPTURE

It is evident that abominable, carnal sins, such as fornication, adultery, and the like, generally arise from sheer blindness of heart, are committed premeditatedly and intentionally, and are of unclean, inflamed passions and carnal lusts, even though the beginning comes by surprise. Of this we have a good example in David, for although he was a man after God's own heart, and by the power of his faith slew the fierce giant, Goliath, whom all Israel dreaded, and rescued the lamb from the jaws of lions and bears, yet he was so captivated in his flesh by the sight of his eyes that it made him a great and terrible sinner. For as soon as he gave in, sin was born in him, and his heart which was a temple of the Holy Ghost heretofore was made so blind and foolish, that he, without hesitation, went from one deadly sin and wickedness to another. Yes, so that he never once, it seems, thought of the Lord who called him to such distinguished honor and had endowed him with such a precious Spirit. For when it was told him of Bathsheba that she was with child by him he sought with trickery to hide his horrid deed. He had Uriah called in from the field and pretended he wished to consult him in relation to the war, and admonished him twice that he should go into his house. Why, can be easily surmised. Afterwards he invited him to a feast, as though he were very fond of him, so that he might make him drunk and so send him to his wife and cover his own shame. But when he failed in all this, he gave this truly noble man an ungodly, treacherous letter, that Joab should place him in such a point, where the battle was the sorest, and then leave him alone so that he might be slain.

Behold, thus one wicked act engendered another in David, because he consented to the lusts of the eyes, and gave place to conceived sin. Yes, he was blinded to such a degree in his inflamed flesh, and was so intimate with sin, that according to the rigor of the Law, had he not himself wielded the scepter, he would have been doubly guilty of the ban of death; first, because he was an adulterer; and second, because he was guilty of innocent blood.

He boldly continued in such abominations as long as no prophet came to him to overtake him courageously with a parable, so that he pronounced his own sentence as being worthy of death. When he heard the word of the prophet who appealed powerfully to his heart, he was moved, and sought God's grace, and without delay turned to God with a broken heart, bitterly wept over his great sin, and confessed to the Lord that he had sinned against Him. He prayed and sighed pitifully saying, Have mercy upon me, O God! according to thy loving kindness, according to the multitude of thy tender mercies, blot out my transgressions; wash me thoroughly from mine iniquity, and cleanse me from my sin. Create in me a clean heart, O God; and renew a right spirit within me; cast me not away from thy presence; and take not thy Holy Spirit from me. So that he was comforted by the prophet who said unto him, The Lord also hath put away thy sin; thou shalt not die. Nevertheless, he had to endure a severe punishment on account of it, for, said Nathan, The sword shall never depart from thine house, and thy wives will be violated in the sight of the sun, because thou hast despised me. Notice he says, because thou hast despised me.

And behold, in this way the wantonness of David led him greatly to despise his God, and became a grievous sin in him. True are the words of James, Then when lust hath conceived, it bringeth forth sin; and sin, when it hath finished, bringeth forth death.

So also in the new reality in Christ. For since we are not to punish the ugly, carnal transgressors with fire, stoning, or sword, as Israel did of old, but only by excommunication, as is well known to all who are taught of God, therefore it behooves us to consign those with their wicked deeds to the place to which the Scriptures consign them, namely, into the death and wrath of God, even as holy Nathan did the bloodguilty and adulterous David. When they then by such a dread, severe sentence pronounced on them, by and according to the Scriptures, by the means of the ban in true love, and they by the grace of God come under conviction, and are with David provoked to true repentance, so that we may see by all their words, works, and conduct that the gracious Father has again received them in faith, and endowed them with His Spirit, and has taken away their sins, then, and not until then (understand well what I say) we have the same word of promise whereby we may comfort them again and proclaim to them the grace of the Lord, namely, The Lord also hath put away thy sin, thou shalt not die; Thy sins are forgiven, go in peace, and similar words of comfort. For that a truly penitent person should be left uncomforted by God or man, is impossible. Oh, reflect on what has been said.

You see, so should we rightly divide the Scriptures, lest we with the world, turn the sin, repentance, and forgiveness of David to a free and easy end as though we are bound to consider as dear brethren, the offensive, carnal sinners, namely, those who are banished of God, because of a mere promise. We want to see such repentance in them that the spirit of the church may be edified. For we must not, with the world, teach and comfort with uncertainties, but like Nathan, on certainties—unless we want to lull sinners to sleep with lies and treat lightly the judgment of God, as has been heard.

## IX. OF PETER'S SUDDEN FALL, AND IMMEDIATE RECOVERY

Dearly beloved brethren, consider this. Even as we have shown that the abominable, carnal sins usually arise from the enkindling of carnal passions, so certain sins may arise unpremeditately when we are unthinkingly surprised. Of this kind we have a good example in Peter; for when the Lord said to him, Simon, Simon, behold Satan hath desired to have thee, that he may sift thee as wheat; but I have prayed for thee, that thy faith fail not; and when thou art converted, strengthen thy brethren, he replied with confidence, Although all shall be offended, yet will not I. Lord, I am ready to go with thee, both into prison and to death, and to give my life for thee.

Peter was ready to go through thick and thin with his Master, he thought, but as soon as he stood alone, he could not endure a single question put to him by a simple maid. He openly forsook the Christ with whom the evening previous he had said he was ready to die. Yes, he was so disturbed and frightened that he began to curse and to swear that he did not know Christ.

O God! there lay the confident, bold Peter, the firm rock, now broken. Although he had been taught by the heavenly Father just previously, and had been honored by Christ, the beloved Son of God, with the promise of the keys of the kingdom of heaven, yet he could not endure the trifling impact of such a flimsy arrow on his shield. Behold, so altogether little, poor, miserable, ill, and impotent is that man (especially in great need) who is not strengthened by the Spirit of God. But what was it? Peter had to learn what that man is who depends upon his own strength, and not in the fear of God, on Christ, and His grace. Besides he had to learn how to be compassionate and merciful toward his poor, fallen brother, who would repent heartily and rise without hypocrisy from his fall.

I do believe that this may justly be called a case of sudden surprise in Peter. For there had not been a single thought in his heart before to deny his Lord and Saviour. And he also rose from his fall at once, and went out and wept bitterly, and on the third day he was again comforted with the Gospel by the holy angels of the Lord.

Now notice what Paul teaches, Brethren, if a man be overtaken (observe that he says, overtaken) in a fault, ye which are spiritual (note this) restore such a one (notice again) in the spirit of meekness (notice once more) considering thyself (ponder this), lest thou also be tempted (notice this finally).

Elect brethren in the Lord, I would then admonish you in Christ Jesus by the words of Paul, and by the fall of Peter by all means to distinguish in the spirit of wisdom, between falling and lying. For he who lies down in sin, to which eternal death attaches, he is already condemned by the Scriptures. But he who falls into it by surprise, to him the prophet says, Shall they fall and not arise? And Paul says, Restore such a one. Notice that. It is, therefore, helpful and proper that we be duly careful (I say, duly careful) and not depress such a poor surprised sinner, who would so gladly be restored and rescued from his deplorable condition; but we must, in Christian meekness, extend to him the hand of love, lift him out of the mire, and help him to bear his burden as much as we can, and as far as our consciences and the Word of God permit. Ah, take heed.

Be not too stern in such a case, lest you also be tempted, as Paul states. Let our high and holy Peter admonish you, in order that you may not lose yourselves in your proud minds. For if a man thinketh himself to be something, when he is nothing, he deceiveth himself. In short, Let him that thinketh he standeth, take heed lest he fall. For the snares are more numerous than we can count. If a man is to escape them he must be dead to sin, regenerate, and truly Christian, constant in prayer, circumspect. He must watch carefully, and must let himself be led by the Holy Ghost, otherwise he is already in the snare of death. Ah! let us reflect upon this.

Let everyone examine himself carefully whether he has, since his conversion, sinned before God, and become a broken vessel. He that thinks it is not so, let him cast the first stone. But he that knows it to be so, let him with Peter strengthen his weak brother, who perhaps has not sinned half so heinously as he.

Since then it is manifest that to fall and to lie down and to boldly transgress with premeditation is not the same thing, therefore will I leave such sins, on account of which the people of the Lord are grieved, if such should come to pass, to the Spirit, unction, reasonableness, piety, fear of God, and love of the brethren, to ponder with wisdom. If they consider it ban-worthy lying down, then let them judge as the Scriptures teach. If not, but only as a sin unwarily committed, then let them restore the sinner or transgressor with the spirit of meekness and love. This is with the faithful apostle, father, teacher, and leader Paul my admonition to all the pious. Full of power and spirit are the words, Considering thyself lest thou also be tempted.


## X. HOW WE SHOULD, ACCORDING TO THE SCRIPTURES, UNDERSTAND THE SAYING OF JAMES, IF ANY OF YOU ERR FROM THE TRUTH

In the first place, the reasonable law of nature teaches us that if one sees the house or goods of his neighbor on fire, or him, his wife, his children, or his cattle sick or ailing, he must willingly help him and in his trouble render him aid in need.

Secondly, Moses says that if a man sees his brother's ox or sheep straying, he may not turn away, but must return them to his brother or put them
up safely.

Thirdly, Christ says also that if a man had a hundred sheep and one of
them should go astray, he would leave the ninety and nine on the mountains
or in the wilderness, to seek that which was lost.

Seeing then that the reasonable law of nature, of Moses, and of Christ
can teach us such great love and kindliness, not merely toward men, but also
in regard to goods and stock, therefore it is proper that we who are born of
the holy seed of love should seek to restore the soul of our neighbor, whose
feet we see upon the pathway of sin which leads straight to death. Thus
James says, Brethren, if any of you err from the truth, and one convert him,
let him know that he who has converted the sinner from the error of his
way, shall save a soul from death, and shall hide a multitude of sin.

We would entreat all pious hearts for Jesus' sake to differentiate rightly
between erring in ignorance and erring on purpose, between lying in death
and walking into death, in order that the above saying of James may be
Scripturally explained and it may not be construed so as to become a false
comfort and support to frivolous and erring sinners. For it is clear that they
are already condemned to death by the Scriptures, as we have frequently
observed. But when any of our Father's little ones, that is, Christ's sheep,
stray in the direction of death so as to turn their ears to false doctrine
adorned with fair words; if they should suffer themselves through their
lusts, to be led from the truth; should begin to set their feet upon the broad
way, and should bow their hearts again to covetousness, pride, and pomp,
and should seek the intimacy of their neighbor's wife, daughter, servant girls,
or the company of frivolous people; if they should become cold and weak in
their faith, calloused to the truth and erring grievously, and should nevertheless imagine that they are traveling on the right way, then we may
not let such erring ones be lost. But we should seek with all our power and
might to bring them back, not with one or two admonitions, as is done with
sectaries, nor with three as in the case of a transgression between brother
and brother, but as often as the Lord gives spirit and grace, till they again
observe the truth and cease from their error and return to the right way; or
until they become as ravening, biting dogs or unclean, filthy swine. This
all regenerate Christians are taught by their anointing and by Scripture.
Yes, my brethren, whoever can reach such a poor erring sinner with the
truth, and return him from the way of error, and so bring him back to the
fold of Christ, he rescues his soul from the death to which he was straying,
and covers a multitude of sins, with which alas, he was already too much
stained.

And covers from whose sight? From men's or from God's? Not from
men, but from God. For it is impossible to hide from men that which they
see happening before their eyes, such as open seduction of women, adultery,

fornication, homicide, open idolatry, drunkenness, etc. The idolatry of Aaron with the golden calf, the misconduct of David with Uriah and Bathsheba, and the denial of Peter are proof of this. For although their sins were covered before God with genuine repentance, nevertheless they were set before the world by the Holy Spirit as admonitions and warnings, and as demonstrations of His grace with all who truly repent. And of such covering of sin David testifies, Blessed is he whose transgression is forgiven, whose sin is covered. Blessed is the man unto whom the Lord imputeth not iniquity.

With this I leave to the godly to reflect whether these words of James so expounded are not left in their power and purity; for those worthy of exclusion are excluded, the erring are brought back, love is kept in force, the penitent are rescued from death, their open shames as well as the secret sins are covered before God, and all runs smoothly, in keeping with Scripture. In true love observe what is the thrust of Sacred Writ.

## XI. HOW THE LAST PART OF THE TWELFTH CHAPTER, AND THE FIRST PART OF THE THIRTEENTH OF SECOND CORINTHIANS ARE TO BE UNDERSTOOD

We learn from Paul's epistle to the Corinthians that there were many contentious or factious persons among them. Some boasted that they were of Cephas, others of Paul, and others still, of Apollos. For this, in fatherly compassion, Paul reproved them in love, and admonished them to be one in Christ. He writes also in the eleventh chapter of the same epistle, When ye come together in the church, I hear that there be divisions among you, and I partly believe it, for there must be also heresies among you, that they which are approved may be made manifest among you. There were also some among them who said there was no resurrection from the dead. Therefore, he also feared that when he came, he would not find them as he desired, nor that they would find him as they desired. For he feared he would find more dissension than unity, more envy than love, more wrath than meekness, more strife than peace, more whispering than rebuking of wickedness, more pride than humility, more tumult than quiet, even as is commonly the case where the high and proud of heart, who neither know nor have the peaceful, humble Spirit of Christ, are highly esteemed, and where those have obtained authority over the plain simple people who regard pompous words more than the spirit of power. This I write in upright, undissembled love, without regard to party and out of plain experience. God grant us grace to see it.

We also find that there were some impenitent ones among them, as well as selfish, covetous, contentious, fornicators, incontinent, and unchaste persons. Therefore, he feared that when he came he would have great sorrow on account of those who had already sinned before, and had not repented of their lewdness and unchastity. For it is manifest that fornication was at that time so common among the Gentiles that the holy apostles had already admonished the brethren of the Gentiles in the general council and rebuked them severely.

From all of this it is evident that at that time many were complacent concerning immorality and that dissensions were so prevalent that it was evident that the apostolic excommunication was not strictly observed, as may be seen from Paul's own words of reproach, Ye are puffed up.

Seeing then, that through their heedless disobedience, they permitted the leaven and the unleavened to exist side by side, therefore the faithful man of God took them to task sharply saying, This is the third time I am coming to you. In the mouth of two or three witnesses shall every word be established. I told you before, and foretell you, as if I were present, the second time; and being absent now, I write to them which heretofore have sinned, and to all others, that if I come again, I will not spare. Ah! take note of this.

These hard words of Paul testify clearly enough, I verily think (seeing that in that time such vile, wicked persons as fornicators, unchaste, sectarians, etc., were tolerated, that they paid little attention to his writings concerning the ban. For it is plain if the historians are trustworthy, that some years had passed before Paul made his last journey to them. That they in the meantime should have tolerated these persons with Paul's consent is manifestly contrary to the Scriptural narrative. Yes, without basis or support. Ah, let us ponder this.

From all of this it is evident that since he rebuked all such ugly shame as fornication, uncleanness, and contention with word and writing and pointed to the ban as has been related, and since the foul leaven which was so disgraceful to the holy, divine Word and the church was not put away from them; therefore it is plain that he wrote and expressed his ultimate meaning with these words: that all those who had previously thus sinned and had not repented, also those who had sinned more recently, but were guilty also; that if he would finally come and find the guilt of either testified to by two or three witnesses he would not spare them. Ah! observe this.

It is also manifest that he did not write this rebuke privately to this one or that, and between him or them, but openly to the whole church in a common epistle to reprove their disobedience therewith; even as we, unworthily, do also in our way, when we write or teach the Word of the Lord. Not a syllable does he utter telling us to admonish once, twice, or thrice, but through plain words he writes publicly that if he came he would let them bear their merited punishment. Firm and immovable are his words not to eat nor to have fellowship with fornicators, adulterers, nor idolaters, etc. Oh, reflect what the Scriptural position is.

## XII. THAT CHRIST'S JUDGMENT MUST BE EXECUTED ACCORDING TO SCRIPTURE, AND HIS KEYS VIEWED CORRECTLY

Elect brethren in the Lord, since I have seen so much error and misapprehension in my day by many touching this point, some of whom in my humble opinion were too rigorous, while others were too lenient, and by which some of our people have been, alas! much saddened; and since I have now faithfully explained the true apostolic excommunication, in pure, unadulterated love without partiality, therefore I am further driven by this same love to offer a few remarks on the keys and their proper use, inasmuch as they pertain to excommunication. I do this so that no one, misled by ignorance, may with Antichrist presumptuously place himself in Christ's seat, nor follow and execute his own judgment, idea, and fulfillment, but those of Christ, his Lord, and the doctrine, ordinance, and commandment of the holy apostles; and that without any regard to the flesh, party, or self-will, lest he reject him whom God saves by His grace, or declare saved him whom He in His righteousness rejects. For to Him alone pertains the right of binding and loosing, as we shall hear more fully below. Therefore, reflect on what we say.

It is to be observed in the first place, that there are two heavenly keys, namely, the key of binding, and the key of loosing; even as the Lord said to Peter, I will give unto thee the keys of the kingdom of heaven, and whatsoever thou shalt bind on earth, shall be bound in heaven; and whatsoever thou shalt loose on earth, shall be loosed in heaven. Matt. 16:19. At another time, after His resurrection from the dead, He spoke in a similar manner to His disciples, Receive ye the Holy Ghost; whosesoever sins ye remit; they are remitted unto them; and whosesoever sins ye retain, they are retained. John 20:22, 23.

In the second place, we must observe that the key of binding is nothing but the Word and the righteousness of God: the directing, commanding, threatening, terrifying, condemning Law of the Lord, by which all are included under the curse, sin, death, and the wrath of God; all who do not by faith receive Christ, the only and eternal means of grace; all who do not hear His voice and follow and obey His will.

On the other hand we must observe that the key of loosing is the abundantly cheering and delightful Word of grace, the pardoning, consoling, and liberating Gospel of peace by which are delivered from the curse, sin, death, and the wrath of God those who with regenerated, new, converted, confident, glad, and believing hearts receive Christ and His Word in power, and with a firm confidence in His innocent blood and death; they who fear, love, hear, follow, and obey Him.

In the third place, it is to be observed that this binding key of Christ is given to His ministers and people so that they by it may declare in the power of His spirit to all earthly, carnal, obdurate, and impenitent hearts their great sins, unrighteousness, blindness, and wickedness, as well as God's wrath, judgment, punishment, hell, and everlasting death and so crush before God, terrify, humble, pulverize, and make them sorrowful, distressed, sad of heart, and small in their own eyes. Wherefore it is compared in its power and virtues to the rod of the oppressor, a hard hammer, the north wind, a sorrowful singing, and with a pure, cleansing wine.

Over against this the key of loosing is given to the end that with it the ministers and people of God may direct such contrite, troubled, dejected, sorrowful, sad, and broken hearts (which are enabled by the former key to feel and see the deep mortal wounds and sores through the spiritual brazen serpent) to the throne of grace; to the open fountain of David; to the merciful, compassionate High Priest, our only and eternal sacrifice of atonement, Christ Jesus; and so heal the sores and stripes, and the venomous wound of the hellish serpent. Therefore it is compared in pertinency to the cheering olive branch of Noah's dove; to the balm of Gilead, to the voice of the turtle dove, to the south wind, the joyful pipe, the sweet-smelling ointment.

In the fourth place, it must be observed that these keys are given to us from heaven by Him who created the heaven, the earth, and the sea with the fullness thereof, the eternal power, Word, and wisdom of the Almighty Father; the King of all glory, our only and eternal Redeemer, Intercessor, Bridegroom, Prophet, and Teacher, Christ Jesus. Therefore we may well fear and tremble in regard to this ban, lest we use it under the influence of flesh and blood, hatred or love, favor or disfavor, enmity or friendship, strife, dissension, or partiality, instead of in the fear of the Lord, as the earnest heavenly command, Word, and will of our Saviour, in an upright and good conscience without respect of persons. For without doubt they are precious keys since they are given us from heaven by such a worthy Friend. Ah! take this to heart.

In the fifth place, it is to be observed that these keys are given to no one but those who are anointed by the Holy Ghost, as Christ said, Receive ye the Holy Ghost. From this it is evident that we must be believing people, a true, penitent, sanctified, sober, chaste, humble, upright, friendly, obedient, devout, peaceful, and a spiritual people. Observe, a regenerate people, who sit with the apostles in the seat of righteousness, and with them pronounce the righteous judgment of the Lord against all stiff-necked, ungodly sinners, and teach, admonish, chastise, punish, and in real power, judge or bind with the Word and Spirit of the Lord, the unbelieving, impenitent, earthly-minded, drunken, adulterous, immoral, unchaste, proud, haughty, wicked, perverse, disobedient, quarrelsome, carnal sinners. For it is more than clear that a carnal man cannot understand the things of the Spirit of God. But they that are spiritual examine and judge all things aright, yet they themselves are judged of no man. Yes, my brethren, it is impossible for one carnal man, or for one quarrelsome person, to teach, instruct, admonish, or rebuke another correctly through the Spirit of Christ or in the power of His Word, or to separate him from the church according to the will of God. For their fruits plainly testify that they are both impenitent and destitute of the Spirit, nature, and disposition of Christ; and they are under both condemnation and the curse.

Therefore fear God and know how or what you judge. For if a man should cause a ban-deserving person, such as a fornicator, drunkard, or any other carnal transgressor, to feel the lash of the ban, while he himself was still wrathful, avaricious, proud, haughty, puffed up, ambitious, unchaste, lying, quarrelsome, impure, envious, or false-hearted, and he should secretly continue in his wickedness, then according to Paul, he would merely be judging his own soul, for he says, Thou art inexcusable, O man, whosoever thou art that judgest: for wherein thou judgest another, thou condemnest thyself. Rom. 2:1.

Therefore, I counsel and admonish all the pious who sit in judgment of a sinner deserving of the ban, that they previously examine well their own conscience, heart, and mind, and see whether or not they have the Spirit of Christ, whether or not they sit in the apostles' seat, and also whether they do it out of pure fear of God in obedience to His Word, and out of sincere love for their brethren, or out of flesh and blood through hypocrisy to please men. For if they have not the Spirit of Christ and do not sit in the seat of the apostles and do not carry the keys of heaven, then their judgment is not of God, and it will destroy more than it builds up. It is basically nothing but the certain judgment of their own souls, as was said. But if they have the Spirit of Christ and sit in the apostles' seat and carry the keys of heaven, then their judgment will doubtless be righteous and be as effective as the judgment of Christ itself, and they will not make themselves guilty against the transgressor by carnal considerations. Those who are born of Christ may judge what I advance.

In the sixth place, it is to be observed that these keys must not be made use of, except in the name of Him who left them in our care and by His power, that is, with the Spirit and Word, for He alone is the King and Prince of His church, the Shepherd, Teacher, and Master of our souls, before whose scepter we must all bow, and whose voice we must hear if we would wish to be saved, as has been heard.

Seeing then that He is both Ruler and the Giver in this matter, and both the binding and the loosing are in His hand, and must therefore be done in His name, with His Spirit and Word alone, as has been related; therefore we may well take heed lest we loose by our reckless self-will or boldness those whom He Himself has bound in heaven, or bind those whom He Himself has loosed in heaven, even as that son of perdition and man of sin, together with all his deceiving and vile prophets, O God, have done for many centuries. O children, take heed.

As far as the key of binding (and this is our evangelical ban) is concerned, it is more than clear that when an open fornicator or adulterer is convicted by two or three witnesses, or a sexual pervert, or an idolater, or a drunkard, or an avaricious person, or a perverse or contrary self-willed person, an impenitent, lazy parasite or a blasphemer, thief, robber, or murderer, is brought before the congregation, they have the judging Word of the Scriptures, by which they may expel him and announce to him by the Spirit of Christ that he is now no longer a member of the body of Christ and has no more promise, but that he shall die the death eternally and forfeit the kingdom of grace. In short, that his final end and lot, unless he sincerely repents, shall be the burning lake of fire, hell, and the devil. For his works plainly show that he is of the wicked one.

Behold, such are those over whom the first key has jurisdiction. For the righteous judgment of God, and His firm binding Word, has sway over them, seeing they forsake Christ, despise His holy covenant and Word, live according to the flesh, and cause dissension and schisms, break the bond of love, divide the pious, disquiet peaceful, quiet hearts, and give occasion for offenses and slanders as experience has frequently taught, and as is known to many others with me, alas! more than plenty. Ah, me! what a severe stroke he receives of God. He is bound by the people of God with this dreadful key and punished by His righteous Spirit with this dreadful announcement. O Father, grant Thy grace.

The same thing applies to the key of loosing in this use of the ban. For if a poor, excommunicated sinner humbles himself before his God, his heart breaking before Him in sorrow, groaning and weeping bitterly; if he should become heartily sorry for his sins and have an earnest desire for the truth, hating the wicked paths of the ungodly, and walking again in the paths of the pious, in short, if he conducts himself so in his whole life that we could not perceive anything in him but that the Spirit of the Lord had again anointed him, and received him in His grace, and if he should wish to be one with the Lord's people, etc., then they have the cheering Word of promise by which they may again bring him to the altar of the Lord, sprinkle him with the spiritual hyssop of God, declare to him the grace of Christ, and so receive him again as a beloved brother in Christ Jesus and greet him with the salutation of His holy peace. For the Lord, said the holy prophet, does not desire the death of the wicked, but that he repent and live.

Forasmuch as it is manifest from all this, and certain that as Jesus Christ alone has the key of David, which unlocks heaven for the truly penitent, unties the knot of unrighteousness, and remits their sins; and on the other hand it is He who closes heaven against the impenitent, carnal sinners, binds them unto His judgment, and retains their sins; seeing that we are nothing but heralds, ministers, and messengers in these matters and can stretch the things neither longer nor shorter, narrower nor wider than is taught us by His Spirit and commanded us in His Word, as has been heard, therefore it is more than evident that they greatly err who in their bold ignorance let themselves think that they may forgive or not forgive the sins of a man—also those against God. Also those are in serious error who with reckless, thoughtless minds dare to expel or ban a man, out of carnal motives, hatred, or bitterness, and not purely through the Spirit and the Word of Christ alone; or on the other hand dare to retain him because of natural affection, friendship, or partiality, contrary to the Word of God, and dare comfort him with uncertainties in his sins, excusing them. For by so doing after the examples of the false prophets, they strenghten the hands of the ungodly, since by retaining them they appear to adjudge them to life, even though they shall not live if they do not repent. Ah! brethren, beware.

I would therefore, brethren and sisters, in the love of Christ, have you one and all faithfully admonished in God that no one presume in this weighty, important, and divine matter, to act more highly or less, more sternly or less, than the Word and Spirit require, whether it be with the binding of the first key in righteousness unto eternal death, or with the loosing of the second key in grace into eternal life; lest, by passing an unscriptural judgment, he offend against God and his neighbor, and so be required with the angel of the pit to undergo the punishment of his pride. Observe this!

Ah! most beloved brethren, how marvelously in my opinion is that man taught of God, who is able in this thing so to keep to the true, royal highway as to properly use the entrusted keys in devout, heavenly wisdom, and with a certain and assured concience, in genuine apostolic fashion, to the welfare of all the pious. Let all who are born of God, who are impartial and pure in heart, reflect with the unction of their spirit what is the ground of my writing and admonition.

## CONCLUSION AND EXHORTATION TO ALL THE PIOUS

Behold, beloved brethren, here you have another little gift contributed with much trouble, pains, and anxiety in the infirmity of my declining years, added with much previous care, sorrow, and trouble to the treasury of the Lord, not of the price of a dog, nor of the hire of a harlot, which was forbidden to Israel; but of the abundant benediction of my God, that is, from the solid basis of His truth. Even if it is not to be compared in value with the gold offered, or silver, metal, silk, precious stones of the sacrifice; yet if it may be reckoned with the ivory[6], rams' skins, goats' hair, etc., then I shall have already found what I sought for. For my desire before God and His church is that the living building of the heavenly tabernacles may go forward to obtain its proper glory, the thing for which I have suffered not[7] a little hardship, affliction, sadness, poverty, and reproach to this hour; so I hope that I may boast, in my weakness, with all the pious ones of God, the apostles and prophets, yes, with Christ Jesus Himself, that the zeal of the Lord's house hath eaten me up.

Therefore, I earnestly desire all the pious who with a steady pure conscience have drunk the water of life out of the fountain of God, not to despise this gift, but with open and penetrating minds to examine, as in the presence of God in Christ, its nature, basis, power, force, and vigor, and with a sound Christian judgment to leave it unbroken in all its parts. For it is my valedictory with which I now bid you final farewell in this matter of the ban, and lay myself down to rest.

[6] Reading *ivoren hout* (ivory) for *vuerenhout* (fiery wood) which makes no sense. *Tr.*
[7] The word "not" has been supplied seeing that the sense seems to require it. *Tr.*

Human favor and honor I have not sought, nor the flesh nor partisan spirit, but the principle of truth, the holy ordinances of the apostles. I have kept and given due praise both to the justice and mercy of God, each in its place. I have inserted nothing new, nor have I changed position, except that I have in consequence of much conversation with the pious and of meditation on certain Scriptures, and also on account of great dangers, happenings, and the abominations to which we have fallen heir, pondered the matter a bit more profoundly. And in order to preclude the offensive scandal somewhat more, I have placed it upon more certain and solid basis, as may be seen.

Seeing we know for certain that the depth of Satan is to some but partially known and as a consequence great injury is done by pernicious wrangling and disputation as may be seen, therefore my earnest request to all who are named after the name of Christ is first of all that they would with wise and sane minds perceive what is the actual nature, character, heart, mind, Spirit, and disposition of Christ, noting how all that which He has commanded, left, and taught His followers, is nothing but pure righteousness, truth, patience, love, and peace. May they also see that they have bowed their knees before Him, and have received the token of His most holy covenant and testimony; that they wish to bury their former sinful life in His death, circumcise their hearts with His sharp Word and Spirit; follow Him, walk in all His ways, and be one with Him in both the inward and outward things, as the Scriptures teach, so that reflecting on His lofty promises they would do His will in power and in truth. For He is not a God who takes pleasure in ugly shadows, ceremonies, images, bread, wine, water, hand and mouth, but in spirit, power, deed, and truth.

My second request is, that they would on the other hand, realize what is the nature of the devil, his character, heart, spirit, mind, and work; what a shrewd, cunning deceiver, shameless, scheming liar, and proud and haughty murderer, what a hateful envier of the honor and truth of God; a falsifier of His holy Word, and a deadly enemy of pious souls, he has been from the beginning; seditious, factious, unruly, schismatic, envious, perverse, and devoid of love; one who can only bring forth hatred, slander, falsehood, deception, suspicion, impure hearts, shame, disgrace. And all this he does in the semblance of the truth. I say, in semblance of the truth, for although it is evident that he is the infernal Satan, Beelzebub, Belial, Behemoth, Leviathan, the angel of the bottomless pit, the prince of darkness, the old serpent, and the devil himself, yet notwithstanding he can transform himself into an angel of light, as Paul informs us.

There is nothing external that can constrain or vex him so long as he can possess the citadel of our hearts, and prevent the entry of Christ's nature, disposition, Spirit, and power. If he can do this he has already gained the point of his craftiness; yes, if a man were baptized by Peter or Paul himself and received the bread of the Holy Supper from the Lord's own hand, and never saw the papal idolatry again, but retained one of the fruits of the devil, whether hatred, or party spirit, envy, bitterness, avarice, revenge-fulness, pride, unchastity, or any other wickedness, we must take knowledge with the Scripture that his spirit is devilish, and his life hypocrisy. For it is evident that the whole man must be regenerated, sincere, true, spiritually minded, godly, devout, holy, subject to Christ. As James said, Whosoever shall keep the whole law, and yet offend in one point, he is guilty of all. Jas. 2:10. Yes, worthy brethren, those who are so taught of God, that they are able truly to distinguish as to nature and doctrine between Christ and the devil, and moreover perceive that the nature of Christ brings life and that of the devil brings death, these will, no doubt, separate themselves from all vain and unprofitable disputation, partisanship, schism, contention, dissension, sedition, and schismatic activities and also from all deadly abomi-nations, sins, and shame. Of this I am fully convinced by the grace of God.

My third request is that they may honestly ponder with what glorious and fair names Christians are honored in the Scriptures, such as children of God, saints of God, beloved, God's elect, regenerate, seed and children of Abraham, seed of peace, plants of righteousness, fruitful grafts of Christ, members of the body of Christ, His flesh and bone, Christ's mothers, sisters, brothers, disciples, guests, friends, sons, daughters, His virgin, bride and spouse, His holy vineyard, army, city, Jerusalem, temple, ark, house and dwelling place, the chosen people of God, His own possession, citizens of heaven, living stones, companions of the saints, apostles and prophets, house-hold of God, kings and priests, doves, sheep, the light of the world and the salt of the earth; and this, so that in the knowledge of these things they may commit themselves before God, the church, and the world in all their conduct, words, and works, both inwardly and outwardly, privately and publicly in such a way that they may by grace with the pious walk worthy of all such glorious names in love, peace, and harmony, and by His fatherly gift may forever escape the severe curse of the ban of which we have treated, and may not with the goats at the left hand, hear the stern sentence, Depart from me, ye cursed, but with the sheep at the right hand hear the cheerful words, Come ye blessed, and may not be numbered in eternity with those who are bound by the ban of the Word, in the power of God, rebukingly called a cursed, godless race, cursed children, children of wrath, and of the devil, servants of sin and perdition, mockers, revilers, wicked, carnal, perverse, unrighteous, ungodly, stiff-necked sinners, dogs, and swine, for whom are re-served the eternal woe, death, fire, lake, and torment. O brethren, take heed!

My fourth request is to all those to whom the Word of the Lord is committed, fellow laborers with me in the ministry, that in all their actions they may so conduct themselves before God and the church, that no man can in truth censure or speak evil of them; as sincere ministers of Christ; faithful and true in all things; men full of the Holy Ghost, born of the incorruptible seed of God; encompassed with heavenly light, transplanted into the good disposition of Christ; partakers of His grace; taught and

anointed of God; having their mind on eternal things; averse to their own
fame, vainglory, and impure, carnal lusts; humble and small in their own
eyes; of a meek and quiet spirit, compassionate, merciful, paternal, patient,
friendly, humble, chaste, given to hospitality, submissive, generous, kind, and
peaceful, well-established in sound doctrine, seeking and acting in accordance
with the good nature, disposition, character, heart, mind, and example of
Christ, confirmed in the Spirit, blameless shepherds, caring for the flock of God,
not by constraint, but willingly, not for filthy lucre's sake, nor for the sake of their
own bellies, but from the heart; not as those who dominate, but as examples to the
church of Christ, so that by their faithful ministry, they may without fear and
shame leap joyfully on the mountain of the Lord and escape unharmed the mouths
of cruel ravenous wolves.

Yes, my brethren, if we could all proceed according to this rule in unity
of spirit, and if the destructive foxes would not enter in along with us, how
soon would the bride of the Lamb shine forth in costly and colorful apparel,
adorned in white and glittering robes, with bracelets, earrings, and necklaces
(that is, in the beauty of her virtues) whereas now in consequences of deceitful
workers, cunning wranglers, and subtle seducers she must at times sit in ugly
rags and be the scorn and derision of man. O God!

The anglish of my soul is at times so great, greater than I can write.
May the mighty God strengthen me. And this because I see that the house
of the Lord has to endure so many offenses, not only from without, but, alas!
also from within. O men! arm yourselves! for the words of Paul are true,
that the ministry of the New Testament is not a ministry of the letter, but
of the Spirit. II Cor. 3:6. It cannot therefore be performed to the glory of
God by the proud, the arrogant, the ambitious, or the self-willed who wish to
perform everything after their own mind, notion, and inclination. These
always pull down more than they build up, and harm rather than help.
This is inevitable since after the doctrine of Paul not profundity of intellect
nor human eloquence, nor a dead letter which they generally have aplenty,
but God, Spirit, truth, power, and the life of which they are destitute is the
thing that matters. Oh, take heed!

Once more, arm yourselves, for true teachers are called in the Scriptures,
the angels of the Lord, and valiant soldiers. Therefore be men; keep the
commandment of God; hold fast and waver not.

Watchmen and trumpeters are they. Therefore, blow your trumpet on
the right note; watch diligently over the city of God; watch, I say, and
neither slumber nor sleep.

Spiritual pillars are they. Oh, stand fast in the truth, bear your burden
willingly, waver not, neither be faint.

Messengers of peace are they called. Ah, brethren, live up to your
name, walk in peace, promote it, and break it not.

Bishops and overseers are they called. Oh, take great care of the flock
of Christ. Take great care of them, I say, and neither destroy nor neglect them.

Shepherds are they called. Oh, keep and feed the lambs of Christ; leave them not nor disdain them.

Teachers are they called. Make known the Word and truth of Christ and neither hide it nor keep silence. Spiritual nurses and fathers are they. Oh, nourish and cherish your young children. Neither grieve nor thrust them away. Spiritual mother hens in Christ are they called. In Christ gather the little chicks and neither scatter them nor peck at them. Stewards of God are they called. Ah, dispense the mysteries of God aright; neither abuse nor disgrace them.

The light of the world are they called. Shine forth in full glory and conceal not the brightness of your virtue.

The salt of the earth are they called. Oh, let the salt penetrate through and through to stay worms and decay.

Ministers are they called in Christ's stead. Ah, brethren, serve but do not lord it.

Let no man glory in any gift, I beseech you. We are receivers, not givers; of grace; it is not of ourselves. Observe; we are servants and not lords. Ah, brethren, bow and submit yourselves.

My elect in love and truth, the joy and delight of my soul, so long as you stand fast in the Lord, abide in the way of peace, and are faithful to your brethren, walk worthy of the vocation unto which you are called, fear your God from the heart, love the brotherhood, discharge your ministry faithfully. Rich is he who will pay you. Watch and pray. Pray, I say, and that with confidence, and the Giver of every good gift will not withhold from you His grace and the spirit of love and wisdom. Doubt not, neither be afraid. Fasten securely the glorious, adorned breastplate of Aaron, Christ Jesus, with its beautiful colors, its twelve pearls, beautifully and properly arranged,[8] to the bosom of your conscience with the two golden chains of the two testaments, and with the two yellow ribbons of true faith and genuine love. Let the feet of your affections be washed clean and pure in the spiritual laver, Christ Jesus, with the living water of His eternal and Holy Spirit. Let the tip of your right ear be touched with the blood of His perfect sacrifice so as to hear His Word aright, and the thumb of your right hand and the great toe of your right foot so as to deal and to walk aright before Him and His church. Let your spiritual miters, girdles, and garments be glorious; so that you may like green olive trees, blossoming vines, and burning torches, and brilliant luminaries, in the firmament of the holy Word, serve in fullness of glory day and night with all the faithful servants of Christ in His holy temple to the glory of God, and for the benefit of Israel may bring forth abundance of fruit. And when He shall appear with all His chosen

---

[8] The Dutch, following the German Bible, has literally, "light and right arranged." See Exodus 28:30. Funk's German edition has "Licht und Recht" (I, p. 368). But in his English edition of 1871 the reading is that of the Hebrew Bible in Exodus 28:30: "its Urim and Thummin" (I, 267).

saints, apostles, and prophets, you may receive the everlasting joy, the promised reward. Sweet, gracious, and full of comfort is the word which the Lord utters, Well done, thou good and faithful servant; thou hast been faithful over a few things, I will make thee ruler over many; enter thou into the joy of thy Lord. Matt. 25:21. Ah, brethren, from the heart, let us be admonished to be faithful to Christ and His church. Take heed.

With this, brethren and sisters, I will now in the peace of Christ, commit you all with one accord into the hand of the King of peace; and with Paul, I entreat you from my heart: If there be therefore any consolation in Christ, if any comfort of love, any fellowship of the Spirit, if any bowels and mercies, fulfill ye my joy, that ye be likeminded, having the same love, being of one accord, of one mind. Let nothing be done through strife or vainglory; but in lowliness of mind let each esteem other better than themselves. Phil. 2:13. For you know right well by whom and to what we are called. Reflect upon this, lest anyone lose himself on account of the shame and abominations of another (bad enough already), nor destroy the good works of Christ, disturb the peaceable, grieve the pious, offend the weak, give excuse to the frivolous, drive the wavering back to the world, disgrace the Word of the Lord and His church, bring fame to the revilers, embolden the bloodthirsty. But let us be so careful in all things that we may finish with joy our course in Christ Jesus, magnify His holy name, delight ourselves in the peace of Christ, strengthen our sick members and young brethren, reprove the disorderly, extend the knowledge of the truth of the Lord, and be to all men a blameless, Christian example. To this end may the eternal God of power grant us all the mighty spirit of His grace with perfect obedience and love in Christ Jesus our Lord. Amen. Ah, chosen children, this is my final farewell to you all. Know God, love the brethren, and beware of dissension.

By me,
MENNO SIMONS

# Reply to Sylis and Lemke

*Antwoort aan Zylis ende Lemmeken*

# 1560

*For other foundation can no man*
*lay than that is laid, which is Jesus Christ.*

I Corinthians 3:11

# Introduction

The last years of Menno's life were darkened by stresses and tensions in the brotherhood, especially on the question of the ban. Who should be shunned? As Menno grew older he became more stringent, perhaps partly under the influence of his fellow bishops, Leonard Bouwens and Dirk Philips, and, by his own testimony, partly through observing the sad outcomes of a mild practice of shunning. Two Mennonite leaders from the Rhineland were particularly annoying to Menno for their vigorous opposition to his strict policy of insisting on marital avoidance. It was their activity which called forth Menno's last tract, this *Reply to Sylis and Lemke,* dated Jan. 23, 1560 (1559, *Old Style*). Once again Menno argues at length for a practice of marital avoidance, a position which the Swiss Brethren had never maintained, and which the Dutch Mennonites soon abandoned.

In the Dutch the full title of this work reads: *A Thoroughgoing Reply, Full of Instruction and Counsel, Aimed at Zylis and Lemmeke's Undeserved and Abusive Libel, Slander, and Insipid and Bitter Name-Calling, Touching Our Position, the Position which is, as We See it, the Unfalsified Doctrine of the Holy Apostles Relative to the Ban, Separation, or Shunning.* In addition to I Cor. 3:11, the title page also contains two Apocryphal quotations, Sirach 23:15 and 20:26.

In the *Opera Omnia Theologica* of 1681, the work is found, fol. 479-90, and in the *Complete Works* of 1871, Part II, pages 283-95. The tract contains little that is new, and its tone leaves something to be desired as far as restraint and mildness are concerned; Menno followed somewhat the bitter style of sixteenth-century polemicists.                                    J. C. W.

1000

# Reply to Sylis and Lemke

## 1560

### *Deuteronomy 13:6*

If thy brother, the son of thy mother, or thy son, or thy daughter, or the wife of thy bosom, or thy friend, which is as thine own soul, entice thee secretly, saying, Let us go and serve other gods, which thou hast not known, thou, nor thy fathers; namely, of the gods of the people which are round about you, nigh unto thee, or far from thee, from the one end of the earth, even unto the other end of the earth, thou shalt not consent unto him, nor hearken unto him; neither shalt thine eye pity him, neither shalt thou spare him, neither shalt thou conceal him; but thou shalt surely kill him; thine hand shall be first upon him to put him to death, and afterwards the hand of all the people. He hath sought to thrust thee away from the Lord thy God, which brought thee out of the land of Egypt, out of the house of bondage. And all Israel shall hear, and fear, and shall do no more any such wickedness as this is among you. Then his father and his mother that begat him, shall say unto him, Thou shalt not live; for thou speakest lies in the name of the Lord. And his father and his mother that begat him, shall thrust him through when he prophesieth.

## *A Thorough Reply*

### *Full of Instruction and Counsel*

A true, pure, and pious mind, unfeigned love of God and neighbor, a true and well-seasoned tongue which speaks nothing but the truth, and a resigned, impartial, and pious heart wherein the Holy Spirit dwells, together with a sure knowledge of Jesus Christ and of His holy Word, I wish Sylis and Lemke to all righteousness, now and forever, from my inmost heart. Amen.

I hear and understand, worthy friends, both by oral and written reports, that you sin against God and against me with untrue, slanderous epithets and fearful, bitter backbiting, things not becoming a Christian, and which I had not in the least expected from you, for I would have thought that you were sufficiently taught of the Lord so that you would not thus cruelly smite your poor brother in his absence, nor that you would defame your faithful friend unheard who according to his small talent has ever sincerely served you and all the pious in Christ—and thank him thus for his faithful service and love. But my good expectation of you has alas been misplaced in this case. My experience with you, alas, is like that of good old Jeremiah when those who were ill disposed toward him counseled saying, Come and let us smite him with the tongue, and let us not give heed to any of his words. Yet the innocence of my hands, the true intention of my labors, the pure love of my anointing, together with the incontrovertible foundation of the sure truth shall be my refuge, a shield and defense against all unreasonable railers and defamers, now and at all times. By the grace of God I am sure of this.

You prove yourselves quite unfriendly and unreasonable with me so far away. You act as though you never have read a syllable of the Word of the Lord. By so doing, you not only make me an abomination and stench (which I deem not important) in the sight of many of those who are not at home in this matter, but you do the same to the holy Word which in my weakness has been preached by me for some time,[1] not altogether without fruit. Thus you frighten away those of little understanding from the right way. You strengthen them in their blindness, and rob them of the true insight and understanding of the ban. Therefore I am forced by duty to send you and your associates, whom you draw away from the light by your cunning, my simple but true reply as brief and clear as possible, in writing, since I cannot come in person. I hope that you may reconsider somewhat and henceforth sin no more in this way, but truly repent of your great error and find grace in that day before the Lord and His righteous judgment. Therefore I pray you carefully to consider what I say.

Understand then first of all, that I am blamed by Sylis of being an unstable weathercock because I have published as he says two tracts which contradict each other. To this I answer, in my humility, it is well known to more than one or two that I have been attacked on all sides by many assertive spirits for more than twenty-three years, and that I have had to withstand many a hard and heavy assault. Yet praise to Him who has kept me, I did not go unsteadily from one church to the other as both of you have done. (Pardon me for saying this, but you drive me to it.) I have remained firm and peaceable in the faith and doctrine with my beloved brethren unto this day as I have shown in the name of the Lord in such dark days. I trust by the grace of God to remain firm and peaceable, so long as I remain in this tabernacle. To which of us this name of unstable weathercock, if so

---

[1] Menno united with the Obbenites in January, 1536, and was ordained within about a year. This was written in January, 1560. *Ed.*

it must be called, is applicable I will leave to the judgment of the sensible reader.

As to the two publications which you seem to take ill of me, this is my simple reply. Eighteen or nineteen years ago when I wrote the first book, I was not well enough enlightened to make the necessary distinctions so that until that time, I included all sins in the rule of three admonitions. This I acknowledge verbally and in writing, and do not deny or hide it. All well-minded servants of God who seek the crucified Christ and not their own honor or flesh are always ready, ever deeper to investigate the sure foundation of truth. And so I, the least of all servants, on account of certain abominations which were in the course of time discovered in the church, and also on account of the miserable disputation and discord which during the past two years has crept in without my fault, have come to a more thoroughgoing study concerning this matter; and I came finally to see plainly that men may not retain those whom God Himself by His Spirit and Word excludes, lest Christ and His church be divided from each other. This is as clear as day.

Therefore it would be advisable for you to season your words somewhat more carefully. For you do not slander and despise me but the Holy Spirit which according to the word of promise has led me, His poor, weak servant and instrument, into His truth, and has discovered unto me the true position in this matter. Dear men, if I on that account am to be called an unstable weathercock because I was not perfectly enlightened from the beginning (I do not even now claim to be perfectly enlightened), then, O Lord, what an unstable weathercock you would call the precious, beloved Peter and others if they were alive today and if you had no more love for them than you have for me. For Peter although taught by the Lord's mouth and enlightened by the Holy Spirit, was nevertheless so unintelligent that he dared not preach the Gospel to the heathen until he was admonished and told to do so by a heavenly vision or revelation from God and had gained inner freedom to teach them.

Terrible is the word that slanderers, defamers, and liars shall have no part in the kingdom of God. Behold, chosen Sylis and Lemke, do not say that you have not been told.

Second, I understand that Sylis has also said that I have published a book from which nothing but hatred, murder, and blasphemy could come.

To this I reply with Christ's own words: Think not that I am come to send peace on earth; I came not to send peace, but a sword. At another place, I am come to send fire on the earth; and what will I, if it be already kindled? From these words and also from experience it is plain that the pure doctrine of Christ and of His holy apostles, truly taught and practiced, is of such a nature that it is followed among hardened and unbelieving people with envy, hatred, falsehood, slander, vituperation, persecution, sedition, murder, misery, and every tribulation.

But should we on this account teach and practice the pure doctrine and

truth anyway? If you answer in the affirmative, you yourselves judge that
we should not suppress the truth on account of danger, if any arise as a
consequence, but that notwithstanding this, it should be taught and practiced.
What kind of spirit is it then that teaches you this objection about hatred,
murder, blasphemy, etc., by which you would frighten poor people away from
the truth, I will leave you to reflect on this in the fear of God. But if you
answer in the negative, you make yourselves simply men of blood, for you
still continue to teach, baptize, and the like, while you hear daily that many
a pious soul is because of it robbed and even murdered. I pray you, learn
to know the spirit of your invective.

Tell me, is not the Word of Christ called the word of the cross? You
verily must answer in the affirmative, for in the kingdom and reign of Christ
upon earth, the command to the believing is only this, to deny themselves
and take up the cross and follow Him. If we love father, mother, husband,
wife, children, property, or ourselves better than Christ, we are not worthy
of Him. Yes, if we do not hate all these we cannot be His disciples. Matt.
10:37. Since this is the way it goes with the Gospel of Christ, therefore
your trivial darts and vapid thunderbolts of hatred, murder, and blasphemy
can not and should not deter me a hair's breadth so long as you do not convince me by binding truth and the power of the divine holy Scriptures that
I, in this matter of the ban or separation, have erred against the Word of
the Lord, or in any manner have abused it. I am the more assured by your
slander, seeing that it is put forth so completely without truth or Scripture,
that the invincible foundation of truth and of the immutable Word of the
Lord is on our side.

But as for blasphemy, this is my brotherly reply. Learn with more
piety to know according to the Scripture what blasphemy or sinning against
the Holy Ghost is. In my opinion it is this, that when the truth of God is
impressed upon the heart of man with such a power of the divine, holy Scripture by the Spirit and finger of His power that we become convinced in
spirit and must confess that it is the undeniable true foundation of truth,
and yet for reason of self-conceit or willfulness we are so bold and stubborn
as to persist in opposing and hating, reviling and slandering, this inspired
and now known truth by our ambitious, factious, proud, and contrary flesh,
ascribing it to the devil, even as the proud Pharisees and scribes ascribed
the glorious miracles and power of Christ to Beelzebub: This the mouth of
the Lord calls blasphemy and sinning against the Holy Ghost, if persisted
in, as I take it, and He declares that it will not be forgiven in this world
nor in the world to come. Oh, dear, take heed!

Such slander and sin is very blasphemy and sin against the Holy Spirit,
as was heard. God, before whom we with all our teachings and doings stand
altogether exposed, knows that I have written the tract which you slander
with a good and assured conscience. All theologians must acknowledge
that it is the truth and Word of the Lord. You do not and cannot controvert

it with Scripture, and you are nevertheless so bold and rash as to call this unvanquished writing of mine a book of fables and heretical doctrine. I leave it to the impartial reader to judge with which of us blasphemy is to be found. Oh, that you would see!

I understand that you call our position concerning the shunning of husband and wife heretical.

I reply: First, Paul says a heretical man is perverse and sins as one who condemns himself.[2] Inasmuch as a heretic is one who is subverted and condemned by himself, therefore I know by the grace of God that I am not worthy of such an adjective, for He who knows and tries all hearts also knows that I never discovered and much less practiced obduracy, contrariness, factiousness, or perversity in my heart, contrary to His Word and will. I am sure that the merciful Father, who alone is the true Father of my soul, will not thus condemn to hell His miserable, weak servant and instrument, nor consider him such a heretic, even though I must hear the scornful slander, not merely from the world but from you also. Oh, dear, no. His name is Our Faithful God, Merciful Father, Deliverer, Emmanuel, etc. Therefore let all under heaven judge, vituperate, and slander His paternal Word, conceived in my open and willing heart, together with the Holy Spirit of His love which leads all souls hungering and thirsting after righteousness to the bread of life and to the true fountain of His living waters. He will doubtlessly refresh me in the heat of this and other assaults and extend to me His hand of consolation. For where is the man who sought Him thus and did not find Him in His grace, and where is the man who trusted in Him and was not helped? Oh, that you would see the frightfulness of your perverse and untimely judgment.

Second, I answer that according to the Scripture true heretics are self-willed, restless, willful, and perverse sectarians who choose, assemble, put forth for themselves out of a favorite spirituality or preference a peculiar position, doctrine, and church contrary to the true foundation of truth in which the true church which counts before God should be founded. With this program they disturb the unity of the pious, extinguish love, destroy peace, and cause much disturbance, trouble, sorrow and distress among those who would gladly walk in the truth. I pray you to learn to know what a heretic really is.

These being the real heretics, necessity requires that we indicate the difference between us, and explain it so that the intelligent reader and hearer may understand and comprehend with which of us perverseness and the heretical position is found. Take heed, not words or appearance but God's Word will be the judge.

In the first place, our position and doctrine is that all obedient children of God, without any respect of persons, must withdraw from and shun all brothers and sisters who walk disorderly and who are disobedient to the

2 Dutch version of Titus 3:11. *Tr.*

institution, ordinance, and doctrine received from the apostles, because it is so commanded of the Holy Spirit in the name of Christ. But your position and doctrine is that a husband and wife, in case one of them deviates from the truth, is free from any such command to shun. You have respect of persons of which the Holy Spirit of wisdom does not command nor imply a single word in all Holy Writ. Mark our first point of difference.

Our second position and doctrine is that the true apostolic ban and the requirement of shunning does not refer merely to the spiritual fellowship as at the Supper, and the handshake, and kiss, and salutation of peace, but also to carnal fellowship, such as eating, having business dealings with, to receive into one's house, etc. But your position and doctrine is (for your deeds show it, which in my opinion proves more than words and confession would do) that shunning applies only to spiritual fellowship and not to natural, secular contact. For it is a well known fact that you allow natural association between a husband and his apostate wife, that you eat with the excommunicated ones, and deal with them—if you have not changed your position. Notice our second point of difference.

Our third position and doctrine is that the second table of the law, namely, the commandment concerning our neighbor, must give way to the first, which is the commandment concerning God. But your position and doctrine (for your actions in regard to husband and wife are my witness) is not that the second table must give way to the first, but the first to the second. As if the Creator must do the will of the creature and the creature not the will of the Creator! Oh, dear me. Mark our third point of difference.

Our fourth position and doctrine is that the Holy Spirit in all matters cares for His own and has therefore commanded us to shun the sectarian and offensive sinners lest with the leaven of their unrighteousness they leaven the pious, or by natural intimacy and conversation and cohabitation, they contaminate the pious and get them involved in their own evil deeds; and also that the apostates may therefore be made ashamed before the Lord and His church, may repent, and be converted. But your position and doctrine go so emphatically against this that you quite bitterly call us marriage-breakers and heretics because we, out of zealous fear of God, follow the command of the holy apostles, and point everyone whose lot it becomes to the surest way according to the Scriptures. You tell the poor common people that it is an abomination in your ears that a husband should shun his wife, or a wife her husband on account of the ban. It is also an abomination to the world that we should baptize the believers and refuse to hear the false preachers. You reprove the Holy Spirit of the love of Christ. You accuse and abuse His holy apostles of a false doctrine as if the leaven of corruption (against which they have faithfully warned us) could not leaven husband or wife; and as if we were at liberty, not according to the rule of the holy Word, to seek the reformation of our consorts.

Our fifth position and doctrine is that the ban without shunning is quite as powerless and futile as a mill without a millstone, and as a knife without a blade. For it is more than clear that the apostolic ban has its real power and effectiveness in the outward shunning. For else the danger of corrupting others, the first and main reason for the ban, would not be averted. Your practice shows plainly that you have and teach a ban without the shunning, and that the same is therefore without effect, since you first except husband and wife from the shunning, and then secondly you eat and do business, etc., with those who are banned. Whereas the Holy Scriptures plainly and pointedly forbid it saying, With such an one ye shall not eat; With such do not keep company, but shun them; Do not have to do with them; Do not greet them, nor take them into your houses. Notice our fifth point of division.

But if you would say that if the pious can freely practice his faith, living with the impious, then there is no need for shunning, I would answer, first, that by such interpretation of the matter you destroy all the plain commandments of Scripture concerning the outward, physical shunning, for instance, not to eat, deal, or lodge. If some liberty should be granted to some, it would be more reasonable to give the whole church liberty to eat and deal with apostates than to give it to husband and wife. For it can do this with less danger than husband and wife who are continuously together, something which the church could easily avoid. This is clearer than day. O men, take heed.

My second reply is that none under heaven can practice his faith while living with his apostate consort. To begin with he would be transgressing all the explicit commandments of the Holy Spirit concerning the ban and shunning. And besides, he would not seek the repentance of his consort in such a manner as the Scripture teaches. And third, he keeps company with one who should, according to the commandment of the Word, be shunned by all pious persons. I will leave to the consideration of all of you if this can be called practicing the faith. Therefore, I pray you again, take heed.

Behold, beloved, if you compare this separation with the doctrine of the Scripture and in the fear of God weigh it in the impartial balance of the holy Word, then it is clear, is it not, that I and my beloved brethren have the fast, unshakable Word to sustain us, and that you have only a vain presumption and a willful opinion. We have a restoring ban that has point and power, whereas you have one that is fruitless, lame, and dead. We have obedience. We seek to save all the distressed souls from the infectious disease of corruption, according to the doctrine and commandment of the holy apostles; but you, contrary to all admonition, doctrine, and the explicit commandment of the holy apostles, leave them to the same corruption, without aid, succor, consolation, assistance, and earnest challenge; looking not at that which is pleasing to the Spirit but only at that which is pleasing to the flesh. It appears then that you are, more than is good for you, covered with that shameful cloak of heresy which you impute to me. If you are sensible, do not miss the point.

Fourthly, I understand that you call us marriage-breakers, telling your followers that of such shunning of husband and wife there can not be found a single example in all the Scriptures. I answer that Moses taught the Israelites that they should not excuse their own wives, sons, daughters, and friends who were as precious to them as their own hearts if they should want to lead them to strange gods, but that they should without mercy slay or stone them. Deut. 13:6-10. Tell me, whose was the responsibility for this situation, Moses' or God's? Not that of Moses, but that of God who had commanded him thus. Thus it is with us also. We teach that the apostate and sectarian should be shunned without respect of person. Yet not we but God who has commanded us to do so in His Word, as has been sufficiently shown. And note this also.

In the second place I reply by asking this question, If one of your number had a dishonest, wicked, thievish, sorcerous, perverted, murderous, incendiary, or suicidal wife and were aware of it, would he continue to live with her? If you say yes, then you must acknowledge that he is an abominable, frightful, murderous rogue to be one flesh with her—something which would not become a servant of Christ very well. But if you say no, you judge yourself, for you in this matter—no adultery or fornication having occurred—are marriage-breakers no less than we are. Once more, take note.

Again I ask, If one of your number had such a wife that he would have to silence his faith with her or practice it not without restraint, should he wish or continue to live with her? If you answer yes, you testify plainly that such perverse and wicked flesh means more to you than Christ Jesus Himself, together with His whole kingdom, truth, Word, promise, blood and death, besides your faith, anointing, love, and the salvation of your souls. If you answer in the negative, I say again that you in this matter in which no proved fornication or adultery has taken place are no less marriage-breakers than we are. Mark this in the third place.

Then in the third place I answer, If this our doctrine must be called marriage-breaking by you, then it is evident that the holy Paul was no less a marriage-breaker than we are, for he said, But if she depart, let her remain unmarried (observe he openly admits separation), or be reconciled to her husband. Seeing then that Paul also allows such separation when it is for betterment, provided they remain unmarried, as is also our doctrine, and you do the same (if I understand your answer correctly), then you are no less marriage-breakers than we are. Therefore I would have you to consider in the fear of God a bit more carefully what kind of a spirit it is that prompts you to make use of such slanderous smear words as marriage-breakers, book of fables, heresy, etc. Venom is deadly and gall is bitter, but much more poisonous and bitter is the tongue which is charged and laden with partiality and hatred. Attend to this.

But as to the before-mentioned argument about an example in Scriptures, this is our answer. First, that all those who take recourse to this argument manifest thereby that they do not believe the Scriptures of the apostles concerning the ban and shunning, and do not understand, and care not to understand the reasons, utility, and effects of the ban, and alas, have but little regard for the explicit commandments concerning the outward, bodily shunning.

Again, we say concerning the opinion that a doctrine without Scriptural example cannot stand in the church of Christ: that then we, all of us, if that is to stand, are badly mistaken, both you and we; because we allow our women to approach the Lord's Supper of which not a letter in the Scriptures can serve as example. But if you should say that our women are believing, therefore they should be admitted to the Supper, along with the believing men, I would retort in similar manner, the pious spouse is believing, therefore he should shun his apostate wife according to the common rule of Scripture as do the other believing ones without exception. Whosoever is intelligent will judge and consider what we assert.

In the fifth place, I understand that Lemke has boasted that he is going to undo more than half of the printed tracts. I reply briefly, to promise mountains of gold and the while not having sand hills to give is usually called boasting. Therefore it would be well not to boast of more than we have Scripture and talent for.

But whosoever will undo our writings must first make good[3] the following ten articles. First, that the first table of the commandment in Christ's kingdom and reign must give way to the second. Second, that the Scripture teaches two kinds of bans or shunnings. Third, that there can be a Scriptural ban without the shunning. Fourth, that the deadly disease of corruption cannot leaven or make unclean husband or wife when they do not shun the apostate mate. Fifth, that it is not required at the hands of the pious spouse earnestly to seek the reformation and repentance of the wicked spouse according to the counsel, doctrine, and commandments of the holy Scripture. Sixth, that the pious spouse is not bound to agree to the separation of his wicked consort. Seventh, that the carnal ban and natural love must be preferred to the spiritual ban and spiritual love. Eighth, that the spiritual marriage promise made to Christ must give way to the physical marriage vow made to human flesh. Ninth, that the Holy Spirit has in Scriptures taught exceptions or respect of persons concerning the ban or shunning. Tenth, that married people are not subject to the explicit commandments concerning the outward or bodily shunning.

Behold, worthy Lemke, whenever you or any of your followers dissolve or untie this knot by virtue of the Scriptures, then we will consider the matter further. We know that no man, no matter who he be, can ever do so with Scripture. Of this before God we are certain. Therefore we let men vituperate and boast as much as they like. Firm and unshakable the doctrine remains,

---

[3] The original has *te niete doen* (annihilate or undo); evidently an error, for the very opposite is intended. *Tr.*

namely, that all pious husbands and wives are bound to shun their wicked spouses according to the common rule, doctrine, and command of the holy Scriptures in collaboration with the congregation, as has been frequently shown on the basis of the holy Word. Whosoever seeks and loves the truth may ponder on that which we say and consider the intent of the Scriptures.

In the sixth place, I understand Lemke to have said that if we were of one mind in regard to the article concerning husband and wife, there would be three or four articles besides about which we could not agree. To which I would say, that I would like to have him put in writing these articles and points of difference and send them to me. If you have the truth and not we, then by the grace of God, I for myself will agree with you. But I would warn you not to call that which is right and pure, wrong and impure, nor that which is wrong and impure, right and pure; and not to allow what the Scripture forbids, nor to forbid that which it allows, as some also alas are in the habit of doing. May not our self-made righteousness nor human opinion and holiness, but the Word of God alone be our guide and way. In love, take heed.

In the seventh place, I understand that Lemke also says that I first came to the Franekers and their followers and agreed with them; and afterwards instructed by his faction, I agreed with them. I truthfully reply to you and to all who repeat your untrue story that I fraternally asked the Franekers when I was in conversation with them if they had any inclinaton to make trouble about the matter of three admonitions in case of patent carnal conduct. To this they answered no. Then I said (after a little discussion concerning secret sins), If that is your doctrine we will not remain divided. Then they thanked the Lord as if we were quite of one mind in regard to the matter. Observing this, I said, Not so, brethren, but I will also talk to the others and see what grace the Lord will give. That this is true I can prove by our beloved brother, Nette Lippes. It is also known to the omniscient Lord whose hand and judgment I cannot escape if I lie and do not write the truth.

Afterwards I came to them and conversed with them and got full satisfaction (praise the Lord for His grace!) concerning the matter of secret sins at which my heart was more happy than I can write, not now doubting in the least but that the matter would come to a good solution, until the time that the Franekers came and showed that they did not abide by the declaration which they had made to me concerning carnal works. This caused sorrow in me as bitter as death. I knew not what to do for sorrow, for there is nothing upon earth I love more than the Lord's church. But I have to see that the leavening spirit of the false parties has so corrupted some. Yes, had not the gracious breath of the Almighty saved me I would probably have gone insane. In short, the Franekers would not agree until they had first consulted Henry Naeldeman. In the course of time said Henry came to us and in love we informed him that we were not those who judged the offensive transgressors thus, but that according to the Word we could not retain those whom He with His Spirit and Word excludes. He was so startled that he openly said before us all that he had never in his life so taken the matter to heart and hoped to place the Franekers on a better footing. I then left the country. Not long afterward he again sent for me. He had studied the matter over, and all we had built up with the Lord's Word was again broken in the poor man. Yes, it is known to me and to the Lord how unstable and childishly he acted once or twice in a short time concerning the matter of husband and wife. What he wrote with his own hand will be my testimony in the matter.

Behold, worthy sirs, here you have the essence of our action in this matter of which you so very unfairly dare to accuse me. I assert it with a good conscience before the eyes of the Lord. If you had acted the part of wisdom in this matter and had not inclined your ears to the backbiting of the unpeaceable ones of the sectarian factions, you would never have so sinned against me with such gross falsehood and slander. Paul's word is surely true: A little leaven leaveneth the whole lump.

In the eighth place I understand that Lemke publishes that I have said to him, The people build upon and look to me so much that I am afraid that the Lord will yet cause me to stumble so that they shall no more look to me or any other man. I reply first, If I should now or any time say to Lemke or to anyone else: The people build upon and look to me so much—then my own mouth would convince me that I would be like unto a fool who is quick to praise himself. I trust that not only the Word of the Lord, but also common sense will teach me better. And as I have experienced it more than once in my life, the spirit of Diotrephes is not yet altogether dead—a spirit which generally clothes itself in a sheepskin sighing and complaining, Oh, oh, the people build upon and look too much to Menno! By this the hearts are turned from love. Therefore I have not said once but perhaps ten times, If the common people should build upon me and look to me so much, then I could wish that the Lord would cause me to stumble sometime (not taking His grace from me altogether) so that they might learn to know not to build their foundation, hope, and consolation upon me, but solely upon the living cornerstone, Christ Jesus, who according to the will of His Father and to His honor has called us in His eternal love and married us by faith into His death and blood—but not to Menno or Lemke. Oh, that they would not garble my words, nor repeat anything but the truth which can stand before God.

Secondly, I answer, If you thus turn to shame the words of my piety whereby I seek only the praise and honor of my Redeemer, which I had not thus expected, then I desire that in love you point out my error according to the truth. For although I am a poor sinner who at times am overcome by my flesh, I yet thank God for His grace that He has to this day saved His poor, weak servant without any grave offense both in doctrine and in life. But if your vision is so poor and dim that you call it stumbling, namely, that I teach according to the Holy Scriptures that we should shun the offensive transgressors until they repent, or that the ban should be used without respect of persons, or that I am ever prepared to accept a better instruction of God or admonition and doctrine of His Holy Spirit, as I have done and given an example in regard to the matter of carnal sins,[4] then I may well console myself that the holy apostles are in this matter no less stumblers than I am. For before God, I do not know but that I teach the essence of their Word unadulterated, and walk in the footsteps of their spirit, so far as I have received grace and strength from my God. Oh, how carnal, foolish, blind, and perverse is the judgment of a person who before his God is led away by partiality and envy! If you fear God, then heed what I tell you.

In the ninth place, I understand that you slander and upbraid our dear brethren in Friesland not a little. I reply briefly: It is not necessary that I should be the brethren's attorney since the merciful Lord has not denied them His grace, Spirit, and gifts. Yet I want to say that the ordinary civil rights provide that we should give both sides a hearing. We read of Alexander the Great, that when one party or one side laid a complaint before him without the presence of the other side or party, he would then shut up one ear so that with it he could give the other side a hearing. Since there was found such fairness among the outright heathen people, and it is the common usage in all civil courts not to judge until a hearing has been granted, therefore you have acted very unscripturally, unkindly, and unchristian by not only giving the one party (and that the party which is separated from the church on account of their contention) a hearing, but besides, accepting them as your beloved brethren, the while rejecting the other party—to the great shame of yourself and your counselors. And you have not given them a hearing face to face, although they frequently and in a brotherly way desired it. At this unkindliness, contrariness, and childish folly, we cannot cease marveling. We think that it is unheard of from people who pass for pious. You still proceed on the reports of partisans with intolerable lying and vituperation and defamation, without any sure knowledge about the matter. And by this violence and wrong you take from us that which I fear you can never restore.

But if you had given both parties a reasonable and Christian hearing, you might have (if you had the gift) passed a just sentence between them, and thus have sought unity and peace between them, according to the intent of the holy Word. But now you have revealed yourselves to all mankind while you see that with your useless, frivolous, and lifeless ban exercised by you and your followers these many years, you cannot stand before the sharpness of the Holy Spirit of Christ and of His strong Word. You do not seek to assert and maintain as much as in you is the desirable unity and peace, nor the unfaltering, abiding truth which is of God, but your own brutish will and willful invention by wrong and violence, dissension, partiality, slander, defamation, and the majority opinion. And know, however, that not such

[4] Menno here refers to the fact that he had changed his mind about the need for three public admonitions in the case of patent sins. *Tr.*

wrong and violence as you promote is to be the judgment and decision in this matter, but the Holy Spirit and Word of Christ Jesus. From the heart, let me tell you.

In the tenth place, I understand that Lemke says that he would rather be banned by our elders than agree with them. I answer, That one of two things is true according to his words. Either he does not know what the ban actually is, or else that these elders are such awful people that they are not worthy of a church. For all the world I would not repeat such a judgment. Even if these elders were such evil people as his words imply, why are you then so contrary (in spite of the fact that your office requires it) as not to show your brotherly service by pointing out to them in accord with the Scriptures their error and abomination even as it becomes you before God and His church to seek their salvation in love? But I presume that you have been so much surprised by the impact of truth that you were therefore afraid to face them. Oh, that you would hear the voice of the Lord and not harden your hearts! It still is the today of grace.

Finally, I must remind you that you came to us in 1556, just before May, and that we conferred for almost two days in a kindly spirit in the fear of God. And Lemke, the morning of his departure, confessed openly before me that he quite agreed with us, although still a bit uneasy about the matter of husband and wife, that he had not acknowleged this before the brethren because they had come as a like-minded group, and that if he had now spoken his mind before all, his word would therefore avail but little in your circles after that. And he said he wished to treat further with you on the way back. This is the way he represented things. He said moreover, If the Overlanders[5] will not allow themselves to be persuaded, and Sylis and Henry will stick with them, then I will, said he, go over to the Netherlanders.

He also said, There are some immigrants at Weert who would gladly come under the Word of the Lord. To whom shall I take these, to Sylis or to the Netherlanders? Besides he desired of me that when we would know just where Sylis stood, then to send one or two faithful brethren to his assistance, that the ban and shunning might in this way be introduced into his church. Yes, dear friends, that he agreed with us in this way he did not only confess to me but also before our beloved brethren Herman van T. and Hans S. in turn. And what is become of all these fine words and promises? Were they not all wind and falsehood? You must say yes, must you not? And yet you do not want it repeated at Cologne and thereabout that you had dealt thus with us. The saddest thing of all is that that which you then confessed to be good and right must now be called deceit and heresy. Whether he who acts so crudely and inconsistently can justly be called an unstable weathercock, I will leave to the intelligence of all reasonable readers to

[5] On the margin we read, Overlanders are called Swiss Brethren in Overland and Moravia. (Tr.) The Overlanders or Upperlanders were South German Swiss Brethren. Ed.

judge. Sylis and Henry wanted to take the matter in advisement and propose it to the Overlanders and they sent a written report, but whether or not you showed it to the elders of your church up there, I do not know. Lemke writes yes, and the brethren write no; and it is said that Sylis says no. There is something contradictory here.

In short, at long last, after long delay and waiting, we did receive a reply from you and the Overlanders, namely, that we should not push the matter of shunning to extremes, for it would be broken anyway, and that there were quite as many Scriptures dealing with marriage as with ban and shunning. Behold, this was the teaching of Scripture by which he explains all apostolic Scriptures concerning this matter and wants to reject them as superfluous!

If I do not write the truth, I am willing to bear my rebuke. In my opinion it has come so far with you before God that I do not know who could ever get along with you. First, you agree with us; afterwards without our knowledge you desert us and join the Overlanders.

Notice, Lemke agrees with us, but the same summer turns his back upon us again and agrees with them again.

Those who had been excommunicated on account of the dissension and scandal, you again accepted as your brethren.

Our elders and big churches you despised and to their requests you replied in an unkind and hostile way saying that you did not come on their account.

The spirit of turbulent agitators you believed behind our backs.

You lie, vituperate, backbite, slander, and call heretical me and my beloved brethren without any truth. I for one have never said an unfriendly word about you, God is my witness, but have ever desired the best for you until the hour of this your intolerable action.

The plain Word of the holy apostles concerning the ban and shunning you reject.

You sustain many frivolous, carnal babblers.

You encourage many restless, unpeaceful dissenters and quarrelers.

You bring heavy sadness upon faithful hearts, who sincerely seek God and His truth.

Many pious children who would gladly obey the Word of God in this regard and so save their souls, you hinder.

You beget many defamers, liars, profaners, and ranters.

In short, you have brewed such beer that if the Lord does not keep you in His mercy, I fear you will stumble over the brewing pot. For beware, if you renounce the Overlanders again, and also those whom you alas have now given the hand of brotherhood, then they will not depict you in very pleasing colors.

And if you remain with them, all intelligent persons must confess that you build your faith in this matter with a sectarian spirit upon human insight, opinion, flesh, and man, and not upon the firm rock and foundation of the divine Word. If you change your doctrine which you have so wrongly practiced and taught in your church, then you will have to hear that you are miserable teachers, that you have deceived many souls, and that you did not know the light of truth. But if you do not, you make it manifest that you do not seek and uphold the souls or the salvation of the church nor the Word of God, but only your own flesh and honor.

If you acknowledge that you have through party spirit with patent injustice so slandered me and have robbed my name of its luster, then a cry from the pious ones will issue against you that you have defamed the reputation of your brethren without their fault, not as faithful servants of Christ, but rather as envious defamers. If you do not acknowledge it, nor do such penance as can pass with God, then the just sentence of His immutable Word will be upon you, that is, that defamers, backbiters, slanderers, and liars have no portion in the kingdom of God and Christ. Awful is the word, Woe unto those who must hear and bear it. Reflect, I pray you, with fear and trembling.

Dear elect men, how perilously you are sailing like a ship that goes tripping along between two rocks. If it avoids the one it will run into the other. Therefore, take heed, take heed, I say, that you may escape the eternal shipwreck of your poor souls and arrive in the haven of eternal peace with the most High. Amen. Amen.

This now is the essence, conclusion, intent, and thrust of my writings to you and yours. First, that you may behold the abomination of your actions in this clear mirror, turn from evil, come before the Lord with a contrite heart, and sincerely pray for His grace. Second, that the simple and plain people who are in this respect held in bondage by you may taste and see that you have fed them not with the bread of their heavenly Father, but with chaff and human opinion. Third, that you may know that I and the pious who are with me dare not by the fear of our God be your brethren, so long as there are not found with you such doctrine, obedience, confession, reconciliation, and repentance as to quiet the church of the Lord and make it to be well pleased with you.

This is written in great sorrow. If you fear God, then take heed and reflect. The God of all grace and the Holy Spirit of peace and of the love of Christ grant you grace that you may read with impartial hearts and that it may bear fruit in you. Amen. Amen. Amen.

By me, Menno Simons, who loves your souls in truth.

*January 23, 1559 [1560, New Style]*

# Letters and Other Writings

*For other foundation can no man
lay than that is laid, which is Jesus Christ.*

I CORINTHIANS 3:11

# Sharp Reply to David Joris

### Antwoort aan David Joris

# 1542

I am altogether ready for the battle: not a carnal one, but a spiritual. Until now I have remained standing over against all my adversaries, undefeated, and have overcome them, because I have been always armed, not with my own weapons but with divine ones, namely, the evangelical doctrine: attacked indeed by many, but vanquished by none. By long usage I have become as well acquainted with this armament and this battle as with the eating of bread. Yes, the evangelical teaching has with me taken the place of breastplate, robe, and cloak. But you, David,* have long since rejected this variety of armament, and have considered it obsolete, and in its place put your new fantasies, rhetorical figures, philosophies, and other tricks and deceptions of Satan, and you are therefore rightly called Antichrist, a man of sin, son of perdition, false prophet, murderer of souls, deceiver, one who tramples on the heavenly doctrines and institutions of Christ, etc.

I am therefore amazed and dazed at the audacity and the arrogance of this your writing: that you, after having dispersed so many blasphemous articles in your books, and having propagated them through so many years, yet do not, thus far, show any penitence, so that you seem even now to wish to defend the same madness. It is evidence of diabolical pride and anti-Christian fury that you dare to put your dreams, your fantasies, enthusiasms, rhetorical figures, and other magic illusions ahead of the wisdom of the Holy Spirit, through which the prophetic and apostolic Scriptures have been given.

It is evidenced in that you, a dunghill of a man, ashes, and a vapor, dare to extol your office above that of Jesus Christ, the Son of God, and to put your doctrine ahead of that of the apostles.

---

* For a brief introduction to the notorious David Joris read in this volume from Harold S. Bender's *Brief Biography of Menno Simons*, V, "Labors in Holstein, 1546-1561." David Joris seems to have been an Obbenite minister before Menno united with the group in 1536. But by about the year 1536 Joris had become so unbalanced, fanatical, and unsound that the Obbenites disowned him. A study of the Davidians reveals what a corrupt sect they were, and justifies the severity of Menno's judgments. For another English translation made by John Horsch, see his *Menno Simons*, 1916, 192, 193. For a Latin text see Blesdijk-Revius: *Historia Davidis Georgii*, 129 ff. See also the *Nederlandsch Archief v. Kerkel. Geschiedenis*, V, 1845, 73-77, and the *Zeitschrift f. die historische Theologie*, 1863, 143-46. The letter is missing in both the *Opera Omnia Theologica* of 1681 and the *Complete Works* of 1871. According to K. Vos (*Menno Simons*, 1914, p. 289), the letter should be dated 1542. Vos also reprints the work in Dutch (*ibid.*, 277-79). J. C. W.

I pass by the disgraceful license to which you and your followers resort when you accommodate yourselves to the ritual and the morality of the papists, the Lutherans, and the Zwinglians, taking part in their religious exercises, not fleeing the fellowship of their banquets, weddings, and funerals, but conforming yourself to all in the matter of conduct.

Also, when, contrary to the teachings of Paul, you condemn marital intimacy with a woman either pregnant or barren, and, under this pretense indirectly commend Jewish polygamy and also practice it, and under the pretext of ascetic discipline introduce other carnal comminglings.

Moreover, your life and that of your followers is no less corrupt and polluted than is your teaching, since in this and other matters of conduct you evince a worldly haughtiness, pride, excess, and so forth.

You make bold to transfer the honor due to the Son of God; treat as obsolete the doctrine of Christ and your own as perfect and abiding. You exalt your anti-Christian office and ministry above that of Jesus Christ and of the apostles. Moreover, under the pretext and pretense of a false humility you set forth and promote a satanic pride, under color of perfect chastity and other virtues, various wickednesses and shamefulnesses. Finally, you transform the status and the form of the Christian life into a worldly one, after the manner of the Lutherans and the papists. Therefore I do not doubt but that you will shortly receive from God (who gives not His honor to another) the reward and end such as John Beukelszoon, the king of Münster, received,[1] and others who before him arrogated to themselves the honor due to the Son of God.

Desist from your writing to me, therefore; spare your paper and ink; for I will after this read nothing sent by you until it appears openly that you have condemned and declared accursed your wicked doctrine and have restored again to the true doctrine of Christ the praise and the reverence due to it.[2]

[1] The reference is to John of Leiden, the notorious leader of the Münster rebellion.

[2] This letter written by Menno to David Joris has come down to us not in the original direct discourse but in the indirect discourse of an ancient reporter. We have thrown it back into the direct discourse form. *Tr.*

# Admonition to the Amsterdam Melchiorites

## Erste Brief aan Amsterdam

## c. 1545

To all the true children of God and partakers of the promise of the kingdom of Christ, grace and peace.*

Beloved in Christ Jesus, I am deeply troubled about you, for I hear that you hunger and thirst after righteousness and that there are so few dispensing it to men—persons who correctly cut the bread of the divine Word for their hungry consciences—so few shepherds who pasture the sheep of Christ aright; so few builders and masons to place the living stones in the temple of the Lord; so few watchmen who guard the city, the new Jerusalem, and blow the trumpet; so few fathers to beget the children of God and so few mothers to nourish these begotten ones. I hear that quite the opposite is the case for those who make bold to assume this function but do not know what the bread is, nor who the children are to whom it belongs. For if they had the bread by which the soul lives, not so many children would starve; for they stand there officially dispensing bread once or twice a week (understand, the bread necessary to the support of the body).[1] Inasmuch as they give the people cockatrices' eggs, therefore observe what the prophet says concerning them: He that eateth of their eggs dieth. Isa. 59:5.

Concerning the shepherds who pose as shepherds of Christ, who pasture the sheep for what they get out of it, as Ezek. 34:8 has it, pasturing themselves—you see how little they bother themselves about the sheep, whether they have pasture or not. Just so they get the wool and the milk, then they are satisfied. They pose as shepherds but they are deceivers. They are very different from the shepherds of which we read in Jeremiah, shepherds after

---

* On Melchior Hofmann and the Melchiorites, see Harold S. Bender's *Brief Biography of Menno Simons*, printed in this volume, especially I, "The Catholic Priest." John Horsch has pointed out that the Melchiorites, although teaching various Protestant doctrines, actually constituted a party within the Roman Catholic Church. Inwardly far from Catholicism, they outwardly attended Catholic services as a matter of "liberty" in an attempt thus to avoid persecution. Menno considered this position seriously unchristian and wrong. The letter before us, dated Nov. 18 (of about the year 1545, according to Vos: *Menno Simons*, p. 289), is an earnest appeal to the misguided Melchiorites to break completely with Roman Catholicism, and to come out clean on the side of Christ and His Word. The letter is printed in the *Opera Omnia Theologica* of 1681, fol. 637-40, and in the *Complete Works* of 1871, Part I, 277-80.　　　　J. C. W.

[1] Menno hints, not without sarcasm, at the mercenary spirit of the priests, who dispense bread daily—that is, physical bread for their own support. *Tr.*

His heart whom the Holy Spirit has sent. These other shepherds have not the love of Christ which Peter had and therefore Christ's commandment to pasture His lambs does not apply to them. They are not commanded, that is, if they are not sent how then can they preach? As you see, they are not God-sent shepherds who lead the sheep into the green pastures of the divine Word. Instead they let them starve. They are not the shepherds who lead them to the sparkling waters, but to the muddy pools which they have prepared with their feet, that is, by their glosses and human notions.

They also parade as builders who build the Lord's house, but they do not know Christ, the cornerstone; they have never added a single stone to the house of the Lord, that is, living stones which are built into a spiritual building, which building is the church of God. Heb. 3:6. Wherever there are two or three stones together, held together with the mortar of love, there they hasten to break down and to destroy them, as you may see verified in all countries and cities. How far removed are they from those of whom Paul says: Ye are God's husbandry, ye are God's building, and we are God's co-laborers; namely, those who build the house of the Lord properly, that is, according to His Word.

If then they are not builders, they must be wreckers. They pretend to be the husbandmen who take care of the vineyard but how they tend it and protect it against foxes and all wild animals, I will leave to every Christian to consider for himself. How they labor for the profit of the Lord of the vineyard and how they give Him His rent or honor, that the Lord of the vineyard knows. How they scourge, persecute, rob, hunt, banish, and kill His children for no other cause than that they neither do nor dare consent to them inasmuch as they see that they themselves are not the true husbandmen, but destroyers—that the Lord of the vineyard knows also.

Yet they pose as watchmen. If they are watchmen, then they are blind watchmen and dumb dogs that cannot bay or bark. Isa. 56:10. Hosea, the prophet, shows what they watch for and how they blow the trumpet. How far they are from the Word of the Lord which says, Son of man, I have made thee a watchman. Ezek. 3:17. Lift up thy voice like a trumpet, and show my people their transgression. Isa. 58:1.

They want to be fathers who bring forth the children of God and then nurture them. But how can they beget children when they have never rightly conceived? Oh, how different they are from the fathers of whom Paul speaks: Ye have not many fathers; for in Christ Jesus I have begotten you through the gospel (I Cor. 4:15); also to the Galatians, My little children, of whom I travail in birth again until Christ be formed in you (Gal. 4:19). Here observe who are the real fathers of the children. Now show me one child they have begotten, namely, one child which was born of God through the Gospel. Paul also says, I have fed you with milk (I Cor. 3:2), even as a nurse cherisheth her children (I Thess. 2:7).

You see, sincerely beloved brethren and sisters in Christ Jesus, if you follow me, that you have few who cut and dispense the sweet bread. It is leaven which they give you. They are not shepherds who pasture the sheep, but wolves that destroy them. They are not builders that build the temple, but such as break down that which was built. They are not husbandmen who tend the vineyard of the Lord and give Him His rent.

They are false husbandmen who scourge, stone, garrote, and kill the servants, as alas you may plainly see. They are not the watchmen who watch over the city of Jerusalem and warn her of the enemy, but they betray the citizens and kill them. They are not fathers nor nurses, but they kill that which was begotten and nourished, even as Pharaoh, king of Egypt, killed the true Israelites which he could lay hold on.

Therefore it is necessary to separate from them and to depart, as we read in Matt. 7:15, Beware of false prophets. As Paul says, Beware lest any man spoil you through philosophy and vain deceit, after the tradition of men, after the rudiments of the world, and not after Christ. Col. 2:8.

The church of Christ is the bride of Christ, and Christ does not want His bride to conceive except of the incorruptible seed. I Pet. 1:23. As Paul says, I have espoused you to one husband, that I may present you as a chaste virgin to Christ. II Cor. 11:2. Yes, so pure Paul wanted the church to be that if there were any who caused divisions and offenses contrary to the doctrine which he had taught, they should be avoided. Yes, if they had any in the church that were drunkards, covetous, fornicators, idolatrous, or proud, they should avoid them and not eat with them. I Cor. 5:11. How then could they have such people as preachers? If they preached any other Gospel than that which was preached unto them, they were accursed. Gal. 1:8.

To the Philippians Paul calls them dogs who taught circumcision. He says: Brethren, be followers together of me, and mark them which walk so as ye have us for an example; for many walk, of whom I have told you often and now tell you, even weeping, that they are the enemies of the cross of Christ; whose end is destruction, whose God is their belly, and whose glory is in their shame, who mind earthly things. Phil. 3:2, 17, 19. Notice what kind of people he is thinking of.

The apostle would have the bride so pure that no dissension was allowed; no drunkards, bandits, idolaters, nor those that taught any other doctrine than he taught. Christ Himself says to the church: Beware of false prophets, which come to you in sheep's clothing, but inwardly they are ravening wolves. Ye shall know them by their fruits. Matt. 7:15.

How then can some say this is a matter of liberty? Of this liberty any sensible Christian may judge. Shall we who declare that we defend the glory of God talk of a matter of liberty where God is blasphemed and His ordinances broken? It was commanded of Aaron to serve in the priest's office; and when Dathan and Abiram wanted to function similarly, was this a matter of liberty? Then why did the earth open its mouth and swallow them? Num. 16:32. The children of Aaron, Nadab and Abihu, were required always to keep the fire burning on the altar. If it was a matter of liberty to put strange fire on the altar, why then did they burn? Lev. 10:1, 3.

Read how the worshipers of the calf, the murmurers and the fornicators, all received their punishment. Num. 25:8, 9. Yes, the man of God at Bethel —how much a matter of liberty was it to him when God had told him not to eat bread or drink water in that place, and then through the lies of the old prophet he did eat and drink contrary to God's command? It was so much a matter of "liberty" that he had to die. I Kings 13.

There are very many such passages in Scripture touching this matter. I will omit them for the sake of brevity. But I wish that every Christian would do as Christ teaches, saying: Search the Scriptures (John 5:39); and as did those of Berea who searched the Scriptures daily. Acts 17:11. If you search the Scripture, it will teach you all right, but if you would be a member of the holy body of Christ, you must follow the Head and obey Him. John 3:36; II Thess. 1:8.

If He commands you to beware of false prophets, are we going to make this a matter of liberty? If the emperor should issue a decree and the subjects changed it into a matter of liberty, what kind of officers would you be, if you did not punish the subjects for not obeying the decree?

Now the Chief Emperor Christ has issued a decree, which decree He has sealed with His blood. In this directive it reads that we must be born again, must repent, deny ourselves, take up our cross, believe on Jesus Christ, and on this faith be baptized in the name of the Father, and the Son, and the Holy Ghost; must obey His commandments, give unto Caesar the things that are Caesar's; and love the Lord with all our heart and with all our strength, and our neighbors as ourselves; not live unto ourselves, but unto Him who died for us and rose again; we must beware of false prophets, and abstain from all appearance of evil. Now say, most beloved, which of these is a matter of liberty? Are we at liberty to be born again or not as we choose? Are we at liberty to deny ourselves, or to believe on Christ, or not? At liberty to be baptized, to give unto Caesar that which is Caesar's and unto God that which is God's? To beware of false prophets and to abstain from all appearance of evil? If these things are matters of liberty, why then does the Lord Jesus say at the end: and teach them to keep my commandments. Matt. 28:19? If He has commanded it, He wants it obeyed. Matters of liberty are neither commanded nor prohibited. For example, Paul's reference to eating and the keeping of certain days. I Cor. 10:28. Yet he commands not to offend the brethren by such liberty.

Well then, dear children, if you confess that Christ Jesus is the Son in His house, then please let Him be wise enough to rule His own house, for He has bought this house with His blood and has led captivity captive and given gifts to men. Some He has made pastors and teachers. Eph. 4:6. And Paul teaches us what they should be like. You trot over to the papistic teachers who you know beforehand are not sent of Christ, and as a consequence, bear no fruit. Are you then obedient unto the voice of the Lord? Oh, no!

The Holy Spirit points out those who are unblamable and you go to those that are blamable both in doctrine and in life. Christ has commanded us to look out for such, and you go to hear them, saying it is a matter of liberty. Therefore judge for yourselves whether you are children of God or not. You say it is a matter of liberty; and I ask, Who gave you this liberty? But Paul says: Ye are not your own, ye are bought with a price; therefore glorify God in your body and in your spirit, which are God's. I Cor. 6:19. With what then will you practice this liberty?

Christ Jesus has also commanded His church to baptize believers on confession of faith. If now I do not believe and do not suffer myself to be baptized in accordance with God's Word, but allow my little children without Scriptural warrant to be baptized, am I then obedient unto the voice of the Lord? Can I then inherit the promise given to the believers? The answer is no.

Christ left with His church the Holy Supper, in bread and wine, as a remembrance of His death. It has been changed into a Romish market. Is a Christian now permitted to observe the deviating, errant, papal, daytime meal, and neglect the Lord's nighttime meal?[2] Judge for yourselves since Paul says ye cannot be partakers of the Lord's table and partakers of the table of Antichrist and the devil. I Cor. 10:21. If we cannot partake of both, then we must neglect one or the other. Well, then, keep your distance!

Now look here, my dear children, I have given you a little lesson in keeping with the little talent which the Lord has given me. Judge for yourselves whether it is a matter of liberty to a married woman to be with another man, yes, even if it were but once a year. Now you are the bride of the Lamb, and you are not allowed to have children by anybody but by Christ in His holy Word. If you are the delightful body of Christ, then you must have the Spirit of Christ; if you are baptized into that body by the Spirit, then you must be obedient unto the Head, namely, Christ. If you are the city, the new Jerusalem, where the inhabitants are of one mind, then you must be obedient unto the King of that great city, namely, Christ. If you are the branches, then you must bear fruit like that of the vine. If you are of the vineyard of the Lord, then you must beware of the foxes. If you are the temple of the lord, then you must be submissive unto your High Priest. If you are the ark of the covenant, then the tables of the covenant written with the finger of God, that is, the commandments of God, must be engraved in your hearts, that all men may read that you are an epistle of Christ. II Cor. 3:2, 3.

Dear children, would that the Lord granted that we might meet face to

---

[2] The early Mennonites, as well as all other non-Catholic groups before their times, were forced to celebrate the Lord's Supper at night. It was perhaps a welcome fact that in Menno's language the Supper was called *Avondmaal* (Evening meal) or *Nachtmaal* (Night meal). In the present passage Menno is contrasting the papist daytime Sacrament with the evening meal or night meal of the early Anabaptists. To preserve the contrast we have translated *Nachtmaal* with "nighttime meal" rather than with such an expression as the Lord's Supper. *Tr.*

face. We trust that we could report to you on all points. Therefore ye that fear God, quit Babylon and go to Jerusalem, and do not allow yourselves to be caught by such frivolous and irresponsible words as, It is a matter of liberty. The drunkard is at liberty to drink a lot of wine and beer, the gambler to gamble, and the fornicator to fornicate—but with all that, they do not have liberty to do it. So also we are at liberty to hear the preaching and to allow infants to be baptized—yet that does not make it permissible.

Herewith I commend my beloved children to the Lord. May the rich Word of His grace enlighten you with His pure knowledge and give you to do His will in all things so that the tumble-down temple may be rebuilt on its true foundation, and that we may achieve the end of faith, that is, the salvation of souls. Amen.

*November 14*                                            MENNO SIMONS

# Earnest Epistle to the Davidians

*Brief aan David-Joristen*

## c. 1546

•-•-•-•-•-•-•-•-•-•-•-•-•-•-•-•-•-•-•-•-•-•-•-•-•-•-•-•-•-•-•-•-•-•-•-•-•-•-•-•-•-•-•-•

A Lost Letter to the Disciples of David Joris.

[An Ancient Résumé Thereof]*

The first part deals with the true religion, of what it consists, and how it is worked out in practice; likewise, concerning the service of idols and whether to have a child baptized or to participate with Christians[1] in any ceremonial act instituted by Christ, even if certain wrong usages have become associated therewith. This is idolatry, as he has it.

The second part opposes his[2] idea and doctrine touching the prohibition of the use of gold, silver, expensive attire, etc., which he[3] calls becoming conformed to the world.

The third part takes up the question whether it is indeed safe and without concern for damage to give credence to him or to any group of people[4] and to follow them, because they are in many places persecuted by the civil magistracy. In the same section there is delineated very soundly the genius, the nature, the intentions, the ethics, and the conduct of a true Christian, especially of the Spirit-taught minister of the New Testament.

The conclusion demands and seeks a sober reply, and complains of the unfairness of the wickedness which they use in judging, reproaching, and banishing, showing with clear and sensible argument how far this, their method of carrying on, is removed from the institution and the usage of the apostles.

This is very nearly the content of the entire letter.

* Menno's letter to followers of David Joris, called Davidians or Davidists, is lost. Someone made a brief summary of the contents at an early date, which summary is herewith translated from the Dutch as it is reproduced by K. Vos in his *Menno Simons*, 1914, p. 280. Vos evidently took it from Bleesdijck: *Christelijcke Verantwoordinghe*, 1607, *voorreden*. The date of the letter is about 1546, according to Vos, *Menno Simons*, p. 289.

J. C. W.

[1] The text can also be translated "in the christening."

[2] That is, David Joris'.

[3] That is, Menno.

[4] The reference seems to be to Menno and his followers. *Tr.*

# Comforting Letter to a Widow

*Brief aan eenige weduwen*

## c. 1549

Much grace and peace, and a kind greeting!*

Fervently beloved sister in the Lord, whom my soul cherishes and loves! Since the Lord has now called you to widowhood, my fatherly faithful admonition to you is, as my dear children, to walk as becomes holy women, and I hope that you may, even as the pious prophetess Anna, serve the Lord in the holy temple, that is, in His church with a new and upright conscience, with prayer and fasting, night and day serving the needy saints, which the virtuous widow of Sarepta in Sidon did for faithful Elijah in the time of drouth and scarcity when she received him in her hospitality and fed him with her tiny bit of meal and oil. So shall the meal of the holy divine Word be not lacking in the vessel of your conscience, and the joyous oil of the Holy Spirit from your soul. And even if the newborn son of your spiritual birth do grow slightly ill, and if, in view of the weakness of the womanly nature, he do stop breathing for a moment, yet will our true Elijah, Jesus Christ, raise him up again by His grace and give you a joyous spirit and gladness, seeing that in His members you receive Him, as the Holy Scriptures teach.

Understand me aright, dear children, I refer to needy saints and to none beyond them. Those who are able to help themselves do not need this your aid and service. True Christians ought not to burden each other with unnecessary expense.

Faithful sister, carry on bravely, fear your God from the heart, crucify your flesh and its lusts, resist the enemy and all his solicitations. In all things conduct yourself piously; do not carelessly cause anyone inconvenience. Take good care of your labor, your household and children. Diligently avoid all immodesty, gossip, pride, and vanity and resolve firmly that you will not be so driven by the flesh that you become like the widows that have left their first faith, have turned aside and have followed the devil, as Paul has it. May the merciful Father ever guard you and keep you from this.

* This letter of comfort is dated simply, May 18. K. Vos in his *Menno Simons* dates it as of about the year 1549. Menno writes with all tenderness which gives evidence of his ability to sympathize. In the *Opera Omnia Theologica* of 1681 the letter is printed on fol. 336, and in the *Complete Works* of 1871, Part II, 113. Cornelius Krahn states (*Menno Simons*, Karlsruhe i.B., 1936, p. 76) that this is the only actual autograph of Menno which is still extant. It is preserved in the Doopsgezinde Bibliotheek, Amsterdam. J. C. W.

This brief greeting written to you in true paternal faithfulness receive in love and ponder it earnestly. All the saints that are with me salute you. Greet all pious friends. Pray for me. The eternal saving power and fruit of the crimson blood of Christ be with my elect and much-beloved sister forever, Amen!

*May 18.*                                   M. S., your brother who loves you fondly.[1]

[1] See the illustrations in this volume for the photographic reproduction of this, the "only extant letter in the handwriting of Menno Simons." The Dutch phrase following *MS* is *uwen Broeder die u mindt lief heeft* (your brother who loves you fondly). *Ed.*

# Exhortation to a Church in Prussia

## Aan eene gemeente in Pruissen

# 1549

━•━•━•━•━•━•━•━•━•━•━•━•━•━•━•━•━•━•━•━•━•━•━•━•━•━•━•━•━•━•━•━•━•━•

To the elect, holy children of God in the land of Prussia, grace and peace.* You know, my dear brethren and sisters in Christ Jesus, what grievous solicitude, care, trouble, labor, and sorrow we experienced in your midst this past summer, as well as how it ended; a matter that still at times causes us to be greatly troubled at heart on your behalf, fearing lest the disturber of all peace and Christian love, that is, that ancient coiled serpent which never ceases his ragings, might by means of the past transaction once more sow his seed among many, and by means of all that follows, these might fall in God's sight and come to shame and our services of some weeks expended in your behalf be lost again; a thing which even though I write thus, I nevertheless hope not.

Nor do we cease in all our prayers to God our heavenly Father in the name of our Lord Jesus Christ to remember you, requesting Him according to His great goodness to have mercy on you all, to give you to drink of His Holy Spirit, and watch and keep you all together with an eternal, uninterrupted peace, love, and unity, according to your good intention and unto His eternal praise and glory. And since we are called to be members of one body in Christ Jesus, therefore brotherly faithfulness requires us at all times to be solicitous for each other's welfare. Therefore I have taken it upon myself with this my brief admonition and to the extent that the Lord gives me grace, fraternally to quicken your God-given faith, love, and obedience, and to serve you according to the humble gift that is mine.

* This letter is lacking in both the *Opera Omnia Theologica* of 1681, and the *Complete Works* of 1871, but it is found in the German edition of Menno's works issued by John F. Funk at Elkhart, Ind., Part I, 1876; Part II, 1881: *Die vollstaendigen Werke Menno Simons,* Zweiter Theil, 652-56. The letter is dated Oct. 7, 1549. It is unknown as to which congregation Menno is addressing, but K. Vos conjectures that it was located in West Prussia. The Prussian congregation of Marcushof-Thiensdorf possessed even in the twentieth century a copy of this letter in the *Oostersch* or Eastern dialect, as well as a German translation (Vos, *Menno Simons,* p. 290). The letter itself indicates that Menno had labored in Prussia for a number of weeks the previous summer, and that he had succeeded in resolving a controversy which had been in progress at the time. He is now concerned that the strife should not break out afresh. He appeals powerfully for a peaceful, forgiving spirit to prevail in the brotherhood. He seeks to show what the possession of true Christian love involves. Above all, it means seeking to walk in peace. J. C. W.

In the first place, I admonish and pray you as my precious brethren and companions in Christ Jesus with faithful hearts to observe and realize how that Christ Jesus, blessed forever, in whose Word we believe, and to whom we have, with body and soul, voluntarily committed ourselves, is by the prophet Isaiah called, a Prince of Peace, and by Paul, a Lord of peace. II Thess. 3:16. Yes, such a Lord and Prince who has left and taught to His own an abundant peace, as He says, My peace I leave with you, my peace I give unto you. John 14:27. Peace be with you. John 20:19. In like manner Paul, his faithful messenger and servant: And let the peace of Christ rule in your hearts to which also ye were called. Col. 3:15. Follow after peace and holiness, without which no man shall see the Lord. Heb. 12:14. As much as in you lieth, be at peace with all men. Rom. 12:18. Seek peace and pursue it. Psalm 34:14; I Peter 3:11. But God hath called us to peace. I Cor. 7:15.

Nor was the entire life of Christ aught but love and peace. For although He came unto His own and His own received Him not, but thrust Him forth from the vineyard and desired Him not; and although (ah, the shame of it) He was reviled and blasphemed by them because of the lovely fruits and services of His divine love bestowed on them, was pursued to the death, and at last was reviled by them and blasphemously called an evildoer; and although He was finally as a malefactor nailed by them to the cross, yet His holy peace remained unbroken, His blessed heart did not become bitter nor cruel, but He prayed the rather for His enemies to His Father in pity for their blindness, for they knew not what they did. Luke 23. Moreover, His bitter death is become to us poor sinners a certain peace and life, even as Paul says, By his cross he has reconciled him that is in heaven and those that are on earth. Col. 1:20.[1]

Seeing then that Christ Jesus is the Prince and the Lord of eternal peace, and since His entire doctrine and life, as also His death has represented, portrayed, and implied naught but peace, as was said, therefore none can be the recipient of His honor and good will, or be given a place in His kingdom save those who have the holy peace of God in their hearts. For His kingdom is the Kingdom of peace; it knows no strife, even as it is written in the prophets that in the kingdom of Christ and in His church they beat their swords into plowshares and sit under their fig tree and vine, and no more raise up their hands unto warfare. Isa. 2; Mic. 4.

Since no one can be in the kingdom and church of Christ who does not dwell there through love and peace, as the Scriptures testify, therefore all those who are so quarrelsome, tumultuous, slanderous, defaming, bitter, wrathful, and cruel of heart may well rouse themselves, be sorry, and repent, for they show in deeds that they do not possess peace, do not heed Christ Jesus the true Prince of peace, nor are in His kingdom, even though they do carry the external appearance of being Christians, and are greeted

[1] Dutch translation. *Tr.*

as brethren. Brother, let each man beware, for the Lord Christ does not judge according to externals as do men, but according to the hidden reality of the heart, which is altogether naked and open before His blessed eyes.

Since then for a long time, alas, a severe quarrel has existed among you; and since you have now again received one another with a kiss of peace and have saluted each other as brethren, therefore I now admonish you as in Christ Jesus to try yourselves rightly as to whether you love your brother with a genuine brotherly love, such as the Scriptures teach, and whether you also in the Spirit of Christ say to your brother, Brother, the peace of the Lord be with you. Ah, brethren, I do greatly fear that in the case of some among you that peace is usually heard upon the lips rather than found in the heart. Let each one be careful to have heart and mouth agree, for he that does verily with his mouth express peace toward his brother but carries hostility toward him in his heart is to my mind a make-believe rather than a true Christian. Therefore let each person take care when he says or does anything toward his neighbor to say or do it as in the presence of God who knows and sees all things.

Dearest brethren and sisters in Christ Jesus, I admonish you in love, and that with the Word of the Lord, that if there are still among you some who are at variance with others—a thing which I however do not hope—that such might leave their sacrifice before the altar (that is, their fasting, prayers, and alms) so long as they are not reconciled and have not agreed. Let the unclean hypocritical heart be far from you.

Let no one have any complaint or grievance concerning his brother even if your poor companion through ignorance or transgression has sinned against you and in that way owes you ten or twenty pence. Do not assail your erring brother so vehemently, but by all means remember how your own account stands before God, namely, that you owe so many thousand pounds and have not a penny with which to pay. If you are to escape your Lord's punishment, prison, and judicial severity, then it must be graciously forgiven, and the crimson blood of Christ must stand in your place. If now you seek to receive gracious pardon for your sins from the Lord, then forgive also your brother if he has transgressed against you in some matter. If now you do not forgive, you will likewise not be forgiven, as Christ Himself says in Matthew 18. Therefore, I admonish you with the holy Paul to be kind to one another, gentle and merciful, and to forgive one another even as God has forgiven you in Christ Jesus.

Worthy brethren and sisters in the Lord, consider the Word of God. Have you not heard and read that he who is angry with his brother is guilty of the judgment, and he that says to his brother, Raca, is in danger of the council, and he that says, Thou fool, is guilty of hell-fire? Do you not know that John says, He that loveth not his brother abides in death, and that he that hateth his brother is a murderer? I John 3. He who seeks vengeance, says Sirach, will experience vengeance at the hand of the Lord, and his sins will surely be unremitted. Forgive your fellow his fault, for in that way your sins will also be forgiven when you pray. The man who is angry with a man, how dare he ask forgiveness with God? He who is like unto a man and shows no mercy, how dare he pray for forgiveness of sins? If he that is flesh nourishes and carries anger, who will forgive his sin and be gracious unto him? Ponder your end, and cease from wrath. Sirach 28.

Dearest brethren, do not think that I have written this admonition with a certain brother's person in mind; not at all. But I have seen with my eyes and heard with my ears the heathen impurity of many a heart; the wicked pride and slander, yes, the cruel and bitter fruits that came forth out of the quarrel. Therefore I admonish you all together herewith in general, and that with this intention: that all the pious which now with a pure heart and in true Christian peace have reached an agreement with their brethren might continue in it forever; and if then there are still some in whose heart the poisonous fang of bitterness still sticks fast, these may, without delay, rouse themselves, do penance, pray God for His grace, thus desire, seek, and practice the very desirable Christian unity, love, and peace with their brethren who have, with them, been called to the way of the cross.

In the second place, I admonish you as my fellow soldiers in the struggle and in the patience of Christ that if you desire to live this afore-mentioned peace with faithful hearts, even as I do not doubt, then promote the genuine Christian love among yourselves, for undoubtedly you know how it behaves itself in all things and what is its nature and disposition. Yes, if you would bend your shoulders to its scepter, and voluntarily join its administration and government, then the holy peace of God would surely constantly abide with you, and grow and increase in you from day to day. For love conducts and behaves itself without reproach, and is careful of its words and works lest it sin against God and give offense to a brother, trouble or sadden him. It is always diligent and eager to go before its neighbor in all righteousness, to teach and instruct him. It gives to no one an incentive to evil, being of a divine nature and hating all unrighteousness, willfulness, and trickery. If it is wronged, whether in words or deeds, it bears it with patience and knows no vengeance. It is gracious and loves the truth; and therefore none can be wronged nor cheated by it. It is kind and gentle, and therefore it treats others in humility and reasonableness, also those who are its enemies and foes so as by such readiness to lead and attract many to the truth, and in that way to win the hearts of the hostile to it and to reconcile them in Christ Jesus. Nor does it think any evil. Therefore it conducts itself before all, privately as well as publicly, with pious and honest heart without any sublety or deceit, even as before God in Christ Jesus.

Moreover, this love is not bitter; therefore it does not reproach a poor brother for his fault, neither does it talk behind his back nor defame him, for it covers a multitude of his sins, even as James and Peter teach and instruct the pious. This love is of God and therefore at all times it behaves according to its divine nature and disposition. It admonishes its neighbor in pure love, comforts those of little faith, raises the weak, teaches the foolish, rebukes the delinquent, bears all that may properly be borne; it receives the destitute, clothes the naked, feeds the hungry and gives the thirsty drink, visits the sick; in a word, its resources are ready to serve all men. If by chance it happens, as happen it does, that a pious Christian impelled by this love errs in human fashion, then this selfsame love is prepared at all times to receive fraternal rebuke and instruction; and it does not puff itself up, but receives it with much thanksgiving, even as it becomes the wise, as Solomon says, Rebuke the wise, and he will love you. For he acknowledges in what spirit and with what intention it is done, and that in it nothing is sought and desired but the praise of God and their own salvation.

Faithful brethren in the Lord, methinks this love is indeed a well-paved road to all brotherly unity and peace. Ah, if only this above-mentioned love had held the helm of your ship, never would it have collided so violently with the shore. My brethren, understand what I am driving at. It is still today, rise up and delay not. And be diligent henceforth in this pure and, genuine love, and that with all your power and ability. So that you may in this way deal with each other in all prudence and considerateness, politeness, fidelity, and piety; may avoid all offense; may flee and avoid all useless bickering and disputations; so that the genuine, evangelical Christian peace may not depart from you in such fashion, but may the rather in all happiness take root, repose, and dwell among you as in the congregation of the saints.

Holy and beloved brethren in the Lord, this I would ask of you at this time and admonish you, with deeply serious hearts: Do consider how you together with all Christians are received and called by the God of peace, under the Prince of Peace, by the messengers of peace, to the body of peace, with the Word of peace, unto the kingdom of peace, out of mere love and grace. Therefore walk in that same peace, so that in that day you may in His grace be able to stand before your God with a confident and happy conscience when body and soul must part. Ah, my brethren and sisters, fear your God with all your heart, and purify yourselves in one another's presence as before God in Christ Jesus, in order that just as many brethren and congregations may have been saddened because of your contentions they may now once more be refreshed and gladdened in Christ Jesus by your lovely reconciliation and Christian peace.

Behold, worthy brethren in the Lord, this my little admonition and exhortation to peace I have written out of an upright heart and intention to you all as to such as are desirous of the genuine Christian peace and who at all times gladly seek[1] the best and the most blessed in my dear brethren and companions. For I hope that I may say with the holy Paul, and that according to the testimony of my conscience, that it is my life if you abide in the Lord. Therefore receive it in such a spirit as I have written you. Therefore I

[1] This verb has been supplied, seeing that the context seems to require it. *Tr.*

desire for the Lord's sake that you read it, and understand it correctly, and judge it in the light of the Word and Spirit of the Lord, so that I may not have labored in vain, and you may find in it instruction, profit, and joy.

The merciful Father grant His grace to that end. Amen.

I commend you to the most High and to the Word of His eternal peace. Wait for His appearance, for He will come as a thief in the night, in the hour when we do not expect it. Happy that man who will not be surprised by Him. I hope after this to hear much happiness concerning you and no sadness. The Lord of peace grant you His peace in all places and in every manner. May that selfsame peace keep your hearts and minds in Christ Jesus. Amen.

All the saints that are with us greet you. And do you greet one another with your hearts, with a holy kiss of love. Peace be with you forever. Amen.

Written by Menno Simons to the Church in Prussia Oct. 7, 1549.

# Doctrinal Letter to the Church in Groningen
## Aan de gemeente in Groningen
## c. 1550

To write such a long article to each and every church is quite impossible
for me.                                                    Menno Simons

Grace and peace :*

It is known to all the churches, dear brethren, that in the countries to
the south a great difficulty has arisen in regard to the deity of Christ, and of
the Holy Spirit, and as a result much unbelief, controversy, and division have
arisen to the great grief and sadness of all the saints. And since it happens
that some person coming from these areas, infected with the matter, causes
trouble, therefore love constrains me to copy the following Scriptures for the
churches and for these reasons:

First, that the as yet uninfected and sound consciences may guard
against all such frightful disputations and inconceivable murmurings lest their
hearts drown in such bottomless depths, to their eternal loss, and bring eternal
shame upon themselves before God. Secondly, that all they who err unknowingly and innocently, being afflicted in their conscience and yet fearing God,
and walking under the cross, might by this our service and written instruction
be saved and set free, to the eternal praise and glory of God, and to the joy
and gladness of all the saints.

I have written this for my dear brethren and companions out of a hearty
love and sympathy, and if but a single troubled, shaken, doubting soul might
be helped along, I shall count that dearer than all else under heaven. Children, keep yourself from contention and division, so that you may grow and
increase in Christ. Shun those who disturb you and incite you to discord,
proposing strange novelties wherewith to hurt and harm the Christian evangelical love, peace, and unity. O my dearest brethren and sisters in the Lord,
take careful heed to what I write in order that the divine honor of God, the

---

* This letter is found in the *Opera Omnia Theologica* of 1681, fol. 391, and in the *Complete Works* of 1871, Part II, 231, 232. It seems to have been written to accompany Menno's
treatise, *Confession of the Triune God*, 1550, which it immediately follows in the *Opera
Omnia Theologica*. It gives evidence both of Menno's soundness in the faith, and of his
earnest desire to save his brethren from the heresy of anti-Trinitarianism. One sees here
once again the warm shepherd heart in Menno. The shortened title is taken from the postscript to the letter.                                                      J. C. W.

heavenly Father, and His blessed Son together with the Holy Ghost, may be preserved. Peace be with you.

MENNO SIMONS

To the brethren in the city and province of Groningen, copied and dispatched by a faithful brother under the direction of John Aertsen. In love receive it.[1]

---

[1] The last section of this tract, a sort of postcript, seems to have been written by Menno when it was suggested, seemingly by John Aertsen, that the tract on the Trinity should be copied and a copy sent to each of the churches in view of the seriousness of the anti-Trinitarian defections. But that was too much of an undertaking for Menno, as he himself says. It seems that the supervision of such copying work was then given to Aertsen who employed "a faithful brother" to do the work. This would explain how the foregoing tract could be referred to in this postscript as the following Scriptures. *Tr.*

# Sincere Appeal to Leonard Bouwens' Wife

## Aan de huisvrouw van Leenaert Bouwens

## 1553

Most beloved in Christ Jesus: Grace and peace.* Worthy and faithful sister in the Lord, my inmost soul is grieved in your behalf more so than I can write. For I understand from our dear brethren that you have difficulty reconciling yourself to the request and prayer of the poor, afflicted, and pastorless church in regard to your beloved husband. I cannot reprove you severely if it be considered in the light of natural considerations rather than spiritual. I also understand from the words of Leonard and Helmicht that you hoped that Leonard would be excused by me from serving.

Dear sister in Christ Jesus, I trust that I by the grace of God sincerely love you with divine love in God and that I am prepared to serve you and all pious people even with my blood if need be. But dear sister, who am I that I should resist the Holy Spirit? You are aware, are you not, that not I but the church, and that without my knowledge, has called him to this service. Since the church so urgently desires him and since he cannot conscientiously refuse, how then shall I oppose it? I can find nothing in Leonard for which I could with Scriptural warrant oppose his call.

Dear sister, I am sorry that I cannot give you your way in this matter, for the sorrow and sadness of your flesh pierces my heart as often as I think of it, but the love to God and our brethren must be considered first of all. You are called to this of the Lord and by the operation of your faith you have yielded yourself to the service, not of your own self but of Jesus Christ and of your brethren as long as you live. I hope that you have done this heartily, cost what it may of money, possessions, and even life. You see, do you not,

*Leonard Bouwens of Sommelsdyk in the Netherlands was ordained an elder in 1551. His wife feared for his life because of the severe persecution of the Mennonites at that time, and wrote a letter to Menno Simons begging him to use his influence with the brotherhood to have her husband released. The letter printed herewith is Menno's reply. He calls upon her, out of love for the church, to allow her husband to serve, regardless of what it might cost. And he comforts her with the thought of the sovereignty of God. Menno's appeal must have been successful, for Bouwens had an unusually fruitful ministry. The list of baptisms which he performed from 1551 until his death totals not less than 10,251 (K. Vos, *Menno Simons*, 1914, p. 130). The letter is printed in the *Opera Omnia Theologica* of 1681, 455, 456, and in the *Complete Works* of 1871, Part II, 449-51. The translation of John Horsch is found in his *Menno Simons*, 1916, 84-86. The letter is dated, 1553.

J. C. W.

how great is the need? Remember the days of your release[1] and obediently and resignedly fulfill that which voluntarily and without constraint you have promised the most High.

O beloved sister, consider your brethren in their helpless and sad condition. The spiritual fathers are become betrayers of our souls; the watchmen, blind leaders; and the shepherds, wolves. The walls of Jerusalem are tumbled down; the stones of the sanctuary are trampled underfoot at the corners of every street. Great is Israel's visitation. As Jeremiah and Ezra we may sigh and weep, and let our tears flow down our cheeks. Our inmost soul must be grieved at the need of our brethren, when we take to heart the great hunger and thirst of many pious hearts, the accursed seduction by the false prophets and the divisive sects, and similar griefs and devastations. Inasmuch then as the merciful Lord has gifted our beloved brother with knowledge of divine things, has enlightened him with His Holy Spirit, and gifted him with speech and wisdom so that the brethren are pleased with him, sincerely love him, and desire his talent, therefore if you for the sake of flesh and blood should oppose this and not acquiesce therein, it would seem to me to be identical with seeing your brethren in danger, in fire or water, and then for your own comfort's sake refusing to help. Dear sister, do love your brethren as Christ Jesus has loved us, even if for the sake of your brethren you should be robbed of your goods. Remember that Christ has for a time left the glory of His Almighty Father and the company of angels that He might obtain an eternal inheritance in heaven. So long as we live we shall have enough of the necessities of life if we fear God, depart from evil, and do the right.

Yes, dear sister, be of good cheer and comfort. The eternal Truth has promised us salvation if we seek the kingdom of God and His righteousness. The necessities of life will be provided for us. If you are solicitous for your husband's natural life, then remember and believe that our life is measured by spans, that life and death are in the hands of the Lord, that not a hair falls from our heads without the will of our Father. He protects us as the apple of His eye.

Elijah and Elisha, David, Daniel, Shadrach, Meshach, and Abednego, Peter, and Paul have all escaped the hands of the tyrant and none could injure a single hair on their head so long as the appointed day and hour were not come. So long as the Lord has more pleasure in our life than in our death they cannot injure us; but when our death is more pleasing to the Lord than our life, then we shall not escape from their hands.

O dear sister, if our beloved brother should not serve our brethren, yet still he has years ago already committed himself to danger of death, tribulation, misery, scorn, persecution, anxiety, robbery, water, fire, and sword. And even if he had not committed himself to the cross by baptism, and could pass

---

[1] The Dutch word *verlichtinge* may mean either enlightenment or release; we have chosen the latter rendering, although the other also makes good sense. *Tr.*

through all cities and populations unmolested, you know not at what moment he would have to put off the tabernacle of clay and appear before his God. Therefore, dear faithful sister, be strong in the Lord, be of good cheer, commend yourself to the most High God who holds heaven and earth in His hand, has given you and your husband body and soul, who has called you by the Word of His grace, who has purchased and delivered you with the blood of His blessed Son, who has washed and sanctified and cleansed you with His Holy Spirit. His mercy is above all His works. He knows your going out and your coming in, your sitting down and your rising up. Yes, you were before Him before you were formed in your mother's womb, for He it is who searches the hearts and reins. He knows what our brethren seek.

Dear sister, strengthen your husband and do not weaken him, for it is required of us that if we love God, we shall also love our brethren. In short, prove yourself to do to your neighbor what Christ has proved to be to you, for by this only sure and immutable rule must all Christian action be measured and judged. Behold, worthy and true sister, as the church calls our beloved brother to the office and service, I cannot conscientiously interfere unless I should love flesh, your flesh, more than Christ Jesus my Lord and Saviour and my sincerely beloved brethren. May the Almighty merciful Father act in this matter according to His divine good pleasure and guide the heart of my beloved sister so as to be resigned to His holy will. I sincerely thank my beloved sister for the gift of your love that you have sent me. The Lord repay you in heavenly riches of eternal glory. My wife greets you with the peace of the Lord. The Lord Jesus Christ be forever with my most beloved friend and sister. Amen.

Your brother in the Lord,
*A.D. 1553*                               MENNO SIMONS

# Instruction of Discipline to the Church at Franeker*
## *Brief aan Freaneker*
## 1555

<hr>

The love of God is true wisdom. Sirach 1:14. For God so loved the world that he gave his only begotten Son, that whosoever believeth in him, should not perish but have everlasting life. John 3:16.

Out of great distress and sorrow of heart I write to you in the year of 1555, because a letter was handed me signed by five brethren of good report, from which I learn, may God better it, that a violent dispute has arisen among some of you concerning the ban. One party insists, if I understand correctly, that no sin or work of the flesh should be punished with excommunication without three admonitions going before, a position with which I cannot agree; for there are some sins, as for instance, murder, witchcraft, incendiarism, theft, and other like criminal deeds, which eventually require and imply punishment at the hands of the magistracy. If now we were to admonish such transgressors before they were expelled, then the unleavened lump of the church would be changed into an ugly leaven before the whole world. Therefore act with discretion, and do not judge such matters involving capital punishment, especially if they are public, as you would other works of the flesh which do not constitute an offense and cause for reproach in the eyes of the world.

The other party urges, if I understand correctly, that all works of the flesh (I Cor. 5) are to be punished with excommunication without any previous admonition at all, and that all penitence must take place outside the church. That doctrine and position is, according to my humble understanding, altogether contrary to the word of Christ, of Paul, and of James. For avarice, pride, hatred, discord, defamation, and contention with one's neighbor, are patent works of the flesh, and work death if not mortified and repented of;

---

*This letter is sometimes spoken of as directed to Hendrik Naaldeman, for he was an elder in the church at Franeker in Friesland. A dispute had arisen in the church at Franeker about whether to admonish all sinning members three times regardless of how awful their sin was, or whether to excommunicate all those who fall into any sin whatever, and also what to do in the case of a believer who in weakness falls into some sin of the flesh. Menno, in great concern, earnestly attempts to answer the several questions, constantly showing the reason for his stand, and appealing to the members of the church in Franeker to dwell together in peace and love. The letter is printed in the *Opera Omnia Theologica* of 1681, fol. 643, 644, also in the *Bib. Ref. Neerl.*, VII, 444-47, and in the *Complete Works* of 1871, Part I, 283, 284. J. C. W.

yet they are not punished without three foregoing admonitions according to the Scriptural requirement. I would that men would consider that even as sin when completed yields death, so also does repentance and a contrite heart together with the ceasing from sin bring forth life once more, as may be seen in the case of David, Peter, the thief on the cross, Zacchaeus, and others.

I also understand that these same brethren are of the opinion that if some brother should secretly have transgressed in some deed or other and then in pain and sorrow of heart should lament to one of his brethren that he has sinned against his God in this way, that then this same brother would be obliged to bring it to the attention of the church and if he should fail to do so that he would then be punished with the transgressor. This is not only un-heard of, but also wholly frightful in my way of thinking. For it is clearly against all Scripture and love. Matt. 18; Jas. 5; Col. 2; Eph. 5.

If the ban was in part instituted for the purpose of repentance, how then, if repentance is already shown (namely, in the contrite sorrowing heart), can excommunication be pronounced against such? O my brethren, cease from such plans, for it tends to destroy and not to reform.

If we were to deal thus with poor repenting sinners whose transgressions are not known, how many would be kept from repentance through shame? God keep me from ever agreeing to or practicing such doctrine.

Lastly, I understand that they hold that if anyone in great weakness falls, and openly acknowledges his fall, they should then consider him a worldly person. This again is unheard-of fanaticism, for if the transgression occurred through weakness, then let us not please ourselves and let us not be too severe with the poor soul lest we come to an even greater lapse.

Not the weak but the corrupt members are cut off, lest they corrupt the others. Of such unscriptural extremism and practices, I want to be clear. I seek to use the ban in a noble, fraternal spirit, in faithful love according to the doctrine of Christ and His apostles, as I have abundantly declared in my writings over five years ago.

My elect brethren, guard against innovations for which you have no cer-tain Scriptural grounds. Be not too severe nor too lenient. Let a paternal, compassionate, prudent, and discreet heart, and the Lord's holy Word be with you at all times. Follow this my brotherly admonition which has been urged in this matter for twenty-one years.

I know no other position that is better. That I have written thus at this time is because I have been constrained by the brethren, as was said above. I have in a pious heart served my beloved brethren without any partiality as becomes us in Christ. For I was asked to state my position which I am at all times willing and prepared to reveal, not merely to the pious only, but also to the whole world, as the Word of God has commanded me. I do not teach nor live out of the faith of others, but out of my own. Oh, if only they were all of one mind with me; how paternally and discreetly would excommunica-tion then be practiced without all offense, whereas now it is sometimes prac-ticed so oddly and strangely.

Herewith, I beseech all the pious for God's sake to pursue peace. And if you have with words collided too roughly against each other, then purify your hearts and be reconciled in Christ Jesus. Remember that you are the Lord's people, separated from the world, and hated unto death. If you are baptized into one Spirit, then fulfill my joy and be of one mind with me in Christ. Build up, and destroy not. Let one instruct the other in love, and do not disrupt, so that blessed peace may be with all the children of God and remain with us unbroken and unto eternal life.

May the Spirit of Christ, rich in peace, protect you all; sound in doctrine moreover; ardent in love and without offense in life, to the edification of His church and to the praise of His holy name.

Signed by me, the one who is lame, your brother and servant, November 13, A.D. 1555.

MENNO SIMONS.

# Encouragement to Christian Believers

## *Liefelycke vermaning aan de verstrooide kinderen*

## 1556

•–•–•–•–•–•–•–•–•–•–•–•–•–•–•–•–•–•–•–•–•–•–•–•–•–•–•–•–•–•–•–•–•–•–•–•–•–•–•–•–•–•–•–•

To all the chosen children of God, dispersed here and there, to the sanctified in Christ Jesus, unknown to me in the flesh, my beloved brethren and companions in the faith, kingdom, and patience of Christ: Grace and peace.*

Dearly beloved brethren and sisters in Christ Jesus, I inform you with great joy that dependable brethren have written and informed me that the merciful, faithful God has granted you the heavenly gift of His divine knowledge, and enlightened you with His Holy Spirit; that your faith has been made active in love, that your hope is quickened and your unity among each other is Christianlike, that your peace is delightful, and that the church of the Lord is increased and extended daily in great power and glory through the grace of God. For these things I thank His fatherly goodness with joyful heart, and I pray His grace, inasmuch as He has called you to the fellowship of His beloved Son, to the imperishable, eternal kingdom of His glory through His holy Gospel, that He may now and henceforth preserve you with the great power of His divine arm in your faith, love, doctrine, truth, and life, without any offense until the end. Faithful is He who has called you, and He will undoubtedly do it, just so you continue to be fervent in prayer and unwavering in purpose, never becoming sleepy nor slothful and so at last return, as did contrary, disobedient Israel, to the fleshpots of Egypt, things against which may the Lord eternally and graciously preserve us.

Since then you are called to such a high and glorious grace as related, and we undoubtedly know with what weak evil flesh we poor children are clothed, and how the wicked sinful nature of Adam has invaded our very marrow, defiled our heart and life; and since moreover, we learn from the Scriptures that our opponent the devil goes about like a roaring lion without holiday or recess, but always watching and waiting for the time that he may devour us, therefore I exhort you as my fellow soldiers in this evil flesh and

---

* This is a letter of encouragement to those of the brotherhood who were facing the danger of persecution and death, but who were manfully going forward in the Christian life. Menno does not seem perturbed by any particular trouble in the church, no discord of any sort, and no vexing problems. The tone of the letter is one of gratitude for God's work in the souls of his readers. The letter is printed in the *Opera Omnia Theologica* of 1681, fol. 130-32, and in the *Complete Works* of 1871, I, pages 176-178. In the original Dutch editions the dates differ: one edition reads June 18, 1556, while the other is ten days later. Both editions were printed at Amsterdam.                               J. C. W.

tent of death that you may keep strict watch inwardly and outwardly over yourselves, that you might trim, teach, purify, warn, and chastise your hearts to the Spirit and Word of God, curb your thoughts, and subdue and extinguish your impure evil desires, in the fear of the Lord, for blessed are the pure in heart. Walk worthy of the Lord and the Gospel to which you have come. Do whatever God has commanded without murmuring. Act so that none may truthfully complain of you. Be sincere children of God, unblamable in this crooked and perverse generation, and shine as beautiful lights and torches in the dark night of this evil world.

Take the Lord Jesus Christ as an example and follow His footsteps; walk as He walked, for to this end did Moses and all the prophets preach, to this end did the Son of God come down from heaven and the holy apostles were sent forth. To this end was baptism and the Lord's Supper instituted by the mouth of the Lord, so that we, admonished by it, might awake, repent, and lead an unblamable, pious life in all righteousness. Be ye holy; for I am holy, says the Lord. Peter says that ye are a chosen generation, a royal priesthood, a holy nation, a peculiar people; that you should show forth the praises of him who hath called you out of darkness into his marvelous light. I Peter 1:16; 2:9. You are guests called to the table of the Lord and have come to the marriage [supper] of the Lamb. You are become His chosen friend and bride. Therefore hear His voice willingly, and whatever is pleasing to Him that do cheerfully. Adorn yourselves with the shining garment of white silk. Be faithful unto death and avoid all strange lovers. Give yourselves wholly to the Lord that He may be your Lord and husband; to chasten, govern, and lead and direct you with His Holy Spirit and Word, and have His perfect work in you. For you are His, and by grace He has received you, espoused you, bought you with His precious blood, reconciled His Father, sanctified you to be priests and kings, and made you to be heirs of His eternal kingdom. Therefore it is proper and right that we should be grateful to such a kind Lord and husband for such gifts, hear Him, lay His Word to heart, and do what is well pleasing to Him.

Little children, fear not, but be comforted in the Lord. For He is such a faithful, pious King, to whom you have sworn and bowed your knees. Not the least of His promises shall fail you. He will be our shield and great reward. Therefore neither doubt nor waver, for it is but a small matter to endure the heat of the sun, tribulation, fear, oppression, temptation, plunder, persecution, prison, and death for a short time. The messenger is already at the door, who will say to us, Come ye blessed, enter into the glory of thy Lord. Then will our brief mourning be changed to laughter, our momentary pain into endless joy. These tyrants with their bloody mandates will have an end and all our persecutors, executioners, and torturers will cease. We will follow the Lamb, adorned in white garments with palms in our hands and crowns upon our head. Neither misery nor pain nor pangs of death will touch us longer, but we will forever exalt, praise, and thank in expressibly great joy and glory the Lamb who sits upon the throne.

Behold, my children, all the truly believing pious hearts comfort themselves with this approaching change. With it they possess their souls in patience, knowing well that their reward is great in heaven, and that on the other hand all the ungodly shall have their portion in the eternal, unquenchable fire, under the intolerable, dreadful sentence of God in the depth of hell, if they do not become converted and repent with all their hearts. Woe, woe, to these wretched people. To what an evil day were they born.

Little children, be courageous in Christ and despair not, for so long as we sincerely have God in our minds, seek, fear, love, honor, and serve Him with an upright pure zeal, walk in the truth, neither world nor flesh, nor tyranny, nor devil, nor sin, nor hell, nor death shall hinder us, but the victory which comes with a firm faith in the blood of Christ will through the grace of God be on our side, and this through the Spirit of Christ which abides in us. With my God, said David, I have leaped over a wall. Psalm 18:29. Paul says, I can do all things through Christ which strengtheneth me.

Christ says, Be of good cheer, I have overcome the world; and thus will they overcome who abide in Christ, even as we may see not only in the prophets and apostles, but also in many pious hearts at the present day in great power and clearness.

I have nothing further to say particularly. But take heed that you walk circumspectly, preserve your wedding garment, have oil in your lamps at all times, lest the Lord meet you in an unexpected time and find you unprepared and naked, and then close the door on you or cast you into outer darkness. With unfeigned, true brotherly love and out of a pure heart, love each other sincerely as those who are regenerated, not of corruptible but of incorruptible seed, out of the Word of the living God, which will abide forever. For love is of God and of a divine nature and conducts itself acceptably before God and man, is long-suffering, compassionate, peaceable, and wrongs no one. In short, love is unblamable and brings forth Christian fruit; it is the spiritual girdle of Aaron and his sons; the girdle of perfection and the fair bond of peace. Oh, how completely blessed is he who is girded with this bond, for he is born of God, he is in God, and God is in him. Yes, where this love is, there we find a true, sincere, and pious Christian. Therefore guard carefully this bond, for if you lose it you will lose Christ Jesus and eternal life.

Beware of false doctrine, of all discord, strife, and dissension, and without wavering adhere to the Spirit of Christ, His Word and example, if you would avoid being deceived. For every spirit that is not satisfied with the Spirit, Word, and example of Christ, and does not conform itself thereto in weakness, is not of God, but is the spirit of Antichrist who would rob you again, and all the pious, of the precious light of revealed truth which so graciously has appeared to us poor children in these abominable last days, and would fain lead you on a crooked path of death under the semblance of Scriptures.

Little children in Christ, be warned. Out of true brotherly love I write to you. The merciful, gracious God grant you to hear, read, and understand it with such hearts that it may bring much fruit among you, and that your fruit may abide unto life eternal. Pray for your poor, unknown brother who loves you in truth. He that continues to the end will be saved. The saving power and joy of the crimson blood of Christ be with you, and with all my elect brothers and sisters to eternity. Amen.

# Instruction on Discipline to the Church at Emden

## Brief aan Emden

## 1556

For other foundation can no man lay than that is laid, which is Jesus Christ. I Cor. 3:11.

With great sadness of heart I inform my dear brethren that I receive one complaining letter after another, touching the relation of husband and wife in regard to the ban; so that I notice great sadness with many—a matter that does not surprise me at all; for from the beginning of my service, yes, more than twenty years, I have been distressed with great fear concerning this matter to this very hour, and cannot bring myself to agree with the extremism which is in evidence in the Netherlands just now.*

Dirk Philips our brother and I counseled with the elders in the past in regard to this matter, in 1547 I believe; and it was resolved and repeated two years ago at Wismar how we should conduct ourselves in this matter according to circumstances. We were to admonish according to the known rule, forcing no one beyond that which his conscience could bear; in all love to bear and to tolerate.

For I hope that every pious person is sufficiently instructed by the Lord to know that if either a husband or a wife should become an adulterer, thief, sorcerer, or a malefactor, so that he would have to endure his punishment at the hands of the magistrates, or in case he would be unable to practice his faith in the fellowship of his apostate spouse, if he were assailed day and night with false doctrine or struck and beaten, and if he went backwards regularly in his faith, and that because of the obstacles placed in his way by the apostate mate, he would have to leave such consort if he would stand up before God and the church and save his soul. But if he or she can exercise his or her faith and is not combated with false doctrine, but is permitted in all

---

* The question of marital shunning was not one easy to be disposed of. Here it raises its threatening head again, much to the grief of Menno who very reluctantly faced the question through much of his ministry. He knew that it was a delicate matter, and that the church ought to be content to teach general principles and not go too deeply into such questions. This letter of 1556 to the church at Emden was another effort to bring peace and quiet to the church. The letter is printed on pages 644, 645 (though unpaginated) in the *Opera Omnia Theologica* of 1681, in the *B.R.N.*, VII, 448-50, and in the *Complete Works* of 1871, Part I, 284, 285. In spite of some charges sometimes made to the contrary, Menno here shows himself as a tender and loving pastor, with a good admixture of mental flexibility.                                              J. C. W.

matters to keep the faith, and is moreover bound in conscience so that he dares not leave such a mate who leaves him free to practice his faith seeing they are one flesh for many years as pertains to married folk, and since the matter is fraught with much danger, everyone carrying flesh and blood with him, then to confront such a soul (that in other respects conducts itself without reproach before God) with the ban—to this may the merciful Lord keep me from giving my consent. In view of this, my heart was filled with sorrow on hearing that a certain length of time was given Swaantje Rutgers in which to leave her husband, or that in case of her failure to leave him, she was to be delivered up to Satan and excommunicated.

O elect brethren, consider well what you are doing! What slandering words you will put into the mouth of the slanderers, and what bad reports will you spread upon the Word of the Lord and His church; how many grieved consciences will you give birth to, yea, how many souls will you separate from the truth and expose to sinister dangers. We never dared press the matter so, for we saw what would be the consequences. Oh, that you would let it go at that. How would I, sorrowful man, be gladdened at that. My heart never shall consent to such indiscreet extremism or agree to such plans.

I desire, according to my humble talents, to teach a Gospel that builds up, and not one that breaks down; one that gives off a pleasant odor, and not a stench, and I do not intend to trouble the work of God with something for which I have no certain Scriptural grounds. I can neither teach nor live by the faith of others. I must live by my own faith as the Spirit of the Lord has taught me through His Word.

Here you have my communication. The Lord grant that you may heed it in all love, peace, and unity; not too sternly nor yet too feebly. Excommunication is instituted for reformation and not for destruction. Oh, that all were of one mind with me in this matter! How sanely and carefully would the ban be practiced then. But as it is, everyone follows his own head, and imagines it to be the Spirit and Scripture.

O Lord, grant Thy Spirit and wisdom to those that are Thine so that they may see and judge rightly, endeavoring to keep the unity of the Spirit in the bond of peace. Brethren, follow my advice for the Lord's sake, for it will cause many souls to rejoice. The Spirit of wisdom be with you unto eternity. Amen. Your brother, the one who is lame,

November 12, 1556

MENNO SIMONS

# Letter of Consolation to a Sick Saint*

## *Aan Griet Rein Edes Wijf*

## c. 1557

My elect and beloved sister in Christ Jesus; much mercy, grace, and peace be to you, most beloved sister whom I have ever sincerely loved in Christ.

From your dear husband's letter I understand that during all the winter you have been a sick and afflicted child, which I very much regret to hear. But we pray daily: Holy Father, Thy will be done. By this we transfer our will into that of the Father to deal with us as is pleasing in His blessed sight. Therefore bear your assigned affliction with a resigned heart. For all this is His fatherly will for your own good, and that you may turn with your inmost being from all transitory things and direct yourself to the eternal and living God. Be comforted in Christ Jesus, for after the winter comes the summer, and after death comes life. O sister, rejoice that you are a true daughter of your beloved Father. Soon the inheritance of His glorious promise will be due. But a little while, says the Word of the Lord, and He who is coming shall come and His reward will be with Him. May the Almighty, merciful God and Lord before whom you have bent your knees to His honor, and whom according to your weakness you have sought, grant you a strong and patient heart, a bearable pain, a joyous recovery, a gracious restoration, or a godly departure through Christ Jesus whom we daily expect with you, my beloved sister and child in Christ Jesus.

Secondly, I understand that your conscience is troubled because you have not and do not now walk in such perfection as the Scriptures hold before us. I write the following to my faithful sister as a brotherly consolation from the true Word and eternal truth of the Lord. The Scripture, says Paul, has concluded all under sin. There is no man on earth, says Solomon, who does righteously and sinneth not. At another place: A just man falleth seven times,

* One of the most beautiful letters of Menno was addressed to the wife of Rein Edes. In the Dutch original her name is given as Griet, and K. Vos states (*Menno Simons*, 1914, 290) that she was Menno's sister-in-law. The occasion for the letter was the information which came to Menno that she was troubled by the depravity within her; she longed for greater holiness, and was disturbed at her inability to attain it. Menno attempts to comfort and strengthen her, reminding her that all the saints of history had the same struggles and the same longings, and directing her to the perfect merits and righteousness of Jesus Christ. In the *Opera Omnia Theologica* of 1681 the letter is printed, fol. 434, and in the *Complete Works* of 1871, Part II, 401, 402. Vos assigns the letter to about the year 1557.                                          J. C. W.

and riseth up again. Moses says: The Lord, the merciful God, merciful and
gracious, longsuffering and abundant in goodness and truth, keeping mercy
for thousands, forgiving iniquity and transgression and sin, before whom there
is none without sin. O dear sister, notice, he says, none are without sin before God. And David says: Lord, enter not into judgment with thy servant;
for in thy sight shall no man living be justified. And we read, If they sin
against thee (for there is no man that sinneth not). We are all as an unclean
thing, and all our righteousness is as filthy rags. Christ also said, There is
none good but one, that is God. The evil which I would not, that I do. In
many things we all offend. If we say that we have no sin, we deceive ourselves, and the truth is not in us.

Since it is plain from all these Scriptures that we must all confess ourselves to be sinners, as we are in fact; and since no one under heaven has
perfectly fulfilled the righteousness required of God but Christ Jesus alone;
therefore none can approach God, obtain grace, and be saved, except by the
perfect righteousness, atonement, and intercession of Jesus Christ, however
godly, righteous, holy, and unblamable he may be. We must all acknowledge,
whoever we are, that we are sinners in thought, word, and deed. Yes, if we
did not have before us the righteous Christ Jesus, no prophet nor apostle
could be saved.

Therefore be of good cheer and comforted in the Lord. You can expect
no greater righteousness in yourself than all the chosen of God had in them
from the beginning. In and by yourself you are a poor sinner, and by the
eternal righteousness banished, accursed, and condemned to eternal death.
But in and through Christ you are justified and pleasing unto God, and adopted by Him in eternal grace as a daughter and child. In this all saints have
comforted themselves, have trusted in Christ, have ever esteemed their own
righteousness as unclean, weak, and imperfect, have with contrite hearts approached the throne of grace in the name of Christ and with firm faith prayed
the Father: O Father, forgive us our transgressions as we forgive those who
transgress against us. Matt. 6.

It is a very precious word which Paul speaks, When we were yet without
strength, in due time Christ died for the ungodly. Yea, when we were yet
ungodly, and thereby He manifests His love toward us. For if, when we were
enemies, we were reconciled to God by the death of his Son, much more, being
reconciled, we shall be saved by his life. Rom. 5:6, 10. Behold, my chosen
beloved child and sister in the Lord, this I write from the very sure foundation of eternal truth.

I pray and desire that you will betake yourself wholly both as to what is
inward and what is outward unto Christ Jesus and His merits, believing and
confessing that His precious blood alone is your cleansing; His righteousness
your piety; His death your life; and His resurrection your justification; for
He is the forgiveness of all your sins; His bloody wounds are your reconciliation; and His victorious strength is the staff and consolation of your weakness,

as we have formerly according to our small gift often shown you from the Scriptures.

Yes, dearest child and sister, seeing that you find and feel such a spirit in yourself desirous of following that which is good, and abhorring that which is evil, even though the remnant of sin is not entirely dead in you, as was also the case in all the saints who lamented from the beginning, as was said, therefore you may rest assured that you are a child of God, and that you will inherit the kingdom of grace in eternal joy with all the saints. Hereby we know that we dwell in him, and he in us, because he has given us of his Spirit. I John 4:13.

I sincerely pray that you may by faith rightly understand this basis of comfort, strengthening, and consolation of your distressed conscience and soul, and remain firm unto the end. I commend you, most beloved child and sister, to the faithful, merciful, and gracious God in Christ Jesus, now and forever. Let Him do with you and with all of us according to His blessed will, whether in the flesh to remain a little longer with your beloved husband and children; or out of the flesh to the honor of His name and to the salvation of your soul. You go before and we follow, or we go before and you follow. Separation must sometime come.

In the city of God, in the new Jerusalem, there we will await each other, before the throne of God and of the Lamb, sing Hallelujah, and praise His name in perfect joy. Your husband and children I commend to Him who has given them to you, and He will take care of them. The saving power of the most holy blood of Christ be with my most beloved child and sister, now and forever. Amen. Your brother who sincerely loves you in Christ.

MENNO SIMONS

# Personal Note to Rein Edes and the Brethren in Waterhorne*

## Aan de broeders in Waterhorne

## c. 1558

·-·-·-·-·-·-·-·-·-·-·-·-·-·-·-·-·-·-·-·-·-·-·-·-·-·-·-·-·-·-·-·-·-·-·-·-·-·-·-·-·-·-·-·-·-·-·-·

My very faithful brother in Christ: Grace and peace be with you.

Elect brethren in the Lord, I have nothing in particular to write to you, except that I wish you would write to me how far the choosing of the brethren in Waterhorne, and of Lebe Pieters has progressed. Not that I would obstruct the choosing of Lebe; but I would have liked to have had a talk with him before he is admitted to office, for my soul will not be quieted concerning the way I was treated last year.

O brother Reyn, if I could only speak with you half a day and make known to you a little of my affliction, sorrow, and sadness, and also of my great solicitude which I bear for the future of the church; what a pleasing soft poultice that would be to my sorrowful soul. But now I must sit here by myself and choke it all down. If the omnipotent God had not preserved me last year as well as now, I would already have gone mad. For there is nothing upon earth which my heart loves more than it does the church; and yet I must live to see this sad affliction upon her. I think much, yet I write and say but little. Help me pray that I may find refreshment, and yet see a gracious outcome for all afflicted souls.

Brethren, beware of discord. Follow after love and peace with all your heart; associate yourself at all times with those who want peace; use few words, and in every respect show yourself to be born of God. O most elect brother, with your ardent prayers assist me in my great affliction. I pray you for Jesus' sake, keep my sorrow to yourself; but if you should speak about it to any one, then know with whom you speak. If all hearts were

---

* On September 1, probably of the year 1558, Menno wrote this letter to his brother-in-law Rein Edes and to the brethren in Waterhorne. In it Menno opens his heart to reveal his sorrow over the ban trouble in the church. The only hope Menno had was in the Lord, and he begs Rein to assist him in prayer with his "ardent prayers." In the last section of the letter Menno timidly expresses the hope that no offense would come from his having made known that he was short in money, that he needed money because butchering time was about to come and he had little wherewith to buy. In the letters of this period Menno frequently makes mention of the fact that he was lame, or that he was a cripple. In the *Opera Omnia Theologica* of 1681 this letter is printed, fol. 392, and in the *Complete Works* of 1871, Part II, 232. J. C. W.

pure, all tongues seasoned with salt, and all the mistakes of last year were honestly and truly acknowledged, how soon would I be found a cheerful man. Anyway, the Lord will be my comforter. May the poor church be saved! O brethren, let us pray.

I did not mean to offend you when I wrote to an unnamed brother lately about the sixty thalers a year. I wrote it because I felt free to do so, seeing that I need it annually. May the merciful Lord send it to me. He knows where. Greet the pious with the peace of the Lord. My daughters greet you. The God of all grace be with you, dearest brother, and with all the pious forever. Amen.

If something should be sent to my support, send it at once. Butchering time will soon be here and I have little wherewith to buy. Brethren, do not think it ill of me; necessity compels me. The cripple[1] who loves you,

MENNO SIMONS

*September 1*

---

[1] We know that in his later years at least, Menno was a cripple, a condition that began with an illness. We know also that his face was slightly twisted. If these defects were related, he perhaps had suffered a stroke. The fact that he was a corpulent man lends further likelihood to this suggestion. *Tr.*

# Pastoral Letter to the Amsterdam Church
## Tweede brief aan Amsterdam
# 1558

+-+-+-+-+-+-+-+-+-+-+-+-+-+-+-+-+-+-+-+-+-+-+-+-+-+-+-+-+-+-+-+-+-+-+-+-+

Much mercy, grace, and peace be unto you!*

The Lord said unto Martha, I am the resurrection, and the life; he that believeth in me, though he were dead, yet shall he live; and whosoever liveth and believeth in me shall never die. John 11:25.

Elect brethren and sisters in the Lord, I hear that the fire of pestilence is beginning to rage in your vicinity. Therefore I am constrained by the love which I bear to you and to all the pious who visit you, who are over-shadowed by the heavenly light and called into the communion of Christ, to write to you a short letter of consolation, so that you may now and at all times diligently watch for the coming of the Lord and prepare your whole life, heart, mind, and conduct for death. For Paul says, It is appointed unto men once to die. Heb. 9:27. And Sirach says, All flesh waxeth old as a garment; for the covenant from the beginning is, Thou shalt die.

If we, with a new, regenerate, and penitent soul, firmly adhere to Christ, truly believe His Word, faithfully follow His footsteps, allow ourselves to be governed by His Holy Spirit, and if we mortify the old, sinful life, yes, in every manner die unto the world, the flesh, and the devil, if we sincerely seek God's kingdom, righteousness, Word, will, truth, praise, and honor, and walk inoffensively in His ways, then we shall live with Him, in Him, and through Him forever (John 11:25), and we shall not be hurt by the second death (Rev. 2:11). This in spite of the fact that we were afore-time dead in sins even as the others, full of covetousness, unchastity, pride, hatred, envy, idolatry, and all wickedness; children of hell and the devil. For unto the truly penitent and believing it is all forgiven through the death of Christ; it is paid by His blood, and reconciled by the unique and atoning sacrifice of His unmerited bitter death. So that Paul says, There is therefore

* In the year 1558 (see Vos, *Menno Simons*, 1914, 289) there was a pestilence in Amsterdam from which people were dying. When Menno learned of this, and thought of his beloved brethren in the city, he wrote this letter which is dated November 14. He attempted to get the church to look at the matter of death calmly, remembering that it is but the entrance into a fuller life. He urged the members of the church not to desist from visiting one another in the time of pestilence. Menno reports that he himself was in the enjoyment of reasonably good health, or as the edition of 1871 says, "tolerable health." In the *Opera Omnia Theologica* of 1681 the letter is printed, fol. 641, 642, and in the *Complete Works* of 1871, Part I, 281, 282.    J. C. W.

now no condemnation to them which are in Christ Jesus, who walk not after the flesh but after the Spirit. For the law of the Spirit of life in Christ Jesus hath made me free from the law of sin and death. Rom. 8:1, 2. Therefore be of good cheer and grateful, and give Him praise who has delivered you by the Word of His might from the power of sin and death, and has called you to the heritage of His glory by the Spirit of His grace. Again, I say, Give Him praise, and that with a godly, pure conscience, and an irreproachable, holy life in faith, being blessed, firm, and untainted in love, alive in hope, and fervent in prayer, adorned with the garment of righteousness, and girded with the beautiful girdle of perfection in the Spirit; having oil in your lamps, being sober and alert, so that when the true Head, the glorious King and Bridegroom of our souls, comes, He may not find you asleep and because of your unpreparedness cast you into eternal darkness and close the door upon you, and so assign you your part with the hypocrites. Once more, be sober and watch, labor while it is day lest the dark night overtake you. Reflect on what this means.

Dear faithful brethren, be strong in the Lord, be of good cheer, be comforted. For your whole life and death is lodged in the hands of the Lord. All your hairs are numbered, and without Him not one shall drop from your head. The number of your days, nay, your life, is measured as by handbreadths by Him. Therefore do not fear but willingly serve each other in time of need. Oh, do not let the visiting of the sick vex you, for by this you shall be established in love, as Sirach says, in chapter seven, verse 35. And it is also the nature of true love to lay down our lives for the brethren. I John 3:16. Reflect on what I advise. One thing you know: that an obedient, virtuous son, servant, or bride, does not fear the coming of the Father, Lord or Bridegroom. These long for their coming. There is no fear in love; but perfect love casteth out fear. I John 4:18.

You are also aware that a tired laborer is desirous of rest, and an afflicted soul of solace. And I have no doubt but that my beloved children are sealed in God with a true conscience; that He is your Father, and that you are His children; that Christ Jesus is your Lord, and that you are His servants; that He is your bridegroom, and that you are His bride; and that for the sake of His blessed name you proclaim and teach it to the whole world for doctrine, instruction, and reproof, that they, repenting, may turn to God; the matter on account of which you must suffer such great misery, trouble, distress, slander, and shame from this untoward and slothful generation, as may be seen everywhere.

Therefore we ought not to dread death so. It is but to cease from sin and to enter into a better life. Nor should we sorrow so about the friends who have fallen asleep in God, as do they who do not look for a reward of the saints. We should rather joyfully lift our head, gird our loins with the girdle of truth, and be taken up to the heavenly Canaan. And so with our only and eternal Joshua, Jesus Christ, take the awarded inheritance, and so be delivered from the laborious way of our hard pilgrimage, so full of trouble, which we must lead through the trackless, cruel waste, so long as we are in this life. And after that we shall rest in peace.

O elect brethren and sisters, how greatly and gloriously are they gifted of God who, in grace, delivered from the body of sin, and from the emptiness of all transitory things, are taken up into the holy tabernacles of peace, summoned to the eternal, holy Sabbath.

The old, crooked serpent shall no longer bite them in their heels. No ache nor ill shall touch them more. Death, the last enemy, is overcome. Their tears are washed away, and their souls are in lasting rest and peace in the Paradise of grace, Abraham's bosom, under the altar of God. They are come from their great tribulation to Mount Zion, in robes of purest white, worshiping before the throne of God and the Lamb, waiting henceforth until the number of their brethren be complete, then to be glorified together with the glory of Christ (Phil. 3:21), to shine forth as the sun, and joyfully to enter into the eternal marriage feast, prepared in heaven for all the chosen ones by the blood and death of Christ.

Ah, me, how altogether holy and blessed are they who are called to this feast of Christ and have arrived at it, clothed in pure, clean garments! Oh, sing the glad and joyful Hallelujah in your hearts, and thank Him who has prepared all this by the Spirit of His love, in eternal grace; who has chosen you to a like precious portion.

Reflect on this and be consoled in these times. I will write no more at present. Fear God from the heart, serve Him in truth, uphold unity, love, peace among yourselves, watch and pray; walk circumspectly, wage your warfare with patience, seek that which is good, be friendly to one another, submit yourselves to your elders and obey them, and remember them and me in your prayers. May the God of peace, our merciful Father, by His blessed Son, Christ Jesus, bless you now and at all times, unto greater righteousness, in fuller love.

Your fellow who loves your souls in truth, at present enjoying reasonably good health.

MENNO SIMONS

*November 14*

For other foundation can no man lay than that is laid which is Jesus Christ. I Cor. 3:11.

# Final Instruction on Marital Avoidance

*Uthtog und affschrifft aan etlicke brodern*

# 1558

●–●–●–●–●–●–●–●–●–●–●–●–●–●–●–●–●–●–●–●–●–●–●–●–●–●–●–●–●–●–●–●–●–●–●–●–●–●–●–●–●–●–●–●–●–●–●

*Extract and Copy of a Letter by Menno Simons Sent to Certain Brethren, Containing and Relating Views Touching Separation of Marriage Partners, Husbands and Wives.**

Concerning the separation of married persons the following is specifically my conviction, position, idea, basis, and conception; yes, my life and death. Namely, we must use and employ the doctrine of separation between man and wife carefully and sanely, according to the decision of the elders and brethren named earlier and in part once more drawn up by our dear brethren Dir[k] Ph[ilips], Le[naert] Bou[wens],[1] and by us ourselves in the presence of many elders. For the Word of the Lord must, according to our plain understanding of it, take in its reach all people without respect of persons, and must not be turned aside in the case of husband and wife. Nor is there anything by which a person is so readily brought down as by his marriage partner, whom by nature he usually loves. Practice and experience witness to it that this is so. He should, moreover, also seek his betterment,[2] his penitence and salvation, no less than the church. For which two reasons (namely, that they may not lead us astray, and that by being shamed they may be helped upon a better way) the Holy Spirit has taught and preserved for us the doctrine of separation in the sacred Scriptures, as we may see and trace in I Cor. 5 and II Tim. 2.

We, therefore, beseech every man for Jesus' sake not to oppose this, not to bicker over it or break the peace. Rather he should allow the doctrine,

---

* This letter of 1558 resembles closely that of 1556 to the church at Emden. Once again Menno laboriously goes over the old ground: Grave sins of the flesh require immediate excommunication; secret sins committed through human weakness are not to be punished with excommunication; etc. This letter also is characterized by the tendency which pervades all of his writings to illustrate Christian truths by the use of Old Testament imagery of one kind or another. Here he portrays the children of God as wearing Aaron's breastplate, being anointed in ear, thumb, and toe, etc. In the *Opera Omnia Theologica* of 1681, and the *Complete Works* of 1871, this letter is missing. It is found in the *Doopsgezinde Bijdragen* for 1894, pages 62-69, from which this translation was made. J. C. W.

[1] In the original autograph these brethren were, for reasons of personal safety, referred to with the first few letters of their names only.

[2] That is, the betterment of the marriage partner. *Tr.*

applied with care and sense and in good order with a view to benefiting, to have its course. This should be done in order that if it should happen to someone, he may, by this teaching, be touched in his heart, and pursue in this instance the most certain and dependable rule of his salvation, because of the impulsion of his own spirit and faith, and not because of human contraint or some person's advice or command.

However, it should always be done with this exception and provision: If there is a devout person, whether man or woman, who is able to live out his faith without being hindered by his excommunicated mate, [let them live together]. I refer to one who feels bound or troubled in his conscience touching the Scriptures which say, They two shall be one flesh, or Let him give to his marriage partner what is his due, or Let no one separate except for the sake of adultery, and whatever passages there may be. Or, if there is someone with whom dangers and other noteworthy matters and offenses weigh heavily (for he knows the nature and tendency of his mate most intimately); in the event that any adultery or fornication or some other evil should result from it, and he fears that he might by his separation and avoidance be the cause thereof, [let them stay together]. Moreover, if there be a houseful of children and he fears that if he does not stay with them they may grow up in evil, and their souls be lost; or if he is worried also about his own ability to practice continence, [let them stay together]. Or if he is deeply concerned about the evil speech and shame that might result from it with the world, and also in part with young and weak new converts, and such difficulties, worries, and offenses over and above these—that then such troubled, concerned, straitened, and weak consciences (provided the person is otherwise pious and without reproach, is truly faithful to the Word of his Lord, walks without offense, yes, lives an exemplary life before God and His Holy Spirit, although in this very perilous matter timid and weak) ought not to be excommunicated. But as a member that is in some aspects weak, he should be instructed in all love after the teaching and example of the holy apostles, be admonished, helped to his feet, comforted, strengthened, and carried in fatherly fashion, ourselves not coming to a fall lest we come to a worse situation.

This then is the construction to which the elders and brethren have agreed, and here you have my position and doctrine touching the matter of the separation of marriage partners. I say once more, after the doctrine and example of the holy apostles, for it is evident that Paul taught in unmistakable terms not to make a distinction between *meats* and between *seasons*. And nevertheless he rebuked very severely those who were ready to find fault with, or accuse, the weak conscience which had been taught differently by the Law (just as in the case of these, with respect to the afore-mentioned passages from Scripture concerning the marriage bond). For the weak conscience could not see it so or understand it thus (without which their troubled conscience in doubt and perplexity could not be sufficiently cleansed). And he says: Let us not therefore judge one another any more, but judge ye this rather, that no man put a stumbling block in his brother's way (compare Rom. 14:13), for he who with such a matter of offense sins against the weaker brother, sins thereby against Christ Jesus. Compare I Cor. 8:12.

This then is our position in this matter, and this is how we teach it. If there are some, however, who deal otherwise, and recklessly press and agitate contrary to the decision and consent of the brethren, men who are not minded to use discretion in the matter, who refuse to take into consideration or put up with any weakness or anxiety, who have no regard for peace or dispeace among the pious, who want to crash straight through everything with their heads—with such we are in disagreement.

Similarly, we are also not in agreement with those who wish to have excommunicated, but not before the third admonition, those who live in open adultery, those who are seducers of women, the murderers, the thieves, the sorcerers, and similar evildoers, who because of their crimes are subject to the sword of the magistrate and are an abomination even to the world.

Moreover, we are not in agreement with those who want all works of the flesh publicly confessed outside the church.[3]

Nor do we agree with those who insist that the transgression and sin of their erring brother, a sin which is unknown to the pious and to the world alike, and which he out of a sorrowful, anguished, and troubled heart has himself made known to his brother—that such a sin must be declared to the congregation, to his humiliation (and the scandalizing of certain other brethren who did not know of it), not making allowance for the fact that he is already penitent and that no one by him has been misled or scandalized, etc. For wherever there is a pulverized and penitent heart, there grace also is (Ezek. 18), and wherever there is a voluntary confession not gained by pressure, there love covereth a multitude of sins. I Peter 4; James 5.

Notice, dear brethren, and ponder with what a careful, fatherly, sympathetic, and prudent mind and spirit our teachers, the holy apostles of God and of Christ, have taught, admonished us . . .[4] children, how they set us an example. How lovingly they have pointed us to the spirit, the nature, and the example of Christ, yes, have conducted themselves over against us as fathers and nursing mothers. Those who walked disorderly they have admonished; those of little faith they have comforted; the weak they have lifted off the ground and carried. Against all harmful policy, bickering, dissension, and so forth, they have continually warned us in fullness of love, knowing full well that nothing comes of these but hatred, envy, division, schism, vituperation, evil speaking, defamation, and bitter evil hearts, even as experience and visible deeds testify.

Only schismatics and those who live offensive carnal lives and who refuse

---

[3] The position which Menno here repudiates is that all who commit carnal sin must be excommunicated before their confession could be heard and then restored back into the fellowship of the church. *Tr.*

[4] At this point a word (or words) have become illegible. *Tr.*

the medications of cure-effecting Christian admonition have the brethren excluded from the Lord's flock, and that with sorrow and pain, by the power of the divine Word and the Spirit of God, lest the unleavened bread of Christ should by them become the leaven of Antichrist. It is also done in order that the disobedient might by such humbling be turned back submissively to the obedience of the Word of Christ, with a penitent and converted heart.

It is therefore our humble admonition that we fear the Lord with solemn fear, and with fervent heart pray for wisdom and grace. We must be willing to bind upon our hearts firmly and securely the portrayed gloriously beautiful breastplate of Aaron, Jesus Christ, who is blessed forever. This breastplate has beautiful colors of yellow, crimson, scarlet, and white, has His Spirit, nature, character, and example of all virtues, is adorned with its twelve costly pearls, along with the Urim and Thummim.[5] It has the two golden chains of the two testaments, as well as the two yellow cords of true faith and love. And so with such adornment we will be ready to enter into the sanctuary of God, the church. We must be prepared to let the clear bright light of Christ and His righteousness, rightly grasped and embraced in the heart, according to the beneficial example, and the salutary and precious doctrine of the apostles, shine before all men. We must be prepared to wash the defiled feet of our human tendencies and affections in the spiritual basin of Jesus Christ, with the water of His Holy Spirit, being ready to have the precious blood of the everlasting sacrifice, Jesus Christ, touched to our right ear so as to hear and understand His Word aright, as well as to our right thumb and toe, so as to perform and walk before Him correctly. We must be prepared to be clothed constantly with the beautiful garment of the dedicated Levites or servants of God, in order that in this way we may in glorious dignity and holiness, giving no offense, serve honorably to the glory of God, the Lord, and to the betterment of Israel. We must be green flowering olive trees, like fruitful vines, like burning torches, and like luminous stars in the noble firmament of the holy, divine Word. Like faithful and irreproachable servants of Christ, in the temple of our God, His church, we must bring forth much fruit, and so receive our full reward in due time together with all the holy apostles and prophets.

May the gracious, merciful Father grant us His grace through Christ our Lord.

*15 December, 1558*

M[ENNO] S[IMONS].[6]

---

[5] Dutch, "light and right." See footnote on p. 997.
[6] The brackets indicate that in the original autograph Menno Simons was, for reasons of personal safety, referred to with the first few letters of his name only. *Tr.*

# Extract from a Letter in Menno's Handwriting

*Brief . . . kort uittreksel*

<hr />

[Undated]*

In the first place, it is our position and confession in regard to non-public sins of which one brother out of the sorrow of his heart has complained to his brother—that the same shall be kept secret and that he who divulges the sin of his penitent brother shall be dealt with as a defamer.

Further, it is our position that a brother is to be admonished to repentance, who has, because of the weakness of his flesh, been overtaken by some sin, if he has not in bold and headstrong fashion lived a long time in sin and in this way dwelt with the brethren as a hypocrite.

* The Amsterdam Doopsgezinde Archives contain the above extract from a letter which Menno wrote with his own hand. This extract is missing in all editions of Menno's works, but was printed by K. Vos in his biography, *Menno Simons,* Leiden, 1914, page 279, from which our translator rendered it into English. The extract simply reaffirms what is well known as Menno's clear and wholesome position in reference to brethren who fall into some sin of the flesh secretly through human weakness, and who are completely penitent immediately.                    J. C. W.

The reporter to whom we owe our knowledge of this extract adds, "as I have been told." The fragment is quite certainly from Menno's hand. In the original it is ascribed, in code (for reasons of personal safety), to a person whose name had five letters, of which the third and the fourth are identical. No Anabaptist elder of the sixteenth century but Menno had a name answering to these particulars; the extract may therefore quite confidently be ascribed to him. *Tr.*

# Two Hymns by Menno Simons

## I. HYMN OF DISCIPLESHIP*
*Mein God, waer sal ic henen gaen*

### c. 1540
*To Be Sung to the Tune: "Where May She Be, This Darling Mine?"*

### I

My God, where shall I wend my flight?
　　Ah, help me on upon the way;
The foe surrounds both day and night
　　And fain my soul would rend and slay.
　　　　Lord God, Thy Spirit give to me,
　　　　Then on Thy ways I'll constant be,
　　　　And, in Life's Book, eternally!

### II

When I in Egypt still stuck fast,
　　And traveled calm broad paths of ease,
Then was I famed, a much-sought guest,
　　The world with me was quite at peace;
　　　　Enmeshed was I in Satan's gauze,
　　　　My life abomination was,
　　　　Right well I served the devil's cause.

### III

But when I turned me to the Lord,
　　And gave the world a farewell look,

* About the year 1540 Menno wrote this first hymn which we have entitled, "Hymn of Discipleship." It has never before been included in any book of Menno's writings, but was published by K. Vos: *Menno Simons*, 1914, pp. 153-56, with introductory discussion on pp. 150, 151. The hymn breathes the spirit of a persecuted preacher who loves the Lord and who has chosen deliberately to suffer affliction with Christ rather than to enjoy the applause of the world for a season. In his usual pattern Menno looks back to the persecuted saints of old, and to Christ Himself, for proof that the true disciple must ever bear the cross of suffering and reproach. But it is a joyful experience to choose the narrow way that leads to life eternal. One needs but to contemplate heaven, the New Jerusalem, to realize that earthly tribulation is but trivial indeed. The translator has preserved the meter and the rhyme pattern of the original. **J. C. W.**

Accepted help against the evil horde,
  The lore of Antichrist forsook;
    Then was I mocked and sore defamed,
    Since Babel's councils I now disdained;
    The righteous man is e'er disclaimed!

### IV

As one may read of Abel, famed,
  Zacharias too—recall it well—
And Daniel too, whom bad men framed
  So that he among fierce lions fell;
    So were the prophets treated, all,
    Christ Jesus too—it is good to recall—
    Nor were the apostles spared this call.

### V

I'd rather choose the sorrow sore,
  And suffer as of God the child,
Than have from Pharaoh all his store,
  To revel in for one brief while;
    The realm of Pharaoh cannot last,
    Christ keeps His kingdom sure and fast;
    Around His child His arm He casts.

### VI

In the world, ye saints, you'll be defamed,
  Let this be cause for pious glee;
Christ Jesus too was much disdained;
  Whereby He wrought to set us free;
    He took away of sin the bill
    Held by the foe. Now if you will
    You too may enter heaven still!

### VII

If you in fires are tested, tried,
  Begin to walk life's narrow way,
Then let God's praise be magnified,
  Stand firm on all He has to say;
    If you stand strong and constant then,
    Confess His Word in the sight of men,
    With joy He extends the diadem!

## VIII

Come hither, bride, receive the crown,
  And neckpiece wrought of burnished gold;
Put on that white and costly gown.
    Thy years shall nevermore grow old.
        From death to life thou didst arise;
        All tears shall vanish from thine eyes;
        No grief nor sorrow more shall rise!

## IX

Now standest thou, Zion, in fairest hue,
  A crown to thee, of grace, is given;
The name of God and Jerusalem new
    Upon thy sides are deeply graven.
        Thou wert abused, yes, stripped quite bare,
        But now art decked in garment fair;
        Art entered to the rest that is there.

## X

Then evil men shall, frightened, see
  As they behold thy splendor mounted,
That these are they—Where shall we flee?—
    Whose life by us was glibly counted
        For folly and for ravings wild;
        We judged these people were beguiled,
        Who live forever, reconciled!

## XI

He who this hymn for us did write,
  And to God's praise sang gladly,
Had conflict oft; with flesh did fight;
    Was tempted sore and sadly.
        Pray God that love in him may rise,
        Let him with Babel ne'er fraternize;
        Then the Home awaits him, in the skies!

## II. PRAYER IN THE HOUR OF AFFLICTION*
### *Een truerich droeuich leyt*
### After 1550
### *To Be Sung to the Tune: "Ah, Joy and Sadness."*

### I

A sad and doleful care,
This news, dear brother, share,
Which God hath now for me prepared.
A chastening He applies,
My inmost heart He tries,
My flesh in sore affliction lies.[1]
His godly wisdom sure
That ever shall endure,
Knows perfectly
That now I lie
In anguish sore.
Help, Lord, I Thee implore
That I by grace once more,
After this grievous blow
May comfort know!

### II

The prophet has averred
With clear and clarion word
That grief is mortal man's reward;
His life ebbs fast away
Till death him low doth lay
With suffering, all the weary way.

---

* The second hymn of Menno was written during a period of bodily affliction, possibly—as our translator suggests—caused by a stroke of apoplexy. K. Vos, who printed this poem in his *Menno Simons*, 1914, pp. 151-53 (introductory information on p. 150), estimates that Menno composed it sometime after 1550, which would be during the last decade of his life. Like any other sick believer Menno is aware of his depravity in the flesh, yet even in his illness he rejoices in the sure fact that he is bearing the cross. Naturally he cries earnestly to God for strength and healing, and especially for grace to persevere. He entreats the brethren for their intercessory prayers that he may again "resume (his) place" as active missioner and elder. As in the first hymn the translator has reproduced both the meter and the rhyme pattern of the original. In neither hymn was Menno's poetry perfect as to form, however. This hymn was never before published in any volume of Menno's writings.                                                  J. C. W.

[1] An ancient authority informs us that this hymn was written by Menno "during a great illness, an illness that left him partly paralyzed, so that he had from then on to use a crutch." The exact nature of this malady is not known. We do know, however, that Menno's face showed partial paralysis in his later days. This combination of symptoms would lead us to suggest that Menno's illness was a case of cerebral hemorrhage, or "stroke." This guess is further justified by the knowledge that Menno was inclined to be corpulent, and, therefore, a candidate for cardiovascular ailment. *Tr.*

Like to a fading flower
So is his fame and power,
Like shade of night
Man takes his flight,
Continues not
In state or constant lot
As God Himself hath taught;
Now I detect that He
Deals so with me.

## III

The Father's chastenings sore
Most gladly I endure
As Micheas did, the saint of yore.
I by His Word confess
To wretched sinfulness,
The sinful lusts of human flesh;
I, born of Adam's seed,
Am sinful-born indeed;
Therefore will I
Right willingly
Chastiséd stand;
Accept all at His hand,
Like Job of storied land,
Till me He to Him takes
And blessed makes.

## IV

Ah, faithful Father, Lord,
My flesh has strength no more,
This earthly house Thou breakest sore.
The vile world hates me quite,
For this Thy witness bright;
Thy cross I bear, with grief not light.
And yet—adversity!
Thy hand Thou lay'st on me,
And presses so
My flesh lays low!
Yet rest I me
Upon Thy promise free
Which ever sure shall be;
And praise Thy majesty
In all eternity!

## V

Ah, Father, God and Lord,
Incline Thy face once more
In this disease and sickness sore;
    Give patience, strength, in grace
    The brightness of Thy face,
    Mid sorrows that come on apace!
That I may constant be,
Whate'er Thy way with me;
    And, not the last,
    My soul hold fast!
Yes, Father, kind,
Preserve in pious mind
Thy sons, who sadness find,
    In faith and doctrine whole,
    So prays my soul!

## VI

I beg my brethren all,
Who've heard the Master's call,
My grief and pain now to recall,
    And then, before God's eyes
    Lay pleasant sacrifice;
    Let pleasing prayer as incense rise;
That I may then again,
Delivered from this pain,
    Behold Thy grace,
    Resume my place,
Serve Christ alway,
Right well the livelong day,
This in my song I pray
    With brethren everywhere,
    In Word-borne prayer.

# Index

viling Menno, 936
Law and order, maintenance of by magistrates, 423, 424
Law, function of God's, 718
Law, whether fulfilled and abrogated, 677
Learned ones, appeal to, 207-12
Learned, subtlety of the, 68
Learning, Menno's attitude toward higher, 790, 792
Leeuwarden, 7, 9, 14, 17, 23, 668
Legalism, charge of, repudiated, 322
Lemke, a deacon, 21
*Lemke, Reply to Sylis and,* 28, 999-1015
Lent, Catholic observance of, 332
*Letter in Menno's Handwriting, Extract from,* 1062
*Letter of Consolation to a Sick Saint,* 1050-52
Letter of Scripture, hypocrites may follow, 963
Letters and other writings of Menno, 1017-68
*Lib. Articulorum* of Zwingli, 695
Lip profession inadequate, 96
Lippes, Nette, 1010
London, Dutch (refugee) church in, 733, 734, 829, 836, 842, 848
Loose, keys to, 990, 992
Lord's day, 680n
Lord's Supper, 6, 8, 13, 24, 94, 142-51, 302, 515, 516, 717-23, 1045
Lord's Supper, a communion of Christ's body and blood, 146
Lord's Supper, eaten at night, 1025
Lord's Supper enjoins brotherly love, 145
Lord's Supper, how observe, 149
Lord's Supper in state churches, 516, 517
Lord's Supper, memorial of Christ's love, 144, 302
Lordship of Christ, 29
Lot, choosing ministers by, 443
Lot, Matthias chosen by, 161
Love, brotherly, a test of true church, 740, 1046

Love constrained Menno to write and teach, 290
Love for God, 973, 1024
Love of Money (See Avarice)
Love, the sum total of Scripture, 917
Lübeck, 21, 22, 23, 25, 26
Lucifer, 298
Lucifer's pride, 119
Luther, *De Sublimiori mundi potestate,* 780
Luther, Martin, 5, 6, 7, 8, 12, 241, 242, 279, 301n, 305, 333n, 400n, 514, 550, 652, 703, 711, 741n, 764, 780, 802, 803, 862
Luther on infant baptism, 126
Luther, writings of, 6, 668, 669, 692, 695, 780
Luther's Bible version, 682, 876
Lutheran abuse of Catholic pope and priesthood, 333, 334
Lutheran clergy, 164
Lutheranism, 322, 333, 334, 399
Lutherans, 175, 207, 234, 732, 741n, 762, 922, 1020
Luxurious life, Menno charged with, 673
Lydia and her house, 282

M. H. G., bailiff and burgomaster, 789
Maccabees, Second, 337, 591, 620
Macedonius, 802
Magistracy ordained of God, 922
Magistracy, request to, 117-20, 190-206, 521, 523-31, 836
(See also, Rulers)
Magistrates entreated for toleration, 523-31; their duties, 193
Magistrates, good, but a few, 299
Magistrates, power of, 677
Major commandments of God, 139
Manasseh's idolatry, 127
Manz, Felix, 28
Maosim, or Maozim, 155
Maoz, 516
Marcushof-Thiensdorf, a Prussian Mennonite Church, 1030n
Mariolatry, 332

CPSIA information can be obtained
at www.ICGtesting.com
Printed in the USA
BVOW06s2014190217
476430BV00015B/19/P

9 780836 195224